EFFECTIVE PSYCHOTHERAPY
A Handbook of Research

EFFECTIVE PSYCHOTHERAPY

A Handbook of Research

Edited and with Commentaries by

ALAN S. GURMAN

University of Wisconsin Medical School

and

ANDREW M. RAZIN

Albert Einstein College of Medicine

Library of Congress Cataloging in Publication Data
Main entry under title:
Effective psychotherapy: A Handbook of Research
    (Pergamon general psychology series; 70)
Includes indexes.
1. Psychotherapists. 2. Psychotherapist & patient.
I. Gurman, Alan S. II. Razin, Andrew M. [DNLM:
1. Psychotherapy. 2. Physician-Patient relations.
WM420 T397]
RC480.8.T48 1977   616.8'914   76-23300

Printed in Gt. Britain by A. Wheaton & Co. Ltd., Exeter.
ISBN 0-08-019508-3 (Hard)

PERGAMON PRESS

OXFORD · NEW YORK · TORONTO · SYDNEY · PARIS · FRANKFURT

U.K.	Pergamon Press Ltd., Headington Hill Hall, Oxford OX3 0BW, England
U.S.A.	Pergamon Press Inc., Maxwell House, Fairview Park, Elmsford, New York 10523, U.S.A.
CANADA	Pergamon of Canada Ltd., 75 The East Mall Toronto, Ontario, Canada
AUSTRALIA	Pergamon Press (Aust.) Pty. Ltd., 19a Boundary Street, Rushcutters Bay, N.S.W. 2011, Australia
FRANCE	Pergamon Press SARL, 24 rue des Ecoles, 75240 Paris, Cedex 05, France
FEDERAL REPUBLIC OF GERMANY	Pergamon Press GmbH, 6242 Kronberg-Taunus, Pferdstrasse 1, Federal Republic of Germany

First edition 1977

Library of Congress Catalog Card No. 76-233300

Printed in Great Britain by A. Wheaton & Co. Ltd., Exeter

ISBN 0 08 019508 3 (hard)
0 08 019507 5 (flexi)

To GERRI and HILARY,
With all our love and gratitude
and
To JESSE,
Just for being

CONTENTS

CONTRIBUTORS

WILLIAM A. ANTHONY, Ph.D.
Associate Professor and Director of Clinical Training
Department of Rehabilitation Counseling
School of Allied Health Professions
Boston University
Boston, Massachusetts

ARTHUR H. AUERBACH, M.D.
Assistant Professor
Department of Psychiatry
University of Pennsylvania
School of Medicine
Philadelphia, Pennsylvania

ALLEN E. BERGIN, Ph.D.
Director
Institute for Studies in Values and Human Behavior
Brigham Young University
Provo, Utah

JURIS I. BERZINS, Ph.D.
Professor and Director of Graduate Studies
Department of Psychology
University of Kentucky
Lexington, Kentucky

JEROLD D. BOZARTH, Ph.D.
Professor and Chairman
Rehabilitation Counseling Department
College of Health Related Professions
University of Florida
Gainesville, Florida

ROBERT R. CARKHUFF, Ph.D.
President
Carkhuff Associates, Inc.
Developers of Human Technology
Amherst, Massachusetts

JOHN L. COLLINS, M.S.
Doctoral Student in Clinical Psychology
Department of Psychology
Brigham Young University
Provo, Utah

MYLES T. EDWARDS, Ph.D.
Evaluation Consultant
Denver Treatment Alternatives to Street Crime (TASC) Project
Denver, Colorado

CHAD D. EMRICK, Ph.D.
Chief Psychologist
Aurora Mental Health Center
Aurora, Colorado
    and
Assistant Clinical Professor of Psychiatry (Clinical Psychology)
University of Colorado Medical Center
Denver, Colorado

IAN M. EVANS, Ph.D.
Associate Professor
Psychology Department
University of Hawaii
Honolulu, Hawaii

DONALD W. FISKE, Ph.D.
Professor
Committee on Methodology of Behavioral Research
Department of Behavioral Sciences
University of Chicago
Chicago, Illinois

SOL L. GARFIELD, Ph.D.
Professor and Director of Clinical Training
Department of Psychology
Washington University
St. Louis, Missouri

ALAN S. GURMAN, Ph.D.
Associate Professor and Director, Psychiatric Outpatient Clinic
Department of Psychiatry
University of Wisconsin Medical School
Madison, Wisconsin

WILLIAM E. HENRY, Ph.D.
Professor and Chairman
Committee on Human Development
Department of Behavioral Sciences
University of Chicago
Chicago, Illinois

KENNETH I. HOWARD, Ph.D.
Professor
Department of Psychology
Northwestern University
Evanston, Illinois
    and
Administrative Research Scientist
Institute for Juvenile Research
Illinois Department of Mental Health
Chicago, Illinois

DAVID W. JOHNSON, Ed.D.
Professor
Department of Social, Psychological and Philosophical Foundations of Education
University of Minnesota
Minneapolis, Minnesota

MARILYN JOHNSON, Ph.D.
Assistant Professor
Department of Guidance and Counseling
Syracuse University
Syracuse, New York

CONRAD C. KRAUFT, Ph.D.
Research Scientist and Assistant Professor
Arkansas Rehabilitation and Training Center
College of Education
University of Arkansas
Fayetteville, Arkansas

MICHAEL J. LAMBERT, Ph.D.
Assistant Professor
Personal Development Center and Department of Psychology
Brigham Young University
Provo, Utah

ix

CAROL L. LASSEN, Ph.D.
Assistant Professor of Psychiatry (Clinical Psychology);
    Director, Adult Psychology Section; and Coordinator,
    Human Sexuality Clinic
University of Colorado Medical Center
Denver, Colorado

LESTER B. LUBORSKY, Ph.D.
Professor of Psychology in Psychiatry
Department of Psychiatry
University of Pennsylvania
School of Medicine
    and
Eastern Pennsylvania Psychiatric Institute
Philadelphia, Pennsylvania

RONALD P. MATROSS, Ph.D.
Research Fellow
Student Life Studies
327 Walter Library
Office for Student Affairs
University of Minnesota
Minneapolis, Minnesota

JIM MINTZ, Ph.D.
Assistant Professor of Psychology in Psychiatry
Department of Psychiatry
University of Pennsylvania
School of Medicine
    and
Chief, Drug Dependence Treatment and Research Center
Veterans Administration Hospital
Philadelphia, Pennsylvania

KEVIN M. MITCHELL, Ph.D.
Associate Professor and Associate Director of Undergrad-
    uate Education
Department of Psychiatry
College of Medicine and Dentistry of New Jersey
New Jersey Medical School
Newark, New Jersey
    and
Adjunct Associate Professor
Graduate School of Applied and Professional Psychology
Rutgers University
New Brunswick, New Jersey

DAVID E. ORLINSKY, Ph.D.
Associate Professor
Department of Psychology
The College of the University of Chicago
    and
Senior Research Scientist
Institute for Juvenile Research
Illinois Department of Mental Health
Chicago, Illinois

BENJAMIN POPE, Ph.D.
Director of Psychology Services
The Sheppard and Enoch Pratt Hospital and the Sheppard-
    Pratt School of Mental Health Studies
    Towson, Maryland

JUDITH G. RABKIN, Ph.D.
Associate Research Scientist
New York State Department of Mental Hygiene
Epidemiology of Mental Disorders Research Unit
New York, New York

ANDREW M. RAZIN, Ph.D., M.D.
Resident
Department of Psychiatry
Albert Einstein College of Medicine
Bronx Municipal Hospital Center
Bronx, New York

JEROME M. SATTLER, Ph.D.
Professor
Department of Psychology
San Diego State University
San Diego, California

BARTON A. SINGER, Ph.D.
Assistant Professor of Psychology in Psychiatry
Department of Psychiatry
University of Pennsylvania
School of Medicine
    and
Senior Staff Psychologist
Veterans Administration Hospital
Philadelphia, Pennsylvania

HANS H. STRUPP, Ph.D.
Professor and Director of Clinical Training
Department of Psychology
Vanderbilt University
Nashville, Tennessee

DONALD M. SUNDLAND, Ph.D.
Associate Professor and Director, The Psychological
    Services Center
Department of Psychology
University of North Dakota
Grand Forks, North Dakota

WALLACE WILKINS, Ph.D.
Associate Professor and Director of Clinical Training
Department of Psychology
University of Maine
Orono, Maine

G. TERENCE WILSON, Ph.D.
Associate Professor and Co-Director, Alcohol Behavior
    Research Laboratory
Graduate School of Applied and Professional Psychology
Rutgers University
New Brunswick, New Jersey

PREFACE

Effective Psychotherapy began in 1971 as a fantasy shared jointly by two close friends whose collaborative writing had begun many years earlier as co-sports editors of their high school magazine. As graduate students at Teachers College, Columbia University, we both became very interested in "the therapist's contribution" and pursued different aspects of this area in our research. The passage of time has made it impossible for us to recall with any sense of certainty "whose idea" the book was. Chances are that we independently had roughly the same thoughts at roughly the same time. In any case, we began to think seriously (meaning we first committed some of our ideas to paper) about this project in June 1972. Our feelings then and now about the need for a book such as this can be described rather straightforwardly. First, we had begun to be concerned about what we saw in many quarters of psychotherapy as increasing trends toward the "technologizing" of treatment. While we were not concerned with the *development* of effective new treatment techniques, including behavioral, chemical, and somatic, we *were* concerned about what we saw as a growing tendency, springing from this development, to consider therapy as consisting *solely* of "the application of the right technique" for "the right patient." While it is debatable whether such a purely technological approach to psychological dysfunction is desirable, if indeed it could be developed (and we doubt that this is possible on a broad scale), we do not now in fact have any systematic technology to apply (except perhaps for a few specific problems such as manic-depressive illness, certain of the sexual dysfunctions, and monophobias). It is our feeling, therefore, that it does not seem any wiser to proceed as though applying "the right technique" is all we need do any more than it does to pretend that there *are* no techniques to apply, but only "a good relationship" to be offered. Both approaches, in our view, are gross oversimplifications of what psychotherapy (by which we mean all treatments of psychological problems) has to offer.

Our second motivation for producing this book stemmed from our recognition of the widespread unwillingness among clinicians to examine systematically the process and effectiveness of the treatments in which they engage daily. Without developing a long exposition of the many possible reasons for this reluctance, let us simply note that one reason is that so much research seems irrelevant if not antithetical to clinical practice. While we have no illusion that this volume will come near solving this problem, we both are clinician-researchers and, as such, we have felt a great need to provide clinicians as well as researchers with an easily consulted, unified synthesis of current critical thinking on the many problems and areas of psychotherapy research that focus on the *therapist's contribution* to the process and outcome of treatment. We obviously cannot, and want not, to force all clinicians to be aware of research issues, but we do hope that this book may prompt more clinicians to make inputs into psychotherapy research—hopefully with the same flexibility and creativity that they bring to their clinical work.

Our third primary motivation for editing this book derived more purely from our perspective and experience as psychotherapy researchers. Stated quite simply, it seemed to us that while scores of researchers were active in the general domain of "the therapist's contribution", most of them (among whom we included ourselves) were largely unaware of what was going on next door. Thus, we saw a need to bring together in one place critical assessments of the major dimensions of "the therapist's contribution" so that the interested researcher could see where we've been and where we might go in order to expand our clinically relevant empirical knowledge. In our letter of invitation to potential contributors we wrote:

> Our own research, and that of others, led us to conclude that although much clearly valuable work has been done on "the therapist," it has been done by researchers with widely varying interests and orientations, and has proceeded in widely varying directions. Our primary goal is to develop a comprehensive synthesis of this work. . . . Except for the introductory section, the emphasis throughout will be on substantive empirical issues. We see the value of the book lying in its delineation of those "therapist factors" that (1) influence the process and outcome of psychotherapy and (2) cut across specific schools, professions, and techniques. Thus, this will not be a book on therapeutic technology,

except in its consideration of the relationship between the technology and the "person" of the therapist.

After several preliminary strategies for organizing the book had been discarded, we hit upon one that excited us. While we hardly expect that the reader will approach this book as he would a novel, our underlying format is a temporal one. After the two introductory chapters in Part I which focus on theoretical and methodological issues, the rest of the book follows a sequence which is intended to be developmental. In Part II, "The Development and Ideology of the Psychotherapist," attention is paid to the question of who become therapists, the nature of their training, and the role of increased experience as a therapist. Psychotherapeutic ideologies are examined next, with a focus on therapists' beliefs about mental illness and the practice of therapy. Moving from background to actual therapy, Part III, "The Conduct and Experience of Psychotherapy," addresses the dimensions of therapist–patient compatability, primarily in terms of "givens" that affect the treatment process and outcome, the nature of the therapist's impact, the therapeutic relationship, and the therapist's experience of therapy as both participant and judge.

Before we had ever contacted our first contributor or signed a publisher's contract, we had naively conceived of the work of book editors as being quite consonant with the early expectations of that role described by Richard Greene (1975, p. v): "My previous idea of an editor's task was to neatly pile up a set of manuscripts written by others, fire a staple gun into the left margin at appropriate intervals, and signal the task as completed." After not very long, we were forced, by all the usual experiences of book editors, to improve our reality testing (is this what our behavioral colleagues mean by flooding?)

We also decided, hopefully not presumptuously, that we had more to add to a multi-authored book such as this than merely reviewing and critiquing manuscripts, reminding people how to use the *APA Style Manual*, and politely harassing delinquent contributors. Thus, we have taken the liberty, which we wish book editors would do more often, of adding our own comments and thoughts to those of our contributors. These *Editors' Footnotes* represent some of our reaction to the content of the chapters and they have the following purposes: (1) to take issue occasionally with a contributor's idea or conclusion on the basis of our own thinking

or additional relevant data of which we were aware, (2) to offer our own views on certain matters, (3) to speculate as to the clinical implications of empirical findings, and (4) to point out the relationship between an author's idea and relevant material found elsewhere in this volume. We have devoted a good deal of thought to these comments, and hope that they do more than serve as so much academic trimming; rather, we hope that they will stimulate further thought in the reader and perhaps generate new research ideas.

We have been extremely fortunate in being able to gather together most of the most creative, productive, and influential writers, thinkers and researchers in the area of psychotherapy research with which this book is concerned. We are deeply indebted to each contributor for the seriousness with which he or she responded to their task.

Others deserve public acknowledgment for their contribution to this project: Drs. Arnold Goldstein and Leonard Krasner, Pergamon's Psychology Editors, for supporting this venture from the beginning; Dr. Norman S. Greenfield, who offered us wise counsel on the vagaries and interpersonal politics of book-editing; Dr. Allen E. Bergin, for useful advice on a number of issues; and Drs. Joseph G. Kepecs, John Neill, William C. Lewis, and James R. Greenley, for graciously reviewing particular chapters for us. Luckily, we received complete and swift cooperation from several publishers and journals to use previously published material: Aldine Publishing Company, the American Medical Association, the American Psychological Association; Division 12 (Clinical Psychology) of the American Psychological Association; Jason Aronson Publishers; Holt, Rinehart & Winston; The Ronald Press; and the University of Minnesota Press.

Finally, we offer special thanks to Cathy Beck and Sally Opgenorth for their unfailing assistance in the myriad of secretarial tasks necessary to produce a book such as this.

Madison, Wisconsin
New York City
February 1977
Alan S. Gurman
Andrew M. Razin

REFERENCE

GREEN, R. *Human Sexuality*. Baltimore: Williams & Wilkins, 1975.

ABOUT THE AUTHORS

ALAN S. GURMAN received his B.A. from Boston University (1967) and his M.A. (1970) and Ph.D. (1971) from Columbia University. After a two-year Postdoctoral Fellowship at the University of Wisconsin Medical School he joined the faculty there and is currently Associate Professor of Psychiatry and Research Associate, Psychiatric Research Institute of Wisconsin. He is also the Director of the Outpatient Clinic and Director of Student Psychiatry. Dr. Gurman, a member of the Executive Committee of the Society for Psychotherapy Research, and author of over thirty articles in psychology, psychiatry and sociology journals, recently edited (with David G. Rice) *Couples in Conflict: New Directions in Marital Therapy* (Aronson, 1975). He also serves as a member of the Editorial Board of *Family Process* and the *Journal of Marriage and Family Counseling*. His primary research interests are in the process and outcome of psychotherapy, currently with a major focus on developing a conceptual model for evaluating the outcomes of marital and family therapy.

ANDREW M. RAZIN received his B.A. from Brown University (1967), and his Ph.D. (1972) from Columbia University. After a two-year Postdoctoral Fellowship at the Yale University School of Medicine, he attended the Albert Einstein College of Medicine, where he received the Rock–Sleyster Award in psychiatry. After receiving his M.D. (1976), Dr. Razin began his psychiatry residency at Einstein. His research interests have been in the outcome and process of psychotherapy, and he has published several articles in psychology and psychiatry journals. He has devoted particular attention to the A-B psychotherapist typology over the past eight years. Most recently, Dr. Razin has begun research on the relationship between personality and coronary artery disease. Clinically, his primary interests have been in the individual and group psychotherapy of adults and adolescents, and in systems-oriented school consultation.

INTRODUCTION

THE publication of this book recognizes the central role of therapist characteristics in the psychotherapies, behavior therapies, and other modes of modifying personality and behavior. From the time of the early recognition of these factors by Sigmund Freud, who recommended suppressing them as much as possible, to the present time where some therapies utilize primarily the therapist's personality and style, we have moved from one extreme to the other: from the notion that *TECHNIQUE* is the key to change to the notion that *PERSONAL and RELATIONSHIP* factors are the more powerful ingredients of the therapy process.

Naturally, the separation of these two major elements in the therapy transaction has never been satisfactorily accomplished. The resolution of transference has never been a purely technical matter, nor has behavior therapy ever been able to achieve the technical purity once anticipated in early visions of a behavioral technology. On the other hand, in the intentionally personal transactions that are the essence of humanistic and encounter therapies, questions continue to arise as to the most efficient technical arrangements under which these presumably therapeutic encounters transpire.

As research evidence and clinical experience have accumulated, the modal opinions of leaders in the field have shifted back and forth on these issues. It seems that, repeatedly, professionals have aspired to invent techniques that can be shown to have specific effects that are separable from the interpersonal business that always occurs during therapy. It has been the persistent hope that these effects would be above and beyond those attributable to the so-called nonspecific factors that operate in all helping relationships.

These hopes have not, so far, been realized. The technical claims of the diverse schools have never been adequately vindicated. Comparative studies continue to show little difference in the outcomes of diverse approaches even though each therapy, by itself, can be shown to have significant effects when compared to no-treatment. If this assessment is correct, then the viewpoint of Jerome Frank is most strongly supported by the evidence—namely, that the effective factors are the same for all therapies and that these are the same as the common ingredients in all types of healing and influence processes that occur in all cultures. From such a conclusion, we readily swing to the view that therapist personal factors are the powerful ones and that techniques merely provide the vehicle or, as Frank states, the "ritual" by which these personal influences are mediated. The technique is thus crucial only to the extent that it provides a believable rationale and *modus operandi* for the change agent, one that is given special credibility either by cultural sanction or by a subgroup with whom the participant identifies.

This is not to say that techniques are irrelevant but that their power for change is pale by comparison with that of personal influence. Such a conceptual view provides a good rationale for the efforts undertaken in this book to capture the broad sweep of the therapist's personal impact as it has been documented empirically. This impact is richly described here and can be seen to be diverse—that is, ranging from very helpful to harmful, and everything in between.

Teasing out the ingredients of this diversity of therapist influences has proved to be a difficult but not impossible task. The growing acceptance by practitioners of the need for rigorous evaluation of outcomes has been a positive development in recent years. Many people have sacrificed a great deal to bring about this improved climate for research on the effects of psychotherapy. None has been more devoted to this goal than Carl Rogers. His courage opened the door to honest assessment of the outcomes of therapy. He and his colleagues also set the stage for the subsequent major development of inquiries into the inner workings of therapy via study of the person of the therapist and the nature of his impact. Today, we face a major hurdle in bringing this step of inquiry to fruition.

The challenge is comparable to that of those who pioneered the evaluation of outcomes. This text takes us a long way in the direction of fulfilling the hope, nurtured by Rogers and others, that some day we would have an objective account of the personal factors that make the difference between constructive change and deterioration.

ALLEN E. BERGIN
Brigham Young University

PART I

Conceptualization and Methodology

CHAPTER 1

A REFORMULATION OF THE DYNAMICS OF THE THERAPIST'S CONTRIBUTION

Hans H. Strupp

In all forms of psychotherapy (including such diverse variants as orthodox psychoanalysis and behavior modification) a psychological influence is brought to bear upon the person who has enlisted an expert's help in effecting change. A person, traditionally called a "patient," is dissatisfied with some aspects of his feelings or behavior and, having recognized his inability to rectify the situation on his own, turns to a professional person ("therapist") for assistance, guidance, and intervention. In broadest terms, the enterprise called "psychotherapy" encompasses a person who has recognized that he is in need of help, an expert who has agreed to provide that help, and a series of human interactions, frequently of highly intricate, subtle, and prolonged character, designed to bring about beneficial changes in the patient's feelings and behavior that the participants and society at large will view as therapeutic.

As a scientific discipline, modern psychotherapy must insist on a public or intersubjectively verifiable outcome. In the past, especially in psychodynamic circles, it was held that change could occur without the kind of consensus stipulated here—for example, a patient might observe change without the therapist sharing that view or without the change being observable by outsiders. I shall insist, by contrast, that at least in principle there must be some way of documenting the occurrence of change, difficult and fallible as such demonstrations may turn out to be. There is no need to define change in restrictive terms, as many behaviorists have done, but it is necessary to stipulate that (1) change must be demonstrable; (2) it must be relatively permanent; and (3) it must be attributable to the interpersonal transactions between patient and therapist.

Simple and straightforward as the foregoing formulation appears to be, it has been extraordinarily difficult to put the criteria into practice, and the failure to do so has been a major factor for the continuing controversy concerning the effectiveness of psychotherapy as a treatment modality. An extensive literature has dealt with the practical and conceptual problems; these need not be reviewed here.

A serious difficulty has been the widespread and long-standing reluctance of therapists to adopt a hard-nosed position on the subject of treatment outcomes, a major reason for the continuing confusion being directly traceable to widely divergent views concerning the purpose and objectives of psychotherapy. As long as there is no clarity on the latter, there can be no clarity about outcomes. Examples of conflicting conceptualizations are: psychotherapy as a method of investigating the patient's intrapsychic and interpersonal dynamics; psychotherapy as a form of treatment for a disorder (analogous to medical treatment); psychotherapy as a vehicle for promoting personality growth and maturity; psychotherapy as a means for helping a person come to terms with philosophical and existential problems; psychotherapy as a form of after-education; and psychotherapy as a technique for modifying behavior. While these objectives are clearly overlapping and not mutually exclusive, they inevitably lead to different therapeutic operations. Most serious and detrimental to the development of the field has been the absence of specifications of what is intended, together with the acceptance of a pragmatic—and often dogmatic—view that a particular approach which the therapist has found congenial is the royal road to the achievement of objectives cherished by him. Since divergent goals predictably lead to different outcomes, it is clear that failure to specify the objectives of psychotherapy creates insurmountable difficulties in evaluating whether a particular outcome has been achieved. Thus, the field has been plagued by prolonged and fruitless controversy as to whether psychotherapy "works," is "effective,"

4

or "does any good." Only in recent years have these conceptual issues been brought fully into focus, but there will undoubtedly remain a long lag in translating the implications into practice.

Traditionally, the vast literature on psychotherapy has centered around more or less precise descriptions of changes in the patient that have then been attributed to a set of operations espoused by the therapist as factors producing the changes; or, there have been elaborate expositions of theories and techniques—that is, descriptions of the independent variable. Only during the last two decades have there been systematic attempts to (1) assess patient changes over time and (2) link these changes to particular therapeutic operations. Because of the enormous clinical, technical, and methodological difficulties inherent in these tasks, progress has been slow, and there are as yet very few if any studies that are immune from criticisms, usually on numerous grounds. Nevertheless, we have witnessed a marked growth in conceptual and methodological sophistication; while particular studies may fall short, there is no longer any doubt concerning the criteria that an acceptable investigation must meet (see below). Consequently, as time goes on, we may expect an increasing amount of enlightened experimental effort that will clarify the basic problems with which the field is still grappling.

Having thus expressed my faith in empirical demonstrations as the final arbiter of the controversies besetting this area of investigation, I hasten to add that a great deal of work needs to be done at the conceptual level. In this chapter I have set myself the task of taking another look at the independent variable in psychotherapy— that is, the nature of the therapeutic influence. Apart from the problem of assessing changes in the patient and determining whether a particular change has been for better or for worse, there is no task equal in importance to an analysis of what the therapist *does* (which always includes who he *is*). In general, it is clear that the therapist "does" something to the patient. He attempts to *influence* him, effect change, or set in motion processes that may result in change. Whether the goal is to produce changes in cognitions, beliefs, feelings, behavior, motivations, etc., there can be no doubt that the therapist's business is the more or less deliberate, self-conscious production of change. Even in insight therapy, the therapist subtly pursues a course of persuasion (Frank, 1973), although it can hardly be termed persuasion in the ordinary sense. He becomes effective through his personal interaction with another individual who at least on some level desires change and is motivated to seek it. By the same token, the patient regards the therapist as an expert who can effect change; regardless of whether he pays for the services, he expects the therapist to work in that direction. The nature of the change desired or attempted may vary widely depending upon circumstances, but unless the therapist views his task as that of a change agent he does not merit the appellation of therapist.

The foregoing implies that *there is no such thing as "nondirective" therapy, a term that is basically self-contradictory and has served largely propagandistic purposes (i.e., to castigate psychoanalysis)*. We must also accept the ineluctable fact that the therapist is a manipulator in one sense of the dictionary meaning. Even if the therapist is committed to the view that the patient must find his own solutions and if he eschews the role of a deliberate influencer or behavior shaper, he cannot—nor should he— escape the realization that his assigned task is to effect or participate in the process of producing personality or behavior change in another person. That is his job; that is his *métier*. To deny this essential core of his function is to rob it of its basic meaning.

To further the inquiry, a basic distinction should be made between the therapist's personality and his actions, between what he *is* and what he *does*. The latter leads to a discussion of instrumental acts or techniques, a topic central to psychoanalysis as a treatment modality as well as to behavior therapy and other approaches; the former, to an examination of the therapist's personal attributes, which are emphasized by client-centered, existential, and humanistic psychotherapy but given less weight by psychodynamic theory. In practice, the two sets of variables necessarily fuse and it becomes extraordinarily difficult to disentangle their respective contribution to process and outcome. Classical analysis, except for its important contribution to the broad concept of countertransference, took the position that it is possible to discuss technique in the abstract, analogous to a surgical procedure. Client-centered therapy and humanistic therapy have largely rejected the instrumental aspects of the therapist's influence and elevated his attitudes, beliefs, values, and human qualities to a position of preeminence. The original psychoanalytic position (echoed by contemporary behavior therapy) that techniques can be discussed apart from the person using them, is manifestly untenable if our focus is on empirical operations; the client-centered and humanistic position, if followed to its logical conclusion, contravenes the basic conception of psychotherapy as a treatment modality.

To be sure, there are many ways in which human beings learn, grow, and mature, and difficulties in living can be overcome by widely different means. There are also many ways in which one person can profit from an interpersonal relationship with someone who is wiser, more mature, and more knowledgeable. Unless, however, the person engaged in the influencing process has therapeutic intent, engages in activities that are designed to produce relatively specific personality and behavior changes in another (i.e. uses "techniques"), and relates these instrumental acts to theoretical constructs, however vague, that activity should not be called psychotherapy. The basic issue at this point is not whether psychotherapists and other influences engage in psychological processes that are essentially identical, nor whether psychotherapy in the hands of a professional who calls himself a psychotherapist achieves results that are quantitatively or qualitatively superior to other kinds of influences, but simply whether sets of definable operations (admittedly modulated by the qualities of the person employing them) lead to specifiable outcomes under reasonably specific conditions—for example, with a patient having particular attributes and difficulties.

In practice, two extremes are conceivable: A set of psychological techniques (e.g., systematic desensitization in simple phobias) is sufficiently powerful so that it makes little difference who administers it.[2] The analogy here is a powerful drug that has curative value regardless of whether it is dispensed by a physician, a pharmacist, a nurse, or the patient's spouse. While the situational context or the patient's beliefs might influence the effect of the drug, these are relatively inconsequential if the drug is potent. The other extreme is represented by a healer who exerts a powerful charismatic effect on individuals who seek his help. In this case it would make little difference whether the healer uses incantations, psychoanalytic interpretations, reassurance, or whether he invites the patient to handle a snake: the "technique" is unimportant relative to the healer's personal influence.

Most psychotherapeutic techniques extant probably fall somewhere between these two poles: they are neither totally dependent on the person using them nor are they totally independent. They are in all likelihood potentiated or diminished by the therapist's personality as well as the situational context in which the transaction occurs. The vast literature on treatment outcomes in psychotherapy, particularly the recurrent finding that there is no single technique that is consistently superior to any other, supports this interpretation. It should also be noted that progress in analyzing the problem has been seriously retarded by the fact that debates relative to the alleged merits of one theoretical system over another have until fairly recently been fought on theoretical and ideological rather than on empirical grounds. Yet, unless differential outcomes can be demonstrated, the polemics are of little practical interest.

FACTORS IN THERAPEUTIC OUTCOMES

Given these complexities, it is hardly surprising that confusion continues to flourish at all levels. Despite decades of persistent debate, the advent of new techniques, theoretical writings, and voluminous empirical studies, the basic issue concerning specific effects as a function of specific interventions remains foggy. The fundamental problem which has proved so utterly refractory is that we are trying to assess the outcome of exceedingly complex human interactions. As scientists, we set ourselves the task of ascertaining whether the therapist's interventions have produced a measureable effect on the patient, with the proviso that the changes must be relatively permanent and stable. We further stipulate that temporary or transient changes are trivial and rule them out as legitimate goals. By defining the problem in this manner, we exclude from further consideration those interpersonal activities (e.g. religious movements, educational experiences, entertainment) in which the *mechanisms* by which a particular outcome is achieved are not a primary concern. To restate the scientific problem: Does a set of specifiable operations have a specifiable outcome?

There is hardly anything remarkable about this formulation, nor would it be worth reasserting were it not for the fact that it is not typically in the forefront of the average clinician's thinking and that it becomes obscured in everyday clinical practice. Leaving aside ideological issues between different schools of psychotherapy, it suffices to note that *all* forms of interventions designated as "therapy" appear to result in beneficial outcomes under *some* circumstances. Such intermittent reinforcements bolster the therapist's belief that he is engaged in a worthwhile and socially useful activity. The problem is not that therapeutic changes occur with a certain frequency—although questions have been raised even concerning this assertion—but to account for the changes in terms of specifiable antecedents (Bergin & Strupp, 1972). There is evidence to show that two-thirds to three-quarters of patients who have undergone a series of structured meetings ("psychotherapy") will characterize the outcome of this experience in more or less laudatory terms (Strupp, Fox, & Lessler, 1969) and they will credit to it various changes in their feelings and behavior. Similarly, therapists of diverse theoretical orientations will testify—perhaps somewhat more cautiously—concerning the outcome of their professional work. While such data have a certain utility, they are subject to distortion and misinterpretation similar to those resulting from tabulations presented by Eysenck (1952, 1965; for an incisive analysis of this issue, see Bergin, 1971). Psychotherapy in this sense is comparable to a chemical compound of unknown composition whose virtues the manufacturer advertises in glowing terms. Should we accept the dispenser's or the user's testimony that the benefits are due to the ingredients the manufacturer is interested in promoting? As research with pharmacological agents has abundantly shown, substantial placebo effects are a regular occurrence in human subjects. More specifically, Shapiro (1971) has documented that placebo effects are by no means restricted to drugs but are a pervasive phenomenon in fields as disparate as surgery and psychoanalysis. In psychotherapy research, improvements of this kind have been considered under the heading of "spontaneous remission" (Bergin, 1971).

Eysenck reasoned that any form of psychotherapy worth its salt must exceed the baseline defined by "spontaneous remission" (really a euphemism for ignorance) or face a verdict of inutility. To attribute placebo effects in psychotherapy to so-called nonspecific factors in the patient–therapist relationship (Frank, 1971, 1972) (e.g., warmth, kindness, respect, understanding, the kindling of hope, provision of an "explanation" for the patient's suffering) is an improvement over calling them "spontaneous remission," but the reformulation remains inconclusive until the effects of the nonspecific factors themselves can be teased apart. The likelihood of accomplishing this feat in the foreseeable future, without creating highly artificial situations, is slight. At any rate, as long as the baseline set by spontaneous remission,

placebo, or nonspecific variables cannot be stringently defined, the assessment of treatment effects remains a highly speculative venture.

It would be a mistake, however, to deplore the placebo effect in psychotherapy as an unwelcome confound, as is true in other areas of research. On the contrary, it may turn out that the effects of psychotherapy are to a very large extent placebo effects. As I noted elsewhere (Strupp, 1973), we can choose to brush off placebo effects as a troublesome interference or we can treat them as an impressive set of phenomena which deserve study and scrutiny in their own right. Since placebo effects are the product of as yet poorly understood human expectations, hopes, attitudes, and beliefs in relation to a treatment procedure as well as to an expert (or healer), it may be said that they fall squarely within the province of the psychotherapist's and the psychotherapy researcher's concern. To state the matter slightly differently, the study of psychotherapy as a scientific discipline is principally a quest for understanding the effects of interpersonal forces operating in a human relationship structured to achieve changes that we choose to call therapeutic. By the same token, the practice of psychotherapy (including its various subforms) relates to the skillful management (manipulation) of interpersonal forces in such a relationship. As noted already, the modern psychotherapist is a deliberate and purposeful influencer or change agent, and psychotherapy is the best developed art of influencing people in therapeutic ways.

With regard to the basic problem of specifiable outcomes as a function of specifiable therapeutic interventions, the field has witnessed significant increments in sophistication in recent years. For example, it has been possible for scientists (Fiske, Hunt, Luborsky, Orne, Parloff, Reiser, & Tuma, 1970) to specify in considerable detail the methodological and psychometric desiderata for well-designed studies in psychotherapy. Some progress has also been made in advancing recommendations for standard (albeit crude) measures to be used in future investigations. Further, problems relating to therapist, patient, situational, and demographic variables have been carefully explored, and issues relating to experimental controls have been illuminated (Paul, 1969). It is apparent, of course, that the requirements for the "ideal" experiment cannot be met in actual practice and that compromises of various sorts are inevitable. While it may be expected that the rigor of investigations will substantially increase in the years to come, it is doubtful that significant progress can be made in isolating the effects of single treatment variables.

PROBLEMS IN OUTCOME MEASUREMENT

As schematically presented in Fig. 1, we are traditionally interested in studying the effect of a main treatment variable, x_1, the effect being changes in the patient's feelings, attitudes, and behavior, m through v. For practical purposes, the number of change indicators is finite, and there exists a certain degree of agreement among specialists regarding the kinds of changes acceptable as "real" and worthwhile. The last statement is hedged because the consensus on criteria of outcome is far from perfect. Indeed, the criterion problem has been one of the perennial stumbling blocks in psychotherapy research. For example,

BASIC INGREDIENTS OF PSYCHOTHERAPY

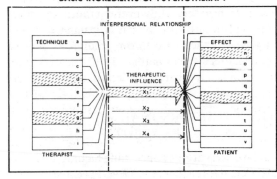

Fig. 1.

it may be agreed that the disappearance of a phobia is a desirable outcome, and the change in symptomatology may be taken as a tangible measure of improvement. On the other hand, it is inordinately difficult to achieve consensus on what might be optimal assertiveness in interpersonal relations, adequate self-esteem, or ego strength. The problem is confounded by the fact that in the final analysis we are usually not concerned with specific behaviors but with the interpersonal contexts in which behaviors are embedded, the subjective feeling states and meanings a behavior has to the patient, his sense of competence, satisfaction, etc. Thus, it is not surprising that most therapists think rather flexibly if not loosely about treatment goals.

Changes resulting from psychotherapy are usually classed under two main rubrics: (1) feelings and cognitive (intrapsychic) changes and (2) behavior. The former are generally assessed by standardized self-report measures

(e.g. the Minnesota Multiphasic Personality Inventory and self-concept scales); the latter, by ratings of the therapist, sometimes complemented by external judges, such as independent clinicians, roommates, dormitory counselors, spouses, etc. The two areas, of course, shade into each other. For example, a patient's overt behavior following therapy may have changed only slightly but he may feel very differently about himself and his behavior with others. Shall our assessment be restricted to behavior in a narrow sense? If not, how can we weight the importance of different factors in the person's total functioning? We are faced with the dilemma that therapeutic changes must somehow be demonstrable in the person's behavior, but observable behavior is too narrow a focus. Behavior therapists (Bandura, 1969; Davison & Wilson, 1973) are beginning to place greater value on cognitive and emotional changes, recognizing their legitimacy. From the early days of psychoanalysis, when behavior change was declared trivial and the thrust of therapy was focused on the resolution of intrapsychic conflicts, the field has come full circle. It is acknowledged that the effects of psychotherapy must be assessed along both subjective and objective dimensions.

Because of a lack of agreement on criteria of outcome and the inevitable intrusion of value judgments, the assessment of psychotherapeutic outcomes has remained one of the major obstacles to progress. Consequently, one study may focus on change in area o, whereas another is concerned with area r. Moreover, what may be rated as improvement in one person may be regarded as deterioration in another.

The last point is particularly troublesome for the researcher because judgments about another person's behavior tend to be suffused not only by the rater's personal values but also by cultural standards.[3] To illustrate: Our culture holds certain values regarding the desirability of a young man's dating behavior. Absence of interactions with members of the opposite sex, regardless of the patient's subjective feelings, tends to be seen as a "symptom." Conversely, a patient may engage in dating but he reports that he is ill-at-ease with a girl, feels he has "nothing to say," and the experience is a strain. Following therapy, the frequency of dating may have increased and now he has a better time. Or, a Don Juan type may decrease the frequency of his flirtations, but the quality of his experiences has improved. Many other combinations are, of course, possible. In short, judging the *frequency* of a behavior can be extremely misleading; conversely, the *quality* of an experience is difficult to assess intersubjectively, although it would be possible to set the latter as a target for therapy. Similar problems are legion.

Research in psychotherapy now insists on the specification of outcome criteria, including predictions concerning the kinds of changes attempted by a therapist. Since changes are typically broad gauged rather than specific, this stipulation is made more easily from the armchair than fulfilled in practice. But from the clinician, too, we have come to expect greater awareness of the precise changes he seeks to produce and the means by which he accomplishes this feat. The field can no longer afford the luxury of two people meeting for seemingly interminable periods of time in the hope that regression will somehow bring elusive transference problems into focus and aid the process of "working through." If the process is to result in maturation, we need to know more precisely what that term means.

Ideally, one would like to test the effects of a technique, d, on a behavior, r. Unfortunately for the researcher, technique d (say, relaxation or a psychodynamic interpretation) does not come neatly labeled or packaged; on the contrary, it is "administered" by a person (the psychotherapist) who, regardless of his theoretical orientation or level of experience, brings to bear on the interaction a wide variety of techniques that are themselves intermingled and fused. There is not—and it is doubtful that there ever will be—a pure technical intervention analogous to a surgical procedure or the injection of a specific drug. Instead, any therapeutic technique is firmly embedded in and thoroughly intertwined with the therapist's personality and the total history of a particular patient–therapist interaction including its current context. It is supported by the therapist's attitudes, values, personal philosophy, etc., which act like a carrier wave from which techniques are inseparable. To count, as was done in the late 1940s, the number of "nondirective" statements occurring in a therapeutic hour—i.e. communications whose outer form seemed to conform to the teachings of nondirective therapy—and to equate such indices with the essence of the therapeutic influence was clearly a miscarriage of empiricism (see Strupp, 1962, for a review).

A similar fallacy, however, pervades the psychoanalytic credo that the nature of the therapist's influence is largely encompassed by interpretations of resistances or unconscious content.

Likewise there is more to behavior therapy than specific techniques such as systematic desensitization or assertive training (Sloane, Staples, Cristol, Yorkston, & Whipple, 1975). In short we are beginning to recognize and take seriously the extraordinary complexity of the therapeutic influence. As shown in Fig. 1, the therapeutic influence, x_1, embodies not only a variety of techniques; it also draws heavily on the totality of the therapeutic relationship and its bidirectional or reciprocal influence (x_2, x_3, x_4, . . .). The participants are enclosed in a complicated interpersonal field (depicted by the border) in which their personalities are deeply enmeshed. While it is true that the major thrust of the influence is unidirectional (see the arrow, x_1), we must not lose sight of its schematic nature. Traditionally, therapists and theoreticians have concerned themselves with the influence of a given technique, g, on a facet of the patient's personality, r. An opponent might focus on technique d, and become interested in effect o. More commonly, however, hypotheses have been formulated in terms of particular techniques and their effects on *unspecified* aspects of the patient's personality. The hopelessness of resolving such dilemmas is readily apparent.

THE INTERPERSONAL RELATIONSHIP AS A THERAPEUTIC FORCE

The observations concerning techniques apply with equal force to what in Fig. 1 is called "Interpersonal Relationship." To this end, we need to replace the boxes labeled "technique" with qualities of the therapist's personality (always in interaction with those of the patient). In the client-centered framework, for example, therapist attributes such as genuineness and empathy have been endowed with curative power with respect to fairly general aspects of the patient's functioning (e.g., self-esteem). Concomitantly, techniques are deemphasized. Nevertheless, it is incontrovertibly true that any form of psychotherapy uses techniques of psychological influence that are more or less deliberately deployed in the context of an interpersonal relationship. The forces operating in the latter, as we have seen, are generally grouped under the headings of "placebo effects," "spontaneous remission," or "nonspecific factors." The problem of analyzing the components of the interpersonal relationship is as urgent (as well as difficult) as that of specifying the influence of particular techniques. An equally pressing, but perhaps more solvable, task is that of studying the relative contribution of the two sets of variables to the outcome of psychotherapy.

There is ample evidence (see Truax & Carkhuff, 1967) that any "good" human relationship—i.e. an interaction characterized by understanding, acceptance, respect, trust, empathy, and warmth—is helpful and constructive. If such a relationship is provided by one person (therapist) for another (patient) who is unhappy, demoralized, defeated, and suffering from the kinds of problems which our society has diagnosed as requiring the services of a specialist in mental health, the outcome will generally be "therapeutic," provided the recipient is able to respond to, or take advantage of, what the therapist has to offer. Some therapists believe that psychotherapy begins precisely at the point where a patient cannot profit from a good human relationship, and the professional is needed specifically by those persons who are chronically unable to seek out and profit from a good human relationship (Bergin, 1971). The position has a certain intuitive appeal but it has never been tested. Arguing against it is the growing literature on nonprofessional therapists which, admittedly in the absence of closely controlled studies and precise measurements, has failed to show substantive differences in favor of professional workers (see Anthony & Carkhuff, Chapter 6, this volume).

If it is conceded that psychotherapy is generally carried out within the framework of a "good" human relationship, questions must be raised about the nature of the professional psychotherapist's contribution over and beyond the provision of a good human relationship. Conversely, if the contribution of a good human relationship to a specific therapeutic outcome is subtracted, what is left over? The development of psychotherapy as a set of theories and as a prestigious profession in the twentieth century is predicated on the assumption that the residue is substantial. Furthermore, a good human relationship, while important, is generally viewed as a *precondition* for the therapist's technical interventions, to which major attention is accorded in theoretical writings and in training programs. Behavior therapy as well as psychoanalysis essentially subscribe to this position. A notable exception is client-centered therapy, which extols the "good" relationship and deemphasizes techniques.

HISTORICAL NOTE

The place of the "good" relationship in psychoanalytic psychotherapy bears closer examination (Freud, 1911–1915; and Editor's Introduction). While Freud recognized that the therapist's personal contribution to the therapeutic relationship transcended "evenly hovering attention," he tended to accept as *selbstverständlich* the therapist's neutrality, understanding, nonjudgmentalness, respect, decency, and the like. He admitted, of course, that these attitudes contributed importantly to the development of the therapeutic alliance and that, in Ferenczi's words, they gave *Tragfestigkeit* (stability) to the relationship. However, the relationship was the ground, not the figure. In psychoanalysis, the figure was seen as the management of psychodynamic factors to which major attention was paid in the technical writings.

When Freud (1910) took explicit cognizance of counterproductive attitudes in the therapist, labeling them "countertransference," he thereby acknowledged that the therapist's attitudes played an important part in the relationship, but he was exclusively concerned with their interference in the progress of therapy. Conversely, he viewed with grave misgivings therapist attitudes that might have a positive influence on the progress of therapy, suspecting them of "countertransference" connotations and detracting from the "pure gold" of analytic interpretations. In essence, then, Freud (and the majority of his followers) had little use for the curative aspects of the good human relationship, which is understandable in the light of the overweening attention lavished upon "technical factors" which were seen as the *raison d'être* of psychoanalytic therapy and its defining characteristic. While Freud was clearly aware that they were powerful therapeutic forces inherent in a good human relationship, he couched this realization in terms that had the effect of delaying their full exploration.[4] These forces, as noted earlier, are of course as much in need of explanation as any other aspect to which one might wish to pay attention.

The trained psychotherapist, whether he be a psychoanalyst or a behavior therapist, will reject as naïve the suggestion that a large segment of the therapeutic influence—that is, the motive power for therapeutic change—might be encompassed by "nonspecific" interpersonal factors which thus far have been highlighted in this exposition. On the basis of his clinical experience, he is deeply convinced that a good human relationship, which he might liken to the laying on of hands, sentimentality, moral treatment, or gross ignorance of the realities of therapeutic work, is severely limited in its therapeutic effects.

Obviously, there are no simple answers, but neither can the problem be ignored.

TWO PRINCIPLES

While every professional psychotherapist has deep commitments to some theoretical framework within which his therapeutic work is embedded, there is no evidence that one set of theoretical assumptions is more satisfactory than another — either in terms of what it permits the therapist to do or the outcomes to which it gives rise. A major investigation (Sloane *et al.*, 1975) failed to demonstrate significant differences between psychoanalytic and behavior therapy, and — at least equally important — suggested that the theoretical assumptions underlying seemingly divergent techniques are not differentiable in terms of demonstrable consequences. On the other hand, there is ample evidence that psychotherapy, by and large, appears to lead to beneficial outcomes (Meltzoff & Kornreich, 1970) and that the assessment of these outcomes is heavily dependent on one's choice of criteria. Furthermore, psychotherapy is always carried out within an interpersonal framework, even when the effects of the personality of the therapist or of the patient's relationship to the therapist are minimized — as in the studies by Lang and associates (1970) in which the patient ostensibly deals only with a computer. In all situations integrated for therapeutic purposes, the patient's attitudes, hopes, and expectations must play a highly significant role whose components must be more fully analyzed. Essentially, this segment of the therapeutic influence activates and capitalizes upon the patient's potential for *trust* in a nurturing figure whose origins are found in early childhood (Strupp, 1970).

We may, therefore, formulate the following principles:

Principle 1: Importance of the interpersonal relationship. All forms of psychotherapy are sustained by "nonspecific" (interpersonal) factors, and an appreciable segment of the therapeutic outcome is attributable to the therapist's interest, understanding, respect, dedication, empathy, and other human qualities which traditionally characterize a "good" human relationship and instill trust. These qualities alone may be expected to lead to personality and behavior changes in the patient which are generally described as "therapeutic."

Principle 2: Equivalence of therapeutic techniques. Identical therapeutic outcomes may be achieved by a variety of therapeutic techniques, all of which are anchored in, and potentiated by, the conditions stipulated in Principle 1. Since all therapeutic techniques are relatively broad gauged in application as well as effect, therapeutic outcomes — at least at the present state of knowledge and in the foreseeable future — cannot be used to validate a set of theoretical assumptions concerning therapeutic change. It follows that "crucial experiments" in psychotherapy are exceedingly unlikely. On the other hand, it is possible that a set of coherent theoretical assumptions may facilitate the therapist's work and perhaps lead to superior outcomes.

The second principle requires further exploration, which will presently be undertaken.

UNIQUENESS OF THE THERAPIST'S CONTRIBUTION

Let us start with the hypothetical situation that therapeutic outcomes produced by highly experienced professional psychotherapists are substantially equivalent to those mediated by untrained individuals (quasi-therapists) who provide a warm, accepting, and kind relationship. In this case (but also if the outcome were different) we would be brought face-to-face with the question concerning the professional psychotherapist's *unique* contribution. It is postulated that this contribution is encompassed by skillful management of an interpersonal relationship for the purpose of achieving therapeutic change. While this formulation may impress the professional psychotherapist as overly general and inclusive, it allows for the possibility that an untrained (in psychotherapy) individual, because of extensive life experience or native talents (or both), has developed skills which are substantially equivalent to those of the trained psychotherapist even though he proceeds on a more intuitive level.

If the repertoire of traditional therapeutic techniques is examined, it emerges that a sizable segment consists of strategies and maneuvers which are to be *avoided*. For example, the therapist is enjoined to avoid power struggles with a patient; he is instructed not to get entangled in the patient's machinations to seek approval, exploit, seduce, become dependent or involved, shirk responsibility, manipulate, etc. He is taught to listen attentively, to leave the initiative with the patient, to help him become aware of his own feelings, attitudes, etc. In short, he is cautioned against participation in neurotic games in which every patient seeks to involve a significant person and which are recognized as constituting the essence of his "illness." On the positive side, he is taught to establish rapport, facilitate the emergence of a therapeutic alliance, and in the context of such a relationship help the patient become aware of his self-defeating interpersonal techniques and the infantile goals he is pursuing.

In the process of acquiring skills in uncovering neurotic stratagems, the therapist is taught not to gratify the patient's neurotic maneuvers but rather to frustrate them by nonparticipation. Further, it is assumed that the process of dealing with the patient's self-defeating neurotic maneuvers will gradually lead to a reexperiencing of basic helplessness and, with it, early traumas. It is hypothesized that once these early experiences are lived through and assimilated, the patient will abandon them and a more mature adaptation will result. Ideally, this is to take place within an atmosphere of understanding and trust, in which the patient experiences at all times and in full measure the therapist's patience, understanding, equanimity, reasonableness, and rationality. He participates nonneurotically in the patient's constructive attempts to grow, master his irrational impulses, and come to grips with the significant problems in his life. Conversely, the therapist seeks to dissect neurotic strategies emerging in the interaction. In other words, the therapist (perhaps unwittingly) encourages and rewards the patient's constructive moves—e.g. efforts to assert himself, master avoidance tendencies, overcome passivity, and the like. Thus, while he encourages and supports adult (a loaded term!) behavior, he tacitly opposes infantile strivings, fantasies, and goals.[5] In other words, he steers, guides, rewards, punishes—that is, he manipulates the relationship toward therapeutic ends.

The burden of the preceding discussion is not to argue that the strategies and maneuvers employed by professional therapists are ineffective. Indeed, there can be little doubt that in the hands of competent individuals whose work is further characterized by persistence and dedication, therapeutic changes may reasonably be expected if patients are carefully chosen. Rather, my point is that *the psychological techniques employed by the professional psychotherapist are cognate to psychological principles by which any person influences the feelings and behavior of another. The therapist's operations may be much more sophisticated, subtle, and indirect, but he has no "special" forces at his command.*

To illustrate, Freud's original insights concerning the effective handling of a therapeutic relationship and the production of change (encompassed by such concepts as transference, countertransference, and the management of resistances) form the bedrock of psychoanalytic psychotherapy. They essentially consist of a humane, rational, and reasonably effective modification of neurotic behavior patterns. The same may be said about the gamut of extant therapeutic approaches, all of which are designed to undercut or extinguish certain kinds of behavior and to replace them with more efficient, adaptive, and satisfying performances. This is not to deny that at certain times and in certain contexts one technique (e.g. implosion, desensitization, a carefully timed interpretation) may be superior to another. In fact, *the art of psychotherapy may largely consist of judicious and sensitive applications of a given technique, delicate decisions of when to press a point or when to be patient, when to be warm and understanding or when to be more remote.*

What a theory of psychotherapy provides is a coherent framework for ordering clinical phenomena. It is a rationale or mythology (e.g. Frank, 1971) which aids the therapist's comprehension and self-confidence and in turn helps the patient to make sense out of his puzzlement and confusion. Accordingly, the therapist's explanations or interpretations may have considerable intellectual appeal to the patient, help him understand his infantile behavior in terms of his life history, and place painful childhood experiences in a new context. However, there is no necessary relationship between such understanding and therapeutic change.

Consequently, I propose a sharper distinction between the process of understanding clinical phenomena as gained through study of the patient's life history on the one hand and the modification of neurotic patterns by means of therapeutic interventions on the other. It appears that, from the beginning, psychoanalytic doctrine has considered the two processes intertwined (if not interchangeable) and postulated that understanding (insight) leads to therapeutic change. It is highly questionable whether such is the case—hard-core evidence is certainly lacking. In addition, there is ample evidence that the search for historical antecedents in and of itself is therapeutically futile (Thompson, 1950). We have learned that what is therapeutically effective is the dissection of neurotic processes and patterns that emerge in the context of the patient–therapist relationship.

This changed emphasis places into focus the study and analysis of interpersonal phenomena arising in the contemporary interaction between the two participants. In this sense, the psychotherapist deals with truly empirical data; while his knowledge of psychodynamic insights helps him understand contemporary transactions in terms of the past, his primary concern is the patient's interactions with significant persons in his current life, including, of course, most prominently, the therapist.

Another distinction is called for between psychotherapy as an educational or growth experience and psychotherapy as a technology for the achievement of behavior change.

The value of the psychoanalytic approach as an educational effort is well recognized and requires little defense, although in recent years it has come under intensified attack from critics who either do not understand its objectives and *modus operandi* or who deliberately reject the proposition that at least for certain patients the searching examination of motivations and their antecedents in a person's life history and the dispassionate analysis of these conflicts may be quite valuable. However, as a model for producing changes in behavior, the psychoanalytic model, despite the foregoing virtues, has been fairly unimpressive. Freud ingeniously and subtly amalgamated the two goals, but in order to do so he had to introduce certain techniques of "behavior management" which do not follow—either logically or technically—from the insight model. Analysts frequently make use of these techniques, but not in a systematic way. The result is a strange mixture of insight-producing and behavior-change strategies which are in great need of disentanglement.

For example, the technique of free association, as generally understood, is a means of gaining access to unconscious conflicts and hidden motivations. If the patient develops trust in the therapist, this also leads, usually by a circuitous route, to the identification and, hopefully, abreaction of traumatic (affectively charged) experiences. The latter, as has been shown by Gestalt therapy, psychodrama, implosive therapy, and other techniques, can often be accomplished by other means, although there remains Freud's seminal insight—dating back to his work with Breuer (Breuer and Freud, 1895)— that the discharge of dammed up affect has a certain, if not decisive, therapeutic effect.

What is not explicitly recognized, however, is that the technique of free association is also an exceedingly effective device for bringing the patient's behavior under the therapist's control. To the extent that analysts understand this, they recognize (although often not explicitly) that they manage (manipulate) the patient's behavior. Moreover, to the extent that they recognize this possibility, they subscribe to the position that effective behavior change occurs primarily when control is temporarily wrested from the patient and assumed by the therapist (Haley, 1963).

The important point, implicit in psychoanalytic formulations, is that the benign experience with the therapist *per se* will not result in a confrontation with repressed affects, but that a confrontation must be forced. This is accomplished through consistent and persistent work on the defenses, which indeed is seen as the central task of the therapeutic endeavor. It is rarely made explicit, however, what "work on the defenses" entails on the empirical level. While the backdrop of the theoretical formulations is presumably kept in mind, work on the defenses may be seen as a form of behavior management; operationally, this constitutes a significant segment of the therapeutic effort. The patient does not abandon a neurotic pattern of behavior (or "symptom") because he is exposed to the therapist's warmth, genuineness, and empathy, or because his expectations of help and succor are aroused by the therapist. To some extent, this is the case, but by and large it does not go very far; indeed, this is where many forms of "supportive therapy" stop. Instead, the patient is brought face-to-face with the reality that he cannot continue in psychotherapy *and* persist in the neurotic strategies he has been accustomed to. In other words, *the therapist structures the situation in bold relief such that the patient is forced either to renounce the helping relationship or to undergo change.*

This formulation somewhat overstates the point because a certain amount of change probably results from the therapist's skill in letting the patient deeply experience and cognitively appreciate the contradictions and futility of his previous attitudes, beliefs, strategies, and behavior. To bring basic issues into sharp relief without directly suggesting alternate courses of action strikes me as a unique therapeutic skill. Instead, the therapist helps the patient identify pieces of the jigsaw puzzle but lets the patient assemble them.

To return to the earlier theme, if the relationship has sufficient positive valence (which it has usually acquired after a period of understanding and support), the patient will opt for the latter alternative. Conversely, he will quit therapy, in which event he will typically rationalize his decision by reference to the therapist's lack of understanding, aloofness, hostility, or incompetence. If the therapist fails to force this kind of a decision, the patient will continue to use the therapeutic relationship to satisfy his dependency needs; he will exploit it in other ways and no change will occur.[6] What needs to be examined is how the therapist forces a choice. Such an examination will make explicit the role of the therapist as a technician of behavior change. As I will attempt to show, the model is substantially identical throughout therapy: It pits the patient's emotional attachment to the therapist (which also includes his "reasonable," "rational," "observing ego") against a symptom, striving, or behavior pattern, and forces a choice between the two.

EXAMPLES OF "BEHAVIOR MANAGEMENT" IN PSYCHOANALYTIC PSYCHOTHERAPY

To illustrate, I shall use four examples, including the management of (1) free associations, (2) infantile needs, (3) a "symptom," and (4) a neurotic behavior pattern.

1. Management of Free Associations

The groundwork for this example has already been laid and needs little further development. When the patient blocks, talks about trivia, or otherwise avoids dealing with "significant" (i.e. emotionally charged) material, the therapist informs him that he is abdicating the "basic rule," which is tantamount to the charge of failing to cooperate. In other words, he is violating the contractual arrangement whose full implications he could not possibly anticipate at the beginning of therapy. Or, we might say that he is not living up to his part of the bargain — to report all of his associations and to pay his bills. The former is really a very complex and contradictory task involving a sustained *active* effort to set aside and oppose reservations, shame, and other conveniences as well as a *passive* effort to report associations without first censoring or screening them. The latter, in effect, involves unlimited trust in the therapist and the security of the situation, the suspension of habitual security operations, and full acceptance of the "basic rule," which means unquestioned obedience to the therapist. None of this the

neurotic patient is prepared or able to do, partly because it entails the arousal of intense anxiety, partly because he has learned to be secretive, self-willed, and stubborn. Only to a limited extent is he clearly aware of what he is doing or the reasons underlying his behavior. The anxiety may relate to the arousal of affect surrounding traumatic experiences and—at least equally important—to the grave threat (never previously verbalized) of unconditionally placing one's fate in the therapist's (=the parent's) hands.

Given this arrangement of forces, the therapist says in effect: "You have ceased to cooperate, and I am showing you, by reference to your observable behavior, why I have come to this conclusion. If you will take an 'objective' look at the situation (appeal to the observing ego), we can both see what is happening. I don't know *why* you are doing this and neither do you. Our joint task is to find out. You have the following choice: You can decide to cooperate with me, thereby furthering the treatment (which is, of course, your reason for coming here), or you can continue as before, which costs you money and is getting us nowhere." A third alternative, usually not verbalized, is for the patient to quit therapy. Thus, it is clear what the patient must do in order to continue therapy, and if all goes well he makes the "right" choice, which the therapist has forced. If the tactic succeeds, the therapist has "analyzed" a piece of resistance, forced the patient to opt in favor of more implicit trust in the therapist, struck a blow to his self-will or narcissism ("I can do it all by myself"), and made him more pliable, obedient, "reasonable," and cooperative. In sum, the patient's "character" has changed, or his "ego" has been strengthened. I submit that this is one of the crucial alterations achievable in psychotherapy, although one should not conclude that a single successful tactic equals character change; as every therapist knows, repetitions are usually necessary, and—more important—a problem often needs to be dealt with from several perspectives and in different contexts.

Why has the therapist succeeded? He has appealed to (a) the patient's motivation to get help from an expert whom he respects, (b) the core of the patient's infantile trust (suggestibility) which listens to a "good" parent who has his best interest at heart, (c) his reasonable, rational ego which wants to cooperate with the therapist, and (d) he has structured the situation such that the patient is compelled to perceive a new *Gestalt* whose implications he can no longer distort, deny, or ignore. However, most important, he has *forced* a change.

Herein lies an important principle: *If one wishes to change a person's behavior, it is done most effectively by some form of manipulation (in the neutral sense) ; conversely, an ineffective way is for the therapist to tell the patient what he is after.*[7] In the foregoing example, the therapist provides only a *partial* explanation (reference to the "basic rule") without telling the patient about the "real" goal—behavior change.

The psychoanalytic psychotherapist's detachment and inscrutability, as advocated by Freud, permits a much more powerful influence than an attitude of "sharing" or "self-disclosing" recommended by other therapists. The former approach places the patient (for whose benefit the influence is ultimately exerted) on the defensive, in a "one-down" position, and forces intrapsychic as well as behavioral change. The therapist, as Haley (1963) astutely noted, arranges the situation so that change is forced. He does not tell the patient: "In order to help you change behavior X or symptom Y, I am going to proceed in the following manner . . ." and then explain his strategy. To do so would merely mobilize the patient's "resistances" and achieve the opposite of the desired result. The same strategy is also effectively used to force the patient to gain "insight" into the reasons for his behavior, by arranging the material so that the patient eventually gets the message, without the therapist's spelling it out. If the therapist is skillful in his task, he has created optimal conditions for "mutative" changes (previously attributed to "transference interpretations"). We cannot ignore the fact that in behavior therapy the therapist frequently explains the strategy he plans to pursue; however, in systematic desensitization, for example, the patient is forced to "opt" for relaxation as opposed to anxiety. In both cases, the patient must *experience* something—it is not the therapist's explanation in cognitive terms that matters.

It seems opportune to note another important reason, rarely mentioned in the literature, for the analytic therapist's distance. The typical neurotic patient is unduly influenced by, and dependent upon, other people's opinions of his feelings and actions, and he is continually alert to cues of approval or disapproval. This constellation forms part of the dependency which successful psychotherapy is designed to modify. Furthermore, such patients are exceedingly sensitive to other people's intrusiveness and their lack of respect for privacy, most of which have their origins in faulty parental attitudes. While the patient may resent intrusions, against which he had erected barriers of furtiveness and secrecy, he craves the very thing he abhors, since it signifies to him closeness, concern, intimacy, love, etc., irrespective of the fact that in his experience these have been counterfeit. By deliberately and consistently staying on the sidelines while permitting (and even forcing) the patient to own his feelings, the therapist manages to foster self-reliance and independence in the patient. Again, he teaches by example and by providing an authentic experience in living. While the patient learns a valuable lesson, the therapist simultaneously disappoints the patient's unspoken, unverbalized, but undeniably real wishes and expectations. The lesson may never be a topic for discussion or formal interpretation, but it is arranged and mediated by the therapist's consistent behavior.

Whether this transaction is truly "psychoanalytic" is perhaps a definitional problem. However, it is clearly grounded in principles of psychodynamics and behavior management. To the extent that he has diagnosed or identified the problem described above and tailored his behavior to bring about therapeutic learning, the therapist is functioning as a skillful change agent. Many therapists, I suspect, are not clearly aware of the kinds of learning they are mediating. Rather, they follow accepted rules (e.g. "analyse resistance first" or "from the surface down"). The result may still be therapeutically useful, since the patient's experience does not necessarily bear a one-to-one relationship to the therapist's intent. A quasi-therapist may intuitively or unwittingly produce a desirable distance between the patient's fear (and wish or expectation) of engulfment, thus also serving a therapeutic function. What is "unique" about the trained therapist's stance in this example— and perhaps in other situations—is his clinical experience with the mechanism I described which permits him to be sensitive to its implications. Therefore, he does not perform mechanically—because an authority has taught him to behave in a particular fashion—but his behavior is based on a clear awareness of neurotic mechanisms, their dynamics, implications, and their management. Regardless of whether one terms this process psychoanalytic, it is part of the therapeutic technology I am concerned with in this chapter. To state the issue another way: I submit that interpretations in the traditional sense may often be trivial whereas the interpersonal learning experience I have sketched is not. It seems to me that an adequate theory of technique must specify the essence of what is learned and the manner in which the learning is mediated, rather than treat it as a by-product. Psychoanalytic theory of technique has many lacunae of this kind.

2. Management of Infantile Needs

As Haley (1963) pointed out, the therapist encourages the patient to relate in "symptomatic" ways, together with the unspoken implication that this paradox will be used to effect therapeutic change. Numerous writers (MacAlpine 1950; Stone, 1961) have illuminated the patient's tendency to "regress" in the therapeutic situation. By encouraging the patient's self-expression while at the same time behaving in nonreciprocal ways, the therapist awakens in the patient a variety of infantile expectations and needs, such as dependency, the wish to be loved and coddled, as well as those affects which revolve around need-gratification and frustrations the patient had come to experience in childhood. In orthodox analysis these feelings are heightened by the therapist's relative remoteness and detachment which create a form of painful sensory deprivation. Since the patient generally becomes attached to the therapist (see Principle 1), the communications of the latter assume importance and significance which can perhaps best be understood by reference to a person in a hypnotic trance. The therapist's words, his approval or implied disapproval, his clarifications and interpretations — indeed every utterance—are experienced as manna from heaven by a patient who goes through the ordeal of reporting his associations for an hour four or five times every week. Since the therapist minimally gratifies emerging primitive needs and fantasies, the patient's continuing wish—and dread—that they somehow might be gratified by the therapist are dashed, with the results that his hopes turn into rage and negativistic behavior, by which in fantasy he seeks to control and punish the therapist for his lack of providing gratification.

The therapist deals with this impasse by focusing sequentially on the oppositional behavior, the underlying rage, the reasons for the rage, and ultimately on the patient's wish, fantasy, or need. Again he pits the reasonable, rational aspects of the therapeutic relationship against the patient's "neurotic" expectations. He thus forces the patient to modify his need by seeking gratification for it in some other relationship, reject it if it can be shown to be infantile and no longer useful in the patient's adult life, or to tolerate in awareness the tension occasioned by an unfulfilled need. He must then take action to satisfy it, abandon it, or modify it. What the therapist no longer permits him to do is to use the relationship with a significant person for the purpose of expressing his need in symbolic or disguised ways. The therapist says in effect: "If you want me to coddle you, baby you, protect you, love you, you must experience the feelings associated with these expectations in my presence and as directed toward me. This is predictably painful but it cannot be helped. Once you have undergone this painful experience, you may realize that your expectations were (a) anachronistic—that is, they may have been reasonable in childhood but are no longer useful; (b) unrealistic—that is, as a mature, independent adult I cannot possibly coddle you, and, if I did, you would be appalled by it and reject it; or (c) based on gross misperceptions of the current situation as well as that prevailing in your childhood, we must understand these distortions. What I will not allow you to do is to act as if you did not have these expectations of me while at the same time expecting me to fulfill them." This is what Freud meant when he said that a conflict must be raised to awareness and fought out on that level.

3. Management of a "Symptom"

Freud, as well as many therapists after him, realized that neurotic avoidance behavior, like a phobia, will not radically change as a result of "analytic" work. In other words, it is possible for a patient to have worked through the childhood antecedents, symbolic meanings, and other neurotic components of a phobia without being able to modify his behavior. In fact, the phobia problem may be seen as a paradigm for the assertion that "insight" in itself is usually not a sufficient condition for behavior change. On the contrary, the patient will typically attempt to use the gratifications available in the therapeutic situation to perpetuate his avoidance of anxiety-provoking situations he needs and (on a conscious level) wishes to master. I submit that such mastery is achieved if the therapist succeeds in pitting the therapeutic endeavor against the patient's anxieties and somehow persuades him that he will further the progress of therapy and maturity by doing what he experiences as unpleasant and anxiety-provoking. In the process he is given reassurance that he can return to the therapist for further work on the problem once the affect bound up with it has been remobilized in the outside world. In essence, this is no different from a parent who puts pressure on his fearful child to brave the cold water while at the same time communicating loving approval of the accomplishment, augmented by the implicit message that the child gains strength and self-confidence in the process so that he is growing up not merely to please the parent but to please himself.

4. Management of a Neurotic Behavior Pattern

The management of a neurotic behavior pattern is intrinsically identical to the management of a "symptom," and nothing new needs to be added. However, since in psychoanalytic psychotherapy neurotic patterns other than circumscribed neurotic symptoms (like a phobia) are typically dealt with, it appears useful to focus special attention on this problem. Every therapist worth his salt realizes that it is pointless to deal in generalities and that intelligent patients are remarkably adept at accepting a theoretical vocabulary which they use as a screen to hide personal and painful implications. The therapist who permits this to happen is inevitably courting defeat (which is really the patient's defeat). Therefore, it becomes important to immobilize as far as possible the patient's defenses and to further the emergence of transference phenomena whose analysis and demolition lead to "true" therapeutic change, as distinguished from pseudo-insights.

To illustrate: a male patient, for example, will recurrently talk about painful interactions with authority figures, situations in which he feels he is not asserting himself sufficiently or adequately. He will castigate his submissiveness and his feeling that he is "putty" in a powerful person's hands. Suppose the boss (with whom he is experiencing many of these problems) approaches the patient and asks him to entertain an important visitor who has unexpectedly come to town. The patient experiences the request as an imposition but because of his neurotic involvement with the boss (submission, rage, resentment, retaliatory fantasies, etc.) feels powerless to decline the request. So he agrees, but inwardly he fumes. Some of the accompanying affect is expressed in the therapeutic hour in the context of discussing the incident with the therapist. The latter may say casually: "I wonder why you did not tell him that you had other plans that evening?" Obviously, this is not a profound interpretation of the patient's dynamics, but it has important implications for the basic problem under scrutiny.

For one thing, the patient may feel that the therapist is on his side, and he may experience his comment as support for the possibility that he *might* assert himself at some future time. He may also feel that the therapist understands the predicament and encourages him to take what the patient considers appropriate action. (In that sense the therapist's comment is a "suggestion" for a course of action, the kind of thing perennially denigrated by orthodox analysts.) The patient may also feel that the therapist considers it acceptable for the patient to assert himself, about which the latter may have had doubts. Further, the patient may feel that if the therapist is not threatened by the patient's emerging assertiveness, perhaps he may also tolerate assertiveness directed at the therapist. Finally, the comment points out to the patient the automatic, irrational, and self-defeating aspects of his behavior.[8] The patient, however, may also be angry at the therapist for bringing to his awareness a fairly mundane possibility which might easily have occurred to him had he not been taken aback and thereby rendered passive by the boss's request. In other words, the problem might have been resolved differently had the patient been confronted with the problem in the abstract. What created the impasse was the patient's automatic and deeply ingrained tendency to acquiesce passively when confronted with a powerful (male) authority figure and then to resent it (a typical passive–aggressive maneuver).

Subsequent scrutiny of this and related incidents which will predictably occur may unearth fantasies about gratifications to be derived from submission to an authority figure (love, acceptance, protection, favors, homosexual implications, etc.). Sooner or later we may also expect that the patient will "act out" the pattern with the therapist in unrecognized ways. In any event, the therapist, having received ample advance warning, will be alert to subtle maneuvers of this kind. When such a maneuver occurs in therapy, when the circumstances are sufficiently clear (that is, the therapist realizes that he has done nothing to provoke submission in the patient and he feels sufficiently confident that the patient cannot misconstrue the situation), when a fair amount of affect is present, and when the patient is sufficiently open (undefended), the therapist can make a "transference interpretation" which summarizes in succinct fashion the various components that have previously been explored and worked through. The crux of the transference interpretation, in analytic terms, is that it is something "apart" from the therapist and the patient–therapist interaction, that it deals with the patient's intrapsychic rather than interpersonal dynamics, and that it contains no specific prescription for action, as would be the case in a suggestion. It is also asserted that "true" therapeutic change is due to the mutative effect produced by interpretations of this kind and that such changes are *intrinsically* different from other kinds of therapeutic interventions.

Undeniably there is nothing as vivid and as meaningful to a patient as present-day events, especially events transpiring in the powerfully charged patient–therapist relationship which continually revives the basic primitive components of the child–parent relationship. At the same time, of course, this relationship models a more mature adult–adult relationship[9] as well as a better child–adult relationship. Critics of psychoanalysis as well as many of its practitioners have frequently misunderstood the fulcrum upon which the therapeutic action turns. *Psychotherapeutic change does not depend on the elucidation of historical antecedents but on the reliving and modification of historically meaningful patterns that come alive in the patient–therapist relationship* in vivo.

FOCUS ON COMMON PSYCHOLOGICAL PRINCIPLES

The questions to be answered are: *What* has changed? *How* has the change been brought about? How can we *document* that change has occurred?

It is apparent that change occurs throughout therapy on many fronts and on many levels. Most important perhaps are inner changes of a cognitive sort—i.e. the patient comes to view himself, others, and the situations in which he functions in a different light. In part, these changes are brought about by more or less direct appeals to the patient's reason. More crucially, however, they are due to the reliving of traumatic experiences and the experiencing of painful affects surrounding present-day neurotic conflicts. All of this is made possible and carried forward by a constructive human experience with an understanding human being who provides a model of a reasonable, rational, and adult human relationship. Conversely, it

seems arbitrary to attribute change to any single class of therapeutic intervention or therapist's attitudes, as has typically been done by the various schools of psychotherapy. All of them are partially correct and it will be the task of the future[10] to delineate more sharply the forces at work. However, in accordance with Principle 2, it is improbable that we will make significant headway by concentrating on the claims advanced by different schools concerning the unique effectiveness of single techniques while ignoring common factors pervading all human interactions established for therapeutic purposes. As Frank (1973) stated: ". . . the therapeutic efficacy of rationales and techniques may lie not in their specific *contents*, which differ, but in their *functions*, which are the same" (emphasis supplied). This seems to be true particularly when we turn from the modification of isolated segments of behavior to the modification of lifestyles, interpersonal strategies, and self-defeating attitudes.

With regard to how change is brought about, I have attempted to show throughout this chapter that it is forged in the crucible of the patient–therapist relationship which, in various and often seemingly diverse ways, pits the patient's attachment to the therapist against the feelings and behaviors the patient unwittingly seeks to perpetuate. In this endeavor various techniques may be used to produce psychological and behavior change.

HIATUS BETWEEN THEORY AND TECHNIQUE

The question of how to document therapeutic change brings us back to a problem raised earlier. For practical purposes, the results of therapy must ultimately be assessed in terms of self-reports of feelings and behavior.[11] In contrast, I am pessimistic about the prospects of our being able to reach consensus on the kind of structural changes that psychoanalysis has considered basic to the therapeutic enterprise. The principal reason for his judgment is the inescapable necessity to insist on empirical referents. On the basis of empirical indicators, it may be possible to make clinical *inferences* concerning structural changes, but scant success along these lines does not inspire hope. To state the matter somewhat differently, there continues to be a vast hiatus between the technical operations of psychotherapy and the theoretical superstructure to which it has traditionally been referred. What is needed is a functional analysis of the technical operations and the changes to which they give rise rather than extrapolations from theoretical formulations, a practice which has been common in psychoanalytic writings but also in behavior therapy (see, for example, the incisive discussion by London, 1972, who makes a similar point).

To return once again to the example cited earlier, as a result of therapeutic interventions, the patient may become more self-assertive and less guilt-ridden when he turns down ("disappoints") his boss, and eventually he may be able to take this situation as a paradigm of other situations in which he must assert himself with authority figures. Or, he may at times acquiesce in the demand characteristics of such a situation but be more clearly aware of the problem and the reasons for his inward rebellion, which he may be able to modulate even if he cannot (because of external rather than internal exigencies) put his learning into action. In the latter case, he may acquiesce but refrain from traversing the previous neurotic cycle of rage, retaliatory fantasies, guilt, self-derogation, depression, and self-pity. Admittedly, clinical observers may have great difficulty in detecting such changes since the patient's observable behavior may provide only very inadequate clues. Thus, despite their well-known limitations, we must rely on the patient's self-report.

It may be argued that "structural" changes must have occurred as well—e.g. changes from "passivity" to "activity," gains in ego strength, etc. However, it is questionable whether such changes can be demonstrated apart from empirical indicators which are—at least potentially— capable of clinical assessment. The difficulties of assessing behavior and attitudinal change are of course formidable in their own right. The kind of behavior under discussion is subtle and not easily discerned by external observers. The patient may believe that a significant change in his behavior has occurred, but one would be hard put to find empirical evidence for it since the change may have been largely intrapsychic (for a notable exception, see Malan, 1975). The value of the change and the degree to which it can be considered an improvement is another matter that presents serious problems for the investigator. Finally, the change may not be the solution of a problem the patient had presented at the beginning of therapy, but perhaps it became isolated as a significant difficulty as therapy got underway. Hence it would prove difficult to obtain "before" and "after" measures of the kind typically used in psychotherapy

research. Despite these difficulties, we have no choice but to (a) define a problem identified as being in need of psychotherapeutic intervention; (b) delineate the techniques brought to bear upon its resolution, keeping in mind the complexities subsumed under Principles 1 and 2; and (c) measure the outcome in terms of empirical indicators, fallible though they be.

NEED FOR DIFFERENTIATION BETWEEN THEORY AND TECHNIQUE

On the basis of everything that has been said, it is likely that insight—i.e. understanding of the mainsprings of one's behavior—is one thing, while psychotherapy and the promotion of behavior change are another. Only if we assume, mistakenly, I believe, that insight and self-understanding are equivalent to, or the basis of, therapeutic change, or that insight leads to therapeutic change can the two be made to coincide. From the patient's vantage point, understanding a complex set of motivations, seeing the errors of one's ways, and recognizing the neurotic components of one's behavior has a certain utility, but it is a limited utility. Conversely, to be an analyst is not synonymous with being a therapist, as Freud unhappily led the world to believe. To the lasting detriment of legions of patients and the public at large, the profession has never learned the difference.[12]

PROSPECTUS FOR A REFORMULATION OF THERAPEUTIC TECHNOLOGY

Perhaps the most incisive operational statement of Freud's view of psychotherapy is found in a passage of his paper on "The dynamics of the transference" (1912):

> This struggle between the doctor and the patient, between intellect and instinctual life, between understanding and seeking to act, *is played out almost exclusively in the phenomena of transference. It is on that field that the victory must be won*—the victory whose expression is the permanent cure of neurosis. (p. 108; emphasis supplied)

Although embedded in an arcane and antiquated theoretical framework, this statement has profound implications for the understanding and future development of psychotherapy as a technique for the therapeutic management of an interpersonal relationship. At this stage, pending a major effort to develop the implications, it must suffice to summarize salient points in brief outline:

1. The most powerful vehicle for producing significant therapeutic change is an emotionally

charged interpersonal relationship. (This does not need to be a one-to-one relationship between a highly trained psychotherapist and a patient nor does it need to be confined to a standard therapeutic office setting.)

2. The effectiveness of psychotherapy is encompassed by the therapist's ability and skill to manage the interpersonal relationship, the kinds of significant emotional experiences he can mediate with the patient, and the patient's ability to benefit from these interventions. (The emphasis in this statement rests on the experiences the patient undergoes, the patient's openness or susceptibility to such experiences, and the therapist's ability to generate, catalyze, or produce them.)

3. Of crucial importance in psychotherapy are the *contemporary* transactions between the patient and therapist. Conversely, it is of minor importance what the patient "remembers" about the past or to "lift the infantile amnesia."[13] Transactions in the here-and-now prominently include reliving and understanding painful affects representing important residues of past experiences, interpersonal struggles for dominance or submission, and scrutiny of maladaptive interpersonal strategies the patient employs toward neurotic ends.

4. The psychotherapeutic experience, if successful, provides important lessons in reasonable, rational, and relatively nonconflictual human living. There are many ways in which such learning can be mediated, "interpretations" of distortions occurring in the patient–therapist relationship being only one, but probably not the most important one. The time has come to reject terms like "*the* transference" as one of many needlessly cumbersome and esoteric psychoanalytic concepts implying special psychological processes requiring special explanatory constructs apart from the dynamics governing all human relationships.

5. The formal techniques of psychotherapy commonly discussed in the literature are instances of techniques commonly used to influence, direct, and guide human behavior. To cite but one example, if a child is afraid of the water, the parent tries to reason with him, takes him by the hand, sets an example of fearlessness, persuades him, etc. Occasionally he may even throw him in or force him to enter the water so he can come to this rescue. Under optimal circumstances, he is benign, respectful, understanding, and kind. The problem for the psychotherapist is that the patient has had a host of unfortunate experiences, as a result of which

he will not readily accept the therapist as a trustworthy helper. It takes time to overcome these "resistances." Due to compounded traumas and other deficiencies in parental guidance, the patient has developed chronic ("characterological") strategies for warding off dangers, intrusions, oppression, etc. Therapy is designed to rectify these. The techniques of psychotherapy serve to alleviate early traumas, to bring troublesome interpersonal strategies into bold relief, to provide guidance and support, and in general to help the patient "grow up." The task is often complicated because human beings are symbol-making and symbol-reacting creatures, and their behavior is influenced by fantasies, distortions, misunderstandings, unrealistic beliefs, expectancies, etc.

Freud's basic insights into the origins of neurotic problems and their potential resolution through a therapeutic relationship have unfortunately been shrouded in and obscured by an unwieldy and archaic theory of instincts, intrapsychic dynamics, mental apparatuses, etc. As a result, sight has been all but lost of what psychotherapy might accomplish. In recent years, progress has been made (though largely outside of psychoanalysis) to take stock of the techniques at our disposal and the manner in which such techniques—not merely free association and interpretations—might be used in optimal ways. In short, there exists a thorough confusion between formulations of intrapsychic dynamics and therapeutic activities directed toward reasonably specific therapeutic ends. The alleged distinction between "psychoanalysis" and "psychotherapy" is a pseudo-problem *par excellence* which bespeaks the prevailing confusion. The alleged distinction between "suggestion" and "analysis" is subject to the same criticism.

6. There are three major techniques for changing human feelings and behavior: (a) a person becomes persuaded that change is in his own interest—that is, he gains "insight" or sees the "errors of his ways"; (b) circumstances are arranged such that he is *forced* to change his behavior; and (c) largely overlapping the former, he undergoes learning experiences which change his expectancies, values, performances, etc. The techniques of all forms of psychotherapy fall under these rubrics. There are no categorical differences between schools, techniques, and therapeutic outcomes nor do they differ intrinsically from other human influence processes. While some techniques may be more effective than others under particular circumstances and with different patients, there are probably def-

inite limits which psychotherapy cannot expect to transcend. One may hazard a guess that the field may not be too distant from these limits. By this I mean that there are upper bounds to what human learning (including "mental healing" as a subform) can achieve. Psychoanalysis has considerably sharpened our understanding of these limits.

7. In accordance with the preceding statements, the psychotherapist's skills are those of an expert in (a) mediating a constructive human experience and (b) identifying, neutralizing, and counteracting those of the patient's tendencies which produce serious emotional entanglements with significant others. While Freud's classical procedure (via the reinstitution and resolution of a quasi-parent–child relationship) represented one approach, there is no reason to suppose that it is the only or the best one, although it does have unique features which commend it for certain patients. Trained psychotherapists are presumably more clearly aware of intrapsychic and interpersonal dynamics such as self-defeating, exploitative, and devious tendencies by which patients unwittingly seek to sabotage interactions designed for therapeutic purposes (beyond interactions with other significant people). Again, Freud, more than any other person, contributed incisive observations about the tactics which patients have learned to use to evade facing reality. As part of the constructive experience mentioned under (a), the therapist sets an example of reasonable, mature adult behavior, and he encourages or models the kinds of interpersonal learning experiences which may serve as corrections and extensions of parental-type influences which are known to have a salutary effect.

In conclusion, *the therapist's ability to understand the genetic origins and psychodynamics of feelings, attitudes, and behaviors is not tantamount to an ability to produce therapeutic change. This, in my estimation, was Freud's cardinal error which has been perpetuated by subsequent generations of psychoanalysts.* To be sure, Freud's revolutionary discoveries have taught us a great deal about the potentialities of psychotherapeutic change as well as its limitations (e.g. Freud, 1937). His views were of course heavily supported by his philosophical belief in the power of man's reason and rationality, with the concomitant conviction that *insight* would somehow subdue irrational strivings (understanding→ control→rational living). To some extent this is true but, as Freud also recognized, the weight of therapeutic change is not carried by reason but by the emotional relationship—i.e. the interpersonal experience between the patient and the therapist.

What the field now needs is a thorough shakedown leading to clearer and more straightforward formulations concerning the effects of more sharply delineated therapeutic interventions (the human influence) and the forces facilitating or impeding therapeutic change (patient factors). To some extent, it may be possible to perfect mechanical (conditioning) techniques for modifying human behavior; to some extent, it may be possible to use pharmacological agents toward these ends; however, in the end it is a significant human experience (kairos, *Erlebnis*) which provides the most powerful therapeutic leverage.[14] Our knowledge of the ingredients of such an experience and how an optimal match between patient and therapist can be brought about is as yet very scant. Indeed, it may not be possible to instrument it in a highly controlled and predictable way. But in the search we may learn a great deal about the limitations of our approaches, the reasons for our failures, and we may emerge with a better understanding of what, at least in principle, are the most propitious conditions (Marmor, 1973). Some modified form of the psychodynamic model will undoubtedly be part of such a framework.

REFERENCES

ALEXANDER, F. & FRENCH, T. M. *Psychoanalytic therapy: Principles and application.* New York: Ronald Press, 1946.

BANDURA, A. *Principles of behavior modification.* New York: Holt, Rinehart & Winston, 1969.

BERGIN, A. E. The evaluation of therapeutic outcomes. In A. E. BERGIN & S. L. GARFIELD (Eds.), *Handbook of psychotherapy and behavior change.* New York: Wiley, 1971. Pp. 217–270.

BERGIN, A. E. & STRUPP, H. H. *Changing frontiers in the science of psychotherapy,* 1972. Chicago: Aldine-Atherton.

BREUER, J. & FREUD, S. Studies on hysteria (1895). *The standard edition of the complete psychological works of Sigmund Freud.* Vol. 2. London: Hogarth Press, 1955. Pp. 1–305.

DAVISON, G. C. & WILSON, G. T. Process of fear-reduction in systematic desensitization: Cognitive and social reinforcement factors in humans. *Behavior Therapy,* 1973, **4,** 1–21.

EYSENCK, H. J. The effects of psychotherapy: An evaluation. *Journal of Consulting Psychology,* 1952, **16,** 319–324.

EYSENCK, H. J. The effects of psychotherapy. *International Journal of Psychiatry,* 1965, **1,** 97–178.

FISKE, D. W., HUNT, H. F., LUBORSKY, L., ORNE, M. T., PARLOFF, M. B., REISER, M. F., & TUMA, A. H. Planning of research on effectiveness of psychotherapy. *Archives of General Psychiatry,* 1970, **22,** 22–23.

FRANK, J. D. Therapeutic factors in psychotherapy. *American Journal of Psychotherapy,* 1971, **25,** 350–361.

FRANK, J. D. *Persuasion and healing.* (2nd Ed.) Baltimore: Johns Hopkins Press, 1973.

FREUD, S. The future prospects of psycho-analytic therapy (1910). *The standard edition of the complete psychological works of Sigmund Freud.* Vol. 11. London: Hogarth Press, 1957. Pp. 139–152.

FREUD, S. Papers on technique (1911–1915). *The standard edition of the complete psychological works of Sigmund Freud.* Vol. 12. London: Hogarth Press, 1958. Pp. 85–173.

FREUD, S. The dynamics of transference (1912). *The standard edition of the complete psychological works of Sigmund Freud,* Vol. 12. London: Hogarth Press, 1958. Pp. 99–108.

FREUD, S. Transference. *The standard edition of the complete psychological works of Sigmund Freud.* Vol. 16. London: Hogarth Press, 1963. Pp. 431–447.

FREUD, S. Analysis terminable and interminable (1937). *The standard edition of the complete psychological works of Sigmund Freud.* Vol. 23. London: Hogarth Press, 1964.

HALEY, J. *Strategies of psychotherapy.* New York: Grune & Stratton, 1963.

LANG, P. J., MELAMED, B. G., & HART, J. A psychophysiological analysis of fear reduction using an automated desensitization procedure. *Journal of Abnormal Psychology,* 1970, **76**, 220–234.

LONDON, P. The end of ideology in behavior modification. *American Psychologist,* 1972, **27**, 913–920.

MACALPINE, I. The development of the transference. *Psychoanalytic Quarterly,* 1950, **19**, 501–539.

MALAN, D. H. Psychodynamic changes in untreated neurotic patients. *Archives of General Psychiatry,* 1975, **32**, 110–126.

MARMOR, J. The future of psychoanalytic therapy. *American Journal of Psychiatry,* 1973, **130**, 1197–1202.

MELTZOFF, J. & KORNREICH, M. *Research in psychotherapy.* New York: Atherton Press, 1970.

PAUL, G. L. Behavior modification research: Design and tactics. In C. M. FRANKS (Ed.), *Behavior therapy: Appraisal and status.* New York: McGraw-Hill, 1969. Pp. 29–62.

SHAPIRO, A. K. Placebo effects in medicine, psychotherapy and psychoanalysis. In A. E. BERGIN & S. L. GARFIELD (Eds.), *Handbook of psychotherapy and behavior change.* New York: Wiley, 1971. Pp. 439–473.

SLOANE, R. B., STAPLES, F. R., CRISTOL, A. H., YORKSTON, N. J., & WHIPPLE, K. *Psychotherapy vs. behavior therapy.* Cambridge, Mass.: Harvard University Press, 1975.

STONE, L. *The psychoanalytic situation.* New York: International Universities Press.

STRUPP, H. H. Patient–doctor relationship: Psychotherapist in the therapeutic process. In A. J. BACHRACH (Ed.), *Experimental foundations of clinical psychology.* New York: Basic Books, 1962. Pp. 576–615.

STRUPP, H. H. Specific vs. nonspecific factors in psychotherapy and the problem of control. *Archives of General Psychiatry,* 1970, **23**, 393–401.

STRUPP, H. H. On the basic ingredients of psychotherapy. *Journal of Consulting and Clinical Psychology,* 1973, **41**, 1–8.

STRUPP, H. H., FOX, R. E., & LESSLER, K. *Patients view their psychotherapy.* Baltimore: Johns Hopkins Press, 1969.

THOMPSON, C. *Psychoanalysis: Evolution and development,* 1950. New York: Hermitage House.

TRAUX, C. B. & CARKHAUFF, R. R. *Toward effective counseling and psychotherapy: Training and practice,* 1967. Chicago: Aldine.

NOTES

1. An earlier version of this chapter appeared in the *International Journal of Psychiatry*, 1973, **11**, 263–327, under the title "Toward a Reformulation of the Psychotherapeutic Influence." Sections are reproduced by permission.

2. *Editors' Footnote.* See Chapter 20 (this volume) by Wilson and Evans for a fuller discussion of this issue in the context of behavior therapy.

3. *Editors' Footnote.* See Rabkin's chapter (Chapter 8) in this volume for a fuller consideration of this issue. Our notes in her chapter represent some of our ideas about this very serious problem, which affects outcome research, definitions of mental health and illness, and certainly the daily practice of psychotherapy.

4. Freud's (1917) formulation of the transference is typical: "what turns the scale in his [the patient's] struggle is not his intellectual insight—which is neither strong enough nor free enough for such an achievement—but *simply and solely his relation to the doctor*" (p. 445; emphasis supplied).

5. More precisely, he seeks to drive a wedge between a wish and fantasied action. He promotes acceptance of the wish or fantasy but discourages action (acting out).

6. Client-centered therapists naively deny the dependency occurs or that it is a salient problem, but they may be correct in saying that the problem is partly iatrogenic. There can be no doubt that psychoanalysts, by encouraging regression in the analytic situation, at the same time fan the patient's strivings for dependency. The purpose, of course, is to "analyze" the dependency when it emerges in "the transference." It is an open question, to what extent this detour is necessary. It is quite possible, for instance, that there are other—more efficient and effective—ways to helping the patient overcome his dependency and other infantile needs. The work by Alexander and French (1946) is one notable example of work designed to question and improve traditional techniques. What is remarkable, however, is the relative lack of comparable efforts. Such has been the persistence of dogma and dogmatism in psychoanalysis!

7. *Editors' Footnote.* For a contrasting view in this volume, see Chapter 15 by Johnson and Matross and Chapter 20 by Wilson and Evans.

8. One might speculate that role-playing the situation with the therapist, as might be advocated by rational–emotive or Gestalt therapists, would achieve the same goal, perhaps in even more dramatic fashion. It is a moot question whether a discussion of the problem and its ramifications in psychoanalytic therapy would facilitate therapeutic learning. It is important to note, however, that in good psychoanalytic practice such discussions do not occur in the abstract but *in the context* of the patient's current emotional experience— a point that is widely misunderstood.

9. An important lesson learned in psychotherapy, particularly in the more intensive variety, is the lesson of human cooperation in achieving *mutual* goals. On a general level, the patient must gain the experience that if he works constructively with the therapist, the latter will provide constructive help. For example, if the patient works hard at overcoming his inhibitions and secretiveness, the therapist will help him to understand the data and "reward" him through interpretations, clarifications of symbolic meanings, etc. Conversely, the therapist responds with silence and minimal communications to resistive maneuverings. The therapist must learn to gauge his participation in terms of this balance or the patient will fail to appreciate the difference. Since patients have typically learned to dominate powerful adults by negativism, passive–aggressiveness, exploitativeness, etc., as a function of having been dominated, oppressed, and exploited by their parents, the lesson of cooperation and mutuality is one of the most important nonverbal kinds of learning mediated by a skilled therapist. It is amazing how little attention (Erikson being an exception) is paid by major theories to this subtle but powerful function of psychotherapy, and yet

it is clearly one of the most important lessons in living that psychotherapy can provide.

10. Freud's (1910) goal as expressed in the following quotation, remains to be realized six decades later: "when we *know* all that we now only *suspect* and when we have carried out all the improvements in technique to which deeper observation of our patients is bound to lead us, our medical procedure will reach a degree of precision and certainty of success which is not to be found in every specialized field of medicine" (p. 146).

11. *Editors' Footnote.* There is a consensus among several authors in this volume (Fiske, for example, and both editors) that the best *single* source of outcome ratings is the patient. We feel, however, that there are potential problems with using only this single source (see Chapter 2 by Fiske, and our footnotes on this issue), so that our inclination is to use multiple (therapist, patient, judge) ratings wherever possible.

12. Freud's celebrated self-analysis is a case in point. He must have concluded (and convinced his disciples) that he changed significantly as a result of the insights he gained. Perhaps he did, having confirmed his anticipated theories, but if psychotherapeutic change is crucially dependent upon a human interaction, Freud could not possibly have been his own therapist. As Bernfeld remarked: "The trouble with self-analysis is the counter-transference." From the vantage point of psychotherapy as an interpersonal process for changing behavior, Freud's self-analysis is as much a miracle as Jesus walking on the waters of the Sea of Galilee. It has become an article of faith. .

13. It is being realized that the clinician's ability to trace the etiology of a phobia or a neurotic disorder to its childhood antecedents does not necessarily imply that therapeutic interventions in order to be effective have to traverse the same historical course in reverse. The theory of psychoanalytic therapy has never succeeded in freeing itself from this crucial working assumption, which in my judgment is a cardinal error. The lack of impressive therapeutic results supports my position.

14. *Editors' Footnote.* There are many, including us, who would disagree with this statement as it now reads. Most, though admittedly not all, work on chemotherapy with psychoses and severe affective disorders has found chemotherapy to be the most powerful single modality. We would agree with Strupp's statement, then, if it were qualified to refer to nonpsychotic disturbances.

CHAPTER 2

METHODOLOGICAL ISSUES IN RESEARCH ON THE PSYCHOTHERAPIST[1]

Donald W. Fiske

THE contribution of the therapist to effective psychotherapy is a matter of great social concern. Psychotherapy is administered extensively at considerable expense. How effective is it? What determines its effectiveness? In particular, what does the therapist contribute? Our society is clearly entitled to expect answers to these questions. Psychology and the related fields represented in the practice of psychotherapy have an obligation to meet such expectations for answers about this application of psychological knowledge.

Research on this topic utilizes the methodology which the discipline of psychology has developed for basic as well as applied investigations. Both kinds of research involve much the same central issues: principles of effective research design, strategies for adequate measurement, adequacy of conceptualizations of major constructs, and linkages between constructs and measuring operations. Thus, in considering the methodological issues in evaluating the therapist's contribution to effective psychotherapy, we are examining issues which are much the same as those involved in the study of personality and some other fields of psychology. The investigation of personality change is but one part of the comprehensive investigation of the domain of personality.

In this chapter, the term methodology is used in a broad sense, with several facets. It refers to specific methods for conducting research, including procedures for making observations and for converting observations to measurements. It also refers to strategies for empirical studies and research programs. It includes consideration of conceptualization and links between constructs and observations. Finally, it embraces statistics and psychometrics. This chapter will address most of these several topics as they bear on the subject matter of this volume. It will not attempt to cover the general principles of research design as applied to psychotherapy research. Discus-

sions of these matters (cf. Fiske, Hunt, Luborsky, Orne, Parloff, Reiser, & Tuma, 1970; Goldstein, Heller, & Sechrest, 1966; Kiesler, 1971) are based on the study of psychotherapy as it is construed and investigated today. The emphasis in this chapter will be on more fundamental, underlying issues, considering the actual phenomena of psychotherapy, including what goes on in treatment and also the patient's behavior before and after treatment and between treatment sessions.

Many of the analytical and evaluative statements made in this chapter have been made by others. What is new is the consideration of the sufficiency of the recommendations and prescriptions as offered in the published literature. For example, will more careful definitions and better attempts at operationalizing the central constructs be enough to enable researchers to make substantial progress in understanding psychotherapy? Can the warmth of the therapist be measured by an objective psychological thermometer (or are those modifiers mutually exclusive to some extent)? Perceived qualities of the therapist fluctuate from patient to patient and from time to time within a session (Gurman, 1973). They also interact with each other. The author is convinced that there is a definite ceiling to what can be reached by even the most diligent and persevering efforts to improve our present approaches to the investigation of therapists and therapy, and that this ceiling is very close to where we are now. Basic research on personality as it is construed today is close to its limit (Fiske, 1974). What major advances have been made in recent decades? *Ad hoc* research on psychotherapy as an applied social problem may have more of a future.

ANALYSIS OF THE QUESTION

The topic of the therapist's contribution is an area of research, not an empirical question.

There can be no exact, unequivocal answer to the question, "What is the contribution of the therapist to effective psychotherapy?" any more than one can answer the question, "How do parents affect the development of their children?" The terms in our question are highly general: what therapists, what patients, what treatments, what outcomes? In this chapter, as in this volume as a whole, the emphasis is on just two of these major components: the therapists and the outcomes.

The central question cannot be directly investigated in a scientific manner. The multiple instances of psychotherapeutic treatment are clearly not a homogeneous class of events. Science studies regularities and replications, not individual occurrences. Many psychotherapists would assert that no therapeutic treatment is exactly the same in all important respects as any other. Yet research has been done, and rightly so. There are regularities and similarities. It is possible to set up categories so that the members of each class are more similar to each other than they are to members of other classes. Patients can be sensibly classified or ordered, quite well on demographic variables and less well on degree of distress and other aspects of their state. Therapists can be described in terms of demographic and background variables, and also in terms of their behavior during therapy. Aspects of outcomes can be assessed by observers in various roles. So, although great precision is not possible, some systematic investigations can be carried out, as the published literature amply demonstrates. The question becomes: What kinds of therapists administering what psychotherapeutic treatments to what kinds of patients produce what kinds of perceived effects, both immediate and ultimate?

The programmatic investigation of therapists' contributions is, however, not merely a matter of establishing a few classes for each component (therapist, treatment, patient, and outcome) and studying each of the dozens of combinations of one instance from each component. There are obviously interactive effects, such as the highly relevant interactions for certain combinations of therapists and patients. Given the enormous complexity of the phenomena under study, what can we do?

Some guidance is provided by recognizing that, while a single empirical study has value, it does not establish any fact or principle. It may provide strong suggestions as to possible relationships, it may increase by one step our subjective confidence in some general proposition, or it may point to variables which appear to

make substantial contributions to the variance. Science builds not on the single study but on sets of studies with similar findings. The goal is replicated findings, with the replications being obtained by varied investigators working in varied settings, and preferably by varied methods of observation and data collection. While that goal is quite remote in psychotherapy research, we must work toward it. One essential and feasible step is to make sure that reports of psychotherapy research contain the information essential to appraising each investigation and to determining the similarities between investigations (Fiske *et al.*, 1970). Another step is the uniform use of some standardized measuring procedures for describing the therapist, the patient, the outcomes (Waskow & Parloff, 1975), and (eventually) the treatment process itself.

The question can also be asked in a different way. Exactly how does the therapist contribute to the effectiveness of treatment? How do the discrete, minute acts of the therapist affect the next actions of the patient? A typical level of conceptualization stresses the experience which the therapist provides the patient, experience which alters his subsequent experiences outside of treatment. Can that initial experience be analyzed into particular sequences of acts, each act being very brief? Such sequences may be a therapist act and the next patient act, or a patient-therapist-patient series. Do certain kinds of sequences, or certain progressions of sequences occur more frequently in treatments which are judged by the usual global assessments to have been more successful? *Although some research has involved judgments about characteristics of whole treatment sessions or of 5-minute segments, almost nothing has been done on moment-to-moment interactions. Is this not where the treating actually takes place?*[2]

CHARACTERISTICS OF THERAPIST AND OUTCOME MEASURES

Measures of the therapist and of the outcome suffer two limitations which are pervasive in personality research—generality and indirectness. The personality of the therapist is assessed in broad terms, such as "committed" or "empathic," without restriction as to time and place. No therapist is empathic under all conditions. No therapist is empathic all the time he is treating or even throughout the treatment of one patient. Measures of empathy are averages or general summaries. It is purely an article of faith to assume that the therapist's empathy at critical moments in treatment is well estimated by the overall score or rating assigned to him.

Similarly, the ex-patient may be asked how much he gained from the treatment. His response to each question of a post-therapy questionnaire is taken as the central tendency of his perception of his improvement. He knows and we know that at times he is now functioning very well, but at times he functions no better than he did before treatment.

We use such general measures for two reasons. We tend to think in simplistic, global terms about people and about consequences of treatment; we also want to economize on respondent time in giving information and on our time in making analyses. But great care must be taken in selecting the procedure for obtaining judgments. Mintz and Luborsky (1971) found that an optimal empathic relationship factor obtained from judgments of whole sessions had only a low correlation with a corresponding factor based on judgments of brief segments from each of these sessions. While general measures may be useful as a first approximation, it is obvious that they conceal a considerable degree of variation and they reduce a mass of information to a single value. What we really want to know is the effect which follows the therapist's conveying to the patient the feeling that he has an empathic understanding of what the patient is saying and feeling, and the effect when the therapist conveys the opposite message.

A measure applied to a whole hour of therapy conceals much variation. For example, the therapist's empathy, warmth, and genuineness fluctuate during a single hour (Gurman, 1973). Perhaps the effectiveness of an hour is determined less by the average value on empathy than it is by the extent of highly accurate empathy. Effectiveness may be even more a function of the degree to which the therapist manifests accurate empathy at particularly appropriate moments—i.e., what Gurman describes as "empathic specificity."

These general measures are not identified with particular moments in time. It is obvious that only what exists at a moment or what occurs at a moment can affect the patient. *It is the effects of the therapist's actions, each at its moment in time, which have any possibility of contributing to the patient's immediate benefit. When we look for relationships between two general variables, we are ignoring the fundamental question of how one characteristic of a therapist's act may contribute to one step toward patient improvement.*

Related to generality is indirectness. Classification of therapists into the A-B typology (see Razin's discussion in Chapter 12, this volume) is done at some time and in some setting far removed from the locus of treatment. We assume that such a labeling is related to what transpires in the treatment process. The significant studies are those that indicate how a personality attribute of therapists is associated with in-treatment behaviors which are highly therapeutic. But if we can identify such behaviors, is it necessary to study the therapist's personality?[3]

Personality Measures as Perceptions and Cognitions

Descriptions of the therapist's personality are based on perceptions and cognitions. The therapist may be asked to report how he perceives some aspect of his behavior. The patient may be asked how he sees the therapist's dispositions. Thus, many of the variables applied to therapists require someone to perceive, cognize, interpret, and label the behavior of the therapist and then to record the result of that complex process. (This requirement holds particularly for the first several categories listed in the Levels of Analysis section, below.)

Even assessments of the therapist's behavior during therapy require perceptions and cognitions as the basis for someone's reported judgment. Ideally, that observer should be the patient: it is presumably the patient's perception and experience of the therapist's warmth, empathy, and genuineness which really matter.[4] Yet patient perceptions may or may not be correlated with perceptions of judges (see Gurman, Chapter 19, this volume). Bergin and Suinn (1975) have noted that even in studies where tape-rated empathy was not related to outcome, patient-perceived empathy may be so related.

Similar processes are involved in most outcome measures. Someone makes a judgment about the ex-patient's ease or dis-ease, his interpersonal relationships, his work effectiveness, etc.

It can be argued with considerable justification that such use of human perception and judgment is quite appropriate in the study of psychotherapy. After all, how a person is seen by others is highly relevant to decisions about the desirability of treatment and evaluations of outcome. These others include significant people in his life, associates on the job, etc. Even a diagnostician's appraisal falls into this category.

And the patient's perception and cognition of himself is, of course, fundamental.

The researcher must recognize the necessity of using judgments in measuring patient status after treatment. He may even go so far as to consider them inevitable. What important aspects of assessed outcome entirely avoid the use of human judgment? Are there any direct and completely objective measures for significant aspects of outcome? The only instances would seem to occur when the therapy is aimed at a specific overt behavior, such as smoking or stuttering. While the remission of a single symptom may be judged with adequate agreement among observers, the assessment of overall symptom relief requires an integrative judgment.

A researcher may wish to argue that he utilizes such judgments for lack of any more adequate procedure, that he takes these data as estimates of some underlying reality. It seems unwise, however, to work conceptually with assumed true variables which are simply too many steps removed from observations to be more than speculative. *The researcher can never feel much confidence that any empirically observed relationship indicates the relationship between two inferred constructs remotely linked to his observed variables.*

The researcher could argue that his true score is defined as the average of an infinite number of ratings of the therapist. Granted that one set of ratings, or the average of a few sets, can provide an estimate for that true score, such an estimate is of limited or unknown quality. Above and beyond these considerations, it is a true score for judgments by the class of raters used; there must be a different true score for other sets of raters. Thus, if a therapist's peers rate him, the concept assessed is not the same as that which is measured by his patients' ratings of him on the same printed scale.

The point is that *most personality assessments are one person's integrative judgments summarizing his perceived experiences with the person described. These assessments are entirely appropriate insofar as the phenomena of personality which we are trying to understand are our own and other people's perceptions and construing of people; most personality phenomena are just that.*

To assert that the patient's and the therapist's personality attributes are the cognitions of people does not deny their reality. It simply states that what is real is how the patient, for example, is perceived by each person with whom he interacts, and by himself. There is a real

patient for each perceiver, but these real patients are only more or less similar to each other: they are not exactly the same; there is no one real patient. We are not talking philosophy here—we are talking psychology. The perceiver's picture of the patient has substantial psychological consequences. It is a major determinant in how the perceiver interacts with the patient.

Limitations of Ratings

Almost instantly when someone perceives another person, he begins to form impressions of that other. Even if these impressions are not verbalized, they undoubtedly affect how he interacts with the other. The impressions are put into words when one thinks about the other subsequently or when one describes the other to a third person. They are also put into words when a researcher asks for descriptions. Words are used in almost every form of data collection in personality. These words are invariably imprecise to some degree; aside from their diverse connotations, their denotations are not specific and objective. They differ greatly from technical terms in the natural sciences. Most importantly, their meanings are not exactly the same for different people—for example, words referring to frequency have a range of interpretations (Hakel, 1968).

Our immediate concern, however, is with the implications for research on the therapist's contributions. The use of human judgments inevitably introduces noise and undependability into the data. Two judges never agree exactly on their perceptions of a person. The degree of agreement appears to increase with the specificity of the rating scale and the availability of direct relevant experience to the judges. When the judgments are based on different sets of experience with the person rated, they become even less consistent.

Psychotherapy research is seriously handicapped when it relies on human integrators for its data. The modest levels of agreement, the relatively limited degree of common variance between raters is important but not necessarily critical. What is critical is the fact that the variance unique to one judge is not random but biased. His particular interpretations of the words used in the rating scale, his reactions to the task of rating the therapist or the patient, and his response sets can all contribute significant distortion to his data. While the researcher must recognize these influences and do all that he can to minimize their effects, he must also accept the inevitability of some influences from this source.

A rating is thus the product of the complex interactions among three components: the rater's perceptions and interpretations of both the task given to him and the particular scales set before him, the past experience on which he is to base his ratings, and his current mental processes as he recalls that experience and relates it to the judgments required of him. The recalling and interpreting of the prior experience can be influenced by such things as expectations. For example, Kent, O'Leary, Diament, and Dietz (1974) report that global evaluations of change in disruptive classroom behaviors were affected by induced expectations, although coding of the nine disruptive behaviors as they were observed on the videotapes were not affected. (Cf. Shweder, 1975, for other evidence that the raters' conceptual framework influences *post hoc* ratings but not immediately recorded behaviors.)

The Measurement of Effectiveness of Psychotherapy

Although this volume is primarily concerned with research on the therapist, some consideration of measuring outcome is needed. Outcome is not a unitary variable. It is an appraisal from some perspective. It can be judged by a professional—one who is involved (the therapist) or one who is not involved (a diagnostician). It can be judged from the perspectives of those who know the patient in his home, at work, or at play. It can be reported by the patient himself. There is a considerable degree of consensus in reports of therapy research on the distinctiveness and the relative independence of outcome judgments from these several perspectives. (Mintz, however, develops a different position in Chapter 22 of this volume.) While some low correlations among appraisals from different viewpoints have been reported (e.g., Berzins, Bednar, & Severy, 1975), it is quite clear that each source of assessment is sufficiently independent of the others to require its separate consideration (Fiske, 1975).

The crucial consequence of distinctiveness among outcome measures is that they are not interchangeable. Measured gain or deterioration (cf. Lambert, Bergin, & Collins, Chapter 17, this volume) differs with the measure used. Each measure has its own pattern of relationships. For example, therapist expectancies have been found to relate particularly to reports of outcome from the patient (Goldstein, 1960); length

of treatment may correlate with therapist appraisal of improvement but not with criterion measures from most other sources (Fiske, Cartwright, & Kirtner, 1964). In addition to the need for standardized outcome measures, Bergin and Suinn (1975) call for "better understanding of the meaning of differing measures" (p. 531).

Rather independent of the categorization of outcome measurements by perspective is the classification by content. Among the pertinent areas are work or occupational adjustment, interpersonal relationships (both intimate and casual), sexual adjustment, symptom status (with special reference to target symptoms and to amount and intensity of negative affect), and insight into one's own mental processes. Although it may not be feasible to assess all of these areas from all perspectives, the researcher must decide which combinations are most pertinent to his purposes (e.g., which ones he would predict to be most influenced by the therapist).

The conditions for assessing outcomes must also be given serious attention. While measures can be derived from the therapy sessions themselves, the researcher cannot be assured that such measures relate highly to measures taken elsewhere. Diagnostic appraisals made from separate assessment sessions within the same institution may be affected by the patient's reactions to the institution. Measurements can also be made in outside settings. The latter may be obtrusive or unobtrusive (Webb, Campbell, Schwartz, & Sechrest, 1966), although it is difficult to see how fully comprehensive assessments could be both unobtrusive and ethical. Other aspects of the problem of measuring outcome are mentioned in Fiske *et al.* (1970, pp. 731–732).

Suppose the researcher seeks to restrict himself to effects which can be linked to the therapist. We have argued earlier that the locus of such effects is the actual interaction during treatment sessions. Judgments about the overall effects of the therapist's behavior during a single hour can be made afterwards by the therapist, although he is such a highly involved and biased reporter that his reports would be difficult to evaluate. The patient cannot be expected to provide useful information about the therapist's effects: while the patient can report his perceptions of the changes which he experienced during the hour as a whole, his attribution of these changes to particular actions or attitudes of the therapist would have quite uncertain validity.[5] For studies of the therapy hour as a whole, the most adequate approach would utilize videotapes, with observers judging characteristics of the therapist's behavior, with additional, independent observers judging the patient's behavior, and then these two sets of judgments being correlated over therapy hours. (For a stimulating study of agreement and disagreement in perceptions of therapy sessions, see Mintz, Auerbach, Luborsky, & Johnson, 1973.)

More promising would be the detailed analysis of videotapes by observers, looking for specific therapist actions and subsequent patient behaviors. Even this analysis has its difficulties. While it is clearly possible to identify sequences of a therapist act and a subsequent patient act, the evaluation of these sequences as beneficial or detrimental would have to be judged rather arbitrarily. There would seem to be no objective way to determine whether a particular patient response was progressive or regressive. (Changes in overt movements have, however, been found by Freedman [1972] to be related to symptomatic improvement in five paranoid patients.) The long-term consequences of a given therapist activity seem equally inaccessible to definitive investigation. The best that can be done is an actuarial study—in treatments judged as more successful by multiple criteria, do certain sequences of therapist-patient acts or patient-therapist acts occur more frequently?

The preceding question illustrates the importance of examining our own assumptions. We tend to think that an action by one person is associated with a subsequent act by another person or, in even more simplistic form, that action causes reaction. As Strupp (Chapter 1, this volume) reminds us, however, the recommended therapeutic technique is frequently avoidance of overt reaction. Hence we might expect to find certain sequences of patient action and subsequent therapist action more frequently in unsuccessful therapy. (Bandura, Lipsher, and Miller [1960] illustrate the analysis of silence and other avoidant therapist behaviors.)

It is curious that the intensive analysis of outcome has been so neglected. There is no chapter in this volume which analyzes outcome or effectiveness of psychotherapy—what we mean by the terms and how effectiveness can be observed and evaluated. The closest material is Chapter 22, on outcome from the perspective of the psychotherapist, and the section on the nature of the psychotherapist's impact (Chapters 13–17). What actual changes in behavior or experience are sought? Is the answer too obvious and well known? (Perhaps, but only in loose, global terms.) Is it highly specific for each patient? (Again, perhaps it is, at the verbal level.)

Are the changes so detailed and so numerous that we simplify the matter by applying broad class labels? (Probably.) Can we make any progress without direct, intensive examination of this matter?

LEVELS OF ANALYSIS

The preceding discussion has come close to the common practice, in writing about psychotherapy, of failing to distinguish among various levels of analysis. Various sections and chapters of this book, for example, consider the therapist from a variety of approaches: his demographic characteristics, his personality, his therapeutic style, etc. It is easy to treat all these attributes as belonging to one general class— descriptions of the therapist. Within that class, one moves all too readily from thinking about style to thinking about early influences on his personality and back to his influence within sessions.

As Singer and Luborsky (Chapter 16, this volume) suggest, however, variables at different levels of analysis must be distinguished. While several such assorted variables may be found to relate to outcome, the inferred course of such determination may be particular to each variable. A personality characteristic of the therapist may affect his nonverbal behavior during treatment. A sociological characteristic may relate to his verbal style. The presumed chain of influence may be indirect. A training experience may affect his attitudes toward a kind of patient, these attitudes affecting his actions within the treatment. The amount of conceptual examination of such implicit chains of contributing factors is all too limited. The empirical investigation of these linkages is even scarcer. (An exception is the study by Bandura, cited by Singer and Luborsky in Chapter 16, relating ratings of the therapist's personality to his responses to patient provocations.)

The investigator planning a study of the relationship between an attribute of the therapist and effectiveness should develop in advance an explicit statement about what the connection might be. He will be inclined to neglect such thinking through, perhaps feeling that the form of linkage (if demonstrated) is obvious. But often we find that what appears obvious is not so self-evident. Consider, for example, the discussion by Wilkins (Chapter 13, this volume) of the two possible relationships between expectations and outcome: the expectancies themselves may produce behaviors contributing to changes in the patient; alternatively, the expectancies may be derived from valid cues which are associated with outcome.

An additional gain from prior speculation about the probable connections is the possibility of improving one's research plan. For example, the method for measuring expectancies or the timing of such measurements might be selected to assist in interpreting the empirical findings. Obviously, the hypothesized type of relationship should help determine the design and analyses. If one believed that therapists' expectancies themselves helped determine outcome, one might randomly assign patients to therapists and then see whether those with the highest average expectancies had more successful outcomes, even though there was no relationship within each therapist's cases between expectancy and outcome. Positive findings would rule out the alternative interpretation.

Levels of Therapist Variables

As later chapters in this volume indicate, research on the therapist has involved a lengthy array of variables. These can be sorted into several classes:

(1) general characteristics: for example, sex, age, ethnic group (see Chapter 3);

(2) psychological attributes assessed outside the treatment room: for example, personality variables, aptitudes, interests (see Chapters 3 and 12);

(3) professional biographic variables: for example, profession, training, experience (see Chapters 3–7);

(4) views about psychotherapy: for example, theoretical orientation, beliefs about mental health and psychotherapy, expectations about patients and outcomes (see Chapters 8, 9, 10, 13);

(5) variables specific to each patient: for example, therapist's perceptions of the patient, his assessments of the patient's personality, and his expectations about potentiality for gain (see Chapters 13, 17, 22);

(6) characteristics of the therapist's behavior during a treatment: for example, variables summarizing the patient's verbal or nonverbal behavior per hour or per total course of treatment (see Chapter 21);

(7) contextual variables: for example, therapist's responses to particular acts or statements of the patient (see Chapter 14).

The preceding list is more illustrative than comprehensive. For example, the analysis of the therapist's behavior during treatment (No. 6)

could be limited to one therapist-patient pairing or could consider the therapist in sessions with various patients.

These categories fall into two main groups. The first four involve descriptions of the therapist himself, while the last three consider the therapist in relation to the patient. The ordering is derived from several separate scales: assumed degree of effect on the patient, relevance to the particular therapist-patient dyad, concreteness-abstraction, and temporal period during which the quality assessed by the variable can be assumed to persist. *Our ultimate concern should be with actions of the therapist during treatment and their effects upon the patient. The therapist's assessment of the patient, his beliefs about psychotherapy, and his age are of interest only insofar as they are related to what he actually does in the treatment interactions and how he and his behavior are perceived by the patient.*

At first glance, studies of the therapist's more enduring general characteristics as related to his successes have an R–R (response–response) form: they are correlational in design. Are more verbal therapists more successful? Are more experienced therapists more successful? The measures of a therapist apply to him as he is during an extended period of time, and his successes occur during a similarly lengthy period. Studies of such relationships are, however, interpreted as S–R (stimulus–response) analyses: it is assumed that the therapist's prior experience should affect his success in his treatment of a particular patient (but cf. Chapter 5). Since it is easy to speculate how prior experience can be useful, little attention is paid to the hard question—exactly what difference does experience make to the therapist's action at a moment,[6] and to whether that action furthers the objectives of the treatment.

Levels of Outcome Variables

Outcome of treatment can be appraised at varying levels of generality:

(1) outcomes for a type of treatment;

(2) outcomes for a specified therapist;

(3) outcomes for one therapist with a particular class of patients;

(4) outcomes for one therapist with one patient;

(5) effects of the therapist during one phase of treatment (e.g., early sessions);

(6) effects during one session;

(7) effects during one portion of a session;

(8) effects of one action by the therapist.

These classes refer to outcomes and effects in the plural because extended and complex treatment does not have a single consequence, whatever the level of analysis.

Relationships

Given such classifications of levels of variables for therapist and for outcome, each joint selection of one level for the therapist variable and one for the outcome variable yields a separate class of research problems, just one class out of many. Findings from studies utilizing one level tell us nothing definite about what might be found using lower levels. Studies measuring outcomes for a particular therapist give no specific information about his outcomes with a particular class of patient; at most, they provide a very rough estimate for any one class and set approximate limits for the range which might be found. Studies on professional variables describing the therapist tell us nothing certain about his position on psychotherapeutic variables. More broadly, findings for variables at one level give no indication what the findings would be if a lower level had been used.

Much the same independence holds for implications to levels above that used in a set of investigations. Even in those instances where data from one level are part of the basis for measures at a higher level, any inference about expected generalizations at the higher level must be tenuous. There is great heterogeneity and specificity in the therapeutic process and in data derived from it.

It is also clear that the probability of finding a relationship depends in part upon the degree to which two variables are proximal. For example, Fretz (1966a) found relationships between scores on "postural" movement factors for the therapist in an interview and subsequent therapist assessment of the quality of the relationship in that interview. In contrast, these movement scores yielded only a chance number of significant correlations with therapist scores on personality inventories taken shortly before the therapy started (Fretz, 1966b). In the first instance, the therapist in his post-interview reports assessed the same time period for which summary scores for movements were derived. In the second, the personality scores for the therapist were based upon his reported judgments, made some days earlier, about himself and his usual behaviors, feelings, etc. Here, the two levels of analysis are distinctly different

(numbers 2 and 6 on the preceding list for therapist variables). Similar findings of relationships for measures pertaining to a single interview and no relationships for personality measures were obtained for the clients in these same dyads.

Most, if not all, of what we have found in studies of psychotherapy should be viewed as actuarial—the more of some specified attribute in the therapist, the more likely that his treatments will be successful. Many of the findings involve a considerable time interval between the measurement of the therapist attribute and the assessment of outcomes. It is assumed, however, that the attribute is pertinent and operates over a more or less indefinite period of time; for example, its effects upon his behavior during treatments continue to occur long after the attribute was measured.

In other studies, scores are obtained to summarize the amount of some therapist activity during an hour and the amount of some patient activity. If we find that the two scores covary, we are all too ready to assume that the therapist behavior contributed to the determination of the patient behavior. Such need not be the case. For example, Butler and Rice (1963) report that the therapist's voice quality converged more toward that of the client during an hour than the patient's voice quality converged toward that of the therapist.

If we want to learn the therapist's contribution to the effectiveness of psychotherapy, we must sooner or later get down to what goes on, moment by moment, in the interactions between therapist and patient. We must decide what patient actions are indicative of effective treatment. This identification may initially be done *a priori*, or it could be done by finding those actions (especially in the later states of treatment) that are related to each of a diverse set of outcome measures. Then we can examine what actions of the therapist preceded the actions we would like to see maximized. It might prove necessary to consider not only therapist–patient pairings of actions but also triads—patient–therapist–patient. It will be tedious and laborious work, but such labor seems unavoidable.

The reader may be inclined to reject out of hand the proposition that we would like to learn what sentences, words, gestures, or glances precede reactions by the patient which represent tiny steps toward the ultimate goal of treatment. The proposition should not be taken too literally. It need not refer to mechanical relationships; it can refer to subtle matters, such as the harmonious timing of the therapist's action. The relationships may be mediated: the therapist's latency in responding and not interrupting may be related to perceptions of his empathy (Hargrove, 1974).

There is certainly no body of empirical research on which to base an argument that such relationships do not exist. The exploratory studies of Scheflen (1966) and of Isaacs and Haggard (1966) seem more encouraging than discouraging. A valuable pioneering study by Charny (1966) also suggests that this level of analysis is promising. He examined 33 minutes of motion picture film recording the 37th interview in one treatment. Classifying the posture configurations of therapist and patient, he found that the proportion of time that the upper body postures were mirror-congruent increased during the recorded period. During such periods, the lexical content of the patient's speech was more interpersonally oriented, positive, and specific. When the two postures were non-congruent, the content was more self-centered, negative, and nonspecific. He suggests that the mirror-congruent posture may indicate a state of therapeutic rapport or relatedness. This is one of very few studies in which the relationship between therapist behavior and concurrent patient behavior has been studied. In addition, Charny looked for relationships between posture and the simultaneous verbal content. Fine-grained synchrony between speech and the body movements of both speaker and auditor has been observed by Condon and Ogston (1967). Molecular acts are an integral part of the processes in behaving.

Within the domain of the patient's verbal content, Luborsky and Auerbach (1969) have found regularities in the thought preceding the appearance of a patient symptom in a treatment session. These appearances are rather rare. If they were not, perhaps that work could be extended to determine whether, toward the termination of successful treatment, that thought context was no longer followed by appearance of the symptom. If so, we would want to ascertain how the therapist had dealt with those patient expressions which had initially preceded the symptom. Perhaps this approach could be used with significant events in therapeutic sessions which appeared with greater frequency than do symptoms. As Garfield emphasizes in Chapter 4 of this volume, we have yet to specify the operations which make for positive change in psychotherapy.

INDICES FOR THERAPISTS AND OUTCOMES

Related to the levels of analysis discussed in the last section is the matter of the data used in studies of therapists' contributions to effective psychotherapy. Once again, what is done in research on this topic is an instance of the methods generally used in research on personality. Several aspects of the nature of the data in psychotherapy research will be examined in this section: the pooling of single observations or judgments, the dependability of the data, and matters of validity.

Pooling of Observations

Where do we get the scores, the numerical values which we enter into our statistical analyses, our correlations or other procedures for determining extent of relationship? Careful scrutiny indicates that in almost every instance the unit of data inserted into these analyses is a summarizing score, combining in some manner a number of discrete observations. The most common summarizing is simply counting the number of instances. To measure the therapist's personality, we may ask him to respond to a number of items in a standard questionnaire, and then we assign him a score, which is the number of his responses that correspond with our *a priori* keying. In studying the therapist's behavior during a session, a judge may be asked to note each instance when the therapist asks a question. We then count the judge's tallies and often average that count with parallel counts for other judges to obtain the final datum for our statistical analysis. Again, a judge may be asked to rate the therapist's warmth in a brief segment of a recorded session. That rating may then be pooled with the judge's ratings for other segments, and also averaged with the overall rating for one or more other judges. Although these examples are all drawn from measurements of the therapist, the same kind of pooling is found in most assessments of his effectiveness. The rare exceptions occur for indices of major events — during the year after treatment, did the patient change jobs, enter a hospital, change his marital status, etc.?

It is not necessary to use such pooled data in psychotherapy research. Our unit of statistical analysis need not be a summary or average score indicating the strength or frequency of a particular quality in the therapist's responses or in the patient's behaviors. The unit can be a sequence of two acts. When the patient makes a provocative remark, does the therapist indicate approval? Another unit could be a provocative remark followed by silence on the part of the therapist. Such a unit is an observed co-occurrence, an association or relationship at the level of basic observations. The frequency of such units can be entered into analyses determining its association with measures of effectiveness or measures of therapist attributes. In the earlier outlines for levels of analysis, the lowest level for both therapist variables and outcome variables refers to data of the kind considered here.

Our concern, of course, is not merely with ways of collecting data; our interest is in the kinds of relationships which can be established by this approach as compared to the standard approach. A standard analysis might determine, for a series of sessions, whether the total frequency of provocative patient remarks was related to the total frequency of therapist statements of approval, for successful cases. The researcher could not tell whether the latter regularly followed the former or not. Much more informative for the researcher would be the observation of frequent sequences of these two behaviors in successful cases, together with infrequent occurrences in unsuccessful cases.

Our standard procedures in pooling separate observations can be interpreted as indicating an implicit recognition of the fact that the phenomena of interest are distinct, momentary acts within the ongoing stream of behaving. The pooling is done for a variety of reasons. First, it is similar to what occurs in the everyday life of everyone—when we think about a person, or about his behavior during an interaction, we summarize in broad descriptive terms (using trait labels or other dispositional words). We usually do not focus on the particular response he made to something another person said. Second, researchers must be practical and economize on effort. They collect data by convenient methods which do not require tedious observing and coding by judges. Third, we tend to distrust the single observation as highly susceptible to error of measurement, stemming from various biases, or as idiosyncratic to some degree, as having some qualities associated with the unique set of circumstances at that moment in time.[7] Finally, we are aware of all the technical considerations developed in test theory for coping with the undependable and almost capricious nature of the response to a single item.

While the observation point may in certain instances be associated with the perception of a single act by the patient, it usually is based on a set of impressions formed from much more lengthy experiences, from observing a segment of a treatment session, from a series of sustained interactions with the subject, etc. For example, after an independent diagnostician has interviewed a patient to assess status after treatment, he may make a rating based on his integration of his impressions of the total interview. Those impressions themselves may come from the patient's summarizing descriptions of his feelings during a period of months. On the other side, the researcher may combine that single rating with other ratings made by the interviewer or with ratings made by an additional interviewer to obtain the datum entered into subsequent statistical analyses.

The pooling process producing the final datum can be done by the researcher or by a judge. We recognize the limitations of asking a judge to make an overall judgment about a quality in the therapist's activity during treatment. We know that, from his reported judgment, we cannot tell on what it is based. Hence we prefer to ask him to make a number of specific ratings which we can later combine as we deem best. While such overt combining can be done mechanically by the researcher, the objectivity of that integrating operation should not mislead the researcher into viewing his final datum as objective; it is based, after all, on the personal perceptions and cognitions used by the judge in making each separate rating. There will inevitably be a degree of uniqueness in the judgments of each judge; no two judges will ever agree exactly, giving the researcher data which are almost perfectly dependable. This consideration brings us to the question of the dependability of measures used in psychotherapy research.

Dependability

The dependability of measures of the therapist and of outcomes must be a matter of strong concern for researchers. One kind of undependability is associated with the particular observer, as has been noted above. Each observer tends to contribute some individuality to his judgments, through his interpretation of wordings in judgment scales and his particular interpretations of the behaviors being judged. Luborsky and his colleagues have studied carefully the agreement between judges. Auerbach and Luborsky (1968) found better agreement on "natural" variables, particularly those with clear behavioral references. Similarly, Luborsky, Graff, Pulver, and

Curtis (1973) report better agreement when the content of the variable had a more specific, less inferential focus. That interpretation has been corroborated empirically by Strupp, Chassan, and Ewing (1966) who obtained a correlation of .71 between observed coefficients of agreement for each of a long list of variables and independent ratings of the degree of inference required to judge the variable. These findings in the psychotherapy area are, of course, quite consistent with those obtained in other areas. The conclusion seems well established: the more specific and overt the behavior to be judged, the better the agreement between judges. This conclusion is one more argument for planning research so as to utilize variables at as low as possible a level of analysis, on the lists presented in the earlier section. Dependability of this form is associated with minimal degrees of inference and also with minimal durations of behavioral sequences to be judged.

The use of extended observations for each rating is also a potential source of undependability. Longer periods provide opportunities for manifestations of variation in the behaviors of the therapist and of the patient. Whether the final datum be a rating or the average of several observations, the more variation in the behaviors observed, the less dependable the datum summarizing them. Less dependable data are simply less useful to the researcher. If the final score is the mean of very varied observations, it is less typical or representative than the mean of a narrow range of observations and, generally speaking, one should expect it to have lower relationships with other measures than would a more dependable index. The sources of unique determinants for each particular observation may be too strong relative to the source of common influence at which the final score is aimed—i.e., the common variance may be only a small proportion of the total variance.

The relationship between agreement and length of observation period is not a simple one. For some kinds of judgments, agreement increases with length of observation but approaches an asymptote after a number of minutes. Such a finding applies only to judges observing the same behavior. Judges observing different samples of behavior may not agree at all (Magnusson, Heffler, & Nyman, 1968). On the other hand, when two sets of judges observe the same person performing the same task at two different times or performing different tasks but with the same group of peers, there is considerable agreement, with apparently higher agreement when both task and peer group are the same for each set of judges' independent bases for judging. Components of variation associated with task and with peer group are but two instances of the generally recognized fact that behavior varies with the context in which it is observed. It is obvious that *outcome ratings made by persons who see the patient in different situations will not agree closely, entirely aside from the contribution associated with the kind of relationship that the observer has with the patient.*

Validity of Measuring Procedures

The ultimate criterion for assessing a measuring procedure is its validity. Agreement between observers, stability of measurements over periods for which consistency is expected, and consistency among the subscores combined into the final datum are of interest primarily because such kinds of reliability set limits to the estimated validity of the measurements. (While the preceding discussion has not used standard psychometric concepts, such as internal consistency, it has indicated how such concepts apply to psychotherapy research.) We do not need to determine the reliability (dependability) of our measurements if we have firm evidence that they are perfectly valid. Of course, we never have such evidence.

For the most part, measures specifically created for psychotherapy research have only face validity:[8] they appear to be getting at whatever is to be measured. In some instances, evidence for convergent or discriminant validation may be offered by the investigator. For example, Berzins et al. (1975) argue that convergence among measures from different sources supports the assertion that the several measures are assessing the global notion of outcome. Systematic consideration of predictive validity is rarely found; the testing of possible predictors of successful outcome does not, strictly speaking, quite fit that concept. Concurrent validity is practically unheard of in this area of investigation.

Among the various usages of validity, the one that really matters is construct validity: does the measure yield empirical relationships (both null and non-null) consistent with those derived from the conceptual framework within which the target construct is embedded? The phrase, construct validity, is foreign to psychotherapy research, a most difficult area for investigation. At least as much as in other personality areas, the theoretical statements are at such a high level of abstraction that one cannot derive unambiguous propositions regarding the expected relationships among operational indices. One gets the impression that researchers are preoccupied with the search for measuring procedures which will have reasonable linkages to their concepts, and do not aspire to very close degrees of coordination. In addition, much of their effort has to be devoted to trying to clarify and explicate their constructs; they have a label for a certain set of impressions and they search for common features among those impressions.

It can be anticipated that many readers will disagree with the emphasis upon dependability and validity and with the focus on objectively observable behaviors during treatment, as recommended earlier. They may assert that psychotherapy deals with meanings, that the work of psychotherapy is primarily verbal, that outcomes should be seen as changes in meanings for the patient. Clearly, each investigator has his own orientation and his own set of values. At this period in the history of psychotherapy research, diversity in orientations increases the likelihood of discovering fruitful relationships and of eventually building some kind of systematic knowledge about the complex phenomena of psychotherapy.

It seems quite clear, however, that an investigator oriented toward the study of meanings has to accept a very limited ceiling on the degree of systematic, consensually accepted knowledge which can be developed about psychotherapy. Most concepts in the area have only verbal definitions, and there is no agreement on those. It is almost certainly true that the personal meanings given a term by different users have substantial areas of incongruence. Given this state of affairs, it is not surprising that there are no standard measures for any psychotherapy concept,[9] and where there are several measures with similar labels, the agreement among the measures is limited. It is also not surprising that there are no general propositions which are accepted by most investigators in this field on the basis of evidence from several studies. The only candidates are negative statements (e.g., measures of outcome obtained from different sources have limited degrees of covariation). The observation made some years ago by Dollard and Auld (1959) is valid today: "Much of the current lack of agreement about the dynamics of psychotherapy can be traced back to a lack of agreement about the basic observations of psychotherapy" (p. 314).

THE DESIGN OF RESEARCH ON THE THERAPIST'S CONTRIBUTION

The nature of psychotherapy makes impossible the use of rigorous experimental designs for research on the contribution of the therapist. One cannot develop a plan in which every component is the same (or truly randomized) for two groups except some one explicit aspect of what the therapist does. In terms of pure experimental rigor, the best that one can do is use quasi-experimental designs. A classic treatment of such designs is that of Campbell and Stanley (1963).

Internal and External Validity

These authors have also introduced the concepts of internal and external validity. Their use of that psychometric term, "validity," is quite appropriate in this context since the validity of a measure and the validity of an experimental design incorporating the measure are intimately related. Internal validity refers to the degree of confidence an investigator can have in the conclusions which he draws about the data in his given study. In particular, it is concerned with factors which may be confounded with the effects of the independent variable. In the instance of concern to this volume, are there factors which make it impossible to conclude that the therapist variable determines the observed values for the chosen measures of effectiveness? The classes of extraneous, confounding variables listed by Campbell and Stanley include effects from history, maturation, testing, instrumentation, statistical regression, selection, experimental mortality, and selection-maturation interaction. For discussions of these and other effects intruding on the validity of designs and measures, see Webb et al. (1966) and Runkel and McGrath (1972).

External validity is concerned with the extent to which the investigator can generalize his conclusions beyond the data from his study. To what populations of subjects, settings, treatment variables, and measurement variables can he generalize? In our case, the question involves populations of patients, of therapists, of treatments, and of measures of effectiveness of treatment. Campbell and Stanley list four factors jeopardizing external validity or representativeness: reactive or interactive effects of testing, interactive effects of selection biases and the experimental variable, reactive effects of experimental arrangements, and multiple-treatment interference. In research on psychotherapy, these effects can enter when the patients are sensitized by the content of pre-treatment measures, when there is an interaction between choice of patient and type of treatment as administered by the therapist, when the therapist and the patient know that they are research subjects, and when there are extraneous treatments such as prior therapy or concurrent counseling with a nonprofessional.

More generally, the representativeness (external validity) of research studies of psychotherapy cannot be claimed with much confidence. We simply cannot measure the variables describing the crucial components with sufficient accuracy to estimate the degree of bias in any single sample. Even more fundamental is the absence of normative data on, for example, therapy in this country. If the investigator uses the therapists at one or a few treatment centers, what criteria can he employ to determine how well they represent therapists in general? Therapists at any one center are almost certain to be more homogeneous than a random sample of therapists, as a consequence of their selection by that center or their choice of that center, their professional discussions, etc. Measures of effectiveness may be more representative and generalizable, provided that they do not involve inferential judgments, especially when the judges have a particular theoretical persuasion.

Intrusiveness

A major dimension of designs for research on psychotherapeutic effectiveness is intrusiveness. To what extent does the research intrude into the natural events of treatment? The problem with intrusiveness is that it is very difficult or expensive to determine how much distortion it contributes. In principle, if one has enough patients and enough resources, one could randomly assign patient–therapist dyads to an intrusive condition and to a condition without that intrusion. In practice, few investigators would be willing to expend resources on such a control, and perhaps with some justification. It could be argued that the effects of an experimental intrusion (such as a measuring procedure given before treatment) are likely to be trivial in comparison with major treatment effects, and that the variance associated with other components would make it difficult to assess with confidence the influence of such an intrusion.

Intrusiveness can take many forms: the therapist knowing he is being studied; the patient knowing he is a subject; the use of auditory, videotape, or motion picture recording; and the introduction of research instruments. Such instruments may be given before and after the entire treatment, or at intervals. (See Chapter 22, this volume, which reports a study in which therapists and patients completed questionnaires after each session.) In psychotherapy research, active intrusion into the treatment session itself has been avoided (although analogue studies have freely used intrusions, manipulations, and even open simulations).

Research on psychotherapy has been conducted with varying degrees of intrusiveness. One major study was intentionally designed to be quite unobtrusive. In the Menninger Psychotherapy Project (Kernberg, Burstein, Coyne, Appelbaum, Horwitz, & Voth, 1972), the therapists and patients were not aware that they were subjects. As these authors point out, this completely naturalistic plan made impossible any kind of controls.

A very common design includes the administration of measuring instruments before and after the series of sessions. When pre-testing is a routine part of the institution's procedures, the design is still naturalistic (although such testing could influence the treatment at that institution). Ordinarily, readministration of tests at the end is not routine. Where testing is routine, and the routine tests are all that will be employed in the research, patient knowledge that he is a research subject need not affect the data. Current ethical practices, however, would at the least require that the patient (and therapist) give their consent to the use of test or other data for research purposes unless an impartial external committee determines that the nature of the research and the way the data will be used do not impinge on the subjects' rights. (See the section on ethics, below.)

Most likely to have intrusive effects are designs requiring the administration of measuring procedures between sessions —usually immediately after a session is over. Whether such intrusions impair or facilitate treatment cannot readily be determined. But the investigator utilizing such designs must recognize that the conclusions which he draws from his obtained data may not generalize to the normal course of therapy which lacks these intrusions.

One way to handle the problem of intrusiveness might be to use two or more experimentally independent procedures having presumably different degrees of intrusiveness. Where the research question makes such a design feasible, the degree of any intrusive effects might be determined and the investigator may be able to generalize somewhat more confidently than he could if he had used only one intrusive procedure.

Analogue and Homologue Research

The ultimate degree of intrusiveness is found in analogue studies where the roles and the treatment are created for research purposes. (See Chapters 4, 15, 17, and 21, in this volume, for examples.) In principle, the strategy of analogue studies looks promising. One identifies a significant component of the therapeutic process and creates a set of experimental conditions which generate phenomena of that kind. The strategy appears to resemble the classical experimental approach of studying a particular kind of phenomena under conditions which minimize or hold constant other effects and thus permit the experimenter to determine the effects associated with his independent variable.

The critical question about analogue studies is the extent to which their findings apply to psychotherapy itself. Is the component which is created in the experimental situation essentially the same process as that occurring in the natural psychotherapy? Does the process take the same course in the experiment as it does in psychotherapy when the several other components are also present? Does that process in its natural occurrences depend heavily on interactions with these other components? For example, in many analogue studies, the subjects are not patients who are seeking help with their problems. Does this condition alter the quality of the experimentally induced process to a significant extent? A decade ago, Bordin (1965) presented a carefully reasoned examination of "simplification as a strategy for research in psychotherapy," which is highly pertinent to the assessment of the analogue approach.

It seems obvious that any generalization of conclusions from analogue studies cannot be applied directly to natural psychotherapy with any degree of assurance. With our limited understanding of psychotherapy, we have difficulty in assessing their relevance. For the present, analogue studies may be most useful as the basis for later research on actual treatment, for studies designed to determine whether the conceptual relationships supported by the analogue research can be found in standard psychotherapy.

The ideal strategy would be homologue research in which the processes deemed essential for psychotherapeutic change were present but could be very readily identified and economically investigated. For example, are there natural interactions which involve the basic defining characteristics of psychotherapy in miniature form—i.e., which last only a few minutes?[10] The author has not seen any experimental work which seems truly homologous. Perhaps the reader can design a homologue study which includes those processes that are essential for psychotherapy as he conceptualizes it.

Related to homologues is the possibility of adapting concepts and methods from related fields of investigation. Since psychotherapy is such a complex matter, researchers must use all the guidance and suggestions that may be provided by research in relevant neighboring areas. Garfield (Chapter 4, this volume) considers the possible contributions from studies of modeling, within the general context of social learning theory. Wilkins (Chapter 13, this volume) brings in studies of expectancy effects in other contexts. Johnson and Matross (Chapter 15, this volume) examine research on interpersonal influence.

Several researchers have noted that traditional verbal psychotherapy is a special case of dyadic interactions, a large class of human behaviors. Particular attention should be paid to the possible applicability of concepts and methods from studies of such interactions. Examples of that orientation can be found in Siegman and Pope (1972), Heller (1971), and Chapters 14 and 15 in this volume.

One specific possibility might be to use the rules for smooth exchanges of speaker and auditor roles in normal interpersonal interactions (Duncan, 1972) as a baseline for investigating possible departures from these general rules in the actions initiated by the patient or even by the therapist. Possible patterns might include elevated frequencies of rule violation by patients, especially in the early stages of therapy or at critical points within each session, and violations by the therapist at points disturbing to him.

Confounding

A major obstacle in psychotherapy research is the confounding of patient and therapist. Within any one treatment dyad, the therapist is reacting to the particular patient and the patient is reacting to that therapist. The therapist can, however, be studied across several such dyads, looking for communalities in his behaviors. On the other side, patient behavior and outcome cannot be examined independently of the particular therapist. Each patient has only one therapist at a time. Even the patient having several courses of treatment, each with a different therapist, is a somewhat different person each time he starts a course of treatment.

It is also difficult to avoid confounding of therapist and treatment. Treatment includes what the therapist does, his actions and inactions within the session. These partake of his individuality. One therapist's application of a therapeutic technique is not exactly the same as another's.

Fortunately for the topic of this volume, the confounding appears to be more serious for studies of patients and treatments than for studies of therapists as they contribute to effectiveness. Thus, if two groups of therapists can be differentiated by some independent assessment, and if patients can be assigned in truly random fashion to therapists in these groups, and if standard measures of effectiveness are administered, it should be possible to relate values of the assessed variable to outcomes. In that design, any differential effects of what the therapist does in treatment, leading to differences in outcomes, are presumed to reflect differences in the variable used to classify the therapists. That presumption could be tested empirically.

The Measurement of Change

An effective treatment effects a positive change. This volume is concerned with the therapist's contributions to such changes. At first thought, the measurement of change appears to be an easy matter—make a measurement before treatment and a measurement after treatment and take the difference. While this simple approach may be satisfactory when each measurement is quite free of errors of measurement (is perfectly reliable), our measurements of changes associated with psychotherapy possess limited reliability.

The measurement of change in an individual, using fallible procedures, turns out to be a highly technical matter and there is still no consensus among experts on the best way to do it, even after a couple of decades of investigation (see Cronbach & Furby, 1970, and Wiley & Harnischfeger, 1973, for two recent analyses). The difficulties are most serious for research designs involving correlations over individuals, for example, over patients, between a predictor and a change measure. Fortunately, there are other reasons why such designs are not suitable

for the topic of this volume. As noted earlier, we cannot profitably study from clinical records the relationship between a measure of outcome and a therapist attribute since the patient's contribution to the therapy-dyad unit would be completely confounded with the therapist's contribution.

An optimal design for studying the contribution of a therapist attribute to effectiveness would involve classifying a number of therapists on that attribute and determining whether the classes differed on one or more outcome measures. For each measure, the average post-treatment status of the several patients treated by each therapist would be determined and entered into the analysis. An absolutely essential condition in this design is the random assignment of patients to therapists.

Strictly speaking, that design investigates only whether there is an association between the attribute and the measure after treatment. It does not evaluate effectiveness defined as positive change. For example, half the patients might improve and half the patients might get worse during the treatment, and the analysis could still indicate an association between the attribute and the status at outcome. Fortunately, the assessment of change for a group as a whole can be made without encountering the problems associated with assessing change for individuals.

For comparing the changes in two groups receiving different treatments, there seems to be no fully adequate substitute for random assignment of patients to the treatment groups. Groups formed on other bases are usually found to have different pre-treatment levels on the major variable for which change is expected. Such differences may be qualitative as well as quantitative. There are complex problems associated with statistical techniques for partialling out the quantitative differences. In some instances, the techniques may produce under-adjustments and lead to erroneous conclusions (see Campbell & Erlebacher, 1970).

The Analysis of Therapist Contributions

It is so easy to think about some aspect of the therapist and some discrete measurements of outcome that the investigator is likely to forget the complexity of the total psychotherapeutic process and avoid the difficult task of considering exactly how the therapist attribute might have its effect. The total process of psychotherapy can be analyzed into a number of processes, at several levels of abstraction. Within the interaction in each session, there are processes going on simultaneously and sequentially. There may be processes extending over more than one session. There are also the processes continuing after each session—the therapeutic work the patient does between sessions. Which processes, and which kinds of processes, are affected by the attribute of the therapist?

The matter is made infinitely more complicated by the fact that these processes are interactive and interdependent, both within those going on at any time and between those at different times. Moreover, we cannot postulate with any assurance that the same kinds of processes occur in every therapist-patient treatment dyad. Any investigator contemplating conceptual and empirical analysis of these phenomena can only hope that he can identify some major processes which account for very substantial proportions of the variance in effectiveness.

Ethical Considerations in Research on Psychotherapy

The motives of psychotherapists include the desire to relieve human suffering and to increase positive, healthy functioning. Those investigating psychotherapy also hope to contribute to such goals by determining what makes treatments effective. Aware of these commendable motives, an investigator may come to believe he can justify any procedural decision which he feels is necessary for his research; even if his experimental procedures may cause his subjects some distress, he can relieve that distress post-experimentally and, besides, he can tell himself that the end justifies the means. The latter assertion is obviously a most dangerous oversimplification. While a surgeon can accept the unavoidable patient discomfort associated with a routine, highly successful operative treatment, a researcher is not in the same position.

It would be presumptuous to present general ethical principles for investigators in this field. We can, however, point out some matters for the researcher to consider. Is it ever justified to generate distress in a patient or subject for research purposes? Is it acceptable to study expectancies in patients by producing positive expectancies in one group and negative expectancies in another? It is hard to imagine when that would be justified. Even though the researcher believes the negative effects would be minor and could be counteracted at a later point, it is highly doubtful that he can have much

confidence in such beliefs. Especially in patients, there is a significant potentiality for subtle long-term harm not detected by the researcher. Similar considerations apply to the development of experimental neuroses and to manipulations which tell subjects that their protocol on a diagnostic instrument indicates maladjustment.

The psychotherapy researcher should not assume that he is able to determine for himself whether his research plans are completely satisfactory from the ethical viewpoint. He must recognize the probability of bias in his judgment and obtain from peers a more disinterested appraisal. (See the "Ethical Principles in the Conduct of Research with Human Participants," APA Ad Hoc Committee on Ethical Standards in Psychological Research, 1973.)

IN CONCLUSION: ONE VIEWPOINT

Elusive Concepts

What does the therapist contribute to the effectiveness of psychotherapy? That question is not researchable. We cannot design a basic research study to answer it. The question is too broad and abstract. It identifies a topic of interest rather than a research problem. As the topic is usually viewed, the field is not ready for definitive investigations. This judgment is based upon the fact that, in one major respect, research on psychotherapy suffers the same handicap as most research on other manifestations of personality—the handicap of elusive concepts. The terms used to portray the therapist's personality and his states during a treatment interview, as well as the terms used to describe the patient's dysfunctions which treatment is intended to remove, are attractive global concepts. These concepts include those which have been developed by the theorists seeking to conceptualize psychotherapy and those which refer to dimensions commonly used by laymen in describing behavior. Those dimensions have been adopted and adapted by psychologists, analyzed verbally, and labeled (sometimes with the dictionary term, sometimes with the theorist's own construction).

Our concepts are beguiling and deceptive. The researcher encountering one of these terms for the first time quickly develops a feeling that he knows the kind of behavior to which it refers. Like all of us, he has interacted with hundreds of persons and has experienced the seemingly infinite variety of their behaviors. Having perceived and cognized this enormous array, he can readily construe certain instances as falling within the scope of this new concept. Yet he typically does not receive the consensual validation for his interpretation of the concept which he obtains for his meaning for "red" or for "skinny." Each concept has a somewhat individualistic meaning for each investigator using it.

More confounding still is the varied use to which the concept is put. A typical personality term may be applied to a group of persons, to single individuals, or to a large group of behaviors which take somewhat different overt form but which can be interpreted as having a common feature. Such a concept is used to summarize a string of perceptions occurring over a period of time. Even the most specific application is usually of the form, "He was acting defensively"—that description being used to characterize several minutes of interaction.

Thus, these concepts are tied to verbal interpretations of behavior, to descriptions attributing intent and other meaning to segments of the stream of behaving. Although they refer to the content of behavior, that content is seen in verbal terms, not as changes in space and time. There is certainly a limit to the consensus which can be obtained between observers who are coding behavior at this level.

Given this state of affairs, it is understandable why our concepts have no coordinating definitions specifying standard operations on which there is general agreement. In their present form, the concepts cannot be well operationalized— we cannot find even a series of operations which, taken together, represent any single major concept adequately. In addition, *the operations being used in psychotherapy research lack the objectivity required of sound scientific procedures. As a consequence of these several considerations, no exact replications of psychotherapy studies exist in the literature, and it is hard to see how there can be any.*

What the literature does show is empirical research on gross variables, each of which is affected by the observers who are providing the data. Most of the findings in published work are reported relationships between variables derived from the perceptions–cognitions of patient, therapist, and others.

Does this description mean that psychotherapy is an art and the psychotherapist is an artisan, as Kiesler (1971, pp. 38–39) has suggested? If one took such a view literally, one would approach the topic with the techniques of the humanities. Kiesler is, however, really referring to the way psychotherapy is practiced (perhaps the way it must be practiced, given our present state of ignorance).

Emphasis on the artistic quality of psychotherapeutic practice must not be used as an excuse for not confronting psychotherapy as a specific set of phenomena with great importance for society, phenomena which we must hope are susceptible to systematic objective study. It has been said that half of scientific progress is asking the right question. Can we identify innovative questions which will reorient us in our investigation of these phenomena?

Retaining the general viewpoint of researchers in this area, we can investigate the role of therapist as perceiver and interpreter of the patient and his presenting difficulties, of the ongoing therapeutic process, and of the outcome of treatment. We can also clarify the role of others (diagnosticians and laymen) in the evaluation of patient status before, during, and after treatment. When we have determined how the perceiver-observer in his particular role contributes to the content of psychotherapeutic concepts and measurement dimensions, we may be in a better position to ask insightful questions about the process of psychotherapeutic treatment.

Much of the last few pages has considered concepts as applied to the therapist, the patient, or to general features of their interaction. What about the analysis of the ongoing process within each session of the treatment? The interview in verbal psychotherapy can be analyzed into two interrelated sequences: there is the verbal exchange—the content of the dialogue—and there is also the flow of nonverbal acts manifested by each participant.

Much analysis has been done on the content (Kiesler, 1973), with rather uncertain and equivocal findings. Such a result, along with limited replication of findings, may be inescapable, although perhaps some small degree of improvement may be possible. A word used by two patients usually has slightly different meanings for the two speakers. A researcher employing judges to classify the content of patients' speech finds only moderate agreement between his observers. These verbal phenomena will always be elusive. The best that can be done is to try to devise concepts and methods of analysis which will yield judgments with the maximal possible level of agreement between observers.

Molecular Acts

Research on nonverbal behavior during psychotherapy has been conducted intensively and perseveringly by several investigators in recent years (e.g., Ekman & Friesen, 1968; Mahl, 1968; Matarazzo, Wiens, Matarazzo, & Saslow, 1968). Much of this work has looked for the communicative meaning of nonverbal acts and their links with verbal behavior. Matarazzo *et al.* (1968), however, have suggested that significant and valid outcome measures might be derived from these nonverbal behaviors.

Most of the research on nonverbal acts during psychotherapy has been concerned with frequencies for interviews and with occurrences for just the patient or just the therapist. There has been little on the sequences of these acts, a topic which has been recommended to the researcher at several earlier points in this chapter. The interaction between two people, in therapy or elsewhere, includes a continuing series of overt acts, acts which may take less than a second to execute. These acts are part of the means by which we communicate and interact with other persons. They occur so rapidly and so naturally, simultaneously with the apparently more central instrumental behavior of speech, that we attend to them only momentarily if at all, a feature which makes them less susceptible to conscious control and manipulation than is the content of our speech. These acts also have the great advantage of accessibility to objective recording and coding, with very high agreement among observers.

The sequences of acts which form the moment-to-moment course of each interview in psychotherapy can be analyzed intensively, both to determine the particular character of that interview and to learn how it compares and contrasts with other dyadic interactions. Are there some patterns of interaction which are associated with benefits from a single interview? Are there some which typify the course of a total treatment which has favorable outcomes?

The possible ways of examining the molecular acts in therapeutic interactions are numerous. Working at that level, the investigator need not be hampered by the broader, summarizing concepts which are commonly used to describe behavior in therapy—concepts such as transference, resistance, defensiveness, incongruity, and lack of openness to experience. He can look at the molecular phenomena and see what is there. He can develop constructs to label the regularities that he discovers. He can formulate hypotheses and test them empirically on new sets of data.

To be highly speculative, even brash, let us consider one possibility. Perhaps one important source of patient distress (as assessed from his reports and those of others) stems from dysfunction in his interpersonal relationships. Perhaps this dysfunction takes the form of difficulty in conducting smooth interactions with others. One kind of difficulty might be associated with the patient making frequent departures from the standard conventions and rules for taking turns in conversations (Duncan, 1972). For example, Duncan has discovered that smooth exchange of the speaking turn occurs when the speaker has given one or more cues signaling that he is relinquishing the turn (and does not give turn-maintaining cues). If the listener attempts to take the speaking turn in the absence of such cues, simultaneous talking is very likely. Simultaneous talking can also occur when the listener starts to speak in the presence of turn-maintaining (floor-holding) cues.

It would seem worthwhile, as suggested earlier, to investigate whether patients tend to practice these rules or violate them. If they seem to ignore the cues of the therapist, the interaction will not flow smoothly because of the presence of simultaneous talking. Continuing to speculate, one might predict that interactions early in treatment would contain more dysfunctioning on the part of the patient and that, with the aid of the model provided by therapist's functioning and with the aid of a favorable situation in which the therapist continues to interact with the patient in spite of the initial unevenness, the patient gradually begins to follow the conventions and rules so that the later interactions are smoother.

The Situation in which Psychotherapy goes on

As part of a theory of interaction, Duncan and Fiske[11] are proposing that each participant in an interaction formulates a notion of the situation and adopts conventions and strategies consistent with that formulation. While the therapist's formulation may be found to be fairly consistent for most of his treatment sessions, the formulation of the patient starting treatment may be somewhat at variance from that of the therapist. The patient may not modify his formulation as he becomes aware of the therapist's one. On the other side, if the therapist does not perceive the incongruity between the two formulations, he cannot either modify his own or attempt to help the patient to modify the patient's. When the patient and therapist maintain separate formulations of the therapy situation, the work of treatment may be found to be seriously handicapped.

The need for congruence between the therapist's and the patient's assumptions about therapeutic interactions has been discussed by Orne and Wender (1968). Writing within the standard framework of psychotherapeutic concepts, they have proposed that patients need a socialization interview to prepare them for what goes on in psychotherapy—i.e., for what the therapist expects the interaction to be like.

The investigation of the therapist's contribution to effective psychotherapy is extraordinarily difficult. Psychotherapy is an extremely complex process. Nevertheless, the investigator in this area has a singular asset—the phenomena can be recorded readily and apparently with little or no effect upon the phenomena themselves. (The two participants meet regularly in the same place and even stay within a relatively small area of the room.) Where else in the field of personality is there such a convenient opportunity for recording and studying important phenomena? In a sense, the situation is highly naturalistic since the treatment occurs whether or not it is being researched. A further advantage for the researcher in this area stems from the nature of the phenomena. Not only are they seen as important by the participants and outsiders (as compared, for example, to casual conversations) but they also involve somewhat structured roles and the nature of the interaction seems to be somewhat varying as the sequence of sessions proceeds.

On the other hand, the investigator who prefers to study the effects of experimental manipulations designed and administered by himself is bound to feel somewhat frustrated by the narrow limits within which he can ethically work on the process of psychotherapy. Similarly, the researcher who attempts simulations which are intended to display essential features of psychotherapy in simpler form or with better controls will find it difficult to do studies with findings that can clearly be generalized to the standard forms of psychotherapeutic treatment.

One product of the extensive research which has been carried out on psychotherapy and on personality in general has been an increase in our understanding of the limitations of our methods for studying the phenomena in these areas. We are becoming aware of the strength of our preconceptions—i.e., of the *a priori* concepts with which we approach these highly significant phenomena. We have acquired considerable knowledge about the fallibility and individuality of the judge whom we use to produce our data by integrating a complex set of impressions. We are

beginning to appreciate the essential role, in science, of intersubjective consensus —consensus on the elementary observations from which any scientific structure is built. With new approaches which enable us to examine the flow of behaving with some detachment, we may be able to develop an objective science of the phenomena now subsumed under the rubric of personality. The study of psychotherapeutic behaviors, of the acts of the therapist and the patient, can build on that science. That study can also contribute to the new science.

REFERENCES

APA Ad Hoc Committee on Ethical Standards in Psychological Research. *Ethical principles in the conduct of research with human participants.* Washington, D.C.: American Psychological Association, 1973.

AUERBACH, A. H., & LUBORSKY, L. Accuracy of judgments of psychotherapy and the nature of the "good hour." In J. M. SHLIEN (Ed.), *Research in psychotherapy.* Vol. 3. Washington, D.C.: American Psychological Association, 1968. Pp. 155–168.

BANDURA, A., LIPSHER, D., & MILLER, P. E. Psychotherapists' approach-avoidance reactions to patients' expressions of hostility. *Journal of Consulting Psychology,* 1960, **24**, 1–8.

BERGIN, A. E., & SUINN, R. M. Individual psychotherapy and behavior therapy. *Annual Review of Psychology,* 1975, **26**, 509–556.

BERZINS, J. I., BEDNAR, R. L., & SEVERY, L. J. The problem of intersource consensus in measuring therapeutic outcomes: New data and multivariate perspectives. *Journal of Abnormal Psychology,* 1975, **84**, 10–19.

BORDIN, E. S. Simplification as a strategy for research in psychotherapy. *Journal of Consulting Psychology,* 1965, **29**, 493–503.

BUTLER, J. M., & RICE, L. N. Adience, self-actualization, and drive theory. In J. M. WEPMAN & R. W. HEINE (Eds.), *Concepts of personality.* Chicago: Aldine, 1963. Pp. 79–110.

CAMPBELL, D. T., & ERLEBACHER, A. How regression artifacts in quasi-experimental evaluations can mistakenly make compensatory education look harmful. In J. HELLMUTH (Ed.), *Compensatory education: A national debate.* Vol. 3. *Disadvantaged child.* New York: Brunner/Mazel, 1970. Pp. 185–210.

CAMPBELL, D. T., & STANLEY, J. C. Experimental and quasi-experimental designs for research on teaching. In N. L. GAGE (Ed.), *Handbook of research on teaching.* Chicago: Rand McNally, 1963. Pp. 171–246. Reprinted separately as *Experimental and quasi-experimental designs for research.* Chicago: Rand McNally, 1966.

CHARNY, E. J. Psychosomatic manifestations of rapport in psychotherapy. *Psychosomatic Medicine,* 1966, **28**, 305–315.

CONDON, W. S., & OGSTON, W. D. A segmentation of behavior. *Journal of Psychiatric Research,* 1967, **5**, 221–235.

CRONBACH, L. J., & FURBY, L. How we should measure "change"—or should we? *Psychological Bulletin,* 1970, **74**, 68–80.

DOLLARD, J., & AULD, F., JR. *Scoring human motives: A manual.* New Haven, Conn.: Yale University Press, 1959.

DUNCAN, S., JR. Some signals and rules for taking speaking turns in conversations. *Journal of Personality and Social Psychology,* 1972, **23**, 283–292.

EKMAN, P., & FRIESEN, W. V. Nonverbal behavior in psychotherapy research. In J. M. SHLIEN (Ed.), *Research in psychotherapy*. Vol. 3. Washington, D.C.: American Psychological Association, 1968. Pp. 179–217.

FISKE, D. W. The limits for the conventional science of personality. *Journal of Personality*, 1974, **42**, 1–11.

FISKE, D. W. A source of data is not a measuring instrument. *Journal of Abnormal Psychology*, 1975, **84**, 20–23.

FISKE, D. W., CARTWRIGHT, D. S., & KIRTNER, W. L. Are psychotherapeutic changes predictable? *Journal of Abnormal and Social Psychology*, 1964, **69**, 418–426.

FISKE, D. W., HUNT, H. F., LUBORSKY, L., ORNE, M. T., PARLOFF, M. B., REISER, M. F., & TUMA, A. H. The planning of research on effectiveness of psychotherapy. *Archives of General Psychiatry*, 1970, **22**, 22–32. Also *American Psychologist*, 1970, **25**, 727–737.

FREEDMAN, N. The analysis of movement behavior during the clinical interview. In A. W. SIEGMAN & B. POPE (Eds.), *Studies in dyadic communication*. New York: Pergamon Press, 1972. Pp. 153–175.

FRETZ, B. R. Postural movements in a counseling dyad. *Journal of Counseling Psychology*, 1966a, **13**, 335–343.

FRETZ, B. R. Personality correlates of postural movements. *Journal of Counseling Psychology*, 1966b, **13**, 344–347.

GOLDSTEIN, A. P. Therapist and client expectation of personality change in psychotherapy. *Journal of Counseling Psychology*, 1960, **7**, 180–184.

GOLDSTEIN, A. P., HELLER, K., & SECHREST, L. B. *Psychotherapy and the psychology of behavior change*. New York: Wiley, 1966.

GURMAN, A. S. Instability of therapeutic conditions in psychotherapy. *Journal of Counseling Psychology*, 1973, **20**, 16–24.

HAKEL, M. D. How often is often? *American Psychologist*, 1968, **23**, 533–534.

HARGROVE, D. S. Verbal interaction analysis of empathic and nonempathic responses of therapists. *Journal of Consulting and Clinical Psychology*, 1974, **42**, 305.

HELLER, K. Laboratory interview research as analogue to treatment. In A. E. BERGIN & S. L. GARFIELD (Eds.), *Handbook of psychotherapy and behavior change: An empirical analysis*. New York: Wiley, 1971.

ISAACS, K. S., & HAGGARD, E. A. Some methods used in the study of affect in psychotherapy. In L. A. GOTTSCHALK & A. H. AUERBACH (Eds.), *Methods of research in psychotherapy*. New York: Appleton-Century-Crofts, 1966.

KENT, R. N., O'LEARY, K. D., DIAMENT, C., & DIETZ, A. Expectation biases in observational evaluation of therapeutic change. *Journal of Consulting and Clinical Psychology*, 1974, **42**, 774–780.

KERNBERG, O. F., BURSTEIN, E. D., COYNE, L., APPELBAUM, A., HORWITZ, L., & VOTH, H. *Psychotherapy and psychoanalysis: Final report of the Menninger Foundation's Psychotherapy Research Project*. Topeka, Kansas: Menninger Foundation, 1972.

KIESLER, D. J. Experimental designs in psychotherapy research. In A. E. BERGIN & S. L. GARFIELD (Eds.), *Handbook of psychotherapy and behavior change: An empirical analysis*. New York: Wiley, 1971.

KIESLER, D. J. *The process of psychotherapy: Empirical foundations and systems of analysis*. Chicago: Aldine, 1973.

LUBORSKY, L., & AUERBACH, A. H. The symptom-context method: Quantitative studies of symptom formation in psychotherapy. *Journal of the American Psychoanalytic Association*, 1969, **17**, 68–99.

LUBORSKY, L., GRAFF, H., PULVER, S., & CURTIS, H. A clinical-quantitative examination of consensus on the concept of transference. *Archives of General Psychiatry*, 1973, **29**, 69–75.

MAGNUSSON, D., HEFFLER, B., & NYMAN, B. The generality of behavioral data II: Replication of an experiment on generalization from observations on one occasion. *Multivariate Behavioral Research*, 1968, **3**, 415–422.

MAHL, G. F. Gestures and body movements in interviews. In J. M. SHLIEN (Ed.), *Research in psychotherapy*. Vol. 3. Washington, D.C.: American Psychological Association, 1968. Pp. 295–346.

MATARAZZO, J. D., WIENS, A. N., MATARAZZO, R. G., & SASLOW, G. Speech and silence behavior in clinical psychotherapy and its laboratory correlates. In J. M. SHLIEN (Ed.), *Research in psychotherapy*. Vol. 3. Washington, D.C.: American Psychological Association, 1968. Pp. 347–394.

MINTZ, J., AUERBACH, A. H., LUBORSKY, L., & JOHNSON, M. Patient's, therapist's and observers' views of psychotherapy: A 'Rashomon' experience or a reasonable consensus? *British Journal of Medical Psychology*, 1973, **46**, 83–89.

MINTZ, J., & LUBORSKY, L. Segments vs. whole sessions: Which is the better unit for psychotherapy research? *Journal of Abnormal Psychology*, 1971, **78**, 180–191.

ORNE, M. T., & WENDER, P. H. Anticipatory socialization for psychotherapy: Method and rationale. *American Journal of Psychiatry*, 1968, **124**, 88–98.

RUNKEL, P. J., & MCGRATH, J. E. *Research on human behavior: A systematic guide to method*. New York: Holt, Rinehart & Winston, 1972.

SCHEFLEN, A. E. Natural history method in psychotherapy: Communicational research. In L. A. GOTTSCHALK & A. H. AUERBACH (Eds.), *Methods of research in psychotherapy*. New York: Appleton-Century-Crofts, 1966.

SHWEDER, R. A. How relevant is an individual difference theory of personality? *Journal of Personality*, 1975, **43**, 455–484.

SIEGMAN, A. W., & POPE, B. (Eds.) *Studies in dyadic communication*. New York: Pergamon Press, 1972.

STRUPP, H. H., CHASSAN, J. B., & EWING, J. A. Toward the longitudinal study of the psychotherapeutic process. In L. A. GOTTSCHALK & A. H. AUERBACH (Eds.), *Methods of research in psychotherapy*. New York: Appleton-Century-Crofts, 1966.

WASKOW, I. E., & PARLOFF, M. B. (Eds.), *Psychotherapy change measures: A report of the Clinical Research Branch Outcome Measures Project*. Washington, D.C.: U.S. Government Printing Office, Department of Health, Education and Welfare Publication No. (ADM) 74–120, 1975.

WEBB, E. J., CAMPBELL, D. T., SCHWARTZ, R. D., & SECHREST, L. *Unobtrusive measures: Nonreactive research in the social sciences*. Chicago: Rand McNally, 1966.

WILEY, D. E., & HARNISCHFEGER, A. Post hoc, ergo propter hoc: Problems in the attribution of change. University of Chicago: *Studies of the Educative Process*, 1973, No. 7.

NOTES

1. Preparation of this chapter was supported in part by NSF Grant GS 3127 A No. 1.

2. *Editors' Footnote*. As Fiske will point out again, the lack of this "molecular" level research constitutes a major gap in psychotherapy research, and the "filling" of this gap (at first, perhaps, with descriptive and methodology-developing research, to be followed by correlative and hypothesis-testing work) should constitute quite valuable research. To study this area properly, however, may require some quite tedious and technically sophisticated methodology, such as frame-by-frame analysis of film, content-filtered audiotape analysis, etc. The findings may be quite rewarding, though, and several family dynamics researchers, among others, have broken some ground with such analyses, so that there is a technology available as well as a group of workers with relevant experience to be consulted.

3. *Editors' Footnote*. Wilkins makes a similar point in Chapter 13 of this volume: why postulate and research a nonobjectifiable, presumably mediating variable (expectancy), when one can as easily, and more parsimoniously, study the well-objectified verb-

al instructions that are presumed to "induce" expectancies and that predict (account for) everything that expectancies predict. Our response to both authors is that, first, the indirectness involved in using constructs such as personality or expectancy is not, of itself, bad, *if* a construct's referents are specific, consistent, objectifiable, and of proven predictive value. Ideally, constructs serve as a conceptual shorthand denoting specific objectifiable data such as high probability of a certain class of behaviors in certain situations. Secondly, they possess the advantages of aiding prediction and theory development. A collection of "pure" objective predictor behaviors must remain just that —unconnected to each other and less utilizable, both statistically and conceptually, as both predictors of other objective data and as links to other constructs (i.e., constituents of theories). Thus, to answer Fiske's question, it may not be absolutely necessary to study the therapist's personality, but from our viewpoint it seems strategically very helpful. Having said all this, let us remind the reader that vital to the use of constructs as advocated above is the careful, detailed "collection" of objective, predictive data that will comprise a construct. Thus, at a concrete, methodological level, the research strategy we advocate does not at all disagree with Fiske's (see Footnote 2).

4. *Editors' Footnote.* Probably this is true, and we *almost* unqualifiedly agree with it. But as clinicians we feel that there are at least brief periods, particularly with schizoid, paranoid, or acutely psychotic patients, when the patient's conscious, elicited (post-session, e.g.) report of his experience is *not* the most accurate in the sense of being clinically "true." Often with these patients, such reports may be based on projections or may involve defensive "anger." Furthermore, such patients may express withdrawal or mistrust as responses to the threat produced by therapist warmth or by these patients' own positive (approach) feelings in response to their therapists. In other words, our clinical experience tells us that often these patients may give untrue "negative" pictures. (We can imagine, though are less familiar with, situations producing distortions in the opposite direction.) This problem is quite knotty for research because, as the reader may have already observed, even acknowledging it requires adherence to a psychodynamic viewpoint —i.e., one that views the unconscious processes described above as important. (We are not considering deliberate, conscious distortion of responses here.) Now even if most latter-day, enlightened behaviorists allow for such a tenet, there is still the great difficulty of "proving" that such distortions occur. Perhaps the only way to do this would be to obtain patients' later acknowledgment that earlier reports were (defensively, e.g.) distorted; of course, eliciting or awaiting such acknowledgment poses its own problems. Of further concern to researchers is the extreme difficulty in deciding who can reliably and validly both indicate when such distortion is occurring and also give the truest picture of the patient when he is not distorting. The therapist might be able to do the former (better than a judge or patient), but the patient is probably best at the latter. Alternative "solutions" to this problem are (1) simply to "live with" the problem and rely solely on the patient, or (2) to use multiple viewpoint (therapist, patient, and judge) process and outcome ratings, not expecting very high agreement among the three.

5. *Editors' Footnote.* Here, Fiske points out still another (see Footnote 4) difficulty in deciding who should rate

the therapy process. His advocacy of using both judges and patients (for different aspects) lends support to the strategy of multiple ratings.

6. *Editors' Footnote.* This is true, but in their discussion of process, Auerbach and Johnson in Chapter 5 of this volume do provide some general leads, if not answers, to the question.

7. *Editors' Footnote.* While we do not really disagree with Fiske about the frequent necessity for pooling (i.e., summing in some way) data, we think that some of the limitations of summing need to be kept in mind. Fiske, for example, notes that we usually do not focus on a particular response in characterizing a person. But often we *do*—i.e., we focus on, or are strongly affected by, one or a few pieces of a person's behavior, often to the point of characterizing him by this behavior. A weakness, then, of data-summing procedures is that nearly all of them fail to valence adequately—i.e., to weigh—events so that their relative importance to the people involved (here, the patient and therapist) is reflected in the numerical values produced. This issue arises even more dramatically in considering Fiske's third point (that we mistrust the single event as idiosyncratic or biased). The point is, of course, well taken, particularly if we consider psychotherapy research a scientific enterprise. But by doing so, we bring to a head the art-vs.-science controversy of psychotherapy. Because to disregard the single event really implies disregarding, among other things, the whole notion of "critical moments" in therapy, a notion much written and talked about by clinicians, but essentially ignored by researchers. And it seems to us that to continue to ignore the different values of behavioral events (i.e., to continue to "count" without "weighing") means that our research will continue to emphasize statistical and methodological feasibility at the expense of clinical and (inter)personal significance. Psychotherapy research will thus run the risk of falling into the rut occupied by much other psychological research —of producing statistically "significant" and methodologically sound findings which are anything but significant in their impact and value. What is needed here, then, are imaginative methodologies that allow quantification of the import as well as the frequency of interpersonal events. This is obviously no small task, but one whose accomplishment might well tremendously vitalize, if not revolutionize, process research. Fiske's suggestion that two-act sequences be used as units of analysis is an important step toward obtaining the significance we describe, but still leaves us with the problem of valencing.

8. *Editors' Footnote.* Client satisfaction (patient report of improvement) probably constitutes a major exception to this state of affairs.

9. *Editors' Footnote.* The situation does not seem quite so bleak to us. The Barrett–Lennard Relationship Inventory, as well as other measures of empathy, warmth, and genuineness, and at least a few diagnostic and interactional style measures (e.g., Leary's and Schutz's), seem to constitute psychometrically sound means of measuring therapeutically relevant concepts.

10. *Editors' Footnote.* But this, in our view, is what analogue research tries to do —capture essential psychotherapy processes in miniaturized, economically feasible methodological situations. Thus, the distinction between sophisticated analogue research and homologue research is not really clear to us.

11. S. D. Duncan, Jr., & D. W. Fiske, *Face-to-face interactions: Research, methods, and theory.* Hillsdale, N.J.: Erlbaum (J. Wiley), 1977.

PART II

The Development and Ideology of The Psychotherapist

CHAPTER 3

PERSONAL AND SOCIAL IDENTITIES OF PSYCHOTHERAPISTS

WILLIAM E. HENRY

PSYCHOTHERAPISTS working in urban contexts represent a confluence of several social and historical forces. Most immediately they stem from specific training backgrounds of a medical character, as with psychiatrists and psychoanalysts, or of a college with graduate specialization, as with psychologists and social workers. Regardless of these differences in training context, they have all entered these training routes selectively, have maximized during their training the available experiences of a clinical nature, and have ended their training with some form of internship or residency providing practical models for their subsequent therapeutic work.

Most of these therapists received their training in the post-1940 period and initiated their practices, whether private or in organizations, in the period after World War II. This period had several features relevant to the development of psychotherapists which helped to mold the profession in the shape which characterized it in the late 1960s and early '70s. Prominent among these forces was the culturally acceptable premise that personal distress and varieties of socially undesirable behavior were somehow psychologically based and that they could be remedied by procedures which examined this psychological base. A change in the moral and ideological climate was effected in the immediate past by the obvious interplay of psychological factors in fear and courage in war, by direct experiences with traumatic neuroses, by the growing influence of psychological (primarily psychoanalytic) modes of thought in many areas. This mode of thought offered the unique and potent advantage of seeming to make sense of many diverse events and, in addition, proposed a solution based upon propositions closely related to the presumed causes. With distress or deviant behavior no longer seen as moral transgressions or as genetic embarrassments, the scene was set for the development of methods and persons prepared to cope with the new explana-

tion and to offer treatment articulated to the growing prominence of this new idea system. While the seeds of these ideas had clearly been around earlier, the upsurge at this time was marked and swept a whole new generation of persons into informed attention to psychological causes.

This increased enthusiasm for a point of view was not left to conversational groupings and intellectual discussion, however, but was rapidly implemented in institutional form, in instructional programs in colleges and universities, in the establishment of clinics and other treatment settings, and in the availability of funds in public and private sectors both for training and for the treatment of patients.

The potential psychotherapist of this period entered into early training, and later practice, in an atmosphere of enthusiasm, in the well-supported conviction that this realm of work was new and exciting. The study of this curious topic was open-ended and led always to some new event or explanation. Old symptoms were seen in new lights as the potentialities for new applications grew. And the extension of training and practice settings led to jobs. The premises which led to new practitioners also led to new patients, as the presumption of psychological need was shared by a significant public. Through this period there developed an increasing formalization, as government agencies were developed both to regulate and fund, as professional associations set standards and began to control forms of entry, and as training settings crystallized their particular forms of training and experience. In the context of increased formalization, there remained considerable new enthusiasm, as inventive therapists of many professions proposed new theories, as adherents to one group came into controversy with adherents of other groups. There evolved a pattern of high involvement, which was increased as one group accused the other of practicing without proper

47

knowledge, or of failing to take into account a psychic event which one group definitely knew to be vital. The new students and the new practitioners participated freely in this ferment and threw themselves with vigor into the examination of the various psychologies of self and others; with each new patient, each came more and more to the conviction of the rightness of his own views and to the development of confidence in his own techniques. More detailed portrayals of the development of psychotherapy, mental health, and manpower in general may be found in Blanck (1963) and in Arnhoff, Rubinstein, and Spiesman (1969).

But clearly not all persons sought training in these fields, nor, for that matter, did even a representative sample of potentially available college youth. As with most professions, and perhaps all occupations, entrance into the field was selective, both in terms of individuals who chose to apply and in terms of the criteria of institutions as to who was an appropriate candidate. The natural history of these processes of choosing and declining, of selecting this person and not that one, is very complex and hard to trace. Some portrayal of those processes and of the personal and social sources of persons in any occupation, however, can be gained by seeing the end result, by the study of those who do actually become members of the occupation. Such a portrayal still lacks some depth, since it is principally cross-sectional and indeed fails both to study the dropouts or to follow over time any group of potential entrants or any cohort of persons, some of whom do and some of whom do not enter the occupation. Still, some perspective is possible by examining different sectors of the field, by retrospective life histories of individuals in various parts of the field, by study of personal motivations for involvement in the area, and by study of the different guiding beliefs and ideologies.

In the present chapter, the effort to understand the sources of therapeutic personnel and some aspects of their personal lives is based upon the study of about 4,000 psychotherapists working in New York, Chicago, and Los Angeles. The sample being discussed represents about 60% of all known psychotherapists in these cities who are members of professions identified as psychoanalyst, psychiatrist, social worker, psychologist. It should be noted that this is not a sample of all persons doing any kind of therapy, although the overlap to such a sample would be considerable, but is a sample from these professional groups. In the case of psychiatrists

and psychoanalysts, we have assumed for selection purposes that all are psychotherapists, though we inquire subsequently about their actual work activities. All are also M.D.s, selected from the official membership list of their association. While some few psychoanalysts exist who are not M.D.s, none were found in this sample. For social workers, we have selected only those for whom we have evidence of some form of therapy practice, whether in agencies or private work. For psychologists, similarly, we have selected only those for whom we have evidence of psychotherapy work. Evidence included statements in professional directories claiming psychotherapy as an activity, as well as memberships in other specifically psychotherapy-oriented organizations. Clearly, other social workers and other psychologists exist who are not principally engaged in psychotherapy and they are excluded from these samples.[1,2] Included within these 4,000 are a subsample of 300 who were more intensively studied by interview methods.

The persons practicing in a given area of work at any given point in time represent a variety of influences. Some of these are of the nature discussed above and include the particular history of the rise or fall of a given area of work. These factors set the scene, so to speak, which individual persons enter in terms of their more particular set of personal histories. Entering the scene of the psychotherapist for a particular person can be perceived in a variety of ways. It is in part a matter of personal motivation—an interest in the kind of work, the opportunity to get relevant training, the encouragement of significant figures, the affinity for particular kinds of problems or persons encountered. And it is in part a matter of the actual training received. The presence or absence of training facilities and their actual character also influence the kind of professional one becomes and tend to direct one's attention to one kind of a problem as opposed to another. The facts of different social histories of individuals and different contemporary prestige systems in occupations suggest that there is a social pathway into particular occupations, a pathway somewhat independent of personal motivations or of specific kinds of training. Professions and occupations do recruit selectively from different social and educational levels as well as from different social and ethnic groups.

In the effort to understand a profession, the sources of its personnel, and the particular identities which they may portray to the persons with whom they interact, no single one of these ways of analyzing the field is sufficient. Personal motivations exist, but they exist in particular social contexts and in persons of particular social histories. Training is or is not available but always is of a character relevant to current social values and is participated in by persons whose motivations and views influence that training and its impact upon the person in training. While there are social coherencies in the backgrounds of persons in given professions, not all persons of those backgrounds enter a given profession and hence other factors are involved in the selectivity that results in the final membership of a group. In presenting these complex influences in the effort to identify psychotherapists, these various influences will be divided into three main areas and presented separately. These are presented as The Social Pathway, The Training Pathway, and The Personal Pathway. Each approach throws a somewhat different light on the field, and each is true in its own terms. Subsequently, an effort will be made to integrate these different facets, to suggest both their total impact upon the field and to show how they relate to the psychotherapist in his contemporary life.[3]

THE SOCIAL PATHWAY

There is a popular stereotype which portrays the psychotherapist (usually identified as a psychiatrist) as Jewish and with a German accent. While other models of the mental health professional exist and are heard occasionally in the film or other popular media, the accented Jewish psychiatrist remains a strong image. The identification of this figure as a representation of the professional psychotherapist is indeed a reasonable one. Not only does it represent symbolically the role of Freud and other early psychoanalysts in the initial emergence of the field, but also it portrays, if in a somewhat extreme form, a significant reality in the field. In our total sample, 34% are Jewish, 9% Catholic, 21% Protestant, and 36% are either agnostic, atheistic, or claim no religious adherence. These figures are in marked contrast to the general population estimate of 66% Protestant, 25% Catholic, and 3% Jewish. The overrepresentation of Jews and the underrepresentation of Catholics become important factors in understanding the field. Of equal interest in this area is the fact that in these data, 51% of the therapists of whatever background or religion claim a Jewish cultural affinity.[4] This implies a considerable sense of cultural homogeneity that is

Jewish in character. Not unexpectedly, this report of affinity is highest for the psychoanalyst, 62%, while 50% of each of the other professions also report such a Jewish affinity. But this should not be taken as a measure of actual religiosity. In fact, a most dominant finding regarding religious position is the strong tendency for all psychotherapists to be less religious than their parents. The 36% who report agnostic, atheistic, or no religion becomes important here as well, as does the sense in which the overrepresentation of Jews suggests not so much a religious position as a form of intellectual and cultural stance. In this regard, there are among the professions some differences which revolve around the degree to which the demand of psychic determinism is characteristic of the philosophical position of the particular profession. Thus, the psychoanalyst and the clinical psychologist tend, on the one hand, to have a more generally psychodynamic orientation[5] and, on the other, to report less religious positions. Psychiatrists and social workers have a more mixed position on the psychodynamic issue and report more religious adherence. These findings are influenced by specific religion, of course, as seen in the generally very low numbers of Catholics throughout all three professions. What Catholics there are here, however, are found more commonly among social workers and psychiatrists, fields again in which a lesser stress upon the psychic determinism permits an easier acceptance of a religious position.

Beyond the question of religion, however, lies the factor of ethnicity itself. If a diversity of values as represented by mixed cultural experiences is at all related to leading one into this field of work, then this sample should portray an ethnic mix out of proportion to the general population. And indeed it does. In reporting the countries to which they trace their origins, only 7.4% mention the United States, while 41% note Eastern Europe, 17% Germany-Austria, 24% Great Britain, and 9% Western Europe.[6] The Eastern European origin is highest among the psychoanalysts (48%), though still relatively high (37%) among the lowest group—social workers. Insofar as these origins reflect cultural values and images, they suggest the high likelihood that psychotherapists have been exposed to more than one set of cultural influences, at least those of the country of origin and those of America. Another aspect of this same cultural mix is the related fact that slightly more than half of all practitioners had foreign-born fathers —again highest for the psychoanalysts (60%)

and lowest for social workers (51%).

One basic social fact shared by our four professions is high socioeconomic status. While there are prestige variations within the professions, in objective measures of social status members of all groups are upper-middle or, in fewer cases, upper class. They have all, of course, had uncommon amounts of higher education. Their positions reflect a general upward social mobility. That is, within each profession the overwhelming majority of practitioners come from the middle class, Class III[7], or lower middle backgrounds, Class IV. Their present social positions in Class II or Class I represent their mobility across social class lines. The amount of mobility to Class II or I positions is greater among psychologists and social workers, reflecting the fact that, in general, the two medical groups are recruited in larger proportions from higher social positions. Within this framework of mobility, it is also true that there is a somewhat greater proportion of males from lower social positions than females, and an overrepresentation of Jews among those who have been upwardly mobile. Despite these variations, upward social mobility is a dominant biographical characteristic of psychotherapists. In this sense, as with religion, the therapists of all professions have a social status different from their parents.

Political biographies of therapists also show a tendency toward change from the positions of their parents. There is a heavy concentration of politically liberal professions in the mental health field. To some extent, this comes from the fact that members are recruited from liberal families, but there remains a strong tendency for these practitioners to have rejected parental political orientation in favor of a more liberal political position.[8] This fact applies equally well to psychoanalysis, psychology, and social work, though here psychiatrists are not considered. There are both more politically conservative persons among psychiatrists, but also a greater tendency for them to have adhered to the position identified for their parents.

Both religious position and political position are concerned with explanations of human behavior and as such should reflect rather similar general orientations among therapists. And in fact among these therapists there is a notable fit. Political adherence to the beliefs of parents is strongly related to adherence to religious beliefs in all four professions. Similarly, those who have changed their political beliefs to a more liberal position are heavily represented among those who have also changed to a more liberal religious position. The importance of these patterns for our purposes resides in the degree to which these positions represent one aspect of a more general attitude toward the social world. These positions contain and in effect summarize a wide range of views on the determinants of behavior, on standards of conduct as well as on views of what behavioral or personality changes are desirable. More liberal positions, and perhaps especially changes in this direction, represent the view that behavior problems can be eradicated through measures which improve underlying social and psychological conditions, and the view that for these changes to be effective, it is necessary that the source of the difficulty be understood. Persons committed to this perspective would appear to be more attracted to notions of psychological determinism and scientific methodology than to notions of indeterminacy, either in persons or in modes of knowing the universe.

Taken together, these elements of social background reflect a particular social world. It is a social world of initial marginality, in terms of ethnicity and culture of origin. And that world becomes more so as we find psychotherapists not only segregating themselves further from the mainstream by advanced education and upward mobility, but to a significant degree abandoning their parental roots by changes in basic values and attitudes as seen in their religious and political stances. These changes are not random, but seem to portray and to be an integral part of a belief system which moves away from formal social conservatism to the relativity of psychological and social determinism. The social pathway to becoming a psychotherapist thus selects and encourages persons who bring to this occupation, and to the interaction with their patients, the orientations and views represented by this order of social marginality and psychological relativity.[9,10]

THE TRAINING PATHWAY

The routes into particular forms of professional training represent long-term developmental processes containing a number of choice points, each of which tends to narrow the range of options until some particular career has been entered.

The point of no return, however, may differ from profession to profession, as may the number of choices open once one has received whatever is considered basic training in the field. The psychotherapists represented in the present study have taken four routes to their present positions—two of which have had more points of overlap than the others. The latter are, of course, the two medically based professions (psychiatrists and psychoanalysts) for whom college is followed by medical school and then by specialization in psychiatry. At this point, the psychoanalyst makes one further choice, or rather, decides to continue for further special training in psychoanalysis while the psychiatrist chooses to go into practice. Each of these steps represents a choice of particular educational and social experiences, and each tends to reduce the options possible for the next choice. Obviously, the therapist anywhere along these lines could actually make a choice to quit and adopt some other line of work, but in fact each higher step in training not only provides more specialized information, it also tends to bind one to the work in question and make one less and less qualified for some other field or work. The psychologist and social worker start the same pathway, college followed by graduate training in their special fields. Like the other two groups, this pathway also involves a further choice, that of specialization in clinical psychology or psychiatric social work after graduate work in psychology and social work. For these latter two groups, the common bond of medical training is missing and the total period of training is shorter. In a sense, the two medical professions also make an earlier choice, since pre-medical work in college most commonly is necessary and characteristic. Thus, the progression of interest and choice in each field is from the general parent field to the more specific. Psychoanalysts and psychiatrists become interested in medicine at around 14 or 15 but not in psychiatry until around age 23, for those who go into psychoanalysis, a further choice is typically made about two years later.

The interest in psychology for the psychologist comes around age 21, followed about two years later by an interest in clinical psychology. Social workers have a somewhat more mixed pattern, though within social work the progression from the more general to the specific still holds. Many social workers were initially interested in medicine (about 15%) or in psychology (about 28%) while they were in college, but tended not to develop an interest in social work until after college. It is only several years later that the specific interest in the psychotherapeutic aspects of social work develop. This delay in part reflects the lessened popular image of social work, as well as the not uncommon tendency for many social workers to have been employed before acquiring their psychiatric social work interest.

The degree to which these professional specialties become organized and more formally institutionalized also influences these patterns of choices. When comparing the age at which the decision is made to enter a profession with the present actual age of the subject, we find the greatest difference in psychology and social work. That is, the younger entrants made their decisions at earlier ages, presumably in part because of the more recently developed and extended training programs available which call attention to these fields and provide ready points of entry. Medicine, as an earlier established field, provides broad messages and notable imageries which are in part responsible for the earlier ages at which future psychiatrists and psychoanalysts make their choice of parent field. The sense in which the state of the field itself influences these choice patterns, as opposed to some more purely personal set of motivations, is also reflected in the stability of the choices made by the entrants. On the one hand, the entrants into the older and more known professions made their choices earlier and contemplated fewer alternatives. Specifically, 49% of psychiatrists and 53% of psychoanalysts claimed that they had considered some other occupations after high school graduation, whereas 83% of clinical psychologists and 74% of social workers considered some other possibilities. The possibility that this pattern is changing as the field provides more options for similar work in related fields is suggested by the fact that this pattern of choices among the medical specialties is broader among the younger entrants. The youngest among our sample thus considered more alternatives than did the older who entered the field when actual alternatives were fewer.

Beyond these general properties of the field lie a number of factors of a more individual nature. Professionals report frequently that specific persons in their environment have influenced their choice. Among this sample of psychoanalysts and psychiatrists, influence was exerted early and from persons close at hand—roughly two-thirds of the persons proposed as having such influence were either parents or relatives. For psychologists and social workers, less than a third of such figures are in these categories. The influencing figures for these groups came at a later age and were more distant figures. Nearly half of the influential figures mentioned by social workers are nonrelatives working in the field, two to three times the frequency of such figures mentioned by the other professionals. Similarly, psychologists identify teachers as the most influential figures. Entrants also identify particular experiences, as opposed to particular persons, as having been influential. Four out of five social workers note a work experience as relevant, about one-third of psychologists identify a formal teaching experience, and an additional fifth a reading experience as having roused their interest. Among psychiatrists and analysts, the general picture is one in which family dynamics were more relevant— i.e., identification with a parent or outside but related figure rather than particular experiences. Psychologists and social workers, on the other hand, were more influenced by experiences or persons in teaching or job roles. For the psychologist, the most important person was not a relative but a teacher, the most important experiences were teaching and reading, and the most important mode of influence was intellectual stimulation. For the social worker, the key figures were nonrelated professional social workers, the crucial experiences were jobs, and the chief mode of influence involved exposure to the field.

Reports of personal motivations for joining these fields seem generally consistent with these forms of influence. Social workers are differentiated from all other professions by the high frequency of their report of the desire to help people, by their need to achieve affiliation with others, and, by their desire to help and understand society. For the psychologist, the dominant reported motive is the desire to understand people. Other important distinctions in these reported motives include the motive to gain an identity, reported in high frequency by the two medical groups, but only minimally by the others. And, in a contrary pattern of distinctions, the motive to understand oneself characterizes the psychoanalysts and psychologists, the two most psychodynamically oriented, from the other two groups.

A similar pattern may be seen in a different kind of motivating factor—the degree to which therapists have themselves undergone therapy. It was suggested earlier that one of the common properties of this set of professions, and of the cultural values during the time of their training, was the prompting to study the self and others and to see psychological motives for behavior. In reporting figures on personal psychotherapy, it is suggested that the prevalence will reflect both

the interest in this form of inner contemplation and a form of socialization which in fact provides practice in the art of examining inner values and experiences. This is also a practice which continues to be reflected in habits of self-examination in later work and in setting a logic for the study of others. This set of experiences also begins to set a pattern for the logic of social interaction and for the development of a set of language patterns.

That the opportunity for such self study is accepted is seen in the fact that 74% of this sample have undergone therapy.[11] Such therapy is commonly encouraged by therapy trainers, but is mandatory only for psychoanalysts. Comparing professions, it is indeed the analysts who most consistently report having had personal therapy—97.5% have. The next most therapized group is the psychologists, of whom 74.7% have had therapy. These two groups are followed by 65% of the psychiatrists and 64% of the social workers. It is also relevant, as a measure of the extent to which therapy may be seen as a kind of model of a lifestyle that 52% of the analysts and 41% of the psychologists have had therapy from two to four times, not merely the once technically encouraged as a training experience. This figure is predictable less among the other groups; 30% of the social workers and 25% of the psychiatrists report added personal therapy.

These figures also parallel what has been suggested as the varying weights given to the psychodynamic stance among these professions— again with the analyst and the psychologist most concerned and the psychiatrist and social worker least. These comparative ranks still hold when one takes into account actual number of hours spent in therapy, rather than merely number of times therapy is entered into. The analysts are clearly the highest, in part because of the greater frequency of their having had full-scale analysis and for the other groups to have therapies of shorter duration. As a form of training experience, personal analysis serves also as a model of subsequent professional practice, partly indeed since so many experience therapy again during their professional careers. These therapy experiences are also significant as a kind of socialization into a particular form of social interaction, a form which comes to account for an important portion of their adult lives.

These more therapeutic forms of training occur at first within the context of the academic programs which characterize these fields and later, for some, within the internship or residency experience, and for those with more than one such experience, within the professional practice years. Some sense of the amount of other experiences within these programs may be gained by comparing the varying lengths of time which are spent in training. In the two medical groups, the mean length of time from the beginning of undergraduate education to the completion of post-residency training is 12.6 years for psychiatrists and 15.1 years for analysts. If one adds the 12 years commonly spent in elementary and secondary school, both have spent a considerable period of a normal life span in educational training—24.6 years for the psychiatrist and 27.1 for analysts. For clinical psychologists, the comparable time is more varied since the amount spent in post-degree internship or special training is less regular. For these psychologists, the 1 year internship is standard and 53% of this sample did just that, others taking internships of from 2 to 8 years. About 34% of the psychologists took some post-PhD work, most commonly in programs for further training in psychotherapy. The mean length of time in these postgraduate training programs is 3.9 years—less than the 5.4 years for the analyst and slightly more than the 3.3 years for the psychiatrist. The formal training program for psychologists places less emphasis upon psychotherapy than does that of psychiatrists; the 34% of psychologists who do elect to take additional training get slightly more than the psychiatrist though still less than the analyst. In overall terms the most extended period for the psychologist is 11.3 years, or, if we add the 12 years previously noted, a total of 23 years.

The route for psychiatric social workers is the shortest of these four professions, and is also less regular with more individual variations. For the majority, it consists of a 2-year graduate program in social work leading to the master's degree. After this, 27% go on to a second graduate program; of those, 60% receive no degree while 40% receive an additional degree. Fifty-seven percent of those receive the MSW, 12% take a master's in another behavioral science, and 30% take a PhD or DSW in social work. The mean length of time in such second graduate programs is 3 years. Post-doctoral work, mainly in university programs, is undertaken by about 17%. Many do enroll in programs conducted in institutes, about 13% of these being psychoanalytic in nature. All in all the mean time for social workers in such post-graduate training is 3.1 years. The overall mean length of training time from undergraduate through completion of post-graduate training, for those who take it, is 7.7 years. The total

time since elementary school, a figure which is given above for other groups, is less meaningful with social workers since their course tends to be more irregular, often with time out for work.

While each of these groups differ in the total years of training, all have significant portions of their training in direct practical contexts. In spite of this, and in spite of the total length of these programs, apparently these professions seldom consider themselves finished. A sizable portion of each profession still considers itself in training, in part by the second and third personal psychotherapy experience and in part in additional formal course work. At the time of this survey, 41% of the analysts, 32% of the clinical psychologists, 29% of the social workers, and 25% of the psychiatrists were then engaged in some educational or training experience. For a significant portion of these professionals, training continues hand in hand with practice.

Some background for these convictions of the worthwhile nature of therapy and therapy-related post-training experience may be seen by examining the value placed by professionals upon their prior training—from their undergraduate college work through the end of formal post-graduate work. Variations occur among the groups, related largely to the differing lengths of major training time and to particular elements of those programs, but several interrelated common features emerge. When formal course work, at whatever level, is compared with clinical work, it is clear that the clinical work is the most highly valued. While at each level many appreciate course work (and at each higher level even the course work becomes more related to practice), it was still the clinical work that was seen as the experience most significant in turning the student into a practicing professional. Each group participates heavily in personal therapy and values it highly; through the training years, as they gradually increase the percentage of their time in therapy-related experiences, they are as groups moving closer to each other. The common core of experiences, of increasing relevance with time, is also ideologically and theoretically of a highly overlapping nature. While each school of psychotherapy emphasizes the unique elements of its particular theory and to a much less degree its techniques, the similarities in fact are far greater than theory would suggest. A psychotherapist of any school relates to the patient in very similar ways, looks for responses from the patient in similar areas, and responds again to the patient stimulus in ways hard to distinguish according to the school of explanation or the professional label the therapist carries.[12]

A central feature of the training pathway has thus been to accommodate entrants from varying backgrounds, to introduce them to subject matter of the parent professions, and gradually to allow these base discipline issues to fade and to become replaced by an increasingly similar sense of involvement in the morals and modes of therapy, in a context where the fashion of relating to the patient has many similar features. Training thus brings to the therapist an emotional stance, an ideological preference for psychodynamic inner events, and a practical preference for personal interactions based upon the therapist-to-patient dialogue.

THE PERSONAL PATHWAY

In the discussion of the social pathway to becoming a psychotherapist, several features of past family and background have been presented. These features are in a sense also personal events since the elements of cultural marginality are clearly posited as having had personal influence upon each therapist and having contributed toward that identity and to the form of interactional expectations which the therapist presents to the patient. In this sense, one thing the therapist brings to the therapeutic scene is the set of values involved in this cultural relativity and the convictions involved in the psychodynamic stance, especially as they demand particular forms of interaction with the patient and as they direct expectations of the kind of thought and behavior that are to come from the patient. They similarly direct the interpretation that the therapist will place upon patient behavior. These expectational sets form a significant portion of the personal environment which the patient enters when he leaves, for specified periods, the world of normal social interchange.

But there is an additional element of potential influence of the therapist that can reside in his own intimate background—the extent to which his own early socialization and development may result in particular orientations which form a part of his therapeutic image. These questions may be approached in part by examining a number of life history events which are commonly associated with issues of early influence upon later personality. The question to which these points address themselves is whether, as psychotherapists, this group of men and women has had patterns of development which are set apart from normal patterns, the extent to which

their own personal pathway to adulthood has been idiosyncratic, deviant, or stressed particular experiences which might suggest the effects of traumatic events, distorted relationships, or special hostilities. In examining such issues, subjects have been asked a large number of questions about their personal lives. In summarizing some of their responses here, it should be noted that there are almost no differences among the four professions, except as specifically noted. The impact of this fact is that despite differing individual routes to therapy training, there appear to have been many common elements in their personal family and early childhood and adolescent lives.

Our therapists report generally positive relationships within their families, though about 39% do say the relation between their parents was not good. Sibling hostilities were minimal, with 60% saying that their experiences were good though mixed, or very good. Only a quarter of them suggest poor relationships with siblings. Dominance patterns among sibs were mixed, but 56% say that they themselves were the dominant sib. This slight emergence of the therapist over his sibs is particularly true of the psychoanalyst, though about equal among the other three groups. Traumatic events as a potential for distress parallel normal expectations. About 37% report some form of death in the family, 33% note some form of illness. About 50% of all therapists had some form of separation, more from mothers than fathers, in childhood or adolescence. National sample figures report about 30% to 40% of such separations up through childhood only. Mental illness in the family appears normal. The figure for this sample is 26%, whereas Srole, Langer, Michael, Opler, and Rennie (1962) report 23% for their midtown Manhattan sample and Leighton (1963) 22% for their rural sample.

In these aspects of early life experiences, there are clearly some persons, about one-fourth, who have experienced some form of upset relation, though indeed in proportions much like other general samples, and hence such proportions in no way set the therapist apart as coming from disturbed backgrounds.

When looked at in later life, these therapists begin to sound not so much like everybody as like a subsample of the college educated. They report that their parents generally avoided discussion of sexual issues, with about one-fourth specifically forbidding the topic and about 16% directly initiating sex discussion. About half say that they got their main early information from peers and most (62%) agree that there were no sudden discoveries but information gradually accumulated over the years. First sex experience is reported to have been in childhood, up to age 14, by 68% of the sample. Another 21% say that their first such experience was between the ages of 14 and 18, and another 11% did not have any sex experience or feeling until after high school. Having asked for a very broad interpretation of sex experiences or feelings, the somewhat surprising element here is only the percentages claiming no such event until after high school. Kinsey, Pomeroy, and Martin (1948) report that only 57% of their *total* sample report sexual experiences in preadolescence, whereas 70% of Kinsey's sample of preadolescents report such experiences. Our therapists are higher than Kinsey's total sample, but about identical with their preadolescent sample. The difference here could be seen as a shift in Kinsey's total sample from 57% in 1948 to 68% in our therapists in the 1960s, suggesting an historical shift toward greater such experience. Our therapist sample, however, is more like the college-educated subsample of Kinsey and hence this comparison is not quite appropriate. In addition, Kinsey's higher figure of 70% is indeed a figure given by subjects closer to the time of occurrence—by preadolescents regarding their preadolescent experience—and might be thought to more truly reflect the facts. That our therapists, now in their adulthood, seem to agree with Kinsey's preadolescents might be plausibly interpreted as reflecting the better memory of the therapists in the light of their professional avowal of the importance of sexuality in personality development.

Roughly half of our sample experienced intercourse by graduation from high school, 16% by age 16, and 45% by age 18. Thirty-three percent did not experience intercourse until college, and 22% not until after college. These figures compare well with Kinsey's college-educated groups, where 16% are reported as having coitus by age 16 and 38% by age 18. Our conclusion is that in general the therapists experienced sex in ways very similar to those of their college campus colleagues going into other occupations. It is true that within our group psychiatrists and social workers were about a year later than the psychologists and psychoanalysts, though they do not report any such differences in other aspects of their early sex experience or information.

In peer relations during these high school and college years, over 80% of this sample report satisfactory experiences both before high school and during it. About half of this 80% actually report their experience as having been very satisfactory. Fifty-eight percent report that they in general had only a few close friends, while 35% say they had many. As with early sex experiences, this pattern of experiences with peers is not visibly distinctive. Where comparisons are possible, the findings are in general agreement.

Intellectual activities during these years were generally positive and fairly extensive, as might be anticipated in this sample of persons who have not only graduated from college but had several years of further graduate work. Three-fourths report intellectual interests beginning in elementary school and the rest during high school. Sixty-five percent did superior work, 21% report merely good work, but only 14% note average or poor work. If there is any difference in the professions here, it is that the psychoanalysts report somewhat more superior performance. The picture which emerges is that of a group of intellectually interested persons with adequate to positive early life and adolescent experiences who differ from a general population mainly in somewhat early interest and delayed sexual activities, a pattern in common with other college-educated groups. There is very little in these personal backgrounds to suggest experiences leading to emotional distress, nothing to suggest major dissociative experiences, personal hostilities, or severe affective deprivations.

While the samples and objectives were not identical, the work of Holt and Luborsky (1958), in which more and less successful psychiatric residents were compared, seems to be in accord with this portrayal. They comment that the better residents were notable for three elements —higher on "genuineness" (as opposed to "facade"), better in social adjustment to coworkers, and freer from "status-mindedness." Kelley and Fiske (1951), in discussing the prediction of performance among clinical psychologists, note a somewhat broader range of attributes which, however, still seem to be in keeping with this general picture. They note the importance of broader interests, adaptability, imagination, desire to understand people scientifically, insight into self, and good quality of their intellectual accomplishments. All of these seem to be signs of a generally positive psychological and intellectual health.

It is true, of course, that several writers think of the psychotherapist as having had a particularly difficult time in early life and see his dedication to therapy as a form of adaptive com-

pensation. Burton (1972), in his comments on
the lives of 12 prominent therapists, sees several
factors of this sort. The therapists whom he
discusses and whose lives are presented through
their own autobiographies, are all highly special
people, being notable contributors to new ideas
in the field. What may be true of them may not
necessarily be true of the more ordinary therapist. In her examination of motivational factors
in psychotherapists, Roe (1969) notes that some
authors do suggest a quest for omnipotence in
psychiatric residents, and Wheelis (1956) sees,
for psychoanalysts, such determining factors as
the need for insight in a struggle for self-mastery
or the need for intimacy. Whether such factors as
the desire for self-mastery or the need for intimacy distinguish psychoanalysts from other therapists, or from other persons with higher education and professional goals, however, is not so
clear. Roe's comments seem to favor the proposition that there is very little evidence in personality research that would permit one to distinguish
the psychotherapist from other persons of graduate education, and broadly social professional
interests. Roe's summary is largely in harmony
with our own conclusions from the present research in viewing psychotherapists as a reasonably balanced group of educated persons with a
positive sense of their own competence and
identity. This does not deny variations in individual styles and other personal attributes, but
does suggest a broad common framework of
approach to the highly personal character of
their psychotherapeutic work.

THE CONTEMPORARY SCENE

The psychotherapeutic encounter is a highly
personalized, circumscribed set of social and
verbal interactions, predicated on a particular
set of assumptions about the nature of behavior,
its variations, and its alteration. As such, it dictates a specialized kind of communication which
directs the conversation and interactions of both
parties. Psychodynamic concepts serve as the
rationale for this interaction and the psychodynamic language sets the terms of the dialogue.
In this sense, this encounter differs from ordinary
interpersonal exchanges. In it the terminology of
everyday social exchange is avoided and a specialized set of terms is used to permit the therapist
to interpret and recognize the meaning of behavior and reported experience. The psychodynamic paradigm provides this context and constitutes a central feature of the verbal and affective
contribution of the therapist to his task.

In another sense, however, the therapist also
brings to the task a particular set of selective
devices. The patient that becomes engaged in
therapy is selected in terms of his availability to
participate in this mode of exchange. Since the
language of the therapist is so specialized and
since he sees the encounter as resting so heavily
upon verbal exchange, it is no surprise that the
therapist attracts persons who speak his own
language.

And in each of these encounters the therapist
also brings to the patient a particular set of
attitudes, within the context of which he conducts the relationship. These attitudes, as suggested by Holt and Luborsky (1958) are those of
an introspective orientation, an intellectual predisposition, and a relativistic perspective upon
behavior. These attitudes further differentiate
the therapy scene from ordinary social life, providing, in psychodynamic words, an ambiance
for the patient in which his behavior and viewpoints are not judged arbitrarily but are rather
examined and reviewed sympathetically and
assigned meaning in a rational context. For the
therapist, too, this form of exchange has formative properties, directing the nature of the responses he makes to and receives from others.
For the therapist, it provides an interactive set
which can be seen to sustain and reinforce the
principal interactive sets learned during his
training period, providing a continuing resocialization in a particular stance toward his
work. And for the therapist, of course, it goes on
all day long, not just for the limited appointment
of an individual patient.

Adherence to this psychodynamic paradigm
sets the psychotherapist apart from other persons. This separation, and the special interpretations of behavior upon which it is based, is part
of the mystique that tends to surround therapists. This kind of distancing is a result of the
fact that therapists see social interaction in highly specialized terms, terms that tend to create
tensions and disjunction in nontherapeutic contexts and to provide a sense of personal comfort
primarily in therapeutic contexts.

The psychotherapist is a person of deep conviction and wholehearted devotion to his patients and to a psychodynamic explanation of
behavior. This firm dedication creates for the
therapist not only a technical professional vocabulary but a lifestyle. It is this lifestyle, with its
assumptions and demands about behavior and
its meaning, and the special constraints which it
places upon personal action, that the therapist
most centrally contributes to the therapeutic

scene. The patient, in entering this world, must suspend belief, at least temporarily, in the terms of ordinary social interaction, and come to review his own life experiences in new ways. That this form of dialogue is helpful to the patient in his subsequent ordinary social living is a basic tenet of the therapist's belief system, one which he attempts to import to the patient through demonstration—that is, through the thoroughness and conviction with which he insists upon his way of examining the patient's life and experience. The degree of success achieved may be partly reflected in the degree to which the patient comes to partake of this conviction and himself adopt the basic psychodynamic paradigm which constitutes the main life way of the psychotherapist.

THOUGHTS TOWARD THE FUTURE

The direction which the future will take in mental health care and in the persons who provide it clearly rests upon a number of factors beyond the character of the field's current principal participants. For one, it will develop in part in relation to the theories of mental health and the treatments in vogue. We have already seen several shifts in these factors, as possession and magic have been usurped by medicine, as psychological causation and theory have supplemented the genetic and, in many sectors, biologic explanation. More recently we have seen several kinds of diffusion of the concept of mental illness. One of these has been the reduction of the implied seriousness by the presentation of the concept of problems of living— clearly a more mundane and frequently occurring upset in ordinary relations. And we have seen a major shift in emphasis, not entirely identified with the problem of living concept but benefiting from it, in the proposal that the causation stated in the psychodynamic paradigm is wrong, and that distressful or merely unwanted behavior, arising, as it is proposed, from injudicious arrangement of rewards and conditions in the social world, may be modified by alternative conditioning systems developed by a behavior modifier.

These two sets of logic have at least two things in common. One, they have altered the degree of seriousness of the mental symptom and defused, as it were, the sense of intensity inherent in the more psychodynamic formulations.[13] Two, they have prompted innovations in treatment concepts and methods. These new concepts and methods have not come only from persons outside the psychodynamic paradigm but have stemmed also from modifications of technique and therapeutic goals from within this group. Each of the four professions dealt with in this chapter has in varying degrees participated in such innovations. Some of these changes have the character of diffusing over several fields— learning and classroom behavior, dental habits, smoking, as well as more traditional mental health symptoms. And some have prompted a diffusion of participants—encouraging housewives and executives, schoolteachers and professors to seek growth experiences—and thus permitting many to change the definition of their distress from that of symptom to that of minor insufficiency, or perhaps only a lack of enriching environment. Such movements have probably also brought many people to the fore who never could and do not now think of themselves as needing mental health care and yet who find worthwhile various of the newer modes of group participation.[14]

As the field of patients/participants has become more mixed, so has the character and background of the therapists/leaders. To a large degree, the newer concepts of treatment—excluding in part some of the developments in the field of drugs—are ones for which there are no apparent and necessary professional routes to training. This has meant that many persons were able to qualify quickly for performance of many skills without having also to qualify for professional status and degrees. Delimited training programs, sometimes merely participation in what is seen as the modal treatment for a given new form, has permitted persons to undertake the therapist role. Similarly, persons with professional training—as psychiatrists, psychotherapists, social workers, pastoral counselors, marriage counselors—have been often quite ready to take on a new mode of treatment by those same routes. Thus, a former housewife or accountant and a former psychiatrist may be offering what is at least superficially the same treatment opportunities.

The significant growth of the field of behavior modification in the past few years has added to the field both more professionals and more persons without professional mental health backgrounds but with special skills in the behavior therapy area. This field differs somewhat from other new modalities in having a background in operant conditioning and concepts of social learning. This difference is probably reflected in the greater development of this field in university teaching and training programs, as well as the somewhat greater tendency for this area to consider research evidence pertinent to their methods and claims.[15]

The field of community mental health, or community psychology, has also added its particular thrust to this mix of mental health relevant issues. Its thrust, of course, has been its only very vaguely achieved goal of introducing the theory that mental health issues and related problems of living occur in, and are produced by, communities—that is, by the particular human relevant values, interaction patterns, options, and constraints presented by a given living space. This image, represented most forcefully by the Community Mental Health Act of 1963 and the attendant establishment of Community Mental Health Centers, both from federal and other agency funds, has had a very unclear impact upon the field. While portraying the theory of social causation, it has hired and used persons who do not believe in it and who instead practice therapies based on the psychodynamic paradigm. While announcing the very sound goals of prevention, as opposed to after-treatment, the movement has hardly been able to demonstrate the meaning and potential of this goal. Constriction in federal funding has meant the abandonment of many sincere efforts in this direction and made extremely difficult the furtherance of these relevant and desirable goals. While the area has raised to public and professional attention the relevance of community living in both its formative and potentially ameliorative dimensions, its future as a movement or its impact upon mental health concepts now seems unclear, even though some of its antecedents in concepts of milieu treatment, open wards, and hospitals remain viable in some areas.

Each of these developments presents its own set of concepts—some looser than others—around which specific procedures could develop. The "growth" movement has sponsored a wide variety of new treatment modes, but very few new concepts and essentially no evidence that any of it works (see especially Lieberman, Yalom, & Miles, 1974). The behavior modification field has presented new concepts, new procedures which can be learned and practiced, and solid evidence that some procedures work (Rimm & Masters, 1974). Each of these areas provides rationales, a kind of built-in paradigm of meaning that could attract practitioners and give a guideline to practice. The Community Mental Health movement provides some useful concepts but at a fairly high level of abstraction and,

in most instances, remote from practitioner action. Its claim on new persons as a system of belief guiding diagnosis and treatment is still very tenuous.

The great advantage of the psychodynamic paradigm has been its hold on patients and therapists alike, a hold based on its claim of total life relevance, its review of past life and meaning systems, and its provision of techniques that appear to work, both for the patient and therapist. One question on future modes of practice may well be just how involving, how "believable," both for client and therapist, other treatment modalities will be. For the various group sensitization experiences, the query is possibly that of how long the draw of the immediacy concept will hold or, phrased differently, will it not be further diffused into interesting forms of parlor games and group get-togethers. Influencing this, of course, will be the question of evidence, formal or mythic, that it "works." For the behavior modification approach, already gaining stable credence in many areas, the main question may be the extent to which it can be shown to deal adequately with diffuse neurotic and character disorders, now the main province of the psychodynamic paradigm, or whether its initial enthusiasm will fade if its successes continue to be principally for highly specific and delimited undesirable behaviors.[16] In denying the more general and personality-related generalness of the psychodynamic paradigm, the behavior theorists run the risk of having no believable alternatives.

If it is true, as proposed in this chapter, that there is a fairly integral relationship between life development and the espousal of the psychodynamic paradigm, the question of future practice in the mental health field may rest in some significant degree on the question of credibility raised above, and in the question of who finds what particular mode of belief desirable—that is, from where do its practitioners come and what form of evidence do they require for their involvement in the development of that mode of treatment.

Some cue may reside in limitations inherent in the psychodynamic paradigm, That is, it seems clear that part of the fact of limited service to some kinds of patients is, in part, built into the system. As it stands now, it seems improbable that either very new concepts of treatment or any major extension in age, ethnic group, or diagnostic category will occur with professionals now trained in the psychodynamic paradigm, even though its appearance under the guise of community mental health or crisis intervention may make it appear so. Surely some of the awkwardness with the community concepts has come not only from its short history and economic difficulties, but from the lack of personnel with any significant belief or training in its particular concepts and methods. And in part it should be noted that this field has not developed any uniquely new and appropriate concepts and methods that could serve as an implementation of a new philosophy. In another sense, of course, its broadest aims almost defined it out of the field in which it was directly located and out of the forms, concerns, and competencies of the people employed to run it. Insofar as its principal constituency was seen to be those not generally treated in private practice, it was a psychology for the poor, the minority, the elderly, though not, interestingly enough, for the children, that other group notably under represented in psychotherapeutic practice. It is not only that these are groups of potential clients with whom community mental health personnel have had no experience, but also that the basic concepts and images are more those of an "enriched" welfare system than they are of a mental health system as it is currently known. One of the real questions for the future will indeed be that of reconciling the desired client with the aims most appropriate for what is perceived to be his problem. Insofar as stable employment and income are crucial issues, insofar as the structure of community life is an issue, the relevant personnel, except coincidentally, are not to be found in mental health systems. Insofar as alcoholism, drug abuse, depression, confusion, and chronic brain syndromes are at issue, then only a very specialized and generally not psychodynamic sector of the mental health world is relevant.

The choice of personnel relevant for various mental health purposes will come to hinge upon the particular goals and target populations at issue. For one thing, it seems obvious that the range of social types needed is indeed greater, for example, than those now practicing within the psychodynamic paradigm. If, for example, the community mental health concept at all implements the prevention theme, it will need persons more familiar with childhood, with educational systems, with leisure and sports, and with normal community living. In this case, the real question is perhaps whether the definition of the purposes and aims will not shift the focus of activities away from mental health and its characteristic personnel and toward more usual educative forms of norm management.

Moving out to the broader community and to the variety of growth experiences available, it is possibly true that a wider and less formally trained group of leaders will arise and be quite adequate for the purpose. As this happens, however, and as the intensity of meaning associated with mental illness is diffused, it seems highly probable that the ideology and contexts of mental illness will be restricted. In this case, and clearly already in progress, these group events will become less associated with ideologies of mental health (as their own literature proposes) and more associated with other forms of cultural innovations, social engineering, and leisure time activities (see especially Laswell, 1969).

What needs to be contemplated, in viewing the future, is the interplay of goals and theories and persons. The field is, in one sense, already too big for itself and has begun to cast off several sectors of its tasks. These sectors, formerly part of some shared core of mental health ideology, need each to be seen as potentially separate and their worthwhileness reviewed, though possibly under some community concept other than mental health.

The other end of this potential split may be developments occurring in the field of drugs, where a less community, less psychodynamic, and more organic logic may prevail, a logic which will suggest its own ends and preselect its own personnel. The psychodynamic paradigm is by no means shattered, however, and while it may become clear that its relevance can be judiciously restricted, its future seems still to reside in its relevance for the middle and upper social range where belief in its merit, the value of introspection, and good verbal skills still persist.[17]

REFERENCES

ARNHOFF, F. N., RUBENSTEIN, E. A., & SPIESMAN, J. C. (Eds.) *Manpower for mental health*. Chicago: Aldine, 1969.

BLANCK, G. S. *The development of psychotherapy as a profession: A study of the process of socialization*. Ann Arbor, Mich.: University Microfilms, 1963.

BURTON, A. *Twelve therapists*. San Francisco: Jossey-Bass, 1972.

CLARK, K. E. *America's psychologists*. Washington, D.C.: American Psychological Association, 1957.

HENRY, W. E., SIMS, J. H., & SPRAY, S. L. *The fifth profession: Becoming a psychotherapist*. San Francisco: Jossey-Bass, 1971.

HENRY, W. E., SIMS, J. H., & SPRAY, S. L. *Public and private lives of psychotherapists*. San Francisco: Jossey-Bass, 1973.

HOLLINGSHEAD, A. B., & REDLICH, F. C. *Social class and mental illness*. New York: Wiley, 1958.

HOLT, R., & LUBORSKY, L. *Personality patterns of psychiatrists*. New York: Basic Books, 1958.

KELLEY, F. L., & FISKE, D. W. *The prediction of performance in clinical psychology.* Ann Arbor: University of Michigan Press, 1951.

KINSEY, A., POMEROY, W., & MARTIN, C. *Sexual behavior in the human male.* Philadelphia: Saunders, 1948.

LASWELL, H. D. The politics of mental health objectives and manpower assets. In F. N. ARNHOFF, E. A. RUBENSTEIN, & J. C. SPIESMAN (Eds.), *Manpower for mental health.* Chicago: Aldine, 1969.

LEIGHTON, D. *The character of danger.* New York: Basic Books, 1963.

LIEBERMAN, M. A., YALOM, I. D., & MILES, M. B. *Encounter groups: First facts.* New York: Basic Books, 1974.

RIMM, D. C., & MASTERS, J. C. *Behavior therapy: Techniques and empirical findings.* New York: Academic Press, 1974.

ROE, A. Individual motivation and personal factors in career choice. In F. N. ARNHOFF, E. A. RUBENSTEIN, & J. C. SPIESMAN (Eds.), *Manpower for mental health.* Chicago: Aldine, 1969.

ROGOW, A. A. *The psychiatrists.* New York: Putnam's Sons, 1970.

SROLE, L., LANGER, T., MICHAEL, S. T., OPLER, M. K., & RENNIE, T. A. *Mental health in metropolis: The midtown Manhattan study.* New York: McGraw-Hill, 1962.

WHEELIS, A. The vocational hazards of psychoanalysts. *International Journal of Psychoanalysis,* 1956, **37,** 171–184.

EDITORS' REFERENCES

BANDURA, A. *Principles of behavior modification.* New York: Holt, Rinehart & Winston, 1969.

FRANKS, C. M., & WILSON, G. T. (Eds.) *Annual review of behavior therapy.* Vol. 1. New York: Brunner/Mazel, 1973.

FRANKS, C. M., & WILSON, G. T. (Eds.) *Annual review of behavior therapy.* Vol. 2. New York: Brunner/Mazel, 1974.

GARFIELD, S. L., & KURTZ, R. A survey of clinical psychologists: Characteristics, activities, and orientations. *The Clinical Psychologist,* 1974, **28,** 7–10.

GOLDSTEIN, A. P. *Structured learning therapy: Toward a psychotherapy for the poor.* New York: Academic Press, 1973.

HERSEN, M., EISLER, R. M., & MILLER, P. M. (Eds.) *Progress in behavior modification.* Vol. 1. New York: Academic Press, 1975.

KANFER, F. H., & GOLDSTEIN, A. P. *Helping people change.* New York: Pergamon Press, 1975.

KEPECS, J. G., & GREENLEY, J. R. *The Wisconsin study of mental health careers.* University of Wisconsin Medical School, 1975.

LORION, R. P. Patient and therapist variables in the treatment of low-income patients. *Psychological Bulletin,* 1974a, **81,** 344–354.

LORION, R. P. Social class, treatment attitudes, and expectations. *Journal of Consulting and Clinical Psychology,* 1974b, **42,** 920.

MAHONEY, M. J. *Cognition and behavior modification.* Cambridge, Mass.: Ballinger, 1974.

O'LEARY, K. D., & WILSON, G. T. *Behavior therapy: Application and outcome.* New York: Prentice-Hall, 1975.

RIMM, D. C., & MASTERS, J. C. *Behavior therapy: Techniques and empirical findings.* New York: Academic Press, 1974.

SLOANE, R. B., STAPLES, F. R., CRISTOL, A. H., YORKSTON, N. J., & WHIPPLE, K. *Psychotherapy vs. behavior therapy.* Cambridge, Mass.: Harvard University Press, 1975.

NOTES

1. Further information on this sample may be found in Henry, Sims, and Spray (1971, 1973).

2. *Editors' Footnote.* One of the key questions that will no doubt strike the reader concerns the generalizability of the findings described in this chapter. The only other large sample systematic study of the sorts of issues and dimensions discussed by Henry that we know of is that of Kepecs and Greenley (1975). Their study represents, in part, an important effort to examine differences between urban and nonurban psychotherapists. Specifically, this study examined a sample of 582 psychiatrists from Chicago ($N = 338$) and Wisconsin ($N = 244$), who were further subclassified as analysts ($N = 11$ from Wisconsin, 135 from Chicago) and nonanalysts ($N = 233$ from Wisconsin and 203 from Chicago). Kepecs and Greenley obtained an acceptable questionnaire return rate (68.3% for Wisconsin psychiatrists; 62.7% for Chicago psychiatrists). At several points in this chapter, we will refer to the findings of Kepecs and Greenley. At the time of this writing, most of their findings had not yet been prepared for publication, so that we are indebted to them for sharing with us a significant amount of their unpublished data.

3. An independent study by Rogow (1970) of data from 149 psychiatrists and 35 analysts conducted in 1966 shows quite similar patterns. It provides in addition, however, some intriguing material documenting their more liberal political views, substantial material on political activities within the two relevant professional associations, and, in particular, details of training curricula. Rogow also provides an analysis of the psychological climate of the 1960s and relates these issues to the values held by psychiatrists and analysts.

4. *Editors' Footnote.* In contrast, Kepecs and Greenley (1975) found only 16% of their nonurban (Wisconsin) psychiatrists claiming a Jewish cultural affinity. Their data on Chicago psychiatrists were nearly identical to those of Henry, and showed 52% claiming such an affinity. In addition, their data showed the following distributions of religious preferences: *nonurban psychiatrists*—Jewish, 12%; Catholic, 25%; Protestant, 30%; none, 34%; *urban psychiatrists*—Jewish, 34%; Catholic, 6%; Protestant, 10%; none, 48%. Thus, a major difference between these two samples appears to be the higher proportion among nonurban psychiatrists of Catholic and Protestant clinicians, 55% vs. Henry's 30%.

5. *Editors' Footnote.* While we are unaware of recent analogous data on psychiatrists and social workers, this clearly is no longer the case for clinical psychologists. In a very recent survey, Garfield and Kurtz (1974) found the distribution of theoretical orientations among clinical psychologists to be: eclectic, 54.97%; psychodynamic (psychoanalytic, neo-Freudian, Sullivanian), 19.06% rational-behavioral (rational-emotive, learning theory), 11.69%; phenomenological (client-centered, existential, humanistic), 7.13%; other, 7.14%.

6. *Editors' Footnote.* Kepecs and Greenley's (1975) data on the ancestry of their psychiatrists showed virtually no difference from the Henry data in the distribution of nonurban respondents—i.e., 59% Eastern European (vs. Henry's 58% total of Eastern European plus Germany-Austria), and 41% Western European (vs. Henry's 33% total of Western European plus Great Britain). Interestingly, they found an even higher (87%) proportion of Eastern European backgrounds among their urban therapists than did Henry.

7. These socioeconomic positions are based on the Hollingshead and Redlich systems in which Class I is upperclass, II—upper-middle, III—intermediate-middle, IV—lower-middle, and Class V—lower class.

8. *Editors' Footnote.* The Kepecs-Greenley (1975) data, on the other hand, show that a smaller percentage of non-

urban psychiatrists come from politically liberal backgrounds (32% and 33% liberal for respondents' fathers and mothers, respectively). Still, the Kepecs-Greenley data appear to support Henry's view that the concentration of political liberals among professional psychotherapists reflects a change from parental political orientations. Thus, Kepecs and Greenley found that while roughly 66% of their nonurban psychiatrists came from politically conservative backgrounds, only 28% of these respondents reported their own political leanings to be conservative. Similarly, and somewhat more strikingly, approximately 50% of urban psychiatrists' parents were reported to have held politically conservative views, while only 13% of these subjects considered themselves to be conservative. Thus, while both groups show a "liberalizing" over generations, the "law of initial values" seems to be operating, such that approximately twice as many nonurban psychiatrists describe themselves as conservative.

9. It may be noted that the psychiatrists studied here were all those listed in directories and that the assumption was first made that all were psychotherapists. However, psychiatrists may be seen as being one of at least two kinds, the more organic-oriented or the psychologic-oriented, as Hollingshead and Redlich (1958) have observed. This distinction is probably operative in our sample returns. We found that in fact the more organic psychiatrists do not perceive their work as "psychotherapy" and hence felt the study was of lesser relevance to them. Organic psychiatrists were thus underrepresented. Experience in the selecting of the smaller sample more intensively interviewed also suggests that they were more resistant to being participants. From this clearly less than adequate sample, it does seem that, in comparison with the psychologic-oriented psychiatrists, the organic psychiatrists work more in institutions than in private practices and are probably both less mobile socially and less culturally marginal. The organic psychiatrist would thus be less likely to have followed this particular social pathway and less a participant in the psychodynamic paradigm.

10. *Editors' Footnote.* As noted in Footnotes 4 and 6, psychiatrists from nonurban areas do not appear to fit the image of social marginality to the extent that urban psychiatrists do. Whether changes in the distribution of theoretical orientations (e.g., the Garfield and Kurtz data noted in Footnote 5) represent a related parallel process is uncertain, but they do suggest an interesting line of inquiry. A study of the "personal pathway" of doctorally trained behavior therapists, for example, would be quite intriguing.

11. *Editors' Footnote.* In this regard, the Kepecs-Greenley data show at least a tendency toward urban-nonurban differences. Among their nonurban psychiatrists, 58% had had therapy at least once, while 80% of the urban psychiatrists had had personal therapy.

12. *Editors' Footnote.* We do not agree with this characterization. See Sundland (Chapter 9, this volume) for an overview of interschool differences and similarities and compare, for example, the chapters in this volume by Strupp (Chapter 1) and Johnson and Matross (Chapter 15) on the nature of the therapist's influence, and Wilson and Evans (Chapter 20) and Mitchell, Bozarth, and Krauft (Chapter 18) on the nature of the therapeutic relationship.

13. *Editors' Footnote.* We believe that there now exists substantial evidence that, in fact, the psychodynamic paradigm has not produced effective therapeutic interventions for a number of common clinical problems that appear more effectively treated in other ways. Bandura (1969), among other social learning theorists, offers a powerfully persuasive alternative framework for viewing the causes of psychological dysfunction and distress. Readers not familiar with psychotherapy based upon

social learning theory may wish to consult any of several excellent recent texts in the field (e.g., Franks & Wilson, 1973, 1974; Goldstein, 1973; Hersen, Eisler, & Miller, 1975; Kanfer & Goldstein, 1975; Mahoney, 1974; O'Leary & Wilson, 1975; Rimm & Masters, 1974). In any case, however, it is inaccurate to imply, as Henry does, that behavioral and other newer systems of psychotherapy have "altered the degree of seriousness of the mental symptom." Behavior therapists, no less than other therapists whose conceptualizations of the nature of psychopathology differ from the psychodynamic paradigm (e.g., family therapists), are quite aware of and sensitive to the phenomenological intensity of their patients' suffering. Clearly, the psychodynamic paradigm can stake no special claim to acknowledging the richness and complexity of human behavior.

14. *Editors' Footnote.* We are not at all convinced that such redefinitions are inherently undesirable; in fact, we would argue that if such terminological changes allow people not to label themselves as "ill" but serve to facilitate their growth by demystifying and destigmatizing change-producing experiences, such labels are to be encouraged.

15. *Editors' Footnote.* While we, too, are disconcerted by the recent flood of people claiming to be well-trained psychotherapists, we fundamentally disagree with Henry on two points he raises here. First, we agree that, as in his example, "a former housewife or accountant and a former psychiatrist may be offering what is at least *superficially* the same treatment opportunities" (emphasis added). But it is clear to us that, on the whole, people of such diverse backgrounds and training experiences do not, in fact, do the same things (see, e.g., Anthony & Carkhuff, Chapter 6, this volume; Emrick, Lassen & Edwards, Chapter 7, this volume). Moreover, if it can be documented that they do different things effectively, we are in favor of such nontraditional diversification and specialization. Second, it is quite inaccurate to characterize behavior therapists as "without professional mental health backgrounds." While recently trained behaviorally oriented clinical psychologists may not, at times, have received their training in the mainstream of *traditional* mental health programs and settings, they clearly have been trained quite professionally.

16. *Editors' Footnote.* For rather persuasive, though preliminary, evidence that such failure probably will not ensue, see Sloane, Staples, Cristol, Yorkston, and Whipple (1975).

17. *Editors' Footnote.* While we agree that psychotherapists are tremendously limited in their ability to respond to different client needs if they attempt to apply uniform treatment strategies in all cases, we do not agree that the psychodynamic paradigm is *inherently* relevant only in the treatment of the "upper social range." Lorion (1974a) recently reviewed the empirical literature on patient and therapist variables in the treatment of low-income patients and concluded that, "Despite extensive theorizing about the more inappropriate expectations held by low-income patients, few actual differences among social groups have been observed. All social classes share expectancies about the nature and duration of treatment" (p. 344). In a study by the same author (Lorion, 1974b) of social class and treatment attitudes and expectations, 90 applicants for outpatient therapy, drawn from Hollingshead's Classes III, IV, and V, showed no between-group differences in help-seeking attitudes. They did *not* anticipate a highly active, supportive, problem-solving therapist and *were* able to differentiate the role of the therapist from that of traditional medical caregiver. Furthermore, they assumed that the therapist's primary function would be to listen. Our position on this issue is that such "patient" expectations usually represent the mote in the eyes of the therapist. While we applaud the efforts of those clinicians (e.g., Goldstein,

1973) who are attempting to broaden the base of treatment approaches for the poor and for the non-YAVIS client, we would encourage such innovative strategies for *all* potential clients, since we favor therapeutic specificity and treatment-tailoring universally. Furthermore, we know of no persuasive empirical evidence that the outcomes of therapy vary as a function of social class. We hope that the future of psychotherapy is not restricted by the use of introspective treatments for the educated only, and "other" therapies for the large majority of people seeking help.

CHAPTER 4

RESEARCH ON THE TRAINING OF PROFESSIONAL PSYCHOTHERAPISTS

SOL L. GARFIELD

THE training of professional psychotherapists encompasses an interesting diversity of professional groups, training centers and settings, value systems and orientations. In one survey of a sample of clinical psychologists, Lubin (1962) reported that a moderate number of orientations were adhered to in psychotherapeutic work, including classical psychoanalytic, neo-analytic, Rogerian, learning theory, and eclectic. Since that time, there has been considerable development of the behavioral therapies, rational-emotive therapy, existential therapy, and several others. As a result, a more recent survey of the theoretical orientations of a sample of clinical psychologists shows a wider range of preferences, with a decline in the number choosing psychoanalytic and neo-Freudian orientations and a clear increase in those favoring an eclectic point of view (Garfield & Kurtz, 1974). With such variability as a fact of life in the field of psychotherapy, it can be expected that any uniformity of procedures and philosophies of training would be difficult to secure. Such differences as exist, for example, between behaviorally oriented therapists and psychoanalysts are bound to lead to differences in training goals and procedures as well as in the actual techniques of therapy and behavior change.

Besides differences in theoretical orientation, there are other differences in the background and professional training of those who are engaged in some form of psychotherapy which make it exceedingly difficult to characterize the training of the "professional psychotherapist." An obvious difficulty at the outset is in defining the professional psychotherapist. About 20 years ago, one might have limited this designation to individuals in the professions of psychiatry, clinical psychology, and psychiatric social work. However, it appears rather unrealistic to do so at the present time. The distinction between counseling and psychotherapy, for example, has become increasingly unclear and a number of individuals designated as counselors of one type or another, or as counseling psychologists, appear to engage in the same types of activities or to be concerned with problems similar to those who refer to themselves as psychotherapists. Does a marital counselor perform differently than a psychotherapist who works with married couples? Operationally, how does pastoral counseling differ from personal counseling or psychotherapy? How does counseling differ from supportive psychotherapy? Distinctions previously made concerning such types of activities no longer appear tenable (Garfield, 1974).

A related problem is also apparent in trying to delimit the "professional psychotherapist" in this age of "nonprofessional" therapists, "para-professionals" and "new professionals." Shall the designation "professional" be limited only to those members of the traditional mental health professions, or to those who, for all practical purposes, are functioning in actuality as professional psychotherapists even if they carry some other labels? Probably, the best example of this issue is to be found in the housewives trained by Rioch (1967, 1971) and her colleagues (Rioch, Elkes, & Flint, 1965) to function primarily as psychotherapists. To the writer's knowledge, this has been the most extensively and systematically studied and evaluated group of psychotherapists to date, and yet they have frequently been designated as nonprofessionals. Various reports of training medical students in psychotherapy are also available (Albrondo, Dean, & Starkweather, 1964; Heine, 1962; Matarazzo, Wiens, & Saslow, 1966). As physicians in training, medical students are clearly budding professionals, but is this type of training to be regarded as professional training in psychotherapy?

Since there is no universally accepted form or definition of psychotherapy, we might anticipate that there will be no commonly accepted form of training. This is essentially so, except that on a formal level one can note broad similarities among a number of programs, such as didactic training, supervision, the use of recorded or videotaped therapy sessions, or the requirements of personal therapy. However, what is taught and emphasized will certainly vary from one orientation and setting to another. This situation presents a problem when it comes to appraising different types of training. For example, is it possible to evaluate the efficacy of a particular form or type of training in psychotherapy without considering the goals, theories, and methods of that particular form of therapy? Consequently, does this mean that each type (school) of psychotherapy training has to be evaluated by means of separate criteria? This also raises the issue of what should be considered adequate criteria for appraising the results of psychotherapy training. In the past, the main criteria of success have been supervisors' judgments rather than performance as measured by therapeutic outcome. In many instances, this leads to the students adopting the patterns and values of their supervisors (Beutler, 1972). If therapeutic outcome were to be used as a criterion of therapeutic training, might we then be able to dispense with those programs or schools which offer either poor results or no data? On the basis of past experience, this does not appear very likely.

An additional issue, previously alluded to, is also raised by the nature of the "basic" profession of the psychotherapist. Psychotherapists in the past have been trained primarily as physicians, psychologists, social workers, etc., and not simply as psychotherapists. Each of these professions has its own distinctive content, training goals, settings, and values. In each of these professions, psychotherapy constitutes only a part (usually a relatively small part) of the total training to which the trainee is exposed.[1] It is, perhaps, only in post-doctoral or post-graduate training programs devoted exclusively to psychotherapy that one has truly professional programs of training psychotherapists. However, such programs train a relatively small number of those who engage in psychotherapy, and they usually require and build upon the previous training the candidate has received in one of the mental health professions.

As a consequence, it is difficult to approach this task with some preconceived formulation or plan of organization. Limits have to be set with reference to what types of training programs should be scrutinized for our immediate purposes. There are a variety of programs for training a multitude of mental health workers which are not specifically or centrally devoted to psychotherapy, although they involve many features of interpersonal behavior which are also emphasized in most systems of psychotherapy. In order to have some reasonable boundaries of operation, most such programs will be excluded from our survey. In a related fashion, many treatises on training and supervision in psychotherapy which are not research-oriented and which contain little in the way of empirical data, also will be passed over. The writer obviously has utilized his own value judgments on what is worth reporting; nevertheless, the small extent of significant empirical research in this area is a factor of some consequence in this regard.

TRAINING PROGRAMS IN PSYCHOTHERAPY

At the present time, then, there exist training programs in several mental health fields which include as part of their training some experience in the area of psychotherapy. These include graduate training programs in psychiatric social work, counseling psychology, clinical psychology, and psychiatry. In addition, there are a variety of post-graduate programs specializing in psychotherapy or psychoanalysis (Rachman & Kauff, 1972). These are offered in different institutional settings, including medical centers, clinic settings, specialized training institutes, and psychoanalytic institutes. In addition to the traditional psychoanalytic training institutes affiliated with the American Psychoanalytic Association, and which generally require the MD degree for admission, there are a number of independent psychotherapy training institutes, particularly in New York City, which do not have such restrictions.

It is difficult to characterize these programs in any systematic way since brief descriptions listing courses and practical work tell little about the actual training operations. Graduate academic programs in psychology usually require some preparation in such areas as personality, psychopathology, and diagnostic appraisal as prerequisites or forerunners of the courses in psychotherapy. In the area of psychotherapy, there will usually be one or more didactic courses in theories or viewpoints in psychotherapy and techniques of psychotherapy prior to some practica in which the student sees a limited number of clients under supervision. The extent, amount, and quality of training vary markedly and it is impossible to make an accurate appraisal of programs solely from their written descriptions.

It can be noted, from a review of brochures describing approved doctoral programs in clinical psychology, that the most typical programs generally include two semesters of formal course work in psychotherapy with some associated practicum training. How the training is provided, however, varies greatly, depending upon the orientation of the faculty and the emphasis upon psychotherapy within the program. In some programs, instruction is provided in both conventional relationship therapies and behavioral therapies, whereas some emphasize one or the other. Additional courses may be provided in such areas as group psychotherapy, family therapy, and psychotherapy with children. Practicum work may be supervised at the university by members of the faculty, or at associated community agencies by agency staff. Use may be made of one-way vision mirrors, audiotapes, videotapes, staff modeling, and so forth. Supervisory sessions may occur in small groups or in supervisor-student dyads. Little in the way of formal appraisal of such training has been made. Evaluations of training tend to be based primarily on the supervisor's appraisals of the student.[2]

Somewhat similar appraisals could be made of the professional training received by psychiatrists and social workers. Psychiatrists, obviously, have taken pre-medical training in which the sciences tend to play an important role. Once admitted to medical school, the would-be psychiatrist may be exposed to a course in psychiatry or behavioral science, but the bulk of the instruction is in the basic sciences of medicine—physiology, anatomy, biochemistry, etc. During his clerkship years and internship, the physician-in-training will again have only relatively brief periods on the psychiatry service and only a part of this training will include work of a psychotherapeutic nature. It is only when the psychiatrist begins his residency training that specific training in psychotherapy may begin; again, it would constitute only part of his training. Similarly, the usual 2-year graduate program for psychiatric social workers includes much instruction in areas other than psychotherapy.

The post-graduate and analytic institutes exhibit a number of similarities to the programs already described, although there is a relatively greater emphasis on personality theory and on a particular theoretical orientation to psychotherapy. In some, there is also a greater emphasis on actual clinical work with clients although various didactic seminars are provided. Since the students in training are already trained professionals, there is a greater focus on specialized topics pertaining to psychotherapy and to the specific orientation of the institute. While many of these programs extend over a period of years on either a part-time or full-time basis, in recent years there have also been a number of training institutes of much briefer duration. This is particularly true of institutes in behavior modification, rational-emotive therapy, and group or encounter types of therapy. In these, there is a relatively greater emphasis on didactic teaching and observation of the therapy expert than there is on actual therapy performance and supervision.

As can be seen from this very brief portrayal of some training programs in psychotherapy, there is considerable diversity on what is taught and how it is taught. As in the field of psychotherapy itself, one cannot discuss a generalized notion of "psychotherapy training." Whereas one training program will include two courses on the writings of Freud, as well as course offerings on dreams, resistance, and transference, another will devote little or no time to such topics.

In this regard, it is interesting to note how professional discipline as well as theoretical orientation influence one's views of what is necessary or desirable in the training of psychotherapists. In two conferences devoted to the training of psychotherapists, there is evident some emphasis on instruction in selected areas of medicine from medically trained psychotherapists, while psychologists tend to emphasize such diverse areas as research training, social psychology, diagnostic testing, and the like (Dellis & Stone, 1960; Holt, 1971). I have made reference to this tendency in order to emphasize how individuals cannot divorce themselves from their own training, even when much of it was not devised to have anything specifically to do with psychotherapy. If one has had a particular course of training, one can usually formulate some justification for it.

There are also differences in training programs with regard to the necessity or importance of personal therapy for the therapist in training. Most analytically oriented training institutes require a specified amount of analysis or personal therapy either before training or to be taken concurrently with the training in psychotherapy. In some instances, the personal therapy must be secured from someone affiliated with the training institute or from someone with the same theoretical orientation (Rachman & Kauff,

1972). Most graduate programs in clinical psychology do not have such a requirement, but faculty members may indirectly influence students to obtain such experience or provide various types of group experience as a means of enhancing the "self-knowledge" of the student. While a few studies have secured some differences between therapists who received or did not receive therapy (Garfield & Bergin, 1971; Strupp, 1955), there are no definitive data on the relationship of the therapist's personal therapy and client outcome. This issue, while debated warmly at the Arden House Conference on Psychotherapy, clearly was not resolved (Holt, 1971). Like many other controversies in psychotherapy, this one has its pros and cons debated on bases other than evidence. However, the issue of the influence of the therapist's personal therapy on his own orientation and procedures in psychotherapy would appear to be one of some importance. Although research data on this topic are very limited, more discussion will follow.

SELECTION OF STUDENTS FOR PSYCHOTHERAPY TRAINING

In discussing this topic, it is difficult not to be somewhat repetitious of comments already made. Relatively few persons are selected specifically for training as psychotherapists. Rather, individuals are selected for graduate or professional training in terms of criteria deemed important by a particular school, faculty, or profession. In the cases of psychology and medicine, it seems reasonably clear that criteria which are not necessarily or directly related to psychotherapeutic competence are used in the selection of students. Among these criteria are high academic performance in college, particularly in areas such as the sciences, and high scores on aptitude tests thought to be related to success in medical or graduate school. While such criteria appear to be related to general intellectual ability, the relationship of the latter to psychotherapeutic ability has yet to be demonstrated—even though we might prefer a bright therapist over a dullard.

Thus, various kinds of intellectual and academic abilities are usually the basic or initial prerequisites for professional programs leading toward the eventual goal of functioning as a psychotherapist. In the case of clinical psychology, interest or proficiency in research may also be an important prerequisite for admission into (and later success in) the program. It is clear that such criteria are not necessarily related to one's success as a psychotherapist, but are geared to the successful completion of programs in medicine and clinical psychology. Individuals who conceivably may have the necessary personal requisites for becoming competent therapists may either not be selected for such programs or may fail somewhere along the road toward successful completion of these programs.

At least several workers in the field have been critical of the criteria used in selecting, as well as training, individuals to become psychotherapists. According to Truax and Mitchell (1971), current selection procedures are exceedingly poor:

> From existing data it would appear that only one out of three people entering professional training have the requisite interpersonal skills to prove helpful to patients. Further, there is no evidence that the usual traditional graduate training program has any positive value in producing therapists who are more helpful than nonprofessionals. In short, current procedures for selection and training are indefensible. (p. 337).

The preceding statement is based largely on studies of therapists and trainees who have been appraised by means of the scales purporting to measure the three necessary therapist attributes of accurate empathy, nonpossessive warmth, and genuineness. One additional study, utilizing the same criteria, can be viewed as lending some slight support to this view (Bergin & Solomon, 1970). In this study, empathic ability of graduate students was slightly negatively related to verbal intelligence and to the psychology subscale of the Graduate Record Examination.

While personal attributes apart from intellectual and academic ability are frequently listed as desirable or necessary qualities of the psychotherapist, they do not appear to be appraised in any thorough or systematic manner as far as admittance to graduate and medical school is concerned. For example, in 1947, the Committee on Training in Clinical Psychology listed the following personality characteristics as those desirable for clinical work: (1) superior ability, (2) originality and resourcefulness, (3) curiosity, (4) interest in persons as individuals, (5) insight into one's own personality characteristics, (6) sensitivity to the complexities of motivation, (7) tolerance, (8) ability to establish warm and effective relationships with others, (9) industry and ability to tolerate pressure, (10) acceptance of responsibility, (11) tact, (12) integrity and self-control, (13) sense of ethical values, (14) broad cultural background, and (15) deep interest in psychology, especially the clinical aspects (American Psychological Association, 1947).

The foregoing list is indeed a formidable one, but apart from intellectual ability, there do not appear to be any systematic procedures employed by most institutions to appraise such personal qualities of applicants. If they are indeed evaluated, such appraisals tend to be based on letters of evaluation and/or personal interviews.[3] Furthermore, little research has been done on selection pertaining to personality variables deemed important for psychotherapy. The large-scale study of clinical psychologists by Kelley and Fiske (1951) produced very little in the way of positive results and the comparable study of psychiatrists by Holt and Luborsky (1958) also secured somewhat disappointing results. In the latter study, it should be remembered, the subjects were psychiatrists in training who had already successfully completed their medical training.

Many writings in the area of psychotherapy have discussed the personal requirements for becoming a psychotherapist. Like the report of the Committee on Training in Clinical Psychology, alluded to earlier, these have mentioned most of the culturally "desirable" features of human personality. The ability to be empathic, to be sensitive to the needs of the client, to be genuinely interested in his welfare, to be able to tolerate stress, and the capacity to develop a warm relationship with the client have been mentioned by a number of writers from diverse schools of thought. Truax and Carkhuff (1967) have summarized some of these statements and believe that the three client-centered conditions of empathy, warmth, and congruence include most of the desired characteristics. However, outside of the research carried out by these and a few other workers, mostly on nonprofessional personnel, scales for measuring these attributes have not been utilized in the selection of candidates for professional training in psychotherapy.

Psychoanalytic and post-graduate training institutions purportedly pay more attention to the personal qualities of their applicants since, among other things, the applicants have already been academically screened and have completed successfully a professional training program. Most apparently require some form of personal interview and a few may require some psychological testing for personality appraisal. Thus, the types of personality evaluation used do not appear to be very extensive, and little in the way of systematic research has been reported.

There have also been more recent attempts at using some form of group or encounter session as an aid in selection, although little research has been reported. In one study, a 16-hour marathon session was evaluated as a possible predictive technique for counselor training (Hurst & Fenner, 1969). Twelve students participated in the group session prior to entering a summer practicum. At the end of the marathon, the two group leaders ranked the 12 participants and each of the latter ranked his peers. The ranking was in terms of which student each person would prefer to refer a friend to for counseling. At the end of the practicum, the students re-ranked their colleagues and these rankings were correlated with their initial rankings. In similar fashion, the rankings of the group leaders were correlated with those of the two practicum supervisors obtained at the end of the practicum. In both instances, the correlations were significantly positive. Unfortunately, conclusions are limited because of small sample size, limited information on the variable rated, the lack of an adequate external criterion of performance as a counselor, and the fact that peer rankings were not correlated with those of the supervisors. Furthermore, in another study, ratings by peers and group leaders generally showed little or no relationship to ratings of counselor facilitative conditions as measured by the Truax scales (McWhirter & Marks, 1972).

On the basis of current selection procedures, therefore, several problems or limitations are apparent. First, would-be psychotherapists are initially selected for professional training on the basis of criteria other than those specifically selected for the field of psychotherapy. Second, the techniques used to select individuals specifically for post-graduate training are both limited and unverified. Finally, the criteria used to designate psychotherapeutic requisites are global, nonoperationally defined, unsystematically appraised in most instances, and lacking in research designed to appraise their importance. Here, again, the practices used cannot be better than the conceptual and research foundations upon which they are based.

RESEARCH ON TRAINING IN PSYCHOTHERAPY

Now that we have been oriented to some of the procedures and programs for training psychotherapists and some of the problems and complexities involved, we will review representative research in this area. Anyone who is familiar with the difficulties encountered in psychotherapy research generally might not be surprised by the rather disheartening conclusions reached by some investigators only a few years ago. Matarazzo *et al.* (1966), reviewing the literature in this area, concluded that there had been essentially no research about the teaching of psychotherapy or the process of supervision. They concluded:

> Many reports of training programs are available and it is evident that many psychotherapists talk about teaching, but few report systematic innovations, comparisons of methods, and/or student skill before and after a course of instruction. Admittedly, the complex behavioral and cognitive changes in *experiential* learning are difficult to define. It is equally or even more difficult to reliably define growth experience, enhanced creativity, therapeutic doctor-patient relationship, and resolution of a countertransference neurosis. (p. 608)

The quotation just cited may not, perhaps, induce exciting expectations on the part of the reader, but it does reflect accurately the fact that research on training in psychotherapy has been sparse and is of relatively recent vintage. For example, of the 2,741 references listed in the research bibliography on psychotherapy compiled by Strupp and Bergin (1967) covering the period through 1967, only 20 references which clearly make some mention of training could be identified by the present writer. This is less than one percent of the total list of research citations. Clearly, research on the teaching and training of psychotherapists is in its infancy.

Furthermore, in perusing eight of the reviews on psychotherapy in the *Annual Review of Psychology* since 1960, only a few scattered references to research on training were found. In fact, training as a topic in psychotherapy generally has received comparatively little attention, and much of it is concerned with rather general treatises concerning who should do psychotherapy, the prerequisites for engaging in psychotherapy, and the like. However, as noted by Matarazzo (1971) in a more recent review, there has been some increase in research in this area. It does appear, though, that perhaps greater attention to actual training procedures has characterized the training of subprofessional or "auxiliary" therapists than has the training of professional therapists. It may well be that when training nonprofessionals to perform therapeutic services, we are more sensitive to the need for accountability in such endeavors than is the case with regard to the training of the more prestigious and accepted professionals.[4] At least these training efforts appear to be focused more directly on the skills which, it is presumed, the would-be therapist needs to learn. It seems evident, also, that not all psychotherapeutic approaches have shared equally in this develop-

ment. Many of them have been content with traditional procedures, have sought little innovation, and have not been overly concerned with evaluating their techniques. The two orientations in psychotherapy which have devoted the most attention to research in training have been the client-centered and, to a somewhat lesser extent, the behaviorally oriented approaches. Before reviewing some of this research, however, let us examine briefly some of the problems involved in research of this type.

The basic variables involved in psychotherapy training would appear to be the student therapist, his teachers and supervisors, the rationale and procedures which are to be taught, the methods of instruction, and the client who receives psychotherapy. One would have to consider all of these aspects of the learning situation in order to secure anything resembling definitive results. The aptitudes and skills of the therapist in training obviously affect his learning rate and proficiency, and not all trainees have similar aptitudes. Nevertheless, very little attention has been paid to this problem in any systematic way. Client-centered therapists have paid more attention to this matter than any other group.

In a similar manner, very little study has been devoted to the particular skills and procedures used by individual supervisors. Not only may supervisors vary widely in their skill in training students, but there may be important student-supervisor interaction effects, with some students being able to profit more from some supervisors than others. However, at present we have mainly clinical discussions of this problem.

With regard to the client being treated, some research is available which does show that the therapist (or therapist-in-training) is very much influenced by the client with whom he is working. Bandura, Lipsher, and Miller (1960), for example, found that hostility directed by the client toward the therapist did not elicit as many positive or approach responses as did hostility which was directed at other persons. Hostile client behavior has also been reported as inducing more anxiety in counselors (Russell & Snyder, 1963) as well as less friendly or avoidant behaviors (Heller, Myers, & Kline, 1963). Manifestations of dependency behavior on the part of the client similarly has led to increased expressions of reassurance and direction from the therapist (Heller *et al.*, 1963; Russell & Snyder, 1963). Bohn (1967) found that while therapist directiveness toward a dependent client was reduced after a course of training, the decrease was not significant.

Another variable involved in the training of psychotherapists, which has been mentioned previously, concerns that of theoretical orientation. While research studies on this topic have produced somewhat conflicting findings concerning the importance of this variable, it certainly cannot be disregarded in any discussion pertaining to training. Even though therapists of the same persuasion may function differently (Glover, 1955; Luborsky & Spence, 1971), and therapists of different orientations perform similarly (Fey, 1958; Strupp, 1969), the basic tenets of the particular school of psychotherapy will influence what is taught and how it is taught. In programs which emphasize a client-centered approach, for example, attention will usually be focused on the therapist-offered conditions of empathy, nonpossessive warmth, and genuineness or congruence. While other therapist orientations which emphasize relationship variables in therapy may also stress similar components, they generally will not utilize the scales and systematic methods developed by client-centered therapists such as Truax and Carkhuff (1967) in such training and they will also focus on other matters.

Differences in concepts and techniques among the various approaches to psychotherapy also present problems in both training and in the evaluation of training effectiveness. In the case of the client-centered and behavioral approaches there is more specificity and also more operational definition of what is to be learned. Thus, training procedures can more easily be devised and appraised. In psychodynamic and relationship approaches, the techniques appear to be more ambiguous and perhaps more complex. Such concepts or procedures as interpretation, transference, resistance, and the like are less precise, more subject to personal judgment, and less easy to appraise. Furthermore, when specific and relatively defined therapeutic techniques or behaviors are selected for more systematic instruction or appraisal, they may not necessarily be the most important variables as far as therapeutic change is concerned. For example, in one interesting study, six major categories of therapist behaviors or "utterances" were defined and appraised (Sakinofsky, Cantor, Green, McFarlane, & Roberts, 1973). Included here were such activities as structuring, classifying, confronting, and expounding. While such behaviors could be defined and rated with some degree of reliability, and while changes over time could be appraised, they constitute just one group of therapeutic variables, and they were not studied in relation to outcome variables. In other words, their significance for effecting change was not appraised, and one does not know if these therapist behaviors are the ones which should be emphasized in training. However, to the extent that this approach can be extended, it does offer real possibilities for operationalizing procedures and appraising them in relation to both training and outcome.

In studies and reports on training more explicit attention has probably been given to teaching procedures and concepts pertaining to the theoretical orientation espoused than to the other variables mentioned. This would appear to have definite implications as far as training is concerned. How orientation-specific are certain procedures used in training psychotherapists and to what extent can they be generalized? While the use of such teaching procedures as audio- or videotape recordings, roleplaying or modeling would appear to transcend theoretical differences, what is stressed or attended to by means of these methods would undoubtedly differ.

Consequently, it would appear difficult to discuss training in psychotherapy without some attention to the basic variables involved. Thus far, however, most of them have received little formal study in this regard, and questions remain, therefore, concerning their particular significance with respect to training.

Ruth Matarazzo (1971), in her excellent review of this area, also referred to some of the problems and difficulties involved in conducting research on the effectiveness of training in psychotherapy, many of which have already been mentioned. Of basic importance, according to Matarazzo, are the need to define the therapeutic variables or procedures which lead to change, to determine whether the students' learning is reflected in changes in the clients, and the adequate measurement of the complex behaviors—cognitive, experiential, and behavioral—which supposedly undergo change in the student-therapist as a result of training. The present writer is clearly in agreement on these matters. Matarazzo also discussed and evaluated research on training deriving from the psychoanalytic school, client-centered therapy, the teaching of psychotherapy in medical schools, specific programs for training professional and lay therapists, training in behavior modification, and the use of special devices in the training of psychotherapists. The present chapter will not duplicate that earlier review. The training of nonprofessionals, which has received considerable attention in recent years, is examined in separate chapters of this volume (Anthony & Carkhuff, Chapter 6; Emrick, Lassen, & Edwards, Chapter 7) and little attention will be devoted here to the teaching of psychotherapy in medical schools. Also, while at times it will be necessary to pay attention to the procedures of a specific orientation, an attempt will be made to focus on techniques or methods which appear to have more general applicability.

As a result of her review, Matarazzo concluded that research on the teaching of psychotherapy was still at an early stage, limited by the state of development of the field of psychotherapy itself. Comments of this sort also were made earlier in this chapter and need little elaboration here. At the same time, Matarazzo did feel that there were some positive trends, such as an increasing emphasis on empiricism, improved techniques of measurement, and the general application of theory and concepts from other areas of psychology to the field of psychotherapy. She also concluded that the client-centered group probably had contributed more to research evaluation in psychotherapy than other schools, that their approach lent itself readily to training in psychotherapy, and that their training programs were the more empirically based and logically developed. The present author tends to agree with these conclusions, although, as will be noted later, he takes a more critical stance toward this latter work.

RECENT RESEARCH FINDINGS AND TRENDS

As has been emphasized in the preceding pages, there are a number of difficulties in attempting to appraise existing research on training in psychotherapy. The kinds of individuals being trained, the length and type of training, the skills or procedures being taught, the theoretical system used, and the supervisors providing instruction, all add complexity to the problem. Programs for masters-level counselors, medical psychoanalysts, and clinical psychologists are all likely to have some unique elements, which may or may not be applicable to the field as a whole.

Consequently, while one can go through the published literature related to training in psychotherapy and abstract and report all of the findings in condensed or summary form, the present writer, after surveying a reasonable sample of research in this area, does not believe this approach is very useful. Many of the studies deal with rather segmented or limited aspects of psychotherapy training; many are limited to a particular orientation; the activities studied are often minor components of psychotherapy; a number involve quasi-therapeutic situations or analogue studies; and others have a small number of subjects, methodological limitations, or findings which, while statistically significant at the .05 level of probability, have very little practical significance. As a result, emphasis here will be placed on studies that appear to have some potential significance or unique interest, that utilize procedures which appear to have general applicability, or that illustrate important problems.

As indicated, the field of psychotherapy reveals both similarities and differences in the various efforts devoted to training its practitioners. Didactic instruction, experiential training, modeling, role playing, observation of performance, practicum experience, and the supervision of learning are among the commonly employed techniques used in most training programs. What is taught, modeled, supervised, and reinforced, however, varies widely, both in substance and in method. Appraisals of training effectiveness in turn are based on and viewed from a particular orientation instead of by means of some independent and objective criteria. At best, one might be able to say that procedures A and B are superior to procedures C and D in training individuals to perform systematic desensitization or to engage in client-centered therapy. If the different therapeutic approaches actually were shown to be efficacious therapies for particular types of problems (e.g., systematic desensitization for phobias), then obviously different training procedures would be plausible and such conclusions would be of definite value. In fact, one logical extension of this view would be to require the would-be therapist to learn several different types of therapy so that he could treat more than one kind of problem. However, while there are some indications of a beginning of such a trend (Abroms & Greenfield, 1973; Brady, 1968; Feather & Rhodes, 1972; Marmor, 1971), the prevailing view appears to be that any given approach is sufficient to handle most problems. As a result, one can say comparatively little about what are the best ways to train psychotherapists in general.

Didactic Versus Experimental Approaches to Training

A fair amount of the work on training psychotherapists and counselors has been devoted to the issue of didactic versus experiential approaches to training. The former, emphasizing more intellectual aspects, as well as perhaps a more authoritarian approach, has been contrasted with the experiential approach stressing the personal growth of the neophyte therapist. The findings concerning the relative effectiveness of these two approaches have been inconsistent, but in view of different training objectives, different levels of students, and different curricular contents, such lack of congruence in findings are not totally surprising. In this reviewer's opinion, it is not really worthwhile to examine this research in great detail since the "either-or" position exemplified in such research leads to rather limited conclusions with regard to training. It is certainly conceivable that many different types of learning experiences, technical acquisitions, and knowledge will have to be utilized in any effective program of training. However, some of the research on this issue can be examined briefly.

While what has come to be termed "experiential learning" has many variants, the emphasis has tended to be on the feelings and experiences of the learner as opposed to the learning of specific information and techniques. Rogers (1957), for example, emphasized the atmosphere of the teaching situation, the relationship between student and supervisor, and the importance of the student's developing his own approach to therapy based on his own experience and personality. Introspection and self-analysis have also been emphasized in such programs, and personal therapy and/or group experience have been seen as means of providing such learning. A few representative studies which have attempted to compare experiential and didactic programs of training can be mentioned to illustrate what is involved. Silverman (1972) compared two groups of graduate students enrolled in a counseling practicum, a course designed to give the students some experience in applying the principles and methods of counseling studied. In this practicum, students did not work with actual clients, but engaged in role playing and observed experienced counselors. In the "experiential-introspective" group, class time was spent in individual and group activities focused on introspection. "The tasks of each member . . . were to learn who he is and is becoming, and to learn counseling primarily through experiencing some of its ingredients" (Silverman, 1972, p. 12). In addition, psychologists were available to these students for individual counseling, and sensitivity training sessions were also conducted. The

task for the members in the "didactic-behavioristic" group "was to assume desired counselor attitudes and behavior through their exposure to the shaping effects of traditional procedures in education." The procedures used included the observation of experienced role models through films, observation, videotapes, role playing, and lecture-discussion sessions. The instructor attempted to reinforce the correct procedures, apparently through verbal means.

Following this semester, the students participated in a course in which they saw actual clients. Rating scales dealing with the counseling sessions and the relationship in counseling were completed by 133 clients and by the 11 counselors in the experiential group and the nine who had undergone didactic training. The results of the clients' responses to the 154 items were then compared for the two groups of counselors. Only six items showed statistically significant differences. The responses of the two groups of counselors on these same 154 items revealed significant differences on nine items. Only one of the latter nine items was also one of the six significant items reported for the analysis of the clients' responses, and was rated in opposite directions in the two sets of ratings. Since these results are very close to chance occurrence, there is little need to review the author's discussion of those items on which differences occurred.

Another study attempted to appraise the importance of the students' preference for the two methods of supervision in affecting outcome (Birk, 1972). Like the previous study, masters candidates in a counselor education program were the subjects and doctoral students in counseling were the supervisors. The outcome measures consisted of ratings on the Empathic Understanding Scale (Carkhuff & Berenson, 1967). The basic experiment, an analogue study, consisted of three 10-minute interviews with a coached client in a videotaped setting. The first and second interviews were followed by a 15-minute supervisory session. Of the 20 subjects who preferred didactic supervision, eight were assigned for such supervision, eight for experiential supervision, and four were assigned to a control group. A similar division was followed for the 20 subjects who expressed a preference for the experiential supervision. In the experiential condition, "an informal discussion atmosphere was maintained." The student was asked for relevant personal experiences, present or past, that might be similar to those of the client and the supervisor explored the student's own feelings while interviewing the client. In the didactic condition, the supervisor specified which student remarks communicated empathic understanding and offered alternative responses for ineffective student responses. Specific suggestions were offered and appropriate student behavior was verbally reinforced.

The findings of this study can be stated briefly. Student preference for one or the other method of supervision had no effect on the criterion. Supervision method did show significant differences, however, and favored the didactic supervision.

Another study differing from those described above was concerned with increasing self-actualization in counselor training by means of a group experience (Eiben & Clack, 1973). The participatory group experience included 12 hours of T-group activity, six hours devoted to sensory awareness, relaxation, and movement activities, eight hours of group decision-making and problem-solving activities, four hours of theoretical input, the viewing of Shostrum's "actualization group" film series, and other activities, including writing songs, constructing collages, and performing pantomimes. In the didactic group, the instructor presented materials pertaining to groups, sensitivity training, and the like. A textbook was used and discussion was limited to questions of the instructor. Both groups were taking a course in group counseling, and the Personal Orientation Inventory (POI) of Shostrum was administered at the beginning and end of the course work. A comparison of the two groups in terms of mean differences of pre- and post-scores showed that the experiential group differed significantly on one of the 12 scales of POI.

Taking these three illustrative studies as a unit, what observations or conclusions can one make? Like many studies of psychotherapy, these, although supposedly studying the same problem, differ in terms of the experimental procedures used and the outcome criteria employed. One must be cautious in generalizing from studies which purportedly are investigating a general class of phenomena, but which in actuality are studying a limited fragment or miniature prototype of the phenomena in question. In many instances, the experimental study is also quite artificial or a very limited amount of time is used to study the phenomena under investigation. If research studies are to have value for the realities of the training situation, then they must bear some definite resemblance to these situations. Experiential training, for example, may include a wide variety of activities, some of which

may be of more direct value than others. We need to be more specific in delineating what we believe are critical aspects of such training, define them operationally, and then study them in situations which bear some correspondence to the actual training situations. Segmental studies are of little value. As in the present instance, the findings secured are frequently inconclusive and offer little in the way of guidelines for practical training.

Specific Training Procedures and Objectives

In this section we shall review some representative reports which deal with specified training objectives or specific training methods. There are a variety of reports in this area concerning the use and adaptation of such techniques as videotapes and the need for setting specific objectives for training. Unfortunately, however, very few have apparently carried out studies to actually evaluate what they recommend as useful. One brief report, for example, describes a videotape technique for examining the process of psychotherapy supervision in which both a videotaped therapy session and the actual supervision are videotaped (Walters, Elder, Smith, & Cleghorn. 1971). In this way, the process of supervision can be studied and discussed. While such an approach appears interesting, no research has been reported on its effectiveness.

Another report which can be alluded to because of the novelty and planned aspects of its program was concerned primarily with teaching medical students basic interviewing skills. The program emphasized a small group setting during a 1-week period (Cline & Garrard, 1973), and utilized a programmed manual, the observation of a skilled interviewer, role-playing exercises, programmed interviewing films, and the interviewing of selected patients. Both the observed interviews and the student interviews were audiotaped for discussion and feedback which followed. The course was assessed in two ways—students' ratings of the course and the use of interviewing films requiring responses from the student at both pre- and post-test intervals. Students' ratings of the program were positive, and statistically significant gains were obtained on responses to the programmed films during the post-test period. While there was no control group used, this study deserves a favorable response for the planned techniques used and the attempts to appraise the teaching program.

Reference can also be made to some other

procedures which have been used and advocated for training purposes. Cleghorn and Levin (1973) have defined a set of specific learning objectives for the training of family therapists, but exact procedures and research evaluations concerning these objectives have not been provided. Strupp and Jenkins (1963) some years ago developed films simulating psychotherapeutic situations and mentioned their potential use for training. However, little in the way of application or research with such standard films has apparently been done. The use of coached clients as a training resource has also been advocated by Whiteley and Jakubowski (1969). They emphasize that the coached client can be programmed so that a number of problems in counseling can actually be experienced and dealt with by the student prior to his work with real clients. Combined with videotapes of such sessions and supervisory feedback, this procedure also appears to have some merit.

Another report investigated the effects of specific verbal interaction analysis training with counseling practicum students (Gade & Matuschka, 1973). In this study, 15 students received the regular practicum training plus 14 hours of training in verbal interaction analysis. The latter specifies categories of counselor direct and indirect influence such as asking questions, giving direction or information, and accepting feelings and ideas of the counselee. Counselee talk is also categorized into response or initiation. The students in the control group received 14 hours of open-ended discussion on counseling techniques in addition to the regular practicum training. The latter, incidentally, is not further specified. Taped segments of early counseling sessions and sessions at the end of 14 weeks of training judged best by the counselees were then rated by judges according to the system of verbal interaction analysis used in training. Significant differences were obtained between the two groups of students. The experimental group showed a significant decrease in counselor talk and an increase in client talk, while the control group showed an increase in counselor talk and no change in client talk. The experimental subjects also showed an increase in the use of indirect counseling response which was not shared by the control subjects. The authors conclude that a semester-long practicum in counseling which includes a 14-hour sequence of verbal interaction analysis "can result in desirable counselor verbal behavior changes," and that "those (trainees) in the traditional client-centered practicum training group became worse" (Gade

& Matuschka, 1973, p. 188). A number of questions can be raised about these conclusions. What is traditional client-centered training? If it is undesirable, why not just use the specific verbal interaction analysis training and drop the rest of it? What is the relation of the verbal behaviors used as criteria in the study to other external outcome criteria? While answers to such questions need to be secured before any real conclusions can be reached, it would appear as if training goals can be reached more readily if they are clearly specified and operationalized.

Another technique which has been used at times in psychotherapy training involves some mechanism whereby the supervisor can offer comments or suggestions to the student while he is engaged with a client. Some years ago, Korner and Brown (1952) described an apparatus whereby the supervisor in another room could observe and listen to the therapy session and yet communicate with the student unnoticed by the client. There have been occasional references to such techniques over the years (Matarazzo et al., 1966; Ward, 1960), even though they apparently have not been very widely used. Two recent reports, however, emphasize their value in training, and it is interesting that no reference is made to the older reports in which such techniques were initially described. One account simply describes the use of a wireless microphone by the supervisor to contact the counselor as he is observed by the supervisor either through a one-way screen or a TV monitor (Cohn, 1973). A pocket-sized FM radio and an ear plug are used. The other is a report of a study of training behavior modifiers to learn eight specific behaviors (Cone & Sheldon, 1973). Two approaches, exposure to videotaped definitions and examples of the eight behaviors, and remote auditory prompting, were compared. Observations were made and recorded by judges at a baseline period, after the experimental procedure, and at a follow-up period a few days later. While the videotape had little overall effect, increases in all eight desired behaviors accompanied the auditory prompting.

Modeling has also been mentioned more frequently in recent years as a training technique for counselors and psychotherapists and has been incorporated into many training programs. Research on its values in training, however, has been more limited, even though considerable research exists on the efficacy of modeling and vicarious learning (Bandura, 1969). In one study of the effects of modeling on group verbal behavior, it was found that modeling by itself was not as effective as modeling used along with specific instructions (Whalen, 1969). In another study, however involving college student volunteers, the findings were somewhat different (Rappaport, Gross, & Lepper, 1973). Where general instructions were used, modeling secured better results than a sensitivity training group and a "no-training" control group. However, when specific instructions were used, all subjects performed equally well. The authors concluded "that for some behaviors and some populations, the same effects may be achieved by structuring an appropriate situation and giving specific instructions as by presenting a modeling film" (Rappaport, Gross, & Lepper, 1973, p. 106). Apparently, Heller (1969) also takes a similar view.

A somewhat related finding was reported also by Bullmer (1972). In his study, a group of subjects who received programmed self-instructional training dealing with terms and concepts pertaining to interpersonal perception showed significant improvement in the accuracy of interpersonal perception. However, since the control group essentially received no training in this area, the actual significance of the results is questionable.

Reference can also be made to two other related studies. In one of these, Miller (1969) used alternative responses by the supervisor to facilitate the use of understanding responses by counselor trainees. When the trainee responded to a tape-recorded client statement, the supervisor offered either an appropriate response as an alternative or verbally reinforced the trainee's response. After five successive understanding responses were given by the student, no further alternatives were given by the supervisor, but verbal reinforcement on a variable ratio schedule was provided for acceptable responses. The group receiving this mode of training made significantly more understanding responses than a group which received random alternative responses without any reinforcement. While the supervisor's alternative responses can be viewed as a form of modeling, this study is clearly not a study of modeling *per se*. There are strong components of verbal reinforcement and feedback, which, nevertheless, are of consequence for learning.

The remaining study concerned the effect of modeling of alternative counselor responses and critical feedback on training in empathic communication (Rasche, 1972). Essentially, both conditions were more effective than control conditions not involving feedback, but a combined condition utilizing both critical feedback and an alternative response was not more effective than either of the two experimental conditions. Thus, feedback or knowledge of results would appear to be important for progress in learning.

Some studies have attempted to appraise certain features of the therapist in relation to specific skills in counseling. Two studies which investigated the relationship of counselor self-actualization on the ability to communicate empathic understanding, positive regard, and facilitative genuineness can be mentioned briefly for illustrative purposes. Foulds (1969) used the Personal Orientation Inventory (POI) as the measure of self-actualization and the Carkhuff (1969) scales to appraise the facilitative conditions in a study of 30 counselors in training. He reported a significant relationship between self-actualization and two of the facilitative conditions. An attempt was then made by Winborn and Rowe (1972) to replicate this study with a sample of 50 comparable subjects. "Whereas Foulds found a total of 24 significant relationships among POI scales and empathic understanding, facilitative genuineness, and total facilitative conditions, only one (attributed to chance) was found in this replication" (Winborn & Rowe, 1972, p. 28). Research based on such self-report measures of self-actualization is bound to be of limited value since such inventories primarily tap the self-view of the individual or what he is willing to divulge at a particular time or place. Expectancy conditions, social desirability, cultural bias, and other factors may all influence the subject's responses. This writer's preference is clearly for some measure which is related to performance rather than self-report. However, with such a construct as self-actualization, it is obviously difficult to get behavioral or performance criteria, and investigators will tend to use whatever measures are readily available.

As has been mentioned before, client-centered research has been facilitated by the emphasis on a limited number of therapists' conditions or attributes which have been appraised by means of relatively brief rating scales. While a fair amount of research on training has been performed, there are justifiable concerns about the adequacy of these facilitative conditions as the ultimate criteria of therapist competence and effectiveness. On the other hand, training with a variety of other traditional approaches to psychotherapy has emphasized largely global concepts and has been subjected to relatively little analysis and research. There have been, however, some attempts to identify specific categories of therapist behaviors and some experimentation with different methods of training. We shall survey some of this work in the next section.

Microteaching and Related Approaches

What has come to be known as microteaching exemplifies the trend to break up complex skills or behaviors such as counseling and psychotherapy into important components. A recent example of this approach is a study of teaching interviewing skills (Elsenrath, Coker, & Martinson, 1972). The goal of the study was to demonstrate the teaching efficiency of an audiotaped programmed approach to increase interviewee verbalization "by (a) increasing the length of silence before responding to interviewee statements, and (b) decreasing the length of their own (interviewer) responses to the interviewee" (p. 151). While the subjects used in this study were undergraduate residence hall assistants and not professional counselors, the procedures conceivably may be of relevance for the latter. In general, the experimental subjects exhibited longer response delays, fewer interruptions, and less total talk time, and their interviewees manifested a larger amount of verbalization. To the extent that the control subjects apparently were given only general instructions for conducting an interview, whereas the experimental subjects had more specific programmed instructions and were reinforced for correct behaviors, the results perhaps are not overly surprising. Nevertheless, the results can be viewed as supporting the notion that complex behaviors can be taught more effectively by emphasizing specific component objectives.

A series of reports and studies of microcounseling have been provided by Ivey and his colleagues (Ivey, 1971, 1974; Moreland, Ivey, & Phillips, 1973). As indicated, the focus is on learning specific single skills in a systematic manner. Recently, a standard paradigm for microcounseling training has been developed as follows:

"1. Videotaping a 5-minute segment of therapy, counseling, or, if a couple or a family, 5 minutes of interaction around a selected topic.
2. Training. (a) A written manual describing the single skill being taught is presented to the trainee(s). (b) Video models of an "expert" therapist or "good" communication illustrating the skill are shown, thus giving trainees a gauge against which to examine the quality of their own behavior. (c) Trainees then view their own videotapes and compare their performance on the skill in question against the written manual and video model. Seeing yourself as others see you is a particularly impactful part of the training procedure. (d) A trainer-supervisor provides didactic instruction and emotional support for the trainees.
3. A second 5- to 10-minute session is videotaped.
4. Examination of the last session and/or recycling of the entire procedure as in step 2 depending on the acquired skill levels of the trainees." (Ivey, 1974, p. 6)

Approximately 1 hour is required for such a cycle of training, while the necessity of going back to step 2 adds another 30 to 45 minutes. Cue discrimination, modeling procedures, and operant reinforcement are utilized in training and the latter focuses on attending and listening behaviors and skills—eye contact, physical attention, and verbal following behavior. After this group of skills has been mastered, Rogerian reflection of feeling is usually the next skill emphasized, although it is taught as selective attention to the client's emotional aspects. "Instead of teaching undefinable empathy and respect, trainees are simply taught to reinforce emotional components of the other person's verbal and non-verbal behavior" (Ivey, 1974, p. 6). Most trainees reach beginning levels of proficiency within a period of 2 hours. In some instances, however, reflection of feeling presents difficulties and consequently trainees have to first learn the skills of "sharing behavior" and "expression of feelings." After they learn how to express themselves and to recognize emotion, they can learn how to listen to others.

The skills mentioned are only a sample of skills systematically learned through microcounseling, but they illustrate the approach. Interpretative skills and "direct authentic mutual communication" are also taught. The latter aims at the mutual exploration of experience and is defined behaviorally so it can be learned more readily. Ivey believes, furthermore, that the skills of helping can be taught not only to professionals and para-professionals, but to practically everyone with profit.

A moderate amount of research has been generated in studying microcounseling. A recent study concerned with teaching 2nd-year medical students interviewing skills is illustrative of the work done (Moreland et al., 1973). Prior to training, 24 students conducted a 20-minute interview with a volunteer patient-interviewee. The middle 10 minutes of each interview were videotaped for later analysis. Twelve subjects were assigned to one of three microcounseling training groups, each of which was led by an advanced psychiatric resident. Each training session was devoted to the learning of one of the six designated basic skills: attending behavior, minimal activity, open-ended questions, paraphrases, reflections of feeling, and summarizations. At end of the sessions, the student read a manual describing the specific skill to be learned and watched a videotaped model depicting it. After this, the student conducted a 6- or 7-minute interview which was videotaped and played back to him. This was also viewed by the instructor and the other students in his group who participated in the critique with the supervisor.

The 12 control subjects were likewise assigned to a group of four which was supervised by a psychiatric resident or faculty member. During six training sessions, each student was similarly observed while he conducted a short interview with a patient. These were not videotaped and the students received no specific instructions in what behaviors to practice. However, they did receive feedback from their instructors which consisted of such recommendations as asking more open questions, talking less, attending more to feelings, and summarizing more frequently. These students also obtained more interviewing experience and supervision since they did not discuss the microcounseling manuals or view model videotapes.

After completion of training, each student interviewed the same patient whom he had seen initially for 20 minutes and again the middle 10 minutes were videotaped. The interval was about 9 weeks. Randomized tapes were then rated by two judges in terms of several categories—e.g., attending behavior, open-ended questions, reflections of feelings, etc. On two of the eight categories rated, attending behavior and reflection of feeling, the microcounseling subjects performed significantly better than the controls. Furthermore, using the Therapist Error Check List (Matarazzo, Phillips, Wiens, & Saslow, 1965), the judges rated each interviewer utterance as good, fair, or poor. The microcounseling students demonstrated a significantly greater increase in good statements and decrease in poor statements than the control group.

A program of training which resembles that of microcounseling, and is usually referred to as Interpersonal Process Recall (IPR), has been developed over a period of years by Kagan and his associates (Kagan, 1971, 1973; Kagan & Schauble, 1969). Their teaching strategy is based on the concept of counselor or therapist developmental tasks. The tasks selected were designed to be specific enough to be grasped and learned by the students, yet of definite relevance for the therapist's interpersonal behavior. The program consists of a sequential progression "beginning with a didactic presentation of concepts, then to simulation exercises to interpersonal affective stress, to video and physiological feedback, to study of self-in-action, to feedback from clients and, finally, to understanding of and skill at dealing with the complex bilateral impacts which occur when two people are in relationship with one another" (Kagan, 1973, p. 44). Although it is believed that 30 to 50 hours are desirable for completion of the program, the methods have been packaged recently in 6 hours of film (Kagan, 1971). A brief description of the program as reported by Kagan (1973) follows.

After a brief introduction concerning the program, the student is presented with Unit I. In this unit, four characteristics of therapeutic response are delineated—"exploratory," "affective," "listening," and "honest labeling." The student is shown vignettes in which an actress-client makes a statement and an interviewer responds to one facet (i.e., cognitive) of her statement. In the next vignette, the client repeats her statement to a second interviewer who responds to a different (i.e., affective) component of her statement. Several client types and interviewer types are presented for each of the four sets of concepts.

The instructor points out the difference between normal social conversation and the response modes used in therapy, and the students practice these modes with a series of simulated clients on film who look directly at them and offer varying verbal statements.

Unit II is deemed more complex. It appears aimed at providing the trainee with practice in labeling feelings and in helping him overcome his own resistance to becoming intimately involved with another person. A number of simulation exercises are used and the student is questioned by his instructor about his own feelings and thoughts in response to them. In addition to small-group discussions of reactions to these simulations, the student can be videotape-recorded as he watches a vignette, and some of the student's physiological responses, such as heart rate, respiration, etc., can also be recorded on the same tape. Unit III, very briefly, consists of the videotaping of the student interviewing a client, following which a supervisor joins him for the playback and discussion. The emphasis appears to be on the student's recalling what his thoughts and feelings were at specific times in the interview.

Unit IV consists basically of the trainee attempting to learn the "inquirer" role displayed previously by the supervisor-instructor so that trainees can then conduct recall sessions with each other. In Unit V, the focus is on learning how clients avoid, deny, suppress, or learn to grow and change. After a session with a client is videotaped, the client is asked to view the videotape with a colleague and to be as frank and open as possible in recalling his thoughts and feelings. Students conduct two or three such sessions with one of them playing the role of the inquirer. Unit VI is a recall session of a videotaped interview in which both client and trainee are asked to recall their feelings and thoughts by an inquirer. "If the inquirer does his job well, he has helped the client and the interviewer not only to talk with each other and to listen to each other in new ways and at more levels, but also has helped each confirm or refute perceptions they had of each other" (Kagan, 1973, p. 49).

References are made by Kagan to several studies which purport to show the effectiveness of this IPR approach. Most of these have been done as doctoral dissertations at Michigan State University, and only a few reports have been published. In one, the results did not substantiate the premise that the IPR techniques would help increase the awareness and effectiveness of practicum students in this program as compared with a control group which received more conventional supervision (Ward, Kagan, & Krathwohl, 1972). In another study, however, the results were generally positive and favored the IPR approach (Spivack, 1972). This approach is certainly innovative and deserving of more evaluative study.

It would appear that, within limits, microcounseling or similar procedures could be used to increase the specificity of what skills are to be taught in psychotherapy and that the measurement of such skills could be facilitated. Such methods have the advantage of specifying and operationalizing what is to be taught in an area which has suffered from ambiguity and the lack of operational clarity. It is possible also that such procedures would increase the efficiency of training. However, some problems remain which, perhaps, can be resolved by future research. Can all of the necessary components be specified and taught separately? And, if so, will they be incorporated into a meaningful and patterned whole by the learner? Research which also utilizes measures of client outcome could provide us with possible answers to such problems.

A Systems Approach to Training

The final portion of this section will attempt to review briefly several papers which have concerned themselves with what is designated as a systems approach to counseling. This approach basically attempts to analyze the operation of a program in terms of the adequacy and efficiency with which program objectives are attained. Such an approach has been used in industry and other organizational settings in order to deal more effectively with the intricacies and complexities of their programs. Hosford and Ryan (1970) describe the systems approach as follows:

> Systems analysis is one approach which has the specific mission of understanding a total program and improving its performance. In essence, it is a methodology or way of applying systems thinking for dealing with complex organizational problems and their changing relationships (Banathy, 1968). The objective of a systems approach to planning is to reduce complex problems and relationships to simple outputs which can be used by the planner in arriving at the "best" decision in terms of effectiveness and efficiency. Only those aspects of the program that are relevant to the objectives which the system is trying to promote are considered; and, therefore, it brings order to investigation and problem-solving. Most importantly, a systems approach forces us to specify what we are trying to accomplish and lets us see immediately what we are not accomplishing (pp. 221–222).

In a recent paper, Zifferblatt (1972) has also presented a rather detailed analysis of counselor-trainer systems from an operant and operations research perspective. According to him, there is a need for the development of comprehensive analytical and evaluation models to guide counselor educators in their decisions pertaining to training. He stresses also the importance of a systems model of continuous evaluation of program objectives rather than simply terminal or outcome evaluation of change and points out the differences between operations research and that of experimental or laboratory research. In the latter, the experimenter "abstracts and simplifies large chunks of the environment," limits the experimental situation so as to study a few selected independent variables, and exerts some control over irrelevant response selection. In contrast, a more technological model seeks to represent the richness and complexity of the actual operational environment.

"In technological analysis, specific system control rather than causal attribution is the priority. It is essential that analysis fully include all parameters of the particular operational environment. The complexity of this environment is deliberately 'captured.' Accomplishment of the mission rather than 'why is it working' is of prime importance" (Zifferblatt, 1972, p. 19).

According to Zifferblatt, counselor (and psychotherapy) training tends to employ analytical models that are based on theoretical validation and causal attribution, rather than on a technological or operational model. Consequently, as appears quite common in psychology, the results secured from different studies supposedly appraising the same phenomena vary widely. "A more useful applied strategy would not attempt to formulate generalizations or causal statements, but would attempt to represent and then maximize what a given system can do with its idiosyncratic curricula, personnel and students" (Zifferblatt, 1972, p. 20). Thus, the systems-oriented approach focuses on the objective or mission of the program and which procedures, staff, and environment can most effectively accomplish the mission.

Zifferblatt (1972) describes a systems approach and provides a number of charts and diagrams to illustrate what is involved with respect to counseling. Generally, such an approach involves establishing objectives, analyzing operations, developing a procedural flow chart to indicate progress and provide feedback, diagramming subsystem operations, collecting and analyzing data, isolating problems, and recycling new inputs into the system.

To illustrate the possibilities of applying such an analytical model, Zifferblatt has utilized an operant approach which he feels is a desirable model for analysis in counselor education. First, the program or system is defined in the light of its mission. Then, if an operant base is employed, the mission must be translated into some sequence of observable and measurable units of behavior. By this means, one is in a better position to appraise specific training procedures in terms of mission objectives. One can examine the specific activities and settings used for training such as readings, lectures, group discussions, laboratory sessions using videotapes, practicum, and so forth, in terms of stated objectives and appraise their value or efficiency. While a systems approach does not necessarily guarantee a successful outcome, Zifferblatt does feel that an "operant-based systems approach . . . does, however, offer a systematic means for us to learn

from our errors and possibly improve the effectiveness of professional training" (p. 29).

While this presentation of a systems approach to counseling and psychotherapy has leaned heavily on the detailed paper of Zifferblatt, others in the field of counselor education have also discussed the possible merits of this approach, as well as reacting to Zifferblatt's paper (Bergland & Quatrano, 1973; Hosford, 1972; Hosford & LeComte, 1973; Hosford & Ryan, 1970; Ryan, 1972; Thoreson, 1969). While some (e.g., Ryan, 1972) have stated that the picture of counselor training is not as bleak as that presented by Zifferblatt, there appears to be strong support for some type of systems approach to training and for the need to evaluate training programs (Whiteley, 1969). What is promulgated for counselor education appears quite applicable to psychotherapy training in general where there has been much less concern and desire for innovation and evaluation. Clearly, the need for performance testing of trainees and system monitoring stressed by counselor educators (Bergland & Quatrano, 1973) is evident in the complimentary area of psychotherapy. This requires evaluating our selection procedures, evaluation during training, and post-training evaluation, as well as evaluating the process of training through system monitoring for both costs and product effectiveness. Such concerns conceivably could do much to improve the quality of psychotherapy training, regardless of the diversity of approaches followed today.

PERSONAL THERAPY FOR THE PSYCHOTHERAPIST

One aspect of psychotherapy training which is mentioned frequently in many discussions of this topic, and which has been alluded to earlier, is the need for personal therapy on the part of the would-be psychotherapist. This issue has generated considerably more discussion than it has research. As indicated previously, psychoanalytic institutes and post-graduate psychotherapy centers generally require some form of personal psychotherapy for their students. As a general rule, most graduate programs in clinical psychology do not have such a requirement although it may be recommended in certain settings or for certain individuals. A number of psychotherapists have sought personal therapy, sometimes for help with their own problems, and frequently because they believed their own training was inadequate or incomplete. On the basis of some surveys of samples of clinical psychologists, it would appear that perhaps more than half have received some form of personal therapy. In one survey, Lubin (1962) reported that 57% of his sample indicated having had personal therapy, with 46% having had 1 year or more of therapy. A more recent, but more limited survey of members of the Division of Clinical Psychology reported that 64.6% of the respondents had undergone some form of personal therapy (Goldschmid, Stein, Weissman, % Sorrells, 1969). Of these individuals, about 50% had 2 or more years of therapy and one-sixth had more than 5 years. Freudian and neo-Freudian orientations covered almost three-fourths of the therapy received.

The results mentioned above are supported also by the findings of a recently published survey of 855 members of the Division of Clinical Psychology. In this survey, 63% of the respondents indicated that they had received some personal psychotherapy (Garfield & Kurtz, 1974). Thus, it appears that perhaps a majority of psychotherapists have themselves undergone some form of personal therapy. What minimal research exists on this topic is too weak to form the basis for any definitive judgment. Nevertheless, it can be looked at briefly.

An early investigation by Strupp (1955) attempted to assess the effect of the psychotherapist's personal analysis upon his techniques. In this study, Strupp attempted to compare the responses of analyzed and nonanalyzed therapists to 27 cards containing brief paragraphs of patient statements taken from published therapeutic interviews. The series of statements included four suicide threats, six transference reactions, and "six complaint statements of a seriously disturbed near-psychotic woman." Strupp hypothesized that analyzed therapists would respond differently to these statements than would nonanalyzed therapists. Although Strupp concluded that two of his three hypotheses concerning differences between analyzed and nonanalyzed therapists were "partially confirmed," the study had a number of methodological weaknesses. While a few comparisons were found to be statistically significant, the overall profiles of the two groups of therapists appear to be more similar than dissimilar. Furthermore, the samples varied in size and experience. Only two of the nonanalyzed therapists were considered to be experienced, whereas 23 of the 30 analyzed therapists were so classified. In addition, inflated Ns appear to have been used in the analyses performed by means of Chi Square. Finally, the hypotheses tested were

derived in large part from a psychoanalytic orientation and although the differences obtained were for the most part quite small, they could simply reflect a somewhat greater adherence on the part of analyzed therapists to analytic procedures. Surprisingly, however, and contrary to predictions, analyzed therapists appeared to respond in a more active manner than their nonanalyzed counterparts.

Unfortunately, there are few other published studies concerning the influence of personal therapy. The writer is familiar with only two other published studies and one very small unpublished report which was mentioned in the proceedings of a conference on training in psychotherapy. In the latter, Derner (1960) made passing reference to some data he had collected from the Adelphi University Clinic. He selected the two top-ranked therapists in training and the two lowest ranked therapists for a period of 4 years. He then compared the eight best therapists with the eight lowest ranked therapists and was surprised to discover that in each instance, half of the group had had therapy and half had not. "In this instance, senior staff judgment as to competence in therapy was unrelated to whether the therapist did or did not have therapy" (p. 133). While Derner rightly points out the modest nature of his data, he does make the point that "Therapists with and without therapy can be effective, and there seems to be no greater effectiveness for those who have had therapy than for those who have not had therapy" (p. 133).

Another small study attempted to relate hours of therapists' personal therapy to some criteria of patient change (Garfield & Bergin, 1971). Because of small sample size, no tests of significance were carried out. However, the data indicated that the clients of those therapists who had no therapy consistently demonstrated the greatest amount of change. These findings are to be interpreted only as suggestive, but they are interesting in relation to the many pronouncements concerning the importance of personal therapy in the training of therapists and illustrate the need for research data even on matters which seem to be widely accepted at a clinical level.

The final study to be discussed here was an investigation of patient and therapist attributes and their relation to improvement in psychotherapy (Katz, Lorr, & Rubenstein, 1958). In brief, therapists' ratings of improvement in two subsamples of 58 patients each had little or no relationship to whether or not the therapist had undergone personal analysis. Years of experience, however, were correlated significantly with the ratings of outcome.

It seems clear that definitive data on the importance of personal therapy for the effective professional functioning of the psychotherapist is not available. As a consequence, decisions on its significance are based on something other than empirical evidence. Most individuals who have undergone personal therapy would appear to stress its value, and, as we have noted, psychoanalytic institutes and most post-graduate psychotherapy training centers require some form of personal therapy. In some, the type of therapy and the specific institutional affiliation of the therapist is also specified. Such requirements appear, however, to be based more on conviction and belief than on scientific evidence, a pattern quite familiar to the field of psychotherapy.

There are also some other issues related to the central one of personal psychotherapy for the psychotherapist, for which no real research data are available. One such issue concerns who should be the therapist of the therapist-in-training, and his role in evaluating that person's progress or suitability. Another concerns the optimal time for personal therapy in the training sequence. Does concurrent personal therapy aid or hinder the training of the would-be therapist, either by focusing on personal problems of the trainee or by giving him too specific a model to imitate? To what extent does requiring that the therapist of the student be a member of the training institution or a card-carrying member of the specific institutional orientation constitute a subtle form of thought control? Clearly, there are many questions for which no adequate answers currently exist.

CONCLUSIONS AND IMPLICATIONS

We thus come to the end of our survey of research on training in psychotherapy. What conclusions and implications can we draw from this survey? With the great diversity which currently exists among approaches to psychotherapy, it would appear difficult to derive generalizations which have general applicability. Clearly, the differences among schools are problems of some importance, particularly when school adherence is based on factors other than scientific evidence. At some point in the history of psychotherapy, the schools will crumble and disappear, vestiges of early historical development, and they will be replaced by scientific principles of behavior change. That wondrous time, however, is not yet upon us, and some of my colleagues even doubt that it ever will be.[5] Thus, we will have to cope with school diversity for the immediate future, at least.

Nevertheless, the writer is willing to hazard a few conclusions and possible implications based on the work reviewed. The first one, which probably is quite obvious at this point, is that the state of training cannot progress very far beyond the state of the field itself. Where ambiguity and confusion reign, it is difficult to have precise, validated, and well-managed procedures. The most critical problem, basically, concerns what is to be taught. *Only after we can first specify the operations which make for positive change in psychotherapy can we go on to develop and evaluate effective means of teaching such skills and procedures.* The objectives must first be stated, then translated into meaningful operations, and later validated. Only then can worthwhile training procedures be developed, utilized, and appraised.

Another conclusion one can probably draw is that much of the training in psychotherapy is of a rather global nature. This is based on personal experience, reading, and observation, rather than on research findings, since little research on training has been reported for most varieties of psychotherapy. Students apparently are taught a variety of theoretical and clinical concepts which are not well defined or validated, and comparatively little attention is paid to the learning of specifically defined skills. This appears to be particularly true of professional as contrasted with nonprofessional training. Does this tendency signify that when a person is a member of a recognized profession, or pursuing a career in such a profession, there is less concern about the mastery of specific skills than is the case when the individual does not have such a professional affiliation or identity? Clearly, specification of what is to be learned not only facilitates learning, but also allows for progress to be gauged more readily. The use of procedures such as those developed for microcounseling and similar approaches would appear to be worth investigation and application. To the extent that what is to be learned is broken into meaningful units, specific concrete examples provided, and checks on the acquisition of skills appraised, it would appear likely that the learning process would become more efficient. As pointed out, however, problems remain concerning what is to be learned.

Another problem evident in most of the training of professional psychotherapists is that significant criteria of patient outcome are not used for evaluating students' progress. Too frequently, either supervisors' ratings or process measures are used rather than measures of client change. Both of these types of measures are of doubtful value if not clearly related to outcome measures. Supervisors' ratings are very widely used because they are easily obtainable and also apparently because the assumption is made that, as therapists, they presumably know what good therapy is. However, this is an assumption which is not necessarily accurate. Supervisors have their own biases, relate differently to different supervisees, and their judgments may be influenced by factors other than therapeutic competence. In one unpublished study, for example, where psychiatric residents were rated on their therapeutic performance by at least three different supervisors, highly significant variation among ratings was obtained.[6] Apart from the apparent limitations of such ratings as measures of therapeutic progress, there is also some question about the possible effects of such discrepant ratings on the therapist-in-training.

Since client change is really the goal of psychotherapy, such kinds of measures should be more frequently used in training programs. Besides providing a more meaningful appraisal of how the therapist-in-training is actually functioning, a focus on what changes are taking place in the client should help the learner from the beginning to attempt to appraise his own therapeutic endeavors along such lines. This type of emphasis may also tend to reduce the pressure on the student to merely please the supervisor or conform to his values, a danger which exists in many conventional programs.

Finally, it can be noted that there have been several new and innovative developments with regard to training in the last few years. There are a number of techniques, approaches, and devices which could be used to improve the quality of training in psychotherapy. Programs of training in counseling psychology and counselor education seem to be much more involved with new developments in training than are programs which train clinical psychologists, psychiatrists, or psychoanalysts. It also appears that there has been no marked attempt on the part of the latter to use and adapt such techniques for the training of professional psychotherapists in their respective programs. Whether there will be changes in this regard remains to be seen. However, a number of new and potentially useful techniques are available for tryout and experimentation, and we shall have to await the future to assess their impact.

REFERENCES

ABROMS, G. M., & GREENFIELD, N. S. A new mental health profession. *Psychiatry. Journal for the Study of Interpersonal Processes*, 1973, **36**, 10–22.

ALBRONDO, H. F., DEAN, R. L., & STARKWEATHER, J. A. Social class and psychotherapy. *Archives of General Psychiatry*, 1964, **10**, 276–283.

American Psychological Association, Committee on Training in Clinical Psychology. Recommended graduate training program in clinical psychology. *American Psychologist*, 1947, **2**, 539–558.

BANDURA, A. *Principles of behavior modification.* New York: Holt, Rinehart & Winston, 1969.

BANDURA, A., LIPSHER, D. H., & MILLER, P. E. Psychotherapists' approach-avoidance reactions to patients' expressions of hostility. *Journal of Consulting Psychology*, 1960, **24**, 1–8.

BERGIN, A. E., & SOLOMON, S. Personality and performance correlates of empathic understanding in psychotherapy. In T. TOMLINSON & J. HART (Eds.), *New directions in client-centered therapy.* Boston: Houghton–Mifflin, 1970.

BERGLAND, B. W., & QUATRANO, L. Systems evaluation in counselor education. *Counselor Education and Supervision*, 1973, **12**, 190–198.

BEUTLER, L. E. Value and attitude change in psychotherapy: A case for dyadic assessment. *Psychotherapy: Theory, Research and Practice*, 1972, **9**, 362–367.

BIRK, J. Effects of counseling supervision method and preference on empathic understanding. *Journal of Counseling Psychology*, 1972, **19**, 542–546.

BOHN, M. J., JR. Therapist responses to hostility and dependency as a function of training. *Journal of Consulting Psychology*, 1967, **31**, 195–198.

BRADY, J. P. Psychotherapy by a combined behavioral and dynamic approach. *Comprehensive Psychiatry*, 1968, **9**, 536–543.

BULLMER, K. Improving accuracy of interpersonal perception through a direct teaching method. *Journal of Counseling Psychology*, 1972, **19**, 37–41.

CARKHUFF, R. R. *Helping and human relations: A primer for lay and professional helpers.* Vol. 1. *Selection and training.* New York: Holt, Rinehart & Winston, 1969.

CARKHUFF, R. R., & BERENSON, B. G. *Beyond counseling and therapy.* New York: Holt, Rinehart & Winston, 1967.

CLEGHORN, J. M., & LEVIN, S. Training family therapists by setting learning objectives. *American Journal of Orthopsychiatry*, 1973, **43**, 439–446.

CLINE, D. W., & GARRARD, J. N. A medical interviewing course: Objectives, techniques, and assessment. *American Journal of Psychiatry*, 1973, **130**, 574–578.

COHN, B. Absentee-cueing: A technical innovation in the training of group counselors. *Educational Technology*, 1973, **13**, 61–62.

CONE, J. D., & SHELDON, S. S. Training behavior modifiers: Getting it going with remote auditory prompting. *Proceedings of the 81st Annual Convention of the American Psychological Association,* Montreal, Canada, 1973, **8**, 905–906.

DELLIS, N. P., & STONE, H. K. (Eds.) *The training of psychotherapists.* Baton Rouge, La.: Louisiana State University Press, 1960.

DERNER, G. F. An interpersonal approach to training in psychotherapy. In N. P. DELLIS & H. K. STONE (Eds.), *The training of psychotherapists.* Baton Rouge, La.: Louisiana State University Press, 1960. Pp. 130–145.

EIBEN, R., & CLACK, R. J. Impact of a participatory group experience on counselors in training. *Small Group Behavior*, 1973, **4**, 486–495.

ELSENRATH, D. E., COKER, D. L., & MARTINSON, W. D. Microteaching interviewing skills. *Journal of Counseling Psychology*, 1972, **19**, 150–155.

FEATHER, B. W., & RHOADS, J. M. Psychodynamic behavior therapy. II. Clinical aspects. *Archives of General Psychiatry*, 1972, **26**, 503–511.

FEY, W. F. Doctrine and experience: Their influence upon the psychotherapist. *Journal of Consulting Psychology*, 1958, **22**, 403–409.

FOULDS, M. L. Self-actualization and the communication of facilitative conditions during counseling. *Journal of Counseling Psychology*, 1969, **16**, 132–136.

GADE, E., & MATUSCHKA, E. Effects of verbal interaction analysis training with counseling practicum students. *Counselor Education and Supervision*, 1973, **12**, 184–189.

GARFIELD, S. L. *Clinical psychology. The study of personality and behavior*. Chicago: Aldine, 1974.

GARFIELD, S. L., & BERGIN, A. E. Personal therapy, outcome and some therapist variables. *Psychotherapy: Theory, Research and Practice*, 1971, **8**, 251–253.

GARFIELD, S. L., & KURTZ, R. A survey of clinical psychologists: Characteristics, activities and orientations. *The Clinical Psychologist*, 1974, **28**, 7–10.

GLOVER, E. *The technique of psychoanalysis*. New York: International Universities Press, 1955.

GOLDSCHMID, M. L., STEIN, D. D., WEISSMAN, H. N., & SORRELS, J. A survey of the training and practices of clinical psychologists. *The Clinical Psychologist*, 1969, **22**, 89–107.

HEINE, R. W. (Ed.) *The student physician as psychotherapist*. Chicago: University of Chicago Press, 1962.

HELLER, K. Effects of modeling procedures in helping relationships. *Journal of Consulting and Clinical Psychology*, 1969, **33**, 522–526.

HELLER, K., MYERS, R. A., & KLINE, L. V. Interview behavior as a function of standardized client roles. *Journal of Consulting Psychology*, 1963, **27**, 117–122.

HOLT, R. R. (Ed.) *New horizon for psychotherapy*. New York: International Universities Press, 1971.

HOLT, R. R., & LUBORSKY, L. *Personality patterns of psychiatrists*. New York: Basic Books, 1958.

HOSFORD, R. E. Systems approach and operations research: Appropriate for evaluating and improving counselor training? *The Counseling Psychologist*, 1972, **3**, 58–63.

HOSFORD, R. E., & LECOMTE, C. Systems intervention applied to counseling. *Journal of Employment Counseling*, 1973, **9**, 108–117.

HOSFORD, R. E., & RYAN, T. A. Systems design in the development of counseling and guidance programs. *Personnel and Guidance Journal*, 1970, **49**, 221–230.

HURST, J. C., & FENNER, R. Extended-session group as a predictive technique for counselor training. *Journal of Counseling Psychology*, 1969, **16**, 358–360.

IVEY, A. E. *Microcounseling: Innovations in interviewing training*. Springfield, Ill.: Thomas, 1971.

IVEY, A. E. The clinician as teacher of interpersonal skills: Let's give away what we've got. *The Clinical Psychologist*, 1974, **27**, 6–9.

KAGAN, N. *Influencing human interactions* (a filmed 6-hour mental health training series and accompanying 186-page instructor's manual). East Lansing, Mich.: Instruction Media Center, Michigan State University, 1971.

KAGAN, N. Can technology help us toward reliability in influencing human interaction? *Educational Technology*, 1973, **13**, 44–51.

KAGAN, N., & SCHAUBLE, P. G. Affect simulation in interpersonal process recall. *Journal of Counseling Psychology*, 1969, **16**, 309–313.

KATZ, M. M., LORR, M., & RUBINSTEIN, E. A. Remainer patient attributes and their relation to subsequent improvement in psychotherapy. *Journal of Consulting Psychology*, 1958, **22**, 411–413.

KELLEY, E. L., & FISKE, D. W. *The prediction of performance in clinical psychology*. Ann Arbor: University of Michigan Press, 1951.

KORNER, I. N., & BROWN, W. H. The mechanical third ear. *Journal of Consulting Psychology*, 1952, **16**, 81–84.

LUBIN, B. Survey of psychotherapy training and activities of psychologists. *Journal of Clinical Psychology*, 1962, **18**, 252–256.

LUBORSKY, L., & SPENCE, D. P. Quantitative research on psychoanalytic therapy. In A. E. BERGIN & S. L. GARFIELD (Eds.), *Handbook of psychotherapy and behavior change*. New York: Wiley, 1971. Pp. 408–438.

MARMOR, J. Dynamic psychotherapy and behavior therapy—Are they irreconcilable? *Archives of General Psychiatry*, 1971, **24**, 22–28.

MATARAZZO, R. G. Research on the teaching and learning of psychotherapeutic skills. In A. E. BERGIN & S. L. GARFIELD (Eds.), *Handbook of psychotherapy and behavior change*. New York: Wiley, 1971. Pp. 895–924.

MATARAZZO, R. G., PHILLIPS, J. S., WIENS, A. N., & SASLOW, G. Learning the art of interviewing: A study of what beginning students do and their pattern of change. *Psychotherapy: Theory, Research and Practice*, 1965, **2**, 49–60.

MATARAZZO, R. G., WIENS, A. N., & SASLOW, G. Experimentation in the teaching and learning of psychotherapy skills. In L. K. GOTTSCHALK & A. AUERBACH (Eds.), *Methods of research in psychotherapy*. New York: Appleton-Century-Crofts, 1966. Pp. 597–635.

MCWHIRTER, J. J., & MARKS, S. E. An investigation of the relationship between the facilitative conditions and peer and group leader ratings of perceived counseling effectiveness. *Journal of Clinical Psychology*, 1972, **28**, 116–117.

MILLER, B. Acquisition of a specified verbal response set among counselor trainees. *Journal of Counseling Psychology*, 1969, **16**, 314–316.

MORELAND, J. R., IVEY, A. E., & PHILLIPS, J. S. An evaluation of microcounseling as an interviewer training tool. *Journal of Consulting and Clinical Psychology*, 1973, **41**, 294–300.

RACHMAN, A. W., & KAUFF, P. F. Directory of postgraduate psychotherapy training facilities. *JSAS Catalog of Selected Documents in Psychology*, 1972, **2**, 116.

RAPPAPORT, J., GROSS, T., & LEPPER, C. Modeling, sensitivity training, and instruction: Implications for the training of college student volunteers and for outcome research. *Journal of Consulting and Clinical Psychology*, 1973, **40**, 99–107.

RASCHE, R. W. The effect of modeling and critical feedback on training in empathic communication. Unpublished doctoral dissertation, Southern Illinois University, 1972.

RIOCH, M. J. Pilot projects in training mental health counselors. In E. L. COWEN, E. A. GARDNER, & M. ZAX (Eds.), *Emergent approaches to mental health problems*. New York: Appleton-Century-Crofts, 1967. Pp. 110–127.

RIOCH, M. J. Two pilot projects in training mental health counselors. In R. R. HOLT (Ed.), *New horizon for psychotherapy*. New York: International Universities Press, 1971. Pp. 294–311.

RIOCH, M. J., ELKES, D., & FLINT, A. A. *National Institute of Mental Health project in training mental health counselors*. Washington, D.C.: U.S. Department of Health, Education and Welfare, Public Health Service Publication No. 1254, 1965.

ROGERS, C. R. Training individuals to engage in the therapeutic process. In C. B. STROTHER (Ed.), *Psychology and mental health*. Washington, D.C.: American Psychological Association, 1957. Pp. 76–92.

RUSSELL, P. D., & SNYDER, W. U. Counselor anxiety in relation to amount of clinical experience and quality of affect demonstrated by clients. *Journal of Consulting Psychology*, 1963, **27**, 358–363.

RYAN, T. A. Response. *The Counseling Psychologist*, 1972, **3**, 32–35.

SAKINOFSKY, I., CANTOR, R., GREEN, A., MCFARLANE, A. L., & ROBERTS, R. An empirical study of the growth of technical skills in psychotherapy training. Paper read at Ninth International Congress of Psychotherapy, Oslo, Norway, June 1973.

SILVERMAN, M. S. Perceptions of counseling following differential practicum experiences. *Journal of Counseling Psychology*, 1972, **19**, 11–15.

SPIVACK, J. D. Laboratory to classroom: The practical application of IPR in a master's level pre-practicum counselor education program. *Counselor Education and Supervision*, 1972, **12**, 3–16.

STRUPP, H. H. The effect of the psychotherapist's personal analysis upon his techniques. *Journal of Consulting Psychology*, 1955, **19**, 197–204.

STRUPP, H. H. Toward a specification of teaching and learning in psychotherapy. *Archives of General Psychology*, 1969, **21**, 203–212.

STRUPP, H. H., & BERGIN, A. E. *Research in individual psychotherapy: A bibliography*. Washington, D.C.: National Institute of Mental Health, Public Health Service Publication No. 1944, 1967.

STRUPP, H. H., & JENKINS, J. W. The development of six sound motion pictures simulating psychotherapeutic situations. *Journal of Nervous and Mental Disease*, 1963, **136**, 317–328.

THORESEN, C. E. The systems approach and counselor education: Basic features and implications. *Counselor Education and Supervision*, 1969, **9**, 3–17.

TRUAX, C. B., & CARKHUFF, R. R. *Toward effective counseling and psychotherapy*. Chicago: Aldine, 1967.

TRUAX, C. B., & MITCHELL, K. M. Research on certain therapist interpersonal skills in relation to process and outcome. In A. E. BERGIN & S. L. GARFIELD (Eds.), *Handbook of psychotherapy and behavior change*. New York: Wiley, 1971. Pp. 299–344.

WALTERS, W. W., ELDER, P., SMITH, S. L., & CLEGHORN, J. M. Psychotherapy supervision—A video-tape technique. *Canadian Psychiatric Association Journal*, 1971, **16**, 367–368.

WARD, C. H. An electronic aid for teaching interviewing techniques. *Archives of General Psychiatry*, 1960, **3**, 357–358.

WARD, R. G., KAGAN, N., & KRATHWOHL, D. R. An attempt to measure and facilitate counselor effectiveness. *Counselor Education and Supervision*, 1972, **11**, 179–186.

WHALEN, C. Effects of a model and instructions on group verbal behaviors. *Journal of Consulting and Clinical Psychology*, 1969, **33**, 509–521.

WHITELEY, J. M. Counselor education. *Review of Educational Research*, 1969, **39**, 173–187.

WHITELEY, J. M., & JAKUBOWSKI, P. A. The coached client as a research and training resource in counseling. *Counselor Education and Supervision*, 1969, **2**, 19–29.

WINBORN, B., & ROWE, W. Self-actualization and the communication of facilitative conditions—A replication. *Journal of Counseling Psychology*, 1972, **19**, 26–29.

ZIFFERBLATT, S. M. Analysis and design of counselor-training systems: An operant and operations research project. *The Counseling Psychologist*, 1972, **3**, 12–31.

NOTES

1. *Editors' Footnote.* An admittedly arbitrary definition of the "professional psychotherapist," but one that would probably receive rather wide consensual endorsement might include the following elements as necessary conditions: (1) that the individual has completed a formal training program that leads to a universally accepted graduate degree (e.g., MD, PhD, EdD, MSW, MA); (2) that this individual received in this program *both* didactic and supervised clinical experiences requiring a substantial degree of comprehension of at least the basics of personality theory, human development, psychopathology, and individual, group, and systems behavior change principles and strategies; and (3) that this individual, regardless of his or her professional discipline, *specializes* in the practice of psychotherapy. While these suggested definitional components are ours, they would appear to be generally consistent with the identification of psychotherapy professionals in the largest empirical study to date in this area (see Henry, Chapter 3, this volume).

2. *Editors' Footnote.* This is a very important fact in that it implies that this phenomenon is based on the *assumption* that since supervisors are (or, not infrequently, have been) also practicing therapists, they know what is "good" therapy and who are the "good" therapists, *independent* of actual patient outcome. The dangers of therapists-in-training thereby receiving evaluations of their performance that vary from supervisor to supervisor cannot be minimized.

3. *Editors' Footnote.* A partial solution to this dilemma might involve selection committees' live observation of "work samples" of promising applicants. Certainly, if the teachers of student therapists believe, as discussed in Footnote 2, that they are capable of evaluating the skill of therapists-*in*-training, they should be willing to go out on a predictive limb by assessing the likely clinical potential of an applicant. Not to do so would imply that experienced therapists, at least under these conditions, do not have a great deal of faith in their own evaluative and predictive abilities.

4. *Editors' Footnote.* We agree, but to be less euphemistic about this issue, we would suggest that this may be the case because it is *assumed* (by both professional therapists and the public-at-large) that (1) the practices of professionals are well understood and demonstrably effective, while (2) "others" need more careful monitoring. Even the most casual reader of the psychotherapy research literature of the last 10 years must have been disabused of the first assumption. In addition, the second implicit assumption is not particularly tenable, as evidenced by Anthony and Carkhuff (Chapter 6) and Emrick, Lassen, and Edwards (Chapter 7) in this volume.

5. *Editors' Footnote.* We are the colleagues to whom Garfield refers. We think this statement represents the author's wish more than likely reality. Furthermore, since there probably always will be "school diversity" (certainly recent scientific advances in psychotherapy research have not dissuaded the creation and continued growth of a plethora of screaming, games-analyzing, and massaging "schools"), the salient issue would seem to us to be how to best maximize the outcomes of specific "schools," styles, and strategies for specific problems, conditions, and situations. This is hardly an original idea, but it is certainly the one we find most in keeping with the pragmatic eclecticism toward which we see and hope the field is constantly moving.

6. J. Geller & A. M. Razin. Supervisory evaluation of psychotherapist competence. Unpublished manuscript, Yale University School of Medicine, 1974.

CHAPTER 5

RESEARCH ON THE THERAPIST'S LEVEL OF EXPERIENCE

ARTHUR H. AUERBACH and MARILYN JOHNSON

WHAT are the effects of a therapist's increasing experience upon the way he/she conducts individual psychotherapy? The question has both practical and theoretical importance. From the practical viewpoint, if we knew more precisely how therapists change in the course of their training and experience, we might more effectively foster desirable changes. There are also significant theoretical reasons for comparing the manner of work and results achieved by inexperienced and experienced therapists. Bergin (1971) and Bergin and Strupp (1972) have pointed out that many findings in the area of therapy research are based on the work of relative beginners. Can generalizations safely be drawn from this group? If there should prove to be important differences between therapy as practiced by inexperienced and by experienced therapists, then many of the conclusions in the field are ill-founded. Bergin (1971) reported a general criticism of psychotherapy research, to the effect that "inexperienced therapists (those captive, conveniently available subjects) are too frequently used ... generalizations from such groups are limited, if not irrelevant."

Comparison of inexperienced and experienced therapists may also illuminate the process of socialization in the role of the therapist. This is an important process, involving as it does more than simply the intellectual content which the beginner must master. In that "more" are probably to be found those nonspecific factors, common to most schools of therapy, which may be more potent change producers than the specific factors emphasized by the various schools (Frank, 1973).

We, of course, start with certain ideas about the differences between experienced and inexperienced therapists. As in all areas of psychotherapy, clinical practice has produced a body of conventional wisdom which research must painstakingly labor to confirm or refute. It is said that beginners in therapy are prone to make certain errors. Matarazzo, Wiens, and Saslow (1966) drew upon texts by Rogers (1942) and Wolberg (1954) as well as their own observations to compile a list of typical errors. They divided these into four categories: (1) errors of focus (e.g., narrow focus or focus on irrelevant material), (2) faulty role definition (e.g., argues—is authoritarian or dogmatic), (3) faulty facilitation of communication (e.g., asking yes, no, or brief answer questions), and (4) other errors (e.g., irrelevant or unprofessional statements). Most supervisors would probably agree that beginners are inclined toward such errors. One of our questions in examining the research literature will be whether the studies verify this impression.

It should be noted that the experienced therapist differs from the inexperienced one in a number of ways. The experienced therapist has been practicing therapy for a number of years and has worked with a large number of clients. But, in addition, he is usually older and has had more life experiences, probably including personal therapy. He has had greater opportunity to integrate the techniques and philosophy of therapy with his own life experiences. For example, he knows from his own struggles that a neurosis is a formidably stubborn and resourceful enemy, which must be met by persistence and patience. In short, the experienced therapist has had greater opportunity for emotional as well as cognitive learning (Rogers, 1957), and this will change his approach to therapy. Some of the changes will be subtle but may nevertheless have important consequences in the delicate process of influencing another human being.

At what point, then, do we call a therapist "experienced"? Clearly, there is no simple answer;[1] we are dealing with a continuous variable. But every study comparing "inexperienced" with "experienced" therapists has had to decide where to draw the line. There has been some variability in this decision. A level of experience which is considered inexperienced in one study may be considered experienced in the next one.

The question arises: Do these differences in definition matter in our comparisons? Can valid generalizations be made from a comparison of studies, some of which treat advanced graduate students as experienced and some as inexperienced therapists? It seems to us that the answer depends on the nature of the relationship between experience and the trait with which it is being compared. For example, consider skill in communication as it is affected by increasing experience. If there is a linear relationship between experience and communication skill, then it should not matter at which two points along the line one chooses to make the comparison. So long as more experienced therapists are compared with less experienced ones, differences will show up, if they are present. However, if communication skill changes in a nonlinear way with experience, then the points chosen for comparison may make a difference.

Unfortunately, at this stage we do not know whether the linear or nonlinear model better represents the true state of affairs. It therefore seemed wise to include all studies we could locate in which there was a reasonably adequate comparison of more and less experienced therapists. Our hope is that when there are sufficient studies of this sort it will be possible to plot the changes which experience brings.

While we do not know for sure how behavior changes as a function of experience, we would expect nonlinearity rather than linearity, and complexity rather than simplicity. It might be that certain behaviors (e.g., directiveness) would be present in the beginner but disappear as he undergoes training. At a later stage, the behavior might reappear, but it would then be handled differently than in the first phase, would spring from different motives, and in general would have a different meaning for both participants. This complexity should be kept in mind in considering the results that we shall survey.

Reviewers of a field have the obligation to evaluate, and the right to criticize, the studies they review. We have exercised the right to criticize only sparingly. It is understood that all research studies in psychotherapy are open to criticism. Either the focus of the study is too narrow, so that the researchers overlook the operation of other variables which might explain their results; or the focus is too broad and the relevant variables are not defined precisely enough; or the n is too small; or the criteria are questionable; or the authors' conclusions do not follow convincingly from the data; or the results

are interesting and apparently well-founded, but one suspects the operation of chance and would like to see the study repeated before giving it full credence. Since these limitations are usually evident, we have not emphasized them.

There is one subgroup of studies—15 dissertation projects—about which certain comments can be made that apply to them as a group, though not specifically to every dissertation. They tend to explore relatively safe topics in familiar territory, to deal with easily measured variables, and to find *some* significant results, even if many correlations must be examined. In addition, they usually study not very experienced therapists, because of their availability. They sometimes make comparisons between 1st-year graduate students as "inexperienced" therapists and advanced graduate students as "experienced" ones. With the dissertations, as with the other studies, our orientation has not been to search for the inevitable shortcomings but to discern converging conclusions that may add to the general body of knowledge.

An interesting situation arises when a number of studies, most of which might individually be criticized, point to a similar conclusion. The reviewer is then likely to conclude that the phenomenon under study is sufficiently prominent that it transcends the limitations of the individual studies. There might be a faint, lingering question whether the convergence of results occurs because researchers find what they *expect* to find, as described by Kuhn (1962). But our first hypothesis would be that convergence points to a real phenomenon, and we have followed that principle in this review.

We have organized the studies comparing experienced and inexperienced therapists under the following headings:

1. *Therapy process*, as studied both in actual therapy sessions and analogue experiments. These studies provide a direct look at the behavior of inexperienced and experienced therapists.
2. *Attitudes* held by experienced and inexperienced therapists. The study of attitudes contributes importantly to understanding the process of socialization as therapists.
3. *Outcome* achieved by experienced and inexperienced therapists.

STUDIES OF THE THERAPY PROCESS

The studies under this heading group themselves into two categories: (a) those having to do with the therapists' patterns of interventions and (b) those concerned with the quality of the therapeutic relationship.

Therapists' Pattern of Intervention

A number of investigators have addressed the question of whether experienced therapists are more active and confrontative than inexperienced therapists. "Active" behaviors refer to directing the course of the session—e.g., by focusing, interpretations, or directive interventions.[2] Activity in this sense does not include reflections or exploratory questions (except that for client-centered therapists, exploratory questions are a relatively active form of intervention). Among the studies that have looked at this issue, the recurrent but not universal finding is that experienced therapists tend to be more active and confrontative.

In an early study, Strupp (1955a) asked therapists of varying orientations and disciplines to respond to a series of written client statements. Responses were assigned to one of nine categories, (e.g., gives reassurance, interprets, shows passive rejection). Within-orientation differences emerged when experienced (more than 5 years) and inexperienced (less than 5 years) therapists were compared. Experienced client-centered therapists used more exploration and less reflection than inexperienced client-centered therapists. Analytic therapists did not show significant experience-related differences, but there was a tendency for experienced therapists to draw from a wider range of responses.

When the data were analyzed by professional discipline, somewhat similar findings emerged: experienced psychiatrists used more interpretations and a larger number of passive rejections, while psychiatric residents used a large number of exploratory responses (Strupp, 1955b).

In Strupp's next study (1958), he asked therapists to make a series of written responses to a film of a client being interviewed. Subjects were 55 psychiatrists and 55 psychologists matched on experience. Among the psychiatrists, experienced therapists differed from inexperienced therapists in the following ways: (1) inexperienced therapists tended to ask more exploratory questions; (2) experienced therapists made more interpretive responses; (3) experienced therapists showed a higher degree of initiative; and (4) experienced therapists changed the dynamic focus of their communications.

In two studies Ornston and her colleagues investigated verbal behaviors of experienced and inexperienced therapists. Ornston, Cicchetti,

Levine, and Fierman (1968) found that experienced therapists made more statements and asked fewer questions than inexperienced therapists. Using the Strupp film method, experienced psychiatrists (2–20 years) and 1st-year residents responded to a filmed client, and their verbal comments were categorized as questions or nonquestions. Overall, experienced therapists used more total words and made more nonquestion statements than inexperienced therapists. The inexperienced therapists made more question than nonquestion statements.

The second study (Ornston, Cicchetti, & Towbin, 1970), using the same procedure, tested the inexperienced therapists from the first study at three points in their first year of training: at the beginning, after 6 months, and at completion of the year. At each point, their verbal behaviors were compared with those of a group of experienced therapists. The initial comparison revealed experience-inexperience differences similar to those in the first study: experienced therapists asked fewer questions and used more words per statement than inexperienced therapists. By the second testing, these differences disappeared and did not reappear in the third testing. It appears that the residents had learned rather quickly to model experienced therapists' behavior. Finally, Ornston et al. (1970) demonstrated that expert therapists could, in 30 of 43 cases, distinguish experienced from inexperienced therapists by reading typescripts of their interviews. The judges, who knew nothing of the results of the previous studies, associated high word/statement ratio and low question/statement ratio with experience in psychotherapy.

Mitchell and Hall (1971) studied the behavior of experienced (2–20 years) and inexperienced therapists (advanced graduate students) in an initial interview. The inexperienced therapists tended to make fewer interventions, and most of their interventions were in the last third of the interview. They rarely confronted the client with his weaknesses or limitations. In this last respect they were similar to one subgroup of experienced therapists but different from another subgroup. It seems that beginning therapists tended to avoid confrontations that might seem aggressive, whereas some experienced therapists felt comfortable with aggressive confrontation.

In an analogue study, Gamsky and Farwell (1966) presented 30 therapists of three experience levels with four actor-clients, two enacting a friendly role and two a hostile role. The experience levels were: (1) no formal psychotherapy training; (2) 1 semester of training; (3) 1 year of experience. From their tape-recorded interviews, therapist responses were scored according to 14 categories. One of the categories was: "Therapist avoids what client was talking about." In general, experienced therapists showed less avoidance than inexperienced therapists, even under hostile-client conditions. However, it should be noted that the "experienced therapists" would be considered relative beginners by most standards.

Campbell (1962) followed up Hoffman's (1959) investigation of counselor interview behaviors. Hoffman had divided therapist activity into 14 behaviors or subroles, examples of which are reflecting, supporting, advising. He found that experienced therapists varied in the patterns of behaviors they used. Campbell studied inexperienced therapists (practicum students) by Hoffman's method and then compared his findings with Hoffman's. The patterns of behaviors used by the two groups showed many similarities. When these behaviors were rank-ordered by frequency, they correlated .63. The difference was that inexperienced therapists did more information-gathering, listening, reflecting, and less participating than experienced therapists.

Not all studies report that experienced therapists are more active and confrontative. Grigg (1961) asked counseling center clients to fill out a Client Observation Report which described their counselors' in-therapy behaviors. Counselors of three experience levels participated: (1) Novices, (2) trainees who had completed a year's internship, and (3) PhDs. The PhDs and trainees allowed the client more control over sessions than did the novices and allowed clients to initiate discussion and made fewer interpretations. The novices gave more advice and suggestions. Clients rated their counseling as equally helpful whether their counselor was experienced or inexperienced. The greater advice and suggestions given by novices conforms to findings from other studies that will be discussed below, and suggests that novices and nonprofessionals conceive of the therapist role as active and advice-giving.[3] There is an important distinction between novices—who have had no or virtually no training—and inexperienced therapists, who have had some training.

In an analogue study, Bohn (1965) asked undergraduate and graduate students in psychology to assume the therapist role in response to tape recordings of three clients: a hostile, a dependent, and a neutral one. At 10 points in each tape, subjects chose a therapist response from one of four alternatives. Two of the alternatives were defined as directive and two as nondirective. It had been expected that counselor directiveness would be related to counselor dominance as measured by the California Psychological Inventory. This proved not to be the case. Directiveness was inversely related to counselor experience—i.e., undergraduates made more directive responses and the graduate students were more nondirective. In addition, the graduate students used a narrower range of responses. They especially favored "restatement of content" and "clarification of feeling." Since the "inexperienced therapists" were undergraduates fulfilling a course requirement, their greater directiveness probably reflects the attitudes of nonprofessionals on how therapy should be conducted.

Parsons and Parker (1968) replicated Bohn's experiment using psychiatrists, senior medical students, and undergraduates. The psychiatrists were found to be less directive than the other two groups, and those psychiatrists with the greatest experience were the least directive. The medical students and undergraduates were equally directive. This finding supports that of Bohn in showing that untrained subjects conceive of the therapist's role as quite directive.

Caracena (1965) examined therapist responses to client dependency statements in the initial stages of therapy. He hypothesized that experienced therapists would show more approach responses (e.g., approval, exploration, labeling, and interpretation) and fewer avoidance responses (e.g., disapproval, ignoring) to dependency statements. Caracena believed that approaches to dependency statements tend to keep clients in therapy in the early stages, and that experienced therapists would have learned this technique. His hypothesis was supported: staff-level therapists showed significantly more approach responses than interns or practicum students.

Schuldt (1966) attempted to replicate Caracena's finding for the first interview of psychotherapy. His results showed a trend in the predicted direction, but it was not statistically significant. Considering the entire course of therapy, there was no difference between experienced (average of 7.5 years) and less experienced (2 years) therapists on approach to dependency expressions. In comparing Schuldt's findings with Caracena's, we note that Schuldt's inexperienced therapists were a little more experienced than Caracena's. Perhaps by the 2nd year therapists learn to approach dependency statements, and subsequent increase in this skill is not significant.

Hill (1975) examined the effects of client sex and therapist sex and experience on therapy behavior. Equal numbers of male and female inexperienced (practicum level) and experienced (at least 2 years of experience) therapists tape-recorded second sessions with a male and a female client. Three segments from the sessions were rated for therapist and client verbal behaviors, therapist empathy, client self-exploration, and therapist and client activity levels. Results showed one main effect involving experience: the inexperienced therapists offered a significantly greater number of "positive confrontations" than did the experienced therapists. "Positive confrontation," which is not defined by the author, presumably consists of pointing out the client's assets. There was a significant triple interaction (client sex by therapist sex by therapist experience) on nine of 13 variables, but they do not add up to a consistent pattern. This is another study which really compares nonexperienced with inexperienced therapists.

Summary of findings on active and confrontative behavior: No firm conclusions can be drawn from these few studies, but certain tentative conclusions suggest themselves: (1) The non-professional conception of therapeutic behavior is active, confrontative, and directive. When untrained students are asked to take the role of therapist, they usually behave this way (Bohn, 1965; Grigg, 1961; Parsons & Parker, 1968). (2) Inexperienced therapists, at least when they are being observed, favor safe interventions—those which do not expose them to criticisms and which cannot be considered mistakes. Thus, their interventions tend to be exploratory, reflective, and brief. They also tend to follow the client's lead rather than take the initiative (Campbell, 1962; Mitchell & Hall, 1971; Strupp, 1958). (3) Experienced therapists are more talkative, commit themselves by use of interpretations and other non-questions, and more often take the initiative (Ornston *et al.*, 1968; Strupp, 1955b, 1958).

Quality of Therapeutic Relationship

It is assumed that with experience comes the ability to establish a good relationship with a client in psychotherapy. The earliest and best-known studies on the importance of the therapist's level of experience were done by Fiedler (1950a, 1950b, 1951). He was interested in learning the characteristics of the ideal therapeutic relationship, and studied therapists of differing orientations and levels of experience. Fiedler (1950a) began by asking therapists to sort a set of statements descriptive of psychotherapy events into six categories, from most to least ideal. While all of the therapists (who included Adlerians, psychoanalysts, Rogerians, and eclectics) were found to have a generally similar notion of the ideal relationship, the experienced therapists agreed with each other more than they did with the inexperienced therapists of their own orientation.[4]

Having arrived at an agreed-upon definition of an ideal therapeutic relationship, Fiedler (1950b) made use of it in studying therapy. He tape-recorded early therapy sessions of experienced therapists (average of 13 years) and inexperienced therapists (average of 2.5 years) of the psychoanalytic, Rogerian, and Adlerian schools. The statements used in making ratings were divided into three broad categories which were descriptive of the therapists: (1) communication, (2) emotional distance, and (3) status role. Trained judges rated the sessions, using the statements from the earlier study. It was hypothesized that the expert therapists would approximate the ideal therapeutic relationship described in the first study, and this was confirmed. Again, the experienced therapists were more similar to one another than to inexperienced therapists of the same schools. It was found that the communication items were most useful in differentiating expert from inexpert therapists of the same school. Experts showed greater ability to understand clients and to communicate their understanding. The above division of the rating items was *a priori*. In his next study, Fiedler (1951) factor-analyzed the ratings made by the judges in the previous study. The factor analysis was done separately for each judge. The tape-recorded sessions from the previous study (Fiedler, 1950b) were scored on the factors and compared. It was found that none of the factors differentiated one school from another, but several of them did differentiate experts from nonexperts. As in the second study, it was the communication factor that most sharply separated the two groups.

Fiedler's findings are satisfying in their clarity and reasonableness. It is gratifying that there should be a consensus on the nature of the ideal therapeutic relationship, and that with experience therapists from different orientations approach this ideal. Indeed, some (but not all) subsequent studies have shown that experienced therapists offer a better therapeutic relationship than do inexperienced ones. In a classic study, Barrett-Lennard (1962) used client and therapist assessments, made after the fifth therapy session, of therapists' offering of facilitative conditions to predict treatment outcome. Both clients and therapists completed Barrett-Lennard's Relationship Inventory, a measure of five therapist conditions: level of regard, empathy, congruence, unconditionality of regard, and willingness to be known. Barrett-Lennard hypothesized that experienced therapists and their clients would perceive their relationship as better on all of the five conditions than inexperienced therapists and their clients would, and that clients of experienced therapists would show greater change in therapy. In addition, he predicted that there would be more client-therapist agreement on the levels of conditions in the experienced therapist-client pairs. The experienced therapists had an average of 5.4 years, and the inexperienced therapists 1 year of experience.[5]

The results showed that clients of experienced therapists perceived their therapists as exhibiting a significantly higher level of regard, empathy, congruence, and unconditionality of regard than did the clients of inexperienced therapists. The experienced therapists felt they offered more empathy and unconditional positive regard. In conjunction with these findings, the inexperienced therapists perceived themselves and were perceived by clients to vary a good deal more than experienced therapists in the given conditions. Experienced therapist-client pairs were significantly more in agreement than inexperienced therapist-client pairs on one of the five conditions: empathy. Thus, the experienced therapist clearly expressed empathy and this expression was understood by the client.

Barrett-Lennard used two outcome criteria —therapist rating of change and length of therapy. He was aware of the limitations of length of therapy as an outcome criterion, but felt that it was worth using, citing earlier studies which showed a correlation between change and therapy length. (In the subsequent review by Luborsky, Auerbach, Chandler, Cohen, and Bachrach [1971], it was indeed found that in 20 out of 21 studies, length of therapy was positively related to outcome, but the meaning of this correlation is open to various interpretations.) Clients of experienced therapists tended to receive higher change ratings than those of inexperienced therapists,[6] and the treatment by experienced therapists was significantly longer than that by inexperienced therapists.

Cartwright and Lerner (1963) explored the effects of clients' need to change and therapists' empathy for clients on improvement in psychotherapy. Results indicated that need to change and improvement were significantly correlated. Empathy was measured as the correlation between the therapist's perception of the client and the client's self-perception. Post-therapy, but not pre-therapy, empathy ratings related to improvement. Given the client's self-description, the therapist's self-description, and the therapist's description of the client, it was possible to calculate (1) the "real" similarity between the two participants (discrepancy between client's self-description and therapist's self-description), (2) the therapist's "assumed" similarity (discrepancy between therapist's self-description and therapist's description of client), and (3) "distance" (discrepancy between real similarity and assumed similarity). These measurements were made after the second session. Experienced therapists made distancing errors in both directions with about equal frequency, but inexperienced therapists tended to see clients as less like themselves than the patient's own views showed them to be. That is, inexperienced therapists distanced themselves from their clients. The authors suggest that "the new therapist is more open to threat and more easily made anxious by seeing clients as similar to himself, and so does more defensive distancing" (Cartwright & Lerner, 1963, p. 143). Experienced therapists can more readily acknowledge similarities between their clients and themselves. In this study experienced therapists were defined as those who had "handled more than five research cases" (p. 143); inexperienced therapists had handled fewer than five research cases.

Kagan (1972) has developed the Interpersonal Process Recall method for use in training therapists. An interview conducted by a therapist-trainee is videotaped; immediately following the interview, the trainee and client independently observe the tape and express what they felt and thought as the interview proceeded. In the recall session, therapist-trainees revealed that they had noted subtle phenomena which they had given no evidence of perceiving during the interview. For example, they may, during the interview, have given no sign of noticing the client's anger toward them, and therefore of course did not deal with it. However, they revealed in the recall session that they were quite aware of the anger at the time. Kagan noted that all trainees perceived much more during the interview than they appeared to. This "feigned clinical naivete" was considered a means of avoiding involvement.

In a study which was primarily concerned with the effect of sex of therapist on client expression of feeling, Fuller (1963) found a relationship between the experience level of therapists and the intensity of feeling expressed by clients. At the beginning of therapy, clients either expressed preference for a male therapist or had no preference (none preferred a female therapist). The degree of feeling expressed by clients was rated from tape-recorded therapy sessions. Therapist experience interacted with assignment to preferred-sex therapist: those clients assigned according to preference expressed more feeling with experienced therapists than with inexperienced therapists. Experienced therapists had an average of 5 years experience, and inexperienced therapists were doctoral students starting their internship.

There have been other studies which support the idea that clients have a more favorable attitude toward experienced therapists. In a replication of an earlier study, Ivey, Miller, and Gabbert (1968) examined client attitudes toward counseling. Clients with more experienced therapists had more favorable attitudes.

Pope, Nudler, Von Korff, and McGhee (1974) examined the effects of expert versus novice interviewers on students in terms of interviewee reactions and productivity of the interviews. Professionals were described by interviewees as more competent and skillful, and novices as more sympathetic, accepting, and sensitive. However, interview productivity did not differ significantly for the professionals and novices.

In considering the reactions of clients to experienced therapists, one must consider the expectations of the client as well as the actual behaviors of the therapist. The client's expectation that he will be involved with an experienced therapist can significantly influence the transaction. Strong and Schmidt (1970) tested this effect in an analogue study by varying pre-interview set (introduction of interviewer as experienced or inexperienced) and interviewer behavior. The actor-interviewer was trained to act either as an expert (confident, organized, responsive to subject, etc.) or as inexpert (unsure of himself, nervous, poorly organized, unresponsive to subject, etc.). The stated purpose of the interview was to discuss need-for-achievement tests with 49 college students who had filled out the Edwards Personal Preference Schedule and guessed at their own need for achievement relative to other college students. The interviewers tried to influence the subject's estimate of his own need for achievement. Following the interview, and one week afterward, students again filled out the EPPS and estimated their relative need for achievement. They also rated the interviewer's expertness and described their reactions to the interview.

Neither role behavior nor introduction alone was sufficient to produce a significant influence on the students, but their combination was effective. Students who expected to see an expert and who did so changed significantly on their self-rating of need for achievement. Subjects perceived the interviewers as intended; they were able to differentiate expert from nonexpert interviewer behavior, regardless of the expectancy condition. In summary, both the expected and the actual role of expert had some effect in influencing the subject, but this effect reached significance only when the expectation of expertness was combined with expert role behavior.

Another study of the effect of pre-session expectancies on receptivity to therapist influence was conducted by Greenberg (1969). Students were given one of four possible sets: therapist was warm and experienced, cold and experienced, warm and inexperienced, or cold and inexperienced. They then listened to a taped, simulated therapy session in which the therapist's warmth and experience were ambiguous, and rated their attraction and receptivity to the therapist. Additionally, they completed a questionnaire on the tape-recorded patient. This questionnaire was actually a vehicle for learning how persuaded the subjects had been by the therapist—that is, how closely their views of the patient approximated the therapist's view, which was known to the subjects.

Subjects instructed to expect experienced therapists rated the therapist as sounding experienced and rated themselves as more attracted and receptive to him than did subjects instructed to expect inexperienced therapists. However, the experience set had no effect on the therapist's persuasiveness. Subjects anticipating a warm therapist, on the other hand, were attracted, receptive, and also persuaded. This was true whether the set was for warmth-experience or warmth-inexperience. Thus, it appears that the set for warmth-coldness was more crucial than was the set for experience level.

Greenberg, Goldstein, and Perry (1970) used the same design with a psychotic inpatient sample, and added an uninstructed control group. Subjects instructed to expect an experienced therapist were no more receptive than those instructed to expect an inexperienced therapist, although they were significantly more receptive than the control subjects. Therapist persuasiveness was not significantly related to any of the instructional variables. The authors speculate that the psychotics' inadequate cognitive functioning may account for the difference in results between this study and those of Greenberg (1969).

Beery (1970) tested Rogers' (1957) hypothesis that therapist unconditional positive regard depends partly on the amount of therapist experience. She asked experienced (mean of ten years) and inexperienced (pre-practicum) therapists to respond to taped actor-clients. Half of the therapists were exposed to a friendly client and half to a hostile client. Beery found that while all therapists responded with greater positive regard to the friendly client, the experienced therapists' unconditional positive regard level was significantly higher than the inexperienced group across both client types. Beery regards Rogers' hypothesis as only partly confirmed. Experienced therapists' positive regard was not truly unconditional, but varied according to client attitude. As a group, however, experienced therapists created a more favorable therapeutic climate—i.e., they were more accepting than inexperienced therapists. Beery speculated that, with experience, therapists are less easily surprised and/or threatened by clients in general, and they learn that reacting positively helps to create a favorable therapeutic climate.

Rice (1965) studied therapist styles of speaking in relation to therapy outcome. Therapist vocal and lexical characteristics were categorized from tape recordings. Three interview types emerged: Type I therapist responses were expressed in commonplace, "garden variety" language. Type II therapist responses were characterized chiefly by a distorted voice quality (e.g., a sing-song effect) and by minimal use of fresh language. Type III therapists used fresh, connotative language and spoke expressively. Type I behavior did not distinguish between experienced and inexperienced therapists. Inexperienced therapists (1–2 years) exhibited significantly more Type II behavior, while experienced therapists (3 or more years) showed significantly more Type III behavior. Type II behavior early in therapy was significantly correlated with unsuccessful therapy outcome, but the expected relationship between early Type III behavior and favorable outcome was not found.

Butler, Rice, and Wagstaff (1962) made a similar study of types of client speech in therapy sessions. They delineated three types, two of which correlated with the amount of experience of the clients' therapists. In factor (type) I speech the client is usually direct and focused, is expressing feeling or analyzing relevant feeling, and is very involved in what he is saying. This speech behavior was associated with the clients of more experienced therapists, who were defined as having had 2 or more years of experience. In factor (type) III speech, the client does not express feelings directly. He discusses ideas and events, and he seems more like an external observer than a participant. The clients of inexperienced therapists (less than 2 years) tended to show this speech pattern. This study is one of the few which has established a link between therapist level of experience and client behavior in therapy. It is encouraging that more experienced therapists can induce their clients to be more direct, focused, and expressive of feeling. Any insight into the means by which experienced therapists affect their clients is welcome. These findings are of sufficient importance to call for replication.

Mullen and Abeles (1971) hypothesized that experienced therapists would be more empathic than inexperienced therapists because the latter are more concerned with satisfying their own needs in therapy and are therefore distracted from full understanding of the client. The inexperienced therapists were practicum students and 1st-year interns, and the experienced therapists were 2nd-year interns and PhDs. Five-minute segments of tape-recorded therapy sessions were rated by judges for non-possessive warmth and accurate empathy. The predicted difference between the two groups was found. Another interesting finding emerged: empathy and warmth were highly correlated for the inexperienced therapists, but not correlated at all for the experienced ones. Evidently some experienced therapists do not feel a need to act warmly toward clients; thus, they may display empathy (understanding) in the absence of warmth.

Mills and Abeles (1965) hypothesized that counselors high in need for nurturance and affiliation would express strong liking for their clients. In addition, such counselors were expected to make approach responses to dependency and hostility statements in clients. Practicum students, interns, and doctoral-level staff psychologists were included in the study. A significant relationship between liking for clients and needs for nurturance and affiliation was found only among the least experienced therapists. Contrary to expectations, those therapists with high nurturant and affiliative needs did *not* show greater approach responses to client dependency statements. However, such therapists did approach client hostility statements significantly more than other therapists. Analysis of the findings according to experience level revealed no consistent pattern.

Cimbolic (1972) studied the effect of counselor race and experience on black clients. Two experienced (3 years) therapists, one white and one black, and two nonexperienced therapists, also black and white, interviewed 17 black college students. The nonexperienced therapists were graduate students in fields unrelated to psychology. After the interviews, the college students rated the counselor's effectiveness, likability, and skill. In addition, trained judges rated tapes of the interviews on four counselor facilitative conditions: empathy, unconditional positive regard, genuineness, and concreteness. Experience, but not race, differentiated the counselors on the basis of student ratings of effectiveness, likability, and skill, with experienced therapists obtaining higher scores. In addition, the experienced therapists offered higher levels of facilitative conditions, except for genuineness. This study compared nonprofessionals with minimally experienced therapists. It should also be remembered that the subjects were not counselees expressing a need for help, but students who were requested to volunteer. The findings should therefore be considered tentative.

Russell and Snyder (1963) studied the anxiety shown by experienced and less experienced therapists in a therapy analogue experiment: actors variously enacted roles of friendly or hostile clients. Therapists showed more anxiety when confronted with a hostile "client," but level of experience had little effect on the amount of anxiety in either the friendly or hostile client condition. It should be noted that there was minimal difference in experience among the therapists, all of whom were graduate students of approximately the same level of training. Their exact range of experience was not stated. They were divided into more and less experienced groups on the basis of a "clinical experience" questionnaire, the items of which were not specified.

Summary of findings on quality of therapeutic relationship: There is a heartening consistency among these findings. With few exceptions, they indicate that experienced therapists do indeed establish better relationships with clients. The studies we have considered arrive at this conclusion through judges' ratings of tape-recorded therapy sessions and through clients' ratings of their therapy. They show that experienced therapists communicate better (Fiedler, 1950b, 1951; Rice, 1965), offer higher levels of positive regard (Barrett-Lennard, 1962; Beery, 1970), of empathy (Barrett-Lennard, 1962; Mullen & Abeles, 1971) and of congruence (Barrett-Lennard, 1962); that they are generally evaluated more favorably by clients (Ivey et al., 1968); that they do not show the inexperienced therapist's tendency to defensively distance himself from the client (Cartwright & Lerner, 1963); that clients express more feeling with experienced therapists, at least when the therapist is of the preferred sex (Fuller, 1963); and that clients of experienced therapists are more direct, focused, involved, and expressive of feeling (Butler et al., 1962). Some studies (Greenberg, 1969; Strong & Schmidt, 1970) have shown that the client's expectation that his therapist is an expert constitutes a significant factor—not so preponderant as to obviate the need for actual expertness, but contributing to the amount of influence on the client. It should also be noted that the beginners' errors delineated by Matarazzo et al. (1966) do in fact occur. At least, these studies give support to that thesis.

THERAPIST ATTITUDES

In this section we examine whether increasing experience is accompanied by changes in therapists' attitudes toward clients, therapeutic techniques, and the therapy endeavor in general. We are searching for insights into the process of socialization in the role of therapist, and are interested in differences between inexperienced and experienced therapists in optimism, the nature of their understanding of clients, and their views of how therapy should be conducted.

As noted above, Fiedler (1950a) studied therapists' concepts of the ideal therapeutic relationship, and found that experienced therapists from different schools agreed with each other more than experienced and inexperienced therapists within a school.

Sundland and Barker (1962) constructed the Therapist Orientation Questionnaire (TOQ) in order to clarify differences in attitude among therapists of varying schools. The TOQ responses of 139 therapists were factor-analyzed. Six factors resulted, and a second-order (general) factor was found which included the majority of the items. It was labeled Analytic vs. Experiential. Therapists were found to cluster by orientation rather than by level of experience. For example, Rogerians, both experienced and inexperienced, were more similar in their views than they were to analysts.

Because this finding contradicted the well-known work of Fiedler, Sundland and Barker reexamined their data, using just the extremely experienced (9 or more years) and inexperienced (2 or less years) therapists' results. Again, therapists of the same orientation were alike regardless of experience. Sundland and Barker suggest that the difference between their results and Fiedler's stems from the different item pools in the two studies. Fiedler's items were so basic that they could be agreed upon by the broad community of therapists; perhaps they can be thought of as lowest-common-denominator descriptors. Sundland and Barker deliberately included more controversial items which were intended to differentiate therapists.

Anthony (1967) followed up 38 of the inexperienced therapists in the Sundland and Barker (1962) study.[8] Four years after the earlier study, these therapists again filled out the TOQ. Anthony studied the 16 "attitudinal areas" of the TOQ that Sundland and Barker (1962) reported. He found that the therapists showed significant changes in 12 areas, in eight of which the changes were in the same direction for Freudians, Rogerians, and Sullivanians. The therapists became more interpretive and thought more about how their clients related to them. They became more personal with clients, and believed more strongly that affect is important in therapy. They assigned more importance to a client's self-understanding, and they formulated more specific therapeutic goals. Unconscious processes became a less important factor. It is of interest that, despite their 4 years of added experience, they expressed feelings of decreased security as psychotherapists. The question arises: Were they truly less secure, or had it become more acceptable for them to express feelings of insecurity which they previously would have denied?

McNair and Lorr (1964) asked 265 therapists to answer a questionnaire based on many of the items in Sundland's and Barker's TOQ. Questionnaire items clustered into three relatively independent dimensions of therapeutic techniques: analytic, impersonal, and directive. Results revealed relationships between therapist technique (as reported on the questionnaire) and professional affiliation, therapist sex, and personal analysis but *not* therapist experience. This lack of correlation between technique pattern and level of experience supports Sundland and Barker's findings.

Berzins, Herron, and Seidman (1971) studied the effects of experience on therapists' conceptions of client roles. Data were obtained from questionnaires completed by 133 male therapists of different disciplines. They were divided into inexperienced and experienced subgroups, the former with a mean of 1.8 years and the latter with a mean of 9.5 years of experience. Therapists were asked to describe the in-therapy behaviors of their typical and of their successful clients. They also completed the A-B Scale and stated their orientation. Factor analyses of patient behavior items produced three patient factors: I-Deferent-Subordinate Patient Role, II-Expressive-Egalitarian Patient Role, and III-Self-Reliant-Dominant Patient Role. Both experienced and inexperienced therapists had typical and successful patients described by all three factors, except that experienced therapists' typical patients were not defined by Factor III.

The authors inferred that those behaviors rated higher on successful than typical patients were good prognostic indicators. The experienced therapists considered Factor II (Expressive-Egalitarian Patient Role) a good prognostic sign. The views of the inexperienced therapists were generally similar. However, the inexperienced therapists also valued characteristics found in Factor III, which included initiating conversation, selecting topics, and generally being verbally active. They valued patients' verbal activity more than their experienced colleagues did. Regarding the correlates of A-B status, inexperienced B therapists' definition of successful clients loaded heavily on Factor III (Self-Reliant-Dominant Client Role). For the experienced therapists, there were no significant correlates of A-B status.

Rice, Gurman, and Razin (1974) explored the relationship between therapist style of behavior in therapy and his/her sex, orientation, and experience. Nearly all of the inexperienced therapists were still in training, whereas the experienced therapists had completed their training. Style was defined by eight factors emerging from a therapist self-report questionnaire. Compared to the inexperienced therapists, the experienced therapists reported themselves as more interested in the client's history, more willing to wait for important material to emerge, more interpretive, more variable in their behavior, and more revealing of themselves and their feelings. Certain of these behaviors also differentiated male and female therapists. Female therapists were more variable in their therapy behavior and more self-revealing. It would seem that, in these two respects, male therapists as they gain experience become more like female therapists, at least as judged by self-report.[9]

A study by Fey (1958) illustrates that sometimes the effect of experience may be confounded with certain changes in the Zeitgeist. Widespread changes in attitudes about therapy (caused, for example, by the rise of a particular therapeutic school) mark a watershed which will differentiate therapists trained before and after it. In 1953, Fey conducted a survey of 34 therapists of different orientations. Rogerians, analysts, young eclectics, and older eclectics answered a 30-item questionnaire which inquired into their in-therapy behaviors and attitudes. He found the expected differences across doctrine, and also found that the young eclectics were much more similar to the analysts than were the older eclectics. "The split between the older and young eclectics corresponds roughly to the pre- and post-World War II training in psychiatry" (p. 407), a period in which psychoanalysis came to the fore.

Brown (1970) found that inexperienced counselors (less than 1 year) at the beginning of counseling tended to see their clients as higher on favorable qualities than did experienced counselors (more than 1 year, including PhDs). The favorable qualities include liking for the client and perceived potential for change. Experienced counselors were more skeptical and pessimistic. The enthusiasm of inexperienced counselors declined somewhat as counseling proceeded, but their satisfaction with the entire experience remained higher than that of the experienced counselors. However, the experienced counselors proved to be better prophets—their initial assessments of client potential for change correlated significantly with their subsequent ratings of improvement ("satisfaction with client progress"). Those of the inexperienced counselors did not correlate significantly.[10]

Somewhat similar findings were obtained by Auerbach (1971), who compared judgments and predictions made by six psychiatric residents and one experienced therapist after witnessing initial interviews with clients. The residents were more optimistic and expressed higher levels of certainty in the accuracy of their predictions than did the experienced therapist. However, their predictions turned out to be less accurate. (None of the predictions in this study correlated significantly with outcome.) We think that these findings reflect the beginner's enthusiasm and also the need for certainty. Having formed an impression of how the client might respond to therapy, residents have a greater need to believe in the accuracy of that impression. The experienced therapist is able to hold his impression tentatively.

Taplin (1968) studied clinical descriptions and dynamic hypotheses as formulated by experienced (post-internship) and inexperienced (less than 1 year) therapists. Segments of therapy were either listened to from tape recordings or observed and heard from videotapes. The subject's task was to describe the client and formulate psychodynamic hypotheses. Taplin found that all therapists included a larger number of descriptive elements when their impressions of the client were based on the videotape rather than on the tape recording. However, the quality of their dynamic hypotheses was essentially the same under both conditions. Quality was rated by two psychological judges.

It is of interest that the quality of hypotheses was not significantly better for the experienced therapists than for the inexperienced therapists, though there was a trend favoring the experienced therapists. It is also interesting that in moving from the audio- to videotape condition, inexperienced therapists showed *increased* confidence in their formulations, while experienced therapists showed *decreased* confidence. It may be that inexperienced therapists, being closer in their mental processes to nonprofessionals, want those cues that lay people typically have in human interaction: sight as well as sound. Experienced therapists, with well-developed clinical schemata in their minds, can categorize clients from the content and paralanguage of their speech. Evidently, the videotape introduced certain distractions which reduced the confidence of the experienced therapists.[11]

Therapists are, of course, influenced by the prevailing cultural climate—for example, changing attitudes toward women. This issue was touched upon by Neulinger, Schillinger, Stein, and Welkowitz (1970). They examined therapists' views of the optimally integrated person. Two samples of psychotherapists, one in the United States and one in Czechoslovakia, completed a questionnaire containing paragraph descriptions of 20 of Murray's needs; instructions were to rank order the 20 needs to describe optimally healthy people. American therapists were asked to describe a healthy male, healthy female, and healthy person. The Czechoslovakian sample described only the healthy person. The average therapist in both samples was 40 years old and had 9.7 years of experience.

Therapists' age and experience were compared to the profiles they constructed. Experience level did not affect the profiles drawn by the Czech therapists, and only one significant relationship occurred in the American sample: older, experienced therapists named aggression as more characteristic of the optimally healthy female than did less experienced therapists. From the viewpoint of changing cultural attitudes, one might have expected that in 1969 younger therapists would accept aggression as part of the healthy female, but it was the older, more experienced therapists who did so. Is it possible that the process of doing therapy broadens the therapist and alters the stereotypes with which he started?

Summary of therapist attitudes: These studies of therapists' attitudes, as revealed mostly by self-report, present us with mixed findings. Two substantial inquiries into therapists' orientation (McNair & Lorr, 1964; Sundland & Barker, 1962) show that experience level does not account for the variance. It seems that when therapists are asked, "What general approach to therapy do you favor?" their answers will depend upon factors other than experience level.

Nevertheless, therapists do report that increasing experience is accompanied by certain changes in attitude. There is considerable congruence between the findings of Anthony (1967), who retested therapists on the Therapist Orientation Questionnaire 4 years after Sundland and Barker, and those of Rice *et al.* (1974), who analyzed their questionnaire results according to therapist experience. With experience, therapists make more interpretations, reveal more of themselves, and are more variable in their behavior. In Anthony's study the therapists reported that they now formulate more specific goals for therapy and are interested in how clients relate to them.

When asked to formulate a description of the good prognostic client (Berzins *et al.*, 1971), experienced and inexperienced therapists were in general agreement, although there was one difference: inexperienced therapists had a greater fondness for verbally active patients who take the initiative in the session and thus, presumably, relieve the therapist of the burden of finding something to say. When confronted with actual clients at the beginning of therapy (Brown, 1970), inexperienced therapists were more inclined to see favorable qualities in the client and to be optimistic about outcome.

Taplin's (1968) finding that the psychodynamic hypotheses written by experienced therapists were somewhat, but not significantly, superior to those of inexperienced therapists is suggestive. It reminds us that the repertoire of dynamic formulations is limited, and that beginners grasp the major, most commonly used formulas rather promptly. One might say that the basic framework of their clinical schemata is laid down rather quickly. The refinements are added more slowly through processes of assimilation and accommodation, resulting in a cognitive structure which is at least partly unique.

Finally, we are reminded by Fey's (1958) study that increasing experience is not necessarily the same phenomenon from one generation to the next. Much depends on *what* is experienced, which is a function of the climate of opinion.

OUTCOME STUDIES

Most of the studies we have reviewed thus far have revealed differences between experienced and inexperienced therapists in their clinical attitudes and their behaviors in therapy and in analogue situations. But the important question is: Do experienced therapists achieve better therapeutic outcome? One would expect them to, but most of the studies we have reviewed fail to give an emphatic yes to the question. We begin with those whose results seem to favor experienced therapists.[1,2]

Scher (1975) hypothesized that therapies characterized by high verbal activity on the part of therapist and client would produce better outcomes than therapies with low verbal activity. Segments of tape-recorded therapies were rated for level of verbal activity. Outcome measures were independent client and therapist ratings of symptom relief and satisfaction with therapy. Verbal activity did not predict outcome, but therapist experience did. Clients of experienced therapists (PhD or at least 2 years of experience) reported greater symptom relief and satisfaction. A significant therapist experience by client sex interaction indicated that experienced therapist-male client pairs and inexperienced therapist-female client pairs reported greater success. The level of experience of the inexperienced therapists is not reported. However, the author states that in some cases there was very little difference between the experience of the two therapist groups.

Cartwright and Vogel (1960) compared the outcome of therapies conducted by experienced and inexperienced client-centered therapists. The experienced therapists had previously handled a mean of 25.8 therapy cases, the inexperienced therapists a mean of one case. TAT and self-description Q-sort measures were administered pre- and post-therapy. The effect of therapists' level of experience on client outcome was striking. Clients in therapy with experienced therapists improved significantly on both tests while those with inexperienced therapists not only did *not* improve significantly on either but bordered on a significant decrease in health on the TAT. This is one of the few outcome studies comparing therapists of different levels of experience in which the outcome criteria included a measure other than therapist and client ratings. However, it should be noted that in this study the contrast was between nonexperienced and not very experienced therapists.

Katz, Lorr, and Rubenstein (1958) studied certain client attributes which had previously been found to predict length of stay in therapy. They were interested in whether these attributes would also predict improvement as measured by therapists' ratings. They did not. There were, however, two significant correlates of therapists' rating of improvement: (1) The therapist's diagnostic classification of the client made at the end of 6 months of therapy—neurotic and psychosomatic cases improved more than character disorders or psychotics. (2) Therapists' years of experience—the more experienced therapists indicated greater improvement in their clients. Katz *et al.* speculated on whether this finding reflects greater competence among the experienced therapists or whether "the standards and perceptions which determine improvement ratings of clients change with increased years in the field" (p. 412).[13]

Myers and Auld (1955) were interested in the outcome of psychotherapy as a function of length of therapy and experience of therapists. They studied the records of treatment cases, using the therapists' notes to gauge outcome. They found that success ratings correlated significantly with length of therapy and that experienced therapists had greater success than residents only with those cases seen more than 10 times. Among clients seen fewer than 10 times, outcome did not differ between the two groups.

Sullivan, Miller, and Smelser (1958) assessed the effects of VA therapist characteristics and client demographic and psychological variables on duration and outcome of psychotherapy. Experienced therapists were defined as those who had had "at least one year of staff work" (p. 2). The other therapists were designated as inexperienced. Experienced therapists tended to keep clients in treatment longer and to rate clients as markedly improved. When it was found that experienced therapists were assigned clients with better prognoses, the authors ex-

amined outcome according to the client-education therapist-experience level combination. It was found that the experienced-therapist well-educated-client combination produced the best outcome. The low-education group outcome was unrelated to level of therapist experience.

Strupp, Wallach, and Wogan (1964) conducted a questionnaire study among 44 clients who had undergone psychotherapy. They had been in therapy with 10 therapists whose median level of experience was 10 years. The 44 clients constituted 58% of those who had been mailed questionnaires. Three-quarters of the respondents indicated considerable or greater improvement in their symptoms.

This is a very satisfactory success for experienced therapists, but it should be compared with Strupp, Fox, and Lessler's (1969) later and similar study of 122 clients seen by 79 therapists in a clinic. These clients represented a 62% return rate of the questionnaire. The therapists were residents in psychiatry, advanced graduate students in clinical psychology, or staff members (psychiatrists or clinical psychologists). The authors did not give the numbers in each category, but they called the population of therapists as a whole inexperienced. The results showed that approximately the same percentage of patients as in the first study reported considerable or greater improvement. The authors state, "there were no appreciable differences [between the two studies] in outcome or quality of the therapeutic relationship; length of therapy or frequency of sessions had no measurable bearing on outcome; and differences in therapeutic competence, as judged by supervisors, were also inconclusive" (p. 119). In attempting to explain these results Strupp *et al.* (1969) offered two speculations: (1) accepting the questionnaire results as valid, they suggest that the young therapists' enthusiasm and infectious optimism may account for their surprisingly good showing; (2) the validity of the questionnaire results may be questioned. The patients in the two groups may have had different internal standards, or frames of reference, when they rated their improvement.

There have been no studies indicating that inexperienced therapists achieved a significantly better outcome. However, Brown (1970), in the study referred to above, noted a tendency for inexperienced therapists to be more satisfied with counseling outcome than were the experienced therapists.

In a large-scale outcome study, Fiske, Cartwright, and Kirtner (1964) examined a number of predictor and criterion variables. Therapists of three levels of experience participated in this study: the experienced therapists had more than 5 years of experience; inexperienced therapists were 1st-year psychology interns. The experience level of the intermediate therapists was not stated but was presumably between these two points. None of the improvement measures correlated with therapist level of experience. The authors were surprised by this lack of correlation and they offered two speculations: (1) Their measure of experience (number of clients seen) may not have been adequate. Nevertheless, in their sample of therapists the number of clients seen was highly correlated with years of experience, which is the usual criterion in all studies of therapist experience. (2) Perhaps experience is a poor index of skill. This is, of course, the crucial question.

When 69 of these clients were followed up 18 months later (Fiske & Goodman, 1965), therapist experience failed to correlate with any client measures.

As noted above, the clients in Grigg's (1961) study rated their counseling experience as equally helpful whether their therapist was experienced or inexperienced.

Feifel and Eells (1963) used a questionnaire to study the reactions to therapy of clients seen in a Veterans Administration Mental Health Clinic. They were interested in what changes the clients felt they had undergone, what had been helpful or not helpful in their therapy, and what suggestions they had for improving therapy. When the results were analyzed according to the experience level of the therapist, no significant differences emerged between the experienced (4 or more years) and inexperienced (less than 4 years) groups.

The University of Pennsylvania Psychotherapy Study (Luborsky, in preparation) included 44 therapists of widely varying experience. For purposes of analysis, they were collapsed into three groups: psychiatric residents, those with about 3 years of experience beyond training, and those with about 10 years of experience beyond training. Outcome measures were obtained from three sources: the client, the therapist, and a clinical judge who interviewed the client before and after therapy.

The surprising result was that therapy outcome showed no correlation with therapist level of experience. This result cannot be explained by any difference in the pre-therapy level of adjustment of the three groups of clients; their adjustment was essentially the same. Our only

clue is that the more experienced therapists treated older clients, and there was a general tendency for older clients to show less change. The main factor determining outcome was the initial psychological health of the client.

Summary of outcome studies: In summary, only five of 12 studies (including Barrett-Lennard, 1962, described earlier) indicate that experienced therapists achieve superior outcome. The others suggest either no difference or that experienced therapists do better only if their clients are better educated. Of the five studies favoring experienced therapists, in one case (Cartwright & Vogel, 1960) the comparison was with very inexperienced therapists who had previously treated an average of one client, and in two studies (Barrett-Lennard, 1962; Katz *et al.*, 1958) the only outcome criteria were therapist's change rating and length of therapy.

We had expected a stronger trend favoring experienced therapists, not only because of our general clinical impression but because Bergin (1971), in his review of 52 outcome studies, found support for the idea that experienced therapists achieve better results. Because of the importance of that survey, some discussion of this approach and the findings is called for. Bergin did not review comparative studies as we have done. Rather, for each of the 52 studies, he determined whether the therapists were experienced or inexperienced, then looked at the reported outcome, and in summary said that 53% of the studies involving experienced therapists yielded positive results, while 18% by inexperienced therapists were positive. But drawing conclusions from 52 diverse studies is a somewhat uncertain process. There is room for varying interpretations of the original research reports on such matters as whether the outcome was in fact positive, negative, or doubtful, and whether the therapists should be called experienced. Bergin did not state his criterion for an experienced therapist. In some of the studies that he counted as successes for experienced therapists, the therapist population contained sizable numbers of psychiatric residents or psychology trainees, whom we would consider inexperienced. In one such study (Feifel & Eels, 1963) the authors themselves compared the outcome achieved by their experienced and inexperienced therapists and found no significant difference.

It should also be remembered that in the comparison of results there may be subtle biases operating against inexperienced therapists. There is the likelihood that, since they are of relatively low status in clinics, they are assigned less healthy clients (Hollingshead & Redlich, 1958). Researchers expect experienced therapists to achieve better results, and furthermore they have to be more considerate of experienced therapists' feelings. These biases and awarenesses may creep into researchers' decisions about experimental design, client assignment, and post-therapy evaluation of clients.

At any rate, if the superior performance of experienced therapists, as concluded from *across*-study comparisons, were a robust phenomenon, it should hold up in *within*-study comparisons. The fact that it does not hold up convincingly must give us pause.[14]

In addition, there is considerable evidence, as noted earlier, that experienced therapists establish better relationships with clients. Why, then, do they not achieve unequivocally better results? The studies we have reviewed do not point to any clear answer, so the field is open for speculation. Ours runs along three lines, having to do with (1) the client's contribution to outcome, (2) what is meant by the better therapeutic relationship established by experienced therapists, and (3) uncertainty in measuring outcome.

It seems that a large part of outcome variance is determined by the assets which the client brings to therapy. There are probably some clients for whom the choice of therapist is not crucial. We are thinking of the least healthy and the most healthy of those who seek therapy. The least healthy will be difficult for anyone to help, and the healthiest can in many cases adjust to an inexperienced therapist who perhaps makes up in interest and enthusiasm what he lacks in skill. For example, this adjustment to an inexperienced therapist would seem quite possible for a client with a basically sound personality who is going through a crisis or loss. With those clients in the middle range of ego strength, the outcome is more uncertain, and it is here that experience probably makes a difference.[15] We know of no research evidence to support this opinion, but our clinical experience has included clients who did not improve significantly with an inexperienced therapist, were transferred to an experienced therapist, and showed definite improvement. These clients were in what we call the middle range of ego strength, with deep-seated problems but also with important assets. They required more than brief therapy—that is, beyond a few months.

In thinking about the effects of experience, one must not confuse the therapist's mastery of his role with influence on the client. With experience, mastery undoubtedly develops, and it is

most gratifying to lose one's early feeling of uncertainty, anxiety, and preoccupation with self in the role of therapist. We naturally assume that this greater sense of competence and well-being will be accompanied by a proportional facility in influencing clients. With some clients, it is, but only with some.[16]

When we speak of the better therapeutic relationships established by experienced therapists, we are usually referring to the measurement of the client-centered triad of facilitative conditions: empathy, unconditional positive regard, and congruence. The measurement of this triad has been an important attempt to understand the therapist's contribution to the interation. But it has become hallowed by usage and has perhaps deceived us into thinking that such measurement tells us all we need to know about the interaction. Of course, this is not true. To measure that triad is to lay a relatively crude yardstick on a process of challenging complexity. Perhaps one of the things experienced therapists learn is to behave in ways that will earn them high ratings on empathy, etc., when they are being tape-recorded. This is an important ability, but other factors may also be important—for example, therapist's motivation or a fortunate personality match between client and therapist.

Outcome measures are, as always, a problem. One suspects that even when ratings are obtained from a number of sources, as in the University of Pennsylvania study, these measurements often include an uncomfortable degree of error variance, which would tend to minimize differences between experienced and inexperienced therapists. It may be that outcome ratings are basically determined by a set of client attitudes toward himself and his therapy which he acquires toward the end of therapy, and which he partially transmits to his therapist. The relationship between this set of attitudes and "true" improvement is perhaps a philosophical question and, in any case, is problematic. This uncertainty about the measurement of outcome throws a disruptive question mark into one's reasoning about its determinants.

With reference to our original question of whether outcome studies based on inexperienced therapists are to be trusted, we unfortunately cannot provide a definite answer. We *can* say that such studies should not be dismissed out of hand, because the evidence indicates that sometimes inexperienced therapists do as well as experienced ones. But sometimes they do not, and it would therefore seem prudent to include experienced therapists in outcome studies.

A FINAL WORD

Our understanding of psychotherapy grows through an interaction of clinical lore and research findings. The studies we have reviewed are generally supportive of the lore on the subject of therapist experience, with one important exception—the view that experienced therapists achieve better results, while it may be true, does not find the unequivocal support that we expected.

That exception aside, these research studies together make up a plausible picture of the effects of increasing experience on the therapist. We can state our summary impressions in the form of a very brief sketch of the career of a hypothetical therapist. Since the sketch is based on the central tendencies of many findings, it is a portrait of the modal therapist. There will be exceptions.

The beginning therapist is anxious in his role and afraid of being found out. He hopes that his client will be sufficiently talkative to remove the spotlight from himself. He feels most comfortable with safe interventions, such as exploratory questions. Other interventions carry the risk of error, the opportunities for which are multiple and varied. Should he modify his natural reaction tendencies? Should he offer the interventions learned from his teachers, in which he may only half believe? And, if so, then from which teacher? His preoccupation with his own role subtracts from the interest that he can devote to his client.

His problem is intensified if he interprets his supervision as a counsel of perfection; he is expected not only to understand the obscure, but to somehow find an appropriate response, and to control his emotions in interacting with the client, while of course not appearing overly controlled. Small wonder that most trainees feel their personal adequacy is on the line with each client. They attempt to manage their anxiety by clinging to therapy systems that seem to offer certainty. At this early stage, most therapists tend not to question the therapy system. If their clients fail to improve, they will find the explanation in their own inadequate performance as therapists.

Increasing experience brings role mastery, in which we can discern several elements. With a reduction in his self-preoccupation, the therapist can turn his attention to the client. His self-protective mechanisms work more efficiently, so that he is less vulnerable to the client's barbs and dissatisfactions. Feeling more secure, the therapist can be warmer with the client when warmth is called for. He now feels freer to say more, commit himself, try new things. His increasing confidence stems partly from the fact that he has a better sense of what might happen. Whereas the beginner often feels that he is in an uncharted wilderness, the experienced therapist has a set of anticipations of possible eventualities, both in therapy and in people's lives. He has learned how these stories turn out.

Alas, they do not always turn out well. The therapist had thought that, having mastered himself, his clients would improve. But some perversely refuse to do so. There follows skepticism, characterized by some loss of faith in his teachers and in the therapy system, and by an awareness that some clients present intractable problems or impossible needs.

We would like to think that the last stage of development is reconciliation, in which the therapist accepts the limitations of his art and his personality, acquires the ability to tolerate uncertainty, and attains an attitude of "detached concern" (Fox & Lief, 1963), in which the detachment and concern are combined in a comfortable and workable proportion.

It is said (Fisher, 1967; McCarley, 1975; Wheelis, 1956) that the stage of reconciliation does not follow inevitably, that it is not easy of attainment, and that it can exact a considerable cost. Hence the vagaries of some therapists' careers, and hence also some of the problems of psychotherapy as a social institution.

But we have wandered too far from the research findings, and indeed beyond the present boundaries of psychotherapy research. A more immediate problem for the field is: What kinds of clients require an experienced therapist, and what kind will do about as well with an inexperienced one? Investigators seeking a challenging problem should find this one sufficiently interesting for the foreseeable future.

REFERENCES

ANTHONY, N. A longitudinal analysis of the effect of experience on the therapeutic approach. *Journal of Clinical Psychology*, 1967, **23**, 512–516.

AUERBACH, A. H. Teaching assessment of patients to psychiatric residents. Paper presented at American Psychiatric Association, Washington, D.C., May 1971.

BARRETT-LENNARD, G. T. Dimensions of therapist response as causal factors in therapeutic change. *Psychological Monographs*, 1962, **76** (43, whole No. 562).

100 EFFECTIVE PSYCHOTHERAPY

BEERY, J. Therapists' responses as a function of level of therapist experience and attitude of the patient. *Journal of Consulting and Clinical Psychology*, 1970, **34**, 239–243.

BERGIN, A. The evaluation of therapeutic outcomes. In A. BERGIN & S. GARFIELD (Eds.), *Handbook of psychotherapy and behavior change*. New York: Wiley, 1971.

BERGIN A., & STRUPP, H. *Changing frontiers in the science of psychotherapy*. Chicago: Aldine, Atherton, 1972.

BERZINS, J., HERRON, W., & SEIDMAN, E. Patients' role behaviors as seen by therapists: A factor-analytic study. *Psychotherapy: Theory, Research and Practice*, 1971, **8**, 127–130.

BOHN, M. Counselor behavior as a function of counselor dominance, counselor experience and client type. *Journal of Counseling Psychology*, 1965, **12**, 346–352.

BROWN, R. Experienced and inexperienced counselors' first impressions of clients and case outcome: Are first impressions lasting? *Journal of Counseling Psychology*, 1970, **17**, 550–558.

BUTLER, J., RICE, L., & WAGSTAFF, A. On the naturalistic definition of variables: An analogue of clinical analysis. In H. STRUPP & L. LUBORSKY (Eds.), *Research in psychotherapy*. Vol. 2. Washington, D.C.: American Psychological Association, 1962.

CAMPBELL, R. Counselor personality and background and his interview subrole behavior. *Journal of Counseling Psychology*, 1962, **9**, 329–334.

CARACENA, P. Elicitation of dependency expressions in the initial stage of psychotherapy. *Journal of Counseling Psychology*, 1965, **12**, 268–274.

CARTWRIGHT, R., & LERNER, B. Empathy, need to change and improvement with psychotherapy. *Journal of Consulting Psychology*, 1963, **27**, 138–144.

CARTWRIGHT, R., & VOGEL, J. A comparison of changes in psychoneurotic patients during matched periods of therapy and no therapy. *Journal of Consulting Psychology*, 1960, **24**, 121–127.

CIMBOLIC, P. Counselor race and experience effects on black clients. *Journal of Consulting and Clinical Psychology*, 1972, **39**, 328–332.

FEIFEL, H., & EELS, J. Patients and therapists assess the same psychotherapy. *Journal of Consulting Psychology*, 1963, **27**, 310–318.

FEY, W. Doctrine and experience: Their influence upon the psychotherapist. *Journal of Consulting Psychology*, 1958, **22**, 403–409.

FIEDLER, F. A comparison of therapeutic relationships in psychoanalytic, nondirective and Adlerian therapy. *Journal of Consulting Psychology*, 1950a, **14**, 436–445.

FIEDLER, F. The concept of an ideal therapeutic relationship. *Journal of Consulting Psychology*, 1950b, **14**, 239–245.

FIEDLER, F. Factor analyses of psychoanalytic, nondirective and Adlerian therapeutic relationships. *Journal of Consulting Psychology*, 1951, **15**, 32–38.

FISHER, K. A. Crisis in the therapist. *Psychoanalytic Review*, 1967, **54**, 81–98.

FISKE, D., CARTWRIGHT, D., & KIRTNER, W. Are psychotherapeutic changes predictable? *Journal of Abnormal and Social Psychology*, 1964, **69**, 418–426.

FISKE, D., & GOODMAN, G. The post-therapy period. *Journal of Abnormal Psychology*, 1965, **70**, 169–179.

FOX, R., & LIEF, H. Training for "detached concern" in medical students. In H. LIEF, V. LIEF, & N. LIEF (Eds.), *Psychological basis of medical practice*. New York: Harper & Rowe, 1963.

FRANK, J. *Persuasion and healing*. Baltimore: Johns Hopkins University Press, 2nd edition 1973.

FULLER, F. Influence of sex of counselor and of client on client expressions of feeling. *Journal of Counseling Psychology*, 1963, **10**, 34–40.

GAMINSKY, N., & FAIRWELL, G. Counselor verbal behavior as a function of client hostility. *Journal of Counseling Psychology*, 1966, **13**, 184–190.

GREENBERG, R. Effects of presession information on percep-

tion of the therapist and receptivity to influence in a psychotherapy analogue. *Journal of Consulting and Clinical Psychology*, 1969, **33**, 425–429.

GREENBERG, R., GOLDSTEIN A., & PERRY, M. The influence of referral information upon patient perception in a psychotherapy analogue. *Journal of Nervous and Mental Disease*, 1970, **150**, 31–36.

GRIGG, A. Client response to counselors at different levels of experience. *Journal of Counseling Psychology*, 1961, **8**, 217–233.

HILL, C. Sex of client and sex and experience level of counselor. *Journal of Counseling Psychology*, 1975, **22**, 6–11.

HOFFMAN, A. An analysis of counselor subroles. *Journal of Counseling Psychology*, 1959, **6**, 61–68.

HOLLINGSHEAD, A. B., & REDLICH, F. C. *Social class and mental illness*. New York: Wiley & Sons, 1958.

IVEY, A., MILLER, C., & GABBERT, K. Counselor assignment and client attitude: A systematic replication. *Journal of Counseling Psychology*, 1968, **15**, 194–195.

KAGAN, N. *Influencing human interaction*. East Lansing: Instructional Media Center, Michigan State University, 1972.

KATZ, M., LORR, M., & RUBINSTEIN, E. Remainer patient attributes and their relation to subsequent improvement in psychotherapy. *Journal of Consulting Psychology*, 1958, **22**, 411–413.

KUHN, T. S. *The structure of scientific revolutions*. Chicago: University of Chicago Press, 1962.

LUBORSKY, L. *Who benefits from psychotherapy?* In preparation.

LUBORSKY, L., AUERBACH, A., CHANDLER, M., COHEN, J., & BACHRACH, H. Factors influencing the outcome of psychotherapy: A review of quantitative research. *Psychological Bulletin*, 1971, **75**, 145–185.

MATARAZZO, R., WIENS, A., & SASLOW, G. Experimentation in the teaching and learning of psychotherapy skills. In L. GOTTSCHALK & A. AUERBACH (Eds.), *Methods of research in psychotherapy*. New York: Appleton-Century-Crofts, 1966.

McCARLEY, T. The psychotherapist's search for self-renewal. *American Journal of Psychiatry*, 1975, **132**, 221–224.

McNAIR, D., & LORR, M. An analysis of professed psychotherapeutic techniques. *Journal of Consulting Psychology*, 1964, **28**, 265–271.

MILLS, D., & ABELES, N. Counselor needs for affiliation and nurturance as related to liking for clients and counseling process. *Journal of Counseling Psychology*, 1965, **12**, 353–358.

MITCHELL, K., & HALL, L. Frequency and type of confrontation over time within the first therapy interview. *Journal of Consulting and Clinical Psychology*, 1971, **37**, 437–441.

MULLEN, J., & ABELES, N. Relationship of liking, empathy and therapist's experience to outcome of psychotherapy. *Journal of Counseling Psychology*, 1971, **18**, 39–43.

MYERS, J., & AULD, F. Some variables related to outcome of psychotherapy. *Journal of Clinical Psychology*, 1955, **11**, 51–54.

NEULINGER, J., SCHILLINGER, M., STEIN, M., & WELKOWITZ, J. Perceptions of the optimally integrated person as a function of therapists' characteristics. *Perceptual and Motor Skills*, 1970, **30**, 375–384.

ORNSTON, P., CICCHETTI, D., LEVINE, J., & FIERMAN, L. Some parameters of verbal behavior that reliably differentiate novice from experienced psychotherapists. *Journal of Abnormal Psychology*, 1968, **73**, 240–244.

ORNSTON, P. CICCHETTI, D., & TOWBIN, A. Reliable changes in psychotherapy behavior among first-year psychiatric residents. *Journal of Abnormal Psychology*, 1970, **75**, 7–11.

PARSONS, L., & PARKER, G. Personal attitudes, clinical

appraisals, and verbal behavior of trained and untrained therapists. *Journal of Consulting and Clinical Psychology*, 1968, **32**, 64–71.

POPE, B., NUDLER, S., VON KORFF, M., & MCGHEE, J. The experienced professional interviewer versus the complete novice. *Journal of Consulting and Clinical Psychology*, 1974, **42**, 680–690.

RICE, D., GURMAN, A., & RAZIN, A. Therapist sex, "style" and theoretical orientation. *Journal of Nervous and Mental Disease*, 1974, **159**, 413–421.

RICE, L. Therapist's style of participation and case outcome. *Journal of Consulting Psychology*, 1965, **29**, 155–160.

ROGERS, C. *Counseling and psychotherapy.* Boston: Houghton-Mifflin, 1942.

ROGERS, C. The necessary and sufficient conditions of therapeutic personality change. *Journal of Consulting Psychology*, 1957a, **21**, 95–103.

ROGERS, C. Training individuals to engage in the therapeutic process. In C. STROTHER (Ed.), *Psychology and mental health.* Washington, D.C.: American Psychological Association, 1957b.

RUSSELL, P., & SNYDER, W. Counselor anxiety in relation to amount of clinical experience and quality of affect demonstrated by clients. *Journal of Consulting Psychology*, 1963, **27**, 358–363.

SCHER, M. Verbal activity, sex, counselor experience, and success in counseling. *Journal of Counseling Psychology*, 1975, **22**, 97–101.

SCHULDT, W. J. Psychotherapists' approach–avoidance responses and clients' expression of dependency. *Journal of Counseling Psychology*, 1966, **13**, 178–183.

STRONG, S., & SCHMIDT, L. Expertness and influence in counseling. *Journal of Counseling Psychology*, 1970, **17**, 81–87.

STRUPP, H. An objective comparison of Rogerian and psychoanalytic technique. *Journal of Consulting Psychology*, 1955a, **19**, 1–7.

STRUPP, H. Psychotherapeutic technique, professional affiliation and experience level. *Journal of Consulting Psychology*, 1955b, **19**, 97–102.

STRUPP, H. The performance of psychiatrists and psychologists in a therapeutic interview. *Journal of Clinical Psychology*, 1958, **14**, 219–226.

STRUPP, H. H., FOX, R., & LESSLER, K. *Patients view their psychotherapy.* Baltimore: Johns Hopkins Press, 1969.

STRUPP, H. H., WALLACH, M., & WOGAN, M. Psychotherapy experience in retrospect: Questionnaire survey of former patients and their therapists. *Psychological Monographs*, 1964, **78**, (whole No. 588).

SULLIVAN, P., MILLER, C., & SMELSER, W. Factors in length of stay and progress in psychotherapy. *Journal of Consulting Psychology*, 1958, **22**, 1–9.

SUNDLAND, D., & BARKER, E. The orientations of psychotherapists. *Journal of Consulting Psychology*, 1962, **26**, 201–212.

TAPLIN, J. Impression of the client as a function of perception mode and clinician experience. *Journal of Counseling Psychology*, 1968, **15**, 211–214.

WHEELIS, A. *The quest for identity.* New York: Norton, 1956.

WOLBERG, L. *The technique of psychotherapy.* New York: Grune & Stratton, 1954.

EDITORS' REFERENCES

BARRETT-LENNARD, G. T. Dimensions of therapist response as causal factors in therapeutic change. *Psychological Monographs*, 1962, **76** (43, Whole No. 562).

BERGIN, A. The evaluation of therapeutic outcomes. In A. BERGIN & S. GARFIELD (Eds.), *Handbook of psychotherapy and behavior change.* New York: Wiley, 1971.

FARSON, R. E. The counselor is a woman. *Journal of Counseling Psychology*, 1954, **1**, 221–223.

HAYDEN, B. Verbal and therapeutic styles of experienced therapists who differ in peer-rated therapist effectiveness. *Journal of Counseling Psychology*, 1975, **22**, 384–389.

NOTES

1. *Editors' Footnote.* We agree that there are no simple definitions of "experienced," and we appreciate that differences between *competence* and *experience* may be impossible to delineate. Nevertheless, we do think it is possible to construct a few broad, if not universally acceptable, guidelines. Primarily from our own clinical work, we would suggest that the experienced therapist: (1) can display a flexibility of technique and approach even within a given avowed school of therapy, based on his ability; (2) can recognize differences between patients' level of functioning, intellectual ability, interpersonal functioning, etc.; (3) will have worked with at least a few patients of each major diagnostic category; (4) will not be preoccupied with his own security and capabilities while with patients (this should be demonstrable as a relative freedom from self-consciousness); (5) will be relatively immune from patient provocations, whether sexual or aggressive; and (6) while no number of years guarantees the presence of the above, will probably have 3 or 4 years of full-time clinical work as a minimal amount of time to acquire such qualities.

In composing this list, we have tried to exclude qualities that a talented but inexperienced therapist would typically embody. Despite our efforts, though, we recognize that many other qualities could be added to the above, and perhaps some could be deleted, but we do feel that a tentative set of guidelines needs a starting point. We also recognize that, while these qualities are all continuous, we have proposed what seems to be a discrete (dichotomous) cutoff. Of course, this is artificial in that both number of years and the qualities comprising "being experienced" are continuous. We feel strongly, though, that at least among clinicians there *is* some useful if not precise information conveyed by referring to someone as "an experienced therapist." What we are proposing, then, admittedly without substantial empirical evidence, is to make this characterization more precise. We are, therefore, suggesting a minimal amount of work experience to insure minimal embodiment of these qualities. Empirical work would be required, of course, to modify the list of qualities, to adjust the minimal number of years, and to investigate further "developmental" changes occurring beyond the minimal level.

2. *Editors' Footnote.* Pope (Chapter 14, this volume) makes what we think is a very useful distinction between activity and directiveness. By the former, he denotes sheer "volume" or "amount" (number or duration) of interventions, while the latter refers to directing or "running things" in sessions. Auerbach and Johnson use the terms nearly synonymously, and this difference should be kept in mind. We prefer Pope's definitions, and will use the terms accordingly (see Footnote 3).

3. *Editors' Footnote.* We suspect, though, that the PhDs here were not *highly* experienced, and that highly experienced therapists might have been more active and/or directive than novices and trainees. That is, there may be a U-shaped relationship between level of activity and experience. Or, it may be—and the following few studies support this—that highly experienced therapists are more active but less directive (than inexperienced therapists). The importance of Pope's distinction (see Footnote 2) may operate here.

4. *Editors' Footnote.* This conclusion, however, is not undisputed, and the reader should consult Sundland's review (Chapter 9, this volume) for further discussion.

5. *Editors' Footnote.* This (5.4 vs. 1) difference in years of

experience, however, is not so great when number of patients treated is used as the criterion (see Gurman, Chapter 19, this volume, or Barrett-Lennard, 1962).

6. *Editors' Footnote.* The clients of experienced therapists received higher change ratings *from their therapists.* There is the possibility, which should be considered throughout this chapter and which probably warrants systematic study as an independent issue, that one effect of experience is to change the therapist's view of the degree and kind of patient change that constitute improvement. Specifically, we suspect that experienced therapists may tend to see improvement more than do inexperienced therapists. If this is so, it may involve developing a keener eye for subtle but important character changes, but may also be part of a "socialization" process of therapists—to come to appreciate "inner changes" which are not manifested by any observable (e.g., behavioral) change, or to come to expect less (i.e., to be more easily contented with smaller changes) than inexperienced therapists.

7. *Editors' Footnote.* We wish simply to emphasize the importance of this point. This link between therapist level of experience and client behavior is, after all, the most important, and, in a sense, the "ultimate" relationship to be examined in all this literature, and we join the authors in calling for replicative study.

8. *Editors' Footnote.* Sundland (Chapter 9, this volume) points out certain critical methodological problems in Anthony's study, and the interested reader should consult Sundland's discussion before accepting Anthony's conclusions.

9. *Editors' Footnote.* This raises the very interesting possibility that females may start with therapeutic qualities that males may take several years to acquire. This notion is supported in part by some nonempirical literature (e.g., Farson, 1954).

10. *Editors' Footnote.* This difference in correlations may in part be due to a self-fulfilling prophecy effect operating among the (more pessimistic) experienced therapists. This point is made by Rabkin (Chapter 8, this volume) in her discussion of psychiatric characteristics of patients.

11. *Editors' Footnote.* If we believe, though, that experienced therapists are more alert to diagnostic cues, then, perhaps the videotape information should be considered to have added nuances and qualifying changes in their formulations rather than "distractions" interfering with their diagnostic skills.

12. *Editors' Footnote.* To these "favorable" studies should be added Hayden's (1975) study which found significant association between experience and facilitativeness and peer-rated effectiveness.

13. *Editors' Footnote.* This observation supports the suspicion we raised in Footnote 6 above.

14. *Editors' Footnote.* Like the authors, we, too, were surprised at the lack of evidence for the commonly assumed superior outcome by experienced therapists. We consider this (apparently now controversial) issue to be one of the most important in psychotherapy research and practice, and we therefore encouraged (with some success) a bit of dialogue between the present authors and Bergin and Lambert. What follows is our summary and assessment of the personal correspondence generated (after the writing of this chapter).

Bergin's (1971) main point was that in deriving empirical conclusions about the effectiveness of psychotherapy, it is more representative, accurate, and useful to examine the work of experienced therapists. (For many reasons, we strongly agree with this.) His analysis of 52 outcome studies (for experience effects) was across-study and not comparative within single studies. As the present authors point out, though, the gross impression (of clear superiority for experienced therapists) that such analysis leaves warrants revision when the studies are each "internally" examined.

Their analysis of the 20 studies cited by Bergin as successes for experienced therapists finds reason to question such conclusions in 10 of these: In four studies, a substantial proportion (15% to 100%) of the therapists had little experience and/or were still in training; in five, no indication of experience level was given; and in two, within-study comparison revealed no outcome difference due to experience level.

In general, we find this analysis very convincing. (Our only possible disagreement is that in one study with unspecified level of experience, our familiarity with the setting would lead us to believe that most therapists were experienced by our own criteria, above.) We think that a problem with Bergin's across-study analysis is that, in many outcome studies (at least 10 here), it is inaccurate to characterize entire pools of therapist-subjects as simply experienced or inexperienced. We thus also agree with the authors' statement below that a robust phenomenon should hold up both in within- and across-study analyses.

Lambert feels that the difference in conclusions is one of degree, not kind, and we agree with this, too. (It should not be forgotten, for example, that although only five of the 12 Auerbach and Johnson studies showed superiority for experienced therapists, none showed the reverse, and that the Bergin analysis' conclusions may have been weakened but clearly not, in our opinion, invalidated.) Nonetheless, the Auerbach and Johnson results are convincing, and we are moved to modify our own thinking, which is primarily clinically and anecdotally based, on the importance of experience level. While we do not now feel that it is inconsequential or trivial in either outcome research (and certainly not in process research) or in daily clinical practice (e.g., patient disposition), we are less inclined to view it as we had previously—as an unquestionably powerful predictor of outcome, and thus clearly more useful and unassailable than perhaps any other therapist factor. We continue to see it as useful, but not substantially more powerful than any of the several other therapist factors important to outcome. And, like these other factors, it suffers in apparent importance when considered alone and independently of the matrix of other therapist, patient, and technique factors. In this light, we are particularly intrigued by suggestions such as the authors' (below) that level of experience may be more important with patients with "middle"—i.e., somewhat tenuous—levels of ego strength. We would enthusiastically welcome and encourage research designs incorporating such thinking as representing substantially sophisticated advances in methodology.

15. *Editors' Footnote.* The possible interactive effects of patient diagnosis and therapist experience level on outcome are very interesting and worthy of study. We are again reminded by this possibility, and by the unconvincing weight of evidence for a clear relationship between experience level (alone) and outcome, that our current state of knowledge about outcome remains quite crude. Once again, the examination of a single variable as a primary determinant of outcome seems to be an inadequate strategy.

16. *Editors' Footnote.* It may be (again, perhaps as part of the socialization process of therapists) that experienced therapists have learned to operate in ways that minimize their exposure to failure, as well as learning skills that increase their competence. The latter may also nourish the former, in that experienced therapists may use their superior (to inexperienced therapists) diagnostic acumen to "select" patients who offer more positive prognoses.

CHAPTER 6

THE FUNCTIONAL PROFESSIONAL THERAPEUTIC AGENT

WILLIAM A. ANTHONY and ROBERT R. CARKHUFF

THE roots of the conflict are clear. On the one hand, our professional sense of concern, based as it is on years of education, tells us it cannot be done—persons without advanced formal training in a mental health profession cannot bring about therapeutic change in individuals who are in need of psychological help. On the other hand, our common sense, based as it is on our collective life experiences, tells us otherwise—we know of individuals with psychological problems who have been successfully helped by various friends and relatives who have not had the benefit of advanced formal training in a mental health profession. This discrepancy between what we know about helping, or therapy based on our common sense, and what we have learned about psychotherapy and helping through long years of schooling has become the focus of increasing concern to the field of mental health.

While the roots of the conflict are clear, the resolution of the conflict is not. The present chapter attempts to resolve the controversies surrounding the issue of the use of so-called "nonprofessionals" by first redefining the term "nonprofessional therapeutic agent" to be indicative of a person who can more accurately and succinctly be referred to as a "functional professional." Next, the economic, social, political, and professional reasons for the increasing use of functional professionals are examined. In addition, recent research findings examining the effectiveness of functional professionals are reported. Based on these research findings, a set of principles is advanced which can serve as guidelines for the selection, training, and use of functional professionals. Lastly, the implications of the functional professional movement on the day-to-day functioning of credentialed professionals are considered.

THE FUNCTIONAL PROFESSIONAL

The term "functional professional" has been coined by Carkhuff (1971a) to identify those individuals who heretofore had been called nonprofessionals, paraprofessionals, companions, volunteers, lay professionals, and subprofessionals. Groups of individuals who have been referred to by these labels include college students, psychiatric aides, community workers, parents, and mental health technicians. Underlying these different terms is the commonality of functions which binds these various groups and labels together into a single entity. Thus, *the functional professional in the mental health field can be defined as a person who, lacking formal credentials, performs those functions usually reserved for credentialed mental health professionals.* In addition, individuals who have credentials in other fields, such as education and corrections, can be appropriately referred to as functional mental health professionals when they are engaging in tasks designed to have an effect on various mental health outcome criteria.

The growing popularity of functional professionals has by no means been limited to the field of mental health. The development of functional professionals in the fields of engineering and science has preceded the recent emergence of functional professionals in mental health. However, most functional professional workers, including mental health functional professionals, have emerged since the mid-1960s (Stevenson, 1973). Examples of functional professionals from these other fields include legal assistants, architectural technicians, physical therapy assistants, teacher aides, physicians' assistants, child development associates, and library technicians.

Thus, the development of functional mental health professionals, corresponding as it does with the emergent use of functional professionals in non-mental health fields, must be, in part, a response to something larger than issues specific to the field of mental health.

The Growth of Functional Professionalism

A number of authors have conjectured as to the reasons for the phenomenal increase in the use of functional professionals within the last decade (Albee, 1967; Guerney, 1969; Skovholt, 1973; Stevenson, 1973). Some of these hypotheses have focused on reasons common to all functional professional fields, while other comments are specific to the growing use of functional professionals within the field of mental health.

Stevenson (1973) has attributed the recent growth in the use of many different kinds of functional professionals to the professional manpower shortages that, at one time or another, have plagued such fields as engineering, health care, teaching, social work, and library work. It was believed that the negative impact of these manpower shortages could be lessened by the functional professionals' taking over some of the more routine professional tasks. In addition, it was hoped that the professional could then use his time efficiently—i.e., concentrating more on those tasks for which advanced educational training was needed. Obviously, economic benefits accrue in having functional professionals perform what were formerly professional tasks, in that functional professionals will perform these tasks for far less money.

Social-political factors have also been hypothesized as part of the underlying force toward functional professionalization. Skovholt (1973) believes that the power and influence of the professional has been undermined by the general demise of authority in our culture. Thus, the trend toward "citizen involvement" in tax-supported organizations has diminished the singular power of the professional. The civil rights struggle, the war on poverty, and consumer rights advocates have all played a part in reducing the professional's felt omniscience and in recognizing the importance of the functional professional's contributions.

Still another possible cause of the widespread growth and use of functional professionals has been the increasing discontent with university-based education. Lengthy years of education are no longer universally valued as the only way to learn how to perform various professional tasks (Skovholt, 1973). More emphasis has been placed on work and life experiences as an alternative learning method.

THE FUNCTIONAL PROFESSIONAL IN MENTAL HEALTH

The field of mental health, in addition to being affected by the same economic, social, and political forces which have influenced the functional professionalization of other fields, has also been subjected to unique pressures which have further facilitated the expansion of functional professionalism. For example, the "disease model" of mental illness, which demands of its adherents a heavily academic training program and reliance on a time-consuming esoteric treatment philosophy has been increasingly criticized (Albee, 1967).[1] In particular, the relevance of the disease model for the treatment of the poor and underprivileged "mentally ill" has been repeatedly questioned. New and more straightforward models of treatment have deemphasized the overwhelming primacy of introspection and insight. A healthier balance between the achievement of insight itself and the ability to *do* something about the insight has been realized. Unlike the more traditional models, these new approaches are primarily ahistorical, emphasize in varying degrees interpersonal interactions and observable behavior change, and do not demand advanced formal schooling (Guerney, 1969).

In addition, the development of the community mental health center concept, along with the recognition that client-change agent similarity can have positive therapeutic effects, has increased the need for functional professionals who come from the same community as the clients. Not only does the community member act as a helper for other community members, but through the process of helping another person, he may also be helping himself (Riessman, 1965).

However, it would appear that the main impetus during the mid-1960s for the emergence of functional professionals in the mental health field was the availability of large sums of federal money for the purpose of preparing unemployed and low-income persons for positions as functional professionals. The two-fold thrust of these federally financed projects was: (1) to provide jobs and income for the "hard core" or multiple disadvantaged, and (2) to fill the unmet needs for staff and services in the helping professions. The concept underlying these federally supported projects for training functional professionals came to be known as the "new careers" concept.

The legislative process which culminated in financial support for the training of functional professionals has been examined elsewhere (Nixon, 1969). It should be fairly obvious that these nationwide demonstration projects in new careers during the late 1960s, resulting as they did in millions of dollars spent in more than 100 different communities, had a tremendous impact on the training and use of functional professionals in the field of mental health.

The Effectiveness of Functional Professionals: An Overview

In 1968, Carkhuff reviewed over 80 articles concerned with the use and effectiveness of functional professionals (Carkhuff, 1968). Based on those studies, Carkhuff (1968) arrived at the following conclusions:

1. Extensive evidence indicates that functional professionals can be trained to function at minimally facilitative levels of conditions related to constructive client change over relatively short periods of time.
2. Functional professionals can effect significant constructive changes in the clients whom they see.
3. In directly comparable studies, selected lay persons, with or without training and/or supervision, have patients who demonstrate change as great or greater than the patients of professional practitioners.

In the past 7 years, no significant body of data has emerged which can seriously challenge those conclusions which were based on the research of the early and mid-1960s. While there are still professionals who criticize either the methodologies or conclusions of the functional professional research (McArthur, 1970; Rosenbaum, 1966; Sieka, Taylor, Thomason, & Muthard, 1971), these same critics have been notably unsuccessful in designing and undertaking their own research in this field.

What apparently has occurred within recent years, however, has been a shift in focus in the functional professional movement. The trend in the literature indicates far less concern with the effectiveness of the functional professional; instead, more attention has been directed toward descriptions of how to develop and use functional professionals within different agency settings (e.g., Christmas, 1969; Christmas, Wallace, & Edwards, 1970; Collins, 1971; Hartog, 1967; Levenson, Beck, Quinn, & Putnam, 1969; Oppliger, 1971; Richards & Daniels, 1969; Rioch, 1966). This emphasis on administrative issues rather than on issues of effectiveness is no doubt due to the infusion of large sums of federal money into the functional professional field. In an attempt to hop on the functional professional "bandwagon," the predominant issue was no longer one of effectiveness, but one of becoming a part of a new popular thrust in mental health. Thus, as is the case in most all of the mental health innovations that have been heavily bankrolled by the federal government, the major concern becomes one of numbers—i.e., numbers of functional professionals hired, numbers of therapeutic contacts made by functional professionals, numbers of new roles filled by functional professionals, etc. This is not to say that these issues are not important; however, it must not be overlooked that the primary issue remains one of client benefits rather than agency frequency counts. What has developed on a wave of popularity must ultimately sail or be swamped on a wave of accountability.

Perhaps another reason for the relative neglect of continued investigation into the effectiveness of the functional professional is that a significant number of credentialed professionals at least give lip service to the advantages of employing functional professionals. While this does not mean that credentialed professionals know how to best select, train, use, and promote functional professionals, it does indicate that many credentialed professionals are at least willing to hire functional professionals. Motivated in part by financial incentives, many credentialed professionals have seemingly accepted the fact that functional professionals can perform many of the tasks heretofore reserved for the credentialed professionals.

Not only are credentialed professionals hiring functional professionals and using them to perform professional tasks, they are also evaluating the services performed by the functional professionals quite favorably. In a massive survey designed to gather information about the utilization of functional professionals in mental health, Sobey (1970) studied the work of over 10,000 functional professionals in 185 government-sponsored mental health programs. Results of the survey indicated that an overwhelming majority of the program directors felt that the service performed by the functional professionals justified the expense of training, supervision, and general agency overhead. In addition, if given the choice, the majority of program directors would prefer to use functional professionals for those functions which credentialed professionals had previously performed. Also, other more circumscribed studies have supported the comprehensive data collected by Sobey (1970), in reporting very favorable ratings of functional professionals by credentialed professionals (Carkhuff & Griffin, 1970; Gould, Smith, & Masi, 1969).

Yet helping outcome, as measured by the

ratings of functional professionals by credentialed professionals, is not a sufficient test of the effectiveness of the functional professional. Favorable ratings may merely reflect the growing acceptance of functional professionals by credentialed professionals. Unfortunately, to be rated as performing as well or better in a field in which the raters themselves have seldom demonstrated a high level of proficiency is certainly not a strong endorsement of effectiveness (Anthony, Buell, Sharratt, & Althoff, 1972; Eysenck, 1952, 1960, 1972; Levitt, 1957).[2]

The Effectiveness of Functional Professionals: The Data

In addition to investigating the efficacy of functional professionals in mental health, other research investigations have examined the mental health outcome of workers from other fields —in particular, education and corrections. That is, teachers and correctional officers may also be considered to be functional mental health professionals when they have been trained to produce changes on criteria which are traditionally thought to be the outcome criteria of the helping professions. Examples of these outcome criteria might be decreases in delinquency, school dropout rate, prison recidivism, etc. and increases in employment, work performance, self-concept, etc.

The issue of functional professional effectiveness will be examined by first analyzing the impact on client change of functional mental health professionals who are typically uncredentialed college students and adults, working as volunteers or for remuneration in mental health settings. The effectiveness of workers from other fields, primarily education and corrections, will also be examined. These studies should shed further empirical light on the basic conclusion emanating from Carkhuff's (1968) earlier review —that the "process of one individual attempting to help another is not the exclusive province of professional helpers."

Directly comparative outcome studies between functional mental health professionals and credentialed mental health professionals have remained a rare commodity. In the last decade, the few studies that have been done have all found the same results. *Regardless of the client outcome criteria studied, in all cases the clients of functional professionals did as well or better than the clients of credentialed professionals* (Poser, 1966; Truax & Lister, 1970; Zunker & Brown, 1966).

These comparative studies represent a wide variation with respect to client population, outcome criteria, and the type of credentialed professional. The client populations sampled included male psychotic inpatients (Poser, 1966), male and female vocational rehabilitation clients (Truax & Lister, 1970), and male and female college freshmen (Zunker & Brown, 1966). Outcome criteria for the psychotic inpatients were six psychological tests, including two psychomotor, two perceptual, and two verbal tests, as well as the Palo Alto Hospital Development Scale (Poser, 1966). Outcome criteria for the vocational rehabilitation clients consisted of ratings made by vocational training supervisors, and included ratings of such behaviors as quality of client work, client cooperativeness in training, and client's ability to learn (Truax & Lister, 1970). Outcome criteria for the college freshmen included course grades, tests of study skills and a measure of client satisfaction with counseling (Zunker & Brown, 1966).

With respect to the type of credentialed professionals studied, Poser (1966) used seven psychiatrists, six psychiatric social workers, and two occupational therapists. The functional professionals were 11 female undergraduate students and two male inpatients. Truax and Lister (1970) employed four experienced masters' level professional counselors. The functional professionals were four secretarial applicants. Zunker and Brown (1966) used four master's level, certified school counselors and contrasted their effects with those of eight upper class undergraduates.

In each investigation, the clients were assigned randomly to treatment personnel. In addition, clients were matched with respect to age, clinical status, length of hospitalization, and pre-test results in the Poser (1966) study. Zunker and Brown (1966) matched their college student clients with respect to age, sex, scholastic ability, study orientation, and high school rank. In the Zunker and Brown (1966) study, the college student clients and counselors were the same sex.

Various criticisms of these comparative studies have been outlined (McArthur, 1970; Rosenbaum, 1966; Sieka *et al.*, 1971); they generally focused on the researcher's failures to control for functional professional —credentialed professional differences for age, sex, and motivation. Concerning sex differences between therapist and client, Zunker and Brown (1966) used only same sex pairs and found the same results. The critics' suggestion that the relatively greater effectiveness of functional professionals could be due to their younger ages and hypothesized higher levels of motivation is in reality a harsh indictment of professional education. Why spend so many years of school learning about psychotherapy if the main therapeutic effects are due to the age and motivation of the therapist?

Regardless of the research criticisms, it is simply amazing that no empirical studies exist which are in opposition to these findings. While few in number, these studies represent a broad sampling of clients, credentialed professionals, and outcome criteria. The unanimity of their results is indeed impressive.

Several recent investigations have assessed the effectiveness of functional professionals in controlled studies. In two of these investigations, the client-functional professional contact usually took place weekly for several hours per week (Stevenson, Viney, & Viney, 1973; Verinis, 1970). These studies were also similar in that the patients were chronic inpatient psychotics seen by untrained functional professional volunteers; however, these studies were dissimilar in the results obtained.

Stevenson et al. (1973) reported no experimental-control differences in ward behavior ratings, while Verinis (1970) reported significant ward behavior rating differences in favor of the treated group. Verinis (1970) also reported five of 18 experimental patients discharged and none of seven control patients discharged. In terms of differences between the two studies which might account for the differences in results, the functional professionals in the Verinis (1970) study used their therapy sessions for "going down to the commissary for a cup of coffee or finding a quiet place on the ward to sit and chat. There were occasional luncheons downtown or visits to the therapist's home, and several of the therapists went to the movies or a concert with their patients." In contrast, the functional professionals in the Stevenson et al. (1973) study "saw themselves doing most of the talking." Few of these functional professionals took their patients for trips outside of the hospital.

Thus, while one possible explanation for the differences in findings in these two studies could be the type of relationship which developed between the functional professional and the patient, perhaps a more parsimonious explanation could be found in the dissimilarities between the patient groups. The patients in the more successful Verinis (1970) investigation were all females with a mean length of hospitalization of approximately 6 years, while the patients in the Stevenson et al. (1973) study had a mean length of hospitalization of 21 years; in addition, 75% of the patients in the Stevenson et al. (1973) study were male. The results of an older controlled group study (Sines, Silver, & Lucero, 1961), which also found no changes in rated ward behavior, may help shed some additional light on a possible explanation. The Sines et al. (1961) procedure involved treatment by psychiatric aides of chronic female patients whose average length of hospitalization was 12 years. The psychiatric aides' training had consisted of didactic seminars about the treatment of mental disorders, combined with a periodic supervisory session to review their treatment plan.

Based on these three controlled inpatient studies, it would appear that a formula for functional professional misuse and failure would be to have untrained lay personnel attempt a kind of "verbal therapy" with extremely chronic patients. In this regard, the lay personnel would appear to be replicating in a rather "watered down" style, a therapeutic technique that apparently did not work very well when tried by professionals. In contrast, the appropriate use of relatively untrained lay personnel would be to have them engage in more supportive friendship-type activities with the chronic patient.

Concerning the use and abuse of the psychiatric aide as a functional professional, it does not appear to make sense to grant him several hours a week with the patient to do whatever the aide believes to be of therapeutic value. It seems that without any additional training which teaches him new skills (Carkhuff & Truax, 1965) or without any greater input into the hospital decision-making process (Ellsworth, 1968), the aide will not have a therapeutic impact on the patient. Most likely, the untrained aide will unsuccessfully attempt to imitate the type of therapy which credentialed professionals use. In contrast, a psychiatric aide who conducts therapy after he has been intensively trained in interpersonal skills (Carkhuff & Truax, 1965) or who is allowed to become actively involved in decisions regarding patient care (Ellsworth, 1968), does seem to have a significant impact on patient outcome as measured by changes in ward behavior, discharge rate, and subsequent rehospitalization rates.

With respect to outpatient studies of severely disturbed patients, a well-controlled investigation of the effect of outpatient functional professional intervention has corroborated the findings of inpatient research—a preferred mode of treatment useful for the functional professional would appear to be a supportive, friendship-type of treatment approach (Katkin, Ginsburg, Rifkin, & Scott, 1971). In this study, the female schizophrenic patients seen by the female volunteers exhibited a 1-year recidivism rate of 11% as opposed to the control group's one year recidivism rate of 34%. Treatment often required that the therapist become involved in many aspects of the patient's daily life.

> She would phone or personally meet with the patient's family members, neighbors, or friends. Frequently, she would contact social agencies as an advocate for the patient and coordinate the efforts of different agencies to better aid the patient. Also, the therapist insisted that the patients keep their appointments, and when they did not, would quickly contact them. In summary, treatment was a form of supportive therapy that was goal-oriented and focused on the interpersonal and social problems of the patient. (p 48)

In an uncontrolled study of the effectiveness of functional professional volunteers, Hetherington and Rappaport (1967) reported on a program designed to ease the psychiatric patient's transition from the hospital to the community. As in the previously mentioned Katkin *et al.* (1971) study, the functional professional volunteers engaged in friendly, supportive activities with their patients, taking them to various community activities or to the volunteer's home. Results of the program indicate a rate of recidivism of 26%, a figure significantly lower than the base rate recidivism figures for that particular hospital as well as for other psychiatric hospitals (Anthony *et al.*, 1972).

Another more systematic outpatient study attempted to utilize indigenous functional professionals in a skills-training role in addition to their role of providing support for the patient in the community (Weinman, Sanders, Kleiner, & Wilson, 1970). The goal of the functional professionals was to "impart social, recreational, and instrumental skills to his patient." Skills training was believed to be an important aspect of the functional professional's outpatient contact because of the investigators' concern that "many chronic patients left to their own desires, or with a tolerant host, often maintain a vegetative existence in the community" (p. 15). In other words, if the patient is to be truly rehabilitated, he must develop the skills to learn to live in the community as independently as possible.

Results of the Weinman *et al.* (1970) study indicated that the functional professional program had a significantly greater number of patients returned to the community than the hospital-based social treatment program. In addition, the 1-year readmission rate for the functional program was significantly less than the 1-year readmission rate for a regular hospital program.

A number of studies have examined the therapeutic impact of college student volunteers on hospitalized psychiatric patients. Initially called "companion programs," these programs consist of the college students spending a certain amount of time each week as "companions" to patients in mental hospitals. The effectiveness of college students as functional professionals is still not resolved. Positive results (Holzberg, Knapp, & Turner, 1967) and negative results (Spiegel, Keith-Spiegel, Zirgulis, & Wine, 1971) have been reported and a survey of the entire field concluded that "it is impossible to draw firm conclusions about the relative effectiveness of college students as therapeutic agents" (Gruver 1971, p. 123). Gruver (1971) indicates that many of these studies of college student volunteers are plagued by the inadequacies characteristic of most studies of psychotherapy. Only a minority of the studies reviewed by Gruver (1971) used control groups, employed pre- and post-testing, and used objective measures of outcome. In sum, all that Gruver (1971) was able to conclude from his review was that the college students themselves profited from the functional professional experience.

The Effectiveness of Functional Professionals: Same Principles

While more recent research supports the three major conclusions of Carkhuff's (1968) review, some additional principles have emerged upon which the mental health field can guide its present thrust toward functional professionalization.

1. *The psychiatric aide can have a beneficial effect on psychiatric patients only when he is given additional training and responsibility.* It does not make sense to merely "turn the psychiatric aide loose" with only a minimum of supervision to do what the aide considers to be of therapeutic value for the patient. Aides can provide a valuable source of functional professionals, but only if properly trained and utilized.

2. *Unselected and untrained lay personnel have not consistently demonstrated their therapeutic effectiveness.* It would seem that in some instances the credentialed professionals' well-intentioned rush to get on the functional professional "bandwagon" has led them to employ as functional professionals

anyone who shows up at their door. Merely because the person has no credentials, is indigenous to the community, and is similar in appearance to the clients being serviced does not guarantee that the person can be an effective functional professional. While those characteristics may give the functional professional an "edge" (Carkhuff, 1968), these attributes do not translate directly into constructive client change. (Selection and training procedures designed to maximize the effects of the functional professional will be discussed later in this chapter.)

3. *The functional professional housewife volunteer has consistently shown herself to have constructive impact on both psychiatric inpatients and outpatients.* These results are so convincing that if the treatment goal is simply to increase the patients' chances of being discharged and/or staying out of the hospital, the use of the functional professional housewife would appear to be a preferred mode of treatment.

4. *The treatment approaches in which functional professionals are most adept would appear to be the ability to develop a friendly supportive relationship with the patient and the ability to train the patient in the skills necessary to function productively in the community.* Obviously, these abilities are not mutually exclusive and could both comprise a part of the functional professionals' contribution to the helping effort.

THE FUNCTIONAL MENTAL HEALTH PROFESSIONAL IN CORRECTIONS: THE DATA

Although the goal of the correctional officer or correctional aide has been primarily defined as securing both the safety of the inmate within the institution as well as the safety of society outside the institution, the current thrust in corrections has become one of rehabilitation. To help achieve this goal, the training of many correctional personnel has been broadened to include mental health training. Recognizing the possibility that credentialed mental health professionals have neither the time nor the ability to make a significant impact on the inmates' rehabilitation, investigations have been undertaken to see if correctional workers can have a positive effect on rehabilitation measures. In addition, as in the field of mental health, volunteers from outside the correctional system have

also been used in an attempt to increase the inmates' rehabilitation potential.

A recent review of the use of functional professional volunteers in corrections has concluded that these agents can have a positive effect on the inmates' rehabilitation (Peters, 1973). All nine studies reviewed by Peters reported a positive effect on recidivism. However, few of these studies are experimental in nature; most merely report a lowering of recidivism rates.

Peters (1973) also reviewed 12 studies which examined the impact of volunteers on inmate measures other than recidivism. These studies have reported noticeable changes on indices of school absenteeism, problem behavior, and feelings toward self, parents, siblings, and police. While many of these studies were uncontrolled, their sheer number provides tentative support for the belief that "usually a volunteer helps the offender have more socially acceptable and personally rewarding feelings and behavior"

A number of studies have investigated the efficacy of training correctional personnel in skills which were first developed for the training of credentialed and functional mental health professionals (Carkhuff, 1969). The effect on inmates of the Carkhuff model of systematic human relations training for correctional personnel has been well documented. In brief, Carkhuff's (1971a) model of systematic human relations training assumes that:

> There are certain dimensions of the human relationship which may be rated to account for effectiveness or ineffectiveness. These dimensions include responsive conditions (responding to another person's experience) such as empathic understanding, respect, and specificity of expression; and initiative dimensions (initiating from one's own experiences) such as genuineness, confrontation, and interpretations of immediacy.[3] Direct translations are made to selection and training on the scales utilized to measure these conditions in helping and human relationships.
>
> In systematic human relations training, a trainee is taken one step at a time, from the simplest form of responsiveness to the most complex communications involving both responsive and initiative behavior. The basic principles involve systematically exposing the trainee to alternate modes of behaving. The process is goal-directed and action-oriented. It provides a work-oriented structure within which creative and spontaneous human processes can take place. Perhaps most important, it emphasizes practice in the behavior which we wish to effect, thus leaving the trainee-helpee with tangible and usable skills which are retained following training. Finally, it offers a built-in means for assessing the effectiveness of the program. (Carkhuff, 1971a, p. 65)

Inmates who have either worked under or been counseled by correctional officers trained in human relations skills have exhibited positive change on a variety of outcome measures, including a 50% reduction in absenteeism and sick calls (Hall, 1973), changes in inmate personality test scores (Day, Matheney, & McGathlin, 1973), reduction in accident rate (Day *et al.,* 1973), increased inmate satisfaction with their correctional counselors (Hall, 1971), and anecdotal effects on a variety of prison conditions (McGathlin & Day, 1972).

Other studies have trained correctional personnel not merely in human relations skills, but also in the ability to train the inmates in all the life skills thus far developed by Carkhuff (Carkhuff, 1972a, b, c, d, 1973, 1974a, b; Carkhuff & Friel, 1974). These life skills include human relations or interpersonal skills, problem-solving skills, program development skills, and career development skills. In a halfway house run by functional professionals, Griffin (1973) reported a recidivism rate of less than 5% as well as other indices of behavioral change such as increases in employment and schooling.

In a county jail setting, Devine, Steinberg, and Bellingham (1973), and Steinberg. (1973), employing the Carkhuff model, trained inmates in a variety of life skills. This training led to pronounced changes in objective measures of the inmates' physical, emotional, and intellectual functioning. In addition, the recidivism rates ranged from 7% to 11% against base-rate data of over 66%. More importantly, however, have been the results which indicate that the level of skills obtained by the inmates prior to release is directly correlated with future recidivism. That is, those inmates who have mastered a high level of skills do not return to jail.

In a demonstration of a police youth diversion program, Collingwood and Wilson (1974) trained personnel without professional degrees in the Carkhuff life skills. They, in turn, trained the youth with whom they worked. They produced a recidivism rate of 6% versus a base recidivism rate of over 50%.

No doubt the most comprehensive use of correctional personnel as agents of inmate rehabilitation has been the changeover of an entire institution for delinquent boys from a custodial to a skills-training orientation (Carkhuff, 1974a). Correctional personnel with no credentials in mental health were trained in the interpersonal, problem-solving, and program development skills developed by Carkhuff (1972a, 1973, 1974b), so that in essence, these correctional personnel became functional mental health professionals. Using their program development skills, the functional professionals developed more than 80 skills-training programs in a variety of physical, emotional, and intel-

lectual areas of functioning.

The results achieved by these correctional personnel were quite dramatic, indicating that, in their capacity as functional professionals, they were able to bring about a kind of inmate change of which credentialed mental health professionals would be justifiably proud. A summary of the various outcome criteria used indicates that the delinquents' physical functioning increased 50%, their emotional functioning 100%, and their intellectual functioning 157%. The physical functioning measure assessed seven categories of physical fitness as developed by the American Association for Health, Physical Education and Recreation. The measure of emotional functioning involved a rating of the juveniles' human relations skills; intellectual functioning was measured by the California Achievement Test. In addition, to the gains in physical, emotional, and intellectual functioning, during a 1-year period elopement status decreased 56%, recidivism rates decreased 34%, and crime in the community surrounding the institution decreased 34% (Carkhuff, 1974a).

The Functional Mental Health Professional in Corrections: Some Principles

1. *The functional professional volunteer in corrections appears to have a positive effect on the inmates with whom he comes in contact.* While much of the evidence supporting this principle is not based on methodologically sound research, it would appear that enough data now exists to encourage the use of volunteers in the corrections field. However, volunteers are still perceived by many correctional line officers as "do-gooders from the outside" who operate without the life and death pressures of full-time correctional personnel. Thus, it would seem that if dramatic rehabilitation gain is to occur, it would have to be brought about by full-time correctional employees.

2. *Interpersonal skills training for correctional officers results in within-institution change in the inmates with whom these trained correctional officers come in contact.* Institutional effectiveness can be improved through the training of correctional officers in human relations skills training programs which were originally designed for mental health functional professionals and credentialed professionals. These training programs do seem to make a difference on a variety of institutional outcome criteria which appear to be related to inmate rehabilitation gain.

3. *Skills-training programs conducted by trained correctional personnel can bring about constructive inmate change on indices related to positive mental health and rehabilitation outcome.* Correctional personnel, trained in a number of life skills and possessing the ability to train inmates in these same skills, can have an impact on various measures which are consonant with the goals of credentialed mental health professionals. The shortage of mental health professionals in corrections would appear to be best overcome by training correctional personnel to become functional mental health professionals. Their impact on outcome indices such as employment, recidivism, and emotional and intellectual growth has been greater than the impact of either volunteers or credentialed professionals. In addition, they represent an existing resource, deficient primarily in the skills training that would provide them with the tools to make a difference on inmate outcome criteria.

THE FUNCTIONAL MENTAL HEALTH PROFESSIONAL IN EDUCATION: THE DATA

As in corrections, the functional mental health professional in education can be a full-time teacher who has received additional training in skills traditionally thought to be the skills of either the credentialed or functional mental health professional. It was hoped that training teachers in these skills which have typically been considered to be related to mental health training would have an effect on student outcome criteria, which have also been traditionally thought to be part of the goals of the field of mental health. The rationale for such a teacher-training emphasis is fairly straightforward. Teachers have the most contact with students; therefore, they have the greatest chance to affect not only students' educational achievement, but also their mental health.

Within the past decade, one particular finding has consistently emerged from the research: a positive relationship exists between the teachers' level of human relations skills and student achievement. Numerous research investigations, in various geographic locations with various types of students at various grade levels and using various educational outcome criteria have reaffirmed the conclusion that the students of teachers who function at high levels of interpersonal or human relations skills learn more than the students whose teachers function at lower levels of these human relations skills (Aspy, 1969, 1972; Aspy & Hadlock, 1967; Aspy & Roebuck, 1974; Berenson, 1971, 1974; Carkhuff & Pierce, 1974; Hefele, 1971).

Using the established relationship between teachers' human relations skills and educational outcome criteria as a research base, a logical extension was to investigate whether teachers at various levels of human relations skills had students who were different in terms of outcome criteria that have been more closely identified in the past as indices of mental health, and thus have primarily been the goals of guidance counselors and other mental health professionals. In an outstanding research investigation on over 5000 students, Aspy and Roebuck (1974) found that the interpersonal classroom functioning of teachers was related not only to measures of student achievement, but also to measures of the students' self-concept and the number of student days absent. In other words, a teacher who is interpersonally skilled in the classroom not only teaches "better," but also performs effectively as a functional mental health professional, capable of having an effect on criteria (e.g., absenteeism, self-concept) that have traditionally been student outcome criteria related to mental health. Aspy (1972) reported the outcome of a training program initiated in an elementary school, which, among other outcomes, exhibited a significant decrease in vandalism and student fights and a significant increase in attendance. In a much larger investigation, Aspy and Roebuck (1974) reexamined the effects of interpersonal skills training for teachers. Results exhibited greater positive student change on indices of absenteeism and self-concept for the students of the trained teachers than for students of the untrained teachers.

In a variation of this training theme, Battenschlag and Rochow (1973) trained teachers of Latino students in interpersonal and career development skills (Carkhuff & Friel, 1974). An evaluation of the training program on student outcome evidenced a decrease in school dropout rate from 27% to 3%, a 66% increase in school attendance, and an increase in parental involvement in school-parent conferences from 5% to 76%.

The Functional Mental Health Professional in Education: Some Principles

1. *Classroom teachers trained in human relations skills can bring about significant change on student mental health outcome criteria.* The

concept of teacher-helper appears to be a viable description of the kind of role which can be filled by a trained teacher. Credentialed mental health professionals (e.g., guidance counselors, school psychologists, child psychiatrists) have traditionally tried to influence student behaviors such as absenteeism, vandalism, dropping out, fighting, and students' feelings about self. While the positive effects of credentialed mental health professionals on these criteria have been difficult to document (Levitt, 1957), the differential effects of teachers on these criteria are fairly clear. In essence, a trained teacher is both an educator and a functional mental health professional, capable of having an effect on both educational and mental health student outcome criteria.

2. *Teacher training must include specific skills training in order to maximize the teachers' impact on mental health outcome criteria.* If, in fact, the teachers' behavior does have an effect on various components of the students' mental health, then it would appear to be extremely sensible to train teachers on those skills which increase the teachers' effectiveness in his or her role as a functional mental health professional. Fortunately, these skills are some of the same skills which also have a positive impact on educational achievement. Thus, interpersonal and career development skills training for classroom teachers would appear to have a two-fold impact on the students—i.e., on both the students' mental health and educational achievement.

While it makes good sense to train the teachers' aides on these same skills (Carkhuff & Griffin, 1970), it makes ultimate sense to train the classroom teacher in these skills. The classroom teacher represents an existing resource who, like it or not, is having a "mental health impact" on the students. To the extent possible, the teacher must be trained so that the impact on the students' mental health is as positive as can be. The classroom teacher, in his or her role as teacher-helper, probably has a greater cumulative effect on our children's mental health than credentialed mental health professionals would ever hope to achieve.

THE SELECTION AND TRAINING OF FUNCTIONAL MENTAL HEALTH PROFESSIONALS: AN OVERVIEW

The goal of the selection and the goal of training are synonymous—the development of effective functional professionals. Despite the rapid growth of functional professionalism, there has been limited research on how best to select and train this new source of practitioners. While descriptions of selection and training procedures abound, there is a paucity of hard data.

In general, it would appear that, with some notable exceptions (Carkhuff, 1971a), the selection and training of functional professionals has not developed much past the early conceptualizations of Pearl and Riessman (1965). On-the-job training and didactic presentations, augmented by individual and group supervision or discussions, remains the traditional approach to training functional professionals. Variations of this training approach, while seldom researched, have been described periodically (Baker, 1972; Christmas et al., 1970; Collins & Cavanaugh, 1971; Euster, 1971; Lynch & Gardener, 1970). In essence, it seems that credentialed professionals are teaching functional professionals to do and think in a manner similar to themselves, thus replicating, to a great extent, the theories and practices which historically have not been very successful in documenting their effectiveness (Anthony et al., 1972; Eysenck, 1952; Levitt, 1957).[4]

While it may be true that the indigenous functional professionals' similar background and experience to the client provides him with some inherent advantages over the typical credentialed professional (Carkhuff, 1968), it has not been shown that these differential background and experiential characteristics are the characteristics which relate to outcome. It seems that similarities between client and care-giver, while helpful in developing a positive first impression, are not the crucial determinants of helping outcome.

The research evidence suggestive of the initial impact of client-counselor social similarities has been summarized by Carkhuff (1972b). While a black counselor working with a black client has an initial advantage over a white counselor, this advantage can be overcome to a great extent by the interpersonal and specialty skills of the counselor (Banks, 1971; Banks, Carkhuff, & Berenson, 1967; Carkhuff & Banks, 1970; Carkhuff & Pierce, 1967). The negative effects of racial differences are mitigated by the helper's skills, and it is the helpers' skills which consistently have been shown to relate to the helpee outcome (Carkhuff, 1972c, 1972d).

Thus, the proponents of functional professionalism cannot consider their job to be done once they have selected functional professionals with characteristics similar to the clients. Client-counselor similarity can be a first step toward effectiveness, but not much more. Nor can the trainers of functional professionals assume their job to be done once the functional professional has received on-the-job experience, didactic presentations, and opportunities for group discussions. No research exists which suggests this training approach makes a difference in terms of observable criteria of client change.

The demise of functional professionalism will no doubt be hastened if systematic selection and training procedures are not developed, researched, and applied. Eventually, the surprise and/or dismay engendered by the findings that functional professionals can help as well as credentialed professionals will dissipate. If selection and training procedures which can demonstrate in observable terms the unique abilities of the functional professional are not forthcoming, the mental health field will stand firm in its old ways. In the place of other criteria, job hiring and, in particular, job promotion and salary will continue to be based on formal educational credentials.

The Selection and Training of Functional Mental Health Professionals: The Data

Logically, the training of functional professionals must occur on those variables which past research has shown to be related to helping outcomes. Likewise, the selection of functional professionals must be based on those variables which past research has shown to be related to training outcome.

Outcome research on functional professionals in mental health, corrections, and education converges on one indisputable finding—mental health outcome is a function of the helpers' skills, and/or the activities in which the helper engages. In terms of helper skills, the skills are typically interpersonal skills and program development skills; in terms of helper activities, the activities are usually either supportive, friendship-type activities, or direct skills-training of clients in those skills which they need to live most effectively.

The notion of training helpers in certain skills which, in turn, allow them to train their clients in those skills is an approach which has been labeled "training as a preferred mode of treatment" (Carkhuff, 1971b, 1971c; Carkhuff & Pierce, 1974).[5] Initially developed as a treatment technique for credentialed professionals (Carkhuff & Bierman, 1970; Pierce, 1973; Pierce & Drasgow, 1969; Pierce, Schauble, & Wilson, 1971; Vitalo, 1971), it quickly became apparent that the skills-training-as-treatment approach could also be an important activity for the functional professional. Numerous investigations have now shown that functional professionals are able to train their clients to function at higher skill levels (Carkhuff, 1970; Carkhuff, 1974a; Carkhuff & Berenson, 1972; Carkhuff & Griffin, 1971; Montgomery, 1973; Weinman et al., 1970).

A most comprehensive demonstration of the training of functional professionals, their subsequent use of the "training as a preferred mode of treatment" approach, and the effect of that training on outcome has been recently reported (Carkhuff, 1974a). In an institution for delinquent boys, a core group of functional professionals was selected and trained in interpersonal and program development skills. This core group then trained the entire staff of the institution. Using their program development skills, the trained staff subsequently developed the physical, emotional, and intellectual skills programs on which the inmates of the institution were trained.[6] As the data mentioned previously in this chapter's section on effectiveness indicated, this use of trained functional professionals as skills trainers demonstrated its efficacy on a variety of outcome measures.

In terms of the other major functional professional activity—providing a friendly, supportive relationship in which the client or student can function—it would appear that the functional professionals' ability to provide this type of environment could be improved through interpersonal skills training. Data presented previously indicated that the helpers' level of interpersonal skills makes a difference in a variety of situations, perhaps because of the atmosphere these skills create. Thus, interpersonal skills training would seem to be an important training focus for several reasons: (1) these skills can help the functional professional create an atmosphere which is conducive to growth; (2) the functional professional can directly train the client in these skills; and (3) the effectiveness of the functional professional's programs may be, in part, a function of his or her interpersonal skills (Aspy & Roebuck, 1974; Mickelson & Stevic, 1971; Vitalo, 1970).

Functional professionals can be trained, however, in more than just interpersonal skills. They have been successfully trained in behavior modification skills (e.g., Bricker, Morgan, & Grabowski, 1972; Gardner, 1972; O'Dell, 1974;

Panyan, Boozer, & Morris, 1970), as well as in a wide variety of other skills designed to teach their clients the important physical, emotional, and intellectual behaviors which their clients need to live, learn and work in the community (Carkhuff, 1974a; Weinman et al., 1970). *In all cases where the goal of functional professional training has been to increase the functional professional's skills, the training outcome was both observable and capable of being documented. Thus, the efficiency of the training experience itself can be evaluated with respect to its ability to change those functional professional behaviors which have been shown to relate to mental health outcome.*

Once the outcome of training has been identified as a certain level of skilled behavior, the selection process loses much of its mystery. In contrast to the selection procedures in graduate education, which have been notably unsuccessful in predicting either future clinical or research expertise (Anthony, Gormally, & Miller, 1974), research into the selection of functional professionals has developed several empirically based principles upon which to guide the selection effort. This success in selection is a direct result of the ability of functional professional trainers to define the goals of the training in objective, behavioral terms. Without this empirical specificity, there could be no effective selection procedures. It is only when we know exactly what criteria we want the training to achieve that trainee selection can become a legitimate and meaningful activity.[7]

A number of research studies have investigated how to select those individuals most likely to profit from skills training and, in particular, interpersonal skills training. The findings unanimously converge on one fundamental selection principle—the best index of a future criterion is a previous index of that criterion (Anthony & Wain, 1971; Anthony et al., 1974; Carkhuff, 1971a; Carkhuff & Griffin, 1970, 1971). The application of that selection principle to functional professional training is as follows: the best index of whether a functional professional can profit from a training experience is an index of the prospective functional professional's present ability to profit from a training analogue experience.

In essence, selection involves allowing the prospective trainee to experience a representative sample of the training program for which he is being considered, and determining the effects of this brief part of the training program through pre- and post-testing of his functioning on the

relevant criterion. To achieve this selection goal, brief standardized training analogue procedures need to be constructed. Anthony et al. (1974) have recently developed a written analogue experience (the Trainability Index) which has accounted for up to 70% of the variance in human relations skills training outcome (Carkhuff, 1971a, 1972a). The Trainability Index consists of having the subject read a brief ($2\frac{1}{2}$ pages) explanation of the concept of empathy, along with examples of various helper responses rated on a 5-point empathy scale (Carkhuff, 1969). Following the description, the subject is asked to respond in writing to five written helpee statements and to rate his own responses on the 5-point empathy scale. A trainability-communication score is obtained by means of trained judges' ratings of the subject's responses on the same 5-point empathy scale (Carkhuff, 1969). The trainability-self-discrimination score is obtained by computing the absolute deviation between the subject's ratings of his responses and the ratings of the trained judges.

Additional training outcome variance can also be studied by correlating various pre-training functional professional behavior with the observable training outcome criteria. For example, Collingwood (1973) has consistently found that measures of physical fitness account for a significant proportion of variance in Carkhuff (1971a, 1972a) human relations skills training.

The Selection and Training of Functional Professionals: Some Principles

1. *Functional professional training goals must be defined in observable, measurable terms.* Without an observable measure of training outcome, there can be no valid assessment of training effectiveness. Thus, the result will be a continued plethora of training program descriptions and a dearth of training program evaluations.

2. *The functional professional training process should be designed to increase the trainees' skills in areas that previous research has shown to relate to mental health outcome.* Defining the training goal in terms of increased functional professional skills will also result in the definition of training goals that are observable and measurable. Because skills training outcome is observable, the trained functional professional will have documented evidence of the attainment of criteria relevant to his performance as a functional mental

health professional. In fact, criteria which assess a person's level of skills are much more relevant to helping outcome than the criteria presently used—i.e., completion of advanced coursework. The functional professional's demonstration of a certain level of skilled behavior following training should become his credentials, certifying his or her ability to have a positive mental health impact on the clients with whom the functional professional comes in contact.

3. *The selection of functional professionals should be based on a training analogue experience.* Future ability to profit from training can be most efficiently predicted from the functional professionals' present ability to profit from a brief aspect of that training. In contrast to the above selection principle, many of the selection procedures currently operating are really no more than screening procedures, just as many of the current training procedures are more similar to orientation tasks rather than systematic training programs.

In summary, selection is a meaningful activity only to the extent that the training goals can be spelled out in observable terms. Without knowing exactly what training outcome is desired, effective selection procedures cannot be developed.

THE FUNCTIONAL MENTAL HEALTH PROFESSIONAL: IMPLICATIONS FOR THE CREDENTIALED PROFESSIONAL

The resolution of the conflict alluded to at the beginning of this chapter is clear. Persons without credentials in mental health can have a positive, measurable effect on individuals in need of help. Client groups with whom functional professionals have demonstrated successful outcome have included psychiatric inpatients and outpatients, college students, elementary and high school students, juvenile delinquents, prisoners, and ex-convicts.

What was a revolutionary idea in the 1960s is more of an accepted fact in the 1970s—whatever enables one person to help another is not the exclusive province of the credentialed mental health professional (Carkhuff, 1968). Volunteers, psychiatric aides, correctional personnel and teachers can all have a constructive impact on many of the same criteria which credentialed mental health professionals try to effect.[8] These outcome criteria have focused primarily on observable measures of outcome, including assessments of institutional discharge and recid-

ivism rates, academic achievement at the elementary, high school, and college levels, behavioral ratings, physical fitness measures, human relations skill ratings, employment rates, school dropout rates, crime rates, and psychological test scores. Few findings in the area of mental health have been replicated as often with such a variety of helpers, helpees, and outcome criteria.

Yet, all is not rosy with the functional professional movement in mental health. While the mutual conflict over whether functional professionals can in fact be helpful has been resolved, new conflicts have arisen. First, some individuals seem to operate on the rather naive assumption that any unselected, untrained functional mental health professional can make a difference. *All the studies which have reported negative results using functional mental health professionals, particularly those studies using college students or randomly selected psychiatric aides, have used either unselected and/or untrained functional mental health professionals.*

The functional mental health professional seems to perform best when he is attempting to develop a friendly, supportive, activity-oriented relationship with the person in need of help and/or when he is training the helpee in important skills. The functional professional's ability to perform these activities can be increased through skills training for the functional professional himself. Unfortunately, as is the case in many mental health innovations which have been bankrolled by the federal government, in the rush to hop on the functional professional "bandwagon," many of these programs did not take the time to systematically select, train, and subsequently evaluate their selection and training efforts.

The reason for this lack of systematic training and selection was no doubt a function of the fact that the credentialed professionals who were doing the training have themselves never systematically been selected or trained on observable, measurable skills. Thus, the training programs which were conceived were relatively watered down didactic seminars plus internship experience in which the credentialed professional himself was educated. Yet this is the very type of training experience which has not enabled the credentialed professional to be a very effective helper (Anthony *et al.*, 1972; Carkhuff, 1968; Eysenck, 1960, 1972; Levitt, 1957). While the product of such functional professional training may be no *less* effective than his credentialed professional mentors, neither will the training product be any better. The implication for the credentialed mental health professional is to either become proficient in training those skills which relate to outcome or to step aside and let those who can demonstrate their training effectiveness do the training for him.

A relatively unselected, untrained functional professional has one main advantage over the typical credentialed professional—he will work for far less money and with far less prestige. It is exactly in this area of salary and status where the major new conflict in the functional professional movement has arisen. Once again, while the roots of the conflict are fairly obvious, a resolution of the inequities in salary and promotional opportunities for the functional professional has not been forthcoming. The recognized need for the development of career ladders for the functional professional has not occurred (Carkhuff, 1971b). While functional professionals are often hired, they are seldom promoted to positions of high salary or responsibility. Academic criteria remain the prime consideration for most of the best jobs in the mental health field (Gould et al., 1969).

When alternatives to academic criteria are allowed, these criteria are often generally stated as "equivalent experience"; yet what is meant by the term "equivalent experience" is never defined (Gould et al., 1969). It would seem that the most viable definition of "equivalent experience" would be the ability to demonstrate a certain level of skills behavior on those skills which have been empirically related to mental health outcome. Until the "credentials" of the functional mental health professional are observable and measurable, the door to advancement will be kept sealed by the professionals with observable academic credentials (irrespective of these educational credentials' undemonstrated relationships to helping outcome). The functional professionals' attainment of skills, which are observable, measurable, and understandable to the layman, represents the most direct and honest route to better salaries and better jobs.

Unfortunately, however, it remains the credentialed professional who can either make or break the functional professional movement. The trained functional professional's demonstrated effectiveness will not be enough, and in some cases may turn out to be too threatening, to bring about fundamental changes in the employment practices of the credentialed professional (Carkhuff, 1974a). While the credentialed professional's resolution of this new conflict is uncertain, the message to the credentialed professional has been stated clearly:

> Rather than to continue to hide the keys to the chastity belt of professionalization, the closely guarded spheres of influence or control based upon credentials, it remains for the professional to recognize the privilege of its violation. Those who can do what professionals now do should spur the professionals on to a definition of professionalization based upon higher levels of creativity in bold, new frontiers. (Carkhuff, 1971a, p. 7)

The functional professional has met one challenge. The credentialed professionals' real challenge has just begun.

REFERENCES

ALBEE, G. W. The relation of conceptual models to manpower needs. In E. L. COWEN, E. A. GARDNER, & M. ZAX (Eds.), Emergent approaches to mental health problems. New York: Appleton-Century-Crofts, 1967.

ANTHONY, W. A., BUELL, G., SHARRATT, S., & ALTHOFF, M. E. The efficacy of psychiatric rehabilitation. Psychological Bulletin, 1972, 78, 447–456.

ANTHONY, W. A., GORMALLY, J., & MILLER, H. The prediction of human relations training outcome by traditional and non-traditional selection indices. Counselor Education and Supervision, 1974, 14, 105–112.

ANTHONY, W. A., & WAIN, H. J. Two methods of selecting prospective helpers. Journal of Counseling Psychology, 1971, 18, 155–156.

ASPY, D. The effect of teacher offered conditions of empathy, positive regard, and congruence upon student achievement. Florida Journal of Educational Research, 1969, 11, 39–48.

ASPY, D. N. Beyond rhetoric. Counseling Psychologist, 1972, 4, 108–110.

ASPY, D., & HADLOCK, W. The effects of high and low functioning teachers upon student performance. In R. R. CARKHUFF and B. G. BERENSON (Eds.), Beyond counseling and psychotherapy. New York: Holt, Rinehart & Winston, 1967.

ASPY, D. N., & ROEBUCK, F. N. Research summary—Effects of interpersonal skills training. National Consortium for Humanizing Education, Interim Report No. 4, Northeast Louisiana University, Monroe, LA. (National Institute of Mental Health Research Grant No. 5 P0 1MH19871), 1974, pp. 153–182.

BAKER, E. J. The mental health associate: A new approach in mental health. Community Mental Health Journal, 1972, 8, 281–291.

BANKS, G. The effects of race on one-to-one helping interviews. Social Service Review, 1971, 45, 137–146.

BANKS, G., CARKHUFF, R. R., & BERENSON, B. G. The effect of counselor race and training upon counseling process with Negro clients in initial interviews. Journal of Clinical Psychology, 1967, 23, 70–72.

BATTENSCHLAG, J., & ROCHOW, R. Human resource development in the school. New Orleans: American Personnel and Guidance Association, 1973.

BERENSON, D. H. The effects of systematic human relations training upon the classroom performance of elementary school teachers. Journal of Research and Development in Education, 1971, 4, 70–85.

BERENSON, D. Effects of trained teachers and learning to learn skills training on students. Final report to Urban League. Springfield, Massachusetts, 1974.

BRICKER, W. A., MORGAN, D. G., & GRABOWSKI, J. G. Development and maintenance of a behavior modification repertoire of cottage attendants through T.V. feedback. American Journal of Mental Deficiency, 1972, 77, 128–136.

CARKHUFF, R. R. The differential functioning of lay professional helpers. *Journal of Counseling Psychology*, 1968, **15**, 117–126.

CARKHUFF, R. R. *Helping and human relations*. Vols. 1 and 2. New York: Holt, Rinehart & Winston, 1969.

CARKHUFF, R. R. The development of effective courses of action for ghetto school children. *Psychology in the Schools*, 1970, **7**, 272–274.

CARKHUFF, R. R. *The development of human resources*. New York: Holt, Rinehart & Winston, 1971a.

CARKHUFF, R. R. Principles of social action in training for new careers in human services. *Journal of Counseling Psychology*, 1971b, **18**, 147–151.

CARKHUFF, R. R. Training as a preferred mode of treatment. *Journal of Counseling Psychology*, 1971c, **18**, 123–131.

CARKHUFF, R. R. *The art of helping*. Amherst, Mass.: Human Resource Development Press, 1972a.

CARKHUFF, R. R. Black and white in helping. *Professional Psychology*, 1972b, **3**, 18–22.

CARKHUFF, R. R. The development of systematic human resource development models. *The Counseling Psychologist*, 1972c, **3**, 4–11.

CARKHUFF, R. R. What's it all about anyway? *The Counseling Psychologist*, 1972d, **3**, 79–88.

CARKHUFF, R. R. *The art of problem solving*. Amherst, Mass.: Human Resource Development Press, 1973.

CARKHUFF, R. R. *Cry twice*. Amherst, Mass.: Human Resource Development Press, 1974a.

CARKHUFF, R. R. *How to help yourself. The art of program development*. Amherst, Mass.: Human Resource Development Press, 1974b.

CARKHUFF, R. R., & BANKS, G. Treatment as a preferred mode of facilitating relations between races and generations. *Journal of Counseling Psychology*, 1970, **17**, 413–418.

CARKHUFF, R. R., & BERENSON, B. G. The utilization of black functional professionals to reconstitute troubled families. *Journal of Clinical Psychology*, 1972, **28**, 92–93.

CARKHUFF, R. R., & BIERMAN, R. Training as a preferred mode of treatment of emotionally disturbed children. *Journal of Counseling Psychology*, 1970, **17**, 157–161.

CARKHUFF, R. R., & FRIEL, T. *The art of developing a career: Student's guide*. Amherst, Mass.: Human Resource Development Press, 1974.

CARKHUFF, R. R., & GRIFFIN, A. H. The selection and training of human relations specialists. *Journal of Counseling Psychology*, 1970, **17**, 443–450.

CARKHUFF, R. R., & GRIFFIN, A. Selection and training of functional professionals for concentrated employment programs. *Journal of Clinical Psychology*, 1971, **27**, 163–165.

CARKHUFF, R. R., & PIERCE, R. M. Differential effects of therapist race and social class upon patient depth of self-exploration in the initial clinical interview. *Journal of Consulting Psychology*, 1967, **31**, 632–634.

CARKHUFF, R. R., & PIERCE, R. M. *Training as a preferred mode of treatment: Introduction to counseling and psychotherapy*. Amherst, Mass.: Human Resource Development Press, 1974.

CARKHUFF, R. R., & TRUAX, C. B. Lay mental health counseling. The effects of lay group counseling. *Journal of Consulting Psychology*, 1965, **29**, 426–432.

CHRISTMAS, J. J. Sociopsychiatric rehabilitation in a Black urban ghetto. *American Journal of Orthopsychiatry*, 1969, **39**, 651–661.

CHRISTMAS, J. J., WALLACE, H., & EDWARDS, J. New careers and new mental health services: Fantasy or future? *American Journal of Psychiatry*, 1970, **126**, 1480–1486.

COLLINGWOOD, T. The human resource development model and physical fitness. In D. W. KRATOCHVIL (Ed.), *The human resource development model in education*. Baton Rouge, La.: Southern University Press, 1973. Chapter 5.

COLLINGWOOD, T., & WILSON, W. Systematic human relations training for youth diversion. Dallas, Texas: Youth Division, Dallas Police Department, 1974.

COLLINS, J. A. The paraprofessional: I. Manpower issues in the mental health field. *Hospital and Community Psychiatry*, 1971, **22**, 362–367.

COLLINS, J. A., & CAVANAUGH, M. The paraprofessional: II. Brief mental health training for the community health worker. *Hospital and Community Psychiatry*, 1971, **22**, 367–370.

DAY, S. R., MATHENEY, K. B., & McGATHLIN, W. B. Training correctional personnel in the helping skills: Atlanta program, 1968–1972. Mimeographed manuscript, Georgia State University, 1973.

DEVINE, J., STEINBERG, H., & BELLINGHAM, R. The Carkhuff Model in Jail. Kalamazoo, Michigan: Kalamazoo County Sheriff's Department, 1973.

ELLSWORTH, R. *Nonprofessionals in psychiatric rehabilitation*. New York: Appleton-Century-Crofts, 1968.

EUSTER, G. L. Mental health workers: New mental hospital personnel for the seventies. *Mental Hygiene*, 1971, **55**, 283–290.

EYSENCK, H. J. The effects of psychotherapy: An evaluation. *Journal of Consulting Psychology*, 1952, **16**, 319–324.

EYSENCK, H. J. The effects of psychotherapy. In H. J. EYSENCK (Ed.), *Handbook of abnormal psychology*, London: Pitmans, 1960.

EYSENCK, H. J. New approaches to mental illness: The failure of a tradition. In H. GOTTESFELD (Ed.), *The critical issues of community mental health*. New York: Behavioral Publications, 1972.

GARDNER, J. M. Teaching behavior modification to nonprofessionals. *Journal of Applied Behavior Analysis*, 1972, **5**, 517–521.

GOULD, K., SMITH, J., & MASI, T. Career mobility for paraprofessionals in human service agencies. MDTA Experimental and Demonstration Findings No. 8, U.S. Department of Labor, 1969.

GRIFFIN, J. *Correctional rehabilitation*. New Orleans, La.: American Personnel and Guidance Association, 1973.

GRUVER, G. G. College students as therapeutic agents. *Psychological Bulletin*, 1971, **76**, 111–127.

GUERNEY, B. G. Why try nonprofessionals? In B. G. GUERNEY (Ed.), *Psychotherapeutic agents: New roles for nonprofessionals, parents and teachers*. New York: Holt, Rinehart & Winston, 1969.

HALL, R. *Helpee perception*. Washington, D.C.: Bureau of Prisons, 1971.

HALL, R. *Human resource development in the Federal Bureau of Prisons*. New Orleans, La.: American Personnel and Guidance Association, 1973.

HARTOG, J. Nonprofessionals as mental health consultants. *Hospital and Community Psychiatry*, 1967, **18**, 223–225.

HEFELE, T. J. The effects of systematic human relations training upon student achievement. *Journal of Research and Development in Education*, 1971, **4**, 52–69.

HETHERINGTON, H., & RAPPAPORT, J. Homecoming: A volunteer program to rehabilitate chronic patients. *Hospital and Community Psychiatry*, 1967, **18**, 171–174.

HOLZBERG, J. D., KNAPP, R. H., & TURNER, J. L. College students as companions to the mentally ill. In E. L. COWEN, E. A. GARDNER, & M. ZAX (Eds.), *Emergent approaches to mental health problems*. New York: Appleton-Century-Crofts, 1967.

KATKIN, S., GINSBURG, M. RIFKIN, M. J., & SCOTT, J. T. Effectiveness of female volunteers in the treatment of outpatients. *Journal of Counseling Psychology*, 1971, **18**, 97–100.

LEVENSON, A. I., BECK, J. C., QUINN, R., & PUTNAM, P. Manpower and training in community mental health centers. *Hospital and Community Psychiatry*, 1969, **20**, 37–40.

LEVITT, E. E. The results of psychotherapy with children. *Journal of Consulting Psychology*, 1957, **71**, 189–196.

LYNCH, M., & GARDENER, E. A. Some issues raised in the training of paraprofessional personnel as clinic therapists. *American Journal of Psychiatry*, 1970, **126**, 1473–1479.

McArthur, C. C. Comment on "Effectiveness of Counselors and Counselor Aides." *Journal of Counseling Psychology*, 1970, **17**, 335–336.

McGathlin, W. B., & Day, S. R. The line staff as agents of control and change. *American Journal of Corrections*, 1972, **34**, 12–16.

Mickelson, D. J., & Stevic, R. R. Differential effects of facilitative and nonfacilitative behavioral counselors. *Journal of Counseling Psychology*, 1971, **18**, 314–319.

Montgomery, C. M. Systematic selection and training of inmate/residents. Mimeographed manuscript, Seagoville, Texas, 1973.

Nixon, R. Congressional actions. In C. Grosser, W. E. Henry, & J. G. Kelley (Eds.), *Nonprofessionals in the human services*. San Francisco: Jossey-Bass, 1969.

O'Dell, S. Training parents in behavior modification: A review. *Psychological Bulletin*, 1974, **81**, 418–433.

Oppliger, S. Volunteers in community programs. *Hospital and Community Psychiatry*, 1971, **22**, 111–112.

Panyan, M., Boozer, H., & Morris, N. Feedback to attendants as a reinforcer for applying operant techniques. *Journal of Applied Behavior Analysis*, 1970, **3**, 1–4.

Pearl, A., & Riessman, F. *New careers for the poor*. New York: Free Press, 1965.

Peters, C. Research in the field of volunteers in courts and corrections: What exists and what is needed. *National Information Center on Volunteerism.* Boulder, Colorado, 1973.

Pierce, R. M. Training in interpersonal communication skills with the partners of deteriorated marriages. *The Family Coordinator*, 1973, **22**, 223–227.

Pierce, R. M., & Drasgow, J. Teaching facilitative interpersonal functioning to psychiatric inpatients. *Journal of Counseling Psychology*, 1969, **16**, 295–298.

Pierce, R. M., Schauble, P. G., & Wilson, F. R. Teaching helper and helpee behaviors in group therapy. *Journal of Research and Development in Education*, 1971, **4**, 94–108.

Poser, E. G. The effects of therapists' training on group therapeutic outcome. *Journal of Consulting Psychology*, 1966, **30**, 283–289.

Richards, H., & Daniels, M. S. Innovative treatment roles and approaches. *American Journal of Orthopsychiatry*, 1969, **39**, 662–676.

Riessman, F. The "helper" therapy principle. *Social Work*, 1965, **10**, 27–32.

Rioch, M. Changing concepts in the training of therapists. *Journal of Consulting Psychology*, 1966, **30**, 289–292.

Rosenbaum, M. Some comments on the use of untrained therapists. *Journal of Consulting Psychology*, 1966, **30**, 292–294.

Sieka, F., Taylor, D., Thomason, B., & Muthard, J. A. critique of "Effectiveness of Counselors and Counselor Aides." *Journal of Counseling Psychology*, 1971, **18**, 362–364.

Sines, L., Silver, R. J., & Lucero, R. J. The effect of therapeutic intervention by untrained therapists. *Journal of Clinical Psychology*, 1961, **17**, 394–396.

Skovholt, T. M. A new manpower boom. *Mental Hygiene*, 1973, **57**, 28–30.

Sobey, F. *The nonprofessional revolution in mental health.* New York: Columbia University Press, 1970.

Spiegel, D., Keith-Spiegel, P. K., Zirgulis, J., & Wine, D. B. Effects of student visits on the social behavior of regressed schizophrenic patients. *Journal of Clinical Psychology*, 1971, **27**, 396–400.

Steinberg, H. *The Kalamazoo story.* New Orleans, La.: American Personnel and Guidance Association, 1973.

Stevenson, E. W., Viney, L. L., & Viney, M. A. The effectiveness of nonprofessional therapists with chronic, psychotic patients: An experimental study. *Journal of Nervous and Mental Disease*, 1973, **156**, 38–46.

Stevenson, G. The paraprofessionals. *Occupational Outlook Quarterly*, 1973, **17**, 3–9.

Truax, C. B., & Lister, J. L. Effectiveness of counselors and counselor aides. *Journal of Counseling Psychology*, 1970, **17**, 331–334.

Truax, C. B., & Tatum, C. An extension from the effective psychotherapeutic model to constructive personality change in preschool children. *Childhood Education*, 1966, **42**, 456–462.

Verinis, J. S. Therapeutic effectiveness of untrained volunteers with chronic patients. *Journal of Consulting and Clinical Psychology*, 1970, **34**, 152–155.

Vitalo, R. L. Effect of facilitative interpersonal functioning in a conditioning paradigm. *Journal of Counseling Psychology*, 1970, **17**, 141–144.

Vitalo, R. L. Teaching improved interpersonal functioning as a preferred mode of treatment. *Journal of Clinical Psychology*, 1971, **27**, 166–170.

Weinman, B., Sanders, R., Kleiner, R., & Wilson, S. Community-based treatment of the chronic psychotic. *Community Mental Health Journal*, 1970, **6**, 13–21.

Zunker, V. G., & Brown, W. F. Comparative effectiveness of student and professional counselors. *Personnel and Guidance Journal*, 1966, **44**, 738–743.

EDITORS' REFERENCES

Bergin, A. E. The evaluation of therapeutic outcomes. In A. E. Bergin & S. L. Garfield (Eds.), *Handbook of psychotherapy and behavior change*. New York: Wiley, 1971.

Bergin, A. E., & Suinn, R. M. Individual psychotherapy and behavior therapy. *Annual Review of Psychology*, 1975, **26**, 509–556.

Gurman, A. S. Some therapeutic implications of marital therapy research. In A. S. Gurman & D. G. Rice (Eds.), *Couples in conflict: New directions in marital therapy.* New York: Aronson, 1975.

Lambert, M. J. Spontaneous remission in adult neurotic disorders: A revision and summary. *Psychological Bulletin*, 1976, **83**, 107–119.

Luborsky, L. B. The latest word on comparative studies: Is it true that all have won so all shall have prizes? Presidential address at the Fifth Annual Meeting of the Society for Psychotherapy Research, Denver, June 1974.

Rachman, S. *The effects of psychotherapy.* New York: Pergamon Press, 1971.

NOTES

1. *Editors' Footnote.* The metaphorical "medical model" of some traditional psychotherapies should not, of course, be confused with the study and treatment of psychological disturbance that is rooted in biochemical and psychophysiological research. Rapid recent scientific advances in the chemotherapeutic treatment of manic-depressive illness and certain of the affective disorders, for example, should serve to remind us that a significant proportion of some debilitating psychological dysfunctions do *not* derive from faulty learning, pathogenic family relationships or other psychosocial transactions.

2. *Editors' Footnote.* It should be noted that the present authors' intent is not to review the efficacy of credentialed professional psychotherapists. Nonetheless, one should be cautious about accepting the two-decade old argument of Eysenck and, more recently, Rachman (1971). It seems to us that the Eysenckian position is no longer considered as persuasive of the nonefficacy of psychotherapy to anyone except Eysenck. Bergin's (1971) penetrating analysis of the issues raised by Eysenck, as well as more recent evaluative reviews (Bergin & Suinn, 1975; Lambert, 1975; Luborsky, 1974) have largely negated Eysenck's arguments. While we do not, of course, believe that a "high" level of proficiency of traditional psychotherapies has been demonstrated, we are convinced that they produce at least moderately positive changes (Bergin,

1971; Gurman, 1975) and that the effects of psychotherapy certainly exceed those of untreated patients (Luborsky, 1974).

3. *Editors' Footnote.* As Mitchell *et al.* (this volume) show, the evidence in support of the predictive utility of nonparticipant judges' ratings of therapeutic conditions, *in the context of psychotherapy conducted by professionals*, is quite inconsistent. This conclusion stands in rather marked contrast to generally held beliefs about the trends in this literature. We find it interesting that more consistently positive trends emerge on the basis of this methodology for assessing helper facilitativeness when nonprofessional therapists' practices are examined. Perhaps certain variables (e.g., therapist prestige) that affect the process and outcome of the therapy done by professionals simply do not enter the clinical picture very saliently for functional professionals. Elucidation of such differences would seem to be an important goal for the future.

4. *Editors' Footnote.* Again, we do not find Eysenck very convincing. Furthermore, the Anthony *et al.* (1972) data are not comparable to those of Eysenck in that they focus on rehabilitation criteria of hospital recidivism and posthospital employment. While such criteria are completely appropriate change indices for hospitalized psychiatric patients, they clearly reflect very different criteria than those emphasizing intrapsychic change, cognitive restructuring, improved self-concept, etc., of the sorts typically used in the study and practice of outpatient psychotherapy.

5. *Editors' Footnote.* While we applaud these research efforts, it should be noted that an important issue addressed but not yet resolved in this approach involves the question of "training as a preferred mode of treatment" *for whom?* Certainly, there are limits to the applicability of any intervention strategy.

6. See Carkhuff (1974a) for a detailed description of the training procedure.

7. *Editors' Footnote.* We agree completely. See Garfield (Chapter 4, this volume) for a discussion of these issues in the context of the training of professional psychotherapists.

8. *Editors' Footnote.* While some of the criteria noted by the authors are common ones in psychotherapy research on professional therapists, most of the criteria employed by a large number of (largely psychodynamically oriented) therapists in actual clinical practice seem not to be included here, and for good reason. That is, functional professionals clearly are able to produce major therapeutic gains with *specific types of patients* when they work toward *specific types of goals*. But these goals, as is well documented in this chapter, often are very different from those of professional therapists. Similarly, the treatment needs of many of the patients treated by functional professionals are often quite different from those of the majority of neurotic outpatients. In sum, while we are very impressed by the effectiveness of functional professionals, we think it is absolutely necessary to keep in mind the differences in patient populations, treatment goals, and outcome criteria that often characterize the actual clinical practices of functional professionals and "credentialed" professionals. Finally, see Emrick, Lassen and Edwards (Chapter 7, this volume) for a provocative analysis of the therapeutic effects of another type of nonprofessional therapeutic agents, peers with similar problems.

CHAPTER 7

NONPROFESSIONAL PEERS AS THERAPEUTIC AGENTS

Chad D. Emrick, Carol L. Lassen, and Myles T. Edwards

This chapter investigates peer therapeutic change agents who function in peer self-help groups. Such groups have generally been ignored by psychotherapy researchers. Members of these groups function in a therapeutic capacity but without professional credentials. They are disturbed by the same or similar psychological problems, or at least identify themselves as similarly troubled. Thus, peer influencers both give and receive psychological assistance in their interactions with peer "clients." To distinguish these agents from professional therapists, we will call them *therapeutic peers* or *peer influencers*. The people these therapeutic peers help will be referred to as *recipients* to differentiate them from patients and clients of professional therapists.

This chapter is not concerned with the many nonprofessional therapeutic agents who do not, in terms of psychological disturbance, have mutually perceived parity with their clients—e.g., volunteers at suicide prevention centers, teachers, well-adjusted children helping maladjusted children (e.g., Guerney, 1970), housewives doing therapy with outpatients (Rioch, Elkes, & Flint, 1963), and a host of other non- and paraprofessionals associated with community, hospital, clinic, or agency projects and programs (see Hurvitz, 1974).[1] Nor are we concerned with social groups formed around certain characteristics and conditions (e.g., homosexuality, physical shortness, single parenthood), "encounter" or "growth" groups, individuals who function as therapeutic peers in professionally directed residential programs (e.g., Odyssey House for drug abusers), or individuals in leaderless groups formed by professional psychotherapists who continue in absentia to exert strong influence over the group's functioning (Seligman & Desmond, 1973).

While Hurvitz (1970, 1971, 1974) has labeled these groups "peer self-help psychotherapy groups," we will refer to the groups simply as peer self-help groups to distinguish them from professionally led psychotherapy groups. We see the therapeutic processes operative in peer groups and professionally led groups as qualitatively different, and our terminology reflects this distinction.

Our review of these groups is divided into three sections. First, we consider Alcoholics Anonymous (AA), the oldest (founded in 1935) and largest of established peer self-help groups. With a membership of some 800,000 (Norris, 1974a, 1974b), AA is more than twice as large as the next largest group of 350,000—Take Off Pounds Sensibly, or TOPS (Stunkard, 1972). AA has served as a model for the establishment of other groups and has been subjected to more empirical evaluation than any other self-help group. It stands as the best prototype available for examining both therapeutic effectiveness and mechanisms of change in such groups.

The second section focuses on some other self-help groups—i.e., Synanon, Phoenix House, Daytop Village, Recovery, Inc., and TOPS, all of which are reasonably well known, have a substantial membership, and have undergone at least some empirical analysis.[2]

The third section is devoted to a relatively new and current self-help group known as consciousness raising (CR). These groups are socially and politically important and yet new enough that no data on their effectiveness have yet been reported. While they are informally organized and have no single national affiliation, they are included here because they are currently very popular, have the potential for involving more participants than any other self-help group, serve as an interesting contrast to AA groups in philosophy, membership, and function, and offer the promise of some significant research.

Several forces have contributed to the self-help movement. One factor is the American "joiner" instinct (Dumont, 1974). Because of America's "pluralistic ethnology" (Dumont, 1974), Americans seem prone to seek a social identity and pride through joining clearly defined groups. The operation of this tendency is clearly manifested in self-help groups where members derive a sense of pride and identity through publicly proclaiming themselves to be "fat" (TOPS), a "junkie" (Synanon), an "alcoholic" (AA), and the like.

Another source of support of the self-help movement is the community mental health movement. Both movements strive to bring closer together the individual receiving help and the one giving it. In self-help groups, the helper and recipient have a similar, clearly defined problem. Mental health centers frequently employ non- and paraprofessionals with cultural, educational, and experiential backgrounds similar to the population they treat (Dumont, 1974; Sobey, 1970).

Also fostering the proliferation of self-help groups has been the increasing concern of Americans with the accountability of helpers to consumers. Rather than remaining dependent on professionals to decide the nature and extent of services provided, some consumers have become sophisticated about means to exercise control over the delivery of mental health services (Dumont, 1974).

Still another factor behind the emergence of self-help groups has been the limited number of professionals available to treat those who ask for help with psychological problems. When two of the earliest and best known self-help groups were formed—AA in 1935 and Recovery, Inc., in 1937—the American Psychological Association (APA) had only about 1500 members (Little, 1975).[3] Although in the last 40 years the supply of professionals has increased,[4] the number remains insufficient to meet all demands for service. In addition, many professionals have focused on one-to-one treatment rather than on family and group work, and have been more concerned with helping patients develop genetic insight than with achieving behavioral change. This appears to have been true particularly in the 1930s, the beginning of the self-help movement, when the influence of psychoanalytic theory on professional practice was especially strong (see Tiebout, 1958). While the last 40 years have seen increased utilization of group (Yalom, 1975) and family (Ferber, Mendelsohn, & Napier, 1972) therapy, many professionals continue to use one-to-one insight-oriented therapy. To the degree that one-to-one therapy has been emphasized, available professionals have underutilized the therapeutic potential of peer influence and have not helped as many people as they might have had they worked more with groups.[5] Also, to the extent that

professionals have not worked directly on behavior change, they have failed to help some people who need to curtail certain behaviors (such as excessive drinking) before therapy can be effective in other ways (see Gerard & Saenger, 1966). In brief, it appears that professionals have failed to meet demands for service because they have been too few in number and have at times failed to utilize the most efficient and appropriate therapeutic strategies. But even if the supply of professionals were ample and these professionals utilized only the most efficient, appropriate approaches to the kinds of problems dealt with in self-help groups, such groups would no doubt continue to flourish. These groups are free or inexpensive compared to professional treatment, and peer influence is powerful. Nonprofessionals have understood this power and have organized groups to maximize it for therapeutic ends.[6]

Two lines of psychological theory and research point to the important influence of peers. One line points to the enormous influence of peers during the childhood and adolescent periods (Muus, 1968; Patterson & Anderson, 1964). This peer influence is particularly important in the early socialization of individuals (Hartup, 1970). Similarly, the influence of therapeutic peers later in life is often another socialization experience. For example, "resocialization" may best describe the events and mechanisms occurring in peer-oriented residential treatment centers for drug addicts.

The second line of theory and research is more general and more complex. It points to the influence of groups in providing individuals with social support, social identity, and social reality (Hollander, 1971). The influence of a group on an individual was vividly demonstrated by Asch (1952) who showed how groups can lead an individual to make obviously erroneous judgments on the relative lengths of lines. Other social influence studies have shown a wide variety of effects such as the degree of involvement in a tenants' organization (Festinger, Schachter, & Back, 1950), the amount of alcoholic beverage consumed, whether drugs are abused, whether help is given to individuals perceived to be in trouble, and the amount of tolerance of pain (see Karlins & Abelson, 1970).

Peer groups represent a special case in that they are considered even more influential than other groups. By definition, there is a basis of similarity between members. In the case of therapeutically oriented peer groups, the similarity lies in the problem or issue which was the basis of the person joining the group. Common experiences and corresponding attitudes about previous social behavior such as drinking, emotional control, drug use, assertiveness, and the like should yield more interpersonal attraction among the members than when these commonalities are absent (Berscheid & Walster, 1969). Though this clearly is to be expected from the results of experimental and descriptive studies, the attraction between members of therapeutic peer groups has not been a focus of research. There *is* evidence that homogeneity of group membership leads to greater cohesiveness (Yalom & Rand, 1966) and that homogeneity and cohesiveness yield greater influence over group members (Deutsch & Gerard, 1955; Yalom, 1975) as well as greater uniformity of membership attitudes (Festinger & Thibaut, 1951; Gerard, 1953).

Attraction between members of a group is not necessarily the same as attraction to or desire to be a member of a group. This latter form of attraction is cohesiveness as considered in the research mentioned above. The link between a person's attraction to the members of a group and his/her attraction to the group itself is implicit in Yalom and Rand's (1966) finding but needs to be definitely established in order to relate the commonality between members of a peer group to heightened influence of the peer group on the members. Attraction and cohesiveness may provide part of the needed explanation for the influence and effectiveness of peer self-help groups.

Indeed, in comparing the influence of peers with nonequals, it appears that people learn better and more readily from peers (Katkin, Risk, & Spielberger, 1966; Krueger, 1971; Sobey, 1970; Zupnick, 1970) and are more likely to imitate peers (DeCourcy & Duerfeldt, 1973; Meichenbaum, 1971). While groups powerfully affect individuals, peer groups do even more so. Given the power of peer influence, it is not surprising that the peer self-help movement is so widespread.

This chapter analyzes the history, structure, therapeutic process, therapeutic change mechanisms, and effectiveness of AA, other major self-help groups, and CR groups.

ALCOHOLICS ANONYMOUS

AA describes itself as "a fellowship of men and women who share their experience, strength and hope with each other that they may solve their common problem and help others to recover from alcoholism," and states that its members' purpose is "to stay sober and help other alcoholics to achieve sobriety."

Members remain anonymous to avoid the potential stigma of membership, their own financial exploitation of AA affiliation, and possible ostracism of family and friends. In addition, anonymity promotes the confidentiality requisite for candid problem discussion.

Before the therapeutic processes in AA are described and analyzed, the organization's history and development will be outlined and its membership characterized.

History and Development

AA was founded in Ohio in 1935 by two chronic alcoholics—a New York stockbroker, Bill W., and an Akron, Ohio surgeon, Dr. Bob S. Convinced that he needed to help other alcoholics in order to keep sober himself, Bill aided Dr. Bob, and together they set about helping other alcoholics. Some months later, Bill started building another self-help group in New York and a third group was formed in Cleveland. Several ideas stemming from the founders' contacts with Moral Rearmament (see Cantril, 1963) guided them. In 1938 and 1939 these ideas were translated into the Twelve Step structure and philosophy of the AA program (see Table 1).

Growth was very slow until around 1940, when several national articles about AA were published. Since then, AA has developed rapid-

TABLE 1. THE TWELVE STEPS OF AA.

1. We admitted we were powerless over alcohol... that our lives had become unmanageable.
2. Came to believe that a Power greater than ourselves could restore us to sanity.
3. Made a decision to turn our will and our lives over to the care of God *as we understood Him.*
4. Made a searching and fearless moral inventory of ourselves.
5. Admitted to God, to ourselves, and to another human being the exact nature of our wrongs.
6. Were entirely ready to have God remove all these defects of character.
7. Humbly asked Him to remove our shortcomings.
8. Made a list of all persons we had harmed and became willing to make amends to them all.
9. Made direct amends to such people wherever possible, except when to do so would injure them or others.
10. Continued to take personal inventory and when we were wrong promptly admitted it.
11. Sought through prayer and meditation to improve our conscious contact with God *as we understood Him,* praying only for knowledge of His will for us and the power to carry that out.
12. Having had a spiritual awakening as the result of these Steps, we tried to carry this message to alcoholics, and to practice these principles in all our affairs.

ly. It has had an average annual growth of more than 10% since 1968, with a current estimated membership of 800,000 (including those not attending meetings) in more than 22,000 groups in over 90 countries (Norris, 1974b). Despite its size, AA remains a movement of nonprofessionals, resisting the pressure of some to turn it into a worldwide professional organization (Norris, 1970).

Membership Characteristics

Contrary to popular opinion, most AA members are middle-class, married, and employed. Of 13,467 members surveyed in 1974 (Norris, 1974a), 55% were aged 31–50, 7.6% were 30 and under, and 36.5% were 51 and over. In other surveys (Bailey & Leach, 1965; Edwards, Hensman, Hawker, & Williamson, 1966, 1967; Kiviranta, 1969), the majority of male respondents were found to be married and living with their spouses, while less than half the women were so situated. Nearly all members were skilled workers and above in terms of occupational level. Most of the AA membership is male.

Research indicates that alcoholics who affiliate with AA are not representative of the total population of alcoholics. This research has been extensively reviewed (Bean 1975b; Leach 1973; Trice & Roman, 1970), and the findings suggest that those alcoholics who join AA are more sociable and affiliative, guilty over past behavior, more chronically and severely problemed, more often middle-class, physically healthier, and more socially stable than those who do not affiliate. These characteristics appear to match the role demands AA places on its members. For example, consistent with members' sociability and affiliativeness, AA requires the alcoholic to interact with others in a group. Similarly, the AA stereotype of the alcoholic as an individual who has been drinking destructively for many years and who has suffered a great deal because of his drinking matches the chronically and severely problemed nature of members. Given that only certain alcoholics—those who find AA consonant with their own characteristics—tend to choose this organization as a form of help, it is a resource of important yet limited applicability to the population of alcoholics.

Therapeutic Procedures

The alcoholic who affiliates with AA generally makes his initial contact during a crisis. Usually two members meet with him; when they invite him to join, he accepts. Once he becomes a member, he chooses one or more "older" members (three on the average) to assist him through the Twelve Step program (see Table 1). Often he selects one of the individuals who responded to his initial call for help. Upon joining, he frequently becomes identified with a particular group. Besides attending the meetings of his own group, which commonly occur weekly, he may go to meetings of other groups. An estimated 25% of members go to at least three meetings per week (Norris, 1974a). Between meetings, the member may call on others at any time for assistance. Survey studies have found the average duration of membership to be about 4 years (Bohince & Orensteen, 1950; Edwards et al., 1966, 1967).

Following these procedures gives the alcoholic a chance to benefit from the therapeutic processes and mechanisms of change operative in AA.

THERAPEUTIC PROCESSES AND MECHANISMS OF CHANGE OPERATING IN AA

In AA change occurs through: (1) self-help through the Twelve Step program, (2) assistance by individual members in one-to-one relationships, and (3) help from groups of members. Each modality entails different processes and mechanisms of change.

Self-help

The Twelve Step program requires the alcoholic to do most of the work himself, although he receives support from others in group meetings and in one-to-one encounters. The mechanisms of change involved can be analyzed from a variety of standpoints, but here we use primarily a cognitive-behavioral model (see Mahoney, 1974). We discuss the steps in numerical order, although members do not always take them in that order (Bean, 1975a).

In taking Step One the newcomer changes the conception of himself from one who controls his drinking to one who cannot. He gives up avoidance and denial of the problem and adherence to the belief that he can meet all challenges (Bateson, 1971). He adopts the belief that there is a Greater Power who can help (Step Two), and he agrees to let Him do so (Step Three). The particular conceptualization of this Power is left to the individual.

He then moves to a specific and complex activity. He makes a list of all persons whom he presently resents or has resented in the past (Step Four) and enters beside each name the behavior of that individual which was antecedent to the resentment, and the negative consequences to him of that behavior. Similar lists are made for fear and for guilt related to sexual behavior. He then works on altering his concepts of the people on the lists. He learns to think of them as sick and in need of understanding and prayer rather than as hostile and stubborn, for example. At the same time, he examines his own actions in terms of how they have contributed to each fear-producing, resentment-provoking, or guilt-inducing situation.

From a cognitive-behavioral viewpoint, this step entails self-analysis of the stimulus conditions for fear, guilt, and resentment which are hypothesized to elicit a drinking response (see e.g., Blane, 1968; Cappell & Herman, 1972), and the shifting of the attribution of the cause of these emotional responses from others to oneself. Since the member is asked to internalize emotional control, it may be that alcoholics who remain in AA are initially more internally oriented than nonjoiners or dropouts. Research on this issue would be interesting.

This change in attribution allows for a change in response to the situations which have in the past led to drink-inducing emotional responses. Now, rather than responding affectively and drinking when abused, threatened, or guilt-ridden, the member assesses what he himself may have done to contribute to the situation, tries to help others, and prays that the Greater Power will also help. A response set or expectancy is acquired which can serve to maintain the new responses: "It is possible for me to help others rather than get drunk when I am abused, anxious or guilty" (see Beck, 1974).[7]

In Step Five, the alcoholic acknowledges these problems to the Greater Power and to another individual. He is urged to choose as a "confessor" someone who will keep strictly confidential what is said: another member, a clergyman, friend, psychologist, etc. This confession can be very cathartic and reduce guilt and anxiety.

Pessimism toward the permanence of catharsis-induced change is dealt with by taking the next two steps. The member first readies himself (Step Six) and then asks (Step Seven) the Greater Power to "remove his shortcomings." If he truly believes the Greater Power can do this, he will feel and act as if his faults can be corrected. As with Step Two, the change mechanism oper-

ating appears to be the introduction of a new belief.

In the next two steps he initiates change by making restitution to those he has hurt in the past. After making a list of everyone he can remember harming (Step Eight), he does whatever he can to make amends and undo the harm caused (Step Nine). Members are cautioned against making amends to individuals if doing so would harm themselves or others. For example, in the interest of protecting the spouse from damaging jealousy, the member may not confess in detail past sexual infidelity. In making restitution, the member usually receives positive social reinforcement for his newly adopted openness, honesty, and constructive behavior. By perceiving himself to be engaged in prosocial behavior, he may come to think of himself as a caring, loving person (see Bem, 1970). This more positive self-perception can reinforce the behavioral changes made.

Step Ten is a repetition of Steps Four and Five; the member continues to identify problems and admit them to himself, others, and the Greater Power. In Step Eleven, he reinforces through prayer and meditation his decision to allow the Greater Power to help (originally done in Step Three). The repetition of these earlier steps helps maintain the changes already accomplished while moving through the first nine steps.

With Step Twelve, the member strives to maintain his newly acquired thoughts, feelings, and actions. He does so in part by helping other alcoholics acquire and maintain sobriety and by working to sustain individual AA groups as well as the AA organization at local, district, and national levels. One-to-one and two-to-one relationships are formed in these helping activities and have much in common with the relationship between a client and his individual professional therapist. The next section analyzes and evaluates the mechanisms of change in these one-to-one and two-to-one relationships.

One-to-One and Two-to-One Relationships

Where possible, these two types of peer relationships are discussed together. The helper is referred to as peer influencer or therapeutic peer and the helpee as recipient. When only two-to-one relationships are discussed, the persons involved are identified as Twelfth Step workers (Twelfth Steppers) and alcoholic in crisis. Participants in one-to-one relationships are referred to as sponsor and sponsoree (baby, pigeon).

Helping Process in Twelfth Step Workers-Alcoholic in Crisis Relationships. Since the majority of AA members join the organization during a crisis, the importance of the interaction between Twelfth Step workers and an alcoholic in crisis cannot be overemphasized. In this delicate interaction, Twelfth Step workers usually do not insist that the alcoholic in crisis admit his alcoholism, but they help him define the nature and extent of his problem and decide what he will do about it. Throughout the contact, Twelfth Steppers attempt to remain accepting, permissive, and unemotional, and seek to develop quick rapport by recounting a brief history of their own alcoholism. Also, they attempt to influence the alcoholic to give up drinking by mentioning that they themselves have recovered through AA. If the alcoholic seems responsive to the AA program, he may be invited to accompany one or both of the workers to an AA meeting. This continues the care initiated during the crisis contact.

Helping Process in Sponsor-Sponsoree Relationships. Once the alcoholic has joined AA, he may become a sponsoree of an "older" member (or sponsor). The importance of this sponsor-sponsoree relationship has been inconsistently assessed. According to Bales (1962, p. 575) the relationship is "the heart of the therapeutic process." Edwards *et al.* (1967, p. 203) believe the importance of the sponsor "can be exaggerated." Regardless of his importance, the sponsor functions variously as a father-confessor or priest, psychotherapist, social companion, and, sometimes, financial helper. However, he does not actually solve problems and thereby avoids the "rescue" game alcoholics typically wish to play in order to escape responsibility for stopping drinking (Steiner, 1971). Without rescuing, he responds to crisis calls at any time in the course of the relationship, usually without regard to the hour they are made.

Potential Benefits in Peer Influencer-Recipient Relationships. It is essential in peer influencer-recipient relationships that *both* helper and helpee benefit from the interchange.

The recipient has been observed to benefit in several ways. For one, he learns to trust another human being. Therapeutic peers are able to foster such trust since they have been alcoholics themselves. The recipient also gains increased hope for recovery since he is interacting with other alcoholics who share his goal of sobriety and have already been helped to reach it through AA.

Throughout the relationship between sponsor and sponsoree, the sponsoree is helped to acquire and maintain sobriety. For example, the sponsor makes suggestions and gives advice about how to avoid drinking relapses, as when he tells the sponsoree how to stay away from frustrating situations which have in the past led to drinking. Also, the sponsor models sobriety-supporting behavior. For instance, he demonstrates an ethical concern for others as he helps the sponsoree without expecting to be paid and tolerates frustration in working with him without retaliating. By learning to be other-oriented, the sponsoree is better able to prevent a relapse due to wounded primary narcissism.

The sponsoree is also helped to begin resocialization. Many alcoholics enter AA as relatively isolated people, although they may be married and employed. Relating to a sponsor gives them the opportunity to work on problems they encounter in intense interpersonal interactions, and they become better equipped to develop and maintain other close relationships in AA and perhaps eventually outside the organization.

Bohince and Orensteen (1950) provide empirical support for the assertion that the sponsoree receives help. One hundred and twenty-five AA members who responded to a request to rank-order four aspects of the AA program ranked "advice and help from sponsor" second only to group meetings.

As noted, the recipient is not the only one who benefits from the peer influencer-recipient encounter. The peer influencer himself (in either the Twelfth Step worker or sponsor role) is helped by developing alternatives to drinking, by receiving reinforcement for sobriety, and by increasing personal strength.

He may seek emotional satisfaction and relief of tension by helping others instead of drinking. In place of buying alcohol for fellow alcoholics and himself, he helps them give it up.

His efforts to maintain sobriety are reinforced in various ways. By telling his drinking history to others, he becomes more accepting of his alcoholism. By persuading others to make a commitment to sobriety, he increases his own similar commitment and his investment to the AA program in general. Seeing others when they are not sober prevents him from idealizing the past, warns him of what he would be like should he return to drinking, and keeps him from engaging in thinking patterns which in the past supported drinking. The inebriation of others can also serve to remind him of how far he has progressed in his struggle against alcoholism. By "rescuing" the recipient, he has in fantasy solved and mastered for a time his own urge to drink. Any time he is tempted to relapse, he can create a "rescue" situation by projecting his wish to drink onto the recipient. In doing this, he has an opportunity to gain once again symbolic mastery over his impulse to drink. This type of symbolic, sobriety-maintaining rescue is, it should be noted, different from the responsibility-avoiding rescue wish of the drinking alcoholic referred to earlier. Finally, in his role as sponsor, the therapeutic peer receives support for his sobriety by being in a situation where he cannot shirk his obligations to sponsorees without threatening his status in the organization.

The personal strength gained by the peer influencer also varies. He finds meaning and purpose for his life and acquires self-respect, status, and prestige by being important to others. He becomes more ethical rather than thinking of himself in an egocentric, narcissistic fashion. He becomes philosophical about failure by stressing that the source of failure of a recipient rests not with him (the peer influencer) but in the battle between the strength of AA and the lure of alcohol. Thus, he acquires the ability to encounter success ·and failure without drinking. He develops useful mechanisms of defense against the inner forces which have in the past led to drinking. Initially, he utilizes undoing, reaction formation, and counterphobia as he helps others stop drinking. When he matures in AA, sublimation operates more centrally. Finally, in his role as sponsor, he acquires skills for relating closely with others by experiencing emotionally involved relationships with sponsorees.

Bohince and Orensteen (1950) reported data relevant to speculations regarding the beneficial effects of the peer influencer-recipient relationship on the peer influencer. Unfortunately, the data pertain only to the sponsor role; however, the findings can probably be generalized to the Twelfth Step worker. They found that 66% of the successful (in sobriety) members had served as sponsors while only 19% of unsuccessful members had participated as sponsors ($p < .001$). The correlation between successful sobriety and sponsorship was significant ($r = .45$, $p < .001$). This finding may indicate, as the researchers concluded, that "chances for success are enhanced considerably through active participation in this aspect of the program" (p. 54). However, since members are expected to have some period of sobriety before becoming a sponsor, it is equally plausible to speculate that the chances for becoming a sponsor are enhanced

through sobriety. Whether there is a causal linkage between sobriety and sponsorship or Twelfth Step work, and the direction of that linkage, can only be determined by further research. We predict that peer influencer activities will be found to strengthen sobriety. Empirical evidence for the therapeutic benefits of helpers dealing with other problems (Fremouw & Harmatz, 1975) is consistent with this prediction.

Potential Harm in Peer Influencer-Recipient Relationships. While potentially mutually beneficial, the relationship between therapeutic peer and recipient also holds destructive possibilities for the participants.

Participants in a long-term sponsor-sponsoree relationship may become overinvolved or overidentified with each other. Excessive involvement may result from the fact that both participants are working toward the same goal,[8] and one or both may turn to drink to escape what is for them an uncomfortably intense relationship.

Overidentification results when the therapeutic peer or recipient (or both) sees the other as more like himself than he really is and loses the objectivity needed for beneficial interchange. Since the participants have a common behavioral problem, excessive identification is very probable. Overidentification may be particularly damaging if it comes from the sponsor. He may, for example, see the sponsoree as like himself in respects other than alcoholism and insist that the sponsoree take the exact approaches he took in combating his own alcoholism. Because he ignores the uniqueness of the sponsoree, he may appear insensitive and rigid. In turn, the sponsoree may reject him, leaving him feeling unappreciated for his well-intentioned efforts.

Although the danger of overattachment exists for both sponsor and sponsoree, excessive attachment can be reduced by interaction with more than one sponsoree or sponsor at a time. In the special case of the newcomer having a close friend or relative already in AA, someone other than the friend or relative can become the sponsor.

The potential for becoming overinvolved or overidentified with a sponsoree may be particularly great for the recently sober alcoholic. Manohar (1973) observed that newly recovering alcoholics (those with less than 12 months' sobriety) in training to be alcoholism counselors tended, compared to counselors with longer sobriety, to be more possessive of their clients, less able to detach themselves and their problems from clients, and more overinvested in the clients' successes and failures. If this finding can be generalized to AA, it suggests that members should wait until they have had at least a year of sobriety before becoming sponsors.

Some potential deleterious effects do not apply equally to the peer influencer and recipient. The sponsor may be "aggressively negative" toward a baby because he depends on the maladjustment of others to maintain his own adjustment (Ripley & Jackson, 1959). Or he may be neglectful or withdraw at a time when the baby needs help the most. Some sponsors may do this because they are insensitive to the needs of the baby, or they may feel their sobriety is being threatened or is at least not being strengthened by involvement with a baby. Neglect or withdrawal may also stem from incompatible pairing of sponsors and sponsorees. Bohince and Orensteen (1950) found that among members who did not benefit from AA, 14% indicated they did not get along with their sponsor. Conversely, a sponsor may be harmful by being too indulgent of the sponsoree's pleas for help. Bean (1975a) noticed that some sponsors preferred the new member who was "dependent, compliant, admiring, and grateful" (p. 11). This tendency may reinforce excessive dependency in the baby, whose sobriety may then be particularly threatened when the sponsor adopts another pigeon. Also, preference for dependent members may occasion sponsors to reject less dependent members to the latter's detriment. Finally, the sponsor may have deleterious effects on a sponsoree by talking more about his own drinking past than his nondrinking present, and thereby being an ineffective model for nondrinking behavior.

Many of the potentially damaging behaviors of sponsors identified here may be a function of inexperience rather than insufficient formal training. This hypothesis is based on findings of research on professional therapists which have shown, at least in some cases, that inexperienced therapists may not be helpful to as many people on the whole and may be more likely to harm clients than experienced therapists (Bergin, 1966, 1971; Caracena, 1965; Meltzoff & Kornreich, 1970).[9] If these findings apply to AA members, they suggest that sponsors will become less harmful and probably more helpful as they acquire experience in the organization.

The peer influencer may himself suffer some unique damage. For example, the sponsor may be hurt by becoming attached to a baby who then "rejects" him either by choosing another sponsor or becoming a sponsor himself. The Twelfth Step worker may be hurt by being called upon to help another when he has little to give.

Some members become Twelfth Step workers very early in their involvement. Bailey and Leach (1965) found that 28.6% of respondents with less than 6 months' sobriety had gone on Twelfth Step calls. This is not surprising since members are required to have only 3 months of continuous sobriety before becoming Twelfth Step workers. While this is not evidence that members fill a Twelfth Step worker role too soon, some alcoholics with only a few months' sobriety are no doubt too vulnerable to help others, and failure —which is inevitable in working with alcoholics—may severely threaten their uncertain sobriety. This will be particularly true if the workers do not possess a philosophical view of failure. At such times, they may resort to drinking along with the alcoholic in crisis.

Comparison of peer influencer-recipient and professional therapist-client relationships. The nature of the relationship between a therapeutic peer and a recipient parallels and differs from the interactions between a professional therapist and the alcoholic client or patient. Dean (1969b) and Hurvitz (1974) have developed lengthy lists comparing professional and peer therapeutic agents in their treatment of a variety of psychological disorders, but here we will compare professionals in their treatment of alcoholism only against those characteristics of the peer influencer-recipient relationship just discussed. This comparative analysis focuses on the treatment of drinking behavior since this is the major goal in AA and should be the primary goal in professional treatment of alcoholism (Tiebout, 1958), with insight being of secondary importance.[10]

Professional therapists vary greatly in theoretical orientation. We are ignoring a great deal of variance among professionals when weighing them against the more homogeneous group of AA peer influencers. A lack of supporting data gives these speculations the status of *hypotheses* based largely on the professional experience, review of the literature, and observations of one of the authors (C.E.).

The Twelfth Step worker and professional crisis worker seem to try to help the alcoholic in crisis in the same manner, by responding quickly to the call for help, aiding him in defining his problems, and exploring with him alternatives for dealing with these problems, including entering some kind of therapeutic program. Like the Twelfth Step worker, the therapist may provide a long-term relationship with the alcoholic.

Of the four roles identified for the sponsor, only two appear to be shared by the professional therapist. Professionals are not usually social companions or financial helpers, but they may function in a priestly capacity. The modern professional has been seen by at least some observers as functioning very similarly to elders and priests in the Middle Ages (e.g., Braginsky & Braginsky, 1974; Steiner, 1972). Also, of course, professionals function as psychotherapists who may have emergency meetings with clients during the course of treatment.

Although sharing some functions, the peer influencer and professional psychotherapist seem to differ in some motivational aspects. The professional helps to fulfill professional responsibility, foster personal growth, perhaps meet therapeutic needs, and gain monetarily, whereas the peer influencer helps in order to maintain his own sobriety and satisfy his desire to help others. Consistent with this difference, the professional, compared to the Twelfth Step worker, tends not to be so immediately and repeatedly responsive to crisis calls; compared to the sponsor, the professional offers a therapeutic relationship which is usually not so open-ended or long-lasting.

Like the peer influencer, the professional provides a relatively intense relationship within which the alcoholic client can learn to handle interpersonal conflicts. The therapist may also win the trust of his client, instill hope, and model an ethical concern for others, although as an alcoholic the peer influencer has an initial advantage over the nonalcoholic professional in winning trust and instilling hope. The professional may also give advice and make suggestions, but he may do less of this if, for example, he is very nondirective.

The two helper types differ in how they influence helpees to reduce or give up drinking. Modeling is a major mode of influence for the therapeutic peer. Since the professional usually has not been alcoholic, he lacks this basis for influence through modeling. Rather, he exerts influence through his general expertise in human behavior. This distinction between the helper types is not so clear-cut with problems other than abusive drinking. Both types may model effective cognitive, affective, and behavioral responses to conflict, and both have a type of expert status—the one through professional training and experience, the other through personal experience.

Consistent with his professional status, the psychotherapist calls for more submission to personal authority than does the peer influencer. Whereas the client must submit to the therapist's personal authority (see Strupp, 1970;

Tiebout, 1949, 1953; Zinberg & Glotfelty, 1968), the AA newcomer is required to submit to a Power greater than himself, which may be both the AA group as a whole and a personal deity. Since the member does not have to surrender to any individual, he may more easily accept a helpee role. Although there are no data to support or reject this speculation, the numbers of alcoholics who enter AA appear to exceed those receiving professional treatment. (There are other reasons, of course, for the larger AA membership; for example, it is considerably less expensive than professional treatment and is usually more open-ended.)

Like the sponsor, the therapist may gain personal strength from being a helper. He may find meaning and purpose for his life and acquire status, respect, and prestige from being important to others. He may strengthen useful defenses such as sublimation through following his therapeutic pursuits.[11] Although he may not benefit from symbolically rescuing himself when helping alcoholics, he may gain from "rescuing" someone significant to him. Burton (1969) has observed that some professionals have a need to fill a "healer role" because they were reared in a family where unresolved emotional problems existed. Henry (1966) has also documented the disturbed family backgrounds of some therapists. By being a healer, the therapist symbolically rescues the troubled family member(s). It would be interesting to determine what percentage of therapists who regularly treat alcoholics have or have had an alcoholic family member and are helped by "rescuing" him through their work.

As noted earlier, sponsors may at times become excessively involved and identified with their babies and vice versa. In one sense overinvolvement may be *less* frequent and intense in professional therapy because the roles of therapist and client are more clearly defined and differentiated than are sponsor and sponsoree roles (Bohince & Ornsteen, 1950). Looked at in another light, however, the client may be *more* susceptible than the sponsoree to overinvestment because the former typically has only one therapist to work with.[12]

Overidentification is probably less likely in professional therapist-patient relationships because the therapist does not have the alcoholism problem in common with the client. Even when the therapist has an alcoholism problem, he may not so readily tell his client about it. Thus, the client cannot use this commonality to form an identification (let alone an excessive identification) with the therapist.

As noted above, a peer influencer may be hostile to a recipient because his adjustment is dependent on the recipient's maladjustment. Conceivably, some professionals may also rely on the maladjustment of others, perhaps with as much frequency. While some sponsors are neglectful of and withdraw from sponsorees when they need help the most, this should happen less often with the professional, although data to support this comparison are lacking. Neglect and withdrawal should be less frequent because professionals are bound by a sense of professional responsibility to work with a client until he either terminates therapy or is transferred to another therapist, even though they may be insensitive to him or mismatched with him. A third criticism of peer influencers—that they may prefer dependent recipients—may apply to some professionals as well. Some studies outside the alcoholism field have found that there are professionals who prefer dependent clients (e.g., Cohler & Shapiro, 1964). Again, there are no data for weighing the relative degree of this problem for the two types of helpers.

Like sponsors, professionals may be emotionally affected by termination of a helpee, particularly if they feel termination is premature or if they have become personally identified with the helpee, which may well happen with the more humanistically oriented therapists.[13] Nevertheless, unlike the sponsor, whose sobriety rests in part on helping others, the therapist's personal adjustment should not be overly vulnerable to any emotional upset encountered.

Issues not yet discussed for either peer influencers or professionals are the training and experience of helpers and the matching of helpers and helpees.

It appears that therapeutic peers and a majority of professionals receive training when, as helpees, they observe their helpers. As novice helpers, both types have some kind of apprenticeship with more experienced helpers. Of course, there is an obvious distinction in the amount of formal training received. While the AA peer influencer has no formal training, the professional therapist has a considerable amount, usually years. How this difference relates to dissimilarities between the two helper types is unfortunately uncertain since at present there is not enough evidence to ascertain clearly whether formal training "does any good" (Meltzoff & Kornreich, 1970, p. 288) for the therapist.[14] Also, the therapeutic peer's lack of formal training may be offset by years of personal experience with alcoholism.

The experience variable appears to be one which does not differentiate peer influencers and therapists. Both helper types are in a position to acquire years of experience over the course of their "careers." Some observations outside the alcoholism field have suggested that with experience professionals diversify their use of therapeutic techniques (Meltzoff & Kornreich, 1970). Does this apply to professionals who treat alcoholics? Do peer influencers also become more flexible in their approach to recipients over time? Or does experience affect peer influencers differently? Research evaluating experienced and inexperienced helpers in the alcoholism field might help to answer these and other questions.

Very little is known about matching helpers and alcoholic helpees. There are currently available *no* specific guidelines for matching therapists with alcoholic clients (see Silon, 1975), let alone peer influencers and recipients. All that is known is that sponsor-baby relationships tend to be same-gender (Bean, 1975b). For both professionals and peer influencers, guidelines should identify specific personal characteristics of both participants, as well as the alignment of these characteristics with the demands made upon each participant by the relationship.

In summary, *professionals are seen as serving some of the same functions as peer influencers, but there are notable differences—namely the motivation for helping alcoholics, the position taken vis-à-vis helpees, the mode of influencing helpees to reduce or stop drinking, and formal training.* Given these differences, one alcoholic may benefit more from a professional, another from a peer influencer, and still another from a combination of helpers, working simultaneously or at different points in the course of recovery. Hopefully, future research will generate guidelines for deciding for each alcoholic who is the best type of helper and what is the most suitable timing of his interventions.

Help in Groups

Procedurally and structurally, AA groups are more striking in their differences than in their similarities to professionally led outpatient small therapy groups. Some structural dimensions which distinguish AA from professionally led groups are leadership of meetings, stability of membership, group size, and frequency and length of meetings. Consistent with the constant leadership changes in AA, group membership is often in continuous flux, and is rarely identical two meetings in a row. AA groups are usually large, having an average of about 25 members per session (Leach, 1973) compared to the typical five to ten members in small psychotherapy groups (Yalom, 1970, 1975). AA members may participate in several groups simultaneously and may attend many meetings each week in contrast to psychotherapy group members who commonly attend only one or two meetings per week and are involved in just one group at a time. Finally, AA group meetings are somewhat shorter, lasting an hour compared to the usual $1\frac{1}{2}$ hours for psychotherapy groups.

Procedural differences between AA and psychotherapy groups include the beginning and ending of meetings and the focus of discussion during meetings. Although the leader or chairman for each AA session has the opportunity to begin and end the meeting any way he chooses, a certain ritual prevails. Most leaders start with a reading from the basic AA text, *Alcoholics Anonymous* (1955), or a recitation of the Lord's Prayer or the Serenity Prayer. They also end the session with one of these prayers. Psychotherapy group sessions open and close in a less structured fashion.

AA meetings follow one of two basic formats: (1) the *discussion meeting*, in which the chairman may "tell his story" of alcoholism and his road to recovery and then open the meeting to general discussion about alcoholism or problems related to alcoholism, or (2) the *speakers' meeting*, in which two or three speakers "tell their stories" of alcoholism and recovery from it. Meetings are of two types: "open," at which anyone interested in alcoholism is welcome, and "closed," at which only alcoholics are present. Both types are non-interactionally focused. This is an important point to keep in mind when analyzing AA groups. Members focus on alcoholism and related problems rather than on their reactions to one another. Professionally led groups, in contrast, pay more attention to interactions among group members or between members and the therapist(s) (Yalom, 1970, 1975).

Given these structural and procedural differences, the conditions for change and therapeutic mechanisms of change operative in these two types of groups probably differ, or at least differ in the centrality of their influence, resulting in dissimilar kinds of experiences offered by the two groups. To test this hypothesis, one of the authors (C.E.) reviewed the literature describing AA groups, searching for direct and indirect references to the 12 "curative factors" Yalom (1970, 1975) identified as essential to the therapeutic process in professionally led psychotherapy groups. These factors include both conditions for and mechanisms of change.

Table 2 shows that, among the 26 studies or publications reviewed, 10 of Yalom's 12 curative factors were mentioned. While this finding suggests that the conditions for and mechanisms of change in AA may be similar to those in psychotherapy groups, it does not speak *per se* about the question of the relative centrality of these conditions and mechanisms in the two groups. Thus, a study was made of how often each curative factor was identified in the studies. For each publication, a score of "1" or "0" was assigned to each of the 12 factors. If one or more comments were made about the factor, the publication received a score of "1" for that factor. If no comments were made, it was given a "0" for the factor. As Table 2 shows, there was considerable variance in the frequency of references made to the factors.

TABLE 2. FREQUENCY OF PUBLICATIONS ($N=26$) REFERRING TO CURATIVE FACTORS OPERATIVE IN AA GROUPS.

Curative factor	Number of publications
Altruism	21
Group cohesiveness	20
Identification	14
Instillation of hope	12
Guidance	12
Universality	10
Catharsis	8
"Insight"	6
Interpersonal learning, "output"	2
Family reenactment	1
Interpersonal learning, "input"	0
Existential awareness	0

If the factors more frequently mentioned play more central roles in AA, then the composition of conditions for and mechanisms of change operating in AA is reflected in the ranking of the factors. To determine whether the composition so indicated matches that for professional groups, the rankings in Table 2 were compared with rankings of the curative factors Yalom (1970, 1975) found for psychotherapy groups. This comparison indicates that the composition of conditions for and mechanisms of change in AA groups does indeed appear to differ from professional groups. Apparently AA groups place more emphasis on guidance, identification, and instillation of hope, and less on interpersonal learning, catharsis, insight and existential awareness.

It should be noted that the rankings for professionally led groups were based on responses of patients to their therapy group experiences, while the rankings for AA were derived from the frequency of references made by observers of AA groups. Nevertheless, this comparison appears to have heuristic value.

The observations of one author (C.E.) are consistent with the assumption that instillation of hope, identification, and guidance operate more centrally in AA than in therapy groups. *Hope* may be strongly elicited when an individual arrives at an AA meeting, because he is confronted with others who have solved the very problem he has and hears them speak about how their lives have been dramatically improved since joining the group. In contrast, professionally run groups are less likely to flood new members with "old" members' testimonials regarding the value of group. In contrast to AA members identifying strongly with sponsors, professionally run groups tend to deemphasize *identification*, placing considerably more emphasis on the unique individuality of each member. While *guidance* plays a minimal role in professional groups in that members are usually encouraged to find their own solutions to problems, people in AA groups are offered a great deal of guidance through the official program guidelines, slogans (e.g., "Easy Does It," "First Things First"), and members advising one another about the best way to "work the program."

Interpersonal learning, catharsis, insight and existential awareness are the factors apparently operating less in AA than in professionally led groups. *Interpersonal learning* may be less central because AA groups are noninteractional in comparison to most psychotherapy groups. AA group participants rarely find out during meetings how they come across to others. Neither do they have much chance to learn how they relate to others or to work out difficulties with a particular individual. In spite of the public confession of past misdeeds, *catharsis* may play a relatively minor role in AA groups. Members have little opportunity to express current feelings, particularly here-and-now reactions to other members, compared to the amount of feeling expression frequently encouraged in interactionally focused professionally led groups. Given the emphasis on behavior change in AA, *insight* (at least of the "genetic" variety) may operate less centrally than in many insight-oriented professionally led groups, although members apparently do quite often gain insight

into the nature and implications of their actions as they listen to other members talk about handling problems. Finally, *existential awareness* may operate less potently in AA. Since meetings are strongly spiritually oriented, members do not have much awareness fostered that as human beings they must ultimately face life alone, although they are taught that people must take ultimate responsibility for their lives.

The remaining curative factors—altruism, cohesiveness, universality, and family reenactment—appear to play similar roles in both psychotherapy and AA groups. Gottlieb and Resnikoff (1974) found that patients looking back at their group experience an average of 39 months after termination rated *altruism* as having been next to most helpful to them. Similarly, a central aspect of AA meetings is members helping one another. In both groups *cohesiveness* appears to be an important precondition for the other curative factors to have impact (Gottlieb & Resnikoff, 1974). The development of cohesiveness may be particularly rapid in AA since members share a problem (alcoholism), a goal (sobriety), and a method (AA's Twelve Steps) for achieving that goal. *Universality* is apparently a factor of only moderate centrality in both groups. It may operate more rapidly in AA where a common problem is clear from the very beginning. Finally, *family reenactment* appears to be a relatively minor component in both groups, although Gottlieb and Resnikoff (1974) found that professionally treated outpatients valued it more an average of 39 months after therapy than they had remembered valuing it while active in treatment. In AA groups, members probably do not acquire much understanding of their families of origin, yet they may well view the group as a better family than the one they grew up in.

It would be interesting and valuable to explore this comparison further by randomly assigning alcoholics to psychotherapy groups and AA groups and, after a certain number of sessions, administering Yalom's instrument for measuring members' perceptions of the curative factors (Yalom, 1970, 1975).

EFFECTIVENESS OF ALCOHOLICS ANONYMOUS

A major goal of this chapter is to evaluate empirically the effectiveness of peer therapy. To address this goal, a comprehensive review of the literature evaluating AA's effectiveness has been made. It should be pointed out that a dispassionate scientific approach to AA has not always been taken, and many unsubstantiated claims have been made about the organization's success. Among the more tendentious are those stating or at least strongly suggesting that AA is more successful than professional treatment for alcoholism (e.g., Bateson, 1971; Johnson, 1971).

In the review to follow, claims such as these give way to empirical data. First, data on AA's effectiveness will be presented. Following this, the best of these data will be compared with relevant data from the outcome literature on the professional treatment of alcoholism.

Four approaches have been taken in evaluating the effectiveness of AA: (1) large-scale questionnaire surveys of members attending meetings; (2) studies of the effects of AA as an adjunct to professional treatment; (3) investigations of members' psychological functioning; and (4) outcome evaluations in which AA was the only known intervention for most alcoholics.

Questionnaire Survey Studies

The surveys (Bailey & Leach, 1965; Edwards et al., 1966, 1967; Kiviranta, 1969; Norris, 1970, 1974a, 1974b) suffer multiple sampling biases. For example, more active members were more likely to receive questionnaires, and in at least one survey (Bailey & Leach, 1965) the sample was biased in favor of higher socioeconomic participants and against relative newcomers. The latter may have refused the questionnaire because they were still suffering from alcohol withdrawal or were uncertain about their commitment to AA.

Another weakness of the surveys is failure to separate the effects of AA from those of professional treatment. In surveys reporting data on the professional treatment experiences of members (Bailey & Leach, 1965; Edwards et al., 1966, 1967), a majority of respondents were found to have had such an experience before or during AA.[15] Other problems with the surveys include failure to establish the reliability and validity of measures, to collect pre-program data for comparison with outcome following AA, and to control for nonprogrammatic variables by randomly assigning alcoholics to AA and one or more comparison or control groups.

Given these methodological problems, the findings on drinking behavior will be merely summarized. Too few data exist on other criteria to make any generalizations. A thorough analysis of all but the latest survey (Norris, 1974a, 1974b) can be found in Leach (1973).

From 32% to 43% of members were found to

have been totally abstinent during several years of membership (Bailey & Leach, 1965; Edwards et al., 1966, 1967; Norris, 1970). Among active participants, 26% to 36% had been abstinent 1–5 or 6 years and another 21% to 26% had been sober 5 or 6 years or more (Bailey & Leach, 1965; Edwards et al., 1966, 1967; Norris, 1970, 1974a, 1974b). Thus, from 46.5% (Edwards et al., 1966, 1967) to 61.4% (Norris, 1970) of the active members had had at least 1 year of continuous sobriety behind them. These abstinence rates are probably higher than those for all members giving AA a fair trial by attending at least five meetings (see Emrick, 1973, 1974). Unfortunately, an unknown number of members who left AA after five or more meetings (nonrapid dropouts) were excluded from these surveys. While the exclusion of such dropouts probably biases the results in a favorable direction, we believe it appropriate for the studies to have excluded rapid dropouts—those attending fewer than five meetings. Our position on dropouts thus appears to be between that of Bergin, who chooses to exclude all dropouts in determining improvement rates, and Eysenck, who excludes none (see Bergin, 1971).[16]

Studies of AA as an Adjunct to Professional Treatment

Twenty-four studies evaluated the relationship between AA involvement and outcome after some form of professional treatment for alcoholism. The basic strategy of these studies was to compare the outcome of alcoholics who had participated in AA before, during, or after some type of professional treatment with the outcome of patients who had not participated in AA, or who had attended meetings less frequently. Among their methodological flaws, these studies assessed the effects of only *self-selected* AA participation on outcome, confounding AA participation with client variables. In addition, the majority of investigations, as with the surveys, failed to establish the reliability and validity of data and collect pre-affiliation data for comparison with outcome. These methodological problems preclude the drawing of definitive conclusions about AA's effectiveness as an adjunct to professional treatment. Nevertheless, the results of the studies are summarized in Table 3.

As Table 3 shows, the most striking characteristic of these findings is their inconsistency. *About half the studies found no relationship between AA involvement and outcome; half found a positive relationship.* These findings suggest that patients who are involved in AA before, during,

TABLE 3. RELATIONSHIPS BETWEEN AA INVOLVEMENT AND OUTCOME WITH TREATMENT OTHER THAN AA.

Time of AA involvement	N studies having data	No relationship[a]	Positive relationship $(p<.01)$[b]	$(.01<p<.10)$[c]
Pre-treatment	7[d]	4		4
Before or during treatment (not differentiated)	3	2		1
During treatment	3	1	2	
During or after treatment (not differentiated)	1			1
After treatment	14[e]	8	6	5
Total	28[f]	15	8	11

[a]Numbers refer to the following studies: (1) *pre-treatment* (Ditman, Crawford, Forgy, Moskowitz, & Macandrew, 1967; Ritson, 1968; Selzer & Holloway, 1957; Tomsovic, 1970); (2) *before or during treatment* (Kissin, Rosenblatt, & Machover, 1968; O'Reilly & Funk, 1964); (3) *during treatment* (Mayer & Myerson, 1971); (4) *after treatment* (Beaubrun, 1967; Belasco, 1971; Davies, Shepherd, & Myers, 1956; McCance & McCance, 1969; Oakley & Holden, 1971; Pattison, Headley, Gleser, & Gottschalk, 1968; Selzer & Holloway, 1957; Wanberg, 1968).

[b]Numbers refer to the following studies: (1) *during treatment* (Gerard & Saenger, 1966; Wattenberg & Moir, 1954); (2) *after treatment* (Beaubrun, 1967; Kish & Hermann, 1971; Ludwig, Levine, & Stark, 1970; Rohan, 1970; Rossi, Stach, & Bradley, 1963; Tomsovic, 1970).

[c]Numbers refer to the following studies: (1) *pre-treatment* (Bateman & Peterson, 1971; Haberman, 1966; Ritson, 1968; Rossi et al., 1963); (2) *before or during treatment* (Baekeland, Lundwall, Kissin, & Shanahan, 1971); (3) *during or after treatment* (Robson, Paulus, & Clarke, 1965); (4) *after treatment* (Belasco, 1971; Davies et al., 1956; Dubourg, 1969; Rohan, 1970; Tomsovic, 1970).

[d]The number of relationships exceeds the number of studies by one because data from two samples are included from Ritson (1968).

[e]The number of relationships exceeds the number of studies by five because there are entries in two columns from each of five studies (Beaubrun, 1967; Belasco, 1971; Davies et al., 1956; Rohan, 1970; Tomsovic, 1970).

[f]This total is inflated since results from three studies (Rossi et al., 1963; Selzer & Holloway, 1957; Tomsovic, 1970) are entered in two different rows. The number of different studies is actually 25.

or after professional treatment may or may not function better. If they do not, they will probably do no worse than patients who are not involved with AA or who go to meetings less frequently. While suggesting that adjunctive AA involvement may sometimes be beneficial, these results need to be questioned because of the methodological problems just adumbrated, especially the confounding of AA involvement with client variables. *Adjunctive participation may have no effect on outcome. Perhaps alcoholics who affiliate with the organization are particularly motivated to stop drinking, and it is this motivation which leads to the better results rather than any active ingredient in the AA program itself.*

Studies of Psychological Functioning of AA Members

Five studies examined the psychological functioning of AA members. Since each has design deficiencies, many of which are shared by the previous two groups of studies, their findings will also be merely summarized.

The studies seem to suggest that AA decreases dependence on others and increases an intrapsychic sense of well-being (Cohen, 1962), leads to more acceptance of oneself as alcoholic and in need of help (Bell, 1970; Bell, Weingold, & Lachin, 1969), decreases self-ideal self-concept discrepancy (Carroll & Fuller, 1969), increases an ethical value orientation—i.e., concern for others as well as oneself (Eckhardt, 1967), and improves perceptual-motor functioning as measured by the Bender-Gestalt (Seiden, 1960). Some or all of these psychological changes may be benefits of AA but, again, AA's role in producing these changes cannot be definitively assessed because of methodological problems.

Outcome Evaluations with AA as the Only Intervention

Five studies evaluated the adjustment of members of one or more AA groups when this was the only help received for most, if not all, the members. Projects such as these are capable of providing the most valid indices of AA's effectiveness, since the effects of AA are not confounded with the effects of professional treatment for at least a majority of subjects, and samples, if properly constructed, include all or are representative of all members of the group(s) under study Fortunately, all but one of the samples among the five studies (C., 1965) were so constructed. Because these projects are capable of giving the best picture of AA's overall effectiveness, they will be reported in some detail. It is important to keep in mind, however, that they are far from ideal and suffer many of the same weaknesses identified for the other studies. Also, since they pertain only to active members, they fail to provide data on the adjustment of alcoholics after leaving AA. Nonetheless, they are the best studies on AA to date.

In the earliest and most comprehensive work (Bohince & Orensteen, 1950), 1,507 Minneapolis alcoholics were studied. They had, over a 3-year period, registered as members of AA while taking a 4-week indoctrination program. Of the 1,507, more than 20% were eliminated from follow-up mostly because they "did not have a maximum opportunity to benefit from the (AA) chapter's services" (p. 10). Of the remaining 1,164, every other one was chosen to receive a questionnaire. Of the 582 questionnaires mailed $1\frac{1}{2}$ to $4\frac{1}{2}$ years after registration, only 231 (39.7%) were returned. While the high no-return rate might have biased the sample in favor of those who had tested AA adequately and had found it helpful, this appears not to be the case, or at least not strongly so, since many non-respondents were among those who had failed to complete the four indoctrination sessions. In fact, 87% of the 121 whose questionnaires were returned unclaimed had failed to complete the sessions. Since they had not given AA an adequate trial, they were, we believe, appropriately excluded from evaluation. Nearly all respondents, on the other hand, had apparently given AA a sufficient test, since 92.6% had at least completed the indoctrination course. Thus, despite the great loss of participants, the sample seems to be fairly representative of those who had actually become involved in the program. Of the final sample, 58.9% had not received pre-AA help for their alcoholism, and only 14.7% were in professional treatment concurrent with AA.

The important findings of this study appear to be: (1) about one-third of participants had been totally abstinent for a mean of $2\frac{1}{2}$ years of active membership, (2) about two-thirds had been abstinent or at least significantly improved in drinking behavior, (3) most members felt they had gotten at least some benefit, and (4) 5% had experienced some hurt.

C. (1965) made a study of 393 participants attending 10 or more meetings of a large AA group in Austin, Texas. Of this group, 31% had been totally abstinent for 1 year or more, 12% had been abstinent for 1 year but later had had a relapse, 17.8% had had one or more relapses during the 1st year, 1.3% were in a mental hospital at follow-up, and the remaining 38% had dropped out before the end of the 1st year and their status was unknown. The large percentage of members not followed up may have seriously biased the sample. Also, not all the members attending 10 or more sessions were identified, because the attendance records were only "fairly good." Thus, the 43% 1-year-or-more abstinence figure is probably not valid. The figure should be somewhere between 43%, the rate based on the total sample, and 69%, the rate based on those followed up. Very likely the true figure is closer to the lower estimate, since the majority of those lost to follow-up probably had not remained abstinent. C. himself estimated the figure to be 47%.

Thorpe and Perret (1959) followed up 278 industrial employees who had been seen in the company's medical department for problems related to drinking and had then been urged to seek one or more of a variety of programs or treatments. Of those choosing AA as the only intervention (N not reported), 48.1% had been abstinent at least a year, 11.5% had been "improved" throughout follow-up, and 40.8% had remained "unimproved." These figures can be compared with those of employees (N not reported) receiving only "medical" treatment (14.5% abstinent, 45.2% improved, 40.3% unimproved), "psychiatric" treatment (14.3%, 50.0%, 35.7%, respectively), "combined" interventions (often including AA) (29.1%, 29.1%, 41.8%, respectively), and "no" treatment (refused) (5.5%, 31.5%, 62.9%, respectively). Since the number of individuals in each group was not reported, statistical comparisons cannot be made. Nonetheless, unquestionably more employees selecting AA had been abstinent than individuals choosing non-AA approaches, and those selecting AA in combination with other interventions had the second best abstinence rate. The percent abstinent or improved was, on the other hand, remarkably similar across all treated groups, being around 60% for all. Since employees were not randomly assigned, the higher abstinence rates for AA participants cannot be attributed to the effects of AA *per se*. The results merely *suggest* that for alcoholics seeking help in response to threat of job loss, AA leads to more abstinence than do other interventions.

In the study by Ditman, Crawford, Forgy, Moscowitz, and Macandrew (1967) 301 court offenders were, upon conviction, randomly assigned to a no-treatment condition, an alcoholism clinic, or AA. Alcoholics assigned to AA had to attend five meetings in 30 days. The alcoholism clinic patients had to "cooperate" with the clinic. Those in the no-treatment group were simply told to return to the court in 6 months. Of those followed up who received AA ($N = 86$), only 31% had no rearrests during 1 year or more after sentencing, compared with 32% for the alcoholism clinic group and 44% for those receiving no treatment. It appears that no treatment was slightly better than being forced to go to AA or an alcoholism clinic. These results suggest that *compulsory* AA intervention and alcoholism clinic treatment are not helpful and may be harmful to chronic municipal court offenders.

In another study of criminal alcoholics, this time with felons, Brown (1963) evaluated the outcome of 40 participants who had been in AA 4 years or more since their discharge from prison. While some had received professional treatment in addition to AA, there was no evidence that a majority had done so. Of the 40 members, 40% had been totally abstinent throughout the period of AA involvement, 10% had had one or more relapses but had been abstinent for at least 5 years, 17.5% had apparently improved though they had had "periodic bouts of drunkenness," and 32.5% had remained unimproved. Altogether, 67.5% had been at least somewhat improved in drinking, a figure similar to those found by Bohince and Orensteen (1950) and Thorpe and Perret (1959). Also, 65% of the group had not returned to a penal institution. This nonrecidivism rate is much higher than that reported by Ditman *et al.* (1967), the difference no doubt resting on the considerable disparity between the two criminal groups.

In considering all the data from these five studies, the following tentative conclusions can be drawn. First, it appears that, *of members giving AA a fair trial, just under half remain abstinent for a year while actively involved in the program* (C., 1965; Thorpe & Perret, 1959). Second, about 30% to 40% of participants are able to remain totally abstinent during a mean of $2\frac{1}{2}$ to more than 4 years of membership (Bohince & Orensteen, 1950; Brown, 1963).[17] Third, about 10% of participants have relapses early in the program but are then able to remain totally abstinent for long periods of time (Bohince & Orensteen, 1950; Brown, 1963). It

appears, then, that *about 40% to 50% of alcoholics who join AA may have long periods of total abstinence while involved in the program.* Fourth and finally, *60% to 68% of members improve to some extent, drinking less or not at all during AA participation* (Bohince & Orensteen, 1950; Brown, 1963; Thorpe & Perret, 1959).[18]

While indeed impressive, these conclusions indicate that AA does not help every alcoholic reduce his drinking or become totally abstinent. Neurotic alcoholics and those with personality disorders appear to do better than psychotic alcoholics (Parker, Meiller, & Andrews, 1960). Members who are not chronic municipal court inebriates seem to have better outcome than those who are (Pittman & Gordon, 1958). Members who are able to maintain satisfactory interpersonal relationships may do better than those who cannot (Button, 1956).

Several other characteristics have been found to be positively associated with successful membership: (1) not having been hospitalized for alcoholism ($p < .001$) (C., 1965); (2) being older (Bailey & Leach, 1965; Bohince & Orensteen, 1950; Ditman *et al.*, 1967); (3) being non-black (Ditman *et al.*, 1967); (4) having had more than 8 years' delay between becoming concerned about drinking and the first AA attendance ($p < .05$) (Bailey & Leach, 1965); (5) having regarded alcoholics as "bums" before becoming a member ($p < .05$) (Bailey & Leach, 1965); (6) having had no "prolonged dry periods" before joining AA ($p < .05$) (Bohince & Orensteen, 1950); (7) not having heard, before becoming a member, that alcoholism is a disease ($p < .01$) (Bailey & Leach, 1965); and (8) not having joined AA to get "inner peace" ($p < .01$) (Bailey & Leach, 1965). For the most part, these results suggest that three pre-AA characteristics may distinguish the successful member from the unsuccessful: better general adjustment, a longer and more severe drinking history, and less acceptance of alcoholism and alcoholics.

Other characteristics found to relate positively with successful membership are: (1) being more active during participation in AA ($p < .05$) (Kissin, Rosenblatt, & Machover, 1968); (2) being more field-independent, as measured by the embedded figure test (Witkin, Karp, & Goodenough, 1959) ($p < .05$) (Kissin *et al.*, 1968); (3) scoring higher on psychometric indices of alleged homosexual orientation ($p < .05$) (Kissin *et al.*, 1968; Machover, Puzzo, Machover, & Plumeau, 1959); (4) spending over two-thirds of one's social life in AA ($p < .05$) (Bailey & Leach, 1965); (5) participating in AA-sponsored retreats ($p<.05$) (Bailey & Leach, 1965); (6) serving drinks to others in one's own home ($p<.01$) (Bailey & Leach, 1965); (7) saying one would not drink even if it could be done safely ($p<.001$) (Bailey & Leach, 1965); (8) having been a sponsor ($p<.001$) (Bohince & Orensteen, 1950); (9) believing one cannot return to social drinking after being an alcoholic ($p<.01$) (Bohince & Orensteen, 1950); and (10) believing that a psychological factor was the main reason for one's drinking ($p<.05$) (Bohince & Orensteen, 1950). Characteristics found to relate negatively with successful membership are: (1) considering alcoholism as a character weakness ($p<.05$) (Bailey & Leach, 1965); (2) having taken barbiturates ($p<.001$), tranquilizers ($p<.01$), or Antabuse ($p<.001$) while in AA (Bailey & Leach, 1965); (3) receiving psychotherapy concurrent with AA ($p<.05$) (Bailey & Leach, 1965); (4) holding "family difficulty" responsible for one's drinking ($p<.05$) (Bohince & Orensteen, 1950); and (5) seeing oneself as restless (Ditman et al., 1967). In general, these findings seem to suggest that successful AA members, compared to failures, become more actively involved in the organization, adopt its beliefs more completely, and follow its behavioral guidelines more carefully.

AA's imperfect effectiveness is reflected in the number of alcoholics who drop out of AA early in the course of involvement. Edwards (1966) noted that 32.5% of 40 alcoholic inpatients were attending AA 1 month after discharge from the hospital, but only 12.5% of them were doing so 1 year after discharge. Bohince and Orensteen (1950) reported that 34.7% of the sample on which relevant data were available had failed to complete four indoctrination sessions and were thus considered rapid dropouts.

While imperfect, how does AA compare in effectiveness with professional treatment for alcoholism? This question will be addressed by comparing drinking outcome data for the two types of help.

Comparison of Drinking Outcome: AA versus Professional Treatment

A clear comparison of AA and professional treatment cannot be made, because there is no way of controlling many important variables between the two approaches—for example, length of help given, time of collecting outcome data, characteristics of the alcoholics receiving help, and characteristics of the therapeutic agents giving help. Nonetheless, there is a handful of data from the professional treatment literature which is similar enough to the AA data to make a comparison, albeit a coarse one. The professional treatment data are limited to those which evaluated patients who had had at least 1 year of treatment,[19] evaluated those patients while at least a majority of them were still in treatment, and collected data on drinking behavior throughout the course of treatment. These data were isolated from 265 outcome studies evaluating psychologically oriented alcoholism treatment (Emrick, 1973, 1974). They are summarized in Table 4. In comparison to these data, the four studies which contributed the best AA drinking outcome data (Bohince & Orensteen, 1950; Brown, 1963; C., 1965; Thorpe & Perret, 1959) evaluated members who had been in the program 1 or more years, evaluated them when at least a majority were still in the program, and collected data on drinking outcome throughout the course of their membership.

As can be seen in Table 4, abstinence behavior for professionally treated alcoholics was evaluated in five samples in four separate studies. During a mean of about 18 months of treatment, a mean of 22.3% of the patients (median = 20.8%, range = 18.5%–27.0%) were totally abstinent. This rate is noticeably lower than the 30% to 40% total abstinence rate for AA members. Since the evaluation period was longer for the AA members than for the patients (mean of $2\frac{1}{2}$ to more than 4 years versus a mean of about 18 months), this comparison is even more favorable to AA than the percentages alone would suggest. *Apparently, AA is more effective than professional treatment in helping alcoholics maintain total abstinence.*

Table 4 also shows that data on total improvement (i.e., drinking at least somewhat less or not at all during treatment) were reported in nine samples in eight separate studies. During a mean of about 29 months of treatment (median ≅ 18 months), a mean of 75.6% of the patients (median = 83.3%, range = 50.0%–100%) were improved in drinking. This total improvement rate is somewhat higher than the 60% to 68% total improvement rate found for AA members. The patients had less opportunity to return to pretreatment drinking levels, since they were evaluated for a shorter period of time than were the AA members (a median of about 18 months versus a median of 27 months for the three AA studies (Bohince & Orensteen, 1950; Brown, 1963; Thorpe & Perret, 1959) reporting total improvement data). Thus, the rate difference may not indicate greater effectiveness for pro-

TABLE 4. DRINKING OUTCOME DURING LONG-TERM (1 YEAR OR MORE) PROFESSIONAL TREATMENT FOR ALCOHOLISM.

Author	Date	Average therapy duration	Time of evaluation	N evaluated	Drinking outcome (in percent)	
					Abstinent[a]	Total improved[b]
Wexberg	1953	18.5 visits	17 months after intake and during treatment	519	—	64.5
Hoff & Forbes	1955	I. 7–10 days inpatient, at least 1 year after care	1½ years since intake and during after care	89	27.0	88.8
		II. Same as I	Same as I	84	20.2	83.3
Pfeffer & Berger	1957	26 months	Mean of 26 months after intake	60	—	91.7
Skála	1957	2–4 months inpatient, 1 year after care	1 year or more after inpatient discharge and during after care	1000	25.0	—
Smith	1958	(Not given)	1 year after inpatient discharge and during after care	24	—	50.0
Scott	1959	2 years	2 years after intake	13	—	84.6
Pattison	1965	15 months	At the end of 15 months	8[c]	—	100
Myerson & Mayer	1966	10 years	10 years after intake	87[d]	—	52.9
Ritson	1968 1969	Inpatient (not reported) plus 1 year after care for 60%	12 months after inpatient discharge	48	20.8	64.6
Wanberg	1968	2 weeks inpatient, 24–48 group therapy sessions in after care	2 years or more after intake and during after care	27	18.5	—

[a] Abstinence refers to absolutely no intake of alcohol throughout treatment.

[b] Total improved refers to all patients who were improved in drinking to any degree (from slight reduction in drinking to total abstinence) throughout treatment.

[c] The evaluation of one patient was not adequately reported so it was excluded.

[d] This figure excludes 13 institutionalized patients who could not be evaluated on drinking behavior.

fessional treatment in helping alcoholics drink less or not at all. Nevertheless, the difference certainly indicates that professional treatment is not less effective in this regard. Since professional treatment appears to be at least as effective in helping alcoholics drink less or not at all, yet is apparently less successful than AA in helping them become totally abstinent, the following tentative conclusion is drawn: *Professional treatment appears to be more effective than AA in helping alcoholics reduce drinking without becoming totally abstinent.*

Although AA *appears* to be more successful than professional treatment in helping alcoholics maintain total abstinence and less effective in helping them merely reduce drinking, it is important to keep in mind that characteristics of the alcoholics involved in making these comparisons were not controlled across the AA-professional treatment split. Alcoholics who choose to go to AA versus those selecting professional treatment probably have, on the whole, greater motivation to work toward the goal of total abstinence, which is AA's sole and unequivocal goal. Professionally treated alcoholics may seek professional treatment in the hope of receiving help to reduce rather than eliminate drinking completely. Hopefully, future research will measure and compare the goals of AA mem-

bers and professionally treated alcoholics and assess how these goals relate to both the selection of helping experience and ultimate outcome status.

The argument could be made that since AA appears to be more effective than professional treatment in promoting long-term abstinence, professionals should cease working with alcoholics. This position could be strengthened by pointing out that AA is much less expensive than professional treatment. There are no professionals to pay, and meetings are free (though most members make small voluntary contributions to their groups). Furthermore, AA is open-ended. Members can continue their involvement in AA indefinitely, with the result that early gains can be effectively maintained (Groves, 1972; Norris, 1974b; Trice, 1958).

With all these advantages to AA, why should professionals treat alcoholics? Our answer lies in the following assumption: Alcoholics who choose AA have certain notions about the kind of help they need and an expectation that AA will provide this kind of help. Alcoholics seeking professional treatment may have different ideas about the kind of help they need, along with expectations that professionals will give such help.

Given that AA may match the personality of

some alcoholics but not others, this organization should work with only certain individuals, while professionals should help others. Uniquely suited to psychotherapy appear to be those who are responsive to professionals, are strongly invested in introspection, view alcoholism as a psychological problem, wish to talk to at most a few people about their alcoholism, choose to keep their battle against alcoholism separate from social activities, and are committed to reducing drinking rather than to becoming totally abstinent. Most appropriate for AA seem to be those who are responsive to peers, drawn toward a spiritually oriented approach, comfortable talking about their alcoholism in front of large groups as well as with many others outside group meetings, and enjoy socializing with reformed alcoholics.[20]

As noted earlier, mixed intervention may or may not help, but it does not appear to be harmful. Appropriate for either approach or a combination thereof seem to be those who share the characteristics of the previous two groups and espouse the position that total abstinence is the desired alternative to problem drinking.

Evidence indicates that alcoholics play an active part in determining the kind of help they receive (see Pattison, Coe, & Doerr, 1973), but AA members and professionals should also do what they can to match alcoholics with the most suitable approach or combination of interventions. Hopefully, both helper types will collaborate in research to develop precise guidelines for such matching.[21]

OTHER SELF-HELP ORGANIZATIONS

This section deals more broadly with peer self-help groups than the preceding, detailed review of Alcoholics Anonymous. Three types of peer self-help groups are reviewed: drug users, former mental patients, and overweight persons. Residential drug treatment programs are given the most attention and more general research issues in the evaluation of addiction therapies are considered.

Synanon, Incorporated

Synanon is a peer self-help group that developed directly out of AA in 1958. There were two major reasons behind the emergence of this group from AA (Randall, 1973). One was a policy decision by AA to accept only alcoholics as members. The other had to do with the limited content of the meetings which formed the basis of the AA program. The early group had two rules: no drugs or alcohol, and no physical violence or threats of physical violence. More recently, rules prohibiting tobacco and requiring "aerobic exercises" of all members have been established (Synanon, 1974).

The current residential membership is about 1,350 men, women, and children (Synanon, 1974). Most residents are formerly active drug addicts and alcoholics (all generally considered as "character disorders"); but there are a considerable number, about 27% as of 1973, who have chosen to live at Synanon because of the style of life it offers.

The total community of Synanon needs to be considered for an adequate understanding of the therapeutic events that occur. Entry is made through a difficult process which requires considerable effort, and then outside contacts are not allowed for about 3 months. During this time, more than average comfort and support is provided, and the individual works at menial tasks. Through good work performance and increased ability at self-expression, a member may advance both in work positions and in residence positions (Patton, 1973).

Synanon members live and work in a mutually supportive communal-type arrangement (Holzinger, 1965). Dederich viewed Synanon as establishing a "climate consisting of a family structure similar in some areas to a primitive tribal structure" (Yablonsky, 1962, p. 51). Since this type of structure is hierarchical and autocratic, the participation in tasks as part of a group provides a new member with a very different experience as compared with the life he or she had formerly been living. This is highlighted by rules prohibiting street talk and requiring members to inform, "rat" or "fink," on each other. These type rules, the tribal structure, the strong norms and attitudes against drugs, and other features of Synanon (such as rewards for industry and honesty) establish an "anticriminal society" consistent with a "differential association" theory (Volkman, 1965; Volkman & Cressey, 1963; Yablonsky, 1962).

When an individual violates one of the above-mentioned rules or acts in some other "bad," unacceptable way, there are two primary forms of punishment. The most severe is ostracism. The individual is expelled from the community for some period of time. A lesser, though still severe form, is the "haircut." Yablonsky and Dederich (1965, p. 215) describe the haircut as "a severe, caustic verbal (public) attack on behavior considered atrocious at Synanon ... the 'offence' is caricatured, exaggerated and severely ridiculed." Other conflicts and disputes are dealt with in encounter groups known as "the game."

The "game" is used as therapy only for new character-disordered members. It is more generally used as a safety valve and form of government (Patton, 1973). Different lengths of time and types of activities are employed in constructing "games" (Nemec, 1974). All members are required to participate in at least one game per week and most average about 30 hours per month. Within the game, there is no formal hierarchy or organization. This equality within "the game" is considered to make possible communal living in the autocratic manner of Synanon (Dederich, 1973).

The goal of the game is the complete expression of a full range of emotions. The content of the game varies, but generally individuality and self-images are ripped apart and rebuilt in stronger form. Confession plays an important role as it does in therapy groups (Volkman & Cressey, 1963). The members see the game as a sport in which the individual fights for his own self-image and identity and in so doing becomes more flexible (Patton, 1973) and resilient (Walder, 1965). Membership varies from game to game so each member is dealt with in a given session.

Maslow (1967) described the "game" as "no crap therapy" in which the members experienced real intimacy, friendship, and respect. Some authors have felt that peers provide each other with more support in such confrontative situations than professionals would patients (Markoff, 1969; Walder, 1965). Maslow felt the major differences between the "game" and group psychotherapy was that in the "game" confrontation started earlier and that "truth" was dished out rather than waiting for the person to get to it. Two other differences between the game and psychotherapy are: (1) no contracts or agreements are explicitly or implicitly made or permitted between participants, and (2) "look good" insights are not rewarded (NIMH, 1969).

Lieberman, Yalom, and Miles (1973) have noted that the Synanon-type group had more deleterious effects than other types of encounter groups. In their study of eight types of encounter groups with college students, one type was an experience at Synanon. Two features distinguish these group events from the regular Synanon "game." The college students had no basis on which to be peers with the Synanon people and were not perceived or accepted as peers. Relatedly, the students were not a part of the larger Synanon community and did not receive its support. As a result, the students were isolated and attacked within the groups they attended.

There are two roles associated with the game that are pertinent to the focus of this volume. One is that of "synamaster." This person utilizes his knowledge of the problems of the group to select members for a "game" (Markoff, 1969). Members may ask to be included in a game to work with certain others. The other role, the "synanist," is directly involved in the game. In a game, the synanist emerges as a leader and then falls back as another person outdoes him (NIMH, 1969). Yablonsky (1962) noted that there are special qualifications to being a synanist: (1) a history of criminal experience with an intuitive knowledge of the problems of others, (2) conversion in Synanon with the view that crime and addiction are wasteful and stupid, and (3) knowledge of the Synanon system through at least 18 months of residence making him difficult to "con." An individual demonstrates these qualities by showing faster progress than his peers (Yablonsky & Dederich, 1965) and through a leadership training program (Benjamin, Freedman, & Lynton, 1966; Patton, 1973; Volkman, 1965). These roles are a differentiation of expertise within "the game" making it distinct from a totally leaderless group.

Peers may not lead each other to positive results, however. Instead, they may foster what we consider to be "dyssocial groups"—that is, a group that is so immersed and isolated in its own values and norms that it is not compatible with the larger society in which it exists. The high degree of conformity and discipline demanded of Synanon residents heightens this possibility. Mueller (1964) has questioned the possible overidentification of Synanon members with sociopathic leaders resulting in beliefs which are not representative of the larger culture. He also notes that the reward structure in Synanon is much more simplified than in the outside world.

Balancing these concerns are the espoused middle-class values of Synanon (Sabath, 1967), the norm to delay impulsive action (Markoff, 1969), and a high value placed on education (Patton, 1973). Also, there is a determined effort to separate the distorted norms and behavior of the game from the everyday life outside the game (Carter, 1973). A goal of Synanon is to create a new social role and career for ex-addicts (Yablonsky & Dederich, 1965). However, this new role and career does not necessarily mean moving outside the Synanon community (Carter, 1973; Casriel, 1963; Cherkas, 1965; Scott & Goldberg, 1973).

Research on Synanon has been hampered by the reluctance of the organization to engage in public evaluation (Casriel, 1963; Preble, 1965). Dederich has felt that even though outcome figures for Synanon would be an order of magnitude better than most other programs, they would still be disheartening and create a potentially negative, self-fulfilling prophecy for new members (Casriel, 1963). Existing data pertains to attendance, dropouts, and graduations but not to comparisons of program components or other variables as in more thorough studies of other programs to be reported later.

As in other residential programs, there is a high dropout rate (50%) within the first 6 months (Holzinger, 1965; Sagarin, 1969). Over time, there is an increasingly high rate of abstention from drugs and alcohol: 47.9% for those remaining 1 month, 66.4% after 3 months, and 86.2% after 7 months (Volkman & Cressey, 1963). Patton (1973) has more recently and more optimistically claimed a dropout rate of 25%. Casriel (1963) reported that 36% return and usually remain, a statistic that vitiates the high dropout rate. Dederich has estimated that 90% of the dropouts return to drugs, while he and others have claimed success rates of 90% for those who remain (Cherkas, 1965; Holzinger, 1965; Yablonsky & Dederich, 1965). Casriel (1963) has noted the cost effectiveness of Synanon by calculating it costs 5% to 10% the total social cost of an addict on the street to maintain one at Synanon.

Phoenix House

Phoenix House is an ongoing therapeutic community operated by the Addiction Services Agency of New York City since May of 1967. In 1973, there were nine Phoenix Houses with approximately 500 residents, most of whom were in their early 20s with a lengthy history of heroin addiction (DeLeon, 1974). Earlier in the program about 40% of the members had been committed by the courts to the New York State Narcotics Control Commission and placed in the program (Nash, Waldorf, Foster, & Kyllingstad, 1974). The program qualifies as a peer self-help group since paid staff are ex-addicts and many staff have risen up through the program itself (Rosenthal & Biase, 1969). However, the program was highly structured in the Synanon model by professional staff. This makes the program considerably different from an autonomous group.

After a preparatory period focusing on motivation and commitment, a new member joins a residential community modeled after Synanon with work groups and encounter groups. A major difference is that there are formal staff positions at Phoenix House. Important features of Synanon are included such as an attainable status system, discipline (Rosenthal & Biase, 1969), and acting as an agent of the system by enforcing rules (Lennard & Allen, 1974). There are a number of different types of encounter group events varying in size, length of meeting, and experience of members (Rosenthal, 1974). The group encounter is to facilitate the work in the residential community. Lastly, members are prepared for reentry with resocialization and vocational training.

Phoenix House has experienced a rise in the dropout rate from 9% in its first 12 months (Rosenthal, 1974) to 64% after 40 months of existence (Nash et al., 1974) and as high as 73% (Biase, 1974b). Nash et al. (1974) found that there was a consistent increase in dropouts over a 2-year follow up of 157 addicts in the program. Checking the program at 12-, 16- and 23-month intervals, they found dropout figures of 34%, 54%, and 64%, respectively. Of the "splittees," 31% left after they had reached the reentry stage having spent at least 18 months in the program. There were two variables clearly related to addicts remaining in the program: type of commitment (voluntary or involuntary) and age. Fifty-nine percent of the voluntary commitments remained in the program 18 months, while only 48% of the involuntary ones did so. Showing even more difference, 64% of those 21 years of age and older remained 18 months while only 40% of those under 21 did so.

Assertions that stress inherent in the program might be the cause of some dropouts found support in a study by DeLeon, Skodol, and Rosenthal (1973). Of 203 residents tested on five personality and emotionality measures, those who dropped out within 6 months (about 58%) had higher psychopathology scores ($p < .05$) on all measures than nondropouts, suggesting that the more disturbed residents leave. DeLeon, Rosenthal, and Brodney (1971) found comparable results on retrospective staff ratings of dropouts and remaining residents. Biase (1974a) found similar results with a sample of adolescents. Of the 37 in his sample, the 59.5% who dropped out within 6 months had significantly higher depression scores ($p < .05$), but there were no differences on anxiety or hostility measures.

There was also some evidence that even dropouts benefited from time in the program. DeLeon, Holland, and Rosenthal (1972) sampled 358 residents of whom 254 (70.9%) dropped out before 18 months in the program. There was a 63% decrease in the arrest rate of the dropout group from before treatment to after treatment. While nonvoluntary residents who dropped out showed a larger decrease in arrest rate after treatment (about 41.6%) than voluntary residents (about 6%), there was still a general decrease in arrest rate depending upon time in the program (less than 3 months = 6.7%; 3 to 11 months ≡ 40% to 50%; 12 or more months ≡ 70%).

Outcome data, aside from the high dropout rates, have been encouraging for the Phoenix House program. Nash et al. (1974) reported that 22% of their selected sample successfully completed the program and another 14% remained in the program after 23 months. Of the graduates, 94.3% did not relapse into addiction within 12 months, and 48.6% were employed on Phoenix House staffs. Addicts remaining in the program for more than 22 months showed a decrease of more than 90% in arrest rate (DeLeon et al., 1972).

Biase (1974b) reported considerable success in drug abstention by residents in the program. Of 2,874 urine specimens, only 4% were positive while less than 1% of these were positive for opiates and most were positive for barbiturates (59.1%). In a random sample of 173 addicts, Biase found a considerably higher success rate than reported by Nash et al. (1974). Forty-four percent achieved reentry phase or graduated. Of those who did not achieve, there were several significant characteristics: more were involuntary commitments, more had past use of opiates other than heroin and past use of stimulants, and more had left the program at least once, usually in the first 12 months of treatment.

Studies of personality and emotionality variables also indicated benefits derived from the program. DeLeon et al. (1973) found that while residents at Phoenix House initially resembled psychiatric patients on psychopathology scores, there was a significant drop ($p < .05$ or better) on all five measures of psychopathology employed after 7½ months in the program. Those results were consistent with the findings of Biase and DeLeon (1969). They found that there was no difference on emotionality scores as a result of either free activity or work activity, but there

was a significant decrease on anxiety, depression, and hostility after encounter group activity. The importance of this study rests not only on these findings but also in the attempt to determine the effects of separate program components.

Daytop Village, Incorporated

Another professionally initiated program is Daytop Village, an acronym for "Drug Addicts Treated on Probation." This program began in 1963 through an NIMH grant to the Brooklyn-Staten Island Second Judicial District of the State Supreme Court of New York. It was consciously modeled on Synanon and located in a suburban setting away from the high level of drug-related activities in the core city (Shelly & Bassin, 1965). In 1965, Daytop Village acquired the status of a nonprofit, nonsectarian, tax-exempt membership corporation with its own board of directors. By 1970, three residential facilities housed 409 men and women.

Theoretically, the program has been open to any nonschizophrenic resident of New York State. Most admissions (51%) have been from the neighborhood facilities of the Special Project Against Narcotics (SPAN) Centers of New York City (Glasscote, Sussex, Jaffe, Ball & Brill, 1972). An estimated 25% to 33% were under some legal pressure to enter as a condition of probation or parole. About 18% of new entries in 1970 were processed directly into the residences. Glasscote et al. (1972) reported residents to be younger, of higher socioeconomic status, and more often white than baseline data from the New York City Narcotics Registry. This racial imbalance was of particular concern to the authors and to the program (Collier, 1972; Glasscote et al., 1972). Of those 16 to 30 years of age, 82% were heroin users or users of mixed drugs.

Daytop considers "encounter" groups as its basic therapeutic tool. Indeed, all therapy is in group settings (Glasscote et al., 1972). The encounter group is heterogeneous by age, sex, and length of treatment. A facilitator does have the tasks of overseeing the group meeting, seeing that each member participates, and interpreting individual or group behavior. These functions are made legitimate through an explicit role. This type of leadership is distinct from the type of leadership found in Synanon groups. The encounter groups have a here-and-now orientation and deal with interactions between members as well as individual problems. Though oriented toward life in the residences, the group may deal with an individual's history of frustrations, hostilities, and so forth. To the present authors, of all the peer self-help groups examined in this review, *these groups seem to most closely resemble professional group psychotherapy sessions.* Other, specialized types of group events are used to focus on particular issues.

Shelly (1966) reported an early evaluation study of the program after 15 months of operation. At that time, all admissions were on probation from the court. Of the 64 men in the study, only eight (12.5%) had dropped out. Six (9.4%) had reached the third stage and were working in the community. Of the rest, 31 (48.4%) were still in the program, while 12 (18.8%) had been returned to the courts and five (7.8%) had been expelled. Compared to a selected control group of addicts on probation, Daytop had fewer people who had not absconded or violated probation (57.8% versus 38.1%, $p < .05$). The two groups did not differ significantly on urine tests, although none of the 809 urine samples for the Daytop group were positive and 5% of the 664 tests on the control group were positive.

A subsequent evaluation by Glasscote et al. (1972) yielded results more consistent with other studies of residential programs. These researchers found that 70% of those who apply at SPAN centers drop out before gaining admission to Daytop. Based on a 1969–1970 sample, a considerable majority (about 80%) of those who do gain admission were thought to drop out in less than 6 months and another 8% drop out after that time.

There is confusion about the number of individuals who reached graduate status. This was due to the Daytop program considering dropouts who remained drug free as graduates. There were 25 in this category while 110 had formally completed the program (the status of two graduates was not reported). Assuming 1,000 admissions, an estimate of successful program completion is about 11% to 13%. Of these "graduates," 10.9% relapsed and 23.4% held regular jobs. The majority of graduates (61.7%) were either working on the Daytop staff or on some other drug program staff (see Scott & Goldberg, 1973). The Daytop program responded to the Glasscote et al. (1972) study with some conflicting data (Collier, 1972). The response reported that there had been 250 graduates by the end of 1971 and that the dropout rate was 50%. Of the dropouts, half were considered to remain drug free, yielding a total "success" rate of 75%. The research team of

Glasscote et al. (1972) questioned these data since they were based upon a sample of 57% of the graduates and 29% of the dropouts. They also questioned the lack of verification of the self-report survey procedures used in the Daytop evaluation.

Recovery, Incorporated

In the field of mental health, an example of a peer self-help group is Recovery, Inc.: The Association of Nervous and Former Mental Patients. This group emerged from psychiatric medicine in 1937 through the efforts of the late Abraham Low, MD. The goal of Recovery (1973, p. 3) is "to prevent relapses in former mental patients and chronicity in nervous patients" which it does through supportive and reeducational activities (Grosz, 1973). In the United States, Canada, and Puerto Rico there are approximately 13,200 members in 1,020 groups. Membership in the organization is voluntary and open to anyone with a present mental disorder or a history of one, and there are nominal dues and charges for materials. There is a board of directors, and a national headquarters provides the support materials and specialized training for group leaders. All Recovery directors, staff, and leaders are patients or former patients. There are no professionals involved, though anyone is welcome to observe a Recovery meeting.

Recovery is considered as an adjunct to treatment as it was initially conceived by Low (1945). He conceptualized an early, behavioristic approach which emphasized cognitive control— i.e., "willpower." Important to his considerations was the resistance physicians encountered, and still do, in trying to "sell the idea of mental health" (Low, 1945, p. 333). Low felt that colleagues or peers could more easily get around this sales resistance and be more convincing to the patient. One of the principal benefits which Recovery is considered to provide is to help the patient be more amenable to accepting the treatment and authority of the physician (Low, 1949). Low developed a systematic method which ignored etiology, diagnosis, and classification while emphasizing self-help in "spotting" and working through problems. A major technique used was a structured group meeting which is still basic to the Recovery method. The Recovery group meetings are informal but are conducted in a prescribed manner by a specially trained group leader who is a patient or former patient.

Two other techniques used are the assignment

of a veteran member to pair up with a new member and the use of telephone calls for mutual aid. The former technique parallels the "sponsor-baby" relationship of Alcoholics Anonymous. The latter technique requires that the phone calls should be focused on the member gaining control, willpower, over his problem, not on discussing it and that the call should not last more than 5 minutes (Carner, 1968), though other calls may be made later in the day.

Recovery seeks to instill hope through a "well-role" model. Since the basic organization is along didactic lines (Wechsler, 1960), the "imparting of information" is one of the primary curative factors at work (Yalom, 1975). Other curative factors that Yalom considers present are "the installation of hope" through testimonials, "universality," "altruism," and some aspects of "cohesiveness." While not mentioning authority as a curative factor, Yalom does consider that both AA and Recovery derive strength from the heavily ritualized tradition in which authority is embedded. Confession or catharsis, referring to a person's acceptance of a stated problem and his/her submission to the Recovery method, is also important (Carner, 1968).

Leaders at group meetings are provided "specialized training" and supervision (Lee, 1971; Shoichet, 1968). The leader clearly sets the agenda, keeps order, and provides interpretations within the Recovery method. Wechsler (1960) considered these leaders to be role models not only in their knowledge of Recovery techniques but also in their social behavior and general level of health. Sagarin (1969) disputed this view and felt ex-patient leaders were deeply distressed and were less than satisfactory role models. The issue of emergent leadership is a particularly apt one in the study of peer groups. It is our view that peer group leaders may perform their roles well and be good models of the work to be done in the group while not necessarily being optimum models of mental health. Since these groups are considered effective (Dean, 1969a; Grosz, 1973), the issues of leadership and role models point to the diversity and flexibility that occur in peer self-help groups. No outcome data were presented in this study.

Only two of the studies reviewed presented data gathered from actual Recovery groups. Wechsler (1960) did not fully report his questionnaire data but did provide some basis of comparison with a more recent study by Grosz (1973). Both surveys were conducted in cooperation with the headquarters of Recovery and local organizations. The most striking difference

was the return rate of questionnaires in the two samples. Clearly, the Grosz study had more support from the organization. Despite this major difference and other probable methodological and procedural differences, the data seem comparable. A large majority of members attend meetings on a weekly basis, and the length of attendance seems to be distributed evenly about 1 year. Approximately half the membership had no prior hospitalization. About a third of the membership reported that they no longer felt they needed to attend meetings in order to function adequately. When research efforts are independent, both in terms of researchers and time of data collection, some confidence may be placed in the results—especially when they are so consistent. The consistency is amazing when one considers that the total size of the organization more than tripled in the decade between studies.

One limitation in both surveys was that only active members were surveyed. It is important to note that dropout data are not available for Recovery groups. Grosz did report that 32% of the members surveyed had dropped out at some time and returned. Even though Recovery is designed as an adjunctive program to therapy, there was no attempt to separate the effects of a Recovery program after professional treatment (68% of sample) or the effects of the program with ongoing professional treatment (60% of sample) nor to employ control conditions with pre- and post-measurement or comparison groups.

There is some concurrence between the membership survey results (Grosz, 1973) and hospital program results (Lee, 1971). Both reported a higher percentage of women (73.0% and 61.4%, respectively) and a high, though not comparable, educational level (high school graduates of 83.0% and 35.2%, respectively). While Lee may have had an intentional group size bias, 76% of the groups studied by Grosz had between six and 20 members, a size which is comparable to the average of 11.6 reported by Lee.

Grosz (1973) has presented data that point to the success of the Recovery program. Before attending Recovery, 52% of the members had experienced one or more hospitalizations, while only 12% were hospitalized after attending. This difference is statistically significant ($p < .001$). Prior to attending a Recovery group, 70% of the members received treatment; after attending, 58% received treatment. *While attendance at Recovery did reduce subsequent hospitalization, it did not significantly reduce treatment for a nervous or mental condition.*[22]

Wechsler (1960) also pointed to several substantive issues in the Recovery program. The program is rigidly based on Low's (1950) work, and its quasi-religious nature may be too inspirational in its presentation. There is no selection of either members or leaders in Recovery groups. Nor are there mechanisms of control of either the content of meetings or deviant behavior though, as noted earlier, there is a strong tradition of authority (Yalom, 1975). Linkage with other aftercare service is up to the individual patient; no organizational procedures do it. The members may be reinforced too much for identifying themselves as "patients" and maintaining the "nervous patient role" (as evidenced from Grosz's, 1973, data as well). Finally, the members are indefinitely kept in a member role since there is no graduation procedure.

TOPS Club, Incorporated

One of the more thoroughly studied peer self-help groups in terms of outcome-effectiveness is TOPS Club (Take Off Pounds Sensibly, Inc., 1974). The organization was founded in 1948, and by 1974 there were more than 32,000 members in some 12,000 chapters throughout the United States and Canada. Membership in the organization is voluntary, and there are annual dues. A national headquarters provides support to the local chapters which are autonomous with their own elected leaders and processes. The TOPS membership is almost all (99%) female with an average age of 42 years and 58% above ideal weight upon joining.

The TOPS program consists of five facets: (1) "medical orientation," (2) "group therapy," (3) "competition," (4) "recognition," and (5) "obesity research" (TOPS, 1974). The medical orientation refers to the requirement that each member consult a physician for weight goals and dietary plan. In this regard, Wagonfeld and Wolowitz (1968) noted that only 3% of the TOPS membership whom they studied were referred to the program by physicians. Similarly, TOPS considers control of emotional factors in obesity to be its major target through the establishment of peer groups, but less than 1% of the membership had consulted mental health resources prior to joining. "Group therapy" refers to the regular meetings and continued contact between members. The central part of each meeting is the weigh-in of all members followed by reactions of the membership to the gain or loss of each person. This portion of the program will receive special discussion later in this section. Other

parts of the meeting are given to speakers and social events such as singalongs or skits related to weight control. Modeled along the lines of AA, the membership maintains contact between meetings through a "buddy system" to provide each other with support. The "competition" and "recognition" facets are closely linked. Both are based on weight loss.

The therapeutic mechanisms at work within TOPS appear to be somewhat different than in other peer self-help groups due to the competitive atmosphere. Following Yalom (1975), "group cohesiveness" with strong social pressure on individual performance appears to be a primary factor. In support of this, "universality," "imparting of information," and "imitative behavior" also occur. The preponderance of middle-aged women in TOPS also indicates a self-selection factor. Wagonfeld and Wolowitz (1968, p. 25) concluded that "after preselection and initial dropout, a group remains which finds TOPS of benefit in maintaining weight loss."

Review of eight medical treatment programs for obesity by Stunkard and McLaren-Hume (1959) indicated that of the 1,368 patients, about 381 (27.8%) had a weight loss of at least 20 pounds and about 109 (7.9%) had a weight loss of 40 or more pounds. Medical management of obesity through a hospital nutrition clinic demonstrated even less success. These data were more complete indicating that of the 100 patients, 97% were women, the median age was 45, and the median percent of excess weight was 44. Of these patients, 12% lost more than 20 pounds, while only one patient lost more than 40. In addition, there was a 39% dropout rate after the first visit to the Nutrition Clinic.

Subsequently, Stunkard, Levine, and Fox (1970) studied a sample of 22 TOPS chapters with 485 members. Despite wide variability between chapters (weight loss of more than 20 pounds by 62% of the most successful chapter and by 10% of the least successful chapter), they found that an average of 28% lost more than 20 pounds and an average of 7.8% lost more than 40 pounds. This compared favorably with the best reports of medical obesity specialists and was superior to the routine, hospital treatment The *nonprofessional self-help groups did as well as professional specialists and better than routine treatment.*

A follow-up study on the same sample after 2 years indicated a striking consistency in the effectiveness of the program over time despite high (72%) turnover (Garb & Stunkard, 1974). Only .2% fewer TOPS members in 1970 had a weight loss of 20 pounds than had the loss in 1968 and that 1.2% fewer had a loss of 40 pounds. The mean weight loss was significantly lower ($p < .01$) for members who dropped out (10.6 pounds) than those who remained ($\bar{x} = 20.0$ pounds).

An interesting and important turn in the research on TOPS groups occurred with the introduction of behavior therapy techniques such as having positive expectations, providing factual information, and review of behavior. Wollersheim (1970) performed an experiment on mildly overweight college females in which one condition simulated the social pressure found in TOPS groups while others experienced behavioral treatment primarily through identifying and shaping the eating behavior, nonspecific treatment, or no treatment. The behavioral treatment condition yielded the greatest weight loss ($p < .05$); the social pressure and nonspecific treatment yielded equivalent weight loss; and subjects in the control condition gained weight. These differences were maintained through a 9-month follow up. Two major limitations of this study were that all experimenters were advocates of psychotherapy based on learning principles and the social pressure condition did not provide the full program represented by actual TOPS groups.

Hall (1972) randomly assigned 14 TOPS members to either a self-control (SC) or an experimenter control (EC) condition for 5 weeks and then reversed treatment condition for another 5 weeks. By examination of the median percentage, weight change before and during treatments revealed that both treatments improved weight loss beyond the baseline during attendance at TOPS groups. Furthermore, while EC was superior to SC initially, when the SC group went onto the EC condition they surpassed the group that was initially on EC and went onto SC treatment. Jordan and Levitz (1973) obtained similar results.

This last study raised interesting possibilities because it indicated that effectiveness of self-help peer groups could be enhanced without the full-time involvement of professional personnel. Levitz and Stunkard (1974) reported an experiment which tested the relative effectiveness of different treatment conditions. They established four different treatment conditions: behavior modification such as recording of eating behavior, replacement of eating with other behavior, reward systems, and changing the act of eating by (1) a trained professional, (2) by a TOPS leader trained in the techniques, (3) nonspecific training in nutrition by TOPS leader provided with the necessary knowledge, and (4) a control treatment of only the regular TOPS program. The 234 TOPS members participated as a member of one of the four TOPS chapters. The experimental treatments took place in the context of the regular meetings. Subjects were closely matched on age ($\bar{x} = 45$ years), previous weight loss ($\bar{x} = 11$ pounds), length of membership ($\bar{x} = 3$ years), and all were female. During the 12-week treatment period, there was little difference between conditions on dropout rates. By the end of the 12-month follow-up, there was a significant difference ($x^2 = 12.35$, $p < .01$) between the attrition rates from the behavior modification treatment groups (38% and 41%) and the other treatment conditions (55% and 67%). The mean weight loss for chapters in which behavior modification techniques were introduced by a professional (-4.2 pounds) was significantly more ($p < .05$) than in the chapter with behavior modification introduced by the regular leader (-1.9 pounds), and significantly more ($p < .001$) than either the chapters with nonspecific, nutrition training ($+0.2$ pounds), or the regular TOPS group ($+0.7$ pounds). Both groups in behavior modification conditions maintained their weight loss throughout a subsequent 9-month follow-up. Unfortunately, a major confounding variable was that the professionals were all male while all other participants in the study were female. The enhancement of peer group effectiveness by professional techniques, whether implemented by professionals or not, remains as a strong finding of this study.

CONSCIOUSNESS-RAISING GROUPS

In recent years another form of self-help group has evolved, known as "consciousness-raising" (CR), "rap," or liberation groups. This form of group structure originated out of the personal and political needs of minority groups. There are now women's CR groups, Gray Panther's groups, Gay Lib groups and Mental Patients' Liberation groups, all of which can be defined as "minority" groups on the basis of social and/ or economic disadvantage. The prototype for all these groups is the women's groups, and this review will confine itself to a discussion of women's CR groups.

CR groups were developed about 1967 by the radical feminist branch of the Women's Movement, in response to the discrimination women experienced, even in civil rights and leftist political organizations (Freeman, 1973; Hole &

Levine, 1971; Morgan, 1970). The philosophy of CR had its roots in the black movement of the 1960s (Hall, Cross & Freedle, 1972; Sherif & Sherif, 1970; Thomas, 1971). Black awareness, black identity, promoting an awareness of the destructive effects of a racist society, and creating one's own definition apart from white society and white values were an integral part of that movement (Caplan, 1970; Dizard, 1970; Thomas, 1971).

The women's liberation movement adopted a portion of that philosophy, but, in addition, institutionalized the process of consciousness-raising in a group movement (Freeman, 1973; Hole & Levine, 1971). Casual observation would suggest that currently there are many women in CR groups who would not particularly identify themselves as feminists, but who join such groups out of a need to combat their social and psychological isolation as women, no matter what their political philosophy may be.

The theory of consciousness raising has a unique emphasis in the annals of psychological theorizing about groups that function for purposes of change. Virtually all writers agree that the function of CR is neither purely personal nor purely political. It is both; it is a medium for personal change and for the concerted effort to change a sexist society (Allen, 1970; Hanisch, 1971; Kirsh, 1974; Pogrebin, 1973). The slogan "The Personal is Political" (Hanisch, 1971) is the metaphor for the CR experience and purpose: that every personal struggle, experience, and problem corresponds with the experiences and problems of other women, and, therefore, that women's problems and their solutions involve the total political and economic society and its change. This review is focused on the potential of such groups for promoting *personal change*, but one cannot understand the function, structure, and mechanisms for change in such groups unless one keeps clearly in mind that the *raison d'etre* for establishing such groups was and remains political change (Allen, 1970; Hanisch, 1971; Hole & Levine, 1971).

Structure and Process

The best experiential description of a CR group is probably by Pogrebin (1973). Guidelines for groups are available from women's movement organizations and in print (*Guide to Consciousness-raising*, 1972).

The typical group ranges in size from six to 15 members. Typically, a group meets once a week at members' homes. One experienced CR member may help to get a group started, and then drop out. No one is designated leader, but typically, as in other groups, leaders emerge within the group. Each meeting usually involves discussion of a topic which is of personal and feminine interest to the members. Examples include discrimination, guilt, relationships with women, body image, work, and sex.

Each group develops its own groundrules such as confidentiality, honesty, regular and punctual attendance, not interrupting, and not monopolizing the conversation. In addition many groups require the step of generalizing from personal experiences to the position of women as a group (Guide, 1972). Many of the groundrules (but not the last) will be recognized as comparable to those in group psychotherapy or T groups (Lieberman *et al.*, 1973; Yalom, 1975).

Allen (1970) has described four developmental stages in CR groups: *opening up, sharing, analyzing*, and *abstracting*. The direction is from the individual and personal to the general and the ideological. *Opening up* involves each woman's attempt to communicate her own feelings to others. *Sharing* occurs when women understand that many of their experiences are not so unique, but that they are common to the women in this group and, by implication, to women in this society. *Analyzing* involves the evaluation of women's oppression and how that oppression can be changed. *Abstracting* is the process of theorizing and of setting priorities for social action. Thus, the progression is (1) ventilation of feelings and communication with others, (2) understanding issues, (3) conceptualization of the problem, and (4) its solution in social terms. The first two of these processes seem quite similar to group therapy and encounter processes, the last two are more sociological and political in emphasis.

An Alternative to Psychotherapy

CR is often proposed as an alternative to traditional modes of therapy. Four distinctions between the two processes are frequently raised in the CR literature, which have implications for outcome, for therapeutic process, and for analysis of change mechanisms:

The therapist versus peer influencer. Strupp (1973) describes therapy as a *learning process* and *an influencing process* which is under the planned direction of a therapist. It is safe to assume that consciousness raising also involves a learning process and an influencing process, but there is a key difference in the role of the professional therapist versus the role of the nonprofessional peer (Mander & Rush, 1974). Roles are defined by function and by expectation. The professional therapist is presumably a behavioral expert, with training and credentials to qualify him or her as an authority. The peer has only the expertise of personal experience to draw upon.

Patient versus group member. Women generally do not go into CR groups defining themselves as "sick" or needing to be "cured" (Hanisch, 1971).[23] Furthermore, that distinction separates CR groups from other peer self-help groups; other groups are designed to meet the needs of those with a specific diagnostic or problem label (e.g., alcoholics, drug abusers). Problems of loneliness, powerlessness, and alienation may lead individuals to join a CR group, but such people apparently define their needs somewhat differently from those who seek the help of a professional therapist.

Goals of change. The direction of change in women's groups is clearly spelled out—it involves competence, assertiveness, autonomy, and positive self-image which does not depend on the approval of the culture (Cherniss, 1972; Kirsh, 1974). By contrast, traditional psychotherapy, and particularly psychoanalytic personality theory, has been bitterly criticized for espousing a conception of women as inherently dependent, docile, nurturing, receptive, altruistic, and self-sacrificing (Chesler, 1971; Gilman, 1971; Koedt, 1970; Weisstein, 1970). Thus, the practice of psychotherapy has been criticized for typically reinforcing the traditional model of womanhood. And the evidence does tend to support the critics' charges that many therapists choose a direction and a therapeutic goal that is antithetical to feminine autonomy. Broverman, Broverman, Clarkson, Rosenkrantz, and Vogel (1970) documented stereotypic differences in clinicians' ideals of mental health for males and for females. The therapeutic consequences implied by that study are that many clinicians are inclined to support less aggressiveness and competence in women than in men, and/or that they actually may encourage passivity and acceptance of women's stereotypic roles in society. (See also, APA, 1975.)

The relationship paradigm. This issue is frequently paired with the preceding goals of change. The process of psychotherapy is criticized for being based on a male-dominated structure, an hierarchical relationship between patient and therapist, which essentially repeats the dominance/submission model in society (Chesler, 1971; Kirsh, 1974; Mander & Rush, 1974). By contrast, CR is described as being based on a relationship among equals which gives validity to the perceptions and experiences of women (Kirsh, 1974). This therapeutic process difference would hold even if the therapist were consciously working toward goals of equality, competence, and autonomy for his client.

Thus, women entering CR groups are probably seeking change but not cure. Their goals are presumably clear and unidirectional, and counter to society's traditional norms for women. For the purpose of fulfilling those goals, they have chosen a group process which is egalitarian and formally leaderless rather than the one-to-one assistance of a professional authority.

Outcome Issues and Suggestive Data

Klein (1976) questions whether traditional therapy outcome criteria are valid for measuring the outcome of feminist interventions, CR or otherwise. She argues that (1) symptom scales frequently used to measure therapy outcome may misinterpret the changes in CR members. Boredom, anxiety, and depression may be positive changes when a bad life situation is recognized and *not* adjusted to. These mood states may then lead to more assertiveness and anger, but ultimately to more satisfaction. Furthermore, (2) target complaint alleviation may be less crucial than *how* complaints are alleviated—i.e., through an autonomous decision or through passive acceptance of a bad situation. (3) Role performance measures often reflect entrenched sex-role stereotypes (e.g., "How well is he doing on his job"; or "How well is she doing as a homemaker and mother?"). *Flexibility* of chosen role is an important feminist outcome consideration. (4) Self-esteem measures are often compared to an ideal standard, but ideal standards often reflect sexist stereotypes. A feminist approach is more likely to attempt to redefine the original oppressive ideal than to work to meet that ideal. In addition, women typically look to men as the source of their value and self-esteem. CR may result in a shift in the source of self-valuing from external to internal, a shift that is likely to be missed with current outcome measurement technology. (5) Interpersonal relationships may change in a direction that appears to be deterioration by traditional standards. The empathic, maternal, and giving woman may become more assertive and aggressive as she attempts to meet her own needs more directly. And her family relationships may become turbulent as she changes lifestyle. Evaluators might tabulate this as a negative outcome; feminists would disagree. (6) Two typical omissions in outcome criteria that Klein would include for CR are changes in body image and increase in political activity.

In summary, the purpose of CR is to seek goals and accomplishments often not encouraged *or measured* by society-bound standards, and therefore comparisons with other forms of cognitive and behavioral change may not be appropriate. Outcome measures should be determined by goals of change, and the goals of change in CR and traditional psychotherapy may differ.

There are no published reports of research exploring psychological change in women as a result of participating in consciousness-raising groups. There are a small number of published reports on comparisons between Women's Liberation members and nonmembers. However, these differences can be attributed to (1) self-selection and/or (2) the influence of CR groups and (3) movement participation. Joesting (1971) reported that Women's Liberation members were significantly higher in risk-taking, originality, and creativity than nonmember comparisons. In an interview study, Cherniss (1972) found that Women's Liberation (WL) members valued autonomy and self-control, freedom, and independence; they lived a life of action, assertiveness, and achievement; they were higher in self-esteem, sense of "specialness," and sometimes had a dramatic flair. Comparison women saw the role of wife and mother as central to their lives and commitment; WL women did not. Cherniss reports that as a result of consciousness-raising, WL participants acquired a new perspective and ideology with which to redefine their world and their experiences. WLs often experienced more stress in their marriages, and spouses as well as participants often changed in assignment of domestic responsibilities. This tends to support Klein's (1976) point regarding outcome assessment.

Diane Kravetz, at the University of Wisconsin, and Morton Lieberman, at the University of Chicago, are currently conducting the most extensive study of CR participation. Utilizing a questionnaire which has been distributed to CR groups nationwide, they are exploring individual background data, reasons for joining CR groups, symptoms, expectations of the group, group structure and standards, and factors which led to goal realization. They hope to compare outcome for women going into traditional therapy groups, feminist therapy groups, and CR groups. Kravetz (1974) hypothesizes that women who go through CR groups, by comparison with those

in traditional groups, will (1) feel more of a sense of equality in interpersonal relationships, (2) claim a personal identity which is independent of their value to men and children, (3) be more trusting of other women, and (4) have a clearer view of social, political, and economic factors that affect their lives.

In an initial report of that work and some other data, Lieberman (1975) compares people who go into sensitivity groups, human potential groups, women's CR groups, and traditional outpatient clinics. *All groups* were higher than the normative population on current stress and symptoms. Of the clinic population, 98% acknowledged seeking help for problems, in contrast with growth center participants (70%), sensitivity training group members (54%), and women's groups (56%). Thus, about half of the women in CR groups were looking for help in alleviating problems and stressful life situations, leaving a sizable proportion that had other motivations for joining. Glaser (1974) reports a possibly related finding: half of the women in their feminist self-help groups also were in other forms of therapy *concurrently*.

Lieberman also finds a major difference among the groups in their *expectation of how change takes place*, even if their goals are similar. Women in CR groups looked primarily for support, not for confrontation or pain.

Possible Change Mechanisms and a Suggested Model

Given a considerable absence of data, what can one conjecture about the efficacy and impact for personal change that CR groups offer? When one considers the current well-known change methodologies, CR seems to be most similar to sensitivity training (or encounter) groups in form, process, and, perhaps, outcome. CR groups, like T groups, can be described as "something more intensive than education, and less reparative and distress relieving than therapy" (Lieberman *et al.*, 1973, p. 211). Both are based on a small-group model, neither is billed as psychotherapy, both are based on humanistic philosophy, and both have *some* similar goals— for example, the growth of human potential. There are also some obvious differences. CR groups are formally leaderless, as compared to the presence of trained leaders in the typical T group. All participants in women's CR groups are of a single sex, and that should make a significant difference in process and in outcome. The expectations of CR members differ from those going into sensitivity groups (Lieberman, 1975).

Nevertheless, the research on encounter groups (Lieberman *et al.*, 1973) probably offers the best analogy to pertinent aspects of CR groups. Some of the conclusions from that study *may* apply to CR groups.

For instance, most T groups provided experiences of openness, closeness, belonging, an opportunity to discover how others perceive one, opportunity for emotional expression, and a trusting atmosphere. Similar experiences develop in CR groups.

Participants in encounter groups considered *feedback, universality,* and *expression of feelings* to be the most important mechanisms of learning within the groups. The literature on CR groups inevitably cites the same dimensions.

In the encounter study, the second most effective groups in positive outcome gain scores were the tape groups—groups run by directions from a recorded tape. One parallel between tape groups and CR groups is that both groups provide specified groundrules or norms and suggestions for exercises and procedures. In both instances the group can use or not use the suggested procedures, but they have a framework to draw from, to modify or reject outright. Neither group has a designated leader, and so leadership emerges within the group. But Lieberman *et al.* (1973) found that the norms established by the groups seemed to predict outcome about as well as leadership style. And groups with more norms and greater peer control tended to have higher outcome yield. Many typical T-group norms also apply to CR, like asking for feedback and giving an honest opinion about another member.

Another very likely parallel is that the major changes which occurred in T groups were in *values, attitudes,* and *self-perception.* Those are exactly the changes cited in the women's literature (Kirsh, 1974).

Finally, in T groups the greatest change occurred in those who achieved new insights. Even self-disclosure was useful only if it was followed by new *cognitive learning.* Assuming a CR group developed according to Allen's (1970) four stages of process, *opening up* represents emotional expression and self-disclosure, *sharing* represents universality, and *analyzing and abstracting* represent a cognitive framework for understanding the experiences and dilemmas of women in this society. The question stands, however, whether conceptualizing about the class, women, provides a framework for *individuals* to gain insights about themselves and to make changes. Cherniss (1972) describes the two processes as correlated.

CR groups can be assumed to be strong in such values as support, sharing, intimacy, cohesiveness, female models, the opportunity for self and other awareness, and rethinking of feminine values. In addition they offer encouragement in the development of self-confidence and skills, in circumstances which are relatively isolated from and unthreatened by society (Allen, 1970; Pogrebin, 1973). Lieberman *et al.* (1973) comment that encounter groups create a culture of their own, separated from the surrounding society, often with their own "counternorms." But ultimately one may internalize those norms and carry them back to the real world. Thus, one could hypothesize that CR may be most useful to the woman who needs some *temporary protection* to express herself, to ventilate anger without punishment, and to discover that she has personal value and ability. The next step is one of generalization to the outside society. This probably requires assertion, the trying-out of new skills, and the gaining of competence. All of that cannot be done in the group. The real step comes *in vivo.* In T groups, too, the investigators found that maintenance of positive change required new strategies on the part of the individual in the real world after the group had terminated. In the case of CR that means strategies to deal with the world of both sexes. Unlike some other peer groups (Synanon, AA), CR groups are not designed to provide a life-long therapeutic environment. They are truly *transitional,* with the intent of inducing enough change in individuals to combat and change the external society.

Our review suggests the outlines of a model for understanding the impact of a CR group (see Fig. 1). We offer this paradigm for its heuristic possibilities, but we would expect that any important data would modify this model.

At step one, an individual has certain *expectations* regarding the helping process. Our assumption is that there is more than one process of influence and personal change, that seeking help from a recognized authority is one such route and seeking help from an equal who has had similar personal experience is another. The peer and the expert each has a different brand of therapeutic credibility, and the least common denominator may be client expectation of what the *process* and the *helping person* will be like (Garfield, 1971; Lieberman, 1975). This would have implications for authority versus

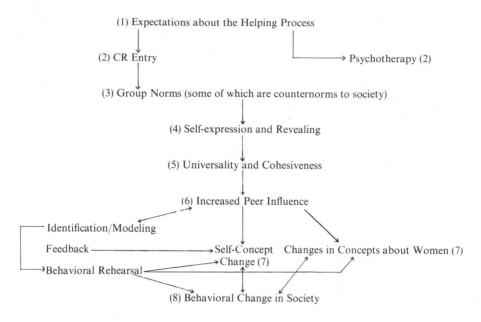

Fig. 1. A model of the mechanisms of impact in CR groups.

equals, therapist self-revealing versus nonrevealing, and participating versus listening and interpreting (Simonson & Bahr, 1974).

Expectations lead to step 2, *CR entry*, or, alternatively, other forms of psychological change or psychotherapy. The CR group establishes step 3, *group norms*. These norms include those provided by social and political pressure, goals, procedures, expectations of other group members, and above all the expectation of establishing a different model for defining womanhood (Cherniss, 1972; Kirsh, 1974). Thus, there are *norms for purposes or goals* and *norms for processes*. Some of these norms or values are clearly *counter norms* to those in the prevailing culture (Lieberman *et al.*, 1973). This is particularly true in the instance of CR groups, since one of its goals is to exert pressure on society to change its values.

One of the norms of CR groups is open *self-expression* or *revealing* of personal experiences, which then leads to the occurrence of that behavior—step 4. Shared personal experience and self-revealing create the potential for step 5, *universality and cohesiveness*, or the realization that one is not alone and there is a bond of mutual understanding with others (Yalom, 1975). Universality and cohesiveness then *increase the power of peer influence*—step 6 (Deutsch & Gerard, 1955; Yalom, 1975).

At this point, the model becomes somewhat more speculative. Peer influence probably instigates two specific categorical changes in attitude, perception and value (step 7). One is a change in concepts regarding *women* and their relationships, the second is a change in attitudes regarding the *self* (Cherniss, 1972).

In addition, peer influence may bring about the process of identification with certain other members of the group. Learning from another according to the modeling paradigm (Bandura, 1971) may in fact further increase the esteem for and influence of the peer group. In addition, it would result in the rehearsal of new behaviors, which presumably further changes one's view of oneself, and perhaps one's view of women generally. Another factor in changing self-perception is direct informational feedback from other members of the group. Also, behavioral rehearsal may be utilized not only as a part of identification and modeling, but may be independently instituted as a means of trying on new coping techniques (Wolpe & Lazarus, 1966). The final step is generalization to the outside world. New attitudes about women and about the self, plus behavioral rehearsal, can result in changes in behaviors in outside relationships and in specified roles (e.g. wife, mother, vocation). One area in which one might expect specific change is the taking of a more active role in society, whether through political or institutional activity (Klein, 1976; Kravetz, 1974). The demonstration of personal and political effectiveness would, in turn, further modify the self-concept.

This model shares a number of factors with other group processes and other peer self-help groups. The factors which may be unique to CR groups are the expectations about the process, some of the norms and their priorities, and the dependent variables, self-concept change, change in concepts of women, and behavioral changes in everyday life.

DISCUSSION

Four issues pertinent to our review of peer therapy will be considered: (1) the therapeutic mechanisms of change operative in peer self-help groups, (2) the development of counter-norms, (3) the matching of expectations of people in need of help with those of helpers, and (4) suggestions for research.

Therapeutic Mechanisms of Change

The therapeutic mechanisms of change operative in self-help groups have been repeatedly identified in this chapter. Table 5 summarizes our impressions concerning the relative importance of these factors in the various groups. Identification and cohesiveness appear to be highly important in all groups. With the possible exception of CR groups, instillation of hope and guidance or advice-giving also seem to be highly important. Catharsis appears to be of high importance in CR groups and Synanon and related groups, of moderate significance in AA, and of low significance in TOPS and Recovery. Interpersonal learning appears to be of high importance in CR groups and Synanon and related groups, but to be of low significance in AA, Recovery, and TOPS. While apparently of high importance in AA, altruism seems to be of only moderate significance in Recovery and Synanon and related groups, and of low significance in TOPS and CR groups. Universality

appears to be of moderate significance in all groups, as does genetic insight—with the exception of Recovery, where it seems to be relatively unimportant, and Daytop Village, where it seems to be of high importance. Family reenactment and existential factors appear to be of low significance in all groups.

With the exception of TOPS, current insight seems to be of high importance in all groups. We have added this category to those of Yalom (1975) to supplement the factor of genetic insight. The latter entails cognitive and related behavioral and affective change regarding largely personal historical material. Most self-help groups focus more on cognitive and related behavioral and affective change concerning members' *current* situation—how members view themselves and the world around them now. In AA, this type of insight involves coming to see oneself as alcoholic, in need of help from a Higher Power, and in control of one's own actions. In the instance of the drug groups (Synanon, Phoenix House, and Daytop Village), current insight includes developing a conceptualization of oneself as responsible for one's own decisions and actions, and learning that life has more rewards if one stays free of drugs and crime. In the case of CR groups, current insight entails a reconceptualization of members' role and identity as women in society. In Recovery, current insight includes members learning to "spot" emotional reactions and reduce dichotomous thinking.

Differing structural parameters of peer groups have implications for these mechanisms of change. The presence of a total community dis-

TABLE 5. COMPARATIVE IMPORTANCE OF THE MECHANISMS OF CHANGE IN SELF-HELP GROUPS.

Therapeutic factor[a]	Group						
	AA	CR	Synanon	Phoenix House	Daytop Village	Recovery	TOPS
Identification	High	High	High	High	High	High	High
Group cohesiveness	High	High	High	High	High	High	High
Instillation of hope	High	?	High	High	High	High	High
Guidance	High	?	High	High	High	High	High
Catharsis	Moderate	High	High	High	High	Low	Low
Interpersonal learning, "input" and "output"	Low	High	High	High	High	Low	Low
Altruism	High	Low	Moderate	Moderate	Moderate	Moderate	Low
Universality	Moderate	Moderate	Moderate	Moderate	Moderate	Moderate	Moderate
Genetic insight	Moderate	Moderate	Moderate	Moderate	High	Low	Moderate
Family reenactment	Low	Low	Low	Low	Low	Low	Low
Existential factors	Low	Low	Low	Low	Low	Low	Low
Current insight[b]	High	High	High	High	High	High	Low

[a]Based on Yalom (1975).
[b]Additional factor added by authors; see text.

tinguishes Synanon and related groups from all other peer groups (although AA members spend much of their social life in contact with AA and its members). Thus, the drug groups have far greater control over the lives of members than do groups with time-limited meetings. There are some disadvantages to such total impact. For example, the commitment to live in a disciplined community appears to contribute to a very high dropout rate early in the therapeutic program. But with commitment to such a program, the potential therapeutic impact is clearly more extensive and intensive. Also, individuals advance in status and responsibility within the community, but may never leave the community, or may leave it only to accept staff or leadership roles in another similar community. Clearly, Synanon and related groups may generate a lifestyle apart from the outside society.

The presence or absence of a formal recognized leader in a group is a second structural parameter which differentiates among peer groups. AA, Synanon and related groups, TOPS, and Recovery all have formal leadership roles. While Synanon has formally designated leadership roles in the total community, leaders merely *emerge* during encounter group meetings. In all these groups, leaders interpret or enforce a code of conduct, a philosophical viewpoint, or a set of psychological principles. AA has designated leaders who administer the operations of chapters, members who run individual meetings, and leaders (sponsors and Twelfth Step workers) who interpret the therapeutic program and guide people through it. TOPS leaders interpret and reinforce the group structure and therapeutic program. Recovery leaders interpret the therapeutic method developed by Low, and guide individual members in its use. By contrast, CR groups reject a hierarchical structure in favor of egalitarianism, which is consistent with their stated purposes.[24]

Counternorms

In any therapeutic group, norms develop pertaining to behavior, expression of affect, and cognitive processes among its members. These norms have an important impact on the therapeutic process and goals of change which become established. We will highlight one aspect of norms —counternorms. Counternorms are norms adopted by a specific group which are in contradiction to the prevailing norms of the surrounding society. The establishment of a separate group or community makes the existence of such norms possible, but these norms will be maintained in the outside society only if they are internalized by the members.

With the exception of TOPS and Recovery, which appear to develop norms in concert with mainstream society, counternorms seem to be an important dimension of peer self-help groups. In AA, the counternorms which develop include total abstinence from alcohol, the identification of oneself as a reformed deviant, and adoption of a 24-hour helper role. In Synanon and related groups, the existence of a separate communal culture with severe disciplinary requirements, and with total abstinence from alcohol and tobacco (in addition to hard drugs), is in opposition to the prevailing norms of American society. Also, these groups emphasize brash honesty and confrontation in interpersonal relationships; and in Synanon, children are raised outside the nuclear family structure. Total abstinence from all drugs is also clearly counter to the prevailing norms of the drug culture, from which most drug abusers came, and in which they held their original membership and cultural identity. In CR groups, an emphasis on the equality of women and men, and on the gaining of personal and political power by women is in contradiction to traditional norms. In addition, open sharing of painful and/or discriminatory experiences, especially with other women, represents atypical behavior in the external society.

The saliency and intensity of these counternorms is increased by a "we-they" flavor which develops in self-help groups. In essence, the self-help group becomes a reference group for its members. This results in strong identification by the members with the norms and values of the group, an identification which is bolstered by heightened cohesiveness.

While most groups develop counternorms, the processes of maintaining such norms varies. It is typical for Synanon and related groups to maintain a separate supportive structure, a lifetime therapeutic milieu to continue the norms. AA and CR members, on the other hand, tend to adopt such norms on a personal scale and then transfer them in practice to the external society; but AA members have the lifetime availability of the group for support, unlike CR members who generally terminate their group contact.

Matching and Expectations

Some observers, having witnessed the success of peer groups, have suggested that professional psychotherapists model their behavior after peer influencers. Hurvitz (1974), the strongest proponent of this view, has hypothesized that (1) "the client [of the professional therapist] should know the therapist as another human being; the therapist should therefore be prepared to reveal as much about himself as he asks the client to reveal" (p. 121); (2) "therapists should be those peers whom the clients select on the basis or criteria they determine. This may include experience with the problem behavior they are attempting to overcome" (p. 121); (3) "psychotherapy should be offered without fees. If psychotherapy is essentially a human relationship that cannot be bought, charging a fee for psychotherapy is a contradiction in terms" (p. 120).

Contrary to the view of Hurvitz and others, we believe that many, if not most, of the differences existing between professional and peer therapists should be preserved. This is because people in need of help appear to have differing expectations, beliefs, and other characteristics which result in their receiving differential benefit from different types of contact. Berzins and Ross (1972), in the only study we are aware of which attempted to identify the characteristics of individuals who respond better to peers and those who respond better to professionals, found that their more disturbed female drug addicts were more responsive to peers than to professionals and were more influenced by peers than were the less disturbed addicts. The better adjusted addicts, on the other hand, responded more to professionals than to peers. If these results can be generalized, they may suggest that the more disturbed individual can most profitably be paired with peer influencers. Assuming that the more disturbed addict, alcoholic, psychotic, and the like, has the greater difficulty with authority figures, it would follow that such a person might work better with peers. Research of real clinical value might come from further study of this possibility.

Whatever differences exist between individuals who respond more to peers and those who are more receptive to professionals, and whatever the explanations for these differences, *both peer and professional helpers appear to be needed, because each is helpful to only some people.*

Consistent with the need to preserve the distinction between professionals and peers, we contend that if professionals are to model any of their practices after peer influencers, they should carefully evaluate the effects of doing so.

Individuals presumably choose whom they will ask to help them, in part according to certain expectations they hold about how the helper will act toward them. Should professionals behave like peers, they might compromise their effectiveness inasmuch as they would be in violation of certain expectations. For example, if a professional were to behave like a peer influencer and tell a client in an early session that he has a drinking problem, sex problem, or other problem that parallels the client's, he might be perceived as inappropriate and therefore unacceptable because he would deviate from the (currently, at least) culturally defined role of the professional therapist as formal, objective, and relatively aloof (Dies, 1973; Truax, Carkhuff, & Kodman, 1965; Weigel & Warnath, 1968).

Results of two psychotherapy analogue studies (Simonson & Apter, 1969; Simonson & Bahr, 1974) tend to support this hypothesis. In both studies, college female volunteers were randomly assigned to listen to one of three 20-minute tapes just before a 1-hour interview with a "therapist." The tape consisted of several segments of a mock first interview between the therapist they were to see and a somewhat disturbed, insomniac "patient" portrayed by an actress. Participants who were told the therapist was a professional were more attracted to the therapist, indicated a greater willingness to self-disclose in the interview, and did self-disclose more if they heard the therapist reveal "nonintimate," "demographic" (not further defined) information about his past than if they heard him make no self-disclosure. They were less attracted, less willing to disclose, and disclosed less if they heard him make "personally revealing [not defined] but not unusual comments" (Simonson & Bahr, 1974, p. 360). Personal disclosure was apparently "frightening or at least disquieting" (p. 362), because "the level of therapist disclosure went too far beyond the subjects' expectations for this professional relationship" (p. 362).

When participants believed the therapist was a paraprofessional, they also anticipated they would disclose more in the interview, found the therapist more attractive, and disclosed more if they were exposed to nonintimate disclosure as opposed to no disclosure. However, contrary to the professional condition, the "paraprofessional's" disclosure of *personal* past material significantly *increased* the participants' anticipated and actual self-disclosure and attraction to the therapist, beyond what had occurred with those hearing only nonintimate disclosure. Apparently, participants were made more comfortable by the paraprofessional's self-disclosure because such behavior was "within the bounds of the subjects' expectations" (p. 362). In this case, what had been "poison" for the professional was "meat" for the paraprofessional. Although these findings pertain to a paraprofessional rather than to a peer influencer, we would predict that similar results would emerge in a study of peer influencers.

Since different expectations seem to attend to the helper role, depending on whether of professional or peer status, professionals must carefully evaluate the effects of fashioning their behavior after peer influencers. The issue here is not whether professional and peer helpers should be similar in *any* way. Because both helper types work with people with psychological problems, they inevitably engage in many of the same behaviors, some of which differ only in timing but not in content. For example, many professionals disclose in a manner much like peer influencers, but usually only some time after the beginning of the helping relationship. Rather, it has been the intent of this discussion to caution against professionals modeling after peer influencers *simply because* a particular practice has been found to be effective for peers.

We take a similar stance on the obverse issue of peer influencers modeling after professionals. What research is available (see TOPS discussion) suggests that peers can increase their effectiveness by using some professional techniques, such as behavior therapy based on learning theory. Other professional characteristics which should be researched and appear to be potentially adoptable by peers are the establishment of clear contracts in the helping process, awareness of and allowance for individual differences, and the use of a wide variety of treatment methods to increase the range of responsiveness to individual needs.

While neither helper type should blindly model the other, they should not ignore the possibility of planned modeling. Barriers against such modeling exist on both sides. The strong ingroup, "we-they" tendency of peer groups may make the entry of professionals to introduce techniques and theory particularly difficult. Likewise, ingroup tendencies on the part of professionals may prevent the application of valuable components of peer therapy to professional treatment. While both helper types may benefit from therapeutic borrowing, we recognize that such borrowing reduces the distinctiveness of the two groups, and, therefore, the availability of alternative modes of help to the individual help-seeker. Also, in our view, the strong "ingroup" status of peer groups contributes to their therapeutic effectiveness through members' enthusiasm and commitment to a method of help. There is something of a dilemma here. Certain benefits and costs accompany either maintenance of the status quo or a reduction of barriers to modeling.[25]

Suggestions for Research

Because of the general paucity of research on self-help groups, there are a myriad of possibilities for future research in this area. We focus on four issues here. First, we consider a major issue to be how best to match therapeutic agents and therapeutic modalities with people in need of help. Descriptive evaluations of individuals who select one modality versus another or who respond more to one type of therapist versus another should be done. With such descriptive studies, helpers will be better able to facilitate the natural self-selection individuals make of helpers and modalities (see Lieberman, 1975).

Second, a more thorough empirical analysis of the relative importance of therapeutic mechanisms among the various self-help groups should be undertaken. Yalom's (1975) 12 factors seem to provide a useful conceptual scheme for this research effort. In addition to these 12 factors, we suggest investigation of a "current insight" dimension. Also, some structural and organizational factors such as leadership roles, experience of leaders, community structure, and the nature of graduation from the group should receive attention.

Third, the choice and selection of outcome criteria for evaluating peer therapy appears to be a major issue. Clearly, peers and professionals do not always share the same goals. For example, successful completion of a program may be the goal of professionals who treat drug addicts, but the goal of Synanon is a drug-free day, not program completion. While AA has total abstinence from alcohol as its only goal, professionals tend to view mere reduction of alcohol abuse as a meaningful pursuit in its own right. Also, professionals work toward genetic insight with alcoholics more than AA does. Similarly, increased political activity is a goal in many CR groups, but this is not shared by most traditional therapists (see Hurvitz, 1973).

The fourth and final issue pertains to the personnel involved in evaluating self-help groups. Most of the research done to date has been performed by professionals from outside the groups. Contrary to this trend have been recent surveys by AA administrators and developments at Synanon where several internal research efforts are underway. Early in Synanon's growth, Dederich was opposed to evaluation research because he feared that documentation of failure might establish a self-fulfilling prophecy for failure (Casriel, 1963). However, the promotion of intellectual pursuits among Synanon members eventually led to internal research projects. Anti-intellectualism is somewhat characteristic of some of the other self-help groups, and may be one cause for the general lack of internal research. While no empirical evidence of anti-intellectualism has been gathered, there have been anecdotal reports of strong anti-intellectual norms in some groups—for example, Recovery, Inc. (Wechsler, 1960).

Another possible factor in the paucity of internal research efforts may be the fear on the part of peer-group members that research may undermine their belief in the absolute success of their approach. It is tempting for some professionals to consider peers as defensive on this issue, yet to do so maintains an elitist, "I'm more objective and open to the truth" stance, which may be particularly objectionable to self-help group members. It is equally plausible to argue that researchers are defensive about conducting research from the outside, because they are apprehensive about finding that peer influencers are as successful, if not more so, than they are. Perhaps this is a reason why professionals have conducted only a limited amount of research in the area.

Both peer influencers and professionals would do well to engage in more evaluation of self-help groups. It may be that peer influencers will be distressed by data indicating that their methods are not perfect, and professionals will be upset by documentation of their failure to corner the therapeutic market. Hopefully this pain will be growth-producing, stimulating a more active constructive interchange between the two helper types.

REFERENCES

Alcoholics Anonymous: The story of how many thousands of men and women have recovered from alcoholism. (New rev. ed.) New York: Alcoholics Anonymous World Services, 1955.

ALLEN, P. *Free space.* New Jersey: Times Change Press, 1970.

American Psychological Association. Report of the task force on sex bias and sex role stereotyping in psychotherapeutic practice. *American Psychologist*, 1975, **30**, 1169–1175.

ASCH, S. E. Effects of group pressure upon the modification and distortion of judgments. In G. E. SWANSON, T. M. NEWCOMB, & E. L. HARTLEY (Eds.), *Readings in social psychology.* (Rev. ed.) New York: Holt, Rinehart & Winston, 1952.

BAEKELAND, F., LUNDWALL, L., KISSIN, B., & SHANAHAN, T. Correlates of outcome in disulfiram treatment of alcoholism. *Journal of Nervous and Mental Disease*, 1971, **153**, 1–9.

BAILEY, M. B., & LEACH, B. *Alcoholics Anonymous pathway to recovery: A study of 1,058 members of the AA fellowship in New York City.* New York: National Council on Alcoholism, 1965.

BALES, R. F. The therapeutic role of Alcoholics Anonymous as seen by a sociologist. In D. J. PITTMAN & C. R. SNYDER (Eds.), *Society, culture, and drinking patterns.* New York: Wiley, 1962.

BANDURA, A. Psychotherapy based upon modeling principles. In A. E. BERGIN & S. L. GARFIELD (Eds.), *Handbook of psychotherapy and behavior change: An empirical analysis.* New York: Wiley, 1971.

BATEMAN, N. I., & PETERSON, D. M. Variables related to outcome of treatment for hospitalized alcoholics. *International Journal of the Addictions*, 1971, **6**, 215–224.

BATESON, G. The cybernetics of self: A theory of alcoholism. *Psychiatry*, 1971, **34**, 1–18.

BEAN, M. Alcoholics Anonymous I. *Psychiatric Annals*, 1975a, **5**, 7–61.

BEAN, M. Alcoholics Anonymous II. *Psychiatric Annals*, 1975b, **5**, 7–57.

BEAUBRUN, M. H. Treatment of alcoholism in Trinidad and Tobago, 1956–65. *British Journal of Psychiatry*, 1967, **113**, 643–658.

BECK, A. T. *Cognitive modification in depressed, suicidal patients.* Paper presented at the Philadelphia Veterans Administration Hospital, February 1974.

BELASCO, J. A. The criterion question revisited. *British Journal of Addiction*, 1971, **66**, 39–44.

BELL, A. H. The Bell alcoholism scale of adjustment: A validity study. *Quarterly Journal of Studies on Alcohol*, 1970, **31**, 965–967.

BELL, A. H., WEINGOLD, H. P., & LACHIN, J. M. Measuring adjustment in patients disabled with alcoholism. *Quarterly Journal of Studies on Alcohol*, 1969, **30**, 634–639.

BEM, D. J. *Beliefs, attitudes, and human affairs.* Monterey, Calif.: Brooks-Cole, 1970.

BENJAMIN, J. G., FREEDMAN, M. K., & LYNTON, E. F. *Pros and cons: New roles for nonprofessionals in corrections.* Washington, D.C.: United States Government Printing Office, Department of Health, Education, and Welfare. 1966.

BERGIN, A. E. Some implications of psychotherapy research for therapeutic practice. *Journal of Abnormal Psychology*, 1966, **71**, 235–246.

BERGIN, A. E. The evaluation of therapeutic outcomes. In A. E. BERGIN & S. L. GARFIELD (Eds.), *Handbook of psychotherapy and behavior change: An empirical analysis.* New York: Wiley, 1971.

BERSCHEID, E., & WALSTER, E. H. *Interpersonal attraction.* Reading, Mass.: Addison-Wesley, 1969.

BERZINS, J. I., & ROSS, W. F. Experimental assessment of the responsiveness of addict patients to the "influence" of professionals versus other addicts. *Journal of Abnormal Psychology*, 1972, **80**, 141–148.

BIASE, D. V. Adolescent heroin abusers in a therapeutic community: Use of the MAACL to assess emotional traits and splitting from treatment. In G. DeLEON (Ed.), *Phoenix House: Studies in a therapeutic community (1968–1973).* New York: MSS Information Corporation, 1974a.

BIASE, D. V. Phoenix Houses: Therapeutic communities for drug addicts: A comparative study of residents in treatment. In G. DeLEON (Ed.), *Phoenix House: Studies in a therapeutic community (1968–1973)*. New York: MSS Information, 1974b.

BIASE, D. V., & DeLEON, G. The encounter group —Measurement of some affect changes. *Proceedings of the 77th Annual Convention of the American Psychological Association*, 1969, 497–498.

BLANE, H. T. *The personality of the alcoholic: Guises of dependency*. New York: Harper & Row, 1968.

BOHINCE, E. A., & ORENSTEEN, A. C. *An evaluation of the services and program of the Minneapolis chapter of Alcoholics Anonymous*. Unpublished master's thesis, University of Minnesota, 1950.

BRAGINSKY, D. D., & BRAGINSKY, B. M. *Mainstream psychology: A critique*. New York: Holt, Rinehart & Winston, 1974.

BROVERMAN, I. K., BROVERMAN, D. M., CLARKSON, F. E., ROSENKRANTZ, P. S., & VOGEL, S. R. Sex-role stereotypes and clinical judgments of mental health. *Journal of Consulting and Clinical Psychology*, 1970, **34**, 1–7.

BROWN, R. F. An aftercare program for alcoholics. *Crime and Delinquency*, 1963, **9**, 77–83.

BURTON, A. The adoration of the patient and its disillusionment. *American Journal of Psychoanalysis*, 1969, **29**, 194–204.

BUTTON, A. D. The psychodynamics of alcoholism: A survey of 87 cases. *Quarterly Journal of Studies on Alcohol*, 1956, **17**, 443–460.

C., B. The growth and effectiveness of Alcoholics Anonymous in a Southwestern city, 1945–1962. *Quarterly Journal of Studies on Alcohol*, 1965, **26**, 279–284.

CANTRIL, H. *The psychology of social movements*. New York: Wiley, 1963.

CAPLAN, N. The new ghetto man: A review of recent empirical studies. *Journal of Social Issues*, 1970, **26**, 59–73.

CAPPELL, H., & HERMAN, C. P. Alcohol and tension reduction: A review. *Quarterly Journal of Studies on Alcohol*, 1972, **33**, 33–64.

CARACENA, P. F. Elicitation of dependency expressions in the initial stage of psychotherapy. *Journal of Counseling Psychology*, 1965, **12**, 268–274.

CARNER, C. Now: Clubs for mutual mental help. *Today's Health*, 1968, **46**, 40–41, 72–73.

CARROLL, J. L., & FULLER, G. B. The self and ideal-self concept of the alcoholic as influenced by length of sobriety and/or participation in Alcoholics Anonymous. *Journal of Clinical Psychology*, 1969, **25**, 363–364.

CARTER, T. The road from heroin junkie to top sales exec. *Sepia*, 1973, **22**, 3.

CASRIEL, D. *So fair a house: The story of Synanon*. Englewood Cliffs, N.J.: Prentice-Hall, 1963.

CHERKAS, M. S. Synanon Foundation —A radical approach to the problem of addiction. *American Journal of Psychiatry*, 1965, **121**, 1065–1068.

CHERNISS, C. Personality and ideology: A personological study of women's liberation. *Psychiatry*, 1972, **35**, 109–125.

CHESLER, P. Patient and patriarch: Women in the psychotherapeutic relationship. In V. GORNICK & B. K. MORAN (Eds.), *Women in sexist society*. New York: Basic Books, 1971.

COHEN, F. Personality changes among members of Alcoholics Anonymous. *Mental Hygiene*, 1962, **46**, 427–437.

COHLER, J., & SHAPIRO, L. Avoidance patterns in staff–patient interaction on a chronic schizophrenic treatment ward. *Psychiatry*, 1964, **27**, 377–388.

COLLIER, W. V. Additional material concerning Daytop Village. In R. M. GLASSCOTE, J. N. SUSSEX, J. H. JAFFE, J. BALL, & L. BRILL (Eds.), *The treatment of drug abuse: Programs, problems, prospects*. Washington, D.C.: Joint Information Service of the American Psychiatric Association and the National Association for Mental Health, 1972.

COOK, J. A., & GEIS, G. Forum Anonymous: The techniques of Alcoholics Anonymous applied to prison therapy. *Journal of Social Therapy*, 1957, **3**, 9–13.

DAVIES, D. L., SHEPHERD, M., & MYERS, E. The two-years' prognosis of 50 alcohol addicts after treatment in hospital. *Quarterly Journal of Studies on Alcohol*, 1956, **17**, 485–502.

DEAN, S. R. Recovery, Inc.: Giving psychiatry an assist. *Medical Economics*, 1969a, **46**, 150.

DEAN, S. R. Self-help group psychotherapy: Mental patients rediscover will power. *Congressional Record*, 1969b, 91st Congress, 1st session, **115**, No. 191, 34978–34980.

DeCOURCY, P., & DUERFELDT, P. H. The impact of number and type of models on claimed success rate and mood of adult alcoholics. *Journal of Genetic Psychology*, 1973, **122**, 63–79.

DEDERICH, C. E. Declaration of Charles E. Dederich on the synanon game. Synanon vs. the Hearst Corporation, No. 651–749, May 3, 1973.

DeLEON, G. Phoenix House therapeutic community: The influence of time in program on change in resident drug addicts. In G. DeLEON (Ed.), *Phoenix House: Studies in a therapeutic community (1968–1973)*. New York: MSS Information, 1974.

DeLEON, G., HOLLAND, S., & ROSENTHAL, M. S. Phoenix House: Criminal activity of dropouts. *Journal of the American Medical Association*, 1972, **222**, 686–689.

DeLEON, G., ROSENTHAL, M., & BRODNEY, K. Therapeutic community for drug addicts, long-term measurement of emotional changes. *Psychological Reports*, 1971, **29**, 595–600.

DeLEON, G., SKODOL, A., & ROSENTHAL, M. S. Phoenix House: Changes in psychopathological signs of resident drug addicts. *Archives of General Psychiatry*, 1973, **28**, 131–135.

DEUTSCH, M., & GERARD, H. B. A study of normative and informational social influences upon individual judgment. *Journal of Abnormal and Social Psychology*, 1955, **51**, 629–636.

DIES, R. R. Group therapist self-disclosure: An evaluation by clients. *Journal of Counseling Psychology*, 1973, **20**, 344–348.

DITMAN, K. S., CRAWFORD, G. G., FORGY, E. W., MOSKOWITZ, H., & MACANDREW, C. A controlled experiment on the use of court probation for drunk arrests. *American Journal of Psychiatry*, 1967, **124**, 160–163.

DIZARD, J. E. Black identity, social class and black power. *Journal of Psychiatry*, 1970, **33**, 195–207.

DUBOURG, G. O. After-care for alcoholics —A follow-up study. *British Journal of Addiction*, 1969, **64**, 155–163.

DUMONT, M. P. Self-help treatment programs. *American Journal of Psychiatry*, 1974, **131**, 631–635.

ECKHARDT, W. Alcoholic values and Alcoholics Anonymous. *Quarterly Journal of Studies on Alcohol*, 1967, **28**, 277–288.

EDWARDS, G. Hypnosis in treatment of alcohol addiction: Controlled trial, with analysis of factors affecting outcome. *Quarterly Journal of Studies on Alcohol*, 1966, **27**, 221–241.

EDWARDS, G., HENSMAN, C., HAWKER, A., & WILLIAMSON, V. Who goes to Alcoholics Anonymous? *Lancet*, 1966, **2**, 382–384.

EDWARDS, G., HENSMAN, C., HAWKER, A., & WILLIAMSON, V. Alcoholics Anonymous: The anatomy of a self-help group. *Social Psychiatry*, 1967, **1**, 195–204.

EGLASH, A. Adults Anonymous: A mutual help program for inmates and ex-inmates. *Journal of Criminal Law, Criminology and Police Science*, 1958a, **49**, 237–239.

EGLASH, A. Youth Anonymous. *Federal Probation*, 1958b, **22**, 47–49.

EMRICK, C. D. *Psychological treatment of alcoholism: An analytic review*. Unpublished doctoral dissertation, Columbia University, 1973.

EMRICK, C. D. A review of psychologically oriented treatment of alcoholism: I. The use and interrelationships of outcome criteria and drinking behavior following treatment. *Quarterly Journal of Studies on Alcohol*, 1974, **35**, 523–549.

FERBER, A., MENDELSOHN, M., & NAPIER, A. *The book of family therapy*. New York: Science House, 1972.

FESTINGER, L., SCHACHTER, S., & BACK, K. *Social pressures in informal groups: A study of human factors in housing*. New York: Harper, 1950.

FESTINGER, L., & THIBAUT, J. Interpersonal communication in small groups. *Journal of Abnormal and Social Psychology*, 1951, **46**, 92–99.

FREEMAN, J. The origins of the women's liberation movement. *American Journal of Sociology*, 1973, **78**, 792–811.

FREMOUW, W. J., & HARMATZ, M. G. A helper model for behavioral treatment of speech anxiety. *Journal of Consulting and Clinical Psychology*, 1975, **43**, 652–660.

GARB, J. R., & STUNKARD, A. J. Effectiveness of a self-help group in obesity control. *Archives of Internal Medicine*, 1974, **134**, 716–720.

GARFIELD, S. L. Research on client variables in psychotherapy. In A. E. BERGIN & S. L. GARFIELD (Eds.), *Handbook of psychotherapy and behavior change: An empirical analysis*. New York: Wiley, 1971.

GERARD, D. L., & SAENGER, G. *Out-patient treatment of alcoholism: A study of outcome and its determinants*. Toronto: University of Toronto Press, 1966.

GERARD, H. B. The effect of different dimensions of disagreement on the communication process in small groups. *Human Relations*, 1953, **6**, 249–271.

GILMAN, R. The femlib case against Sigmund Freud. *New York Times Magazine*, Jan. 31, 1971, 10–47.

GLASER, K. *Women's self-help groups*. Workshop on research on therapy with women: Traditional and alternative models. Fifth Annual Meeting of the Society for Psychotherapy Research, Denver, June 1974.

GLASSCOTE, R. M., SUSSEX, J. N., JAFFE, J. H., BALL, J., & BRILL, L. (Eds.), *The treatment of drug abuse: Programs, problems, prospects*. Washington, D.C.: Joint Information Service of the American Psychiatric Association and the National Association for Mental Health, 1972.

GOTTLIEB, A., & RESNIKOFF, R. *A long-term follow-up study of group psychotherapy patients*. Paper presented at the Colorado Psychiatric Society Midsummer Meeting, Snowmass-at-Aspen, July 1974.

GROSZ, H. J. *Recovery, Inc. survey*. Chicago: Recovery, Inc., 1973.

GROVES, D. H. Charismatic leadership in Alcoholics Anonymous: A case study. *Quarterly Journal of Studies on Alcohol*, 1972, **33**, 684–691.

GUERNEY, B. G., JR. Alfred Adler and the current mental health revolution. *Journal of Individual Psychology*, 1970, **26**, 124–134.

A guide to consciousness-raising. *Ms.*, 1972, **1**(1), Whole Issue.

HABERMAN, P. W. Factors related to increasing sobriety in group psychotherapy with alcoholics. *Journal of Clinical Psychology*, 1966, **22**, 229–235.

HALL, S. M. Self-control and therapist control in the behavioral treatment of overweight women. *Behaviour, Research and Therapy*, 1972, **10**, 59–68.

HALL, W. S., CROSS, W. E., JR., & FREEDLE, R. Stages in the development of black awareness: An exploratory investigation. In R. L. JONES (Ed.), *Black psychology*. New York: Harper & Row, 1972.

HANISCH, C. The personal is political. In J. AGEL (Ed.), *The radical therapist*. New York: Ballantine, 1971.

HARTUP, W. W. Peer interaction and social organization. In P. H. MUSSEN (Ed.), *Carmichael's manual of child psychology*. Vol. 2 (3rd ed.). New York: Wiley, 1970.

HAYMAN, M. Current attitudes to alcoholism of psychiatrists in Southern California. *American Journal of Psychiatry*, 1956, **112**, 485–493.

HENRY, W. E. Some observations on the lives of healers *Human Development*, 1966, **9**, 47–56.

Historical statistics of the United States, colonial times to 1957. Washington, D.C.: United States Bureau of the Census, 1960.

HOFF, E. C., & FORBES, J. C. Some effects of alcohol on metabolic mechanisms with applications to therapy of alcoholics. In M. G. SEVAG, R. D. REID, & O. E. REYNOLDS (Eds.), *Origins of resistance to toxic agents*. New York: Academic Press, 1955.

HOLE, J., & LEVINE, E. *Rebirth of feminism*. New York: Quadrangle, 1971.

HOLLANDER, E. P. *Principles and methods in social psychology*. (2nd ed.) New York: Oxford University Press, 1971.

HOLZINGER, R. Synanon through the eyes of a visiting psychologist. *Quarterly Journal of Studies on Alcohol*, 1965, **26**, 304–309.

HURVITZ, N. Peer self-help psychotherapy groups and their implications for psychotherapy. *Psychotherapy: Theory, Research and Practice*, 1970, **7**, 41–49.

HURVITZ, N. Peer self-help groups. *Radical Therapist*, 1971, **1**, 5.

HURVITZ, N. Psychotherapy as a means of social control. *Journal of Consulting and Clinical Psychology*, 1973, **40**, 232–239.

HURVITZ, N. Peer self-help psychotherapy groups: Psychotherapy without psychotherapists. In P. M. ROMAN & H. M. TRICE (Eds.), *The sociology of psychotherapy*. New York: Aronson, 1974.

JOESTING, J. Comparison of women's liberation members with their nonmember peers. *Psychological Reports*, 1971, **29**, 1291–1294.

JOHNSON, N. "Innovative group programs": What is Al-Anon? *National Catholic Guidance Conference Journal*, 1971, **15**, 188–191.

JORDAN, H. A., & LEVITZ, L. S. A pilot study: Behavior modification in a self-help group. *Journal of the American Dietetic Association*, 1973, **62**, 27–29.

KARLINS, M., & ABELSON, H. I. *Persuasion: How opinions and attitudes are changed*. New York: Springer, 1970.

KATKIN, E. S., RISK, R. T., & SPIELBERGER, C. D. The effects of experimenter status and subject awareness on verbal conditioning. *Journal of Experimental Research in Personality*, 1966, **1**, 153–160.

KIRSH, B. Consciousness-raising groups as therapy for women. In V. FRANKS & V. BURTLE (Eds.), *Women in therapy*. New York: Brunner-Mazel, 1974.

KISH, G. B., & HERMANN, H. T. The Fort Meade alcoholism treatment program: A follow-up study. *Quarterly Journal of Studies on Alcohol*, 1971, **32**, 628–635.

KISSIN, B., ROSENBLATT, S. M., & MACHOVER, S. Prognostic factors in alcoholism. *Psychiatric Research Reports*, 1968, **24**, 22–43.

KIVIRANTA, P. *Alcoholism syndrome in Finland*. Helsinki: Finnish Foundation for Alcohol Studies, 1969.

KLEIN, M. H. Feminist concepts of therapy outcome. *Psychotherapy: Theory, Research and Practice*, 1976, **13**, 89–95.

KOEDT, A. The myth of the vaginal orgasm. In L. B. TANNER (Ed.), *Voices from women's liberation*. New York: Signet, 1970.

KRAVETZ, D. *Psychotherapy and consciousness-raising groups*. Workshop on research on therapy with women: Traditional and alternative models. Fifth Annual Meeting of the Society for Psychotherapy Research, Denver, June, 1974.

KRUEGER, D. E. Operant group therapy with delinquent boys using therapist's versus peer's reinforcement. *Dissertation Abstracts International*, 1971, **31**(11-B), 6877–6878.

LEACH, B. Does Alcoholics Anonymous really work? In P. G. BOURNE & R. FOX (Eds.), *Alcoholism: Progress in research and treatment.* New York: Academic Press, 1973.

LEE, D. T. Recovery, Inc.: Aid in the transition from hospital to community. *Mental Hygiene*, 1971, **55**, 194–198.

LENNARD, H. L., & ALLEN, S. D. The treatment of drug addiction: Toward new models. In G. DELEON (Ed.), *Phoenix House: Studies in a therapeutic community (1968–1973)*. New York: MSS Information, 1974.

LEVITZ, L. S., & STUNKARD, A. J. A therapeutic coalition for obesity: Behavior modification and patient self-help. *American Journal of Psychiatry*, 1974, **131**, 423–427.

LIEBERMAN, M. A. Some limits to research on T-groups. *Journal of Applied Behavioral Sciences*, 1975, **11**, 241-249.

LIEBERMAN, M. A., YALOM, I. D., & MILES, M. B. *Encounter groups: First facts.* New York: Basic Books, 1973.

LITTLE, K. B. Report of the executive officer: 1974. *American Psychologist*, 1975, **30**, 611–615.

LOW, A. A. The combined system of group psychotherapy and self-help as practiced by Recovery, Inc. *Sociometry*, 1945, **8**, 332–337.

LOW, A. A. Recovery, Inc., a project for rehabilitating post-psychotic and long-term psychoneurotic patients. In W. H. SODEN (Ed.), *Rehabilitation of the handicapped: A survey of means and methods.* New York: Ronald Press, 1949.

LOW, A. A. *Mental health through will-training: A system of self-help in psychotherapy as practiced by Recovery, Incorporated.* Boston: Christopher, 1950.

LUDWIG, A. M., LEVINE, J., & STARK, L. H. *LSD and alcoholism: A clinical study of treatment efficacy.* Springfield, Ill.: Thomas, 1970.

MACHOVER, S., PUZZO, F. S., MACHOVER, K., & PLUMEAU, F. Clinical and objective studies of personality variables in alcoholism. III. An objective study of homosexuality in alcoholism. *Quarterly Journal of Studies on Alcohol*, 1959, **20**, 528–542.

MACHOVER, S., PUZZO, F. S., & PLUMEAU, F. E. Values in alcoholics. *Quarterly Journal of Studies on Alcohol*, 1962, **23**, 267–273.

MAHONEY, M. J. *Cognition and behavior modification.* Cambridge, Mass.: Ballinger, 1974.

MANDER, A. V., & RUSH, A. K. *Feminism as therapy.* New York: Random House, 1974.

MANOHAR, V. Training volunteers as alcoholism treatment counselors. *Quarterly Journal of Studies on Alcohol*, 1973, **34**, 869–877.

MARKOFF, E. L. Synanon in drug addiction. *Current Psychiatric Therapies*, 1969, **9**, 261–272.

MASLOW, A. H. Synanon and eupsychia. *Journal of Humanistic Psychology*, 1967, **7**, 28–35.

MAYER, J., & MYERSON, D. J. Outpatient treatment of alcoholics: Effects of status, stability and nature of treatment. *Quarterly Journal of Studies on Alcohol*, 1971, **32**, 620–627.

McCANCE, C., & McCANCE, P. F. Alcoholism in North-East Scotland: Its treatment and outcome. *British Journal of Psychiatry*, 1969, **115**, 189–198.

McGINNIS, C. A. The effect of group-therapy on the ego-strength scale scores of alcoholic patients. *Journal of Clinical Psychology*, 1963, **19**, 346–347.

MEICHENBAUM, D. H. Examination of model characteristics in reducing avoidance behavior. *Journal of Personality and Social Psychology*, 1971, **17**, 298–307.

MELTZOFF, J., & KORNREICH, M. *Research in psychotherapy.* New York: Atherton Press, 1970.

MORGAN, R. Introduction: The women's revolution. In R. MORGAN (Ed.), *Sisterhood is powerful.* New York: Vintage, 1970.

MOWRER, O. H. Integrity groups: Principles and procedures. *Counseling Psychologist*, 1972, **3**, 7–33.

MUELLER, E. R. Rebels—with a cause: A report on Synanon. *American Journal of Psychotherapy*, 1964, **18**, 272–284.

MULLAN, H., & SANGIULIANO, I. *The therapist's contribution to the treatment process: His person, transactions, and treatment methods.* Springfield, Ill.: Thomas, 1964.

MUUS, R. E. *Theories of adolescence.* (2nd ed.) New York: Random House, 1968.

MYERSON, D. J., & MAYER, J. Origins, treatment and destiny of Skid Row alcoholic men. *New England Journal of Medicine*, 1966, **275**, 419–425.

NASH, G., WALDORF, D., FOSTER, K., & KYLLINGSTAD, A. The Phoenix House program: The results of a two year follow-up. In G. DELEON (Ed.), *Phoenix House: Studies in a therapeutic community (1968–1973)*. New York: MSS Information, 1974.

NEMEC, R. New games at Synanon. *Southland Sunday, The Long Beach Independent, Press Telegram*, Aug. 18, 1974. (Reprint by Synanon News Service).

NIMH. *Directory of narcotic addiction treatment agencies in the United States: 1968–1969.* Washington, D.C.: National Clearinghouse for Mental Health Information, 1969.

NORRIS, J. Alcoholics Anonymous. In E. D. WHITNEY (Ed.), *World dialogue on alcohol and drug dependence.* Boston: Beacon Press, 1970.

NORRIS, J. L. *A.A.'s 1974 membership survey.* Paper presented at the North American Congress on Alcohol and Drug Problems, San Francisco, December 1974a.

NORRIS, J. L. *General survey. General Service Board of Alcoholics Anonymous, Inc.* Paper presented at the North American Congress on Alcohol and Drug Problems, San Francisco, December 1974b.

OAKLEY, S., & HOLDEN, P. H. ARC: Follow-up survey 1969. *Inventory, N.C.*, 1971, **20**, 2–4, 19.

O'REILLY, P. O., & FUNK, A. LSD in chronic alcoholism. *Canadian Psychiatric Association Journal*, 1964, **9**, 258–261.

PARKER, J. B., MEILLER, R. M., & Andrews, G. W. Major psychiatric disorders masquerading as alcoholism. *Southern Medical Journal*, 1960, **53**, 560–564.

PATRICK, S. W. Our way of life: A short history of Narcotics Anonymous, Inc. In E. HARMS (Ed.), *Drug addiction in youth.* Oxford: Pergamon Press, 1965.

PATTERSON, G. R., & ANDERSON, D. Peers as social reinforcers. *Child Development*, 1964, **35**, 951–960.

PATTISON, E. M. Treatment of alcoholic families with nurse home visits. *Family Process*, 1965, **4**, 75–94.

PATTISON, E. M., COE, R., & DOERR, H. O. Population variation among alcoholism treatment facilities. *International Journal of the Addictions*, 1973, **8**, 199–229.

PATTISON, E. M., HEADLEY, E. B., GLESER, G. C., & GOTTSCHALK, L. A. Abstinence and normal drinking: An assessment of changes in drinking patterns in alcoholics after treatment. *Quarterly Journal of Studies on Alcohol*, 1968, **29**, 610–633.

PATTON, T. *The Synanon philosophy.* San Francisco: Synanon Research University Press, 1973.

PFEFFER, A. Z., & BERGER, S. A follow-up study of treated alcoholics. *Quarterly Journal of Studies on Alcohol*, 1957, **18**, 624–648.

PITTMAN, D. J., & GORDON, C. W. *Revolving door: A study of the chronic police case inebriate.* Glencoe, Ill.: Free Press, 1958.

POGREBIN, L. C. Rap groups: The feminist connection. *Ms*, 1973, **1**(9), 80–104.

PREBLE, E. Some questions are put to Synanon. *Bulletin: New York State District Branches, American Psychiatric Association*, 1965, **8**, 7, 12.

RAMSAY, R., JENSEN, S., & SOMMER, R. Values in alcoholics after LSD-25. *Quarterly Journal of Studies on Alcohol*, 1963, **24**, 443–448.

RANDALL, D. Synanon—Born while AA slept. *24: The Magazine of Living the Way—Twenty four Hours at a Time*, July 1973.

Recovery, Inc. *Recovery, Inc.—What it is and how it developed*, pamphlet. Chicago: Recovery, Inc., 1973.

RIOCH, M., ELKES, D., & FLINT, A. *A pilot project in training mental health counselors.* Washington, D.C.: U.S. Government Printing Office, Public Health Service Publication No. 1254, 1963.

RIPLEY, H. S., & JACKSON, J. K. Therapeutic factors in Alcoholics Anonymous. *American Journal of Psychiatry*, 1959, **116**, 44–50.

RITSON, B. The prognosis of alcohol addicts treated by a specialized unit. *British Journal of Psychiatry*, 1968, **114**, 1019–1029.

RITSON, B. Involvement in treatment and its relation to outcome amongst alcoholics. *British Journal of Addiction*, 1969, **64**, 23–29.

ROBSON, R. A. H., PAULUS, I., & CLARKE, G. G. An evaluation of the effect of a clinic treatment program on the rehabilitation of alcoholic patients. *Quarterly Journal of Studies on Alcohol*, 1965, **26**, 264–278.

ROGERS, C. Characteristics of a helping relationship. *Canada's Mental Health*, 1962, **27**, 1–18.

ROHAN, W. P. A follow-up study of hospitalized problem drinkers. *Diseases of the Nervous System*, 1970, **31**, 259–265.

ROSENTHAL, M. S. The Phoenix House therapeutic community: An overview. In G. DeLeon (Ed.), *Phoenix House: Studies in a therapeutic community (1968–1973)*. New York: MSS Information, 1974.

ROSENTHAL, M. S., & BIASE, D. V. Phoenix Houses: Therapeutic communities for drug addicts. *Hospital and Community Psychiatry*, 1969, **20**, 27–30.

ROSSI, J. J., STACH, A., & BRADLEY, N. J. Effects of treatment of male alcoholics in a mental hospital: A follow-up study. *Quarterly Journal of Studies on Alcohol*, 1963, **24**, 91–108.

RYBACK, R. S. Schizophrenics Anonymous: A treatment adjunct. *Psychiatry Medicine*, 1971, **2**, 247–253.

SABATH, G. Some trends in the treatment and epidemiology of drug addiction: Psychotherapy and Synanon. *Psychotherapy: Theory, Research and Practice*, 1967, **4**, 92–96.

SAGARIN, E. *Odd man in:* Societies of deviants in America. Chicago: Quadrangle Books, 1969.

SCHEFF, T. J. Reevaluation counseling: Social implications. *Journal of Humanistic Psychology*, 1972, **12**, 58–71.

SCODEL, A. Inspirational group therapy: A study of Gamblers Anonymous. *American Journal of Psychotherapy*, 1964, **18**, 115–125.

SCOTT, D., & GOLDBERG, H. L. The phenomenon of self-perpetuation in Synanon-type drug treatment programs. *Hospital and Community Psychiatry*, 1973, **24**, 231–233.

SCOTT, E. M. Joint and group treatment for married alcoholics and their spouses. *Psychological Reports*, 1959, **5**, 725–728.

SEIDEN, R. H. The use of Alcoholics Anonymous members in research on alcoholism. *Quarterly Journal of Studies on Alcohol*, 1960, **21**, 506–509.

SELIGMAN, M., & DESMOND, R. E. Leaderless groups: A review. *Counseling Psychologist*, 1973, **4**, 70–87.

SELZER, M. L., & HOLLOWAY, W. H. A follow-up of alcoholics committed to a state hospital. *Quarterly Journal of Studies on Alcohol*, 1957, **18**, 98–120.

SHELLY, J. A. Daytop Lodge—Halfway house for addicts on probation. *Rehabilitation Record*, 1966, **7**, 19–21.

SHELLY, J. A., & BASSIN, A. Daytop Lodge—A new treatment approach for drug addicts. *Corrective Psychiatry and Journal of Social Therapy*, 1965, **11**, 186–195.

SHERIF, M., & SHERIF, C. Black unrest as a social movement toward an emerging self-identity. *Journal of Social and Behavioral Sciences*, 1970, **15**, 41–52.

SHOICHET, R. Recovery Incorporated. *Canadian Family Physician*, 1968, **14**, 13.

SILON, E. L. *Attitudes about alcoholics and alcoholism: Development of an assessment instrument.* Unpublished master's thesis, University of Denver, 1975.

SIMONSON, N., & APTER, S. *Therapist disclosure in psychotherapy.* Paper presented at the meeting of the Eastern Psychological Association, Philadelphia, April 1969.

SIMONSON, N. R., & BAHR, S. Self-disclosure by the professional and paraprofessional therapist. *Journal of Consulting and Clinical Psychology*, 1974, **42**, 359–363.

SKÁLA, J. The fight against alcoholism in Czechoslovakia and the part played by health workers. *British Journal of Addiction*, 1957, **54**, 59–70.

SMITH, C. M. A new adjunct to the treatment of alcoholism: The hallucinogenic drugs. *Quarterly Journal of Studies on Alcohol*, 1958, **19**, 406–417.

SMITH, P. L. Alcoholics Anonymous. *Psychiatric Quarterly*, 1941, **15**, 554–562.

SOBEY, F. *The nonprofessional revolution in mental health.* New York: Columbia University Press, 1970.

Statistical Abstract of the United States: 1974. (95th ed.) Washington, D.C.: United States Bureau of the Census, 1974.

STEINER, C. *Games alcoholics play: The analysis of life scripts.* New York: Ballantine, 1971.

STEINER, C. M. Radical psychiatry. In H. M. RUITENBEEK (Ed.), *Going crazy: The radical therapy of R. D. Laing and others.* New York: Bantam Books, 1972.

STRUPP, H. H. Specific vs. nonspecific factors in psychotherapy and the problem of control. *Archives of General Psychiatry*, 1970, **23**, 393–401.

STRUPP, H. H. *Psychotherapy: Clinical, research, and theoretical issues.* New York: Aronson, 1973.

STUNKARD, A. New therapies for the eating disorders: Behavior modification of obesity and anorexia nervosa. *Archives of General Psychiatry*, 1972, **26**, 391–398.

STUNKARD, A., LEVINE, H., & FOX, S. The management of obesity: Patient self-help and medical treatment. *Archives of Internal Medicine*, 1970, **125**, 1067–1072.

STUNKARD, A., & McLAREN-HUME, M. The results of treatment for obesity: A review of the literature and report of a series. *Archives of Internal Medicine*, 1959, **103**, 79–85.

SUOMI, S. J., HARLOW, H. F., & McKINNEY, W. T. Monkey psychiatrists. *American Journal of Psychiatry*, 1972, **128**, 927–932.

SUSSMAN, M. B. Psycho-social correlates of obesity: Failure of "Calorie Collectors." *Journal of the American Dietetic Association*, 1956, **32**, 423–427.

Synanon, Inc. *Fact sheet.* Unpublished manuscript, Marshall, Calif., 1974.

Take Off Pounds Sensibly, Inc. *What is TOPS*, pamphlet. Milwaukee: TOPS, Inc., 1974.

THOMAS, C. W. *Boys no more.* Beverly Hills: Glencoe Press, 1971.

THORPE, J. J., & PERRET, J. T. Problem drinking: A follow-up study. *Archives of Industrial Health*, 1959, **19**, 24–32.

TIEBOUT, H. M. The act of surrender in the therapeutic process: With special reference to alcoholism. *Quarterly Journal of Studies on Alcohol*, 1949, **10**, 48–58.

TIEBOUT, H. M. Surrender versus compliance in therapy with special reference to alcoholism. *Quarterly Journal of Studies on Alcohol*, 1953, **14**, 58–68.

TIEBOUT, H. M. Direct treatment of a symptom. In P. H. HOCH & J. ZUBIN (Eds.), *Problems of addiction and habituation.* Vol. 13. *Proceedings of the American Psychopathological Association.* New York: Grune & Stratton, 1958.

TIMMENS, J. M. A program for the rehabilitation of alcoholics in a combat division overseas. *Medical Bulletin U.S. Army, Europe*, 1965, **22**, 382–385.

TOMSOVIC, M. A follow-up study of discharged alcoholics. *Hospital and Community Psychiatry*, 1970, **21**, 94–97.

TRICE, H. M. Alcoholics Anonymous. *Annals of the American Academy of Political and Social Science*, 1958, **315**, 108–116.

TRICE, H. M., & ROMAN, P. M. Sociopsychological predictors of affiliation with Alcoholics Anonymous: A longitudinal study of "treatment success." *Social Psychiatry*, 1970, **5**, 51–59.

TRUAX, C. B., CARKHUFF, R. R., & KODMAN, F. Relationships between therapist-offered conditions and patient change in group psychotherapy. *Journal of Clinical Psychology*, 1965, **21**, 327–329.

VOLKMAN, R. Differential association and the rehabilitation of drug addicts. *British Journal of Addiction*, 1965, **61**, 91–100.

VOLKMAN, R., & CRESSEY, D. R. Differential association and the rehabilitation of drug addicts. *American Journal of Sociology*, 1963, **69**, 129–142.

W.G.W. Alcoholics Anonymous. *New York State Journal of Medicine*, 1950, **50**, 1708–1710.

WAGONFELD, S., & WOLOWITZ, H. M. Obesity and the self-help group: A look at TOPS. *American Journal of Psychiatry*, 1968, **125**, 249–252.

WALDER, E. Synanon and the learning process: A critique of attack therapy. *Corrective Psychiatry and Journal of Social Therapy*, 1965, **11**, 299–304.

WANBERG, K. W. A pilot follow-up study of alcoholism patients. *Journal of the Fort Logan Mental Health Center*, 1968, **5**, 101–106.

WATTENBERG, W. W., & MOIR, J. B. Factors linked to success in counseling homeless alcoholics. *Quarterly Journal of Studies on Alcohol*, 1954, **15**, 587–594.

WECHSLER, H. The self-help organization in the mental health field: Recovery, Inc., a case study. *Journal of Nervous and Mental Disease*, 1960, **130**, 297–314.

WEIGEL, R. G., & WARNATH, C. F. The effects of group therapy on reported self-disclosure. *International Journal of Group Psychotherapy*, 1968, **18**, 31–41.

WEISSTEIN, N. "Kinder, kuche, kirche" as scientific law: Psychology constructs the female. In R. MORGAN (Ed.), *Sisterhood is powerful*. New York: Vintage, 1970.

WEPPNER, R. S. Matrix House: Its first year at Lexington, Ky. *HSMHA Health Reports*, 1971, **86**, 761–768.

WEPPNER, R. S. Some characteristics of an ex-addict self-help therapeutic community and its members. *British Journal of Addiction*, 1973, **68**, 73–79.

WEXBERG, L. E. The outpatient treatment of alcoholism in the District of Columbia. *Quarterly Journal of Studies on Alcohol*, 1953, **14**, 514–524.

WITKIN, H. A., KARP, S. A., & GOODENOUGH, D. R. Dependence in alcoholics. *Quarterly Journal of Studies on Alcohol*, 1959, **20**, 493–504.

WOLLERSHEIM, J. P. Effectiveness of group therapy based upon learning principles in the treatment of overweight women. *Journal of Abnormal Psychology*, 1970, **76**, 462–474.

WOLPE, J., & LAZARUS, A. A. *Behavior therapy techniques*. New York: Pergamon Press, 1966.

YABLONSKY, L. The anticriminal society: Synanon. *Federal Probation*, 1962, **26**, 50–57.

YABLONSKY, L., & DEDERICH, C. E. Synanon: An analysis of some dimensions of the social structure of an antiaddiction society. In D. M. WILNER & G. G. KASSENBAUM (Eds.), *Narcotics*. New York: McGraw-Hill, 1965.

YALOM, I. D. *The theory and practice of group psychotherapy*. New York: Basic Books, 1970.

YALOM, I. D. *The theory and practice of group psychotherapy*. (2nd ed.) New York: Basic Books, 1975.

YALOM, I. D., & RAND, K. Compatibility and cohesiveness in therapy groups. *Archives of General Psychiatry*, 1966, **15**, 267–275.

ZINBERG, N. E., & GLOTFELTY, J. A. The power of the peer group. *International Journal of Group Psychotherapy*, 1968, **18**, 155–164.

ZUPNICK, S. M. The effects of varying degrees of a peer-model's performance on the extinction of a phobic response in an individual or group setting. *Dissertation Abstracts International*, 1970, **31** (6-B), 3719.

NOTES

1. *Editors' Footnote.* The reader should note the very different sort of "nonprofessional" therapeutic agent discussed in the preceding chapter by Anthony and Carkhuff.

2. A number of peer self-help groups have been excluded from our review because (1) they lack empirical evaluation—Diet Workshop, Integrity Groups (Mowrer, 1972), Reevaluation Counseling (Scheff, 1972), Weight Watchers, and numerous groups bearing the name Anonymous: Bad Checks, Checks, Convicts, Crooks, Delinquents, Disturbed Children, Dropouts, Ex-convicts, Fatties, Families, Gamblers (Scodel, 1964), Illegitimates, Mothers, Narcotics (Patrick, 1965), Neurotics, Overeaters, Parents, Parents of Youth in Trouble, Psychotics, Recidivists, Schizophrenics (Ryback, 1971), Smokers, and Suicides (see Sagarin, 1969, for an account of many of these groups); (2) they have been evaluated but are small and relatively unknown—e.g., Matrix House (Weppner, 1971, 1973); or (3) they are of limited significance and not empirically evaluated—Adults Anonymous (Eglash, 1958a), Calorie Collectors (Sussman, 1965), Forum Anonymous (Cook & Geis, 1957), and Youth Anonymous (Eglash, 1958b).

3. While membership size of the APA is not a direct indicator of the number of mental health professionals in America since only a fraction of psychologists provide direct service and psychologists are only one of several disciplines in the mental health field, the size is at least an indirect index of the number of such professionals available.

4. During the last 40 years APA membership increased 26-fold—1975 membership = 40,000 (Little, 1975) while the U.S. population did not even double—1935 population = 127 million (*Historical Statistics of the United States, Colonial Times to 1957*, 1960); 1975 population = 208 million (*Statistical Abstract of the United States: 1974*, 1974).

5. *Editors' Footnote.* Accessibility to professional therapists, however, is not the only issue here. Modalities of psychotherapy other than traditional, one-to-one encounters (e.g., family therapy) also represent a different conceptualization of both the nature of psychopathology and of the conditions required for effective treatment. In this limited but important sense, some of the newer professional therapies, then, have a degree of commonality with the peer self-help groups described in this chapter.

6. Interestingly enough, observations have been made of animal peers helping one another. Suomi, Harlow, & McKinney (1972) found that when 6-month old, severely socially isolated male monkeys were exposed to 3-month old socially appropriate female monkeys, the males behaved at 1 year in a manner "virtually indistinguishable from the therapists" (p. 930), and at 2 years showed "virtually complete recovery" (p. 931). The experimenters concluded that ". . . gentle physical contact and model-serving exhibited by the therapists" (p. 931) were the major forces leading to recovery. As with human peer influencers, these monkey therapeutic agents ". . . received no formal training, nor were they reimbursed for their efforts by so much as one extra pellet of monkey chow" (p. 931).

7. *Editors' Footnote.* This description of Step Four sounds rather idealistic; it implies a quality of sought-after near-saintliness that we doubt is often achieved. It would, indeed, be interesting to know whether AA dropouts are more likely to occur at this step than at others; we would suspect so.

8. Consistent with this, Sobey (1970) found that former mental patients who worked as counselors in National Institute of Mental Health funded projects tended to overidentify with clients and lose objectivity in their therapeutic activities.

9. *Editors' Footnote.* See Auerbach and Johnson (Chapter 5, this volume) and our footnote 14 in that chapter for a provocative reanalysis of the presumed superior efficacy of experienced therapists.

10. *Editors' Footnote.* This is a controversial point, especially since most professional therapists, in our experience, tend to see the development of insight, in both genetic and functional terms, as of primary importance, with decreased drinking behavior presumed to be contingent upon such cognitive-affective changes. We can see no way of deciding, except in the most extreme cases, which goal "should" be primary; but we think that professional therapists do owe it to their (here, alcoholic) clients to be quite explicit, from the beginning, about their values and goals.

11. That the therapist can grow in his work with people has been noted particularly by those who operate within a humanistic/existentialist framework. According to them (e.g., Mullan & Sangiuliano, 1964; Rogers, 1962), he not only can, but must grow if he is to be an effective therapist.

12. Sometimes the patient does have more than one therapist, as for example, when he has two group therapists or a group therapist and another individual therapist.

13. *Editors' Footnote.* On the other hand, such therapists presumably are more attuned to people's needs for growth experiences and since they often view even "premature" terminations as evidence of client growth and acceptance of responsibility, we would suspect that these therapists would be *less* likely to suffer the consequences of untoward countertransference reactions, especially around the issues of loss and separation.

14. *Editors' Footnote.* In his chapter in this volume, Garfield (Chapter 4) reaches a similar, but somewhat more optimistic, conclusion.

15. Only Bailey and Leach (1965) analyzed, and then only to a very limited extent, the impact of a professional treatment experience on outcome with AA.

16. *Editors' Footnote.* This is a recurrent methodological issue that often generates much heat but little light. The "exclusion" advocates argue, in a common-sense fashion, that such patients should not be counted since they have not really undergone the treatment in question and it is, therefore, unjust (to the treatment) to consider it to have failed. "Inclusionists," on the other hand, argue that part of a treatment method's potency must include its ability to keep its patients in treatment, so that early dropouts do, in this sense, constitute therapeutic failures. We ourselves disagree on this matter, yet see no better resolution presently available than to encourage researchers to decide what side of this particular fence they are on before beginning their investigations; post hoc positions often appear suspect. Moreover, we wish researchers would not merely "drop" such subjects, but would follow them up as well, for the purpose of learning more about the experience of "premature terminators." The authors' decision to use an in-between position seems to be a reasonable compromise.

17. The 30% to 40% abstinence figure is very similar to the total abstinence figure of 30% to 40% Bailey and Leach (1965), Edwards *et al.* (1966, 1967), and Norris (1970) found for several years of membership in their questionnaire survey studies. The figure for the surveys is somewhat more favorable, because it covers a longer period of time (several years versus a mean of only $2\frac{1}{2}$ to more

than 4 years). This difference is not surprising, since the surveys were biased in favor of the more active members.

18. Seven studies, which Leach (1973) saw as evaluating AA's effectiveness, have been excluded from this review. In four (McGinnis 1963; Ramsay, Jensen, & Sommer, 1963; Smith, 1941; Timmens, 1965) AA data were inseparable from professional treatment data. The fifth (Machover, Puzzo, & Plumeau, 1962) was not an outcome study. The sixth and seventh (Hayman, 1956; W. G. W., 1950) reported impressionistic evidence rather than hard outcome data.

19. Readers interested in comparing AA outcome rates with drinking adjustment data for patients active in treatment of less than a year can find such data in Emrick (1973). These data have been excluded here because of their incompatibility with AA rates: The data represent behavior covering a much shorter period of time than do AA rates.

20. Bailey and Leach (1965) found that 77.1% of the members surveyed ($N = 873$) spent more than 50% of their "social life" in AA and 43.2% spent more than two-thirds of their "social life" in it.

21. *Editors' Footnote.* As in the case of the "functional therapeutic agents" discussed in the preceding chapter by Anthony and Carkhuff, we are again impressed by the power of nonprofessionals to effect *certain kinds of changes with certain kinds of clients.* As we noted in the preceding chapter (Footnote 8), it is necessary to keep in mind that the question of "professionals versus nonprofessionals" is as misguided as the old saw about whether psychotherapy is effective. As Emrick *et al.* note, the goals (abstinence versus controlled social drinking) of AA are quite different from those of many professional therapists.

22. *Editors' Footnote.* But this does not constitute evidence for the failure of Recovery since, as the authors point out above, "One of the principle benefits which recovery is considered to provide is to *help the patient be more amenable to accepting the treatment and authority of the physician*" (emphasis ours). Moreover, we would argue that since most Recovery members have severe and chronic conditions, staying out of the hospital yet *in* treatment is a very good outcome and perhaps the most that can, in many cases, be hoped for.

23. *Editors' Footnote.* While women in CR groups may not, in general, define themselves in this way in the context of or for the purpose of entering CR groups, it should be noted here (as the authors later point out) that there is evidence (Glaser, 1974) that as many as half the members of (some) CR groups are also involved in professional psychotherapy concurrently.

24. *Editors' Footnote.* While CR members may be philosophically opposed to a formalized hierarchical structure, this in no way precludes the inevitable emergence of one or more leaders within these groups, since it is an inherent property of group process that leadership functions are not distributed equally. Scientific study of the natural, albeit implicit, "election" of group leaders in groups, such as CR, that forthrightly deny the existence of such a phenomenon, would be most welcomed.

25. *Editors' Footnote.* We are generally in agreement with this position, but would add that, again, the specificity issue once more must reign. We would support further empirical study of the "borrowing" of specific treatment components for specific treatment conditions.

CHAPTER 8

THERAPISTS' ATTITUDES TOWARD MENTAL ILLNESS AND HEALTH

JUDITH G. RABKIN

Introduction

ATTITUDES of others toward the mentally ill constitute a major dimension of their experience. Once it becomes public knowledge that a person has spent time in a mental hospital, or even that he has received outpatient treatment, the attitudes of those whom he encounters in his daily living are usually affected, for the most part negatively. It is now generally acknowledged that the label of mental illness leads to a lowered status in the public view, as reflected in increased difficulties in the search for jobs, friends, or a place to live. Despite the current emphasis on early release from mental hospitals, ex-patients often are handicapped in their efforts to be accepted back into their communities and to become reintegrated in ongoing social and economic transactions.

Mental health professionals are generally aware of the role of public opinion in shaping the social environments of present or former patients, and many recognize that these attitudes also are associated with the legal and economic conditions which determine the treatment facilities and options available to most patients. Even if they have not read the research literature, administrators and clinicians quickly learn that the relatives and neighbors of patients have a real impact on their fate; for example, the willingness of families to accept home a hospitalized relative materially influences the probability and timing of his discharge.

What is perhaps less often considered by mental health workers is the effect of their own attitudes about mental illness and health on the experiences of the patients they encounter. Mental patients, characteristically quite sensitive to the evaluations of those with whom they associate in the course of their daily routine, are particularly influenced by those of the mental health workers concerned with their treatment and rehabilitative programs. Such workers, who are assigned by society an authoritative

position in relation to the patients in their care, often control their very destinies. Their attitudes toward mental illness in general, their expectations about who will profit from treatment and what sort of treatment is suitable for what kind of patient, their conceptions of suitable therapeutic goals, and their definitions of mental health all inevitably play integral roles in the initiation and outcome of therapeutic endeavors. Such attitudes help to determine who is accepted for treatment, the kind of treatment program selected, its duration, and even its outcome. Accordingly, a systematic delineation of mental health workers' attitudes about mental illness and health is warranted in the course of understanding the total therapeutic process.

Professional attitudes about mental illness and health are best understood in relation to public attitudes, especially when it is considered that most psychiatric patients are themselves laymen and typically share the attitudes of their families and friends. In this chapter, a preliminary section summarizes research concerning public attitudes toward mental illness; virtually no work has been done to determine public conceptions of mental health. The second section is devoted to a review of findings about therapists' attitudes toward mental illness, including their personal and occupational characteristics associated with variations in attitudes. This section is followed by a review of patient characteristics which influence therapists' attitudes. The fourth section is concerned with the considerably smaller group of studies of therapists' attitudes and beliefs about mental health. The chapter concludes with suggestions for future research in the field.

Definitions and Populations

Although the terms "mental illness" and "mental patient" are variously interpreted by professionals as well as laymen, in the realm of

162

attitude studies they characteristically refer to psychiatric hospitalization. Most attitude scales in wide use, such as the Opinions About Mental Illness Scale (OMI) of Cohen and Struening (1962), state in instructions to respondents that the term "mental patient" refers to hospitalized patients only. While there is undoubtedly some extension to either clinic or private outpatients, or to those simply regarded as eccentric by the individual respondent, it is reasonably accurate to conclude that, in studies of attitudes toward mental illness, the term refers to those who are presently hospitalized or have been so in the past.

The term "mental health" is far less specific. Since no formal attitude questionnaire about mental health has been developed, investigators in the area have relied on such measures as adjective checklists and semantic differential scales. While researchers generally do not equate "mental health" with the simple absence of symptoms, it is often difficult to tell whether they (and respondents) are thinking about "good adjustment" in the sense of social conformity, or a more elite notion of personal maturity and development. Hopefully, a consensual definition will evolve as more work is done in the area.

The term "therapist" as used in this chapter refers to all mental health workers who spend time with patients. This broad usage is dictated by two considerations. First, the large majority of hospitalized mental patients seldom, sometimes never, see an individual psychotherapist in an ongoing treatment program, and many psychotherapists have little if anything to do with the severely disturbed patients to whom the term "mental illness" refers. Consequently from a practical standpoint, most attitudinal studies concerning mental illness and health have dealt with more numerous, more involved, and more available groups of mental health workers, ranging from aides, who constitute the largest single occupational group, to students, administrators, and clinicians.

PUBLIC ATTITUDES TOWARD MENTAL ILLNESS

Despite longstanding awareness of the discrepancies between what people say and what they do, the link between attitude and behavior has been regarded as sufficiently meaningful to warrant extensive research regarding public attitudes toward mental illness. Since the late 1940s, when the first studies were designed, there has emerged a substantial body of research concerning the delineation of attitudes held by the public. A brief review of this work will provide a framework for evaluating attitudes of mental health workers toward mental health and illness. I will summarize the early major studies of attitudes about mental illness in the 1950s, subsequent trends that developed during the 1960s, and the present status of the field.

Major Early Studies[1]

A classical experimental study of opinions about mental illness was conducted in a rural Canadian town in 1951 by Cumming and Cumming (1957). They planned to evaluate such attitudes and their mutability by testing residents before and after a 6-month educational program. However, their message that normal and abnormal behavior are not qualitatively distinct was seen as so offensive that the community eventually rejected the entire program. Instead of changing initially negative attitudes toward mental illness, the Cummings demonstrated instead the unfeasibility of trying to modify a specific attitude in a direction at variance with the system of values prevailing within a community.

An extensive 6-year survey was conducted during the 1950s by Nunnally (1961) to see what the public knew and felt about mental illness and treatment. Summarizing his results, he reported that "as is commonly suspected, the mentally ill are regarded with fear, distrust and dislike by the general public" (p. 46). The stigma associated with mental illness was found to be very general, both across social groups and across attitude indicators, with little relation to demographic variables such as age and education. "Old people and young people, highly educated people and people with little formal training—all tend to regard the mentally ill as relatively dangerous, dirty, unpredictable and worthless" (p. 51). A strong negative halo surrounds the mentally ill—"they are considered, unselectively, as being all things bad" (p. 233). However, these "bad" attitudes were not held because of existing information or even misinformation about mental illness by the public, but rather because of *lack* of information.

Shirley Star's contributions (summarized in a report of the Joint Commission on Mental Illness and Health, 1961, p. 75) to the field were both methodological and substantive. She formulated the six case history descriptions often referred to as the Star vignettes. The cases include a neurotic depressive, a paranoid, and a simple schizophrenic, alcoholic, phobic-compulsive, and juvenile conduct disorder. Using these vignettes, she found in the early 1950s that only the most extremely disturbed behavior was recognized as such by the majority of her respondents, that they tended to resist calling anyone "mentally ill," and did so only as a last resort.

Whatley (1958) investigated the social consequences of psychiatric hospitalization, adapting for this purpose a social distance scale which has since been widely used. He showed that people tend to keep a distance between themselves and former mental patients, creating for the latter a type of social isolation which enhances their problems of social readjustment after being away.

In the course of their massive study of social class and mental illness in New Haven, Hollingshead and Redlich (1958) found that higher social status was associated with more knowledge about psychiatrists and psychiatric treatment, greater willingness to seek such help, and greater competence in arranging for it. Lower social status was related to lack of information, resistance, and sometimes open antagonism to psychiatric intervention. The lower the class, the more likely that mental illness was seen as a feared somatic disease.

In short, by 1960, it was unambiguously established that mental patients were dimly regarded in the public view. The label was feared; people tended to overlook behavior that professionals regarded as pathological, evidently as a mechanism of denial rather than because of greater tolerance for deviance. When the label was authoritatively assigned, the person so labeled was stigmatized and shunned. People did not subscribe to the medical model of mental illness as often as mental health professionals would have liked, and furthermore were generally outspoken about the discomfort and anxiety evoked in them by the subject of mental illness and the presence of a person so labeled.

Subsequent Trends: The 1960s

During the 1960s, many workers in the field of attitude studies seemed to belong to one of two categories of conceptual orientation. One group tended to regard mental illness in the traditional psychiatric framework of a medical model. They were encouraged by their findings that an increasing proportion of the public believes that mental illness is an illness like any other, and that more and more respondents

identified case history descriptions as indicating mental illness. These investigators were typically optimistic in their appraisals of the effects of public education programs on public attitudes about mental illness. In contrast, other investigators subscribed more or less explicitly to a psychosocial or social deviance model of mental illness and characteristically shared the orientation of the community psychiatry movement in which primary prevention and early outpatient treatment are emphasized. They continued to find evidence of stigma and fear in the attitudes of the public about mental illness. These divergent evaluations seem at least partly due to differences in underlying ideologies and research strategies leading to dissimilar expectations regarding amount and direction of attitude change seen as necessary or desirable.

Crocetti, Lemkau, and their colleagues represent the more optimistic view regarding public attitude change. They categorically reject the general proposition that "the mentally ill are stereotyped, stigmatized and punitively rejected by society" (Crocetti, Spiro, & Siassi, 1974). They tend to interpret the findings of their own and others' studies quite liberally, and feel that other investigators have selectively underemphasized reports of public tolerance of mental illness. As an example, they mention two early studies, one by Cumming and Cumming (1957) summarized above and in many other reviews, published under the pessimistic title of "Closed Ranks," and the other by Woodward (1951) more hopefully entitled "Changing Ideas of Mental Illness and its Treatment." Woodward found in his survey that "people no longer see mental illness as a result of sin or the devil, that it is merely evil or willful misbehavior and that punishment is the only solution." While all would probably agree that the devil is seldom invoked in contemporary discussions about mental illness, abandonment of such Victorian conceptions hardly signifies eager acceptance, either. It becomes a matter of taste and interpretation whether one regards studies such as Woodward's as evidence of public acceptance of the mentally ill.

Crocetti and his colleagues (Crocetti & Lemkau, 1965; Crocetti, Spiro, & Siassi, 1971) and others (Bentz & Edgerton, 1970, 1971; Meyer, 1964; Ring & Schein, 1970; Rootman & Lafave, 1969) have conducted a series of studies in which three Star vignettes and a social distance scale are presented to various groups in order to see how frequently the vignettes are identified as describing mental illness, and to get an estimate of preferred social distance regarding mental patients. In general, results have been analyzed in simple proportions; thus, one study reported that 69% of the sample identified the case description of the paranoid as mentally ill, while another study found that 91% did. These investigators have concluded that the public is becoming increasingly able to identify case descriptions as being mentally ill, to regard medical care as the appropriate treatment for mental illness, to see mental illness as an illness like any other, and to be less concerned than formerly about keeping at a social distance from ex-patients. The cumulative impact of these studies does indeed demonstrate an increase during the 1960s in public acceptance of the medical model of mental illness and a less extreme rejection of those labeled mentally ill.

Another series of studies also conducted during the 1960s provides less ground for optimism about public tolerance and enlightenment regarding mental illness. A major contributor to this position has been the sociologist D. L. Phillips. His earlier studies (1963, 1964) showed that consultation with mental health professionals, as opposed to clergymen or family doctors, led to greater social rejection, as did greater visibility of disturbed behavior, especially if the disturbed person was male. Phillips also ingeniously demonstrated (1966) that a history of psychiatric hospitalization, apart from any present manifestation of difficulty, had a stigmatizing effect in the public view; from these results, he concluded that the public does not really believe that mental illness is a transient condition. Other sociologically oriented studies lent support to Phillips' observations. Tringo (1970) sought to establish a hierarchy of preference in the public view among various categories of the disabled, ill, and stigmatized. He adapted from Bogardus (1925) a social distance scale with a 9-point response range, the extremes of which were "would marry" and "would put to death." Of the 21 disability groups ranked, the four that consistently were assigned lowest place by all respondents were ex-convict, mental retardation, alcoholism, and mental illness in last place of all.

Approaching the problem of stigma from another viewpoint, Farina (1971, 1973) has considered the effect of a past psychiatric history of employability on judgments of competence and likability. Using previously unacquainted pairs of male college students in a laboratory setting, Farina showed that merely believing that a partner had been told that he, the subject, was a mental patient, led this subject to act in a manner that alienated his partner. In fact, the partner had not been so informed. In another design, Farina demonstrated that those who bore the label of mental patient, even when they were really normal, felt less comfortable, performed more poorly on a simple manual task, and were seen by others as more anxious than subjects not so labeled.[2] In a carefully designed field study of employment interviewers, Farina and Felner (1973) found that job applicants who acknowledged a prior psychiatric hospitalization were offered fewer jobs and were treated less cordially by the interviewers.

As a group, these studies do not consider the issue of whether the stigma of mental illness has diminished in the United States; they simply demonstrate that prejudice toward those labeled mentally ill continues to be seen among members of the general public.

Comment

In reviewing the findings of the last 20 years to evaluate how much public opinion has changed and where it stands today, several major points seem to emerge from the prevailing controversies. First, regardless of one's ideological point of view, it seems evident that people are better informed about mental illness now than in the past.

A second point is that the message "mental illness is an illness like any other" has been widely disseminated; people seem to accept it as the "correct" thing to believe. In this sense Crocetti and his colleagues are accurate in reporting the propagation of the medical model. But the public, as Sarbin and Mancuso (1972) vigorously point out, seems ultimately unconvinced of the explanatory value, or at least the implications, of this conceptual framework. Ex-mental patients are simply not perceived with the same trust, good will, and restoration of the former "normal" status that is reassigned to ex-medical patients. This continued differentiation between mental and physical illness is reflected in an item presented in a community survey in New York City (Elinson, Padilla, & Perkins, 1967) to which 77% of their respondents agreed: "Unlike physical illness which makes most people sympathetic, mental illness tends to repel most people," while only 16% of these respondents themselves confessed to being repelled by mental illness. It seems, then, that people "know" they should regard mental illness as an illness like any other, but their feelings are not regularly shaped by this conviction.

As a general overview of the status of public attitudes toward mental illness in the early 1970s, it seems reasonable to endorse Halpert's (1969) conclusion that people are distinctly better informed and disposed toward mental patients than they have been, but a major portion of the population continues to be frightened and repelled by the notion of mental illness. Today, as in times past, when people encounter the description or presence of someone who has been labeled mentally ill, they are not pleased to meet him.

DETERMINANTS OF THERAPISTS' ATTITUDES TOWARD MENTAL ILLNESS

While mental health professionals are generally better informed than the public at large about matters such as etiology and outcome of various psychiatric disorders, there remain extreme divergences of belief and opinion even among the most highly trained. Mental health workers with positions of less prestige, such as aides, attendants, and nursing assistants, tend to have attitudes that are virtually indistinguishable from those prevailing in their home communities; such workers are not necessarily better educated or more enlightened about mental illness than are their blue-collar neighbors. To them, mental illness often appears as a fearful, stigmatizing, and dehumanizing condition from which recovery is doubtful. At the other extreme, professionals with post-graduate training have much more positive, optimistic attitudes which are often shared by the well-educated, upper class layman who lacks some of the understanding but not necessarily the tolerance of the professional. Consequently, it is not fruitful to deal with all mental health workers as a single population in examining their attitudes toward mental illness. Instead, variations in the attributes, training, and experience of members of the mental health professions will be considered in relation to their attitudes. A preliminary review of results associated with these variables, based on samples of the general public, will be followed by a summary of studies of therapist variables as they relate to their attitudes about mental illness.

Characteristics of Laymen Associated with Attitudes toward Mental Illness

Members of the general public can be differentiated on the basis of their age, education, occupation, race, ethnicity, social class, and exposure to mental patients; each of these variables has been related to variations in attitudes toward the mentally ill. Investigators have observed a strong and consistent relationship between the age and education of respondents, their degree of prejudice in general, and rejection of the mentally ill in particular (Bates, 1968; Bordeleau, Pelletier, Panaccio, & Tetreault, 1970; Clark & Binks, 1966; Freeman, 1961; Lawton, 1964, 1965; Middleton, 1953; Ramsey & Seipp, 1948). The older the individual and the less educated he is, the more unsympathetic, intolerant, rejecting, and distant are his attitudes about the mentally ill. This is true among hospitalized mental patients also; evidently the condition of patienthood does not significantly alter beliefs and judgments (Bentinck, 1967; Giovannoni & Ullman, 1963; Manis, Houts, & Blake, 1963). With respect to social class, higher status groups are more apt to regard deviant behavior as a manifestation of mental illness than are lower class groups who tend to overlook disturbed behavior or regard it as bad and serious but not mentally ill. Once lower class members decide that someone is indeed mentally ill, however, they are more intolerant and rejecting than others (Dohrenwend & Chin-Shong, 1967; Hollingshead & Redlich, 1958). As Dworkin (1969) observed among her working-class subjects, they typically conceive mental illness as a dichotomous condition with no intermediary stages between being crazy and normal; if crazy, it is assumed that the individual is irrational and incompetent in all areas of functioning.

Race and ethnicity have been linked to attitudes largely in terms of the extent to which various ethnic groups are acquainted with and share middle-class American values generally. The lower in status and less assimilated the group, the more authoritarian and restrictive are their attitudes toward the mentally ill (Crocetti & Lemkau, 1965; Edgerton & Karno, 1971; Fournet, 1967). Low occupational rank has been associated with the reduced likelihood of ascribing deviant behavior to mental illness (Guttmacher & Elinson, 1971). However, menial employment typically characterizes the recent immigrant, the uneducated, the people with low social status, and it may be these factors which account for most of the attitudinal differences observed. In short, it seems that those who are better off in our society are more inclined to tolerate deviance, including mental illness, than those whose lives are less secure, comfortable or financially rewarding.

Characteristics of Therapists Associated with Attitudes Toward Mental Illness

Occupational category. Analyses of characteristics of mental health workers affecting attitudes about mental illness have focused primarily on comparisons between occupational groups. Personnel with lower status—such as aides, nursing assistants, and maintenance and kitchen workers—are generally found to be more authoritarian and restrictive in their attitudes toward mental patients, while those with post-graduate training are typically more aware of the strengths patients possess, are more liberal and tolerant in their attitudes, and more optimistic about their prospects for recovery.

Cohen and Struening (1962, 1963, 1964, 1965) conducted a series of studies concerning attitudes of mental health workers by occupational category. They devised the Opinions about Mental Illness Scale (OMI), a 51-item questionnaire that yields for each respondent scores on five factors: authoritarianism, benevolence (which refers to an unsophisticated paternalism), social restrictiveness, mental hygiene ideology, and interpersonal etiology. Working within the Veterans Administration Psychiatric Hospital system, they studied members of 19 occupational categories in 12 hospitals and grouped them empirically into four clusters in terms of their OMI responses. Blue-collar workers including aides, maintenance and kitchen workers, scored high on authoritarianism and social restrictiveness. Their attitudes were not benevolent and they did not advocate the concepts of mental hygiene ideology or interpersonal etiology. White-collar workers, including technicians, nurses, dentists, and nonpsychiatric physicians, scored low on authoritarianism. The third cluster, consisting of psychologists and social workers, endorsed attitudes that were the converse of those of blue-collar workers: low on authoritarianism and social restrictiveness, high on mental hygiene ideology and interpersonal etiology. These were the most tolerant respondents, clergymen, constituting the fourth group, showed patterns similar to but less extremely positive than the third group. Psychiatrists did not fit into any cluster, but resembled clergymen more than the other groups.

Cohen and Struening also reported that, while occupational groups differed significantly from each other in their attitudes, the climate in any given hospital was largely determined by the attitudes of aides and nurses, because they comprised the large majority of the staff. Patients in hospitals with a strong authoritarian-restrictive atmosphere spent fewer days in the community in the 6 months after date of admission than did patients in other hospitals, when variables such as symptom pattern at admission were controlled for. The extent of authoritarian and benevolent attitudes was found to vary across hospitals in different geographical locations for nurses and aides, probably according to the local subculture, but did not vary for professionals.

Another extensive and well-designed study dealing with Veterans Administration personnel in 27 hospitals was conducted by Klett and Lasky (1962), who administered a modification of Gilbert and Levinson's Custodial Mental Illness Ideology Scale (CMI) and a Chemotherapy Attitude Scale (CAS) to 79 nursing assistants, 76 nurses, 103 psychiatrists, 86 psychologists, and 45 social workers. Each scale was separately factored and professional groups were ranked in terms of their mean scores on each of five CMI factors and six CAS factors. The pattern of observed differences between staff occupational groups was fairly consistent, especially on the CMI and especially for nursing assistants. Nursing assistants expressed the view that mental patients need to be closely regulated, restricted, and cared for physically because they are irresponsible and incompetent. As might be expected, they favored the use of drugs as the primary treatment modality.

Although more moderate in their position, nurses' attitudes were more like those of the nursing assistants than the attitudes of any other group except that nurses regarded patients as more capable than did the nursing assistants. Psychologists and social workers held similar attitudes regarding chemotherapy and mental illness, both generally contrary to those of nursing assistants. Psychiatrists occupied a middle ground among the staff groups; they were more aware of the side effects, disadvantages, and limitations of chemotherapy than any other group. The authors suggest that the differences in amount and nature of formal education, particularly regarding theories of psychopathology and the philosophy of its treatment, probably contribute to these differences in attitudes held by various occupational groups. Other factors may include the nature of occupational responsibilities and amount of direct patient contact. In all, the results of this investigation serve to validate the findings of Cohen and Struening, at least within the population of Veterans Administration neuropsychiatric hospital personnel.

Recently, a third large-scale study was conducted by Creech (1974), designed to evaluate the attitudes toward mental illness held by staff members at a state hospital and five community mental health centers in North Carolina. A total of 348 mental health workers responded to Cohen and Struening's OMI and Ellsworth's Opinions about Mental Illness-Staff Opinion Survey (OMI-SOS), from which Creech used a factor called "nontraditionalism-accountability." This attitude dimension reflects endorsement of warmth and engagement with patients and conviction that patients can shape events rather than being the passive victims of either childhood trauma or congenital determinants of disorder. Creech analyzed the factor scores of his respondents by occupational group, with results comparable to those of Cohen and Struening and Klett and Lasky: aides and clerical workers scored high on the factors of authoritarianism and social restrictiveness and low on the others, while the converse was true for groups with post-graduate training. All groups scored rather low on interpersonal etiology, although in the earlier studies of Cohen and Struening, scores on this factor were high among occupational groups with more advanced training. It seems likely that this attitude dimension, which emphasizes the psychoanalytic notions of childhood trauma and lack of parental love as basic contributors to latter disorder, has become less popular in the last decade as the social psychiatric perspective with its emphasis on contemporary transactions and sources of stress has become increasingly accepted.

Creech also compared parallel occupational groups working in the state hospital and at the community mental health centers. Personnel in the latter setting tended to be less authoritarian and restrictive and more inclined to accept the ideas of mental hygiene ideology and nontraditionalism than their hospital counterparts. Creech suggests that this may be due to differences in degree of pathology seen at the two settings, or because younger and better trained people seek employment in mental health centers in view of greater opportunities for innovative programs and career development.

A third analysis undertaken by Creech was between his two samples and the standardization population of Cohen and Struening which consisted of Veterans Administration personnel whose attitudes were investigated more than a decade earlier. Both hospital and community respondents in the present sample have lower means than the standardization population on all of the OMI factors except that of mental

hygiene ideology, where their mean scores were higher. Unfortunately, we cannot tell if these differences are due to a generalized modification of attitudes over the past 10 years or whether they are attributable to the occupational settings of the respondents. However, it is apparent that the scores of the present sample are more homogeneous within occupational category than were those of the Veterans Administration population.

Findings consonant with those of the foregoing studies have been reported by Appleby, Ellis, Rogers, and Zimmerman (1961), Reznikoff (1963), Reznikoff, Gynther, Toomey, & Fishman (1964), Wright and Klein (1966), Williams and Williams (1961), and Vernallis and St. Pierre (1964). Appleby et al. (1961), using the Custodial Mental Illness Ideology Scale (CMI), OMI, and a Q sort to measure role conception, found that professional staff members differed from aides and administrative personnel in being less authoritarian and more humanistic. Reznikoff (1963) investigated attitudes toward psychiatrists, hospitals, and psychiatric treatment held by nurses and aides, using a 12-item "Multiple Choice Attitudes Questionnaire" he constructed. He found nurses generally more favorable in their attitudes toward psychiatrists and psychotherapy than aides, and supervisory personnel more favorable than others within each group. He was subsequently unable to replicate these findings, however.

Wright and Klein (1966) found professional staff more accepting than aides and other employees with less education and less formal training, although hospital personnel as a group were more accepting than members of the local community—a small Southern town. Williams and Williams (1961) found that student nurses were less authoritarian and scored lower on a measure of anomie than aides, as measured by two scales they constructed. The student nurses were also more "modern" in their attitudes about the symptoms and stigma of mental illness.

Attitudes of volunteer workers at the Veterans Administration hospital in Topeka were compared with those of other hospital employees (Vernallis & St. Pierre, 1964). Their responses were most similar to those of male aides: they were not receptive to the ideas of mental hygiene ideology, and were more socially restrictive than white-collar and professional workers, although they accepted, like most of the staff, the concepts of interpersonal etiology as the major origins of disturbed behavior.[3]

Personal Characteristics of Therapists. In

addition, and at times related to attitudinal variations associated with occupational category, a number of personal characteristics of mental health workers have been found to be linked with their attitudes. In their direction and influence, these relationships are parallel to those found in studies of members of the general public. Such characteristics include the variables of age, education, experience with mental patients, and specific training.

Middleton (1953), using a 47-item Prejudice Test with a dichotomous agree-disagree format, found that better-educated, younger, and more intelligent hospital employees were less prejudiced than others. This matches the more general finding that age and extent of prejudice are positively related. He also reported that the more experienced workers were more prejudiced, a fact which logically follows since more experienced workers were typically older. Like Middleton, Lawton (1964, 1965) using the OMI, found that authoritarianism and social restrictiveness were positively related to age and years of service. He also found a negative correlation between social restrictiveness and education. Similarly, Clark and Binks (1966) reported that greater education and younger age were associated with more liberal attitudes about mental illness. Perry (1974), studying attitudes of nearly 500 psychiatric aides in a Texas mental hospital, again found a progressive increase in the strength of the "unfavorable" attitudes of authoritarianism and social restrictiveness over a range of experience from zero to 19 years. At the same time, the strength of positive attitudes related to the modern mental health movement was found to decrease with length of experience. In contrast, Reznikoff (1963) found low but significant correlations between positiveness of overall attitudes and years of experience for both nurses and aides. Cohen and Struening (1962) did not find age highly correlated with any of their factors on the OMI, but education was negatively correlated with authoritarianism and social restrictiveness, and positively correlated with mental hygiene ideology and interpersonal etiology factors.

Berg (1974), using the OMI in a study of 380 mental health workers in Alaska, found attitudinal variations related to size of community of residence, type of program, amount of education, amount of training, and occupational category. Workers who lived in small Alaskan communities tended to be more authoritarian and socially restrictive, as did case workers in community alcoholism treatment projects re-

gardless of locale, health workers with only high school education, and health aides. More training and more education were associated with more liberal and tolerant attitudes: social workers and physicians scored lowest on authoritarianism and social restrictiveness factors. Training did not seem to overcome the effects of limited education on attitudes, since health workers with high school education or less were found to be highly authoritarian despite specialized training.

Baker and Schulberg's (1967) Community Mental Health Ideology Scale (CMHI), a single-factor measure of degree of acceptance of community mental health beliefs, has been used to rank professional and lay groups in terms of their adherence to this socially directed and politically liberal attitude dimension. In their initial study, the authors found that the highest scores, reflecting greatest agreement, were obtained by clinical and community psychologists, followed in descending order by occupational therapists, psychiatrists, and psychoanalysts in private practice. In a study of community mental health center personnel in Texas, Langston (1970) extended these findings to a broader range of occupational categories. His sample also included social workers who obtained scores even higher than psychologists, who were followed in turn by occupational therapists, nurses, clerical staff, psychiatrists, aides, and orderlies. In addition to the relationship between occupation and attitudes, Langston found positive correlations between degree of acceptance of community mental health ideology and years of liberal arts education, and also with length of time employed in a mental health center. Poovathumkal (1973) found that 24 black paraprofessionals working at community mental health centers in Chicago obtained scores on the CMHI Scale much lower than those reported elsewhere for professionals. However, these scores were not related to the respondents' ages or length of experience.

In another study, Baker and Schulberg (1969) found that lay members of local mental health boards obtained higher scores than the mean of national random samples of mental health professionals. In terms of its relationship to other belief dimensions, community mental health ideology scores have been found to be negatively correlated with measures of political-economic conservatism and dogmatism, empirically demonstrating the "liberal" nature of this point of view. As expected, younger respondents among the professional samples had higher CMHI scores, probably reflecting both their less traditional political and professional views and also the greater likelihood of exposure to this comparatively new ideological position during their training.

Myers (1973) has surveyed psychiatrists and medical psychoanalysts on the attending staff of a private nonprofit psychiatric hospital in Philadelphia in 1961 with 89 respondents, in 1965 when 109 responded, and in 1972 when 149 responded. Over the years, an increasing proportion of his sample described themselves as eclectic in their practice; the number currently in analytic training has declined. Respondents were asked to evaluate different types of therapy in terms of their primary effectiveness with different categories of patients. For neurotic patients, insight therapy has declined in valued importance from 1961 to 1972 among both psychiatrists and analysts. For the treatment of schizophrenics, an increased number of both groups regard drugs as the most effective element of treatment; this increase seems to have come largely from those who had valued the social milieu and hospital program most highly. The analysts were more positive about psychotherapy, particularly "insight" than the remainder of the staff, and a little less so about drug usage though still in favor of it as an auxiliary tool. Myers notes that the declining enthusiasm among psychiatrists for the therapeutic effectiveness of the social milieu coincided with a marked growth of interest and activity in the therapeutic community among the paraprofessional staff members.

For the treatment of affective disorders, most respondents felt that drugs were most effective, psychoanalysts more so than the others. Other findings include increased respect for behavior therapy among psychiatrists and analysts, and a shared belief in the value of social milieu therapy as an adjunctive method (although, as noted, fewer regarded this as the most effective primary form of treatment). In their expectations regarding future developments in the field, respondents in 1962 looked forward to increased understanding of intrapsychic and interpersonal phenomena; in 1972 they anticipated that the most significant advances would lie in the realm of biochemical treatment. In general, fewer differences between psychiatrists and psychoanalysts were observed than might have been expected, especially regarding their shared attitudes about the constructive role of behavior therapy, drugs, and directive therapy for schizophrenic patients and those diagnosed as character disorders.

One group of healers not usually considered as members of the mental health professions are nevertheless consulted about many problems we would consider emotional or psychological. Members of this group are Puerto Rican spiritualists; their attitudes about mental illness and the nature of their clientele have been examined by Lubchansky, Egri, and Stokes (1970). In New York, where one of nine residents is Puerto Rican, spiritualists probably carry as large a caseload of mentally ill Puerto Ricans as do the established psychiatric resources; many patients consult both. In this study, 20 spiritualists were interviewed separately. Each was presented with six of Star's case history descriptions and was asked for his diagnostic impression and suggestions for alleviating the described difficulties. They were also asked a series of questions about their conceptions of mental illness. The authors concluded that the spiritualists have idiosyncratic conceptions of mental illness, compared to usual psychiatric notions, that they tend to describe it in terms of the less visible behaviors (e.g., disorganized thinking), and consider the possibility of change in the illness over time. Although many elements of their thinking resemble those of the standard psychiatric perspective, the phraseology in which their views are expressed and their derivation of illness from spirits has the effect of discouraging professional interest in their work.

Lubchansky et al. (1970) found that mental illness is typically defined by spiritualists as the handiwork of evil spirits. Prescriptions are offered which include both changes in behavior and ritualistic procedures. The use of trance and dissociation are preferred techniques for carrying out the prescription. Somatic language is used by patients and spiritualists, though both understand it to have implications beyond the literal terms employed. In short, spiritualists as mental health workers have particular beliefs and methods which overlap with those of traditional professionals but which are particularly suited to the cultural heritage of those they serve.

In summary, among mental health workers as among members of the general public, those who are younger, in the mainstream of American middle-class culture, more highly trained, and of greater social and professional status tend to be less socially restrictive and less authoritarian in their attitudes about mental illness and mental patients. Among therapists with post-graduate training, there presently seems to be a wider range of attitudinal variation among psychiatrists, extending from radical young residents to the very conservative and traditional, while clinical psychologists and social workers tend to be more homogeneously liberal in their outlooks.

The distinct attitudinal patterns that have been differentiated for categories of mental health workers cannot be attributed solely to occupational differences, since members of these categories differ significantly in terms of demographic variables. It seems likely that just as attitudes are shaped by age, education, and social class, so choice of occupation is largely dictated by these variables (see Henry, Chapter 3, this volume).

Changing Attitudes About Mental Illness

Many studies of student and staff attitudes about mental illness have been designed in relation to efforts at attitude modification. Hospital and clinic administrators and educators in professional schools are often eager to encourage more favorable attitudes among present and prospective staff members and students. Practical experience with patients, in-service training programs, and classroom instruction have each been employed as a vehicle for inducing attitude change. Several dozen studies of this nature have been carried out; most have looked for and found changes in questionnaire responses rather than in observable behavior. (For an extensive review of this literature, see Rabkin, 1972.) Cumulatively, their findings suggest that *neither academic instruction nor contact with patients by themselves are sufficient conditions for attitude change in the absence of predisposition or motivation to improve attitudes toward the mentally ill.* Given such motivation, however, positive changes occur; thus, scores on the OMI factors of authoritarianism and social restrictiveness typically decline, while those on the factors of benevolence, mental hygiene ideology, and interpersonal etiology increase. (Such changes are regarded as improvements.) Greater understanding and acceptance are facilitated when the mental patient is seen in a role that can be perceived as representing "normal" behavior. Accordingly, events like joint camping trips are apt to be far more conducive to attitude change on the part of the psychiatric aides who accompany the patients than exposure to them in their forlorn and not-quite-human conditions of hospitalization.

Direction of Attitude Change

Before concluding this discussion of the relation between characteristics of mental health workers and their attitudes about mental illness, it seems important to mention an issue regarding scientific values. In several of the foregoing studies, investigators indicated either directly or by implication that there are "good" or "desirable" attitudes toward mental illness and that there are "bad" attitudes. Desirable attitudes are typically thought to be those reflecting the middle-class values of liberalism, tolerance, and humanism, as seen in positive endorsement of the OMI factors of mental hygiene ideology and interpersonal etiology. High scores on authoritarianism and social restrictiveness are viewed as regrettable. It has been recommended by several investigators that mental health workers be selected and trained accordingly; prospective employees who score low on social restrictiveness, for example, would be preferred to those who scored high.

However, these evaluations seem to be based at least as much on moral as on practical considerations. It is true that some studies have suggested that in institutions where a pronounced authoritarian atmosphere prevails, patients tend to have longer hospital stays (e.g., Cohen & Struening, 1965), although it has not been demonstrated whether such patients recover more slowly or whether an authoritarian atmosphere is associated with more stringent criteria for discharge. In any case, as Kish, Solberg, and Uecker (1971) have observed, the correspondence between attitudes and effectiveness in job performance does not depend on the inherent virtue of the former but on the situational demands of a particular treatment setting. Such demands have been found to vary considerably, not only between hospitals (Meltzer & Smothers, 1967) but even between wards in the same institution. Similarly, Lawton (1965) pointed out that humanistic values are desirable for personnel working in settings with therapeutic or humanistic demands. But high scores on authoritarianism and social restrictiveness may actually be associated with better role performance in settings with primarily custodial demands, of which there are many. Consequently, criteria for "good" attitudes and "good" performances must depend on the health worker's actual setting, the kinds of patients, and types of disorders that are involved.[4]

Characteristics of Patients that Influence Therapists' Attitudes

Over the last several years it has become increasingly apparent that mental health professionals as well as the public make a variety of distinctions in their responses to disturbed behavior. Attitudes are influenced by personal characteristics of the individual manifesting the behavior in question, the particular symptoms, degree of unpredictability and diagnostic category involved, the visibility of the disturbed behavior, and the extent to which violence is an issue. In deciding on the suitability of a prospective patient for treatment, professionals are also notably influenced by their estimates of his motivation for change, and his prior psychiatric history.

Personal characteristics. In studies of public attitudes, personal characteristics of the individual described in a case presentation have been shown to influence the likelihood and extent of his social rejection. Males, for example, are more heavily stigmatized for deviant behavior than are females (Linsky, 1970; Phillips, 1964). Social class has long been recognized as a determinant of public tolerance for deviance; the lower the social status of the deviant person, the more likely is his rejection and exclusion from the community (Bord, 1971; Goffman, 1961; Linsky, 1970). Linsky found that members of low-status ethnic and racial groups and those lacking social ties in the community are also more apt to be excluded for acting deviantly than are others. One might observe in passing that these are the groups that are heavily over-represented in state and county mental hospital populations.

Like the public in general, mental health professionals have decidedly more positive attitudes toward middle- and upper class patients than those of lower status. *It often seems that the most basic qualification of a patient regarding both the probability of being accepted for treatment and the type of treatment offered is that of social class.* As Myers and Schaeffer (1954) noted some time ago, "the higher the patient's social class and position in the community, the greater his chances of being accepted for therapy, of being assigned to a relatively experienced therapist occupying a high status position within the clinic, and of maintaining contact with the clinic (p. 88). Hollingshead and Redlich (1958) found that social class was more highly correlated than was clinical diagnosis with acceptance for treatment, choice of treatment offered, and its duration. Rudolph and Cumming (1962), focusing on the function of social agencies, reported that the more sophisticated an agency's therapeutic methods, the higher its status in the community, and the more qualified its workers, then the more highly selected and higher in status is

the population that agency serves. One has only to compare the characteristics of patients being treated at psychoanalytic institutes with those seen at the clinics of public hospitals to appreciate the accuracy of this observation. As Gordon (1965) observed, "agencies with the most qualified workers also tend to 'discover' the most 'unmotivated' clients, and the most 'clients who are not yet ready for service.'" Schneiderman (1965) reinforces these findings with the observation that members of the lowest social class are the least adequately served in health and welfare enterprises, that they are considered as poor service risks in programs presumably set up to meet their needs, and consequently are getting less attention from mental health services than are their working-class or middle-class neighbors. Ryan (1969) also found, in the Boston Mental Health Survey conducted between 1960 and 1962, that among people identified as emotionally disturbed, those least likely to receive help were the poor, the young and elderly, and multi-problem families. Of course, lower class members lack the financial resources to seek treatment from private sources; even if they have access to insurance, they generally lack the information and social skills needed to arrange for private treatment.

In recent summaries of patient and therapist variables in the treatment of lower class patients, Lorion (1973, 1974) reported that therapists often lack a sense of rapport with lower class patients, perceive them as inarticulate and suspicious, interested "merely" in symptomatic relief, too apathetic and passive in the treatment situation, and harboring alien values. It is often expected that such patients will not profit from treatment, and that assigning them to individual psychotherapy represents an unproductive use of limited time. (See also Hollingshead & Redlich, 1958; Stein, Green, & Stone, 1972.) Lorion further noted that therapists tend to view with lack of enthusiasm members of both social classes IV and V, following the Hollingshead index, and that this represents a significant error in anticipation since Class IV members are in fact far more apt to share middle-class values and outlooks than are Class V members, and are accordingly more amenable therapeutic candidates.

However biased or inaccurate such attitudes may be, they are understandable in light of the extensive investigations of interpersonal attraction, which is one of the branches of attitude research. Positive relationships between attraction felt for a person and the similarity of his beliefs, attitudes, values, personality characteristics, and interests to those of the respondent who is judging his attractiveness have been found so consistently in the literature that analysts of the field conclude that further demonstrations are quite unnecessary (Fishbein & Ajzen, 1972).

Not only does social class affect the probability of acceptance for treatment, but it also influences the type of treatment offered and its duration. The higher the social position of the patient, the greater the likelihood that analytic rather than supportive or biochemical measures will be recommended (Hollingshead & Redlich, 1958; Myers & Schaeffer, 1954; Winder & Hersko, 1955). Attrition rates and therapeutic results are related to therapists' attitudes toward treating low-income patients (Lorion, 1974). In general, termination of services by therapists increases as social class declines (Schneiderman, 1965), but this occurs less often among therapists who prefer to work with low-income patients or those coming from a lower class background (Lorion, 1974). The voluntary dropout rate of lower class patients is also higher than it is for others (Baum, Felzer, D'Amura, & Shumaker, 1966; Coles, Branch, & Allison, 1962; Lorion, 1973; Rosenthal & Frank, 1958).

There is evidence to suggest an interaction between diagnostic classification and social class, with higher rates of severe disorders more frequent in lower social classes (Dunham, 1965; McDermott, Harrison, Schrager, & Wilson, 1965; Srole, Langer, Michael, Opler, & Rennie, 1962). Both social class membership and severity of illness are often related to experience of the therapist; the less severe the illness, and the higher the social standing, the more likely that the patient will get an experienced therapist (Lorion, 1973). Actually, the therapists who decide about the treatment suitability of lower class patients and who are responsible for providing it are usually still in training; the majority of the foregoing studies are based on studies of attitudes of residents rather than those of senior members of the field. While experienced psychiatrists may be available for advice and supervision, they are seldom found in the "front lines" of public clinics where lower class patients seek psychiatric services. In all, it is not surprising that Sullivan, Miller, and Smelser (1958) conclude that "those persons who are least equipped to meet life's challenges are the ones who stand to gain least from psychotherapy" (p. 7).

Clearly, low social class standing has a major negative impact on therapists' attitudes about the feasibility and outcome of treatment. Most prospective patients, however, especially those seen at teaching facilities and in private practice, possess somewhat greater social status. Even among this population, therapists as a group have very decided and generally homogeneous expectations and preferences about the kinds of patients they prefer to work with.

Both personal and psychiatric characteristics of patients influence therapists' attitudes toward them. Personal factors include those that are given (such as age) and achieved (such as education and occupation). After considering personal characteristics regarded as desirable by therapists, aspects of psychiatric condition (such as symptoms, prior psychiatric history, and level of motivation) will be reviewed.

Over the years, especially during the 1950s, many studies were published describing the "good therapy prospect," those with whom therapists prefer to work. Some of these characteristics are products of lifelong development such as intelligence, verbal facility, capacity for insight, and educational and occupational achievement (Auld & Myers, 1954; Meltzoff & Kornreich, 1970; Stieper & Wiener, 1965). Age is also a factor; therapists prefer to treat adolescents, college students, and young and middle-aged married adults (Rogow, 1970). These preferences have prevailed since Freud expressed interest in the qualities of youth, education, sophistication, and strength of character in his patients, despite lack of research evidence that any one of these characteristics is a necessary condition for remaining or succeeding in psychotherapy. As Strupp (1973) has appropriately concluded, therapists' "clinical judgments are not medical assessments of a disease process but rather a mixture of moral approval (or disapproval) coupled with a prognostication of whether the client, as a function of the therapist's influence, is likely to change, grow up—become a mature adult, as defined by our culture" (p. 522).

In summary, patients who are young, physically attractive, well-educated, members of the upper middle class, intelligent, verbal, willing to talk about and take responsibility for their problems, possessing considerable ego strength, and showing no signs of gross pathology are those who are welcomed as good therapeutic candidates. Such patients have previously demonstrated past success in coping with social and economic aspects of living, and enter psychotherapy actively with the expectations of succeeding there too. As Stieper and Wiener (1965) somewhat acidly point out, the good psychotherapy prospect is "the kind of patient also sought to insure successful outcome in brain-cutting, shock treatment, and virtually any other type of therapy (and who is also the best prospect for spontaneous remission)" (p. 48). Strupp (1963) makes an equally cogent point when he notes that it is hard to say whether therapy is effective, because therapists invest their best efforts when these conditions prevail, or whether the conditions themselves contribute to favourable outcome.

Psychiatric Characteristics. Aside from the socioeconomic and personal qualities of prospective patients, another major set of factors influencing therapists' attitudes concerns the nature of the presenting disorder in terms of symptoms, diagnosis, degree of unpredictability, and prior psychiatric history.

With respect to public attitudes toward disturbed behavior, it has been observed that people respond differently to various kinds of symptoms. Physical symptoms like headaches and ulcers seem more respectable than behavioral ones like phobias and obsessions. When the disturbed behavior includes violence as a major component, this symptom pattern is, understandably, quickly rejected apart from any question of the seriousness of the psychopathology. Seemingly incomprehensible behavior, such as hearing voices, is more objectionable than behavior which seems within normal understanding but too extreme, such as manic episodes. The public also tends to reject disturbed behavior that is socially visible, even if it is not very incapacitating for the patient. In our culture it is less acceptable to behave in a disruptive, bizarre, or troublesome fashion than to act depressed or detached. Thus, a paranoid schizophrenic is more often identified as mentally ill than a simple schizophrenic, an acting-out child more often than a withdrawn one (Lemkau & Crocetti, 1962; Phillips, 1964; Yamamoto & Dizney, 1967). The more socially threatening the behavior, the greater the social rejection (Blizard, 1970).

Members of the general public also tend to regard a history of psychiatric treatment, especially hospitalization, as a reason for maintaining social distance from the ex-patient. Phillips (1966) found that, when presenting the description of a normal man with and without the additional information that he had been formerly hospitalized, subjects identified him as normal in the latter case but did not want to have anything to do with him in the former. Farina

et al. (1971) found in an experimental setting that the experimenter was seen as less adequate and was liked less by those subjects who had been led to believe that he had been in a mental hospital.

The public seems willing to regard as normal a much broader range of behavior than experts would so define. It may thus be presumed that it is not eccentricity or deviance *per se* that is troubling as much as certain characteristics which seem exclusively attributed to mental patients. Chief among these are the characteristics of unpredictability and lack of accountability, which refers to the attribution of responsibility for behavior (Bord, 1971; Cumming & Cumming, 1965; Johannsen, 1969; Nunnally, 1961). As Nunnally observed, "because unpredictable behavior is frightening and disruptive, much societal machinery is devoted to making the behavior of individuals predictable to others."

In brief, the public finds particularly objectionable behavior that entails mystifying symptoms, that is socially visible or includes violence, and that is unpredictable. Therapists share most of these attitudes to a greater or lesser extent. Such attitudes among therapists probably result from more complex considerations than seemingly comparable attitudes among members of the general public, however. For example, therapists are better informed about the realistic prognostic implications of such factors as nature of onset, degree of precipitating stress or duration of illness, as well as the expected outcomes associated with different symptom configurations. Therapists understandably prefer to work with patients for whom treatment will make a difference; their own sense of competence and perhaps their reputation are involved, as well as their humanistic concerns about helping others.

Investigators have largely neglected to consider the relationship between each therapist's declared attitudes (about mental illness and mental patients) and his information (or misinformation) regarding outcomes associated with various patterns of disturbance. As a result, findings of therapists' attitudes concerning various patient characteristics consist of an unknown blend of affective components (e.g., fear of bodily harm from a violent patient), intellectual understanding (e.g., violent, agitated behavior of recent sudden onset has a better outlook than a pattern of long-standing detachment), and possibly inaccurate beliefs (e.g., schizophrenics are usually hopeless). In other words, the *interpretation* of therapists' attitudes toward psychiatric characteristics is a complex and largely undone task, although such attitudes have been systematically investigated.

In general, therapists have distinct preferences regarding the kinds of difficulties they wish to work with therapeutically. Most prefer to work with patients who are comparatively healthy to begin with, whose behavior is reasonably predictable, and who have neurotic symptoms. In a study of the effect of patient diagnosis on therapists' attitudes (Stein et al., 1972), 20 residents at a psychoanalytically oriented hospital were presented with four case history vignettes, each followed by questions regarding the patient's likability, prognosis, degree of discomfort evoked in the respondent, and the respondent's interest in treating him or of becoming friendly had they met socially. All of the residents preferred to treat the neurotic patients rather than the schizophrenic ones, showed more interest in becoming friendly with them, and regarded them as having a more favorable prognosis. Schizophrenic patients were seen as more potent and active, which may account for the residents' reluctance to treat them, according to the authors. "Not surprisingly, the less impulsive, more predictable patient is the one who is not only defined as healthier but also the one preferred as a patient" (p. 305).

Rogow (1970) conducted an extensive study of the values of psychiatrists and the role of these values in psychotherapy. He mailed elaborate questionnaires to every 30th name in the American Psychiatric Association Directory and the American Psychoanalytic Association Directory. With a 40% return, he got responses from 149 psychiatrists and 35 psychoanalysts for a total of 184. Among other questions, he asked what diagnostic categories were preferred in treatment; both groups named neuroses as their first choice. Analysts next preferred to treat patients with characterological problems while psychiatrists preferred to treat schizophrenics. Both groups agreed that alcoholics were the least desirable patients because of recidivism, missed appointments, and low percent of cure. For psychiatrists, the second least desirable group of patients was homosexuals; for analysts, schizophrenics. Rogow concludes that therapists generally prefer patients most likely to respond well to the kinds of treatment they provide.

Like members of the general public, therapists regard severity of disturbance as a major factor in their treatment decisions; among professionals as well as nonprofessionals, the sickest patients are usually least preferred. Conse-

quently, severity of illness is often inversely related to experience of the therapist, since senior members who can afford to be more selective than inexperienced therapists seldom choose to see severely disturbed patients, especially in office settings (Lorion, 1973). Severity of illness is regarded by therapists as a "legitimate" basis for treatment decisions and is seen as a professionally acceptable reason in the sense that it seems determined by cognitive realities rather than prejudices or biases. In contrast, it is the author's impression that few therapists can comfortably acknowledge that they do not wish to see a given patient because he is dull, boring, inarticulate, lower class, or unattractive.

As a result of its apparent respectability, severity of illness sometimes may be presented as justification for professional decisions when in fact other factors are major determinants. This was vividly demonstrated in a study conducted by Mendel and Rapport (1969) of determinants of the decision to hospitalize patients appearing in psychiatric admitting offices. They found that the professional staff members responsible for such decisions believed that symptom severity was a major consideration in determining which patients to hospitalize; they also believed that a history of prior hospitalization was largely irrelevant. Contrary to these beliefs, the authors found that patients who were actually hospitalized were indistinguishable from those who were not on the basis of symptom severity, but far more had a prior history of psychiatric hospitalization.

Psychiatrists also seem influenced by the degree of nonconformity of disturbed behavior, according to a study by Manis, Hunt, Brawer, and Kercher (1965), in which conceptions of mental illness held by a random survey of public respondents and by a panel of psychiatrists in private practice were compared. Respondents were asked to rate 10 different types of behaviors, each represented by two items, to indicate degree of mental illness. Half of the behavioral types were intended to portray disruptiveness (e.g., aggressive, bizarre, manic), and the others, disturbed but not troublesome behavior (e.g., withdrawn, persecutive). Contrary to expectations, ranking of the 10 types was found to be substantially similar for both public and professionals; the investigators had assumed professionals would be more influenced by degree of severity and the public, by the social disruptiveness of the behaviors described. As they discovered, "nonconformist" behavior (bizarre, persecutive, emotional) was seen as most indicative of mental illness and more ordinary behaviors (conformist, manic, depressive) as least indicative of mental illness. Although the authors do not utilize the concept, it seems that the amount of mystification (obscuring of origin) entailed in the symptomatology may be the general factor underlying their notion of nonconformist behavior. As noted earlier, actions that appear qualitatively distinct from the normal are generally seen as more objectionable than that which seems simply an exaggerated level of action common to us all.

In contrast to the similarity of opinions about mental illness between the public and professionals observed by Manis *et al.* (1965), Dohrenwend and Chin-Shong (1967) found that mental health experts were indeed more sensitive than the public regarding the severity of withdrawn behavior, as well as anti-social behavior, which is the category that lower class samples tend to regard as most pathological.

A history of psychiatric hospitalization is a handicap for the patient in his dealings with both the public at large and with mental health professionals. As Mendel and Rapport (1969) discovered, such a history facilitates professional decisions regarding readmission. Members of the public regard hospitalization as the most stigmatizing form of psychiatric treatment and view ex-hospitalized. patients with continued suspicion. *Evidently neither professionals nor laymen are firmly convinced that "mental illness is a disease like any other" from which one can totally recover, since previous episodes influence current appraisals.*[5] The experience of Senator Eagleton during the 1972 presidential campaign exemplifies this point; there was no way he could convincingly demonstrate his present mental health in the light of his psychiatric record which included three hospitalizations more than 5 years earlier. In short, a history of psychiatric hospitalization influences therapists regarding selection of subsequent treatment plans, enhancing the probability of rehospitalization, and diminishing the likelihood of acceptance in individual psychotherapy in office practice.

Length of hospitalization has only sometimes been found to influence professional evaluations of the patient. Koppel and Farina (1971) designed a study to investigate the effect of length of hospital stay on psychiatric judgments regarding diagnosis, estimates of severity of disorder, and treatment plans. Fifty-four psychiatrists were asked to rate three case history vignettes which varied in terms of severity,

ambiguity of description, and length of hospital stay which was described as being either 2 weeks, 2 months, or 2 years. Results showed no direct effect of hospital time on psychiatrists' perceptions of the variables under study. On the other hand, Greenley (1972) did find that psychiatrists' estimates of patients' impairment were significantly related to length of hospitalization. However, the decision to discharge a patient was determined more by the patient's and particularly the family's desires for discharge than by the psychiatrist's estimate of psychiatric impairment.

The variable of patient motivation—eagerness to be helped—is another psychiatric characteristic commonly believed to influence therapists' attitudes. Wallach and Strupp (1960) designed an elaborate study to verify this assumption. Eighty-two experienced psychiatrists were each presented with two case histories of neurotic patients with alternate forms identical in all respects but that of motivation, which was described as either good or poor. Each description was followed by a 27-item questionnaire regarding clinical impressions, treatment plans, and attitudes toward the patient. Although the data analysis consisted, unfortunately, of numerous *t* and *chi-square* tests which generally excluded the study of possible interactions and higher order factors, several interesting findings were nevertheless revealed. As predicted, a positive correlation was found between ascribed motivation and perception of the patient as having more insight and greater ego strength. These relationships are important since estimated capacity for insight emerged as a key variable entering into prognostic judgments, the therapist's eagerness in accepting the patient for psychotherapy, and his self-rated ability to empathize with the patient.

It has been hypothesized that patients described as being highly motivated would elicit a more positive attitude on the therapist's part than patients described as poorly motivated. Because the two case histories varied in degree of disturbance, and the positive correlation between motivation and attitude was found only for the less disturbed case, the authors concluded that patient motivation for treatment positively influences the therapist's attitude only when the degree of disturbance is not too great. Therapist attitude was found in itself to predict judgments; when their attitudes were more positive, therapists rated patients as having more ego strength and insight and diagnosed them more often as psychoneurotic rather than personality disorders. According to this study, then, greater apparent motivation attributed to the patient, which is partly based on severity of disorder, leads to a more favorable attitude in the therapist who perceives the patient as having more ego strength and greater insight.

These perceptions may be crucial to the patient's subsequent experiences since the therapist's initial impression of a patient often has the character of a self-fulfilling prophecy. Strupp (1963), for example, has observed that therapists generally reveal their expectations concerning the course and outcome of treatment in the style and manner of their communications, and that more positive attitudes on the part of the therapist are associated with more empathic transactions.

In general, Wallach and Strupp demonstrated that therapists prefer patients who are eager to be helped, able to be helped, and who are not too disturbed. This essentially summarizes the major psychiatric characteristics of patients that materially influence therapists' attitudes toward them, their diagnoses, treatment, and probable outcomes.

EMPIRICAL STUDIES OF THERAPISTS' CONCEPTIONS OF MENTAL HEALTH

Despite the extensive literature encompassing theoretical discussions of the concepts of normality and mental health, relatively little work has been designed to determine how these concepts are defined by either the general public or by mental health clinicians and administrators. Elaborate public surveys have been undertaken to delineate attitudes toward mental illness, mental patients, and psychiatric prognoses but they did not simultaneously inquire about popular conceptions of positive mental health. The few studies that have been conducted generally have asked various groups of mental health professionals to use behavioral or trait-descriptive labels, in the form of Q sorts and checklists, to indicate those attributes believed to characterize a normal or well-adjusted person. Some investigators broadened this approach to include requests for descriptions of related concepts such as "preferred patient" and "cured patient." The data-analytic methods used in most of these studies have been simple, often too simple, so that interactions between variables and complex relationships could not emerge despite the likelihood of their presence. Even more problematic is the intrusion of the variable of social desirability into attempts to define mental health; it is often unclear whether the confusion lies in the minds of the respondents or in the design of the study. What follows is a summary of those studies which seem comparatively straightforward in this respect, after which the issue of the role of social desirability in evaluations of mental health will be considered.

In a survey of psychotherapists' conceptions of adjustment and mental health, Goldman and Mendelsohn (1969) sent four 300-adjective checklists and a personal history questionnaire to psychologists, social workers, and psychiatrists randomly selected from their respective national directories. Each was asked to describe four concepts by means of Gough's Adjective Checklist: yourself, the kind of adult male you work with best, an adult male patient who has successfully completed therapy, and an adult male who has made a satisfactory adjustment to himself and his environment. These four concepts were intended to represent descriptions of oneself, preferred patient, cured patient, and normal man.

Of 1,200 therapists to whom materials were sent, 421 provided usable data. Results were presented as lists of the 25 adjectives most commonly selected to describe each of the four concepts studied, followed by lists of the 12 adjectives that differentiated most between pairs of concepts. The data analysis was unfortunately limited to simple percentages of the sample that checked each item, and repeated measurements *chi-square* tests to demonstrate significant differences between responses in pairs of concepts. The 24 scales customarily used for scoring the Adjective Checklist were not used on the grounds that they were standardized for self-descriptions only, but no other method was substituted to reduce the 300 adjectives into conceptually meaningful factors or clusters. As a result, most of the information gathered in the study was not used at all, and conclusions regarding underlying patterns must be at best tentative. Characteristics of the therapist, gathered in the personal history questionnaire, were not related to their checklist responses, and were utilized simply to demonstrate that the study's respondents are representative of the professions to which they belong in terms of demographic, educational, professional, and theoretical characteristics. We are given no information about consistency of preference across concepts; for example, does a therapist who describes himself as adaptable prefer an adaptable patient and does he attribute this capacity to a cured patient or normal man? We have no information about the 275 items that were checked less frequently for each concept; perhaps it would be worthwhile to consider the adjectives *not* as commonly checked for the various concepts. In general, there is a substantial loss of information due to the chosen means of data analysis and reporting, which is particularly regrettable in view of the excellent sampling carried out.

Despite these deficiencies, the authors provide valuable profiles of therapists' conceptions of normality, therapeutic impact, and social adjustment. As a group, the therapists described themselves as reliable and competent people who are intelligent, considerate, and understanding. They seemed to agree that stability, objectivity, and a willingness to help should be major components of therapists' behavior.

Preferred patients, those with whom therapists say they work best, are described as imaginative, sensitive, well-motivated, reliable, and anxious. Aside from the anxiety, there is little pathology; these are not people who generally would be seen as mentally ill. Cured patients resemble preferred patients except that they are seen as having more self-confidence, contentment, and stability and are not anxious. The cured patient, as described by therapists, is comfortable with himself and his environment.

A normal adult male is described as possessing all the positive but none of the negative characteristics of the other three concepts; "he is reality-oriented, socially effective, self-accepting, free of inner conflict, and concerned with the welfare of others" (Goldman & Mendelsohn, 1969, p. 168). But in contrast to the self, preferred, and cured portraits, the normal man is described as more affectively involved in his relationships.

Goldman and Mendelsohn feel that their sample displayed relatively high levels of agreement in describing these concepts, despite the profusion of inconsistent definitions found in the literature. They attribute their results to the nature of the questions they asked, their use of theoretically neutral language, and their emphasis on outcome rather than method. They conclude that the extent of agreement regarding normal behavior here attained indicates that "it is possible to derive an empirical criterion of 'positive mental health,' at least as this elusive concept is conceived by specialists in the field" (p. 171).

Broverman and her associates (Broverman, Broverman, Clarkson, Rosenkrantz, & Vogel, 1970; Broverman, Vogel, Broverman, Clarkson, & Rosenkrantz, 1972) have conducted a series of interlocking studies concerning the sex-role stereotypes prevailing among various groups differing in age, sex, religion, marital status, education, and occupation. To measure conceptions of sex roles, they designed a 122-item questionnaire encompassing bipolar alternatives (e.g., "not at all aggressive"/"very aggressive"); respondents were asked to what extent each item characterized an adult man or adult woman. In brief summary, three major findings emerged. First, they discovered a strong consensus among disparate groups about the differing characteristics of men and women. Perceived male traits form a cluster of related behaviors including competence, rationality, and assertiveness, while the positively valued feminine traits concern warmth and expressiveness. Second, characteristics ascribed to men are positively valued more often than those ascribed to women. Finally, they observed that the sex-role definitions are incorporated into the self-concepts of both men and women, are considered "desirable" by college students and "ideal" by both men and women (Broverman et al., 1972). In other words, *the assignment of behaviors to masculine or feminine roles is widely seen as socially desirable, and even though male characteristics are valued more than female characteristics, female respondents share these views.*

Most relevant to the present discussion is a study carried out by Broverman et al. (1970) comparing these sex-role stereotypes with clinical judgments of health made by mental health professionals. The authors proposed and demonstrated two hypotheses: first, that clinical judgments about the traits characterizing healthy adults will differ as a function of the sex of the person judged, and second, when sex is not specified, the ideal of adult mental health will more often resemble that regarded elsewhere as masculine. The subjects in this study consisted of 79 practicing clinicians aged 25 to 55, male and female. They were divided into three groups: one group was asked to describe a healthy adult male by means of their Stereotype Questionnaire, another was asked to describe a healthy adult female, and the third, to describe a healthy adult person.

The authors found that male and female clinicians in each group did not differ from each other in their responses. Together, they strongly agreed on behaviors which characterize healthy men and women, conforming to the socially desirable stereotypes obtained from nonprofessional groups. Only four items out of 122 showed a divergence between social desirability ratings by nonprofessionals and mental health ratings by professionals.

No differences were found between the concept of mental health for "man" and "person," but significant differences emerged between the concepts of "woman" and "person." The authors conclude that a double standard of health exists for men and women, that the general standard of health applies only to men, while healthy women are perceived as significantly less healthy by general adult standards. They suggest that this double standard stems from clinicians' acceptance of an "adjustment" notion of mental health—that health consists of a good adjustment to one's environment and that a well-adjusted woman accepts the behavioral norms for her sex even though these behaviors are less socially desirable and less healthy by general standards. Thus, clinicians' description of the healthy woman as "more submissive, less independent, less objective, more easily influenced, more emotional, more easily excitable in minor crises" is as the authors note, "a most unusual way of describing any mature, healthy individual" (Broverman et al., 1972, p. 5). It seems most easily understood as a portrayal of the way things are rather than the way they ought to be. But, as the authors conclude, the cause of mental health may be better served if both men and women are encouraged toward maximum development rather than acceptance of prevailing restrictive sex roles.

Neulinger (1968) has reported findings similar to those of Broverman et al. (1970) with respect to the clinical perception of different standards of mental health for men and women. He drew upon a method developed by Blatt (1964) which consists of ranking 20 paragraphs, each representing one of Murray's manifest needs. Blatt obtained "ideal" ranks by asking judges, who were clinical psychology graduate students, to place the paragraphs in the order most descriptive of the "optimally integrated personality." The top-ranked needs were achievement, affiliation, counteraction, and autonomy. He then asked 116 male scientists to describe themselves by ranking the paragraphs. Respondents whose descriptions were closer to the ideal scored higher on separate measures of ego strength, and lower on the F Scale and on a test of manifest anxiety.

Given this preliminary validation of the method, Neulinger asked 114 psychotherapists (psychiatrists, psychologists, and social workers,

two-thirds of whom were male) to rank each paragraph from most to least descriptive of the "optimally integrated personality," for both males and females. His data analysis consisted of assigning a mean rank to each need and comparing those obtained for the male "optimally integrated personality" with those of the female "optimally integrated personality." He found that, while the ranks were correlated, there were significant differences between means on 18 of the 20 needs. The highest ranks assigned to the male "optimally integrated personality" were for the needs of sex, affiliation, dominance, and achievement, while those for the female were for affiliation, sex, and nurturance. Neulinger concluded that distinct conceptions of mental health exist for males and females, and that the optimal male role is still perceived as the more dominant, the female more submissive, by psychotherapists as well as most other Americans.

Direct confirmation regarding the existence of sex-role stereotypes among therapists is provided by a recent survey conducted by Roche Laboratories (1974). Questionnaires on attitudes about Women's Liberation were sent to every sixth American psychiatrist concerned with patient care, and the following statement and questions were included:

Some advocates of Women's Liberation complain that, although psychiatry in general tries to help women make a better adjustment to their life situations, in effect psychiatrists are inducing women to adapt to a social stereotype . . .

Question 1: Do you believe that most psychiatrists have a stereotype of "normal healthy male" role and "normal healthy female" role?

yes: 73%   no: 27%

Question 2: Do you believe that psychiatrists . . . attempt to influence their patients to "adjust" to the psychiatrists' own stereotypes?

yes: 65.5%   no: 34.5%

Analysis of these responses showed no difference in response by type of practice, but the percent of "yes" responses was inversely correlated with age. Clearly, *there is a striking consensus among psychiatrists regarding the wide prevalence of sex-role stereotypes held by them; a majority also acknowledges that these stereotypes influence therapeutic activities and goals.*

A major issue associated with the task of

defining conceptions and attitudes toward mental health is to differentiate between prevailing notions of socially desirable behavior and what is considered optimally effective or healthy. It thus becomes relevant to inquire to what extent efforts to define and evaluate concepts of mental health are actually tapping opinions about social-desirability. Several investigators have become aware of this methodological problem,[6] and their findings suggest that it remains largely unresolved.

Studies by Kogan, Quinn, Ax, and Ripley (1957), Wiener, Blumberg, Segman, and Cooper (1959), Cowen (1961), and Broverman et al. (1970) have all found a strong relationship between behavioral ratings based on social desirability compared to ratings of the same behaviors in terms of mental health or adjustment. Kogan et al. (1957) found a correlation of +.89 between health-sickness ratings and social desirability ratings made on behavioral samples of 24 hospitalized mental patients and 24 normal college students. They concluded that assessments of health seem to be based more on cultural stereotypes than on factors related to mental health and illness, since the two measures evidently refer to the same underlying variable.

Wiener et al. (1959) sought to delineate and compare the concepts of psychological adjustment held by social workers and psychologists. Their method, using a Q sort of 100 items earlier employed by Rogers and Dymond, was to ask professionals about the relative importance of various behaviors in their conception of the adjusted person, and to compare these sorts to estimates of social desirability of the behaviors involved. Twenty-eight clinical psychologists, 14 social workers, and 21 college students completed judgments for the Adjustment Scale Q sort according to how each thought "a well-adjusted person would sort these cards." Another 16 psychologists rated the social desirability of each of the 100 items.

The adjustment ratings of these groups were highly correlated, ranging from +.91 to +.95, with more variability seen within groups than between them. These results demonstrate high agreement among clinicians regarding their notions of the behavior a well-adjusted person is expected to report. All groups rated as most characteristic of good adjustment those items concerning personal responsibility, emotional maturity, and comfortable relationships with others. All 10 items considered least characteristic of the well-adjusted person were the same for the two professions, though in slightly

different order within these 10 places. These items dealt with feelings of failure, helplessness, being unable to cope, and having no self-respect.

The implications of these findings are somewhat obscured by the observation that the Q sorts for adjustment and for social desirability were correlated +.88. That is, instructions to rank behaviors based on the concept of adjustment produced ratings strikingly similar to those obtained when psychologists were asked to rank them on the basis of social desirability. It seems likely that the judges regarded the social desirability of behaviors as a major determinant in their classifications of adjustment. The authors suggest that the nature of the relationship between social desirability and adjustment will be better understood if it can be demonstrated that well and poorly adjusted people respond differently to the Adjustment Q sort despite the role of social desirability, or that poorly adjusted Ss produce the same sorts but display behavior incongruent with their verbal reports. In summary, this study reveals no significant differences in the concepts of adjustment expressed by psychologists and social workers, and demonstrates a high degree of overlap in behavior ratings based on the concepts of adjustment and of social desirability.

Cowen (1961) asked 67 college students to rate trait-descriptive adjectives in terms of their social desirability, and compared these with ratings made by clinicians of the same adjectives in terms of their normality-abnormality. He found a correlation of +.92. While he suggested the possibility that there really is little difference between what is clinically normal and culturally desirable, he seemed more inclined toward the explanation that clinicians as well as the lay public are influenced in their assessments of normality by the "insidious contamination" of social desirability stereotypes.

Broverman et al. (1970) reported that their comparisons of social desirability ratings of behavioral adjectives by samples of the general public and clinical ratings of the same adjectives by a sample of clinicians showed the same strong association reported by other investigators. They would agree with Cowen (1961) and Kogan et al. (1957) that clinicians are too heavily influenced by prevailing normative standards of behavior and that a greater distinction must be made between behavioral characteristics that are seen generally as socially desirable and those that reflect healthy functioning. Certainly there is an overlap between the concepts, but the specific qualities of each must be acknowledged.

Comment

Perhaps because these studies necessarily begin with a descriptive approach, they fail to get at the essential qualities of positive mental health regarded as crucial by theorists. Major mental health concepts have been classified by Jahoda (1958) in six groups: autonomy, environmental mastery, accurate perception of reality, self-actualization, self-regard, and integration; these concepts have not been directly measured in the foregoing studies. The investigators of professional attitudes toward mental health have, in general, simply presented large and unorganized lists of descriptive terms, varying in level of abstraction, which therapists consider indicative of healthy adjustment. No single concept or cluster of concepts has been delineated as necessary or sufficient for such definition. The criterion itself has varied from one study to the next, with some respondents asked to select behavioral terms describing the "well-adjusted person," others asked to portray the "optimally integrated personality," and others, to describe a normal adult man or woman or cured patient. It has not been shown that these criterion terms are equivalent, and the lack of difference in descriptions associated with each may merely derive from the level of generality involved. Certainly, subsequent studies must focus on delineation of the major factors underlying the behavioral adjectives used, and more precise efforts are needed to define the contexts and parameters of health and illness as therapists see them.

The results available from these studies do succeed in demonstrating, perhaps unintentionally, a major point regarding the strong relationships between personal and social values and concepts of mental health.[7] Among theorists, it has been increasingly recognized that health cannot be described in absolute terms, that its definition is influenced by the social context as well as the priorities of the observer. While Freud tended to use polar terms, his concept of health represented an ethical ideal, not a realizable state attainable by any individual. Hartmann (1958), a major psychoanalytic theorist, acknowledged that mental health is "in part, a very individual matter" and that its criteria are affected by social and political factors. Haley (1963), from an entirely different theoretical vantage point, noted that "the ills of the individual are not really separable from the ills of the social context he creates and inhabits" (p. 2).

The notion of an interaction between definitions of mental health and social factors seems generally accepted in principle today; most would agree that certain social conditions such as pervasive poverty and a socially disorganized setting together with a lack of power to alter one's surroundings would almost surely preclude the development of optimal mental health. However, there is a crucial difference between relating definitions of mental health to social *conditions* and replacing them with social *values*. We refine our definition of health by recognizing the interaction between the individual's potential development and his social context; here, the separate components are accurately identified and their interaction evaluated. We are merely narrowing our definition of health, on the other hand, by using the concept interchangeably with that of socially desirable behavior. Here the separate components—what is healthy and what is desirable or typical—are simply confounded, as has been convincingly demonstrated in the foregoing studies by the authors' or respondents' widespread inability to differentiate between behavior labeled socially desirable and that labeled healthy or normal. While it seems both necessary and desirable to consider together the first set of concepts, those of health and the social context, there seems little to be gained in using the concept of mental health interchangeably with that of social desirability. It would seem more helpful to regard social desirability as one of several dimensions of mental health, and devote more attention to elaborating other components that independently contribute to its fuller understanding.

CONCLUSIONS

Since therapists' attitudes toward mental illness and mental patients have received far more attention and systematic investigation in the literature than have therapists' attitudes about mental health, the two areas will be considered separately in these concluding remarks.

Evaluations of public and professional attitudes about mental illness have been conducted for nearly 30 years, in the course of which several major findings have emerged. In studies of public attitudes it has been demonstrated repeatedly that a negative, stereotyped notion of mental illness prevails, and that the label of mental patient usually leads to markedly diminished status in the eyes of the community. During the 1960s, large-scale programs of public education bore the compound message that mental illness is an illness like any other, that it can strike anyone, that its victims are entitled to physicians' care, and that the illness can be conquered. These efforts have had measurable impact on American thinking about mental illness; more recent studies have convincingly shown growing public awareness of these tenets.

Unfortunately, the framework of this educational campaign, based as it is on the medical model of illness, seems to be increasingly divergent from contemporary views of mental illness, its origins, and treatment goals. As the psychosocial or transactional model of health and disorder gains increasing acceptance among the upper ranks of mental health professionals, especially those working in community settings, attention is being shifted from childhood or congenital etiological conceptions to an emphasis on current sources of stress in the generation of disturbed behavior.[8] Treatment efforts are being conceptualized in terms of reduction of external stress as well as the development of more adaptive coping behavior. In this context, the traditional notions of illness and cure no longer apply. It seems, ironically, that just when the lower and middle echelons of mental health workers and the public generally are becoming acquainted with conceptualizations of mental illness formulated in traditional medical-psychiatric terms, an increasing number of those with post-graduate training have moved to a social-psychiatric framework in their conceptualizations and attitudes about mental illness.

Even among mental health clinicians, changes are occurring in conceptualizations of mental illness. Where once the psychodynamic theories embodied in the OMI factor of interpersonal etiology were widely accepted among the most liberal and progressive therapists, now these notions of early childhood trauma as causative agents in the development of later mental illness, where the patient is seen more or less as the victim of his past, are less pervasive. As expressed in Ellsworth's OMI-SOS nontraditionalism factor, more clinicians have come to regard the mental patient as accountable for his own rehabilitation and seek to enlist his active cooperation and participation in the therapeutic process. On questionnaires in current use, this attitude dimension of nontraditionalism seems to be the area in which greatest change is occurring in terms of increasing acceptance among students in post-graduate training and among young professionals.

In seeking potentially fruitful areas of study to further understand therapists' attitudes about mental illness, several guidelines can be drawn from the literature. First, it has been established

that such attitudes have several component parts, and measures must account for this multidimensional structure. There seems no further need to measure attitudes of mental health workers by occupation; these attitudes have been adequately identified. It has also been satisfactorily demonstrated that personal characteristics of the therapist and of prospective patients influence his attitudes toward mental illness generally and his judgment about the therapeutic management of the particular patient. In general, univariate correlational studies of attitudes toward mental illness have provided a helpful and necessary descriptive basis for the more complex and analytic studies that should constitute the next phase of research in this area.

At the present time, further work is indicated in terms of relating observed attitudes to a broad range of categories of variables, such as behavioral acts of the respondent, other of his attitudes and beliefs, and the effect of attitudes on those to whom they are addressed. In the present context, an important area of study concerns the correspondence of expressed attitudes on the part of the therapist and treatment outcome. While the work of Ellsworth (1965) and of Cohen and Struening (1964, 1965) provide imaginative leads, little basic information has been gathered to document the impact of various attitudes on different kinds of patients. One formulation might be expressed in the following way: In what kinds of social-attitudinal structures do patients most effectively develop the social competence and adaptive skills which will help them lead more productive lives? Another approach to the general area might be to inquire in what kinds of treatment climate a given mental health worker with specified attitudes about mental illness will be able to function most effectively. A related topic would be the investigation of different types of patients and the treatment philosophies and attitudes most suitable to their prompt recovery. We also ought to know how major differences in attitudes toward the causes and treatment of mental disorders among treatment team members, administrators, and clinicians influence the effectiveness of mental health programs. In general, studies of interactions between patient, staff, and program attitudes and assumptions represent a more complex level of understanding, and depend on the prior delineation of direct relationships between attitudes and behaviors.

The foregoing questions are not intended to categorize exhaustively the work to be done, but rather to indicate several important aspects of the field which are presently receiving little attention in the literature.

Attitudes Toward Mental Health

In this area, work at the descriptive level has just begun. No instruments have been developed to evaluate attitudes about mental health; indeed, even an operational definition is lacking. Though it is inelegant and imprecise, respondents understand and agree when "mental illness" is operationalized by reference to hospitalization status. An equivalent empirical referent is not available for the concept of "mental health." It is probably because an adequate conceptual definition of health has not been developed that we have no operational definition.

A major handicap in efforts to define health is the tendency of so many people to overlook the issue of values. Where health begins and ends on a continuum from well-being to death is a matter of social values, societal standards, and the exigencies of everyday living. Even broad conceptual definitions involve attitudes and values about the nature of growth and functioning. For example, the World Health Organization definition of health as "a state of complete physical, mental and social well-being, and not merely the absence of disease or infirmity" (WHO, 1958), though seemingly innocuous, runs counter to at least two perspectives about health. According to one view, organisms are constantly exposed to new stimuli, new problems and challenges, and are perpetually in flux. From this standpoint, "complete well-being" sounds not like health, as one acerbic critic pointed out, but like coma. From another perspective, health indeed *is* defined by many as relative freedom from any disorder or impairment in functioning (Gardner, 1968); this is the traditional medical and psychiatric "antonym" model which continues to be widespread among both laymen and psychiatrists (Sabshin, 1968).

Apart from the conceptualization of health as the relative absence of disease, which does not seem particularly helpful to the practicing psychotherapist or to those working in community-centered programs, two other broad dimensions of mental health have been proposed by contemporary writers. One concerns good adjustment in the statistical sense of normality, and the other refers to a more elite notion of health based on achieved levels of psychological maturity. Examples of the latter include the idea of self-actualization and the psychoanalytic notion of optimal balance between intrapsychic forces.

Such concepts, which contribute to the idea of a state of positive mental health above and beyond the absence of illness, have been cogently criticized by Loevinger (1968) in terms of their value as criteria for mental health. She has noted that these are the hallmarks of maturity and that characteristically they develop with age. Since health is *not* a function of age, it cannot conceptually be represented by factors such as these. Further, they are relevant dimensions primarily at the upper end of the ego-development continuum, while a direct relationship between ego development and mental health is found only at the lower end of the continuum. One may conclude that concepts of this nature do not seem to lend themselves to a general definition of mental health applicable to broad populations.

The other category of concepts meant to define mental health concerns good adjustment. As the studies reviewed above demonstrate, the term "good adjustment" is often used interchangeably with "socially desirable behavior." This equation brings to the notion of adjustment a glib, superficial, unthinking quality which detracts from its acceptability as a therapeutic goal. Adjustment has been criticized by representatives of minority and underprivileged groups who feel that the social order itself is to blame for the stresses experienced by those for whom they speak, and it is society that calls for readjustment, not their clients. From a moral standpoint, it has also been argued that adjustment within a corrupt or evil system (e.g., National Socialist Germany) is itself a form of evil.

While such criticisms have merit, the concept of adjustment still can be a useful one. When defined in terms of personal and social competence (cf., Smith, 1968; White, 1959), the term begins to suggest constructive courses of action for research workers, therapists, and community workers alike. Maladjustment may be seen as a complex of behavioral deficits and negative attitudes including such components as social defeat, poor skills and little knowledge, passivity, hopelessness, and a sense of being unable to control one's destiny. Maladjustment seen in such terms leads to the formulation of problems which can be defined at the individual level and whose solution can be undertaken without waiting until society itself is reorganized. In parallel terms, adjustment can be given an operational definition by focusing on component parts such as a sense of control over one's fate (which has been studied under the label "internal vs. external locus of control"—Beckman, 1972), acquisition of social skills and knowledge, and so forth.

Through sophisticated statistical methods, it has been demonstrated that a person's attitude about mental illness is not a unitary concept, but consists of five or more component dimensions (e.g., Cohen & Struening, 1962). It seems evident that a person's attitude about mental health is equally complex. Indeed, the concept of mental health is no more unitary than that of mental illness; as Smith (1968) has wryly noted, "mental health" is not a theoretical concept but at best a chapter heading! The words do seem to refer to various aspects of human personality and behavior among which the health-disease continuum is only one. Accordingly, it would seem potentially valuable to work with subsets under the general heading of mental health, seeking empirical referents for concepts which contribute to the general notion of adjustment.

REFERENCES

APPLEBY, L., ELLIS, N. C., ROGERS, G. W., & ZIMMERMAN, W. A. A psychological contribution to the study of hospital structure. *Journal of Clinical Psychology*, 1961, **17**, 390–393.

AULD, F., & MYERS, J. Contributions to a theory for selecting psychotherapy patients. *Journal of Clinical Psychology*, 1954, **10**, 56–60.

BAKER, F., & SCHULBERG, H. C. The development of a community mental health ideology scale. *Community Mental Health Journal*, 1967, **3**, 216–225.

BAKER, F., & SCHULBERG, H. C. Community mental health ideology, dogmatism, and political-economic conservatism. *Community Mental Health Journal*, 1969, **5**, 433–436.

BATES, J. Attitudes toward mental illness. *Mental Hygiene*, 1968, **52**, 250–253.

BAUM, O., FELZER, S., D'AMURA, & SHUMAKER, E. Psychotherapy, dropouts and lower socioeconomic patients. *American Journal of Orthopsychiatry*, 1966, **36**, 629–635.

BECKMAN, L. Locus of control and attitudes toward mental illness among mental health volunteers. *Journal of Consulting and Clinical Psychology*, 1972, **38**, 84–89.

BENTINCK, C. Opinions about mental illness held by patients and relatives. *Family Process*, 1967, **6**, 193–207.

BENTZ, W. K., & EDGERTON, J. W. Consensus on attitudes toward mental illness. *Archives of General Psychiatry*, 1970, **22**, 468–473.

BENTZ, W. K., & EDGERTON, J. W. The consequences of labeling a person as mentally ill. *Social Psychiatry*, 1971, **6**, 29–33.

BERG, L., HELMICK, E., MILLER, S., NUTTING, P., & SHORR, G. Health worker opinions about mental illness in Alaska. Mimeo. Summary published in *Clinical Psychiatry News*, July 1974, **2**:7, 10 entitled, Mental health workers performance affected by attitudes toward illnesses.

BLATT, S. J. An attempt to define mental health. *Journal of Consulting Psychology*, 1964, **28**, 146–153.

BLIZARD, P. The social rejection of the alcoholic and the mentally ill in New Zealand. *Social Science and Medicine*, 1970, **4**, 513–526.

BOGARDUS, E. A. Measuring social distances. *Journal of Applied Sociology*, 1925, **9**, 299–308.

BORD, R. Rejection of the mentally ill: Continuities and further developments. *Social Problems*, 1971, **18**, 496–509.

BORDELEAU, J., PELLETIER, P., PANACCIO, L., & TETREAULT, L. Authoritarianism–humanism index in a large mental hospital. *Diseases of the Nervous System*, 1970, **31** (II, Suppl.), 166–174.

BROVERMAN, I., BROVERMAN, D., CLARKSON, F., ROSENKRANTZ, P., & VOGEL, S. Sex-role stereotypes and clinical judgments of mental health. *Journal of Consulting Psychology*, 1970, **34**, 1–7.

BROVERMAN, I., VOGEL, S., BROVERMAN, D., CLARKSON, F., & ROSENKRANTZ, P. Sex-role stereotypes: A current appraisal. *Journal of Social Issues*, 1972, **28**, 59–78.

CLARK, A. W., & BINKS, N. M. Relation of age and education to attitudes toward mental illness. *Psychological Reports*, 1966, **19**, 649–650.

COHEN, J., & STRUENING, E. L. Opinions about mental illness in the personnel of two large mental hospitals. *Journal of Abnormal Social Psychology*, 1962, **64**, 349–360.

COHEN, J., & STRUENING, E. L. Opinions about mental illness: Mental hospital occupational profiles and profile clusters. *Psychological Reports*, 1963, **12**, 111–124.

COHEN, J., & STRUENING, E. L. Opinions about mental illness: Hospital social atmosphere profiles and their relevance to effectiveness. *Journal of Consulting Psychology*, 1964, **28**, 291–298.

COHEN, J., & STRUENING, E. L. Opinions about mental illness: Hospital differences in attitude for eight occupational groups. *Psychological Reports*, 1965, **17**, 25–26.

COLES, N., BRANCH, C., & ALLISON, R. Some relationships between social class and practice of dynamic psychotherapy. *American Journal of Psychiatry*, 1962, **118**, 1004–1012.

COWEN, E. The social desirability of trait descriptive terms: Preliminary norms and sex differences. *Journal of Social Psychology*, 1961, **53**, 225–233.

CREECH, S. K. Differences in attitudes about mental illness among health personnel in an area program, 1974, *Mimeo*.

CREECH, S. K. Opinions about mental illness in the personnel of a state psychiatric hospital and community mental health centers, 1974, *Mimeo*.

CROCETTI, G., & LEMKAU, P. On rejection of the mentally ill. *American Sociological Review*, 1965, **30**, 577–578.

CROCETTI, G., SPIRO, H., & SIASSI, I. Are the ranks closed? Attitudinal social distance and mental illness. *American Journal of Psychiatry*, 1971, **127**, 1121–1127.

CROCETTI, G., SPIRO, H., & SIASSI, I. *Contemporary attitudes toward mental illness.* Pittsburgh: University of Pittsburgh Press, 1974.

CUMMING, E., & CUMMING, J. *Closed ranks: An experiment in mental health.* Cambridge, Mass.: Harvard University Press, 1957.

CUMMING, J., & CUMMING, E. On the stigma of mental illness. *Community Mental Health Journal*, 1965, **1**, 135–143.

DOHRENWEND, B. P., & CHIN-SHONG, E. Social status and attitudes toward psychological disorder: The problem of tolerance of deviance. *American Sociological Review*, 1967, **32**, 417–433.

DUNHAM, W. *Community and schizophrenia.* Detroit: Wayne State University Press, 1965.

DWORKIN, G. Teaching the boys in the back rooms: A program for blue-collar workers. *Mental Hygiene*, 1969, **53**, 258–262.

EDGERTON, R., & KARNO, M. Mexican–American bilingualism and the perception of mental illness. *Archives of General Psychiatry*, 1971, **24**, 286–290.

ELINSON, J., PADILLA, E., & PERKINS, M. *Public image of mental health services.* New York: Mental Health Materials Center, 1967.

ELLSWORTH, R. B. A behavioral study of staff attitudes toward mental illness. *Journal of Abnormal Psychology*, 1965, **70**, 194–200.

FARINA, A., & FELNER, R. Employment interviewer reactions to former mental patients. *Journal of Abnormal Psychology*, 1973, **82**, 268–272.

FARINA, A., GLIHA, D., BOUDREAU, L. A., ALLEN, J., & SHERMAN, M. Mental illness and the impact of believing others know about it. *Journal of Abnormal Psychology*, 1971, **77**, 1–5.

FISHBEIN, M., & AJZEN, I. Attitudes and opinions. *Annual Review of Psychology*, 1972, 487–544.

FOURNET, G. Cultural correlates with attitudes, perception, knowledge and reported incidence of mental disorders. *Dissertation Abstracts*, 1967, **28** (1B), 339.

FREEMAN, H. E. Attitudes toward mental illness among relatives of former patients. *American Sociological Review*, 1961, **26**, 59–66.

GARDNER, E. A. Concepts of mental disorder. In S. B. SELLS (Ed.), *The definition and measurement of mental health*. Washington, D.C.: Public Health Service, 1968. Pp. 2–28.

GIOVANNONI, J. M., & ULLMAN, L. P. Conceptions of mental health held by psychiatric patients. *Journal of Clinical Psychology*, 1963, **19**, 398–400.

GOFFMAN, E. *Asylums*. New York: Doubleday Anchor, 1961.

GOLDMAN, R., & MENDELSOHN, G. Psychotherapeutic change and social adjustment: A report of a national survey of psychotherapists. *Journal of Abnormal Psychology*, 1969, **74**, 164–172.

GORDON, S. Are we seeing the right patients? *American Journal of Orthopsychiatry*, 1965, **35**, 131–137.

GREENLEY, J. G. Alternative views of the psychiatrist's role. *Social Problems*, 1972, **20**, 252–262.

GUTTMACHER, S., & ELINSON, J. Ethno-religious variation in perception of illness. *Social Science and Medicine*, 1971, **5**, 117–125.

HALEY, J. *Strategies of psychotherapy*, New York: Grune & Stratton, 1963.

HALPERT, H. Public acceptance of the mentally ill: An exploration of attitudes. *Public Health Reports*, 1969, **84**, 59–64.

HARTMANN, H. *Ego psychology and the problem of adaptation*. New York: International Universities Press, 1958.

HOLLINGSHEAD, A., & REDLICH, F. C. *Social class and mental illness*. New York: Wiley, 1958.

JAHODA, M. *Current concepts of positive mental health*. New York: Basic Books, 1958.

JOHANNSEN, W. J. Attitudes toward mental patients: A review of empirical research. *Mental Hygiene*, 1969, **53**, 218–228.

Joint Commission on Mental Illness and Health (Eds.) *Action for mental health*. New York: Basic Books, 1961.

KISH, G., SOLBERG, K., & UECKER, A. The relation of staff opinions about mental illness to ward atmosphere and perceived staff roles. *Journal of Clinical Psychology*, 1971, **27**, 284–287.

KLETT, C. J., & LASKY, J. J. Attitudes of hospital staff members toward mental illness and chemotherapy. *Diseases of the Nervous System*, 1962, **23**, 1–5.

KOGAN, W., QUINN, R., AX, A., & RIPLEY, H. Some methodological problems in the quantification of clinical assessment by Q array. *Journal of Consulting Psychology*, 1957, **21**, 57–62.

KOPPEL, I., & FARINA, A. Hospitalization time and psychiatrists' perceptions of mental patients. *Journal of Clinical Psychology*, 1971, **27**, 59–61.

LANGSTON, R. Community mental health centers and community mental health ideology. *Community Mental Health Journal*, 1970, **6**, 387–392.

LAWTON, M. P. Correlates of the opinion about mental illness scale. *Journal of Consulting Psychology*, 1964, **28**, 94.

LAWTON, M. P. Personality and attitudinal correlates of psychiatric-aid performance. *Journal of Social Psychology*, 1965, **66**, 215–226.

LEMKAU, P., & CROCETTI, G. An urban population's opinion and knowledge about mental illness. *American Journal of Psychiatry*, 1962, **118**, 692–700.

LINSKY, A. Who shall be excluded: The influence of personal attributes in community reaction to the mentally ill. *Social Psychiatry*, 1970, **5**, 166–171.

LOEVINGER, J. The relation of adjustment to ego development. In S. B. SELLS (Ed.), *The definition and measurement of mental health*. Washington, D.C.: Public Health Service, 1968. Pp. 162–180.

LORION, R. P. Socioeconomic status and traditional treatment approaches reconsidered. *Psychological Bulletin*, 1973, **79**, 263–270.

LORION, R. P. Patient and therapist variables in the treatment of low-income patients. *Psychological Bulletin*, 1974, **81**, 344–354.

LUBCHANSKY, I., EGRI, G., & STOKES, J. Puerto Rican spiritualists view mental illness: The faith healer as a para-professional. *American Journal of Psychiatry*, 1970, **127**, 312–321.

MANIS, J. G., HUNT, C. L., BRAWER, M. J., & KERCHER, L. C. Public and psychiatric conceptions of mental illness. *Journal of Health and Human Behavior*, 1965, **6**, 48–55.

MANIS, M., HOUTS, P. S., & BLAKE, J. B. Beliefs about mental illness as a function of psychiatric status and psychiatric hospitalization. *Journal of Abnormal and Social Psychology*, 1963, **67**, 226–233.

McDERMOTT, J., HARRISON, S., SCHRAGER, J., & WILSON, P. Social class and mental illness in children. *American Journal of Orthopsychiatry*, 1965, **35**, 500–508.

MELTZER, M. L., & SMOTHERS, J. M. Assessing attitudes toward mental health concepts. *Hospital & Community Psychiatry*, 1967, **18**, 245–250.

MELTZOFF, J., & KORNREICH, M. *Research in psychotherapy*. New York: Atherton Press, 1970.

MENDEL, W. M., & RAPPORT, S. Determinants of the decision for psychiatric hospitalization. *Archives of General Psychiatry*, 1969, **20**, 321–328.

MEYER, J. Attitudes toward mental illness in a Maryland community. *Public Health Reports*, 1964, **79**, 769–772.

MIDDLETON, J. The prejudices and opinions of mental hospital employees regarding mental illness. *American Journal of Psychiatry*, 1953, **110**, 133–138.

MYERS, J. M. Psychiatrists evaluate treatment: 1961–1972. Mimeo. Summary published in Sandoz' *Psychiatric Spectator*, 1973, **9**, 15.

MYERS, J., & SCHAEFFER, L. Social stratification and psychiatric practice: A study of an out-patient clinic. *American Sociological Review*, 1954, **19**, 307–310.

NEULINGER, J. Perceptions of the optimally integrated person: A redefinition of mental health. *Proceedings of the 76th Annual Convention of the American Psychological Association*, 1968, 553–554.

NUNNALLY, J. *Popular conceptions of mental health: Their development and change*. New York: Holt, Rinehart & Winston, 1961.

PERRY, R. J. The effect of long-term experience on the attitudes of psychiatric aides. *Journal of Community Psychology*, 1974, **2**, 166–173.

PHILLIPS, D. L. Rejection: A possible consequence of seeking help for mental disorders. *American Sociological Review*, 1963, **28**, 963–972.

PHILLIPS, D. L. Rejection of the mentally ill: The influence of behavior and sex. *American Sociological Review*, 1964, **29**, 679–687.

PHILLIPS, D. L. Public identification and acceptance of the mentally ill. *American Journal of Public Health*, 1966, **56**, 755–763.

POOVATHUMKAL, C. Community mental health ideology standing of paraprofessionals. *Community Mental Health Journal*, 1973, **9**, 108–115.

RABKIN, J. G. Opinions about mental illness: A review of the literature. *Psychological Bulletin*, 1972, **77**, 153–171.

RABKIN, J. G. Public attitudes toward mental illness: A review of the literature. *Schizophrenia Bulletin*, Issue No. 10, Fall 1974, 9–33.

RABKIN, J. G. The role of attitudes toward mental illness in evaluation of mental health programs. In E. L. STRUENING & M. GUTTENTAG (Eds.), *Handbook of evaluation research*. Vol. II. Beverly Hills, Calif.: Sage, 1975, pp. 431–482.

RAMSEY, G. V., & SEIPP, M. Attitudes and opinions concerning mental illness. *Psychiatric Quarterly*, 1948, **22**, 428–444.

REZNIKOFF, M. Attitudes of psychiatric nurses and aides toward psychiatric treatment and hospitals. *Mental Hygiene*, 1963, **47**, 354–360.

REZNIKOFF, M., GYNTHER, M. D., TOOMEY, L. C., & FISHMAN, M. Attitudes toward the psychiatric milieu: An inter-hospital comparison of nursing personnel attitudes. *Nursing Research*, 1964, **13**, 71–72.

RING, S., & SCHEIN, L. Attitudes toward mental illness and the use of caretakers in a black community. *American Journal of Orthopsychiatry*, 1970, **40**, 710–716.

ROCHE LABORATORIES. Report of a survey of psychiatric opinion on the social issue—'Women's Liberation.' Psychiatric Viewpoints Report. Nutley, N.J.: Hoffman-LaRoche, 1974, p. 10.

ROGOW, A. *The psychiatrists*. New York: Putnam's Sons, 1970.

ROOTMAN, I., & LAFAVE, H. Are popular attitudes toward the mentally ill changing? *American Journal of Psychiatry*, 1969, **129**, 261–265.

ROSENTHAL, D., & FRANK, J. D. The fate of psychiatric clinic out-patients assigned to psychotherapy. *Journal of Nervous and Mental Diseases*, 1958, **127**, 330–343.

RUDOLPH, C., & CUMMING, J. Where are additional psychiatric services most needed? *Social Work*, 1962, **7**, 15–22.

RYAN, W. (Ed.) *Distress in the city*. Cleveland: Case Western Reserve University Press, 1969.

SABSHIN, M. Toward more rigorous definitions of mental health. In L. M. ROBERTS, N. S. GREENFIELD, & M. H. MILLER (Eds.), *Comprehensive mental health: The challenge of evaluation*. Madison: University of Wisconsin Press, 1968. Pp. 15–27.

SARBIN, T., & MANCUSO, J. Paradigms and moral judgements: Improper conduct is not disease. *Journal of Consulting and Clinical Psychology*, 1972, **39**, 6–8.

SCHNEIDERMAN, L. Social class, diagnosis and treatment. *American Journal of Orthopsychiatry*, 1965, **35**, 99–105.

SMITH, M. B. Competence and 'mental health:' Problems in conceptualizing human effectiveness. In S. B. SELLS (Ed.), *The definition and measurement of mental health*. Washington, D.C.: Public Health Service, 1968. Pp. 99–114.

SROLE, L., LANGER, T. S., MICHAEL, S. T., OPLER, M. K., & RENNIE, T. A. *Mental health in the metropolis: The midtown study*. New York: McGraw-Hill, 1962.

STEIN, L., GREEN, B., & STONE, W. Therapist attitudes as influenced by A–B therapist type, patient diagnosis, and social class. *Journal of Consulting and Clinical Psychology*, 1972, **39**, 301–307.

STIEPER, D., & WIENER, D. *Dimensions of psychotherapy: An experimental and clinical approach*. Chicago: Aldine, 1965.

STRUPP, H. The outcome problem in psychotherapy revisited. *Psychotherapy: Theory, Research and Practice*, 1963, **1**, 1–13.

STRUPP, H. *Psychotherapy: Clinical, research and theoretical issues*. New York: Aronson, 1973.

SULLIVAN, P., MILLER, C., & SMELSER, W. Factors in length of stay and progress in psychotherapy. *Journal of Consulting Psychology*, 1958, **22**, 1–9.

TRINGO, J. L. The hierarchy of preference toward disability groups. *The Journal of Special Education*, 1970, **4**, 295–306.

VERNALLIS, F. F., & ST. PIERRE, R. G. Volunteer workers' opinions about mental illness. *Journal of Clinical Psychology*, 1964, **20**, 140–143.

WALLACH, M., & STRUPP, H. Psychotherapists' clinical judgments and attitudes toward patients. *Journal of Consulting Psychology*, 1960, **24**, 316–323.

WHATLEY, C. Social attitudes toward discharged mental patients. *Social Problems*, 1958–59, **6**, 313–320.

WHITE, R. Motivation reconsidered: The concept of competence. *Psychological Review*, 1959, **66**, 297–333.

WIENER, M., BLUMBERG, A., SEGMAN, S., & COOPER, A. A judgment of adjustment by psychologists, psychiatric social workers and college students, and its relationship to social desirability. *Journal of Abnormal and Social Psychology*, 1959, **59**, 315–321.

WILLIAMS, J., & WILLIAMS, H. M. Attitudes toward mental illness, anamia and authoritarianism among state hospital nursing students and attendants. *Mental Hygiene*, 1961, **45**, 418–424.

WINDER, A. E., & HERSHO, M. The effect of social class in the length and type of psychotherapy in a Veterans' Administration Mental Hygiene Clinic. *Journal of Clinical Psychology*, 1955, **11**, 77–79.

WOODWARD, J. L. Changing ideas of mental illness and its treatment. *American Sociological Review*, 1951, **16**, 443–454.

World Health Organization. *Constitution of the World Health Organization*. Geneva: W.H.O., 1958.

WRIGHT, F., & KLEIN, R. A. Attitudes of hospital personnel and the community regarding mental illness. *Journal of Counseling Psychology*, 1966, **13**, 106–107.

YAMAMOTO, K., & DIZNEY, H. F. Rejection of the mentally ill: A study of attitudes of student teachers. *Journal of Counseling Psychology*, 1967, **14**, 264–268.

EDITORS' REFERENCES

COIE, J., COSTANZO, P., & COX, G. Behavioral determinants of mental illness concerns: A comparison of "gatekeeper" professions. *Journal of Consulting and Clinical Psychology*, 1975, **43**, 626–636.

NOTES

1. This section briefly summarizes a more extensive recent review by the author (Rabkin, 1974).

2. *Editors' Footnote.* This finding demonstrates, to us at least, the great power of the stigma of "mental illness": it seems to be very quickly and easily internalized, even by a fictitious bearer of the label.

3. *Editors' Footnote.* Another study of interoccupational (as well as rural-urban) differences in concerns about mental illness is that of Coie, Costanzo, and Cox (1975).

4. *Editors' Footnote.* The issue of "good" and "bad" treatment goals, attitudes, and performances, highlights the confounding or perhaps inextricable intertwining of "therapeutic" aims on the one hand and social, moral, political, and religious aims on the other. As such, the issue is really a part of the problem of the separability of social values from therapeutic values. Both Rabkin and we discuss this issue below (Footnote 7) where it presents itself in the problem of defining "mental health" apart from social desirability.

5. *Editors' Footnote.* Professionals and laymen may not view mental illness as a disease like any other. But this conclusion does *not* seem to be warranted by their beliefs about recovery from it. Surely both clinicians and laymen are aware of the many chronic physical diseases from which recovery either never or only partially occurs, and which appropriately influence current appraisals by virtue of the number and severity of previous episodes. We think that the best demonstration that mental illness

is not viewed as a disease like others lies in the stigma almost uniquely attached to it.

6. *Editors' Footnote.* We (and obviously Rabkin, too) think that this is much more than a methodological problem for researchers. It raises the very serious question (answered by the above survey results?) of whether therapists are anything other than societal adjustment promoters. Footnote 7 discusses the issue of confounding of social desirability and mental health.

7. *Editors' Footnote.* We think that there are at least two probably inseparable problems here. One is definitional: What is meant by each of the terms "mental health," "normal," "adjustment," and "socially desirable"? The second problem is the inseparability of notions of mental well-being from those of social desirability. The following represents our attempt to deal with both these issues.

Conceptually at least, it *is* possible to distinguish the terms: There *is* something about being mentally healthy that is not the same as being socially desirable, morally upright, "normal," or well-adjusted. And we think that operational distinction of these similar but not identical terms can be approximated.

We would like to see "normal" used to mean "unexceptional," in the statistical sense of simply denoting where some majority of people lie on a dimension. This means that, depending on the dimension, "normal" could refer to a lower, upper, or middle group of subjects (for continuous variables), or to one of two or more discrete groups (for discrete variables). This usage, of course, differs from the popular one in which "normal" (good) is opposed to "abnormal" (bad); we are not proposing an attempt to change this usage, but are proposing that for professional research and clinical precision this definition will be useful, especially if the following is also adopted.

Mental health-illness is best considered a set of *bi*polar dimensions. This means that the absence of symptoms and obvious problems is *not* one end of the scale but rather a point nearer the middle of the distribution. One implication, then, is that some proportion of individuals "exceed" a symptom-free state (being "self-actualized" or similarly described), and are "abnormal" statistically. "Normal" and "mentally ill" (symptomatic) will refer *roughly* to middle and lower regions of the distribution. We say "roughly" because such a distribution may well *not* be bell-shaped. In fact, given the large extent of symptomatology popularly "tolerated" as "normal" (in the several studies that Rabkin describes above), we suspect that the statistical majority of people are not nearly symptom-free, and that an accurate distribution of mental illness-health would be positively skewed.

We think "social adjustment" is best used to refer to one's success, as defined by the absence of overt symptoms and conscious discontent, in a given situation (family, work, community, for example). This definition avoids equating adaptational success with mental health (stressing only overt "problems," the existence, if not the etiology, of which a person would clearly be conscious), and it avoids evaluating the social setting. One may thus be "well adjusted" to a destructive social setting at a great cost to one's mental health, which cost, however, remains covert. Conversely, one may be "poorly adjusted" to such a setting and be quite mentally healthy.

Finally, "social desirability" should denote that class of traits and behaviors that makes a person consciously *liked* by the individuals and institutions of his social setting. We distinguish "liked" from "valued" here, thinking that a person may well be one but not the other (e.g., a family scapegoat who is consciously disliked but highly valued). A well-adjusted person, it should be clear, will most likely be socially desirable, and it may be operationally impossible to distinguish the two concepts.

A knottier and more serious problem, though, is the overlap between social desirability and mental health. Rabkin very alertly points out this problem many times in the chapter, and we strongly agree with her and others that, although some degree of overlap is probably inevitable, the two concepts can and should be better distinguished *operationally*.

Up to this point, we have tried to map out broad domains without attempting the obviously difficult empirical task of specifying the contents of each domain. And, while we will not attempt to do so for "mental health," we nevertheless have some thoughts on the reasons for the social desirability-mental health overlap.

First, we think that there are at least a few well-standardized means of describing and quantifying behavior at the lower (symptomatic) end of the scale. The lack of agreement among these measures is probably something we can live with, either temporarily (if some comprehensive schema can be devised which will subsume these dimensions. analogously to subtests of an intelligence test) or even relatively permanently, if we simply cannot or will not try to integrate conceptually and operationally the different kinds of disturbance that exist.

One reason for such difficulty in agreement and integration is that different definitions of mental health-illness arise from different theories, which in turn arise from different philosophical-moral-social worldviews. This is perhaps to say no more than that personality theories are products of their times and places. We think this is largely true and that it constitutes one of the major reasons for the confounding of mental health and social desirability. But it may at the same time hold a clue for disentanglement. If we have several different culturally based ideas of mental health, each heavily influenced by the needs and wishes of a particular subgroup at a particular point in history, can we not benefit by some sophisticated, broad, cross-cultural analysis aimed at refining or distilling the concept of mental health-illness by specifying what is common to the various definitions and eliminating areas of disagreement?

A second, and probably more important, reason for the confounding is simply that mentally ill people have disturbances in their social functioning which probably correlate at least roughly with their degree of intrapsychic disturbance, or can even be said to *constitute* (part of) their mental illness. That is, it seems inevitable that at least part of the definition of mental illness *is* social malfunctioning. We cannot and should not shy away from this, but instead should try to specify the social malfunctioning that is *not* peculiar to the person's subculture. That is, we should define as mentally ill-social malfunctioning those behaviors and traits that are relatively "culture-independent," and which would therefore be socially malfunctional in nearly any community or subculture. The cross-cultural refining we propose above should serve usefully here.

A third source of confounding is that all sorts of deviance tend to get labeled as mental illness, from political dissent to criminal behavior, to social and economic radicalism. It seems to us that at any given time and place in recent history, there have been mental health professionals who have supported such "diagnoses." After all, clinicians are in large part products of their cultures no less than their theories are, and it is obviously quite easy to blur any distinctions between what constitutes a liked or upright (adjusted) person in one's subculture and a mentally healthy one, especially in the absence of clear criteria for the latter category.

Now we would readily admit that clinicians, especially in working with more seriously or chronically disturbed patients, may be quite cognizant of this problem of confounding. Yet, because of their patients' poor prognosis, they consciously decide to aim for "adjustment" as a major therapeutic achievement. In fact, such clinical work may be very common, and we really have no quarrel with realistically appraising such a clinical situation and acting accordingly. What we are discussing, however, is the intellectual integrity and conceptual development of our whole psychotherapeutic enterprise.

One further thought concerns Rabkin's criticism (below) of "elite" notions of mental health "above and beyond" the absence of illness. She offers two criticisms: first, that such criteria as self-actualization are measures of maturity and are thus age-dependent; second, that they have little applicability to broad populations. While both statements are probably true, we nonetheless feel that such concepts have usefulness. If the age-dependence of these definitions limits their applicability to adults, then at least we may have a starting point for defining the healthy adult. And the current inapplicability of these concepts to large numbers of people should not rule out their use as "ideals"—perhaps rarely attainable, in and of themselves, but useful as guidelines which may help, by "downward" extrapolation, in the formulating of more broadly applicable concepts and operational criteria. We furthermore feel that these "elite" concepts are useful in demonstrating the areas and degrees to which different environments (familial, community, cultural) prevent or promote individual development.

This brings us to our final point—namely, that every environment we know of has its "cost" in terms of individual mental health. While we mentioned above the possibility of being healthy in a destructive environment, we must of course remember that most people are harmed by destructive environments, and many become perpetuators of very similar kinds of destructiveness. Clearly, then, our attempt to separate social desirability from mental health should not be seen as an attempt to deny that social influences can and do *make* (and not just *define*) mental illness, which persists beyond the time and place of its genesis.

8. *Editors' Footnote.* We do not wholly agree with this appraisal. While psychosocial or transactional models are currently favored by many theoreticians and clinicians to account for many clinical problems, there is currently also a reascendancy of medical illness theory. Furthermore, this work, on biogenic amines in schizophrenia, for example, constitutes more than a mere borrowing of medical terminology to construct models of some of the psychoses and affective disorders. It seems increasingly likely that distinctive biochemical and neurophysiological substrata for these problems will be identified in the near future. It may be then that for certain disorders—the neuroses, for example—transactional social models may replace illness models, but the reverse seems to be happening for other disorders.

CHAPTER 9

THEORETICAL ORIENTATIONS OF PSYCHOTHERAPISTS

Donald M. Sundland

In this chapter we will discuss how theoretical orientations (TØs) of psychotherapists are measured, acquired, and to what they are related. As the results of these studies are presented, the methodological issues of design and data analysis will be commented upon.

After a review of some of the basic TØ measurement problems and a comprehensive description of most of the instruments that have been used to measure TØ, the chapter will present a developmental analysis of TØs and their correlates. First, I will review the existing evidence relating to those antecedent conditions which may influence the adoption of TØs and then discuss concurrent conditions that are associated with adherence to varying theoretical positions. Finally, the chapter will consider a range of consequences associated with the adoption of TØs, focusing primarily on therapeutic outcome and issues involved in the matching of both clients and therapists and co-therapists.

MEASUREMENT OF THERAPISTS' ORIENTATIONS

In the field of TØ measurement we have the same problem as in any measurement task. The questions that are posed strongly influence the results. An example—an experimenter concludes that there are no differences between psychotherapists because they all have the same answer to his questionnaire item: "Effective psychotherapy is based on shooting the patient in the head." (It certainly solves all the patient's problems, has predictable results, etc.) A weakness in the classic Fiedler (1950a, 1950b) studies was the omission of items focusing on points of controversy between TØs, while the benchmark Sundland and Barker (1962) study was deficient in its omission of items about which "expert" therapists agreed.

Types of Data: Nominal

In the TØ area we deal mostly with nominal data, relying on "school" names—Adlerian, Sullivanian, behavioral, etc.—or with the ordinal data derived from scores on some measurement instrument, such as the Therapist Orientation Questionnaire (TOQ) (Sundland & Barker, 1962) and the AID (McNair & Lorr, 1964).

One example of nominal data was obtained by Wildman and Wildman (1967), who surveyed a random sample of the Clinical Psychology Division of the American Psychological Association. Of the 400 surveys sent, they obtained only 100 usable returns. The respondent was presented with a list of 36 therapeutic systems and asked to rank his top three choices. Another 24 returns had to be discarded for failure to follow directions. With the remaining 76 respondents, they weighted the top three choices, 5:2:1, respectively. Their top 11 systems, with weighted scores in parentheses, were: very eclectic (161), Freudian psychoanalysis (94), client-centered therapy (68), Sullivan (63), learning theory therapy (32), experiential (22), directive therapy (20), rational psychotherapy (13), existential (12), and Frommian and psychobiologic (both 11).

Goldschmid, Stein, Weissman, and Sorrells (1969) also did a questionnaire study of members and fellows of the Clinical Psychology Division. Based on 244 responses, they found that the four most frequent responses were eclectic (24%), neo-Freudian (17%), behavioristic (12%), and Freudian psychoanalytic (12%). Almost 60% had been using their present TØ for seven or more years. Some changes in TØ over the years were reported by 70% of the respondents.

Without knowing what their decision rules were for the placement of their respondents into the various TØs, it is not possible to speculate on why Goldschmid et al., found a lower percentage of "eclectics" than Wildman and Wildman (1967) or Garfield and Kurtz (1974). Their data with regard to changes in TØ are interesting in view of the fairly high percentage of therapists who report change.

As another example of the nominal approach, Garfield and Kurtz (1974) surveyed 855 clinical psychologists and found a wide distribution of

TØ (see Table 1). These data clearly point to the
futility of using TØ labels.[1] A minority of the
field identify with any one of eight specific labels;
the majority choose a label, "eclecticism," that
by its meaning disavows specificity. While we
can be sure that psychoanalytic therapist A
differs from psychoanalytic therapist B to some
extent, eclecticism by its nature indicates diverse
ideological stances. Most of the TØs found by
Wildman and Wildman (1967) are still found in
this survey with a trend toward more eclecticism.
*One may ask therapists to label themselves, but
over half will disavow any systematic, organized,
articulated theory held in common with others.*

TABLE 1. THEORETICAL ORIENTATIONS OF CLINICAL
PSYCHOLOGISTS[a]

TØ	Frequency	Percent
Eclectic	470	54.97
Psychoanalytic	92	10.76
Learning Theory	85	9.94
Other	61	7.14
Neo-Freudian	45	5.26
Sullivanian	26	3.04
Humanistic	15	2.92
Existentialist	24	2.81
Rational-Emotive	25	1.75
Rogerian	12	1.40
TOTAL	855	99.99

[a]From Garfield and Kurtz (1974). Copyright 1974 by the
American Psychological Association Division of Clinical
Psychology. Reproduced by permission.

There is some evidence discussed later in this
chapter that these "school" labels coexist with
attitudinal differences that seem to fit with the
theoretical differences. In studies dealing with
psychotherapy, the TØ of the therapists is a
crucial variable. Given only one minute to
assess TØ, labels offer, at least, something;
something which, in this case, seems better than
nothing. Sometimes, even this is not done. For
example, Waskow and Bergman (1962) used
three groups of therapists from different institutions and *assumed* a cohesiveness in TØ among
the therapists at each institution: University of
Chicago Counseling Center (client-centered);
Menninger Foundation (orthodox Freudian);
and National Institutes of Health (a neutral,
eclectic group). Therapists were never actually
asked to label themselves.

A novel approach to the nominal scaling of
therapists is described by Gamboa and Koltveit
(1973). They assessed not only the counseling
attitudes of their therapists, but also some of
their personality characteristics and their relative effectiveness with five types of delinquent
youth.

Types of Data: Ordinal

The ordinal data in this area consist of questionnaires dealing with therapeutic issues. Sometimes the focus is on the behavior of the therapist,
actual or desirable; sometimes on the attitudes,
values, and goals of the therapists which underlie their behavior as therapists. Some of the
studies have dealt with "captive" populations,
for example, colleagues or friends of colleagues;
others have used "random" samples. We will
first discuss the problem of response bias in these
latter studies and then examine some of the TØ
measures themselves and the results obtained in
using them.

Response Bias

Response bias poses a moot or, in the least, a
very expensive question to answer. As indicated
in a later section, we have found certain TØ
attitudes to be related to some therapists' characteristics (Sundland, 1972). It seems reasonable
that the means of the respondent group are *not*
unbiased estimates of the total sample or the
sampled population. What the bias is we can
estimate but not prove. If older respondents have
higher scores on factor X, this does not prove
that older nonrespondents would also obtain
higher scores on factor X. We therefore have no
way of adjusting the respondent sample, even
after we show that they are younger than the
total sample. In the two studies just mentioned
(Garfield & Kurtz, 1974; Wildman & Wildman,
1967), it is possible that eclecticism is not as
rampant as it appears, but that perhaps eclectics
are more cooperative in answering questionnaires.

With regard to profession, there are some data
on the variation in response rates to mailed questionnaires. Kissinger and Tolor (1965) report
the following response rates for a short questionnaire sent to 100 persons randomly selected
from each of several groups: clinical psychologists (55%), diplomates in clinical psychology
(54%), psychiatrists (38%), psychoanalysts (19%),
and psychiatric social workers (42%).

In a national survey of psychotherapists,
Goldman and Mendelsohn (1969) randomly
selected 1200 therapists from among psychiatrists, clinical psychologists, and psychiatric
social workers. Of this group, 186 could not be
reached, 443 responded, and of these 421 provided usable data. By profession, 29% ($n=144$)
of psychiatrists, 60% ($n=143$) of clinical psychologists, and 60% ($n=134$) of psychiatric
social workers responded.

In a recent study I sent questionnaires to several groups of psychotherapists. The response rates were as follows: pastoral counselors (41%), psychologists (29%), psychiatrists (19%), psychoanalysts (11%), social workers (15%), Gestalt therapists (23%), members of the American Academy of Psychotherapists (32%), transactional analysts (29%), rational-emotive therapists (42%), and respondents to the 1961 TOQ study (Sundland & Barker, 1962) (24%).

Naturally, response rate varies with the arduousness of the task. It also seems clearly to vary with profession. Psychologists, ministers, and social workers tend to respond more frequently, while psychiatrists and psychoanalysts have low response rates. We are only in the 30% to 50% response range with the clear possibility of some bias between the attitudes of responders and nonresponders.

Instruments Used in Measuring Therapists' Orientations

Wolff (1956) interviewed a number of psychotherapists using a standard schedule and reported some descriptive data. His conclusion heralded the findings of the later quantitative study of Sundland and Barker (1962): "Thus, there are two types of psychotherapy, the one following a preconceived system of thought, operating with formulas of interpretation, the other based upon an evolving personal relationship" (p. 206).

Fey's Questionnaire. Fey (1958) constructed a simple questionnaire describing issues commonly arising in the conduct of psychotherapy. This form contained 27 items, scored on a 1–5 scale, and was sent to 36 therapists, of whom 34 participated. In addition to his 27 questionnaire items, Fey scored "doctrine"—Rogerian, analytic, eclectic; years experience; the number of "3" answers and the number of "1" and "5" answers. His data analysis was clever and thorough. He found seven Rogerians, five analysts, and 22 eclectics. He split the latter group on years of experience—young eclectics (1–9 years) and older eclectics (10–24 years). He summed the scores within each group, found the averages and correlated each therapist with these "models." The Rogerians were more homogeneous—as shown by their higher average correlation coefficients—the analysts were least.

He also factored the questionnaire into four oblique factors and selected the purest items to obtain scale scores. He then compared his four groups on these scale scores and found that all four scales were sensitive to the variable,

doctrine, and that two scales were sensitive to the variable, experience. Finally, Fey expressed some appropriate reservations about his data in terms of his limited sampling of therapists and of questionnaire items. This paper formed an important part of the genesis of the work that Sundland and Barker (1962) soon began.

Fourteen years later as a co-author (Rice, Fey, & Kepecs, 1972), Fey continued his study of TØ. As before, his approach was not as attitudinal as was Sundland and Barker's (1962), but was more behavioral. Rice et al. used an assessment measure having 23 adjectives or short phrases. With a sample of 50 therapists, these 23 items were intercorrelated and factor-analyzed, using a principal components-varimax rotation procedure. This yielded six factors (no mention was made as to the decision rule used to determine the number of factors). The authors report the six "styles" of in-therapy behaviors and the key self-descriptive phrases (items which "load" highly on that factor) to be: (I) *blank screen* (passive, unchanging, unprovocative, anonymous, and cautious); (II) *paternal* (businesslike, patient, interpretive, interested in patient's history, and impartial); (III) *transactional* ("here-and-now," casual, relationship oriented, interpretive, spontaneous); (IV) *authoritarian* (theory-oriented, persistent, definite, goal-oriented, guiding, businesslike); (V) *maternal* (talkative, explanatory, supportive, guiding, interpretive); and (VI) *idiosyncratic* (critical, unspontaneous, encourages conformity, nonprovocative, talkative). No data are provided on the distribution of the answers to the 23 items, or their means, only the means of "transformed scores" on the factors. This leaves the reader adrift as to the homogeneity of the therapist sample, how skewed scores on an item were, etc.

The questionnaire gives us a handy way of cutting the TØ pie. Compared with the factors reported by Sundland and Barker (1962), Factor I looks like their activity factor, Factor II smacks of the psychoanalytic orientation, while Factor III has some of the experiential flavor. The rest of the factors of Rice et al. (1972) do not appear comparable to those of Sundland and Barker (1962).

Rice, Gurman, and Razin (1974) used this questionnaire in another study. They obtained responses from 47 male and 39 female psychotherapists. The intercorrelation matrix was factor-analyzed using a principal components method, followed by a varimax rotation. Previously (Rice et al., 1972) six factors had been found; this time there were eight. They report that each of the six found a corresponding one among the current eight, but do not offer any statistical basis for this statement. They conjectured that the two additional factors are related to having more female therapists in this sample than in the earlier one and to the increased influence of phenomenological schools of therapy from 1967 to 1972 (the time span of the two studies).

The eight factors and their key items were: (I) *low activity level* (cautious, passive, and talkative [negative loading]); (II) *directed focus* (focus on the relationship, challenging, interpretive, and guiding); (III) *cognitive goal emphasis* (goal-oriented, guided by theory, and explanatory); (IV) *traditional* (interested in history, patient/willing to wait, and interpretive); (V) *rigid/mechanical* (consistent during session, anonymous, and businesslike); (VI) *feeling-responsiveness* (casual, spontaneous, and provocative); (VII) *judgmental* (critical/disapproving, encourage conformity, and persistent); and (VIII) *supportive* (supportive, businesslike, and guided by theory [negative loading]).

Therapist Orientation Questionnaire. The Therapist Orientation Questionnaire (TOQ) (Sundland & Barker, 1962) was composed of 133 items designed to reflect evenly both poles of 13 scales on attitudes and methods about which psychotherapists disagreed. The results were based upon the replies of 139 subjects. Factor-analytic procedures of Wherry (1959) and Wherry and Winer (1953) gave orthogonal factors. In generalizing the findings it is important that two limitations be kept in mind. First, there is the limitation of the sample of therapists—namely, psychologists interested in psychotherapy. A second limitation refers to the sampling of items. It is possible that there were important categories of attitudes and methods which were left out of the questionnaire. For example, informal behavior and interruptive activity were included in the next study (Sundland, 1972) and found to form primary factors. It was very unfortunate that we did not include the three factors that Fiedler (1950b) had found: communication, proper emotional distance, and status concerns. Even though these items were used on an early form and found not to discriminate between therapists, it would have been desirable to include them in the larger scale study to confirm this finding and to compare them with Fiedler's (1950a) finding that "expertness" was related to these three factors.

The 13 attitudinal scales were: (1) *frequency of activity* (talkative, active); (2) *type of activity*

(depth of interpretation); (3) *emotional tenor of the relationship* (impersonal versus a warm, personal approach); *Structure of the relationship*—the intercorrelations of these items indicated a split into the following three groups: *spontaneity in the therapeutic relationship* (spontaneous, unreasoned), *planning of the therapeutic relationship* (planned behavior of therapist), and *conceptualization of the therapeutic relationship* (therapist thinks about the patient's relationship with him); (5) *goals of therapy* (has goals); (6) *therapist's security* (therapist's own security in the therapy situation); (7) *theory of personal growth* (a "life force" urging to mental health); (8) *nature of therapeutic gains*—this is another subtest which, from the table of intercorrelations, it was decided to divide into two parts: *cognitive therapeutic gains* (understanding is important), and *learning process in therapy* (process is verbal and conceptual); (9) *topics important to therapy* (discussion of childhood is important); (10) *theory of neurosis* (ineffectual conscience versus a too strong one); (11) *criteria for success* (social adjustment is important); (12) *theory of motivation* (unconscious processes are important); and (13) *curative aspect of the therapist* (training versus personality).

The 13 original scales yielded 16 scores due to splitting two of the scales. These 16 scores gave six first-order factors and one second-order factor. One of the most interesting and surprising findings of the analysis was that there was a general factor which cut across the majority of the scales. In terms of these items this general factor was considered the most significant single continuum upon which to compare therapists. For convenience, one pole of the general factor was labeled the "analytic" pole—i.e., in the broad sense of attending and responding, not as an abbreviation for "psychoanalytic." The other pole of the general factor was labeled the "experiential" pole, congruent with its emphasis upon nonrationalized, nonverbal experiencing. In terms of the subtests with the higher loadings, the "analytic" pole stressed conceptualizing, the training of the therapist, planning of therapy, unconscious processes, and a restriction of therapist spontaneity. The "experiential" pole deemphasizes unconscious processes and accepts therapist spontaneity.

Rosso and Frey (1973) suggest a theoretical model for describing TØs that is somewhat related to the factors found in this study. Frey (1972) used the schemes proposed by Patterson (1966) (with theories differentiated on a rational-cognitive to affective continuum) and London (1964) (theories based on insight or action goals). Frey proposed a four-celled model combining these two schemes: rational-insight and rational-action, affective-insight and affective-action. The rational-affective continuum seems similar to Sundland and Barker's (1962) general factor of analytic versus experiential. Sundland and Barker's scheme has been more geared toward what the therapist is doing and why he does it. Therapists' goals are not made explicit. It would be desirable for therapists to indicate what goals they strive for and the relative importance they ascribe to different goals. Perhaps by using such a fairly simple scheme, as Rosso and Frey propose, we would be in a better position to match clients' and counselors' goals.[2]

TOQ—1961 Study. The initial results of the Therapist Orientation Questionnaire were reported by Sundland and Barker (1962). While this paper was in the process of publication, we decided to expand the sample on which these results were based to include psychiatrists and psychiatric social workers and to revise the questionnaire slightly at the same time. Since we were going to revise the questionnaire, we felt it was necessary to obtain another psychologist sample. Questionnaires were sent to a random sample of 249 psychologists who listed psychotherapy as a first or second interest in the 1960 American Psychological Association Directory. There was an estimated total number of 3,300. At the same time, using the 1959 National Association of Social Workers Directory and membership in Division P (Psychiatric), questionnaires were sent to a group of psychiatric social workers. Sampling 53 pages, 389 names were obtained from an estimated total of 4,600 then practicing psychotherapy. Of these, 199 answered a Preliminary Questionnaire (PQ) that they were currently practicing psychotherapy. These 199 were sent a TOQ. The 1959–1960 American Psychiatric Association Directory was used to obtain a random sample of 150 members, who were sent the PQ. Since 80% of the 71 respondents answered that they were currently practicing psychotherapy, it was decided to have no selection rules for psychiatrists. Two hundred and seventy-seven questionnaires were sent to a random sample from an estimated group of 8,800. All questionnaires were followed up 6 weeks later with a letter.

The TOQ was considered unscorable if the person was not presently engaged in psychotherapy or if he omitted more than 10% of the answers or if he wrote in too many qualifications. It was possible to obtain at least 100 scorable questionnaires from each of the three professional groups. Where more than 100 questionnaires were received from a group, it was randomly reduced to exactly 100. Thus, we obtained a sample of 100 respondents from each of the three groups.

The questionnaire was based on the one reported in Sundland and Barker (1962) with some revisions and additions. There were 24 dimensions which we felt might play a role in distinguishing psychotherapists from one another (see Table 2). This enlargement of the number of dimensions was based on discussions with colleagues who had seen a preprint of the Sundland and Barker (1962) paper.

TABLE 2. A PRIORI DIMENSION NAMES FOR THE THERAPIST ORIENTATION QUESTIONNAIRE (1961).

1. Affective therapeutic goals	14. Personal involvement
2. Curative aspects of therapy	15. Planned therapeutic relationship
3. Social goals	16. Spontaneous therapeutic relationship
4. Cognitive therapeutic goals	17. Type of activity
5. Conceptualizing therapeutic relationship	18. Theory of therapy
	19. Theory of motivation
6. Deliberate directiveness	20. Theory of neurosis
7. Emphasis on ego control	21. Theory of personal growth
8. Expression of personal involvement	22. Therapist's security
9. Frequency of activity	23. Use of psychoanalytic techniques
10. Have goals for therapy	24. Variety of therapists behaviors
11. Interruptive activity	
12. Learning theory	
13. Medical responsibility	

A number of different factor-analytic procedures were performed on these data. Although the problem of deciding how many factors to use proved to be quite a source of difficulty, by using Horn's (1965) procedure to suggest the number of factors to extract and rotate, I obtained 10 factors which seemed useful in a revision of the TOQ and took the content of the items into account. Table 3 presents the factors and their polar descriptions.[3]

These factors are similar to the three factors reported by McNair and Lorr (1964). Factor (A), the psychoanalytic factor, is like Factor 5. Factor (I), "impersonal versus personal techniques," is a mixture of Factor 8 ("informal behavior is *not* all right"), Factor 6 ("emotional uninvolvement is important"), Factor 7 ("therapist feels secure"), and Factor 3 ("training and nonspontaneous behavior is important"). In our analysis, however, Factor 3 also has the planning and conceptualizing of the case, which are split off into McNair and Lorr's Factor (D),

TABLE 3. THERAPIST ORIENTATION QUESTIONNAIRE FACTORS: 1961 STUDY.

Factor	Positive Pole	Negative Pole
1.	Social goals are important and directiveness should *not* be avoided	Social goals are *not* important and deliberate directiveness should be avoided
2.	Affective gains are *not* most important	Affective gains are most important
3.	Training, planning, and conceptualizing	Personality, spontaneous, and nonconceptualizing
4.	Learning process in therapy is verbal and conceptual, and cognitive gains are most important	Learning process in therapy is nonverbal and emotional, and understanding is not important
5.	Necessity for discussing childhood, use of psychoanalytic techniques, and unconscious motives are important	Discussion of childhood is not necessary, psychoanalytic techniques are not used, and unconscious motives are not important
6.	Activity and involvement of the therapist are *not* desirable	Activity and involvement of the therapist are desirable
7.	Therapist feels very secure	Therapist admits to some insecurity
8.	Informal behavior by the therapist is *not* all right	Informal behavior by the therapist is all right
9.	Growth is *not* inherent	Growth is inherent
10.	Interrupting the patient is *not* acceptable	Interrupting the patient is acceptable

"directive techniques." Also, in "D" are Factor 1 ("social goals and deliberate directiveness") and Factor 10 ("it is acceptable to be nontalkative and noninterruptive"). McNair and Lorr's questions focused on the behavior of the therapist and left out the theoretical issues: Factor 2 ("affective gains are *not* important"), Factor 4 ("the learning that takes place is verbal and conceptual in nature and cognitive gains are most important"), and Factor 9 ("growth is *not* inherent"). These are theoretical positions that the therapist may hold, which underlie some of his behavior, but are not directly equivalent to behavior.

The correlations between the 10 factors suggested two clusters: A—Factors 1, 4, and 7; and B—Factors 5, 8, and 10. These clusters were uncorrelated with one another (.083). In addition, there were two factors (3 and 6) which were correlated with each other (.36) and with both of the clusters, and there were two factors (2 and 9) that were not significantly correlated with either of the clusters. Research is continuing with two sets of the two clusters, one set: OA (orthogonal A) and OB (orthogonal B), the simple, orthogonal clusters, and the other set: CA (correlated A) and CB (correlated B), which correlate .69 with each other, where Factors 3 and 6 have been added to both OA and OB. Cluster OA consists of Factors 1 (social goals—important, be directive), 4 (learning process—verbal and conceptual, cognitive gains—important), and 7 (therapist—secure). Cluster OB has Factors 5 (childhood discussion, psychoanalytic techniques, unconscious motivation), 8 (informal behavior is *not* all right), and 10 (nontalkative and noninterruptive). The common factors were 3 (training, planning, and conceptualizing) and 6 (activity and involvement *not* desirable).

When we sent out the TOQ in 1961, we had included a Personal Data Questionnaire (PDQ), the results of which have not been previously published. Seven variables were studied: (1) profession, (2) had private control analysis, (3) years of experience, (4) works in private practice, (5) hours per week doing psychotherapy, (6) had personal therapy, and (7) "school." Since there are 14 TOQ scores, the comparison of each of these on the seven PDQ variables yielded 98 analyses of variance. Considering the number of comparisons, I chose to adopt an alpha level of .01. Overall, there were 16 F tests significant at the .001 level and eight significant at the .01 level. Group means were compared by use of a t test. Differences between the means are considered significant only if they exceed the .01 level.

Comparing the three professions yielded seven significant differences: six at the .001 level and one at the .01 level. The social workers (SW) scored higher than the psychiatrists (MD) or psychologists (PSY) on Factor 1 (social goals are important and directiveness should *not* be avoided). This seems to be a reasonable result and one that could have been predicted. Whether their preferences led them to choose these professions, or vice versa, is uncertain.

The SWs were highest on Factor 3 (training, planning, conceptualizing) and the PSYs were lowest. On Factor 5 (discuss childhood, use psychoanalytic techniques, unconscious important), the SWs were lower than the MDs and PSYs. With regard to Factor 6 (activity and involvement—*not* desirable), the PSYs had lower scores than the MDs and SWs. The other three significant differences are on the cluster scores and add very little to the information obtained from the first-order factors.

Comparing therapists who had had private control versus those who did not, we found two significant differences: Factor I (social goals and directiveness), "private controls" had the lower score, and Factor 5, the psychoanalytic factor, those with the private control had a very much higher score. This gives some construct validity to both these factors.

The third comparison was between groups of varying levels of experience. There were no F tests significant at the .01 level or better; one was significant at the .05 level and was most likely a chance result.

Compared with the rest of the group, private practitioners had a lower mean on Factor 1 and on Factor 5, and on cluster OB they were higher. This is similar to the "private control" findings; social goals are not stressed but psychoanalytic tenets and techniques are valued. The data for five levels of hours per week doing psychotherapy yielded only one significant difference, again on Factor 5, such that part-time practitioners tended to adhere less to some psychoanalytic tenets.

Contrasting those therapists who had had personal therapy with those who had not, the former had a lower score on Factor 1 (social goals are not emphasized) and a much higher score on Factor 5 (psychoanalysis valued).

If we ignore the clusters, in the 60 comparisons on the 10 factor scores, there were 11 significant differences, nine of which were on Factors 1 and 5. On Factor 1 (social goals), PSYs and MDs were low and SWs were high, and "private controls," private practitioners, and those with personal therapy were all low. On Factor 5 (psychoanalysis) MDs were high and SWs were low, "private controls," private practitioners, full-time workers, and those with personal therapy were all high.

There were nine significant F tests for "schools" and 106 significant t tests. Table 4 lists the latter. Only a few will be commented on. Four (Nos. 3, 5, 6, 8) of the five factors which were significant are all in Cluster CB (only Factor 10 is missing). So the results on CB summarize many of the differences.

In brief, the experientialists (experiential eclectic and experiential) differ from most everybody else and the orthodox Freudians are at the other extreme, also holding views that differ from all the rest. This is a repetition of the general factor reported earlier.

The findings on Factor 2 (affective gains—*not* important) show the experiential group at the low end (denying the *not*), while the diagnostic group affirms this position. The eclectics and psychobiologicalists also have high means but

TABLE 4. SIGNIFICANT DIFFERENCES BETWEEN "SCHOOLS" ON THERAPIST ORIENTATION QUESTIONNAIRE FACTORS.

Factor	
2	$6 < 1, 2, 3, 10; 4, 5 < 2$
3	$4, 6 < 1, 2, 3, 5, 7, 8, 9, 10; 1 < 9$
5	$2, 6, 8 < 1, 5, 7, 9; 4 < 9$
6	$4 < 1, 5, 8, 9; 6 < 1, 2, 3, 5, 7, 8, 9$
8	$1, 2, 4, 6 < 9; 6 < 5, 7, 9$
OA	$1, 3, 4, 5, 6, 7 < 8; 4 < 2, 8$
CA	$4, 6 < 1, 2, 3, 5, 7, 8, 9, 10; 1 < 8$
OB	$2, 3, 4, 6, 8, 10 < 9; 2, 4, 6 < 5; 6 < 1, 7$
CB	$4, 6 < 1, 2, 3, 5, 7, 9; 6 < 8, 10; 1, 2, 3, 8 < 9$

Note.

1: Cultural Analysts	6: Experiential
2: Diagnostic	7: Modified Analysts
3: Eclectics	8: Other
4: Experiential Eclectics	9: Orthodox Freudian
5: Freudian Eclectics	10: Psychobiological

are too few in number for the t test to be significant.

TOQ—1972 Survey. Using this factor analysis as a basis, the TOQ was shortened. A form of the TOQ was prepared containing 61 items from the 1961 form, the 10 factors mentioned above, and 43 new items. Some of these were from the Wallach and Strupp (1964) study and others were based on colleagues' suggestions. The Personal Data Questionnaire was also revised to take into account that group therapy is more common now than 10 years ago.

In June 1972 these two questionnaires were sent to several random samples of psychotherapists: pastoral counselors ($N = 362$), psychologists ($N = 800$), psychiatrists ($N = 494$), psychoanalysts ($N = 106$), psychiatric social workers ($N = 758$), Gestalt therapists ($N = 123$), the total membership of the American Academy of Psychotherapists ($N = 545$), transactional analysts ($N = 99$), rational-emotive therapists ($N = 120$), and most of the respondents to the 1961-TOQ study ($N = 252$) reported above. The results of this survey are now being analyzed.

Usual Therapeutic Practices Scale. Wallach and Strupp (1964) present a study of therapists' preferences for and attitudes toward basic therapeutic practices. They constructed a 17-item scale of the therapist's Usual Therapeutic Practices (UTP) (see Table 5). They had two samples: (A) 59 medical psychotherapists at North Carolina Memorial Hospital and (B) 248 psychotherapists (91 psychiatrists, 157 psychologists), a random, nationwide sample from a mailing of 300 questionnaires to each profession.

They performed principal-axis factor analyses on the correlation matrices of each sample. These analyses were rotated using a varimax procedure. Four factors are discussed—*Factor I*: personal distance; *Factor II*: intensive (psychoanalytic,

TABLE 5. USUAL THERAPEUTIC PRACTICES QUESTIONNAIRE[a].

1. Generally tend to be active.	10. Keep all aspects of my private life out of therapy.
2. Find it difficult to cope with patient's hostility.	11. Technique varies a good deal from patient to patient.
3. Tend to be more effective with some patients.	12. Usually willing to grant extra interviews.
4. Rarely express own feelings in treatment.	13. Consider psychotherapy much more an art than a science.
5. Rarely answer personal questions.	14. Almost never answer personal questions of opinion.
6. Verbal interventions are usually sparing and concise.	15. A warm, giving attitude is the most important characteristic of a good therapist.
7. If asked by my patient, would be willing to talk with a relative.	16. Therapist should be more like a "blank screen" than a person in therapy.
8. Prefer to conduct intensive rather than goal-limited therapy.	17. Prefer patients not to develop intense feelings about me.
9. Almost never let silences build up during the therapy hour.	

[a]Adapted from Wallach and Strupp (1964). Copyright 1964 by the American Psychological Association. Reproduced by permission.

uncovering) psychotherapy; *Factor III*: verbal interventions; *Factor IV*: view of psychotherapy as an artistic and artful activity, flexible as opposed to rigid.

Wallach and Strupp view their first factor as similar to Sundland and Barker's (1962) general factor. As reported earlier, Fey (1958) also factored his data (using a different method and rotational criteria) and found a similar factor on which 16 of his 30 items had loadings of +.40 or larger. Fiedler (1950a, 1951) also sees "emotional distance" as an important dimension. This appears as Cluster OA and Common Factor 6 in the most recent analysis of the TOQ. The robustness of this dimension of therapeutic activity certainly gives credence to its validity.

The AID Scale. Shortly following this paper, McNair and Lorr (1964) reported the results of another study of therapists' preferences regarding treatment techniques. They hypothesized three dimensions: (A) a psychoanalytically oriented approach, (I) the therapist's affective responses to patients: impersonal versus warm, and (D) a directive, active approach to treatment. Their 49 items came primarily from the TOQ, a few from Fey (1958), and some were their own. The AID (analytic-impersonal-directive) Scale was administered to 192 male and 73 female therapists from 44 Veterans Administration Mental Hygiene clinics. There were 67 psychiatrists, 103 psychologists, and 95 social workers. The answers were indicated by degree of agreement or disagreement on an 8-point scale with no undecided category. The responses were intercorrelated and the resulting correlation matrix was analyzed by a multiple group factoring procedure (Guttman, 1952). The three hypothesized dimensions were found defined by 10, 11, and 10 items, respectively. The factor

scores were intercorrelated yielding, A-I: .44, A-D: .32, and I-D: .24.

In terms of the latest TOQ analysis presented earlier, these dimensions—A, I, and D— correspond to the Cluster OA and the Common Factors 3 and 6. The items of Cluster OB were omitted in their questionnaire as relating to theoretical bias and personality more than technique.

McNair and Lorr derived eight configural pattern scores by dichotomizing each of their three scales at their medians. The resulting patterns were compared on sex, profession, personal therapy, and experience. This is an interesting approach to developing a typology of psychotherapists, particularly with regard to effects on patients.

Another questionnaire based on the TOQ was the Therapist Orientation Sheet (Paul, 1966), which contained 24 attitudinal and 20 technique scales. This was used both descriptively (Paul, 1966; Paul & Shannon, 1966) and as a measure of attitudinal change (Paul & McInnis, 1974).

Other TØ Measures. Weissman, Goldschmid, and Stein (1971) used a maximum-likelihood factor analysis to analyze the use of 27 therapeutic techniques by their 244 respondents. They had a 6-point scale ranging from "with every patient" to "never" and found nine factors as shown in Table 6.

They related their nine factors to five "themes" reported by Lionells (1966) and to the TØs of respondents. Lionells (1966) presented five "themes"—egalitarian, dogmatist, normalist, pragmatist, and authoritarian—as underlying therapeutic behavior. Factor I and, to a lesser degree, Factor VIII primarily resemble the egalitarian theme (an interpersonal relationship

TABLE 6. FACTOR ANALYSIS OF SPECIFIC THERAPEUTIC TECHNIQUES
PRESENTLY EMPLOYED WITH LABELS BY LIONELLS[a]

Loading	Item No.	Technique Item
		Factor I—Egalitarian
.96	9	I talk about myself and my problems.
.47	4	I talk freely about my personal feelings.
.40	5	I interact freely with the patient socially.
.37	10	I use didactic methods (e.g., reading assignments).
.34	8	I give negative reinforcement (e.g., scolding, shock).
		Factor II—Normalist
.96	6	I see patient's family.
.55	25	If there is a spouse, I see the spouse also.
		Factor III—Dogmatist
.58	24	I reward the patient (e.g., gifts, praise, tokens, etc.).
.51	14	I relabel symptoms.
.49	8	I give negative reinforcement (e.g., scolding, shock).
.48	7	I explain my therapeutic plans and goals.
.44	23	I specify the length of our contacts.
.42	15	I use operant conditioning.
.39	21	I role play with the patient.
.32	10	I use didactic methods (e.g., reading assignments).
		Factor IV—Authoritarian
.67	12	I reflect the patient's feelings.
.64	13	I interpret the patient's thoughts and feelings.
.55	11	I analyze and interpret dreams.
.40	3	I let the patient do most of the talking.
		Factor V—Normalist
.64	17	I use play techniques if the patient is a child.
.58	18	I see the parents if patient is a child.
		Factor VI—Pragmatist
.65	22	I use psychodrama with patients.
.62	21	I role play with patients.
.53	20	I hypnotize the patient.
.32	16	I use relaxation techniques.
		Factor VII—Dogmatist
.68	16	I use relaxation techniques.
.38	15	I use operant conditioning.
		Factor VIII—Egalitarian
.59	19	I work with a co-therapist.
.45	26	I sometimes touch, hold, or embrace patient.
.40	4	I talk freely about my personal feelings.
.30	5	I interact with the patient socially.
		Factor IX—Pragmatist
.51	2	I give patient my home phone number.
.50	1	I plan activities for the patient.
.40	10	I use didactic methods (e.g., reading assignments).
.30	11	I analyze and interpret dreams.

[a]From Weissman et al. (1971). Copyright 1971 by the American Psychological Association. Adapted by permission.

between equals). Factors III and VII relate to the dogmatist theme (systematic problem solving). Factor IV relates to the authoritarian theme (formalistic expert manner). Factors II and V bear on the normalist theme (integrating into social environment). Factors VI and IX relate to the pragmatist theme (nonformalistic use of techniques). The nine factors then served as dependent variables against which present orientation could be compared by means of analysis of variance. None of the Fs for techniques were found to be significant.

It is hard to explain the difference between the findings of this study and those of Sundland and Barker (1962), and the later results of the 1961 TOQ study presented above. We can note that they had nine orientation categories. Nowhere do they indicate the Ns for each TØ. They do present data that the N used was less than the total sample of respondents. It is possible that by using both "school" labels and "names of influential authors," we arrived at more cohesive TØ groups. Also our items are worded with regard to the therapist's *belief* about the most desirable way to behave rather than an estimated frequency of his own behaviors.

All of the above approaches used a measure-based typology rather than a criterion-based typology. For example, therapists can be grouped by their scores on TOQ factors or by their success rate with schizophrenic patients. The following work, which combines these two approaches, has been developed in California for the Community Treatment Program for delinquent youth (Gamboa & Koltveit, 1973; Palmer, 1973). Unfortunately, the original papers are internal communications of the California Youth Authority and not readily accessible. Gamboa and Koltveit (1973) classify a worker through an individual, taped interview. The interview deals with the relationships with clients, personal themes in the lives of the counselors, the type of desired counseling relationship, and counseling methods. This leads to five types of counselors: Type A—less concerned with setting controls and limits, gives structure, not easily threatened by primitive client behavior; Type B—mild, passive, modest, patient, maintains good rapport, role models for clients; Type C—formal and distant, sets controls, firm, direct and outspoken, personal-change and activity-oriented; Type D—easygoing, focuses on introspective, affective material, personally involved with clients; and Type E—firm, hostile and aggressive, quick-thinking, consistent, interested in client's dynamics.

Based on these descriptions, the following is a partial list of their rating characteristics: (1) sets controls and limits; (2) comfortable with traditional (affective) counseling; (3) gives structure; (4) reticent about expressing feelings; (5) degree of socialization; (6) desires rapport/intimacy; (7) expresses hostility; and (8) seeks personal changes in client. These seem to be a mixture of counseling attitudes (1, 2, 3, 6, 8) and personal traits (4, 5, 7) of the workers. The expression of feelings (4, 7) did not seem like therapeutic maneuvers, but rather character traits of the counselor.

Group Therapy Questionnaire. All of the above measures of TØ deal with individual therapy. Wile, Bron, and Pollack (1970) report on a Group Therapy Questionnaire (GTQ) which was designed to detect leadership styles of group therapists. The GTQ contains descriptions of 20 group therapy situations and asks each S to choose from a list of responses, what he might do as a group leader. The Ss' choices are scored for 15 qualities of therapy leadership.

Their 15 scales are: (1) directive, (2) nondirective, (3) group-oriented, (4) individual-oriented, (5) group mind (talks to group as if it were a single person), (6) outside group events, (7) silence, (8) authoritarian, (9) interpretation (an *enriched* description of events or an explanation of the *causes* of the events), (10) question, (11) interpretation question (asks members to describe or explain what is going on in the group), (12) feeling question, (13) member feeling (points out some member's feeling), (14) leader feeling (describes own feelings), and (15) supportive (approval or reassurance).

The authors determined the scoring of all the suggested responses and then compared this pooled judgment with an independent scorer. The interscorer reliability estimates varied from .66 to .99, with 10 scales being above .80.

The GTQ, of course, faces the same difficulty as TØ measures for individual therapy. Of all possible group situations, which ones are to be chosen? Of the many possible scoring scales, which ones are to be used? Were the authors biased toward a limited approach to group therapy? Some events typical in Gestalt therapy, psychodrama, or transactional analysis do not seem covered.[4]

ANTECEDENT CONDITIONS INFLUENCING THE ADOPTION OF THEORETICAL ORIENTATIONS

The design problem is very thorny here. What among many life experiences have been the significant influences? What effects do demographic variables, training, supervision, personal therapy, and doing therapy have on a developing therapist's TØ? The data have yet to be collected or reported in the available literature. What follows reflects the limited existing data, both published and unpublished, and some ideas.

Demographic Variables

In the McNair and Lorr (1964) study, most of the sex differences were accounted for by the higher impersonal (I) scores of the females ($t = 2.01$, $p < .05$) and are confounded with profession since 57 of the 73 women were social workers. The authors suggest the higher "I" scores may reflect a tendency to be more reserved with patients of the opposite sex (since most of the VA patients were men).

The paths toward psychotherapy have been detailed in Henry, Sims, and Spray (1971), who found that "these professionals are a culturally homogeneous group but also a culturally marginal one." They were overrepresented by people with Jewish backgrounds, from urban settings, political liberals, and "religious apostates."[5] Unfortunately, they do not report data on the TØs of these psychotherapists. Their findings are somewhat limited by their sampling procedure: "All generalizations about the mental health professionals are intended to pertain only to Chicago, Los Angeles and New York City and should be evaluated from this perspective" (p. 212). Another methodological criticism is that they did not compare their sample of psychotherapists with nontherapists from the same cities. It may be that all their statements about psychotherapists are merely descriptions of educated citizens of these cities.

Rice et al. (1974) examined their eight "style" factors for the influence of sex and experience. They found that the male and female therapists differed across two factors: female therapists described themselves as more varying in their therapy behavior, less "anonymous," and more "judgmental."

Profession

As mentioned earlier, in the McNair and Lorr study (1964) a pattern score analysis of profession (psychiatrist, psychologist, and social worker) was done. Unfortunately it is confounded with sex for the social workers. For the other two professions, there are two clear findings. Psychiatrists (24 of 67) endorse an HHH (H-High) pattern indicating a psychoanalytic approach, an impersonal way of relating, and having control of the course of therapy. The

psychologists, as might be expected in 1962, chose the Rogerian pattern LLL (L-Low) (31 of 103). As can be seen, there are no monolithic endorsements by either professional group and all professions had people of all eight possible configural patterns. Earlier we reported on differences between professions found in the 1961 TOQ study.

Supervisor's TØ

Wile et al. (1970) used their Group Therapy Questionnaire (GTQ) to assess the effect of a training seminar on group counseling trainees ($N = 39$). The seminar was held over a 3-day period. The GTQ was given at the beginning of the 1st day and at the end of the 3rd day. A control group showed no changes over a 3-day period. Eight scales showed before-after changes in the seminar group. But the scales are *not* independent and the changes in the experimental group can be mostly accounted for by the substantial increase in "silence" responses. Through discussion with the trainees and instructors, it was determined that the two group process experiences were the most forceful ones in the seminar. The leader of these experiences was relatively silent. This seemed to influence the trainees so that they increased their use of the nondirective and silence categories on their post-seminar GTQ answers.

Based on this *post hoc* finding, Wile et al. (1970) conducted an experiment which used two groups of lower division students from two introductory psychology classes. The experimental group ($N = 25$) participated in two sensitivity training exercises where the leader—the class instructor—remained almost entirely silent. The control group ($N = 21$) had two sessions where the instructor picked the discussion topic and provided some direction to the discussion. The GTQ was given before the two sessions and also 2 weeks following the sessions. The control group showed no significant changes, while the experimental group significantly increased its use of silence and of nondirective responses. The authors mention that in five other training seminars changes on the GTQ have been found, with a different pattern each time.

These findings dovetail with those of Sundland and Garfield (1974) showing the modeling effects of the TØ of clinical supervisors. Their results were found only after a good deal of searching and need further confirmation. They are consistent with social learning theorizing that

200 EFFECTIVE PSYCHOTHERAPY

imitation is, in part, a function of the perceived status of the role model (Bandura, 1969).

Weismann et al. (1971), utilizing the same data as Goldschmid et al. (1969), report on whether present T∅ is guided by the T∅ dominant in the therapist's training: only 19 of the 116 psychologists remained in the orientation in which they had been trained. These findings are consistent with those of Lionells (1966), who found that a therapist's present T∅ is related to personality and cognitive belief system.

These authors also examined the T∅s most influential in the training of their respondents by means of an analysis of variance of orientation and technique scores. The two significant findings, on Factors II and VII (Table 6), showed the Rogerian training orientation produced higher mean factor scores than did neo-Freudian or Freudian training orientations. These results indicate that training orientation does not predict the kind of techniques that will subsequently be utilized, although one may question whether their factors were the best data to provide these answers.

The following unpublished study by Sundland and Garfield (1974) is presented here more to show the reader how complicated a data analysis can get than for the substantive results. This is a very simple study from the data collection and purpose points of view. Perhaps it is due to the complexity of the data analysis that we have yet to find reports of such studies in the journal literature. Hopefully the following will clarify the problem.

We administered the 1962 long form of the TOQ to 10 therapy supervisors and their 31 student trainees at the start of a year's practicum in therapy. At the end of the year, it was re-administered to the trainees. The question was: Have students become more similar to their supervisors, as measured by the TOQ?

We scored the TOQ for all people and occasions and computed the Cluster OA and OB scores. Movement toward a supervisor was defined as a score becoming numerically more similar to the supervisor's. On Cluster OA, psychoanalytic approach, the trainees more often moved away from than toward their supervisors. On Cluster OB, social goals/cognitive processes, the trend is almost the reverse, but in neither case does it reach a level of statistical significance. It seemed that the individual supervisor did not affect his trainee. Did the trainees move toward the mean position of the supervisor group? On Cluster OA, there was no movement toward this mean but on Cluster OB, a Wilcoxon

signed-ranks test yields a probability of .087. A further thought was that maybe those supervisors who were department members had more visibility, so that their views would be better known by the students and might be thought of as being more important. There was still no significant movement on Cluster OA, while on Cluster OB the significance increased (p = .002).

We can look at the combination of the two cluster scores by means of distance measures. The trainees' scores moved closer to those of their own supervisor 17 times and further away 12 times (ns, Sign Test), while compared to the scores of the Director of the Clinical Program, 22 moved closer, while only nine moved further away (p = .02; Sign Test).

An improved design for this problem would be to have repeated T∅ measures of both trainees and supervisors, measure supervisor status, and perhaps also the T∅s of trainees' personal therapists. The analysis would be based on normalized factor scores with movement being measured relative to the trainees' own supervisor and also to those seen as influential.

One published study of the effects of a supervisor's T∅ (as assessed by Sundland and Barker's TOQ) on the T∅s of student therapists was a dissertation by Vickers (1974). She hypothesized that when a supervisor is perceived as offering high levels of facilitative conditions, as measured by the Barrett-Lennard Relationship Inventory (RI) (Barrett-Lennard, 1962), his student therapist will change his T∅ more readily in the direction of this supervisor's T∅ than will a student therapist who perceives his supervisor as offering low levels of facilitative conditions. Using 22 supervisors and 34 student therapists, the supervisors were divided at the median into two facilitative groups—"high" and "low." "High-facilitative" supervisors tended to be experiential, but their student therapists became more analytic. The results suggest that the supervisor's impact on the novice therapist's theoretical framework is minimal.

The distribution of the supervisors on the RI is important in understanding these results. Did Vickers' median cut a homogeneous group at an arbitrary middle? Some power of a statistical test is lost when scores are grouped that have a metric to them. Also, it may be that "high-facilitative" supervisors train students to be "high-facilitative" student therapists but not ones that espouse their supervisors' T∅. A causative factor in "becoming more analytic" may have been the therapeutic milieu of New York City!

Training Programs

Two groups ($n=21$ each) of nonprofessional trainees were given job-related education in behavioral principles and procedures of both Milieu and Social-Learning treatment programs for chronic mental patients (Paul & McInnis, 1974). One group obtained sequential training with professional staff first conducting classroom instruction, followed by on-the-job training. A second group was given abbreviated classroom instruction by professional staff, tied in with clinical observation with experienced technicians. The Therapist Orientation Sheet (TOS) (Paul, 1966) was administered before and after the academic portion of the training programs.

The TOS has two sections, the first being 24 5-point bipolar attitudinal items relating to activity, relationship, goals, etc., of treatment; the second section being 20 specific therapeutic techniques such as reflection and clarification of feelings or interpretation of content. These 44 items were rated as to frequency of use from "never" to "almost always." There were five "attitude" scores: active/informed, structured/ nonpermissive, personal/change oriented, rational planning, and client discomfort/verbal process. The "technique" section also gave five scores; reflect/clarify/question; interpretation; suggest/reassure/listen; interpersonal reinforcement; and information/contingency.

A complex analysis of variance (training groups X pre-post training assessments X scores) was computed for each section of the TOS. For the attitude section, only the "score" main effect was significant, indicating no differences between the groups or between the pre-post times of assessment. For the technique section, differences were found to exist prior to training, but these changed so that at the end of the training periods no differences still existed.

The TOS-attitude scores of the trainees were related to those of the professional instructors by means of correlations and D^2s (sum of squared deviations). Two-way analyses of variance (training groups X pre-post assessments) were calculated for each measure: D^2 and r scores. No overall or differential effects were related to either of the two factors for the correlations. The D^2 scores showed a significant groups X pre-post interaction ($F=4.98$; $df=1/40$; $p<.05$). Group 1 was initially closer to the instructors and moved away somewhat, while Group 2, which had been more deviant, moved closer to the instructors after training. A parallel analysis of the TOS-technique scores found no

significant effect for either the correlations or the D^2 scores.

This study shows a good use of TØ measures and methods of data analysis and provides some initial results for certain types of training with nonprofessional mental health workers. Since the groups were not chosen to reflect differences in TØ, the lack of differences between them is to be expected. The pre-post effect found could be merely a regression toward the mean, and a control group that received no training would have been desirable. Obviously, we have barely scratched the surface of measuring the effect of training programs and trainers on the attitudes held by mental health workers, in general, and specifically, professional psychotherapists.

Personal Therapy

McNair and Lorr (1964) found that therapists with considerable (300 + hours) personal therapy had higher analytic scores. They further report that the data indicated that the psychologist subsample accounted for the finding, the trend being less pronounced for psychiatrists and not evident among social workers. We can speculate that this resulted because most of these therapists' therapists were psychoanalytically oriented. This finding dovetails with the one reported earlier from the 1961 TOQ study: those with personal therapy deemphasized social goals and valued psychoanalysis.[6]

Experience

One of the most researched characteristics has been the effect of *experience* as a therapist on TØ. This has been done by comparing two groups of therapists with differing amounts of experience, except for the one longitudinal study of Anthony (1967). Strupp and Bergin (1969) note, "It must also be considered that therapy is a transaction in which the patient may also affect and change the therapist. No one seems to have studied this problem in a systematic way" (p. 34). Several studies have investigated the influence of patients on the *behavior* of therapists (Houts, MacIntosh, & Moos, 1969; Moos & Clemes, 1967; Van der Veen, 1965), but none has addressed the issue of how patients influence counselors' attitudes, specifically those dealing with psychotherapy. The following studies relate only to the global concept "experience as a therapist." Anecdotally, it is clear that working with only college students as clients produces a TØ distinctly different from working exclusively in a mental institution with severely disturbed patients. Further, moving from one work experience to another will sometimes drastically alter a therapist's TØ, at least in some respects. The details of this process have yet to be elucidated.

The focal study in this area is the one by Fiedler (1950b), who found that experts of differing TØs were more like each other than like neophytes of their own approach. He had reputed "expert" and nonexpert psychoanalytically oriented, nondirective, Adlerian, and eclectic therapists describe the "ideal therapeutic relationship" by sorting a set of statements. His items were represented by three factors: (1) understanding and communicating with patients, (2) maintaining an emotionally proper distance, and (3) avoiding status concerns. Unfortunately, he used a narrow range of items and very few therapists ($N = 13$).

In the next study, Fiedler (1950a) used the composite ratings of the 75-item Q sort from his previous study to judge the rating of an audio recording of a therapy interview of each of 10 therapists having differing TØs and levels of experience. He concluded that the relationships created by expert psychotherapists more closely approximated the "ideal therapeutic relationship" than relationships created by nonexperts. The therapeutic relationship created by experts of one school resembled more closely that created by experts of other schools than it resembled relationships created by nonexperts within the same school.

Strupp (1958b) compared four experienced and four inexperienced Rogerian and three experienced and four inexperienced analytically oriented psychologist-psychotherapists on their responses to 27 patient statements. The responses were classified by the Bales system of interaction process analysis. He found no differences between experience levels for the psychoanalytic group, but the Rogerians showed a decrease in the use of reflective responses with more experience. He concluded that reliance on a single technique is a product of inexperience. Or, stating the other side of the same coin, with experience comes diversity.

Meltzoff and Kornreich (1970) take Strupp to task for his statistical method. They point out that he used the difference between proportions of responses rather than of the proportion of people. Pooling all the responses disregards interindividual variability, or sampling error—the main source of error in the experiment. It seems to me that another problem was the lack of independence of his scoring categories. The responses were scored as one of several classes. The appropriate statistical test would have been an overall *chi*-square rather than separate tests for each subdivision. Having found 75% of the Rogerian responses and only 15% of the non-Rogerian responses to be scored for "clarifies," this in turn created significant differences for some of the other scoring categories. Strupp's conclusions, although they sound most reasonable, still require a true test.

Fey (1958) found that his "older eclectics" were more resourceful, supportive, and had a greater "expedient virtuosity in dealing with... patients from moment to moment" (p. 408) than his "young eclectic" group. His experience split was less-than-10-years versus more-than-10-years.

Sundland and Barker (1962) challenged Fiedler's (1950b) conclusion that experts are more like other experts than like neophytes of their own TØ. They found, among inexperienced (less than 6 years) and experienced (6 or more years) Rogerians, Sullivanians, and Freudians, that the differences between therapists were better accounted for by their TØ than by their amount of experience. The subtest profiles of the experienced and inexperienced therapists within each TØ are similar, and the profiles of experienced therapists of different TØs are not similar. McNair and Lorr (1964) reported that experience did not relate to either technique configural pattern scores or to technique factor scores. It appears that there is a limit to the generalizability of Fiedler's conclusion. Agreement or disagreement is generated, at least in part, by item-selection of the researcher rather than being a characteristic of the therapists themselves.

Anthony (1967) described the results of re-administering the TOQ four years later to the 60 therapists who were in the "low experience" group of the Sundland and Barker (1962) study. Thirty-eight therapists responded. He reported the results for the three "schools": Freudian, Rogerian, and Sullivanian. Unfortunately most of the scoring was incorrectly done. A "Scoring Key for Revised Dimensions of the January 1960 Therapist Orientation Questionnaire" scored "positive" items 5 to 1, going from "strongly agree" to "strongly disagree." The reverse had been done in Sundland and Barker (1962). Anthony was given the scores and not the questionnaires themselves. Thus, the data for the experienced subjects were scored in the reverse way from when they were inexperienced. This is only not true for the dimensions, theory of personal growth, therapist's security and theory of motivation, which had been reversed for statistical reasons.

Meltzoff and Kornreich (1970) quote this study at some length because it is a "unique longitudinal" one: "Freudians shifted from being least to most probing, and Rogerians from most to least interpretive" (p. 392). It is doubtful that people change that much in 4 years. Are Rogerians more interpretive than Freudians?

Wile et al. (1970) used their Group Therapy Questionnaire to measure differences between counselors of grossly different levels of experience. Their high group ($n=42$) had 15 years or more of experience and their low group ($n=41$) had less than 1 year. An unfortunate confounding is that the groups also differed in professional background. "The experienced group was composed of 5 psychologists, 3 psychiatrists, 12 social workers, 7 registered nurses, 6 pastoral counselors, 4 school counselors, 2 probation officers, and 3 people from other professions. The inexperienced group contained 11 social workers, 27 deputy probation officers, 1 psychiatric resident, and 2 school counselors" (p. 369). What influence did the high proportion of inexperienced deputy probation officers have on the results?

They found that the experienced group made a greater number of silence responses and fewer individual and question responses. It seems consistent with their training that deputy probation officers would talk, focus on individuals rather than the group, and ask questions.

Rice et al. (1972) calculated an analysis of variance for repeated measures on the six factor scores of "style" for their 25 experienced (E) versus the 25 inexperienced (IE) therapists. They found no significant main effects or interaction, but that E therapists did have a greater variance —i.e., both higher and lower scores—than the IE therapists. They suggest that this finding reflects a more "differentiated" therapy style for the E therapists.[7]

This is congruent with Fey's (1958) finding that experienced eclectics were more variable than inexperienced eclectics. In a personal account, as a comment on the Rice et al. (1972) article, Whitaker (1972) describes himself as moving through developmental stages as a therapist. The first he calls, "my pornographic period: My impotence as a therapist made it safer to watch and listen and to respond only to prove I was present and to prevent the patient from discovering how little I knew" (p. 14). From this he moved to a maternal—total acceptance—

period, then to a paternal—authoritative, yet kindly—period. The next was a transactional period with frequent use of a co-therapist. Finally, he sees his current style as a mixture of all previous ones. Thus, in a personal way, Whitaker exemplifies these findings.

Rice et al. (1974) found three significant differences, each at the .05 level, on their eight "style" factors between experienced ($n=31$, completed their formal professional training) and inexperienced ($n=55$, 52 of whom were still in training) therapists. Experienced therapists were found to be (1) more interested in history, (2) more patient, (3) more interpretive, (4) more varying in their behavior, and (5) more revealing of themselves and their feelings than inexperienced therapists. They point out that the first three of these might reflect the fact that the experienced therapists were older and had been taught to hold these views in their own training. The last two results further support Strupp (1955), Fey (1958), and Rice et al. (1972) mentioned above.

CONCURRENT CONDITIONS RELATED TO THEORETICAL ORIENTATION

What present behaviors are related to a therapist's TØ? Logically, we can divide the answers to this question into two parts: Measures of the therapist as-a-person and as-a-therapist. There are very few studies which have addressed this question.

Personality Traits of Therapists

The relationship between therapists' personality characteristics and their TØ has received scant attention. Allen (1966) used 31 male therapists who answered an abbreviated version of the Therapist Orientation Questionnaire (TOQ). He used only those seven scales which dealt directly with therapist's behaviors and omitted those dealing with theoretical issues. They also answered a somewhat abbreviated form of the California Personality Inventory (CPI), consisting of 324 items and yielding 11 scale scores. Allen condensed these into four classes: (I) measures of poise, ascendancy, and self-assurance (dominance, capacity for status, self-acceptance); (II) measures of socialization, maturity, and responsibility (responsibility, socialization, communality); (III) measures of achievement potential and intellectual efficiency (achievement via conformance, achievement via independence, intellectual efficiency); and (IV) measures of intellectual and interest modes (psychological mindedness and flexibility).

Using these CPI "classes" as predictor variables, he computed multiple correlation coefficients for each of the seven TOQ technique scales. A significant relationship was found for frequency of activity, deliberate directiveness, spontaneity in the therapeutic relationship, and interpretive activity. For the latter three, Psychological mindedness/flexibility (PM/F) accounted for the major part of the variance. For frequency of activity, dominance/capacity for status/self-acceptance was the major predictor. The other three TOQ scales were not predicted significantly by these CPI classes. It is noteworthy that "use of psychoanalytic techniques" correlated significantly with "achievement via conformity."

Allen concluded that the more specific the technique in question, the less predictable it is from the therapist's personality characteristics. The PM/F scores were those which were most powerful in predicting the therapist's self-described behavior in the interview room. The higher the PM/F score, the less likely the therapist was to direct his clients or to be spontaneous, interpretive, and active.

This would fit with a view of therapy in which the therapist uses his sensitivity in a nondirective, planned way. Unfortunately, high PM/F scores are typified as "observant, spontaneous, perceptive...insightful, adventurous, confident." One would think that high spontaneity on the CPI would predict high spontaneity in the therapeutic relationship, but this was not found. We see here the pitfall of factor labeling. The CPI factor is composed of many items. The labels are given in an attempt to simplify and clarify. They often do, but not in this instance.

Patterson, Levene, and Breger (1971) report a study relating personality to TØ: behavior therapy or client-centered. Unfortunately the results pertinent to TØ are based on a factor analysis of at least 27 measures with only 13 Ss taking these measures. With this ratio of measures to subjects, the loadings on the factors will vary greatly from sample to sample. Two factors were found. Behavior therapy was associated with a common sense conceptualization of mental illness and personality traits of dominance, extroversion, self-confidence, and low social maturity. A client-centered TØ was related to achievement needs, desire for status, psychological mindedness, and some lack of self-acceptance.

While of a clinical nature, the observations reported by Weiss (1973) serve as a starting point in an almost completely neglected area. Weiss writes that, "It is unclear as to whether the reported differences reflect the extent to which (a) the department's commitment to a particular orientation shapes and stimulates the student's involvement in that direction or (b) the program hinges upon its compatability with his personality configuration" (p. 149). Weiss interviewed 20 analytically oriented student psychotherapists (AO) and 20 student behavior therapists (BT), inquiring about their interests, goals, and projected professional activities. From these interviews, he also made clinical observations of their personality characteristics.

Only 17% of the AO students, as compared to 46% of the BT students, expressed an interest in future research work. Conversely, 61% of the AO students, but only 37% of the BT students, had a desire for a future clinical practice. Regarding research content, the AO student chose relevant but global topics, while the BT students preferred rigor and laboratory-oriented topics. The AO student focused on understanding how the patient felt about himself and others, while the BT student looked at external details, specifics, and on the quantitative aspects of behavior. The AO student seemed more interpersonally sensitive, while the BT student was geared to think about ideas and overtly observable phenomena. This finding seemed to Weiss similar to William James' distinction between tough- and tender-minded orientations.

In describing themselves and their work, the AO students seemed more humble, or perhaps less secure, while the BT students seemed confident, sometimes to the point of arrogance. Freedom, autonomy, and choice-making capacities were valued by the AO group, while the BT group opted for symptom remission and other overt behavioral changes. Weiss' assignment of the TØs of the students was questionably based on the reputations of their doctoral programs. As mentioned earlier, some check on the orthodoxy of the students would have been desirable.

Values and Attitudes

Welkowitz and Schillinger (1969) sought to develop typologies of therapists. They had 80 therapists (psychologists and psychiatrists) respond to Morris' (1956) Ways to Live Scale (WTL), to the Strong Vocational Interest Blank (SVIB) an occupational interest inventory, and the AID scale (McNair & Lorr, 1964). Using a 37-item modification of the original 49-item AID scale, they found 12 factors. The WTL and SVIB data yielded 5 and 12 factors, respectively. These 29 factor scores were then intercorrelated and factored. This gave a 12-factor solution in which the AID in combination with the WTL and SVIB defined 5 other factors. These were described as follows: Factor 1—conventionality, security, lack of rebelliousness, belief in self-restraint, and desire for an orderly process in psychotherapy; Factor 2—conservative, authoritarian, anti-analytic; Factor 3—artistic, interested in humanities and social science, personal as a therapist; Factor 4—receptive and concerned with persons and nature, analytic as a therapist; and Factor 5—aloofness, self-centered, impersonal, and nonanalytic as a therapist.

Rothman (1971) related therapists' TØs to their A-B status. She hypothesized that A therapists would tend to have an "experiential" TØ, and that B therapists would have an "analytic" TØ. Thirty male doctoral level counselors completed a Whitehorn and Betz A-B scale and the Sundland and Barker TOQ. The TOQ was scored for only the General Factor-Experiential versus Analytic. Contrary to her hypothesis, she found no correlation ($r = -.02$) between TOQ scores and A-B scores.

Based on interviews, Weiss (1973) had concluded that there were value differences between analytically oriented student therapists and those espousing a behavior therapy point of view. The next study quantifies some of his conclusions. Garfield and Kurtz (1975) administered an Ideology Scale, which was based on the work of Commoner (1972), Shaffer (1953), and Strauss, Schatzman, Bucher, Ehrlich, and Sabshin (1964). One subscale asks about psychoanalytic-psychodynamic issues (PsD), a second about attitudes toward learning theory-behavior modification (BM), and the third measures beliefs along an intuitive-objective dimension (IO). The scores of the three subscales are somewhat related as shown by their intercorrelations: PsD vs. BM: $r = -.50$; PsD vs. IO: $r = .39$ (IO was scored in the intuitive direction); BM vs. IO: $r = -.42$. The subjects were grouped by TØ. The rank-order correlations between these subscales for the means of the 10 groups are all greater than $\pm .90$, suggesting again that there is an underlying unity to these attitudinal dimensions.

They also analyzed these data by means of discriminant function analyses. Significant differences were found on all three subscales when those who ascribed to the psychoanalytic, neo-Freudian, and Sullivanian schools were compared to those choosing the learning theory label. Next a humanistic group (humanistic, existential, and Rogerian) was compared with the psychoanalytically oriented group, and the former had a significantly higher mean on the subscale measuring preferences for a learning theory-behavior modification approach. Comparing the humanistic group with the learning theory group, significant differences are again found on all three subscales. They also report significant differences between academicians-researchers and clinicians. It may be that there was a confounding between the humanistic group and the academicians. A comparison of the humanistic academicians and the humanistic clinicians would have been desirable.

The first two subscales basically refer to attitudes concerning theoretical therapeutic issues and thus mainly serve to clarify what the choice of a "school" label means. The intuitive-objective subscale has a broader, philosophical significance. More work could be done in this area, using available and validated measuring instruments.

These relationships between TØ and a therapist's other personal characteristics are of only academic interest if these TØ attitudinal differences are not reflected in differential therapeutic outcome.

Attitudes Concerning Therapy

Fiedler (1950b) investigated the concept of the "ideal therapeutic relationship" (ITR). He operationalized this using a Q sort by which therapists described what they thought an ITR would be. Thirteen therapists of diverse levels of reputed expertness and "schools" participated. Using a factor analysis (Holzinger's bifactor method) of the intercorrelations between therapists, he found a single factor. Generally, the intercorrelations of the "experts" were higher than those of the nonexperts, indicating the greater agreement by them on what constituted an ITR. He saw these results as indicating that there was general agreement on the most effective type of therapeutic relationship. These results are valid *only* for his items, which had a narrow range of content. This finding is often quoted without attending to this fact.[8]

Sundland and Barker (1962) compared TØ, as determined from the psychologist-therapists' choices of "schools" and "authors" with factor scores on the TOQ. The subjects, grouped into

Freudians, Sullivanians, and Rogerians, accounted for more than 80% of the sample. These groups differed significantly ($p < .05$) on nine of the 16 scales. Usually, the Sullivanian group occupied a middle position. They were closer to the Freudians in emphasizing planning, conceptualizing, having goals, and in inhibiting spontaneity. They were nearer the Rogerians in liking a personal approach and in stressing the personality of the therapist. This position of the Sullivanians—between the experiential Rogerians and the analytic Freudians—seems well summarized by the concept of the "participant observer." Sundland (1972) developed more data along these lines from a multiprofessional sample, and obtained results which similarly showed experientialists to differ from psychoanalysts. Another way of looking at Sundland and Barker's (1962) findings, though, is that even on a questionnaire constructed to be sensitive to issues among TØs, there were still seven out of 16 scales which did not distinguish between these three "schools."

Wilcox (1960), using the same data as reported by Sundland and Barker (1962), compared Freudians ($N = 50$), Rogerians ($N = 48$), and Sullivanians ($N = 50$), who were 82% of the total respondents. They ranked what goes into making a "good" therapist: formal training, broad experience in living, desirable personality characteristics, and personal therapy. The average ranking for each of the three TØ groups was: Freudians—therapy, training, personality, and experience; Sullivanians—personality, training, therapy, and experience; and Rogerians—personality, training, experience, and therapy. Only the rankings of the Freudians conform with Wilcox's expectations based on the literature.

Wallach and Strupp (1964) compared four TØs: orthodox Freudian, psychoanalytic-general, Sullivanian, and client-centered, using the four factors they had found from the responses to their questionnaire. Significant Fs (.05 level) were obtained for all factors but Factor I. The orthodox Freudians were highest in preference for intensive therapy and keeping verbal interventions at minimum. The Sullivanians had the lowest mean score on the latter, preferring active interpersonal involvement. The client-centered group saw psychotherapy as an art and did not prefer intensive therapy. The psychoanalytic groups were found to be most dissimilar from the client-centered group, confirming the Sundland and Barker (1962) findings reported earlier.

In another study of this type, Rice *et al.*, (1974) compared factor scores of "style." They grouped their Ss as follows: analytic ($n = 34$), phenomenological ($n = 26$), and rational-behavioral ($n = 15$). Using an analysis of variance design, Groups X Factors, they found no main effects and a highly significant interaction ($F = 2.26$, $df = 14$, 576, $p < .005$). They report that rational-behavioral (B) therapists had the highest activity level and the highest degree of cognitive, goal-oriented, theory-guided behavior. Analytic (A) therapists were more "interested in history," "patient," "willing to wait" in therapy, and more interpretive than B or phenomenological (P) therapists. P therapists were more along these lines than B therapists. P therapists described themselves as more varying in their therapy behavior and less "anonymous" than A or B therapists. P therapists reported a greater "feeling emphasis" in therapy than A or B therapists.

At least on self-report data, therapists are consistent in what they say they do and what we would expect from their chosen "school" of therapy. The study of whether they really behave in those ways has yet to be done.[9]

Somewhat related to the above group of studies was Wyrick's (1971) investigation of therapists' personal involvement with patients and their TØ. Questionnaires measuring personal involvement and TØ were administered to a sample of psychologists engaged in psychotherapy. Therapists scoring high on personal involvement tended to hold subjective, humanistic, experiential orientations. Those scoring low endorsed an objective, empirical, behaviorial orientation.

TØ was related to therapists' expectancies of patients' role behaviors by Berzins, Herron, and Seidman (1971) and was surprisingly found to be absent. TØ was assessed from influential authors and related-to-"schools." Three categories were formed—insight (Freud), relationship (Rogers), and action (Wolpe). Their 133 therapists split 42%, 38%, and 15%, respectively. In four factor analyses of patient behavior such as: "places you on a pedestal," "displays freedom of expressiveness," "leads the way in introducing topics," there were three factors containing these items but no TØ item. Profession and TØ formed fourth and fifth factors with most psychologists ($n = 84$) being in the relationship group and most psychiatrists ($n = 29$) being in the insight group. They also analysed their data to find which behaviors were felt to be good prognostic indicators. TØ loaded on one of these for their experienced Ss but not on any of the factors for the inexperienced group. For the former group, there was a factor of verbal initiative which was valued positively by relationship-oriented therapists but not by insight-oriented therapists.

Therapists' Actual In-Therapy Behavior

Using his ITR Q sort, Fiedler (1950a) had each of 10 taped interviews rated by four judges. He formed a composite ITR by pooling the ratings of the four "most expert" therapists from his earlier study (1950b). Each interview was conducted by a different therapist; there were five reputed expert and five nonexpert; four nondirective, four psychoanalytic, and two Adlerian. The Q sort contained items dealing with three dimensions: communication, status, and emotional distance. He found, using the composite ITR as a criterion, that experts came closer to this ideal than nonexperts, especially on the first dimension, communication: the ability to understand, communicate, and maintain rapport with the client. The dimensions of status (feeling inferior, equal, or superior to the patient) and, to some extent, emotional distance were related to T$\emptyset$. The Adlerian and some of the psychoanalytically oriented therapists tended to place themselves in a more tutorial role, whereas nondirective therapists tended toward the opposite direction. Using these data, Fiedler (1951) factor-analyzed the intercorrelations among ratings of the 10 therapists. There were no factors which separated T$\emptyset$s from each other.

Many criticisms could be made of these studies: very few subjects were used, the use of the Q technique is open to criticism (Sundland, 1962), the item populations were neither random nor constructed to elicit T$\emptyset$ differences, etc. The most unfortunate aspect of these studies is that they have been uncritically accepted by some as proving that T$\emptyset$ does *not* affect an expertly conducted therapeutic relationship. The correct conclusion is that there are *some* similarities between therapy sessions conducted by expert therapists but that there are also clear differences.

Strupp (1957a), using a multidimensional system that he developed to analyze therapist behavior (Strupp, 1957b), compared nine published interviews of Wolberg, an analytically oriented therapist, with three of Rogers, a client-centered therapist. Some clear differences in the verbal behavior of these two therapists emerged, which were consistent with the theories espoused by each. Wolberg showed a variety of activities with "interpretation" and "exploration" being significant proportions, whereas Rogers used "clarification" almost to the exclu-

sion of any other activity. Although not part of his "system," Strupp (1957a) mentions that "both therapists conveyed ... respect for their patients ... appeared to be warm, accepting, and noncritical; both encourage the patient's expression of feelings; and both ... seemed to engender a feeling of greater self-acceptance in their patients" (p. 307).

While they did not report the T$\emptyset$ of their therapists, Houts et al. (1969) describe a study that bears indirectly on the question of whether T$\emptyset$ influences a therapist's behavior with clients. Therapists rated how they believed the patient and therapist should behave during psychotherapy to achieve the patient's goals. Independently, judges rated these behaviors from tapes of therapy sessions. The seven therapist behaviors used in this study were: (1) suggest new ways of looking at her problems, (2) tell her what to do about her problems, (3) help her to understand why her personality is the way it is, (4) speak to other people with whom she has difficulties, (5) mostly listen to what she has to say, (6) encourage and support her in what she wants to do, and (7) give her medicine. The main conclusions were that therapists were more influenced by their patients than patients were by their therapists, and that differences among therapists are more evident in how therapists *think* than in how they or their patients behave. While these conclusions are justified for *this* set of questions, as stated, they are unwarranted generalizations.

Cohen (1974) classified therapists' responses into 10 content categories: causing, blaming/praising, feeling, labeling, believing, intending, probing, problem solving, supportive, and other. She had 16 psychiatrists, residents and experienced, with two patients each. For each patient, four 4-minute portions randomly chosen were coded from a 50-minute interview. Her results pertinent to this chapter were that psychoanalytically oriented therapists asked significantly more questions and made fewer supportive responses than non-Freudians. Most of the experienced therapists were Freudians.

Raskin (1974) reports a study in which six expert therapists of different T$\emptyset$s were judged by 83 therapists on a set of 12 therapist behavior variables: cognitive, experiential, empathic, therapist-directed, equalitarian, warm and giving, unconditional positive regard, congruent, emphasizes unconscious, systematically reinforces, self-confident, and inspires confidence. Overall, Raskin concludes: "These expert therapists, then, who give themselves different labels, are experienced here as indeed different from one another, while seen as least unlike in the dimensions of genuineness (congruence) and of self-confidence" (p. 14).

Raskin also reports a factor analysis of the 12 dimensions based on the intercorrelations of the means for the six experts. He found two factors: Factor 1 has high positive loadings on self-confidence, cognitive, therapist-directed, and systematically reinforces, and has high negative loadings on experiential and equalitarian; Factor 2 has its high loadings on inspires confidence, empathic, and congruent. Factor 1 seems similar to the "general factor"—analytic versus experiential—found by Sundland and Barker (1962). Factor 2, on the other hand, is similar to Fiedler's (1950a, 1950b) "ideal therapeutic relationship" and needs to be included in future studies of TØ.

Summarizing a number of the findings mentioned above, it seems likely that for some therapist behaviors TØ does not matter, yet it seems very clear that for other therapist behaviors TØ is predictive. To put this another way, *in some respects therapists behave similarly, often influenced by the particular client with whom they are interacting, even though the rationale that they give themselves, their colleagues, and their patients may be dissimilar; in other respects, therapists behave dissimilarly in ways that are consonant with the TØ that they hold.*

Therapists' Simulated In-Therapy Behavior

Strupp (1958a) used a sound film that was interrupted at 28 pre-selected points. The therapist-viewers were asked to respond and their responses were analyzed by the system developed earlier (1957b). Again he found that reflection-of-feeling was the major (67%) response of the client-centered therapists (CC), whereas it was only a minor (17%) response for analytically oriented therapists (AO). There were many other differences—CC showed greater reluctance to set therapeutic goals than AO; areas in the patient's living to avoid or single out were rarely mentioned by the CC group, but were by the AO group. The CC group "encouraged or fostered a 'corrective emotional experience' by conveying respect or clarifying feelings . . . [the AO group] . . . tended to advocate interpretation and other procedures such as reassurance and firmness, in which the therapist uses his role to induce changes in attitudes and actions" (p. 268).

In his two studies Strupp (1957a, 1958a)

showed that TØ labels led to different therapist behavior in vivo and vitro.

Wrenn (1960) used written selections from counseling sessions in which the response of the counselor was omitted. He mailed this to 54 therapists of different TØs asking them to fill in the responses of the counselor. There was a high degree of similarity in responses, mostly focusing on the "core of the client's statement" and on the feeling aspects. The only category that captured the TØ differences was the more frequent use of "reflection" by the phenomenologists and eclectics than by the analysts.

This technique seems fruitful, but to which client responses is the therapist asked to respond? It seems likely that to some client responses there will be no TØ differences, while with others TØ will guide the therapists' responses. Rice (1974) and Greenberg (1974) reported a methodology for finding these latter "critical patient remarks."

Therapists' Rating Behavior

How does TØ influence a therapist's rating behavior? Waskow and Bergman (1962) hypothesized that "raters might view as more warm and accepting those responses which seem 'better' in light of their own theoretical orientations" (p. 484). They had 10 therapists from the University of Chicago Counseling Center (client-centered), 10 from the Menninger Foundation (psychoanalytic), and 10 college graduates beginning training as therapists from National Institutes of Health (neutral) rate every therapist response from a therapy session on a 7-point scale of emotional tone: warm, accepting versus cold, rejecting. Separately, two judges categorized the responses as: following, leading, or neither. Agreement was achieved on 24 leading and 29 following responses, "neither" responses being eliminated. Twenty of each "leading" and "following" were randomly chosen. The data analysis was based on these 40 selected responses. They report: "The findings indicate that good agreement could be obtained in ratings of the warm, accepting/cold, rejecting dimension, and that there was no appreciable influence due to the theoretical orientation of the raters, to the leading or following nature of the therapist responses, or the interaction of these two variables" (Waskow & Bergman, 1962, p. 484).

Since Strupp's (1958a) finding with regard to response differences of psychoanalytic versus client-centered therapists showed the latter to be much more often reflective—that is, following—it seemed reasonable to find an evaluative bias with regard to this quality of the therapist responses between these groups. While warm-cold is on the good-bad semantic continuum, it may be that psychotherapists such as Bach (1975) could differentiate and rate a response as "warm" but not "good," that is, maximally therapeutic.

In the rating of the behavior of six expert therapists, Raskin (1974) divided his therapist-judges by their own TØ. He found three groups: analytically oriented ($n=20$), client-centered ($n=23$), and eclectic ($n=28$). He computed *chi*-squares for each of the 12 ratings of each of the six experts and appropriately interprets his analyses as indicating that the TØs of the judges did not seem to affect their ratings. This supports the finding of Waskow and Bergman (1962) that the TØ of a therapist-rater does not influence his rating behavior.

In addition to rating the experts, the judges were also asked to rate themselves and the "Ideal Therapist" on the 12 variables. He grouped the judges by experience level into more experienced (6 or more years, $n=42$), and less experienced (less than 6 years, $n=41$). He found that most of the analytically-oriented judges were experienced and most of the eclectics were inexperienced. Because of this, he analyzed this data *within* a given experience category. For the self-ratings, he found that the three orientations do not mostly describe themselves differently. The client-centered judges tended to see themselves as less directive and cognitive, and the eclectic judges described themselves as more directive and reinforcing.

The parallel analysis of the ideal therapist ratings yielded three significant findings. In the more experienced group, the client-centered therapists esteemed less directive behavior by the therapist, the analytics hold a middle ground and the eclectics prefer more directiveness. Also in this group, eclectic judges preferred more systematically reinforced behavior, while the other groups were equal to each other and chose less. Finally, in the less experienced group, the analytic more often esteemed therapist behavior that emphasizes unconscious, while eclectics had a middle position, and client-centered therapists least favored this type of behavior.

As can be seen, the results for the self-rating and the ideal-rating have much in common. Given this set of data, it would have been more efficient and powerful to use a four-way analysis of variance: Experience X Orientation X Object (Self/Ideal) X Rating Dimension.

Recall of Therapy Session

Gottsegen (1967) compared the professed activity level of some group therapists with their ability to recall what went on in the group session. The directive (D) scale of the AID was used to measure activity level (Gottsegen, 1975). From a preliminary sample of 65, she chose the 15 highest and the 15 lowest on the "D" scale. They were then equated for their recall ability. Using the therapy groups of the participating group therapists, an independent observer scored each group member's interactions as they happened during the session. The accuracy of the recall of the group therapists was then assessed. She found that (1) low-active therapists recalled more accurately the interactive content of group therapy sessions than high-active therapists; (2) therapists, regardless of their activity level, were more accurate in their recall of the interactive material produced by the low-active members in the group; and (3) there was no difference between high- and low-active therapists in their recall accuracy of social-emotional types of material.

Therapists' Work Practices

Wilcox (1960), using the same data reported in Sundland and Barker (1962), reported on the therapeutic practices of 148 psychotherapists. The following results were significant at the .05 level. More often, Freudians had more years of training in therapy than either of the other two groups, had a Freudian supervisor, and had had 400 or more hours of personal therapy. Freudians spent more of their work week in the practice of therapy. A surprising finding was that 60% to 70% of *all* three groups reported doing some weekly diagnostic work. From the literature, fewer Rogerians would have been expected to be doing diagnostic work. Also there was no difference in the weekly frequency with which patients were seen. As expected, the Freudians more often saw their patients for longer than 1 year.

CONSEQUENT CONDITIONS RELATED TO THEORETICAL ORIENTATION

Has all this been an intellectual exercise? Yes, we can measure TØ. Yes, some behaviors of therapists seem rather consistently related to therapists' TØs. But are these behaviors important? Is the process or outcome of therapy influenced by the TØ of the therapist? Theoretically, either the client or the counselor could change as a result of their therapy sessions, so we will look at three facets of the experience: process, client outcome, and therapist outcome.

Process Outcome

The studies discussed in the previous section, Therapists' Actual In-Therapy Behavior, dealt with the effect of TØ on the therapist's behavior during the therapy sessions. What about the clients? Does the therapist's TØ modify the way clients behave? We have no data on this. Only the phenomenology of the experience has been studied—that is, how a therapist's TØ influences the client's *experience of their therapy relationship*. Howard, Orlinsky, and Trattner (1970) studied the TOQ and the Therapy Session Report (TSR) (Orlinsky & Howard, 1967). The TSR[10] contains 147 items covering (a) topical areas of dialogue, (b) problematic concerns, (c) the feelings of patient and therapist, (d) modes of interpersonal behavior, (e) modes of self-experience in the patient, (f) the exchange process linking patient wants, therapist aims, and patient satisfactions, (g) the development of the session as an interpersonal act, and (h) evaluation of the session. These 147 items were factor-analyzed and found to yield 46 factors. The paper reported on only 41 factor scores; the other five scores did not focus on the patient-therapist interaction.

Twenty-one therapists participated. They came from different professional backgrounds and most were experienced therapists (more than 5 years). The 104 patients were all female. They tended to be single, working, of at least high school education, and having had psychotherapy previously. The diagnoses were made by the psychiatrist during the intake process. These were: (a) depressive reaction, $n=46$; (b) anxiety reaction, $n=17$; (c) personality disorder, $n=28$; (d) schizophrenic, $n=13$.

The TOQ was scored by a system that they developed for their sample of therapists. This gave five scores for clusters of items: psychoanalytic orientation, impersonal learning versus personal relationship, therapist's role responsibility, patient's inner experience, and therapist directiveness. They also retained a single item as a separate score. Thus, they had six scores on the therapists. As mentioned above, there were also 41 scores from the TSRs of the patients. The correlation of these with the six therapist scores yielded a matrix with few significant correlation coefficients.

Previous research had indicated that the diagnostic type of patient might influence these results and so separate analyses were done for the four patient types. This created four correlation matrices, each having 246 correlation coefficients (41×6). Each one of these could have a chance expectation of about 12 coefficients reaching the .05 level. They found 19 for the schizophrenic group, 16 for the anxiety reactions, 8 for the depressive reactions, and 6 for the personality disorders. Of the 49 significant correlations, 16 were with the single retained item: "My own attitudes toward some of the things my patients say or do stop me from really understanding them" (p. 265).

Their main conclusion was that TØ makes a slight impact on patients' therapeutic experiences. They point out that the relatively high experience level of therapists may have lessened the effect of TØ differences on the relationships they created with their patients.

It would have been desirable if the homogeneity of their therapists' TØs had been mentioned. A truncated distribution may sometimes mask a relationship that exists when the full range of variation is present.

Their correlation matrices on the separate patient groups yield a chance, if somewhat bimodal, distribution of significant correlations, the average of which, 12.25 ($49 \div 4$), is clearly not significantly different than the expected *mean* of 12.30 ($246 \div 20$). One should apply the mean to the total experiment rather than to each correlation matrix separately (Ryan, 1960). This, of course, merely adds a stronger emphasis to their main conclusion.

When a factor analysis is performed on a correlation matrix of 45 items, based on only 21 subjects, the solution is very unstable. The most powerful data analysis would have been to use all 45 TOQ items against all 46 TSR factors, and then search for patterns of relatedness. The availability of computers and their capacity for rapid conversion of immense amounts of data allow us to do this kind of searching. A caveat for the researcher is to recognize that he is generating hypotheses rather than confirming them. Since there were no specific hypotheses in this study, this would have been a desirable approach.

Both of these sets of data (Therapists' Actual In-Therapy Behavior and Process Outcome) deal with the process from only one side or the other and omit the dyadic relationship between client and counselor.

Client Outcome

Heine (1953) reported on research with 24 subjects, of whom eight had been treated by therapists from one of three schools of psychotherapy—psychoanalytic, nondirective, and Adlerian. The clients described changes resulting from therapy and the events which had occurred during therapy that were related to these changes using prepared statements—120 for each. He found that patients described similar changes regardless of the "school" of their therapist. It may be that therapists of various schools are working toward similar goals for their patients, employing different means. Patients selected different therapeutic factors which they felt accounted for the changes, and within any one school tended to report similar factors as being responsible. Of the 120 statements, only 20 significantly differentiated between schools. Unfortunately, 23 years later this potentially seminal study has not been replicated, revised, or expanded.

Ellis (1957) reported on a comparison of orthodox psychoanalysis, psychoanalytically oriented psychotherapy, and rational psychotherapy. The patient groups were fairly well matched and contained both neurotic and borderline psychotic clients. Ellis was the therapist for all cases, and the comparison was made from retrospective notes. He had routinely rated cases on termination with regard to improvement. He found that significantly more clients treated with rational analysis showed considerable improvement and significantly fewer showed little or no improvement than clients treated with the other two techniques.

Ellis pointed out that while he was doing the two earlier forms of therapy, he was just as convinced of their potency as the rational-emotive therapy that he later developed. It seems reasonable to question this, presumably he was motivated to change due to some dissatisfaction with the earlier psychoanalytic approaches. It is possible that this dissatisfaction affected his therapy, or at least his expectations and/or ratings of patient improvement.

Shlien, Mosak, and Dreikurs (1962) report on a comparison of client-centered and Adlerian therapists within a time-limited structure. Patients were seen for a maximum of 20 interviews at a suggested rate of two per week. Fifteen client-centered therapists saw 20 patients and eight Adlerians saw 20 patients. Improvement was assessed by means of the self-ideal self (S-I) correlation using an 80-item modified Butler-Haigh Q sort, which was given before therapy,

after seven sessions, on termination, and after a follow-up period "averaging" 12 months.

Some of the salient findings were: while Adlerian and client-centered therapists have points of agreement, there are also differences, which show up sharply in the actual conduct of the therapist. Based on the improvement in the S-I correlation, the structure of time limits will promote certain similar effects even where the therapists are distinctly different in their behavior. There were also certain clusters of Q sort items which differentiated Adlerian and client-centered effects in the self-sorts at posttherapy.

The authors did not specify these "clusters," but their focus was on the efficacy of the time-limited structure rather than on a comparison of the two therapeutic approaches.

Matching Therapists and Clients. An aspect of client outcome involves the matching of therapists and clients to enhance the efficacy of the therapy process (see Berzins, Chapter 10, this volume). Heine (1966) made some opening remarks at a symposium entitled, "Therapies, Therapies, Therapies: Another Search for the Essentials." He called for matching patients and therapists, pointing out that the past work in this area has been compromised by the largely erroneous belief that training in a particular theory and technique eliminates individual stylistic differences. He said that it is possible at this point to study the therapist who stresses cognitive elements in his relationship with patients in contrast to the empathizer; the active versus the passive therapist; the existential approach versus a genetic-diagnostic approach, etc., working with patients who are symmetrical or asymmetrical with respect to these salient characteristics.

During this time, workers in the California Treatment Project, dealing with delinquent youth, were using this idea but it was not reported in the general literature until later. Palmer (1973) reports using the counselor-type procedure of Gamboa and Koltveit (1973) for matching counselors with types of delinquent youth. Between 1961 and 1969, 686 youths were matched with a counselor and, to serve as a control group, 328 were not. Palmer reports that 53% of each group did equally well (or poorly) whether matched or not; 36% did better with a matched counselor, and 10% did better under the control conditions. He also found that matching gave a lower rate of parole revocation or court recommitment over a 15-month parole period—23% for "closely matched" boys as compared with 49% for those not closely matched. Presumably this favorable showing did not hold for girls, who were 21% of the sample. Also, it is unclear on what dimension "*closely matched*" was measured.

A follow-up after discharge from parole again showed a favorable effect of matching—50% for matched and 74% for nonmatched youths, the criterion being "arrest rate subsequent to favorable discharge." Palmer also points out that matching has a favorable effect on the "matched" counselors, who stay on the job longer, perhaps because of their greater success with their selected work sample. There is also less pressure on the matched counselor to be able to work with *all* types of clients. A further concept that Palmer suggests is that of "negative matching," the planned avoidance of specific client-counselor pairings where it is predicted that this will be discordant.

This concept of negative matching was employed in a dissertation by Dougherty (1972). He utilized the TØ of therapists to predict outcome ratings with groups of patients homogeneous with respect to "personality." The first step was the development, by the use of factor-analytic techniques, of a set of 11 psychological variables measuring personality characteristics, needs, values, and orientations to therapy. Therapists and patients who had ended their psychotherapeutic relationship were split into groups with regard to these 11 variables by means of a cluster-analysis technique. This procedure gave three "personality" groups each of patients and therapists and two groups of therapists, homogeneous with respect to their TØ. Using therapists' ratings of outcome as the criterion, regression analyses were performed for each of the eight groups on the attributes of their therapy partners. Five regression equations were obtained to predict outcome of certain patient-therapist dyads.

During the following year, patients and therapists were categorized into the homogeneous groups previously defined, using a weighted distance function. Two groups of therapists were found through calculations of predicted outcome with all applicable predictive equations:

> O therapists, who were predicted as "optimally" beneficial with certain types of patients, Group II patients, and D therapists, who were predicted as likely to rate their therapy outcomes as poor ("deterioration" match) with another type of client, Group I patients. Seven patients each from Group I and II were assigned D and O therapists. Ten other Group I patients were assigned randomly to other therapists and 14 patients, selected randomly, were assigned to D therapists as control

groups to the deterioration match for the effects of patient-type and therapists-type respectively. Identical controls for the optimal match were provided by randomly assigning 30 Group II patients to other therapists and assigning 14 patients, randomly selected, to O therapists (p. 6074).

The mean therapist outcome ratings in the deterioration matched group were significantly lower than the ratings for the optimal match and either control group. Those patients who were expected to be rated poorly, in fact, were. The outcome ratings for the optimal match group were not significantly better than the two control groups, although in the predicted direction. A problem is that we really do not care how the therapist rates the outcome; our concern is whether the patient changes for the better.

So the negative matching concept mentioned by Palmer (1973) proved to have the more powerful, albeit negative, effect in this study. This picks up the theme of Bergin (1963) and Truax and Carkhuff (1964) that therapy can be for better or for worse and points to a way of predicting the "for worse." As we come to better understand and utilize this negative matching, the frequency of iatrogenic deterioration should lessen.

Matching Co-Therapists. Another "matching" problem presents itself when two therapists work together as co-therapists. Rice *et al.* (1972) present a technique for using TØ scores in this situation. From their "style" questionnaire, they obtained TØ factor scores, and each therapist's factor scores were correlated with the average of the self-descriptions of the six therapists with whom he chose to conduct co-therapy. Some *tentative* ideas as to possible compatible and incompatible pairings of co-therapy "style" were given by these correlations. These data were analyzed separately for the experienced and inexperienced therapists and showed different patterns of preferences for the two groups. The five significant results ($p < .01$) were that for experienced therapists there was a negative relationship between their factor I (Blank Screen) scores and the idiosyncratic scores of their choices. For the inexperienced group, there was a negative relationship between their Factor II (paternal) scores and the idiosyncratic scores of their choices. The reverse was true for their Factor III (transactional) scores. Also related to the latter was a negative relationship with their choices' Factor III scores showing a preference for therapists unlike themselves on this factor. Finally, they preferred a co-therapist like themselves on Factor V (maternal). Rice *et al.* also found that experienced therapists seemed to want a somewhat restrained co-therapist, while inexperienced therapists desired an active co-therapist. These results are complex to conceptualize but straightforward if we are only concerned with defining compatible co-therapy styles.

A design problem was that they used the "chosen" co-therapists *actual* scores rather than how the "chooser" sees the "chosen." The chooser's preference is based on *his* perception of the chosen, rather than that person's perception of himself. It would have been interesting to have found the correspondence between these perceptions. Possibly this too would be a measure of compatability.

Another problem is that they look only at the "shape" of the relationship between a chooser and his average "chosen." Level is at least as important. To give a simple numerical example: a chooser has scores 5, 7, 5, 7, 5, 7; if his "chosen" has scores 1, 3, 1, 3, 1, 3, the correlation is perfect (1.0) and the mean absolute difference is 4.0; if "chosen" has scores 6, 6, 6, 6, 6, 6, the correlation is 0.0, but the mean absolute difference is 1.0. There are two different meanings for "closeness" of a *set* of scores, and it is certainly arguable in this case which is most desirable: "shape" or "level" (Cronbach & Gleser, 1953).

Rice *et al.* (1972) had 39 couples for whom they had "therapy effectiveness" ratings by each of the co-therapists. Given the "desired" type of co-therapist for each therapist, they could have tested the hypothesis that co-therapy is more effective when the co-therapists are wanted by each other. Also this T$\emptyset$ measure is just one of many possible measures to predict effective co-therapist pairings.[11] Whether T$\emptyset$ compatability is more important than, for example, interpersonal behavior compatability, is an empirical question.

In another report, Rice, Razin, and Gurman (1976) used their "style" questionnaire to compare 12 married (to each other) (M) and 12 not married (NM) co-therapist pairs. These co-therapists were also categorized as experienced (E) and inexperienced (IE) on the basis of the number of clients with whom they had worked. For the purposes of this chapter, the specific results are mostly not relevant, but the methodology is, since it shows another way of using T$\emptyset$ as a dependent variable.

The findings relevant to T$\emptyset$ came from the analyses of variance of each of the eight style factors, using marital status and experience level as main effects in a 2 × 2 design. There were two significant findings: M co-therapist pairs had higher scores on Factor IV, showing them to be more interested in history, patient/willing to wait, and interpretive, than NM co-therapists; E pairs had higher scores on Factor VI, indicating a self-perception as more "casual" and "spontaneous" in relating to clients than IE pairs. Rather than analyzing each factor separately, a repeated measures design over all eight factors (2 × 2 × 8) would have been more powerful and comprehensive.

They went on to examine the similarities between the pairs using the "style" questionnaire, items and factors, as the measures for comparison. In this way it would be as if they had taken any attitude inventory and were determining whether marital status or experience level was related to the degree of similarity between pairs of co-therapists. The fact that the attitudes being measured are those concerning psychotherapy is incidental unless related to some other criteria such as client outcome.

Therapist Outcome

It is logically clear that psychotherapy is a two-way street and that both therapist and patient influence one another. Compared to the number of studies of client outcome, those dealing with therapist "outcome" are very few indeed. The reports discussed earlier dealing with "experience-as-a-therapist" and T$\emptyset$ do, of course, fall within this class.

As we have emphasized throughout this chapter, the questions asked control the answers produced. Clearly, experience has some effect on T$\emptyset$. Most consistently, across studies, the effect is to develop a belief in a diversity of therapeutic interventions, an expedient virtuosity (Fey, 1958; Rice *et al.*, 1972; Rice *et al.* 1974; Strupp, 1958b; Whitaker, 1972). Experienced therapists were also similar to each other in their rating of the "ideal therapeutic relationship" (Fiedler, 1950a, 1950b). While experience mattered for these studies, the level of experience was found to be unrelated to other attitudes regarding therapy as measured by scores on T$\emptyset$ questionnaires (McNair & Lorr, 1964; Sundland & Barker, 1962). On a more specific level, several researchers have found that in-therapy behaviors of therapists are influenced by the patients with whom they are interacting (Houts *et al.*, 1969; Moos & Clemes, 1967; Van der Veen, 1965).

A powerful method to study this phenomenon would be a multivariate design with classes of therapists (defined by TØ) and classes of patients (defined by gender, problem, level of ego functioning, etc.) as the independent variables and classes of effects on therapists (using a variety of measures, such as TØ, attitudes about people, values, interpersonal behavior, etc.) as the dependent variables. This design would allow us to answer such questions as: does working with college students influence therapists to be pessimistic (or optimistic) about the future of the human race? The next step then would be to study how *these* attitudes feed back and modify the therapeutic relationship and the changes that occur in the client's behavior.

SUMMARY

The basic TØ dimension was described by Wolff (1956): "... there are two types of psychotherapy, the one following a preconceived system of thought, operating with formulas of interpretation, the other based upon an evolving personal relationship." This exemplifies one of the two basic dimensions that TØ research has isolated—that is, the *ideological* dimension of analytic versus experiential (Patterson, 1966; Sundland & Barker, 1962). The second dimension is behavioral—namely, activity level (Sundland & Barker, 1962).

Since most therapists see themselves as eclectics (Garfield & Kurtz, 1974; Goldschmid et al., 1969; Wildman & Wildman, 1967), it does not seem useful to employ "school" names as measures of TØ for random samples. Even samples selected for their adherence to specific "schools" frequently show both similarities and differences in their theoretical belief systems and self-reported behavior (Fey, 1958; Fiedler, 1950a, 1950b; Rice et al., 1974; Sundland, 1972; Sundland & Barker, 1962; Wallach & Strupp, 1964).

The above comments and those that follow are limited to the individual therapy of non-psychotic, nonhospitalized adults. Wile et al. (1970) have designed a Group Therapy Questionnaire that has some utility as a group therapy TØ measure. It is mostly atheoretical and focuses on the behavior of the therapist rather than his theory as to why he would behave in particular ways.

It seems clear that a therapist's TØ is not a static belief system but one that may change (Weissman et al., 1971). What are the roles that various systems play in shaping the TØ that is chosen? The experimental evidence is sparse.

Looking back on his own TØ changes, Whitaker (1972) describes a growth process influenced by his contacts with colleagues, clients, and his own personal therapy. This gives some phenomenological data. More objectively, we find that differences with regard to TØ among psychologists, psychiatrists, and social workers were found on four of the 10 first-order factors of the 1961 revision of the Therapist Orientation Questionnaire (TOQ) (Sundland, 1972). In brief, social workers, more than psychologists and psychiatrists, emphasized social goals, the training of the therapist, and a planful approach to working with a patient. On the other hand, they placed less emphasis on discussing childhood and on the use of psychoanalytic techniques. Psychologists endorsed a less active and involved approach than did the other two professional groups. Presumably, the professional choice preceded the TØ acquisition, but a more definite answer must await a longitudinal study.

Gender, personal therapy (the therapist's own), supervisor's TØ, and experience as a counselor have also been shown to be somewhat related to differences among therapists' TØs. Experience as a counselor is the influence that has been most adequately studied. The only longitudinal study (Anthony, 1967) contains statistical errors that obscure the results. All later studies were foreshadowed by Fey (1958), who found that with experience therapists become more resourceful, supportive, and varied in their moment-by-moment interaction with the client. This is basically what Whitaker (1972) described about himself. He changed over the years from being technique-oriented in a very narrow way to doing what occurs to him to fit the momentary encounter between himself and his client.

The generality of the relationship between effectiveness and increased flexibility is quite important. As people gain experience, they rely less on rules laid down for them by others and more on a differentiated assessment of what particular situations require. Or perhaps the ability to do this is what distinguishes the more effective person from the less effective. Kelly (1955) describes creativity as a sequence of alternating the processes of loosening and tightening concepts of effective behavior. The more effective therapist would, in this process, tend to become eclectic in his application of therapeutic techniques, rather than taking a Procrustean approach to working with clients. But "more effective" would need definition, since some effective therapists remain very technique-centered even after extensive experience (Perls, 1969).

Effective therapists, irrespective of TØ, behave similarly in some ways; for example, they appear confident, express concern and caring, communicate clearly, are empathic, etc. Frank (1961) has written that the crux of therapy is the faith that the therapist expresses by word and deed that the client can modify his behavior to achieve his goals in life, and that he, the therapist, can facilitate this modification.

While relatively little work has been done on how a TØ is acquired, we find even less relating TØ to other characteristics of therapists. Allen (1966) found that a "class" of California Personality Inventory scale scores, psychological mindedness/flexibility, was related to several TOQ (Sundland & Barker, 1962) technique scales: frequency of activity, deliberate directiveness, spontaneity in the therapeutic relationship, and interpretive activity. It seemed to him that the more specific a technique was, the less predictable its use was from the therapist's personality traits. This fits in with the general problem of predicting behavior: the more specific the behavior, the poorer the prediction. We can predict "introverted behavior," but not how the person will respond to: "Hello!"

In contrast to this objective study, Weiss (1973) reported some impressions of the personalities of analytically oriented (AO) students versus those in a program known for its behavior therapy (BT) approach. The AO students were more involved with their own and their patients' psychodynamics, were interpersonally sensitive, and modest; the BT students focused on specific behavior, external details, ideas, and seemed sure of themselves. These differences remind one of William James' comparison of tough and tender-minded philosophies.

The values and philosophical ideas that a therapist holds and his TØ are all parts of a belief system, hopefully a coherent one. Welkowitz and Schillinger (1969) and Garfield and Kurtz (1975) describe studies that touch on this area. The former study is a complex set of data consisting of a TØ measure, the AID (McNair & Lorr, 1964), an attitudinal measure, the Strong Vocational Interest Blank, and a measure of values, the Ways to Live Scale (Morris, 1956). Five factors were found that combined these three facets. The latter study showed that beliefs scaled along an intuitive-objective dimension related to "school" choices of clinical psychologists: psychoanalytic and humanistic therapists tended toward the intuitive end, while learning theory therapists leaned toward the objective pole. The dynamic interaction between the therapist's *Weltanschauung* and his TØ has been researched only slightly. Clearly, the philosophical ideas are present first. Do they remain unchanged by the training and practical experiences of the therapists? Do they guide the novice therapist in his choice of TØ? These and many other questions in this area remain unanswered.

While little has been done relating TØ to the broader views of therapists, there has been a fair amount of work relating TØ (as measured by "school" labels) to therapists' views of therapy. This is in the nature of construct validity and for the most part there has been good congruence: Freudians have answered as one would expect, as have Sullivanians and Rogerians (Sundland & Barker, 1962; Wallach & Strupp, 1964; Wilcox, 1960); analytic, phenomenological, and rational-behavioral groups of therapists have also responded as expected (Rice *et al.*, 1974).

In the literature there are many papers dealing with quantified distinctions among therapists—for example, the A-B variable. Researchers seem to prefer a variable whose theoretical meaning is unclear, but whose value is easily measurable, over theoretically meaningful variables which are somewhat more time-consuming to measure. While ease of measurement is an *important* practical consideration in enlisting cooperation from subjects, it should not be an overweening one.

Extremely important and lacking have been data showing that therapists' beliefs are matched by their behaviors. If a therapist believes that "discussing childhood, working with dreams, and analyzing the transference" are important, does he do it more than another who does not think that these therapist behaviors are important? Does a therapist who values activity actually interact more than a "passive" therapist? The importance of this issue cannot be overstated. *Professed orientation may have little or no practical importance unless it denotes specifiable classes of actual therapist behavior with patients. It is the behavior of a therapist, not his endorsement of items on a questionnaire, that affects the outcome of treatment.*[12]

One of the major determinants of the events of therapy, of course, are the goals sought by the therapist. These goals may be influenced to an important extent by a therapist's private belief system. Some TØ positions seem clearly to hold that behavioral change is crucial and insight is secondary while others endorse the opposite position.

The proof of the pudding, of course, is in the eating. If TØ really matters, it should be related to the outcome of therapy with clients. Howard *et al.* (1970) related to TOQ and their Therapy Session Report (Orlinsky & Howard, 1967). They found there to be little covariation between the two measures. Heine (1953) found that clients treated by therapists of different "schools" reported similar changes for different reasons. In general, this makes sense; there are many ways to facilitate more effective modes of living. So here, too, the research questions that are asked may influence the conclusions drawn. Does TØ matter with regard to improving decision-making ability, emotional expressiveness, interpersonal sensitivity, stuttering, etc.? We need to look at specific behavior changes and assess the effectiveness of producing these changes by therapists of particular TØs.

One of the goals of a mature science of psychotherapy is the matching of patient and therapist in such a way as to maximize the effectiveness of what transpires. Using a cross-validation design with a sophisticated set of measures for clients and counselors, Dougherty (1972) found that TØ was related to a *lack* of improvement for particular therapist-patient pairs as predicted, but that when matched for predicted improvement, there was no significant effect as compared to control groups. This study used results from one year to predict profitable matching for the following year. Building on a feedback system extending over many years, Palmer (1973) showed that treatment of delinquent boys could be improved by using a complex matching procedure that combined TØ and other therapist characteristics (Gamboa & Koltveit, 1973). These multivariate designs linking outcome to patient-therapist combinations, as defined by TØ and other variables, point the way for professional and social progress in the field of psychotherapy.

Thus we come to a crucial point of psychological research. There is little likelihood that researchers can design a perfect study. Research needs to be programmatic with replications and near replications. This is often done in the animal or learning field, but almost never with therapy. Bergin and Strupp (1970) modified the position they took in Strupp and Bergin (1969) recommending colloborative research. While asserting that the time is *not* ripe for massive centrally coordinated studies, they point to the need to wed clinical research to clinical practice, to improve communication among researchers, and to develop small-scale collaborative projects. They see "limited promise" in further studies comparing one TØ with another. Rather, "the task of the researcher is to document, with increasing precision, the conditions under which a therapeutic strategy or set of techniques forming part of that strategy is relatively effective or ineffective" (Bergin & Strupp, 1970, p. 22).

The time has long since past to dispose of the vague, fuzzy "school" designations of TØ. There are many useful TØ measures available. These supply scores which can be used either descriptively in psychotherapy research or as one of the variables. It is inappropriate to present psychotherapy research omitting the sex and experience level of the therapists. Some specification of their scores on major TØ dimensions such as analytic-experiential and active-passive should also be standard.

REFERENCES

ALLEN, D. H. Some relationships between therapist personality characteristics and techniques employed in therapy. Doctoral dissertation, University of Maryland, 1966. *Dissertation Abstracts International*, 1967, **27**, 3280B–2381B (University Microfilm No. 67-2375).

ANTHONY, N. A longitudinal analysis of the effect of experience on the therapeutic approach. *Journal of Clinical Psychology*, 1967, **23**, 512–516.

BACH, G. R. The narcissistic core: The "nice" therapist and the suicidal patient. *Voices: The Art and Science of Psychotherapy*, 1975, **10**, 61–65.

BANDURA, A. *Principles of behavior modification.* New York: Holt, Rinehart & Winston, 1969.

BARRETT-LENNARD, G. T. Dimensions of therapist response as causal factors in therapeutic change. *Psychological Monographs*, 1962, **76**, No. 43 (Whole No. 562).

BERGIN, A. E. The effects of psychotherapy: Negative results revisited. *Journal of Counseling Psychology*, 1963, **10**, 244–250.

BERGIN, A. E., & STRUPP, H. H. New directions in psychotherapy research. *Journal of Abnormal Psychology*, 1970, **76**, 13–26.

BERZINS, J. I., HERRON, E. W., & SEIDMAN, E. Patients' role behaviors as seen by therapists: A factor-analytic study. *Psychotherapy: Theory, Research and Practice*, 1971, **8**, 127–130.

COHEN, W. D. Relationships of selected psychiatrist and patient characteristics to psychiatrist's attributional and nonattributional responses in individual psychotherapy. Doctoral dissertation, University of Pennsylvania, 1974. *Dissertation Abstracts International*, 1974, **35**, 1905B (University Microfilm No. 74-22, 824).

COMMONER, G. The interpreter effect: Variations in judgments of scientific articles as a function of ideological commitment. Doctoral dissertation, Washington University, 1972. *Dissertation Abstracts International*, 1973, **33**, 3911B–3912B (University Microfilm No. 73-5026).

CRONBACH, L. J., & GLESER, G. C. Assessing similarity between profiles. *Psychological Bulletin*, 1953, **50**, 456–473.

DOUGHERTY, F. E., III. Patient–therapist matching: An

empirical approach toward the improvement of psycho-therapy outcome. Doctoral dissertation, Vanderbilt University, 1972. *Dissertation Abstracts International*, 1973, **33 (12-B)**, 6074 (University Microfilm No. 73-14, 505).

ELLIS, A. E. Outcome of employing three techniques of psychotherapy. *Journal of Clinical Psychology*, 1957, **13**, 344–350.

FEY, W. F. Doctrine and experience: Their influence upon the psychotherapist. *Journal of Consulting Psychology*, 1958, **22**, 403–409.

FIEDLER, F. E. Comparison of therapeutic relationships in psychoanalytic, nondirective, and Adlerian therapy. *Journal of Consulting Psychology*, 1950a, **14**, 436–445.

FIEDLER, F. E. The concept of the ideal therapeutic relation-ship. *Journal of Consulting Psychology*, 1950b, **14**, 239–245.

FIEDLER, F. E. Factor analyses of psychoanalytic, non-directive and Adlerian therapeutic relationships. *Journal of Consulting Psychology*, 1951, **15**, 32–38.

FRANK, J. D. *Persuasion and healing*. Baltimore: The Johns Hopkins Press, 1961.

FREY, D. Conceptualizing counseling themes: A content analysis of process and goal statements. *Counselor Education and Supervision*, 1972, **11**, 243–250.

GAMBOA, A. M., JR., & KOLTVEIT, T. H. I-Level: A differ-ential counseling system. *Personnel and Guidance Journal*, 1973, **52**, 83–89.

GARFIELD, S. L., & KURTZ, R. A survey of clinical psy-chologists: Characteristics, activities, and orientations. *The Clinical Psychologist*, 1974, **28**, 7–10.

GARFIELD, S. L., & KURTZ, R. Clinical psychologists: A survey of selected attitudes and views. *The Clinical Psychologist*, 1975, **28 (3)**, 4–7; 23.

GOLDMAN, R. K., & MENDELSOHN, G. A. Psychotherapeutic change and social adjustment: A report of a national survey of psychotherapists. *Journal of Abnormal Psy-chology*, 1969, **74**, 164–172.

GOLDSCHMID, M. L., STEIN, D. D., WEISSMAN, H. N., & SORRELLS, J. A survey of the training and practices of clinical psychologists. *The Clinical Psychologist*, 1969, **22**, 89–107.

GOTTSEGEN, G. B. The relationship between group psycho-therapist professed activity level and awareness of group psychotherapy interaction. Doctoral dissertation, New York University, 1967. *Dissertation Abstracts*, 1967, **28 (3-B)**, 1194 (University Microfilm No. 67-11, 103).

GOTTSEGEN, G. B. Personal communication, January 8, 1975.

GREENBERG, L. *A method of studying active ingredients of psychotherapy: Application to Gestalt therapy*. Paper presented at the Fifth Annual Meeting of the Society for Psychotherapy Research, Denver, June 1974.

GUTTMAN, I. Multiple group methods for common factor analysis: Their bases, computation, and interpretation. *Psychometrika*, 1952, **17**, 209–222.

HEINE, R. W. A comparison of patients' reports on psycho-therapeutic experience with psychoanalytic, non-direct-ive, and Adlerian therapists. *American Journal of Psychotherapy*, 1953, **7**, 16–22.

HEINE, R. W. Opening remarks. *Symposium: Therapies, therapies, therapies: Another search for the essentials*. Paper presented at the 74th Annual Convention of the American Psychological Association, New York, 1966.

HENRY, W. E., SIMS, J. H., & SPRAY, S. L. *The fifth profes-sion: Becoming a psychotherapist*. San Francisco: Jossey-Bass, 1971.

HORN, J. L. A rationale and test for the number of factors in factor analysis. *Psychometrika*, 1965, **30**, 179–185.

HOUTS, P. S., MACINTOSH, S., & MOOS, R. H. Patient–therapist interdependence: Cognitive and behavioral. *Journal of Consulting and Clinical Psychology*, 1969, **33**, 40–45.

HOWARD, K. I., ORLINSKY, D. E., & TRATTNER, J. H.

Therapist orientation and patient experience in psycho-therapy. *Journal of Counseling Psychology*, 1970, **17**, 263–270.

KELLY, G. A. *The psychology of personal constructs*. New York: Norton, 1955.

KISSINGER, R. D., & TOLOR, A. The attitudes of psycho-therapists toward psychotherapeutic knowledge: A study in differences among professions. *Journal of Nervous and Mental Disease*, 1965, **140**, 71–79.

LIONELLS, M. *Themes of therapy: A study of the effects of personality and ideology on therapeutic style*. Unpub-lished doctoral dissertation, University of Chicago, 1966.

LONDON, P. *The modes and morals of psychotherapy*. New York: Holt, Rinehart & Winston, 1964.

McNAIR, D. M., & LORR, M. An analysis of professed psychotherapeutic techniques. *Journal of Consulting Psychology*, 1964, **28**, 265–271.

MELTZOFF, J., & KORNREICH, M. *Research in psychotherapy*. New York: Atherton Press, 1970.

MOOS, R. H., & CLEMES, S. R. A multivariate study of the patient–therapist system. *Journal of Consulting Psy-chology*, 1967, **31**, 119–130.

MORRIS, C. *Variations of human values*. Chicago: University of Chicago Press, 1956.

ORLINSKY, D. E., & HOWARD, K. I. The good therapy hour: Experiential correlates of patients' and therapists' evaluations of therapy sessions. *Archives of General Psychiatry*, 1967, **16**, 621–632.

PALMER, T. B. Matching worker and client in corrections. *Social Work*, 1973, **18**, 95–103.

PATTERSON, C. H. *Theories of counseling and psychotherapy*. New York: Harper & Row, 1966.

PATTERSON, V., LEVENE, H., & BREGER, L. Treatment and training outcomes with two time-limited therapies. *Archives of General Psychiatry*, 1971, **25**, 161–167.

PAUL, G. L. *Insight versus desensitization in psychotherapy: An experiment in anxiety reduction*. Stanford: Stanford University Press, 1966.

PAUL, G. L., & McINNIS, T. L. Attitudinal changes asso-ciated with two approaches to training mental health technicians in milieu and social-learning programs. *Journal of Consulting and Clinical Psychology*, 1974, **42**, 21–33.

PAUL, G. L., & SHANNON, D. T. Treatment of anxiety through systematic desensitization in therapy groups. *Journal of Abnormal Psychology*, 1966, **71**, 124–135.

PERLS, F. S. *Gestalt therapy verbatim*. Lafayette, Calif.: Real People Press, 1969.

RASKIN, N. J. *Studies of psychotherapeutic orientation: Ideology and practice*. Research Monograph No. 1, American Academy of Psychotherapists, Orlando, Florida, 1974.

RICE, D. G., FEY, W. F., & KEPECS, J. G. Therapist expe-rience and "style" as factors in co-therapy. *Family Process*, 1972, **11**, 1–12.

RICE, D. G., GURMAN, A. S., & RAZIN, A. M. Therapist sex, "style," and theoretical orientation. *Journal of Nervous and Mental Disease*, 1974, **159**, 413–421.

RICE, D. G., RAZIN, A. M., & GURMAN, A. S. Spouses as co-therapists: "Style" variables and implications for patient–therapist matching. *Journal of Marriage and Family Counseling*, 1976, **2**, 55–62.

RICE, L. *A method of studying active ingredients of psycho-therapy: Application to client-centered therapy*. Paper presented at the Fifth Annual Meeting of the Society for Psychotherapy Research, Denver, June 1974.

ROSSO, S. M., & FREY, D. H. An assessment of the gap between counseling theory and practice. *Journal of Counseling Psychology*, 1973, **20**, 471–476.

ROTHMAN, L. K. Toward a theoretical conceptualization of the Whitehorn–Betz A–B Scale. *Journal of Consulting and Clinical Psychology*, 1971, **36**, 442.

RYAN, T. A. Significance tests for multiple comparisons of

proportions, variances, and other statistics. *Psychological Bulletin*, 1960, **57**, 318–328.

SHAFFER, L. F. Of whose reality I cannot doubt. *The American Psychologist*, 1953, **8**, 608–623.

SHLIEN, J. M., MOSAK, H. H., & DREIKURS, R. Effect of time limits: A comparison of two psychotherapies. *Journal of Counseling Psychology*, 1962, **9**, 31–34.

STRAUSS, A., SCHATZMAN, K., BUCHER, R., EHRLICH, D., & SABSHIN, M. *Psychiatric Ideologies and Institutions.* Glencoe, Ill.: The Free Press, 1964.

STRUPP, H. H. An objective comparison of Rogerian and psychoanalytic techniques. *Journal of Consulting Psychology*, 1955, **19**, 1–7.

STRUPP, H. H. Multidimensional comparison of therapist activity in analytic and client-centered therapy. *Journal of Consulting Psychology*, 1957a, **21**, 301–308.

STRUPP, H. H. Multidimensional system for analyzing psychotherapeutic techniques. *Psychiatry*, 1957b, **20**, 293–306.

STRUPP, H. H. Performance of psychoanalytic and client-centered therapists in an initial interview. *Journal of Consulting Psychology*, 1958a, **22**, 265–274.

STRUPP, H. H. The psychotherapist's contribution to the treatment process. *Behavioral Science*, 1958b, **3**, 34–67.

STRUPP, H. H., & BERGIN, A. E. Some empirical and conceptual bases for coordinated research in psychotherapy: A critical review of issues, trends, and evidence. *International Journal of Psychiatry*, 1969, **7**, 18–90.

SUNDLAND, D. M. The construction of Q sorts: A criticism. *Psychological Review*, 1962, **69**, 62–64.

SUNDLAND, D. M. *The number of factors in factor analysis.* Unpublished manuscript, University of Missouri Medical School, 1966.

SUNDLAND, D. M. *Therapist Orientation Questionnaire, Up-to-Date.* Paper presented at the Third Annual Meeting of the Society for Psychotherapy Research, Nashville, June 1972.

SUNDLAND, D. M., & BARKER, E. N. The orientations of psychotherapists. *Journal of Consulting Psychology*, 1962, **26**, 201–212.

SUNDLAND, D. M., & GARFIELD, S. L. *Therapy supervisors and the theoretical orientations of their students.* Unpublished manuscript, Washington University, 1974.

TRUAX, C. B., & CARKHUFF, R. R. For better or for worse: The process of psychotherapeutic personality change, in *Recent advances in the study of behavior change.* Montreal: McGill University Press, 1964.

VAN DER VEEN, F. Effects of the therapist and patient on each other's therapeutic behavior. *Journal of Consulting Psychology*, 1965, **29**, 19–26.

VICKERS, K. H. Supervisory effects on novice therapists' therapeutic style and orientations. Doctoral dissertation, Adelphi University, 1974. *Dissertation Abstracts International*, 1974, **35 (5-B)**, 2452–2453 (University Microfilm No. 74-24, 647).

WALLACH, M. S., & STRUPP, H. H. Dimensions of psychotherapist's activity. *Journal of Consulting Psychology*, 1964, **28**, 120–125.

WASKOW, I., & BERGMAN, P. Does "theoretical orientation" influence ratings of "warmth-acceptance"? *Journal of Consulting Psychology*, 1962, **26**, 484.

WEISS, S. L. Differences in goals, interests, and personalities between students with analytic and behavior therapy orientations. *Professional Psychology*, 1973, **4**, 145–150.

WEISSMAN, H. N., GOLDSCHMID, M. L., & STEIN, D. D. Psychotherapeutic orientation and training: Their relation to the practices of clinical psychologists. *Journal of Consulting and Clinical Psychology*, 1971, **37**, 31–37.

WELKOWITZ, J., & SCHILLINGER, M. *Development of typologies of psychotherapists: A factor analytic study.* Paper presented at the First Annual Meeting of the Society for Psychotherapy Research, Highland Park, Illinois, June 1969.

WHERRY, R. J. Hierarchical factor selections without rotation. *Psychometrika*, 1959, **24**, 45–51.

WHERRY, R. J., & WINER, B. J. A method for factoring large numbers of items. *Psychometrika*, 1953, **18**, 161–179.

WHITAKER, C. A. A longitudinal view of therapy styles where N = 1. *Family Process*, 1972, **11**, 13–15.

WILCOX, R. C. *The relationships of personal background variables to psychotherapists' orientations.* Unpublished masters thesis, Ohio State University, 1960.

WILDMAN, R. W., & WILDMAN, R. W., II. The practice of clinical psychology in the United States. *Journal of Clinical Psychology*, 1967, **23**, 292–295.

WILE, D. B., BRON, G. D., & POLLACK, H. B. Preliminary validational evidence for the group therapy questionnaire. *Journal of Consulting and Clinical Psychology*, 1970, **34**, 367–374.

WOLFF, W. *Contemporary psychotherapists examine themselves.* Springfield, Ill.: Thomas, 1956.

WRENN, R. L. Counselor orientation: Theoretical or situational? *Journal of Counseling Psychology*, 1960, **7**, 40–45.

WYRICK, L. C. Relationships between theoretical orientation, therapeutic orientation, and personal involvement with patients. Doctoral dissertation, University of Arizona, 1971. *Dissertation Abstracts International*, 1971, **32 (3-B)**, 1866 (University Microfilm No. 71-24, 366).

EDITORS' REFERENCES

LIEBERMAN, M. A., YALOM, I. D., & MILES, M. B. *Encounter groups: First facts.* New York: Basic Books, 1973.

FISCHER, J., PAVEZA, G. J., KICKERTZ, N. S., HUBBARD, L. J., & GRAYSTON, S. B. The relationship between theoretical orientation and therapists' empathy, warmth, and genuineness. *Journal of Counseling Psychology*, 1975, **22**, 399–403.

GURMAN, A. S. Attitude change in marital cotherapy. *Journal of Family Counseling*, 1974, **2**, 50–54.

GURMAN, A. S. Couples' facilitative communication skill as a dimension of marital therapy outcome. *Journal of Marriage and Family Counseling*, 1975, **1**, 163–174.

SLOANE, R. B., STAPLES, F. R., CRISTOL, A. H., YORKSTON, N. J., & WHIPPLE, K. *Psychotherapy vs. behavior therapy.* Cambridge, Mass.: Harvard University Press, 1975a.

SLOANE, R. B., STAPLES, F. R., CRISTOL, A. H., YORKSTON, N. J., & WHIPPLE, K. Short-term analytically oriented psychotherapy versus behavior therapy. *American Journal of Psychiatry*, 1975b, **132**, 373–377.

NOTES

1. *Editors' Footnote.* For research purposes, yes. Still, one should keep in mind the professional-political purposes and functions of such labels. While we are hardly gladdened by the isolationist entrenchment of some therapy "schools," we believe that a continuing active dialogue about "ideal" therapeutic philosophies and treatment strategies is an intellectually satisfying state of affairs.

2. *Editors' Footnote.* We doubt that this particular scheme would be sufficient for the task; see Berzins (Chapter 10, this volume) for a comprehensive discussion of the complexities in "matching" research.

3. Copies of this revised TOQ and the scoring key can be obtained from the author upon request.

4. *Editors' Footnote.* In addition, the benchmark study of Lieberman, Yalom, and Miles (1973) identified seven basic types of encounter group leaders' ideological orientations. See Lambert, Bergin, and Collins (Chapter 17, this volume) for a concise descriptive summary of these styles of group leadership.

5. *Editors' Footnote.* See Henry (Chapter 3, this volume) for a fuller description of this project.
6. *Editors' Footnote.* As in Garfield's chapter (Chapter 4) in this volume, again we see evidence of the dearth of empirical attention that has been paid to the personal therapy of professional psychotherapists. It is now generally acknowledged publicly (see Lambert *et al.*, Chapter 17, this volume) that some therapists do make some patients worse. Now that the therapist's omnipotence has been demystified, perhaps someone will be courageous enough to dispassionately examine some of the many important issues involved in therapists' own personal therapy.
7. *Editors' Footnote.* This inference seems to be largely consistent with the developmental sketch of the effects on therapists of increasing experience proposed independently by Auerbach and Johnson (Chapter 5, this volume).
8. *Editors' Footnote.* Because Fiedler's research is considered by many to be a classic study and is cited again and again, we want to underscore Sundland's comments here.
9. *Editors' Footnote:* An important step in this regard has been taken by Sloane, Staples, Cristol, Yorkston, and Whipple (1975a, 1975b) who, in their excellent comparative outcome study of behavior therapy and psychodynamically oriented therapy, examined "contrasting elements" and "elements in common" between these two treatment approaches. In some important ways, the actual *behavior* of these therapists was quite consistent with what one would predict from their theoretical orientations (e.g., behavior therapists were more active, directive, and talkative and defined therapeutic goals and treatment strategies more focally than their dynamically oriented colleagues, while the latter were more interested in childhood memories, explained symptoms symbolically, and interpreted resistance more frequently). Rather surprisingly, on the other hand, these two groups of therapists did not differ in frequency of interpretations. While the generalizability of this study is questionable because of the small therapist sample (three therapists per approach) and the within-treatment variability of therapist style (e.g., Joseph Wolpe and Arnold Lazarus were two of the three behavior therapists), we recommend reading the report of this landmark research.

10. *Editors' Footnote.* See Orlinsky and Howard (Chapter 21, this volume) for a full description of this methodology.
11. *Editors' Footnote.* In addition, Gurman (1974, 1975) has found, in the context of marital therapy, significant negative relationships between co-therapists' experience level differences and patient-couples' attitude change and changes in their ability to interact empathically, warmly, and spontaneously. While attitudinal differences about how to do therapy (T∅) may influence the outcomes of such treatment, it is likely that issues of status and competition between co-therapists constitute higher order levels of influential factors.
12. *Editors' Footnote.* One of the classes of therapist behavior that has occupied a central research role *vis-à-vis* outcome has involved relationship-enhancing behavior, most often studied in terms of empathy, warmth, and genuineness (see Mitchell, Bozarth, & Krauft, Chapter 18, this volume). Two recent studies, published after this chapter was completed, have examined the relationship between theoretical orientation and therapists' levels of functioning on these dimensions. Fischer, Paveza, Kickertz, Hubbard, and Grayston (1975) rated the empathy, warmth, and genuineness offered by experienced ($\bar{x} = 7$ years of practice) psychodynamic, behavioral, and humanistic therapists in a single interview with a pseudo-client. No significant differences among therapists of these three orientations were found. Unfortunately, the generalizability of these findings is limited by the low (52%) rate of positive response to the authors' mail solicitation. In the Sloane *et al.* study (1975a, 1975b), referred to in Footnote 9, behavior therapists and psychodynamically oriented therapists were equal on rated warmth, but the behavior therapists received higher empathy and congruence ratings. None of these therapist qualities was related to outcome—an increasingly common finding (see Mitchell *et al.*, Chapter 18, this volume). As noted in Footnote 9, the likely within-orientation variability of the small sample of therapists used in this study makes the meaning of these findings uncertain. Nevertheless, these two studies are important first steps in attempting to measure what therapists of diverging orientations actually *do* in real clinical interactions.

PART III

The Conduct and Experience of Psychotherapy

CHAPTER 10

THERAPIST–PATIENT MATCHING

Juris I. Berzins

INTRODUCTION

Therapist-patient matching is a concept with loose denotative boundaries. The most acceptable general definition reflects the idea that certain therapist-patient pairings are more desirable than others. The empirical delineation of this problem requires an understanding of the conditions under which, regardless of the characteristics of therapists and patients considered separately, the *interaction* of these characteristics proves decisive for the processes or outcomes of psychotherapy.

Just as psychotherapy itself may be justified on scholarly, ethical, or curative grounds (Rychlak, 1965), a concern with therapist-patient matching may be justified in similar ways. The scholarly researcher or practitioner may proceed from a concern with parameters of interpersonal compatibility in dyadic influence situations, from a commitment to a bidirectional view of causality in therapist-patient dyads, or even from an abstract preference for construing dyads as the smallest meaningful unit of analysis in psychotherapy research. Ethical justification of a concern with therapist-patient matching would emphasize principally the importance of avoiding "psychonoxious" mismatches—*primum non nocere*—in the conduct of therapy. To the curatively oriented psychotherapist or researcher, the effort expended in matching needs, above all, to have strong instrumental consequences—i.e., it should lead to better outcomes than prior or adventitious procedures. Pragmatic justification may also include such ingredients as a systems-analytic commitment to the improvement of the delivery of mental health services, and a preference for a pragmatic theory of truth—leading to the use of only those techniques or matching strategies that, regardless of the reasons, have been shown to work empirically.

Although most theorists, practitioners, and researchers seem favorably disposed toward the idea of therapist-patient matching, at least in principle, there is at present no organized body of knowledge that could serve as an effective guide for implementing matching strategies, and no ideological movement is clearly ascendant in this area. Rather, the very idea of matching elicits a wide spectrum of reservations among practitioners. Probably the strongest opposition comes from humanistically and experientially oriented psychotherapists who recoil from the very notion of "mechanical" matching of persons; in them it evokes visions of computerized dating or mate-selection services, or some other routinized, impersonal process that would divest psychotherapy of its intrinsic spontaneity, excitement, and meaningfulness. While relationship-oriented therapists may favor a focus on the personal qualities (e.g., warmth, empathy, genuineness) of the therapist, they tend to deemphasize the contributions of the patient (e.g., Truax & Carkhuff, 1967) and the role of specific techniques in facilitating favorable outcomes. On the other hand, while behavior modification enthusiasts may strongly endorse the application of research results to clinical practice and the general idea of matching specific technical interventions with the patient's maladaptive behavioral "responses," they prefer to relegate personality variables to the domain of error or nuisance variance in making psychotherapy more effective (e.g., Bandura, 1971, p. 696).[2] The spectrum of reactions to the notion of therapist-patient matching thus appears to range from beliefs that science should not tamper with art to beliefs that art should not attenuate science.

Ideology aside, the goals implicit in theories and research concerned with optimizing therapist-patient pairings, like the determination of the "drug of choice" for a particular illness in medicine, certainly seem unimpeachable. In typical clinical settings, where a relatively small number of therapists sees a large number of patients, the assignment of patients to therapists is accomplished by asking which therapist has

Therapist-Patient Matching

a vacancy, whose turn it is in the rotation, what the demands of teaching or training needs are, or what the intake interviewer's or the secretary's intuitions regarding the therapist of choice for a particular patient might be. Despite impressive advances in the field of psychometric assessment, moreover, very few clinical settings conduct pre-therapy testing of patients with a view toward determining which therapist or which technique would be optimal for the patient. While, given the vastness of our ignorance, adventitious assignment procedures and the failure to evaluate systematically the relation of patients' characteristics to subsequent outcomes with a particular technique or therapist may not constitute instances of malpractice, it is clear that the accountability of the therapeutic professions would be enhanced by the development of systematic guidelines for pairing patients with therapists and techniques so as to increase the probability of favorable outcomes.

Informal Beliefs Regarding Therapist-Patient Pairing

Although most therapists readily concede that they perform better with some patients than with others, their training regimen has not included special attention to the conditions under which their emergent skills wax and wane relative to the types of patients encountered. Most of us have been trained to "universalize" ourselves, to behave as though we could be of decisive benefit to almost any patient with whom we happen to be doing psychotherapy. On the other hand, each of us has encountered perplexing "problem cases," patients who made us squirm and who managed to call attention to our blind spots with ineffable ease. How a trainee or supervisor conceptualizes dealings with such problematic patients (e.g., in terms of personal needs or conflicts of the therapist, countertransference or the intrinsic "untreatability" of the patient) is not the issue here; the point is that we encounter such problematic patients with some frequency. Moreover, even if the clinicians in a particular setting may be informally conversant with each other's peculiar strengths and weaknesses, the reassignment of the problem patient to another trainee or therapist is seldom considered. Rather, the original therapist persists, trying to effect a breakthrough and a cure, guided by the assumption that with further effort and supervision, an ostensible mismatch will turn into a match.

To their credit, patients often resolve stalemates by leaving therapy or by asking to be assigned to someone else. Each experienced therapist has heard many patients describe strange and even bizarre dealings with the two, three, or more therapists they have consulted in the past. Interestingly, in these accounts as in successful therapy (cf. Sloane, 1974) patients usually emphasize the interpersonal characteristics of their prior therapists rather than specific interventions or techniques. In comparing therapists, patients refer to a whole host of potentially researchable matching variables— e.g., personality dimensions, likability, age, sex, ethnicity, tone of voice, etc. The listening therapist, however, has often been taught to dismiss patients' characterizations of prior therapists as probable extensions of the patient's pathology, as instances of parataxic distortion or manipulative ingratiation, and the like.

Therapists' reluctance to consider matching important also seems rooted in their belief that psychotherapy, even under nonoptimal conditions, cannot be harmful to the patient. The very notion of "psychonoxious" therapeutic interventions, to be sure, has a short history in the literature, and the practitioner is perhaps entitled to a skeptical attitude toward the generality of "deterioration effects" (Bergin, 1971). But even a reasonable probability that *some* therapist-patient pairings are ineffectual or psychonoxious suggests that psychotherapy research must move beyond the separate assessment of therapist and patient characteristics to serious investigation of the interaction of these characteristics (Kiesler, 1966, 1971; Strupp & Bergin, 1969).

The Inchoate Nature of Relevant Theory and Research

It is a sad but fair observation that the serious student of therapist-patient matching must proceed relatively unencumbered by theoretical propositions regarding how to conceptualize dyadic therapeutic interactions, let alone how to conduct research that could improve clinical practice. Although the "relevant" literature is vast, comprising literally hundreds of investigations in which some juxtaposition of therapist characteristics, techniques, and patient characteristics has been effected, most of these studies have not been designed so as to elucidate interactive phenomena (e.g., factorial designs including several different "types" of therapists, technical interventions, and patients).

Accordingly, this chapter addresses, in a

highly selective fashion, several theoretical positions that seem especially relevant to therapist-patient matching, methodological issues whose resolution may expedite research into this matter, and empirical studies that are representative in the sense of exemplifying problems or promising solutions. Finally, an attempt is made to suggest useful future directions for research on therapist-patient matching.

THEORETICAL AND METHODOLOGICAL ISSUES

Review of Selected Theories Relevant to Therapist-Patient Matching

Sullivan's Interpersonal Psychiatry. The theoretical antecedents of the idea of therapist-patient matching seem best embodied in Harry Stack Sullivan's interpersonal psychiatry (Sullivan, 1965). Sullivan saw "personality" as an intrinsically interpersonal product, shaped by the evaluations of significant others, and including a large number of "personifications," chief among which is the self-concept (self-system, self-dynamism), a self-personification that owes its origins as well as its current organization to interpersonal relations. In Sullivan's fluid, dynamic, situational view of dyadic interaction, psychotherapy could not be properly understood in terms of the separate characteristics of two individuals (therapist and patient) but rather in terms of the interpersonal situation "integrated by" the prepotent needs of both individuals. These integrating tendencies were broadly classified as conjunctive or disjunctive—i.e., they drew people together or drove them apart. Especially relevant to the notion of matching is Sullivan's conception of the "tensions" associated with interpersonal needs (e.g., security, intimacy) which could be complementary or antagonistic.

According to Sullivan's theorem of reciprocal emotion, the reciprocal needs of therapist and patient could be gratified or aggravated in the therapeutic situation. Regardless of how strong a particular need might be in one of the participants, dyadic interaction will necessarily involve the complementary or antagonistic nature of the other participant's needs. In other words, neither the needs of the patient nor of the therapist can be viewed apart from the particular situation in which the needs seek conjoint expression. In the parlance of analysis of variance, individual needs or "traits" such as dependency, which could be considered sources of "main effects," cannot be viewed apart from the

potential "interaction effects" which conjoin the needs in a particular interpersonal situation. Although Sullivan's extreme emphasis on the situationality of interpersonal events (e.g., his tendency to denigrate the notion of personal individuality), if followed slavishly, could lead investigators to minimize or even overlook the importance of relatively stable emotional-social response dispositions or "traits" in dyadic interactions, it should be understood that an emphasis on the interactional nature of person and situation variables primarily requires one to examine each particular therapist-patient pairing as a single unit.

The facilitation of conjunctive (complementary) therapist-patient pairings leads logically to the notion of matching. While Sullivan himself would not have been likely to assess the participants' needs through psychometric devices prior to the inception of therapy, he was keenly aware of variables that affect or could affect the match between therapist and patient. For example, he not only delimited his own therapeutic interactions largely to young, male, "reactive" or catatonic schizophrenics but he also surrounded such patients with pre-selected aides on the rationale that their needs should not aggravate those of the patient even in casual interactions on the ward. Sullivan, thus, seemed informally aware of which personal-social characteristics of therapists would facilitate or hinder therapy with these patients. Although, in the main, Sullivan appears to have believed that "like cures like"—e.g., male schizophrenics require male therapists, paranoids should not be exposed to undue warmth—he was nevertheless clearly concerned with the effects of each individual's behavior on the other under particular pairing conditions.

Because of this emphasis, Sullivan appears to have provided at least the rudiments of a theoretical framework for therapist-patient matching more than the other, largely "intrapsychic" theorists of his day. While his ideas regarding complementary and antagonistic needs may lack specificity, his view of interpersonal relations has inspired a number of relevant refinements in recent theory and research (see below) and may form the core of future paradigms for understanding interpersonal events (Swensen, 1973).

Leary's Interpersonal Diagnosis of Personality. In an attempt to systematize and extend Sullivan's ideas, Leary (1957) and his colleagues at the Kaiser Foundation developed a comprehensive framework for classifying or "diagnosing" persons in terms of their predominant interpersonal behaviors or "reflexes." After extensive observation and coding of clinical and nonclinical interactions, Leary formulated an operational model of interpersonal behavior, according to which behaviors in interpersonal situations were categorized with respect to two orthogonal bipolar dimensions, Dominance-Submission (the vertical dimension) and Love-Hate (the horizontal dimension).

Placing the two dimensions at right angles to each other, Leary organized interpersonal behaviors into a circumplex (circular arrangement) containing eight major subcategories, two in each quadrant (see Fig. 1). In the quadrant formed by the nodal points Dominance (12 o'clock) and Love (3 o'clock), for example, were placed Managerial-Autocratic and Responsible-Hypernormal behaviors (the term after the hyphen denotes an extreme form of the behavior in question); proceeding clockwise around the circle, we encounter the remaining octants—Cooperative-Overconventional, Docile-Dependent, Self-effacing-Masochistic, Rebellious-Distrustful, Aggressive-Sadistic, and Competitive-Narcissistic. Each octant "diagnosis" was further subdivided into two separate "reflexes." For example, the Managerial-Autocratic octant was comprised of the reflex to "manage, direct, lead" and the reflex to "guide, advise, teach." Each reflex, in line with Sullivan's theory of reciprocal emotion, was presumed to "pull" its complement from the other person—e.g., a managerial reflex should provoke obedience.

In ordinary dyadic interactions, individuals were generally thought to reciprocate each other's affective orientation directly (i.e., love elicits love and hate elicits hate) and to complement each other's stance on the Dominance-Submission dimension (i.e., dominance elicits submission and vice versa). Since both therapist and patient can be classified by various measures into the appropriate quadrants, octants, or reflexes, the implications for therapist-patient matching are straightforward. Leary and his colleagues, however, did not pursue this matter systematically.

Carson's Extensions of Interpersonal Theory. Beginning, like Leary, with Sullivanian theories regarding interpersonal relations, Carson put forth a brilliant extension of Leary's contributions.[3] In his book *Interaction Concepts of Personality* (Carson, 1969), he reviewed the impressive empirical support that the circumplicial ordering of interpersonal behavior had received in widely diverging data sources, and proposed that a parsimonious theory of interpersonal relations could be organized around the classes of behaviors denoted by the four main quadrants of the Interpersonal Circle—namely, friendly dominance (F-D), friendly submission (F-S), hostile submission (H-S), and hostile dominance (H-D). Although an adequate presentation of Carson's *tour de force* would require exposition of the "interaction outcome matrices" that integrate the four-quadrant perspective with that of social exchange theory, with reformulations of learning and communications theories, and a whole host of original observations about psychopathology and psychotherapy, for the present we may note that the quadrants of the interpersonal circle yield four intrinsically *complementary* combinations (F-D and F-S, F-S and F-D, H-D and H-S, H-S and H-D) and four *anticomplementary* combinations (F-D and H-D, H-D and F-D, F-S and H-S, H-S and F-S) whenever two persons interact.

Since, like Leary, Carson considered patients to hold extreme or rigid self-definitions (i.e., unlike "normals," patients often restrict themselves to a relatively small segment of the Interpersonal Circle but engage in intense degrees of behavior within that segment), it would seem that, once a patient's predominant quadrant placement were ascertained, a complementary therapist could be readily provided. Anticomplementary pairings could be avoided since, under anticomplementary pairing conditions, therapeutic communication would be difficult to establish and dropouts may occur. On the other hand, given initially satisfactory (complementary) pairing conditions, the therapist's subsequent main task is to *avoid prolonged complementary reciprocation* of the patient's interpersonal overtures since doing so would "confirm" the patient's rigid or constricted self-concept and little therapeutic change could be expected. Giving credit to patients' skill in eliciting complementary responses from therapists as from nontherapists, Carson in effect endorses the therapist's being able to "move" the patient from his or her predominant orientation by countering the patient's bids for complementary behaviors with asocial responses (Beier, 1966) or with any behavioral strategy that precludes the therapist's being caught in the "disturbance-perpetuating maneuvers of his patient" (Halpern, 1965). The generally effective therapist, therefore, should be able to move to any segment of the Interpersonal Circle at will, an ability Carson suggests is equivalent to

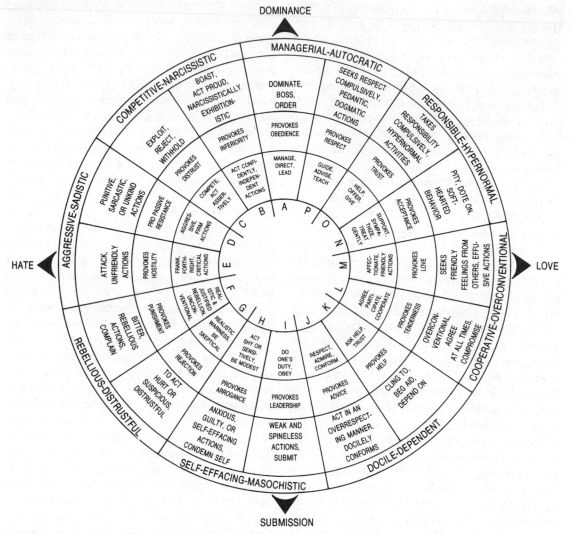

Figure 1. The Interpersonal Circle. Adapted from T. Leary, *Interpersonal diagnosis of personality*. Copyright © 1957, The Ronald Press Company, New York.

maximum personal adjustment.

While this chameleon-like flexibility on the part of therapists may indeed facilitate progress in long-term therapy, Carson's specification of the parameters of *initial* therapist-patient compatibility offers a sophisticated and testable perspective on therapist-patient pairings.

Schutz's Interpersonal Compatibility Theory. Schutz (1958) advanced a theory of interpersonal compatibility that also has direct relevance to therapist-patient pairing, even though the theory was meant to have much broader applicability. Interpersonal compatibility was thought to depend on three classes of needs—inclusion, control, and affection. Whereas the need for inclusion refers to a generalized tendency to include versus exclude other persons in social interactions, the needs for control and affection refer basically to the same constructs as the

Leary-Carson dominance-submission and love-hate axes of the Interpersonal Circle. In each of the need areas, Schutz distinguished between the need to express (originate) and to want (receive) behaviors; each individual can thus be characterized with regard to expressed inclusion, wanted inclusion, expressed control, wanted control, expressed affection, and wanted affection. From an examination of the implications of these six individual characteristics for dyadic (and group) interaction, Schutz delineated three types of compatibility.

Reciprocal compatibility exists when each participant's level of expressed behavior matches the other's level of wanted behavior, across the three need areas. For example, reciprocal compatibility would be denoted by the pairing of a therapist whose need to express control is matched by the patient's need to receive control, and the patient's need to control is matched by the therapist's need to receive control. Incompatibility increases to the extent that one participant's expressed behavior becomes discrepant (too high or too low) with respect to the other's receptiveness and vice versa.

The second type of compatibility, *originator compatibility*, refers to dyadic complementarity with regard to who shall originate and receive behaviors across the need areas. If both participants prefer to be originators (e.g., both therapist and patient show higher levels of expressed control than wanted control), a type of "competitive" incompatibility results; if both are primarily receivers, "apathetic" incompatibility results.

The third type of compatibility is designated *interchange compatibility*. It refers to the extent to which both participants assign the same "importance" to the need areas. For example, if the patient is more concerned with affection than is the therapist (or vice versa), the relationship would not be as compatible as when both participants are equally concerned with (expressed and wanted) affection. Ideally, therefore, the participants' preferences across the need areas should be as similar as possible.

Although these three types of compatibility are not wholly consistent with those based on the Interpersonal Circle, their assessment was operationalized by Schutz's Fundamental Interpersonal Relationship Orientation (FIRO) inventory whose psychometric features will be examined subsequently. At this point, however, it may be sufficient to note that Schutz's formulations in principle afforded psychotherapy researchers propositions that could have received extensive empirical examination.

Carkhuff-Berenson "Levels" Theory. The traditional client-centered position on the effective ingredients in psychotherapy has stressed the role of therapist-offered "core conditions" (accurate empathy, nonpossessive warmth, genuineness) with the rationale that if therapists were able to offer high levels of these facilitative conditions, patient change would follow more or less automatically. In their neo-Rogerian departure from this tradition, Carkhuff and Berenson (1967) shifted to a dyadic conception emphasizing the facilitative conditions offered by *both* participants.

In other words, both therapist and patient may be rated on the Carkhuff-Berenson measures of "core dimensions" (empathy, respect, genuineness, concreteness). Employing 5-point rating scales for these dimensions and averaging the ratings, one can obtain overall scores for each participant. On each scale, the midpoint (3) refers to a "minimally facilitative" level; below that scale point the responses of the "first person" detract from those of the "second person"; above the point, the responses of the first person add to those of the second. The most interesting feature of this formulation concerns the predicted levels of client gain as a function of the facilitative levels both participants bring to the situation (Carkhuff & Berenson, 1967, p. 52). Given a Level 1 (retarding) therapist, for example, who is paired with a Level 3 (minimally facilitative) patient, the predicted gain is minus two. By implication, therefore, a Level 3 patient needs to be paired with at least a Level 4 therapist to experience any gain whatsoever! Although patients are not considered to exceed Level 3, whereas therapists can theoretically attain Level 5, data compiled by the authors on various groups of "helpers" suggest that almost no group exceeds a mean value of 2, presumably indicating the "psychonoxious" style of the average helper.[4]

Closely examined, the Carkhuff-Berenson formulation reduces to the proposition that therapists should be "healthier" than their patients. Whatever the ultimate validity or fate of the details of this seemingly noncontroversial proposition, it does implicitly suggest that pretherapy assessment of the facilitative levels of both participants should be explored so as to preclude inadvertent mismatches that lead directly to "deterioration effects" in patients.

Millon's Theory of Psychopathology. In a comprehensive attempt to provide clinicians with a coherent theory within which to view psychopathology and treatment, Millon (1969) developed a parsimonious scheme for conceptualizing subgroups of patients, and has created a number of distinctions that offer promise for rational pairing of patients with therapists and techniques of intervention. Following a critique of traditional nosologies, Millon presented a scheme for dividing psychopathological phenomena into four major categories (personality patterns, symptom disorders, behavior reactions, biophysical defects), the first three of which require brief exposition.

Millon proposed that a set of eight basic personality patterns could be generated from conjoint consideration of (a) the primary *source* from which patients obtain positive reinforcements and avoid aversive consequences (i.e., no source = "detached" patterns; other persons as source = "dependent" patterns; self as source = "independent" patterns; conflict between sources = "ambivalent" patterns), and (b) the *style of instrumental behaviors* employed by persons to secure these reinforcements (active versus passive instrumental styles). Combining sources and styles, Millon termed the resulting personality patterns asocial (detached, passive), avoidant (detached, active), submissive (dependent, passive), gregarious (dependent, active), narcissistic (independent, passive), aggressive (independent, active), conforming (ambivalent, passive), and negativistic (ambivalent, active). In the order listed, the patterns closely resemble the traditional nosological categories: asthenic, schizoid, passive-dependent, hysterical, (no equivalent for narcissistic), antisocial, obsessive-compulsive, and passive-aggressive or explosive personality; seven of the eight patterns also correspond well to Leary's octant diagnoses.

The theory also includes specific propositions regarding continuities between the eight basic personality patterns, which represent mild degrees of disturbance, and more severe levels of decompensation. At moderate levels of decompensation, the detached patterns are designated schizoid; the dependent patterns, cycloid; the independent patterns, paranoid; and the ambivalent patterns, either cycloid or paranoid. At marked levels of decompensation, the corresponding labels are schizophrenic, cyclophrenic, paraphrenic, and cyclo- or paraphrenic.

Symptom disorders and behavior reactions (the second and third categories of psychopathology) differ primarily in that symptom disorders (e.g., phobic or conversion disorders) represent accentuations or exaggerations of certain features of the basic personality patterns whereas behavior reactions (e.g., fear reactions) do not. Rather, behavior reactions may represent learned maladaptive responses to narrowly circumscribed stimulus events or responses to transient situational stresses. Therefore, a so-called phobia may be conceptualized as learned *or* as coextensive with a person's basic personality pattern, depending on an accurate etiological assessment.

Since the eight personality patterns are based primarily on interpersonal variables, it follows that therapists' personality variables should be decisive in the modification of the basic personality patterns or of the symptom disorders that are coextensive with them; technique variables, on the other hand, should be more decisive in the treatment of behavior reactions. If a phobic disorder is determined to be an accentuation of, say, a passive-dependent (submissive) personality pattern, interpersonal, intrapsychic, or phenomenological approaches that emphasize the therapist-patient relationship might be entirely appropriate; should a phobia *not* be an exaggeration of a personality pattern, desensitization or flooding techniques would be more appropriate than relationship therapy.

Although Millon's theory, as he stresses repeatedly, requires empirical validation and likely revision, its eclecticism (it endeavors to integrate biophysical, intrapsychic, phenomenological, and behavioral data sources), convergence with much available clinical theory and research, testability, and specificity offer promise for subgrouping patients, syndromes, and symptoms in ways that directly specify appropriate interpersonal and technical interventions.

Basic Conceptual and Analytic Models

The preceding brief overview of selected theories illustrates only a few promising conceptual beginnings. Taken together, they suggest the importance of assessing empirically the interaction of therapist-patient needs, interpersonal "reflexes" or Interpersonal Circle quadrant placements, levels of facilitative conditions, and the "fit" between particular therapeutic interventions and patients' personality characteristics and/or symptoms. Other reviewers undoubtedly would have selected a different set of theoretical leads; little consensus exists on "important" positions in this area.

Probably the major obstacle to moving from theory regarding dyadic compatibility in psychotherapy to empirical confirmation or disconfirmation is our ignorance of the relative importance of single therapist, technique, or patient variables, let alone their interactive combinations. The selection of important matching variables requires theoretical precision and scope which are not currently available. Consequently, partial and often crude notions prevail.

The research methodology available for empirical tests of particular propositions, on the other hand, is quite advanced, and even highly complicated multivariate analyses can be executed within minutes. The following section surveys the main issues in designing psychotherapy studies which lead to implications for matching patients with therapists.

Methodological Issues

Any research design which facilitates an assessment of therapist-patient interaction effects, in addition to therapist and patient main effects, is useful for the empirical delineation of matching variables. Designs that vary only therapist and/or patient variables, without assessing their interaction, give no information regarding optimal therapist-patient pairings; designs that assess only therapist-patient interactions do not permit an evaluation of the separate contributions of therapist and patient main effects, which conceivably could explain more variance in eventual outcomes than the interaction effects. Ideally, therefore, the appropriate design should include conjoint assessment of the more important therapist (or treatment) variables, patient variables, and their interaction, each term evaluated relative to one or more measures of outcome.

The simplest model satisfying these requirements calls for a crossed factorial design incorporating a minimum of two levels of some therapist or technique variable (e.g., introverts vs. extraverts, desensitization vs. implosion, leading vs. reflective interventions) and two levels of some patient variable (e.g., introverts vs. extraverts, hysterics vs. obsessionals, process vs. reactive schizophrenics). Should an analysis of variance for this 2×2 factorial arrangement disclose, with regard to some measure(s) of outcome, a significant interaction effect in the absence of main effects, one would conclude that (a) both types of therapists were equally competent or effective, (b) both types of patients were equally responsive to treatment, but (c) while one type of therapist excelled with one type of patient, the other type of therapist excelled with the other. Obviously, the future assignment of patients to therapists could be guided directly by these hypothetical results (assuming their replicability and generalizability).

In the preceding example, it should also be apparent that the interaction effect need not take the form of a perfect "X" to be useful for matching; even if only one of the two types of therapists shows differential outcomes with the two types of patients, these therapists could be spared the task of treating the "less suitable" type of patient. Similarly, given a significant interaction effect, it is not necessary that therapist and patient main effects be nonsignificant, since it would be quite appropriate to pair even relatively ineffective therapists with patients with whom they would be less likely to fail.

While factorial designs thus facilitate direct translation of empirical findings into practical assignment strategies, it should be noted that in most clinical settings the therapist supply is relatively small even though patients are plentiful. This imbalance constrains the design of studies since the number of therapists within cells is too small to assume that their individual idiosyncrasies can be "washed out," or, put another way, that the sample adequately reflects therapist population values on the variables investigated. Given this possibility, it is desirable to nest specific therapists (i.e., the particular therapists working at a particular clinical setting) within levels of the therapist variable. The incorporation of this random factor in the design permits the evaluation of both idiosyncratic interaction effects (i.e., therapist-patient interactions that appear to "work" with these particular therapists) and potentially generalizable interaction effects. Although the latter are ordinarily of greater scientific interest, idiosyncratic interaction effects can nevertheless be employed to develop matching strategies for the particular setting in which the study was conducted, especially if the therapists in question are likely to remain on the premises for some time.

Finally, it is of course possible to employ a larger number of matching variables, as well as a greater number of "levels" of each variable, within the same investigation. Without large-scale collaborative efforts involving a number of clinical settings, however, considerations of necessary cell sizes usually preclude complex factorial designs.

Large samples of therapists and patients are required also in attempts to utilize multiple regression procedures to develop therapist-patient matching strategies. Multiple regression, however, is particularly useful when large therapist and patient samples can be assessed on a large number of potential matching variables prior to therapy. Although there is no inherent limit to the number of therapist and patient variables included in the eventual regression equation, the important methodological requirement is that the equation include, beyond coefficients for each therapist and patient variable, coefficients based on the cross-products (therapist score X patient score) of the variables selected. The importance of single and interactive predictor terms can be simultaneously evaluated, and the most predictive set of terms can be selected by various stepwise procedures.

Although multiple regression approaches are constrained by the generic need for large numbers of therapists and patients to ensure adequate ranges of variation on the variables of interest and to guard against the shrinkage that inevitably accompanies attempts to cross-validate beta weights on new samples, the interactive (cross-product) terms that emerge as significant can again be used as direct guides to matching patients with therapists. Moreover, the simultaneous evaluation of a large number of potential matching variables, which is not practical in the otherwise rigorous analysis of variance designs, makes multiple regression a useful tool for appraising the relative importance of different matching variables.

Consequently, multiple regression procedures appear desirable primarily for the selection of "important" interactive variables, whereas factorially designed analyses of variance appear best for the experimental evaluation of these interactive variables under relatively controlled circumstances (e.g., by systematic assignment of patients and therapists to the cells of the design).

With regard to dependent variables, it is obviously desirable to include multiple measures of outcome (or process) so as to assess the patterning of different dimensions of outcome across the time period of the study and beyond (cf. Kiesler, 1971), to evaluate agreements and disagreements associated with different vantage points or "sources" (e.g., therapist, patient, independent judge, relative), and hopefully to arrive at relatively consensual measures of improvement that could be used as criteria for actual attempts to match patients with therapists (Berzins, Bednar, & Severy, 1975). Multiple outcome measures, when used in conjunction with factorial designs, are readily analyzed via multivariate analyses of variance (Cooley & Lohnes, 1971), which evaluate the outcome measures as a set and which take the usual redundancies (intercorrelations) among outcome measures into account. Multiple outcome measures, of course, can also be employed in extending the multiple regression model to that of canonical correlation—i.e., one may relate sets of therapist-patient predictor variables to sets of outcome variables (Berzins et al., 1975; Cooley & Lohnes, 1971; Veldman, 1967).

From an overall design perspective, the factorial grid model advocated by Kiesler (1969, 1971) appears to hold the greatest promise for an effective approach to therapist-patient matching. Kiesler recommends that investigators include in the same design at least two homogenous subgroups of patients (e.g., hysterics, phobics, obsessionals) to whom at least two different therapist interventions (e.g., implosion, desensitization, covert sensitization) are administered and with whom at least two different types of therapists are paired. In addition, Kiesler urges that investigators employ more than one dependent variable or measure of change, each measure coordinated theoretically with the types of patients treated, changes expected for each type of patient, rate at which change is expected to occur, frequency of interventions required to produce changes, the locus of changes within therapy hours and in the patient's milieu, and the number of repeated measures determined by theoretical expectations for particular patients or problems. Although, in some respects, the grid model is more a catalog of our ignorance than a call to action (Eron & Callahan, 1969), the central question it raises—which therapists' behaviors or characteristics produce which kinds of changes in which kinds of patients?—will need to be answered empirically before therapist-patient matching strategies can be implemented.

Conceptual Issues

Supposing we agree with Kiesler and decide to pair, within a factorial design, at least two types of therapists or interventions with each of two or three types of patients in our next study. Where do we begin? It would obviously help to know in advance which background, clinical, or individual difference variables in therapists and patients would be likely to yield interaction effects. Kiesler (1966) himself has shown that current theories of psychotherapy fall considerably short of providing testable propositions regarding "important" therapist personality and technique dimensions that should interact with the characteristics of various subgroups of patients. Although hypotheses regarding interpersonal compatibility formulated by social psychologists (e.g., the relation of attitude similarity to interpersonal attraction) (e.g., Byrne, 1971) may receive support in nonclinical settings, their applicability to clinical settings is still relatively unexplored (Harari, 1971) and may require extensive modification (e.g., Beutler, Johnson, Neville, Elkins, & Jobe, 1975). For example, the intriguing attempts by Goldstein (1971) and his colleagues to extend relationship-enhancing phenomena from the laboratory to clinical populations have shown that certain extrapolations may be effective with YAVIS (young, attractive, verbal, intelligent, successful) (Schofield, 1964) patients but ineffective with non-YAVIS patients.

If deductions from current clinical and nonclinical theories do not furnish investigators with "important" matching variables, it must also be acknowledged that inductions from the accumulation of interaction effects emerging from separate empirical studies have not proven superior in this regard. Prior reviews of research in this area have extracted only a small number of promising variables for therapist-patient matching (cf. Luborsky, Chandler, Auerbach, Cohen, & Bachrach, 1971; Strupp & Bergin, 1969). These variables usually refer to the degree of therapist-patient similarity in such areas as socioeconomic status, expectancies, cognitive styles, interest, values, or personality variables. In none of these areas, however, are the empirical findings so solid as to demand revisions in theory or practice, or to suggest the feasibility of systematic pairing of patients with therapists.

In fact, the majority of studies conducted with implications for matching in mind have not departed far from common sense. As Meltzoff and Kornreich (1970) have observed, most studies of dyadic compatibility in psychotherapy have examined variants of the common sense notions that "it takes one to know one" (similarity) or its converse, that "opposites attract" (complementarity). As we noted earlier, however, such notions can coexist peacefully when it is appreciated that therapist-patient similarity may be helpful on some dimensions (e.g., on the love-hate axis of the Interpersonal Circle) but complementarity optimal on others (e.g., on the dominance-submission axis). Similarly, while similar socioeconomic status might facilitate communication in psychotherapy whereas dissimilar status might retard it, similarity with respect to "unresolved neurotic conflicts" presumably should activate therapists' blind spots and prove counterproductive.

The empirical assessment of therapist-patient similarity, complementarity, or some curvilinear association between participants' scores seemingly requires that both participants be measured on the same instruments. The selection of independent variables for their "symmetrical" applicability to both participants presupposes that the variables are equally important for therapist and patient. An "asymmetrical" conception of the matching problem would hold, in contrast, that some variables are more important for therapists than for patients and vice versa. For example, therapists' techniques have no direct counterpart in the domain of patient behaviors (although some may wish to debate this point); patients' diagnoses also (hopefully) have no counterpart in therapist behaviors.[5] Yet both therapists' techniques and patients'

diagnoses are highly relevant to the attainment of therapeutic objectives. Since both symmetrical and asymmetrical approaches may lead to the emergence of significant interaction effects, they are equally appropriate in matching research. This distinction between symmetrical and asymmetrical studies, however, is employed here to organize the review of the literature into two sections.

REVIEW OF THE LITERATURE

Symmetrical Matching Variables

In the studies described in this section both participants are assessed on the same variable or variables prior to therapy, so as to permit an evaluation of the relation of therapist-patient similarity to the process or outcome of therapy. Somewhat arbitrarily, the independent variable domains have been categorized into (a) background characteristics, (b) expectancies, preferences, and values, (c) personal constructs, (d) Interpersonal Circle behavior categories, and (e) personality characteristics.

Participants' Background Characteristics. Few investigators would wish to expend the effort required to conduct parametric studies of the effects of systematically varying the participant's age, sex, marital status, socioeconomic status, etc., across therapist-patient dyads. In themselves, and especially when considered singly, most demographic variables seem psychologically uninteresting (although easily measured), and such variables are usually employed as "control" variables to examine the homogeneity or comparability of groups rather than as independent variables.

Considered in various combinations, however, demographic variables refer to the participants' similarities and differences in the most obvious respects and thus have a bearing on both the therapist's and patient's "social stimulus value" and the ease with which first impressions may facilitate or hinder initial therapeutic communications. The potency of certain demographic variables is undeniable when we consider the finding that, in some comprehensive care centers, 52% of black clients drop out after only one interview (Sue, McKinney, Allen, & Hall, 1974).

The demographic characteristics of patients as a group are much more diverse than those of therapists, of course. In major urban centers, practicing therapists are preponderantly males (about seven of every ten) in their forties who have moved from backgrounds of lower middle-class status to at least upper middle status (Goldman & Mendelsohn, 1969; Henry, Sims, & Spray, 1971). While therapists as a group appear to be remarkably homogeneous, despite differing professions of origin or work situations (Henry et al., 1971), the patients who secure their services are comprised of at least two major demographic subgroups: (1) the YAVIS patients (Schofield, 1964) whose backgrounds are predominantly metropolitan, collegiate, and relatively affluent, and who are overrepresented in the consulting rooms of private practitioners and college clinics, and (2) the non-YAVIS, rather older, poorer, less well-educated group of patients that forms the clientele of comprehensive care centers. (A third group, largely middle class in origin, is relatively invisible to professional therapists because it seeks out the clergy.) Interestingly enough, in all three groups of patients the proportion of women exceeds that of men (Howard & Orlinsky, 1972).

Probably the most pervasive assumption regarding demographic variables and dyadic compatibility is that therapist-patient similarity in socioeconomic status is desirable. In support of this assumption, Carkhuff and Pierce (1967) found, for example, that similarity in interviewer-interviewee socioeconomic status (as well as race) facilitated patients' self-disclosure in an analogue study. Another widespread assumption is that, in view of their relatively privileged (even if achieved rather than inherited) socioeconomic status, therapists prefer YAVIS and reject non-YAVIS patients. Even if the rejection of non-YAVIS patients may not be blatant, it might involve the denial of the best available treatment services on the grounds that these patients hold inappropriate attitudes toward psychotherapy (Hollingshead & Redlich, 1958). Although earlier research has adduced some evidence that the social classes differ in attitudes toward or expectancies regarding psychotherapy (e.g., Overall & Aronson, 1963; Williams, Lipman, Uhlenhuth, Rickels, Covi, & Mock, 1967), recent reviews and findings (see Lorion, 1974a, 1974b) suggest that these differences may have disappeared in more recent samples. There is every reason to suppose, however, that therapists' continued belief that non-YAVIS patients lack the proper attitudes, expectancies, or motives toward psychotherapy could serve as sources of dyadic incompatibility.

In view of the fact that most therapists are men and most patients women, it is surprising that few investigators have considered that same versus opposite sex pairings might be relevant to variations in outcome; the method sections of many articles do not even specify the gender of participants. If we assume participants' gender to make a major difference in early sessions, some evidence exists that opposite sex dyads may communicate more effectively than same sex dyads (e.g., Brooks, 1974; Cartwright & Lerner, 1963; Fuller, 1963), although non-significant results have also been noted (Mendelsohn, 1968; Mendelsohn & Geller, 1963). Although gender per se may be a weak determinant of the ultimate outcome of therapy, its obvious relation to sex-role expectations and stereotypes in clinical settings (e.g., Broverman, Broverman, Clarkson, Rosenkrantz, & Vogel, 1970) makes it an important variable for empirical reexamination in this era of changing conceptions of "appropriate" sex roles.

Variables such as age and marital status are also relatively weak when considered separately. When combined with other demographic variables, however, they may indicate salient "life positions" or roles that have potent implications for matching. Although such research is still embryonic, a hint of the sort of specificity that is desirable is provided by an interesting descriptive study (Howard, Orlinsky, & Hill, 1970). Howard et al. classified female patients by age (young vs. mature), marital status and parental status, and examined their satisfactions with therapy (in four categories—catharsis, mastery-insight, encouragement received, and "nothing") when they were paired with therapists also classified as to sex, age, marital and parental status. Although the number of dyads per cross-classification was small, several suggestive patterns emerged. For example, when the therapist was herself an older mother, female patients who were young mothers responded negatively, but young single women positively, to the pairing conditions. While the results of this study may not be reliable or generalizable, they do suggest that, whenever sample size is adequate (as in comprehensive care centers), meaningful cross-classification of dyads on multiple demographic dimensions should be explored for its relevance to outcome.

Overall, although there is scant evidence that demographic variables (with the possible exception of those related to social class and sex matching) are significantly related to outcome (cf. Meltzoff & Kornreich, 1970), parametric studies are necessary to clarify their relation to initial therapist-patient communication, patient acceptance by therapists, and continuance in therapy.[6]

Participants' Expectancies, Preferences, and Values. Two types of expectancies have been differentiated in the literature—prognostic expectancies and participant role expectancies (Goldstein, 1962). Prognostic expectancies refer to the amount (or rate) of improvement, gain, or symptom relief the patient is expected to undergo. These expectancies have often been regarded as central to the explanation of improvement associated with psychotherapy (Goldstein, 1962), especially as regards the so-called placebo effects (Frank, 1961; Shapiro, 1971), although their conceptual and empirical status has been sharply questioned recently (Wilkins, 1973).[7]

Participant role expectancies refer to the kinds of personal attributes or behaviors that the participants expect to be appropriate during therapy sessions. Role expectancies are difficult to distinguish from preferences, although the latter may include more evaluative or need-determined components. Since both participants entertain prognostic and role expectancies, it is not surprising that many writers and reviewers have stressed the proposition that "mutuality of expectations" (or preferences) should significantly affect the process and outcome of therapy (Bordin, 1955; Borghi, 1968; Fiske, Hunt, Luborsky, Orne, Parloff, Reiser, & Tuma, 1970; Goldstein, 1962, 1968; Lennard & Bernstein, 1960, 1967; Levitt, 1966; Strupp & Bergin, 1969). From a matching perspective, however, there is very little empirical support for this proposition because investigators have seldom assessed both participants on the same measures. In the area of prognostic expectancies, for example, only one study appears to have assessed both participants' expectancies of patient improvement (Goldstein, 1960). In that small-scale study, neither patient expectancy, therapist expectancy, nor the "closeness" of their expectancies related to an index of outcome (patient-perceived change). More frequently, prognostic expectancies have been construed as either patient or therapist variables but not both.

In the area of role expectancies, several attempts have been made to delineate the predominant therapist-patient roles envisaged by patients (e.g., Apfelbaum, 1958; Garfield & Wolpin, 1963; Mendelsohn, 1968; Overall & Aronson, 1963; Rickers-Ovsiankina, Berzins, Geller, & Rogers, 1971; Williams *et al.*, 1967) and preferred by therapists (e.g., Berzins, Herron, & Seidman, 1971; Goldman & Mendelsohn, 1969). In principle, a number of "mutualities"

could thus be readily examined—e.g., therapist-patient agreement regarding appropriate patient roles, therapist roles, or both, as they relate to process or outcome measures. Generally, however, the focus has been on patient expectancies and no direct measurement of therapists' expectancies or preferences has been undertaken; rather, therapists have been *assumed* to prefer certain patient behaviors—e.g., active participation rather than passive acceptance of guidance. Given this assumption, some evidence exists that mutuality of expectancies facilitates continuance in therapy (Clemes & D'Andrea, 1965; Heine & Trosman, 1960; Overall & Aronson, 1963). Evidence from studies that have assessed *both* participants' role expectancies and have included measures of outcome, however, is equivocal. A study that examined both participants' role expectancies in a college counseling center (Mendelsohn, 1968) found no relation of expectancies or of therapist-patient mutuality to outcome measures. Although the period of counseling was extremely brief (two or three sessions), Mendelsohn concluded that the importance of expectancies may be exaggerated. However, another study that assessed therapist-patient "convergence" (moving toward agreement) with regard to appropriate therapist techniques found that convergence scores correlated significantly with patients' global improvement ratings (pre-post change scores) and with therapists' global improvement ratings (changes from the 5th week to post-therapy) in a sample of 32 neurotic outpatients (22 women) treated by five therapists (Schonfield, Stone, Hoehn-Saric, Imber, & Pande, 1969). While, overall, the available evidence does not accord mutuality of expectancies a major role in determining outcomes, it is too scant for the conclusion that the issue has been tested adequately.

Even if research has not established that the mutuality of expectancies importantly influences outcome, it is undeniable that many patients enter therapy expecting behaviors and attributes that therapists do not possess or will not deliver, and that many therapists hold similar expectancies regarding patients. Since patients' concerns with role-related issues appear to be highest in early sessions (Alexander & Abeles, 1968; Lennard & Bernstein, 1967), procedures have been developed to structure patients' expectancies even prior to the first interview (e.g., the role induction interview developed by Hoehn-Saric, Frank, Imber, Nash, Stone, & Battle, 1964) or to increase patients' attraction to therapy (Goldstein, 1971). Once therapy has been initiated, therapists have also been urged to engage in exploration and structuring of patients' expectancies (Goldstein, 1962; Rotter, 1954), to tailor therapies so as to be congruent with social class-linked expectancies (Goin, Yamamoto, & Silverman, 1965; Goldstein, 1973), and to select techniques in a flexible and innovative fashion (e.g., Lazarus, 1971). Regardless of whether one accords greater weight to patients' preferences (e.g., Begley & Lieberman, 1970; Boulware & Holmes, 1970; Ziemelis, 1974) or to therapists' preferences (e.g., Lee & Temerlin, 1970), clearly empirical research with implications for matching will need to encompass both.

Whereas participants' expectancies may often be "worn on the sleeve," their value systems or moral stances are more difficult to detect immediately and tend to emerge as therapy proceeds. Perhaps for this reason, there has been little research into the compatibility of participants' values at the beginning of therapy. In any case, the measurement of values has not achieved a high degree of refinement; for example, some investigators have employed the Strong Vocational Interest Blank for this purpose.

The caliber of the initial efforts in this area may be illustrated by Cook's (1966) study. The values of 42 counselor trainees and 90 clients (54 males) being seen in brief counseling in a college clinic were assessed prior to therapy on the Allport-Vernon-Lindzey Study of Values; dyadic similarity indices (Cronbach's D^2) were calculated and categorized into thirds (most similar, intermediate, least similar). The dependent measures consisted of raw change scores on four concepts (me, the ideal student, my future occupation, education) evaluated by clients before and after therapy. The concepts were rated on 15 scales drawn from the evaluative dimension of the semantic differential. Although the intermediate category of value similarity dyads showed the most change, the changes involved the last two concepts (future occupation, education) rather than the self (me). Cook himself acknowledges that the effort has been "a rather modest approach to a profound problem."

A more recent study attempted to relate both values and indices of social class to the duration of psychotherapy (Pettit, Pettit, & Welkowitz, 1974). To assess values, the Allport-Vernon-Lindzey Study of Values, Morris' Ways to Live Scale, the Strong Vocational Interest Blank, and Neulinger's Optimal Personality Integration Scale were administered to a total of 104 therapists and 249 patients (sexes unspecified) forming 256 dyads. After preliminary analyses, the various test subscales were reduced to six major interest factors (e.g., Rotary Club vs. aesthetic interest, authoritarian-submissive vs. independent, transcendentalism vs. concrete-rational, etc.). Factor scores were then assigned to each participant, and dyadic difference scores, along with Hollingshead's two-factor index of social position, were employed as predictors of the duration of therapy. (Incidentally, the patients' value factor scores, especially scores on the authoritarian-submissive factor, significantly predicted social class standing; therapists' value factor scores, in contrast, did not, perhaps due to their greater homogeneity.) Although no single dyadic difference score on the value factors nor the index of social position were predictive of the duration of therapy, two major effects emerged from the series of multiple regression analyses: dyadic difference scores on the authoritarian-submissive factor interacted with the index of patients' social position in a linear as well as a curvilinear manner. The lower the patient's social class and the higher the patient's tendency to submit to authority (relative to that of the therapist), the longer the duration of therapy. The curvilinear component indicated that, while for middle and upper classes, the discrepancy on the authoritarian-submissive factor bore no relation to the duration of therapy, in the lower social classes the discrepancy predicted duration. For the latter patients, the greater their tendency to submit to authority (relative to that of their therapists), the longer the treatment. Although this study involved unusual boundary conditions (e.g., participants' preferences regarding assignments were solicited and honored by clinic staff), failed to report and analyze effects associated with participants' gender, and included no measures of outcome, it illustrates the degree of methodological sophistication needed for explorations of values (and socioeconomic variables) in large-scale parametric studies (e.g., in comprehensive care centers).

Studies that do not measure participants' values at the outset of therapy but rather assess the appealing proposition that, in the course of therapy, patients tend to adopt their therapists' values (e.g., Rosenthal, 1955; Welkowitz, Cohen, & Ortmeyer, 1967), are not related to the matching question and fall outside the scope of this review.

Participants' Personal Constructs and Other Cognitive Variables. How similarly therapist and patient conceptualize important aspects of their respective worlds seems a salient issue for therapist-patient matching. An examination of recent research reveals, however, that very little solid evidence is available in this area.

Edwards and Edgerly (1970) investigated the relation of participants' "cognitive congruence" to the outcome of brief counseling. To operationalize cognitive congruence, the investigators required both participants to rate 12 concepts on scales drawn from the evaluative dimension of the semantic differential; raw difference scores between dyad members were then summed across concepts, ranked, and three equal-sized "congruence" groups (low, medium, high) were formed, evidently pairing each of eight therapists with two patients at each congruence level. Indices of outcome were derived from patient change scores of the evaluative dimension and on the Dymond Adjustment Index; changes in therapist-patient congruence were examined also. While the results suggested that patients in the low-congruence (most dissimilar) dyads changed the most, presumably arguing for the desirability of pairing cognitively dissimilar participants, the results are reported in a highly abbreviated and unclear form, the use of raw difference scores makes regression effects especially likely in low-congruence dyads, and the congruence categories interacted with specific therapists (who were not nested), making generalization of the results virtually impossible.

Hypothesizing that "differentiation compatibility" was essential to improvement in psychotherapy, Carr (1970) obtained measures of participants' differentiation levels prior to therapy. The latter were assessed by Carr's Interpersonal Discrimination Test which provides a measure of the number of interpersonal discriminations a person makes among a number of stimulus persons along the person's own conceptual dimensions. An unspecified number of medical student therapists saw 24 (mostly neurotic and female) patients for 12 weeks. Differentiation-level difference scores (therapist minus patient) were computed and three groups formed (therapist more differentiated than patient, both about equal, patient more differentiated than therapist). Carr expected the dyads showing approximately equal differentiating scores to improve the most. When those dyads were compared with the two incongruent groups, they indeed showed greater improvement according to patient ratings and a measure of symptom reduction. The results thus suggested that participants' similarity with respect to differentiation levels is better than dissimilarity.

Probably the most extensive and sophisticated investigation of the role of therapist-patient similarity in personal constructs was conducted by Landfield (1971). Employing George Kelly's personal construct theory and his Role Construct Repertory (REP) Test to assess similarity in personal constructs, Landfield examined three hypotheses related to premature termination, three hypotheses related to improvement, and one to therapist-ascribed pathology. Eight therapists (seven males) saw various small to moderate sized samples of college clinic patients of both sexes, the samples variously subdivided for analysis according to prematurity of termination and length of therapy. According to the results, continuance was enhanced if (a) participants perceived each other as meaningful figures, (b) participants saw each other's construct dimensions as meaningful, and (c) participants' constructs had similar content. Improvement categories (applicable to stayers only) were derived from pre-therapy and terminal interview transcripts rated by three expert judges. Support for the hypotheses regarding improvement indicated that outcomes were better when (a) participants organized their personal constructs differently, (b) participants showed converging construct systems over time, and (c) patients shifted their "present selves" toward therapists' "ideal selves" (the latter framed in the patient's language system). Contrary to prediction, however, therapist-patient similarity in content of personal constructs tended to evoke *negative* patient descriptions from therapists.

The thrust of Landfield's outcome results generally supported the proposition that "maintenance of interpersonal communication requires, in addition to some minimal degree of shared meaningfulness, a difference in the organizational structures of a client and his therapist" (Landfield, 1971, p. 66). Although the replicability of the results has not been established, Landfield's book warrants close study by any student of cognitive compatibility in psychotherapy. Among its virtues are its multidimensional conception of personal constructs (hand and computer scoring manuals are provided), nonsimplistic thinking about initial and later stages of therapy, and distinctions between content and structure (organization) of personal constructs.

Although carried out in the context of group therapy with alcoholic patients, a study by McLachlan (1972) also warrants mention since it presents a quasi-developmental theory regarding "conceptual levels" (CL) that is relevant to dyadic compatibility in psychotherapy. Conceptual levels are thought to range from a dependence on authority to independence and self-assertion; low CL patients presumably should receive at least moderate structure in therapy, whereas high CL patients should be encouraged toward autonomy. Although no direct measure of the degree of structure provided by high and low CL therapists was taken, high CL therapists paired with high CL patients and low CL therapists paired with low CL patients showed better improvement scores (according to patients) than did the incongruent pairings.

Participants' Interpersonal Circle Behavior Categories. In their classic analogue study, Heller, Myers, and Kline (1963) examined the hypotheses, based on Leary's Interpersonal Circle, that dominance evokes submission (and vice versa) but that friendliness evokes friendliness and hostility evokes hostility. A total of 34 graduate student interviewers (sexes unspecified) saw, in counterbalanced order, four "patients" who in fact were actors selected and trained to enact the patient roles corresponding to the four main quadrants of the Interpersonal Circle (friendly-dominant, hostile-dominant, friendly-dependent, hostile-dependent). Interviewers' behaviors in response to these standardized client roles were rated on the Leary Interpersonal Checklist by trained observers; the interviewers thus could also be classified with regard to the degree of dominance and friendliness shown during the interview. With only minor qualifications, both hypotheses received significant support: patient dependency evoked more interviewer dominance than did patient dominance, and patient friendliness evoked more interviewer friendliness than did patient hostility.

In further exploration of the dominance-submission (DOM) and love-hate (LOV) axes of the Interpersonal Circle, Swensen (1967) reported an intriguing series of pilot studies. In one study, Minnesota Multiphasic Personality Inventory profiles obtained from clinical psychology graduate students and the 79 patients (sexes unspecified) they treated were scored, according to a method suggested by Leary (1957), so as to determine DOM and LOV quadrant placements for both participants. Measures of outcome (improved vs. unimproved) were supplied by two raters who evaluated therapists' pre-post case summaries. Improvement proportions were higher when dyad members were complementary on the DOM dimension (therapist domin-

ant, patient submissive, or vice versa) and similar on the LOV dimension (although, contrary to Leary and Carson, Swensen had expected complementarity on the LOV dimension to enhance outcomes). Although, from the perspective of Leary and Carson, 62% of all pairings had involved favorable conditions, 82% of the compatibly paired patients (opposite on DOM, similar on LOV) improved whereas only 55% of the incompatibly paired patients (similar on DOM, opposite on LOV) did.

The desirability of having therapists and patients occupy different quadrants of the Interpersonal Circle was also suggested by another analysis in which Swensen scored published transcripts of sessions conducted by three well-known therapists (Rogers, Ellis, Wolberg) according to another scheme provided by Leary (1957). Assuming the transcripts to represent instances of successful therapy, Swensen showed that in each dyad the therapist and patient occupied different quadrants (e.g., the "responsible-hypernormal" Rogers was paired with a "self-effacing-masochistic" patient).

In a related study, Mueller and Dilling (1968) conducted content analyses of therapy interviews (fifth to seventh sessions) involving 19 dyads (male therapists, patients' sex unspecified). Although the Leary scoring system could not be applied reliably to all quadrants, therapist-patient rank-order correlations, based on behaviors in the reliably rated quadrants, indicated that therapists' friendly-dominant behaviors were positively related to patients' friendly-submissive behaviors (consistent with interpersonal theory) and that participants' hostile-dominant behaviors were also positively related (partially contrary to theory).

In an analogue study, Beery (1970) presented (on tape) a female patient exhibiting either a friendly or a hostile attitude to 16 experienced and 16 inexperienced therapists. Although Beery's primary interest lay in examining the unconditionality of therapists' regard for patients as a function of patient affect and therapist experience, the results, consistent with Heller *et al.* (1963) and interpersonal theory, showed that the patient's affect tended to elicit its match from therapists (i.e., the friendly patient tape elicited more acceptance from therapists than did the hostile tape).

Finally, Crowder (1972) contrasted the proportions of behaviors that successful and unsuccessful groups of therapists and patients emitted in each quadrant of the Interpersonal Circle in early, middle, and late portions of therapy. Comparisons of 15 successful and 10 unsuccessful dyads (sexes unspecified) revealed a number of differences—e.g., in late sessions, therapists in success dyads emitted more friendly-dominant and less hostile-dominant behaviors than did therapists in failure dyads. Even though Crowder's design failed to examine therapist-patient interaction effects and did not consider sequential aspects of participants' interchanges, the study reminds us of the need for longitudinal research that would clarify the manner in which participants move across quadrants of the Interpersonal Circle as a function of initial pairing conditions (cf. Carson, 1969).

Participants' Personality Characteristics. The studies reviewed in this section employ independent variables derived mainly from three personality assessment devices and are organized accordingly.

Minnesota Multiphasic Personality Inventory (MMPI). Although this widely used instrument for assessing varieties and degrees of psychopathology would, almost by definition, seem inappropriate as a measure of therapists' personality characteristics, the possibility that global therapist-patient profile similarity might be related to outcome led Carson and Heine (1962) to conduct a study with 60 medical student therapists (52 males) and their 60 outpatients (35 females). Even though patients' profiles showed a mean elevation of 65.6 on the nine clinical scales (MF excluded), versus therapists' 54.6, a difference that exceeds one standard deviation, Carson and Heine calculated dyadic profile similarity indices (Cronbach's D^2) and related the similarity scores to a composite measure of outcome (supervisors' assessment of improvement, occupational adjustment, etc.). Analysis of variance of outcome scores across five groups of dyads representing increasing degrees of profile dissimilarity yielded a significant F ratio; the pattern of mean scores suggested a curvilinear association between similarity and outcome—i.e., moderately dissimilar dyads achieved the best outcomes.

When Lichtenstein (1966) attempted to replicate these results, however, neither the original nor any new patterns emerged, despite close duplication of Carson and Heine's procedures and comparable therapist-patient samples. Moreover, Carson and Llewellyn (1966) also were unable to reproduce the original results. It seems safe to conclude that global indices of participants' MMPI profile similarity are not useful in matching research. This conclusion,

of course, in no way minimizes the research potential of the instrument itself. For example, Swensen (1967), whose use of the MMPI in the Leary framework was cited earlier, rescored the Carson-Heine data so as to estimate dyadic scores on the DOM and LOV dimensions and deduced from the pattern that greater improvement appeared to be associated with dyadic complementarity on the DOM and LOV dimensions.

Wogan (1970) employed the MMPI in a different fashion. He obtained pre-therapy factor scores on a number of MMPI dimensions (anxiety, repression, withdrawal, subtlety, etc.) in a sample of 82 inpatients (55 women) treated by 12 psychiatric residents (10 men). The dependent measures were comprised of three patient-based and three therapist-based post-therapy factors. This methodologically sophisticated study employed a multiple regression design which included not only therapist and patient factor scores but also therapist X patient cross-product terms (e.g., therapist anxiety X patient anxiety) as predictors of each outcome variable. Disregarding results that applied only to therapist or client predictor variables, Wogan found that therapist-patient similarity on the subtlety factor (based primarily on participants' scores on the K and L scales) retarded the patients' progress, and that dyadic similarity on the repression factor decreased the patient's liking for the therapist. Wogan cogently suggested that similarity in defensive styles may be counterproductive.

Although some investigators may have abandoned the MMPI on the basis of the inconclusive results of the Carson *et al.* studies cited above, and although the MMPI appears less appropriate for therapists than for patients, Wogan's and perhaps also Swensen's data suggest that configural components of MMPI profiles (e.g., factor scores, Leary quadrants) could well prove relevant to matching. Because of its popularity in clinical settings, the MMPI can also be used to form homogeneous subgroups of patients whose differential responsiveness to various therapeutic interventions of therapist types could be studied systematically (cf. Kiesler's Grid Model).

Fundamental Interpersonal Relations Orientation Scale (FIRO-B). Schutz's (1958) theory regarding interpersonal compatibility, reviewed earlier, led directly to the FIRO-B instrument, whose scoring system yields scores for "reciprocal," "originator," and "interchange" compatibility for each dyad. An overall compatibility index ("K") can also be obtained. Although the latter index has been used in several studies, its continued use is inappropriate in light of the fact that, whereas reciprocal and interchange compatibility scores can take only positive values (zero denoting maximum compatibility on all three scales), scores for originator compatibility can have both positive and negative values. As Mendelsohn and Rankin (1969) have pointed out, the composite "K" score is inappropriate if, as one type of *incompatibility* increases, overall compatibility is also said to increase.

Evidently without having considered this scoring artifact, Sapolsky (1965) obtained the FIRO-B scores of three psychiatric residents (two men) and their 25 female inpatients, and related the "K" index to several dependent variables (e.g., supervisors' ratings of patient improvement, measures of perceived similarity). Sapolsky reported a significant correlation between dyadic "K" scores and improvement ratings; compatibly paired patients also felt more understood and considered themselves to be more similar to their therapists than did incompatibly paired patients. Since separate correlations for reciprocal, originator, and interchange compatibility were not reported, however, the results must be judged inconclusive.

In a college counseling center, Mendelsohn and Rankin (1969) administered the FIRO-B to 11 counselors (six males) and 115 counselees (73 males) prior to the inception of short-term vocational and personal counseling. Dependent measures consisted of scores derived from a cluster analysis of a post-therapy questionnaire. FIRO-B compatibility scores were found to be totally unrelated to improvement scores among male clients. In the 42 dyads involving female clients, however, five (of 10 possible) compatibility scores related significantly to outcome. Curiously, originator and interchange compatibility in the control area was positively related to outcome but reciprocal and interchange compatibility in the inclusion area, and reciprocal compatibility in the affection area, were *negatively* associated with outcome scores. Whatever the interpretation of these findings, supplementary analyses disclosed that an *ad hoc* compatibility score composite could be formed by multiple regression (not to be confused with "K," which was totally unrelated to outcome in both patient sexes) which yielded a multiple R of .54 ($p < .001$) with improvement scores among female clients.

Gassner (1970) conducted the only study that employed FIRO-B scores to select matched and mismatched dyads for experimental purposes, albeit on the basis of the flawed "K" index. Her therapists were 24 theological students (22 males) engaged in twice-weekly pastoral counseling with some 150 (largely psychotic) inpatients for a period of 12 weeks. From the pool of patients, 24 compatible, 24 incompatible, and 24 no-treatment controls were selected. (The groups were balanced for sex and other characteristics.) The dependent measures included a nurse-rated Behavioral Adjustment Scale (MACC), a Client Personal Reaction Questionnaire (CPRQ), and a Therapist Personal Reaction Questionnaire (TPRQ). Three-week changes on the nurse-rated MACC did not differentiate the groups. At 3 and 11 weeks of therapy, however, compatibly paired patients evaluated the therapy relationship more favorably than did incompatibly paired patients (on the CPRQ). A supplementary analysis showed that these differences in attraction to the therapist were principally due to compatibility on the reciprocal and interchange components of "K" (i.e., originator compatibility was unrelated to CPRQ scores). The TPRQ showed no reliable effects.

Obviously, these studies admit no sweeping conclusions. Although each study reported some "positive" results, variations in dependent measures, therapist professions and sexes, and patient characteristics make comparisons difficult. At best, the FIRO-B scales, purged of the "K" index, may have some bearing on the compatibility of dyads involving female patients.

Myers-Briggs Type Indicator (MBTI). This instrument is based on Jungian theory and assesses characteristic preferences in cognitive and perceptual orientation on four bipolar scales (judgment vs. perception, sensation vs. intuition, thinking vs. feeling, extraversion vs. introversion).

In a short-term college counseling center, Mendelsohn and Geller (1965) administered the MBTI to counselors and 129 counselees. Employing Cronbach's D^2 as the index of dyadic similarity across the four MBTI dimensions, Mendelsohn and Geller divided the dyads into groups of low, medium, and high similarity. The dependent variables were comprised of three cluster scores (evaluation, comfort-rapport, therapist competence) derived from the post-therapy ratings of patients. (Refreshingly, the analyses assessed the effects of same versus opposite sex matching as well as differences between freshman and nonfreshman clients.) The results suggested a curvilinear association between MBTI similarity and the evaluation of counseling—i.e., the medium similarity group reported the most favorable appraisals of counseling, especially among nonfreshman and opposite-sex dyads. Like Carson and his colleagues in their study of MMPI profile similarity, however, Mendelsohn (1968) could not replicate these results. Although the replication sample was drawn from the same clinical setting (71 dyads), the medium similarity group showed the lowest rather than the highest evaluation scores. Therefore, although MBTI similarity has been found (Mendelsohn, 1966; Mendelsohn & Geller, 1967) to be predictive of the duration of counseling, its relation to outcome appears nil.

Other Personality Tests. One final study warrants mention because it illustrates a number of problems. Bare (1967) administered the Gordon Personal Profile and the Gordon Personal Inventory to 47 counselors and 208 clients (sexes not specified); 140 of the clients also completed the Edwards Personal Preference Inventory. These instruments provided a total of 23 different measures of participants' personality characteristics. Four outcome ratings were obtained from both participants after 10 weeks of counseling. Two measures of counselor-client similarity were employed as predictors of the 10-week ratings: (a) the absolute difference between participants' percentile scores on each personality measure and (b) the directional difference score obtained by subtracting the client's percentile score from that of the counselor. Although the correlational analyses suggested that counselor-client dissimilarity on such variables as original thinking, vigor, and responsibility was predictive of positive outcomes, alternative interpretations cannot be ruled out because important procedural details are missing. For example, if the percentile scores used to form indices of similarity were based on the same (e.g., general population) norms, one would expect counselors as a group to score higher than clients on such variables as original thinking. Since counselors' original thinking scores related positively to all eight criterion ratings, as did both the absolute and relative dyadic difference scores, it seems reasonable to infer that effective counselors were generally higher in original thinking than the less effective counselors. In other words, the effects attributed to counselor-client dissimilarity may be attributed to individual differences among counselors.

Symmetrical Matching Variables: Overview

In most of the studies reviewed, the essential procedure has been to assess both participants on the same pre-therapy variable or variables in the hope that some degree of level of dyadic similarity would prove predictive of patients' responses to therapy. Since almost any pattern of results emerging from this paradigm can "make sense" in retrospect, the need for theoretically anchored predictions and replication of single studies cannot be stressed too strongly.

As noted in connection with the interpretation of Bare's (1967) study, some effects which seem dyadic may not be dyadic at all. Probably the most serious methodological obstacle to clear interpretation of results in this group of studies involves the investigators' persistent use of ambiguous indices of similarity (e.g., Cronbach's D^2 and raw difference scores). Because the D^2 index does not permit the investigator to determine whether effects attributed to therapist-patient "similarity" may not in fact be due to therapist or patient scores alone, its use in deriving implications for matching is problematic at best. After all, an effect emanating from one or the other (but not both) participants has no bearing on differential assignment but only on therapist and patient selection (e.g., firing incompetent therapists or preferentially selecting "good" patients). In matching research, factorial analyses of variance and multiple regression models that include therapist-patient cross-product terms are clearly preferable to global similarity indices.

In considering the substantive import of this group of studies, it does appear that dyadic similarity with respect to some background variables (e.g., social class) and their correlates (e.g., role expectancies or preferences) may facilitate the initial stages of therapeutic communication and enhance patient continuance. Although in some of the studies therapist-patient similarity was assumed rather than measured directly, and although various speculations regarding "appropriate" patient attributes may reflect therapists' preferences for YAVIS and rejection of non-YAVIS patients, the available evidence points to the need for large-scale parametric studies of participants' background variables, considered in various meaningful combinations (e.g., Howard *et al.*, 1970), preferably in settings that include large proportions of non-YAVIS patients (e.g., comprehensive care centers).

Since the modal therapist-patient dyad appears to be comprised of a male therapist and a female patient, such parametric studies should devote particular attention to possible sex-matching effects. Although sex differences a-bound in the literature (Carlson, 1971; Maccoby & Jacklin, 1974), some investigators do not even report the gender of participants, fail to consider that compatibility variables may operate differentially in the sexes, and neglect to analyze data for sex-matching effects. We surely do not need to add a "unisex" assumption to Kiesler's (1966) catalogue of uniformity assumption myths in psychotherapy research. It is also a significant fact that the sex-role orientations of therapists and patients, which, after all, are not necessarily predictable from a knowledge of gender, have been almost totally excluded from the matrix of variables thought to have a bearing on the processes and outcomes of therapy.

Of the independent variable domains examined in this review, however, the classification of therapists and patients into the quadrants or categories of the Interpersonal Circle seems the most promising beginning toward a serious investigation of therapist-patient pairings. Although supportive evidence is not yet extensive, this approach entails a comprehensive sampling of interpersonal behaviors, rather than a narrow focus on some particular attitude or personality trait, and has the advantage of being guided by theoretical propositions (Carson, 1969; Leary, 1957).

Asymmetrical Matching Variables

The asymmetrical perspective on the matching problem holds that, in designing studies, some variables are more important for therapists than for patients and vice versa. On the therapist side, such independent variables as therapeutic techniques, modalities, orientations, styles, or behavioral dispositions seem closely related to what the therapist actually does during therapy sessions; on the patient side, such variables as diagnosis, prognosis, symptom patterns, expectancies, and so on, most obviously warrant consideration. To be potentially useful for matching, the research design must simply conjoin two or more levels of a therapist variable with two or more levels of a patient variable, so as to detect significant interaction effects.

It should be noted that studies of the relative efficacy of several therapeutic approaches or techniques in alleviating some particular problem in a group of patients (college students afflicted with snake phobia or speech anxiety seem most popular in recent years) offer only limited data for matching purposes unless the patient group is subdivided in some meaningful manner (e.g., high vs. low anxiety, introverts vs. extraverts) or unless two or more distinct clinical groups are studied (e.g., hysterics vs. obsessionals). To illustrate, Meichenbaum, Gilmore, and Fedoravicius (1971) contrasted the efficiency of desensitization, rational-emotive "insight" therapy, and the two combined (relative to placebo and waiting list controls) in group therapy with speech-anxious volunteer patients. While the results suggested that the two main treatment modalities were equivalent (but superior to control procedures) across multiple outcome measures at post-therapy and follow-up points, Meichenbaum et al. conducted a post hoc analysis which added a new dimension to the results. Namely, when patients in the treatment groups were subdivided as to whether their speech anxiety was specific to speech situations or whether it was a part of generalized interpersonal anxiety, desensitization yielded better results with the specific anxiety subgroup than did rational-emotive techniques whereas the opposite pattern applied to patients with generalized anxiety. If replicable, such findings have direct implications for matching.

Another example of a design matching therapists' techniques with patient variable is provided by DiLoreto (1971). He contrasted the efficacy of desensitization, rational-emotive therapy, and client-centered therapy (with placebo and noncontact control groups) in alleviating interpersonal and general anxiety in introverts and extraverts. Recruited from a larger pool of undergraduates who wanted help for interpersonal anxiety and who qualified as introverted or extraverted on the Myers-Briggs Type Indicator, 100 volunteers (58 females) were treated in groups of five by six male therapists. Each therapist explicitly favored the approach he employed in treatment and was required to treat one group of introverts and one group of extraverts for a maximum of nine sessions. The design was a 5 (three treatment and two control groups) × 2 (specific counselors nested within treatments) × 2 (patients' intro- vs. extraversion) factorial. Multiple outcome measures were examined for pre-post and follow-up changes in self-reported anxiety levels. While subjects in all three treatment groups showed more improvement than controls, systematic desensitization appeared equally effective with introverts and extraverts, whereas rational-emotive therapy favored introverts and client-centered therapy extraverts, respectively.

The remainder of this section is devoted largely to (a) a brief review of research into the interaction hypothesis associated with the so-called A-B therapist distinction and (b) a description of the Indiana Matching Project, a study that has not been previously reported in the literature (see Footnote 1).

The A-B Interaction Hypothesis. Although a comprehensive review of research involving the A-B therapist variable and its relation to therapeutic outcomes is provided by Razin (Chapter 12, this volume), and earlier reviews that reach generally "positive" conclusions (e.g., Carson, 1967; Razin, 1971) or "negative" ones (e.g., Chartier, 1971; May, 1974) are available elsewhere, the so-called interaction hypothesis (IH)—that A-type therapists perform better with schizophrenic patients while B-type therapists perform better with neurotics—so clearly exemplifies the notion of therapist-patient matching that at least some aspects of its history require review.

The distinction between "A" and "B" therapists originated with Whitehorn and Betz, who studied therapist variables associated with differential success in the treatment of inpatient schizophrenics (see summaries by Betz, 1962, 1967). Psychiatric residents at the Johns Hopkins Hospital were ranked retrospectively according to their success in treating schizophrenics; therapists with high rates were designated A-types, while therapists with low rates were termed B-types. The identification of A and B therapists in subsequent research was facilitated by a 23-item "A-B" scale derived from the Strong Vocational Interest Blank (SVIB). Items included in the scale were simply those SVIB items that significantly distinguished the Whitehorn-Betz more effective (A) from less effective (B) therapists.

The major impetus to further research, however, was afforded by one of many possible interpretations of the results of a study of the relation of the A-B distinction to the treatment of neurotic outpatients in the Veterans Administration setting (McNair, Callahan, & Lorr, 1962). McNair *et al.* found that, with neurotic patients, the B-type therapists outperformed A-type therapists—a clear reversal of the Whitehorn-Betz findings. (Although Whitehorn and Betz claimed that A and B therapists did not differ with neurotic patients at Johns Hopkins, no supportive data were ever presented.) While many alternative explanations of this reversal were adduced (Lorr & McNair, 1966; McNair *et al.*, 1962) one intriguing hypothesis suggested itself—perhaps A-type therapists work better with schizophrenics and B-types with neurotics.

This interaction hypothesis (IH) obviously did not emerge from a factorially designed study pairing both types of therapists with both types of patients. It was an appealing guess.

Nevertheless, following Kemp's (1966) pioneering attempt to test the IH in a psychotherapy analogue experiment, a large number of analogue studies have paired A and B quasi-therapists or "helpers" with stimulus materials or, occasionally, live patients exemplifying schizoid or neurotic symptom patterns. The assumption that, if the A-B distinction refers to an individual difference (interest or personality) dimension, results consistent with the IH should emerge even in highly contrived "helping" situations met with a surprising degree of support (e.g., Anzel, 1970; Barnes, 1972; Berzins & Seidman, 1968, 1969; Carson, Harden, & Shows, 1964; Dublin & Berzins, 1972; Green, 1971; Sandler, 1965; Scott & Kemp, 1971; Segal, 1970; Seidman, 1971; Trattner & Howard, 1970; Welch, 1971). While reviews of these studies have noted problems with extrapolation from the laboratory to the clinic, the empirical rather than theoretical nature of the A-B distinction, the differences in independent and dependent measures from study to study, and so on, the relevance of the A-B variable to dyadic compatibility—even if it had never been clearly established in clinical settings—seemed undeniable to researchers in this area. The "addictive" nature of this conclusion has led to a profusion of studies, ranging from tests of the IH in traditional clinical settings (e.g., Berzins, Ross, & Friedman, 1972; Beutler, Johnson, Neville, & Workman, 1972; Beutler, Johnson, Neville, Workman, & Elkins, 1973) to investigations of the relation of mothers' A-B status to their success in alleviating their children's enuresis, employing Mowrer's conditioning procedures (James & Foreman, 1973); B-type mothers significantly outperformed A-type mothers!

Although the empirical power of the A-B variable to "produce results" continues to generate research, its conceptual or theoretical status remains elusive. A factor analysis of the responses of 95 nationally prominent male therapists to the Kentucky version of the Whitehorn-Betz scale disclosed that high scores, characteristic of B-types, resulted from (a) an affinity for manual hobbies ("being handy with tools"), (b) an interest in technical, complex, precision-requiring vocations, or (c) both (Geller & Berzins, 1976). In terms of personality correlates, the B pole or the A-B score distribution has been associated with risk-taking, dominance, variety-seeking, pursuit of sensual-esthetic enjoyments, and counter-dependence in samples of practicing therapists, male and female college students, and even college clinic patients (Berzins, Barnes, Cohen, & Ross, 1971; Berzins, Dove, & Ross, 1972). A plausible hypothesis regarding what all these characteristics have in common is that they involve aspects of psychological masculinity-femininity or the personological correlates of sex-role orientation (Dublin, Elton, & Berzins, 1969; Goodwin, Geller, & Quinlan, 1973; Johnson, Neville, & Workman, 1969; Lorr & McNair, 1966), although the conceptualization as well as measurement of the latter have undergone important revisions recently (cf. Bem, 1974; Spence, Helmreich, & Stapp, 1975).[8] However obliquely, the interactive results associated with therapists' A-B status and patients' schizoid versus neurotic status may make manifest the relevance of therapists' sex-role orientations to dyadic compatibility in psychotherapy.

The Indiana Matching Project. This project represented a 4-year (1967–1971) attempt to develop, implement, and evaluate a therapist-patient matching procedure (algorithm) in a college clinic devoted to short-term, crisis intervention oriented psychotherapy (Berzins, 1974; see Footnote 1). Given a setting in which therapists were devoted to the philosophy that patients' problems were to be modified in 3 to 4 weeks, the selection of matching variables was guided by these boundary conditions. To obtain brief but relevant measures on patients, measures of the "avoidance of others" role (complaints of interpersonal anxiety and avoidance), the "turning against the self" role (depressive and somatic complaints), the "dependency on others" role (approval- and advice-seeking expectancies), and the "turning toward others and self" role (audience- and relationship-seeking expectancies) were developed through factor-analytic and rational procedures. Eight patient predictor scores tapping the four roles were thereby derived from a total of only 50 Likert-type items. Pre-therapy assessment of these variables was obtained on a total of 751 (391 male, 360 female) patients. Since the 10 project therapists (six men, four women) were relatively homogeneous with regard to therapeutic philosophies and goals, therapists' predictor scores were based on the Personality Research Form (Jackson, 1967), administered to therapists at entry into the project. Rather than employing scores on some or all of the 20 content scales of that instrument, each project therapist was characterized by his or her standardized component score, derived from a principal components analysis of the data of 158 professionals, on each of six personality dimensions (impulse expression, ambition, acceptance, dominance, caution, abasement). Therapists' predictor scores thus focused on their relatively stable personality characteristics, while patient predictor scores were keyed primarily to salient situational factors.

Once random patient assignment was assured (including random administration of "placebo compatibility" instructions to some patients before therapy), the 10 project therapists saw from 29 to 145 patients each (mean = 75.1), typically for about 3 weeks. Following the terminal session, both participants completed short post-therapy rating scales (seven therapist ratings, six patient ratings). The 13 ratings were subsequently intercorrelated and reduced to three principal components (patient improvement, therapist self-appraisals, patient-experienced rapport). The first component score, patient improvement, was designated as the criterion measure for evaluating the efficacy of the pairing conditions. (Incidentally, the criterion score exhibited the desirable feature of inter-source consensus; the zero-order correlation between participants' ratings of patient improvement was approximately .50, $p < .0001$, in both patient sexes.)

The patient improvement scores were analyzed in a series of analyses of variance employing a 3-factor partially hierarchical factorial design (therapists trichotomized on each personality dimension; three therapists nested within each level; patients dichotomized at the median of each patient symptom or expectancy measure). Analyses were conducted separately for dyads involving male and female patients. For each patient sex, therefore, there were eight possible main effects for patients, six possible main effects for therapists, and 48 possible therapist-patient interaction effects. The results disclosed several replicable main effects—for example, therapist acceptance and caution and patient advice-seeking were associated with greater improvement in both patient sexes. The results also revealed 14 therapist-patient interaction effects, seven for dyads involving male and seven for dyads involving female patients. The interacting variables differed for patient sexes, however.

When the patient variables involved in the interaction effects were organized according to the four role orientations, favorable therapist-patient pairings in both patient sexes and in three of the role orientations (avoidance of others, turning against the self, and dependency on others) suggested dyadic complementarity along a superordinate dominance-submission dimension. Favorable pairings generally conjoined submissive, inhibited, passive patients with dominant, expressive, active, cue- and structure-emitting therapists, and sometimes vice versa, suggesting that improvement in brief psychotherapy was facilitated by pairing patients with therapists whose personalities embodied ingredients that complemented the patients' needs, deficits, expectations, or interpersonal stances. Results involving the fourth role orientation (turning toward others and the self), however, indicated that such complementarity applied to dyads containing male patients whereas "similarity" (e.g., verbally forthcoming female patients improved more with spontaneous and forceful therapists) applied to dyads involving female patients. Although the main sweep of these results appeared conceptually consistent with Leary's (1957) and Carson's (1969) interpersonal theories, the Indiana project was not designed to test specific hypotheses associated with these theories. Rather, the results were intended to generate guidelines for future therapist-patient pairings in this clinic.

To take an illustration from dyads involving male patients, "accepting" therapists performed better with male patients who had high (rather than low) pre-therapy scores on the interpersonal anxiety scale, whereas "rejecting" therapists showed the opposite pattern. (Therapists moderate on the acceptance dimension performed equivalently with the two groups of patients.) Therefore, even if "rejecting" therapists *generally* obtain lower levels of improvement than accepting therapists (i.e., the main effect cited above), their future performance should be "less poor" when their patients are *low* in interpersonal anxiety. The obverse should apply to "accepting" therapists: they should perform better with patients who score high rather than low on interpersonal anxiety. (With patients low on interpersonal anxiety, accepting and rejecting therapists in fact performed indistinguishably.) It follows that, given an interpersonally anxious patient, the appropriate match is a therapist who is at least moderate in acceptance; given a patient low in interpersonal anxiety, it does not matter whether the therapist is accepting or rejecting. Should it be pragmatically or ethically impossible to "purge" the clinic staff of "rejecting" therapists, to them should go patients with low levels of interpersonal anxiety!

To move from this illustration to a formal algorithm or assignment procedure for future patients, it should be noted that each project therapist in fact can be represented by a six-element profile (high, moderate, or low on each of the six personality dimensions) and each patient can be represented by a profile of up to eight (high vs. low) predictor score elements. It is then easy to recast the empirically determined interaction effects into a matrix which specifies the hypothesized favorability or compatibility of pairing any set of patient characteristics with any set of therapist characteristics.

In the data involving male dyads, for example, the obtained interaction effects conjoined the six therapist dimensions with five (of eight) patient predictor measures. Each future patient can be classified as high or low on each of the five scales; each classified element "predicts" one or more compatibly paired therapist elements. Similarly, each therapist in the clinic or the community can be classified as high, moderate, or low on each of the six personality dimensions; each profile element predicts one or more compatibly paired patient characteristics. By weighting both sides of the equation algebraically—e.g., by summing the predicted compatibility scores—a matrix is derived which pairs all possible patient predictor profiles (32 in this case) with all possible therapist personality profiles. (In practice, however, the permutations of therapist profiles can be restricted to the small number of therapists who are likely to participate in further patient assignments.) It remains only to subdivide the distribution of predicted compatibility scores into decision-relevant categories—for example, assign, assign if necessary, do not assign. The algorithm is now operational and can be implemented by a secretary or research assistant only minutes after a patient has filled out the 50-item pre-therapy instrument.

When the matching algorithm was actually implemented at the Indiana clinic in 1971, all therapists were informed that henceforth all patients would be "research-tailored" for them, so as to equalize expectations of favorable outcomes. After one semester, the data obtained from seven therapists and their 109 patients were evaluated to assess the predictive validity of the algorithm. Since mismatches (cases associated with the "do not assign" category for a particular therapist) were curtailed administratively, the essential comparison contrasted 73 "assign" dyads with 36 less optimally paired dyads (32 "assign if necessary" and four "do not assign" pairings). The analyses revealed that optimally paired dyads indeed showed higher improvement scores than did the less optimally paired dyads; patient-experienced rapport scores also showed a significant difference in the same direction. In the case of four therapists, each of whom had seen at least 12 optimally paired patients during the semester, the improvement scores of optimal pairings exceeded not only those of less optimal pairings but also those of patients that these therapists had seen in the prior phases of the project. Although the therapists involved in this validity study had also furnished data leading to the construction of the algorithm, thereby constraining generalization to other therapist populations, the algorithm had proven predictive of the effects of new patient pairings.

Incidentally, from its inception, the project had included an interest in assessing the effects of simply telling patients, after pre-therapy testing but prior to the first session, that they had been matched with the "therapist of choice." After all, if such "placebo compatibility" instructions were effective, why construct cumbersome matching algorithms? Periodic analyses of accumulating data, however, suggested that placebo compatibility instructions comprised a weak and irrelevant manipulation. A final contrast of 265 dyads in which the patients had received placebo compatibility instructions with 486 dyads in which patients had not received such instructions disclosed no significant differences or trends with respect to patient improvement, nor did the placebo variable interact with levels of algorithm-based compatibility. Although a trend-level ($p < .10$) effect suggested that therapists who had been assigned placebo patients tended to appraise *themselves* more positively and to see the patients slightly longer than therapists paired without placebo instructions to patients, the failure of the placebo instructions to relate to patient improvement suggested that their effects cannot be substituted for empirically or theoretically based attempts at matching patients with therapists. (Auxiliary analyses had also indicated that patient improvement did not vary significantly with therapist sex, therapist-patient sex matching, therapist case load—i.e., full vs. part-time—therapist experience at entry into the project, or experience gained in the course of the project.)

Overall, the Indiana Matching Project showed the feasibility of implementing a clinic-wide scheme for assigning patients to therapists so as to maximize compatible and minimize incom-

patible pairings. The construction of the algorithm, like the selection of matching variables, undoubtedly entailed certain arbitrary decisions, and it should be noted that replication and cross-validation in similar or comparable clinical settings is difficult to accomplish. Despite such difficulties, however, the implementation of matching procedures based on empirical findings with matching variables appropriate to particular clinical settings remains an important objective, especially in large-scale clinical systems such as comprehensive care centers.

Other Asymmetrical Matching Variables

It is obviously beyond the scope of the present review to examine exhaustively the many recent studies in which some set of therapist or treatment variables have been conjoined with a set of patient variables, and in which interaction effects have emerged. Psychotherapy research, however, appears to be moving both in the directions associated with Bergin's and Strupp's calls for greater specificity in defining meaningful treatment, therapist, and patient dimensions (Bergin & Suinn, 1975; Strupp & Bergin, 1969) and the directions suggested by Kiesler's Grid Model (Kiesler, 1969, 1971). Whereas Paul (1966), for example, clearly specified the techniques of systematic desensitization in his classic study, he failed to do likewise for "traditional" therapy. Subsequent researchers (e.g., DiLoreto, 1971; Meichenbaum *et al.*, 1971) have remedied this neglect with regard to several systematic "insight" approaches. Thus, while we may not have made much progress in discovering just which therapist and patient variables are truly decisive for the outcomes of psychotherapy, more variables are being included simultaneously in the same design than in the past, and we can hope that such comparative efforts will bear fruit.

The most popular current approach appears to be comparing two or more different treatment modalities (rather than therapist personality characteristics) relative to two or more subgroups or types of patients. With regard to the latter, the attention paid to Rotter's internal-external locus of control construct as a patient variable (Rotter, 1966; see also Rotter, 1975) warrants particular mention. The intuitively appealing notion that patients who believe that important reinforcements are attributable to their own efforts (internals) and patients who attribute important reinforcements to chance, luck, and the like (externals) should require different therapeutic approaches or should respond differentially to a particular treatment modality is gaining impetus (e.g., Abramowitz, Abramowitz, Roback, & Jackson, 1974; Best, 1975; Best & Steffy, 1971, in press; Friedman & Dies, 1974). Best's (1975) study, for example, examined the effects of tailoring treatment procedures to clients' internal-external beliefs so as to facilitate abstinence from smoking; prior to the first formal treatment session, internals were exposed to stimulus satiation aversion procedures, whereas externals were encouraged to conduct situational analyses of environmental cues that influence their smoking. Abramowitz et al. (1974), on the other hand, considered directive group therapy techniques appropriate for externally oriented patients, and nondirective ones for internally oriented patients. Interaction effects conjoining treatment modality and client characteristics were significant in both studies.

Asymmetrical Matching Variables: Overview

The asymmetrical perspective on matching holds that the independent variables employed to detect potential interaction effects need not be the same for therapist and patient. Although the major attention in this section was devoted to asymmetrical studies that divided therapists according to personality rather than treatment variables, recent trends toward increased specificity in defining treatment modalities and patient subgroups were noted as promising. If matching research is to affect clinical practice, however, its results will need to be more impressive than they have been thus far. Apart from the Indiana Matching Project and the few other attempts to match dyads prior to therapy, most of the research can be regarded as strictly exploratory.

The obvious challenge to psychotherapy researchers is to intensify their search for promising matching variables and to coordinate them with the unique boundary conditions of particular clinical settings. It seems likely that this quest will involve a multiplicity of therapist-patient variable combinations rather than the supremacy of some "definitive" set of findings; matching variables that enhance treatment with YAVIS patients need not be the same as those that enhance results with non-YAVIS patients (cf. Goldstein, 1971). A liberal view of future research would emphasize the need for both clinical and laboratory analogue studies examining interpersonal compatibility variables in both YAVIS and non-YAVIS patient contexts.

Just as the interactive variables that facilitate initial therapist-patient communication need not be the same as the variables that determine the quality of outcomes among patients who stay in therapy, it seems entirely appropriate to consider the symmetrical and asymmetrical perspectives as equally useful for further research. Certain variables (e.g., socioeconomic similarity, compatible Interpersonal Circle quadrant combinations) may be more important in early therapy, whereas others (e.g., therapists' technical interventions; patients' symptom patterns) may become important later. Therefore, it would seem advisable to combine the symmetrical and asymmetrical perspectives in the same design.

To institute actual matching, however, we need not only know what pre-therapy measures are important but we need to have confidence that the criterion measures against which the effects of matching are evaluated are trustworthy. As we have argued elsewhere, outcome measurement needs to encompass as much consensus among sources of evaluation (e.g., therapists, patients, independent judges) as possible (Berzins et al., 1975).[9]

CONCLUSIONS AND RECOMMENDATIONS

On both theoretical and empirical grounds, our understanding of interactive variables in psychotherapy barely exceeds common sense. Whether the independent variables be the same for therapist and patient (symmetrical perspective) or different (asymmetrical perspective), the available evidence does not justify modifications of current, admittedly adventitious, procedures for pairing patients with therapists.

Among theoretical leads, the conceptualization of therapeutic interactions in terms of the dimensions and categories of the Interpersonal Circle seems the most promising, although the central proposition that dyadic similarity on the LOV dimension and complementarity on the DOM dimension facilitate therapeutic communication or outcomes has not been tested rigorously in short- or long-term therapy. Among methodological recommendations, the structure of Kiesler's Grid Model, with its emphasis on studying temporal changes in homogeneous therapist-patient dyads, seems the most constructive, if abstract, guide for further matching research. Although the entire field of psychotherapy research suffers from a lack of coordination between theory and empirical data and an absence of trustworthy measures of outcome, recent trends toward tailoring treatment modalities so as to be differentially effective with various subgroups of patients suggest that increases in both theoretical and empirical specificity are likely.

While it seems clear that studies of global therapist-patient similarity have been conceptually simplistic and empirically flawed (especially with regard to similarity indices that do not permit separation of interactive and main effects), there is no intrinsic reason for preferring asymmetrical variable designs over symmetrical ones. Rather, they should be combined whenever possible. Important symmetrical variables such as participants' gender, Interpersonal Circle quadrant placement, socioeconomic status, expectancies, and others, can be combined factorially with asymmetrical variables such as treatment modalities, therapists' personality dimensions, patients' diagnoses, symptom patterns, etc., depending on their salience in particular clinical settings.

With regard to the asymmetrical approach, the attention devoted to tailoring treatment modalities to specific patient characteristics will need to be extended into an appraisal of the match or interaction between therapists' personality and technique variables. Even though therapists are in small supply in many settings, collaborative research could clarify the personological grounds for therapists' preferences for (or aversion to) such techniques as confrontation, self-disclosure, implosion, aversive conditioning, and so forth. Further attention to symmetrical variables could take as its keynote the need for more comprehensive sampling of interpersonally salient behaviors. In this regard, the categories of the Interpersonal Circle encompass a wider variety of potentially relevant behaviors than do single individual difference dimensions, (e.g., beliefs in internal-external control).

In considering promising individual difference variables for further matching research, it becomes apparent that interpersonal theory can be amalgamated with recent developments in sex-role theory and research. As long as masculinity-femininity was confounded with gender and sex-role stereotypes (Constantinople, 1973), sex roles were considered to vary along a single bipolar dimension ranging from "sex-appropriate" to "sex-reversed" placements, depending on the person's gender; one could not be classified as *both* masculine and feminine ("androgynous"). New conceptions of sex roles, however, construe

masculinity and femininity as dual (not opposite) components of human behavior, involving distinctions between agency and communion (Bakan, 1966; Block, 1973), instrumental and expressive orientations (Parsons & Bales, 1955), or dominance and nurturance. If, like the DOM and LOV axes of the Interpersonal Circle, masculinity and femininity are considered independent (orthogonal) coordinates for cross-classifying interpersonal behaviors, then traditionally masculine sex-typing can be seen as an emphasis on "masculine" and a repudiation of "feminine" components of one's behavioral repertoire; feminine sex-typing, in turn, over-emphasizes femininity and repudiates masculinity. An androgynous person accepts both masculine and feminine aspects of the self, whereas an "indeterminate" person endorses neither. In terms of the Interpersonal Circle, masculine-type persons, regardless of gender, would place in the hostile-dominant quadrant; feminine-typed persons, in the friendly-submissive quadrant; androgynous persons, in the friendly-dominant quadrant; and indeterminates, in the hostile-submissive quadrant. Thus conceptualized, the sex-role orientations of therapists and patients (hitherto implicated to some extent in research with the A-B variable) could be assessed directly and examined for their dyadic significance in symmetrical studies. Indeed, the behavioral flexibility associated with the androgynous orientation (Bem, 1974) is strongly reminiscent of Carson's (1969) sketch of the effective therapist who can move to various positions of the Interpersonal Circle at will. Several new measuring instruments are available for assessing sex roles as independent variables (Bem, 1974; Berzins & Welling, 1974;[10] Spence et al., 1975).

If we grant that a fully functioning, androgynous person can be "*both* masculine and feminine, *both* assertive and yielding, *both* instrumental and expressive—depending on the situational appropriateness of these various behaviors" (Bem, 1974, p. 155), then measures of psychological androgyny can also be examined as dependent (outcome) variables in psychotherapy research. Although hyperfeminine women often receive assertiveness training or encouragement from their therapists, hypermasculine men are seldom considered to require "love" or "nurturance" training. But if traditional sex-typing engenders deficits in both sexes (Bem, 1974), psychotherapy theory, research, and practice will have to move toward a more androgynous conception of healthy behavior.

Finally, even if future research should disclose

more powerful interactive variables, the crucial issue confronting all attempts to match patients with therapists or therapies is the pragmatic matter of incremental validity. To what extent will the matching algorithm improve upon the usual outcomes yielded by a clinical system, and to what extent will matching improve on the results that could be obtained by replacing the less competent therapists in that system with more competent ones?

REFERENCES

ABRAMOWITZ, C. V., ABRAMOWITZ, S. I., ROBACK, H. B., & JACKSON, C. Differential effectiveness of directive and nondirective group therapies as a function of client internal-external control. *Journal of Consulting and Clinical Psychology*, 1974, **42**, 849–853.

ALEXANDER, J. F., & ABELES, N. Dependency changes in psychotherapy as related to interpersonal relationships. *Journal of Consulting and Clinical Psychology*, 1968, **32**, 685–689.

ANZEL, A. A-B typing and patient socioeconomic and personality characteristics in a quasi-therapeutic situation. *Journal of Consulting and Clinical Psychology*, 1970, **35**, 102–115.

APFELBAUM, B. *Dimensions of transference in psychotherapy*. Berkeley and Los Angeles: University of California Press, 1958.

BAKAN, D. *The duality of human existence*. Chicago: Rand McNally, 1966.

BANDURA, A. Psychotherapy based upon modeling principles. In A. E. BERGIN & S. L. GARFIELD (Eds.), *Handbook of psychotherapy and behavior change: An empirical analysis*. New York: Wiley, 1971.

BARE, C. E. Relationship of counselor personality and counselor-client similarity to selected counseling success criteria. *Journal of Counseling Psychology*, 1967, **14**, 419–425.

BARNES, D. F. A and B college students as interviewers of schizophrenic and neurotic inpatients: A test of the interaction hypothesis. Unpublished doctoral dissertation, University of Kentucky, 1972.

BEERY, J. W. Therapists' responses as a function of level of therapist experience and attitude of the patient. *Journal of Consulting and Clinical Psychology*, 1970, **34**, 239–243.

BEGLEY, C. E., & LIEBERMAN, L. R. Patient expectations of therapists' techniques. *Journal of Clinical Psychology*, 1970, **26**, 112–116.

BEIER, E. G. *The silent language of psychotherapy*. Chicago: Aldine, 1966.

BEM, S. L. The measurement of psychological androgyny. *Journal of Consulting and Clinical Psychology*, 1974, **42**, 155–162.

BENJAMIN, L. S. Structural analysis of social behavior. *Psychological Review*, 1974, **81**, 392–425.

BERGIN, A. E. The evaluation of therapeutic outcomes. In A. E. BERGIN & S. L. GARFIELD (Eds.), *Handbook of psychotherapy and behavior change: An empirical analysis*. New York: Wiley, 1971.

BERGIN, A. E., & SUINN, R. M. Individual psychotherapy and behavior therapy. *Annual Review of Psychology*, 1975, **26**, 509–556.

BERZINS, J. I. Matching patients with therapists: Conceptual, empirical, and pragmatic perspectives. Paper presented at the fifth Annual Meeting of the Society for Psychotherapy Research, Denver, Colorado, June 1974.

BERZINS, J. I., BARNES, D. F., COHEN, D. I., & ROSS, W. F. A reappraisal of the A-B therapist "type" distinction in terms of the Personality Research Form. *Journal of Consulting and Clinical Psychology*, 1971, **36**, 360–369.

BERZINS, J. I., BEDNAR, R. L., & SEVERY, L. J. The problem of intersource consensus in measuring therapeutic outcomes: New data and multivariate perspectives. *Journal of Abnormal Psychology*, 1975, **84**, 10–19.

BERZINS, J. I., DOVE, J. L., & ROSS, W. F. Cross-validational studies of the personality correlates of the A-B therapist "type" distinction among professionals and nonprofessionals. *Journal of Consulting and Clinical Psychology*, 1972, **39**, 388–395.

BERZINS, J. I., HERRON, E. W., & SEIDMAN, E. Patients' role-behaviors as seen by therapists: A factor-analytic study. *Psychotherapy: Theory, Research, and Practice*, 1971, **8**, 127–130.

BERZINS, J. I., ROSS, W. F., & FRIEDMAN, W. H. The A-B therapist distinction, patient diagnosis, and outcome of brief psychotherapy in a college clinic. *Journal of Consulting and Clinical Psychology*, 1972, **38**, 231–237.

BERZINS, J. I., & SEIDMAN, E. Subjective reactions of A and B quasi-therapists to schizoid and neurotic communications: A replication and extension. *Journal of Consulting and Clinical Psychology*, 1968, **32**, 342–347.

BERZINS, J. I., & SEIDMAN, E. Differential therapeutic responding of A and B quasi-therapists to schizoid and neurotic communications. *Journal of Consulting and Clinical Psychology*, 1969, **33**, 279–286.

BERZINS, J. I., & WELLING, M. The Berzins–Welling PRF-ANDRO Scale. Unpublished manuscript, University of Kentucky, 1974.

BEST, J. A. Tailoring smoking withdrawal procedures to personality and motivational differences. *Journal of Consulting and Clinical Psychology*, 1975, **43**, 1–8.

BEST, J. A., & STEFFY, R. A. Smoking modification procedures tailored to subject characteristics. *Behavior Therapy*, 1971, **2**, 177–191.

BEST, J. A., & STEFFY, R. A. Smoking modification procedures for internal and external locus of control clients. *Canadian Journal of Behavioral Science*, in press.

BETZ, B. J. Experiences in research in psychotherapy with schizophrenic patients. In H. H. STRUPP & L. LUBORSKY (Eds.), *Research in psychotherapy*. Vol. II. Washington, D.C.: American Psychological Association, 1962.

BETZ, B. J. Studies of the therapist's role in the treatment of schizophrenic patients. *American Journal of Psychiatry*, 1967, **123**, 963–971.

BEUTLER, L. E., JOHNSON, D. T., NEVILLE, C. W., ELKINS, D., & JOBE, A. M. Attitude similarity and therapist credibility as predictors of attitude change and improvement in psychotherapy. *Journal of Consulting and Clinical Psychology*, 1975, **43**, 90–91.

BEUTLER, L. E., JOHNSON, D. T., NEVILLE, C. W., & WORKMAN, S. N. "Accurate empathy" and the A-B dichotomy. *Journal of Consulting and Clinical Psychology*, 1972, **38**, 372–375.

BEUTLER, L. E., JOHNSON, D. T., NEVILLE, C. W., WORKMAN, S. N., & ELKINS, D. The A-B therapist type distinction, accurate empathy, nonpossessive warmth, and therapist genuineness in psychotherapy. *Journal of Abnormal Psychology*, 1973, **82**, 273–277.

BLOCK, J. H. Conceptions of sex role: Some cross-cultural and longitudinal perspectives. *American Psychologist*, 1973, **28**, 512–527.

BORDIN, E. S. The implications of client expectations for the counseling process. *Journal of Counseling Psychology*, 1955, **2**, 17–21.

BORGHI, J. H. Premature termination of psychotherapy and patient-therapist expectations. *American Journal of Psychotherapy*, 1968, **22**, 460–473.

BOULWARE, D. W., & HOLMES, D. S. Preferences for therapists and related expectancies. *Journal of Consulting and Clinical Psychology*, 1970, **35**, 269–277.

BROOKS, L. Interactive effects of sex and status on self-disclosure. *Journal of Counseling Psychology*, 1974, **21**, 469–474.

BROVERMAN, I. K., BROVERMAN, D. M., CLARKSON, F. E., ROSENKRANTZ, P. S., & VOGEL, S. R. Sex-role stereotypes and clinical judgments of mental health. *Journal of Consulting and Clinical Psychology*, 1970, **34**, 1–7.

BYRNE, D. *The attraction paradigm*. New York: Academic Press, 1971.

CARKHUFF, R. R., & BERENSON, B. G. *Beyond counseling and therapy*. New York: Holt, Rinehart & Winston, 1967.

CARKHUFF, R. R., & PIERCE, R. Differential effects of therapists' race and social class upon patient depth of self-exploration in the initial clinical interview. *Journal of Consulting Psychology*, 1967, **31**, 632–634.

CARLSON, R. Where is the person in personality research? *Psychological Bulletin*, 1971, **75**, 203–219.

CARR, J. E. Differentiation similarity of patient and therapist and the outcome of psychotherapy. *Journal of Abnormal Psychology*, 1970, **76**, 361–369.

CARSON, R. C. A and B therapist "types": A possible critical variable in psychotherapy. *Journal of Nervous and Mental Disease*, 1967, **144**, 47–54.

CARSON, R. C. *Interaction concepts of personality*. Chicago: Aldine, 1969.

CARSON, R. C., HARDEN, J. A., & SHOWS, W. D. A-B distinction and behavior in quasi-therapeutic situations. *Journal of Consulting Psychology*, 1964, **28**, 426–433.

CARSON, R. C., & HEINE, R. W. Similarity and success in therapeutic dyads. *Journal of Consulting Psychology*, 1962, **26**, 38–43.

CARSON, R. C., & LLEWELLYN, C. E. Similarity in therapeutic dyads: A reevaluation. *Journal of Consulting Psychology*, 1966, **30**, 458.

CARTWRIGHT, R. D., & LERNER, B. Empathy, need to change, and improvement with psychotherapy. *Journal of Consulting Psychology*, 1963, **27**, 138–144.

CHARTIER, G. M. The A-B therapist variable: Real or imagined? *Psychological Bulletin*, 1971, **75**, 22–33.

CLEMES, S., & D'ANDREA, V. Patients' anxiety as a function of expectations and degree of initial interview ambiguity. *Journal of Consulting Psychology*, 1965, **29**, 397–404.

CONSTANTINOPLE, A. Masculinity–femininity: An exception to a famous dictum? *Psychological Bulletin*, 1973, **80** 389–407.

COOK, T. The influence of client-counselor value similarity on change in meaning during brief counseling. *Journal of Counseling Psychology*, 1966, **13**, 77–81.

COOLEY, W. W., & LOHNES, P. R. *Multivariate data analysis*. New York: Wiley, 1971.

CROWDER, J. E. Relationship between therapist and client interpersonal behaviors and psychotherapy outcome. *Journal of Counseling Psychology*, 1972, **19**, 68–75.

DILORETO, A. O. *Comparative psychotherapy: An experimental analysis*. Chicago: Aldine-Atherton, 1971.

DUBLIN, J. E., & BERZINS, J. I. The A-B variable and reactions to non-immediacy in neurotic and schizoid communications: A longitudinal analogue of psychotherapy. *Journal of Consulting and Clinical Psychology*, 1972, **39**, 86–93.

DUBLIN, J. E., ELTON, C. F., & BERZINS, J. I. Some personality and aptitudinal correlates of the "A-B" therapist scale. *Journal of Consulting and Clinical Psychology*, 1969, **33**, 739–745.

EDWARDS, B. C., & EDGERLY, J. W. Effects of counselor-client cognitive congruence on counseling outcome in brief counseling. *Journal of Counseling Psychology*, 1970, **17**, 313–318.

ERON, L. D., & CALLAHAN, R. (Eds.) *The relationship of theory to practice in psychotherapy*. Chicago: Aldine, 1969.

FISKE, D. W., HUNT, H. F., LUBORSKY, L., ORNE, M. T., PARLOFF, M. B., REISER, M. F., & TUMA, A. H. Planning of research on effectiveness of psychotherapy. *American Psychologist*, 1970, **25**, 727–737.

FRANK, J. D. *Persuasion and healing*. Baltimore: Johns Hopkins Press, 1961.

FRIEDMAN, M. L., & DIES, R. R. Reactions of internal and external test anxious students to counseling and behavior therapies. *Journal of Consulting and Clinical Psychology*, 1974, **42**, 921.

FULLER, F. F. Influence of sex of counselor and of client on client expressions of feeling. *Journal of Counseling Psychology*, 1963, **10**, 34–40.

GARFIELD, S. L., & WOLPIN, M. Expectations regarding psychotherapy. *Journal of Nervous and Mental Disease*, 1963, **137**, 353–362.

GASSNER, S. M. Relationship between patient-therapist compatibility and treatment effectiveness. *Journal of Consulting and Clinical Psychology*, 1970, **34**, 408–414.

GELLER, J. D., & BERZINS, J. I. The A-B distinction in a sample of prominent psychotherapists. *Journal of Consulting and Clinical Psychology*, 1975, **44**, 77–82.

GOIN, M. K., YAMAMOTO, J., & SILVERMAN, J. Therapy congruent with class-linked expectations. *Archives of General Psychiatry*, 1965, **13**, 133–137.

GOLDMAN, R. K., & MENDELSOHN, G. A. Psychotherapeutic change and social adjustment: A report of a national survey of psychotherapists. *Journal of Abnormal Psychology*, 1969, **74**, 164–172.

GOLDSTEIN, A. P. Therapist and client expectations of personality change in psychotherapy. *Journal of Counseling Psychology*, 1960, **7**, 180–184.

GOLDSTEIN, A. P. *Therapist-patient expectancies in psychotherapy*. New York: Pergamon Press, 1962.

GOLDSTEIN, A. P. Maximizing expectancy effects in psychotherapeutic practice. *Interactional Journal of Psychiatry*, 1968, **5**, 397–400.

GOLDSTEIN, A. P. *Psychotherapeutic attraction*. New York: Pergamon Press, 1971.

GOLDSTEIN, A. P. *Structured learning therapy: Toward a psychotherapy for the poor*. New York: Academic Press, 1973.

GOODWIN, W. B., GELLER, J. D., & QUINLAN, D. M. Attitudes toward sex roles among A and B psychotherapists. *Journal of Consulting and Clinical Psychology*, 1973, **41**, 471.

GREEN, M. H. The effectiveness of A and B college males as interviewers, as response-biasers and verbal conditioners with schizophrenic and neurotic patients. Unpublished doctoral dissertation, University of Kentucky, 1971.

HALPERN, H. M. An essential ingredient in successful psychotherapy. *Psychotherapy: Theory, Research and Practice*, 1965, **2**, 177–180.

HARARI, H. Interpersonal models in psychotherapy and counseling: A social-psychological analysis of a clinical problem. *Journal of Abnormal Psychology*, 1971, **78**, 127–133.

HEINE, R. W., & TROSMAN, H. Initial expectations of the doctor-patient interaction as a factor in continuance in psychotherapy. *Psychiatry*, 1960, **23**, 275–278.

HELLER, K., MYERS, R. A., & KLINE, L. V. Interviewer behavior as a function of standardized client roles. *Journal of Consulting Psychology*, 1963, **27**, 117–122.

HENRY, W. E., SIMS, J. H., & SPRAY, S. L. *The fifth profession*. San Francisco: Jossey-Bass, 1971.

HOEHN-SARIC, R., FRANK, J. D., IMBER, S. D., NASH, E. H., STONE, A. R., & BATTLE, C. C. Systematic preparation of patients for psychotherapy. I. Effects on therapy behavior and outcome. *Journal of Psychiatric Research*, 1964, **2**, 267–281.

HOLLINGSHEAD, A. B., & REDLICH, F. C. *Social class and mental illness*. New York: Wiley, 1958.

HOWARD, K. I., & ORLINSKY, D. E. Psychotherapeutic processes. In P. MUSSEN & M. ROSENZWEIG (Eds.), *Annual review of psychology*. Vol. 23. Palo Alto, Calif.: Annual Reviews, 1972.

HOWARD, K. I., ORLINSKY, D. E., & HILL, J. A. Patients' satisfactions in psychotherapy as a function of patient-therapist pairing. *Psychotherapy: Theory, Research and Practice*, 1970, **7**, 130–134.

JACKSON, D. N. *Personality Research Form Manual*. Goshen, N.Y.: Research Psychologists Press, 1967.

JAMES, L. E., & FOREMAN, M. E. A-B status of behavior therapy technicians as related to success of Mowrer's conditioning treatment for neurosis, *Journal of Consulting and Clinical Psychology*, 1973, **41**, 224–229.

JOHNSON, D. T., NEVILLE, C. W., & WORKMAN, S. N. A-B therapy scale: MMPI and 16 PF correlates for male and female psychiatric inpatients. Paper presented at the meeting of the Southeastern Psychological Association, New Orleans, February 1969.

KEMP, D. E. Correlates of the Whitehorn–Betz AB scale in a quasi-therapeutic situation. *Journal of Consulting Psychology*, 1966, **30**, 509–516.

KIESLER, D. J. Some myths of psychotherapy research and the search for a paradigm. *Psychological Bulletin*, 1966, **65**, 110–136.

KIESLER, D. J. A Grid Model for theory and research in the psychotherapies. In L. D. ERON & R. CALLAHAN (Eds.), *The relationship of theory to practice in psychotherapy*. Chicago: Aldine, 1969.

KIESLER, D. J. Experimental designs in psychotherapy research. In A. E. BERGIN & S. L. GARFIELD (Eds.), *Handbook of psychotherapy and behavior change: An empirical analysis*. New York: Wiley, 1971.

LANDFIELD, A. W. *Personal construct systems in psychotherapy*. Chicago: Rand McNally, 1971.

LAZARUS, A. A. *Behavior therapy and beyond*. New York: McGraw-Hill, 1971.

LEARY, T. *Interpersonal diagnosis of personality*. New York: Ronald Press, 1957.

LEE, S. D., & TEMERLIN, M. K. Social class, diagnosis, and prognosis for psychotherapy. *Psychotherapy: Theory, Research and Practice*, 1970, **7**, 181–185.

LENNARD, H. L., & BERNSTEIN, A. *The anatomy of psychotherapy*, New York: Columbia University Press, 1960.

LENNARD, H. L., & BERNSTEIN, A. Role learning in psychotherapy. *Psychotherapy: Theory, Research and Practice*, 1967, **4**, 1–6.

LEVITT, E. E. Psychotherapy research and the expectation-reality discrepancy. *Psychotherapy: Theory, Research and Practice*, 1966, **3**, 163–166.

LICHTENSTEIN, E. Personality similarity and therapeutic success: A failure to replicate. *Journal of Consulting Psychology*, 1966, **30**, 282.

LORION, R. P. Patient and therapist variables in the treatment of low-income patients. *Psychological Bulletin*, 1974a, **81**, 344–354.

LORION, R. P. Social class, treatment attitudes, and expectations. *Journal of Consulting and Clinical Psychology*, 1974b, **42**, 920.

LORR, M., & McNAIR, D. M. Methods relating to evaluation of therapeutic outcome. In L. A. GOTTSCHALK & A. H. AUERBACH (Eds.), *Methods of research in psychotherapy*. New York: Appleton-Century-Crofts, 1966.

LUBORSKY, L., CHANDLER, M., AUERBACH, A. H., COHEN, J., & BACHRACH, H. M. Factors influencing the outcome of psychotherapy: A review of quantitative research. *Psychological Bulletin*, 1971, **75**, 145–185.

MACCOBY, E. E., & JACKLIN, C. N. *The psychology of sex differences*. Stanford, Calif.: Stanford University Press, 1974.

MAY, P. R. A. A brave new world revisited: Alphas, betas, and treatment outcome. *Comprehensive Psychiatry*, 1974, **15**, 1–17.

McLACHLAN, J. C. Benefit from group therapy as a function of patient-therapist match on conceptual level. *Psychotherapy: Theory, Research and Practice*, 1972, **9**, 317–323.

McNAIR, D. M., CALLAHAN, D. M., & LORR, M. Therapist "type" and patient response to psychotherapy. *Journal of Consulting Psychology*, 1962, **26**, 425–429.

MEICHENBAUM, D. H., GILMORE, J. B., & FEDORAVICIUS, A.

Group insight versus group desensitization in treating speech anxiety. *Journal of Consulting and Clinical Psychology*, 1971, **36**, 410–421.

MELTZOFF, J., & KORNREICH, M. *Research in psychotherapy*. New York: Atherton, 1970.

MENDELSOHN, G. A. Effects of client personality and client-counselor similarity on the duration of counseling: A replication and extension. *Journal of Counseling Psychology*, 1966, **13**, 228–234.

MENDELSOHN, G. A. Client-counselor compatibility and the effectiveness of counseling. Unpublished manuscript, University of California, Berkeley, 1968.

MENDELSOHN, G. A., & GELLER, M. H. Effects of counselor-client similarity on the outcome of counseling. *Journal of Counseling Psychology*, 1963, **10**, 71–77.

MENDELSOHN, G. A., & GELLER, M. H. Structure of client attitudes toward counseling and their relation to client-counselor similarity. *Journal of Consulting and Clinical Psychology*, 1965, **29**, 63–72.

MENDELSOHN, G. A., & GELLER, M. H. Similarity, missed sessions, and early termination. *Journal of Counseling Psychology*, 1967, **14**, 210–215.

MENDELSOHN, G. A., & RANKIN, N. O. Client-counselor compatibility and the outcome of counseling. *Journal of Abnormal Psychology*, 1969, **74**, 157–163.

MILLON, T. *Modern psychopathology*, Philadelphia: Saunders, 1969.

MUELLER, W. J., & DILLING, C. A. Therapist-client interview behavior and personality characteristics of therapists. *Journal of Projective Techniques and Personality Assessment*, 1968, **32**, 281–288.

OVERALL, B., & ARONSON, H. Expectations of psychotherapy in patients of lower socioeconomic class. *American Journal of Orthopsychiatry*, 1963, **33**, 421–430.

PARSONS, T., & BALES, R. F. *Family, socialization, and interaction process*. New York: Free Press, 1955.

PAUL, G. L. *Insight vs. desensitization in psychotherapy*. Stanford, Calif.: Stanford University Press, 1966.

PETTIT, I. B., PETTIT, T. F., & WELKOWITZ, J. Relationship between values, social class, and duration of psychotherapy. *Journal of Consulting and Clinical Psychology*, 1974, **42**, 482–490.

RAZIN, A. M. The A-B variable in psychotherapy: A critical review. *Psychological Bulletin*, 1971, **75**, 1–21.

RICKERS-OVSIANKINA, M. A., BERZINS, J. I., GELLER, J. D., & ROGERS, G. W. Patients' role-expectancies in psychotherapy: A theoretical and measurement approach. *Psychotherapy: Theory, Research and Practice*, 1971, **8**, 124–126.

ROSENTHAL, D. Changes in some moral values following psychotherapy. *Journal of Consulting Psychology*, 1955, **19**, 431–436.

ROTTER, J. B. *Social learning and clinical psychology*. Englewood Cliffs, N.J.: Prentice-Hall, 1954.

ROTTER, J. B. Generalized expectancies for internal versus external control of reinforcement. *Psychological Monographs*, 1966, **80**, No. 1 (Whole No. 609).

ROTTER, J. B. Some problems and misconceptions related to the construct of internal versus external control of reinforcement. *Journal of Consulting and Clinical Psychology*, 1975, **43**, 56–67.

RYCHLAK, J. F. The motives to psychotherapy. *Psychotherapy: Theory, Research and Practice*, 1965, **2**, 151–157.

SANDLER, D. *Investigation of a scale of therapeutic effectiveness: Trust and suspicion in an experimentally induced situation*. Doctoral dissertation, Duke University (Ann Arbor, Mich.: University Microfilms, 1965. No. 66-1382).

SAPOLSKY, A. Relationship between patient-doctor compatibility, mutual perception, and outcome of treatment. *Journal of Abnormal Psychology*, 1965, **70**, 70–76.

SCHOFIELD, W. *Psychotherapy, the purchase of friendship*. Englewood Cliffs, N.J.: Prentice-Hall, 1964.

SCHONFIELD, J., STONE, A. R., HOEHN-SARIC, R., IMBER,

S. D., & Pande, S. K. Patient-therapist convergence and measures of improvement in short-term psychotherapy. *Psychotherapy: Theory, Research and Practice*, 1969, **6**, 267–272.

Schutz, W. C. *FIRO: A three-dimensional theory of interpersonal behavior*. New York: Holt, Rinehart & Winston, 1958.

Scott, R. W., & Kemp, D. E. The A-B scale and empathy, warmth, genuineness, and depth of self-exploration. *Journal of Abnormal Psychology*, 1971, **77**, 49–51.

Segal, B. A-B distinction and therapeutic interaction. *Journal of Consulting and Clinical Psychology*, 1970, **34**, 442–446.

Seidman, E. A and B subject-therapists' responses to video-taped schizoid and neurotic prototypes. *Journal of Consulting and Clinical Psychology*, 1971, **37**, 201–208.

Shapiro, A. K. Placebo effects in medicine, psychotherapy, and psychoanalysis. In A. E. Bergin & S. L. Garfield (Eds.), *Handbook of psychotherapy and behavior change: An empirical analysis*. New York: Wiley, 1971.

Sloane, R. B. Short-term analytically oriented therapy versus behavior therapy. Paper presented at the Fifth Annual Meeting of the Society for Psychotherapy Research, Denver, Colorado, June 1974.

Spence, J. T., Helmreich, R., & Stapp, J. Ratings of self and peers on sex-role attributes and their relation to self-esteem and conceptions of masculinity and femininity, *Journal of Personality and Social Psychology*, 1975, **32**, 29–39.

Strupp, H. H., & Bergin, A. E. Some empirical and conceptual bases for coordinated research in psychotherapy: A critical review of issues, trends, and evidence. *International Journal of Psychiatry*, 1969, **7**, 18–90.

Sue, S., McKinney, H., Allen, D., & Hall, J. Delivery of community mental health services to black and white clients. *Journal of Consulting and Clinical Psychology*, 1974, **42**, 794–801.

Sullivan, H. S. *Collected works*. New York: Basic Books, 1965.

Swensen, C. H. Psychotherapy as a special case of dyadic interaction: Some suggestions for theory and research. *Psychotherapy: Theory, Research and Practice*, 1967, **4**, 7–13.

Swensen, C. H. *Introduction to interpersonal relations*. Glenview, Ill.: Scott, Foresman, 1973.

Trattner, J. H., & Howard, K. I. A preliminary investigation of covert communication of expectancies to schizophrenics. *Journal of Abnormal Psychology*, 1970, **75**, 245–247.

Truax, C. B., & Carkhuff, R. R. *Toward effective counseling and psychotherapy*. Chicago: Aldine, 1967.

Veldman, D. J. *Fortran programming for the behavioral sciences*. New York: Holt, Rinehart & Winston, 1967.

Welch, R. D. The effectiveness of A and B college males as models and interviewers with schizophrenic and neurotic patients. Unpublished doctoral dissertation, University of Kentucky, 1971.

Welkowitz, J., Cohen, J., & Ortmeyer, D. Value system similarity: Investigation of patient-therapist dyads. *Journal of Consulting Psychology*, 1967, **31**, 48–55.

Wilkins, W. Expectancy of therapeutic gain: An empirical and conceptual critique. *Journal of Consulting and Clinical Psychology*, 1973, **40**, 69–77.

Williams, H. V., Lipman, R. S., Uhlenhuth, E. H., Rickels, K., Covi, L., & Mock, J. Some factors influencing the treatment expectations of anxious neurotic out-patients. *Journal of Nervous and Mental Disease*, 1967, **145**, 208–220.

Wogan, M. Effect of therapist-patient personality variables on therapeutic outcome. *Journal of Consulting and Clinical Psychology*, 1970, **35**, 356–361.

Ziemelis, A. Effects of client preference and expectancy upon the initial interview. *Journal of Counseling Psychology*, 1974, **21**, 23–30.

EDITORS' REFERENCES

Razin, A. The A-B variable and therapist persuasiveness. *Journal of Nervous and Mental Disease*, 1974, **159**, 244–255.

Seidman, E., Golding, S., Hogan, T., & Lebow, M. A multidimensional interpretation and comparison of three A-B scales. *Journal of Consulting and Clinical Psychology*, 1974, **42**, 10–20.

NOTES

1. Because the results of the Indiana Matching Project, described briefly in this chapter, have not yet been published elsewhere, the author wishes to acknowledge his gratitude to his collaborators in that research, William H. Friedman and Wesley F. Ross. A full description of the project is in preparation. Special thanks are extended also to Martha A. Welling for her editorial and substantive contributions to the preparation of this chapter.

2. *Editors' Footnote*. While this was true of early behavior therapists, more recently the views of behaviorists have changed tremendously. See Wilson and Evans (Chapter 20, this volume).

3. For the most recent three-dimensional extension of Leary's model, see Benjamin (1974).

4. *Editors' Footnote*. This is an important point, demonstrated in the chapters of Gurman and of Mitchell, Bozarth, and Krauft in this volume, both of which show the surprisingly low levels of facilitativeness found among therapists in most studies.

5. *Editors' Footnote*. Berzins' distinction between symmetric and asymmetric studies is quite useful, as will be seen toward the end of the chapter. We think it is much more than a semantic distinction, and that the major, if not sole, basis for it is the consideration of "personality" in symmetric research versus "roles" in asymmetric research. Thus, for example, any therapist *could* have a diagnosis, or even a presenting problem, if he assumed the role of a patient, as could a patient use techniques if he were a therapist in a different situation. "Personality" or symmetric characteristics, though, cannot be so characterized.

6. *Editors' Footnote*. See, in contrast, Sattler (Chapter 11, this volume) for a detailed examination of therapist and patient racial factors influencing the process and outcome of psychotherapy.

7. *Editors' Footnote*. See Wilkins (Chapter 13, this volume) for a very comprehensive and persuasive critical consideration of these issues.

8. *Editors' Footnote*. Characterizations of the A-B dimension as primarily based on masculine-feminine sex-role differences have, however, been criticized as oversimplistic by Seidman, Golding, Hogan, and Lebow (1974), whose work is discussed in Razin's chapter in this volume.

9. *Editors' Footnote*. While we, of course, agree that outcome measures need to be trustworthy, it is not at all clear to us that there exists, or ought to exist, high degrees of consensus among patients, therapists, and judges rating process or outcome. Fiske and Gurman in their chapters, in this volume for example, and Razin (1974) argue that, although perhaps low-moderate correlations are to be expected, there are important differences among these viewpoints which should not allow for very great similarity of assessments, no matter how internally reliable the measures used.

10. This recently developed instrument, the Berzins-Welling PRF ANDRO scale, permits investigators to derive separate masculinity and femininity scores from the items of Form A or AA of the Personality Research Form (PRF) (Jackson, 1967). PRF data originally collected for other purposes can consequently be reex-

amined in sex-role terms. The theoretical definitions of the ANDRO scale constructs closely resemble those of Bem's (1974) Sex Role Inventory (BSRI). The cross-validated correlation between the ANDRO and BSRI androgyny difference scores (femininity minus masculinity) is .76 in a combined sample of 199 college men and 374 women. Information on the ANDRO scale may be obtained from the author.

CHAPTER 11

THE EFFECTS OF THERAPIST–CLIENT RACIAL SIMILARITY

JEROME M. SATTLER[1]

PSYCHOTHERAPEUTIC relationships are probably the most intimate contacts occurring within behavioral science. When the element of race is added to the psychotherapeutic relationship, more complex and challenging patterns arise. Group therapeutic procedures introduce even more complex patterns of racial grouping because many combinations can occur when both clients and therapists vary in racial backgrounds.

Although the focus of this chapter is on the Black client in psychotherapy, counseling, and social work, many of the dynamics described also pertain to other interracial and interethnic relationships. I use the term "psychotherapy" to represent the disciplines of psychotherapy, counseling, and social work and the designation "therapist" to represent the respective practitioners because I believe that these disciplines are all engaged in similar kinds of helping procedures, and that the dynamics of traditional psychotherapeutic relationships also arise in counseling and social work.

Therapists working with Black clients need special awareness of their own and their client's feelings about blackness and whiteness (including an understanding of potential transference and countertransference reactions) and an understanding of how psychotherapeutic theories and techniques may serve the special needs of Black clients. Many sources of information are needed to meet these needs, and this chapter, with its focus on research literature, is but one small step toward guiding the reader to an appreciation of some of the dynamics involved in psychotherapy with Black people. Gardner's (1971) excellent review of primarily nonresearch literature covering the therapeutic relationship under varying conditions of race is an additional good source of information.

Psychotherapy has sometimes been characterized as a racist tool which provides an opiate to Black people and merely serves to lull them into accepting passively their inferior economic and political status (cf. Statman, 1971). While I believe that this indictment has some merit, I also believe that psychotherapy has the potential to make a valuable contribution to Black people in their struggle for growth, political influence, and economic well being. For that potential to be actualized, it is important that the therapist be willing and able to examine with special care and sensitivity himself, his procedures, the institutions in which he works, and both the dominant and nondominant cultures. Even then his knowledge provides him only the tools necessary to attempt the construction of trusting and helping relationships. The ultimate test of these tools and his skills in using them will be found in the face-to-face interaction with Black clients.

The studies covered in this chapter represent a broad, diversified group. I have included studies and reports that shed some light on psychotherapy, counseling, and casework with Black clients, even though some of the studies do not deserve the label "research" and should be read simply as descriptive pieces of information. Because the area of psychotherapy with Black clients is relatively new and because the number of research reports is still limited, I believe that it is most appropriate to consider the experience of all workers in the field.

The organization of the studies deserves some comment. A number of studies have focused on more than one dimension, so that their placement in a particular section is somewhat arbitrary. In addition, studies pertinent to more than one section have been cited in both sections. The chapter begins with some pertinent background material related to interracial therapeutic relationships, and primarily focuses on the White therapist's reactions to Black clients, interviewing research, and factors involved in interracial communication. This section is followed by sections that review research literature on analogue and field diagnostic studies, analogue and field preference studies, archival studies of differential treatment of Black and White clients, and analogue studies of individual therapy and field studies of individual and group therapy.

The research studies, especially those dealing with the effectiveness of therapy, focus on Black clients who were willing to make contact with White therapists and with White institutions. Therefore, the findings should not be generalized to all Black persons, but only to those who are open to Black–White encounters. The research covers many different kinds of helping agents who have varied types of relationships with their clients. Some of the conflicting findings therefore may be a function of the depth of the relationship that exists between the therapist and client. There are major differences between intensive psychotherapy and less intensive guidance-types of situations.

Time differences should be taken into account in evaluating the research literature. Until the middle and, especially, the latter part of the 1960s, there was almost no possibility in the South of White counselors working with Black students or Black counselors with White students. Since that time, there has probably been even greater opportunity for such patterns of interaction in the South than in the North. In the past, preferences and attitudes in the North could be assessed on a more or less limited basis cross-racially, whereas in the South there was almost no possibility of such evaluation. Now there is such a possibility. Few, if any, of the preference studies reviewed were conducted in the South, while some of the individual and group therapy reports came from the South. While both chronology and geography are important in interpreting preferences and attitudes, the available studies are too few in number to come to firm conclusions about these factors. Because of the rise of the Black Power movement in the latter half of the 1960s, it is possible that if some studies were repeated today the results would be markedly different.

RACISM, COUNTERTRANSFERENCE, AND COMMUNICATION

Black Americans are bicultural and bidialectical, and far from being either deficient or merely different in culture often possess a richer repertoire of lifestyles than middle-class Whites (Valentine, 1971). The cultural diversity existing within the Black community makes any generalizations about Black clients suspect. However, the pattern of race relations in our country is likely to have had similar effects on Black people, regardless of their particular individual cultural style.

The withering effect of racism has been cited as the major and overriding psychiatric problem of Black individuals (Pierce, 1974). The family patterns developed in the inner city, which may be adaptive for occupational and economic survival, also are likely to be ones that are unsuitable to the task of socialization of children for achievement in the middle-class culture (Rodman, 1968). The Black Power movement has developed as one attempt to eradicate racism (Pinderhughes, 1969) and a remarkable fact of the movement is that it begins to legitimize psychologically the fact of being Black. The movement should help to rectify some of the negative imagery attached to blackness in the years since slavery (Pierce, 1968; White, 1970).

Psychiatric literature has had a long history of promulgating cultural stereotypes regarding the inferiority of American Blacks. Szasz (1971a) has observed that psychiatry and psychoanalysis have used their specialized jargons to justify the systematic subjugation of Black people. Szasz (1971b) also noted that one of the first articles to appear concerning Blacks was by Cartwright (1851), who proposed that the effort of the Negro slave to gain his freedom by running away was merely the symptom of a serious mental disease. In the past, derogatory characterizations were crude and blatant, involving statements that Negroes are at a much lower cultural level than Caucasians, with a simple dream life and an inability to grasp subjective ideas (Lind, 1914, 1917); that Negroes are superstitious, changeable in impulse and emotion, and lacking in the ability to comprehend abstractions (O'Malley, 1914); that Negroes are irresponsible, unthinking, easily aroused to happiness, and happy-go-lucky (Green, 1914); and that Negroes show a comparative lack of self-consciousness, draw a fainter line of demarcation between will and destiny, illusion and knowledge, and dreams and facts, and make less distinction between hallucinations and objective existences than do more civilized races (Lewis & Hubbard, 1931). As Thomas noted (1962), some of these derogatory stereotypes were cited with approval as late as 1947 in an article by Ripley and Wolf (1947).

The anxiety, insecurity, latent prejudice, and other reactions to contemporary Black–White relations that are experienced by White therapists in their work with Black clients may be transmitted to the client in any of a number of different ways.[2] These reaction patterns, which are technically called "countertransference reactions,"[3] are also in part dependent on the individual Black client's reactions to the therapist ("transference reactions") and to the client's view of Whites (in general). The following are some specific types of countertransference reactions that may impede the therapeutic relationship.

Paternalism and "Great White Father" syndrome. In discouraging the Black client for "his own good" from setting high achievement goals, we have a form of the "White man's burden" type of paternalism (Seward, 1972). Therapists who try to infantilize the client, especially clients who are apathetic, depressed, and powerless, increase the client's feelings of impotence and dependency (A. M. Jackson, 1973). Similarly, therapists who respond positively to Black clients who act in an "Uncle Tom" manner are reinforcing self-destructive behavior (Bloch, 1968). The therapist who is a member of a minority group that has been subject to discrimination should avoid the paternalism implied in suggesting that the client and his group should follow the examples of the therapist's group if they are to be successful in advancing their group (Gardner, 1971).

The "Great White Father" syndrome is characterized by the therapist's need to demonstrate his power and authority and to prove that he is different from other Whites that the Black client has known (Vontress, 1973a). The therapist communicates, on one level, that he can help the client only if the client will put himself in his hands and, on another level, that the client must be dependent upon him if he is to avoid catastrophe.

Overidentification. Too great an identification with the client may impede the therapist's ability to render any assistance, and may occur as a result of the therapist's own experiences of social rejection (Seward, 1972).

Overconcern. Overconcern for the client's welfare may be an attempt to atone for the sins of Whites or for the therapist's own guilt about a residue of prejudice toward Blacks (Vontress, 1971). The guilt can become a kind of entrapment in that the attempt to relate compassionately to the real oppression of Blacks may place the therapist in a position of losing clinical objectivity: by viewing all Blacks as victims, the therapist adds an additional dimension to the client's personal pathology (Cooper, 1973).

Excessive sympathy and indulgence. The tendency to be excessively sympathetic and indulgent with Black clients is illustrated when the therapist has one standard of achievement for Whites and a lower one for Blacks (cf. Ginsburg, 1951; Vontress, 1973a).

Reactive fear. The recent emergence of a new Black consciousness and the surfacing of anger have affected the countertransference reactions of White therapists, who now are likely to experience reactive fear and a lessened sense of competence. Such countertransference reactions could impede the therapist's ability to distinguish the client's realistically grounded feelings of hostility from hostility arising from emotional disturbance. The unaccustomed stresses for the White therapist may bring to the surface repressed fantasies that Black people are uncontrollable savages. Stresses experienced by the therapist may lead him to overcompensatory behavior (making antitherapeutic concessions to the client's demands) or to rationalized forms of racist aggression in the guise of therapy (Bernard, 1972). Not confronting the client with his behavior, skirting issues that evoke hostility, and concentrating on social issues are other ways of handling Black clients who are activists (A. M. Jackson, 1973). In addition, some White therapists may have difficulty in allowing Black clients to select the Black Power model (Kincaid, 1969).

Inhibition. White therapists may show a variety of inhibitory reactions, including inhibiting their own aggressiveness and assertiveness, in order to avoid feeling or acting like a boss; denying White capabilities, privilege, and power, which is in effect an apology for being White; withholding negative feelings toward Black clients for fear of hurting them, representing, perhaps, an overcompensation for prejudiced feelings of being all-powerful in comparison with Blacks; avoiding issues that may be painful to the client; and restraining spontaneity for fear that whatever they say or do may be taken as proof of their prejudice (A. M. Jackson, 1973; Samuels, 1972).

Projection. The racist therapist will discover that Black clients are untreatable by him because they respond negatively to him (Adams, 1970).

Sexual anxiety. Myths concerning sexuality and aggression may complicate the countertransference dynamics (Adams, 1950; Bernard, 1953; Bloch, 1968). Perhaps the most problematic combination for a good therapeutic relationship is a White female therapist and a Black male client (Kadushin, 1972; Vontress, 1971). This combination intensifies all of the threats to masculine pride involved in the subordinate position of client and may evoke, for the White female therapist, all of the menacing mythology of interracial sex.

Research in the area of interviewer racial effects indicates that interviewers' race affects respondents' replies (Sattler, 1970, 1973). Respondents inhibit their replies or give replies that conform more to the existing social or racial stereotypes to different-race interviewers than to same-race interviewers. The social class status of Black and White respondents is related to their replies: lower class respondents are more likely to be sensitive to the interviewer's race than middle- and upper class respondents. These findings are open to a number of different interpretations. First, respondents may try to avoid generating threat and hostility from the interviewer. Black respondents, in particular, may experience tension and fear before White judgment and criticism. A simpler explanation of these findings is that the respondents desire to avoid offending a polite stranger. Second, Black respondents may feel that they should profess discontent to Black interviewers. Finally, Schuman and Converse (1971) suggested that there may be a simultaneous White and Black interviewer effect: "The presence of a White or Black interviewer may simply serve to stimulate racially 'appropriate images'" (pp. 58–59). Thus, interviewer effects may be partly a frame-of-reference phenomenon.

The research findings also indicate that racial interviewer effects were usually nonsignificant when the interviewer had a second role relationship with the respondent, such as psychiatrist-patient or teacher-student. These second roles not only are carried out in settings different from those found in survey interviews, but also have higher status than the status associated with the role of interviewer qua interviewer. Therefore, responses are less likely to be influenced by interviewer racial characteristics when interviewers occupy a high-prestige status role.

Research findings from the area of interracial communication and from other areas of interpersonal communication also are probably applicable to the psychotherapeutic relationship. The following generalizations have been adopted from Porter's (1974) review of such literature.

1. There is an extreme scarcity of directly relevant research concerned with interracial communication, in both individual and group conditions.

2. Racial membership differences may be less important than assumed attitude or belief differences in determining the quality of therapy.

3. Some Whites and some Blacks may behave in an overly compliant manner in biracial situations. When this occurs, communication between therapist and client is interfered with.

4. Similarities between therapist and client must be perceived as relevant if the communications are to be accepted.

5. A communication is more likely to be accepted and acted upon if the receiver perceives that his acceptance will lead to positively valued outcomes. Thus, even though the client views the therapist as different from himself, he still will tend to accept the therapist's communications if he believes that something will be gained from doing so.

6. The establishment of trust can improve the quality of communications, even when there are obvious differences between therapist and client. Trust can be developed when the client perceives that the therapist possesses expert knowledge, is a person who can be relied upon, and is a person who has good intentions toward the client.

In addition to the dimensions of interracial communication derived from Porter's (1974) review, it appears that such communication can be facilitated when the communicators share a common coding system (both verbal and nonverbal), when there is proximity of source and receiver coupled with a genuine desire of the communicators to transcend boundaries, and when the therapist, in particular, is able to grasp and appreciate the client's viewpoint and is willing to accept the possibility of a perspective other than his own (Smith, 1971). Understanding in the communication process will require the capacity to respond to nonverbal as well as to verbal cues. Studies by Willis (1969), Baxter (1970), Banks (1973), and Fugita, Wexley, and Hillery (1973) suggest that there may be a relatively low degree of immediacy behaviors—behaviors that increase mutual sensory stimulation between persons (Mehrabian, 1972)—within the Black subculture. Close contact allows for tactile, olfactory, and thermal information that is not as readily available to individuals interacting under more distant conditions. The above findings, if replicable, suggest that Blacks may rely, to varying degrees, on different channels of information and may employ different communication mechanisms from Whites. These results have implications for psychotherapy in that close spacings between members of a group may be more anxiety arousing for Blacks than for Whites.

A misreading of verbal and nonverbal cues in

interracial communication may help to sustain stereotypic interpersonal judgments and contribute to conflict in interracial encounters (LaFrance, 1974). Therapists must be aware that if they attempt to persuade the Black client to change his patterns of communication or style, they are making an ethnocentric value judgment. Such judgments have a devastatingly coercive effect on the behavior and identity of Black people (and other minority groups) "to the extent that they have either ended up despising their own group and themselves or paying a heavy social and psychological price in having to defend their other cultural values against the massive onslaught of majority opinion" (Kochman, 1971, p. 8). A successful therapeutic interaction will require the therapist to be able to accept and to understand the verbal and nonverbal communication patterns of Black clients.

These summary considerations of racism, countertransference, and interracial communication have been presented in order to establish a broad-spectrum context in which to view the existing empirical research on the effects of therapist-client racial similarity, to which we now turn.

THE THERAPIST AS DIAGNOSTICIAN

Every day countless diagnostic decisions are being made in hospitals, clinics, counseling centers, and other mental health centers throughout the country. Diagnostic decisions are always difficult under the best of circumstances, and when we have a situation in which a White professional is required to diagnose Black clients, certain personal elements in the interaction are likely to rear their ugly heads. These elements are as much a part of the Black client's repertoire as they are of the diagnostician's. The Black client's manner of dealing with Whites (or representatives of the establishment or power structure) will be expressed in the interaction. We also have to consider how the clinic's policies affect the diagnostic process and, of course, the attitudes of the larger society as a whole toward mental illness, toward those who differ from the majority group, and toward those who question society's values. Research studies can help us in determining the extent to which mental health personnel have been or may be biased in their work with Black clients. Diagnostic decisions are especially important for therapy because diagnoses can determine the type and extent of treatment that the client receives.

To study whether diagnostic and treatment bias exists, two procedures have been used. One consists of constructing a case history, varying the client's race or sex or social class or degree of psychopathology or combinations of these variables, and then giving it to raters who are asked to make various clinical and diagnostic judgments about the case. This type of study is an analogue study, referring to the fact that the situation depicted is "hypothetical," yet mirroring to some degree what actually may happen in clinical situations. Analogue research is valuable because it provides information about the value judgments held by mental health personnel and the cues that they may use in making clinical decisions.

A second method of studying bias is to examine the actual diagnostic decisions made by mental health professionals for Black and White clients. The studies generated by this procedure are more difficult to control than analogue studies because they are either archival studies (using past records of patients) or field studies (working within a specific setting with a specific type of client population). These data are important, however, because they reflect the actual practices of mental health workers. It is necessary to consider that the value of an analogue study depends on the believability of the case—that is, whether the material or situation is simultaneously applicable to a Black client as well as a White client. Another potentially important variable is the rater's clinical background, especially with respect to experience in working with both Black and White clients. Unfortunately, in most of the studies reviewed below there was no attempt to compare the clinical estimates of Black and White mental health professionals. In addition, none provided information about the raters' professional experience with Black clients.

Analogue Studies of Clinical Judgment

Psychiatrists were the focus of two investigations. In one study a case describing a nonpsychotic patient, who had been referred to an inpatient facility of a large psychiatric hospital for evaluation, was sent to 102 psychiatrists (race unspecified) (Schwartz, 1974). The psychiatrists were requested to make a variety of clinical judgments about the patient, such as degree of maladjustment and prognosis. Some cases described a Black patient, others a White patient, with the patient's sex also being varied. Severity of maladjustment ratings and prognostic ratings were not affected by the patient's race. Of the four patients described, the Black male patient was judged to be least suitable for insight-oriented treatment. The two White patients were judged as being more suitable for inpatient treatment than the two Black patients, whereas the two Black patients were viewed as being more attractive than the two White patients. Overall, the ratings did not show any consistent bias against patients identified either as Black or as female.

In another study, 16 White 1st-year psychiatric residents in New York City rated a case history of either a Black or a White 27-year-old twice-married female whose chief complaint was that of having recurrent nightmares (Blake, 1973). The Black patient received significantly more diagnoses of schizophrenia than the White patient. However, the patient's race did not enter into other ratings, such as favorableness of prognosis, adequacy of ego functions, raters' interest in offering treatment, and anticipated success of treatment.

Social workers served as the subjects in another series of investigations. A case history describing a client (sex not reported), who was either Black or White, of the middle or low socioeconomic class, with severe or mild psychopathology, was sent to 360 professional social workers (race unspecified) employed by the State of California, who were asked to make various clinical judgments (Fischer & Miller, 1973). The Black clients were rated as having less psychopathology than the White clients, with the lower class White clients being rated as the most disturbed. The severely disturbed White lower class client was rated as being least suitable for treatment and least liked, while the mildly disturbed Black upper class client was rated as being the most suitable for treatment and the best liked. The client's race did not affect ratings on items measuring "social emphasis in treatment" or on those measuring "tenor of relationship." Overall, Black clients were judged more positively than White clients. The investigators suggested that the current social movement among Black people—such as the emphasis on civil rights, Black studies in universities, and Black independence—and the raters' sympathetic predisposition toward this movement, coupled with their sensitivity toward and awareness of the negative effects of racism, could account for the more positive judgments of the Black client—a "leaning over backwards" effect.

When 12 Black and 22 White social workers (sex not reported) rated a case history of a White 16-year-old pre-delinquent boy, the rater's race was not a factor in judgments of treatment potential or of psychological adjustment (Seligman, 1968). Another sample of 35 White social workers rated a similar case history of a Black adolescent. A comparison of the ratings given to the two cases indicated that treatment and psychosocial adjustment ratings were similar. However, the Black adolescent was more frequently recommended for individual interviews than for family interviews, whereas the recommendations for the White adolescent were more equally distributed between family and individual interviews. A second case describing a 30-year-old Black housewife was presented to the entire group of raters, but the client's race was not varied. For this case, the raters did not differ in their judgments.

Vail (1970) studied the effects of the clients' race and social class (middle or lower) on the treatment potential and treatment strategy judgments made by 99 female student social workers and 71 female experienced social workers (race unspecified). The social workers read a protocol describing an initial interview with a female client who had come to an agency for marital counseling. Treatment potential ratings were not affected by the client's race or social class or by the raters' level of experience. Treatment strategy recommendations, however, were influenced by the client's social class, with more social workers recommending supportive therapy for the lower-class client than for the middle-class client. Because of methodological difficulties, such as noncomparability of lower- and middle-class scripts and failure to use analysis of variance procedures, the findings must be accepted with caution.

Another investigation focused on the ways in which the client's race mediates clinical estimates of prognosis in psychotherapy (Goldstone, 1971). The raters were 22 White male advanced graduate students enrolled in a clinical psychology doctoral program at Purdue University. The raters were shown pictures of clients together with information about the client's degree of anxiety, verbal ability, ego-strength, and insight. The raters made prognostic ratings for 50 Black and 50 White clients. Instructional set was manipulated by informing half of the raters that the study concerned the effects of the client's race on clinical judgments.

The client's race was found to interact with the personality descriptions in subtle ways in affecting prognostic ratings. For example, when clients were described as being a very poor risk or as having a low level of anxiety, White clients received a better prognosis than Black clients. In these cases being Black was viewed as an additional handicap. In contrast, when the clients were described as being good therapy risks, Black clients received a more favorable prognosis than White clients. Perhaps raters believed that a Black individual who is functioning well must be an exceptionally good risk. Being Black became a significant factor at both ends of the prognostic continuum. Other interesting findings were that the Black clients were judged to need less verbal ability than White clients for effective functioning and that the ratings were less complex when the raters knew that race was a variable in the investigation than when they did not know. Overall, the results suggested that for the majority of raters the cues used to make prognostic ratings were probably different for each race.

A study of group therapists revealed some interesting information about their attitudes toward interracial groups (Rosenbaum, Snadowsky, & Hartley, 1966). At an annual group therapy meeting, a questionnaire was passed out to those attending, which asked the therapist to decide whether or not to place in an ongoing group of Southern White clients a Black college graduate businessman. The 85 therapists (race and sex unspecified) who completed the questionnaire were from various geographical regions, and represented the professions of medicine, psychology, and social work. Only 35% of the therapists were in favor of having the Black businessman directly join the group. The remainder either would first consult the group (46%) or would not have an integrated group (19%). Therapists' decisions were not related to their place of residence. The findings indicate that, for the specific situation described, therapists consider the client's race to be an important factor in the composition of a therapy group.

This survey was conducted over 10 years ago, and it would be of interest to learn whether similar responses would be given in the 1970s and whether the responses would differ according to (a) the geographical location of the group, (b) the composition of the group (e.g., a Black group admitting a White member versus a White group admitting a Black member), (c) the race of the therapist described in the situation and the race of the raters, and (d) the raters' racial attitudes. These clinical judgment studies suggest that the client's race on occasion affects mental health workers' clinical estimates. However, the ways in which the workers' judgments are affect-

ed by the clients' race are by no means clear. In many of the studies few significant differences were found in the ratings given and in the recommendations made for Black and White clients. When significant differences were reported, Black clients were sometimes rated as healthier and sometimes as more pathological than White clients. In cases in which Black clients were described as being a fairly good risk they were viewed as having a better prognosis than their White counterparts. At the other end of the continuum, however, no consistent findings appear. Raters appear to believe that Black male clients are less suitable for insight therapy than either Black female clients or White clients and that verbal ability is not as important a prognostic sign for Black clients as it is for White clients. Therapists appear to be sensitive to the formation of interracial groups, at least a group in which there are Southern White members.

These results suggest that the raters' background, the client's presenting problems, social class, and sex, or some combination of these and other variables interact with the client's race to affect clinical judgments. Although the available studies of Black clients are few and findings are by no means definitive, it appears that clinicians believe that the most suitable Black client for psychotherapy is a mildly disturbed, middle-class female, while the least suitable Black client is a severely disturbed, lower class male. Not surprisingly, these dimensions differentiating good and poor risk Black therapy clients are similar to those that have been found in studies of White clients (Strupp, 1971). A mildly disturbed, fairly good risk Black middle-class female patient may be judged by some clinicians as having a better prognosis than White patients of either sex. The available data are too limited to permit meaningful inferences about rater background characteristics (e.g., race, professional affiliation, location of practice, or sex) that may be related to their clinical judgments.

Archival and Field Diagnostic Studies

We now turn to reports of the actual clinical practices that are found in hospitals and clinics. The first four studies shown in Table 1 were conducted by examining case records, with the findings reflecting the procedures used by the hospital or clinic during the time period covered by the records. In such cases there is no control for changes in the professional staff or in the

TABLE 1. ARCHIVAL AND FIELD DIAGNOSTIC STUDIES OF CLINICAL JUDGMENT

Author	Location	Subjects			Facility	Results
		N	Sex	Race		
de Hoyos & de Hoyos (1965)	Not reported	26	M	Black	Hospital	Psychiatrists, nurses, social workers, and psychologists recorded fewer symptoms for Black patients than for White patients.
		62	F	Black		
		26	M	White		
		62	F	White		
Dorfman & Kleiner (1962)[a,b]	Philadelphia	94	M, F	Black	Mental health center	Psychiatrists' diagnoses and recommendations for hospitalization not related to patient or psychiatrist race or to their interaction.
		94	M, F	White		
Krebs (1971)	Baltimore	27	M	Black	Psychiatric clinic	Diagnoses not related to patient race or sex.
		87	F	Black		
		47	M	White		
		112	F	White		
Lane (1968)[c]	Cleveland	50	M	Black	Public hospitals	More Black than White patients were classified as process schizophrenics. Process diagnoses were received by 75% of the Black patients, while 25% received reactive diagnoses. For White patients, there was a more even distribution: 53% process, 47% reactive. Classification differences were more pronounced between Black and White males than between Black and White females.
		50	F	Black		
		50	M	White		
		50	F	White		
Lowinger & Dobie (1966)[a,d]	Detroit	35	M, F	Black	Outpatient and inpatient psychiatric clinic	Diagnoses essentially identical for both Black and White patients; Black patients rated as significantly more attractive and more dependent than White patients. On six other attitude factors (communication-ego strength, therapist discomfort, patient aggression and acting out, acceptability for treatment, patient-therapist similarity, and therapist's liking of patient), Black and White patients were similarly rated.
		276	M, F	White		

Note. M = male, F = female.

[a] A sex breakdown for subjects was not given.

[b] Records were selected of three White psychiatrists and two Black psychiatrists.

[c] Based on files of consecutive first admissions to several public hospitals. Patients were between 16 and 40 years of age and were classified as process or reactive schizophrenics by means of the Phillips Symptom Checklist.

[d] Clinicians were 14 White resident psychiatrists and two Black resident psychiatrists. No separate analyses were done for the White and Black psychiatrists.

hospitals' or clinics' policies. In the fifth study resident psychiatrists rated patients on various dimensions after an initial interview. Because most of the findings are based on retrospective analyses of case records, they may be less powerful than results obtained from direct interviews. Nevertheless, the findings are important because they shed light on the psychiatric interview, which, in turn, can play a decisive role in determining a patient's therapeutic program.

The results of these archival and field studies suggest that White mental health professionals do not, for the most part, appear to be differentially biased in the diagnostic decisions they make for Black and White patients. De Hoyos and de Hoyos (1965) hypothesized that the underrecording of symptoms in the records of Black patients, which may be an indirect measure of the diagnostic process, was a manifestation of the social distance that likely exists between White mental health professionals and Black patients. An alternate explanation is that the Black patients themselves may have preferred to limit their interactions with the White professional staff, thereby leading to an under-recording of symptoms. Only one of the four case record diagnostic studies reported direct evidence of differential diagnostic decisions based on the patient's race (Lane, 1968). However, as we shall see below, these findings are difficult to interpret.

Lane offered three explanations for her findings. One was that the findings were valid—that is, the Phillips scale is a valid measure of differences in schizophrenic behavior in Black and White patients. A second explanation is somewhat opposed to the first—namely, that the scale is a valid measure of differences in normal patterns of behavior but not of differences in schizophrenic behavior. A third possibility is that the scale reflects biases of the interviewing psychiatrists. Bias could occur because on the scale behavior indicative of aggressiveness toward oneself is rated as reactive, whereas aggressiveness toward others (and withdrawn behavior) is rated as process. Bias could operate if the psychiatrists perceived the Black patients as more threatening and aggressive than the White patients or if during the interview they induced hostility in the Black patients. Data that would compare the performance of Black psychiatrists with that of White psychiatrists would help in clarifying this third possibility. Another consideration is that because the scale was not validated on Black groups it may be open to bias: the behaviors and values included in process-reactive rating scales may not be equally meaningful criteria of process and reactive schizophrenia for both White and Black groups.

Comparison of Analogue with Archival and Field Diagnostic Studies

The trends resulting from clinical judgment studies and from the archival and field diagnostic studies are similar. The diagnostic judgments of clinicians (who in most of the studies were likely White) are not systematically biased in favor of or against Black clients. However, the results from both types of studies indicate that the patient's race does play, at times, some subtle role in affecting clinical judgments. The manner in which such judgments are affected is still open to much further study.

PREFERENCES FOR BLACK AND WHITE THERAPISTS

Preference studies provide useful information about the attitudes and expectations held by individuals toward Black and White therapists. Three different types of studies have been used to assess preferences. In one type, referred to as an analogue study, videotapes or a case history depicting Black and White therapists interacting with clients are presented to subjects who then are asked to select the most preferred therapist. A second type of study, referred to as a modeling study, is an indirect measure of preference in the sense that subjects must choose a model to imitate or to guide their behavior. Only those studies in which subjects were exposed to adult Black and White models, via a videotape or tape recording, are reviewed because adult models are more likely to represent "therapists" than peer models. The third type of study directly asks subjects to state their preference for a Black or for a White therapist by means of a questionnaire or interview.

Analogue Preference Studies

Analogue preference studies are summarized in Table 2. These studies, as a group, indicate that the counselor's style or the counseling technique used are more important variables than race in determining students' preferences. Racially similar pairings were sometimes preferred by students, particularly when the counselor's style or counseling techniques were not variables in the investigation. Students' preferences also are dependent in part on their level of dogmatism and place of residence. Highly dogmatic Black students and White students from Appalachia tended to prefer same-race counselors to a greater extent than less dogmatic Black students and White students from the North.

The four preference studies in Table 2 suffer from having only one counselor of each race and sex and only one counselee-actor, thereby limiting the generalizability of the findings. The preference-study investigators, too, do not appear to be concerned with the experimenter's race because they fail to describe the experimenter, although the experimenter's race may affect the subjects' choices (Sattler, 1970, 1973).

In studies in which the subjects chose one of a number of counselors no information is obtained about their attitudes toward all of the counselors. Similarly, studies that do not permit a "no preference" choice force the subjects to make a preference that in reality may not mirror their true beliefs. When only one counselor is presented for each group and sex, there is no way to isolate whether or not the choices reflect individual differences among the counselors or whether it

TABLE 2. ANALOGUE STUDIES OF PREFERENCES FOR BLACK
AND WHITE THERAPISTS

Study	Location	N	Sex	Age	Race	Therapists	Black subjects	White subjects
							Results	
Gamboa (1971)	Ohio Youth Commission	40 40	F F	12 to 18 12 to 18	Black White	One Black male and one White male[a]	Counselor's race and warmth did not affect preferences.[b]	Same findings as noted for Black girls.[c]
Riccio & Barnes (1973)	Columbus, Ohio	60 60 60	M, F M, F M, F	Senior high school Senior high school Senior high school	Black Northern White Appalachian White	One Black, one Northern White, and one Appalachian White of each sex[d]	A Black counselor was preferred by 88%.[e]	A White counselor was preferred by 61%.[e]
Silver (1972)	New York City	122 122	M, F M, F	High school High school	Black[f] White[f]	Two Black and two White counselors[g]	Directive counselor was preferred to the non-directive counselor, regardless of the counselor's race.[h]	Same findings as noted for Black subjects.[h]
Stranges & Riccio (1970)	Columbus, Ohio	36 36 36	M, F M, F M, F	Adults Adults Adults	Black Northern White Appalachian White	One Black, one Northern White, and one Appalachian White of each sex[i]	Trainees preferred the Black counselors.	Significant preference patterns did not emerge.

Note. M = male, F = female.

[a]The counselors videotaped a 2-minute interview, which varied in degree of warmth, with an Oriental female actress-counselee.

[b]The girls rated on a 7-point scale their willingness to visit the counselor for vocational, personal-social, and educational counseling.

[c]White girls were more willing to visit a counselor to discuss personal-social and educational matters than Black girls.

[d]Counselors videotaped a 5-minute interview with a 16-year-old Black female client; only her voice was heard.

[e]Individual counselor traits played a more important role than did their racial identity. Nearly 43% of all the subjects preferred the Black male counselor, with the next highest choice being the Appalachian female counselor (22%). A majority of the Northern White male students preferred the Black male counselor.

[f]The students were classified as closed-minded (dogmatic) or open-minded (nondogmatic) on the basis of the Rokeach Dogmatism Scale.

[g]Case histories were presented to subjects which described clients counseled by a Black or a White counselor who used a directive or a nondirective approach.

[h]Disregarding counselor's style, students preferred a same-race counselor. Closed-minded (dogmatic) Black students had a significantly higher preference for Black counselors than open-minded (nondogmatic) Black students. Both open- and closed-minded students preferred the directive counselor. It is evident from a reading of the scripts why the directive counselor was overwhelmingly preferred to the nondirective counselor. The client was described as going for counseling to obtain information about selecting a college. The directive counselor provided lists of schools, selected a number of schools for the client to consider, and guided the client, whereas the nondirective counselor made no attempt to guide the client, merely reflecting the client's feelings and thoughts.

[i]Counselors videotaped a 5-minute interview with an actor-counselee (race and sex of counselee not reported); only the voice was heard (A. C. Riccio, personal communication, July 1975).

was their race or sex that was the key element in the subjects' choices. The race and sex of the client-actor, too, may affect the subjects' choices and may interact with the race and sex of the counselor; however, these variables have not received attention in any of the analogue preference studies shown in Table 2.

Modeling Studies

Modeling procedures can be used to ameliorate specific undesirable behaviors in both children and adults (Bandura, 1969). The therapist serves as a model for the client; within the therapeutic situation, the therapist's actions provide information for the client. Although the modeling studies reviewed here have not taken place within a therapeutic or counseling context, the results are informative about the influence of the model's race on the behavior of Black and White subjects.

A study by Shapiro (1973) sheds some light on the relative merits of Black and White role models in influencing the occupational choices of 120 11th- and 12th-grade Black girls living in the San Francisco Bay area. The experimenters were two Black female graduate students. One Black female and one White female served as actresses who recorded material, elicited in an interview with a professional White male announcer, about eight occupations, half of which were masculine and half were feminine. After listening to a tape recording, accompanied by a photograph of the speaker (in actuality 10 different photographs were presented of women aged 21 to 27 years), the girls completed a questionnaire. A control group, not exposed to the models, also completed an occupational questionnaire.

Neither the race of the model nor the sex-labeling of the occupations was a significant factor in affecting the girls' recall of information about the jobs or about the model, or in their acceptance of the models or jobs. However, girls with high aspirations relative to their peers and those with high levels of vicarious experiences with race discrimination were more influenced by the Black model than by the White model. The results suggest that the girls found Black occupational models more relevant when occupational information was salient to them. Overall, both Black and White models were effective and were significantly better than no role models in enabling the girls to learn about the jobs.

A variety of tasks have been used to study imitative behavior of Black and White children and adolescents, including sorting behavior, aggressive behavior, self-reward standards, cognitive and motor performances, guessing behavior, and selecting pictures. In five studies the model's race was not a significant variable in affecting the imitative behavior of either Black or White children (Breyer & May, 1970; Kunce & Thelen, 1972; Rosenbaum, 1972; Thelen & Fryrear, 1971b; Thelen, Roberts, & Coverdell, 1973). In one study on aggressive behavior the model's race was not a significant variable for Black children but it was for White children, with White children imitating the Black model more than the White model (Thelen, 1971). In four other studies Black and White children imitated the White models more than the Black models (Cook & Smothergill, 1973; Havelick & Vane, 1974; Liebert, Sobol, & Copemann, 1972; Thelen & Fryrear, 1971a). Elementary school and high school aged children were represented in studies reporting significant modeling effects and in those reporting nonsignificant modeling

effects. In none of the studies cited above did Black children imitate Black models to a significantly greater degree than White models.

Previous research has shown that imitation depends on such factors as the age and sex of the subjects, the class of responses investigated, and the characteristics of models, observers, and tasks (Breyer & May, 1970; Cook & Smothergill, 1973). In addition, complex cognitive operations are involved in modeling, including the subject's phenomenology of the situation (e.g., perceptions and cognitions), and these operations have not been clearly delineated in the above studies. While few of the many factors involved in biracial modeling situations have been systematically investigated, there are trends that emerge from the available studies. The results suggest that White adult figures have prestige value for Black children and that Black adult figures have prestige value for White children. The greater imitation of White than of Black models by Black children, when it occurred, might be accounted for by the fact that Black children have little opportunity to see adults of their own race, particularly when they are in a White school environment.[4] Consequently, they may not be as prone to imitate the behavior of Black adults to the same degree as that of White adults.

The modeling results pertain to highly limited and circumscribed behaviors. In other types of situations, especially in social situations, Black models may be more influential for Black subjects than White models. The prestige of the model may depend on the particular problem the person might have, so that in some cases a White model might be more effective and in others a Black model. Because this type of research still needs to be done, it is premature to make any general conclusions about the effects of the racial characteristics of models on subjects' behaviors.

Questionnaire and Interview Preference Studies

One of the major difficulties in evaluating questionnaire and interview preference studies is that there is often no way of determining how much contact the subjects had had with counselors or therapists prior to the study. This is especially true for studies evaluating high school and college students. Another complicating factor is that the data in some studies were obtained by interviews and in others via questionnaires. In comparing these studies it is difficult to discern how the different data-collection methods might have affected the respondents' replies. Finally, some studies show that changes in preferences occur as a direct result of contact with therapists.

The above factors as well as others suggest that attitude preference studies must be viewed with caution, especially studies in which the subjects have had limited, if any, contact with therapists. The preference choices obtained in a survey or interview may not reflect what actually occurs in situations wherein the client chooses a therapist. A social desirability factor may be a potent force in affecting the clients' responses in attitude preference studies. That is, clients may feel obliged to state their preference in a manner that they think conforms to the norms of their group or to the interviewer's expectations (Sattler, 1970). When the respondent becomes a client and must choose a therapist because of personal needs, a social desirability factor may be of less importance than when he is asked to make a choice in a survey situation where he is not in the position of a client. Nevertheless, attitude preference studies are valuable because people do act upon their attitudes—and attitudes give rise to actions.

Table 3 summarizes the results of 20 attitude preference studies of adults who have been in psychotherapy, of high school and college students, of the general public, and of agency clients. With one exception (Pohlman & Robinson, 1960), Black subjects were clearly identified. In 10 of the other 19 studies the Black subjects clearly reveal a preference for Black therapists or state negative opinions about White therapists. In nine studies, Black subjects have no preference for either a Black or a White therapist, react similarly as White subjects do to their therapist, have a variable pattern of preferences, or even prefer a White therapist to a Black therapist. Even in some of those studies in which Black subjects preferred Black therapists, there were indications that therapy conducted by White therapists was beneficial to them and that they preferred a competent White professional to a less competent Black professional.

Attitudes toward therapy are dependent on the subjects' social class, with middle-class Blacks having attitudes similar to those of middle-class Whites. The self-referent racial designation terms (e.g., "Black," "Negro," or "Afro-American") preferred by Black subjects were not systematically related to their counselor-racial preferences. A sex factor also was found, with Black female students expressing more difficulty with White female counselors than

with White male counselors. Counselor effectiveness becomes an important factor in students' preferences, with Black students, in particular, being favorably inclined toward competent White counselors. A comparison of Black high school and college students indicates that those in college tend to have less favorable attitudes toward White counselors than those in high school.

The findings of studies in which subjects had participated in therapy do not appear to be different from those in which they had not participated. Some studies show that as a result of contact with White therapists Black clients may change their attitudes toward them, sometimes in a positive direction and sometimes in a negative direction. In considering other professionals, however, Black people have a strong preference for a Black minister. A possible explanation for this choice is that the single most formidable and influential Black institution since slavery was the Black church, serving as the major socializing vehicle for most Blacks until the present generation (Mithun, 1973). Currently, the Black church still serves as a primary communication link for the Black community, especially in times of crises, and as a major vehicle for advancement in the civil rights movement.

The therapist's race appears to be of minimal importance to White subjects. White subjects may feel free not to state a racial preference because they believe that it would be rare for them to encounter a Black therapist or because of the operation of a social desirability factor—the White subjects' desire to appear benevolent. The results from attitude surveys also may be a true reflection of the beliefs of White subjects.

Two other reports, not included in Table 3, provide information about the attitudes of high school students toward their counselors. Similar expectations toward their counselors were held by 313 Black and 367 White inner-city male and female 11th- and 12th-grade high school students, residing in a major Northern metropolis. The students expected their counselors to be of prime help with educational-vocational problems but not with personal-social problems (Pallone, Hurley, & Rickard, 1973). At least one Black counselor served on the staff of each of the four schools surveyed, with an overall ratio of 1 to 6 of Black to White counselors. When 85 Black and 300 White high school students in Portland were asked whether or not their counselors (four White male counselors, four White female counselors, and one Black male

TABLE 3. QUESTIONNAIRE AND INTERVIEW STUDIES OF PREFERENCES FOR BLACK AND WHITE THERAPISTS

			Subjects				Results	
Study	Location	N	Sex	Age	Race	Therapists	Black subjects	White subjects
					Clients in Therapy			
Goldberg (1973)[a,b]	San Francisco area	12 11	F F	Adult Adult	Black White	21 White therapists	No consistent pattern emerged: Some preferred a Black therapist, others a White therapist, and others had no preference.	White clients usually had no preference, although some had reservations about working with a Black therapist.
Warren, Jackson, Nugaris, & Farley (1973)[a,b,c]	Denver	20 20	M, F M, F	Adult Adult	Black White	All therapists were White	A Black therapist was preferred by 31%.[d]	Preferences of White parents were not studied.
					High School Students			
Barnes (1970)[e]	Columbus, Ohio	90 90	M, F M, F	Senior high school Senior high school	Black White	Not indicated	A Black counselor was preferred by 53%.[f]	There was no preference by 77%.[f]
Burrell & Rayder (1971)[e]	Lansing, Michigan[g]	10 40	M, F M, F	High school High school	Black White	Only White counselors; there were no Black counselors on the staff	Less favorable attitudes toward counseling than Whites, although the mean rating of 2.80 was just slightly below the average of the 5-point rating scale.[h]	Mean rating was 3.45, indicating a favorable average rating.
Gamboa (1971)[e]	Ohio Youth Commission	40 40	F F	12 to 18 12 to 18	Black White	Not indicated	Majority had no race or sex preference, but they did prefer a younger to an older counselor.	Same findings as noted for Black girls.
Mims, Herron, & Wurtz (1970)[e]	Detroit suburbs	161 1947	M, F M, F	Junior high school Junior high school	Black White	White male, White female, and Black male counselors on school staff	Black males had positive attitudes toward their counselors.[i] Black females had unfavorable attitudes toward White female counselors, but favorable attitudes toward all male counselors.	Male and female students had positive attitudes toward their counselors.
					College Students			
Backner (1970)[e]	City College of New York	129 174 30	M, F M, F M, F	College College College	Black[j] Black[j] Black[j]	Integrated counseling staff	Majority of students indicated that they can work with White counselors and that the counselors were helpful.[k]	

TABLE 3 (cont.)

Study	Location	N	Sex	Age	Race	Therapists	Black subjects	White subjects
							Subjects	**Results**
Brown, Frey, & Crapo (1972)[e]	San Francisco Bay area	50	M	Junior college	Black	20 full-time White counselors and two part-time Black counselors on staff[l]	Students held positive attitudes toward their counseling experience.[m]	
		30	F	Junior college	Black			
Jackson & Kirschner (1973)[e]	Newark[n]	391	M, F	Freshman college	Black	Not indicated	A majority of the students preferred a Black counselor.[o]	
McCreary (1971)[e]	Southern Illinois University	56	M, F	College	Black	Not indicated	For four problem areas, 80% to 93% preferred a Black counselor.[p]	For four problem areas, 26% to 64% preferred a White counselor.[p]
		31	M, F	College	White			
Pohlman & Robinson (1960)[e]	Ohio State University	109	M, F	College	Not reported	Not indicated	Black students apparently were not sampled to any great extent.	Neutral ratings were given for a Negro counselor and for a Jewish counselor.[q]
Thomas (1970)[e]	Los Angeles	80	M, F	Upper division and 1st-year graduate	Black	Not indicated	For problems of a personal nature, students preferred a Black militant counselor.[r]	
Wolken, Moriwaki, & Williams (1973)[e]	Los Angeles area	24	F	Lower class	Black	Not indicated	Almost three-quarters of the two groups preferred Black therapists.[s]	About one-quarter of the group preferred a White therapist.[s]
		20	F	Middle class	Black			
		25	F	Middle class	White			
					General Public			
Brieland (1969)[b]	Chicago	295	F	Adult	Black	Not relevant to study	A majority of those interviewed by Black interviewers preferred a Black helping person, whereas a majority of those interviewed by White interviewers had no preference.[t]	
		85	M	Adult	Black			
Dubey (1970)[b]	Cleveland	353	M, F	Over 25	Black	Not relevant to study	Between 77% and 84% had no preference for the race of a professional or business man and 56% had no preference for a minister's race.[u]	
		187	M, F	16 to 24	Black			
					Agency Clients			
Barrett & Perlmutter (1972)[b]	Philadelphia	12	F[v]	Adult	Black	Black and White counselors in agency	Most (83%) preferred Black counselors upon entering program.[w]	
Harrison (1973)[b]	Detroit	75	M	Adult	Black	Black and White counselors in agency	Attitudes were favorable toward both White and Black counselors upon entrance into program.[x]	
		116	F	Adult	Black			

TABLE 3(*cont.*)

Study	Location	N	Sex	Age	Race	Therapists	Black subjects	White subjects
					Subjects		**Results**	
Stokely (1966)[b]	Cincinnati	18 2	F M	Adult Adult	Black Black	Not indicated	One client preferred a Black worker, 11 had no preference, and eight preferred a White worker.	
Witbeck (1946)[b]	Chicago	31 3	F M	Adult Adult	Black Black	Black caseworkers	Eleven had no preference, one preferred a White caseworker, and 22 preferred a Black caseworker.	
Yashko (1970)[e]	Philadelphia	20	F	Adult	Black	Not indicated	Only two mothers preferred a Black social worker.[y]	

Note. M = male, F = female.

[a]Survey conducted after clients had had at least three individual therapy or counseling sessions.

[b]Results obtained by interview.

[c]The sample consisted of matched parental groups attending a child guidance clinic.

[d]Other findings were that in the Black parents' group 40% believed that the White therapists' lack of understanding and lack of contact with Black people was a hindrance to therapy, between 23% and 31% believed that a White therapist could not like a Black person, and 80% would return to the same clinic for treatment.

[e]Results obtained by questionnaire.

[f]The subjects in the Barnes (1970) and Riccio and Barnes (1973) (cited in the Analogue Preference Studies part of this section) studies are the same, permitting an analysis of preference changes. After viewing the videotapes, the Black students changed their preferences for a Black counselor from 53% to 88%, while the White students changed their preferences for a White therapist from 23% to 61%.

[g]L. F. Burrell, personal communication, July 1975.

[h]Number of interviews and length of time since students had seen counselors were not controlled.

[i]Black males preferred White male counselors.

[j]Eighty percent of the sample of minority students were Black.

[k]Those with effective White counselors placed much less stress on the counselors' racial background than those with less effective White counselors. The students preferred a counselor under 35 years of age, of the same sex, having experiences with similar students, and having good counseling skills. Results are based on three different surveys. Preferences were assessed both pre- and post-counseling.

[l]Only students who had seen counselors participated in the study. All students had seen only the White counselors.

[m]There was some suggestive evidence that females felt more comfortable and talked more in the counseling sessions than males. No differences in attitudes toward counseling were found in high and in low achievers.

[n]G. G. Jackson, personal communication, July 1975.

[o]Preferences for a Black counselor were as follows: 53% of the 300 students designating themselves as Black, 69% of the 27 students designating themselves as Afro-American, and 29% of the 52 students designating themselves as Negro.

[p]The four problem areas studied were sexual adjustment, vocational choice, social adjustment, and study habits. A majority of the White students preferred a White counselor with whom to discuss sexual problems.

[q]Since Ohio State University is predominantly a White institution, it was assumed that most of the students in the class were White.

[r]This was a preliminary study; complete data were not reported. Students indicated that they would talk to White counselors about problems involving academic difficulties, financial need, or employment opportunities, although even in these areas they believed that it would be difficult to confer with White counselors.

[s]The Black and the White middle-class groups had similar attitudes toward therapy. The middle-class Black students had significantly more positive attitudes toward therapy than the lower class Black students.

[t]The five helping persons were physician, caseworker, teacher, lawyer, and leader of parents' child-care discussion group. The question was, "If both were equally good, would you prefer that they be Negro (Black, Colored) or White?" When asked whether it would make a difference if the White helping person were better qualified, a majority said that it would to both Black and White interviewers. Preferences were not related to self-descriptions (Negro, Black, or Colored).

[u]The seven occupations studied were agency director, social worker, nurse, doctor, storeowner, druggist, and minister. The questions were asked in the following format: "Would you rather go to an agency where the director is Negro or to one where the director is White?"

[v]F. Perlmutter, personal communication, August 1975.

[w]After meeting with both White and Black counselors, only 25% had a preference for a Black counselor. Trainees indicated that knowledge of their problems was the crucial element, not the counselor's race.

[x]After being in the program for a period of 6 to 8 months, attitudes became less favorable toward White counselors, regardless of the race of the counselor who worked with the trainees in the program. The trainees apparently became pro-Black rather than anti-White.

[y]Of all the qualities of a social worker studied (age, sex, marital status, religion, or race), race was of least importance.

counselor) encouraged them to go to college, no significant differences emerged in the two ethnic groups, with almost three-quarters of the students being encouraged to go to college (Barney & Hall, 1965).[5]

Comparison of Analogue, Modeling, and Questionnaire and Interview Studies

A comparison of the various types of preference studies covered in this section indicates that other things being equal many Black subjects prefer Black therapists to White therapists. However, a competent White professional is preferred to a less competent Black professional and the therapist's style and technique are more important factors in affecting Black clients' choices than the therapist's race. Preferences also are associated with the clients' (a) temperament, with highly dogmatic Black students preferring same-race counselors to a greater extent than less dogmatic Black students and (b) location, with White students from Appalachia more likely to prefer a same-race counselor than those from the North. Middle-class Blacks have similar attitudes toward therapy as do middle-class Whites. Finally, in modeling situations White adults serve as powerful figures for Black children and Black models are prestigious figures for White children. The overall results indicate that a simple unequivocal answer cannot be given to the question, "Do Black people prefer Black therapists or counselors?"

Because none of the analogue or questionnaire and interview preference studies was conducted in the Deep South, the results should not be generalized to this area. Further, almost all of these studies occurred in the late 1960s and early 1970s. Consequently, there is no way of knowing whether the results apply to other eras and how generalizable they are to future eras. Preference study results probably reflect to some extent the pattern of race relations that exists in various parts of the country and therefore serve as clues to intergroup relations.

ARCHIVAL STUDIES OF DIFFERENTIAL TREATMENT OF BLACK AND WHITE CLIENTS

The treatment process in the field of mental health involves a number of different stages. First, there is the question of whether or not the individual comes to a mental health facility. If he comes, what kind of treatment is offered to him? Further, once in treatment does he continue to keep appointments or does he drop out? The studies reviewed here help us determine how the client's ethnic group is related to the various phases of treatment. Unfortunately, the studies do not permit an evaluation of the effects of the treatment staff, because most failed to describe the racial composition of the staff.

Table 4 summarizes the results of 17 studies concerned with differential treatment of Black and White clients. The studies primarily focus on outpatients at mental health clinics, although a few also surveyed inpatient facilities; children were studied in only two of the 17 investigations (Weiss & Dlugokinski, 1974; Williams & Pollack, 1964).

The archival studies of differential treatment of Black and White clients reveal some striking findings. Black clients usually are underrepresented in mental health facilities; when offered treatment, they usually, but not always, after the initial interview have higher dropout rates than White clients; they are assigned less often to individual therapy than are White clients; once in therapy they are likely to have higher dropout rates than White clients; and when hospitalized usually are discharged more quickly than White patients. The one major exception to these findings was in a specialized treatment facility for alcoholics in the South in which an intensive treatment program was equally effective for both White and Black alcoholics (Lowe & Alston, 1974).

Singer (1967) offered a number of intriguing hypotheses to account for his findings, hypotheses that likely pertain to many of the other differential treatment findings. The higher drug/lower psychotherapy rate as well as the greater homogeneity of treatment and quicker discharge for Blacks that Singer and others found might be attributable to the psychiatrists' choosing that form of treatment necessary to return the patient to the group of which he is a member—the patient is normed against his own group. The psychiatrists thus may have been influenced by "sociological realism" (the problems of Blacks are more social than psychiatric). The psychiatrists also may have been fatalistic (regardless of the amount or quality of treatment, the poor social conditions in the Black community will contribute to the patients' readmission). Finally, it is possible that the Black patient collaborates in the decision to employ shorter, less intensive treatment by making fewer demands on himself in order to leave the hospital (he experiences fewer differences between the hospital and his own environment than Whites). Only further

TABLE 4. ARCHIVAL STUDIES OF DIFFERENTIAL TREATMENT OF BLACK AND WHITE CLIENTS

Study	Location	N	Facility	Results
Adler, Goin, & Yamamoto (1963)	Los Angeles	Not reported	Outpatient psychiatric clinic	Patients' ethnic background (non-Spanish White, Spanish American, or Black) not related to failure to keep appointment rates.
Cripps (1973)	Denver	209 Black and Chicano[a] 1775 White	Hospital-based community mental health center	Voluntary patients—a higher proportion of Blacks than Whites received inpatient care, whereas the proportions were similar for outpatient care. Involuntary patients—the proportions receiving inpatient and outpatient care were similar. The percentage of involuntary admissions was 26% of the White patients and 56% of the Black patients ($p < .05$).[b]
Gibbs (1975)	Stanford University	87 Black 3000 Non-Black	University mental health clinic	In the 1st year of the survey Black students were significantly overrepresented in the clinic population, whereas in the 2nd and 3rd years they were underrepresented, but these differences were not significant.[c] Termination rates by mutual agreement among the Black students were similar to those among the general population of students.[d]
Hughes (1972)	Bay Area of California	42 Non-White[e] 259 White	Mental health clinics and private practice[f]	Client race was unrelated to duration of treatment, although non-White clients were less positive than White clients about the effects of treatment.
Kadushin (1969)	New York City	Not reported	Eight mental health clinics	Less than 5% of all clients seen were Black, with the exception of one facility where 20% were Black. The overall percentage was far below the general population rate for the area studied.
Krebs (1971)	Baltimore	70 Black F[g] 17 Black M 95 White F 31 White M	Mental health clinic	A disproportionate number of Black females, in comparison with the other groups, were assigned to crisis therapy rather than to long-term therapy. Black women also attended therapy at significantly lower rates than the other three groups.[h]
Lowe & Alston (1974)	Deep South	118 Black 699 White	Alcoholism clinic section of a mental health institute[i]	No pattern of discrimination was found in the delivery of services, with treatment more often being influenced by social and medical factors than by race.[j]
Mayo (1974)	New York City	59 Black 919 Non-Black	Inpatient hospital	Black patients received less individual psychotherapy than Whites (25% of Blacks vs. 80% of Whites). Black patients also received less electroconvulsive therapy, less group therapy, spent less time in the hospital, and were more often discharged without referral to other sources.
Overall & Aronson (1963)	Not reported	27 Black 13 White	Outpatient psychiatric clinic	Race was not related to rate of return for treatment.
Raynes & Warren (1971)	Boston	88 Black 160 White	Psychiatric clinic	Once referred for treatment, a significantly higher proportion of Blacks than Whites failed to keep their first appointment (46% of Blacks vs. 34% of Whites).
Rosenthal & Frank (1958)	Baltimore	76 Black[k] 308 White	Outpatient psychiatric clinic	Referral rate for psychotherapy during a 3-year period was disproportionately higher for White than for Black clients.[l] Of those seen in therapy, almost twice as many White clients as Black clients had six or more interviews. Rate of refusal to accept psychotherapy and improvement rate were not significantly different for the two groups.[m]

TABLE 4 (*cont.*)

Salzman, Shader, Scott, & Binstock (1970)	Boston	21 Non-White 430 White	Walk-in psychiatric clinic	Non-Whites had higher dropout rates (i.e., failure to return for a second interview) than Whites (24% of non-Whites vs. 3% of Whites).
Singer (1967)	Philadelphia	160 Black 160 White	Inpatient hospital	Black patients, in comparison to White patients, spent less time in the hospital, were given less intensive forms of treatment, were more likely to be given drugs as the only form of treatment, and were given more optimistic prognoses.[n]
Sue, McKinney, Allen, & Hall (1974)	Seattle	959 Black 1190 White	Seventeen community mental health clinics	Black clients, in comparison to White clients, attended fewer sessions (4.68 vs. 8.68), terminated more often after the first session (50% vs. 30%), and were more likely to be seen by nonprofessionals. However, there was no evidence that the Black clients received more inexpensive or inferior types of treatment.
Weiss & Dlugokinski (1974)	Oklahoma City[o]	15 Black 85 White	Outpatient psychiatric clinic	Race was not related to the number of treatment sessions received by the children.
Winston, Pardes, & Papernick (1972)	New York City	19 Black 19 White	Inpatient hospital	Medication use and length of hospitalization were similar in the two groups, with Black patients having a better rate of improvement than White patients. Overall, Black patients were treated as successfully with individual and milieu therapy as were White patients. All therapists were White, with patients being assigned to therapists in rotation.
Williams & Pollack (1964)	Chicago	Not reported	Child guidance clinic	Black children more frequently than White children were involved in cases that were closed before intake procedures were completed.[p]
Yamamoto, James, & Palley (1968)	Los Angeles	149 Black 387 White	Outpatient psychiatric clinic	Individual or group psychotherapy was received by approximately one-third of the Black patients and by approximately one-half of the White patients. Black patients also were more likely to see the therapists only briefly.[q]

[a]No breakdown was given for Blacks and Chicanos.

[b]Cases seen from 1965 to 1971. Only first admissions were selected. Each patient had been in treatment for 90 days or more.

[c]Cases seen from 1968 to 1972.

[d]Students from professional and middle-class families tended to remain in therapy for longer periods and terminated by mutual agreement more frequently than did students from non-middle-class backgrounds.

[e]The non-White group was composed of Black, Latin, Asian, American Indian, and Philippino.

[f]There were 61 therapists in the study who used individual-dynamic or insight-oriented approaches. All therapists were White (59% males, 41% female), except for one Latin female therapist. The therapists were either trainees in psychology or social work (64%) or professionals in psychiatry, psychology, or social work (36%).

[g]F = female, M = male.

[h]Three therapist variables—gender, profession, and experience—were not related to the patients' rates of attendance in therapy.

[i]Approximately 10% of the therapeutic staff were Black (G. D. Lowe, personal communication, March 1975).

[j]The variables studied included diagnostic services, group attendance, days in treatment, and medical clinic visits. Clinic policies, such as immersing patients in as many programs as possible, may have contributed to the lack of bias that was found.

[k]Table 2 in Rosenthal and Frank lists 81.3% and 19.7% for White and Black groups. These percentages add up to 101. In Table 4 I arbitrarily decided to correct their figure to 80.3%.

[l]Cases seen from 1952 to 1954.

[m]Other demographic data indicated that the better educated and those in the upper income range also were referred more frequently for psychotherapy than their less fortunate counterparts.

[n]Cases seen from 1959 to 1962.

[o]S. L. Weiss, personal communication, July 1975.

[p]Cases seen from 1951 to 1957. The investigators interpreted the results as indicating that there may have been some bias in the selection of treatment cases, with clinic policy rather than family choice being the prime consideration. The modal profile of a child seen for therapy was that of a preadolescent, middle-income. While Jewish male who was from an intact small family.

[q]A majority of the Black patients (61%), but less than 5% of the White patients, believed that the therapists were prejudiced.

study will enable us to determine which of the above hypotheses, if any, are correct.

Cripps (1973) attempted to account for the higher percentage of inpatient care found among the Black than among the White voluntary patients by suggesting that a set for inpatient treatment of Black patients may have developed among the staff because of the high incidence of court-ordered care. This explanation, however, does not appear to be justified because there was no difference in the proportions of Black and White involuntary patients receiving inpatient care. If a set for inpatient treatment were present among the staff, why should the set differ for Black and White patients?[6] Another reason offered was that Black patients may volunteer for treatment mainly to receive hospital care.

Krebs (1971) offered various explanations to account for the lower attendance rates reported for the Black women in his sample. The Black women's difficulties in keeping their appointments may have been due to the fact that more Black women than White women were employed. More Black women who failed to keep appointments also were on medical assistance than those who kept their appointments (a relationship not found for the White women); however, there was no apparent explanation for this relationship. The therapists also may have rejected the Black women, although there was no evidence to confirm this hypothesis.

Hughes (1972) also reported that his sample of therapists did not differ consistently in their ratings of White and non-White clients on major outcome factors. However, the therapists believed that they understood their White clients better than their non-White clients. Therapists who had had personal therapy were more effective in their work with non-White clients than those without personal therapy; however, personal therapy was not a significant variable in their work with White clients. While client's race was not a significant variable in psychotherapy outcome, it was important in the therapists' subjective opinions of their own level of comfort in the relationship.

Gibbs (1975) also reported that the problems of the Black college students generally were similar to those of the White students. However, Black students were more likely to experience stress in areas related to ethnic identity and socioeconomic status and to cultural attitudes and behavior patterns resulting from their dual marginality—they are part of the Black culture as well as part of the White culture of the campus, but in neither do they feel completely accepted. Those from middle-class integrated backgrounds tended to be defensive about their familiarity with the majority norms and guilty over their advantages. Those from lower class backgrounds expressed anxiety about competing with middle-class Whites and about being accepted by the campus community; they also expressed ambivalence toward middle-class Black students.

In the Sue *et al.* (1974) survey Black clients represented a different type of group than White clients: Black clients tended to be unmarried, have low income and educational levels, and have more males than females represented in the sample, whereas the opposite pattern existed for White clients. The investigators concluded that there was subtle discrimination against Blacks in the mental health system studied, as reflected by the assigned personnel and number of agency contacts. This conclusion does not appear to be warranted on the basis of their findings. Nonprofessionals may be equally effective or even more effective than professionals with Black clients (Cowen, 1973; Grosser, 1969) and there was *no* evidence that the Black clients received inferior forms of treatment. The number of agency contacts may be a function of clients' choice rather than an indication of discrimination.

Studies conducted at the Los Angeles County General Hospital shed some light on how therapists' cultural stereotypes may be related to their treatment decisions. First, we look at the attitudes of therapists toward various ethnic groups, and then observe how these attitudes are related to the amount of time the patient spends in therapy. In one study 16 psychotherapists (race and sex unspecified) on the outpatient psychiatric service were interviewed about their attitudes toward five ethnic groups (Blacks, Jews, Japanese-Americans, Mexican-Americans, and Chinese-Americans), and also completed the Bogardus Social Distance Scale (Bloombaum, Yamamoto, & James, 1968). When interviewed, the therapists replied that they believed that Blacks, in comparison with the general population, were more superstitious (31% of the therapists), more changeable in impulse or emotion (50% of the therapists), more lacking in the grasp of abstract ideas (31% of the therapists), and more unable to demarcate between illusion and fact (25% of the therapists). Stereotypes toward the other ethnic groups also were found.

On another series of questions, 79% of all the responses indicated that the therapists believed that individuals who are subject to oppression and discrimination have various psychological difficulties as a result of such discrimination. On the Bogardus Scale, the level of social distance expressed was low, showing tolerance for the ethnic groups studied. However, Blacks were least often preferred for intermarriage. Overall, the results showed that therapists maintain unfavorable stereotypes toward Blacks and toward other ethnic groups.

When the therapist staff at the Los Angeles County General Hospital clinic was divided according to their degree of prejudice, Yamamoto, James, Bloombaum, and Hattem (1967) found that the eight high-prejudiced therapists saw male and female Black patients for a smaller number of therapeutic sessions (8% of the Black patients—6 of 76—were seen for six or more sessions) than six low-prejudiced therapists (27% of the Black patients—15 of 55—were seen for six or more sessions). Approximately 30% (95 of 322) of the White patients were seen for six or more treatment sessions, with the number of treatment sessions not being related to the therapists' level of prejudice. In this study all therapists were White (sex not reported). The results suggest that the therapists' attitudes toward Blacks also play a role in the therapeutic relationship.

THE EFFECTIVENESS OF THERAPY

We now turn to analogue and field studies, either in an individual or group context, that have investigated the therapeutic relationship in the initial interview or in longer term relationships. In all of the analogue research both White and Black therapists were studied, whereas in most of the field studies only White therapists were represented, a fact which probably reflects the underrepresentation of Black therapists in the mental health field. Further, it is unfortunate that none of the studies in this section investigated the interaction effects of client's and therapist's sex on outcome measures.

Analogue Studies of Individual Therapy

The individual therapy analogue studies primarily focus on the effects of the therapist's race in the initial interview with both Black and White subjects in seven studies and with only Black subjects in three studies (see Table 5). In many of the studies the therapists had had minimal training, and in only one was their level of experience investigated systematically. The studies provide almost no information

about the extent of the therapists' experience with Black clients.

The subject sample sizes were rather small, ranging from a low of eight to a high of 64, while the therapist sample sizes ranged from one to seven for Black therapists and from two to nine for White therapists. Considering the difficulty investigators are likely to have in obtaining therapists who represent both races, the sample sizes are reasonable. Some studies fail to cite the sex of the subjects and therapists, thereby preventing the evaluation of sex effects in the initial interview.

Another consideration in evaluating these studies is the composition of the samples. In six studies the subjects were college students, while in the others they were high school students, schizophrenic patients, or agency clients. As far as I can determine, the high school and college student subjects either were volunteers or were selected by the experimenters from regular classes or programs; they were not "clients" at a mental health clinic or counseling center. Consequently, it is difficult to know if these findings are generalizable to clients (or patients) in mental health facilities.

In evaluating these analogue research studies it is necessary to consider the relationship that might have existed between the counselors and subjects prior to the experiment. On college campuses, especially, Black students may belong to Black student organizations and maintain close contacts. If a Black student is chosen to be a counselor in an experiment, he may have had contact with the subjects prior to the experiment. It behooves investigators to describe how the counselors were selected and the extent of their prior association with the subjects. Perhaps in these types of analogue studies the subjects and counselors should be asked routinely if they know each other. This holds both for White and Black subjects and for counselors. If this information is not provided in the research report (e.g., Banks et al., 1967; Tanney, 1973), there is no way of evaluating the possible contamination that exists in the experiment.

The results of the analogue studies suggest that the therapist's race is for the most part not a significant variable in affecting the subject's performance and reactions in these types of nonclinical initial interviews.[7] In six of the nine initial interview studies White and Black therapists obtained similar kinds of reactions from the subjects. However, depth of self-exploration was occasionally more intense in racially similar pairings. The conflicting results concerning the effects of the therapist's experience and the willingness of Black subjects to return to see a White counselor (Banks *et al.*, 1967; Cimbolic, 1972) may be in part a function of the location of the studies (Northeast vs. Midwest) and the counselor and subject samples.

TABLE 5. ANALOGUE STUDIES OF INITIAL INTERVIEWS OF INTERRACIAL THERAPY AND COUNSELING

Study	Location	Subjects				Therapists			Results
		N	Sex	Age	Race	N	Sex	Race	
Banks (1972)	Lexington, Kentucky[a]	16	M	High school[b]	B[c]	4	M	B	Racially similar pairings resulted in greater subject self-exploration and increased rapport than racially dissimilar pairings. Social class, however, was not a significant factor in affecting self-exploration or rapport. Counselors high in empathic ability obtained greater self-exploration and increased rapport than those low in empathic ability.
		16	M	High school[b]	W[c]	4	M	W	
Banks, Berenson, & Carkhuff (1967)	University of Massachusetts	4	M	College	B	1	M[d]	B[e]	The two inexperienced counselors obtained higher levels of facilitative conditions than the two experienced counselors. All subjects stated that they would return to see the Black counselor for a second session, while only one-third said they would return to see one of the White counselors.
		4	F	College	B	1	M[d]	W[e]	
Bryson & Cody (1973)	Southern Illinois University[f]	16	M, F	College	B	4	M, F	B	Overall, the White counselors understood both Black and White subjects better than did the Black counselors. However, Black counselors understood Black subjects better than White subjects, while White counselors understood White subjects better than Black subjects. Black and White subjects had similar levels of understanding of their counselors.
		16	M, F	College	W	4	M, F	W	
Carkhuff & Pierce (1967)	South	8	F	Adult[g]	B	2	F	B[h]	Same race and social class pairings resulted in greater depth of self-exploration than opposite race and social class pairings. The effects of race were not dependent upon the level of social class in both patient and therapist.
		8	F	Adult[g]	W	2	F	W[h]	
Cimbolic (1972)	University of Missouri	8	M	College	B	2	M	B[i]	Level of experience, but not race, was related to counselor effectiveness, likability, and level of skill, with experienced counselors achieving the highest ratings. All subjects said that they would be willing to return to see at least one of the White counselors for future counseling.
		9	F	College	B	2	M	W[i]	
Ewing (1974)	Not reported	13	Not reported	Pre-college	B	3	Not reported	B	Counselor's race did not affect subjects' reactions, with all mean ratings being highly favorable. Counselors rated favorably by White subjects also were rated favorably by Black subjects. Black subjects, in comparison with White subjects, indicated that they would more likely return to see the White counselors.
		13	Not reported	Pre-college	W	8	Not reported	W	
Grantham (1973)	East	37	M, F	College	B	2	F	B	Subjects preferred the Black counselors over the White counselors. However, subjects' depth of self-exploration was not related to the counselor's race.[j]
						3	M	B	
						3	F	W	
						6	M	W	

TABLE 5 (cont.)

Study	Location	Subjects				Therapists			Results
		N	Sex	Age	Race	N	Sex	Race	
Mullozzi (1972)[k]	Illinois	15	Not reported	Adult	B	7	Not reported	B	Both Black and White subjects perceived their counselors in similar ways on three of the four Barrett-Lennard Relationship Inventory scales. On the level of regard scale, White counselors were rated lower by Black subjects than by White subjects. White counselors perceived themselves as being more congruent with and more understanding of their White subjects than of their Black subjects, while Black counselors perceived themselves as being more empathic in their understanding of White than of Black subjects.
		15	Not reported	Adult	W	8	Not reported	W	
Tanney (1973)	University of Maryland	12	M	College	B	3	Not reported	B	Neither the counselor's race nor the subjects' socioeconomic status and level of dogmatism was significantly related to the subjects' reactions to the interview. However, the Black subjects consistently rated the interview experience more favorably than did the White subjects.
		12	M	College	W	3	Not reported	W	
Young (1973)[l]	University of Illinois	32	M	College	B	2	M, F	B	None of the variables studied (subject's race, therapist's race, and therapist's sex) were significant (at or below the .05 level) on any of the Barrett-Lennard Relationship Inventory scales.
		32	M	College	W	2	M, F	W	

Note. Abbreviations are as follows: M = male, F = female, B = Black, W = White.
[a] Location obtained from W. M. Banks, personal communication, July 1975.
[b] Eleventh and twelfth graders.
[c] Lower and middle class.
[d] Sex of counselors obtained from R. R. Carkhuff, personal communication, September 1969.
[e] The Black counselor was inexperienced, while one White counselor was relatively inexperienced and two were experienced.
[f] Location obtained from Bryson (1973).
[g] These were hospitalized schizophrenic patients, with half of each racial group in the upper class and half in the lower class.
[h] These were lay counselors who had completed a mental health training program. In each racial group two were of the upper class and two of the lower class.
[i] There was one experienced and one inexperienced counselor in each racial group.
[j] Depth of self-exploration was related to the counselor's sex, with female counselors obtaining greater depth than male counselors. Counselor's sex, however, was not related to the subjects' level of satisfaction.
[k] Professional counselors working in various agencies in Illinois had their next Black and their next White client, who were able to read at approximately a ninth-grade level, complete the Barrett-Lennard Relationship Inventory (the four Inventory scales are level of regard, empathic understanding, unconditionality of regard, and congruence) after the first counseling session. The counselors also completed the Inventory at the same time. Most of the counselors were of the middle class, whereas most of the clients were of the lower class.
[l] This study is technically not an initial interview study because excerpts of a standard psychotherapy dialogue were used. Actors, whose voice patterns were ambiguous as to racial identity, recorded prepared scripts. The subjects listened to the recorded excerpts and then rated, assuming the position of the client, the therapeutic relationship via means of the Barrett-Lennard Relationship Inventory. Before listening to the excerpts, the subjects were given a case folder containing a description and pictures of the therapist and the client. The client-actor's race always corresponded to the subject's race.

Interestingly, White therapists in their work with Black clients occasionally were better at facilitating self-exploration than Black therapists, and Black therapists occasionally perceived themselves to be more empathic with White clients than with Black clients. A study of the counselors' reactions is also important because while the clients may not be affected by the counselors' race, the counselors themselves may believe that the client's race affects the counseling relationship. This belief may have effects in long-term relationships, if not in the initial interview. The position that Blacks prefer to be counseled only by Blacks or that White therapists cannot be effective in working with Black clients does not receive support from these initial interview analogue studies.

Grantham (1973) also found that the counselors' ability to comprehend nonstandard Black English was not related to the subjects' level of satisfaction or depth of self-exploration. However, Grantham pointed out that the subjects did not use nonstandard Black English in the interview. Conceivably, they were able to respond with the language that was appropriate for the interview. When scores were adjusted for the level of facilitative conditions offered by the counselors, the subjects seen by White counselors showed greater depth of self-exploration than those seen by Black counselors. This latter finding, according to Grantham, suggests that in the initial interview Black counselors may be more concerned with establishing identity with Black clients than with moving immediately into the exploration of personally relevant clinical material.

Banks *et al.* (1967) observed that in the counseling of Black college students the counselor's race and counseling orientation may be more important variables than level of counselor experience. This conclusion was based on the fact that one of the experienced White counselors espoused a trait-and-factor orientation to counseling and that facilitative conditions were higher with the inexperienced Black counselor than with the experienced White counselors. However, their conclusion must be viewed with caution for a number of reasons. First, the total number of subjects was small ($N = 8$). Second, there was only one Black counselor and only one White counselor with a trait-and-factor orientation. Finally, because the Black counselor was an undergraduate college student apparently attending the same university as the subjects, there is no way of determining whether he personally knew the Black students who were participating in the experiment and whether their acquaintanceship, if it existed, affected the students' replies.

The studies in this section would have benefited from a more careful reporting of experimental methodology. Sometimes it is difficult to know whether or not the subjects perceived the situation as an experiment or as a normal part of their college or high school or hospital activity. Some reports also do not mention the experimenter's race or sex or what part the experimenter played in the experiment. Investigators need to attend to such details if their findings are to be meaningfully interpreted.

Field Studies of Individual Therapy

The field studies of individual therapy reviewed here have not employed extensive out-

come measures. In fact, the last three reports failed to use any objective indices. In addition, *none* of the studies used control groups; consequently, these studies do not provide direct evidence of the effectiveness of therapy. However, the first five studies provide useful information about therapy outcome and attitudes toward therapy of Black and White clients, who were seen for the most part by White therapists, while the last five studies focus on Black clients only, with two of them studying Black and White therapists.

An elaborate and extensive research investigation conducted in a mental health center located in a large Midwestern city over a period of several months was reported by Lerner (1972). The study employed a variety of client prognostic and descriptive factors (e.g., race, age, social class, prior hospitalization, prior psychotherapy, severity of psychological impairment, authoritarianism, Rorschach pattern, and initial in-therapy behavior) and therapist measures (experience, democratic values, predictive empathy, concurrent empathy, expectation of success, initial liking, initial understanding, initial interest, evaluation of own experience as a client, and Whitehorn-Betz A-B classification). A new scale, the Rorschach Psychological Functioning Scale, was developed for the investigation. Changes on the scale, therapists' outcome ratings, and clients' outcome ratings were the three measures used to study improvement.

Of the original group of 45 clients, 30 males and females completed the therapy sessions and constituted the sample for the study. Their mean age was 30 years (range of 16 to 57 years); 17 were Black and 13 White. Many of the clients were poor, from the lower class, and were rated as severely disturbed before treatment began. There were 15 White therapists in the initial study, eight with experience (five female, three male) and seven with minimal experience (three female, four male), and 14 had at least one case in the final sample.

Measures of improvement were highly favorable. Scores obtained from the Rorschach Psychological Functioning Scale indicated that 23 of the 30 clients showed a gain in psychological functioning following psychotherapy. Ratings made by the therapists indicated that 29 of the 30 patients improved, while 20 of the 30 clients rated themselves as improved. There were no significant differences in outcome between Black and White clients. On the average, good results were achieved in less than 9 months and required less than 30 hours of face-to-face contact between client and therapist. Unfortunately, because 11 different client factors and 10 different therapist factors were not significantly related to improvement scores (corrected measures on the Rorschach Psychological Functioning Scale), there is no way of knowing what client or therapist factors were associated with improvement. The study demonstrated that lower class Black and White adults who are severely disturbed can and do benefit from psychotherapy conducted by White therapists.

In interviews with 12 Black and 11 White women, predominantly lower socioeconomic class residents of the San Francisco area who were seen by White therapists for at least three individual therapy sessions, Goldberg (1973) found that the two groups did not significantly differ in their expectations regarding treatment, identification of the helpful aspects of treatment, perceptions and evaluations of the therapists, or reasons for terminating treatment. However, the Black women had more presenting problems and less ambivalence about seeking treatment than did the White women. After treatment, the Black women, but not the White women, had fewer problems than when they began treatment. All of the White women and a majority of the Black women were seen at mental health clinics sponsored by the city of San Francisco. The study demonstrated that the White therapists were able to work effectively with low socioeconomic class Black women.

A study of the attitudes toward psychotherapy of matched groups of 20 Black and 20 White parents who had completed at least three therapy sessions with White therapists in a Denver child guidance clinic indicated that the two parent groups had similar attitudes toward treatment, including the perceived helpfulness of therapy, expectations toward therapy, and perceived attitude of therapist toward the patient (Warren, Jackson, Nugaris, & Farley, 1973). On selected individual questionnaire items, however, Black parents tended to perceive therapy as less beneficial than did the White parents. Ambivalence characterized the Black parents' view of the White therapists. The therapists were seen as supportive, yet not involved with the struggles of Black people and not understanding of their needs. Race was often not discussed in therapy. A reduction of reported negative attitudes may have occurred because the community lacked mental health facilities manned by a Black staff and because the parents may have believed that it was necessary to form an alliance with the White staff. The investigators concluded that although the Black parents had problems working with the White therapists, they were not as great as previously postulated.

Overall and Aronson (1963) studied the extent to which lower class male and female clients, the majority of whom were Black (27 of 40), would return for treatment after an initial interview conducted by student therapists (race and sex not reported) in their 4th year of medical school. The setting was an outpatient university hospital psychiatric clinic (location not reported). A study of the clients' attitudes toward therapy (i.e., the therapist's behavior in the initial interview), measured via a questionnaire administered before and after the initial interview, indicated that the greater the discrepancy between the clients' expectations for the interview and their actual perceptions of the interview, the less likely they were to return for treatment. Race was not a factor in distinguishing those who returned for treatment from those who did not. The clients expected that the therapists would assume an active but permissive role in a medical-psychiatric type of interview. When these expectations were not fulfilled, they tended not to return. Overall and Aronson suggest that the clients' expectations be considered during the first hour so that they can be reeducated as to both their own and the therapist's role in treatment.

The interrelationships among several variables, including parents' race, social class, and expectations of psychotherapy, and length of child's therapy, were studied in a sample of 100 cases (85 White, 15 Black) seen at an outpatient psychiatric clinic in Oklahoma (Weiss & Dlugokinski, 1974). On the staff were nine mental health professionals (five White males, three White females, and one Black female).[8] Prior to the formal intake interview, the same questionnaire developed by Overall and Aronson (1963) was administered to the parents. Black parents differed from White parents in expecting more active and supportive treatment, although these expectations were not related to their child's length of stay in treatment. The two groups did not differ in their expectations regarding the therapist's focus on organic problems or on emotional material or on the degree of responsibility the child assumes for treatment. Social class, but not race, was significantly related to the number of treatment sessions, with children from higher social classes staying in treatment longer.

Walker (1973) studied the effectiveness of an

Adlerian counseling approach (defined as offering direction and structure by the therapist) and a self-emergent counseling approach (defined as the therapist being reflective and client-centered) with low socioeconomic Black subjects, ages 16 to 21, who were living in Atlanta, Georgia, and were enrolled in an educational program. Each orientation was represented by two White male counselors who individually counseled four Black male and four Black female counselees for a total of four 30-minute interviews. The Adlerian approach proved to be the more efficient counseling procedure (noted by longer responses, more references to affect, and more positive responses). However, there is no way of knowing whether the Adlerian approach would be as effective when used by Black counselors or whether Black and White counselors would be equally effective.

After five individual counseling sessions, nine White male professional counselors and nine minimally trained Black peer counselors, of both sexes, were equally effective in obtaining higher levels of trust and self-disclosure with 19 male and female Arizona State University Black college students (Williams, 1974).[9] An impressionistic review of the case histories of clients seen in a New York City Community Service Society project indicated that treatment was not affected by the racial differences between the Black clients and their White social workers (Aronow, 1967). In a predominantly Black Los Angeles high school, White counselors, after a semester of work with 17-year-old Black students, reported that they considered themselves to be ineffective (Phillips, 1960). Black counselors, in contrast, found the students to be relaxed and willing to discuss problems. There was a total of 12 students in the study.

Silverman (1971), in interviews with 17 Black clients (13 had dropped out and four had successfully completed treatment at various mental health facilities) and their White therapists, reported that, for the most part, neither the clients nor the therapists considered the therapists' race to have been an important factor in therapy, although both groups were aware of racial differences. The therapists, in particular, were vigilant in looking for any clues that might be revealing of the client's attitude toward the therapist's race. (Location of study and gender breakdown of clients and therapists were not reported.)

The findings from these field studies, with one exception, are unequivocal. Black clients report that they have benefited from treatment received from White therapists, who have used, as far as can be determined, traditional forms of therapy. Because these studies have been limited to mental health centers, clinics, and schools, the results cannot be generalized to patients in mental hospitals.

Studies of Group Therapy

The relevant group therapy reports include observations of work with schizophrenic and other psychiatric patients, adolescents, and mentally retarded children and cover interracial as well as intraracial groups. These studies, for the most part, were not well controlled, did not include the therapist's race as a variable, and did not provide outcome measures. However, the reports are still useful in giving some picture of what occurs when White therapists work with Black clients in a group. In the two reports clearly covering Black group therapists, the therapists were either school counselors or lay counselors.

The effects of assertive and passive leadership on Black and White schizophrenic patients hospitalized in Louisiana were studied by Levinson and Jensen (1967). One White female therapist served as the group therapist for four eight-member groups each composed entirely of White or of Black patients that met twice a week for 5 consecutive weeks. For the most part, the therapist's behavior and patients' race were not related to various measures of group behavior. For example, amount or frequency of speech and amount of hostility expressed were similar in both assertively led and passively led groups. However, in the assertively led group Black patients directed more speech to the therapist than did White patients and were more satisfied than the Black patients in the passively led group.

In an interracial group of three Black and three White male patients, the Black patients were more verbally active than those in an intraracial group of six Black male patients (Murray, Brown, & Knox, 1964). The two groups met with a White male psychiatrist for one hour once a week for a period of 4 weeks in a Southern psychiatric hospital.

Heckel (1966) studied the effects of White therapists' background (Southern or Northern) on 20 hospitalized psychiatric male patients (six Northern White, seven Southern White, and seven Southern Black) who participated in one of three interracial groups. The Southern White therapists led two groups and the Northern

White therapist led one group (sex of therapists and location of study not reported). Measures of verbal behavior and group interaction, obtained for the first three meetings of each group, were for the most part not significant, with therapists' and patients' verbal behaviors being similar in each group. Because the study failed to include groups led by Black therapists or groups composed of all-Black patients or of all-White patients, there is no way of evaluating the effects of group composition or the therapist's race on group processes. From his experiences, Heckel observed that for interracial groups to be successful, patients must work through their communication problems.

Swanson (1973) investigated the effects of group counseling techniques on the self-concept (measured by the Tennessee Self-Concept Scale) of 34 pregnant, unwed, lower class, inner-city Black adolescents (location not reported). Three White, relatively inexperienced co-therapist teams of graduate students in counselor education (composed of two females, one female and one male, and two males) led biweekly groups for 10 meetings. Each pair of co-therapists led one structured group (specific topics were assigned to the group by the therapists) and one nonstructured group. Neither the sexual composition of the therapist team nor the group structure significantly affected self-concept scores. The counselors believed that 10 counseling sessions were not sufficient to bring about changes in self-concept; they also reported that the girls failed to develop trust and confidence in the group.

Neither vocational counseling nor traditional counseling significantly changed the personality or interest-inventory scores of 72 average ability Black male seventh- and eighth-grade Ohio students who were seen in small groups led by White male counselors over a 16-week period (Kehres, 1972). However, teachers reported that those seen for group counseling had more constructive behaviors than those with no counseling. After a 10-week counseling period with three racially mixed groups of 10 fifth- and sixth-grade West Virginia elementary school students (sex not reported), the counselor's race (gender unspecified) and the counseling process did not significantly affect attitude and self-esteem scores (Owen, 1970).

The effects of the race of lay male counselors (four Black and four White) on various measures of personality and temperament were studied in a design in which the counselors were assigned two groups of three Black eighth-grade boys who were in an Oakland, California school (Heffernon, 1970; Heffernon & Bruehl, 1971). The two groups were matched for IQ, reading level, and attendance in school. The counselor introduced himself either as a trained counselor or as someone interested in helping young people with problems. Group meetings were held weekly for 8 weeks, except for individual meetings during the sixth and seventh sessions.

There were no significant changes in any of the groups on the Mooney Problem Check List, Barrett-Lennard Relationship Inventory, and on an adjective checklist for real- and ideal-self. However, on an item giving the students a choice during the fifth session of either going to a counseling session or to the school library, all of the 20 students of the Black counselors chose to attend the counseling session rather than go to the library, while only 11 of the 23 students of the White counselors chose to go to the counseling session. (Some students did not complete all sessions.) Interestingly, all the students of one White counselor who had had substantial previous experience with Black people also chose the counseling session. The results indicate that although the counselors' race did not affect paper-and-pencil measures of personality and temperament, it did have some effect on preference for counseling. The Black adolescent students responded more favorably to Black than to White lay counselors, although one White lay counselor also was responded to favorably.

Snyder and Sechrest (1959) studied the feasibility of group therapy with young adult defective delinquents in a Pennsylvania institution. There were two nine-member White groups, two nine-member Black groups, and one 18-member White and Black no-treatment group. Nine subjects dropped out before the study was completed. The groups were led by a White male staff psychologist and met once weekly for 1-hour sessions over a 13-week period. Those in therapy showed improved institutional adjustment, and no differences were observed in the adjustments of Black and White group members.[10]

Mann (1969) studied the effectiveness of group counseling (location of study not reported) for 12 White and 24 Black mentally retarded boys, ages 9 to 13 years. Interracial groups of six students met for 12 1-hour counseling sessions with a male counselor (race not reported) and three additional groups served as controls. Group counseling significantly improved self-concept scores, deportment, reading, and arithmetic, and significantly reduced anxiety for both the Black and the White students.

The group therapy studies of hospitalized psychiatric patients indicate that the patients' race is not a significant factor in affecting group processes in White-therapist led groups. Black patients prefer an assertive White group therapist to a passive one and are more verbally active in an interracial group than in an intraracial group. When objective paper-and-pencil personality and temperament measures were used with adolescent groups, no changes usually were reported for both Black and White students with either Black or White therapists. Group therapy, however, does appear to improve the adjustment of mentally retarded persons of both races.

Comparison of Analogue and Field Studies of Individual and Group Therapy

The results of the nonclinical initial interview analogue studies and of the studies of actual therapy point to the same conclusion. Students, mentally retarded, and hospitalized Black psychiatric patients frequently do benefit from the therapeutic services offered to them by White therapists and counselors. This conclusion does not mean that White therapists are as effective as Black therapists, especially in long-term therapeutic contacts. There are still too few studies available comparing the effectiveness of Black and White therapists with Black clients over extensive periods of time. However, in the initial interview it appears that Black students, for the most part, react to Black and White counselor-interviewers in similar ways.

COMMENT ON RESEARCH STUDIES

The research studies and reports, while not well controlled in many instances, reveal some important trends. White therapists have been effective helping agents with a variety of Black clients and patients. Because of the paucity of research with Black therapists, we do not know whether Black therapists are more effective than White therapists with Black clients. In nonclinical initial interview studies Black and White therapists usually obtain similar kinds of responses from Black and White subjects.

When White therapists have empathic ability, use techniques that meet the client's needs, and have had experience with Blacks, they are likely to be especially effective with Black clients. Therapists from the North may be more successful than those from the South with certain populations. The therapist's level of experience has not been found to be systematically related to the client's level of improvement. Some of the studies clearly demonstrate that individual differences among therapists are important determinants of subjects' choices and behaviors. Black clients who are militant or dogmatic (findings are not consistent on this variable) or who have had vicarious experiences with discrimination prefer or work better with Black therapists than with White therapists. However, middle-class Black clients are more likely than lower class Black clients to have attitudes toward therapy that resemble those of middle-class White clients. Therapists are sometimes more concerned with race difference than are clients.

In comparison with the studies of individual and group therapy, a different picture emerges from studies of actual practices of clinics and hospitals. *Black persons do not partake in the utilization of mental health services as extensively as do White persons. They have higher dropout rates, receive less individual therapy, and are given quicker discharges.* The reasons for these differential treatments are not clear. It is unlikely that diagnostic bias is one such reason because studies indicate that clinicians are usually not biased in the diagnoses they give to Black patients. Although clinicians do take into account the patient's race in making a variety of clinical judgments, the direction of these judgments is by no means systematic. The results may reflect prejudice on the part of the institutional staff, a belief that standard treatment programs are less effective with Black clients, or Black clients' unwillingness to use existing services or agencies. It will be interesting to see if changes occur in the treatment of Black clients when clinics and hospitals have Black professionals on their staffs and governing bodies.

When asked about their racial preferences for mental health professionals, Black respondents tend to prefer Black professionals over White professionals. However, this generalization must be tempered with other findings which indicate that competent White professionals are preferred to less competent Black professionals and that in many situations Black respondents have no racial preference. White respondents, in contrast, do not appear to have strong racial preferences for mental health professionals. Perhaps White respondents desire to be magnanimous or to "lean over backwards"; or they may realize that in actual practice Black therapists are rarely found, so that their choice has few consequences; or they may genuinely have no preferences. Answers will come only when integrated staffs are available in all agencies and in all communities. Then we will be able to study a variety of patterns of racial interaction between clients and therapists.

The research literature reveals a paucity of research on comparative treatment procedures, on short- or long-term studies using Black therapists, and on differential effectiveness of Black and White therapists with Black and White clients. A number of studies fail to describe the racial and sexual makeup of the treatment staff, rendering it difficult, if not impossible, to establish the pertinence of the findings to the racial membership of the staff. All reports dealing with Black clients, whether they be case reports or research studies, should specify the race, sex, and professional status of the treatment staff; the location of the study; the race, sex, age, and social status (if possible) of the clients (or subjects); and the race and sex of the experimenter. Studies evaluating therapist race effects should attempt either to sample therapists randomly from each racial group or to match therapists carefully; in either case, it is essential that adequate sample sizes be used if the results are to be generalized. This is especially important in analogue studies using videotapes, where more than one therapist of each racial group should be used. Studies should describe carefully how the subjects were recruited. A few reports use the term "counselee," yet these "counselees" actually appear to be students who were recruited by the experimenter. A careful use of descriptive terms is called for in describing the "subjects" of the investigation. Investigations of both the therapists' and clients' reactions to the interview or to the therapeutic relationship would add considerable information to many research studies. Investigators also should provide information about the therapist's experience with the ethnic groups that are studied.

The initial interview and analogue experiments, while extremely helpful, may not mirror what actually occurs in practice. The results of such experiments perhaps reflect the generalized attitudes of the respondents, but an actual face-to-face encounter may elicit perceptions and behaviors different from those that occur in an experiment. During the therapeutic process, subtle changes in the practices of the therapist occur as a result of interacting with the client, and the client in turn may react differently as a result of the therapist's behavior. There is no substitute for planned studies and field studies that examine the work of experienced therapists over a period of time. It will be important to see

if, as a result of the Black Consciousness movement, changes will occur in preference studies as well as in other studies investigating Black-White relationships.

All types of research in interracial therapy are needed, and only a few of the many possible areas are considered here. From a broad perspective, we need to study the interaction of psychotherapy and the social system and ways psychotherapists can help to promote needed social changes rather than merely attempt to help people who have been hurt as a result of the lack of that change (Spanner, 1970). Research is needed that will identify more systematically specific client variables involved in treatment decisions (e.g., sex, socioeconomic status, education, and militancy), critical elements necessary in the training of therapists to work with Black clients, characteristics of therapists that are related to positive outcomes with Black clients, and effective treatment procedures (Lorion, 1973, 1974).

Thus, for example, we need studies to evaluate the effectiveness of individual- versus group- versus community-treatment approaches with Black client populations, the therapist's level of experience with Black culture as a factor affecting his work with Black clients, the importance of discussing race in the first few sessions when the therapist is White and the client is Black, and the nonverbal and paralinguistic channels that transmit complex racial attitudes in interracial interactions. Concerning the latter point, videotapes showing the therapist-client interaction can be analyzed for such variables as gaze, smiling, eye contact, and posture and compared within and across race and sex combinations (cf. Powell & Dennis, 1972). Also needed are studies that compare the effectiveness of Black-therapist Black-client with that of White-therapist Black-client, Black-therapist = White-client, and White-therapist White-client relationships.

Clinical judgment studies are a promising area for future research, as are studies of actual diagnostic and treatment decisions that are made for Black clients by mental health professionals. Especially needed are studies that investigate the diagnostic, treatment, and prognostic judgments of both White and Black professionals made for Black and White patients who come from different social classes and have different kinds of psychopathology. The raters' degree of racial prejudice should be measured whenever possible. Medical records are an interesting source of data by which to study the effects of race on clinical processes. These effects should also be investigated via records obtained from Black mental health professionals.

CLINICAL RECOMMENDATIONS

Psychotherapy should help to identify and nurture those attitudes, aspirations, and motivations that can be used productively by Black clients (Gordon, 1964). Clients should be encouraged to strive for goals that represent a greater use of their capacities and potentials, with young Blacks in particular encouraged to further their educational and vocational aspirations. Black clients need to develop a sense of pride and self-confidence and to learn to feel needed, wanted, useful, satisfied, and satisfying (Anderson & Love, 1973; Pierce, 1974). These goals can be achieved, in part, by helping them to develop a sense of power—the ability to make decisions that can determine their lifestyle and the way their community develops (see Hopkins, 1972). In accomplishing these goals they can realize that they have more control of their own destiny, having multiple, positive options at their disposal to use in reducing racist behaviors in the culture (Pierce, 1974). Agencies, in particular, should use their resources to provide opportunities for Blacks to secure power in their community.

Realistic therapeutic goals must be formulated within the limits of the client's environment (Lorion, 1973). Ignoring the social reality of a client's existence while attempting to implement change may be self-defeating, especially when the environment into which a client must return will not accept such change (Thomas & Sillen, 1972). Under such conditions, it may be a sign of health for a client to refuse change and withdraw from treatment. Using minority group status, like socioeconomic status, as a basis for limiting treatment has no basis whatsoever in reality as the research findings clearly show. The very factors used to rationalize exclusion of minority group and poor individuals from treatment justify their need for therapy (Lorion, 1973).

The Black community, especially, needs improved quantity and quality of direct services. The rarity of Black therapists within Black communities reduces the early recognition of symptoms of mental illness, informal mental health education, and linkages to resources (J. J. Jackson, 1973). Experienced, skilled, and expert Black mental-health professionals and nonprofessionals are needed. Training programs for both Black professionals and nonprofessionals need to be expanded (Comer, 1973; Pierce, 1972) as documented in a recent survey of over 90 clinical and counseling-psychology programs (Boxley & Wagner, 1970). Less than one-half of one percent of the faculty in these programs were of minority group origin (non-White) and less than two percent of the students in the programs were Black, while other ethnic groups combined were less than one-half of one percent of the student population. These statistics suggest that it will be a long time before Black Americans (and other minority groups) will have their mental health needs met by professionals indigenous to their culture.

The therapist, regardless of race, who desires to work with Black clients must be committed to this population (Katz, 1971) and must affirm the integrity of the Black client (Kincaid, 1969). He would do well to find out as much as he can about the living situations of his prospective clients and their responses to personal problems (Sundberg, 1974). This, in part, will require a proper assessment of social factors. For example, Black families, in spite of many difficulties, remain intact—with or without two parental figures—and it is the therapist's responsibility to see strengths where they exist and to encourage their maximum development and utilization (Shannon, 1970).

In interracial psychotherapy, as well as in our society as a whole, communication problems can be reduced and a better society fostered by having both Whites and Blacks (and other groups as well) strive for biculturalism (Kochman, 1971): an acceptance and understanding of each other's language, customs, and mores.[11] The Black client needs to feel confident in assuming a national loyalty, while building on the strengths of his subcultural identity (Kupferer & Fitzgerald, 1971). Our culture (and psychotherapeutic practices when they follow cultural dictates) must change from forcing everyone into the same White mold to the celebration of differences: the "White American way" is not the only correct way (Kochman, 1971; Thomas, 1970).

The White Therapist, in particular, should be aware of cultural attitudes of Blacks and Whites toward each other and focus on them when it seems therapeutically indicated (Rosen & Frank, 1962; Vontress, 1967). He will need to confront the issue of race with the Black client (Cohen, 1974; Comer, 1973; Rosen & Frank, 1962; Stiles, Donner, Giovannone, Lochte, & Reetz, 1972). The therapist should learn whether or not the client accommodates to the political and social system, fights against it, or simply exists with the system. The client who is overly accommodating to the system needs help in achieving a new level of self-esteem, so that he does not compromise himself, whereas the client who is just existing needs to be motivated to fight back (Shannon, 1970).

The therapist must understand the "Black Norm" if he is to achieve even a modest degree of success with Black clients (Grier & Cobbs, 1969). This norm includes a profound distrust of White people; use of protective mechanisms to guard against mistreatment by societal representatives; sadness and an intimacy with misery as a result of mistreatment; and questioning laws that do not respect them and are designed to protect White people. These norms are adaptive devices developed to cope with a particular environment and do not reflect pathology. The therapist, Grier and Cobbs advise, should not attempt to remove these traits by treatment.

Helping Black Clients with Rage

One aim of psychotherapy is to help the Black client work constructively with rage, because the problem of rage is a central one (Halpern, 1970). The expression of rage or anger serves a number of purposes (Stiles et al., 1972). First, it is a realistic reaction to the injustices in the client's life. Second, it has an educational function in instructing the White therapist about the scope and depth of the Black experience. Third, it serves as a test of the therapist's capacity to understand his society's pervasive repression and the resultant rage that Blacks have developed toward Whites. The therapist can attempt either to reduce the rage or to use it to help the client become more aware of himself. Halpern (1970) advocates helping the client use his rage for constructive, self-realizing purposes; it should be addressed, not denied or repressed.

The Therapist as a Social Change Activist

Many writers have advocated that therapists who desire to work with Black clients must become agents of social change in the wider community of which they are a part, and by so doing they have a means of stimulating natural and adaptive change in their clients (Banks & Martens, 1973; Berg, 1974; Gordon, 1968; Hawkins, 1973; Mayfield, 1972; Mitchell, 1971; Pearl, 1970; Thomas, 1969). Mayfield (1972), in particular, observed that "if the goals of community mental health programs are to be achieved in black communities, mental health practitioners must speak out against and try to change social and economic systems that bind black people in the vermin infested human dumping grounds so many of them call home" (p. 108). Professional energies should be directed toward altering the economic system that reinforces poverty in Black communities. Inner-city economic realities, especially, must be considered in developing treatment plans for Black clients. For example, self-respect and dignity, which in large part develop from job satisfaction, are tenuous qualities in the chronically underemployed Black community. The therapist must "distinguish between powerlessness that originates within the individual and powerlessness that is imposed on the individual from without. If the powerlessness is derived from within, the worker may be able to help by using individual therapy techniques. However, if the client's despair is derived from his inability to get a response from an impossible system, then the worker has the professional and moral obligation to help change that system." (Mayfield, 1972, p. 109).

If the therapist subscribes to the social change-activist philosophy, he is likely to run into a number of difficulties. We have seen that the therapist's paternalism and "doing" for Blacks may be a source of difficulty in the therapeutic relationship. The therapist is likely to be poorly equipped to help in the resolution of political, economic, and social issues (Steisel, 1972).[1][2] Further, once he leaves the confines of the individual or group therapeutic relationship, he no longer is able to practice his unique skills. Is there any solution to his dilemma? My answer is that the therapist must walk a tightrope, juggling his therapeutic skills and latent social change skills simultaneously. Opting exclusively for either alternative will be of less significance and importance than interweaving both skills. A better fabric will be woven by helping the individual Black client recognize the sources of his difficulties and at the same time helping to restructure society by eliminating those forces that have generated discrimination and have limited individual achievement.

Training of White Therapists

During training, White therapists should have some practicum and internship experiences in Black communities (Butts, 1972; Vontress, 1974). Therapists need to study verbal and nonverbal indices, emanating from themselves as well as from the client, that reveal racial attitudes. An acquaintance with nonstandard Black English and the "body language" of the Black client will provide the therapist with information and will facilitate communication. Personal psychotherapy dealing with the therapist's racist distortions and negative countertransference reactions is also recommended (Adams, 1970). Training programs need to acquaint therapists with techniques enabling them to bring about changes in the social, political, and economic system in aid of the Black client (see Gunnings, 1971; Steisel, 1972).

Suggested Therapeutic Procedures

The research findings do not provide much guidance as to the kinds of therapeutic procedures that are most effective with Black clients. However, traditional techniques have been reported to be effective in a number of different studies with lower class Black (and White) clients. These findings are particularly noteworthy because traditional forms of psychotherapy have been accused of being almost irrelevant for lower class Black clients (Fishman & McCormack, 1969; Grosser, Henry, & Kelly, 1969; Hunt, 1960). Still, the studies do report higher dropout rates among Black than among White clients, and it may be that in these cases other therapeutic techniques were called for. Traditional approaches might be suitable, for example, for Black clients who are willing to engage in a verbal dialogue, or who have middle-class backgrounds, or who are able to assume a longer term perspective, or who believe that a resolution of their intrapsychic conflicts may facilitate a healthier outlook.

For Black clients who live in destructive environments, analytically oriented therapy, which emphasizes intrapsychic factors and encourages the adjustment of the individual to his environment,[13] may not be appropriate (Gordon, 1964). Some Black clients may have limited tolerance for the long verbal interactions that occur in analytically oriented therapy and in nondirective therapeutic approaches (Gordon, 1968; Vontress, 1973a). Nondirective approaches may be threatening because the signals in the interaction frequently are ambiguous (Haettenschwiller, 1971). The therapeutic relationship implies some admission of inadequacy and Black clients who already feel inadequate vis-à-vis the White institution may be further threatened by therapy (Haettenschwiller, 1971). Because of these reasons, work with Black clients

requires a flexible range of therapeutic procedures. As Lorion (1974) pointed out: "If patients enter treatment with negative attitudes and inappropriate expectations, the burden of responsibility rests with the mental health professional to use procedures that will maximize the probability that available services will be used by the patient" (p. 352).

Useful suggestions and promising approaches have appeared, as noted below, to make therapy more viable and less threatening to lower class Black clients. These represent insights and experiences of many therapists working with Black clients, but they are not based, for the most part, on research findings. Other innovative approaches therapeutically beneficial and acceptable to Black clients and staff also should be considered. Modifications in therapeutic techniques should be rationally adapted to the varieties of cultural value orientations that exist among Black clients (cf. Spiegel, 1959).

1. The therapist should have an informal and open-door policy, attend to problems immediately without the formal structure of appointments,[14] be available to rap without the client having a "present problem," and make services available in the evening (cf. Davis & Swartz, 1972). Professional and nonprofessional personnel and the full spectrum of therapeutic approaches (e.g., individual, group, family, crisis, and activity) should be available to Black clients (cf. Comer, 1973). The reports of Bauman and Grunes (1974), Brooks (1974), Davis and Swartz (1972), Kaplan and Roman (1973), and Taber (1970) describe innovative treatment programs which have incorporated many of the above suggestions. Family therapy, which may be particularly relevant for lower class Black clients, is described in reports by, for example, Minuchin (1974) and Minuchin, Montalvo, Guerney, Rosman, and Schumer (1967).

2. Black clients, particularly those who are from the lower class, may benefit from role-induction procedures introduced prior to the start of psychotherapy (Strupp & Bloxom, 1973). Such procedures are necessary because lower class clients tend to have limited information about psychotherapy, poor motivation stemming from apathy or feelings of helplessness, defensive inhibitions and reluctance to examine self, and misconceptions about problems of living and their amelioration through psychotherapy. Role-induction procedures can be introduced via an interview (Doster & McAllister, 1973; Heller, 1969; Lennard & Bernstein, 1967; Orne & Wender, 1968), film (Strupp &

Bloxom, 1973), or tape recording (Truax, 1966) and are designed to produce a better alignment between the client's feelings, attitudes, and expectations about psychotherapy and the actual experiences faced as a client. The role-induction procedure can be conceived as a general learning experience leading to more realistic expectations concerning the process of therapy and the meaning of improvement. Strupp and Bloxom (1973) have demonstrated that a filmed role-induction procedure was successful in helping lower income Black and White clients in group psychotherapy.

3. The therapist may need to use active therapeutic techniques, being directive, confrontive, and persuasive in helping the client (Harper & Stone, 1974). This approach may be necessary because some lower class Black clients want and need immediate results. The techniques should be functional, never ignoring the most pressing issues of the moment (Grier & Cobbs, 1971), and the discussion concrete and structured (Gordon, 1968; Vontress, 1973b). In the early phases of treatment specific and active intervention, such as assurance, advice, symptom relief, environmental manipulation, and medication may be useful (Yamamoto & Goin, 1966). These types of interventions, even though they may be regarded as "inferior" treatment methods by some members of the mental health establishment, should be used whenever they are deemed appropriate because they may be more relevant for some lower class clients than more traditional forms of therapy.

4. The therapist may need to be open and direct, providing unequivocal feedback regarding the relationship (Haettenschwiller, 1971).

5. The content of therapy may need to be tied closely to the current experiences of the client, with opportunities for the client to test decisions by direct actions (Gordon, 1968).

6. Verbal activities may need to be brief, interspersed with opportunities for motor behavior—such as role-playing, rehearsals of planned actions, or therapist-client interchanges during the course of some shared activity (Gordon, 1968). Role-playing uses a physical, action-centered motor style and may stimulate introspection (Riessman, 1964).

Goldstein (1973) describes a set of treatment procedures ("Structured Learning Therapy") combining modeling, role-playing, and social reinforcement for use with lower and working-class inpatients and outpatients. The procedures also can be useful in the training of nonprofessionals. Extensive research studies support the utility of the treatment procedures. While no specific mention is made of Black clients in the research reports, his program should be useful in treating Black clients.

7. The therapist may need to provide necessary labels for the client's actions and experiences because the client may have difficulty in so doing. The client also should be helped to learn about the actions and behaviors that are appropriate to the word referents occurring in the therapy session (Gordon, 1968).

8. In some cases therapy may be short-term, with intermittent return visits as necessary, and geared toward dealing with crisis situations (Jacobson, 1965; Rosenthal & Langee, 1970; Sager, Brayboy, & Waxenberg, 1970). Because crisis therapy is brief, limited in breadth and depth of exploration, and focused in the here and now, it may appeal readily to the expectations of lower class clients. Crisis therapy not only has value in its own right but may constitute the opening phase of longer term treatment.

9. Therapeutic contacts may need to occur in the client's home, neighborhood, or job situation (Behrens, 1967; Chappel & Daniels, 1972; Davis & Swartz, 1972; Gordon, 1968). Brief home visits can increase understanding of the client's home life and family dynamics, increase trust, and perhaps arouse the client's interest in therapeutic procedures. Home visiting provides a way of reaching an apparently unmotivated, isolated, but needy population of Black inner-city inhabitants.

10. The therapist should represent the client, not the institution (Williams & Kirkland, 1970) and intervene as necessary with welfare agencies, housing authorities, courts, schools, and employers (Sager et al., 1970). Extensions into community, political, and social realms may be necessary if therapists are to be effective.

11. Community mental-health programs in the Black community must be committed to social action and change (Pierce, 1972).[15] The programs must be relevant and responsive to the needs of the community that are served. The key is *relevancy*: successful mental health programs must maintain the same orientation and framework that exist in the Black community. The inclusion of community people in decision-making and decision-reviewing activities can help insure the formulation and development of new programs based on community needs (Banks & Martens, 1973; Comer, 1973).

12. The therapist should support and establish, where feasible, practical, mental health clinics "without walls" that go directly into the

community and involve it in the clinic's decision-making processes, especially with respect to program planning (Fishman & McCormack, 1970). In such a clinic there would be professional and nonprofessional personnel, decentralized services, and integration of services with other agencies. The treatment programs are more concrete, relevant, and meaningful, especially for inner-city residents. Training programs and job opportunities can replace verbal forms of therapy as a means to enhance self-confidence and coping ability.

CONCLUDING COMMENT

There are many difficulties and some advantages in a White-therapist Black-client relationship. In spite of the numerous difficulties that have been postulated for a White-therapist Black-client relationship, the research literature indicates that in many instances White therapists are effective with a variety of Black clients, including children, adolescents, college students, the poor, and the severely disturbed. White models also are prestigious sources for Black children. These findings should not make us complacent, for many difficulties are still present in the White-therapist Black-client relationship. Therapists may be prejudiced, even if less than the general population, and antipathy between the races is a fact, but an expert in human relations who is perceived to be an expert by the client can effect change, regardless of the racial client-therapist combination.

Writers have advocated that Black clients be treated only by Black therapists (Baughman, 1971; Franklin, 1971; Gunnings, 1971; Mitchell, 1970; Thomas, 1970; Vontress, 1971; Williams & Kirkland, 1970). The main arguments center on the disparity between middle-class White therapists and lower-class Black clients, leading to communication and rapport difficulties, and difficulty in the White therapist's ability to understand the Black clients' frame of reference —the Black experience. Even well-intentioned White therapists may encounter hostility and suspicion, reducing their effectiveness. The general sociocultural climate of race relations affects the therapeutic relationship, and, given the less than favorable atmosphere that exists in some sections of our country, interracial therapy is likely to suffer. Perhaps in today's polarized climate there are Black clients who can work successfully only with a Black therapist (Bernard, 1972). White therapists may be unable to treat Black clients effectively because they feel too intimidated, apologetic, biased, or inexperienced with interracial therapy.

The contention that only Black therapists can adequately treat Black clients is as much a racist notion as the contention that Black therapists cannot treat White clients (Bernard, 1972; Butts, 1972; Shapiro & Pinsker, 1973; Silverman, 1971; Smith, 1968). Setting special standards for a person because he is Black and insisting that only another Black can understand him "is to make him less than equal, to deprive him of his humanity, and thereby to continue to keep him down" (Silverman, 1971, p. 36). There is no doubting the fact than an understanding of Black history, sociology, psychology, and language can be of significant aid to the therapist in his work with Black clients and such knowledge should be acquired whenever possible. However, White therapists claiming lack of experience in the inner city and ignorance of the Black experience as reasons for being unable to work with Black clients are making feeble excuses: they can easily find in that very rhetoric a rationale for inaction (Pallone et al., 1973). Special preparation for work with Black clients is desirable and important but it by no means is an absolute necessity. *In the final analysis, success in interracial therapy is dependent on the therapist's possession of competence, sensitivity, warmth, understanding, energy, sense of timing, fairness, and a host of other interpersonal skills and abilities that can be brought to bear in the therapeutic relationship; being Black or White will not automatically guarantee either success or failure* (Cytrynbaum, 1972; Harper & Stone, 1974; Sager et al., 1970).

REFERENCES

ADAMS, P. L. Dealing with racism in biracial psychiatry. *Journal of the American Academy of Child Psychiatry*, 1970, **9**, 33–43.

ADAMS, W. A. The Negro patient in psychiatric treatment. *American Journal of Orthopsychiatry*, 1950, **20**, 305–310.

ADLER, L. M., GOIN, M., & YAMAMOTO, J. Failed psychiatric clinic appointments: Relationship to social class. *California Medicine*, 1963, **99**, 388–392.

ANDERSON, N. J., & LOVE, B. Psychological education for racial awareness. *Personnel and Guidance Journal*, 1973, **51**, 666–670.

ARONOW, A. *The Negro client's use of casework treatment.* Unpublished master's thesis, Smith College School for Social Work, 1967.

BACKNER, B. L. Counseling black students: Any place for whitey? *Journal of Higher Education*, 1970, **41**, 630–637.

BANDURA, A. *Principles of behavior modification.* New York: Holt, Rinehart & Winston, 1969.

BANKS, D. L. *Proxemic behavior as a function of race and sex.* Paper presented at the meeting of the American Psychological Association, Montreal, August 1973.

BANKS, G., BERENSON, B. G., & CARKHUFF, R. R. The effects of counselor race and training upon counseling process with Negro clients in initial interviews. *Journal of Clinical Psychology*, 1967, **23**, 70–72.

BANKS, W. M. The differential effects of race and social class in helping. *Journal of Clinical Psychology*, 1972, **28**, 90–92.

BANKS, W. M., & MARTENS, K. Counseling: The reactionary profession. *Personnel and Guidance Journal*, 1973, **51**, 457–462.

BARNES, K. D. Preferred school counselors and specified relationships between them and their counselee-selectors. Doctoral dissertation, Ohio State University, 1970. *Dissertation Abstracts International*, 1970, **31**, 1571A (University Microfilms No. 70-19, 291).

BARNEY, O. P., & HALL, L. D. A study in discrimination. *Personnel and Guidance Journal*, 1965, **43**, 707–709.

BARRETT, F. T., & PERLMUTTER, F. Black clients and white workers: A report from the field. *Child Welfare*, 1972, **51**, 19–24.

BAUGHMAN, E. E. *Black Americans: A psychological analysis.* New York: Academic Press, 1971.

BAUMAN, G., & GRUNES, R. *Psychiatric rehabilitation in the ghetto: An educational approach.* Lexington, Ky.: Heath, 1974.

BAXTER, J. C. Interpersonal spacing in natural settings. *Sociometry*, 1970, **33**, 444–456.

BEHRENS, M. I. Brief home visits by the clinic therapist in the treatment of lower-class patients. *American Journal of Psychiatry*, 1967, **124**, 371–375.

BERG, K. R. Six years of experience as a white community psychologist in a black community. In G. ROSENBLUM (Chair), *Community psychology: Treatment and research with racial and ethnic minority groups.* Symposium presented at the meeting of the American Psychological Association, New Orleans, September 1974.

BERNARD, V. W. Psychoanalysis and members of minority groups. *Journal of the American Psychoanalytical Association*, 1953, **1**, 256–267.

BERNARD, V. W. Interracial practice in the midst of change. *American Journal of Psychiatry*, 1972, **128**, 978–984.

BLAKE, W. The influence of race on diagnosis. *Smith College Studies in Social Work*, 1973, **43**, 184–192.

BLOCH, J. B. The white worker and the Negro client in psychotherapy. *Social Work*, 1968, **13**, 36–42.

BLOOMBAUM, M., YAMAMOTO, J., & JAMES, Q. Cultural stereotyping among psychotherapists. *Journal of Consulting and Clinical Psychology*, 1968, **32**, 99.

BOXLEY, R., & WAGNER, N. N. Minority group membership in clinical and counseling psychology training programs: A survey. *Proceedings of the 78th Annual Convention of the American Psychological Association*, 1970, **2**, 551–552 (Summary).

BREYER, N. L., & MAY, J. G., JR. Effects of sex and race of the observer and model on imitation learning. *Psychological Reports*, 1970, **27**, 639–646.

BRIELAND, D. Black identity and the helping person. *Children*, 1969, **16**, 170–176.

BROOKS, C. M. New mental health perspectives in the black community. *Social Casework*, 1974, **55**, 489–496.

BROWN, R. D., FREY, D. H., & CRAPO, S. E. Attitudes of black junior college students toward counseling services. *Journal of College Student Personnel*, 1972, **13**, 420–424.

BRYSON, S. L. The relationship of race to level of understanding in the initial counseling interview. Doctoral dissertation, Southern Illinois University, 1972. *Dissertation Abstracts International*, 1973, **33**, 4824A (University Microfilms No. 73-6190).

BRYSON, S. L., & CODY, J. Relationship of race and level of understanding between counselor and client. *Journal of Counseling Psychology*, 1973, **20**, 495–498.

BURRELL, L., & RAYDER, N. F. Black and white students' attitudes toward white counselors. *Journal of Negro Education*, 1971, **40**, 48–52.

BUTTS, H. F. Black psychiatrist uses racial myths to speed therapy. *Roche Report, Frontiers of Psychiatry*, 1972, **2**, (8), 1–2, 6.

CARKHUFF, R. R., & PIERCE, R. Differential effects of therapist race and social class upon patient depth of self-exploration in the initial clinical interview. *Journal of Consulting Psychology*, 1967, **31**, 632–634.

CARTWRIGHT, S. A. Report on the diseases and physical peculiarities of the Negro race. *New Orleans Medical and Surgical Journal*, 1851, **7**, 691–715.

CHAPPEL, J. N., & DANIELS, R. S. Home visiting: An aid to psychiatric treatment in black urban ghettos. *Current Psychiatric Therapies*, 1972, **12**, 194–201.

CIMBOLIC, P. Counselor race and experience effects on black clients. *Journal of Consulting and Clinical Psychology*, 1972, **39**, 328–332.

COHEN, A. I. Treating the black patient: Transference questions. *American Journal of Psychotherapy*, 1974, **28**, 137–143.

COMER, J. P. The need is now. *MH*, 1973, **57**, 3–6.

COOK, H., & SMOTHERGILL, D. W. Racial and sex determinants of imitative performance and knowledge in young children. *Journal of Educational Psychology*, 1973, **65**, 211–215.

COOPER, S. A look at the effect of racism on clinical work. *Social Casework*, 1973, **54**, 76–84.

COWEN, E. L. Social and community interventions. *Annual Review of Psychology*, 1973, **24**, 423–472.

CRIPPS, T. H. Sex, ethnicity, and admission status as determinants of patient movement in mental health treatment. *American Journal of Community Psychology*, 1973, **1**, 248–257.

CYTRYNBAUM, S. Race of teacher, task and affective interaction in southern black college classes. Doctoral dissertation, University of Michigan, 1971. *Dissertation Abstracts International*, 1972, **32**, 6639B (University Microfilms No. 72-14, 834).

DAVIS, K., & SWARTZ, J. Increasing black students' utilization of mental health services. *American Journal of Orthopsychiatry*, 1972, **42**, 771–776.

DE HOYOS, A., & DE HOYOS, G. Symptomatology differentials between Negro and white schizophrenics. *International Journal of Social Psychiatry*, 1965, **11**, 245–255.

DORFMAN, E., & KLEINER, R. J. Race of examiner and patient in psychiatric diagnosis and recommendations. *Journal of Consulting Psychology*, 1962, **26**, 393.

DOSTER, J. A., & MCALLISTER, A. Effect of modeling and model status on verbal behavior in an interview. *Journal of Consulting and Clinical Psychology*, 1973, **40**, 240–243.

DUBEY, S. N. Blacks' preference for black professionals, businessmen, and religious leaders. *Public Opinion Quarterly*, 1970, **34**, 113–116.

EWING, T. N. Racial similarity of client and counselor and client satisfaction with counseling. *Journal of Counseling Psychology*, 1974, **21**, 446–449.

FISCHER, J., & MILLER, H. The effect of client race and social class on clinical judgments. *Clinical Social Work Journal*, 1973, **1**, 100–109.

FISHMAN, J. R., & MCCORMACK, J. Mental health without walls: Programs for the ghetto, *Current Psychiatric Therapies*, 1969, **9**, 245–256.

FISHMAN, J. R., & MCCORMACK, J. "Mental health without walls": Community mental health in the ghetto. *American Journal of Psychiatry*, 1970, **126**, 1461–1467.

FRANKLIN, A. J. To be young, gifted and black with inappropriate professional training: A critique of counseling programs. *Counseling Psychologist*, 1971, **2**, 107–112.

FUGITA, S. S., WEXLEY, K. N., & HILLERY, J. M. *Black-white differences in nonverbal behavior in an interview setting.* Paper presented at the meeting of the Midwestern Psychological Association, Chicago, May 1973.

GAMBOA, A. M., JR. Race and counselor climate as selected

factors in the counselor preference of delinquent girls. Doctoral dissertation, Ohio State University, 1971. *Dissertation Abstracts International*, 1971, **32**, 1853A (University Microfilms No. 71-27, 472).

GARDNER, L. H. The therapeutic relationship under varying conditions of race. *Psychotherapy: Theory, Research and Practice*, 1971, **8**, 78–87.

GIBBS, J. T. Use of mental health services by black students at a predominantly white university: A three-year study. *American Journal of Orthopsychiatry*, 1975, **45**, 430–445.

GINSBURG, S. W. The impact of the social worker's cultural structure on social therapy. *Social Casework*, 1951, **32**, 319–325.

GOLDBERG, M. The black female client, the white psychotherapist: An evaluation of therapy through clients' retrospective reports. Doctoral dissertation, California School of Professional Psychology, San Francisco, 1972. *Dissertation Abstracts International*, 1973, **33**, 3302B (University Microfilms No. 72-33, 287).

GOLDSTEIN, A. P. *Structured learning therapy: Toward a psychotherapy for the poor*. New York: Academic Press, 1973.

GOLDSTONE, M. G. Differences in prognosis for psychotherapy as a function of client race. Doctoral dissertation, Purdue University, 1970. *Dissertation Abstracts International*, 1971, **31**, 4992B–4993B (University Microfilms No. 71-2603).

GORDON, J. E. Counseling the disadvantaged boy. In W. E. AMOS & J. D. GRAMBS (Eds.), *Counseling the disadvantaged youth*. Englewood Cliffs, N.J.: Prentice-Hall, 1968. Pp. 119–168.

GORDON, M. M. *Assimilation in American life*. New York: Oxford University Press, 1964.

GRANTHAM, R. J. Effects of counselor sex, race, and language style on black students in initial interviews. *Journal of Counseling Psychology*, 1973, **20**, 553–559.

GREEN, E. M. Psychoses among Negroes: A comparative study. *Journal of Nervous and Mental Disease*, 1914, **41**, 697–708.

GRIER, W. H., & COBBS, P. M. *Black rage*. New York: Bantam Books, 1969.

GRIER, W. H., & COBBS, P. M. *The Jesus bag*. New York: McGraw-Hill, 1971.

GROSSER, C. Manpower development programs. In C. GROSSER, W. E. HENRY, & J. G. KELLY (Eds.), *Nonprofessionals in the human services*. San Francisco: Jossey-Bass, 1969. Pp. 116–148.

GROSSER, C., HENRY, W. E., & KELLY, J. G. Prologue. In C. GROSSER, W. E. HENRY, & J. G. KELLY (Eds.), *Nonprofessionals in the human services*. San Francisco: Jossey-Bass, 1969. Pp. 1–11.

GUNNINGS, T. S. Preparing the new counselor. *Counseling Psychologist*, 1971, **2**(4), 100–101.

HAETTENSCHWILLER, D. L. Counseling black college students in special programs. *Personnel and Guidance Journal*, 1971, **50**, 29–35.

HALPERN, F. Psychotherapy in the rural south. *Journal of Contemporary Psychotherapy*, 1970, 2(2), 67–74.

HARPER, F. D., & STONE, W. O. Toward a theory of transcendent counseling with blacks. *Journal of Non-White Concerns in Personnel and Guidance*, 1974, **2**, 191–196.

HARRISON, D. K. *Similarity-dissimilarity in counselor-counselee ethnic match: An investigation of the attitudes of black counselees toward white counselors*. Paper presented at the meeting of the American Psychological Association, Montreal, August 1973.

HAVELICK, R. J., JR., & VANE, J. R. Race, competency, and level of achievement: Relationship to modeling in elementary school children. *Journal of Psychology*, 1974, **87**, 53–58.

HAWKINS, H. C. A message to white counselors in metropolitan schools. *Michigan Personnel and Guidance Journal*, 1973, **4**, 56–60.

HECKEL, R. V. Effects of northern and southern therapists on racially mixed psychotherapy groups. *Mental Hygiene*, 1966, **50**, 304–307.

HEFFERNON, A. W. The effect of race and assumed professional status of male lay counselors upon eighth-grade black males' perceptions of and reactions to the counseling process. Doctoral dissertation, University of California, Berkeley, 1969. *Dissertation Abstracts International*, 1970, **31**, 1575A (University Microfilms No. 70-17, 478).

HEFFERNON, A. W., & BRUEHL, D. Some effects of race of inexperienced lay counselors on black junior high school students. *Journal of School Psychology*, 1971, **9**, 35–37.

HELLER, K. Effects of modeling procedures in helping relationships. *Journal of Consulting and Clinical Psychology*, 1969, **33**, 522–526.

HOPKINS, T. J. The role of community agencies as viewed by black fathers. *American Journal of Orthopsychiatry*, 1972, **42**, 508–516.

HUGHES, R. A. *The effects of sex, age, race, and social history of therapist and client on psychotherapy outcome*. Unpublished doctoral dissertation, University of California, Berkeley, 1972.

HUNT, R. G. Social class and mental illness: Some implications for clinical theory and practice. *American Journal of Psychiatry*, 1960, **116**, 1065–1069.

JACKSON, A. M. Psychotherapy: Factors associated with the race of the therapist. *Psychotherapy: Theory, Research and Practice*, 1973, **10**, 273–277.

JACKSON, G. G., & KIRSCHNER, S. A. Racial self-designation and preference for a counselor. *Journal of Counseling Psychology*, 1973, **20**, 560–564.

JACKSON, J. J. "Help me somebody! I's an old black standing in the need of institutionalizing!" *Psychiatric Opinion*, 1973, **10**, 6–16.

JACOBSON, G. F. Crisis theory and treatment strategy: Some sociocultural and psychodynamic considerations. *Journal of Nervous and Mental Disease*, 1965, **141**, 209–218.

KADUSHIN, A. *The social work interview*. New York: Columbia University Press, 1972.

KADUSHIN, C. *Why people go to psychiatrists*. New York: Atherton, 1969.

KAPLAN, S. R., & ROMAN, M. *The organization and delivery of mental health services in the ghetto: The Lincoln Hospital experience*. New York: Praeger, 1973.

KATZ, B. EAC: A store-front counseling agency in an inner-city ghetto. *New York State Personnel and Guidance Association Journal*, 1971, **6**, 31–43.

KEHRES, R. J. Differential effects of group counseling methods with black male adolescents. Doctoral dissertation, University of Akron, 1972. *Dissertation Abstracts International*, 1972, **33**, 1440A–1441A (University Microfilms No. 72-26, 284).

KINCAID, M. Identity and therapy in the black community. *Personnel and Guidance Journal*, 1969, **47**, 884–890.

KOCHMAN, T. Cross-cultural communication: Contrasting perspectives, conflicting sensibilities. *Florida FL Reporter*, 1971, **9**, 3–16, 53–54.

KREBS, R. L. Some effects of a white institution on black psychiatric outpatients. *American Journal of Orthopsychiatry*, 1971, **41**, 589–596.

KUNCE, J. T., & THELEN, M. H. Modeled standards of self-reward and observer performance. *Developmental Psychology*, 1972, **7**, 153–156.

KUPFERER, H. J., & FITZGERALD, T. K. *Culture, society, and guidance*. Boston: Houghton Mifflin, 1971.

LAFRANCE, M. Nonverbal cues to conversational turn taking between black speakers. In J. W. JULIAN (Chair), *Dyadic communication*. Symposium presented at the meeting of the American Psychological Association, New Orleans, August 1974.

LANE, E. A. The influence of sex and race on process-reactive ratings of schizophrenics. *Journal of Psychology*, 1968, **68**, 15–20.

LENNARD, H. L., & BERNSTEIN, A. Role learning in psychotherapy. *Psychotherapy: Theory, Research and Practice*, 1967, **4**, 1–6.

LERNER, B. *Therapy in the ghetto: Political impotence and personal disintegration.* Baltimore: Johns Hopkins University Press, 1972.

LEVINSON, D. A., & JENSEN, S. M. Assertive versus passive group therapist behavior with southern white and Negro schizophrenic hospital patients. *International Journal of Group Psychotherapy*, 1967, **17**, 328–335.

LEWIS, N. D. C., & HUBBARD, L. D. Manic depressive reactions in Negroes. In Association for Research in Nervous and Mental Disease, *Manic-depressive psychosis.* Baltimore: Williams & Wilkins, 1931. Pp. 779–817.

LIEBERT, R. M., SOBOL, M. P., & COPEMANN, C. D. Effects of vicarious consequences and race of model upon imitative performance by black children. *Developmental Psychology*, 1972, **6**, 453–456.

LIND, J. E. The color complex in the Negro. *Psychoanalytic Review*, 1914, **1**, 404–414.

LIND, J. E. Phylogenetic elements in the psychoses of the Negro. *Psychoanalytic Review*, 1917, **4**, 303–332.

LORION, R. P. Socioeconomic status and traditional treatment approaches reconsidered. *Psychological Bulletin*, 1973, **79**, 263–270.

LORION, R. P. Patient and therapist variables in the treatment of low-income patients. *Psychological Bulletin*, 1974, **81**, 344–354.

LOWE, G. D., & ALSTON, J. P. Hospital structure and racial discrimination. *Journal of Alcohol and Drug Education*, 1974, **19**, 29–37.

LOWINGER, P. L., & DOBIE, S. Attitudes and emotions of the psychiatrist in the initial interview. *American Journal of Psychotherapy*, 1966, **20**, 17–34.

MANN, P. H. Modifying the behavior of Negro educable mentally retarded boys through group counseling procedures. *Journal of Negro Education*, 1969, **38**, 135–142.

MAYFIELD, W. G. Mental health in the black community. *Social Work*, 1972, **17**, 106–110.

MAYO, J. A. Utilization of a community mental health center by blacks: Admission to inpatient status. *Journal of Nervous and Mental Disease*, 1974, **158**, 202–207.

MCCREARY, B. P. *Race as a determinant of counselor preference.* Unpublished master's thesis, Southern Illinois University Rehabilitation Institute, 1971.

MEHRABIAN, A. *Nonverbal communication.* Chicago: Aldine-Atherton, 1972.

MIMS, J., HERRON, L., JR., & WURTZ, R. E. *Parallel pigmentation and counselee satisfaction.* Unpublished research report, Ferndale, Michigan Public Schools, 1970.

MINUCHIN, S. *Families and family therapy.* Cambridge, Mass.: Harvard University Press, 1974.

MINUCHIN, S., MONTALVO, B., GUERNEY, B. G., JR., ROSMAN, B. L., & SCHUMER, F. *Families of the slums: An exploration of their structure and treatment.* New York: Basic Books, 1967.

MITCHELL, H. The black experience in higher education. *Counseling Psychologist*, 1970, **2**, 30–36.

MITCHELL, H. Counseling black students: A model in response to the need for relevant counselor training programs. *Counseling Psychologist*, 1971, **2**, 117–122.

MITHUN, J. S. Cooperation and solidarity as survival necessities in a black urban community. *Urban Anthropology*, 1973, **2**, 25–34.

MULLOZZI, A. D., JR. Interracial counseling: Clients' ratings and counselors' ratings in a first session. Doctoral dissertation, Southern Illinois University, 1972. *Dissertation Abstracts International*, 1972, **33**, 2175A–2176A (University Microfilms No. 72-28, 546).

MURRAY, D. C., BROWN, J., & KNOX, W. Verbal participation of Negro psychotics in combined as contrasted to all-Negro groups. *International Journal of Group Psychotherapy*, 1964, **14**, 221–223.

O'MALLEY, M. Psychosis in the colored race: A study in comparative psychiatry. *American Journal of Insanity*, 1914, **71**, 309–337.

ORNE, M. T., & WENDER, P. H. Anticipatory socialization for psychotherapy: Method and rationale. *American Journal of Psychiatry*, 1968, **124**, 1202–1212.

OVERALL, B., & ARONSON, H. Expectations of psychotherapy in patients of lower socioeconomic class. *American Journal of Orthopsychiatry*, 1963, **33**, 421–430.

OWEN, I. Adlerian counseling in racially mixed groups of elementary school children. *Individual Psychologist*, 1970, **7**, 53–58.

PALLONE, N. J., HURLEY, R. B., & RICKARD, F. S. Black students and school counselors: Rhetoric and reality. *School Counselor*, 1973, **20**, 259–267.

PEARL, A. The poverty of psychology—An indictment. In V. L. ALLEN (Ed.), *Psychological factors in poverty.* Chicago: Markham, 1970. Pp. 348–364.

PHILLIPS, W. B. Counseling Negro pupils: An educational dilemma. *Journal of Negro Education*, 1960, **29**, 504–507.

PIERCE, C. M. Problems of the Negro adolescent in the next decade. In E. B. BRODY (Ed.), *Minority group adolescents in the United States.* Baltimore: Williams & Wilkins, 1968. Pp. 17–47.

PIERCE, C. M. Psychiatric problems of the black minority. In G. CAPLAN (Ed.), *American handbook of psychiatry.* Vol. 2. *Child and adolescent psychiatry, sociocultural and community psychiatry.* (2nd Ed.) New York: Basic Books, 1974. Pp. 512–523.

PIERCE, W. D. The comprehensive community mental health programs and the black community. In R. L. JONES (Ed.), *Black psychology.* New York: Harper & Row, 1972. Pp. 398 405.

PINDERHUGHES, C. A. Understanding Black Power: Processes and proposals. *American Journal of Psychiatry*, 1969, **125**, 1552–1557.

POHLMAN, E., & ROBINSON, F. P. Client reaction to some aspects of the counseling situation. *Personnel and Guidance Journal*, 1960, **38**, 546–551.

PORTER, L. W. Communication: Structure and process. In H. L. FROMKIN & J. J. SHERWOOD (Eds.), *Integrating the organization: A social psychological analysis.* New York: Free Press, 1974. Pp. 216–246.

POWELL, E. R., & DENNIS, V. C. *Application of an anthropological technique to desegregated schools.* Paper presented at the meeting of the American Educational Research Association, Chicago 1972.

RAYNES, A. E., & WARREN, G. Some distinguishing features of patients failing to attend a psychiatric clinic after referral. *American Journal of Orthopsychiatry*, 1971, **41**, 581–588.

RICCIO, A. C., & BARNES, K. D. Counselor preferences of senior high school students. *Counselor Education and Supervision*, 1973, **13**, 36–40.

RIESSMAN, F. Role-playing and the lower socio-economic group. *Group Psychotherapy*, 1964, **17**, 36–48.

RIPLEY, H. S., & WOLF, S. Mental illness among Negro troops overseas. *American Journal of Psychiatry*, 1947, **103**, 499–512.

RODMAN, H. Family and social pathology in the ghetto. *Science*, 1968, **161**, 756–762.

ROSEN, H., & FRANK, J. D. Negroes in psychotherapy. *American Journal of Psychiatry*, 1962, **119**, 456–460.

ROSENBAUM, E. Effects of race of observer, examiner, and model on imitation of a school-like task. Doctoral dissertation, University of Wisconsin, 1971. *Dissertation Abstracts International*, 1972, **32**, 4428A (University Microfilms No. 72-1053).

ROSENBAUM, M., SNADOWSKY, A., & HARTLEY, E. Group

psychotherapy and the integration of the Negro. *International Journal of Group Psychotherapy*, 1966, **16**, 86–90.

ROSENTHAL, A. J., & LANGEE, H. The development of a service-oriented psychiatric program in a disadvantaged area. *American Journal of Psychiatry*, 1970, **126**, 1436–1443.

ROSENTHAL, D., & FRANK, J. D. The fate of psychiatric clinic outpatients assigned to psychotherapy. *Journal of Nervous and Mental Disease*, 1958, **127**, 330–343.

SAGER, C. J., BRAYBOY, T. L., & WAXENBERG, B. R. *Black ghetto family in therapy: A laboratory experience.* New York: Grove Press, 1970.

SALZMAN, C., SHADER, R. I., SCOTT, D. A., & BINSTOCK, W. Interviewer anger and patient dropout in walk-in clinic. *Comprehensive Psychiatry*, 1970, **11**, 267–273.

SAMUELS, A. S. The reduction of interracial prejudice and tension through group therapy. In H. I. KAPLAN & B. J. SADOCK (Eds.), *New models for group therapy.* New York: Dutton, 1972. Pp. 214–243.

SATTLER, J. M. Racial "experimenter effects" in experimentation, testing, interviewing, and psychotherapy. *Psychological Bulletin*, 1970, **73**, 137–160.

SATTLER, J. M. Racial experimenter effects. In K. S. MILLER & R. M. DREGER (Eds.), *Comparative studies of blacks and whites in the United States.* New York: Seminar Press, 1973. Pp. 7–32.

SCHUMAN, H., & CONVERSE, J. M. The effects of black and white interviewers on black responses in 1968. *Public Opinion Quarterly*, 1971, **35**, 44–68.

SCHWARTZ, J. M. Psychiatrists' treatment decisions as a function of patient race and sex. In N. HAAN (Chair), *Clinician value and client sex, race, and social-class effects on clinical decisions.* Symposium presented at the meeting of the American Psychological Association, New Orleans, September 1974.

SELIGMAN, M. R. The interracial casework relationship. *Smith College Studies in Social Work*, 1968, **39**, 84.

SEWARD, G. H. *Psychotherapy and culture conflict in community mental health.* (2nd Ed.) New York: Ronald Press, 1972.

SHANNON, B. E. Implications of white racism for social work practice. *Social Casework*, 1970, **51**, 270–276.

SHAPIRO, B. A. N. Effects of race and sex role stereotyping on acceptance of and learning from occupational role models. Doctoral dissertation, Stanford University, 1973. *Dissertation Abstracts International*, 1973, **33**, 7022A (University Microfilms No. 73-14, 976).

SHAPIRO, E. T., & PINSKER, H. Shared ethnic scotoma. *American Journal of Psychiatry*, 1973, **130**, 1338–1341.

SILVER, C. Counselor-client compatability: A comparison of dogmatism and race in inner-city college-bound client decision-making. Doctoral dissertation, St. John's University, 1972. *Dissertation Abstracts International*, 1972, **33**, 2723A–2724A (University Microfilms No. 72-31, 041).

SILVERMAN, P. R. The influences of racial differences on the Negro patient dropping out of psychiatric treatment. *Psychiatric Opinion*, 1971, **8**, 29–36.

SINGER, B. D. Some implications of differential psychiatric treatment of Negro and white patients. *Social Science and Medicine*, 1967, **1**, 77–83.

SMITH, A. L. Interpersonal communication within transracial contexts. In L. L. BARKER & R. J. KIBLER (Eds.), *Speech communication behavior: Perspectives and principles.* Englewood Cliffs, N.J.: Prentice-Hall, 1971. Pp. 305–320.

SMITH, P. M., JR. Counselors for ghetto youth. *Personnel and Guidance Journal*, 1968, **47**, 279–280.

SNYDER, R., & SECHREST, L. B. An experimental study of directive group therapy with defective delinquents. *American Journal of Mental Deficiency*, 1959, **64**, 117–123.

SPANNER, F. E. The psychotherapist as an activist in social

change: A proponent. In F. F. KORTEN, S. W. COOK, & J. I. LACEY (Eds.), *Psychology and the problems of society.* Washington, D.C.: American Psychological Association, 1970. Pp. 58–62.

SPIEGEL, J. P. Some cultural aspects of transference and counter-transference. In J. H. MASSERMAN (Ed.), *Individual and familial dynamics, science and psychoanalysis.* Vol. 2. New York: Grune & Stratton, 1959. Pp. 160–182.

STATMAN, J. Community mental health as a pacification program. In J. AGEL (Ed.), *The radical therapist.* New York: Ballantine, 1971. Pp. 210–218.

STEISEL, I. M. Paraprofessionals—Questions from a traditionalist. *Professional Psychology*, 1972, **3**, 331–334; 340–342.

STILES, E., DONNER, S., GIOVANNONE, J., LOCHTE, E., & REETZ, R. Hear it like it is. *Social Casework*, 1972, **53**, 292–299.

STOKELY, B. M. *Crow Jim: Its effect upon Negro clients' use of casework treatment when the worker is white.* Unpublished master's thesis, Smith College School for Social Work, 1966.

STRANGES, R. J., & RICCIO, A. C. Counselee preferences for counselors: Some implications for counselor education. *Counselor Education and Supervision*, 1970, **10**, 39–45.

STRUPP, H. H. *Psychotherapy and the modification of abnormal behavior: An introduction to theory and research.* New York: McGraw-Hill, 1971.

STRUPP, H. H., & BLOXOM, A. L. Preparing lower-class patients for group psychotherapy: Development and evaluation of a role-induction film. *Journal of Consulting and Clinical Psychology*, 1973, **41**, 373–384.

SUE, S., McKINNEY, H., ALLEN, D., & HALL, J. Delivery of community mental health services to black and white clients. *Journal of Consulting and Clinical Psychology*, 1974, **42**, 794–801.

SUNDBERG, N. D. *Toward research evaluating cross-cultural counseling.* Unpublished manuscript, University of Oregon. 1974.

SWANSON, D. D. The effects of behavioral group counseling on the self-concept of pregnant Negro teenagers using male and female co-counselors. Doctoral dissertation, State University of New York at Buffalo, 1972. *Dissertation Abstracts International*, 1973, **33**, 3312A (University Microfilms No. 72-27, 273).

SZASZ, T. S. The Negro in psychiatry: An historical note on psychiatric rhetoric. *American Journal of Psychotherapy*, 1971a, **25**, 469–471.

SZASZ, T. S. The sane slave. *American Journal of Psychotherapy*, 1971b, **25**, 228–239.

TABER, R. H. A systems approach to the delivery of mental health services in black ghettos. *American Journal of Orthopsychiatry*, 1970, **40**, 702–709.

TANNEY, M. F. The initial impact of racial differences on clients: An analogue study. Doctoral dissertation, Ohio State University, 1972. *Dissertation Abstracts International*, 1973, **33**, 5527B (University Microfilms No. 73-11, 588).

THELEN, M. H. The effect of subject race, model race, and vicarious praise on vicarious learning. *Child Development*, 1971, **42**, 972–977.

THELEN, M. H., & FRYREAR, J. L. Effect of observer and model race on the imitation of standards of self-reward. *Developmental Psychology*, 1971a, **5**, 133–135.

THELEN, M. H., & FRYREAR, J. L. Imitation of self-reward standards by black and white female delinquents. *Psychological Reports*, 1971b, **29**, 667–671.

THELEN, M. H., ROBERTS, M. C., & COVERDELL, S. A. Model's race and S's race in imitation of cognitive and motor tasks. *Psychological Reports*, 1973, **33**, 485–486.

THOMAS, A. Pseudo-transference reactions due to cultural stereotyping. *American Journal of Orthopsychiatry*, 1962, **32**, 894–900.

THOMAS, A. P., & SILLEN, S. *Racism and psychiatry.* New

York: Brunner/Mazel, 1972.

THOMAS, C. W. Black-white campus and the function of counseling. *Counseling Psychologist*, 1969, **1**, 70–73.

THOMAS, C. W. Different strokes for different folks: A conversation. *Psychology Today*, 1970, **4**, 49–53, 78, 80.

TRUAX, C. B. *Counseling and psychotherapy: Process and outcome.* (Final Rep. Vocational Rehabilitation Administration Research and Demonstration Grant 906-P.) Fayetteville: University of Arkansas, Arkansas Rehabilitation Research and Training Center, June 1966.

VAIL, S. The effects of socioeconomic class, race, and level of experience on social workers' judgments of clients. *Smith College Studies in Social Work*, 1970, **40**, 236–246.

VALENTINE, C. A. Deficit, difference, and bicultural models of Afro-American behavior. *Harvard Educational Review*, 1971, **41**, 137–157.

VONTRESS, C. E. Counseling Negro adolescents. *School Counselor*, 1967, **15**, 86–91.

VONTRESS, C. E. *Counseling Negroes.* Boston: Houghton Mifflin, 1971.

VONTRESS, C. E. Counseling: Racial and ethnic factors. *Focus on Guidance*, 1973a, **5**, 1–10.

VONTRESS, C. E. *Racial and ethnic barriers in counseling.* Paper presented at the meeting of the American Psychological Association, Montreal, August 1973b.

VONTRESS, C. E. *Cross-cultural counseling in perspective.* Paper presented at the meeting of the American Personnel and Guidance Association Convention, New Orleans, April 1974.

WALKER, P. L. The effect of two counseling strategies with black disadvantaged clients. Doctoral dissertation, Georgia State University, 1972. *Dissertation Abstracts International*, 1973, **33**, 4106A–4107A (University Microfilms No. 73-4345).

WARREN, R. C., JACKSON, A. M., NUGARIS, J., & FARLEY, G. K. Differential attitudes of black and white patients toward treatment in a child guidance clinic. *American Journal of Orthopsychiatry*, 1973, **43**, 384–393.

WEISS, S. L., & DLUGOKINSKI, E. L. Parental expectations of psychotherapy. *Journal of Psychology*, 1974, **86**, 71–80.

WHITE, J. L. Guidelines for black psychologists. *Black Scholar*, 1970, **1**, 52–57.

WILLIAMS, B. M. Trust and self-disclosure among black college students. *Journal of Counseling Psychology*, 1974, **21**, 522–525.

WILLIAMS, R., & POLLACK, R. H. Some nonpsychological variables in therapy defection in a child-guidance clinic. *Journal of Psychology*, 1964, **58**, 145–155.

WILLIAMS, R. L., & KIRKLAND, J. The white counselor and the black client. *Counseling Psychologist*, 1970, **2**, 114–117.

WILLIS, F. N., JR. Initial speaking distance as a function of the speakers' relationship. *Psychonomic Science*, 1969, **5**, 221–222.

WINSTON, A., PARDES, H., & PAPERNICK, D. S. Inpatient treatment of blacks and whites. *Archives of General Psychiatry*, 1972, **26**, 405–409.

WITBECK, G. B. *Attitudes of Negro clients toward Negro caseworkers.* Unpublished master's thesis, Smith College School for Social Work, 1946.

WOLKEN, G. H., MORIWAKI, S., & WILLIAMS, K. J. Race and social class as factors in the orientation toward psychotherapy. *Journal of Counseling Psychology*, 1973, **20**, 312–316.

YAMAMOTO, J., & GOIN, M. K. Social class factors relevant for psychiatric treatment. *Journal of Nervous and Mental Disease*, 1966, **142**, 332–339.

YAMAMOTO, J., JAMES, Q. C., BLOOMBAUM, M., & HATTEM, J. Racial factors in patient selection. *American Journal of Psychiatry*, 1967, **124**, 630–636.

YAMAMOTO, J., JAMES, Q. C., & PALLEY, N. Cultural problems in psychiatric therapy. *Archives of General Psychiatry*, 1968, **19**, 45–49.

YASHKO, M. A. Relationship problems in interracial casework. *Smith College Studies in Social Work*, 1970, **41**, 81–82.

YOUNG, A. H. Race of psychotherapist and client and perception of variables relevant to therapy outcome. Doctoral dissertation, University of Illinois at Urbana-Champaign, 1972. *Dissertation Abstracts International*, 1973, **33**, 5506A (University Microfilms No. 73-10, 093).

EDITORS' REFERENCES

BANDURA, A. *Principles of behavior modification.* New York: Holt, Rinehart & Winston, 1969.

SATTLER, J. Racial "experimenter effects" in experimentation, testing, interviewing, and psychotherapy. *Psychological Bulletin*, 1970, **73**, 137–160.

NOTES

1. The author wishes to express his thanks and gratitude to Ralph Mason Dreger, George C. Gross, Alan S. Gurman, Herbert Harari, William A. Hillix, John Holt, Steve Perry, and Andrew M. Razin for their valuable criticism and suggestions.

2. Space limitations do not permit a discussion of the dynamics of the Black-therapist White-client relationship.

3. *Editors' Footnote.* The following list of pitfalls seems to cover nearly every "reaction" a White might have to a Black. This is not to impugn the validity of the list, but it seems noteworthy that the list seems to cover mistakes in nearly every direction and its opposite, suggesting two things to us. One is that a therapist free of all these would be a nonexistent saint. Therefore, real, living therapists ought perhaps to content themselves with recognizing their own "impulses" in these directions and be able and willing to acknowledge them openly with their patients and/or work on them in their own supervision, for example.

   The second suggestion is that "reaction" in nearly any direction can be detrimental if extreme enough, and that the therapist in an interracial situation ought therefore be alerted to any strong reaction he feels and spend some time and effort examining it.

4. *Editors' Footnote.* This is an interesting issue, for at least two reasons. First, modeling behavior is supposed to be enhanced by perceived similarity between subject and model (Bandura, 1969). Here, there apparently are other factors which override the obvious dissimilarity between Black children and White adults. What these factors might be forms the second point of interest in this issue. Sattler's explanation (the paucity of Black adults in the schools) seems problematic. We doubt, from our own experience, that there is such a paucity, at least in urban schools. In addition to the substantial number of Black teachers and administrators, there are many paraprofessionals, volunteers, and special program staff who are Black. But even if there were such a paucity, a more likely explanation seems to us to be that White adults are seen as powerful, prestigious figures, and model power and prestige are also important facilitators of modeling.

5. The location of the study and the racial and gender composition of the staff were obtained from O. P. Barney, personal communication, July 1975.

6. *Editors' Footnote.* There is a more "malignant" interpretation for more frequent hospitalizations of Blacks: underlying (unconscious or conscious but not promulgated) White fear of Black violence, as part of the "crazy nigger" myth.

7. *Editors' Footnote.* This is interesting and surprising in view of the clear documentation (Sattler, 1970) of

experimenter race effects on subjects' performance in many other (test) situations.

8. Location of the study and number of professionals obtained from S. L. Weiss, personal communication, July 1975.

9. B. M. Williams, personal communication, July 1975.

10. Location of institution and therapist race obtained from R. T. Snyder, personal communication, July 1975.

11. *Editors' Footnote.* If mutual acceptance and understanding constitute "biculturalism," we have no disagreement about its desirability or even feasibility. To us, however, the term denotes *adoption* of two sets of language, customs, and mores, and we have great reservations about the feasibility and desirability of such biculturalism. We do not feel there is any substantial disagreement with Sattler here, but we prefer a more specific term that would make this distinction clear.

12. *Editors' Footnote.* An excellent point. We feel that the magnitude of the kind of change being called for in this discussion cannot be overestimated. Calls for social activism in other professions often appeal to the social consciousness that members of the group (doctors, teachers, e.g.) ought to have, but only rarely have professions been asked to change their roles to include such activism as a major task.

In fact, the "interweaving" of (activist and therapeutic) skills that Sattler calls for below strikes us as a very difficult enterprise. It would complicate and intensify the conflict between White therapist tendencies toward paternalism ("doing for") on the one hand, and attempts to allow the client as much autonomy and freedom to grow as possible, on the other hand. Our own opinion, which we realize may conflict with that of many community-oriented therapists, is that activist and therapist activities are two very different enterprises which are

ideally engaged in *separately.* This whole issue is controversial and deserves a lengthier discussion than we can give.it here, but we would like to point out at least one problem: that political, social, and economic ideologies must by definition be part of such activism and that we see no realistic way of changing the training of therapists to include activist skills without promoting a particular ideology. Such a situation runs the risk of aligning a profession with political ideology.

13. *Editors' Footnote.* Whether or not analysis or analytically oriented therapy is useful to Blacks, we think it unfair to characterize analysis as encouraging adjustment to one's environment. Granted its intrapsychic emphasis, there is no evidence that we are aware of that it promotes such "adjustment" any more than other types of therapy.

Of interest here, however, is the evidence that "externalizers" of Locus-of-Control may do better with directive than nondirective therapy. If we assume (admittedly without evidence) that poor Blacks are more often "appropriate" (given their socioeconomic situation) externalizers than middle-class Whites and Blacks, then, on this basis, there may be empirical reasons for using directive therapies with such patients.

14. *Editors' Footnote.* Again, we ask the reader to appreciate the degree of role change being discussed here (and in the following modifications).

15. *Editors' Footnote.* If we have seemed in our above notes to be somewhat hesitant to endorse some of Sattler's proposals, let us here state that we wholeheartedly endorse the direction, spirit, and aims of these changes. Specifically, we feel it very appropriate that therapists be activists in the development and continuity of mental health and related programs in Black communities, as Sattler here proposes.

CHAPTER 12

THE A–B VARIABLE: STILL PROMISING AFTER TWENTY YEARS?

ANDREW M. RAZIN

In 1954, Whitehorn and Betz first differentiated therapists whose schizophrenic patients improved most from therapists whose schizophrenic patients improved least. The former therapists were labeled "As," and the latter, "Bs." In a series of attempts to find systematic differences (in therapeutic style, "personality," etc.) between these more and less effective therapists, Betz and Whitehorn (1956) found that the two groups of therapists generated different vocational interest patterns on the Strong Vocational Interest Blank (SVIB). Literally every "A-B" study since then (with the exception of Whitehorn and Betz' validation attempts) has defined As and Bs on the basis of their SVIB response patterns.

The many studies that have followed fall into three groups: clinical process and outcome studies, analogue or pseudotherapy studies, and correlational studies relating the A-B variable to other "personality" dimensions. (In addition, since several versions of the A-B scale, of varying length, content, and psychometric quality, have been generated, there has also evolved a small body of research comparing the several scales.)

Several major reviews have appeared in the area, and, although these have each had distinct viewpoints to present, they have been very careful, generally fair and comprehensive, astute and informative. What follow are essentially brief capsule comments on these reviews, which are in no way intended as comprehensive summaries. (Readers interested in the substantive issues mentioned should consult the original reviews.)

Carson (1967) was the first to attempt to integrate the diverse A-B literature, and the title of his review article ("A and B therapist 'types': A possible critical variable in psychotherapy") reflects the cautious optimism found in his conclusions. He was particularly concerned with defining the A-B variable personologically, and, noting the factors then known to

be associated—e.g., disinterest in mechanics—he concluded that the A-B variable is a powerful, though indirect, measure. At this point in A-B history, there was already much confusion and disagreement to be found in the research literature, and Carson made some valuable efforts at reconciling some of the existent discrepancies. Thus, for example, he pointed out that "paradoxical discomfort" diminished or disappeared as dyadic contact was extended to resemble actual psychotherapy more closely.

In 1969, more comprehensive reviews were submitted (by coincidence, nearly simultaneously) by Razin and Chartier, who therefore divided the area, so that Razin concentrated on actual clinical studies and on personality characteristics, while Chartier focused on analogue studies. The reviews appeared together in 1971. Razin's (1971) viewpoint was not too different from Carson's. He found work in the area to be riddled by discrepancies and methodological flaws, but nevertheless concluded that the differential therapeutic effectiveness of As and Bs was not a fluke or artifact. He concluded, for example, that work on clinical outcome had produced an unclear, yet intriguing (still promising?) picture that warranted further pursuit. He also concluded that some order *could* be imposed on the personality data, and he pieced together a picture of As as open to unusual perceptions, flexible, and able to communicate to schizoid patients acceptance of bizarre behavior and experiences. Furthermore, he argued that there is a commonality among A-occupations and A-items on the SVIB—namely, *persuasiveness*, a dimension which had received some independent (non A-B) support as a determinant of therapy outcome. He discouraged further correlational personological studies, and urged further work on actual in-therapy behavior to define "A-Bness" operationally in that situation.

Chartier (1971) took a more skeptical stance.

He sharply criticized much of the analogue work (1) for extrapolating from tenuous assumptions, particularly regarding the interaction hypothesis, so that such work, he concluded, had contributed very little support or clarification; (2) for the use of such simplifications as college student "therapists," an example of research emphasis being dictated by the availability of technique; and (3) for the general inconsistency of evidence. Despite his more critical stance, his recommendations were quite similar to Razin's in calling for clear demonstration of the A-B interaction effect in an actual clinical setting, after which laboratory (analogue) research should pursue more specific questions. He also pointed out that the widespread use of ataractic drugs *since* the collection of the Whitehorn and Betz data may have produced a current state of affairs wherein medication effects are much more potent than, and thus obscure or obliterate, any A-B differences; under such conditions, demonstration of the "interaction hypotheses" (see below) would constitute an elaborate, wasteful enterprise.

May's (1974) review of outcome studies is still more critical, and, as it is the most recent review, and thus covers previous reviews as well as newer research, a relatively detailed consideration of it seems warranted here. In general, it is very astutely written and presents often cogent arguments for skepticism regarding much of the A-B outcome research. In particular, May has found many statistical errors and ambiguities, and, quite commendably, has apparently gone to great lengths to obtain and reanalyze old data. He represents many of the original (Whitehorn & Betz, e.g.) findings as much less positive—i.e., less supportive of A-B differences— than they had been. He raises many of the criticisms already cited by previous reviewers, as well as a few new ones—for example, bias in the evaluation of outcome in the original Whitehorn and Betz studies, and contamination of psychotherapy effects (on outcome) with insulin shock effects, in these same studies.

But if May is correct—and he may well be— in concluding that Razin (1971) was overly generous in his review, it seems that May's consideration may be unfairly critical in places.[3] Stylistically, his review tends to minimize positive findings by, for example, giving relatively little attention to legitimate cross-validations by Whitehorn and Betz (1960), and by maximizing attention to negative findings by repeating the same criticisms in several places. Specifically, he is quite uncritical of the Stephens

and Astrup (1965) study which purported to reanalyze (more carefully) the Whitehorn and Betz data and which reported essentially null results. Their study, however, is itself open to serious criticisms (see, e.g., Razin, 1971) which May ignores. Later, May refers to the Berzins, Ross, and Friedman (1972) study as failing to support the B hypothesis (that Bs do better than As with neurotics). This is not clearly so. Of the three outcome measures in that study, one showed clear significant support for the interaction hypothesis (which, obviously, includes the B hypothesis), one showed nonsignificant support, and one showed no support. Furthermore, May's description of the Shader, Grinspoon, Harmatz, and Ewalt (1971) study as elegant seems strikingly uncritical, as will be shown below, where this study is considered in detail. In his discussion, he concludes that neither the A hypothesis (that As do better with schizophrenics) nor the B hypothesis (that Bs do better with neurotics) has received support, and to substantiate this conclusion, he states that neither the Beutler, Johnson, Neville, and Workman (1972) nor the Grinspoon, Shader, and Ewalt (1972) studies found A-B differences. Beutler *et al.* did not find differences in patient outcome but did find significant interaction hypothesis support on empathy, and Shader *et al.* (1971) did find significant A > B outcome differences in their drug-plus-psychotherapy group.

Also in May's discussion, he cites Razin's suggestion that B therapists may do better in a treatment atmosphere where "B-like" goals define success, and he claims to "put the shoe on the other foot," pointing out that the same should hold for As in an "A-like" atmosphere, and that the positive Whitehorn-Betz results may therefore be due to an expectancy effect. I do not at all disagree with that suggestion; of course, there are really shoes on both feet— i.e., any particular set of institutional goal-expectancies may be found to exert effects in any treatment setting. The existence of such effects (i.e., the expectancy of A-like or B-like goals somehow producing A > B, or B > A, differential outcome) not only reminds me of the absolute necessity of specifying outcome criteria, but also implies that outcome research ought to enlarge its focus to include the study of such expectancies and the parameters through which they exert their effects. (See, e.g., Wilkins, Chapter 13, this volume.)

Finally, it should be remembered that May's review is exclusively devoted to clinical outcome, with virtually no attention to analogue or personological research. It is, of course, the outcome area that has been weakest over the years, in terms of providing consistent, sound evidence.

In addition to these major reviews, there has been a series of briefer reviews and comments. Cartwright (1968) leveled a series of criticisms at the analogue research, pointing out that the use of undergraduate Ss provides no guarantee that they (As and Bs) are both (1) alike on physician, psychologist, and public administrator SVIB profiles, and (2) different on lawyer, CPA, printer, math-science teacher profiles, as were the residents in the Whitehorn-Betz studies. There is, thus, incomplete data on Ss who may not, in fact, have been "true" As and Bs. She urged designs which, among other things, allow Ss to react to a variety of patient types. (The reader with particular interest in analogue A-B research is encouraged to consult the Chartier and Cartwright reviews for excellent, detailed consideration of the many pitfalls involved therein.)

Meltzoff and Kornreich (1970) critically summarize the early Whitehorn-Betz work, pointing out still another source of data contamination: C. Astrup, in classifying patients as "process" or "non-process," used discharge improvement ratings (i.e., outcome data) in making his diagnostic decisions. They conclude that subsequent research has never really affirmed the original findings, and that the relationship of the SVIB items to (differential) outcome therefore remains hypothetical. Furthermore, "if the hypothesis could be supported, it would seem likely that underlying these (SVIB) interests one could find personality, social class, and other background variables that were primary determinants of the interest patterns" (p. 306).

Kemp (1970) provides another review, which is briefer, much less critical, and more speculative. He concludes that patient-therapist matching warrants greater attention, that optimal matching may depend on complementarity rather than similarity, and that the A-B dimension may be more closely related to therapeutic activity level than to the Rogerian facilitative conditions.

Krasner and Ullmann (1973), in their personality text, agree (p. 177) with Howard and Orlinsky (1972), who conclude that the A-B variable has been elusive, generated a great deal of perplexity, and is probably much less worthwhile pursuing than other person-relevant characteristics or specific, overt "influencers'" behaviors.

More recently, Heaton, Carr, and Hampson (1975) survey some of the A-B literature and suggest (1) that "true" Bs may be a vanishing breed, to be found in adequate numbers among therapists trained before 1960, but in diminishing numbers among younger therapists; (2) that there are many complexities (e.g., involving sex and socioeconomic status of patients) and contradictions in the A-B area; but (3) that greater specificity of hypothesis and designs, rather than overall skepticism, is called for in this area.

Most recently, Franco (1975) reviewed the area, attempting to provide a theoretically coherent personality description of As and Bs. He concludes that As are less defensive, more open to their own emotional experiences, and thus perhaps more "available" to schizophrenics.

The present chapter is an attempt to assess the status of the A-B variable after more than 20 years of research. It will focus primarily on work appearing between the 1971 reviews and mid-1975, but will also include some prior research which was not obtainable at the time of these earlier reviews. Within that domain, it represents a comprehensive review, including all known A-B research in the process, outcome, analogue (pseudo-therapy), and personality characteristics areas.

Before proceeding to consider the research itself, though, it might be useful for the reader to acquaint himself with some of the terms that have become part of the jargon of the A-B research literature. The most common of these are:

AVOS, TAO, TAS. These terms refer to research subjects, usually patients, pseudo-patients, or interviewers, described as "avoidant of others," "turning against others," and "turning against self." The terms are used as roughly synonymous with "schizoid," "personality (or character) disorder," and "neurotic," and are especially common in the analogue literature. Although the AVOS-TAS distinction is most commonly used, all three terms have actual empirical origins in the symptom checklist research of Phillips and Rabinovitch (1958).

Complementarity, Complementary Pairings. These terms refer to therapist-patient dyads in which A-therapists are paired with schizophrenic, schizoid, or AVOS patients, and B-therapists are paired with neurotic, or TAS patients. The rationale for considering such dyads complementary is described immediately below (Interaction Hypothesis).

The Interaction Hypotheses. The interaction hypothesis very specifically refers to the (unproven) notion that the complementary dyads described above are more effective therapeutically than are oppositely paired dyads. "Effectiveness" is variously defined in different studies to refer to anything from outcome in actual therapy to amount of information gathered in an analogue interview. The interaction hypothesis developed after McNair, Callahan, and Lorr (1962) published data suggesting that in an outpatient, presumably neurotic, patient population, Bs obtained better outcome than As. In conjunction with the earlier Whitehorn-Betz findings of opposite results with schizophrenics, then, an interaction effect was hypothesized, sought, and variably found. The Razin (1971), Chartier (1971), and May (1974) studies provide detailed, critical reviews of much of this work.

Similarity, Dissimilarity. In the context of this chapter, these terms will be used to denote therapist-patient dyads in which both partners are of similar A-B status—i.e., both As or both Bs; dissimilar dyads are those in which one partner is an A, and the other a B. These terms should be distinguished from the term "complementary," defined above.

SVIB. The Strong Vocational Interest Blank was one of the measures on which Whitehorn and Betz sought to differentiate their more effective (A) and less effective (B) therapists. Twenty-three items emerged from statistical analyses as significantly differentiating, and these items came to be known as *the* "A-B scale," which, importantly, came to *define* therapists as As and Bs, replacing the original defining criterion of differential outcome with schizophrenics.

Actually the above description is a gross oversimplification. There have been *many* A-B scales, of varying item length, many with additional items not from the SVIB (but from the MMPI, for example). In fact, a major methodological problem has been the profusion of scales, which are not psychometrically equivalent. There have been a few studies comparing the several scales (Chartier, 1974; Kemp & Stephens, 1971; Seidman, 1972), and, fortunately, a consensus emerges from these comparative studies. The 23-item scale appears "strongest" in the sense of correlating with other variants; there are at least two other variants that correlate well with other scales; and there is one variant, the Campbell, Stevens, Uhlenhuth, and Johansson (1968) revision, which correlates poorly with the 23-item scale and the other variants, and which seems to be measuring something different than the others. In this chapter,

then, studies using the Campbell scale will be described as such. Recently, Stephens, Shaffer, and Zlotowitz (1975) constructed still another revision, which is discussed below (see "A-B Scale Comparisons").

May (1974) provides a very well-detailed, critical examination of this problem, and researchers contemplating work in this area should carefully consider the issues and findings in his paper as well as in the above comparative studies.

RECENT A-B RESEARCH

The review that follows considers work within the areas of outcome and process, analogue studies, and personality research. Within each of these three areas, I have attempted to further categorize and group studies wherever possible, but because so many studies deal with multiple or overlapping issues, this was often impossible. The discussion which follows this section will provide coherent consideration of each issue singly.

Outcome and Process: Inpatient Outcome

Shader *et al.* (1971) describe two studies, with some lack of detail. In the first, the A-B scores—using the Campbell *et al.* (1968) scale—of 18 senior psychiatric staff at the Massachusetts Mental Health Center (MMHC), all experienced and analytically oriented, were examined for their relationship to improvement rates of chronic schizophrenics after 2 years of treatment. No significant A-B differences were found. (Samples were too small for formal therapist X drug analyses, but the two patients who improved most had thioridizine and A-therapists, while the two patients who improved least had placebo drug and B-therapists.) For the second study, 1st-year residents' work (over an 8-week period) with acute schizophrenics was examined (These younger therapists were significantly more often As than were the senior staff.) Their thioridizine-treated patients improved more than did their placebo-treated patients. Within the thioridizine group, those with A-therapists improved significantly more than those with B-therapists; within the placebo group, there were no A-B differences. As tried more than Bs to establish verbal-teaching relationships. Apparently, no two-factor data analyses were performed. Additionally it might be noted that, in the first study, improvement was positively related to therapists' attempts to have patients discuss anger; no such relationship was found in the second study.

The major flaw in the report of this study is the lack of *psycho*therapeutic methodological information. There is no mention of the number of patients in either study, of how they were diagnosed, or of how improvement was determined; nor is there mention of the therapist N in the second study, the (A-B) classification criteria (cutoff scores) for therapists in either study, or of demographic data (therapist sex, e.g.) of patients or therapists in either study. Some of this information is found in the book (Grinspoon *et al.*, 1972) which describes the entire much larger schizophrenia research project, of which "the therapist variable" was only a part. Here it is seen, for example, that A-B classification was done using the Campbell *et al.* (1968) cutoffs; and that there were 20 chronic schizophrenics whose diagnoses were quite carefully made: each had spent 3 years prior to entering the study at the Boston State Hospital, was there diagnosed schizophrenic, *and* was diagnosed as chronic schizophrenic by three senior psychiatrists at MMHC. Acute schizophrenics were referred, based on a diagnosis of acute thought and affective disorder, *and* were diagnosed as acute schizophrenics by three senior psychiatrists at MMHC. Improvement (outcome) was determined with even greater care, via an extensive series of at least six measures (some homemade), incorporating the assessments of nurses, ward staff, therapists, and others. It is not clear (even in this extensive report), though, which of these was (were) used in A-B analyses, nor could I find therapist Ns for the second study (described above) or any therapist demographic data.

Commendably, the authors also reveal that the senior staff involved in the first (chronic patient) study included many (most?) who were very unhappy about being called upon (coerced?) by the superintendent of the facility to work with the chronic patients. These therapists were "glad when the whole thing was over" (p. 21). This contrasts sharply with the very enthusiastic 1st-year residents in the second (acute patient) study, among whom, interestingly, significant A-B differences did emerge. This suggests that these residents may have closely resembled Whitehorn and Betz' original (active, enthusiastic) As, a possibility consistent with the authors' conclusion: while "our data are clearly insufficient to clarify the therapist variable . . . we would now add that the degree

of improvement [effected by anti-psychotic drugs] may vary as a function of therapist type" (p. 247). Despite this important statement, however, the authors do treat psychotherapy as a homogeneous variable, and their attention to the details of psychotherapeutic parameters is minimal.

As May (1974) points out, this *is* an elegant study. It is extensive, detailed, and meticulously designed and reported, but it is so in nearly every area *except* psychotherapy parameters. Also May's description of the results for the "psychotherapy alone" condition as "contrary" to the A-hypothesis (p. 14) warrants qualification. First, there was no "psychotherapy alone" condition; there was a "psychotherapy-plus-placebo" condition, which, given the repeated demonstration of placebo effects, is obviously not the same as psychotherapy alone. Second, the results were null—i.e., they showed no significant differences, not "contrary." Finally, May's conclusion that the results with drugs here contradict those of Whitehorn and Betz— i.e., here As did better with drugs, while, in Whitehorn and Betz' studies, "Bs did better" (p. 14)—suffers from two problems: (1) it represents a surprising homogenization by May of "drugs," in that it makes no distinction between insulin and phenothiazines; (2) in Whitehorn and Betz (1957), Bs with insulin "did better" than Bs without insulin, *not* better than As with insulin.

To return to the issue of therapist enthusiasm briefly, it is worth noting the comments of Karon and Vanden Bos (1972). Finding psychotherapy superior to chemotherapy in changing thought disorder, they point out that supervisor, ward staff, and therapist attitudes and beliefs about the likely efficacy of the treatment modality (e.g., psychotherapy) which they are employing, and about its appropriateness for the particular patients involved, can have profound effects on the outcomes obtained using the modality. Furthermore, they point out that being required, without special recompense, to take part in research, or to administer treatments one dislikes (e.g., ECT), can also have striking effects on the outcomes obtained.

With this in mind, it is interesting to consider Klem's (1971) dissertation, in which the Ss were the participants in group counseling sessions aimed at "enhancing awareness and communications skills." Eight or nine Ss were in each of six groups, three led by one psychologist and three by another. The groups met for a total of 16 hours as part of a 4-week training institute.

After the institute, all Ss rated all of their group peers on the Relationship Inventory (see Gurman, Chapter 19, this volume). Klem's hypothesis, that dissimilar dyad ratings (As' ratings of Bs and Bs' of As) would be higher than similar dyad ratings, was supported only for empathy and congruence (not for self-disclosure, level and unconditionality of regard, or for total score). These results aside, though, what is relevant to our present discussion is the additional finding that in those groups led by the psychologist who was an A, A-members were rated higher than were Bs by their peers on empathy and congruence, while in the three groups led by the other psychologist, who was a B, Bs were rated higher on congruence. While an N of two group leaders is obviously too small to be conclusive, the weight of all the above discussion strongly suggests that leadership (supervisory or institutional), peer (therapist), and co-worker (nurse, ward staff) attitudes and expectations about treatment goals and modalities can exert a very potent effect on the outcomes obtained in a given setting. The above discussion also has bearing on the issue of institutional expectancies discussed in connection with May's (1974) review earlier. While this conclusion is by no means startling and is certainly not new to clinicians, it warrants emphasis for two reasons: (1) this piece of clinical lore has been largely undocumented empirically. The few pieces of data grouped together here represent almost all the "hard" data that I am aware of; (2) there is, therefore, as stated above, a real need not only to examine systematically the effects of "institutional character" (if we may so dub the conglomerate of all these attitudes and expectations) on therapeutic outcome, but also, perhaps, to explain existent discrepancies in outcome in several areas—for example, failures to replicate early client-centered results in non-client-centered settings (see Mitchell et al., Chapter 18, this volume).

In another, quite rigorously executed study of inpatients, Bowden, Endicott, and Spitzer (1972) found no evidence of differential A-B effectiveness. Thirty-six therapy trainees (psychology interns and psychiatric residents at the New York State Psychiatric Institute) were given the 23-item A-B scale, which was scored three different ways for data analysis. Patients ($n = 55$ at final "follow-up") were assigned by rotation, and were excluded from the study if they fell into alcoholic, retarded, drug dependent, antisocial personality, and organic categories, or if their frequency of therapy sessions was too

low. The Spitzer Psychiatric Status Schedule (PSS), whose reliability and validity has been demonstrated, was given on admission, generating an initial rating and at two "follow-ups" (at 1 month and at 3 months). Outcome was defined by PSS score changes over the two periods. Of the 122 correlations between therapist variables (A-B status, supervisor rating, own analysis, liking for patients, etc.) and patient PSS change, only four (none A-B measures) attained the .05 significance level, whether all patients or only schizophrenics were considered. Data on each therapist's "average patient" yielded similar results. Only "supervisor's rating" showed a consistent relationship with outcome.

There are a few criticisms to be made. It is not clear how diagnosis was determined; the therapist distribution was very much skewed toward the "A" end; no (therapist X patient) interaction effects (and no main effects within the "neurotic" category) were examined, and therapists all seemed to be inexperienced. Moreover, it seems curious that fewer correlations than chance would predict attained "significance"; not only did just four of 122 therapist versus outcome correlations attain significance, none of the 17 intercorrelations of the therapist variables attained significance. It is surprising that almost no attributes of the therapists seemed to be related to their differential outcome. It is not clear whether the limited variation in level of experience precluded consideration of it as a predictor, but if it also failed to predict outcome, the authors' findings would seem still more curious. Finally, as the authors and as Betz (1972) point out, one to three months is a very short time for any substantial change to appear in schizophrenic patients, particularly chronic schizophrenics, who comprised half the patient sample.

Despite these problems, the study is carefully done and throws serious doubt on the predictive power of the A-B variable. It is quite tempting to join Bowden et al. (1972) in concluding that the advent of phenothiazines and changes in the meaning of A-B scale item responses have virtually wiped out formerly found A-B differences.

Beutler et al. (1972) had raters examine typescripts of the initial sessions of inpatients (at Duke University's Highland Hospital) for "accurate empathy." Therapists were eight psychiatrists, identified as As or Bs by the Kemp (1963) version of the A-B scale (the four As saw 14 neurotics and nine schizophrenics; and the four Bs saw four neurotics and nine schizophrenics).

Two measures of outcome were made: the therapist's post-treatment evaluation and the length of hospitalization. Apparently because of small cell size, the authors pooled the B-therapist neurotic patient sample with the A-therapist schizophrenic patient sample into one group, and pooled the remaining two samples to form a second group. The authors found no significant differences between these two groups on either improvement measure; likewise, empathy ratings were also unrelated to improvement. They did find, however, that the first pooled group (As with schizophrenics and Bs with neurotics) showed higher empathy than the second group (opposite pairings). To the authors' appropriate criticism of their own outcome data (4-point scale) as crude, four more should be added: the use of only eight therapists; the lopsided distribution of patient types among As and Bs; the unidentified means and source of diagnoses; and the failure of their design to allow for testing main (therapist, patient) effects. Furthermore, patients were diagnosed *at discharge* (improvement could have changed diagnoses); and the sex, orientation, level of experience, etc., of the therapists' and the hospital's orientation are all unmentioned. These flaws lead one to question the validity of both their positive process finding (that the client-centered theoretical constructs are related to the A-B variable) and the negative outcome finding.[4]

In May's (1968) very comprehensive study of five different treatment methods of inpatient schizophrenia, the psychiatric residents involved completed A-B scales, but I could find no mention in his book of an examination of the relationship between A-B status and any other parameters. Apparently, though, May will be reporting on the relationship of A-B to outcome in the near future.

Outcome and Process:
Outpatient Outcome

In an extensive, long-range outpatient study aimed primarily at delineating the differential effects of several tranquilizing drugs, Koegler and Brill (1967) examined 12 A and five B psychiatry residents and their 300 nonpsychotic patients. Patient selection was not random, but was deemed representative of the clinic population. Diagnoses included neurosis, psychosomatosis, personality disorder, and borderline schizophrenia. Each therapist saw one or two patients at least once a week (for an unspecified number of sessions) in psychoanalytically ori-

ented therapy. Outcome was measured by five scales, including a Q sort completed by patients and a patient evaluation of outcome. The authors report that although the small number of Bs made statistical analysis difficult they were able to complete *t* tests, none of which showed any relationship between A-B and outcome.

The methodology in this study warrants comment, particularly because it typifies several other of the "drug-oriented" studies. In these, careful attention is usually paid, for example, to insure double-blinding and to detailed specification of the drug regimens, but the reader often finds it difficult or impossible to find very basic information on the *psycho*therapy parameters in the design. Here, for example, we are told that 30 therapists completed an A-B scale. The particular scale used, the cutoffs for A and B designation, and the means of therapist selection are all unidentified. Furthermore, even the total therapist N is unclear (is it 17, or were there also some AB—i.e., intermediate-scoring—therapists?). Finally, the quite heterogeneous diagnostic spectrum is never broken down for separate analyses (e.g., of neurotics), so that it is quite possible that the unspecified numbers of borderline patients in this sample, although they were outpatients, were much more similar to the AVOS or schizoid than to the TAS or neurotic patients in other studies. In brief, many of these studies are characterized by little or no attention to *psycho*therapeutic parameters in the design and/or in the reporting of the research. Now, obviously, one cannot be faulted for choosing to study chemotherapy rather than psychotherapy. Nor should chemotherapy researchers be faulted for failing to use good psychotherapy research design. The level of methodological and statistical complexity needed to study both areas well is probably impossible to realize in most situations. A serious problem is created, however, because "psychotherapy" then comes to be reported and viewed as a homogeneous entity, and important distinctions within this "entity" are lost. Furthermore, such studies are (often cumulatively) cited—for example, by May (1974) and May and Tuma (1965)—as convincing evidence of the predictive inutility not only of the A-B variable but of *psycho*therapy parameters in general. It is quite clear that, in certain situations (e.g., with chronic schizophrenia) certain chemotherapies are much more potent than psychotherapies, and the reverse apparently holds in other situations (e.g., neurotic depression). But relative potency is not the issue here. Rather, the issue is that "psychotherapy," no less than "drugs," is a heterogeneous class of interventions, the many parameters of which need to be specified, studied, and reported in detail if appropriate conclusions are to be drawn in a given study.[5]

Berzins, Ross, and Friedman (1972), after executing a long series of analogue studies (described below), most of which supported the interaction hypothesis, found further support in an outcome study of brief therapy. Using a 19-item modified A-B scale, they selected from the 12 therapists at the University of Indiana Student Health Service the three highest and three lowest scores. The groups were fairly evenly matched for age, experience, theoretical orientation, professional training, and numbers of neurotics and schizoids treated; there was one female therapist in each group. These therapists diagnosed their (26 neurotic and 31 schizoid) male patients at the beginning of treatment, which was apparently nearly always brief and crisis-oriented. Of the three outcome ratings, the first—therapist's rating of own effectiveness—yielded a significant interaction effect in the expected direction; the second—patient-rated improvement of presenting problems—yielded nonsignificant interaction support; the third—patient-rated rapport—showed no interaction hypothesis support but found neurotics to report higher rapport than schizoids. The authors fairly successfully discount one alternate hypothesis, that the results were due to idiosyncrasies of the particular therapists used. Their data on a second alternate hypothesis, that As were more successful with prognostically better categories of patient (in order of severity: schizoid, passive-aggressive personality, neurotic reaction, adjustment reaction) were ambiguous. With the exception of quite small therapist sample size, no major flaws in design appear, and the study does seem to bear witness to the utility of Berzins' previous analogue studies.

In a study giving peripheral consideration to the A-B variable, O'Brien, Hamm, Ray, Pierce, Luborsky, and Mintz (1972) randomly assigned 100 consecutive discharged schizophrenics, all using phenothiazines, to group or individual outpatient therapy with one of 16 therapists (six psychiatrists, four medical students, and six social workers). Patients were rated independently of their assigned therapists and were generally found to do better "clinically" in group than in individual therapy, regardless of all therapist variables.

Uhlenhuth and Duncan (1968a, 1968b) dis-cuss a project in which they assigned 105 senior male and female medical students one patient each for 9 to 10 weeks of once per week therapy. Patients included 65 neurotics, 26 personality disorders, seven psychotics, and seven situational disorders; both they and the therapists completed unidentified A-B scales. Change in subjective distress constituted the outcome dimension. The first report (1968a) simply documented that medical student therapists can effect relief of subjective distress. The second report (1968b) found that several patient variables (e.g., initial level of depression, optimism about outcome) predicted outcome, as did certain therapist variables; being born of a very young or very old mother, and an SVIB pattern resembling psychiatrists. A-B scores were not related to outcome *nor* to psychiatrist pattern similarity on the SVIB. Furthermore, there was no support for any patient-therapist interaction effects.

Uhlenhuth and Covi (1969) also examined a number of determinants of relief of subjective distress in first interviews. The 179 therapists (145 medical students, 10 residents, and 24 senior psychiatrists) were those who first encountered, interviewed, and diagnosed all the 179 patients (79 neurotic, 49 schizophrenic, 37 personality disorder, and 14 situational disorder) seen at the Phipps Clinic in 1962–63. Outcome consisted of pre-post therapy changes on a symptom checklist, the Bendig Anxiety Scale, systolic blood pressure, pulse rate, and respiration rate. In addition to several patient determinants of change (on the checklist, which was deemed most important) therapist B status, regardless of diagnosis, correlated significantly with distress relief. The authors conclude that the ambulatory schizophrenics here may have been less disturbed than those in the early Whitehorn-Betz work, and that therapist variables play a particularly important role very early in therapy, with relationship variables becoming more important later.[6]

In the only study yet to examine the A-B variable in behavior therapy, James and Foreman (1973) examined improvement rates in 36 enuretic children (5 to 16 years old; 12 female, 24 male) as a function of several "therapist" variables, where the "therapists" were the children's mothers. James served as "consultant" to the mothers in the use of a Mowrer-type conditioning device. Viewing enuresis as a neurotic problem, the authors hypothesized that Bs, because of their mechanical interests, would be more successful, and, as hypothesized, B-mothers (as well as mothers who were conscientious, or more positively reinforcing in style) were more successful than their opposites. Eysenck (1975) criticized the authors (1) for defining enuresis as a neurosis; (2) for concluding that (A and B) mothers could have possibly differed in their execution of such a routinized, mechanical task; and (3) for failing to study personality differences between successful and unsuccessful children, differences which he claims have a genetic origin. Eysenck's first two criticisms, and the genetic emphasis of his third criticism make little sense to James and Foreman (1975) or, for that matter, to me. He is quite correct, however, in scoring the authors' failure to find or even speculate about children's personality differences and the relationship between these and maternal (A-B) and other personological differences. Wilson and Evans (Chapter 20, this volume) appropriately criticize the authors' failure to consider *behavioral* correlates of the more effective B-mothers, as well as their acceptance of the A-B interaction hypothesis as established. In sum, this is an interesting study, whose hypothesis, however, is based on oversimplified reasoning, and which provides no satisfactory information (e.g., on the personological or behavioral meaning of B-status in mothers, or on children's perceptions of A- and B-mothers) to explain the results they obtained.

Outcome and Process: "Facilitative" Conditions

In addition to the Klem (1971) and Beutler et al. (1972) studies described above, the following studies all considered one or more of the four "facilitative" client-centered conditions: empathy, warmth, genuineness, and unconditionality of regard.

Gray's (1969) dissertation[7] investigated the A-B dimension in the therapy of diagnosed passive-aggressive patients. The A-B scores of 40 male therapists, each working with one male and one female passive-aggressive outpatient, were studied in relation to therapeutic progress. No A-B differences on progress or on any of the several therapeutic interaction variables were found (although several interactional variables— e.g., therapist's confidence, warmth, and empathy—related to progress).

Scott and Kemp (1971) examined 25 male senior medical student-therapists' first sessions with neurotic outpatients (17 female and eight male) for empathy, genuineness, warmth, and depth of self-exploration (DX). As and Bs were

identified by the Kemp (1963) scale, and ratings of taped segments were done at the University of Arkansas laboratory by the Truax procedures (Truax & Carkhuff, 1967). There were no significant A-B differences on warmth, genuineness, or empathy. Bs, however, did elicit higher DX ratings supporting one "half" of the interaction hypothesis. In this study, too, means and sources of diagnoses are unclear; moreover, the "therapists" were quite inexperienced and there were no schizophrenic patients to test the other "half" of the interaction hypothesis. Nevertheless, the authors' suggestion that the A-B variable and the identified therapeutic "relationship" variables operate independently seems supported. Likewise, in a dissertation, Muehlberg (1971) found no relationships, in a sample of 50 therapists, between the A-B variable and a questionnaire rating of level of facilitative interpersonal functioning, which purportedly tapped empathy, respect, genuineness, concreteness, and therapist self-disclosure.

Braun's (1971) dissertation examined several dimensions (patient perceptual flexibility, degree of insight, socioeconomic status, and therapist levels of empathy and experience), of which the A-B dimension was but one, in a Veterans Administration hospital outpatient neurotic population treated by psychologists, social workers, and clinical psychology trainees. There were no significant A-B differences on any dimensions.

Using what seems to be the same sample of 141 practicing therapists as in Bednar and Mobley (1969; also described in Razin, 1971), Bednar and Mobley (1971) examined the patient preferences of 18 As and 14 Bs currently treating schizophrenics or neurotics. Therapists were classified A or B by their scores on the Campbell et al. (1968) A-B scale revision; their mean A-B scores were at least two standard deviations apart. Nineteen schizophrenic and 18 neurotic patients (identified by the Spitzer PSS) were about equally distributed among As and Bs. Therapists completed likability ratings on these patients after initial and final sessions. Also, 106 therapists returned semantic differential scales rating work with the two types of patient, and 115 returned modified Fiedler's Least Preferred Coworker scales measuring the therapist's self-esteem and esteem for the patient with whom he had the greatest difficulty establishing a therapeutic relationship.

Likability data showed that As initially like both types of patient, particularly schizophrenics, more than do Bs, but that, by termination, all the ratings equalize, except for Bs' ratings of neurotics, which dropped from initial to final session. The semantic differential data revealed no A-B differences, but did find both types of therapist to prefer working with neurotics. The Least Preferred Coworker data found no A-B differences in self-esteem or esteem of patient. Nor did the combined (self- and patient-esteem) score, "assumed similarity," which purportedly measures warmth, acceptance, and permissiveness, show any A-B differences. The authors conclude that As and Bs do not differ in their preferences for schizophrenic or neurotic clients. A somewhat earlier study by Bednar (1970) had examined 20 As and 27 Bs (the extreme quartiles of a sample of 165 practicing therapists) treating 26 schizophrenics and 21 neurotics. There were no differences in perceived overall level of offered therapeutic relationship (measured by the Relationship Inventory) attributable to (A vs. B) therapist type, (schizophrenic vs. neurotic) patient diagnosis, or (patient vs. therapist) perception of the relationship. Bednar and Mobley (1971) conclude from all these findings that As and Bs do not differ with respect to therapeutic conditions offered, orientation toward interpersonal relationships, and attitudinal sets toward, or likability of, schizophrenic or neurotic patients.

Tanley's (1973b) dissertation also examined therapist-offered facilitative conditions in a sample of 45 crisis phone volunteers. He found that in compatible pairs there was greater facilitativeness.

Kennedy's (1973) dissertation examined A-B status similarity between 15 male clinical psychology trainees and their male outpatients. Measures included patient ratings of therapists' empathy, genuineness, and respect, therapist and patient ratings of themselves and each other on a 10-scale interpersonal adjective checklist, and therapist liking for clients. Contrary to Kennedy's hypothesis that A-B similarity between patient and therapist would lead to greater "effectiveness" and liking, he found that A-B dissimilarity was associated with higher patient and rater ratings of therapists' facilitative functioning, and with patient ratings of the therapist resemblance of a (stereotyped) "good" therapist. Patient-therapist A-B similarity was, however, associated with patient-therapist adjective checklist similarity.

Outcome and Process: Influence and Control

In an attempt to illustrate, but not systematically compare, A-B differences in therapeutic

intervention, Segal (1971b) excerpted therapy transcript segments of neurotic patients being treated by 2A and 2B clinical psychology graduate students. These segments were selected as exemplary, from the sessions of 20 male therapists, of moderate experience level (3 to 6 years). Using the segments, Segal characterizes As as more active, direct, and interpretive, involving themselves with their clients, and providing clients with a frame of reference. Bs are described as less directive and interpretive, and as encouraging greater self-exploration by their clients. With an unsystematized selection procedure and no control over bias in the characterizations of As and Bs, the study obviously cannot be considered, nor was it intended to be, a piece of "hard" research. It is nevertheless of interest in raising the issue of As' actively "leading," directive behavior. Of course, Whitehorn (1961, 1964) and Betz (1966) have also, at different times and in different ways, stressed the importance of "therapeutic leadership" but very little research relating this dimension to the A-B variable exists.

One study which did explore this area was Alpert's (1973) dissertation, which examined 48 outpatients, equally divided between MMPI diagnoses of schizoid and neurotic, who were assigned to 24 psychiatric residents (12 As and 12 Bs). She hypothesized that, in optimally paired (As with schizoids, Bs with neurotics) dyads and in positive expectancy dyads, therapists would show more behavior consistent with an influential role, and that patients would show more behavior consistent with receptivity to therapists' influence. Expectations were induced by telling each therapist that one of the two patients assigned him had been "specially paired" with him and that the other was a control. Clearly negative results emerged, however. In A-with-neurotic and in B-with-schizoid dyads, there were higher (therapist and patient) ratings of progress after 16 weeks, more positive patient perceptions of therapists, more positive patient in-therapy behavior (as rated by observers), more therapist behavior consistent with a healer-influencer (as rated by therapist), and more favorable content-filtered tape ratings of therapists (as rated by observers). Alpert concludes that factors other than patient symptomatology (outpatient status, socioeconomic status, e.g.) determine A-B differential response, and that these were responsible for A-B differences found in earlier work.

Razin (1974) also examined the issue of therapist influence. Concluding in his 1971 review that A-occupations and A-items on the original SVIB seemed to have in common an element of persuasiveness, he hypothesized that As were more persuasive therapists than Bs. In a fairly detailed design, he had 21 therapists (15 male, six female; mean experience level: 6 years; two psychiatrists, six psychologists, four social workers, and nine psychiatric residents), each tape-record three sessions with a neurotic outpatient and three sessions with a schizoid or schizophrenic outpatient. Therapists, patients, and a reliable rater each rated therapists on three measures of persuasiveness: patients' acceptance of therapists' "messages," therapists' embodiment of four correlates of persuasiveness, and therapists' "general" persuasiveness. Of the nine measures thus generated, only two (message acceptance rated by rater, and total-of-four correlates rated by therapist) showed significant A-B differences. Although the other seven measures all showed nonsignificant A-B differences, Razin concluded that the results were essentially null or at most mildly supportive of the hypothesis.

In light of these studies, my current thinking on persuasiveness or influence and the A-B dimension is that As would perhaps *like to be* persuasive or influential, though they apparently do not succeed any more than do Bs. This conclusion is in part derived from personological A-B research and will be discussed in greater detail in the personality characteristics section below.

Outcome and Process: Other Process Dimensions

Powell's (1969) dissertation hypothesized that, in a group of 20 senior medical students (10 A, 10 B) seeing outpatients (10 A, 10 B) in first interviews, dissimilar (A with B) dyads would be more effective than similar (A with A, B with B) dyads. Effectiveness was measured in five ways: patient and therapist attitudes toward the encounter, patient depth of self-exploration and degree of intimacy of relating, and degree to which patient expectations were met. No significant support for the hypothesis occurred on any of these, although therapists were more active in complementary pairings. A-patients, moreover, were higher on depth of self-exploration and on intimate relating.

Howard, Orlinsky, and Trattner (1970) assessed the effects of therapist theoretical orientation and A-B status on outpatient experience of therapy. The 21 therapists were mostly experienced, of both sexes, and represented the three major therapy professions. Their 104 patients were all seen in weekly sessions and were all female, diagnosed depressed (46), anxiety reaction (17) and personality disorder (28), and schizophrenic (13). Patient experience was assessed on several dimensions by the Therapy Session Report, and therapist orientation was assessed by the Therapist Orientation Questionnaire. Across all diagnostic groups, therapist orientation made little impact on patient experience. Among the schizophrenic and anxiety groups, however, there were several significant relationships between patient experience factors and therapist orientation. The A-B dimension, though, bore virtually no relationship to patient experience in any of the diagnostic groups. The authors conclude that the absence of A-B effects might be attributable to the use of an all female patient population and/or schizophrenics who were ambulatory; they surmise that A-B effects may be present in only specific situations with very limited populations.

Kriegsfield's (1971) dissertation examined 56 therapists treating 1,012 outpatients. He hypothesized that therapists who were As, or who valued self-control and restraint, or who were analytic, impersonal and nondirective, would see lower class patients for shorter durations, fewer sessions, and with more cancellations than would oppositely characterized therapists. He found no support for any of the three hypotheses.

In a study of therapist-viewed patient role behavior, Berzins, Herron, and Seidman (1971) examined a male therapist population ($n = 133$) and found that inexperienced B-therapists may see their most "successful" patients as more verbally autonomous or self-directed than do inexperienced A-therapists. Among experienced therapists, however, the A-B scale bears no relationship to any of the five factors otherwise related to therapist experience level or patient-role ("typical" vs. "successful").

Geller and Berzins (1976) polled a national sample of 134 prominent therapists. Obtaining an excellent return rate (95 Ss, 71%) and good internal consistency on their A-B scale, they assigned therapists to one of four orientation categories: insight, which included primarily analysts (46%); relationship (18%); action, which included all the behaviorists in the sample (23%); and "other," which included primarily therapists who were explicitly eclectic (13%). They found that those therapists reputed for effectiveness with schizophrenics and those effective with neurotics did not tend significantly to be scored as As and Bs, respectively. The orientation data, however, indicated that Bs tend to espouse relationship orientations, which stress therapist-patient involvement, affective interchange, expressive spontaneity, genuineness, self-disclosure, and confrontation. Interestingly, the B group included several members of the client-centered group (Jourard, Rogers, Truax), the Esalen Institute (Perls, Schutz), and the "Atlanta group" (Warkentin, Whitaker). The intermediate, AB, group included a large number of eclectic therapists. Factor analysis of the A-B scale items yielded two factors: manual interests and engineering interests, which were moderately ($r = .40$) correlated with each other, and on which Bs scored higher. Examining therapists' reactions to feedback, the authors found that, as predicted, therapists classified as As or Bs (and thus "typecast") were more resistant to accepting the research implications of their A-B status, than were ABs.

The authors conclude that, in light of recent trends depicting Bs as more risk-taking, variety-seeking, and complexity-seeking, their findings suggest that the Bs in this prominent population may "need" or seek the complex, exciting, interpersonal patient inputs that characterize their therapy, while As may have greater tolerance — e.g., with chronic schizophrenics—for communications and behaviors with which Bs rapidly become impatient.

While this study is quite interesting (if not conclusive), it seems to suffer from a sampling problem. Aside from the issue of deciding what constitutes "prominence," it is implicit here that each of these therapists is very effective clinically, using his particular orientation, modality, and/or patient group. But fame does not equal success rate, and the usual outcome data that we demand for nonfamous therapists are, of course, not here. Furthermore, at least some of these "therapists" are prominent by virtue of their scholarly (theoretical or research) written work, as opposed to their clinical work. In fact, we can argue that this is true of virtually the whole sample, and that almost no one becomes famous (at least not nationally so) solely by being a superb therapist, but by writing and/or by being "charismatic," provocative, or unusual. (Incidentally, the relationship of therapist charisma to positive outcome is one that has been assumed to exist, but has been largely unexplored, except by Frank [1961] and other workers of a comparative or anthropological orientation.) The present sample, then, although it obviously includes some excellent clinicians,

also includes some who are primarily non-clinicians and furthermore excludes many excellent clinicians who are simply not famous. It is thus not clear what dimensions are being tapped by "prominence."

Analogue Research: "Facilitative" Conditions

In Vaughn's (1969) dissertation, clinical psychology graduate students listened to tape recordings of TAS and AVOS patients and were instructed to respond as though they, the students, were the therapists. As with AVOS, and Bs with TAS, patients were judged to be warmer, more empathic and (on one of three measures of activity) more active therapeutically. No A-B differences emerged in comfort, and, surprisingly, both therapist types rated AVOS patients as more likable, more interesting, and more like themselves than were TAS patients.

Seidman (1971) selected 20 A and 20 B male undergraduates (from those who fell into the extreme quartiles of an A-B distribution and who volunteered after being informed of the nature of the study) in order to get Ss with interests and motivations similar to actual therapists'. He showed these Ss videotapes of AVOS and TAS patients and had them respond at interruption points. Hypothesizing an interaction effect on facilitative conditions, Seidman employed independent raters who were moderately reliable on respect and empathy (r's $= .67, .72$) but less so on congruence ($r = .49$). A further problem arose in the validation procedure, where TAS patients successfully came across as TAS but AVOS patients were seen as suspicious and angry, but not really avoidant of others. Results showed significant interaction effects, as hypothesized, on respect, empathy, and length of response, though not on congruence. Later in the study, As (more than Bs) reported that in general their reaction to stress was to turn toward others, while Bs more often (though nonsignificantly) reacted by avoiding others. Seidman also found respect, empathy, response length, and congruence to be highly interrelated and concluded that they comprise an interchangeable constellation of approach behaviors. He speculates that the advantage of the complementary dyads may lie in (1) the availability of a model who is different from the patient and whom the patient comes to resemble, and (2) the existence of fewer therapist "blind spots" (than in a similarity dyad).

Complementary pairings may in fact be more "effective," but it is not really clear that As are more "approaching" and Bs more avoidant. There is confusion in the literature about this; even in this study, for example, it is not apparent that greater verbal productivity (response length) indicates "approach." Such verbosity could indicate anxiety or obsessiveness on the part of the respondent, or an attempt to control the patient. Furthermore, the whole issue of complementarity/similarity is made problematic in the literature by assumed or imprecise equating of the dimensions involved. Thus, for example, A-Bness has been equated with approach-avoidance, with TAS-AVOS, and neurosis-schizoidia (or schizophrenia). The recent reviews of Heaton *et al.* (1975) and Franco (1975), despite their efforts to clarify this problem, are not, in my opinion, at all successful in their attempts. In fact, no conclusive evidence exists that any of these dimensions is even nearly identical to the A-B dimension. In the absence of such evidence, it is incumbent on the author and the reader of any study involving similarity/complementarity to be clear that the correspondence between the A-B dimension and any other dimension is at most partial, and that the terms "similar" and "complementary" thus have limited, or even misleading, functions.

Hoffnung and Stein (1970) presented 20 A and 20 B male introductory psychology students with one-sentence requests for help written in one of four ways: ambiguous, neurotic, schizophrenic, or neutral. The authors hypothesized that As with schizophrenics and Bs with neurotics would show greater depth-directedness, empathy, unconditional regard, personal involvement, congruence, and verbosity. The independent reliable raters found As > Bs on depth-directedness, congruence, and empathy; there was no support for any of the above interaction hypotheses, except for the empathy data. The authors also found that As gave more symbolic interpretations, regardless of patient type, while Bs responded more to literal elements. As also used a greater number of "feeling" words, regardless of patient type. Within the neurotic patient group, As "tried harder" to understand patients' feelings.

Stern and Bierman (1973) attempted to relate A-B status to facilitative variables in 20 graduate students (sex unidentified). Ss were in the final week of an "intensive facilitative communication workshop," and each served as "helper" and "helpee" for half-hour interviews in which the helper was instructed to communicate empathy and promote helpee self-exploration. Reliable raters using tape excerpts, found A

helpees to be higher on experiencing and self-revelation. "Significant others'" perceptions of Ss showed As to be more unconditional in their regard (as measured by the Barrett-Lennard Relationship Inventory [RI]) and Bs to be more reactive to, and to concentrate on, specific external events. No significant A-B differences emerged on several other variables, including helpee self-exploration; helper empathy and respect; focusing, RI empathy, regard, congruence, and RI total score.

The authors discuss these findings as consistent with earlier personological A-B research, but, with the number of statistical tests exceeding the number of subjects, and with the large number of nonsignificant results, this set of results is best considered null.

Kulberg and Franco (1975) had 60 male undergraduates, randomly paired into (A-A, A-B, B-B, AB-A, AB-B, AB-AB) dyads, instructed to talk to each other about their feelings, problems, and relationships. After this, Ss completed the Barrett-Lennard Relationship Inventory and a scale measuring perceived similarity to partner. In addition, moderately reliable raters evaluated tape recordings of the Ss for empathy and regard. It was hypothesized that perceived similarity, but not A-B similarity, would predict higher levels of facilitative conditions offered. A-B similarity, however, bore no relationship to facilitative conditions offered; rather, Bs were rated by partners (though not by raters) as higher on both conditions, regardless of partner types; As, on the other hand, gave their partners highest ratings on empathy and regard. Subjectively perceived similarity, though, did relate positively to empathy and regard—i.e., a S who saw his partner as similar to himself tended to see the partner as empathic and positively regarding. (These Ss' ratings, however, were not supported by raters' ratings.)[8] The authors conclude that some personality aspect other than the A-B dimension formed the basis for perceived similarity.

Analogue Research: Perceptions of, and Reactions to, "Patients"

Frahm's (1966) dissertation presented tape recordings of "talkative" and of "silent" clients of 10 A- and 10 B-therapists. He hypothesized that As listening to talkative clients and Bs listening to silent clients would like these clients better and would rate them as less disturbed and as producing less discomfort. The results, however, showed no A-B differences; both therapist types liked the talkative clients more and saw them as less disturbed.

Cohen's (1967) dissertation presented 10 written statements (five describing schizophrenic patients and five describing neurotic patients) to 30 male professional therapists (psychiatrists, psychologists) and to 30 male undergraduates. She examined these Ss' expectancies of outcome and process, finding no significant patient X therapist interaction effect but did find A-B differences (regardless of Ss' professional status) on all 10 statements.

In Shows' (1967) dissertation, the relationship between the A-B dimension and field-independence was examined. He had 80 male undergraduates paired into 40 dyads that were assigned communication tasks: picture discrimination, word association, and adjective ratings. He found that As with field-dependents and Bs with field-independents found these partners to be more sympathetic and easier to understand than did oppositely paired Ss; similarly, field-dependents with As, and field-independents with Bs found their partners more interesting. As rated both types of partners as more forgiving and indulgent than did Bs, and both field-dependents and field-independents saw Bs as more dignified than As. Finally, both As and Bs found field-independents easier to talk with. Recalling that As have been found to be more field-dependent, we can view these results as supporting a "similarity" hypotheses for affect—i.e., that partners paired similarly versus complementarily on the field-independence, AB, or both dimensions show more mutual positive effect.

Jacob and Levine (1968) attempted a virtual replication of the Carson, Harden, and Shows (1964) experiment, in which there was a near-significant finding that, with "compatible" dyads (As with distrusting-hostile-harm expecting [DHH] Ss, Bs with trusting-friendly-help expecting [TFH] Ss), more information was gathered in interviews than with incompatible dyads. Here, the authors hypothesized that interviewers would more accurately predict the self-descriptions of their compatible interviewees (As with DHH, Bs with TFH) than those of their incompatible interviewees. Ss were 40 male interviewees and 40 male interviewers, who were extreme scorers on an A-B scale given to 250 undergraduates. The authors found no significant main or interaction effects involving interviewer or interviewee A-B status; a near-significant main effect of (DHH vs TFH) interviewee "set" emerged: all interviewers predicted DHHs' self-descriptions better than they did

TFHs'. (The authors conclude that DHH descriptions are simply easier to predict.) There was, thus, a failure to replicate the Carson et al. findings.

Berzins and Seidman (1968) has Ss respond "helpfully" to "patients" and found that compatible dyads (As with AVOS, Bs with TAS) experienced greater ease in responding and greater satisfaction than incompatible dyads (see Razin, 1971, for a complete description). The authors later (Berzins & Seidman, 1969) had reliable raters examine these "helpful responses" to discover behavioral differences underlying the differential satisfaction. Raters examined length, form, interactive characteristics, and content of responses. On both length and form data, there were significant interaction effects, such that compatibly paired therapists gave longer responses, and more often of declaratory sentence form, than did oppositely paired therapists. Also, the emotional quality of responses was judged more positive and less negative in "compatible" dyads than in opposite pairs. On the content ratings, there were no main or interaction effects on acceptance. There were significant interaction effects on the relevance and assertiveness data, such that, in "compatible" dyads, responses were judged more assertive, but less relevant, than in opposite pairings. Nearly all of these effects were maximal on the first trial—i.e., after less than 1 minute of listening to the "patient." Several of the dependent measures were intercorrelated, and the authors attempt to integrate the findings under an "information-processing" model, according to which, compatibly paired "therapists" behaved as though they had assimilated and processed enough information to be able to produce long, positive, declarative responses, which they felt to be satisfying and helpful. Incompatibly paired "therapists" behaved as though they needed more information, engaging in shorter, negative, inquiring responses which they saw as less satisfying and less helpful. The authors suggest that the dysphoric sounding TAS patient and disorganized AVOS patient may constitute "blind spots" for As and Bs, respectively, since As' similarity to TAS patients (e.g., dysphoria and intrapunitiveness) and Bs' need for cognitive clarity may make work with these patients threatening. They suggest that pairing on the basis of dissimilar reactions to stress may maximize therapeutic effectiveness.

Kirkpatrick's (1969) dissertation had 28 A and 27 B undergraduates rate themselves on an interpersonal checklist, watch a film on a TAS or a TAO (turning against others, or personality disorder) patient, and rate the patients on the checklist. He found that As more than Bs saw both patient types as intrapunitive, submissive, and dependent. As also saw TAO patients as less friendly and less soft-hearted than did Bs. Finally, As rated themselves as similar to TAS patients, and Bs rated themselves as similar to TAO patients.

Anzel's (1970) five-factor (A-B status X student vs. therapists X AVOS vs. TAS patient X severity of patient disturbance X patient SES) analogue utilized 48 male therapists (psychologists, psychiatrists, psychiatric residents) from several facilities and 80 male undergraduates. These Ss listened to tapes of alleged "psychiatric interviews" involving "patients" who varied on AVOS-TAS symptoms, SES, and severity. (A validation procedure showed these dimensions to have been effectively manipulated.) There were no main A-B effects on S-rated similarity to patient, interest in patient, comfort with patient, prognosis, appropriateness for therapy, motivation, severity, psychosis, or social likability. (The other factors yielded several main effects, not detailed here.) Of the several significant multifactor analyses, many were too complex to detail here. Briefly, these analyses indicated that all three patient variables were in some way related to A-B status, and that the existence of therapist-student differences suggests that the use of the former as research Ss should therefore yield more accurate information about therapy. Furthermore, there was some evidence that As saw AVOS patients and Bs saw TAS patients as more severely disturbed than did oppositely paired Ss. The assumption that severity ratings are positively related to perceived need for help was supported by the finding that As saw AVOS patients and Bs saw TAS patients as more motivated. The relationship of patient SES to A-B status of Ss was more complex, but among therapists, As seemed to respond more favorably to (e.g., rate higher prognoses for) upper class and severely disturbed patients, while Bs respond more favorably to lower class and mildly disturbed patients. The study also seems to have shed some light on earlier "paradoxical discomfort" findings—namely, that the paradoxical discomfort phenomenon occurs only when the patients were of the lower SES.

For its exhaustiveness, for features such as validation of the intended portrayal of patients, and for its more easily interpreted findings, the study is commendable. One wishes, though, that the more complex analyses (e.g., four-way ANOVAs) were either eliminated or more simply presented. Finally, the frequently significant therapist-student X A-B interactions cast doubt on Berzins' "invariance hypothesis" (that A-B findings remain essentially the same across populations). It may be that such effects do not appear on the personality traits Berzins identified, but do appear in measures of attitudes toward and perceptions of different patients.

Dublin and Berzins (1972) examined "verbal non-immediacy," which has been researched elsewhere, quantified into scales, and is defined as the attenuation of the directness and intensity of the communicator's interaction with the object of his communication. As such, its presence purportedly indicates avoidance and/or negative affect. The authors introduced "longitudinal" and "change" aspects in the research by informing subjects (36 A and 36 B male undergraduates) that they were seeing a videotaped "patient" (actually an actor) in his third, and again in his 25th, sessions, and that the patient had improved, deteriorated, or not changed between the two sessions. Ss were instructed to respond "helpfully" at interruption points in the videotapes. As hypothesized, reliable raters found that As with schizophrenics, and Bs with neurotics, were more immediate. They also found that As gave longer responses (measured by number of words or length of time) than Bs. Furthermore, the immediacy differences tended to be seen later in the "relationship," while response length differences tended to be seen earlier, although the overall effect of the longitudinal dimension was unclear. Interpretation of results is complicated by the incompletely successful portrayal of the AVOS patient. Nevertheless, the authors conclude that greater immediacy, which may involve a more subtle congruence than Rogerian congruence, may underlie As' success with schizophrenics, and may require some time to be seen in the therapy relationship.

Friedman's dissertation (1971) had 109 male undergraduates act as pseudotherapists listening to tapes of "patients." He found As were more emotional and more accepting, regardless of patient type. Also, the formal qualities of As' responses—i.e., declarative sentence patterns—changed with the level of affect and amount of confusion displayed by the patient (Bs did not change). Finally, in response to patients producing confused material, As either approached or avoided, but, unlike Bs, did not show ambivalence. He concludes that As are more helpful in response to confused material and that, consistent with previous findings, they are in general more accepting, emotional, and flexible.

Goodwin's unpublished (1971) study examined 83 practicing male therapists' responses to AVOS and TAS tape recordings and hypothesized that As with schizophrenics and Bs with neurotics would, as measured by a post-test questionnaire, like their patients more, want to work with them more, feel more comfortable and compatible with them, find it easier to respond helpfully to them, and be more satisfied with their verbal interventions than they would in opposite pairings. Goodwin found some limited support for the interaction hypotheses (on liking, satisfaction with response) but also some disconfirmation (on desire to work with patient, compatibility). Interpretation of these data is further complicated by the near-significance $(p < .10)$ of all but one of these findings, by the use of three different A-B scales, and by the significant order-of-presentation effects. A significant main effect—that therapists were more satisfied with response to TAS patients—also emerged, but on only one AB scale. Level of experience was found unrelated to A-B status.

Barnes' (1972) dissertation hypothesized (1) that Bs, being more risk-taking, variety-seeking, and counterdependent, would look forward to encountering state hospital inpatients more than would As; (2) that during actual interviews "optimal" pairs (As with schizophrenics, Bs with neurotics) would exceed opposite pairs on patients' self-disclosure, interviewer nonverbal immediacy, and interviewer confrontation; and (3) that after the interview participants in optimal pairs would show more positive reactions. Twenty A and 20 B undergraduates each conducted two 20-minute interviews, one with a schizophrenic and one with a neurotic state hospital inpatient. All three hypotheses were supported.

Fancher, McMillan, and Buchman (1972) examined the relationships among accuracy in person perception, accuracy in role-taking, and the A-B dimension. Noting that there is a documented inverse relationship between a rational, intellectualized approach and accuracy in person perception (and even between psychological training and such accuracy), they hypothesized that As, being more intuitively and less rationality-oriented, should do better on a person-perception task and on a role-taking task. Their Ss were 30 male undergraduates. A "programmed case" format was used to test accuracy on person perception, and a complicated role-taking task was used to assess role-taking ability. Only near-significant support for the hypotheses emerged. Interesting, however, were judges' perceptions of As and Bs in their role-taking performances. As tended to be seen as more angry, hesitant, rude, nervous, shy and stubborn than Bs, who were seen as more businesslike, calm, and self-confident. Furthermore, accuracy in person perception was highly correlated with some of these traits: anger, impatience, rudeness. The authors correctly argue that this correlation did not result simply because the role-taking situation happened to call for more of these negative affects. Rather, as they point out, it seems that the tendency to dramatize anger is a characteristic of Ss who are accurate in person-perception and also characteristic of Ss who are As. They conclude that these results support earlier characterizations of Bs as rational, and that the negative affects and interpersonal difficulties or fears that characterized As' performances suggest an easy access to such feelings, which may underlie As' greater empathy with those experiencing such feelings (schizoids?). At several points, though, the authors state or assume that A > B differences in empathy are consistently found. This is not clearly so. Furthermore, their findings are subject to at least one other interpretation—that As were rated higher on negative affects and interpersonal difficulties because they "projected" these qualities onto the characters of the roles they played. That is, the results may indicate not merely an easy access to such feelings, but an "excess" of them: As may be more fearful and hostile.

Stein, Green, and Stone (1972) had 37 1st-, 2nd-, and 3rd-year psychiatry residents write brief case histories on likability, discomfort, interest in treating, interest in friendship, and prognosis. To control for and study patient SES effects, the authors had each resident rate four "patients": a neurotic lower-class patient, a neurotic middle-class patient, a schizophrenic middle-class patient, a schizophrenic lower-class patient. Only likability ratings yielded a significant interaction effect (with Bs liking neurotics more); neither the other four ratings nor three semantic differential scales yielded any significant A-B results. Several main effects of diagnosis emerged, with both As and Bs displaying greater interest in treating neurotics and in becoming friendly with them, and assigning them better prognoses. On the semantic differential, both As and Bs rated schizophrenics as more potent and more active. Also both As and Bs preferred to treat middle-class patients and assigned them better prognoses. The authors conclude that the A-B scale is of little value in predicting differential attitude toward schizophrenic and neurotic patients, and suggest that training seems to eliminate many of the observed A-B differences.

Chartier and Weiss (1974) had 6 A and 6 B male "therapists in training" predict the actual responses and other behavior of a schizophrenic patient and a neurotic patient, based on limited information (a brief social history and a taped interview excerpt) and, again, after receipt of more complete diagnostic information (psychological test results). Two of three dependent measures showed no A-B differences; the third, however, found As more perceptive than Bs, primarily with schizophrenics, while both were comparable with neurotics. Interestingly, more complete information significantly increased Bs' perceptiveness to equal As', suggesting that Bs may overcome an initial disadvantage with schizophrenic patients upon receipt of more complete diagnostic information.

Johnson and Smith (1974) hypothesized that since As seemed to be more attuned to subtle and (therefore?) nonverbal channels of communication, As and Bs should react differentially to communications in which verbal and nonverbal channels are incongruent. That is, As should react more to the nonverbal and Bs to the verbal content. Fifty-eight male undergraduates were studied via both a paper-and-pencil test and videotape observation of an actor, neither of which yielded A-B differences. These results suggest that if, as other findings indicate, As are more attuned to subtle or incidental cues, "subtle" should not be equated with "nonverbal". In fact, as we have seen (and as Johnson and Smith apparently do not acknowledge), As are probably more comfortable with and attuned to verbal modalities.

Analogue Research: "Patient" Reactions to As and Bs

Shardlow (1968) used a diagnostic interview format in her dissertation, incorporating four A and four B clinical psychologists, each interviewing two schizophrenic and two neurotic patients. Each patient was interviewed twice, once by an A and once by a B. (For these features, and for the careful means of categorizing both therapists and patients, this study is commendable.) After the interview, the therapist asked the patient to summarize his problems as completely as possible in 3 minutes. The small N precluded

formal statistics, but independent judges did find As to be more effective in eliciting summaries, regardless of patient type. Furthermore, schizophrenic patients perceived As, and neurotic patients perceived Bs, more positively than vice versa. No differences were found between As and Bs on assignment of personality characteristics to schizophrenics or neurotics.

In Blank's (1968) dissertation, 75 patients viewed therapist-patient interactions involving A- and B-therapists acting with different degrees of affect. In the 75 patients' written reactions to the A- and B-therapists they viewed, Blank found neither A-B differences in productivity nor greater response to As from "low adjustment" patients. He did find that patients respond more "actively" to Bs, and that A-therapists with low affect were liked best, while Bs with low affect were liked least. Finally, As "approach" was preferred over Bs, and primarily because of the content (vs. affect) of As' behavior; in general, As' *content* was the more important determinant of emotional response toward them, and Bs' affect was the more important determinant of response toward them.

In an analogue design using aides, Berzins, Ross, and Cohen (1970) also duplicated the procedure used by Carson *et al.* (1964): 40 addict patients, whose A-B scores fell in the extreme thirds of the distribution, had either "distrust" or "trust" sets "induced" (verbally) regarding interviews they were about to have with 40 similarly selected aides, who were instructed to gather "in depth" information on six "personal" topics and six "neutral" topics from patients. Reliable raters found "compatibly" paired aides (As with distrusting Ss, and Bs with trusting Ss) to obtain more self-disclosure on personal topics and on overall self-disclosure than did incompatibly paired aides. No such effect occurred with self-disclosure on neutral topics or on number-of-topics covered. A-aides explored more personal topics than did B-aides. A dissimilarity hypothesis, that dyads of opposite A-B status would outperform dyads with the same A-B status, was not confirmed; in fact, it was nearly significantly ($p < .10$) reversed. Patient A-B status was generally unrelated to performance measures. Positive post-experimental ratings, by both interviewer and interviewee, coincided with high self-disclosure scores.

Aside from their ambiguity, the results of the study are open to several objections to their validity. There is good reason to believe that the sets were not really induced. DHH patients were more self-disclosing than TFHs; post-experimental ratings of "trust" revealed no differences between the groups; and the previously determined "acceptability for psychotherapy" scores seemed to predict self-disclosure much better than did "induced-set."

Welch (1971) and Green (1972) had each of 12 A and 12 B male undergraduates meet with two actual AVOS patients and two TAS patients to interview them and to administer three learning tasks (modeling, response-biasing, and verbal conditioning). Welch's dissertation was based on the modeling data. He found TAS to disclose more in the interview than AVOS, and also to learn more modeling, though not significantly so. As who administered learning tasks first and then interviewed, and Bs who did interviews first and then learning tasks, both elicited very poor self-disclosure. Welch offers the questionable explanation that As, with their "verbal" orientation, and Bs, with their practical orientation, each had greater *initial* feelings of ineptness (in the above sequences) which somehow led to poorer subsequent interview performance by As and poorer concurrent interview performance by Bs.

Green's dissertation was based on the interview biasing and verbal conditioning data. She found As with AVOS and Bs with TAS to disclose more deeply than opposite pairs. This was true, however, only for those Ss who interviewed first; Ss who did learning tasks first got opposite results. Another complication in her findings is that, for those Ss who anticipated mental health careers (MH Ss), the anticipated interaction effect was found on the biasing task: As biased AVOS and Bs biased TAS patients more. In the non-MH Ss, though, opposite results obtained. These complexities make it very difficult to interpret any of the findings. Of tangential but nonetheless substantial interest are the findings that non-MH Ss got better patient disclosure than did MH Ss, were seen by raters as warmer, and by patients as less nervous, possessing superior life-skills, and liking patients more. Furthermore, non-MH Ss did better on biasing and verbal conditioning tasks.

Lynch (1974) had 6 A and 7 B police officers each interview one black male ghetto citizen presumed to be "distrustful" toward police officers, with the goal of eliciting personal information. But the interviewer and interviewee selection procedures were necessarily somewhat biased, and interviewees must, in fact, have been trustful enough to take part in the study. Contrary to Lynch's hypothesis, Bs (rather than As) were better liked by interviewees (and non-

significantly trusted more) and showed greater liking for interviewees than did As. Also, on post-session semantic differential scales, citizens interviewed by As rated themselves as less active and less potent than those interviewed by Bs. Reliable raters found no differences in number of areas explored, nor in depth of self-exploration; A-B differences also failed to appear in nine other interviewer ratings and six other interviewee ratings. The number of nonsignificant findings, as well as other methodological problems, must therefore reduce the positive findings to a suggestive level. Lynch interprets the results as conflicting with the many findings of As' greater functioning with distrustful Ss, but it should be repeated that distrust was assumed here, and, without specific information on the citizens, we could as easily assume them to be neurotic. Lynch also sees his results as consistent with findings of Bs' greater effectiveness with lower class Ss. Finally, he notes that, since most interviewees were As, there is here some evidence supporting what he calls the "complementary hypothesis"—actually, the dissimilarity hypothesis (see distinction above).

Analogue Research: Effects of "Patient" A-B Status

There have been several studies examining the A-B variable in patients (or interviewees), in nearly every case also examining therapist (or interviewer) A-B status, and then attempting generate findings attributable to therapist-patient A-B similarity or dissimilarity. In addition to the studies below, the Shows (1967) and Berzins *et al.* (1970) studies above are also concerned with these issues.

Boyd (1970) examined the effects of A-B status in master's-level high school counselors engaged in career development interviews with high school senior boys. He used the 80-Item Campbell A-B scale to identify the 14 counselors and the 14 students (both samples were skewed somewhat in the B direction). One A- and one B-client were randomly assigned to each counselor for recorded interviews. The Hill Interaction Matrix was used to assess subject orientation and therapeutic impact of interview statements. Reliable raters found no effects of counselor type or of client-counselor similarity on interview content, but did find that client type affected the nature of the interaction in that B-clients generated a greater percentage of "personal" comments, challenging comments, and comments requiring more personal commitment; furthermore, dyads with B-clients did more work in assessing alternatives to proposed action. The only counselor effect was that A-counselors' interviews contained more statements. Boyd concludes that B-clients generate conversations which are more personal, confrontative, and speculative, and that, to some extent, counselor behavior is under client control.

Bennington's (1972) dissertation had 40 undergraduate males (20 A, 20 B) each paired with two of each other, so that each S "interacted dyadically" with one A and one B. He hypothesized that Bs could be more "transmitting-oriented" and As were more "receiving-oriented," and that there would be differential response to A and B partners. No differences emerged on any of eight content-free measures, and only mild evidence of differential response emerged: with A partners, Ss (whether A or B) responded with more words, more unsuccessful interruptions, and fewer successful interruptions.

Magaro and Staples (1972) examined patient A-B status and pre-morbid adjustment in relation to verbal and nonverbal dyadic interaction. An A-B scale was verbally administered to 65 diagnosed chronic schizophrenic inpatients, and 8 As and 8 Bs were chosen from the extreme scorers. The two A-most and two B-most scorers were designated patient-therapists, and there were, in addition, two control-therapists: experienced male psychology (graduate?) students. Each of these six therapists saw one A and one B patient. The design was balanced for pre-morbid adjustment. Patient-therapists were instructed that they were to help the patient they would be speaking with and that the experience "should be helpful to both of you." Reliable raters assessed the verbal measures (speaking time, number of verbal responses) and nonverbal measures.

Overall, B patients spoke longer than did As, especially when B patients were paired with B therapists or with control-therapists. Control-therapists elicited more talk than did patient-therapists. Patients with good pre-morbid adjustment spoke longer than those with poor adjustment. The following interaction effects were observed. A-patients with B-patient-therapists talked the least of any dyad type and scored highest on preoccupation with self: these patients seemed to be silent and withdrawn. B-patients with A-control-therapists talked second most, presumably because control As were able to influence B-patients to decrease avoidance and withdrawal behavior and increase verbal behavior. B-patients with B-control-therapists were apparently the most successful dyads, talking the longest, smiling at the therapist most, and showing no disinterest by yawning. A-patients had difficulties in all conditions. The authors conclude that the A-B dimension is valuable as another basis, in addition to pre-morbid adjustment, for classifying patients. Such classification, they conclude, could have value in suggesting appropriate treatment (e.g., the treatment of A-patients with good pre-morbid adjustment should emphasize social-interaction, while Bs with good pre-morbid adjustment would be less in need of such emphasis and could be assigned to vocational-milieu, or minimal staff, wards with high degrees of patient decision-making).

Portnoy and Resnick (1972) hypothesized that A-B-dissimilar dyads would perform better than similar dyads on a verbal conditioning task. Using two A and two B male undergraduates as Es, and 20 male As and 20 male Bs as Ss randomly assigned to each other, the authors had Es reinforce particular word usages by Ss in a sentence construction task which followed a 15-minute "conversation." Contrary to hypothesis, there was no significant interaction effect of E types. A-type Ss, though, did show greater conditioning than Bs, who actually decreased their frequency of reinforced word use. The authors conclude that their results support the Pollack and Kiev (1963) findings of As' greater responsiveness to stimulus attributes of the perceptual field, including, and perhaps especially, incidental cues. They also found the results consistent with the greater verbal facilities of As (Dublin, Elton, & Berzins, 1969).

In an attempt to differentiate As' postural and gestural communications from Bs' Smith (1972) selected the "extreme-scorers," 20 As and 20 Bs, from 225 male undergraduates and randomly assigned to them to one of four conditions: A-interviewer with A-interviewee, B-interviewer with B-interviewee, A-interviewer with B-interviewee, and B-interviewer with A-interviewee. Interviewers were instructed to get to know the interviewee as well as possible in a 12-minute interview. Interviewees were told that the study was one of the process of interviewing and that they would be asked about themselves. Moderately reliable female raters scored both interviewers and interviewees on ease in responding, enjoyment, liking of partner, knowing (or being known by) other, feeling at ease, involvement in interview. Seven postural and eight gestural categories, distinguishable and common in occurrence, were also reliably rated. Smith hypothesized that As would be more variable in gesturing than Bs, and two of the seven measures (hand-gestures and negative nods) confirmed this. Smith failed to point out, however, that on four of the seven measures, Bs were more variable (though nonsignificantly) than As. Smith's review of literature classifies all the postural and gestural behaviors as "conjunctive" (affiliative) or "disjunctive" (disaffiliative), and his second hypothesis was that As, in consonance with research showing them to be cautious and inhibited, would show more caution and inhibition in their postural and gestural behavior. Smith cites the significant B>A score on quasi-courtship behavior as confirming this. Ss' own ratings on the six dimensions identified above showed Bs to enjoy the interview more. Smith concludes from these data that Bs are more conjunctive. Calculation of the number of statistical tests from which these two "significant" findings were drawn indicates that the first was one of 15 tests, and that the second was one of six tests; the overall findings, then, two "significant" tests out of 21 computed, barely exceeds chance expectations. No effects of role (interviewer vs. interviewee) were found, nor were any effects of dyadic (dis-)similarity of A-B status found. However, AA dyads were found least conjunctive and BB dyads most conjunctive, of all four combinations. Smith takes this as (further?) evidence of Bs' greater conjunctivity and affiliativeness. While Smith's findings confirm other recent characterizations of As and Bs, they themselves are statistically weak, and there is little that emerges conclusively from the study.

Personality Research: Perceptual and Cognitive Dimensions

Pardes, Winston, and Papernick (1971) examined field-dependence in a group of 26 inpatients and 32 therapists (psychiatry residents and "allied" staff) in an acute treatment setting. Across the whole (patients plus therapists) group, there was a slight B>A difference on field-dependence. This study appears, then, to conflict with the earlier Pollack and Kiev (1963) data. Here, however, the Campbell A-B scale was used (see SVIB discussion in Introduction), both males and females were used, and patients were used in addition to therapists, unlike the Pollack and Kiev study. (No separate therapist-only data are given here.)

Portnoy and Resnick's (1972) finding (see analogues, above) that As verbally conditioned

much better and that social reinforcement for Bs became aversive, confirms earlier findings of As' greater comfort, and perhaps aptitude, with verbal material, as well as findings of As' greater responsiveness to unobvious social cues. Bs' reactions might be interpreted as evidence that they sense and resent controlling, direction, or structuring more than do As. This would be improved with their self-perception of independence.

Schubert and Wagner (1975) hypothesized that (1) As would show more creativity than Bs, (2) As would show more personal involvement with people in general, and (3) As would show greater femininity and verbal orientation. Using 59 male undergraduates, they found nonsignificant A>B differences on 11 of 12 creativity measures, and one significant A<B difference. (They interpreted these results as confirmatory.) They also regarded the second hypothesis as supported, by virtue of A-B findings on MMPI scales Hy, social presence, social status, dominance, leadership, and defensiveness, as well as the B>A finding on the Si scale. Here a sample of 237 undergraduate males were used. Finally, they regard the third hypothesis as supported. Using the $N=237$ sample as well as another $N=608$ sample, they found As>Bs on the Mf scale and Bs>AS on quantitative orientation. This study, however, suffers from questionable statistical methodology and probably oversimplistic interpretation would be more conservative. There is at most tentative support for the notions of As' greater creativity, personal involvement, and verbal orientation, and moderate support for the notion of As' greater "femininity" and greater level of "maladjustment."

Finally, Hasenfus, Martindale, and Kaplan (1975) found that A psychology graduate students showed greater EEG alpha wave activity, suggesting greater free-floating attention than Bs under three conditions (listening to a clinical interview, talking about the interview, and relaxing).

Personality Research: Defensive Patterns and Psychopathology

In Kirkpatrick's (1969) analogue dissertation (described above) As' and Bs' self-ratings on an interpersonal checklist did not differ significantly, but As rated themselves as similar to TAS patients, and Bs rated themselves as similar to TAO patients.

In a group of 63 male undergraduates, Segal (1971a) found no relationship between A-B status and the R-S (repression-sensitization) scale, which identifies predominantly avoidant behavior at one pole and approaching (intellectualizing, obsessional, sensitizing) behavior at the other. Tanley (1973a) also attempted to relate A-B status to R-S. He used 180 male and female undergraduates (with no male-female R-S differences) and found essentially no correlation.

As indicated in the above consideration of the Fancher *et al.* (1972) analogue, there is evidence that As may have more ready "access to" fearful, angry, and other "negative" affects, and there is at least a strong suggestion that such access is due to As actually having such feelings more often.

In a study of the A-B variable in patients, Johnson, Workman, Neville, and Beutler (1973) examined the MMPI and Sixteen Personality Factor (16 PF) scores of 53 male and 90 female inpatients. They found virtually no correlation between females' A-B status and MMPI or 16 PF. Males' scores, however, showed As to have more feminine interests and to be more depressed, obsessive-compulsive, socially isolated, anxious, and less defensive (MMPI data). As were also emotionally less stable, had poorer self-control, greater general emotionality and psychiatric pathology, and were more imaginative, inner-directed, apprehensive, depressive, inconsiderate, and anxious (16 PF data). The authors conclude that the A-B scale measures different things in males and females, and that A patients display more test pathology than do B patients. The latter conclusion is supported by Berzins, Ross, and Friedman's (1972) finding that patients' A-B scores were much more in the A-direction than were normal undergraduates'.

Finally, Franco and Magaro (1975) studied the relationships among A-B scores, field dependency, feeling reactivity, facilitation versus inhibition of emotional experience, and paranoid versus nonparanoid status in 24 acute male inpatients. Eight were paranoid schizophrenics, eight were nonparanoid schizophrenics, and eight were "controls"—i.e., nonpsychotics (neurotic depressive or character disorder)—as determined by a double diagnostic criterion methodology. With five major variables, the results were predictably complicated and not at all uniform or as expected. Summarizing these simply, we note that for the paranoids the predictions were upheld: As were more feeling-reactive and more emotionally facilitative (as had been found by Silverman, Buchsbaum, & Stierlin, 1973). Among nonparanoids, though,

these findings were reversed. Furthermore, although nonparanoids were, as predicted, more field-dependent, they scored much more highly in the B-direction of the A-B scale. The authors suggest that the nonparanoid schizophrenic is cognitively undifferentiated and therefore open to an overendorsing response bias, but, as they point out, this explanation does not account for all the discrepancies in their findings. One can hardly disagree with their exhortation that the paranoid versus nonparanoid distinction need be made in research with schizophrenics, given the great heterogeneity in the diagnosis. Hopefully, the complexity of the results in this study can be reduced and made more interpretable by further work incorporating such distinctions, especially if such research attempts to interrelate fewer variables.

Personality Research: Other Intrapsychic, Trait, and Interpersonal Dimensions

Kenworthy's (1968) dissertation attempted to find "construct validity" for the A-B dimension. He examined data on several tests taken by 107 senior medical students who designated psychiatry as their specialty: their verbal (V) and quantitative (Q) scores on the MCAT (Medical College Admission Test); the Allport-Vernon-Lindsey Study of Values (AVL), and unspecified scales of the Edwards Personal Preference Schedule (EPPS). On the AVL, As were higher on aesthetic and lower on economic values. On the MCAT, As' and Bs' scores were approximately equal on both V and Q, but As' V scores were greater than their Q scores. On the EPPS, As scored lower than Bs on succorance and on order, but higher than Bs on autonomy. Kenworthy concludes that the findings support the original Whitehorn-Betz description: As appear more individualistic, independent, outspoken, self-sufficient, nonconforming, and unconventional; Bs seem more conforming, more passive and retiring, less assertive, and have greater need for order. As Kenworthy's abstract gives no information on the statistical methodology and we do not know the total number of scales on which As and Bs were compared, we, therefore, do not know the overall significance of the above findings.

Rothman (1971) attempted to relate the A-B scores on 30 experienced male doctoral level "counselors and counselor educators" at the University of Florida to (1) developmental histories of "socially-independent-nonconforming" behavior (Bs) and to (2) "experiential-personal-spontaneous-unplanned" therapy orientations (for As) versus "analytic-impersonal-nonspontaneous-planned" orientations (Bs). Developmental history was measured by a questionably constructed Biographical Information Blank, and therapeutic orientation was measured by the Sundland and Barker Therapist Orientation Questionnaire (see Chapter 9, this volume). Neither hypothesis was supported. In fact, there was a significant reversal on the second: Bs appeared more independent-nonconforming. In Kennedy's (1973) dissertation (above), however, B-*patients* were seen by their therapists (regardless of therapist A-B status) as managerial. And B-therapists were seen by their patient as more responsible and "hyper-normal."

In an unpublished paper, Welch and Berzins (1968) examined Rosenzweig Picture Frustration scores (of 100 male and 100 female undergraduates at the University of Kentucky) for extrapunitiveness-intropunitiveness. Ss' A-B scores placed them in an A, AB (middle), or B group. Four fairly reliable judges found As to be least extrapunitive, *not* significantly less, though, than Bs who were next, but significantly less than ABs, who were most extrapunitive.

McGuigan and Seidman (1971) examined the relationships between A-B status and self-esteem and social competence. They had 65 male undergraduates complete the Tennessee Self-Concept scale and Lanyon's (social competence) questionnaire, which taps a stereotyped cultural ideal for college students, stressing extroversion, activity, and decision-making at the expense of thinking and reflection. Only a near-significant ($p < .10$) relationship between overall self-esteem and A-B status emerged, although several of the Tennessee subscales showed significant B > A differences. On social competence, moreover, a significant B > A difference also emerged. The authors saw this latter difference as related to B's "defensive distortion" and greater need for social desirability, which itself was *not* related to A-B status. They speculate that Bs' greater competence and sex-role adequacy may threaten schizoids. It should be noted, however, in noting the social competence data, that the scale used taps cultural stereotypy to an undetermined extent; thus, while Bs may "really" be more socially competent, the finding of greater competence here may be (totally?) due to the Lanyon scale's overlap with other scales that find Bs > As on cultural stereotypy.

Berzins, Barnes, Cohen, and Ross (1971) examined A-B differences on the Personality Research Form (PRF), a multidimensional, 440-item schedule with apparently excellent psychometric qualities. Two samples were studied: one consisted of 223 male undergraduates at the University of Kentucky, the other was a "cross-validation sample" of 50 male professionals (psychologists, psychiatrists, social workers) at clinical settings in Indiana and Wisconsin. The outer quartiles (40 As, 51 Bs) of the college group and the outer quartiles (13 As, 12 Bs) of the professional group were selected for examination of PRF scores. Univariate analyses characterized Bs as oriented toward thrill-seeking or risk-taking (low harm-avoidance), concerned with sensory, physical enjoyment (high sentience), tending to present themselves in a positive light (high desirability), dominant or ascendant (high dominance), and persistent (high endurance). Opposite positions on these five scales characterized As, who emerged as inhibited, cautious, unconcerned with sensory pleasures, lacking self-esteem, submissive, and lacking stamina. Multiple discriminant analyses found As to score high on exhibition, harm-avoidance, nurturance, and autonomy scales; the authors label this complex amalgam "cautious self-expression." The more internally consistent B amalgam involved high scores on sentience, dominance, play, and understanding; the authors call this "openness to complex experience." The univariate results "converge" in characterizing Bs as high on social ascendancy and on cognitive ascendancy, and characterizing As as cautious, socially inept, and restricted in cognitive scope.

Although there were several college versus professional differences found on the PRF, three (harm-avoidance, sentience, dominance) of the five dimensions that differentiated undergraduate As and Bs also differentiated professionals. The authors conclude (1) that the major linear correlates of A-B status apply to professionals as well as to undergraduates, and (2) that the results firmly support the characterization of Bs as approximating cultural "masculine adequacy," and As as conforming poorly to such cultural expectations.

A validation (Berzins, Dove, & Ross, 1972) was attempted with four new samples: 94 male professionals, 661 male students, 114 male outpatients, and 720 female students. Despite marked intersample differences on the A-B scale and PRF profiles, the validation was largely "successful": once again, regardless of sample, As emerged as cautious, submissive, uninclined to seek variety or sensual pleasure for its own sake, and succorant; Bs were risk-taking, dominant, variety-seeking, sentient, and "counter-dependent." The authors add to their previous conclusions that the harm-avoidance scale is the best single predictor of A-B status in all the samples and warrants consideration in therapy research.

Nerviano (1973) studied the relationship between A-B status and the PRF in male alcoholic outpatients at a VA hospital. He found replication on four of the five "core" correlates (harm-avoidance, dominance, change, and sentience, but not succorance) that Berzins, Barnes, et al. (1971) had found to distinguish As and Bs. Here, as earlier, As were more cautious, uninclined to seek sensory "thrills," change-avoidant and submissive; Bs were adventurous, sensation-seeking, change-seeking, and more dominant.

Goodwin, Geller, and Quinlan (1973) hypothesized that As would describe themselves in socially desirable "feminine" terms, and Bs in socially desirable "masculine" terms. Using a previously developed Rosenkrantz Stereotype Questionnaire, they found no relationship between A-B status and masculine traits, but did find a significant relationship for feminine traits, which were more often self-attributed by As. Goodwin et al. emphasize that As need not (here, they do not) attribute less "masculinity" to themselves, so much as more "femininity," and that such traits (gentleness, kindness, affectionateness, for example) may underlie As' greater success with schizophrenics, whose mothering has reportedly been so pathogenic.

Personality Research: A-B Scale Comparisons

Seidman's (1972) work on A-B scale comparison found with male undergraduates the 80-item AB-R scale (Campbell et al., 1968) to add reliability, by virtue of its greater length, but its correlation with the other two commonly used scales, the UK-19 (Schiffman, Carson, & Falkenberg, 1967) and the original 23-item scale (WB-23), is poor. The UK-19 and WB-23, on the other hand, correlate well with each other (.79–.85). He concludes that the AB-R is tapping something different than the other two and should not continue to be used.

In 1974, Seidman, Golding, Hogan, and LeBow (1974) found similar results after dropping several Ss from the 1972 sample for psychometric reasons. In this study the authors attempted to conceptualize and clarify the A-B dimension by examining A-B scales in relation to the Personality Research Form (PRF), the Ruch and Ruch Employee Attitude Survey, and Lanyon's Social Competence Scale. (The AB-R showed correlations with these measures that were different—at times, even reversed—from those derived by correlating the UK-19 or WB-23 with these measures. Again, the authors emphasize, the AB-R must be measuring something different, and they urge that researchers classify Ss on both the AB-R and the WB-23, or UK-19, as an aid in preventing and reconciling discrepant results). They subjected the test battery to a two-step principal component analysis, and a multiple discriminant-function analysis was calculated for extreme As and Bs. Of the eight second-order components generated (social ascendance and management, verbal versus quantitative ability, adventuresomeness, service-oriented and dependency, aesthetic-intellectual, humble outdoorsman, works with concepts and things and emotionally controlled, and business management and scales interests), Bs scored high on concepts and things, business management, humble outdoorsman, and verbal ability; As scored high on service-orientation. The authors conclude that As are characterized by a "people" orientation, based perhaps on the potential gratification of their own needs for support, nurturance, and reassurance. Bs are characterized by interest and ability in dealing in a disciplined and cognitively well-differentiated way with abstract ideas and concepts, with mechanical things, with technical details, with nature, and with themselves, at least in a self-critical way. Bs also have skill in comprehension of written or spoken language. The two orientations may be considered social-interpersonal and impersonal, cognitively complex, and oriented toward concepts and things.

Considering these findings in the light of previous data, the authors note that the masculinity-femininity distinction represents an oversimplification and that the above emphasis on cognitive structure (Bs) versus people-orientation (As) represents a more precise distinction. Regarding earlier findings of A-B verbal aptitude, the authors point out that the inconsistency between their findings and the earlier ones is more apparent than real. They interpret these (Berzins, Friedman, & Seidman, 1969; Dublin et al., 1969) findings as indicating greater verbal inclination or expressiveness and not the more formal ability to use words in thinking and to discover relationships.

The authors conclude by recommending a change in research strategy whereby the current scales are dropped as *the* definition of an under-lying dimension. Instead, they should serve to identify provisionally Ss who are then charac-terized multidimensionally, as here, which in-dividuals are then observed and described in interpersonal interactions. This approach seems much sounder and more productive than the pattern of study that has in fact characterized A-B research for 20 years, and this particular study should be considered a very commendable first step in the prescribed direction, with sophisticated statistics and logic and thoughtful consideration of work in the entire area.

Chartier (1974) also compared several A-B scales (10-, 13-, 15-, 23-, 31-item versions), using 19 male therapists in training and concluded that, although intercorrelations were high among the five versions (.55–.94), the 10-item version was particularly poor and the 23-item (WB-23) particularly good, in terms of correlating with all other versions. He then recommends use of the WB-23, but suggests that use of several different measures, in a multiple-criterion selec-tion procedure, may be best in light of the non-existence of a truly standardized A-B scale.

Most recently, and perhaps most significantly in the area of A-B scale construction and mean-ing, Stephens *et al.* (1975) have accomplished what appears to be a very careful and successful major overhaul of A-B scaling. They obtained and reanalyzed all of the 67 male therapists' SVIB data, and their 511 schizophrenic patients' improvement data, from the original Whitehorn and Betz work. Reanalyzing, they note several deficiencies in some or all of the previously used scales. Thus, for example, the use of the same scale for male and female therapists is particul-arly problematic, as 12 of the WB-23 items actually have negative correlations with patient improvement percentage (PIP) for the female therapists in the original sample. Also, the statistical bases for item selection were often unclear or inappropriate; internal consistency reliability is low, or, in the case of the AB-R with its higher reliability, validity is low; item scoring has been dichotomous despite trichotomous question format; improvement rates and item response preference systematically changed be-tween 1947 and 1961, suggesting a spurious positive correlation between the two; and the derivation of WB-23 involved several computa-tional errors.

To examine the influence of other variables on outcome (PIP), the authors intercorrelated PIP, date of beginning residency, percent of process schizophrenics, percent of male schizophrenics, and percents of insulin coma-treated patients, ECT treated patients, and chemotherapy-treated patients. Only data of beginning residency correlated with PIP.

To summarize their scale construction pro-cedure briefly, they selected those SVIB items which correlated well (> .15) with PIP, showed high internal consistency, and were statistically free from contamination by other variables. After deriving several alternative scales, they arrived at and refined the "SSZ-46," which cor-relates .77 with PIP (vs the .51 correlation of the WB-23), and the "SSZ-61," which correlates .81 but has lower internal consistency.

Finally, they factor-analyzed the SSZ-46 and found five principal factors: I: verbal-conceptual (As) versus manual-practical (Bs) (the authors claim that this factor forms the basis for any validity the WB-23 may have); II: sales (As) versus scientific (Bs); III: social concern (As); IV: artistic (As) versus business-oriented (Bs); and V: "uninterpretable" (production manager, aviator, engineer and banker). They conclude that their SSZ-46 scale is clearly superior to previous scales in all respects; that A-B scales are multidimensional; that none of the scales have clear meaning with female therapists; and that, despite the correlation with short-term improvement, there is no evidence (in the orig-inal patient sample) of any relationship between A-B status, even as measured by the new, more highly correlating SSZ-46, and long-term (5- to 14-year follow-up) psychiatric status. In fact, however, even short-term improvement cor-relates only .24 with long-term status, so that this last conclusion needs to be carefully con-sidered and not overly weighted.

DISCUSSION

The mass of studies described in the above review can productively be used as material to provide partial resolutions to the many issues raised by the years of research in this area. What follows, then, is a series of the most important issues and questions in A-B research, each followed by an assessment of its status.

Clinical Outcome with Inpatients

Considering not only the research reviewed here, but also the earlier research that followed the original Whitehorn-Betz work, *we find virtually no study showing A > B differences, or interaction hypotheses effects, in the clinical out-come of inpatients.*

The one possible exception is the Shader *et al.* (1971) finding that with acute schizophrenics, treated by psychiatric residents and also receiving phenothiazines, As do better. (In the several other treatment categories in this study, no A-B differences emerged.) While it should be noted that no more than five such studies have been reported, the conclusion seems unavoidable that there has been essentially no successful independent replication of the original Whitehorn-Betz findings.

Clinical Outcome for Outpatients

Of the eight studies considered here, four found no A-B differences in outpatient outcome or "progress." Three studies found support for B>A effectiveness, though the findings were limited either in statistical magnitude or in generalizability (because of the circumstances in which they occurred—for example, with mothers of enuretic children or medical students relieving subjective distress in one interview). One study found *un*complementary dyads (As with neurotics, Bs with schizoids) to have better progress than complementary dyads. There is thus in this area only very weak evidence of differential A-B effectiveness—that Bs are more effective than As with outpatients. The strength of even this evidence, moreover, must be limited by the diagnostic heterogeneity of outpatients. Though they are most often considered neurotic, outpatients fall into many diagnostic categories and are thus by no means identical with neurotics. *There is, then, only scant evidence that Bs are more effective than As with neurotics. Furthermore, such differential effectiveness seems less likely to be found in circumstances resembling usual ongoing therapy and more likely to be found in therapeutically unusual situations and/or where "therapist" training is minimal.*[9]

Therapeutic Process: Therapeutic Facilitative Conditions

Research on the relationship between the A-B variable and the facilitative conditions of empathy, warmth, genuineness, and unconditionality of regard has been almost exclusively limited to outpatients. Nine relevant clinical studies are considered here, of which five, including a variety of therapists, report no A-B differences on the one or more facilitativeness variables measured. One of these five studies examined patient types in interaction with therapists and found no interaction effects on

any of the four variables. Two additional studies (one done with crisis-phone volunteers and the other with first-session changes) found complementary pairs to be higher on facilitative conditions, while the last two studies found that A-B dissimilar Ss' mutual ratings (i.e., As' ratings of Bs, and Bs' ratings of As) were higher on facilitative conditions than were A-B-similar ratings (As' of As, Bs' of Bs).

There is thus no strong evidence that As and Bs are different in their facilitativeness (as defined by the four conditions), but there is suggestive evidence that patients' diagnosis or A-B status may bring about interaction effects such that complementary or A-B-dissimilar dyads *may* function with greater facilitativeness. These conclusions are supported by the five analogue studies of facilitative conditions. Three of these found conflicting therapist main effect A-B differences and one found B>A differences, while all three which studied the interaction hypothesis found varying degrees (mild to moderate) of support for it.[10]

Therapeutic Process: Therapist Roles, Orientations and Behavior

Two clinical studies found As to be more active, directive, and/or teaching, while a third provides very marginal evidence that As may be more persuasive. One of these studies also found As to be more interpretive. Other findings suggest that Bs favor strong involvement, affective interchange, spontaneity, self-disclosure, and confrontation by the therapist. One study found no A-B difference on therapist self-disclosure and another found no difference in therapeutic orientation.

Four relevant analogue studies together suggest that A-Ss are perhaps better at assuming certain therapist-like roles, that they "try harder" to understand "patients'" feelings, and that they use more feeling words, more symbolic interpretations, longer responses, and more statements per session, while Bs respond to more literal elements of "patient" communications to them. Two other analogue studies found that in complementary dyads "therapists" gave longer responses, used more declarative sentences, had more positive emotional tone in their responses, were more assertive (though less relevant), and more "immediate" in their communication.

The net impression, then, adorned perhaps with a bit of speculation, is that As are probably *not* more influential, but perhaps would *like to be.* They are thus more likely to adopt "teachy" or "preachy" stances as attempts to control or influence patients, attempts which may often be countertherapeutic. This thinking is supported by an analogue that found the partners of As to respond with more words, fewer successful interruptions, and more unsuccessful interruptions, as though these partners were trying to counter As' attempts. Furthermore, it should be remembered, though it rarely seems to be, that the A-B scale is derived from the SVIB, a self-report measure of interests and occupations which Ss *would like to* engage in. In this light, then, it should not be surprising that As *try to* assume "influential" or controlling roles.

Bs seem more inclined to "mix it up" with patients, although apparently not from an intrusive or "one-up" stance. As the personality studies indicate, they are probably more likely to come across as "regular guys." Finally, as with facilitativeness, there *may* be some enhancement of therapist communicative qualities in complementary pairings.

Therapeutic Process: Therapist Perceptions of, and Reactions to, Patients

One clinical study reports *initial* A > B preference for both neurotic and schizophrenic outpatients; this difference, however, disappears as therapy proceeds. It furthermore notes no A-B differences on therapist self-esteem, esteem of patient, or assumed similarity to patient. Another study reports a similar absence of differences: in confidence in ability to help the patient and awareness of own reaction to patients.

There are many more analogue than clinical studies in this area. Two of these suggest that, at least in early therapy, As are more perceptive of patients; a third study, however, found no main or interaction effect A-B differences in ability to predict interviewees' self-descriptions. In the nine analogues examining A-B differences in reactions to patients, main effect A-B differences failed to emerge, in five studies, on similarity to patient, interest in patient, comfort with patient, disturbance rating, prognosis rating, preference for talkative or silent patient, reaction to nonverbal versus verbal content in incongruent communications, and assignment of personality characteristics to schizophrenic or neurotic patients.

In five of the nine analogues, though, A-B differences were found: with As rating both TAO and TAS "patients" (or partners) as more intrapunitive, submissive, dependent, forgiving, and indulgent; seeing TAO patients as less friendly than did Bs; responding more flexibly, emotionally, and acceptingly; and preferring upper class and more disturbed patients. One analogue found Bs to show greater liking than As of lower class Ss. Finally, three analogues found interaction effects: in compatible dyads, "therapists" reacted more positively after the interview, rated patients as more likable (though not, in this one study, more comfortable, more interesting to treat, more interesting as a friend, or having a better prognosis), and saw patients as more disturbed, though more motivated.

The appropriate conclusion here seems to be that, *in ongoing therapy, there are no consistently demonstrable A-B differences in perceptions of, or reactions to, patients.* On this issue, however, the analogue data do not wholly agree with the clinical data, and I interpret this disagreement in two ways. One is that although many A and B personality characteristics may be found to be consistent across professional and nonprofessional samples, professional (A or B) therapists are obviously different from (A or B) undergraduate Ss. This distinction and the above results, then, simply though strongly suggest that *professional training tends to override any A-B-determined differences in differential reactivity to different patient personalities.* The second interpretation, not at all contradictory to the first, is that *even with training such A-B differences that do appear tend to do so very briefly and in the very early parts of therapy.* This tendency is one that I have suspected to be the case for some time; it is discussed further below under "therapist-patient A-B Similarity."

Therapeutic Process: Patient Self-Exploration

Four outpatient studies considered the dimensions of patient self-exploration, self-disclosure, and/or insight. Their findings are conflicting or null. Of two studies done with medical students in first interviews, one found As > Bs on depth of self-exploration and intimate relating (but found no interaction effects) while the other found Bs > As. A third study found no A-B differences in patient insight, and the fourth found members of A-B-similar dyads to rate their partners as more self-disclosing. One analogue found As more effective in eliciting patients' summaries (regardless of patient type), while another found no A-B differences in self-disclosure. In interpreting these findings, we must of course remember that conflicting results are not necessarily null results, and that it is thus remotely possible that very precise specification of clinical circumstances might demonstrate that in different situations each therapist type is better able to elicit self-exploration. Still, the most reasonable conclusion is that there are no A-B-attributable differences in patient self-disclosure.

Therapeutic Process: Patient Reactions and Behavior

Three outpatient studies together indicate no A-B differences in patient's experiences of therapy (regardless of diagnosis), in duration of therapy, or in number of sessions, number of cancellations, reactions to first encounter, or degree to which expectations were met in a first encounter. One study found a "negative" interaction effect. In "uncomplementary" dyads, outpatients reported more positive perceptions of therapists.

Six analogues concerning interviewee, or "patient," reactions were reviewed. No A-B-attributable differences emerged in learning by modeling, degree of verbal conditioning, content of interview; in written productivity (in actual patients' responses to observation of therapist-patient interaction); in responsiveness among low-adjustment patients; and in degree of biasing of patients by therapists. Several positive findings also emerged from this group of studies, but these were inconsistent. Bs were seen as more dignified, and elicited more activity from patients, but As' "approach" was preferred. *There thus seem to be no clearly or consistently demonstrable patterns of different patient reactions to As and Bs.*

Personality: Needs, Values, and Life-Orientations

Ten studies fall in this domain, and they produce a substantially unconflicted composite picture. As are described as valuing personal authenticity and more likely to show a service orientation, wherein their social-interpersonal focus ("people orientation") is exerted. They are perhaps more creative, though less concerned with sensory pleasure. Finally, they consistently espouse more (culturally) stereotypical "feminine" interests and self-descriptions.

Bs are described as endorsing "economic" values, more likely to show an orientation to "nature," wherein their relatively impersonal, concept-oriented focus is exerted. They are much more sentient—i.e., seeking sensory experiences and pleasures—and tend not to espouse "feminine" interests and/or tend to espouse "masculine" interests.

Although most of these data are from studies using undergraduate Ss, they essentially agree or dovetail with data from studies using professionals or psychiatry-bound medical students.

Personality: Interpersonal Style

Some caution must be exercised in interpreting the data on this issue, as nearly all of the nine relevant studies used self-report measures versus, for example, partners' or judges' ratings of Ss in actual interpersonal interaction. There is thus the possibility that the following conclusions really describe differences in the ways in which As and Bs *think* they are seen or would *like* to be seen.

With this limitation in mind, though, we again find a consistent picture emerging. As seem inhibited, submissive, and cautious, especially in self-expression. They are less competent socially and less conforming. Under stress, they may turn against themselves in an intropunitive fashion. Bs, consonant with their above-described values and orientations, seem consistently to fill a culturally defined role of "masculine adequacy." They are more thrill-seeking, risk-taking, socially ascendant, managerial or dominant, and try to present themselves in a positive light. They conform much more to social norms and are thus, for example, reported in one study to be seen by their patients as "hypernormal." Under stress, they tend more to turn away from or against others and to be extrapunitive. One writer describes this amalgam of social desirability-seeking through "masculine" normality as counterdependent. The one study in this group that failed to show A-B differences examined "developmental history" by utilizing a questionable methodology.

Personality: Cognitive and Perceptual Dimensions

Nine studies, whose data are primarily from undergraduates, together coherently present As as more "verbally oriented" (for example, they verbally condition more easily, show higher verbal than quantitative test scores, and are perhaps more "comfortable" functioning in verbal modalities). Bs, however, may be better able to conceive of and use language as a set of formal symbols. As may be more "inner-oriented," imaginative, creative, in general oriented toward and comfortable with unobvious "incidental" percepts, and perhaps able to generate more free-floating attention, especially in clinical situations. (No A-B differences emerged in terms of being more transmission- or reception-oriented.) Bs are cognitively more complex and seek cognitive variety and complexity in their experiences.

Personality: Psychopathology and Defensive Structure

Seven of eight studies, most using undergraduate Ss, consistently portray As as more disturbed. Qualitatively, this difference is seen in As' greater anxiety, depression, obsessive-compulsiveness, social isolation, apprehensiveness, and access to negative affects; they show lower self-esteem, stamina, and persistence. They are probably less defensive, however, than Bs, and also more socially aware, perhaps acutely so.

Although there is good evidence that As see themselves as more like TAS (than AVOS or TAO) patients, the above data (especially the characterization in Fancher et al., 1972) suggest a more schizoid than neurotic picture of marginality, panneurosis, withdrawal, exquisite sensitivity, and perhaps greater paranoia. And, while this impression, of course, does not mean that As are clinical schizoids, it does suggest that As are more schizoid than Bs, perhaps clinically so in patient A-B studies such as Johnson et al. (1973), but subclinically so among nonpatients. Refining patient diagnostic categories (for example, to distinguish paranoid from nonparanoid schizophrenics) may yield different, even conflicting, A-B relationships for each clinical subpopulation.

Patients' versus Nonpatients' A-B Scores

The above discussion brings us to the question of whether the A-B variable means something different among patients than among nonpatients. There is no evidence in any study reviewed here or previously of such differences. On the contrary, as is indicated above, the personality differences emerging from studies using different types of Ss tend much more to complement each others' characterizations.

A and B Patients in Interviews

Two analogue studies' designs permitted examination of main effect patient A-B status. In Magaro and Staples (1972), where A and B

chronic schizophrenics were paired with A or B patient-"therapist," or with A or B control-therapist, A-patients had difficulties communicating in all pairings. In a second study, B counseling clients' conversations (with their counselors) were marked by more personal comments, more challenge, and more active work. Both these findings are consistent with the personality findings described above.

Therapist-Patient A-B Similarity

Two clinical and nine analogue studies examined therapist-patient A-B score similarity as a predictor of process. The results are somewhat mixed. Four analogues together found no differences in interview content, degree of verbal conditioning, pattern of verbal conditioning, pattern of nonverbal communication, or empathy and regard. The two clinical studies and one analogue, however, found greater facilitativeness (each on at least some conditions) in A-B dissimilar dyads. Yet the four other analogues found that A-B similarity was associated with increased patient responsiveness, greater degree of information-gathering, greater similarity on adjective checklist self-ratings, and probably also with viewing one's partner as more sympathetic, easier to understand, and more interesting. In sum, these results do not seem coherent, and no interpretation of them is apparent.

Early versus Late A-B Differences

There are at least four studies (one clinical, three analogue) documenting A-B differences very early in "therapy," which later disappeared or diminished: As giving longer responses, being more perceptive than Bs, especially with schizophrenics, and showing greater preferences for both neurotic and schizophrenic patients. Moreover, complementary dyads had longer therapist responses, more positive emotional tone, and more assertiveness. In addition, there are the medical student studies finding B > A differences in one-session subjective distress relief, in contrast to the generally null outcome studies in longer term therapy.

To the extent, then, that the very early moments of therapy have any importance, the A-B variable may have some value, although, again, it cannot be overemphasized that, if, as most therapy does, the therapy goes beyond a few moments or one session, subsequent events, according to the vast bulk of available evidence, seem to override any effects of the A-B variable.

Now if all this is correct, and I believe that it is, then there is a potentially valuable insight that the body of A-B research may have heuristically provided—namely, that the early moments of therapy may constitute a period in which the therapist's "personality" and/or compatibility between the therapist's and the patient's "personalities" are more important (perhaps, in some cases, crucially important) than techniques or professional training. This is a possibility which, if actual, should have general applicability well beyond A-B research and may be of particular value in crisis-intervention therapy, therapy with client populations traditionally considered "poor candidates," walk-in or "hot-line" interventions, etc. Furthermore, investigation of such early therapy moments may be vital to future research on patient-therapist matching.

SUMMARY AND CONCLUSIONS

In the 20 years since Whitehorn and Betz first reported distinguishing therapists who were most successful with schizophrenics (As) from those who were least successful (Bs), and later reported that certain Strong Vocational Interest Blank items could serve as the basis for this distinction, a continuous flow of studies has appeared. While this flow has been almost unfailingly constant, the quality of work and results has not been. Fortunately there have also appeared several astute reviews to punctuate and occasionally influence the direction of this flow. Carson (1967), for example, expressed cautious optimism that a promising, possibly critical variable was emerging. It takes little imagination to conceive of the appeal of a simple, 23-item scale purporting to predict who will be successful with schizophrenics; furthermore, so the evidence was interpreted, this scale could at the same time predict success with neurotics by those who were unsuccessful with schizophrenics. Thus, the (therapist type X patient diagnosis) "interaction hypothesis" was born and rapidly adapted. Unfortunately, this eagerly welcomed newborn was soon to utter the most remarkable and often confusing things.

Cartwright's (1968), Razin's (1971), and Chartier's (1971) reviews pointed out some of the many logical and methodological flaws in the area, and, in general, the research in the late 1960s and early 1970s has been of a higher, more rigorous quality than that preceding it. But these more rigorous attempts at demonstrating A-B differences in outcome of actual therapy have, with few exceptions, failed. Until about 1970 or 1971, however, the analogue research continued to promise; significant interaction effects continued to emerge. Moreover, work on differential personality correlates also continued to show consistent, replicable differences (e.g., As were less field-independent, more "feminine" by cultural stereotype standards, more open to unusual perceptions, less daring, and more verbally oriented).

My involvement with the A-B variable has been marked by initial optimism and encouragement, as reflected in my 1971 review; this optimism, however, has progressively diminished and turned to skepticism about the A-B research quest. Nevertheless, in undertaking this review, I have sought neither to fall in with the total skepticism of May (1974) nor to embrace a position of continued uncritical optimism. Rather, it made most sense to try to discern the specific areas in which the A-B variable might have utility. Completion of this review, however, which was undertaken as an open-minded, even eager search that left no stone unturned (e.g., including every known doctoral dissertation and unpublished study, and even older studies unavailable at the time of the 1971 review) reveals only a scant few areas of possible clinical utility.

In long-term clinical outcome, it seems that the time for fulfilling promises has just about elapsed. The A-B variable is clearly not the predictive panacea many hoped it would be. It has really not predicted outcome very consistently or very often, no true replication of the original Whitehorn-Betz work has been done, and many (e.g., Bowden et al., 1972) doubt that it can be.

The picture in clinical process is almost, though not quite, as totally negative. All the relevant data being considered, there is the suggestion that early in therapy, with complementary dyads, with untrained "therapists," and/or in clinical situations unlike traditional ongoing therapy, there may be some enhancement of process and even short-term outcome. Again, however, I must repeat that such differences do not seem to endure the usual course of therapy.

It has also become clear, on the other hand, that the variable, whatever it measures, is *not* an artifact or a fluke. The personality correlate literature has continued to be relatively consistent, and, in fact, has fleshed in some of its earlier sketching. For example, there is consistent evidence of As' social marginality (which, in pre-phenothiazine 1954, may have been important in reaching chronic schizophrenics). And there is evidence that, while As are more comfortable with verbal modalities, Bs are better able to deal with language as a set of formal logical symbols and probably seek and enjoy such cognitively complex activity.

At this point, then, it seems clear that skepticism should no longer be suspended and that the status of the A-B variable can be fairly summarized as follows:

1. It is not a fluke, as some contend; it does correlate with, and thus predict, a consistent constellation of personality differences (between As and Bs).

2. While these differences are replicable and may have real value for theory and research in personality, *the A-B variable is not a powerful predictor of any important process or outcome parameters in real, ongoing therapy.*

3. Other variables, such as therapist level of experience and severity or chronicity of patient disturbance, are simply more powerful.

4. Situations that do not resemble traditional therapy *may* have some use for the A-B variable. The clinically relevant differences that do occur are based on brief encounters, early sessions, and/or untrained change agents. Perhaps, then, modalities using very brief encounters, such as suicide hot-lines, other brief crisis interventions, and college-student-therapist programs (particularly where therapy staff may have little formal training and may thus rely on their "personality" rather than on specific, learned therapeutic ideologies or techniques) may find some potential clinical value in the A-B variable, especially if a rapid triage mechanism is part of the intervention system.

5. Such initial encounter differences are possibly heightened by complementary dyadic pairings, so that, in the above clinical situations, there may be some utility for the A-B variable in providing one parameter for increasing compatibility. Again, though, complementarity, like the A-B variable itself, has at most trivial effects in longer courses of therapy.

REFERENCES

ALPERT, G. Therapeutic effects of therapist-patient matching and positive therapist expectancies. *Dissertation Abstracts International*, 1973, **33B**, 3924.

ANZEL, A. A/B typing and patient socioeconomic and personality characteristics in a quasitherapeutic situation. *Journal of Consulting and Clinical Psychology*, 1970, **35**, 102–115.

BARNES, D. A and B college students as interviewers of schizophrenic and neurotic inpatients: A test of the interaction hypothesis. Unpublished doctoral dissertation, University of Kentucky, 1972.

BEDNAR, R. Therapeutic relationship of A-B therapists as perceived by client and therapist. *Journal of Counseling Psychology*, 1970, **17**, 119–122.

BEDNAR, R., & MOBLEY, M. A-B research findings: Methodological considerations, new data, and interpretation. Unpublished manuscript, Arkansas Rehabilitation Research and Training Center, 1969.

BEDNAR, R., & MOBLEY, M. A-B therapist perceptions and preferences for schizophrenic and psychoneurotic clients. *Journal of Abnormal Psychology*, 1971, **78**, 192–197.

BENNINGTON, K. Communicative behavior and the A-B dimension. *Dissertation Abstracts International*, 1972, **32B**, 5432.

BERZINS, J., BARNES, D., COHEN, D., & ROSS, W. A reappraisal of the A-B therapist "type" distinction in terms of the Personality Research Form. *Journal of Consulting and Clinical Psychology*, 1971, **36**, 360–369.

BERZINS, J., DOVE, J., & ROSS, W. Crossvalidational studies of the personality correlates of the A-B therapist "type" distinction among professionals and nonprofessionals. *Journal of Consulting and Clinical Psychology*, 1972, **39**, 388–395.

BERZINS, J. I., FRIEDMAN, W. H., & SEIDMAN, E. Relationship of the A-B variable to psychological symptomatology and psychotherapeutic expectancies. *Journal of Abnormal Psychology*, 1969, **74**, 119–125.

BERZINS, J., HERRON, E., & SEIDMAN, E. Patients' role behaviors as seen by therapists: A factor-analytic study. *Psychotherapy: Theory, Research and Practice*, 1971, **8**, 127–130.

BERZINS, J., ROSS, W., & COHEN, D. The relation of the A-B distinction and trust-distrust sets to addicts self-disclosures in brief interviews. *Journal of Consulting and Clinical Psychology*, 1970, **34**, 289–296.

BERZINS, J., ROSS, W., & FRIEDMAN, W. The A-B therapist distinction, patient diagnosis and outcome of brief psychotherapy in a college clinic. *Journal of Consulting and Clinical Psychology*, 1972, **38**, 231–237.

BERZINS, J. I., & SEIDMAN, E. Subjective reactions of A and B quasi-therapists to schizoid and neurotic communications: A replication and extension. *Journal of Consulting and Clinical Psychology*, 1968, **32**, 342–347.

BERZINS, J., & SEIDMAN, E. Differential therapeutic responding of A and B quasi-therapists to schizoid and neurotic communications. *Journal of Consulting and Clinical Psychology*, 1969, **33**, 279–286.

BETZ, B. Bases of therapeutic leadership in psychotherapy with the schizophrenic patient. *American Journal of Psychotherapy*, 1963, **17**, 196–212.

BETZ, B. The problem solving approach and therapeutic effectiveness. *American Journal of Psychotherapy*, 1966, **20**, 45–56.

BETZ, B. Studies of the therapist's role in the treatment of the schizophrenic patient. *American Journal of Psychiatry*, 1967, **123**, 963–971.

BETZ, B. A-B therapist variable: Commentary on Bowden's paper. *Journal of Nervous and Mental Disease*, 1972, **154**, 287–288.

BETZ, B., & WHITEHORN, J. C. The relationship of the therapist to the outcome of therapy in schizophrenia. *Psychiatric Research Reports*, 1956, No. 5, 89–105.

BEUTLER, L., JOHNSON, D., NEVILLE, C., & WORKMAN, S. "Accurate empathy" and the A-B dichotomy. *Journal of Consulting and Clinical Psychology*, 1972, **38**, 372–375.

BLANK, G. An experimental study of the effects of patients' perceptions of different types of psychotherapeutic approaches on patients' responses in psychotherapy. *Dissertation Abstracts International*, 1968, **29B**, 362.

BOWDEN, C., ENDICOTT, J., & SPITZER, R. A-B therapist variable and psychotherapeutic outcome. *Journal of Nervous and Mental Disease*, 1972, **154**, 276–286.

BOYD, R. Whitehorn-Betz A-B score as an effector of client-counselor interaction. *Journal of Counseling Psychology*, 1970, **17**, 279–283.

BRAUN, J. The empathic ability of psychotherapists as related to therapist perceptual flexibility and professional experience, patient insight, and therapist-patient similarity. Unpublished doctoral dissertation, Fordham University, 1971.

CAMPBELL, D. P., STEVENS, J. H., UHLENHUTH, E., & JOHANSSON, C. B. An extension of the Whitehorn-Betz A-B scale. *Journal of Nervous and Mental Disease*, 1968, **146**, 417–421.

CARSON, R. C. A and B therapist "types": A possible critical variable in psychotherapy. *Journal of Nervous Mental Disease*, 1967, **144**, 45–54.

CARSON, R. C., HARDEN, J. A., & SHOWS, W. D. The A-B distinction and behavior in quasi-therapeutic situations. *Journal of Consulting Psychology*, 1964, **28**, 426–433.

CARTWRIGHT, R. Psychotherapeutic processes: The qualities of effective dyads. *Annual Review of Psychology*, 1968, **17**, 387–416.

CHARTIER, G. A-B therapist variable: Real or imagined? *Psychological Bulletin*, 1971, **75**, 22–33.

CHARTIER, G. Classification of therapists on the A-B variable. *Journal of Consulting and Clinical Psychology*, 1974, **42**, 617.

CHARTIER, G., & WEISS, L. A-B therapists and clinical perception: Support for a "Super A" hypothesis. *Journal of Consulting and Clinical Psychology*, 1974, **42**, 312.

COHEN, T. A-B distinction and therapist expectancies in a quasi-therapeutic situation. *Dissertation Abstracts International*, 1967, **28B**, 1693.

DELK, J., & RYAN, T. Sex role stereotyping and A-B therapist status. *Journal of Consulting and Clinical Psychology*, 1975, **43**, 589.

DUBLIN, J., & BERZINS, J. A-B variable and reactions to non-immediacy in neurotic and schizoid communications: A longitudinal analogue of psychotherapy. *Journal of Consulting and Clinical Psychology*, 1972, **39**, 86–93.

DUBLIN, J. E., ELTON, C. F., & BERZINS, J. I. Some personality and aptitudinal correlates of the "A-B" therapist scale. *Journal of Consulting and Clinical Psychology*, 1969, **33**, 739–745.

EYSENCK, H. Some comments on the relation between A-B status of behavior therapists and success of treatment. *Journal of Consulting and Clinical Psychology*, 1975, **43**, 86–87.

FANCHER, R., MCMILLAN, R., & BUCHMAN, N. Interrelationships among accuracy in person perception, role taking, and the A-B variable. *Journal of Consulting and Clinical Psychology*, 1972, **39**, 22–28.

FRAHM, P. A and B therapists evaluate talkative and silent clients: An analogue study. *Dissertation Abstracts International*, 1966, **27B**, 1621.

FRANCO, E. A-B requiem: An integrative review and alternatives in the study of the therapist's personality. Paper submitted to *Psychological Bulletin*, 1975.

FRANCO, E., & KULBERG, G. Content analysis of the natural language of A and B males in a dyadic interaction. *Journal of Consulting and Clinical Psychology*, 1975, **43**, 345–349.

FRANCO, E., & MAGARO, P. The relationship and meaning of A-B, field-dependency, and emotional openness in paranoid and non-paranoid schizophrenics. Paper submitted to *Journal of Consulting and Clinical Psychology*, 1975.

FRANK, J. *Persuasion and healing: A comparative study of psychotherapy*. Baltimore: Johns Hopkins Press, 1961.

FRIEDMAN, H. A-B "therapist" types and responses to "patient" communications varying in clarity and affect.

Dissertation Abstracts International, 1971, **32B**, 2633.

GELLER, J., & BERZINS, J. The A-B distinction in a sample of prominent psychotherapists. *Journal of Consulting and Clinical Psychology*, 1976, **44**, 77–82.

GOODWIN, W. "A" and "B" psychotherapists responses to schizoid and neurotic patient prototypes. Unpublished manuscript, Yale University, 1971.

GOODWIN, W., GELLER, J., & QUINLAN, D. M. Attitudes toward sex roles among A and B psychotherapists, *Journal of Consulting and Clinical Psychology*, 1973, **41**, 471.

GRAY, J. Correlates of the A-B scale in the therapy of passive-aggressive patients. *Dissertation Abstracts International*, 1969, **30B**, 832.

GREEN, M. The effectiveness of A and B college males as interviewers, as response-biasers, and as verbal conditioners with schizophrenic and neurotic patients. *Dissertation Abstracts International*, 1972, **33B**, 915–916.

GRINSPOON, L., SHADER, R., & EWALT, J. *Schizophrenia: Pharmacotherapy and psychotherapy*. Baltimore: Williams & Wilkins, 1972.

HASENFUS, N., MARTINDALE, C., & KAPLAN, C. Alpha amplitude and hemispheric asymmetry in A and B type clinical and experimental psychologists. Paper presented at the Sixth Annual Meeting of the Society for Psychotherapy Research, Boston, June 1975.

HEATON, R., CARR, J., & HAMPSON, J. A-B therapist characteristics *vs.* psychotherapy outcome: Current status and prospects. *Journal of Nervous and Mental Disease*, 1975, **160**, 299–309.

HOFFNUNG, R., & STEIN, L. Responses of A and B subjects to normal, neurotic, schizophrenic, and ambiguous communications. *Journal of Consulting and Clinical Psychology*, 1970, **34**, 327–332.

HOWARD, K., & ORLINSKY, D. Psychotherapeutic processes. *Annual Review of Psychology*, 1972, **23**, 615–668.

HOWARD, K., ORLINSKY, D., & TRATTNER, J. Therapist orientation and patient experience in psychotherapy. *Journal of Counseling Psychology*, 1970, **17**, 263–270.

JACOB, T., & LEVINE, D. AB distinction and prediction of interviewee self-descriptions based on a quasi-therapeutic interaction. *Journal of Consulting and Clinical Psychology*, 1968, **32**, 613–615.

JAMES, L., & FOREMAN, M. A-B status of behavior therapy technicians as related to success of Mowrer's conditioning treatment for enuresis. *Journal of Consulting and Clinical Psychology*, 1973, **41**, 224–229.

JAMES, L., & FOREMAN, M. James and Foreman reply. *Journal of Consulting and Clinical Psychology*, 1975, **43**, 87–88.

JOHNSON, D., WORKMAN, S., NEVILLE, C., & BEUTLER, L. MMPI and 16 PF correlates of the A-B therapy scale in psychiatric inpatients. *Psychotherapy: Theory, Research and Practice*, 1973, **10**, 270–272.

JOHNSON, W., & SMITH, E. Responsivity to incongruent verbal and non-verbal communications and A-B therapist type. *Perceptual and Motor Skills*, 1974, **38**, 1066.

KARON, B., & VANDEN BOS, G. The consequences of psychotherapy for schizophrenic patients. *Psychotherapy: Theory, Research and Practice*, 1972, **9**, 111–119.

KEMP, D. E. Personality and behavior in psychotherapeutic relationships: Correlates of a scale of therapeutic effectiveness. Unpublished doctoral dissertation, Duke University, 1963.

KEMP, D. Routinizing art: Implications of research with the A-B scale for the practice of psychotherapy. *Journal of the American College Health Association*, 1970, **18**, 238–240.

KEMP, D., & STEPHENS, J. Which AB scale? A comparative analysis of several versions. *Journal of Nervous and Mental Disease*, 1971, **152**, 23–30.

KENNEDY, J. A-B therapist and client matching: A process study of the A-B variable in actual clinical situations. *Dissertation Abstracts International*, 1973, **33B**, 3308.

KENWORTHY, J. Personality correlates associated with effectiveness in psychotherapy. *Dissertation Abstracts International*, 1968, **29B**, 3488.

KIRKPATRICK, P. A further exploration of the A-B "type" distinction. *Dissertation Abstracts International*, 1969, **30B**, 849.

KLEM, R. The A-B variable and interpersonal perceptions in peer dyadic interactions. *Dissertation Abstracts International*, 1971, **32B**, 3641.

KOEGLER, R., & BRILL, N. *Treatment of psychiatric outpatients*, New York: Appleton-Century-Crofts, 1967.

KRASNER, L., & ULLMANN, L. *Behavior influence and personality: The social matrix of human action*. New York: Holt, Rinehart & Winston, 1973.

KRIEGSFIELD, M. An investigation of the relationship of some psychotherapist variables to the outcome of treatment with patients of different social classes. *Dissertation Abstracts International*, 1971, **31B**, 4339.

KULBERG, G., & FRANCO, E. The effects of A-B similarity and dissimilarity in a dyadic interaction. *Psychological Reports*, 1975, in press.

LYNCH, D. A-B type and the relationship between police officers and ghetto citizens. *Community Mental Health Journal*, 1974, **10**, 434–440.

MAGARO, P., & STAPLES, S. Schizophrenic patients as therapists: An expansion of the prescriptive treatment system based upon pre-morbid adjustment, social class and A-B status. *Psychotherapy: Theory, Research and Practice*, 1972, **9**, 352–358.

MAY, P. *Treatment of schizophrenia*, New York: Science House, 1968.

MAY, P. A Brave New World revisited: Alphas, Betas, and treatment outcome. *Comprehensive Psychiatry*, 1974, **15**, 1–17.

MAY, P., & TUMA, A. Treatment of schizophrenia. *British Journal of Psychiatry*, 1965, **3**, 503–510.

MCGUIGAN, S., & SEIDMAN, E. A-B type status, self-concept, and social competence. *Journal of Clinical Psychology*, 1971, **27**, 493–494.

MCNAIR, D. M., LORR, M., & CALLAHAN, D. M. Patient and therapist influences on quitting psychotherapy. *Journal of Consulting Psychology*, 1962, **27**, 10–17.

MELTZOFF, J., & KORNREICH, M. *Research in psychotherapy*. New York: Atherton Press, 1970.

MUEHLBERG, N. The Strong Vocational Interest Blank as a measure of effective therapeutic communication. Unpublished doctoral dissertation, State University of New York at Buffalo, 1971.

NERVIANO, V. Crossvalidation of some personality correlates of the A-B scale among male alcoholics. *Psychological Reports*, 1973, **32**, 1338.

O'BRIEN, C., HAMM, K., RAY, B., PIERCE, J., LUBORSKY, L., and MINTZ, J. Group versus individual psychotherapy with schizophrenics. *Archives of General Psychiatry*, 1972, **27**, 474–478.

PARDES, H., WINSTON, A., & PAPERNICK, D. Re-examination of the A-B field dependence relationship. *Archives of General Psychiatry*, 1971, **24**, 465–467.

PHILLIPS, L., & RABINOVITCH, M. Social role and patterns of symptomatic behaviors. *Journal of Abnormal and Social Psychology*, 1958, **57**, 181–186.

POLLACK, I. W., & KIEV, A. Spatial orientation and psychotherapy: An experimental study of perception. *Journal of Nervous and Mental Disorders*, 1963, **137**, 93–96.

PORTNOY, S., & RESNICK, J. Similarity and complementarity with the A-B scale in verbal conditioning. *Journal of Consulting and Clinical Psychology*, 1972, **39**, 152–155.

POWELL, T. An investigation of the effectiveness of therapist-patient dyads in an initial psychotherapy interview under conditions of A-B complementarity and similarity. *Dissertation Abstracts International*, 1969, **31B**, 3712.

RAZIN, A. A-B variable in psychotherapy: A critical review. *Psychological Bulletin*, 1971, **75**, 1–22.

RAZIN, A. The A-B variable and therapist persuasiveness. *Journal of Nervous and Mental Disease*, 1974, **159**, 244–255.

ROTHMAN, L. Toward a theoretical conceptualization of the Whitehorn and Betz A-B scale. *Journal of Consulting and Clinical Psychology*, 1971, **36**, 442.

SCHIFFMAN, H., CARSON, R., & FALKENBERG, P. A psychometric analysis of Whitehorn-Betz A-B scale. Unpublished paper, Duke University, 1967.

SCHUBERT, D., & WAGNER, M. "A" therapists as creative and personally involved with other people. *Journal of Consulting and Clinical Psychology*, 1975, **43**, 266.

SCOTT, R., & KEMP, D. The A-B scale and empathy, warmth, genuineness, and depth of self-exploration. *Journal of Abnormal Psychology*, 1971, **77**, 49–51.

SEGAL, B. Further investigation of personality correlates of the A-B scale. *Psychotherapy: Theory, Research and Practice*, 1971a, **8**, 37.

SEGAL, B. Illustrations of therapeutic interventions of A and B therapists. *Psychotherapy: Theory, Research and Practice*, 1971b, **8**, 273–275.

SEIDMAN, E. A and B subject therapists' responses to videotaped schizoid and intropunitive neurotic prototypes. *Journal of Consulting and Clinical Psychology*, 1971, **37**, 201–208.

SEIDMAN, E. Which AB scale? An extension. *Journal of Nervous and Mental Disease*, 1972, **155**, 105–109.

SEIDMAN, E., GOLDING, S., HOGAN, T., & LEBOW, M. A multidimensional interpretation and comparison of three A-B scales. *Journal of Consulting and Clinical Psychology*, 1974, 42, 10–20.

SHADER, R., GRINSPOON, L., HARMATZ, J., & EWALT, J. The therapist variable. *American Journal of Psychiatry*, 1971, **127**, 1009–1012.

SHARDLOW, G. The Whitehorn-Betz A-B scale as related to differential motivational effectiveness and interpersonal perception. *Dissertation Abstracts International*, 1968, **29B**, 1181.

SHOWS, W. Psychological differentiation of the A-B dimension: A dyadic interaction hypothesis. *Dissertation Abstracts International*, 1967, **28B**, 3885.

SILVERMAN, J., BUCHSBAUM, M., & STIERLIN, H. Sex differences in perceptual differentiation and stimulus intensity control. *Journal of Personality and Social Psychology*, 1973, **25**, 309–318.

SMITH, E. Postural and gestural communication of A and B "therapist types" during dyadic interviews. *Journal of Consulting and Clinical Psychology*, 1972, **39**, 29–36.

STEIN, L., GREEN, G., & STONE, W. Therapist attitudes as influenced by A-B therapist type, patient diagnosis, and social class. *Journal of Consulting and Clinical Psychology*, 1972, **39**, 301–307.

STEPHENS, J. H., & ASTRUP, C. Treatment outcome in "process" and "non-process" schizophrenics treated by "A" and "B" types of therapist. *Journal of Nervous and Mental Disorders*, 1965, **140**, 449–456.

STEPHENS, J., SHAFFER, J., & ZLOTOWITZ, H. An optimum A-B scale of psychotherapist effectiveness. *Journal of Nervous and Mental Disease*, 1975, **160**, 267–281.

STERN, M., & BIERMAN, R. Facilitative functioning of A-B therapist types. *Psychotherapy: Theory, Research and Practice*, 1973, **10**, 44–47.

TANLEY, J. Relationship between repression-sensitization and A-B therapist types. *Journal of Clinical Psychology*, 1973a, **29**, 109.

TANLEY, J. Uses of personality and interest measures in predicting crisis phone counselor effectiveness. *Dissertation Abstracts International*, 1973b, **33B**, 3964.

TRUAX, C., & CARKHUFF, R. *Toward effective counseling and psychotherapy: Teaching and practice*. Chicago: Aldine, 1967.

UHLENHUTH, E., & COVI, L. Subjective changes with the initial interview. *American Journal of Psychotherapy*, 1969, **23**, 415–429.

UHLENHUTH, E., & DUNCAN, D. Subjective change with medical student therapists. I: Course of relief in psychoneurotic outpatients. *Archives of General Psychiatry*, 1968a, **18**, 428–438.

UHLENHUTH, E., & DUNCAN, D. Subjective change with medical student therapists. II: Some determinants of change in psychoneurotic outpatients. *Archives of General Psychiatry*, 1968b, **18**, 532–540.

VAUGHN, R. Investigation of the therapeutic behavior of type A and type B psychotherapists. *Dissertation Abstracts International*, 1969, **30B**, 2427.

WELCH, R. The effectiveness of A and B college males as models and interviewers with schizophrenic and neurotic patients. *Dissertation Abstracts International*, 1971, **32B**, 2413.

WELCH, R., & BERZINS, J. The A-B therapist "type" distinction and reactions to pictorial frustration. Unpublished manuscript, University of Kentucky, 1968.

WHITEHORN, J. Alienation and leadership. *Psychiatry*, 1961 (supplement), **24**, 1–6.

WHITEHORN, J. Human factors in psychiatry. *Bulletin of the New York Academy of Medicine*, 1964, **40**, 451–466.

WHITEHORN, J. C., BETZ, B. A. A study of psychotherapeutic relationships between physicians and schizophrenic patients. *American Journal of Psychiatry*, 1954, **111**, 321–331.

WHITEHORN, J. C., & BETZ, B. A. A comparison of psychotherapeutic relationships between physicians and schizophrenic patients when insulin is combined with psychotherapy and when insulin is used alone. *American Journal of Psychiatry*, 1957, **113**, 901–910.

WHITEHORN, J. C., & BETZ, B. Further studies of the doctor as a crucial variable in the outcome of treatment of schizophrenic patients. *American Journal of Psychiatry*, 1960, **117**, 215–223.

EDITORS' REFERENCES

BARRETT-LENNARD, G. T. Dimensions of therapist response as causal factors in therapeutic change. *Psychological Monographs*, 1962, **76**, No. 43 (Whole No. 562).

BEDNAR, R., & MOBLEY, M. A-B therapist perceptions and preferences for schizophrenic and psychoneurotic clients. *Journal of Abnormal Psychology*, 1971, **78**, 192–197.

CARKHUFF, R. R. *Helping and human relations: A primer for lay and professional helpers*. Vol. 1, *Selection and training*. New York: Holt, Rinehart & Winston, 1969a.

CARKHUFF, R. R. *Helping and human relations: A primer for lay and professional helpers*. Vol. 2, *Practice and research*. New York: Holt, Rinehart & Winston, 1969b.

KENNEDY, J. A-B therapist and client matching: A process study of the A-B variable in actual clinical situations. *Dissertation Abstracts International*, 1973, **33B**, 3308.

KLEM, R. The A-B variable and interpersonal perceptions in peer dyadic interactions. *Dissertation Abstracts International*, 1971, **32B**, 3641.

KIESLER, D. J. Some myths of psychotherapy research and the search for a paradigm. *Psychological Bulletin*, 1966, **65**, 110–136.

KULBERG, G., & FRANCO, E. The effects of A-B similarity and dissimilarity in a dyadic interaction. *Psychological Reports*, 1975, in press.

ROGERS, C. R. (Ed.) *The therapeutic relationship and its impact: A study of psychotherapy with schizophrenics*. Madison, WI: University of Wisconsin Press, 1967.

STERN, M., & BIERMAN, R. Facilitative functioning of A-B therapist types. *Psychotherapy: Theory, Research and Practice*, 1973, **10**, 44–47.

NOTES

1. The author is indebted to Drs. Alan Gurman and George Chartier for their valuable comments and advice on this chapter.

2. *Editors' Footnote.* As co-editors, we each have written "editors'" footnotes for the other's chapter. Thus, Alan S. Gurman is responsible for the notes in this chapter.

3. In addition to the examples that follow, there are several minor ones, one of which I feel warrants at least parenthetical mention: My review describes the original Whitehorn and Betz work as utilizing randomized patient-therapist pairing. May (1974, p. 15) flatly denies that this occurred. But Betz explicitly described random assignment and actually carried out (1963) statistical tests which showed no systematic differences in pairing.

4. *Editors' Footnote.* Three other critical issues are brought to mind by this study. First, it now appears that patients' *perceptions* of the client-centered "conditions" are far more consistently predictive of therapeutic outcome (see Gurman, Chapter 19, this volume) than are judge-rated conditions (see Mitchell, Bozarth, & Krauft, Chapter 18, this volume). Second, evidence exists (Rogers, 1967) that with schizophrenic patients congruence is the most salient among the three facilitative conditions. Finally, it should be noted that, on clinical grounds, it is understandable that empathy may fail to enhance the quality of the therapeutic relationship and, thereby, be positively correlated with outcome, with patients whose interpersonal relationships are marked by ambivalence, mistrust and fear: for many such patients, to be understood is to be threatened.

5. *Editors' Footnote.* It may well be that, among many other possible reasons, this "homogeneity myth" (Kiesler, 1966) is one of the supreme culprits working against the potential influence of therapy research on therapeutic practice. The absence of crucial descriptive data of the actual (vs. intended or assumed) process of therapy in a given study provides ample fuel to an already burning flame of nonapplicability that exists among some clinicians. Perhaps a "truth in publishing" code should be developed which would require that any published research on the process or outcome of psychotherapy must explicate enough of at least the central tendencies of what actually occurred in treatment that a reader wishing to replicate the study would be able to do so in a way that is believable to practicing therapists. Journal articles would thereby, no doubt, become longer, but might have more impact in the real world.

6. *Editors' Footnote.* The general format of this hypothesis, that the same variables may have differential impact at different stages of therapy, is appealing. We doubt, however, that "relationship variables" *become* salient late or later in therapy. In fact, we would argue that relationship variables, if in fact they are more important at any one phase of treatment than others, would have their primary impact *early* in therapy, as suggested by the paradigm of Carkhuff (1969a, 1969b) and Mitchell *et al.* (Chapter 18, this volume). More likely, relationship variables probably need to be "steady state," serving initially as the necessary conditions for client self-disclosure and self-exploration and later as the autonomy-fostering attachment context within which and without which risk-taking and exploratory behavior can be initiated.

7. While I have attempted to be as comprehensive as possible in including relevant unpublished dissertations, it would have been nearly impossible to examine each of these in great detail. I deemed it more informative to present a large number of dissertations relatively briefly and uncritically, rather than a few in great detail. Thus the descriptions and discussions of most dissertations are based on abstracts, and may thus often read more like telegraphic bulletins than detailed reviews.

8. *Editors' Footnote*. This is not surprising in light of the evidence adduced by Gurman (Chapter 19, this volume) that judge-rated and patient- (or participant-) rated facilitative conditions, with the possible exception of empathy, share little common variance.

9. *Editors' Footnote*. The conclusions reached in this and the last subsection seem to be among the most solid, convincing, and probably controversial of any that have been unearthed and pieced together either in this volume or in psychotherapy research in general. Razin's thorough review and analysis of the A-B literature, in addition to its major contribution to clarifying this domain *per se*, should serve well to remind psychotherapy researchers (and psychotherapists) that the search for an oasis of simple and "magical" predictors of therapeutic outcome is one guaranteed to lead but to an empty well. The power of single variables is meager in investigating the rich and complex process of psychotherapy.

10. *Editors' Footnote*. Among the nine naturalistic studies, three (Bednar & Mobley, 1971; Kennedy, 1973; Klem, 1971) tapped the facilitative conditions with the Relationship Inventory (RI) of Barrett-Lennard (1962). Two of these three studies (Kennedy, 1973; Klem, 1971) found A-B *dis*similarity associated with higher patient ratings of facilitative functioning. In addition, both of the analogue studies in this domain (Kulberg & Franco, 1975; Stern & Bierman, 1973) produced at least some significant results. Thus, four of the five studies using the RI found either interaction effects or A-B differences, whereas only four of 10 (clinical and analogue studies combined) that used judge(tape)-ratings yielded any significant results. While the salience of even these positive findings is, as Razin notes, not strong, it appears that the RI is relatively stronger than the independent judge, tape-rating strategy, in terms of unearthing *some* A-B differences and interaction effects. This analysis of therapist facilitativeness and the A-B variable appears, then, to be supportive of trends noted elsewhere in this volume—i.e., of the greater predictive utility, regarding therapy outcome, of the RI (Gurman, Chapter 19, this volume) than of independent judges' ratings of therapist "conditions" (Mitchell *et al.*, Chapter 18, this volume).

CHAPTER 13

EXPECTANCIES IN APPLIED SETTINGS

WALLACE WILKINS

INTRODUCTION

The study of therapist expectancies represents the intersection of two areas of contemporary psychological investigation: the study of variables contributing to effective psychotherapy and the general psychological study of the expectancy effect.

In addition to therapist behavioral and personality traits shown in other chapters of this volume to effect differential therapeutic change, therapist cognitive variables have been identified as playing a contributory role in the process and outcome of therapy. Data presented by Fontana, Gessner, and Lorr (1968), for example, showed that for one of the professional groups studied, treatment recommendations were more consistently related to inferences which therapists made about the client than they were to the complaints actually communicated by the client. Temerlin and Trousdale (1969) found that even when clinicians were specifically instructed to attend to and report only observable information, their descriptions of a client were rich with events which were assumed and inferred, but not observed. Among the myriad of cognitive events occurring throughout therapy, therapist expectancies have been a focus of recent psychotherapy investigations.

Not only is therapist expectancy only one of the many therapist variables which may affect outcome, but the therapy setting is only one of the many situations in which expectancy effects may be found to occur. As pointed out by Rosenthal (1969), it may be useful to consider clinical interactions as a special case in the class of general social interactions and to consider the possibility that the principles governing general social interactions may be applied to account, in part, for events occurring in clinical interactions. In addition to the role of therapist, the wide variety of applied functions served by the clinician include those of diagnostician, educator, and institutional consultant. Unless it is assumed that the psychological processes operating in the therapy setting are different from those operating in extratherapy settings, not only is the information emerging from those extratherapy settings directly relevant to the professional functioning of the clinician, but the theoretical and methodological advances made in extratherapy investigations may be applied to further the understanding of events occurring in the therapy settings.

It is the endeavor of this chapter (1) to provide a comprehensive survey of the empirical investigations of expectancies in the variety of situations in which the clinician functions, (2) to discuss the methodologies employed in those studies as they bear upon theoretical issues, (3) to discuss the therapeutic implications of laboratory investigations of expectancies, and (4) to identify processes and mechanisms through which prognostic information delivered to the therapist may be translated into actual client change. Topical sections in which methods and results of studies are reviewed will, in general, be followed by discussion of relevant conceptual and methodological issues and by a critical evaluation of the evidence on the basis of the issues discussed.

REVIEW OF FINDINGS IN APPLIED SETTINGS

Therapist Expectancies

In several early psychotherapy investigations, results have shown that expectancies of client improvement are reliable across therapists and reliably correlated with some other therapist ratings. Correlations between expectancies and measures other than therapist reports have, however, been mixed. Strupp (1958), for example, conducted an analogue study in which observers viewed a film of a client-therapist interaction, rated the client on a variety of dimensions, and reported how they would have responded to the client at various points during the interview. Prognostic ratings were most reliably correlated with therapist positive attitude toward the client ($r = .39$; $p < .01$) and with client emotional maturity ($r = .41$; $p < .01$), ego-strength ($r = .37$; $p < .01$), self-observation ($r = .36$; $p < .01$), insight ($r = .38$; $p < .01$), and social adjustment ($r = .28$; $p < .01$). Observers reporting favorable prognoses were more likely to accept the client's focus without attempting to shift it and were less likely to respond in a "cold" manner than were observers reporting unfavorable prognoses. Observers whose prognostic ratings were noncommittal indicated the greatest "warmth," the most initiative, and the fewest silences in their vicarious responses.

Strupp and Williams (1960) found ratings of expected improvement to be reliable across two different interviewers ($r = .53$; $p < .05$) and to be most strongly correlated in a negative direction with ratings of client defensiveness ($r = -.67$ and $-.64$; $p < .01$) and in a positive direction with ratings of client capacity for insight ($r = .71$ and $.84$; $p < .01$), client motivation for therapy ($r = .78$ and $.87$; $p < .01$), and therapist liking for the client ($r = .55$ and $.66$; $p < .01$).

Garfield and Affleck (1961) found prognostic ratings of clients whose cases were presented at intake staffings to be highly reliable across staff members (mdn $r = .88$), to be most strongly correlated in a negative direction with ratings of client defensiveness (mdn $r = -.53$), and to be most strongly correlated in a positive direction with ratings of therapist positive feelings toward the client (mdn $r = .66$) and therapist interest in treating the client (mdn $r = .65$). Prognostic ratings were also found to be reliably associated with the outcome measure of duration of therapy—high-prognostic clients remained in therapy longer than low-prognostic clients. This latter finding was not confirmed, however, by Affleck and Garfield (1961), who found that while a high degree of consensus occurred among the prognostic predictions ($r = .79$, $.61$, and $.53$; $p < .01$) and ratings staff members made of clients, none was reliably related to duration of therapy.

Goldstein (1960) found therapist expectancies of client change to be uncorrelated with client reports of change during therapy. In spite of the lack of reliable correlation between therapist expectancies and client reports, a *post hoc* data analysis showed that therapists of clients who reported improvement had significantly higher initial expectancies than therapists of clients who reported becoming worse. In addition, therapist expectancies of improvement measured after the 10th and 15th sessions were correlated with duration of psychotherapy ($r = .60$ and $.76$, respectively, $p < .05$)—clients whose therapists expected greater personality change participated in more therapy sessions than clients whose therapists expected less change.

Heller and Goldstein (1961) measured client attraction toward therapy and therapist expectancies of client change during therapy. Therapist expectancies measured during early sessions were found to be significantly and positively correlated with post-therapy client attraction to therapy ($r = .54$: $p < .05$) and with pre-to-post change in attraction ($r = .62$; $p < .05$).

Hill (1969) found client satisfaction with therapy to be related to therapist goals; clients of male therapists with relatively low goals were less satisfied than clients of male and female therapists with higher goals.

Lanning (1971), however, failed to find a reliable relationship between expectancies and other therapy measures. While trainee therapists expected to establish a therapeutic relationship similar to the relationship they had with their supervisors, their ratings of expectation of the client-therapist relationship were unrelated to ratings made by their clients.

To those studies yielding mixed results may be added two experiments which showed significant effects in a direction opposite to predictions derived from an expectancy effect interpretation. Anderson and Rosenthal (1968) investigated the separate effects of assigning institutionalized retardates to a one-to-one tutorial relationship and delivering expectancy instructions to their counselors. In that study, the counselees whose counselors received "late-bloomer" expectancy instructions were found to improve significantly in self-help scores on a measure of social competence. Contrary to predictions, however, "late bloomers" assigned to the one-to-one tutorial condition were found to decrease significantly on a measure of reasoning.

McNeal, Johnston, and Aspromonte (1970) employed weighted demographic variables to predict length of hospitalization in an inpatient psychiatric setting. This information was withheld from the hospital staff for half of the randomly assigned patients. For the other half, the staff was informed of the expected length of hospitalization and was reminded of that information during the patients' hospitalizations. The investigators found that the presentation of prognostic information, *per se*, did not affect the length of hospitalization. However, the results did reveal an effect in the direction opposite to the expectancy-effect hypothesis:

when the staff was given prognostic information, prognoses were significantly less accurate than when prognostic information was withheld from the staff—staff-informed-short-stay patients left later and staff-informed-long-stay patients left earlier than their respective control patients.

In other studies, the interactive effect of therapist expectancies with process events have been studied. In a major investigation of therapy process variables, Lennard and Bernstein (1960) measured expectancies reported by therapists and clients prior to and during therapy and also examined the relationship of those expectancies to other events in the client-therapist interaction. The therapists' activity level expectancies were found to correspond with actual activity level and both therapist and client were in general agreement that the client would do the most talking throughout therapy; however, considerable discrepancy was found between therapist and client expectancies regarding the specific content of material to be dealt with. This finding was coupled with the finding that greater discrepancies in expectancies were associated with greater discussion of the client-therapist relationship rather than extratherapy material relevant to the client. Throughout therapy, the behavior of the therapist appeared to be influenced more by the actual interaction with the client than by the therapist's expectancies of that interaction.

This latter trend was confirmed in an experiment designed by Kumar and Pepinsky (1965) to assess the interaction of expectancy-related, pre-therapy information about a client and actual contact with the client on therapists' ratings. The presentation of pre-therapy information describing the client as either hostile or friendly was reported to have its intended effect on graduate student therapists and these initial expectancies were maintained if the client behaved in a manner which confirmed them. The investigators reported, however, that if client behavior was discrepant from pre-therapy information, subsequent therapist ratings were determined primarily by the behavior of the client rather than the previous information.

In an analogue experiment relevant to the events occurring in the therapeutic situation, Trattner and Howard (1970) identified E, S, and communication variables through which an expectancy effect may occur. The Es were classified as A or B (see Chapter 12, this volume, for a review of the A-B therapist variable), schizophrenic Ss were classified as high or low on a measure of social competence, and voice analyses were made of their verbal interaction during a standard laboratory task. The results showed that expectancy information delivered to A Es affected the performance of low-social-competence Ss more than the same information delivered to B Es and that B Es biased the performance of high-social-competence Ss more than A Es. In addition, voice ratings showed that A Es were rated as higher on the dimension of social control when they tested low-social-competence Ss and B Es were higher on social control with high-social-competence Ss.

A summary analysis of the results of these studies does not yield very strong support for the popular assumption that therapist expectancies function as determinants of client change. While some correlational studies have found therapist goals, expectancies, and prognostications to be reliable across therapists (Affleck & Garfield, 1961; Garfield & Affleck, 1961; Strupp & Williams, 1960) and to be related to other therapist ratings (Garfield & Affleck, 1961; Strupp, 1958; Strupp & Williams, 1960), to client attitudes toward therapy (Heller & Goldstein, 1961; Hill, 1969), to duration of therapy (Garfield & Affleck, 1961; Goldstein, 1960), and to client-reported improvement (Goldstein, 1960), none has shown a reliable association between therapist expectancy and symptom reduction measured independently of client ratings.

While experimental manipulations designed to affect therapist expectancies have not always been found to affect outcome, even when expectancy information has been found to have an effect, the direction of the effect is not always predictable. Reversal effects have been found in studies by Anderson and Rosenthal (1968) and McNeal et al. (1970).

The results of a nontherapy, picture-rating task (Trattner & Howard, 1970) are suggestive of possible processes involved in the effect of pre-therapy information on client behavior. However, even if it is assumed that therapist expectancies have some effect on therapist behavior, the analyses made by Kumar and Pepinsky (1965) and Lennard and Bernstein (1960) indicate that therapist behavior is influenced more by interaction with the client than by therapist expectancies.

Diagnostician Expectancies

To the degree that diagnostic methods and scoring procedures are not perfectly standardized, unreliability occurring in diagnostic results may be accounted for by factors other than examinee characteristics. Attempting to identify the extent to which diagnostic methods may be selectively vulnerable to the influence of non-examinee factors, Plumb and Charles (1955), Sattler, Winget, and Roth (1969), Schwartz (1966), and Walker, Hunt, and Schwartz (1965) have documented considerable disagreement in the scoring of ambiguous intelligence test responses—even by highly experienced scorers and even when the responses are rated by those scorers as needing no further inquiry for clarification.

In addition to the situational and interpersonal variables which have been shown in reviews by Masling (1960) and Sattler and Theye (1967) to affect the outcome of projective and intelligence testing, a study presented by Temerlin and Trousdale (1969) demonstrates that the unreliability in diagnostic conclusions may be attributable, in part, to information designed to influence diagnosticians' expectancies. In that study, in which various groups of mental health professionals were asked to provide a diagnosis from a tape-recorded interview, the information presented to diagnosticians about the interviewee's mental status prior to playing the tape was found to have a profound effect on the diagnoses emerging from this analogue clinical situation.

Procedures designed to influence diagnostician expectancies have also been shown to affect judgments emerging from the more standard clinical instruments used in personality and intellectual assessment. In some of these studies, researchers have not only asked whether or not expectancy effects occur in the diagnostic situation, but also whether those effects occur during the administration phase or during the scoring phase of psychodiagnosis and whether or not there are identifiable diagnostician behaviors which mediate the expectancy effect.

Personality Assessment. The effect of expectancies in personality assessment has been studied through the use of Rorschach and Holtzman projective inkblot tests and through the use of word-association procedures.

Masling (1965) found graduate student examiners to generate a greater animal-to-human response ratio during Rorschach administration when they were informed that experienced examiners produced more animal responses than when they were informed that experienced examiners produced more human responses. Further analysis of the verbal interaction during

testing showed that examiners given the animal information commented more after both animal and human responses than did examiners given the human information. The proportion of comments following human and animal responses did not differ between the two groups of examiners, however.

Using advanced undergraduates as examiners, Marwit and Marcia (1967) examined the effect of expectancy on number of responses given to achromatic Holtzman inkblots. Members of one group of examiners were told to expect either a high number of responses or a low number. Members of another group were given no pre-testing information, but were divided on the basis of their own reports according to whether they expected a high or low number of responses. In both grouping procedures, expectancies of higher levels of responses were associated with higher actual response productivity.[1] Consistent with a learning theory interpretation, the investigators noted that differences between high and low groups were minimal on the first trial and increased across trials. Performance differences, however, were not associated with the number of questions asked by the examiner, nor were they associated with examiner differences on a measure of acquiescence.

From an experimental design in which the effects of two different expectancy instructions delivered prior to Rorschach administration were confounded, Marwit (1969) reported some effects on the productivity and content of Rorschach responses, as well as on examiner ratings of test reports, but did not find support for the hypothesis posed that examiners model the behavior expected of the examinee. In an attempt to locate the occurrence of that expectancy effect during Rorschach administration or scoring phases, Marwit (1971) asked an independent group of judges to provide a second set of test reports from the same protocols generated in the Marwit (1969) study. Because statistically nonsignificant differences were found between the two sets of test reports based upon the same set of protocols, Marwit (1971) accepted the null hypothesis and concluded that the expectancy instructions in the Marwit (1969) study had resulted in biased protocols, not just scoring errors on the part of the examiners to whom the expectancy information had been delivered.

Strauss (1968b) also presented evidence for the occurrence of bias in personality interpretation resulting from information presented to examiners prior to Rorschach administration. However, in contrast to the significant effects associated with examiner expectancies found by the above investigators, Strauss (1968a) and Strauss and Marwit (1970), using different dependent measures, different expectancy instructions, and different situations in Rorschach administration, did not find support for the expectancy effect.

In a word association task administered to freshmen by advanced undergraduate and graduate students, Silverman (1968) found response latencies of Ss to be affected by information delivered to Es. While the data presented indicated that some of the differences were due to scoring errors, the investigator suggested the possibility that the results could have been due to actual performance differences by the examinees.

Similarly, Johnson and Adair (1970), using advanced undergraduates as examiners, found that scoring errors did not account for all of the significant bias effect observed in their word-response-latency study. When taped latencies were measured by independent scorers, the biasing effect approached an acceptable level of statistical significance, indicating that the actual protocols were affected somewhat by the instructions delivered to Es.

Intellectual Assessment. Evidence has also been presented showing that expectancy information can have an effect on events occurring in the administration and scoring phases of intelligence testing. Data reported by Schroeder and Kleinsasser (1972) indicate a pronounced effect of expectancy information on test administration. In that study, when the same examiner was responsible for both administration and scoring, expectancy instructions were found to have an effect significant at the .05 probability level on the Information and Similarities Subtests of the WISC and a near-significant effect on the Vocabulary Subtest. The investigators noted that the effect occurred primarily on ambiguous responses. When the protocols were scored by uninformed, independent scorers, the expectancy effect was reduced only somewhat to a less pronounced .07 probability level.

Several experimenters have also found evidence for an expectancy effect when expectancy information is presented to Ss who are asked only to score protocols previously prepared for the scorer. In such an experiment, Sattler, Hillix, and Neher (1970) found evidence for an expectancy effect on WISC Vocabulary and WAIS Comprehension, Similarities, and Vocabulary Subtests. Employing undergraduate scorers, Simon (1969) found expectancy instructions to

affect WISC Vocabulary scores to a significant degree. In a similar experiment with graduate student scorers, Egeland (1969) found expectancy instructions to be associated with significant differences on WISC Comprehension and Similarities scores, but not with Vocabulary scores. In the Egeland (1969) study, it was also found that while high-expectancy information inflated IQ scores above a no-information condition, low-expectancy information did not reliably depress scores below those in the no-information condition.

Contrary to these findings supporting an expectancy effect interpretation, pre-diagnostic information did not have a significant effect on Stanford-Binet scores in a study reported by Saunders and Vitro (1971). Auffrey and Robertson (1972) found nonsignificant scoring differences attributable either to expectancy instructions or to scorer experience; they also found novice scorers to be, in general, more variable.

Graduate student examiners in an experiment conducted by Hersh (1971) received referral information of either a positive or negative nature about Headstart children to be tested with the Stanford-Binet. On the basis of what appears to be an unbalanced and inappropriate factorial analysis in which Stanford-Binet scores associated with either positive or negative referral information were compared to Peabody Picture Vocabulary Test scores with no referral information, the author concluded that support for a reliable expectancy effect had been documented. The data presented do not warrant that conclusion, however. Nor was referral information found to have a significant effect on length of testing nor on examiner warmth as rated by a blind observer. That information did have a significant effect, however, on the age at which testing was begun on the Stanford-Binet.

Nor did Sattler and Winget (1970) find evidence for an expectancy effect in their balanced design in which expectancy information delivered to diagnosticians was varied along with the behavior of stooges employed as examinees who memorized either a high or low IQ script of WAIS responses for the testing session.[2] While examiner ratings and credit awarded for ambiguous responses were relatively unaffected by the expectancy messages, the behavior of the examinees was found to exert a significant influence on those dependent measures.

Summary. While there is some evidence to the contrary, the results of a substantial body of experimental evidence show that differential pre-diagnostic information can have a reliable effect on diagnostic outcome in both personality and intellectual assessment. Further, both the administration and scoring phases of diagnostic procedures appear to offer opportunities for the differential information to have its effect. *As in the case of therapist expectancies (Kumar & Pepinsky, 1965; Lennard & Bernstein, 1960), however, pre-diagnostic information appears to have a relatively insignificant effect on diagnostic results when compared with the effect of the behavior of the diagnostee (Sattler & Winget, 1970).*

Teacher Expectancies

Intensive interest was drawn to the area of teacher expectancies by the classic experiment reported by Rosenthal and Jacobson (1968). In that study, a group of randomly selected students pre-tested on a test of nonverbal intelligence was included in a list which teachers were informed contained the names of students who would show intellectual "blooming," or a marked increase in academic progress during the year. Students were then retested on several occasions by the teachers on measures which included the same scale used in the pre-test. The data presented by the investigators showed significant increases in IQ scores for "bloomers" in the first and second grades over and above the IQ scores of "nonbloomer" controls.

As a consequence of the more thorough scrutiny which followed a fairly widespread initial acceptance of the results and implications of the Rosenthal-Jacobson (1968) study, it has become the target of extensive criticism on methodological, statistical, and inferential grounds. Attempts to verify the original findings through replication have failed to find significant effects attributable to the delivery of differential information (Claiborn, 1969; Fielder, Cohen, & Feeney, 1971; Fleming & Anttonen, 1971a, 1971b; Gozali & Meyen, 1970; Jose & Cody, 1971). Indeed, partial evidence for a reversal effect was presented by Evans and Rosenthal (1969) who found that while male "bloomers" gained more on a measure of reasoning ability than did male "nonbloomers," female "bloomers" gained less than female "nonbloomers."

The Rosenthal-Jacobson (1968) methodology of having the classroom teachers conduct the IQ testing was criticized by Pellegrini and Hicks (1972), who presented data showing that an expectancy effect occurred only when teachers were familiarized with the specific outcome measure employed—a finding which the investigators interpreted as reflecting a specific coaching of pupils in relation to the outcome criteria rather than a valid change in intellectual functioning.

Gephart (1970), Gephart and Antonoplos (1969), Snow (1969), and Thorndike (1968) have also presented critical arguments calling the validity of that study into question, and Elashoff and Snow (1971) have presented a detailed and comprehensive analysis of the Rosenthal-Jacobson (1968) study along with pro and con discussions by other reviewers.

Measures of teacher expectancies taken after contact with students were found by Palardy (1969) to be correlated with actual pupil achievement. Brophy and Good (1970) found teacher expectancies to be correlated not only with pupil performance but also with teacher behavior expressed toward pupils; the high-expectancy-high-achieving pupils received, for example, proportionally less teacher criticism, more information following wrong answers, and more praise following right answers than did pupils of whom teachers had low expectancies.

Schrank (1968) found that when college prep students were randomly assigned to five groups which teachers were told represented different ability levels, differences in math grades between the highest and the lowest bogus ability groups approached statistical significance. In a subsequent study by Schrank (1970), when teachers were informed that students were randomly assigned to groups, an inconclusive pattern of results was reported. Saunders and DiTullio (1972) found that the delivery of "late bloomer" information about emotionally disturbed pupils did not reliably affect teacher ratings of the pupils' classroom behavior; however, that information delivered to teachers did affect peer acceptance ratings of the pupils in one of the four grades included in the study.

In addition to attempting to demonstrate the occurrence of a teacher expectancy effect, several investigators have attempted to identify mechanisms and processes through which the effect may occur.

In a classroom analogue study conducted by Beez (1968), student teachers were observed during a 10-minute training session on a task of symbol learning with Headstart children; the teachers had been informed on a random basis that the children had high or low potential. Not only did the "high-potential" students outperform "low-potential" students after the training sessions, but observations of the interaction revealed that teachers gave more training trials to "high-potential" students, while with "low-potential" pupils they spent more time engaged in explanations, examples, and nonteaching activities.

Meichenbaum, Bowers, and Ross (1969) found that quantity of teacher attention did not change after "late bloomer" instructions were delivered to teachers about a small group of delinquents enrolled in an operant-oriented educational program. While the quality of the attention delivered by the teachers changed, the nature of that change varied from teacher to teacher. "Late bloomer" instructions were also followed by increases in performance on objective exams and a decrease in frequency of classroom misbehavior.

Conn, Edwards, Rosenthal, and Crowne (1968) found teacher expectancies to be associated with a different effect depending upon the accuracy with which pupils were able to judge emotionality portrayed in voices.

Rothbart, Dalfen, and Barrett (1971) found that information presented to teacher trainees describing high school students as having either high or low potential resulted in significant differences among teacher ratings of the potential of the students and near-significant differences in amount of teacher attention delivered to students and amount of student verbal output. Reliable differences were not observed, however, on amounts of positive and negative reinforcement delivered by teachers to the two groups of students.

In a study of expectancy effects in teacher training, Haberman (1970) delivered high- or no-expectancy information to trainees about their supervisors and high- or no-expectancy information to supervisors about their trainees. It was found that the information had no significant effects on the mutual ratings made by trainees and supervisors after training.

In summary, many studies have failed to demonstrate an expectancy effect. Evidence, however, has been presented in some classroom investigations (Conn et al., 1968; Meichenbaum et al., 1969) and in an analogue study (Beez, 1968), under some circumstances, information presented to teachers about their students can influence subsequent student performance. Considering the methodological criticisms and replication failures of the original study by Rosenthal and Jacobson (1968), it appears that this effect is not powerful enough to produce reliable changes in IQ. *As in the studies on therapist expectancies, the direction of the effect that prior information has on academic behavior is not always predictable (Conn et al., 1968; Evans & Rosenthal, 1969; Meichenbaum et al., 1969).*

ACTUARIAL AND DETERMINISTIC USAGES OF THERAPIST EXPECTANCIES

In spite of an absence of strong empirical support, therapist expectancies have become, for many researchers and therapists, a construct providing an appealing and almost self-evident explanation for events occurring in the therapy situation. Unencumbered by the establishment of empirical boundaries, the uncritical acceptance and indiscriminant use of this construct has resulted in the attribution of qualities to therapist expectancies which cannot possibly be supported by existing data. Expectancies were employed by Uhlenhuth, Canter, Neustadt, and Payson (1959), for example, to account for the results of a study which was designed specifically to prevent expectancy effects from occurring. In a study by Lerner and Fiske (1973), even though expectancies were not measured, a *post hoc* expectancy effect interpretation was invoked to explain a failure to find statistical significance between client characteristics and improvement.

Reviews by Frank (1968) and Rosenthal and Jacobson (1968) illustrate the potential importance of the therapist expectancy construct as an abstract theoretical device through which the findings from a diverse set of investigations may heuristically be integrated, but this use of the construct, too, requires empirical validation.

Conceptual advancements in the theoretical function of the therapist expectancy construct may be made by discriminating between major ways in which it has been employed and by identifying the minimum methodological procedures and controls which are required to support each of its major usages: the actuarial, or predictive, usage and the deterministic, or causal, usage.

The issue, as stated in a different context by Bootzin (1969), is whether and under what conditions expectancy and therapy outcome are correlated because of the expector's sensitivity to cues predictive of the outcome (actuarial usage) or because the expector actually influences the outcome (deterministic usage).

A consideration of the methodological and outcome conditions indicates that there are difficulties in accepting either the actuarial or deterministic usage of the therapist expectancy construct.

Actuarial Usage of Therapist Expectancies

In a very practical sense, the measurement of therapist expectancies, along with other therapist characteristics, may serve as actuarial data employed simply to predict probable outcomes of therapy.

Rosenthal and Jacobson's (1968) Type IIB1b expectancy (see Table 1) occurs as a consequence of knowledge of past events related to outcome and is a predictor, not a cause, of a future outcome. Drawing upon an analogy presented elsewhere (Wilkins, 1973b), a stated expectancy of rain based upon the observation of dark clouds, thunder, and lightning may be more appropriately employed as an actuarial predictor of rain than as a causal explanation accounting for the rain. To the degree that therapist expectancies are correlated with therapy outcome, they may be used to account for statistical variance in outcome studies and may be used as a variable to consider in the assignment of clients to therapists in order to optimize the probability of client change.

TABLE 1. TYPOLOGY OF RELATIONSHIPS BETWEEN PROPHECIES AND SUBSEQUENT EVENTS.

Type I. No Relationship Between Prophecy and Event
   A. And no relationship is claimed
   B. But a relationship is claimed

Type II. Some Relationship Between Prophecy and Event
   A. The relationship is negative
     1. But not due to the prophecy
     2. And due to the prophecy
   B. The relationship is positive
     1. But not due to the prophecy
       a. coincidental
       b. prophecy is due to related past events
     2. And due to the prophecy

From Rosenthal and Jacobson (1968). Copyright by Holt, Rinehart, and Winston. Reprinted by permission.

To validate the actuarial usage of therapist expectancies, it is necessary only to demonstrate a reliable and replicable correlation between the operations defining expectancy and the operations defining outcome. In this sense, it is the concurrent and predictive validities of therapist expectancy which are at issue.

There is considerable evidence from studies conducted in the therapy, diagnostic, and classroom settings that knowledge about expectancies is informative of other events occurring prior to, concurrent with, and after the measurement of expectancies. It is also evident from the same body of evidence that expectancies are not always related to other events and that the investigators reporting strong relationships have not identified and described the parameters involved sufficiently enough to allow other investigators to replicate their findings. Indeed, in some replication attempts in the therapy setting (Anderson & Rosenthal, 1968; McNeal et al., 1970) and in the classroom (Evans & Rosenthal, 1969; Conn et al., 1968; Meichenbaum et al., 1969), the procedures employed have resulted in surprising reversals with no clear understanding of why. As a consequence, the predictive validity of measured expectancies cannot, at present, be considered to be very high.

These studies, taken together, also suggest that therapist expectancy is probably not a powerful enough phenomenon to emerge as a main effect across a very wide range of situations. The most promising direction for increasing the predictive validity of this variable appears to be in those studies in which expectancies are studied not only as a main effect, but as they interact with other variables involving characteristics of the therapist, the client, and the outcome measures employed. Correlational therapy studies such as those conducted by Lennard and Bernstein (1960, 1966) and Hill (1969) attest to the increase in concurrent and predictive validities which may occur when the interactive effect of therapist expectancies or goals and other therapy process variables are studied. The same may be said of the therapy analogue experiment conducted by Trattner and Howard (1970) and the classroom experiment by Conn et al. (1968) which showed the expectancy effect to be moderated by client, therapist, or pupil characteristics.

In addition, as pointed out by Strauss (1968a), a demonstration of an expectancy effect employing some dependent measures does not imply that other measures may be similarly affected. Since specific dependent measures may be differentially sensitive to events associated with the delivery of expectancy information, the predictive validity of expectancies may be enhanced by limiting predictions to the particular measures shown to be influenced by expectancies. The study by Anderson and Rosenthal (1968) attests to the increase in the predictive validity of expectancies when generalizations concerning the effect are limited to particular outcome measures. This case is further supported by the classroom study by Pellegrini and Hicks (1972) and by the diagnostic studies conducted by Marwit (1969), Schroeder and Kleinsasser (1972), Egeland (1969), and Sattler *et al.* (1970), which show that the predictive validity of expectancies can be increased if predictions are limited to specific outcome measures.

Deterministic Usage of Therapist Expectancies

In their second usage, the implication is not only that therapist expectancies are predictive of therapy outcome, but that client change occurs *because* of the expectancies held by the therapist. The use of expectancies in this manner is, in the typology presented by Rosenthal and Jacobson (1968), Type IIB2 (see Table 1) in which therapist expectancy is not considered to be a passive predictor of outcome, but an active contributor to and determinant of the occurrence of the expected outcome.

Predictive validity of the therapist expectancy construct serves as a necessary, but not a sufficient condition, for the establishment of expectancy as a determinant of therapy outcome. For causal characteristics to be attributed to the therapist expectancy construct, other conditions must be met which involve the operations employed to define and validate therapist expectancies and the issue of whether or not those operations occur independently of other events which could possibly account for therapy outcome.

Independence of Therapist Expectancies: Correlational Studies. While the correlational studies reviewed in earlier sections may be used to form an empirical foundation for the actuarial usage of therapist expectancies, support for the attribution of causality to expectancies may not be derived from these studies, since their designs do not preclude the possibility of other factors accounting for the results. Two major interpretive constraints which preclude the attribution of causality to expectancies on the basis of those correlational studies involve the issues of (1) the independence of expectancies from outcome measures and (2) the independence of expectancies from other therapist characteristics.

Independence of therapist expectancies from outcome measures. A necessary condition for the attribution of causality to therapist expectancies is to preclude events related to outcome measures from influencing measures of expectancy. In the therapy studies by Goldstein (1960), Heller and Goldstein (1961), Hill (1969), Lennard and Bernstein (1960) and in the classroom studies by Brophy and Good (1970) and Palardy (1969), some goals and expectancies of outcome were assessed after the therapist or teacher had interacted with clients or pupils. Under such measurement conditions, the strong possibility emerges that rather than expectancies necessarily causing client change, client change in behavior occurring prior to the measurement of expectancies caused those expectancies (as argued by Goldstein, 1960), or that both expectancy and client behavior were caused by some other factor. The possibility that either event may have occurred would preclude a definitive causal statement.

Independence of therapist expectancies from other therapist characteristics. In the therapy studies conducted by Brophy and Good (1970), Goldstein (1960), Heller and Goldstein (1961), Hill (1969), Lanning (1971), Lennard and Bernstein (1960), and Palardy (1969) and in one of the groups studied in the diagnostic investigation by Marwit and Marcia (1967), expectancies were measured as an organismic variable. As pointed out by Edwards (1968, pp. 258–260), unless expectancies are induced independently of other therapist characteristics, it may be as legitimate to attribute the cause of outcome to any other variable correlated with expectancies as it is to attribute it to expectancies. In relation to the typology of expectancies presented by Rosenthal and Jacobson (1968) studies of this type do not rule out the possibility of a Type IIB1a (see Table 1) event occurring—an event in which the expectancy and the outcome are correlated but coincidental, the event being caused by some factor other than expectancy.

In identifying therapist variables associated with client improvement, the exploration of therapist organismic variables is an important area of psychotherapy investigation in its own right. Since some other therapist characteristic correlated with therapist expectancy may actually affect client behavior, however, therapist expectancy measured as an organismic variable may not definitely be said to cause client behavior.

Independence and Validation of Therapist Expectancies: Experimental Studies. In order to circumvent the interpretive constraints inherent in correlational measurement, other investigators have employed procedures designed to instill expectancies independently of other variables which, if not controlled for, may affect outcome measures. Given that the effect of other causal variables are ruled out by their balanced or random distribution across different expectancy conditions, effects emerging from these designs may legitimately be attributed to the procedures designed to instill differential expectancies. These procedures have typically involved the delivery of bogus information about the clients, diagnostees, or students prior to and independent of their interaction with the holders of the expectancies. Except for the influence of chance events, these procedures eliminate the likelihood of Types IIA1, IIB1a, and IIB1b (see Table 1) events (Rosenthal & Jacobson, 1968) from intervening to account for a reliable relationship between expectancy and outcome.

While the random or controlled assignment of client and therapist to different expectancy conditions rules out some of the interpretive constraints in the attribution of causality to expectancies, further issues involving the independence and validation of expectancies must be considered.

Independence of expectancy-instilling procedures from outcome measurement. For causal statements about the effect of therapist expectancies on client behavior to be made on the basis of experimental evidence, the measurement of client change must be a process independent of the delivery of expectancy information to the therapist. This condition cannot be met if the measure of outcome is based on reports or evaluations made by the therapist to whom expectancy information has previously been delivered—such as the teacher ratings employed by Saunders and DiTullio (1972)—or by any other evaluator who is not experimentally blind as to which clients were assigned to which expectancy conditions. The results of the study by Horenstein, Houston, and Holmes (1973) attest to the possibility that therapists' evaluation of outcome is different from the evaluation made by other judges. Indeed, data presented by Jose and Cody (1971) showed that even in classes in which teachers reported "late bloomers" as having improved, the "late bloomers" were actually found to have improved less than their "nonbloomer" counterparts on independent measures of reading and arithmetic. Rothbart *et al.* (1971) pointed out that their dependent measure using teacher ratings of students may have simply reflected the success of the experimental manipulation rather than an independent measure of student performance.[3]

Pellegrini and Hicks (1972) also documented the possibility of artifacts occurring in the study of teacher expectancy effects when teachers are familiar with the outcome measures even if the teachers themselves do not actually perform the outcome measurement.

The issue of the independence of expectancy-instilling procedures from outcome measurement was also raised in the diagnostic setting by Marwit (1971): Do expectancy instructions delivered to the examiner actually affect the behavior of the examinee, the examiner's scoring and interpretation of examinee performance, or both? The above studies show that when outcome is not measured by a procedure that is independent of the delivery of expectancy information, the strong possibility exists that expectancies may affect the measurement procedure, not necessarily actual client or pupil performance. While such an event is of importance, especially as it relates to expectancy effects in the diagnostic setting, causal inferences about the effect of expectancies on actual client or pupil behavior must be attenuated. In the therapy setting, definitive conclusions about the causal effect of expectancy information on client change may be drawn only if the measurement of client change is a process independent of therapist evaluations. At a minimum, designs which allow the individual to whom expectancies were delivered to evaluate outcome obscure the locus of any expectancy effects and can easily be avoided methodologically.

Validation of expectancies. Given that therapy outcome is measured independently of the procedures designed to instill expectancies and given that those procedures are delivered independently of the events occurring in the client-therapist interaction, outcome differences may legitimately be attributed to those *procedures*. To attribute causal characteristics to the actual *expectancies* which the *procedures* are designed to instill requires, however, a validation of those procedures as to their effectiveness in instilling the intended expectancies.

If the presence of therapist expectancy is not validated by procedures other than therapy outcome, their definition and identification is entirely circular; on the basis of client change, the therapist is said to have held certain expectancies and, circularly, the client is said to have changed because the therapist held certain expectancies.

Validity checks are perhaps even more crucial in studies in which an expectancy effect does not occur or in studies demonstrating a reverse effect. *If there is no independent check on expectancies, it is impossible to determine whether the information did not instill the intended expectancies or whether the intended expectancies were instilled, but did not have the predicted effect on the outcome measure. It appears quite inapprop-*

riate to conclude that expectancies have no effect on a dependent measure if a check is not made to insure that differential expectancies have been instilled.

Zegers (1968) has pointed out that the assumption that instructions have their intended effect on expectancies is questionable, since adequate measurement of initial expectancies is frequently omitted in experimenter-bias type research. In the therapy analogue experiment by Trattner and Howard (1970), the results of which are consistent with an expectancy-effect interpretation, procedures validating the instillation of intended expectancies or biases were omitted, as they were omitted in the experiments by Anderson and Rosenthal (1968) and McNeal *et al.* (1970) demonstrating reversal effects. The same is true of the diagnostic experiments supporting an expectancy-effect interpretation which were conducted by Egeland (1969), Johnson and Adair (1970), Marwit (1969), Marwit and Marcia (1967), Masling (1965), Sattler *et al.* (1970), Sattler and Winget (1970), Saunders and Vitro (1971), Schroeder and Kleinsasser (1972), Silverman (1968), and Simon (1969). Similarly, validity checks were not included in the experiments in which evidence for teacher expectancy effects was reported (Beez, 1968; Conn *et al.*, 1968; Meichenbaum *et al.*, 1969; Pellegrini & Hicks, 1972; Saunders & DiTullio, 1972) and in those failing to find statistically significant support for an expectancy-effect interpretation (Fielder *et al.*, 1971; Fleming & Anttonen, 1971a, 1971b; Gozali & Meyen, 1970; Schrank, 1968).

In addition, the results of three studies which have included expectancy validity checks in their methodology attest to the inappropriateness of simply assuming that because expectancy information was delivered it instilled the intended expectancy. Employing a retrospective assessment of teacher expectancies after outcome measures had been taken, Jose and Cody (1971) found in the majority of teachers that expectancies were unaffected by the "late bloomer" information presented. Evans and Rosenthal (1969) and Rosenthal and Jacobson (1968) also reported remarkable inaccuracies in teachers' memories of which children had been described as "late bloomers."

While those studies show that the presentation of expectancy information cannot always be assumed to have actually affected expectancies, another body of research shows that even when the presence of intended expectancies has been validated, an expectancy effect has not been demonstrated. The validity check employed in Claiborn's (1969) study of the effect of teacher expectancies on measures of intelligence indicated that teachers could remember, after a 2-month period of time, which students had been described as "late bloomers"; however, those descriptions were unrelated to the outcome measure of intelligence. The validity check employed by Kumar and Pepinsky (1965) was reported to have induced the intended expectancies; however, outcome measures were reported to be affected primarily by the behavior of the client, not by therapist expectancies.

When Fleming and Anttonen (1971b) asked teachers to assess the accuracy of previously delivered expectancy information after interaction with pupils had occurred, the results showed that the high-expectancy information was rated as less accurate than realistic information about pupils. These results, together with their failure to find support for an expectancy effect, indicate that pupil performance had a more potent effect on the teachers than did the expectancy information.

Similarly, validation procedures employed by Strauss (1968a) verified that while the intended diagnostician expectancies had been instilled, neither the expectancy-instilling procedures nor the measured diagnostician expectancies had a reliable effect upon the dependent measures employed. Strauss and Marwit (1970) also reported that successful validation procedures had been conducted in their diagnostic experiments; however, no reliable effects of expectancies on outcome were found.

Hersh (1971) reasoned that because positive and negative referral information produced a significant difference as to the age level at which testing was begun on the Stanford-Binet,[4] the initial difference could be taken as validation of the instillation of differential expectancies. Scores analyzed through an inappropriate statistical design, however, indicated that the differential information did not appear to reliably affect Stanford-Binet performance.

Very little support for the expectancy effect can be derived from studies in which validity checks are not made independently of events occurring in the teacher-pupil interaction. For example, in Claiborn's (1969) validation procedure of measuring teacher expectancies months after teacher-pupil interaction had begun, even if the experimental manipulation had reliably affected pupil progress, a possibility which the method did not preclude is that pupil progress could have determined the outcome of the expectancy validation measurement rather than teacher expectancy determining student progress. The same may be said of the retrospective expectancy assessment procedures employed by Evans and Rosenthal (1969), Jose and Cody (1971), and Rosenthal and Jacobson (1968), and the dependent measure interpreted by Rothbart *et al.* (1971) as a check on the experimental manipulation.

Special additional problems for interpretation occur when a validity check reveals that not all therapists presented with expectancy information had the expectancies instilled. At this juncture, the investigator has the choice of eliminating those therapists from subsequent analyses of the data or retaining the data generated by them. Either choice imposes constraints on attempts to attribute the cause of subsequent results to therapist expectancies. If the therapists not holding the proper expectancies are eliminated, assumptions of randomization cannot be met since those therapists remaining are a select group characterized not only by the proper expectancies but also by any other trait which happens to be correlated with the instillation of the proper expectancies. While outcome differences between groups could be tested, the causal attribution of those differences to expectancies would be attenuated since the possibility exists that the outcome could have been determined by one of the correlated events rather than expectancies. On the other hand, if the data generated by the therapists without the proper expectancies are retained and included in the statistical analyses, attribution of causality to expectancies is untenable.

The Utility of Therapist Expectancies

It should be noted that when the conditions necessary for the attribution of causality to therapist expectancies are met by the induction of expectancies independent of other therapist characteristics and by the measurement of outcome independent of expectancy-instilling procedures, therapist expectancy becomes a superfluous explanatory construct accounting for nothing more than that which may be explained by observable events alone. When expectancy-instilling procedures are delivered independently of other events occurring in therapy, causality stated in terms of the observable expectancy-related *procedures* is as scientifically complete and inclusive as causality stated in terms of the unobservable *expectancies* which the procedures are said to instill. Some investigators have made their causal statements in

terms of the procedures employed rather than in terms of expectancies (Auffrey & Robertson, 1972; Strauss, 1968b). Since the conclusions drawn in those diagnostic experiments were limited to the effects of prior information, not expectancies, no validity checks as to the presence of expectancies were necessary to support their causal statements. Indeed, an expectancy interpretation would have been superfluous in that the data for which expectancies could account were already accounted for by the observable procedures employed as independent variables.

Since expectancy, as a causal explanation, is a superfluous construct,[5] it appears that its importance does not lie in its deterministic usage. The actuarial usage of therapist expectancies does, however, appear to hold significant implications for therapy research, practice, and training. To the degree that therapist expectancy is prognostic of therapy outcome, the measurement of therapist expectancies is important in the identification of conditions under which client change occurs. That information may be of value in the assignment of clients to therapists who hold relatively high prognostic expectations, rather than to therapists who hold expectancies predictive of less therapeutic change.

Secondly, that information may be of value in the identification of the therapist behaviors which do cause client change. To the degree that therapist expectancies are prognostic of client change, an approach toward the identification of beneficial therapist endeavors may be made by identifying behavioral differences between therapists and within the same therapist when high or low expectancies of improvement are held. Circumventing entirely the issue of attributing causality to expectancies, *the important question is not necessarily how therapist expectancies cause client change but, rather, how therapists behave differently when they hold different expectancies.*

Thirdly, information regarding the actuarial usage of expectancies and the identification of differential therapist behaviors under high- and low-expectancy conditions may hold important training implications. Therapists may be encouraged to identify and employ the *behaviors* which produce client improvement rather than learning the adage "It makes little difference what the therapist does—as long as the therapist expects the client to improve, improvement will occur," an adage which appears to be a direct logical extension of the deterministic usage of expectancies.

DETERMINANTS OF EXPECTANCIES: IMPLICATIONS OF LABORATORY INVESTIGATIONS FOR THERAPIST EXPECTANCIES

In light of the potential importance of therapist expectancies, both as a prognostic indicator of therapy outcome and as a vehicle through which differential therapist behavior in high- and low-prognostic situations may be identified, the controlled investigation of the events which affect expectancies emerges as a potentially important area of empirical inquiry. Since most of these controlled experimental investigations have dealt with the performance expectancies held by students in the psychological laboratory rather than outcome expectancies of therapists in the therapy situation, caution must be observed in generalizing the findings to account for events occurring in the therapy setting. While the *results* emerging from the laboratory studies may be of only indirect relevance to the understanding of therapist expectancies, the *theoretical issues* explored in the laboratory are of direct relevance to the issues involving therapist expectancies, and the *methodologies* employed in the laboratory studies may serve as research models for the direct investigation of therapist expectancies.

Paralleling the study of the determinants of observable behavior, investigations have been undertaken to identify the stimulus events which lead to the acquisition, maintenance, generalization, and extinction of expectancies.

Acquisition and Maintenance of Expectancies

Results of experiments show that expectancies may be acquired and maintained by the difficulty of the task in which the S is engaged, by the presentation of information predictive of future events, by information feedback about past events, and by information about the value of the occurrence of an event.

Actual Task Difficulty. Feather (1966, 1967, 1968) and Feather and Saville (1967) found that difficult tasks in which Ss were engaged produced lower performance and lower expectancies of subsequent performance than did easy tasks, and Feather (1961) reported a decrease in performance expectancies in the face of repeated failure at a task.

These studies show that actual task difficulty has a causal effect on both performance and expectancy. Since performance and expectancy are correlated events in these studies, however, causal relationships among expectancy, performance, informational aspects which task difficulty convey, and performance feedback cannot be identified. The causal effect of performance feedback and of the informational aspects of task difficulty on expectancy have been identified in other experimental designs in which those events are varied independently of performance and expectancy.

Prior Information. Several different types of information presented to Ss prior to performing a task have been shown to affect performance expectancies. Feather (1961, 1963c, 1965a, 1965b, 1966) showed that initial performance expectancies were significantly influenced by presenting Ss with fictitious norms and/or bogus difficulty estimations which were presumably based on the performance of other Ss similar to the S about to perform the task. While similar information presented by Feather and Saville (1967) was found to have an effect in the predicted direction, it did not approach statistical significance. Zegers (1968) also found that initial expectancies concerning the effectiveness of a laboratory procedure were significantly influenced by false norms presented to Ss.

Significant effects were reported by Crandall, Solomon, and Kellaway (1955), Irwin (1953), and Marks (1951) when information was presented to Ss in the form of objective probabilities of occurrence of an event.

The generalizability of these trends to non-laboratory settings is supported by the reports presented by Kumar and Pepinsky (1965) in the therapy setting and by Strauss (1968a) in the diagnostic setting. These studies indicate that when expectancies are assessed soon after the delivery of expectancy information, that information can be found to have an effect. With the exception of the study by Claiborn (1969), however, reports on expectancies in the classroom setting, by Evans and Rosenthal (1969), Jose and Cody (1971), and Rosenthal and Jacobson (1968), indicate that the effect of expectancy information is much more difficult to detect after a relatively long delay after its delivery.

Information Feedback of Prior Performance. Several laboratory investigations have also found expectancies of subsequent performance on a task to be markedly affected by the delivery of information about the S's own previous performance on that task. In order to circumvent the interpretive constraints inherent in correlation between actual performance and performance feedback, in these studies information feedback is arranged to occur independently of actual performance through the use of bogus information.

Experiments by Cottrell (1965), DeSoto, Coleman, and Putnam (1960), Diggory, Riley, and Blumenfeld (1960), Feather (1963a), Jessor and Readio (1957), Mischel (1958), Schwarz (1966), and Simon, Shaw, and Gilchrist (1954) showed that performance feedback affected expectancies and estimates of later performance. Also, level of aspiration was found by Diggory and Morlock (1964) to be affected by feedback of past performance. Rychlak and Eacker (1962) reported greater expectancy changes following a series of negative feedback trials than a series of trials during which positive feedback was delivered. The direction of those changes was not reported, however. Feather (1963b) found that when Ss attempted to solve an impossible task, which they were told was possible but very difficult to solve, expectancies of success increased significantly during early trials before returning to a level below initial expectancies. In addition, confidence ratings made by Ss indicated that they became more confident of their expectancies as the failure trials progressed. Feather (1963a) also reported greater expectancy variability under conditions of failure feedback than under success conditions.

In a different context, Harvey and Clapp (1965) found that the evaluation expectancies of Ss who received relatively favorable evaluations from another person became significantly more positive than the evaluation expectancies of Ss who received relatively unfavorable evaluations.

Value of Outcome. Several experiments have shown that the *desirability* of outcome, as well as information concerning the *probability* of an outcome, affects expectancies of its occurrence. In Marks' (1951) experiment, the expectancies of the occurrence of a positive outcome were significantly higher than the expectancies of a negative outcome occurring at the same level of objective probability. Crandall *et al.* (1955) and Irwin (1953) reported similar significant findings while Diggory *et al.* (1960) and Jessor and Readio (1957) found partial support for the hypothesis that the expectancy of an outcome is higher if the value of its occurrence is higher. Worell (1956) was unable to replicate that pattern of results, however, within the range of values employed in that experiment.

Modification and Extinction of Expectancies

It is evident from the studies in the previous section that reports of expectancies can be determined by information presented prior to engaging in a task and by information feedback of task performance. Additional studies have shown that expectancies can be modified by the presentation of more recent feedback which is inconsistent with pre-task information or earlier information feedback.

In studies conducted by Feather (1965a, 1965b, 1966), pre-task information affected expectancies of success only on early trials, after which expectancies were realigned with actual performance regardless of the level of pre-task expectancy information. After expectancies concerning the effectiveness of a laboratory procedure were instilled through the delivery of information, Zegers (1968) found that Ss' expectancies were maintained by subsequent confirmatory information, but were modified significantly by subsequent disconfirmatory information.

When the effects of prior and recent performance feedback are compared directly, further evidence for a recency effect emerges. Schwarz, Gold, and Seeman (1970), for example, found that when feedback of success was replaced by failure feedback, the previously established expectancies of success were significantly reduced.

An expectancy manipulation check performed by Cottrell (1965) indicates that after the presentation of consistent performance feedback across several trials, the presentation of inconsistent feedback on one trial has very little effect on subsequent expectancies. Rychlak and Eacker (1962) also found expectancies to be relatively unchanged by only one trial of inconsistent feedback when it followed several trials of consistently high or consistently low feedback. Studying the effect of inconsistent feedback on expectancies on a trial-by-trial basis, however, Church, Millward, and Miller (1963) found predictions of an event occurring on a future trial to be significantly higher if the event had occurred on the previous trial than if the event had not occurred on the previous trial.

Not only does the effect of information feedback appear to be more potent than prior information, but several studies have shown that the effect of recent information is to reduce or eliminate personality differences correlated with initial expectancies. For example, initial expectancies of success were found by Feather (1965b) to be correlated with some personality traits; however, expectancies reported after engaging in a task were not reliably correlated with personality traits, but were significantly correlated with performance on the task.

Schwarz (1969) found personality to be related to pre-task expectancies but not to performance expectancies after the delivery of feedback. While pre-task expectancies were correlated with post-feedback expectancies, the results of that study showed post-feedback expectancy level to be a function of a significant interaction involving initial expectancy level, number of feedback trials, and the specific sequence of success-failure feedback. In the study of Zajonc and Brickman (1969) in which Ss were grouped according to whether they had high or low pre-feedback performance expectancies, the introduction of feedback all but eliminated differences in expectancies between those two groups.

James and Rotter (1958) showed the skill-chance dimension to be an important factor in the extinction of expectancies. When Ss were instructed that outcome was essentially a matter of chance, resistance to extinction was greater after partial reinforcement than under continuous reinforcement, but this difference which is consistent with operant conditioning formulations was not observed when Ss were instructed that outcome was a matter of S's skill.

The findings emerging from the laboratory studies reviewed in this section show that while expectancies are determined by information delivered prior to engaging in a task, they are readily modifiable by information acquired during the task. These strong trends imply that the *information acquired during interaction with a client may have a greater influence on therapist expectancies than any pre-therapy information about the client.* The report by Kumar and Pepinsky (1965) supports this implication in that counselor ratings after a counseling analogue interview were determined more by the behavior of the interviewee than by prior information about the interviewee. In the diagnostic setting, Sattler and Winget (1970) also found examinee behavior to have a more potent effect on outcome than the delivery of expectancy information. In addition, descriptions provided by Saunders and Vitro (1971) serve as anecdotal evidence that discrepancies between pre-diagnostic expectancy information and diagnostee performance were resolved in favor of diagnostee performance by at least two of the six diagnosticians.

An additional implication of these findings is that *any event which precludes exposing the therapist to information inconsistent with previous information will lead to a perpetuation of expectancies based on that previous information about the client.* Differential treatment selection in favor of high-prognostic clients is one such event which precludes the opportunity for exposure to expectancy disconfirming information about low-prognostic clients and, thus, may lead to a perpetuation of low expectancies of improvement.

Generalization of Expectancies

From the laboratory investigations reviewed in previous sections, it may be concluded that information feedback about performance on a task affects expectations of future performance on the same task. Additional research has also been conducted to determine the extent to which information feedback received on one task affects performance expectancies on different tasks.

Jessor (1954) found not only that success and failure feedback on one task altered expectancies of performance on other tasks, but evidence was also documented for a gradient of expectancy generalization. Significantly more Ss changed performance expectancies if the subsequent task was similar to the original task than if the subsequent task was dissimilar.

In an experiment by Rychlak (1958), Ss received consistent feedback of success or failure either on one trial of one task, on four trials of the same task, or one trial of each of four different tasks. The results showed that expectancies of performance on a subsequent task were relatively uninfluenced by the amount of feedback previously received, *per se*, but were significantly influenced by the number of situations in which feedback had been received. Expectancies of performance on a new task were more resistant to change for Ss who had received consistent feedback on four different situations than for Ss who had received the same amount of feedback in only one situation.

In an experiment reported by Mischel (1958), Ss were asked to indicate performance expectancies on two tasks, were given feedback on one task which was below their expectancy, and were given the opportunity to alter their reported expectancies of performance on the second task. The Ss who made their initial predictions under private circumstances were found to lower their expectancies significantly more than Ss whose initial expectancies were made publicly.

Heath (1959) found that feedback of success or failure on one task influenced those expectancies of performance on other tasks and also that Ss who were more familiar with the tasks showed less generalization of expectancies across the tasks than Ss who were unfamiliar with the tasks. In Heath's (1961) experiment, not only was feedback of performance on one task found to have a significant effect on expectancies on a different task, but the particular reference group with which S's performance was compared had a significant effect on the shape of the gradient of generalization across the dimension of task similarity.

Lack of independence between measures of expectancy and measures of task similarity prevent an uncritical acceptance of Heath's (1959, 1961) findings, however. In a further study in which measures of expectancy and task familiarity were conducted independently, Heath (1962) presented evidence which confirmed previous findings that success and failure feedback raise and lower expectancies on similar tasks more than on dissimilar tasks. Failure feedback led to greater generalization of expectancies to other tasks in that study than did feedback of success.

Generalizing the results of these laboratory investigations to the therapy setting, it appears that a therapist's previous experience with clients may function as a source of information affecting expectancies of other clients and that the greater similarity there is between a previous client and a future client, the greater the expectancy generalization is from one client to another. *If expectancies based on previous contact with similar clients function like expectancies founded on the delivery of information feedback, they, too, may be easily attenuated by exposure to discrepant information through client contact.*

Lanning (1971) found that ratings made by counselor trainees about their relationship with their supervisors were significantly correlated with their expected relationships with future clients. These results indicate that, for new therapists, expectancies of therapy process events may be based upon and generalized from the events occurring in their own therapy supervisory relationship.

PROCESSES AND MECHANISMS INVOLVED IN THE TRANSLATION OF EXPECTANCY INFORMATION INTO CLIENT CHANGE

Necessary and Recommended Research Procedures

Regardless of whether the investigator chooses to attribute the causes of client change to the expectancy-instilling *procedures* or, with proper controls, to therapist expectancies, simply demonstrating the expectancy effect does not specify the processes or mechanisms through which prognostic information affects actual client change. Those research endeavors demonstrate when and under what conditions expectancy effects occur, but neither how they occur nor what differential therapist behaviors account for differential client change under high- and low-expectancy conditions.

The procedures necessary for the identification of how prognostic information affects client change consist, essentially, of an elaboration of the model presented by Brophy and Good (1970): a systematic, two-stage program of interrelated experiments involving an identification of (1) which therapist behaviors are affected by which kinds of expectancy information and (2) which therapist behaviors affect which kinds of client change. The intersection of those two sets of therapist behaviors may be considered to be the mechanisms through which expectancy information is translated into client change.

The first stage leading to an identification of which kinds of expectancy information affect which therapist behaviors requires the manipulation of expectancy information as an independent variable and the measurement of therapist behavior as a dependent variable.[6]

While that single measurement of therapist expectancy is sufficient to reach conclusions about the effect of information on expectancy *per se*, measurement designs showing the most promise in the heuristic identification of the expectancy effect are those in which an effect of expectancy information on therapy outcome is demonstrated and in which therapist behaviors are measured concomitantly during therapy intervention. In addition to demonstrating an effect of expectancy information on therapy outcome and in addition to identifying which therapist behaviors are affected by the expectancy information, these designs would also show which of the therapist behaviors measured during intervention were correlated with outcome. Observation and measurement strategies such as those employed in the therapy setting by Anderson and Rosenthal (1968) and Trattner and Howard (1970), in the diagnostic setting by Hersh (1971), Marwit (1969), Marwit and Marcia (1967), Masling (1965), and Sattler and Winget (1970), and in the educational setting by Beez (1968), Claiborn (1969), and Meichenbaum *et al.* (1969) may be used as models in this endeavor.

In order to draw definitive conclusions about

which particular therapist behaviors affected by expectancy information actually function as the mechanisms through which expectancy information affects client change, it is not sufficient to demonstrate merely that the presentation of differential expectancy information causes differential therapist behavior and a correlated differential client improvement. Therapy outcome and therapist behavior may be correlated without being causally related. Therefore, what is required in the second stage of the investigatory sequence endeavoring to identify the mechanisms of the expectancy effect is the manipulation of those therapist behaviors found to correlate with client change as independent variables and the validation that they, indeed, do affect the dependent variable of client improvement.

While their results were not definitive in relation to actual client improvement, an excellent model for this second step of investigation is the experiment conducted by Michaux and Lorr (1961), in which frequency of contact was varied as an independent variable by assigning clients on a random basis to be seen by therapists on a twice-weekly, weekly, or bi-weekly basis. Their results showed that frequency of contact had a significant influence on treatment goals reported by the therapists but not, however, on therapist outcome ratings.

Unsupported Hypotheses

While the definitive, two-stage research strategy aimed at identifying the therapist variables through which expectancy information affects therapy outcome has yet to be systematically conducted, several hypotheses have already been presented to provide a theoretical account for the expectancy effect.

Covert Processes. In this description of how expectancy-instilling procedures result in client change, it is simply suggested that the processes are covert and unobservable. While it is logically tenable to assume that covert processes occur in the therapy setting, these processes are, by definition, outside the realm of empirical investigation. The assumption of the philosophy of science that events be publicly observable precludes the investigation of covert events and, therefore, precludes the scientific validation of this theoretical model.

Self-Fulfilling Prophecy. As articulated by Brophy and Good (1970), Palardy (1969), Rosenthal and Jacobson (1968), and Simon (1969), the self-fulfilling prophecy implies that holding a certain expectancy of an outcome causes the holder of the expectancy to behave in a manner which causes or increases the probability of the occurrence of the expected outcome. In this approach, it is assumed that the expectancy is not merely a predictor of an outcome, but that the expected outcome would not have occurred without the intervention of the expector.

Not only is differential client change predictable on the basis of the self-fulfilling prophecy hypothesis, but the direction of the differential effect is also predictable. For the self-fulfilling prophecy hypothesis to remain a viable description of the events occurring in therapy, it must be shown that clients associated with high therapist expectancy of improvement actually improve more than clients associated with lower therapist expectancies. Reversal effects reported by Anderson and Rosenthal (1968), Evans and Rosenthal (1969), and McNeal *et al.* (1970), however, indicate that the self-fulfilling prophecy model is inadequate as either an explanation or a description of the events involved in the expectancy effect.

These reversals in the effect of expectancies on outcome are not exclusive to the therapy and classroom settings. Bootzin (1969), for example, reported a significant reversal in a study of experimenter effects in the laboratory. As reviewed by Barber and Silver (1968), in laboratory studies by Friedman, Kurland, and Rosenthal (1965), Marcia (1961), Persinger (1963), Rosenthal, Friedman, Johnson, Fode, Schill, White, and Vikan (1964), and Rosenthal, Persinger, Mulry, Vikan-Kline, and Grothe (1964, Experiment 1), treatment differences were reported in a direction opposite to that which experimenters were led to believe should occur. This reversal was reported at a statistically significant level in studies by Rosenthal, Persinger *et al.* (1964, Experiment 2) and White (1962). Referring to the Rosenthal-Jacobson (1968) typology presented in Table 1, the inability to distinguish between a self-fulfilling prophecy (Type IIB2) and an anti-self-fulfilling prophecy (Type IIA2) by any other criteria except on the basis of the outcome which the prophecies are circularly said to produce, calls into question the concept of the self-fulfilling prophecy as a cause of outcome and even as a metaphor for cause-effect sequences.

Communication of Therapist Expectancies to the Client. In this theoretical model, it is hypothesized that the therapist outcome expectancies are communicated to and instilled into the client and that a particular outcome occurs because the client expects it to occur (Frank,

1968; Goldstein, 1960, 1962b). At the extreme, as presented by Bednar (1970, pp. 651–652), is the position that the specific procedures employed in therapy are actually irrelevant—as long as the therapist imparts certain beliefs to the client, improvement will occur.

For that sequential chain of theoretical events to be a valid description of the expectancy effect process, it must be shown, at a minimum, that client expectancies of improvement affect actual client improvement. While this is a widely held contention in psychotherapy theory (Frank, 1959, 1968; Goldstein, 1962a, 1962b) recent reviews by Wilkins (1973a, 1973b) show that the evidence supporting that contention is inadequate both conceptually and empirically. Indeed, results reported by Marcia, Rubin, and Efran (1969) and McGlynn and Williams (1970) show that Ss in some experimental groups who receive a high-expectancy communication actually improve somewhat less than Ss who received a low- or no-expectancy communication.

In addition to the absence of strong support for the effect of the communication of expectancies in the therapy setting, the results of expectancy communication experiments conducted in the classroom have also been contradictory. When Meichenbaum and Smart (1971) communicated "late bloomer" information to academically borderline students about themselves, those students not only predicted that they would perform higher than students exposed to control procedures, but they actually did perform better. Further data indicated that while there were no reliable differences between the groups of students in study behavior or in their evaluation of the course, the "late bloomers" did report greater interest in the course content and greater relevance of the course.

Beyer (1971), however, reported statistically nonsignificant effects of the communication of academically prognostic information to students, and Beyer and Oetting (1970) found a reversal effect in that students in a remedial course who were told that they would do quite well in school actually performed less well than students who did not receive that information.

In summary, there does not appear to be sufficient evidence to warrant the conclusion that therapist expectancies contribute to client improvement via being communicated to the client.

Empirical Foundations for the Development of Theories

Current trends from therapy research may be integrated with findings emerging from the psychological laboratory to provide an empirical foundation for hypotheses about events involved in the translation of expectancy information into client change.

I. *Effects of expectancy information on quantity and quality of client-therapist interaction.* An examination and integration of the existing evidence from applied and laboratory investigations suggests several processes through which prognostic information may affect the client-therapist interaction. Differential therapeutic benefit will occur, for example, if therapist expectancies result in differential selection for therapy between high- and low-prognostic clients. Even assuming unbiased selection of high- and low-prognostic clients for therapy, different therapist expectancies may also result in differential client change if expectancies are associated with differences in the quantity, quality, and frequency of therapeutic interactions to which clients are exposed.

A. *Treatment selection per se.* Correlational studies conducted by Garfield and Affleck (1961) and Strupp and Williams (1960) show therapists to be more interested in treating clients of whom they have relatively high expectancies of improvement. This differential selection in favor of high-expectancy clients appears to be one instance of a more general decision-making pattern described in Feather's (1959a) theoretical model and supported by evidence presented by Feather (1959b): the probability of attempting to obtain a goal increases as the probability of success increases.

Assuming that psychotherapy is effective in producing improvement, to the degree that high-prognostic clients are more likely to receive therapy than low-prognostic clients, benefit will occur differentially in favor of high-prognostic clients simply by virtue of exposure to therapy.

In addition to the effect which treatment may have on the client, the selection of a client for therapy may affect the therapist (1) by the possibility of exposing the therapist to expectancy-disconfirming information and (2) by the events shown in psychological experiments to follow from commitment to a course of action.

1. *Exposure to expectancy-disconfirming information.* As a consequence of interaction with the client, the therapist may be exposed to information which is inconsistent with previously held expectancies. One group of laboratory investigations shows that under such conditions expectancies are likely to become realigned and correspond to the recent information. Other

studies have generated results which bear relevance to possible changes in affective state and changes in performance resulting from the presentation of disconfirming information.

a. Modification of prior expectancies. A consistent trend emerging from previously reviewed laboratory investigations shows that when prior expectancies are in conflict with recently presented information, there is a marked tendency for the expectancies to be modified by the more recent information (Feather, 1965a, 1965b, 1966; Zajonc & Brickman, 1969; Zegers, 1968). A qualification of this trend emerged in Cottrell's (1965) study, which showed that the presentation of only one trial of inconsistent feedback after several trials of uniformly consistent feedback was not sufficient to produce changes on the measure of expectancy employed. The presentation of the one trial of inconsistent feedback was, however, sufficient to produce reliable changes in behavior.

The findings presented by Feather (1963b) also indicate that Ss are less confident of expectancies on early trials of a task. As such, initial expectancies may be considered to be relatively susceptible to change.

An implication of this trend for the therapy setting is that if initial expectancies are inaccurate and if, in interacting with the client, the therapist is presented with information which contradicts pre-therapy information, subsequent expectancies will be aligned more appropriately with the information acquired through the client-therapist interaction.

The results of studies in the therapy setting support this generalization. Eells (1964), for example, found an overall positive correlation between therapist preferences for client traits and selection for treatment; however, in the study by Kumar and Pepinsky (1965), when initial expectancies of an unattractive client were disconfirmed by the client's behavior, not only were the expectancies of the therapist realigned to the client's behavior, but therapists were more willing to engage in further interaction with the client. Accounts of diagnostic experiments reported by Sattler and Winget (1970) and Saunders and Vitro (1971) also support the interpretation that recent information has a more potent effect than prior information in applied settings.

Even though therapist initial expectancies may be easily modifiable, they would be more likely to be maintained if events occurred which precluded exposure to the disconfirming information. If low-prognostic clients are selected less often for treatment, not only are they eliminated from receiving the possible benefits of therapy, but therapist expectancies are more likely to be perpetuated in the absence of disconfirming information.

To the degree that therapist expectancies are predictive of therapy outcome, it may be concluded that events which expose the therapist to expectancy-disconfirming information have an enhancing effect on therapy outcome with low-prognostic clients while, on the other hand, events which preclude exposure to expectancy-disconfirming information, such as differential therapy selection in favor of high prognostic clients, have an interfering effect on therapy outcome with low-prognostic clients.

b. Expectancy disconfirmation and affective state. In an experiment by Feather (1965a), Ss attempted a difficult task after having received information that the task was either easy or moderately difficult to solve. The results showed that Ss receiving information that the task was easy reported higher initial expectancies of success and greater anxiety and disappointment during the task than Ss who had been told that the task would be difficult.

These results have direct implications for the effect of expectancy-disconfirmation in relation to high-prognostic clients, but not necessarily in relation to low-prognostic clients. The results of a classic laboratory experiment by Carlsmith and Aronson (1963) do, however, offer suggestive implications for expectancy-disconfirmation in relation to both types of clients. In that experiment Ss were asked to predict, on the basis of cues presented to them, whether they would receive a bitter or sweet solution and were asked to rate the taste of the solution they actually received. It was found that the sweet solution was rated as significantly less sweet and the bitter solution significantly more bitter under conditions of expectancy disconfirmation than when expectancies were confirmed. Both measures suggest a more negative affective state when expectancies are disconfirmed than when they are confirmed. Sampson and Sibley (1965) were able to replicate only the findings for the sweet solutions reported by Carlsmith and Aronson (1963), however. In addition, Keisner (1969) found that expectancy disconfirmation produced more bitter ratings of the bitter solution and less sweet ratings of the sweet solution only in conditions in which Ss' performance was made public, not when performance was kept private. The investigator suggested that the generality of the conclusions presented by Carlsmith and

Aronson (1963) should be limited to settings in which both expectancy and outcome are public. These events may or may not occur in the therapy setting.

The limited generalizability of the findings presented by Carlsmith and Aronson (1963) is further indicated by the results of the experiment conducted by Harvey and Clapp (1965). The Ss were asked to rate how they expected to be evaluated by another person and were then presented with those evaluations, which were arranged to deviate from S's expectancy in either a more favorable or more unfavorable direction. While magnitude of deviation from reported expectancy, *per se*, did not affect Ss' subsequent evaluation expectancies, the direction of deviation did. Deviations in a favorable direction produced more positive self-descriptions than did deviations in an unfavorable direction-regardless of whether Ss' expectancies were relatively high or low prior to reception of the evaluative information. In that instance in which the direction of the expectancy-disconfirming information, not exposure to disconfirmation *per se*, affected positive or negative self-evaluations, the results are more parallel to those reviewed in the previous section on the modification of expectancies than they are to the results presented by Carlsmith and Aronson (1963).

c. Expectancy disconfirmation and performance strategy. In another classic laboratory study by Aronson and Carlsmith (1962), Ss received several trials of consistent feedback that they were performing either very well or very poorly on a choice task and, then, on one predesignated trial, Ss received feedback which was either consistent or inconsistent with the prior information. Independent of the specific content of that information, when asked to repeat that trial, Ss altered their responses more after receiving inconsistent information than after receiving information consistent with previous performance. That is, not only did Ss who were previously performing well change their responses when they were told they performed poorly on the predesignated trial, but also Ss who were previously performing poorly changed more of their responses when they were told that they had performed well on that trial—a paradoxical response which could only have worsened their performance.

While the results of this study are intriguing, it has received criticism on methodological, statistical, and theoretical grounds, and attempts to replicate the findings have yielded inconsistent results and results which are difficult to integrate

with the original findings (Brock, Edelman, Edwards, & Schuck, 1965; Cottrell, 1965; Kornreich, 1968; Lowin & Epstein, 1965; Moran & Klockars, 1967; Silverman & Marcantonio, 1965; Ward & Sandvold, 1963; Waterman & Ford, 1965).

Sarason (1961) found performance deterioration to be moderated by personality variables when Ss performed on difficult tasks after they had been told the tasks should be easy for them to solve. Employing the same task and expectancy manipulation, Feather (1965a) found a statistically nonsignificant trend that Ss who were told of, and expected, a moderately difficult task performed better on the difficult task than Ss who had been told that the task was easy. Feather (1965a) also found a significant interaction between expectancy information and personality on performance, but in a direction opposite to that reported by Sarason (1961).

d. Implications for expectancy disconfirmation in applied settings. In integrating the results of experiments in which the effects of expectancy-disconfirming information have been studied, there is a marked trend indicating that exposure to disconfirming information has the effect of realigning expectancies to recently presented information (Feather, 1965a, 1965b, 1966; Zajonc & Brickman, 1969; Zegers, 1968). While the possibility of negative effects of disconfirmation on affective state (Carlsmith & Aronson, 1963) and on performance (Aronson & Carlsmith, 1962) should not be ignored, the current evidence indicates that the generalizability of the results of the experiment by Carlsmith and Aronson (1963) are quite limited (Harvey & Clapp, 1965; Keisner, 1969; Sampson & Sibley, 1965) and that the results of the experiment reported by Aronson and Carlsmith (1962) are not readily replicable (Brock *et al.* 1965; Cottrell, 1965; Kornreich, 1968; Lowin & Epstein, 1965; Moran & Klockars, 1967; Silverman & Marcantonio, 1965; Ward & Sandvold, 1963; Waterman & Ford, 1965).

It remains an important issue to determine not only if expectancy disconfirmation affects the therapist differentially in relation to high- and low-expectancy clients, but also to determine if any of these behavioral differences are in the direction of perpetuating previous expectancies. Design considerations in the experiment by Aronson and Carlsmith (1962) indicate, at most, that a therapist may behave differently in relation to high- and low-prognostic clients, and not necessarily that the therapist, given a less restricted set of behavioral alternatives than that imposed by the statistical design employed by Aronson and Carlsmith (1962), will behave in a manner to confirm previous expectancies. Anecdotal descriptions provided by Saunders and Vitro (1971) show that some examiner behavior resulting from discrepancies between pre-diagnostic expectancy information and examinee performance may, indeed, be of benefit to the low-expectancy examinee.

The results of an investigation reported by Kumar and Pepinsky (1965) conducted on these issues in an applied setting indicate that counselor ratings of counselees were determined primarily by counselee behavior; however, the confirmation-disconfirmation variable was reported to have moderated the effect of client behavior on counselor ratings.

The suggestive results of the diagnostic experiments conducted by Sattler and Winget (1970) are also of relevance: while examinee behavior was shown to have a more potent effect on outcome than did the delivery of expectancy information, the interaction of those two independent variables approached statistical significance.

2. *Commitment to therapy.* Not only does selection offer the opportunity for exposure to additional information about clients, but the results of several laboratory studies attest to possible positive effects of treatment selection on therapist attitudes even prior to actual client-therapist interaction. A study by Mirels and Mills (1964) showed that prior to a forced or chosen interaction with an unpleasant person, Ss rated that person as more pleasant and more competent than under conditions in which Ss would not have interacted with the unpleasant person. Darley and Berscheid (1967) also found that Ss evaluated other individuals more positively if they were informed that they would be interacting with the other person than if the information they received indicated that there would be no opportunity for interaction.

Similarly, Aronson, Carlsmith, and Darley (1963) found that when Ss were informed that they would be required to engage in an unpleasant task and then were given a choice to engage in either the unpleasant task or a neutral task, proportionately more Ss actually chose the unpleasant task than did Ss who were not informed that they would be required to engage in the unpleasant task.

Anticipation of future contact with another person was shown by Gergen and Wishnov (1965) to increase the presentation of one's own positive characteristics to that person. Kanfer,

Duerfeldt, Martin, and Dorsey (1971) also found Ss to be more observant of a model performing a task when they were instructed that they would be required to perform that task.

Tentative support for the generalizability of the results of laboratory experiments to the therapy setting may be found in the study reported by Strupp and Williams (1960). Although assumptions of randomization were not met in that study, the results suggest that contact with a client may increase the therapist's expectancies of improvement; interviewers of a client reported significantly higher expectancies of client improvement than did nonparticipant observers of the interview.

B. *Quantity of task-oriented interactions.* In addition to the effects of differential treatment selection *per se*, trends emerging from the literature show that therapist expectancies and therapy outcome may be associated via differential amounts of therapeutic interaction delivered to high- and low-prognostic clients.

While Affleck and Garfield (1961) failed to find a reliable correlation between therapist prognostic measures and duration of therapy, the results of studies by Garfield and Affleck (1961) and Goldstein (1960) did show that clients of whom therapists expected the greatest change participated in more therapy sessions than clients of whom therapists expected less change.

Some support for the association between expectancy and quantity of performance emerges from the psychological laboratory if speed and persistence may be interpreted as indices of quantity. Feather (1963a) found that under conditions which led to a low expectation of personal success, Ss completed experimental tasks more slowly than under conditions leading to a high expectancy of success. Feather (1963b) also found that Ss who reported higher initial expectancies of success persisted longer on laboratory tasks which they were repeatedly unsuccessful in solving. That correlation between initial expectancy and persistence was not observed by Feather (1961), however, except through significant interaction with motivational measures.

In an experiment by Rothbart et al. (1971), the difference between the amount of attention delivered by teacher trainees to students described as high-potential and that delivered to low-potential students approached statistical significance in the predicted direction, as did the difference in amount of verbalization between the two groups of students.

Beez (1968) found not only that pre-interaction expectancy information had a significant effect on subsequent pupil performance but also that teachers presented high-expectancy pupils with more task-oriented problems and spent more time in task-oriented activity with them than with low-expectancy pupils.

The two previous experiments indicate that when high-expectancy information results in greater quantity of interaction than low-expectancy information, greater outcome is associated with the high-expectancy information. The study by Anderson and Rosenthal (1968), however, suggests that high-expectancy information does not always result in a greater quantity of contact and that when less contact results from high-expectancy information, high expectancies may be associated with less improvement on some outcome measures. In that study, it was shown that "late bloomers" received less attention from their counselors than did "nonlate bloomers" and that one group of "late bloomers" deteriorated on a measure of reasoning. In the same study, possibly as a consequence of receiving less attention from their counselors, "late bloomers" improved on a measure of self-help more than did "nonlate bloomers."

C. *Frequency of interaction: Masses versus spaced trials.* In addition to the effects of *treatment selection per se* and *quantity* of interaction, the *frequency* of interaction with a client may have an impact on the therapist's expectancies of that client. Suggestive evidence was presented in an experiment by Michaux and Lorr (1961) in which it was found that the frequency with which a client was scheduled for therapy sessions—twice-weekly, weekly, or bi-weekly—had a significant effect on the therapists' treatment goals. Contrary to clinical lore, supportive goals were relatively higher in incidence and reconstructive goals were relatively lower in incidence with clients scheduled for twice-weekly sessions, while the reverse trend was evident for the bi-weekly group.

Investigations into the effects of massed versus spaced trials on the modification of performance expectancies on laboratory tasks also have strong implications for the operation of expectancies in the therapy situation. With total feedback held constant, increases in the temporal distance between the presentation of information and the measurement of expectancies have been shown in several laboratory investigations to significantly attenuate the effect of that information.

Thus, Schwarz et al. (1970) found that expectancies of performance were higher if they were measured immediately after a series of success feedback trials than if they were measured after a delay. When Ss were given low-performance feedback on early trials and were subsequently presented with high-performance feedback, Phares (1961) found that expectancies were significantly lower if high-feedback trials were spaced over a 12-day period than if the same number of feedback trials were delivered during 1-day or 5-day periods. The author also noted that the performance expectancies which were lower after temporal delay were raised after a few massed trials for the 5-day group.

In a balanced design in which success feedback following initial failure feedback or failure feedback following initial success feedback was delivered in massed or spaced trials, Phares (1964b) also presented clear evidence that expectancies are significantly more influenced by recent information feedback if trials are massed rather than spaced over 24 hours. Data presented by Phares (1964a) and Schwarz (1966) also documented the facilitating effect of massed trials over spaced trials occurring after 24-hour delays in aligning expectancies and performance with recent information feedback. In the Schwarz (1966) study, delay was also found to produce significantly greater variability in performance expectancies than massed trials.

Rychlak and Eacker (1962), however, found relatively little expectancy change attributable to the variable of delay when delay was only of an 8-minute duration.

Clear trends emerge from those studies indicating that if information is presented which is inconsistent with previously held expectancies, the impact of that new information is reduced by the imposition of delay between trials. These findings are particularly relevant to the events occurring in the therapy setting, in that the manner in which therapy is normally conducted resembles an arrangement of spaced trials rather than massed trials, a condition which has been shown to be most conducive to the maintenance of prior expectancies even when expectancy-disconfirming information is presented. As a consequence of the spacing of therapy sessions, the expectancies of therapists toward high- and low-prognostic clients are more likely to be perpetuated in the face of contradictory information than they would be under conditions of a massed trial arrangement of therapy sessions.

To the degree that therapist expectancies are actuarially related to therapy outcome, greater gain may be predicted for high-prognostic clients than low-prognostic clients under these conditions than under conditions of a more massed trial arrangement. In addition, *to the degree that low-prognostic clients are seen less frequently than high-prognostic clients, therapist initial expectancies of low-prognostic clients are less amenable to modification by the presentation of contradictory information and are more likely to be perpetuated than are the initial expectancies of high-prognostic clients.*

D. *Quality of interaction.* While previously reviewed studies indicate that expectancy-instilling procedures may be associated with client change via differences in treatment selection, frequency of contact, and quantity of task-oriented trials, there is also evidence that those procedures may affect client change via differences in the quality of the client-therapist interaction. The ratings and reports made by observers in a therapy analogue study described by Strupp (1958) showed that those observers of a filmed interview who had relatively high expectancies of therapeutic gain for the client would be more likely to accept the client's focus without attempting to shift it and would be less likely to respond to the client in a "cold" manner than were observers of the interview who had relatively low expectancies.

In addition to that correlational evidence, the results of the classroom experiment conducted by Meichenbaum *et al.* (1969) offer suggestive evidence for the occurrence of qualitative differences in the therapeutic situation associated with differential therapist expectancies. The numbers of teachers and pupils in that experiment were small and the findings were inconsistent from teacher to teacher; however, three of the four teachers were observed to engage in more positive or less negative interactions with high-expectancy students than with low-expectancy students. The high-expectancy students of one teacher who decreased positive interactions with them following expectancy instruction showed less improvement than control students.

On the other hand, while the quantity of teacher attention delivered to students described as either high- or low-potential approached significance in the experiment conducted by Rothbart *et al.* (1971), the positive or negative quality of attention delivered to the two groups of students did not differ.

The laboratory experiments by Brock *et al.* (1965), Lowin and Epstein (1965), Moran and Klockars (1967), and Waterman and Ford (1965) showed that the delivery of failure feedback results in poorer recall of past performance than does the delivery of success feedback. These findings suggest the possibility of qualitative differences in therapist performance under different expectancy conditions mediated by differential recall.

II. *Expectancy, goal-setting, and therapy outcome.* Not only do the procedures designed to instill expectancies contain information predictive of an outcome, but they may also contain motivational or incentive properties related to the attainment of the predicted outcome. Zajonc and Brickman (1969) have described the lack of conceptual, empirical, and methodological clarity between expectancies and aspirations. Those authors noted that while the concept of expectancy places a relative emphasis on cognitive processes and the concept of aspiration implies the presence of motivational processes, both cognitive and motivational aspects are contained in each. To the degree that expectancy-instilling procedures contain motivational properties, a predicted outcome may function as a goal, performance standard, or criterion for the evaluation of the performance of the individual to whom expectancy procedures are delivered.

Review of laboratory findings. While considerable attention has been paid to the effects of performance on goal-setting, Bryan and Locke (1967), Locke (1966a, 1966b, 1967a), and Locke and Bryan (1966a, 1966b, 1967) have contended that goal-setting functions as a cause, not just a consequence, of performance. The studies conducted to test that contention not only contain information relevant to expectancy theory, but also provide the methodological models for the investigation of events related to expectancies in the therapy setting.

After high- and low-task performers had been identified, Bryan and Locke (1967) instructed the high performers to continue to do their best, while low performers were instructed to reach specific goals established for them. This procedure not only brought the performance of the low performers within the range exhibited by the high performers, but also improved the attitudes toward the task held by the low performers.

Locke (1966a) and Locke and Bryan (1966b, 1967) found that Ss who set high performance standards performed significantly better than Ss who did not. In addition, a sequence of investigations by Locke (1966b, 1967a) and Locke and Bryan (1966a, 1967, 1969) in which performance standard was manipulated as an independent variable showed that performance was consistently superior when Ss were given high performance standards than when Ss were given low performance standards or instructions simply to do their best. Even when the probability of reaching a high standard of success was quite low, the setting of that standard led to higher performance. Locke and Bryan (1967) also noted that trying to reach a specific goal was a primary source of task interest for Ss and found that Ss given specific goals were more interested in the task than Ss who were not instructed to reach predetermined goals.

Zajonc and Brickman (1969) showed that simply requiring Ss to state their performance expectancies, regardless of whether the expectancies were high or low, led to a significant improvement in performance in comparison to Ss who were not required to state their expectancies. A positive correlation between expectancies and actual performance was also found in that study.

While Locke (1966b) reported a linear relationship between level of goal and performance within the ranges of tasks employed, Dey and Kaur (1965) found evidence for an inverted-U relationship between performance and performance standards presented in the form of false norms. Increasing performance standards led to a monotonic increase in performance up to a point, after which increasing the false standards produced less than optimal performance.

Indirect evidence for the incentive function of expectancy-instilling procedures has been presented in a study by Pellegrini and Hicks (1972). In criticizing the classroom expectancy study by Rosenthal and Jacobson (1968), they pointed out that the teachers not only received expectancy information, but as a consequence of conducting the pre-treatment assessment, they were familiar with the specific measure to be used in evaluating outcome. This familiarity may have offered a direction for the coaching of behavior related to that specific dimension rather than representing a general improvement in student functioning. The data Pellegrini and Hicks (1972) presented in their own study showed, as predicted, that evidence for expectancy effects occurred only when teachers were informed of the specific outcome measures employed.

Implications of goal-setting for therapy outcome. A demonstration by Locke (1967b) sheds light on possible processes through which the incentive properties of expectancy-instilling procedures may affect therapy outcome. When Ss were instructed to stop performing when a specific goal had been reached, Ss with high goals performed better than Ss with low goals. While the results of this study may seem trivial

in themselves, when they are considered within the context of other studies by Locke (1966a, 1966b), Locke and Bryan (1967, 1969) and Zajonc and Brickman (1969), they suggest the possibility that performance may continue until expectancies or goals are reached, after which the S may, in effect, stop performing. If this process is operating in the therapy setting, it implies that *therapists with relatively low goals or expectancies of client change may stop performing after less change than therapists with relatively high expectancies.*

An additional implication of goal-setting in the therapy situation concerns whether or not goals are even specified for some clients. The findings reported by Zajonc and Brickman (1969) show that simply requiring Ss to state performance expectancies improves performance regardless of whether expectancies are high or low. If goals tend to be specified for high-prognostic clients and not for low-prognostic clients, the therapist's interactions with low-prognostic clients parallel the "do your best" strategy which has been shown to be associated with relatively low performance and less interest in the task.

While the possibility of less than optimal performance resulting from very high goals (Dey & Kaur, 1965) should not be overlooked, evidence presented by Locke (1966b, 1967a) and Locke and Bryan (1966b, 1967, 1969) shows that even if high goals are not reached, simply having high goals leads to higher performance. Graphs presented by Feather (1964) also indicated that when payoffs were contingent upon actual performance rather than contingent upon reaching a stated goal, performance was maintained at a high level even though it consistently fell below stated aspiration level.

III. *Personal control over expected events.* Information presented to Ss as to the degree to which their own behavior can affect the occurrences of an expected event has been shown in laboratory investigations to influence expectancies as well as performance related to expectancies. Two approaches may be used to assess the degree to which the dimension of personal control over an event affects expectations of that event. One strategy is to compare Ss' predictions of the occurrence of events which are contingent upon their own performance with their prediction of events which occur independently of their own performance. In the other research strategy, Ss are instructed that performance outcome is determined either by their own skill or by chance factors over which they have no control.

Expectancies of performance-contingent versus performance-noncontingent events. Data presented by DeSoto et al. (1960) showed that with information about performance held constant, Ss' predictions about their own performance were higher than their predictions of the performance of another person. While the effects of competition were confounded with the effects of personal control in a study by Church et al. (1963), in the condition in which outcome was contingent upon S's performance, expectancies were significantly higher and influenced significantly more by recent information than in the condition in which outcome was not contingent upon S's performance.

Consistent with the direction of the findings of the two previous studies, Diggory and Morlock (1964) also found levels of aspiration for one's own performance to be slightly higher than performance feedback on previous trials. Similarly, Feather (1963a) found that Ss' expectancies of their own performance were consistently above the level of success-failure feedback which they received and, also, that these overestimations were greatest for Ss receiving the lowest level of success feedback.

Skill versus chance instructions. In this group of investigations, the variable of personal control is manipulated by instructing Ss that performance on a task is determined essentially by chance factors or, conversely, that performance on a task reflects on S's skill. In such an experiment, Feather (1967) found that the level of success expected on the first trial of a task was greater under chance instructions than under skill instructions, but that the level of success expected after a number of trials was greater under skill instructions. In that study, measures of motivation to achieve success and avoid failure increased across trials in the skill condition but not in the chance condition. In another study by Feather (1959b), however, the skill-chance variable was found to have relatively little effect on Ss' choice to engage in a high-probability-of-success or a low-probability-of-success task.

Phares (1957) found that expectancies under skill instructions were more aligned with feedback than expectancies under chance instructions. James and Rotter (1958) showed that while the difference in the rate of extinction between continuously and partially reinforced expectancies in the chance condition was consistent with operant conditioning formulations, extinction of expectancies in the skill condition was not.

In addition to having a reliable effect on expectancies, skill-versus-chance instructions were shown by Phares (1962) to have an effect on actual performance: thresholds for tachistoscopically presented words previously paired with electric shock were significantly lower when Ss were instructed that escape from shock was a matter of skill in word detection rather than being instructed that escape was essentially a matter of chance.

Attribution of personal control in applied settings. Several studies have been conducted to determine the conditions which lead one to attribute the cause of an event to oneself or to some other source. The results of these studies show that if an intervention is followed by a change, particularly by a change indicating success or improvement, Ss will attribute the cause of that change to themselves.

Schopler and Layton (1972), for example, found that Ss rated themselves as having been significantly more influential if the performance of another person changed after S's intervention than if the performance of another person did not change, particularly by a change indicating perhaps more importantly, if the performance of the other person improved after S's intervention, there was a greater tendency for Ss to attribute the cause of the change to themselves than if the performance of the other person decreased after intervention.

Similarly, Johnson, Feigenbaum, and Weiby (1964) found that, if previously poor performing students improved after interaction with a teacher, the teachers attributed the cause of the change to themselves, but if students continued to perform poorly, the causes of the performance were attributed to the students. In addition, those teachers had more positive sentiment for pupils who improved after interaction with the teacher.

These findings are consistent with the trends noted by Locke (1965) in a post-experiment questionnaire in which Ss were asked the reasons for their liking or disliking of a task. The Ss who liked a task tended to attribute their liking to their own personal characteristics, such as skill, while Ss who disliked the task attributed their dislike to aspects of the task, events external to their own performance.

The results of these studies not only indicate that post-intervention change and, particularly, post-intervention improvement are attributed to oneself, but they also open the possibility that expectancy information communicated in the applied setting may be confounded with information concerning personal control over therapy outcome. From the direction of the results of the above studies, it would appear that low-prognostic information would, if anything, be most likely to be accompanied by information of low therapist control, while high-prognostic information would be accompanied by information indicating relatively high therapist control. Indeed, *if a therapist receives information that a client has not shown improvement in the past, and if the reasons for the lack of success are attributed to client characteristics, the therapist's expectancies and behavior might be quite different than if the reasons for a laek of past success are attributed to characteristics of the therapists who have intervened in the past.* In that expectancy information and information regarding personal control are confounded, the dimension of personal control may account, in part, for the variance previously attributed only to expectancies.

If the results of the previously cited laboratory experiments by Church *et al.* (1963), DeSoto *et al.* (1960), and Feather (1963a) may be generalized to the therapy setting, they suggest that *if a therapist receives information that treatment outcome for a particular client is an event over which the therapist has relatively little control, expectancies of improvement will be lower than if the therapist is informed that treatment outcome is within the therapist's control.*

Feather's (1967) laboratory study suggests that if outcome is under the therapist's control, motivation to achieve success and avoid failure would increase across trials, while the results presented by Phares (1962) indicate that, in that condition, the therapist may be more vigilant in seeking out and observing other task-related information. In addition, the laboratory data presented by Church *et al.* (1963) and Phares (1957) also suggest that if the therapist is informed that improvement is under his control and if recent information feedback about the client contradicted prior information, therapist expectancies would be more aligned with the recent information than if outcome was not under the control of the therapist.

The dimension of personal control over therapeutic outcome also holds implications for client selection, for therapists may be more likely to select for treatment those clients whose improvement is contingent upon intervention as opposed to clients whose change will be determined by extratherapy factors.

SUMMARY

Very little evidence exists to support the popular assumption that therapist expectancies play a contributory role in causing therapeutic change. Expectancy-related information about a client appears to have neither a predictable effect on the direction of client change nor as powerful an effect on the therapist as does client behavior. Therapist expectancies have, however, been shown to be correlated with a variety of other events occurring in the therapy setting. Nor does expectancy-related information appear to have a predictable effect in the educational setting; that information has, however, been shown to have replicable effect during the administration and scoring phases of personality and intellectual assessment.

In relation to the deterministic usage to which therapist expectancies have been put, no correlational or experimental study has both (1) established the independence of therapist expectancies from therapy outcome and from other therapist characteristics and (2) validated the presence of the assumed expectancies. There is not, at present, empirical support for the attribution of causal characteristics to therapist expectancies. Indeed, once all of the conditions necessary for causal attributions have been met, therapist expectancies explain no more than can be explained by appealing to observable events alone.

While there is not, at present, definitive support for the actuarial usage of therapist expectancies, that usage appears to hold promise as a predictor of therapy outcome, as a variable to consider in the assignment of therapists to clients, and as an event the study of which may lead to the heuristic identification of effective therapist conduct. The most promise of the actuarial usage of therapist expectancies does not appear to be as a main effect but as a factor interacting with other observable events, such as client characteristics or the particular outcome measure employed.

The methodologies and findings of controlled laboratory investigations appear to be of considerable significance to the identification of events which affect expectancies in applied settings. That evidence shows that expectancies are acquired and maintained by the presentation of predictive information, by the actual difficulty level of a task, by information feedback, and by the value of a particular outcome. Expectancies instilled in one situation have been shown to be generalizable to other situations and appear to be relatively easily modifiable by the presentation of information discrepant with the previously held expectancies. There does not appear to be reliable evidence for possible negative effects on affective state or performance resulting from expectancy disconfirmation.

The processes through which expectancy-related information may affect therapy outcome may be identified by a programmatic research strategy aimed at identifying the intersection between those therapist behaviors, measured as a dependent variable, which are affected by expectancy-related information and those therapist behaviors, varied as independent variables, which affect client change. While no definitive research has been conducted to identify these processes, several possible mechanisms have been presented. There is little empirical support for the notions that client improvement is influenced by processes involving covert events, by self-fulfilling prophesies, or by the communication of therapist expectancies to the client. Trends emerging from empirical investigations do, however, suggest that expectancy-related information may affect therapy outcome via treatment selection *per se*, via the quantity, frequency, and quality of therapeutic interactions, via differential goal-setting in relation to high- and low-prognostic clients, and via events related to the dimension of personal control of the therapist over expected events.

REFERENCES

AFFLECK, D. C., & GARFIELD, S. L. Predictive judgments of therapists and duration of stay in psychotherapy. *Journal of Clinical Psychology*, 1961, **17**, 134–137.

ANDERSON, D. F., & ROSENTHAL, R. Some effects of interpersonal expectancy and social interaction on institutionalized retarded children. *Proceedings of the 76th Annual Convention of the American Psychological Association*, 1968, **3**, 479–480.

ARONSON, E., & CARLSMITH, J. M. Performance expectancy as a determinant of actual performance. *Journal of Abnormal and Social Psychology*, 1962, **65**, 178–182.

ARONSON, E., CARLSMITH, J. M., & DARLEY, J. M. The effects of expectancy on volunteering for an unpleasant experience. *Journal of Abnormal and Social Psychology*, 1963, **66**, 220–224.

AUFFREY, J., & ROBERTSON, M. Case history information and examiner experience as determinants of scoring variability on Wechsler Intelligence tests. *Proceedings of the 80th Annual Convention of the American Psychological Association*, 1972, **7** (Part 2), 553–554.

BARBER, T. X., & SILVER, M. J. Fact, fiction, and the experimenter bias effect. *Psychological Bulletin*, 1968, **70** (6, Part 2), 1–29.

BEDNAR, R. L. Persuasibility and the power of belief. *Personnel and Guidance Journal*, 1970, **48**, 647–652.

BEEZ, W. V. Influence of biased psychological reports on teacher behavior and pupil performance. *Proceedings of the 76th Annual Convention of the American Psychological Association*, 1968, **3**, 605–606.

BEYER, H. N. Effect of students' knowledge of their predicted grade point averages on academic achievement. *Journal of Counseling Psychology*, 1971, **18**, 603–605.

BEYER, H. N., & OETTING, E. R. Effect of encouragement and reassurance on students' performance in remedial English. *Journal of Educational Research*, 1970, **64**, 59–60.

BOOTZIN, R. R. Induced and stated expectancy in experimenter bias. *Proceedings of the 77th Annual Convention of the American Psychological Association*, 1969, **4** (Part 1), 365–366.

BROCK, T. C., EDELMAN, S. K., EDWARDS, D. C., & SCHUCK, J. R. Seven studies of performance expectancy as a determinant of actual performance. *Journal of Experimental Social Psychology*, 1965, **1**, 295–310.

BROPHY, J. E., & GOOD, T. L. Teachers' communication of differential expectations for children's classroom performance : Some behavioral data. *Journal of Educational Psychology*, 1970, **61**, 365–374.

BRYAN, J. F., & LOCKE, E. A. Goal setting as a means of increasing motivation. *Journal of Applied Psychology*, 1967, **51**, 274–277.

CARLSMITH, J. M., & ARONSON, E. Some hedonic consequences of the confirmation and disconfirmation of expectancies. *Journal of Abnormal and Social Psychology*, 1963, **66**, 151–156.

CHURCH, R. M., MILLWARD, R. B., & MILLER, P. Prediction of success in a competitive reaction time situation. *Journal of Abnormal and Social Psychology*, 1963, **67**, 234–240.

CLAIBORN, W. L. Expectancy effects in the classroom : A failure to replicate. *Journal of Educational Psychology*, 1969, **60**, 377–383.

CONN, L. K., EDWARDS, C. N., ROSENTHAL, R., CROWNE, D. Perception of emotion and response to teachers' expectancy by elementary school children. *Psychological Reports*, 1968, **22**, 27–34.

COTTRELL, N. B. Performance expectancy as a determinant of actual performance: A replication with a new design. *Journal of Personality and Social Psychology*, 1965, **2**, 685–691.

CRANDALL, V. J., SOLOMON, D., & KELLAWAY, R. Expectancy statements and decision times as functions of objective probabilities and reinforcement values. *Journal of Personality*, 1955, **24**, 192–203.

DARLEY, J. M., & BERSCHEID, E. Increased liking as a result of the anticipation of personal contact. *Human Relations*, 1967, **20**, 29–40.

DeSOTO, C. B., COLEMAN, E. B., & PUTNAM, P. L. Predictions of sequences of successes and failures. *Journal of Experimental Psychology*, 1960, **59**, 41–46.

DEY, M. K., & KAUR, G. Facilitation of performance by experimentally induced ego motivation. *Journal of General Psychology*, 1965, **73**, 237–247.

DIGGORY, J. C., & MORLOCK, H. C. Level of aspiration, or probability of success? *Journal of Abnormal and Social Psychology*, 1964, **69**, 282–289.

DIGGORY, J. C., RILEY, E. J., & BLUMENFELD, R. Estimated probability of success for a fixed goal. *American Journal of Psychology*, 1960, **73**, 41–55.

EDWARDS, A. L. *Experimental design in psychological research*. New York : Holt, Rinehart & Winston, 1968. (3rd. Ed.)

EELLS, J. F. Therapists' views and preferences concerning intake cases. *Journal of Consulting Psychology*, 1964, **28**, 382.

EGELAND, B. Examiner expectancy : Effects on the scoring of the WISC. *Psychology in the Schools*, 1969, **6**, 313–315.

ELASHOFF, J. D., & SNOW, R. E. *Pygmalion reconsidered.* Worthington, Ohio: Jones, 1971.

EVANS, J. T., & ROSENTHAL, R. Interpersonal self-fulfilling prophesies: Further extrapolations from the laboratory to the classroom. *Proceedings of the 77th Annual Convention of the American Psychological Association,* 1969, **4**, (Part 1), 371–372.

FEATHER, N. T. Subjective probability and decision under uncertainty. *Psychological Review,* 1959a, **66**, 150–164.

FEATHER, N. T. Success probability and choice behavior. *Journal of Experimental Psychology,* 1959b, **58**, 257–266.

FEATHER, N. T. The relationship of persistence at a task to expectation of success and achievement related motives. *Journal of Abnormal and Social Psychology,* 1961, **63**, 552–561.

FEATHER, N. T. The effect of differential failure on expectation of success, reported anxiety, and response uncertainty. *Journal of Personality,* 1963a, **31**, 289–312.

FEATHER, N. T. Persistence at a difficult task with alternative task of intermediate difficulty. *Journal of Abnormal and Social Psychology,* 1963b, **66**, 604–609.

FEATHER, N. T. The relationship of expectation of success to reported probability, task structure, and achievement related motivation. *Journal of Abnormal and Social Psychology,* 1963c, **66**, 231–238.

FEATHER, N. T. Level of aspiration behaviour in relation to payoffs and costs following success and failure. *Australian Journal of Psychology,* 1964, **16**, 175–184.

FEATHER, N. T. Performance at a difficult task in relation to initial expectation of success, text anxiety, and need achievement. *Journal of Personality,* 1965a, **33**, 200–217.

FEATHER, N. T. The relationship of expectation of success to need achievement and test anxiety. *Journal of Personality and Social Psychology,* 1965b, **1**, 118–126.

FEATHER, N. T. Effects of prior success and failure on expectations of success and subsequent performance. *Journal of Personality and Social Psychology,* 1966, **3**, 287–298.

FEATHER, N. T. Valence of outcome and expectation of success in relation to task difficulty and perceived locus of control. *Journal of Personality and Social Psychology,* 1967, **7**, 372–386.

FEATHER, N. T. Change in confidence following success or failure as a predictor of subsequent performance. *Journal of Personality and Social Psychology,* 1968, **9**, 38–46.

FEATHER, N. T., & SAVILLE, M. R. Effects of amount of prior success and failure on expectations of success and subsequent task performance. *Journal of Personality and Social Psychology,* 1967, **5**, 226–232.

FIELDER, W. R., COHEN, R. D., & FEENEY, S. An attempt to replicate the teacher expectancy effect. *Psychological Reports,* 1971, **29**, 1223–1228.

FLEMING, E. S., & ANTTONEN, R. G. Teacher-expectancy effect examined at different ability levels. *Journal of Special Education,* 1971a, **5**, 127–131.

FLEMING, E. S., & ANTTONEN, R. G. Teacher expectancy or My Fair Lady. *American Educational Research Journal,* 1971b, **8**, 241–252.

FONTANA, A. F., GESSNER, T., & LORR, M. How sick and what treatment: Patient presentations and staff judgments. *American Journal of Psychotherapy,* 1968, **22**, 26–34.

FRANK, J. D. The dynamics of the psychotherapeutic relationship: Determinants and effects of the therapist's influence. *Psychiatry,* 1959, **22**, 17–39.

FRANK, J. D. The influence of patients' and therapists' expectations on the outcome of psychotherapy. *British Journal of Medical Psychology,* 1968, **41**, 349–356.

FRIEDMAN, N., KURLAND, D., & ROSENTHAL, R. Experimenter behavior as an unintended determinant of experimental results. *Journal of Projective Techniques and. Personality Assessment,* 1965, **29**, 479–490.

GARFIELD, S. L., & AFFLECK, D. C. Therapists' judgments concerning patients considered for psychotherapy. *Journal of Consulting Psychology,* 1961, **25**, 505–509.

GEPHART, W. J. Will the real Pygmalion please stand up. *American Educational Research Journal,* 1970, **7**, 473–475.

GEPHART, W. J., & ANTONOPLOS, D. P. The effects of expectancy and other research-biasing factors. *Phi Delta Kappan,* 1969, **50**, 579–583.

GERGEN, K. J., & WISHNOV, B. Others' self-evaluations and interaction anticipation as determinants of self-presentation. *Journal of Personality and Social Psychology,* 1965, **2**, 348–358.

GOLDSTEIN, A. P. Therapist and client expectation of personality change in psychotherapy. *Journal of Counseling Psychology,* 1960, **7**, 180–184.

GOLDSTEIN, A. P. Participant expectancies in psychotherapy. *Psychiatry,* 1962a, **25**, 72–79.

GOLDSTEIN, A. P. *Therapist-patient expectancies in psychotherapy,* New York: MacMillan, 1962b.

GOZALI, J., & MEYEN, E. L. The influence of the teacher expectancy phenomenon on the academic performances of educable mentally retarded pupils in special classes. *Journal of Special Education,* 1970, **4**, 417–424.

HABERMAN, M. The relationship of bogus expectations to success in student teaching (or Pygmalion's illegitimate son). *Journal of Teacher Education,* 1970, **21**, 69–72.

HARVEY, O. J., & CLAPP, W. F. Hope, expectancy, and reactions to the unexpected. *Journal of Personality and Social Psychology,* 1965, **2**, 45–52.

HEATH, D. Stimulus similarity and task familiarity as determinants of expectancy generalization. *Journal of Experimental Psychology,* 1959, **58**, 289–294.

HEATH, D. Instructional sets as determinants of expectancy generalization. *Journal of General Psychology,* 1961, **64**, 285–295.

HEATH, D. Reinforcement and drive level as determinants of expectancy generalization. *Journal of General Psychology,* 1962, **67**, 69–82.

HELLER, K., & GOLDSTEIN, A. P. Client dependency and therapist expectancy as relationship maintaining variables in psychotherapy. *Journal of Consulting Psychology,* 1961, **25**, 371–375.

HERSH, J. B. Effects of referral information on testers. *Journal of Consulting and Clinical Psychology,* 1971, **37**, 116–122.

HILL, J. A. Therapist goals, patient aims and patient satisfaction in psychotherapy. *Journal of Clinical Psychology,* 1969, **25**, 455–459.

HORENSTEIN, D., HOUSTON, B. K., & HOLMES, D. S. Clients', therapists', and judges' evaluations of psychotherapy. *Journal of Counseling Psychology,* 1973, **20**, 149–153.

IRWIN, F. W. Stated expectations as functions of probability and desirability of outcome. *Journal of Personality,* 1953, **21**, 329–335.

JAMES, W. H., & ROTTER, J. B. Partial and 100% reinforcement under chance and skill conditions. *Journal of Experimental Psychology,* 1958, **55**, 397–403.

JESSOR, R. The generalization of expectancies. *Journal of Abnormal and Social Psychology,* 1954, **49**, 196–200.

JESSOR, R., & READIO, J. The influence of the value of an event upon the expectancy of its occurrence. *Journal of General Psychology,* 1957, **56**, 219–228.

JOHNSON, R. W., & ADAIR, J. G. The effects of systematic recording error vs. experimenter bias on latency of word association. *Journal of Experimental Research in Personality,* 1970, **4**, 270–275.

JOHNSON, T. J., FEIGENBAUM, R., & WEIBY, M. Some determinants and consequences of the teacher's perception of causation. *Journal of Educational Psychology,* 1964, **55**, 237–246.

JOSE, J., & CODY, J. J. Teacher-pupil interaction as it relates to attempted changes in teacher expectancy of academic ability and achievement. *American Educational Research Journal*, 1971, **8**, 39–49.

KANFER, F. H., DUERFELDT, P. H., MARTIN, B., & DORSEY, T. E. Effects of model reinforcement, expectation to perform, and task performance on model observation. *Journal of Personality and Social Psychology*, 1971, **20**, 214–217.

KEISNER, R. H. Affective reactions to expectancy disconfirmations under public and private conditions. *Journal of Personality and Social Psychology*, 1969, **11**, 17–24.

KORNREICH, L. B. Performance expectancy as a determinant of actual performance: Failure to replicate. *Psychological Reports*, 1968, **22**, 535–543.

KUMAR, U., & PEPINSKY, H. B. Counselor expectancies and therapeutic evaluations. *Procedings of the 73rd Annual Convention of the American Psychological Association*, 1965, **1**, 357–358.

LANNING, W. L. A study of the relationship between group and individual counseling supervision and three relationship measures. *Journal of Counseling Psychology*, 1971, **18**, 401–406.

LENNARD, H. L., & BERNSTEIN, A. *The anatomy of psychotherapy: Systems of communication and expectation.* New York: Columbia University Press, 1960.

LENNARD, H.L., & BERNSTEIN, A. Expectations and behavior in therapy. In B. J. BIDDLE & E. J. THOMAS (Eds.), *Role theory: Concepts and research.* New York: Wiley, 1966.

LERNER, B., & FISKE, D. W. Client attributes and the eye of the beholder. *Journal of Consulting and Clinical Psychology*, 1973, **40**, 272–277.

LOCKE, E. A. The relationship of task success to task liking and satisfaction. *Journal of Applied Psychology*, 1965, **49**, 379–385.

LOCKE, E. A. A closer look at level of aspiration as a training procedure: A reanalysis of Fryer's data. *Journal of Applied Psychology*, 1966a, **50**, 417–420.

LOCKE, E. A. The relationship of intentions to level of performance. *Journal of Applied Psychology*, 1966b, **50**, 60–66.

LOCKE, E. A. Motivational effects of knowledge of results: Knowledge or goal setting? *Journal of Applied Psychology*, 1967a, **51**, 324–329.

LOCKE, E. A. Relationship of goal level to performance level. *Psychological Reports*, 1967b, **20**, 1068.

LOCKE, E. A., & BRYAN, J. F. Cognitive aspects of psychomotor performance: The effects of performance goals on level of performance. *Journal of Applied Psychology*, 1966a, **50**, 286–291.

LOCKE, E. A., & BRYAN, J. F. The effects of goal-setting, rule-learning, and knowledge of score on performance. *American Journal of Psychology*, 1966b, **79**, 451–457.

LOCKE, E. A., & BRYAN, J. F. Performance goals as determinants of level of performance and boredom. *Journal of Applied Psychology*, 1967, **51**, 120–130.

LOCKE, E. A., & BRYAN, J. F. Knowledge of score and goal level as determinants of work rate. *Journal of Applied Psychology*, 1969, **53**, 59–65.

LOWIN, A., & EPSTEIN, G. F. Does expectancy determine performance? *Journal of Experimental Social Psychology*, 1965, **1**, 248–255.

MARCIA, J. E. The need for social approval, the condition of hypothesis-making, and their effects on unconscious experimenter bias. Unpublished masters thesis, Ohio State University, 1961.

MARCIA, J. E., RUBIN, B. M., & EFRAN, J. S. Systematic desensitization: Expectancy change or countercontioning? *Journal of Abnormal Psychology*, 1969, **74**, 382–387.

MARKS, R. W. The effect of probability, desirability, and "privilege" on the stated expectations of children. *Journal of Personality*, 1951, **19**, 332–351.

MARWIT, S. J. Communication of tester bias by means of modeling. *Journal of Projective Techniques and Personality Assessment*, 1969, **33**, 345–352.

MARWIT, S. J. Further notes on the effect of pretest expectancies on the psychological test report. *Journal of Personality Assessment*, 1971, **35**, 303–306.

MARWIT, S. J., & MARCIA, J. E. Tester bias and response to projective instruments. *Journal of Consulting Psychology*, 1967, **31**, 253–258.

MASLING, J. The influence of situational and interpersonal variables in projective testing. *Psychological Bulletin*, 1960, **57**, 65–85.

MASLING, J. Differential indoctrination of examiners and Rorschach responses. *Journal of Consulting Psychology*, 1965, **29**, 198–201.

McGLYNN, F. D., & WILLIAMS, C. W. Systematic desensitization of snake-avoidance under three conditions of suggestion. *Journal of Behavior Therapy and Experimental Psychiatry*, 1970, **1**, 97–101.

McNEAL, B. F., JOHNSTON, R., & ASPROMONTE, V. A. Effect of accurate forecasts on length of hospital stay of psychiatric patients. *Journal of Consulting and Clinical Psychology*, 1970, **35**, 91–94.

MEICHENBAUM, D. H., BOWERS, K. S., & ROSS, R. R. A behavioral analysis of teacher expectancy effect. *Journal of Personality and Social Psychology*, 1969, **13**, 306–316.

MEICHENBAUM, D. H., & SMART, I. Use of direct expectancy to modify academic performance and attitudes of college students. *Journal of Counseling Psychology*, 1971, **18**, 531–535.

MICHAUX, W. W., & LORR, M. Psychotherapists' treatment goals. *Journal of Counseling Psychology*, 1961, **8**, 250–254.

MIRELS, H., & MILLS, J. Perception of the pleasantness and competence of a partner. *Journal of Abnormal and Social Psychology*, 1964, **68**, 456–459.

MISCHEL, W. The effect of the commitment situation on the generalization of expectancies. *Journal of Personality*, 1958, **26**, 508–516.

MORAN, G., & KLOCKARS, A. J. Dissonance and performance alteration: Critique and empirical reexamination. *Journal of Social Psychology*, 1967, **72**, 249–255.

PALARDY, J. M. What teachers believe, What children achieve. *Elementary School Journal*, 1969, **69**, 370–374.

PELLEGRINI, R. J., & HICKS, R. A. Prophecy effects and tutorial instruction for the disadvantaged child. *American Educational Research Journal*, 1972, **9**, 413–419.

PERSINGER, G. W. The effect of acquaintanceship on the mediation of experimenter bias. Unpublished master's thesis, University of North Dakota, 1963.

PHARES, E. J. Expectancy changes in skill and chance situations. *Journal of Abnormal and Social Psychology*, 1957, **54**, 339–342.

PHARES, E. J. Expectancy changes under conditions of relative massing and spacing. *Psychological Reports*, 1961, **8**, 199–206.

PHARES, E. J. Perceptual threshold decrements as a function of skill and chance expectancies. *Journal of Psychology*, 1962, **53**, 399–407.

PHARES, E. J. Additional effects of massing and spacing on expectancies. *Journal of General Psychology*, 1964a, **70**, 215–223.

PHARES, E. J. Delay as a variable in expectancy changes. *Journal of Psychology*, 1964b, **57**, 391–402.

PLUMB, G. R., & CHARLES, D. C. Scoring difficulty of Wechsler Comprehension responses. *Journal of Educational Psychology*, 1955, **46**, 179–183.

ROSENTHAL, R. Unintended effects of the clinician in clinical interaction: A taxonomy and a review of clinician expectancy effects. *Australian Journal of Psychology*, 1969, **21**, 1–20.

ROSENTHAL, R., FRIEDMAN, C. J., JOHNSON, C. A., FODE, K., SCHILL, T., WHITE, R. C., & VIKAN, L. L. Variables affecting the experimenter bias in a group situation. *Genetic Psychology Monographs*, 1964, **70**, 271–296.

ROSENTHAL, R., & JACOBSON, L. *Pygmalion in the classroom: Teacher expectation and pupils' intellectual development.* New York: Holt, Rinehart & Winston, 1968.

354 EFFECTIVE PSYCHOTHERAPY

ROSENTHAL, R., PERSINGER, G. W., MULRY, R. C., VIKAN-KLINE, L., & GROTHE, M. Changes in experimental hypotheses as determinants of experimental results. *Journal of Projective Techniques and Personality Assessment*, 1964, **28**, 465–469.

ROTHBART, M., DALFEN, S., & BARRETT, R. Effects of teacher's expectancy on student-teacher interaction. *Journal of Educational Psychology*, 1971, **62**, 49–54.

RYCHLAK, J. F. Task-influence and the stability of generalized expectancies. *Journal of Experimental Psychology*, 1958, **55**, 459–462.

RYCHLAK, J. F., & EACKER, J. N. The effects of anxiety, delay, and reinforcement on generalized expectancies. *Journal of Personality*, 1962, **30**, 123–134.

SAMPSON, E. E., & SIBLEY, L. B. A further examination of the confirmation or nonconfirmation of expectancies and desires. *Journal of Personality and Social Psychology*, 1965, **2**, 133–137.

SARASON, I. G. The effects of anxiety and threat on the solution of a difficult task. *Journal of Abnormal and Social Psychology*, 1961, **62**, 165–168.

SATTLER, J. M., HILLIX, W. A., & NEHER, L. A. Halo effect in examiner scoring of intelligence test responses. *Journal of Consulting and Clinical Psychology*, 1970, **34**, 172–176.

SATTLER, J. M., & THEYE, F. Procedural, situational, and interpersonal variables in individual intelligence testing. *Psychological Bulletin*, 1967, **68**, 347–360.

SATTLER, J. M., & WINGET, B. M. Intelligence testing procedures as affected by expectancy and I.Q. *Journal of Clinical Psychology*, 1970, **26**, 446–448.

SATTLER, J. M., WINGET, B. M., & ROTH, R. J. Scoring difficulty of WAIS and WISC comprehension, similarities, and vocabulary responses. *Journal of Clinical Psychology*, 1969, **25**, 175–177.

SAUNDERS, B. T., & DiTULLIO, W. M. The failure of biased information to affect teacher behavior ratings and peer sociometric status of disturbing children in the classroom. *Psychology in the Schools*, 1972, **9**, 440–445.

SAUNDERS, B. T., & VITRO, F. T. Examiner expectancy and bias as a function of the referral process in cognitive assessment. *Psychology in the Schools*, 1971, **8**, 168–171.

SCHOPLER, J., & LAYTON, B. Determinants of the self-attribution of having influenced another person. *Journal of Personality and Social Psychology*, 1972, **22**, 326–332.

SCHRANK, W. R. The labeling effect of ability grouping. *Journal of Educational Research*, 1968, **62**, 51–52.

SCHRANK, W. R. A further study of the labeling effect of ability grouping. *Journal of Educational Research*, 1970, **63**, 358–360.

SCHROEDER, H. E., & KLEINSASSER, L. D., Examiner bias: A determinant of children's verbal behavior on the WISC. *Journal of Consulting and Clinical Psychology*, 1972, **39**, 451–454.

SCHWARTZ, M. L. The scoring of WAIS Comprehension responses by experienced and inexperienced judges. *Journal of Clinical Psychology*, 1966, **22**, 425–427.

SCHWARZ, J. C. Influences upon expectancy during delay. *Journal of Experimental Research in Personality*, 1966, **1**, 211–220.

SCHWARZ, J. C. The contribution of generalized expectancy to stated expectancy under conditions of success and failure. *Journal of Personality and Social Psychology*, 1969, **11**, 157–164.

SCHWARZ, J. C., GOLD, G., & SEEMAN, G. A comparison of massed and spaced extinction of expectancies for success. *Journal of Experimental Research in Personality*, 1970, **4**, 129–134.

SILVERMAN, I. The effects of experimenter outcome expectancy on latency of word association. *Journal of Clinical Psychology*, 1968, **2**, 60–63.

SILVERMAN, I., & MARCANTONIO, C. Demand characteristics versus dissonance reduction as determinants of failure-seeking behavior. *Journal of Personality and Social Psychology*, 1965, **2**, 882–884.

SIMON, J. R., SHAW, M. E., & GILCHRIST, J. C. Some effects of prearranged performance scores upon level of aspiration. *Journal of Experimental Psychology*, 1954, **47**, 10–12.

SIMON, W. E. Expectancy effects in the scoring of vocabulary items: A study of scorer bias. *Journal of Educational Measurement*, 1969, **6**, 159–164.

SNOW, R. E. Unfinished pygmalion. *Contemporary Psychology*, 1969, **14**, 197–199.

STRAUSS, M. E. Examiner expectancy: Effects on Rorschach experience balance. *Journal of Consulting and Clinical Psychology*, 1968a, **32**, 125–129.

STRAUSS, M. E. The influence of pre-testing information on Rorschach based personality reports. *Journal of Projective Techniques and Personality Assessment*, 1968b, **32**, 323–325.

STRAUSS, M. E., & MARWIT, S. J. Expectancy effects in Rorschach testing. *Journal of Consulting and Clinical Psychology*, 1970, **34**, 448.

STRUPP, H. H. The psychotherapist's contribution to the treatment process. *Behavioral Science*, 1958, **3**, 34–67.

STRUPP, H. H., & WILLIAMS, J. V. Some determinants of clinical evaluations of different psychiatrists. *Archives of General Psychiatry*, 1960, **2**, 434–440.

TEMERLIN, M. K., & TROUSDALE, W. W. The social psychology of clinical diagnosis. *Psychotherapy: Theory, Research and Practice*, 1969, **6**, 24–29.

THORNDIKE, R. L. Review of "Pygmalion in the classroom." *American Educational Research Journal*, 1968, **5**, 708–711.

TRATTNER, J. H., & HOWARD, K. I. A preliminary investigation of covert communication of expectancies to schizophrenics. *Journal of Abnormal Psychology*, 1970, **75**, 245–247.

UHLENHUTH, E. H., CANTER, A., NEUSTADT, J. O., & PAYSON, H. E. The symptomatic relief of anxiety with meprobamate, phenobarbital and placebo. *American Journal of Psychiatry*, 1959, **115**, 905–910.

WALKER, R. E., HUNT, W. A., & SCHWARTZ, M. L. The difficulty of WAIS comprehension scoring. *Journal of Clinical Psychology*, 1965, **21**, 427–429.

WARD, W. D., & SANDVOLD, K. D. Performance expectancy as a determinant of actual performance: A partial replication. *Journal of Abnormal and Social Psychology*, 1963, **67**, 293–295.

WATERMAN, A. S., & FORD, L. H. Performance expectancy as a determinant of actual performance: Dissonance reduction or differential recall? *Journal of Personality and Social Psychology*, 1965, **2**, 464–467.

WHITE, C. R. The effect of induced subject expectations on the experimenter bias situation. Unpublished doctoral dissertation, University of North Dakota, 1962.

WILKINS, W. Client's expectancy of therapeutic gain: Evidence for the active role of the therapist. *Psychiatry*, 1973a, **36**, 184–190.

WILKINS, W. Expectancy of therapeutic gain: An empirical and conceptual critique. *Journal of Consulting and Clinical Psychology*, 1973b, **40**, 69–77.

WORELL, L. The effect of goal value upon expectancy. *Journal of Abnormal and Social Psychology*, 1956, **53**, 48–53.

ZAJONC, R. B., & BRICKMAN, P. Expectancy and feedback as independent factors in task performance. *Journal of Personality and Social Psychology*, 1969, **11**, 148–156.

ZEGERS, R. A. Expectancy and the effects of confirmation and disconfirmation. *Journal of Personality and Social Psychology*, 1968, **9**, 67–71.

EDITORS' REFERENCES

JOSE, J., & CODY, J. J. Teacher-pupil interaction as it relates to attempted changes in teacher expectancy of academic ability and achievement. *American Educational Research Journal*, 1971, **8**, 39–49.

MARWIT, S. J., & MARCIA, J. E. Tester bias and response to projective instruments. *Journal of Consulting Psychology*, 1967, **31**, 253–258.

MEICHENBAUM, D. H., BOWERS, K. S., & ROSS, R. R. A behavioral analysis of teacher expectancy effect. *Journal of Personality and Social Psychology*, 1969, **13**, 306–316.

NOTES

1. *Editors' Footnote.* Later in this chapter, in his discussion of the utility of therapist expectancy, Wilkins argues that the observable procedures used to instill an unobservable expectancy will explain and account for everything an expectancy accounts for, and that the whole concept of expectancy therefore becomes superfluous. This is an interesting point, which we will comment on (Footnote 5), but here we would like to note that Marwit and Marcia demonstrate that a given expectancy can apparently be "instilled" in more than one way—i.e., by instructions and as well by a set of life experiences probably not specifiable at the time of research. Importantly, the expectancy derived by whatever means is associated with the same outcome. This is obviously not a very startling set of facts. It is important, though, because it suggests that, although Wilkins' argument is logically and scientifically impeccable, practically expectancy is a valuable construct because it represents a final common pathway with predictive utility for any number of antecedent events, many of which are unspecifiable.

2. *Editors' Footnote.* In this study, however, Ss' behavior was staged and thus immune to agent (tester) influences and presumably invariant. If expectancy effects operate via the induction of *client* changes in behavior, the methodology of this study (while it convincingly demonstrates the relative power of actual client behavior) thus precluded an important possible mechanism for the operation of expectancy effect. It is perhaps better regarded as a demonstration of the power of disconfirmatory information.

3. *Editors' Footnote.* It impresses us as a very striking "success" of manipulation that teachers should persist in their expectancy-induced perceptions despite evidence of contrary objective performance. The reader will most likely conclude, by the time he finishes this chapter, that Wilkins very astutely, thoroughly, and convincingly demonstrates that expectancies simply do not exert the kind of sweeping effects on therapy and educational outcome suggested by earlier empirical and other literature. One of our conclusions, though, is that, under certain circumstances, expectations do effect behavioral changes in agents (teachers, therapists, diagnosticians, etc.) that *may*, in turn, effect changes in their clients. That is, we still feel that there may be very limited, but nonetheless potentially demonstrable, expectancy effects on client behavior. We thus think that the reader is likely to come away with a balanced impression if, in the face of all the disconfirmatory data, he also notes the several instances where expectancies do surprisingly persist and/or affect agent behavior in ways not immediately apparent.

In the present (Jose and Cody, 1971) case of "late bloomers," for example, it is clear that from a formal scientific viewpoint no expectancy effect occurred. But *practically* speaking, we think that expectancy "effects" have been demonstrated; we find it hard to imagine, for example, that such persisting impressions among teachers (or therapists or diagnosticians) will have no consequences for their clients. In the real world, these agents do often make decisions about their clients' careers and dispositions, and we thus think that the demonstration of even the persistence of an expectancy should not be considered trivial.

4. *Editors' Footnote.* This to us is a good example of a nontrivial, practical consequence (see Footnote 3) of an expectancy—a change in the behavior of an agent that would easily affect clients in important ways.

5. *Editors' Footnote.* This is an interesting, provocative point with which we do not wholly agree. It is true from a black-box empiricist viewpoint that observable procedures are as inclusive a causal explanation of expectancy-related behavior as is an unobservable expectancy. But if there are several "procedures" (sets of prior events) which can instill the same expectancy, then expectancy has value not only as a shorthand for stating that procedures are as inclusive a causal explanation of expectancy- For expectancy also, then, has deterministic value as a mediating variable (if its "existence" is demonstrable) or event along a final common pathway. Furthermore, it has inferential scientific value, for we may tentatively assume (if A through N is a long enough list) that several, or perhaps any, procedures which instill this given expectancy will tend to produce the same behavioral outcome.

Furthermore, as we have pointed out (Footnote 1), many (perhaps most) of the really important expectancy-shaping "procedures" are cumulated life experiences which are lost to us at any one moment at which we may choose to study expectancies' effects. And, as we also point out in the earlier note, there is at least a bit of evidence (Marwit & Marcia, 1967) supporting our "multi-procedure" line of reasoning.

6. *Editors' Footnote.* This is a crucial point. Apparently, the same expectancy can bring about very different agent behaviors, which in turn can bring about very different outcomes (Meichenbaum *et al.*, 1969). This suggests, not surprisingly, that there is an interaction between expectancy and other factors (e.g., agent "personality") in evolving outcome. Wilkins' two steps are quite necessary, then, because expectancy may well be a two-edged sword, which can, for example, promote both helping and harming agent behaviors such as increased or decreased patient contact. (Could much of the failure to document clear expectancy effects be attributed to a mutual "canceling out" of opposite effects?) More precise delineation, therefore, of the chain of events (both behavioral and cognitive) leading to outcome is necessary before conclusions, positive or negative, about expectancy can be considered definitive.

CHAPTER 14

RESEARCH ON THERAPEUTIC STYLE

BENJAMIN POPE

DEFINITIONAL ASPECTS

The domain of the present chapter is that of therapist *style*. A person positioned at the geographical center of the territory so designated would have no difficulty in making a number of general statements about the character of the area in which he stands. But if he were given the task of demarcating its borders, he could accomplish it only with great difficulty and after considerable negotiation with spokesmen for the territories that surround him. Since such multilateral negotiations are not practical, under present circumstances, an attempt will be made, instead, to define the assigned region in a manner that will facilitate minimal overlap with adjoining areas.

What then is to be included in a chapter dealing with therapeutic style? Kiesler (1973) refers to *stylistics* as a component of psycholinguistics applied to psychotherapy process studies. He goes on to characterize it as "... the study of individual differences in the selection of words in various contexts" (p. 8). This aspect of verbal style was brought home to the present author recently when he was asked to review an article submitted to a psychology journal. Although the article was reviewed under the usual conditions of author anonymity, the identity of the author was apparent to the reviewer from the imprint of such aspects of verbal style as idiosyncratic preference for certain words and forms of sentence structure. One attribute of style is quite evidently its idiosyncratic character.

The linguist studies style in verbal communication only. But not all aspects of verbal communication serve equally well as vehicles of style. Mahl (1963) subdivides speech into its lexical and nonlexical aspects, and locates style not exclusively but most clearly in the *nonlexical* aspects. For Mahl, the most significant locus of style is not the manifest content of what is said, but rather how it is said. The mode or style of communicating content is sought in *nonlexical linguistic* indexes such as grammatical aspects of language and in *nonlexical, extralinguistic* aspects of speech such as rate of speech, duration of utterances, and speech disruptions.

It is in the nonlexical channels of verbal behavior that one hears the relatively uncontrolled expression of affect that the speaker may not intentionally wish to communicate. Thus, a therapist attuned to the emergence of anxiety in a patient is most likely to hear it in verbal rate and speech disruption rather than in the manifest content of the message. These are the modalities of speech which express affect directly. Such expressiveness is considered to be a second attribute of style, on a par with its idiosyncratic character.

The ambiguity of the term "style" becomes increasingly evident as one separates out its definitional ingredients. For example, what is meant precisely by the term "expressiveness"? Although the concept has thus far been applied to linguistic and extralinguistic aspects of speech only, Dittman (1963) speaks without hesitation about *expressive movement*. He postulates and partially demonstrates that movement expresses something inside the person such as affect, mood, or tension. In this sense stylistic expressiveness (now attributed to both verbal and nonverbal communication) performs a discharge function; through expression, it reduces the level of tension or mood within the organism. But discharge is not the sole function of expressiveness. Almost by semantic definition, it refers to communication as well. Thus, when a person becomes agitated in an interview situation he may express his psychological condition through elevated motility, increased verbal rate, and flustering of speech; in doing so he may be momentarily discharging the tensions within. But, wittingly or unwittingly, he is simultaneously making his condition known to his dyadic partner—i.e., he is communicating it. In the process of communicating he is influencing the other person, evoking his support, or eliciting some other reaction. In an interpersonal sense, therefore, the interviewer's expressiveness performs an instrumental (Dittman, 1963) function as well. It need hardly be added that the three functions of expressiveness are by no means independent of each other. Thus, the discharge of tension may very well be facilitated by its communication to others.

If therapist style is idiosyncratic, and performs expressive and instrumental functions, it must cut a broad swath indeed through therapy process studies. It appears more relevant to process than outcome because it occurs at the immediate interface between the two participants in an interview, as they interact with each other. Its impact on both communication and relationship will therefore be the focus of most studies reviewed in the present chapter.

The stylistic differences between proponents of different therapeutic schools have been considerably explored (Matarazzo, 1965). Without benefit of formal investigation, one may obtain an impression of stylistic contrasts by reading the verbatim transcripts of interviews representing a psychoanalytic (Nemiah, 1961), a Sullivanian (Will & Cohen, 1953), and a Rogerian (Seeman, 1957) orientation. These interviews contrast markedly in the content elicited from the interviewee. Just as decided are the following stylistic differences between the interviewers. The psychoanalytically oriented interviewer (Nemiah, 1961) lets his patient tell his story in his own way. To grant the interviewee the latitude needed to do so, the interviewer's questions are ambiguous in character. Although not passive, the interviewer is permissive, directing the course of the interview through selective attention rather than through a more directive form of guidance. The following words describing the psychoanalytically oriented interview are stylistic references: "ambiguous," "permissive," but not "passive."

The words that describe the style of the Sullivanian interview (Will & Cohen, 1953) are somewhat different. The therapist is more "active" and "productive" than the first one, without being more "directive." Above all, he is more personally "expressive." In the Rogerian interview (Seeman, 1957) the therapist limits himself to "reflective" remarks, remaining moderately "productive" while expressing an "accepting" and "empathic" attitude.

The first group of studies below will be based on multidimensional systems of stylistic analysis. In these, the authors strive for comprehensiveness, for breadth rather than for the definitional specification of stylistic variables. These were the earliest investigations in therapeutic style, applied to the gross comparison of therapy schools. It was only later that investigators worked with single dimensions of style, more rigorously defined and directed toward nicer comparisons than those based on therapist school of allegiance.

MULTIDIMENSIONAL STUDIES

With the emergence of nondirective counseling in the early 1940s, psychotherapy research began to focus on its process and particularly on the style of the therapist. While much had been said in the early 1940s about the principles and goals of nondirective therapy, it was not until somewhat later that investigators developed systems for describing the therapy process that could be used for differentiating the nondirective orientation from other approaches. The early studies in this area were contained within linguistic channels and were based on content.

The first Rogerian researcher to develop a content-analytic scheme for studying the process of psychotherapy was Porter (1943). Extending and modifying Porter's scheme, Snyder (1945) constructed one which achieved a greater utility and a much broader application over a period of several years. Only his counselor categories will be presented in brief form at this point; they include *lead taking* (structuring, forcing client to choose and develop topic, directive questions which require the giving of factual information, nondirective leads and questions which encourage the client to enlarge on his communication), *nondirective response-to-feeling* (simple acceptance, restatement of content or problem, clarification or recognition of feeling), *semidirective response to feeling* (interpretation), and *directive counseling categories* (approval and encouragement, giving information or explanation, proposing client activity, persuasion, disapproval, and criticism).

The language designating the above categories is dated by now, but the focus of the scheme on the issues of counselor lead and directiveness remains currently relevant. The system was applied to typed verbatim transcripts of psychotherapy interviews. In his 1945 study, based on 48 therapy interviews obtained from six clients and four nondirective counselors, Snyder's purpose was to assess the relative efficacy of directive and nondirective therapist style. His four counselors utilized clarification of feeling in approximately half of their statements. In reaction, their clients expressed understanding and insight in 12% of their responses at the beginning of therapy, but increased this category to 30% at the end. The most frequent response to a nondirective lead by a counselor was the client's statement of his problem. On the other hand, the client was seldom induced to express his problems by the counselor's structuring of the interview, direct questioning or clarification of feeling, and almost never by interpretation, persuasion, or disapproval and criticism. Although the results were not all congruent with principles of nondirective therapy, Snyder (1945) felt that they were sufficiently so for him to conclude: "The facts of the present study clearly support the theory that it is the nondirective elements of this type of treatment which produce the favorable change in the client's behavior. What directive elements exist are unfavorably received" (p. 203).

In the beginning, then, therapist style was demonstrated to relate to therapist orientation. Moreover, Snyder (1945) operationalized the directive and nondirective approaches and demonstrated the greater efficacy of the latter.

Five years after Snyder's first study, Fiedler appeared to challenge his major thesis of a stylistic distinction between therapists adhering to different schools of orientation with his classic work on the ideal therapeutic relationship (Fiedler, 1950a, 1950b). First (1950b) he asked therapists from the psychoanalytic, Adlerian, and nondirective schools to describe their concepts of an ideal therapeutic relationship by means of a Q-sort assembly of 75 statements. What emerged was a high level of agreement among Ss from the various schools. A finding that Fiedler made much of was the higher level of congruence between experienced rather than inexperienced therapists, regardless of school of allegiance. Indeed two experienced therapists from different schools were more likely to agree with each other than were an experienced and inexperienced therapist within the same school.

In a second study (1950a) Fiedler asked an analogous group of therapists to use the same Q sort as an instrument for rating recordings of actual therapist behavior. The results were essentially the same. Experienced therapists of the three schools evaluated therapist behavior in the same way, differing, however, from inexperienced therapists in their own schools. A subsequent factor analysis (Fiedler, 1951) yielded one general relationship factor out of the intercorrelations of the 75 items of the Fiedler Q sort.

This has been designated as an accurate empathy factor (Kiesler, 1973), on which the following items are some of those that were positively loaded:

"Is able to participate completely in the patient's communication."

"Comments are always right in line with what the patient is trying to convey."

"Really tries to understand the patient's feelings" (Kiesler, 1973, p. 341).

The inconsistency between the Snyder and Fiedler studies is not surprising since the two authors sampled different aspects of therapist behavior. The stylistic elements rated by Snyder related to directive and nondirective categories of verbal response. In fact, they were highly salient to the central element in nondirective practice. By contrast, Fiedler's array of therapist behaviors emphasized general aspects of relationship not as likely to differentiate between the processes emphasized by the three schools investigated. Historically, the studies by Snyder and Fiedler are significant because they posed a central problem that researchers in the realm of therapy style and process grappled with for nearly two decades—i.e., the relative weights of therapist school of allegiance and therapist experience in determining style of therapist behavior. Most of the multidimensional studies reviewed below addressed themselves to this problem.

Strupp's work (1958, 1960) dominated the scene in the late 1950s. During this period, his efforts were directed toward the descriptive study of therapeutic style with an approach that was largely exploratory. His system consisted of two basic categories for classifying a therapist's communication—*Type of Therapeutic Activity* and *Dynamic Focus*. Under *Type of Therapeutic Activity*, Strupp included such major techniques as facilitating communication ("Go on"), exploratory operations ("Tell me what you can about your father"), interpretive operations ("You reacted to your teacher as you often have toward your father"), structuring remarks ("My practice will not be to instruct you on how to conduct your life, but rather to listen to your thoughts and feelings and to respond when I feel I have something helpful to say"), direct guidance ("I don't think you should ask your wife to stay home from work whenever you think you may be catching a cold"), activity not clearly relevant to the task of therapy ("You can reach Annapolis by taking the Mountain Rd"), and other responses not classifiable. (The examples are the present author's and not Strupp's.) *Dynamic Focus* appears to consist of two, apparently confounded dimensions. One pertains to the therapist's tendency either to go along with the patient's topical focus through remaining silent, passive acceptance, reflecting of feeling, and nondirective questions, or on the contrary, to take the initiative in changing the topical focus. The second dimension pertains to topical content, including such categories as asking for additional information about a topic under discussion and changing the focus to past events, present events, and the therapist-patient relationship. In addition to the two basic sets of categories there are three intensity scales— *depth-directedness* (noninferential to highly inferential statements), *therapist initiative* (similar to directiveness), *and therapeutic climate* (coldness-rejection to warmth-acceptance). In the above process system the concern appeared to be more with overall comprehensiveness than with the refinement of the separate dimensions.

In the first study based on this system reported by Strupp (1958) the therapist sample was a completely medical one. The procedure followed in gathering data was as follows. A film of an initial interview with a male phobic patient was shown to groups of Ss. At 28 points within the interview, the film was stopped and Ss were asked to respond to the question: "What would you do?" The Ss, all psychiatrists, were requested to cast themselves in the role of the filmed patient's therapist and write their response on a record blank provided them.

In the context of the initial interview the Ss, in general, tended to use responses that evoked information from the patient, avoiding highly inferential communications. As to the experienced-inexperienced distinction, the experienced rather than inexperienced psychiatrists asked fewer exploratory questions, gave more interpretation communications (at a higher level of inference, with a focus on interpersonal events in the patient's life), showed a higher level of initiative, changed the focus of communication more, and tended to be slightly warmer. With reference to the apparently greater warmth of more rather than less experienced psychiatrists, it should be noted that the rating of warmth and coldness was accomplished with a great deal of uncertainty and no reliability check because of the absence from the protocol data used of important non-verbal cues of affect. In general, with experience came a reduced emphasis on interrogatory remarks and a greater degree of interpretation

and activity. Finally, Strupp compared his more and less experienced groups on one additional variable, an overall evaluation of each protocol on empathy, and found no significant differences between them.

Since *experience* may interact with the professional discipline to which a therapist belongs, the above findings for psychiatrists were compared with analogous ones for psychologists. Unlike the psychiatrists, who manifested several stylistic differences based on experience, the psychologists demonstrated only two. Like the psychiatrists, the psychologists demonstrated an increase of warmth with experience. In addition, the number of communications in which the psychologist appeared as an expert or an authority also increased with experience, a finding which did not occur in the psychiatrist data.

Other comparisons between the two disciplines were made after they were equated for length of experience and personal analysis. In contrast to psychologists, psychiatrists asked a significantly larger number of exploratory questions, used less reflection of feeling in the Rogerian sense, and changed the focus of the interview more. The above differences appear to reflect a more marked Rogerian orientation among psychologists than psychiatrists.

To further clarify the stylistic character of Rogerian psychotherapy, with the discipline of the therapist kept constant, Rogerian therapists (all psychologists) were compared with psychologists who represented a psychoanalytic orientation. In general, the Rogerian psychologists assumed a more positive attitude to the patient than those with a psychoanalytic orientation; a greater number of them judged the patient's prognosis with therapy to be favorable and rated their personal reaction to the patient as positive. The greater tendency of Rogerian rather than analytical psychologists to stay within the patient's frame of reference was noted in the more frequent reluctance of the former group to set up therapy goals, to refer to countertransference as a factor in treatment, and to emphasize any specific areas of living in treatment.

Rogerians were more frequently reluctant than analytical therapists to encourage specified patient attitudes or behaviors. By contrast, analytical therapists were more likely to prompt the patient to develop a sense of responsibility and increased socialization, and to discourage such attitudes and behaviors as intellectualization, obsessive-ruminations, helplessness, and other symptomatic and maladaptive forms of behavior. Although there was no difference between the two groups on activity-passivity, the analytical therapists tended to recommend therapist firmness with the patient, a response lacking in the Rogerian group. In contrast to analytical therapists, few Rogerians paid attention to such clues as gestures, body movements, patient style of speaking, and interpersonal relationships with significant others. Instead, the Rogerians were preeminent in their attention to patient feelings and attitudes, without specifying the channels of communication through which such attitudes and feelings were to be expressed. Most pointedly, the client-centered group tended to emphasize the reflection and clarification of feeling, while the analytical group advocated interpretation, reassurance, and firmness.

None of the contrasts between the Rogerian and analytical groups of therapists comes as any surprise; all are congruent with the theoretical orientations and practices advocated by both groups. What Strupp has contributed is a carefully etched description of stylistic behaviors advocated by psychotherapists of both persuasions.

Several authors have used multidimensional rating systems to distinguish between good and poor therapy hours. For example, Orlinsky and Howard (1967) characterized good psychotherapy hours as "...experiential in manner...." Such hours were "actively collaborative and generally warm and affectively both expressive and involving. Moreover, the manner of therapeutic work in the 'good' therapy sessions was essentially symmetrical; that is, similar for both patient and therapist, rather than sharply differentiated" (Orlinsky & Howard, 1967, p. 630).

Conceptualizing the psychotherapeutic interview as a dyadic communication system, Lennard and Bernstein (1960) compared those interviews in which patients felt communication flowed easily with those they rated as difficult, a comparison which is roughly analogous to that between good and poor therapy hours. In the sessions rated as easy, rather than difficult, therapist and patient verbal output was greater, the number of interactions between the two members of the dyad was greater, and therapists were somewhat more productive in relation to the productivity of the patients. Therapists asked fewer questions and their statements were less ambiguous (i.e., more specific). Patients tended to change the topic less frequently.

Therapists communicated more affective statements both in absolute terms and relative to the number of affective expressions by the patients. In brief, patients preferred therapy sessions in which the therapist was active, productive, avoided a high level of interrogation and ambiguity, and was emotionally expressive.

It was inevitable that at some point in the use of multidimensional schemes in process research questions would be raised about the comparability of dimensions similarly labeled and, indeed, about the meaning of the dimensions used. These questions led to a series of unidimensional studies, less comprehensive and less directly clinical in character, but more illuminating of the stylistic components in the therapeutic interview. Moreover, the unidimensional (or two or three dimensional) studies often went beyond procedures based on the rating of linguistic content in naturalistic interviews to the experimental manipulation of variables in psychotherapy analogue studies. These will be considered later under a number of different headings. For now, the focus will be on a number of investigations, still multidimensional, still complex, and directly clinical, but utilizing factor analysis as a means of bringing a degree of simple structure into the confusing assemblies of redundant ratings.

An early study in the above-designated group (Sundland & Barker, 1962) stated its objectives in the following terms: "...the first, to develop an economic and comprehensive measure of psychotherapeutic orientation; the second to obtain actuarial information about the methods and attitudes of psychotherapists" (Sundland & Barker, 1962, p. 201). The authors elicited responses from 139 members of the American Psychological Association who were active in psychotherapy. They used a questionnaire entitled the Therapist Orientation Questionnaire, consisting of 133 items pertaining to therapist attitudes and methods to which the Ss responded by scoring each item on a 5-point Likert-type scale. Factor analysis was used to validate the *a priori* placement of items in subtests with titles such as, "Frequency of Activity," "Type of Activity," "Emotional Tenor of Relationship," and others. The most illuminating finding was the emergence of a general, second-order factor which cut across the majority of scales, with one extreme labeled the *analytic* pole and the other, the experiential pole. The former pole is characterized by subtests that emphasize "...conceptualizing, the training of the therapist, planning of therapy, unconscious process, and a restriction of therapist spontaneity. The experiential pole de-emphasizes conceptualizing and unconscious process stressing instead the personality of the therapist, an unplanned approach to therapy, and therapist spontaneity" (Sundland & Barker, 1962, p. 205).

The above data were also used to test the perennial hypotheses that psychotherapist style would vary with school of allegiance and with experience. All respondents were assigned to one of three schools, designated Freudian, Rogerian, and Sullivanian. The greatest difference in attitude, as measured by the scale used, occurred between the Freudians and Rogerians. Limiting the report of findings to stylistic variables only, one notes that the Freudians emphasized the use of interpretation, the usefulness of conceptualizing causation, the therapist's impersonality and inhibited spontaneity. By contrast, the Rogerians placed a great deal more emphasis on spontaneity. With the Freudians and Rogerians as two poles of a continuum, the Sullivanians fell somewhere in between. They were closer to the Freudians than the Rogerians in stressing planning and conceptualization and closer to the Rogerians in their preference for personal expressiveness. When experience was used as the basis of comparison, there was only one significant difference: the less experienced group espoused a self-actualizing theory of personal growth to a greater degree than the more experienced group did. The authors concluded: "In terms of the attitudes measured here the differences between therapists are clearly better accounted for by their theoretical orientation than by their amount of experience" (Sundland & Barker, 1962, p. 208).

While still dealing with the problem of delineating stylistic dimensions in psychotherapist behavior, Lorr (1965) used as his data the perceptions of therapists by their clients. Borrowing from previous investigators (Apfelbaum, 1958; Fiedler, 1950b; Leary, 1957), Lorr constructed a questionnaire based on eight hypothesized dimensions, including 65 statements. The inventory was administered to 523 patients in individual therapy in 43 veterans' clinics. In each response the patient indicated how often the therapist exhibited the behavior described (almost never, sometimes, usually, nearly always). The responses of the patients were intercorrelated and the following five orthogonal factors extracted, all descriptive of therapist style of relationship: *understanding* ("Seems to know exactly what I say"; "Seems to understand how I feel"; "Understands me even when I don't

express myself well"), *accepting* ("Shows a real interest in me and my problems"; "Makes me feel that he is one person I can really trust"; "Shows a real liking and affection for me"), *authoritarian* ("Is full of advice about everything I do"; "Tells me what to do when I have difficult decisions to make"; "Seems to try to get me to accept his ideas and opinions"), *independence encouraging* ("Expects an individual to shoulder his own responsibilities"; "Encourages me to work on my problems in my own way"), and *critical-hostile* ("Becomes impatient when I make mistakes"; "Acts smug and superior as though he knew all the answers"; "Gives me the impression that he doesn't like me").

Later, Lorr and McNair (1966) reported several relationships between the above dimensions in therapist style and outcome variables. Thus, patient ratings of therapist *understanding* and *accepting* correlated positively with patient ratings of their own improvement; they also correlated at a somewhat lower level but still significantly with therapist ratings of patient improvement. On the other hand, patient ratings of therapists on the *authoritarian* and *critical-hostile* dimensions, correlated negatively with patient self-ratings of improvement and satisfaction in treatment. Because the above variables overlap with those used by Fiedler (1950b) in characterizing the good therapeutic relationship, they provide some additional support for Fiedler's conceptualization of the ideal therapeutic relationship.

Reference was made above to the study by Apfelbaum (1958) dealing with transference parameters. This investigation will be summarized briefly at this point because it resembles the Lorr (1965) study in two ways: (a) it is concerned with therapist style as it applies to his relationship with the patient, and (b) it is based on the patient's perceptions of the therapist's role. The author asked each of 100 individuals seen in a university outpatient psychiatric clinic to Q sort statements pertaining to patients' expectations, pre-therapy, about the role behavior that they expect their prospective psychotherapists to manifest. Ratings for the various items were intercorrelated, and then cluster-analyzed with the following three types of therapist role behavior emerging:

1. The *nurturant* therapist is supportive, protective, and willing to guide the patient, actively helping him in his problem areas.

2. The *model* therapist is an interested, tolerant listener, tending to be permissive and nonjudgmental. While he is not prone to evaluate

his patients or respond to them critically, neither is he particularly protective. Basically, he is perceived by his patients as well adjusted, interested, but not highly responsive.

3. The therapist as *critic* is judgmental and expects his patients to show a high level of responsibility. Of the three types, the *critic* is least benign, largely lacking in permissiveness or supportiveness.

Apfelbaum's (1958) findings about the correlates of the patients' perceptions of three styles of therapist relationship were not extensive. Moreover, the evidence he produced addressed itself to problems that were quite different from those with which the other studies in the present series were concerned. Thus, Apfelbaum (1958) found that those patients who expected a *model* therapist demonstrated lower dropout rates than the others who anticipated *nurturant* and *critical* therapists. On the other hand, those with *nurturant* expectations of the therapist, who remained in therapy, stayed longer than the others. Since all Ss had taken the MMPI, it was possible to obtain MMPI correlates of the three patterns of expectation. Patients with both *nurturant* and *critical* expectations started psychotherapy with higher maladjustment scores and more distress than those who expected their therapists to demonstrate *model* behavior.

Returning to the Lorr investigations, it is noted that McNair and Lorr (1964) developed an additional 57-item inventory, most of which was borrowed and modified from Sundland and Barker (1962). In this instance therapist style was investigated in the area of technique and communication rather than relationship. Three postulated factors included items descriptive of a psychoanalytical style (A), an impersonal style (I), and an active, directive style (D). Respondents indicated degree of agreement or disagreement on 8-point scales, in response to the items in the inventory (entitled AID). The Ss were male and female psychotherapists—psychiatrists, psychologists, and social workers. The responses to all items were intercorrelated and factor-analyzed with the result that the three postulated factors were confirmed. Items loaded on the psychoanalytic factor (A) included the interpretation of unconscious motives and slips of the tongue, the analysis of resistance, and a focus on events in childhood. Those loaded on the impersonal factor (I) referred to an impersonal approach, an invariant unresponsiveness, and a greater evaluation of therapist technique than therapist personality. Directiveness (D) was characterized by a major emphasis on treatment planning, a downgrading of patient goals and an imposition of the therapist's own, an emphasis on the social adjustment of the patient, and the assumption of an active therapist role. Again, the later article by Lorr and McNair (1966) reported correlations of the above self-ratings of therapists with training and experience. "Each professional group exhibited distinct preferences for one or two of the patterns; suggesting a strong relation between therapeutic approach and training of therapist... As expected, therapists who had some personal analysis were more likely to endorse... patterns characterized by high scores on the analytic factor. Experience of therapists was unrelated to the techniques they endorsed" (p. 587).

The dimensions of the preceding study, derived from psychotherapist behavior patterns known to vary with therapeutic school were quite similar to those developed in another investigation. Wallach and Strupp (1964) prepared a 17-item Likert-type scale dealing with various aspects of a therapist's usual practice. The S (a therapist) responded by rating his level of agreement or disagreement with each practice. As in the immediately preceding studies, therapists' responses were intercorrelated and factor-analyzed with four factors emerging: *maintenance of personal distance* ("The therapist avoids answering questions about his personal life and private opinions"), *preference for intensive psychotherapy* ("The therapist prefers an intensive, uncovering, psychoanalytic form of therapy"), *preference for keeping verbal interventions to a minimum* ("The therapist avoids personal expressiveness, limiting himself to concise remarks with a therapeutic function"), and *a perception of psychotherapy as an artistic and flexibly artful activity* ("The therapist does not permit himself to be governed by rigid rules of procedure, but responds instead with personal spontaneity") Three of the four factors discriminated significantly between therapists with divergent orientations. "It will be noted that Orthodox Freudians were highest in maintaining personal distance, preference for intensive psychotherapy, keeping verbal interactions at a minimum, and lowest in considering therapy as an artistic activity. The client-centered group was distinct in considering psychotherapy as an art and in their lack of preferences for intensive therapy" (Wallach & Strupp, 1964, p. 123).

Shostrom and Riley (1968) played down the importance of therapist school, asserting "... that in actual practice every therapist may be described as an 'emerging eclectic,' in that he appears to pick up and to utilize parameters to which he himself may not even consciously subscribe" (p. 629). Without negating the possibility that differences between schools of psychotherapy may be etched by certain stylistic parameters, the authors preferred to place their emphasis on the general applicability of the parameters. They utilized a series of three films (Shostrom, 1966) recording the work of Carl Rogers (client-centered), Frederick Perls (Gestalt), and Albert Ellis (rational-emotive) with the same patient. These were rated on a set of variables pertaining to therapist style and behavior. In a series of two such rating studies, Rogers scored highest on *caring* ("The therapist's attitude of loving regard for the individual, whether expressed by unconditional warmth or aggressive critical caring") and *feeling* ("Helping the person to experience in a psychologically safe relationship, feelings which he has heretofore found too threatening to experience freely") (Shostrom & Riley, 1968, p. 629); Perls scored highest on *encountering* ("Providing the experience of encounter between person and therapist, each of whom is being and expressing his real feelings") (Shostrom & Riley, 1968, p. 629), *feeling*, and *interpersonal analyzing* ("The analyzing by the therapist of the person's perceptions or manipulations of the therapeutic relationship, and therefore of his interpersonal relationships in life") (p. 629); and Ellis scored highest on *value-reorienting* ("The reevaluation by the therapist of the person's loosely formulated value orientations... which enables the patient to commit himself to examined and operational values") (p. 629), and *pattern analysis* ("The analyzing of unworkable patterns of functioning and assisting in the development of adaptive or actualizing patterns of functions for the individual") (p. 629). Thus, the three schools were, in fact, stylistically differentiated although, in accordance with the authors' predictions, all the parameters did apply in some degree to the work of the three prototypical therapists.

A study by Rice, Gurman, and Razin (1974) provided additional data about therapist style in relation to level of experience and theoretical orientation, and, additionally, included findings related to the sex of the therapist. A sample of 86 therapists, of both sexes, contrasting levels of experience, and theoretical preferences designated as *analytic* (Freudian, Adlerian, analytically oriented), *phenomenological* (client-centered, Gestalt, existential), and *rational-behavioral* (rational-emotive, behavioral) were asked to complete a 23-item "... self-report therapist-style

questionnaire..." used in a previous study (Rice, Fey, & Kepecs, 1972). The questionnaire contained items descriptive of the respondent's style of response in a psychotherapy interview, including such attributes as talkative, supportive, guided by theory, critical, focusing on relationship, cautious, and others. The responses were intercorrelated and factor-analyzed; eight orthogonal factors were extracted.

The results for therapist experience, theoretical orientation, and sex were given in terms of the eight factors. In the present summary, factor titles are replaced with the individual questionnaire items that are loaded on the factors, since these seem to be more descriptive of actual therapist behavior. Thus, experienced therapists rated themselves as more interested in history, more patient, more willing to wait for information, more interpretive, more variable in their interview behavior, and more affectively expressive than inexperienced therapists. Among the three above-designated psychotherapist orientations, those with an analytical bent emphasized history and interpretation; those with a phenomenological leaning underscored personal feelings and lack of anonymity; and those with a behavioral-rational orientation stressed high activity level, a cognitive and goal-directed focus. Women therapists described themselves as more variable than men in their psychotherapy behavior, less given to impersonal anonymity, and more judgmental.

From the studies in this section, it is evident that multidimensional systems of coding and describing style have effectively differentiated between subgroups and types of therapists—male and female, experienced and inexperienced, and therapists adhering to different theoretical orientations. The controversy about the relative salience of theoretical orientations versus level of experience has long since lost its point. Those systems that emphasize general aspects of relationships appear to differentiate level of experience more pointedly than they do theoretical orientation. Those that emphasize the parameters of behavior that are theory- or school-specific understandably differentiate between theoretical orientations.

A final study in the present section dealing with multidimensional systems is included because of the range of variables studied simultaneously (Tourney, Bloom, Lowinger, Schorer, Auld, & Grisell, 1966). The actual therapy sessions of 10 psychiatric residents with both schizophrenic and psychoneurotic patients were observed by two experienced psychotherapists.

Audiotapes of the sessions were later played back and rated on a number of therapist and patient variables, scored with a 9-point Likert-type rating scale. All patient and therapist variables were intercorrelated separately for the psychoneurotic and schizophrenic patients. Two of the therapist style variables were composites, one designated as *errors of commission* and one as *errors of omission*. Errors of commission were consequences of therapist overactivity, including excessive probing, interruption of patient, excessive questioning, inaccurate or untimely interpretations, inappropriate advice and direction, and provocation of the patient. Errors of omission were consequences of therapist underactivity, including insufficient questioning and failure to provide support when needed, to give appropriate interpretations, to express empathy and understanding. Clearly these two composite categories of therapist style are highly evaluational in character. The following were the correlates of both forms of error. For both groups of patients, errors of commission correlated positively with therapist anxiety and hostility, and negatively with depression. The finding about depression was significant only for the schizophrenic patients. Thus, the errors of commission were a consequence of activating emotions—anxiety and hostility. Errors of omission also correlated positively with therapist anxiety in the interviews conducted with the neurotic patients but not with the schizophrenic patients. For both groups of patients, errors of omission correlated positively with therapist depression. The crucial contrast between the errors of commission and omission was the negative correlation of the former with therapist depression and the positive correlation of the latter, apparently supporting the authors' view of both types of errors as relating to an activity-passivity dimension.

The two kinds of errors correlated differentially with the responses of the two patient groupings. To errors of commission, psychoneurotic patients responded with hostility (i.e., positive correlations between therapist errors of commission and patient resistance and hostility), and schizophrenic patients, with anxiety and withdrawal (i.e., a positive correlation with patient anxiety and a negative correlation with patient verbal productivity). In contrast to their reactions to therapist errors of overactivity, the two types of patients responded as follows to therapist errors of underactivity. The psychoneurotic patients tended to manifest an increase in verbal activity and anxiety at a significant but not a strong level. The schizophrenic patients also manifested an increase in verbal productivity, associated however with an increase in thought disorder, hostility to others, but a decrease in their own depression. The neurotic patient was less affected by errors of both types than the schizophrenic patients. The schizophrenic was more manifestly disorganized by errors of omission (i.e., by the therapist's underactivity) than by errors of commission (i.e., therapist overactivity).

The study investigated therapist style as expression of affect. For example, how did patients react when the therapist was rated as anxious? Neurotic patients became angry with and resistive to the therapist; schizophrenic patients, more disorganized and anxious, less talkative and friendly. When the therapist was rated as hostile, neurotic patients reciprocated with hostility and negative feeling toward the therapist; schizophrenic patients became silent, anxious, and paradoxically more friendly to the therapist. Clearly, the schizophrenic patients responded in a maladaptive and often inappropriate manner. Depression in the therapist evoked both depression and negative feeling in the neurotic patients; in the schizophrenic patients, negative feeling, but most markedly, a thought disorder. In general, schizophrenic patients were more sensitive than neurotics to therapist style as the expression of affect. With therapist negative affect, they became more withdrawn and disorganized. By contrast, with therapist positive affect they demonstrated a decrease in thought disorder, anxiety, and hostility and an increase in positive feeling. Neurotic patients responded to the therapist's positive feeling with their own. But in other respects they were not greatly affected.

Clearly, therapist style both as activity level (and its associated errors) and as affective expression are of marked clinical importance in the therapist-patient interaction. The sections that follow will deal with individual stylistic parameters, focusing on their pragmatic effects and their relevance to therapist expressiveness.

STUDIES ON THE PRAGMATICS OF SOME ASPECTS OF THERAPIST STYLE

The Directive-Nondirective Dimension

It may appear unnecessarily redundant to begin the present section like the previous one with a discussion of therapist directiveness. But there is a difference between the two approaches to the same topic. In the previous section composite scales were used to distinguish between therapy schools designated as directive or nondirective. In the present section, directiveness is studied as a dimension in the therapeutic interaction. What are its attributes? How does the client respond within the interview to therapist directiveness? To what client behavior does the therapist respond with directiveness? The methodology of research will move from content analysis to the experimental analogue of psychotherapy.

Directiveness has been defined operationally in many of the early studies prompted by the client-centered orientation. Thus, Berdie (1958) developed a content analysis scheme for studying the counseling process which contained interviewer categories at varying levels of directiveness. The following may be assumed to exemplify low levels of directiveness: "nondirective leads: a request to the client to express himself, without the therapist specifying the topic" and "restatement of content or feeling: repetition of the idea expressed by the client which does not reorganize the statement in such a manner as to reveal more clearly the client's feeling or idea." By contrast, high levels of directiveness are exemplified by the following categories: "interpretation: therapist responses that either indicate relationship (one aspect must be inherent in the client's preceding statement) or respond to feelings that have not been expressed by the client" and "advice: recommending following a course of action" (Kiesler, 1973, p. 297). Bergman (1950) operationalized directiveness more concisely as structuring or interpreting, and nondirectiveness as simply the reflection of feeling. Although there is a drift in the definitional emphasis given directiveness as one moves from one study to another, most authors would agree that high therapist directiveness may be defined as high initiative and lead. It is characterized by the frequent use of inputs which arise outside of the client's frame of reference.

In some studies therapist directiveness emerges as an independent variable with a unidirectional main effect, without interactional complications. Thus, Bergman (1950) found, based on the content analysis of counseling interviews, that directive counselor statements (i.e., structuring or interpreting) discouraged client self-exploration and nondirective statements (i.e., reflection of feeling) enhanced both self-exploration and insight.

A later and more complex investigation (Ashby, Ford, Guerney, & Guerney, 1957) studied the effects of therapist style on client behavior within a framework that allowed for an interaction between therapist and client variables. The therapists, six clinical psychology graduate students, were trained to use two contrasting therapy styles, designated as "reflective" (restatement of content, reflection of feelings, nondirective leads, and nondirective structuring responses) and "leading" (directive leads, interpretations, directive structuring, information giving, and persuasion). The clients, all psychoneurotic, were randomly assigned to the six therapists and the two styles, each client continuing in treatment for a minimum of four sessions. In general, there was some support for the expectation that the two styles of therapy would have different effects on the clients. But the interaction between therapist style and type of client proved to be even more striking. Those clients who were more defensive before treatment behaved more defensively in treatment with a leading (i.e., directive) but not with a reflective (i.e., nondirective) therapist. Similarly, clients who were more aggressive pre-therapy reacted more defensively in the leading rather than the reflective therapy. By contrast, clients who manifested a greater need for autonomy reported feeling less defensive in leading therapy. Thus, the two styles of treatment affected different types of clients differentially.

Although the next study (Abramowitz, Abramowitz, Roback, & Jackson, 1974) deals with group rather than individual therapy, it is reviewed here because it also found that directive versus nondirective therapy styles had differential effects on varying types of clients. The setting of the study was an interuniversity clinic serving two neighboring campuses. The patients were students who had responded to campus notices announcing the formation of groups with the objectives of improving personal adjustment and interpersonal relationship skills. The leader of the four groups formed was one of the authors, a clinical psychologist on the staff of the interuniversity clinic. Three of the groups were conducted along directive lines ("...the therapist was to structure sessions, steer discussions, and make interpretations..."). In the fourth, designated a "problem discussion" group (the nondirective group) the leader was less dominant, functioning as a moderator: "Rather than to structure meetings, his prescribed role was to encourage intermember discussion of presenting concerns" (Abramowitz et al., 1974, p. 850). To assess the possible differential effect of therapist approach on different types of clients, all participating Ss were assigned to an *internal* or *external locus* of *control* category (Rotter, 1966) depending on whether they scored above or below the group median on the *I-E* variable. The outcome scales to which the clients responded provided a means of comparing the relative efficacy of directive and nondirective modes of treatment for the *internal* and *external* Ss. As expected, the *external* Ss did relatively better in directive rather than nondirective groups, while the *internal* Ss did relatively better in the nondirective group. Since the externals tend to believe that the events in their lives are determined by outside forces, they are more responsive to group leaders who adopt an active, powerful role. The *internals* believe in the efficacy of their own initiative and are less responsive to external power and control. It is, therefore, not surprising that they should find a less active and controlling leader more congenial.

A second study dealing with the interaction of therapist directiveness and patient locus of control was conducted by Friedman and Dies (1974). These authors arranged two forms of behavioral treatment (i.e., automated desensitization and standard systematic desensitization) and nondirective discussion-oriented counseling on a continuum of decreasing directiveness: "The prediction was that internally controlled individuals would respond more favorably to counseling in which they control the course of therapy, whereas externals would react well to the more structured treatment in which control of the therapy session is other determined" (Friedman & Dies, 1974, p. 921). The Ss were introductory psychology students, selected because of high test anxiety. One group of Ss, consisting of matched pairs scoring both at the high and low extremes of the I-E Scale (Rotter, 1966), was assigned to discussion-oriented counseling, another to systematic desensitization, a third to automated desensitization, and a last group to a no-treatment control condition. The focus of the study was not on outcome but on S perception of and attitude toward the psychotherapy process. As expected, *external* Ss felt that they retained too much control of therapy in both the discussion-oriented counseling and systematic desensitization conditions. By contrast, *internal* Ss felt that they had just the right amount of control in the counseling condition with not quite enough control in systematic desensitization. In all three conditions *internal* Ss would have "chosen more client control" with

significantly greater frequency than *external* Ss. Clearly, then, *internal* and *external* Ss perceive and evaluate therapist directiveness in different ways.

In the 1970s the inquiries of the 1940s into the relative merits of the directive versus the nondirective schools seem remote and simplistic. Today the focus in the study of the directive-nondirective dimension is on its relative effectiveness for specific purposes, specific types of patients, and as practiced by specified therapists. As in other areas of psychotherapy research, the emphasis is less ideological and more pragmatic.

Therapist directiveness-nondirectiveness has been the subject of a number of experimental analogue investigations. Gordon (1957, p. 406) studied "... the effects of therapist Leading and therapist Following on hypnotically induced repression and on neurotic interpersonal functioning". Gordon proposed the following hypotheses: "Those who use Leading techniques tend to regard the lifting of repressions as the aim of therapy. Those who use Following techniques ... focus instead on the improvement in the patient's present interpersonal functioning as the aim of therapy" (p. 406). Male college students who emerged as good hypnotic Ss in three screening and training sessions were retained for the study. The design called for the hypnotic induction of a traumatic experience, with repression of the experience consequent on the suggestion under hypnosis that the S would not be able to recall it when he awoke, but that he would be troubled by it. He was given leave, under hypnosis, to spend the subsequent interview in trying to determine what was bothering him. Because it was suggested that the hypnotically induced perpetrator of the trauma resembled the therapist, it was anticipated that a negative transference reaction (i.e., a hostile reaction) would develop to the therapist, during the posthypnotic therapy hours. The therapists, advanced graduate students in clinical psychology, were trained to conduct both leading and following interviews; each therapist conducted one of each. As anticipated, the results indicate a tendency for leading therapy sessions to be superior to following sessions for the lifting of the hypnotically induced repression. Contrary to anticipation, there was no significant advantage for either form of therapy in the evocation of affect expression—transference hostility in this instance. A direct translation of these analogue findings into psychotherapeutic terms would prompt one to conclude that a directive (i.e., analytic) form of treatment is more effective than a nondirective form in uncovering repressions. By contrast, the asserted efficacy of nondirective treatment in evoking expressions of feeling and, therefore, in changing the patient's interpersonal functioning was not demonstrated.

In another experimental analogue Wiener (1955) set out to determine the relative effectiveness of two verbal counseling techniques, designated as *reassurance-interpretation* (the interviewer reassured stress-induced Ss that their thoughts and feelings were quite normal; he also interpreted some reactions of the S as indicative of feelings not yet reported), and *catharsis-reflection* (the interviewer responded to similarly stress-induced Ss by a simple acceptance of their feelings and their reflection to encourage further expression of affect). The Ss were undergraduate college volunteers from advanced psychology courses. The experimental induction of stress was accomplished by the raising of some questions about the adjustment of each experimental S on the basis of a previously administered Rorschach examination. Utilizing a number of outcome criteria, the two treatment groups combined showed greater recuperation from the stress than two control groups, but there were no significant differences between the reassurance-interpretation (i.e., directive) and catharsis-reflection (i.e., nondirective) groups.

While most process studies on psychotherapist directiveness have dealt with it as an independent variable, its role as a dependent variable is not without interest. Is directiveness as a form of therapist behavior evoked more frequently by certain types of clients than by others, and by certain forms of client behavior? The answer to both of these questions is in the affirmative in the studies that follow.

Parker (1967) found that male therapists' verbal behavior on a directive-nondirective continuum was significantly related to the sex of the client being interviewed. His therapists gave significantly more nondirective responses to female clients than to male clients. Heller, Myers, and Kline (1963) observed that client dependence evoked dominant (i.e., directive) interviewer behavior and client dominance evoked passive (i.e., nondirective) interviewer behavior. The latter study was an experimental analogue of the initial interview in a university counseling center. Graduate students, in training as interviewers in the counseling center were asked to interview "clients" applying for admission to the center. Actually, the "clients" were actors who were trained to portray four types of client roles: dominant-friendly, dominant-hostile, dependent-friendly, and dependent-hostile. The friendly-hostile client dimension is not relevant at the moment, but the dominant-dependent dimension is. Observers rating the interviews judged that "...dominant client behavior...evoked significantly more interviewer dependence than was the case for dependent clients..." (Heller *et al.*, 1963, p. 120). If one can hazard translating interviewer dominance to interviewer directiveness, one could conclude that a dependent client is more likely to evoke directive interviewer behavior than a dominant client. The two preceding studies suggest that directiveness is not necessarily a stable invariant trait within the interviewer; it may well vary in response to type and behavior of interviewee.

Finally, in a further test of this impression, Bohn (1967) investigated the responses of students in a graduate psychology course on psychological counseling to three tape recordings of simulated initial interviews. The tapes represented three client types, called "the typical client," "the hostile client," and "the dependent client." The procedure followed was similar to the one originally used by Strupp (1958). During selected silences on the tape, the S responded by selecting a counselor response from a group of four presented in multiple choice format. The alternatives had been scored for directiveness according to a system derived from Snyder (1945). The taped interviews were administered to the Ss before and after the course in psychological counseling. During both pre- and post-course evaluations, the dependent client elicited a significantly higher level of directiveness from the interviewers than the "typical" client. The hostile client's evoked directiveness fell in between that of the dependent and "typical" client.

Interpretation

In the early investigation of directiveness, therapist interpretation tended to be assimilated into the directive-nondirective continuum, on the directive or "semi-directive" side (Snyder, 1945). As one would expect, interpretation was given a negative connotation in the client-centered value system. Thus, Rogers asserted: "It is always best to deal with attitudes already expressed. To interpret unexpressed attitudes is definitely dangerous" (Rogers, 1942, p. 205). In direct contrast, interpretation is considered to be the major instrumentality of therapeutic movement in the psychoanalytic system. According to Bernstein (1965), interpretation is used to make the unconscious conscious, to provide the patient with an insight or a solution, to allay anxiety, to provide support, to overcome resistance, to facilitate communication, to produce changes in extratherapeutic behavior, to inhibit acting out, and for many other purposes. Clearly then, for the psychoanalytically oriented therapist, interpretation is a multipurpose instrument with a diversity of consequences. It need hardly be added that psychotherapists of other persuasions and many psychotherapy researchers disagree with several of the above claims for interpretation. This section provides a consideration of the meaning or definition of interpretation, its attributes, and its sequelae in the interactional process of psychotherapy.

Snyder's (1945) definition of interpretation is characteristic of its operational description when it is consigned to the directive-nondirective continuum: "Responses in which the counselor points out patterns and relationship in the material provided. The category is always used when causation is implied or indicated. 'You do this because....' If the counselor attempts even vaguely to say 'why' the client does or feels something, it is considered interpretation" (Kiesler, 1973, p. 417). Thus, in making an interpretation about the behavior of the patient, the therapist goes beyond the personal information communicated to him; he makes a causal *inference* about this information.

The analyst would not object to the designation of inference as an attribute of interpretation. But he would hasten to add that the inferences made pertain to motives, experiences, images, and thoughts beyond the patient's awareness. Thus, the therapist as interpreter amplifies and translates the signals from the patient's unconscious. He knows that "... the patient's utterances are frequently allusions to other things..." and "... endeavors to deduce what lies behind the allusions and at the proper time to impart this information to the patient." He considers that his task is "to infer what the patient has forgotten from what the patient tells him and to reconstruct the patient's past" (Bernstein, 1965, p. 1178). In a word, his interpretations are based on inferences directed toward experiences or cognitions that are beyond the patient's awareness. In the terms of Dollard and Auld (1959), the therapist provides the patient with *verbal labels* for unconscious experiences, thus making them manageable.

The studies that investigate the effects of the psychotherapist's interpretations on immediate patient responses reflect the contradictory anticipations of adherents of the client-centered and psychoanalytic schools. This does not imply that all researchers were necessarily partisans of any one school but rather that they tended to deal with questions posed by the schools. Investigators have dealt with such matters as the impact of interpretation on client verbal productivity, self-exploration, resistance, and therapeutic movement.

Though not adhering specifically to the client-centered school, Kanfer, Phillips, Matarazzo, and Saslow (1960) reported findings that were broadly congruent with the Rogerian view of the effect of interpretation on the interview process. They investigated the effect of interpretation as a therapist category without reference to its content. Following the opinions of previous authors (Auld & White, 1959; Speisman, 1959), they anticipated that the formal aspects of interpretation, regardless of its veracity or content in a particular instance, would affect the patient's interactional pattern in the interview. In their own words, "the basic hypothesis of the present study is simply that interpretations, as a global category of interviewer's behavior, differ from exploratory or information seeking statements in their immediate effect on the interviewee's verbal output, in time units, regardless of their differing content or their role in the interview strategy" (Kanfer *et al.*, 1960, p. 529). The Ss were female volunteers from the nursing staff and the student nurses at the University of Oregon Medical School. All Ss participated in a single initial interview which dealt with such topics as vocation, family, friends, and social and recreational activities. The nurses were subdivided into three experimental groups and two control groups. For all groups, the interviews consisted of three periods, the first of 15 minutes duration, the second and third of 10 minutes duration each. In the control groups the interviewer (the senior author) utilized exploratory information-gathering questions in the three interview periods. In the experimental groups, the first and third periods were similarly exploratory and information-gathering; the second period was interpretive. The results clearly point to a significant drop in mean duration of interviewee utterance in the second (interpretive) period of the experimental interviews in contrast to the first and third periods (exploratory). No such drop occurred in the control interviews, which were exploratory throughout. Regardless of content, the effect of interpretive style was the immediate inhibition of interviewee productivity.

Although the results of this study are striking, it should be noted that they say very little about the therapeutic effects over time of therapist interpretations. Instead, they are limited to the immediate interactional consequences of this category of interviewer remarks. Indeed, after the end of the experiment, the authors (Kanfer et al., 1960) asked each S to recall the most vivid statement made by the interviewer. The experimental Ss all mentioned an interpretation; the control Ss could not recall a single, most memorable statement. Moreover, the experimental Ss discussed the recalled interpretive statements as though they had unleashed a process of self-exploration. Thus, interpretation appeared to have one effect on the immediate interviewee response and quite another in a more protracted sense. However, only the former was experimentally supported.

In the Kanfer et al. (1960) investigation interviewer interpretation appeared to function as an inhibitor of speech when measured in duration units. It is therefore puzzling to note that in a series of three later investigations (Adams, Butler, & Noblin, 1962; Adams, Noblin, Butler, & Timmons, 1962; Noblin, Timmons, & Reynard, 1966) interpretation was used effectively as a reinforcer of pre-selected verbal responses. To be sure, the context for interpretation in the latter investigations was not an interview, but a Taffel-type of verbal conditioning experiment. In all three, hospitalized schizophrenic patients were the Ss. A standardized pack of cards was used, each card containing two pronouns at the top, one first person (I or we) and the other third person (he, she, they). At the bottom of each card, a sentence fragment was printed. A complete sentence could be formed by attaching one of the two pronouns to the sentence fragment below. The object of the experiment was to condition the S's use of the first-person pronoun. The reinforcer was a psychoanalytically derived interpretive statement. In the first two investigations (Adams, Butler, et al., 1962; Adams, Noblin, et al., 1962) the interpretations were pre-selected to relate to the content of the stimulus sentences. In both, the frequency of selecting the first-person pronoun was raised significantly when "correct" choices were followed by interpretations.

The third study of the series was designed to test the assumption that the content of the interpretation, particularly its "truth status" was crucial to its efficacy. A procedure was followed which scrambled the interpretations so that they were randomly related to the content of the sentences on the cards. "The learning curve for the Ss receiving 'shuffled interpretations' were quite similar to that of Ss who received the logically fitting interpretations following 'correct' responses. The data support the hypothesis that the 'truth status' or relevance of interpretations is *not* the central factor in whether interpretations lawfully modify verbal behavior in a verbal conditioning situation" (Noblin et al., 1966, p. 418).

From the preceding studies, it would appear that interpretation as a stylistic category tends to inhibit verbal productivity in an initial interview, but paradoxically serves as a reinforcer of verbal learning in a verbal conditioning situation.[1] More congruent with the first finding than with the second is the belief, derived from client-centered anticipation, that interpretation is likely to evoke client resistance. This belief was challenged by Auld and White (1959) who failed to find that therapist interpretations were followed by patient resistive remarks.

The psychoanalytic origin of interpretation as a process category has prompted an interest in depth as a major attribute of interpretation. In its psychoanalytic sense an interpretation is assumed to proceed beyond the current limits of awareness of a patient. "Depth of interpretation is a description of the relationship between the view expressed by the therapist and the patient's awareness. The greater the disparity between the view expressed by the therapist and the patient's own awareness of these emotions, the deeper the interpretation" (Raush, Sperber, Rigler, Williams, Harway, Bordin, Dittman, & Hays, 1956, p. 44). Based on this definition, a 7-point graphic rating scale of depth of interpretation has been developed (Harway, Dittman, Raush, Bordin, & Rigler, 1955) marked by the following items, among others, arranged in the order of low to high depth (Harway et al., 1955, p. 249):

"Therapist merely repeats the material of which the patient is fully aware."

"Therapist connects for the patient two aspects of the content of the previous patient statement."

"Therapist response deals with information about material completely removed from the patient's awareness."

Not necessarily in conflict with the above definition of depth of interpretation, but with a somewhat different emphasis, is another based on the concept of plausibility: "It was hypothesized that judgments relating to depth of interpretation are implicitly derived from (and hence should be correlated with) the rater's subjective estimate (i.e., prediction) of how 'plausible' the interpretion is to the patient: deep interpretations will be considered more 'implausible' than shallow interpretations" (Fisher, 1956, p. 249). In the study that followed, 60 therapist statements were selected because they met the author's criterion of interpretation and varied widely in depth. The raters were psychiatrists, psychologists, and psychology graduate students, organized into subgroups of 10, each instructed to rate each statement for either depth of interpretation or plausibility to the patient. The graduate students' plausibility ratings correlated .88 with psychologists' depth ratings; psychologists' plausibility ratings correlated .84 with psychiatrists' depth ratings. Therefore, depth and plausibility appear to refer to the same attribute of interpretation.

Fisher (1956, p. 255) perceived depth as close to the social psychological concept of distance, defined as "... the discrepancy between two persons' opinions." Thus, if the therapist expresses an opinion (i.e., makes an interpretation) that is close to the opinion held by the client, the distance between therapist and client is small; the interpretation is plausible to the client and is therefore shallow. By contrast, if distance is great and plausibility is low, the interpretation is deep.

In general, the larger the distance between the therapist and client (i.e., the less plausible the interpretation), the greater the likelihood that the interpretation will not be accepted by the client. From this, Fisher (1956) is led to predict that "... deep interpretations should be rejected by the patient more frequently than shallow interpretations" (p. 255). This anticipation accords completely with predictions based on the Rogerian approach, according to which deep interpretations are likely to be followed "... (a) by a reduced frequency of insight and (b) by an increased frequency of rejection by the client of these therapist responses" (Collier, 1953, p. 325). This attitude is not discordant with the psychoanalytically based one that the premature "communication of interpretations may be wasted because they are unacceptable to the patient, or they may drive the patient out of treatment because of the resistances they evoke or because of the relief that results from the insight obtained" (Bernstein, 1965, p. 1179).

Basing himself on Fenichel's (1941) view of the role of interpretation Speisman (1959, p. 93) studied the proposition that "deep interpreta-

tions lead to the most resistance, moderate interpretations lead to the least resistance, and superficial interpretations fall between the other two levels as to their influence on resistance." Depth of interpretation was measured by an adaptation of the scale developed by Harway et al. (1955); resistiveness by two verbal categories, one designated *exploration* (a positive, nonresistive category and the other *opposition*. Patient statements assigned to the opposition category expressed doubt, negativism, and denial toward the therapist or therapy. The data consisted of verbatim transcriptions of taped therapy interviews of psychoneurotic patients, rated by advanced graduate students and faculty members in clinical psychology. The original proposition was borne out. Both superficial and moderate interpretations were followed by more exploratory and fewer oppositional patient statements than were deep interpretations. Moreover, there was less resistance after moderate rather than superficial interpretations. Following Fenichel (1941), the author concluded that moderate interpretations relate to experiences that are close to consciousness. They provoke cognitive restructuring by the patient without evoking the kind of blocking or opposition that is prompted by deep interpretation. In an earlier study Dittman (1952) found that "deeper" rather than "superficial" therapist responses tended to be associated with progressive rather than regressive movement in therapy. (The results did not attain a five percent level of significance). However, the "deeper" category included both moderate and deep interpretations as they would have been classified by Speisman (1959). Both of the last two authors interpret their findings to be supportive of the position taken by Fenichel (1941) rather than Rogers (1942)—i.e., the therapist should go slightly beyond the preconscious level in his interpretations rather than limit himself to restating that of which the patient is already aware.

Therapist Activity Level

It would be difficult to define therapist activity level without reference to other stylistic variables. For example, Howe and Pope (1961b) found it necessary to invoke ambiguity, lead, and inference, as three attributes of activity level. A highly active therapist remark is low in ambiguity, high in lead, and high in inference. In this regard, consider their following three descriptions of therapist response (p. 511):

"1. Therapist gives a general, unfocused invitation to talk.

2. Therapist asks the patient to describe the last occasion when a pattern of symptoms occurred.

3. Therapist explores the patient's feelings about something just reported by the patient."

As one proceeds through the above sequence of responses, ambiguity decreases, and both lead and inference increase. In a word, activity level increases. It should be noted that the above definition of activity level relates to certain lexical attributes of therapist style that have both informational (ambiguity and inference) and interactional (lead) implications.

The studies that follow are based on the above definition of activity level. Howe and Pope (1961b) constructed two parallel 11-point scales for rating the activity level of therapist remarks. Thirty Board-certified psychiatrists were asked to rate 50 descriptions of therapist verbal responses. Those items that were scored reliably were retained, and their scale values computed by averaging the ratings of all the Ss. The following three items occur at low, medium, and high points on the first of the two scales (p. 513).

"Therapist uses a single word or syllable to give the patient an invitation to continue."

"Therapist focuses upon an objective, factual aspect of patient's life (age, job, salary)."

"Therapist suggests that what the patient has just said is inconsistent with certain other things said earlier by the patient."

With the use of the above scale, the authors (Howe & Pope, 1961a) investigated the dimensionality of the concept of therapist activity level. Experienced psychiatrists were asked to make semantic ratings of 10 therapist responses, representing the entire range of the Activity Level Scale. These ratings were based on 40 bipolar adjectival scales, most of which were selected because they had some connotative reference to ambiguity, lead, and inference. Other adjectives were selected because they had established relevance to the three semantic differential dimensions—evaluation, potency, and activity (Osgood, Suci, & Tannenbaum, 1957). The first factor to emerge from the intercorrelation and factor analysis of the ratings was one of professional evaluation, marked by such bipolar adjectives as wise-foolish, acceptable-unacceptable, skillful-unskillful, and sensitive-insensitive. The concept of activity-passivity appeared only in a modest second factor, characterized by such adjectival variables as colorful-colorless, vibrant-still, precise-vague, strong-weak, and active-passive. The first factor accounted for 33% of the total variance; the second, 18%. It may be that ratings based on therapist categories lexically defined must contend with the ubiquitous presence of a primary evaluative factor, regardless of the specific dimension on which the ratings are made. At any rate, such a finding would be consistent with the position of Osgood et al. (1957).

When a group of psychiatrists and clinical psychologists classified 50 therapist responses, already independently rated for activity level, into five other therapist response categories, these arranged themselves into the following sequence of increasing activity level: simple facilitation, exploration, clarification, interpretation, approval, and reassurance. Thus, there is a systematic association between activity level and a number of conventional categories of therapist response.

For the most part, studies that attempt to correlate interviewer activity level, as lexically defined, with interviewee response are disappointingly meager in their findings. With the initial diagnostic rather than the psychotherapy interview in mind, Finesinger (1948) regarded the interviewer's low activity level as a means of encouraging the patient to unfold his story spontaneously, following his own associative path. In a sense, low interviewer activity was thought to ensure the *projective character* of the interview, and thus its diagnostic usefulness. This expectation notwithstanding, the one study that attempted to establish a relationship between therapist verbal activity level and diagnostic utility of patient verbal response (Howe & Pope, 1962) obtained negative results.

One might be led to conclude that content-based or lexical measures of therapist style possess some flaws that doom them to failure as instruments for illuminating communication interactions within the interview. Such a conclusion might be prompted further by the many positive results that are obtained in studies that utilize a direct, behavioral measure of activity—i.e., duration of speech or productivity. However, before dismissing lexical measures, the studies in the section dealing with therapist specificity should be examined. Meanwhile, a series of investigations based on activity level as speech duration or productivity follows.

The utility of therapist activity level defined as gross productivity or output in the description of the interview will now be examined. Lennard and Bernstein (1960), both associated with Columbia University's Bureau of Applied Social

Research, have made an important contribution in this endeavor. They have rather impressively applied concepts and methods from the social sciences to the process of psychotherapy, focusing on the verbal interaction between the interviewer and the interviewee. These authors have described their approach to the study of the psychotherapeutic interview in the following terms: "From the perspective of the social sciences, the focus in the study of therapy can be upon therapy as a system of action (verbal communication), upon therapy as a system of expectation, and upon the interrelations between communications and expectations" (p. 4). Although a dyadic communication system is channelled through variables at different levels simultaneously, the present focus will be on therapist activity level as a single dimension within the system. The interviewer's activity level is an important referent in the anticipatory role expectations with which both patient and therapist approach the psychotherapeutic encounter. It is equally relevant to any examination of the verbal interaction between the two.

In the Lennard and Bernstein (1960) studies eight therapies (four therapists with two patients each) were recorded over a period of 8 months, resulting in more than 500 therapy interview protocols. The two most frequently used indexes of activity level as gross productivity were average number of clause units per session and therapist proportion of the total output of the session.

The authors broke down role expectations of both participants in an interview into the following components: "Who shall speak, how much, about what, and when?" (Lennard & Bernstein, 1960, p. 154). They found that nearly all the patients they studied anticipated that the interviewee would do most of the talking during psychotherapy; with this, the interviewers agreed. However, complementarity between interviewers and interviewees regarding activeness was limited to the general premise stated above. With reference to specifics, there was considerable disagreement. For example, interviewers and interviewees tended to have discrepant expectations regarding the role of each in the initiative for and control of communication during the interview. Disagreement about the content of communication (the subject matter to be covered) was similarly prevalent. The therapists and patients disagreed about the relevance of approximately one-half of the topics about which the investigation inquired. In general, patients tended to exclude certain topics from discussion, while the therapists were more broadly accepting.

Whenever dissimilarity with reference to activity level expectations arose, the therapist would attempt to reduce the resulting instability by introducing into the interview a "primary system reference." This term refers to any remark by the therapist that has the aim of making the patient aware of what is required of him regarding both type and level of activity. Thus, the patient is taught how to engage in a reciprocal role relationship as defined by the therapist.

The naturalistic movement of a dyadic communication system that remains viable is toward stability. Consider the following tendencies toward equilibrium found by Lennard and Bernstein (1960) and summarized by Matarazzo (1965).

1. The relative quantities of therapist and patient speech move toward a stable and fixed ratio, maintained over a psychotherapy interview series, but varying over different patient-therapist pairs. In the group of patients and therapists studied by Lennard and Bernstein (1960) the patients were four times as productive verbally as the therapists, when the interview as a whole was the unit. Single patient verbalizations averaged about five times the length of the preceding interviewer remarks. The generality of this ratio is noted in its occurrence in other studies conducted under different circumstances. Thus Matarazzo, Wiens, Matarazzo, and Saslow (1968) found patient to therapist duration of utterance ratios of 5 to 1 and 6 to 1 in a sample of initial interviews. These are average figures and do not necessarily remain invariant over time. In fact, Lennard and Bernstein found two contrasting patterns in the psychotherapy sequences they studied. In one the ratio of therapist output to that of total interview output did indeed remain constant, without fluctuation. In another there was a tendency for the ratio of the therapist output to fluctuate around an overall mean. When the ratio was below the mean during one session, it tended to rise above the mean in the next session. As in the motion of a pendulum, equilibrium in the interview was not static but, instead, a fluctuating or dynamic steady state over time.

2. Within the relative stability of each therapist's activity level, there were certain interactional fluctuations relative to the verbal output of the patient. When the patient increased his output, the therapist reduced his. Conversely, when the patient decreased his output, the thera-

pist increased his. Thus, there was a tendency toward an overall constant level of verbal productivity for any given psychotherapy dyad. However, there are exceptions to this steady state model of the interview which will be considered below.

3. Some therapists demonstrated greater flexibility and greater capacity to vary their verbal activity level than others.

While the viability of a dyadic communication system is noted in its stability, equilibrium is by no means inevitable. Lennard and Bernstein (1960) found that strain in the interview was frequently a consequence of low therapist activity level. Thus, when they divided their four therapists into two who were more active and two who were less active, they noted that there were no broken appointments among the patients of the two more active therapists and 10 broken appointments among the patients of the two less active therapists. In addition there were frequent expressions of "situational dissatisfaction" by patients in the typescripts of the less active therapists and almost none in those of the more active therapists. No tests of significance of the preceding two impressions were given. However, the third body of evidence regarding the strain engendered by low therapist activity level was statistically documented and evaluated. Patients were asked to compare the ease and satisfaction of communication in any given hour with that experienced over the preceding two weeks. To a significant degree, they rated interviews in which the therapist was relatively active as the ones in which communication went more easily than those in which the therapist was relatively inactive. In general, the patients preferred those sessions in which the therapist spoke more frequently and at greater length. It may be assumed that they found the more highly active therapists more reinforcing than the more passive ones. As to why this should be so, the results of the following two studies provide some evidence. Truax (1970) found a positive relationship between duration of therapist utterance and his independently rated accurate empathy. Similarly, Pope, Nudler, VonKorff, and McGee (1974) found a positive association between interviewer productivity (i.e., number of words uttered) and his independently rated warmth. It seems plausible that interviewees are likely to perceive their more active therapists in the same way that the raters did—i.e., as more empathic and warmer. The reinforcing effect of high interviewer activity level may also be a consequence of the amount of feedback it gives to the interviewee.

It should be noted that there is no evidence here to justify the view that the long-term goals of psychotherapy are necessarily better served by high therapist activity. Rather, the evidence points only to lesser strain, and the easier flow of communication with high rather than low therapist verbal activity. It is conceivable that a therapist may deliberately choose to increase the strain experienced by the patient within a particular therapy hour by maintaining a low level of activity.

Moreover, an increase in therapist activity level is not always associated with an analogous increase in patient activity. In some interview situations the *synchrony* model does indeed obtain; in others the communication model may be quite different. The results in the Heller, Davis, and Myers (1966) investigation accord with the synchrony model. The purpose of the study, in the authors' words ". . . was to examine the interaction of interviewer affect and activity level in a laboratory interview in which the behavior of the interviewer could be standardized and controlled" (p. 501). Each of 12 graduate students in speech and theater was trained to conduct one of the following four types of interviews: active-friendly, passive-friendly, active-hostile, and passive-hostile. The active interviewer spoke often and verbosely; the passive interviewer, infrequently and laconically. The interviewees (introductory psychology students) in the active conditions did indeed use the time available to them for speaking significantly more than those in the passive conditions. The most inhibiting condition for the interviewee was that of interviewer silence, the condition which produced least interviewee speech. The authors concluded that their findings were at variance with what they designated as ". . . the nonresponding, noninteracting model presented by Freud and the early writing of Rogers . . . ." (Heller *et al.*, 1966, p. 507) and agreed with those in the studies reported by Matarazzo (1965).

The interview used by Matarazzo and his group leading to their early synchrony findings was not a psychotherapy but rather an occupational interview with applicants for positions as policemen and firemen. Without marring its functional character, Matarazzo and his colleagues inserted into the naturalistic interview an experimental analogue. The interview was divided into three 15-minute segments. During the first period, the interviewer spoke in 5-second comments; during the second period, he increased the duration of each utterance to 10 seconds; and during the third period, he reverted to 5-second remarks. During these segments, the interviewees tracked the interviewer's pattern with average speech durations of 24.3, 46.9, and 26.6 seconds, respectively ($p < .01$). In a second study, the interviewer's pattern was reversed; he started with 10-second remarks, dropping their duration to 5 seconds in the second period, and increasing them again to 10 seconds in the third segment. Again the interviewees tracked the interviewer's pattern, with remarks that averaged 41.1, 22.8, and 48.2 seconds, respectively. The case for synchrony as the interactional model for the activity levels of both interviewer and interviewee appeared to be solidly established.

However, the apparently ubiquitous character of the synchronous relationship between interviewer and interviewee activity level was placed under question by a naturalistic psychotherapy study later conducted by Matarazzo and his colleagues (Matarazzo et al., 1968). Seven uncontrolled psychotherapy sequences were tape-recorded and observed. Three of the four authors conducted the psychotherapies, two treating two patients each and the third treating three patients. For the seven patients, the number of psychotherapy sessions ranged from 11 to 50. In the studies discussed above, which manifested synchrony so strikingly, the interviewer's input was experimentally manipulated and considered to be the independent variable. The design was therefore a unidirectional one, with the action proceeding from the interviewer to the interviewee. In the free psychotherapy situation, the communication situation was quite different; the process was one of dyadic interaction in which the two participants reciprocally affected each other. The data used were the mean durations of patient and therapist utterances in individual therapy sessions. If synchrony were present, it would be reflected in significant positive correlations between therapist and patient mean durations across sessions. In fact, such positive correlations did not occur. Three of the correlations were near zero (.03, .07, and .19); the other four were negative ($-.14$, $-.18$, $-.34$, $-.42$), with the last one significantly so. Thus, instead of synchrony, there appeared to be a tendency toward an inverse relationship. When the patient increased his output, the therapist reduced his; when the patient decreased his verbalization, the therapist increased his. This inverse model would accord with what Matarazzo et al. (1968) referred to as a "thera-

peutic set," and what Lennard and Bernstein (1960) spoke of as balance or equilibrium in a dyadic communication system. It is also completely congruent with the finding by Heller et al. (1963) that dependent and passive interviewees evoked a relatively high level of activity from interviewers while dominant interviewees evoked interviewer passivity. They concluded that in an interactional psychotherapy situation, high patient output would be associated with low therapist output, and low patient output with high therapist output.

It would appear that expectations regarding the occurrence of synchronous communication should be governed by situational factors. Thus, in the above studies the unidirectional process in an experimental analogue of the initial interview promoted synchrony;[2] the free interaction of the two participants in a psychotherapy exchange did not. Additionally, one might expect certain variables to be more responsive to situational factors than others. Thus, mean reaction time latencies and interruption behavior of both therapist and patient remained synchronously related in the seven psychotherapy series, as they did in the earlier analogue studies (Matarazzo et al., 1968). It may be that verbal activity level is more situationally responsive than latency and interruption.

The situational responsiveness of interviewer and interviewee activity level (number of words uttered) was studied in another investigation (Pope et al., 1974) based on a replicated comparison of the interviewer behavior of professionals and complete novices. In each of the two component studies the interviewees were 16 female freshman students; 16 interviewers were professionals (psychiatrists and 3rd-year resident psychiatrists) and 16 were novices (sophomore students with no training in interviewing). Each interviewer conducted only one interview, but each interviewee was seen twice, once by a professional and once by a novice. "It was anticipated that when students interview students, interviewer and interviewee productivity will be positively correlated, that is, will manifest *synchrony*. When professionals interview students, an *inverse* or *reciprocal* relationship should occur" (Pope et al., 1974, p. 682). The above prediction was based on the view of the "nonprofessional" interview as a communication system that is relatively non-role-differentiated, akin to a conversational encounter, with a spontaneous mutuality of response. By contrast, the "professional" interview would be governed by an operating principle that prompts the interviewer to say little when the interviewee is productive, and relatively more when the interviewee's productivity flags. The results bore out the first prediction; there was one significant ($p < .05$) and one borderline ($p < .10$) positive correlation between interviewer and interviewee productivity for the two groups of "nonprofessional" interviews. The evidence for the inverse model in the "professional" interview was less consistent. There was indeed a highly significant negative correlation between interviewer and interviewee productivity for the first group of interviews, but a failure to replicate it, in the second.

In conclusion, the studies based on lexically defined therapist activity level failed to produce significant results. By contrast, therapist activity level objectively defined as quantity of verbal output has proven to be an illuminating variable, with significant findings in both the therapeutic and initial diagnostic interviews, and for both experimental analogue and naturalistic investigations. The failure of the lexical approach to the study of activity level may be a consequence of its dependence on a variable that lacks unidimensionality. For example, it will be recalled that the Howe and Pope (1961b) definition of therapist activity level referred to three attributes or semantic dimensions—lead, inference, and ambiguity. In the section that follows only the last dimension—therapist ambiguity (or specificity)—will be considered, to determine whether a reduction in the dimensionality of a variable increases its utility in the investigation of the interviewer-interviewee verbal interaction.

Therapist Ambiguity-Specificity

A study by Pope and Siegman (1962) appears to confirm the above contention. The data consisted of the verbatim transcripts of 12 naturalistic psychiatric interviews. Its objective was to determine the relationship between both *activity level* and *specificity* in therapist remarks and such aspects of patient verbal behavior as productivity (clause units) and speech disturbances (Mahl, 1956) in immediately following patient responses. Therapist remarks were rated for activity level with the Howe and Pope (1961b) scale, discussed above, and for specificity with a scale developed by Lennard and Bernstein (1960). No significant findings for activity level occurred, but predicted negative correlations between therapist specificity and patient productivity were obtained in nine out of 12 interviews;

similar negative correlations between therapist specificity and patient speech disturbance were found in six out of eight interviews. Thus, therapist message or informational ambiguity (the converse of specificity) was positively associated with patient productivity (clause units) and with an index that purported to measure anxiety (Mahl's Speech Disturbance Ratio). It should be noted that the Speech Disturbance Ratio used included both ah and non-ah disturbances of speech (Mahl, 1956). These were later separated, with only the non-ah ratio retained as an index of anxiety (Mahl, 1963).

The positive association of therapist ambiguity and patient productivity accorded with the psychoanalytically based concept of the projective interview. Thus, Bordin (1955) spoke about ambiguity in psychotherapy as fostering the type of associational flow that circumvents the patient's ordinary defenses (as it does in a projective device) bringing into the therapy interview "his major conflictual feelings no matter how unaware he is of them" (Bordin, 1955, p. 13). Structure and specificity from the therapist would tend to obstruct the above process, especially when irrational thoughts and feelings are at issue.

Nor would psychoanalytic theory find it inconsistent that patient productivity would be associated with anxiety under the condition of therapist ambiguity. Such an expectation "assumes that people try to defend themselves against anxiety associated with conflictual impulses by denying to awareness or distorting those stimuli associated with the impulse. When the stimuli are ambiguous, the discriminative processes necessary for defense are hampered and greater anxiety will result" (Bordin, 1955, p. 13). Thus, specific therapist inputs such as narrowly focused questions would provide the patient with the discriminant stimuli needed to activate his defenses. Ambiguous inputs would lack such stimuli and would therefore foster the expression of anxiety-arousing communication.

The Lennard and Bernstein (1960) model of the psychotherapeutic interview as an informational exchange system provides a different theoretical foundation for the positive association between therapist ambiguity and patient productivity, although it does not address itself to the possible correlation of therapist ambiguity and patient anxiety. Lennard and Bernstein (1960) speak about a reciprocal relationship between the information put into the communication system by each member of the therapy dyad. The informational input of the therapist is determined by the ambiguity of his remarks. Thus, an ambiguous remark which does not restrict the options available to the interviewee for replying has low informational stimulus value; a specific remark has high informational value. The informational input of the interviewee is measured in his productivity. Since the therapist's task is that of prompting or eliciting information from the patient, his productivity is not crucial, but the ambiguity of his inputs is. In accordance with the principle of informational reciprocity advanced by the authors, ambiguous therapist remarks (remarks with low informational stimulus value) should be followed by relatively long patient responses, and specific therapist remarks by relatively brief patient responses. The same principle of reciprocity and, indeed, the findings of Lennard and Bernstein (1960) would lead one to expect that unproductive patient responses would be followed by specific therapist communications, and relatively productive patient responses by ambiguous therapist communications. Pope and Siegman (1962) were only able to confirm the therapist-to-patient component of the reciprocal relationship; the patient-to-therapist component was not significant in their data.

In the relationships described above, only message or informational ambiguity is involved. This aspect of therapist ambiguity is a major stylistic dimension, germane to the therapist-patient verbal interaction. But it is by no means the only form in which ambiguity may occur in the interview. Bordin (1955) refers to interviewer ambiguity as a variable related to the degree to which an interviewer defines himself or the situation to an interviewee: "It is possible to conceive of three especially relevant areas in which these definitions can take place: (a) the topics it is appropriate to discuss with him, (b) the closeness and other characteristics of the relationship expected; (c) the therapist's values, in terms of the goals he assumes he and the patient should work toward . . . ." (p. 10). The first and third area relate to informational or message aspects of ambiguity. Under (a), consider the contrast between the analyst who instructs his patient to speak of anything that occurs to him, and the behavior therapist who might ask his patient to give him a precise, blow-by-blow account of a recent angry exchange with his wife. Under (c), compare the analyst who begins the therapy session in silence with the practitioner of desensitization who tells the patient that the goal on a particular day is to complete training in deep muscle relaxation. Finally,

under (b), contrast the mute psychoanalyst, seated behind the patient, with the client-centered practitioner, facing his client and engaging in a spontaneous, "genuine," egalitarian exchange. It need hardly be added that in each of the above instances the first example in each pair is the ambiguous one; the second, the specific one.

Therapist ambiguity may be defined more pointedly in informational terms. In developing their 11-point empirical scale for assessing therapist specificity (the converse of ambiguity), Siegman and Pope (1962) utilized the informational definition of specificity advanced by Lennard and Bernstein (1960). Messages sent by the interviewer to the interviewee differ in the degree to which they limit the range of possible patient response. For example, the therapist remark, "Just start by saying anything that occurs to you," does not limit the patient's response to any specific subject area and may therefore be said to have low informational specificity (high ambiguity). By contrast, the question, "How old is your sister?" sets definite and narrow limits on the range of possible alternatives for the patient's reply. It may, therefore, be said to have high informational specificity (low ambiguity). In the studies that follow the informational definition of ambiguity governs the investigations carried out.

One additional comment is needed about the Pope and Siegman (1962) study reviewed above. The second finding of the study—i.e., the positive association between therapist ambiguity and the early Mahl (1956) Speech Disturbance Ratio—was considered, tentatively, as evidence that therapist ambiguity promotes patient anxiety. However, speech disturbances as scored by Mahl were viewed as indicative of cognitive uncertainty rather than anxiety in a study by Brenner, Feldstein, and Jaffe (1965). These authors determined the occurrence of speech disturbances when subjects were asked to read passages varying in their approximation to written English. They found a negative correlation between a passage's level of approximation to written English and the level of speech disturbance it elicited. Thus, speech disturbance has been variously assumed to be indicative of either anxiety or cognitive uncertainty. The meaning of patient speech disturbance as a consequence of therapist ambiguity was therefore itself ambiguous. Both anxiety and cognitive uncertainty were thought to be possible sequelae of therapist ambiguity.

To further test the consequences of interviewer ambiguity and, more particularly, to clarify the role of interviewee anxiety and/or cognitive uncertainty in resulting verbal behavior, an experimental analogue of the initial interview was devised (Pope & Siegman, 1962; Siegman & Pope, 1965). Both interviewer specificity as measured by the Siegman and Pope (1962) scale and the anxiety arousing effect of the interviewer's topical focus, were independently manipulated in an experimental interview. (The latter variable is not of immediate concern.) The Ss were 50 junior and senior students at a university-based school of nursing. Again, ambiguous rather than specific interviewer remarks were associated with high interviewee productivity (number of words spoken). Regarding the occurrence of either (or both) anxiety and cognitive uncertainty, it should be noted that Mahl no longer considered his first Speech Disturbance Ratio (1956) as an index of anxiety. He had removed the category termed ah (the expression ah and allied hesitation expressions) from the ratio, designating the remaining speech disturbances as components of the non-ah ratio (Mahl, 1956). Ah, sometimes referred to as the "filled pause ratio," is on its face an expression of hesitation. The non-ah ratio has been assumed to be indicative of the flustered speech of anxiety. In the results of the second investigation, therapist ambiguity was associated with a high ah ratio, but was not significantly related to the non-ah ratio. In sum, therapist ambiguity was associated with both high interviewee productivity and the type of hesitation and caution that reflects interviewee uncertainty. Interviewee anxiety did not occur. In a second experimental analogue study (Pope & Siegman, 1968), dealing only in part with interviewer ambiguity, the preceding results were replicated.

The findings regarding interviewee productivity and hesitation were replicated in quite a different kind of investigation (Pope, Blass, Cheek, Siegman, & Bradford, 1971). In this instance the Ss were not nursing students but psychiatric inpatients, interviewed three times by the same interviewer, in one low-specificity, one high-specificity, and one uncontrolled interview. The low-specificity (ambiguous) interviews did indeed evoke significantly greater productivity than high, with uncontrolled interviews falling between the two. Low-specificity interviews also evoked high interviewer hesitation and caution (long reaction time, high silence quotient, and slow rate of speech). Thus, the association between interviewer ambiguity and both interviewee productivity and uncertainty, as

reflected in several indexes of caution and hesitation, has been noted in experimental analogues of the interview, in semi-naturalistic interviews, and partially in an early naturalistic psychotherapy study.

A study conducted by Heller (1968) appeared to contradict the above findings regarding the relationship between interviewee productivity and interviewer ambiguity. However, Heller created interviewer ambiguity through the distortion of his speech by a throat microphone and a voice-distorting machine. He found that interviewee talk time was higher in the clear than in the distorted condition, but self-referent remarks (an index of self-disclosure) were more numerous in the distorted condition. It is difficult to make a meaningful comparison of the Heller study with those by Pope and Siegman, since Heller's ambiguity referred to both reduced informational input and a distortion of language as such, which may well constitute a threat to the entire communication system.

Pope, Siegman, and their colleagues distinguish between interviewee anxiety as reflected in flustered speech (non-ah ratio) and cognitive uncertainty as noted in hesitation and caution (ah ratio, rate of speech, silence, reaction time). They considered only the latter to be a consequence of interviewer ambiguity. But their findings conflict with clinical impression and some findings of other investigators.

Sullivan (1954) was forceful and very specific in his observation about the association between therapist ambiguity and patient anxiety: "Were any of us to be interviewed about a significant aspect of our living by a person who gave us no clues as to what he thought and how we were doing, I think we would be reduced to mutism within a matter of minutes" (p. 103). The mutism was considered to be a result of a paralyzing sort of anxiety.

Sullivan's clinical impression was supported by an investigation carried out by Dibner (1953), based on semi-naturalistic diagnostic interviews he conducted at the point of admission to a psychiatric service in a general hospital. Four clinicians were instructed to interview five patients in an ambiguous manner and five in a structured manner. The experimentally manipulated ambiguity of the interviewer was clearly informational in character, and would in fact rate at a low point on the Siegman and Pope (1962) Specificity Scale. Patient anxiety was measured with ratings of speech disturbance, GSR conductance level, an introspective report by the patient, and global ratings of anxiety by a clinical judge who audited the interview tape recordings. The ambiguity achieved by each interviewer was determined by a measure of the structure provided by the interviewer's verbalizations (objective index) and by the patients' ratings of their perceptions of interviewer structure. Four of the anxiety measures correlated positively with the objective index of therapist ambiguity, and two with the patients' subjective ratings. Thus, Dibner did indeed find a positive relationship between therapist ambiguity (the opposite of structure) and patient anxiety.

However, the Dibner position regarding therapist ambiguity and patient anxiety was contradicted by a later investigation (McCarron & Appel, 1971) again using GSR amplitude as a measure of anxiety arousal. This study was based on two analyses. In one a 21-year-old patient with a schizoid personality disturbance was studied across a series of 12 weekly psychotherapy sessions. His therapist was a psychiatrist with more than 10 years of clinical experience. In the second analysis based on an initial interview the Ss were 12 patients with a variety of problems; their therapists were six male psychiatrists and six male medical students. The therapist remarks were distributed among four categories—reflection, interrogation, interpretation, and confrontation—arranged in the order of low to high specificity as defined by Lennard and Bernstein (1960). Both in the psychotherapy series and in the group of initial interviews, GSR amplitude in both patient and therapist was found to increase with the stimulus specificity of the therapist verbalizations. Clearly, specificity, and not ambiguity, as in the Dibner (1953) study, evoked anxiety in patient and therapist. Specificity appeared to impart a quality of stimulus potency to interviewer remarks. Both the Dibner (1953) and the McCarron and Appel (1971) investigations found significant associations between interviewee anxiety and interviewer ambiguity, although the direction of relationship in one study was the opposite of that in the other. Both investigations are in conflict with those of Pope, Siegman, and their colleagues (Pope & Siegman, 1962; Pope & Siegman, 1968; Pope et al., 1971; Siegman & Pope, 1965) in which no association between interviewer ambiguity and interviewee anxiety occurred.

A possible reason for this conflict may be the failure of the Dibner (1953) and the McCarron and Appell (1971) studies to control for topical focus. That topics vary considerably in their anxiety-arousing effects was demonstrated by

Siegman and Pope (1965) when they manipulated therapist ambiguity and topical focus independently. As indicated above, the former was associated with cognitive uncertainty (ah ratio). The association of the latter with anxiety (non-ah ratio) will be considered below, in the section dealing with the expressive style of the therapist. This evidence regarding the anxiety-arousing effect of topical focus would suggest that the confounding of topic with other communication variables remains a major flaw in interview research.

As Bordin (1955) implied, the study of therapist ambiguity need not be limited to lexical or message aspects of the communication system. Situational or relationship ambiguity is the subject of the two studies that follow. In one (Siegman & Pope, 1972), situational or relationship ambiguity was created by placing a screen between the interviewer and interviewee. It was assumed that the barrier posed by a screen would indeed create a condition of relationship ambiguity because the "... interviewer's feelings and attitudes about the interviewee are encoded primarily in such non-verbal cues as smiling, head nodding, and other body movements. By monitoring these non-verbal interviewer cues, the interviewee obtains information about the adequacy of his responses and the impression he is making upon the interviewer" (p. 48). When such information is cut off by a screen, one may assume that a condition of interpersonal ambiguity results. The presence of the screen had the effect of significantly reducing the verbal productivity (number of words spoken) of experimental Ss below that of control Ss, decreasing the rate of speech, and increasing the ah ratio (filled pauses). Thus, unlike message ambiguity, relationship ambiguity decreased productivity, but like message ambiguity, increased verbal indexes of hesitation and uncertainty.

In order to assess the possibility that the above results were artifactual consequences of the presence of the screen, rather than sequelae of relationship ambiguity, the procedure was varied somewhat in a second investigation. In the second experimental condition the interviewees faced away from the interviewer, so that they could not see him, while he had an angular view of them. In this experimental analogue of the psychoanalytic situation the interviewer's non-verbal reinforcing cues were reduced, as in the case of the interposition of the screen. In the control condition the interviewees faced the interviewer in the usual manner. Again, interviewee productivity was significantly lower and hesitation greater in the experimental than in the control condition. However, the significant indexes of hesitation varied somewhat from those that were significant in the previous study. Thus, the ah ratio was again greater in the ambiguous rather than the control condition, but the speech rate difference dropped out, being replaced by a slower reaction time.

Thus, whether it occurs in the interviewer's messages or in situational aspects of the relationship between himself and the interviewee, ambiguity is associated with interviewee hesitation and uncertainty. The drop in interviewee productivity under conditions of relationship ambiguity, but not message ambiguity, may be a consequence of the threat that the former poses to the communication system. A similar possibility was considered previously in relation to Heller's (1968) findings regarding distorted interviewer speech.

Finally, there are the comments by Frank (1961) about the association between a therapist's ambiguity and his persuasive power over the patient. Many therapists maintain an aura of ambiguity about the goals of treatment; they imply that they know what the patient's problems are but that the patient can only benefit from treatment if he discovers them for himself. The patient is compelled to strive for an unspecified cure and lacks cues regarding his progress toward its attainment. Since the patient remains dependent on the therapist for a reduction of the ambiguity in the situation, he is highly susceptible to the therapist's influence.[3] This picture may be somewhat overdrawn, but it is not a basically inaccurate description of the manipulation of ambiguity in traditional psychotherapy.

EXPRESSIVE STYLE OF THERAPIST

In the preceding section the instrumental functions of some dimensions in therapist style were investigated. In the remainder of this chapter the focus will be on therapist's expressive behavior. Note, however, that the distinction between instrumental and expressive communication is not as clear as one might wish. "Expressive speech or words are said to convey emotion in contrast to the semantic or syntactic aspects of words and speech which are said to impart meaning.... One ends up with the antithesis in sociology between 'instrumental' (problem solving) and 'expressive' (affective) behavior and, in psychology, with the contrast between 'cogni-

tion' and 'emotion'" (Spiegel & Machotka, 1974, p. 25). The instrumental nature of such dimensions as directiveness-nondirectiveness and interpretation is indeed evident. Nor is there any difficulty in recognizing the relevance of certain linguistic and paralinguistic forms of communications to the expression of affect. Thus, tone of voice, tempo of speech, and its flustering may be correlated with the expression of certain emotions or psychological states. But the research studies summarized below will indicate that expressive communication is not limited in its effect to the release of inner psychological states, their display, and the eliciting of resonant emotional responses from the person to whom communication is directed. Within the context of the interview, it may also perform certain instrumental roles. However, the characteristic that appears to distinguish expressive from other forms of speech is its primary relevance to the communication of affect.

General Expressiveness

At a later point, the investigation of the therapist's communication of specific emotions will be reviewed. For the present, the concern will be with therapist emotional expressiveness as a generality. Such expressiveness may occur in both linguistic and paralinguistic components of speech, but possibly more in the latter than the former.

Linguistics deals with words and syntactical structures. The sounds of language "... are those that are essential for the production of the words of a language. For example, if I want to say the word 'tin' it is absolutely essential that I produce a 't' sound..."(Markel, 1969, p. 5). By contrast, paralinguistics consists of "... all sounds not essential to word formation ... Language is always accompanied by nonlanguage. That is, whenever a speaker is producing sounds to form words he is also producing sounds which are not essential to form words..." (Markel, 1969, p. 6). Clearly, language attains a higher level of institutionalized structure than paralanguage; the latter is more readily adaptable to the expression of idiosyncratic feeling or experience than the former and is therefore better suited for expressive rather than instrumental speech. The following are some paralinguistic categories: intonation patterns (pitch and juncture in speech), "tone of voice," vocal differentiators (laughing, crying, breaking), tempo of speech (Pittenger & Smith, 1957) and vocalizations (e.g., pauses and speech disturbances).

Paralinguistic expressions have no referential meaning in themselves but contribute to the auditor's impression of "how" something is said.

Nevertheless, one cannot entirely deny the contribution of language to the therapist's expressive style. For example, Lennard and Bernstein (1960) gave considerable attention to the therapist's linguistic references to affect in the psychotherapeutic interview and how they articulated with those of the patient. Basing themselves on eight psychotherapeutic dyads (four therapists with two patients each) over their first 50 sessions, they found that the therapists increased the frequency with which they inquired into patient verbalizations about feelings as the therapy proceeded. Congruently, the patients increased the frequency with which they spoke about their feelings. When Lennard and Bernstein divided their psychotherapy protocols into three successive time intervals, they noted an increasing synchrony over each successive interval. Thus, the correlation between percentage of patient and therapist propositions dealing with affect was .23 over the first two sessions, .43 over the fifth and sixth sessions, and .70 over two sessions from the third and fourth months.

With the division of individual sessions into three 15-minute segments, the authors found that there was an increase in communication about affect between the first and second segments, and a drop again between the second and third.[4] The drop was probably a consequence of the tendency of communication to veer in the direction of arrangement-type talk about such matters as fees and appointment time as the end of an interview approaches. The sequential pattern within the interview was more marked for the therapist than for the patient.

Another therapy process study (Isaacs & Haggard, 1966) investigated the relationship between therapist interventions containing affective words and the meaningfulness of patient response. Therapist and patient statements were classified into those containing *affect words* (directly expressing joy, sadness, love, hate, loneliness), *emotionally toned words* (either mixtures or amalgams of affective and cognitive elements or such ambiguous emotions as worry, upset, disturbance), and *nonaffective* words. A meaningfulness scale for patient responses was developed by submitting 50 patient statements to 20 experienced therapists for rating on a 5-point scale tracing a meaningfulness dimension. On relating the affect and nonaffect groups of therapist interventions to the immediate responses of patients, as scored on the meaningfulness scale,

the affect group was found to be more evocative of meaningful patient response than the non-affect group. Additionally, the similarity of the present and the preceding study regarding the interviewer-interviewee synchrony in the communication of affective words is striking. There was a *rho* of .80 between interviewer and interviewee overall level of affective statement across interviews in the work by Isaacs and Haggard (1966).

The next investigation differs from the preceding two in its use of a paralinguistic rather than a linguistic approach to the study of therapist expressiveness.

The objective of Duncan, Rice, and Butler (1968) in their research on therapist paralinguistic attributes was to explore ". . . the relationship between the therapist's designation of therapy hours as either peak or poor and his voice quality during these hours" (p. 566). They had assumed that when voice quality and content were not congruent the listener gave greater credence to the former rather than the latter. Each of nine experienced therapists was asked to select a peak interview from his first 20 sessions (all taped) with one patient, and a particularly poor interview from his first 20 sessions (also taped) with another patient. Thus, the basic data consisted of nine peak sessions and nine poor sessions selected on the basis of the therapists' own criteria of excellence and inferiority. From the various paralinguistic categories outlined by Trager (1958), the following were chosen because they were considered to be particularly germane to the psychotherapy process: (a) intensity of voice including such gradations as overloud, normal, and oversoft; (b) pitch height encompassing overhigh, normal, and overlow pitches; and (c) vocal lip control (i.e., control of vocal cords) which may range from overtight to open, the latter associated with softness and warmth of tone. In addition, three types of verbal nonfluencies were used—unfilled hesitation pauses, filled hesitation pause (ah) and repeats.

Through a process of factor analysis, three paralinguistic interview types emerged, the first associated with peak interviews, and the remaining two with poor hours. The peak interviews were characterized by such attributes of interviewer speech as oversoft intensity, oversoft pitch, open vocal cord control, unfilled hesitation pauses, and repeats. In this type of interview the therapist would sound "serious, warm, and relaxed. In those moments when open voice was present, the therapist would sound especially close, concerned, and warm" (Duncan et al., 1968, p. 569). Two paralinguistic patterns were associated with poor hours. In one the major characteristic was a forced overloud intensity together with overhigh pitch at some times and oversoft intensity at other times. "In this type of interview the therapist's voice would sound dull and flat, rather uninvolved. When his voice took on more energy, he would seem to be speaking for effect, editorializing" (Duncan et al., 1968, p. 567). The third pattern, also associated with poor hours, included all three nonfluencies, but predominantly filled pauses.

The authors concluded that groups of paralinguistic variables, rather than the variables taken singly, distinguish between effective and ineffective psychotherapist behavior. In addition they remarked: "It may prove highly profitable to take non-verbal behaviors of this nature into account in evaluating the reinforcement characteristics of any interpersonal interaction, whether it be social, therapeutic, or experimental" (Duncan et al., 1968, p. 570).

Finally, there is an important group of studies within the client-centered framework (Butler, Rice, & Wagstaff, 1962; Rice, 1965) that uses both linguistic and paralinguistic variables to investigate therapist and client expressiveness. Only the aspects dealing with therapist expressiveness will be reviewed here. The rationale of the authors is that an expressive therapist has a stimulating impact on a client, evoking a strong response from him and thus prompting him into new experiences (Butler et al., 1962). "The effect of a stimulating therapist is to arouse or re-arouse within the individual more associations, images, trains of thought, etc.... It seems obvious that the stimulus (therapist communication and behavior) with the greatest connotative range, with the most far-reaching reverberations within the organism, results in a maximum of satisfying experience" (p. 188). The authors imply that a stimulating therapist style is an important condition for therapeutic change.

Rice (1965) set out to develop and test a process language, both lexical and vocal, for describing therapist style. The system she designed consisted of three categories:

1. *Freshness of words and combinations. Fresh, connotative words* have "a metaphorical quality with high imagery, auditory and kinaesthetic as well as visual" while *ordinary language* consists of commonplace words and phrases.

2. *Voice quality.* An *expressive voice* manifests high energy, which is controlled but not constricted. There is a wide range of pitch, emphatic and appropriate to the communication. A *usual voice* demonstrates a moderate level of energy and a limited pitch range. A *distorted voice* shows marked pitch variation with a declamatory emphasis which connotes a speaking for effect rather than for the spontaneous expression of meaning.

3. *Functional level.* This refers to the "... expressive stance..." of the therapist. If it is one of inner exploring, the focus is on the client's immediate *inner experience*. If it is an *observing* stance, it prompts the therapist to join the client in "... observing and analyzing the self as an object...". In an *outside focus* the therapist responds to something outside the client, but from within the client's frame of reference.

The data on which the study was based consisted of taped interviews of 20 client-therapist pairs, all selected from the files of the University of Chicago Counseling Center, a clinic with a Rogerian orientation. Five advanced graduate students audited the tapes (two students for each tape), and rated 30 therapist responses per tape, 10 consecutive responses being selected from equal thirds of the interview. Through a process akin to factor analysis (Butler et al., 1962), three interview types were separated out, each characterized by a different pattern of therapist expressive behavior. In Type I the therapist style was ordinary, characterized by commonplace words and phrases, a usual voice quality, and an observing functional level. Type II interviews were, again, noted for commonplace (not fresh) language and a self-observational functional level. However, their most prominent attribute was a distorted voice quality. Finally, Type III interviews were characterized by fresh, connotative language, an expressive voice quality, and a functional level of inner exploration. The third type of interview in contrast to the first and second was associated with the most stimulating of the three therapist expressive styles and was expected to be most evocative of positive therapeutic change. One measure of change was based on a questionnaire completed by the therapist at the termination of therapy. The other four were client measures, including a questionnaire paralleling the therapist's, a client change measure based on a Q sort, and two MMPI-based client change measures—the Taylor Manifest Anxiety Scale and the Barron Ego Strength Scale. Type II interviews were negatively associated with successful outcome on two of the five measures. By contrast, Type III interviews were positively correlated with successful outcome on three of the five outcome measures. The author concluded that "...style of participation is related to...favorableness of case outcome" (Rice, 1965, p. 160). The expressive style of the interviewer most conducive to positive therapeutic change (i.e., Type III) was an active one, marked by fresh, connotative language, expressive voice quality, and a focus on inner exploration.

The Expression of Specific Emotions

Although there is considerable literature dealing with the verbal expression of specific emotions, most of it focuses on the interviewee rather than the interviewer. This need surprise no one since the communication of such feelings as anxiety, hostility, or depression by the patient is considered to be central to the psychotherapeutic process. The therapist's task is to prompt such communication. However, his capacity to elicit emotional communication is not unrelated to the emotional tone of his own speech. The preceding section presented some evidence that general affective expressiveness by the therapist has a stimulating and evocative effect on the patient. In view of this it should not be long before interviewer style, as defined by his expression of specific emotions, will become an object of considerable inquiry. For the present, the extant studies in this area are few. To review these, it will first be necessary to summarize briefly, but in considerable imbalance with the major focus on therapist style, some of the research on patient affective communication, in order that the relevant concepts and instruments of study be made explicit.

By way of introduction, there will be a look at a study that ranged over three specifically designated affects—anxiety, anger, and depression—in 15-tape-recorded interviews of a patient in intensive psychotherapy (Eldred & Price, 1958). Avoiding the technical specifics of a microlinguistic analysis of· their data, the research group pursued an impressionistic clinical course. After the four auditors participating in the study listened, both privately and as a group, to many psychotherapy interviews, they developed "... the hypothesis that passages which communicate certain kinds of feeling states to the auditors have *over-all* vocalization patterns which are significantly different from the vocalization patterns in the rest of the interview" (Eldred & Price, 1958, p. 116). The group selected the following paralinguistic variables as the channels in which they listened for the above-designated affects:

"(1) Alterations of pitch (overhigh pitch and overlow pitch).

(2) Alterations of volume (overloudness and oversoftness).

(3) Alterations of rate (overfastness and overslowness).

(4) Break-up (much break-up or little break-up . . .)"

The last variable pertains to the disruption of the smooth flow of speech. Later in this section, similar variables will be designated as pauses and speech disruptions.

The four auditors listened to the 15 tapes as a group, following on typescripts, and characterizing interviewee passages agreed upon as expressive of specific emotions, with the above parameters. Following this impressionistic procedure, they arrived at a consensus about the paralinguistic features of three basic emotions and two additional emotional variants.

Anxiety was always marked by increased break-up (i.e., flustering) of speech. In other respects it varied over time. Sometimes patient anxiety was associated with overhigh pitch, overloudness, and overfastness; at other times, the opposite characteristics were found. *Suppressed anger* had a pattern of overhigh pitch, overloudness, overfastness, and high break-up. *Overt anger* was similar to suppressed anger in its overhigh pitch, overloudness, and overfastness. But, unlike suppressed anger, it lacked a high level of break-up. In his overtly angry moods the patient spoke fluently, without disruption. The patient's passages designated as *suppressed depression* were characterized by overlow pitch, oversoftness, and overslowness, associated with increased break-up. In his *overtly depressed* passages the patient's communication was similarly marked by overlow pitch, oversoftness, but without the increased break-up of suppressed depression. Although this study in intuitive and qualitative rather than rigorously controlled and quantitative, it presented rather vividly some strikingly discernible paralinguistic differences between specified emotions in the patient's speech.

Because of its central role in personality theory and in communication, anxiety is the affect that has received most intensive scrutiny in psychotherapy research. The literature on the expression of anxiety reflects rather clearly the two basic and sometimes contending approaches to the study of affect in speech—the linguistic and the paralinguistic routes. Gottschalk (Gottschalk & Gleser, 1969) has pursued the former course; Mahl (1959), followed by others (Siegman & Pope, 1972), pursued the latter.

Gottschalk and his group (Gottschalk, Winget, Gleser, & Springer, 1966) based their advocacy of the use of linguistic content for the assessment of transient feelings such as anxiety and hostility, on the following assumptions:

1. "The relative magnitude of an affect can be validly estimated from the typescript of the speech of an individual, using solely content variables" (Gottschalk et al., 1966, p. 96).

2. From verbal content alone, it is possible to assess the strength of a transient feeling. This strength varies directly as: (a) the relative frequency of the verbal themes that are related to specific affects and (b) the weight assigned to each. "Higher weights have tended to be assigned to scorable verbal statements which communicate affect that, by inference, is more likely to be strongly experienced by the speaker" (Gottschalk et al., 1966, p. 67). The more directly the statement relates the affect to the speaker, the more intensely he is assumed to experience it. Additionally, a greater personal involvement is weighted more than a lesser one (e.g., an unmodulated statement about a feeling is given greater weight than a statement followed by its denial). An ordinal measure of the magnitude of the affect is calculated by obtaining the product of the frequency of occurrence of specified categories of verbal statements and the weights assigned to them.

The thematic categories in the anxiety scale include death, anxiety, mutilation, separation, guilt, shame, and diffuse or nonspecific anxiety. This anxiety scale is a sophisticated example of the use of linguistic content in the assessment of affect. While it has been widely used in the study of interviewee communication, there are no investigations known to the author in which it was applied to interviewer speech. However, one study in which the scale was used did encompass the verbal communication of both psychotherapist and patient, exploring the emotional congruence between the two. The data were obtained from a taped psychotherapy interview, the second of two selected from a psychotherapy series for intensive analysis by a number of researchers, all interested in the application of psycholinguistics to the investigation of communication in psychotherapy (Gottschalk, Springer, & Gleser 1961). In the interview under consideration the content of the therapist's remarks pertained to shame and nonspecific anxiety. The same two themes dominated the patient's verbalizations, as assessed by the Gottschalk anxiety scale. That patient-therapist

emotional congruence did indeed occur was evident again in the earlier interview. There, five of the six therapist comments focused on hostility; synchronously, the patient's verbalizations were given high hostility ratings with another linguistically based Gottschalk affect scale.

Emotional congruence or synchrony in the interview has been noted by other authors. Reference has already been made to the finding by Lennard and Bernstein (1960) that there is increasing congruence between therapist and patient propositions dealing with affect as therapy proceeds during the first 4 months. In an experimental analogue of the initial interview (Heller, Myers & Kline, 1963), four student actors were trained to play the roles of hostile and friendly clients. The interviewers were 34 graduate students, instructed to conduct initial intake interviews with "clients" on the waiting list of a university counseling center. As anticipated, the interviewers demonstrated greater hostility, as assessed by observers' ratings on an interpersonal checklist, when the "clients" were hostile rather than friendly, and greater friendliness when the "clients" were friendly. Borrowing a phrase from Jones and Thibaut (1958) the authors described the psychotherapy interview as a "reciprocally contingent interaction" and concluded that their findings support this view.

Returning from the above digression to the literature dealing with the assessment of anxiety in verbal communication, the focus will now move from studies dealing with linguistic cues of anxiety to others investigating paralinguistic cues. On the basis of clinical observation, Sullivan (1954) remarked that "... much attention may profitably be paid to the telltale aspects of intonation, rate of speech, difficulty in enunciation....". In this observation, Sullivan anticipated the later research emphasis on paralinguistic cues of emotion in patient speech. Thus, Mahl (1963) listed such extralinguistic variables as rate of speech and its duration as vehicles of affective expression. But the categories that were by far of greatest interest to him were those indicative of speech disturbance. (See previous reference to his non-ah ratio in the discussion of therapist ambiguity.) His first speech disturbance ratio included the following categories: filled pauses (i.e., ah and allied hesitation expressions); sentence changes that interrupt the flow of speech and correct either the form or content of the utterance; superfluous repetition of one or more words; stutters; omission of parts of words, usually occurring during sentence change and repetition; sentence incompletion, in which a partial sentence is left dangling without correction; tongue slips including neologisms; the transposition of a word from an appropriate to an inappropriate position in a sentence; the substitution of an unintended for an intended word; and intruding incoherent sounds. Initially, all the above forms of speech disturbance were assumed to be indicative of anxiety (Mahl, 1956). Later, Mahl (1959) concluded that ah and similar expressions of hesitation were not related to the expression of anxiety. Since all other categories continued to be associated with anxiety in speech his verbal index of anxiety came to be known as the non-ah ratio.

In an early study (Mahl, 1956) based on a single psychotherapy series the therapist acting as judge divided six psychotherapy interviews into high- and low-anxiety segments. In order that his judgments might not be contaminated by the attributes of speech that were to be the dependent variables, all speech disturbances, silences, and other hesitations were removed from the typescripts. Speech disturbances, scored independently by another person, were significantly more frequent in the high- rather than the low-anxiety segments of patient speech. In a later follow-up experimental analogue study Kasl and Mahl (1958) assessed the speech disturbance levels of 25 experimental Ss, all male college students, during two successive interviews—the first functioning as a control for the second, which was an experimentally manipulated "anxiety" interview. Ten additional control Ss, also male college students, were given two successive control interviews. The rate of speech disturbance increased significantly during the "anxiety" interview.

Mahl (1963) regarded flustered speech as a stylistic or expressive variable reflecting the discharge of feeling. He contrasted this discharge function with certain resistive linguistic expressions such as "I don't know . . ." and "I can't. . . ." He noted that speech disturbances and such verbalizations as the above were likely to occur together in an interview, but the functions of the two were not the same. The former served to discharge emotion or drive and the latter to express a conscious sort of verbal resistance. Thus, he maintained a distinction between the expressive function of paralinguistic variables and the consciously controlled, defensive functions of linguistic variables.

But a close reading of the Mahl non-ah ratio dispels the notion that non-ah is purely an ex-

pressive index. Part of it does indeed appear to channel the discharge of anxiety as affect or drive (i.e., repetition, stutter, tongue slip, and intruding incoherent sound). But other speech disturbance categories appear to play the role of censor or editorial revisionist of what has already been or is in the process of being said, (i.e., sentence incompletion, omission, and sentence correction). Actually, Mahl and Schulze (1964) accepted this dual function of speech disturbances in their later work, emphasizing both the direct effect of anxiety noted in some categories of speech disturbances and the defense against the experienced anxiety noted in other categories.

Siegman and Pope (1972) took the position that anxiety may be regarded as a drive that would tend simultaneously to activate and disrupt speech. This view seemed to encompass in a parsimonious manner a number of paralinguistic findings that might otherwise appear contradictory. Thus, Kanfer (1958, 1960) had found verbal rate to accelerate in response to shock-conditioned tones and anxiety-arousing interview topics. Based on this finding and the view of anxiety as drive in the experimental literature, Siegman and Pope (1965) had predicted that an increase in anxiety level would bring an increase in verbal output both in terms of words uttered and rate of speech. Simultaneously the activation of competing response tendencies would result in an increase in speech disturbances.

These predictions were tested in an experimental analogue study based on the initial interview already discussed in the section on therapist specificity-ambiguity (Siegman & Pope, 1972). The Ss were 50 female nursing students, all interviewed by one of the authors, who followed a standard interview outline. Eight questions pertained to the topic of school experiences and eight other questions to family relationships. For the population studied, the former topic was demonstrated to be neutral in character and the latter, moderately anxiety-arousing. Within each topical segment, half of the questions were of high specificity and half of low (i.e., ambiguous). That anxiety did indeed function as a drive was noted in the greater productivity of the interviewee (number of words uttered), higher speech rate, and shorter reaction time associated with the anxiety-arousing rather than the neutral topical area. The last two findings were only at a borderline level of significance. The activating effect of anxiety was noted further in its association with low hesitation (low ah ratio) but only in the high- rather than low-specific segments of the interview. Thus, the impact of anxiety-arousing content was most pronounced when the interviewer zeroed in with specific questions. Simultaneous with anxiety's function as an activator of speech was its additional function as a disruptor of speech. This was noted in the higher non-ah ratio occurring in interviewee speech in the anxiety-arousing rather than neutral segment of the interview.

The basic paralinguistic pattern associated with interviewee anxiety, noted above, was observed in two further studies (Pope, Blass, Siegman, & Raher, 1970; Pope, Siegman, & Blass, 1970). However, there was some variation in the precise paralinguistic variables for which significant results were obtained from one study to another. The first of the above two studies was naturalistic in character. The paralinguistic correlates of both anxiety and depression in speech were investigated in a series of 10-minute monologues taped by six psychosomatic patients. The daily vicissitudes of anxiety and depression in the patient sample were determined by two nurses with research training using a rating method described by Bunny and Hamburg (1963). For each of the six patients, eight high- and eight low-anxiety days and eight high- and low-depression days were selected. Several paralinguistic attributes of speech in the monologues taped on the selected days were scored and analyzed. (Note that the monologues were taped daily over an extended period of time without reference to the days selected later for the study.) The activation effect of anxiety was observed in the higher speech rate and the lower silence quotient on high- rather than low-anxiety days; its disruptive effect was evident in the higher non-ah ratio on high-anxiety days. If anxiety may be viewed as an activator of speech, it was reasoned that depression may be regarded as a retarder. This anticipation was borne out in the lower speech rate and the higher silence quotient on the high- rather than the low-depression days.

The last study referred to above (Pope, Siegman, & Blass, 1970) was a second experimental analogue of the initial interview, and again demonstrated that anxiety both activates speech (increases the interviewees' verbal output) and disrupts it (increases the non-ah ratio).

The preceding studies deal with paralinguistic indexes of anxiety in the speech of patients and interviewees. The author knows of only two investigations in which interviewer style of expression of anxiety was investigated. The study by Pope, Nudler, VonKorff, & McGee,

(1974) was a comparison of the interviewer behavior of complete novices and experienced professionals in conducting initial interviews. The novices were male and female sophomore students who were about to begin their training as mental health workers but who had neither experience nor training as interviewers at the time the investigation was carried out. The experienced professionals were staff psychiatrists and 3rd-year psychiatric residents in a private psychiatric hospital, matched with the novices for sex. The interviewees were female college freshmen. Under the circumstances of the study, one would have expected the novice interviewers to be more tense and anxious than the experienced interviewers. That they were perceived by the interviewees as more tense was evident in their post-interview ratings of the interviewers. That the differential perception of the two groups of interviewers by the interviewees may have been based, in part, on each group's expressive style, was evident in the significantly higher level of speech disturbance (non-ah) for the novice rather than the professional interviewers. This finding is neither unexpected nor startling, but it does add to the construct validity network supporting the use of speech disturbance as an index of anxiety.

In a study by Russell and Snyder (1963) the behavior of the client was the independent variable and counselor response was the dependent variable. The goal was the investigation of the relationship between client hostility and interviewer anxiety in an experimental analogue of the counseling interview. The "clients" were two male actors, selected from an undergraduate course in theatre arts, and carefully trained to perform two "client" roles—one friendly, positive, and helpful, and the other, hostile, and negative. The counselors were 20 graduate students in counselor training. There were four criteria of counselor anxiety. The first two, palmar sweating and eyeblink rate, were physiological in nature and not particularly relevant to the current discussion of therapist style. However, the third and fourth were more congruent with the stylistic variables under examination in the present chapter. At the end of each interview, the "client" completed a 60-item scale rating counselor anxiety. Finally, the authors developed a composite scale containing 16 criteria for assessing verbal anxiety. Six experienced counselors listened to the taped interviews recorded by the counselor Ss and judged the verbal anxiety level of each with the use of the scale. The most frequently occurring criteria in the verbal anxiety scale were speech disturb-ances, such as unfinished sentences, repetition of words and phrases, stuttering, and blocking. Others were "tone of voice" variables such as poor voice quality and tremulousness. The remaining criteria included both inept inter-actions (interrupting, premature interpretations, unnecessary reassurance) and counselor avoid-ance of "client" content (changing the subject and not responding to the "client's feelings"). On three of the four criteria, hostile "client" behavior evoked greater counselor anxiety than friendly client behavior. Two of these are relevant to the present discussion. Thus, in their post-interview ratings of the counselors the "clients" perceived greater counselor anxiety in "hostile" rather than "friendly" interviews. However, the sharp-est discriminations between the two types of interviews occurred in the ratings of verbal anxiety, with the highest counselor anxiety again occurring in the "hostile" interviews.

A place in the present chapter has been reserved for the well-known investigation by Bandura, Lipsher, and Miller (1960) because of its focus on interviewer hostility anxiety. Twelve advanced clinical psychology graduate students, all of whom were rated for hostility anxiety in their extra therapy behavior by colleagues who knew them well both socially and profession-ally, served as interviewers. The various criteria of therapist hostility anxiety were then correlated with the approach and avoidance behavior of the interviewers to patient expression of hostil-ity. Only two criteria of several were significantly related to the therapist's intra-interview behav-ior. Thus, therapists who expressed hostility directly in their social lives, rather than indirect-ly, were more likely to respond to patient expres-sion of hostility with approach reactions (ap-proval, exploration, instigation of patient hostile talk, and labeling of patient affect) than with avoidance (disapproval, change of topics, silence, ignoring of patient affect, and mislabeling of expressed patient affect). In addition, therapists with a strong need for approval were more likely to avoid the patients' hostility than were thera-pists low in need for approval. Since therapist approach to patient communication may be expected to be reinforcing, it was anticipated that it would lead to the continued expression of this feeling by the patient. In fact, this was the case. In a complementary way, therapist avoid-ance of hostile topics led the patient to terminate discussion of them. Thus, interviewer hostility anxiety as a form of social response was opera-tive in the interview in the form of avoidance of patient hostility, with the consequent inhibition of the patient's exploration of his angry feelings.

The above studies have dealt with the expres-sion of specific negative feelings such as anxiety, depression, and hostility. In the concluding section of this chapter the focus will be on the expression by the therapist of such positive feelings as warmth and permissiveness. While research on therapist warmth is discussed else-where in this volume (Mitchell, Bozarth, & Krauft, Chapter 18; Gurman, Chapter 19) the studies reviewed here are derived from a different tradition and conceptual framework than those relating to the Truax-Carkhuff facilitative con-ditions in psychotherapy. It is therefore expected that there will be little, if any, overlap.

First, some of the ways in which warmth is specified in the psychotherapy literature will be reviewed. Raush and Bordin (1957) derived their definition of therapist warmth from concepts of personality development and psychoanalytic ego-psychology. In their view warmth consists of three components, which they designated as commitment, effort to understand, and spon-taneity. A therapist's commitment is noted in his assignment of a specified period of time to the patient and an undisturbed place to meet. In addition "... he commits his skills and his efforts at understanding and aiding the patient; he also commits to the patient a relationship in which the patient's needs and interests are dominant, and in which the therapist's personal demands are minimized" (p. 357). A therapist's commitment is most evident when he provides support and gratification to a patient with a long-term ego deficit, as in chronic schizo-phrenia, or with a transient paralysis of the ego, as in acute anxiety or depression.

As an aspect of warmth, the therapist's effort to understand is not independent of his active commitment to the patient. Nor does it lack some overlap with the concept of empathy. But empathy includes both the process and its end result—the accuracy with which the therapist perceives the patient. In a discussion of therapist warmth, it is only the process that is of interest—the therapist's efforts to achieve rapport with the patient and to enter into his contextual world. This may be communicated to the patient "... by attentive and unintrusive listening, by questions indicative of interest, by sounds of encourage-ment, by any of the verbal or nonverbal cues which say in effect, 'I am interested in what you are saying and feeling—go on'" (Raush & Bordin, 1957, p. 360). The third ingredient of warmth (therapist spontaneity) appears to be similar to the kind of general expressiveness that Rice (1965) and her colleagues associate with positive psychotherapy outcome. Central to therapist spontaneity is his readiness to be emotionally expressive in the interview situation. Raush and Bordin assume that "... a more spontaneous therapist will ... interact with more expression of affect than will a less spontaneous one" (p. 362).

In their definition of therapist warmth, Strupp, Fox, and Lessler (1969) followed a more empirical course. Their discussion of warmth occurred within the context of a study which elicited from former patients ratings of their impressions of both the psychotherapy process and of their former therapists. In the words of the authors "... we asked the patients to speak for themselves and to assess the over-all value of their experience" (Strupp et al., 1969, p. xv). This the patients did by indicating the degree of their agreement with a number of questionnaire statements descriptive of psychotherapy and psychotherapists as these might apply to their erstwhile therapists. Their responses were then intercorrelated and factor-analyzed, with two of the emerging factors of particular relevance to the present discussion. Indeed, one was designated as *therapist warmth* and the other as *therapist interest, integrity, and respect*. The two factors correlated positively with each other ($r = .55$), demonstrating a considerable degree of overlap. Moreover, the therapist traits associated with the two factors correlated positively and significantly with the patients' own judgments about the positive therapeutic change that they experienced.

The warm therapist was "... always keenly attentive ... having a manner that patients experienced as natural and unstudied, saying or doing nothing that decreased the patient's self-respect, at times giving direct reassurance ... and leaving no doubt about his 'real' feelings" (Strupp et al., 1969, p. 80). Though an empirical course was followed, the definition that emerged in this study is similar to that developed by Raush and Bordin on clinical and speculative grounds.

It would be safe to assume that there would be a broad consensus among clinicians that warmth is a positive force within the interview. Indeed, several authors have found that interviewer warmth does indeed facilitate interviewee communication in the forms of gross productivity and of verbal fluency (Pope & Siegman, 1972; Pope et al., 1974). However, several other authors have questioned the assumption that interviewer warmth necessarily promotes meaningful communication (Ganzer & Sarason, 1964; Heller, 1972; Heller et al., 1966; Sarason & Winkel, 1966).

In the Pope and Siegman (1972) research the *S*s were 32 junior and senior female nursing students (ages ranged from 20 to 22) who were each given two interviews, one warm and the other cold. The interviewers were two female clinical psychology interns, in their mid-20s. Each interviewer conducted both warm and cold interviews. The warm-cold manipulation was achieved by arousing contrasting warm and cold interviewee expectations regarding the interviewers, before the two succeeding interviews, and by varying the interviewers' behavior to accord with interviewee expectations. As predicted, warm interviews evoked a significantly higher productivity (i.e., mean number of words per response) than cold interviews. However, the warm-cold effect interacted with warm-cold sequence. Thus, the greater productivity associated with warm rather than cold interviews held only when the warm interview was the first in a sequence of two. When the cold interview was first, its inhibiting effect continued into the second (warm) interview, eliminating the productivity difference between the two. In a later study by Pope et al. (1974) in which experienced interviewers were compared with novices, interviewer warmth, as scored with the Non-Possessive Warmth Scale (Truax & Carkhuff, 1967) correlated positively with interviewee productivity (i.e., number of words spoken), but only in the interviews conducted by the novices.

In an earlier investigation Allen, Wiens, Weitman, & Saslow (1965) had failed to obtain a positive relationship between interviewer warmth and interviewee speech duration length (i.e., productivity). The method, however, was different in several respects from the procedure followed by Pope and Siegman (1972). The *S*s were 40 men applying for civil service positions as policemen or firemen who were in fact given employment interviews. The interviewer's behavior was not included in the warm-cold manipulation. The latter was based entirely on the creation of warm and cold sets, in random order, but equally distributed among the 40 *S*s. The warm-set *S*s read a paragraph descriptive of the interviewer they were to meet shortly, identical in content to the one read by the cold-set *S*s, with the exception that the words "very warm" were used to characterize the interviewer rather than the words "very cold." As indicated above, there was no difference in average length of

388   EFFECTIVE PSYCHOTHERAPY

interviewee utterance as between warm and cold interviews. However, the average interviewee reaction time, between the completion of the interviewer's utterance and the beginning of the interviewees' responses, was significantly shorter for the Ss given a warm rather than a cold set. Finally, returning to the Pope and Siegman (1972) study, cold interviews elicited higher non-ah speech disturbance ratios from the interviewees than the warm interviews, but only in high rather than low specific segments of the interviews. The evidence thus far tends in the direction of greater productivity, more rapid reaction time, and greater verbal fluency in response to warm rather than cold interviewers.

For the most part, these results are not directly challenged by the research reviewed below, but the negative findings of the studies that follow about interviewer warmth do create a climate of skepticism about the earlier positive ones. The first study is clearly relevant to the interview interaction, although it was designed in a verbal conditioning format (Ganzer & Sarason, 1964). The Ss were 40 male undergraduate students selected from an introductory psychology class. All Ss were put through an interview-like procedure in which they were told that the interviewer was interested in learning how students think and feel about themselves. One-half of the Ss was both greeted and later instructed in a hostile manner by the E; the other half was treated in a friendly way. In the interview analogue that followed, all Ss were reinforced for making negative self-references. As it turned out, those who were given the hostile treatment by the E were more self-disclosing in their more frequent use of negative self-reference than those treated in a friendly manner—i.e., they demonstrated a greater amount of conditioning. One may assume that the interview analogue in the Ganzer and Sarason study resembled a verbal conditioning experiment more than an interview. Yet it is difficult to avoid the possible implications of this experiment for interviewee self-disclosure. Is it conceivable that a cold interviewer rather than a warm one is more likely to promote the self-disclosure of negative psychological information? That such may be the case was suggested by Sarason and Winkel (1966), who found that the less favorably an interviewee rated an interviewer (i.e., more hostile), the more likely he was to speak to him in a personally revealing manner.

Partly as a consequence of these findings, Heller (1972) developed the hypothesis that moderately stressful interviews were more likely to evoke more self-disclosing communication than nonstressful interviews, particularly when an interviewee's defensive style permits him to be openly communicative about personal matters.

In one of his studies (Heller et al., 1966) each of 12 male interviewers was trained to play one of four experimentally controlled roles—that of an active-friendly, passive-friendly, active-hostile, or passive-hostile interviewer. Additionally, there was a group of interviewers that remained completely silent after they gave the Ss initial instructions. The Ss (interviewees) were introductory psychology students, both male and female. The effect of therapist activity-passivity in this study has been considered at an earlier point in the present chapter. The results were unambiguous with reference to the clear preference of the Ss for friendly rather than hostile interviewers. This preference was determined by asking each S to complete an inventory giving his reaction to the interview, and the interviewer, immediately after the completion of the experimental interview. The best liked interviews were the active-friendly ones; and the least liked, the passive-hostile ones. The silent interviews evoked preference scores that fell in between those for the hostile and friendly groups. However, there was no relationship between interviewer warmth and interviewee verbal behavior. Unlike Pope and Siegman (1972), Heller et al. (1966) failed to obtain a significant association between interviewer warmth and interviewee productivity (speaking time). Nor did they find any correlation between warmth and interviewee self-disclosure of pathology. The authors concluded that "there was no indication that verbal behavior during the interview changed in any way as a result of friendliness" (Heller et al., 1966, p. 506).

These findings were largely negative with reference to interviewer warmth, but they neither negated nor supported Heller's concept of the optimum, moderately stressful interview. Actually, his view about this matter was based on an interaction between type of interviewee and the degree of stress in an interview, as will be evident in the next three studies.

Heller and Jacobson (1967) selected 96 male and female Ss on the basis of their high- and low-dependency scores on the EPPS and asked them to talk about themselves in 30-minute personal interviews. There were three interview conditions. In the *friendly* condition the interviewers were trained "... to appear friendly, expressive, and encouraging by smiling appropriately, nodding, leaning toward the subject, and maintaining eye contact." In the *reserved* condition they did not smile, were nonexpressive, leaned away from the subject, and maintained minimum eye contact. In the *no-interviewer* condition subjects were given initial instructions to talk about themselves, after which they were left to respond to a tape recorder, with no other person present in the room. As in previous studies, friendly interviewers were best liked by all Ss. However, the verbal responses of Ss to the different interview conditions varied with the interviewee type. High-dependent males talked about themselves most often and their problems —i.e., they were most self-disclosing—in the *reserved* condition. By contrast, low-dependent (i.e., independent) males talked about themselves least in the reserved condition, a finding that contradicted the anticipations of the investigators. Similarly, independent females made their fewest problem references in the reserved condition. These findings do not offer strong support for Heller's hypothesis. There was, indeed, evidence that one group of Ss was prompted most toward self-disclosure by reserved interviewers, but the investigators had incorrectly predicted the specific groups of Ss that would react in this way.

The contrast between the responses of varying interviewee types to friendly and reserved interviewer styles was more emphatically evident in a later investigation (Heller *et al.*, 1968). Friendly and reserved interviewer styles were structured into single interviews so that style sequence followed a friendly-reserved-friendly (FRF) pattern in one group of interviews, and a reserved-friendly-reserved (RFR) pattern in another group. There were two groups of interviewees—college students and patients—both encouraged to speak about themselves. The two groups of Ss responded to the two interviewer style sequence patterns in sharply contrasting ways. The college students were more verbally productive in the RFR sequence than in the FRF sequence, and were less disturbed than the patients by the reserved condition, when it came first. The degree to which they were able to speak in a self-disclosing manner about themselves or their problems was not affected by the changes of interviewer style within interviews. The patient group was more productive and more self-disclosing in the FRF rather than the RFR sequence. In this instance the moderate stress of a reserved interviewer style stimulated the verbal responsiveness of one group of interviewees, inhibiting that of another.

Finally, there will be a brief reference to an investigation of the effect of therapist permissiveness on a patient's galvanic skin response (Dittes, 1957). It is selected as a means of ending this chapter because it provides an intra-organism view of the psychological effect of interviewer warmth on the interviewee.

Dittes' (1957) definition of interviewer permissiveness overlaps considerably with the Raush and Bordin (1957) concept of warmth. Thus, the permissive therapist is attentive, attempts to understand the patient, and does not intrude or force his opinions on the patient. Therapist permissiveness is characterized by the absence of critical, punishing behavior that often occurs in stressful interpersonal relationships. The typed transcripts of the final 43 hours of therapy with a 36-year-old male neurotic patient were rated on a 4-point permissiveness scale defined in terms of therapist understanding, gentleness, and overall acceptance. Therapist permissiveness showed a significant negative relationship with frequency of galvanic skin response. As therapist permissiveness increased within and across interviews, the patient's GSR frequency decreased, and thus, presumably his tension. Moreover, the therapist's permissiveness helped the patient to mitigate his embarrassment or anxiety whenever he communicated self-disclosing information that tended to arouse such feelings. Thus, embarrassing sex statements were accompanied by a GSR more frequently in hours that were scored low on permissiveness than in other hours scored high. The Dittes (1957) study is an intensive investigation of a single individual. It does not address itself to the kind of interactional problem raised by Heller and his colleagues. It does, however, demonstrate the psychological impact of warmth or permissiveness regardless of the ultimate view that will be taken of this therapist variable from an interactional perspective.

SUMMARY AND CONCLUSIONS

The summary that follows is an integration of research findings that have met two criteria: (a) resistance to erosion over time and (b) a significant level of clinical relevance. The multidimensional studies with which the chapter started, based on naturalistic psychotherapy interviews, are largely concerned with evaluating ideological conflicts between different schools of psychotherapy, particularly the nondirective and the psychoanalytic (Snyder, 1945; Strupp, 1958, 1960). Another controversy to which multidimensional studies have been directed occurs between the proponents of the primary salience for therapist style of school of allegiance versus that of the therapeutic relationship (Fiedler, 1950a, 1950b). Multidimensional scales are comprehensive, but lacking in definitional clarity. It was inevitable that a number of investigators would attempt to bring greater clarity of definition and economy of structure into these scales through factor analysis. In one study (Sundland & Barker, 1962) a general stylistic factor emerged, with an *analytic* pole at one extreme and an *experiential* pole at the other. Evidently the psychoanalytic versus nondirective dichotomy survived the rigorous sorting of individual scale items in the factor analysis. Another study (Apfelbaum, 1958) with impact on the conceptualization of therapist role, generated three factors, descriptive of three different patterns of therapist relationship behavior: the nurturant therapist, the permissive and nonjudgmental therapist, and the judgmental critic.

Unlike the multidimensional studies which are for the most part naturalistic in character, those based on single dimensions are either naturalistic investigations or experimental analogues of the therapy interview. In these studies, the stylistic dimension itself tends to become a focus of investigation. Hence, there is concern with its definition and with such related matters as the channel of communication (e.g., lexical, paralinguistic) through which it is expressed.

When the interest in nondirectiveness as a school yielded to an interest in nondirectiveness as a stylistic dimension, studies became less concerned with proving the superiority of one school over another and more involved with investigating this variable in the therapy interaction. In two experimental analogue studies (Ashby *et al.*, 1957; Friedman & Dies, 1974) the investigators demonstrated that directive and nondirective styles of treatment affected different types of clients differently. The first of these found that clients who were highly defensive before treatment responded more defensively to a leading rather than a reflective therapist. The second demonstrated that *S*s with an internal locus of control preferred a nondirective counseling situation to a structured, automated, desensitization session, while *S*s with an external locus of control had the reverse order of preference. That the level of therapist directiveness is responsive to certain traits and behaviors of the patient is noted in two additional analogue studies (Heller *et al.*, 1963; Parker, 1967). In the

second (Parker, 1967) male therapists gave significantly more nondirective responses to female than to male clients. In the first (Heller *et al.*, 1963), client dependence evoked directive interviewer behavior and client dominance evoked passive behavior.

If directiveness is relevant only to the interviewer, activity level (in the sense of gross productivity) applies equally to both interviewer and interviewee. In a number of naturalistic studies (Lennard & Bernstein, 1960) activity level as gross verbal output was used to demonstrate some of the attributes of the interview as a dyadic communication system. For example, increasing stability over a psychotherapy sequence was noted in the movement toward a fixed ratio between therapist and patient verbal output. Synchrony between therapist and patient activity level (i.e., productivity) was observed in several analogue studies (Heller *et al.*, 1966; Matarazzo, 1965). In these investigations the effect of therapist activity level was unidirectional because it was the experimentally manipulated independent variable. Synchrony failed to occur in a naturalistic psychotherapy study (Matarazzo *et al.*, 1968) in which both therapist and patient productivity were free to vary. Instead, there was a tendency toward an inverse relationship between therapist and patient productivity. That the character of the interaction affects the occurrence of synchrony was noted in yet another study (Pope *et al.*, 1974). When both interviewer and interviewee were students with low social distance between them, synchrony did indeed occur. But it was consistently absent when the interviewer was a more socially remote professional.

Therapist ambiguity-specificity is another variable that is particularly apt for investigating the psychotherapy interview as a communication system. In both a naturalistic study (Pope & Siegman, 1962) and a number of experimental analogues (Pope & Siegman, 1965; Pope & Siegman, 1968; Siegman & Pope, 1965) therapist ambiguity was associated with high patient productivity and cognitive uncertainty (i.e., a high ah ratio). This relationship is congruent with the view of the therapy interview as an informational exchange system (Lennard & Bernstein, 1960) with a reciprocal relationship between therapist and patient informational input. Low therapist input (high ambiguity) elicits high patient productivity; high therapist input (high specificity) elicits low patient productivity.

The focus of the present chapter changes

appreciably when it moves from the pragmatics of specific stylistic variables to therapist expressiveness. While some investigators seek the expression of affect in linguistic aspects of speech (Gottschalk *et al.*, 1966), most assume that paralinguistic categories, free of the constraint of referential meaning, are particularly emphasized in the expression of emotion. A good example of a linguistic system for scoring anxiety in verbal communication is a scale developed by Gottschalk *et al.* (1966), consisting of such categories as death, mutilation, guilt, shame, and diffuse anxieties. The psychoanalytic lineage of the Gottschalk approach can be traced in the linguistic categories it employs. Possibly the most widely known paralinguistic index of anxiety is the Mahl (1956) speech disturbance ratio, later known as the non-ah ratio (Kasl & Mahl, 1958). Several investigations (Kanfer, 1958, 1960; Pope *et al.*, 1970; Siegman & Pope, 1965, 1972) have assumed that anxiety functions as a drive, both activating speech through increasing verbal rate and productivity and simultaneously disrupting it (i.e., elevating the non-ah ratio). In the preceding studies anxiety was investigated in interviewee speech, but in only two was it observed in the speech of the interviewer. One (Pope *et al.*, 1974) demonstrated a higher level of speech disturbance in novice rather than professional interviewers, and another (Russell & Snyder, 1963) showed that hostile behavior by clients elicited higher counselor anxiety (as reflected in his speech) than friendly client behavior.

In conclusion, it is evident that the investigation of therapeutic style is, in fact, the study of therapy process. Stylistic variables are not decorative embellishments on the process of therapy; they are the components of process. They provide the student of psychotherapy with dimensions that transcend ideological and theoretical boundaries. Since stylistic dimensions are embedded in the psychotherapeutic interaction, they are more palpably related to communication and relationship within the interview than to outcome. In the end, our capacity to apply information about therapist style to the practice of psychotherapy will depend both on our knowledge of its main effects and on its interactions with interviewee and situational variables.

REFERENCES

ABRAMOWITZ, C. V., ABRAMOWITZ, S. I., ROBACK, H. B., & JACKSON, C. Differential effectiveness of directive and nondirective group therapies as a function of client internal-external control. *Journal of Consulting and Clinical Psychology*, 1974, **42**, 849–853.

ADAMS, H. E., BUTLER, J. R., & NOBLIN, C. D. Effects of psychoanalytically derived interpretations: A verbal conditioning paradigm. *Psychological Reports*, 1962, **10**, 691–694.

ADAMS, H. E., NOBLIN, C. D., BUTLER, J. R., & TIMMONS, E. O. The differential effect of psychoanalytically derived interpretations and verbal conditioning in schizophrenics. *Psychological Reports*, 1962, **11**, 195–198.

ALLEN, B. V., WIENS, A. N., WEITMAN, M., & SASLOW, G. Effects of warm-cold set on interviewee speech. *Journal of Consulting Psychology*, 1965, **29**, 480–482.

APFELBAUM, B. *Dimensions of transference in psychotherapy*. Berkeley, Calif.: University of California Publications, 1958.

ASHBY, J. D., FORD, D. H., GUERNEY, B. G., JR., & GUERNEY, L. F. Effects on clients of a reflective and a leading type of psychotherapy. *Psychological Monographs*, 1957, **71** (24, Whole No. 453).

AULD, F., & WHITE, A. M. Sequential dependencies in psychotherapy. *Journal of Abnormal and Social Psychology*, 1959, **58**, 100–104.

BANDURA, A., LIPSHER, D., & MILLER, P. E. Psychotherapists' approach-avoidance reactions to patients' expressions of hostility. *Journal of Consulting Psychology*, 1960, **24**, 1–8.

BERDIE, R. F. A program of counseling interview research. *Educational and Psychological Movement*, 1958, **18**, 255–274.

BERGMAN, D. V. *The relationship between counseling method and client self-exploration*. Unpublished masters thesis, University of Chicago, 1950.

BERNSTEIN, A. The psychoanalytic technique. In B. B. WOLMAN (Ed.), *Handbook of clinical psychology*. New York: McGraw-Hill, 1965. Pp. 1168–1199.

BOHN, M. J. Therapist responses to hostility and dependency as a function of training. *Journal of Consulting Psychology*, 1967, **31**, 195–198.

BORDIN, E. S. Ambiguity as a therapeutic variable. *Journal of Consulting Psychology*, 1955, **19**, 9–15.

BRENNER, M. S., FELDSTEIN, S., & JAFFE, J. The contributions of statistical uncertainty and test anxiety to speech disruption. *Journal of Verbal Learning and Verbal Behavior*, 1965, **4**, 300–305.

BUNNY, W. E., & HAMBURG, D. A. Methods for reliable longitudinal observations of behavior. *Archives of General Psychiatry*, 1963, **9**, 280–294.

BUTLER, J. M., RICE, L. N., & WAGSTAFF, A. K. On the naturalistic definition of variables: An analogue of clinical analysis. In H. H. STRUPP & L. LUBORSKY (Eds.), *Research in psychotherapy*. Washington, D.C.: American Psychological Association, 1962. Pp. 178–205.

COLLIER, R. M. A scale for rating the responses of the psychotherapist. *Journal of Consulting Psychology*, 1953, **17**, 321–326.

DIBNER, A. S. *The relationship between ambiguity and anxiety in a clinical interview*. Unpublished doctoral dissertation, University of Michigan, 1953.

DITTES, J. E. Galvanic skin response as a measure of patient's reaction to therapist's permissiveness. *The Journal of Abnormal and Social Psychology*, 1957, **55**, 295–303.

DITTMAN, A. T. The interpersonal process in psychotherapy: Development of a research method. *Journal of Abnormal and Social Psychology*, 1952, **47**, 236–244.

DITTMAN, A. T. Kinesic research and therapeutic process: Further discussion. In P. H. KNAPP (Ed.), *Expression of the emotions in man*. New York: International Universities Press, 1963. Pp. 140–160.

DOLLARD, J., & AULD, F., JR. *Scoring human motives: A manual*. New Haven: Yale University Press, 1959.

DUNCAN, S., JR., RICE, L. N., & BUTLER, J. M. Therapist's

paralanguage in peak and poor psychotherapy interviews. *Journal of Abnormal Psychology*, 1968, **73**, 566–570.

ELDRED, S. H., & PRICE, D. B. A linguistic evaluation of feeling states in psychotherapy. *Psychiatry*, 1958, **21**, 115–121.

FENICHEL, O. *Problems of psychoanalytic technique*. Albany, N.Y.: The Psychoanalytic Quarterly, 1941.

FIEDLER, F. E. A comparison of therapeutic relationships in psychoanalytic, nondirective, and Adlerian therapy. *Journal of Consulting Psychology*, 1950a, **14**, 435–436.

FIEDLER, F. E. The concept of an ideal therapeutic relationship. *Journal of Consulting Psychology*, 1950b, **14**, 239–245.

FIEDLER, F. E. Factor analysis of psychoanalytic nondirective, and Adlerian therapeutic relationships. *Journal of Consulting Psychology*, 1951, **15**, 32–38.

FINESINGER, J. E. Psychiatric interviewing: Principles and procedure in insight therapy. *American Journal of Psychiatry*, 1948, **105**, 187–195.

FISHER, S. Plausibility and depth of interpretation. *Journal of Consulting Psychology*, 1956, **20**, 249–256.

FRANK, J. D. The role of influence in psychotherapy. In M. I. STEIN (Ed.), *Contemporary psychotherapies*. New York: Free Press, 1961. Pp. 17–41.

FRIEDMAN, M. L., & DIES, R. R. Reactions of internal and external test-anxious students to counseling and behavior therapies. *Journal of Consulting and Clinical Psychology*, 1974, **42**, 921.

GANZER, V. J., & SARASON, I. G. Interrelationships among hostility, experimental conditions and verbal behavior. *Journal of Abnormal and Social Psychology*, 1964, **68**, 79–84.

GOLDMAN-EISLER, F. Hesitation and information in speech. In C. CHERRY (Ed.), *Information theory*. London: Butterworth, 1961. Pp. 162–173.

GORDON, J. E. Leading and following psychotherapeutic techniques with hypnotically induced repression and hostility. *Journal of Abnormal and Social Psychology*, 1957, **54**, 405–410.

GOTTSCHALK, L. A., & GLESER, G. C. *The measurement of psychological states through the content analysis of verbal behavior*. Berkeley, Calif.: University of California Press, 1969.

GOTTSCHALK, L. A., SPRINGER, M. J., & GLESER, G. Experiments with a method of assessing the variations in intensity of certain psychological states occurring during two psychotherapeutic interviews. In L. A. GOTTSCHALK (Ed.), *Comparative psycholinguistic analysis of two psychotherapeutic interviews*. New York: International Universities Press, 1961. Pp. 115–138.

GOTTSCHALK, L. A., WINGET, C., GLESER, G., & SPRINGER, K. The measurement of emotional changes during a psychiatric interview: A working model toward quantifying the psychoanalytic concept of affect. In L. A. GOTTSCHALK & A. AUERBACH (Eds.), *Methods of research in psychotherapy*. New York: Appleton-Century-Crofts, 1966.

HARWAY, N. I., DITTMAN, A. T., RAUSH, H. L., BORDIN, E. S., & RIGLER, D. The measurement of depth of interpretation. *Journal of Consulting Psychology*, 1955, **19**, 247–253.

HELLER, K. Interview structure and interviewer style in initial interviews. In A. W. SIEGMAN & B. POPE (Eds.), *Studies in dyadic communication*. New York: Pergamon Press, 1972. Pp. 9–28.

HELLER, K., DAVIS, J. D., & MEYERS, R. A. The effects of interviewer style in a standardized interview. *Journal of Consulting Psychology*, 1966, **30**, 501–508.

HELLER, K., & JACOBSON, E. A. Self-disclosure and dependency. *The effects of interviewer style*. Unpublished research, Bloomington, Ind., 1967.

HELLER, K., MYERS, R. A., & KLINE, L. V. Interviewer behavior as a function of standardized client roles. *Journal of Consulting Psychology*, 1963, **27**, 117–122.

HELLER, K., SILVER, R., BAILEY, M., & DUDGEON, T. *The interview reactions of patients and students to within-interview changes in interviewer style*. Unpublished research, Bloomington, Ind., 1968.

HOWE, E. S., & POPE, B. The dimensionality of ratings of therapist verbal responses. *Journal of Consulting Psychology*, 1961a, **25**, 296–303.

HOWE, E. S., & POPE, B. An empirical scale of therapist verbal activity level in the initial interview. *Journal of Consulting Psychology*, 1961b, **25**, 510–520.

HOWE, E. S., & POPE, B. Therapist verbal activity level and diagnostic utility of patient verbal responses. *Journal of Consulting Psychology*, 1962, **26**, 149–155.

ISAACS, K. S., & HAGGARD, E. A. Some methods used in the study of affect in psychotherapy. In L. GOTTSCHALK & A. AUERBACH (Eds.), *Methods of research in psychotherapy*. New York: Appleton-Century-Crofts, 1966.

JONES, E. E., & THIBAUT, J. W. Interaction goals as bases of inference in interpersonal perception. In R. TAGIURI & L. PETRULLO (Eds.), *Person perception and interpersonal behavior*. Stanford, Calif.: Stanford University Press, 1958. Pp. 151–178.

KANFER, F. H. Effect of a warning signal preceding the noxious stimulus on verbal rate and heart rate. *Journal of Experimental Psychology*, 1958, **55**, 73–86.

KANFER, F. H. Verbal rate, eye blinks, and content in structured psychiatric interviews. *Journal of Abnormal and Social Psychology*, 1960, **61**, 341–347.

KANFER, F. H., PHILLIPS, J. S., MATARAZZO, J. D., & SASLOW, G. Experimental modification of interviewer content in standardized interviews. *Journal of Consulting Psychology*, 1960, **24**, 528–536.

KASL, W. V., & MAHL, G. F. Experimentally induced anxiety and speech disturbance. *American Psychologist*, 1958, **13**, 349.

KIESLER, D. J. *The process of psychotherapy*. Chicago: Aldine, 1973.

LEARY, T. *Interpersonal diagnosis of personality*. New York: Ronald Press, 1957.

LENNARD, H. L., & BERNSTEIN, A. *The anatomy of psychotherapy*. New York: Columbia University Press, 1960.

LORR, M. Client perceptions of therapists. *Journal of Consulting Psychology*, 1965, **29**, 146–149.

LORR, M., & McNAIR, D. M. Methods relating to evaluation of therapeutic outcome. In L. A. GOTTSCHALK & A. AUERBACH (Eds.), *Methods of research in psychotherapy*. New York: Appleton-Century-Crofts, 1966. Pp. 573–594.

MAHL, G. F. Disturbances and silences in patient's speech in psychotherapy. *Journal of Abnormal and Social Psychology*, 1956, **53**, 1–15.

MAHL, G. F. Exploring emotional states by content analysis. In I. POOL (Ed.), *Trends in content analysis*. Urbana, Ill.: University of Illinois Press, 1959. Pp. 89–130.

MAHL, G. F. The lexical and linguistic levels in the expression of the emotions. In P. H. KNAPP (Ed.), *Expression of the emotions in man*. New York: International Universities Press, 1963. Pp. 77–105.

MAHL, G. F., & SCHULZE, G. Psychological research in the extralinguistic area. In T. A. SEBEOK (Ed.), *Approaches to semiotics*. The Hague: Mouton, 1964. Pp. 51–124.

MARKEL, N. N. *Psycholinguistics: An introduction to the study of speech and personality*. Homewood, Ill.: Dorsey Press, 1969.

MATARAZZO, J. D. The interview. In B. B. WOLMAN (Ed.), *Handbook of clinical psychology*. New York: McGraw-Hill, 1965. Pp. 403–450.

MATARAZZO, J. D., WIENS, A. N., MATARAZZO, R. G., & SASLOW, G. Speech and silence behavior in clinical psychotherapy and its laboratory correlates. In J. M. SHLIEN (Ed.), *Research in psychotherapy*. Washington, D.C.: American Psychological Association, 1968. Pp. 347–394.

McCARRON, L. T. & APPEL, U. H. Categories of therapist verbalizations and patient-therapist autonomic response. *Journal of Consulting and Clinical Psychology*, 1971, **37**, 123–134.

McNair, D. M., & Lorr, M. An analysis of professed psychotherapeutic techniques. *Journal of Clinical Psychology*, 1964, **28**, 265–271.

Nemiah, J. C. *Foundations of psychopathology*. New York: Oxford University Press, 1961.

Noblin, C. D., Timmons, E. O., & Reynard, M. C. Psychoanalytic interpretations as verbal reinforcers: Importance of interpretation content. In A. P. Goldstein & S. J. Dean (Eds.), *The investigation of psychotherapy*. New York: Wiley, 1966. Pp. 416–418.

Orlinsky, D. E., & Howard, K. I. The good therapy hour: Experiential correlates of patients' and therapists' evaluations of therapy sessions. *Archives of General Psychiatry*, 1967, **16**, 621–632.

Osgood, C. E., Suci, G. J., & Tannenbaum, P. H. *The measurement of meaning*. Urbana, Ill.: University of Illinois Press, 1957.

Parker, G. V. Some concomitants of therapist dominance in the psychotherapy interview. *Journal of Consulting Psychology*, 1967, **13**, 313–318.

Pittenger, R. E., & Smith, H. L., Jr. A basis for some contributions of linguistics to psychiatry. *Psychiatry*, 1957, **20**, 61–78.

Pope, B., Blass, T., Cheek, J., Siegman, A. W., & Bradford, N. H. Interviewer specificity in seminaturalistic interviews. *Journal of Consulting and Clinical Psychology*, 1971, **36**, 152.

Pope, B., Blass, T., Siegman, A. W., & Raher, J. Anxiety and depression in speech. *Journal of Consulting and Clinical Psychology*, 1970, **35**, 128–133.

Pope, B., Nudler, S., VonKorff, M. R., & McGee, J. P. The experienced professional interviewer versus the complete novice. *Journal of Consulting and Clinical Psychology*, 1974, 42, 680–690.

Pope, B., & Siegman, A. W. The effect of therapist verbal activity level and specificity on patient productivity and speech disturbance in the initial interview. *Journal of Consulting Psychology*, 1962, **26**, 489.

Pope, B., & Siegman, A. W. Interviewer specificity and topical focus in relation to interviewee productivity. *Journal of Verbal Learning and Verbal Behavior*, 1965, **4**, 188–192.

Pope, B., & Siegman, A. W. Interviewer warmth in relation to interviewee verbal behavior. *Journal of Consulting and Clinical Psychology*, 1968, **32**, 588–595.

Pope, B., & Siegman, A. W. Relationship and verbal behavior in the initial interview. In A. W. Siegman & B. Pope (Eds.), *Studies in dyadic communication*. New York: Pergamon Press, 1972. Pp. 69–89.

Pope, B., Siegman, A. W., & Blass, T. Anxiety and speech in the initial interview. *Journal of Consulting and Clinical Psychology*, 1970, **35**, 233–238.

Porter, E. H., Jr. The development and evaluation of a measure of counseling interview procedures. *Education and Psychological Measurement*, 1943, **3**, 105–126.

Raush, H. L., & Bordin, E. S. Warmth in personality development and in psychotherapy. *Psychiatry*, 1957, **20**, 351–363.

Raush, H. L., Sperber, Z., Rigler, D., Williams, J., Harway, N. I., Bordin, E. S., Dittman, A. T., & Hays, W. L. A dimensional analysis of depth of interpretation. *Journal of Consulting Psychology*, 1956, **20**, 43–48.

Rice, D. G., Fey, W. F., & Kepecs, J. G. Therapist experience and "style" as factors in co-therapy. *Family Process*, 1972, **11**, 1–12.

Rice, D. G., Gurman, A. S., & Razin, A. M. Therapist sex, "style," and theoretical orientation. *Journal of Nervous and Mental Diseases*, 1974, **159**, 413–421.

Rice, N. Therapist's style of participation and case outcome. *Journal of Consulting Psychology*, 1965, **29**, 155–160.

Rogers, C. R. *Counseling and psychotherapy*. Boston: Houghton-Mifflin, 1942.

Rogers, C., & Rablen, R. *A scale of process in psychotherapy*. Mimeographed manual, University of Wisconsin, 1958.

Rotter, J. B. Generalized expectancies for internal versus external control of performance. *Psychological Monographs*, 1966, **80** (Whole No. 609).

Russell, P. D., & Snyder, W. U. Counselor anxiety in relation to amount of clinical experience and quality of affect demonstrated by clients, *Journal of Consulting Psychology*, 1963, **27**, 358–363.

Sarason, I. G., & Winkel, R. Individual differences among subjects and experimenters and subjects' self descriptions. *Journal of Personality and Social Psychology*, 1966, **3**, 448–457.

Seeman, J. *The case of Jim*. Nashville, Tenn.: American Guidance Service, 1957.

Shostrom, E. L. *Three approaches to psychotherapy*. Santa Ana, Calif.: Psychological Films, 1966.

Shostrom, E. L., & Riley, C., M. D. Parametric analysis of psychotherapy. *Journal of Consulting and Clinical Psychology*, 1968, **32**, 628–632.

Siegman, A. W., & Pope, B. An empirical scale for the measurement of therapist specificity in the initial psychiatric interview. *Psychological Reports*, 1962, **11**, 515–520.

Siegman, A. W., & Pope, B. Effects of question specificity and anxiety arousing messages on verbal fluency in the initial interview. *Journal of Personality and Social Psychology*, 1965, **4**, 188–192.

Siegman, A. W., & Pope, B. The effects of ambiguity and anxiety on interviewee verbal behavior. In A. W. Siegman & B. Pope (Eds.), *Studies in dyadic communication*. New York: Pergamon Press, 1972. Pp. 29–68.

Snyder, W. U. An investigation of the nature of nondirective psychotherapy. *Journal of General Psychology*, 1945, **33**, 193–223.

Speisman, J. C. Depth of interpretation and verbal resistance in psychotherapy. *Journal of Consulting Psychology*, 1959, **23**, 93–99.

Spiegel, J., & Machotka, P. *Messages of the body*. New York: The Free Press, 1974.

Strupp, H. H. The psychotherapist's contribution to the treatment process. *Behavioral Science*, 1958, **3**, 34–67.

Strupp, H. H. *Psychotherapists in action*. New York: Grune & Stratton, 1960.

Strupp, H. H., Fox, R. E., & Lessler, K. *Patients view their psychotherapy*. Baltimore: The Johns Hopkins Press, 1969.

Sullivan, H. S. *The psychiatric interview*. New York: Norton, 1954.

Sundland, D. M., & Barker, E. N. The orientation of psychotherapists. *Journal of Consulting Psychology*, 1962, **26**, 201–212.

Tourney, G., Bloom, V., Lowinger, P. L., Schorer, C., Auld, F., & Grisell, J. A study of psychotherapeutic process variables in psychoneurotic and schizophrenic patients. *American Journal of Psychotherapy*, 1966, **20**, 112–124.

Trager, G. L. Paralanguage: A first approximation. *Studies in Linguistics*, 1958, **13**, 1–12.

Truax, C. B. Length of therapist response, accurate empathy, and patient improvement. *Journal of Clinical Psychology*, 1970, **26**, 539–541.

Truax, C. B., & Carkhuff, R. R. *Toward effective counseling and psychotherapy*. Chicago: Aldine, 1967.

Wallach, S., & Strupp, H. H. Dimensions of psychotherapists' activities. *Journal of Consulting Psychology*, 1964, **28**, 120–125.

Wiener, M. The effects of two experimental counseling techniques on performances impaired by induced stress. *The Journal of Abnormal and Social Psychology*, 1955, **51**, 565–572.

Will, O. A., & Cohen, R. A. A report of a recorded interview in the course of psychotherapy. *Psychiatry*, 1953, **16**, 263–282.

EDITORS' REFERENCES

GURMAN, A. S. Instability of therapeutic conditions in psychotherapy. *Journal of Counseling Psychology*, 1973, **20**, 16–24.

NOTES

1. *Editors' Footnote*. It occurs to us that interpretations, and probably other "core" interventions (i.e., those that involve the therapist directly in an area or problem of core importance to the patient) are probably all reinforcing by virtue of the heightened affective ("drive") state in the patient that accompanies such interventions.
2. *Editors' Footnote*. It should be remembered that the therapy "analogue" interview, in which a unidirectional process (interviewee "following" interviewer) was found, was actually a job interview. Surely, in such a situation, applicants will be eager to pick up on and mimic behavioral cues, including speech patterns, of the interviewer who may hold the interviewee's economic future in his hands.
3. *Editors' Footnote*. Interestingly, Johnson and Matross (Chapter 15, this volume) can be read as arguing that the therapist derives much of his influence by *reducing*, not maintaining, ambiguity. Perhaps a mixture of "revealing and yet concealing" provides a tantalizing (partially reinforcing?) situation that heightens all the more the patient's susceptibility to the therapist's influence.
4. *Editors' Footnote*. This pattern closely parallels that found by Gurman (1973) for "facilitative conditions." One may speculate that this is more than coincidence and that the therapist's change in level of facilitativeness determines the extent of communication about affect.

CHAPTER 15

INTERPERSONAL INFLUENCE IN PSYCHOTHERAPY: A SOCIAL PSYCHOLOGICAL VIEW

DAVID W. JOHNSON AND RONALD MATROSS

THERAPY AND INFLUENCE

Like all cooperative relationships, psychotherapy is based upon mutual influence. Clients come to therapists for help and ask to be influenced; therapists seek to influence clients in giving them help; clients influence the way in which the therapist gives help. Therapists influence clients, clients influence therapists.

The mutual influence between the therapist and the client is not surprising, as all human interaction involves influence. It is not possible to discuss relationships among persons without discussing influence. Persons influence each other continually in many ways. They take turns talking, they put aside individual interests to discuss mutual interests, they adjust expressions of attitudes to take into account the reactions of other persons, they speed up or slow down their activity to stay coordinated with others. Persons who are interacting are constantly influencing and being influenced by each other.

Influence is significant and central in social interaction because of human interdependence and the central role of cooperative efforts in human societies. In their relationships persons depend on each other for information and help in accomplishing their goals. In order to accomplish his goals a person often finds it necessary to influence other persons who may either frustrate or facilitate his aims. If a person is unwilling to influence others, he will find himself frustrated and dependent on the actions of others. Moreover, if the person refuses to be influenced by others, they may find him unrewarding and withdraw from their relationships with him. Cooperative relationships are based upon mutuality of goals and mutual influence in achieving goals. The more cooperative the relationship, the more mutual influence persons will have on each other.

Within therapy, the therapist will wish to influence the client in many ways: through providing information; interpreting; changing client perceptions, values, attitudes, and behaviors; teaching skills and social competencies; and changing the client's attributions concerning past and present behaviors. There is ample evidence that a therapist can influence a client during therapy. Verbal conditioning and reinforcement studies have demonstrated that a therapist's remarks can affect the client's remarks (Bierman, 1969; Strong, 1968). Psychological interpretations in therapy can lead the client to adopt the therapist's view of the client's actions (Levy, 1963; Strong, 1970). Clients will follow therapists' elaborate instructions in undergoing systematic desensitization (Wolpe & Lazarus, 1966). Therapist reflection of feelings leads clients to adopt the therapist's feeling content and affective language and engage in deep personal exploration (Strupp & Bergin, 1969; Truax & Carkhuff, 1967). Given the cooperative nature of psychotherapy and the central role of influence within psychotherapy, this chapter will review the relevant research in social psychology and therapy and present the current theoretical approaches to examining influence within the therapy relationship.

AVERSION TO THE USE OF DIRECT INFLUENCE

Although influence is pervasive in all human relationships and although it has played a significant role in the lives of all members of succeeding civilizations from antiquity to the present, some psychotherapists find the planned use of direct influence aversive. There are multiple ways in which one's behavior is influenced; education, government, law, interpersonal expectations, religion, social norms, organizational role requirements, and even advertising influence our behavior. But the thought of a therapist consciously planning how best to influence a client may seem to violate the client's freedom of choice and self-direction.

London (1969) states that in our society there are at least three rules which oppose influencing others' behavior: (1) the rule of noncoercion, which states that people should not be forced to do what others want but should be free to refuse them; (2) the rule of explication, which says that people should not be seduced into compliance but should be told what is wanted of them; and (3) the rule of self-direction, which says that people should be free to decide for themselves how they want to guide their lives. Especially within the humanistic movement in psychology there is a concern that psychotherapists have a great deal of power and may abuse it while planning how a client should change (Johnson, 1973a). For these psychotherapists, the words "power" and "influence" have negative connotations, and they frequently say they do not wish to have power over other persons (including clients).

This point of view confuses the use of influence with manipulation. All human interaction involves mutual influence; manipulation is a certain type of influence. *Manipulation*, as we refer to it here, is the managing or controlling of others by a shrewd use of influence, especially in an unfair or dishonest way, and for one's own purposes and profit (*Webster's English Dictionary*). Manipulation is influencing others in ways they do not fully understand and with consequences which are undesirable for them but highly desirable for oneself. It is using power for one's own benefit at the expense of others. People characteristically react with anger, resentment, and retaliation when they find that they have been manipulated. *In proceeding through this chapter the reader should keep in mind that it focuses upon the constructive use of influence to increase the client's goal accomplishment and well-being: the use of manipulation is destructive to therapy and should be avoided.* This issue will be further discussed in the section on ethics at the end of this chapter.

VIEWS OF INFLUENCE

For those who have experienced psychotherapy, either as a therapist or as a client, the therapeutic relationship often seems qualitatively different from other relationships. Attempts to explain therapeutic influence in terms of general influence theory may therefore appear simplistic and reductionistic. It should be noted, however, that any attempts to conceptualize therapy must always be retrospective approximations (Meehl, 1954). No model of therapeutic

interaction can capture all the nuances of the ongoing process as it occurs. Because of their post facto nature, theories about therapy will necessarily be more rational and less rich than the actual events. Thus, social psychological views of therapeutic influence should not be summarily dismissed merely because they were not originally developed in clinical contexts. Some conceptions will of course be clearer and more useful approximations of clinical phenomena than others, and this point will be a leitmotif throughout this chapter.

As has the study of psychotherapy, the study of general social influence has been approached from fundamentally different perspectives, each with long epistemological traditions. Two basic orientations to the study of influence may be distinguished. The first is the *trait/factor* approach. The principal assumption of the trait/factor approach is that human behavior and interaction can be ordered along continua of relatively enduring and discrete characteristics (Pepinsky & Pepinsky, 1954). Influence is viewed as a function of the characteristics of the person exerting the influence, the person receiving the influence, and the influence attempt itself (Hovland, *et al.*, 1949). This perspective can be traced to Aristotle, whose *Rhetoric* can be considered the first text in social psychology. Aristotle dealt at some length with the characteristics of an effective influencer and gave detailed advice on the techniques of persuasion. A more recent antecedent of modern trait/factor views of influence is the individual differences tradition pioneered by Galton, Binet, Spearman, and Cattell.

The general purpose of all trait/factor theories is to identify factors which explain why an individual is as he is, how he became so, and how these factors maintain him so, despite circumstances, fortune, and opportunities (Gendlin, 1964). This viewpoint is *static* in that it focuses more on continuity than on change; *atomistic*, in that it assumes that complex phenomena can be analyzed into their component parts; *historical*, in that it assumes that causation of present behavior is a function of genetic and experiential factors acting cumulatively over relatively long periods of time; and *inductive* in that it stresses accounting for empirically observed phenomena more than seeking empirical validation for general theoretical statements.

The major application of the trait/factor approach to influence was the Yale Attitude Change Program, led by Carl Hovland immediately after World War II (Hovland, Lumsdaine,

& Sheffield, 1949). Most of the research in this program focused on the areas where trait/factor view is strongest—namely, the analysis of the effects of a single attempt to influence delivered through the mass media. In situations where a politician is giving a speech to an audience, an announcer is delivering a television commercial, or a health official is warning the public about a health danger, the findings from the Yale program are quite useful. In each of these situations the contact between the communicator and receiver of the communication is brief and not repeated, and the communication is one way with no interaction between the two parties. Because single instances of one-way communication are essentially static, a trait-oriented theory is quite helpful. However, in settings where there is repeated face-to-face interaction, with two or more individuals continually interactive, the Yale approach has been weak both logically and empirically.

In contrast to the trait/factor view of influence is the *dynamic/interdependence* view of influence. The principal assumption of this approach is that human behavior at any given time is best understood in terms of forces acting on the individual at that time. Influence is understood to be a product of the changing relationship between two individuals rather than a function of the static and discrete characteristics of the influencer and influencee. The basis of influence is *interdependency*. Two persons are interdependent and influence each other to the extent that they each mediate the attainment of important goals for the other person (Cartwright, 1959; Thibaut & Kelley, 1959). Since interdependence involves (a) the current progress of the individual toward his goals, (b) the costs of that progress, and (c) the availability of goal mediation in alternative relationships, the degree of influence in the relationship is continually changing. From this point of view, *power is a property of the social relation, not an attribute of a person.*

The main progenitor of current dynamic views of influence was Kurt Lewin's "topographical" psychology. Lewin, in turn, was part of a tradition including Brentanos' Act Psychology, James' concept of the stream of consciousness, and the Gestalt view of perception and learning. The dynamic/interdependence view can be described as *phenomenological* in its stress on immediate experience and contemporaneous causation, *holistic* in its attempts to account mutual influence, and *deductive* in its attempts to apply and validate molar principles.

The dynamic/interdependence approach to influence has generally proven itself to be more useful than the trait/factor approach in accounting for ongoing interactions. It is the major focus of current social psychological theorizing and research on influence and power. No single unified program unites the several dynamic views (e.g., Cartwright, 1965; Gruder, 1970; Raven & Kruglanski, 1970; Thibaut & Kelley, 1959), but they have been applied to a number of influence phenomena in dyads and groups. An important aspect of this approach has been to place influence within cooperative and competitive relationships (Deutsch, 1949, 1962a).

Since psychotherapy involves an ongoing, ostensibly cooperative, face-to-face relationship, and not a single, static attempt to influence, one can make a prima facie case for the notion that a dynamic/interdependence view of influence has more applicability to therapy than a trait/factor view. In fact, however, nearly all the existing social psychologically oriented studies as well as many of the other studies of psychotherapy have explicitly or implicitly employed a trait/factor viewpoint. This chapter will review these studies and then present a synthesis of findings and hypotheses from dynamic/interdependence views of influence as they might be applied to psychotherapy. Finally, attention will be given to the methodological and ethical issues related to the application of social influence concepts to therapy.

YALE ATTITUDE CHANGE APPROACH

Immediately following World War II the study of attitude acquisition and change became an ascendant topic in social psychology. Much of the research stemmed from Carl Hovland's wartime studies of propaganda and was organized around the theme sentence, "Who says what to whom with what effect?" This sentence was usually broken down into the investigation of variables relating to source (the characteristics of the communicator), message (the characteristics of the communication), and receiver (the characteristics of the person receiving the message). Like other trait/factor orientations, the Yale research approach was quite empirical and inductive. While not atheoretical, it focused more on the definition of research areas and the complete investigation of these areas than on the evolution of molar principles from which numerous specific hypotheses could be derived. Hovland and his associates searched eclectically for theories relevant to the problem being studied rather than for issues relevant to a theory being validated. They made the assumption that people are rational in the way they process information and are motivated to attend to a message, learn its contents, and incorporate it into their attitudes.

Consideration of the Yale attitude change approach is essential to this chapter because it has had more impact on psychotherapy research historically than has any other portion of the social psychology literature. All but a handful of the extant social psychologically oriented psychotherapy studies have used either the concepts, findings, or methods of the Yale researchers. This section will present brief summaries of the findings from the social psychology literature and review the psychotherapy studies relevant to the study of the effects of source, message, and receiver characteristics.

Source Effects: Credibility

Aristotle noted that an effective communicator must be a man of good sense, good will, and good moral character. Following Aristotle's notions, most of the research on personal characteristics of the communicator has focused on the dimension of credibility. The credibility of a communicator consists of his perceived ability to know valid information and his motivation to communicate this knowledge without bias. More specifically, research (Giffin, 1967; Johnson, 1973) has demonstrated that credibility depends upon the primary determinants of:

(1) objective indicants of *expertness* relevant to the topic under discussion—e.g., PhD, affiliation with a prestigious organization;

(2) *reliability* as an information source; this refers to the perceived character of the communicator, such as his dependability, predictability, and consistency;

(3) *motives and intentions* of the communicator; communicators who argue against their own self-interest or who appear not to be attempting to influence a receiver tend to be regarded as more trustworthy than communicators who overtly attempt to influence in the direction of obvious self-interest;

(4) the expression of *warmth and friendliness*;

(5) *dynamism* of the communicator; a confident, forceful, and active communicator tends to be regarded as more credible than a self-conscious, listless communicator;

(6) the *majority opinion* of other people concerning the expertness and trustworthiness of the communicator.

A number of investigators have sought to determine whether the factors listed above affect the credibility of psychotherapists and whether therapist credibility affects client attitude change. The majority of these studies have been analogue experiments involving college student volunteer subjects, male graduate students interviewers, post-interview ratings of interviewer characteristics, and a single attempt to modify a target self-referring attitude.

Table 1 presents a summary of the findings from analogue experimental studies of interviewer credibility. Bergin (1962) attempted to modify subjects' self-ratings of masculinity-feminity through varying the credentials and dress of the interviewer and the behavior and setting of the interview. The highly credible

TABLE 1. SUMMARY OF RESULTS[a] OF ANALOGUE EXPERIMENTS ON INTERVIEWER CREDIBILITY.

Independent Variables	Perception of Interviewer	Attitude Change
Credentials		
Bergin (1962)	+	*
Binderman et al. (1971)	0	*
Strong & Schmidt (1970a)	+	0
Expert Behavior		
Strong & Schmidt (1970a)	+	0
Credentials and Expert Behavior		
Sprafkin (1970)	+	0
Strong & Schmidt (1970a)	+	+
Trustworthy Content		
Strong & Schmidt (1970b)	*	0
Trustworthy Content and Manner		
Kaul & Schmidt (1971)	+	†

[a] + = Significant positive relationship.
* = Partial significant positive relationship.
0 = No significant relationship.
† = Not tested.

interviewer was introduced as an experienced and knowledgeable PhD psychologist, was dressed in a white coat, administered a number of complex psychological tests, and conducted the interview in an impressive office. The low-credibility interviewer was introduced as a high school student with no knowledge of personality assessment, was dressed casually, gave no tests, and conducted the interviews in a dingy basement. The interviewers were found to be significantly more credible and influential when presented as highly credible than when they were presented as low in credibility. Using a much less extreme operationalization of credibility (PhD vs. grad) Binderman, Fretz, Scott, and Abrams (1972) found no effects on ratings of the interviewer credibility and only partial effects on a measure of attitude modification (compared to low-credibility interviewers, highly credible interviewers produced more attitude changes in a socially desirable direction but not in a socially undesirable direction). Sprafkin (1970) operationalized credibility through a combination of interviewer credentials and organized, confident behavior and found effects on perceived expertness of the interviewer, but subjects' attitudes were unaffected.

Using interviewer nonverbal and verbal behaviors which had been found to be perceived as reflecting high and low expertise (Schmidt & Strong, 1970), Strong and Schmidt (1970a) crossed interviewer credentials with interviewer behaviors. They found that a combination of expert behaviors and credentials produced more change in subjects' ratings of their achievement motivation than did a combination of inexpert behaviors and lack of credentials with a trend for the behavior of the interviewers to be more influential than were interviewer credentials. Both credentials and interviewer behavior individually influenced the subjects' perception of interviewer expertise but neither affected opinion change singly. Comparing expert behaviors with untrustworthy behaviors under conditions of high or low confidentiality, Strong and Schmidt (1970b) found no differences in changes in subjects' self-ratings of their achievement motivation but did find significant differences in the subjects' ratings of the trustworthiness of the interviewers. Kaul and Schmidt (1971) found that nonverbal behaviors as well as the content of messages affected subjects' perceptions of interviewer trustworthiness.

From these studies, it may be concluded that differences in interviewer credibility affect college students' attitude change only when the differences are extreme or when interviewer credentials are paired with highly credible-interviewer behaviors. These findings are congruent with the dynamic/interdependence view of influence which emphasizes that influence depends more upon the relationship than upon the personal qualities of the potential influencer. The findings of Strong and Schmidt (1970a) that interviewer behavior tended to be more influential than interviewer credentials further supports the relationship approach to influence. Some support for the importance of creating a positive perception of therapist credibility, however, is provided by a study by Beutler, Jobe, & Elkins (1974) in which measured credibility was correlated with attitude change and improvement of hospitalized clients receiving psychotherapy. Therapist credibility was positively related to self-rated improvement of patients discharged after a mean of 16.5 weeks of treatment but not with changes in patient attitudes toward a variety of life situations or with therapist ratings of client improvement.

It should be noted, furthermore, that the studies appearing in Table 1 represent attempts to change subjects' attitudes in the first 20 or 30 minutes of an interview. Even in crisis intervention therapy, most therapists would not exert direct influence attempts on client's attitudes so quickly. As Goldstein (1971) has suggested, a more important goal in the initial stages of therapy is to "hook" the client, creating a positive perception of the therapist so that the client will reappear for later therapy when changes can be induced.

Source Effects: Attractiveness

While credibility received the most attention from the Yale group, other investigators have studied another source variable—communicator attractiveness. A great deal of social psychological research has focused upon the determinants and consequences of interpersonal attraction. The following factors have been demonstrated to be determinants of how attractive one person appears to another:

1. *Cooperativeness and goal facilitation* (Johnson & Johnson, 1974a, 1975). Persons like others who are cooperating with them and facilitating their goal accomplishment.
2. *Physical appearance* (Berscheid & Walster, 1974). Other personal attributes being equal, physically attractive people tend to be liked better than homely people.
3. *Liking* (Byrne, 1969). If one person knows that he is liked by another, he is apt to reciprocate that liking.
4. *Similarity* (Byrne, 1969). Although the point is controversial, considerable evidence suggests that persons who perceive themselves to be similar in basic evaluative attitudes and other characteristics tend to like each other.
5. *Competence* (Blanchard, Weigel, & Cook, in press). Persons who are perceived to be competent in important areas tend to be liked.
6. *Warmth* (Johnson, 1971a). Warm, friendly people tend to be liked.
7. *Familiarity and propinquity* (Berscheid & Walster, 1969; Watson & Johnson, 1972): Although the point is equivocal, some

findings suggest that a person likes others with whom he is familiar. "To know them is to love them."

The crucial assumption for the application of attraction research to psychotherapy is that client liking for the therapist will increase the client's susceptibility to therapist influence attempts. Within the social psychological research on attitude change there is a large amount of evidence that a person's attitudes will be more influenced by others he likes (McGuire, 1969a). Thus it may be hypothesized that a *therapist who is liked will be more influential than will a therapist who is disliked.*

Many of the variables relevant to therapist attractiveness were tested in quasi-therapeutic settings in an extensive series of experiments by the Syracuse University Research Group, led by Arnold Goldstein (see Goldstein, 1971, for a detailed review). The primary focus of this research was on determinants of client attraction to the therapist in the initial stages of therapy. It was hypothesized that early liking for the therapist indirectly affects outcome through such mediating variables as patient self-disclosure, self-exploration, and resistance. The more attracted a patient is to the therapist initially, the more likely he is to return for further therapy and to participate fully and willingly in the process. A noteworthy feature of the research program was a systematic plan of experimenting on a given topic first with YAVIS (young, attractive, verbal, intelligent, successful) college student volunteers, secondly with YAVIS counseling clients, and finally with non-YAVIS psychiatric inpatients.

The majority of the Syracuse studies examined the effects on attraction of subjects' pre-interview expectations about the interviewer's characteristics, variables most directly related to the therapist's reputation among potential clients. The paradigm for these experiments involved giving subjects varying information about the characteristics of an interviewer immediately before they participated in an initial interview or listened to a taped therapy session. Following the interview or listening session, the subjects rated their attraction to the interviewer on a variant of the Client's Personal Reaction Questionnaire (Ashby, Ford, Guerney, & Guerney, 1957), shortened and modified for use with non-YAVIS subjects. The revised instrument had subjects rate on a 5-point scale how characteristic each of 39 statements was of their feelings toward their interviewer. Items assessed both positive subjective reactions (including respect,

admiration, and confidence) and negative subjective reactions (including anger, resentment, and criticism). Items were summed to yield an overall indication of how positively the subject viewed the interviewer.

Table 2 summarizes the findings regarding the effects on post-interview client attraction of pre-interview sets toward the interviewer. With YAVIS subjects, attraction to the interviewer was significantly affected by pre-interview statements about the interviewer's warmth (warmth > cold); statements about the interviewer's credentials (experienced PhD psychologist > inexperienced graduate student); and the apparent reactions of peers toward the interviewer (hearing a previous client or other subjects indicate

TABLE 2. SUMMARY AND FINDINGS ON THE EFFECTS OF INTERVIEWER CHARACTERISTICS ON PATIENT ATTRACTION TO INTERVIEWER.

Interviewer Characteristics	Attraction to Interviewer	
	Yavis College Students	Non-Yavis Inpatients
Reputed Liking	0	0
Reputed Competence	0	0
Expert Credentials	+	0
Reputed Warmth	+	+ (tape listening)
		0 (interview)
Attitude Similarity	0	0
Previous Client Reactions	+	0
Peer Reactions	+	not tested

high attraction for the interview > hearing them indicate low attention). Tested variables *not* clearly affecting the attraction of YAVIS subjects to their interviewers were: (1) presumed interviewer liking (telling the individual that he was matched with an interviewer who liked clients like him versus telling him no match on liking was possible); (2) presumed interviewer competence with similar clients (telling the individual that he was matched with an interviewer who was previously successful with clients like him versus telling him no match could be made); and (3) presumed attitudinal similarity between interviewer and interviewee (giving the individual a measure of attitudes and telling him that he and his interviewer agreed on many or few of the items). Thus, it would appear that at least certain aspects of the therapist's reputation influence his attractiveness in an initial interview with YAVIS subjects. With non-YAVIS subjects, however, only statements about the interviewer's warmth affected their attraction toward the interviewer; this effect was found when they listened to a taped interview but not when they participated in an actual interview.

One variable studied by the Syracuse group which did clearly affect the attraction of non-YAVIS clients to their therapists was not part of the reputation of the therapist but was an aspect of the behavioral interaction between patient and therapist. Psychiatric inpatients were matched with a group of pastoral counselors according to their interpersonal compatibility as assessed by Schutz's (1958) FIRO-B Scale. The FIRO-B assesses compatibility of two people in terms of their needs to originate and receive behaviors relevant to the dimensions of inclusion, affection, and control. Each counselor conducted 24 therapy sessions over a 12-week period with a patient who was a high compatibility match with him and a patient who was a low compatibility match with him. Administrations of the Client's Personal Reaction Questionnaire after the 3rd and 11th weeks indicated that patients in the high-compatibility relationships were significantly more attracted to their therapists on both occasions than were patients in the low-compatibility relationships. Thus, the one study in the Syracuse series which focused on the therapist's behavior, albeit indirectly, was the one which produced the most positive results with non-Yavis patients.

Not associated with the Syracuse studies were three analogue studies which varied therapist behavior on attractiveness dimensions. Patton (1969) found that warm and attentive behaviors by an interviewer produced significantly more subject liking for the interviewer than did cold and inattentive behaviors, but no differences were found on the measure of attitude change. Schmidt and Strong (1971) found similar results using warmth, attentiveness, and similarity in likes and dislikes as the behavioral operationalization of interviewer attractiveness. Increasing the strength of this operationalization by adding high credentials to the attractive interviewer and a lack of credentials to the unattractive interviewer, Strong and Dixon (1971) found significant differences in both subject liking for the interviewer and in subject attitude change. From these studies, it can be hypothesized that *warm and attentive behaviors by a therapist result in client liking for the therapist, but it is unclear whether such liking leads to increased therapist ability to influence the client's attitudes.*

Source Effects: Summary and Conclusions

While there is evidence that interviewer credibility and attractiveness affects subjects' reactions to the interviewer, the data linking liking for the interviewer and interviewer ability to modify subjects' attitudes are not very promising. Most of the studies reviewed have adopted with little modification the extra-interview reputational independent variables used in the social psychology experiments of the 1950s and early 1960s. The uneven results of the studies of the effects of the therapist's reputation along with the sparse but promising results of examinations of therapist behavior in the initial interview suggest that further studies of therapist credibility and attractiveness should shift more heavily to the examination of what the therapist does, rather than what qualities are reputed to 'characterize the therapist. For voluntary clients, the reputation of the therapist may be a critical factor in the client's choice of a therapist. Once the client has engaged a therapist, however, the client's reappearance and subsequent progress is likely to depend more on the quality of the therapeutic interaction than on aspects of the therapist's reputation. *Since therapeutic influence is a fluctuating variable occurring within an ongoing relationship, further research on the effects of the therapist's reputation on influence does not seem warranted.*

Message Effects

Without a message there can be no influence on attitudes and behavioral patterns. Like Aristotle, the Yale researchers were deeply concerned with the nature of arguments, their logical coherence and emotional appeal, and the language used by the communicator to get these aspects of the message across. As with the studies of source variables, most of the message research in social psychology traditionally has focused on single influence attempts outside the context of a face-to-face interaction with the communicator. The basic findings (Aronson, 1972; McGuire, 1969c; Watson & Johnson, 1972) from research on message variables are:

1. In general messages which inspire fear tend to be persuasive with receivers who have high self-esteem, but not with low self-esteem receivers. High-fear appeals with specific instructions for action tend to be more persuasive than high-fear appeals without these instructions.

2. With intelligent receivers, communications which acknowledge opposing viewpoints (two-sided messages) are more persuasive than one-sided communications. With less intelligent receivers, one-sided messages tend to be more effective than two-sided messages.

3. When a communicator is highly credible, the greater the discrepancy between the position he advocates and the receiver's initial position, the greater the change. If a communicator is not credible, he will be most effective with mildly discrepant positions.

Virtually all the studies of message effects within psychotherapeutic and quasi-therapeutic settings have examined the effects of message discrepancy, and more specifically the possible interactions between communicator characteristics and message discrepancy. The rationale for the presumption of an interaction between credibility and discrepancy derives from cognitive dissonance theory (Aronson, Turner, & Carlsmith, 1963; Festinger, 1957). It is assumed that discrepant messages induce cognitive dissonance, which individuals seek to eliminate. The greater the discrepancy the greater the dissonance aroused. A person can reduce his dissonance by (a) changing his opinion to make it congruent with the advocated position, (b) changing the communicator's opinion, (c) seeking social support for his position, or (d) derogating the communicator. From dissonance theory, it can be predicted that highly credible interviewers will influence subject attitude change most with messages highly discrepant from the subject's current attitudes while interviewers with low credibility will influence most with messages of low discrepancy. Bergin (1962) in a therapy analogue study confirmed such a prediction but later studies have not replicated Bergin's results. Binderman et al. (1972) found that the more discrepant the interviewer's message from the subject's present attitude the more the resulting subject attitude change, regardless of the credibility of the interviewer. Bergin, however, used a much more extreme operationalization of credibility than did Binderman and his associates.

Patton (1969) and Strong and Dixon (1971) extended the dissonance theory prediction to the study of attractiveness and discrepancy. Patton found that the unattractive interviewers produced similar attitude changes with both high- and low-discrepancy messages, while the attractive interviewers were more effective with the high-discrepancy message. Strong and Dixon found no significant difference between the success of high- and low-attractive interviewers in changing the subjects' attitudes; their results indicated that a moderate discrepancy tended to be more effective than low- and high-discrepant messages in changing subjects' attitudes.

Each of the experimental studies of therapist characteristics and message discrepancy has produced differing results. Conclusions are difficult to state because each of the studies employed different dependent variables, different definitions of discrepancy, and different operationalizations of therapist characteristics. Further complicating the picture are correlational studies of attitude discrepancy by Beutler (1971), Beutler, Johnson, Neville, and Workman (1972), and Beutler et al. (1974). These studies did not directly manipulate the actual presentation of messages but assessed the effects on change of therapy-related attitudes of initial discrepancy between patient and therapist on these attitudes. Should selected patient attitudes converge with those of the therapist, it could be assumed that the therapist was presenting persuasive communications. In each of these correlational studies both therapists and patients were given an attitude inventory early in therapy. Patients were then divided into groups according to how discrepant their responses were from those of their therapist. Late in therapy the attitude inventory was readministered to subjects. Change scores were computed, and differences between discrepancy groups were assessed. Although using a variety of measures, treatments, settings, and therapists, each of the studies in this series found a positive linear relationship between initial patient-therapist attitude discrepancy and later attitude change. When therapist credibility was studied in conjunction with discrepancy (Beutler et al., 1974), the effects on attitude change were congruent with the experimental findings of Binderman et al. (1972) and contrary to those of Bergin (1962). Regardless of therapist credibility, a linear relationship between discrepancy and change held. Again, however, methodological differences make comparisons with other studies uncertain.

Message Effects: Conclusions

Clearly, many of the social psychological findings regarding message effects have not been examined within a psychotherapeutic context. Although message discrepancy has been considered in several studies, topics such as fear appeals and one-sided versus two-sided arguments have received little attention. Additional message variables may not have been studied because they are simply not relevant to therapy. The generalization of findings developed in studies of ways to change nonemotional buyer preferences and political opinions to the change of highly involving self-referring attitudes may be quite hazardous (Argyris, 1969; Beutler, 1972). Further studies of therapist influence attempts might productively use the experimental methods of developed for social psychological studies of messages, but apply them to techniques and hypotheses derived from clinical theories. For example, social influence techniques might have much in common with suggestion techniques derived from hypnosis (Haley, 1963). Attempts to integrate the two approaches in well-controlled experiments might be a step toward a deeper understanding of principles of influence possibly underlying both.

Receiver Effects

Within social psychology, a multitude of personality characteristics and other individual difference variables among the receivers of persuasive communications have been examined for their effects on the acceptance of persuasion. From the variety of findings, the most salient and consistent are the following:

1. *Self-esteem* (McGuire, 1969c; Watson & Johnson, 1972). When self-esteem is manipulated experimentally, the most frequent result is that receivers with low self-esteem are more persuasable than receivers with high self-esteem. When long-term self-esteem has been measured and correlated with persuasion, the clear negative relationship is less frequent and pronounced.

2. *The receiver's present attitudes* (Watson & Johnson, 1972). Receivers may refuse to listen to messages which disagree with their present attitudes or they may misinterpret what the communicator is stating. Additionally, attitudes which are more central to the individual's self-conception appear to be more difficult to change than do less central attitudes (Rokeach, 1968).

3. *Forewarning* (Watson & Johnson, 1972). Forewarning receivers of the communicator's intention of converting them to his point of view creates resistance to his message.

4. *Role playing* (Watson & Johnson, 1972). Actively role-playing a previously unacceptable position increases its acceptability to the receiver.

5. *Innoculation* (McGuire, 1964). Having receivers practice defending their position and then giving them additional arguments to support their attitudes decreases their susceptibility to influence attempts.

6. *Distraction* (Baron, Baron, & Miller, 1973).

Receivers are generally more susceptible to influence when they are distracted during the communicator's statement of his message.

7. *Intelligence* (McGuire, 1969b, 1969c). Intelligence and influence are negatively related in the middle and upper portions of the IQ distribution and positively related in the lower portion.

As is the case with message variables, studies of receiver variables in actual or analogue therapeutic contexts are sparse in comparison with studies of source variables. The firmest data relating patient variables to the acceptance of the therapist's influence are those provided by the Syracuse group (Goldstein, 1971). In general the reputational variables which enhanced the therapist's attractiveness and influence with YAVIS students and clients did not have the expected effect with non-YAVIS inpatients. Exactly which aspect of the YAVIS/non-YAVIS difference was responsible for the lack of generalization is unclear. However, some social psychological evidence would suggest that differences in intelligence may be the most important factor. Some support for this conjecture is furnished by the results of a study of pre-interview liking statements by Davidoff (1969). In a *post hoc* analysis she found that patients with relatively high functioning intelligence and a relatively more favorable prognosis were more attracted to the interviewer than were patients with lower levels of intelligence and less favorable prognoses. Less intelligent patients may require an approach to therapeutic influence quite different from that used with more intelligent patients.

The present attitudinal state of the client has received very little attention but remains potentially quite important. Beutler *et al.* (1974) found that assessment of attitudes of medium centrality (religious and philosophical beliefs) allowed somewhat better prediction of improvement and change than did assessment of attitudes of high centrality (self-referring attitudes) and low centrality (social-political beliefs). Contrary to previous social psychological findings (Rokeach, 1968), centrality was not linearly related to change.

The effects of social support for the interviewee's present attitudes were investigated experimentally by Meland (1974). He found that previous social support for an interviewee's attitudes makes the task of inducing attitude change more difficult. On the positive side, strong therapist support for constructive change might help the client maintain the change against subsequent social pressure to revert.

Receiver Effects: Conclusions

Current knowledge of client variables related to therapist influence is very slight. While some study of client variables may yield useful information (the Syracuse group's repetition of a number of experiments with both YAVIS and non-YAVIS subjects is the best example), the study of client behaviors such as role playing and inoculation procedure may be much more fruitful. The relationship between the therapist and the client, however, remains the most important area to study as it relates most directly to current approaches to the study of influence.

An Assessment of Studies Derived from the Yale Attitude Change Program

Although alluding to a number of different theories, almost all of the studies using social psychological concepts owe their primary derivation to the Yale Attitude Change Program. Consequently they share many of the same strengths and weaknesses of the Yale program and trait/factor approaches in general. Most of the studies share the Yale program's emphasis on well-controlled experimentation, allowing inferences about causality. They also share the weakness of not being well integrated, either theoretically or historically. Several investigations have addressed similar topics, each with different measures, different contexts, and little consideration of other work in the area. For instance a credential (PhD) is the operational definition of credibility in one study, (Binderman et al., 1972), expertness in another (Strong & Dixon, 1971), and status, a contributor to attractiveness, in another (Goldstein, 1971). More importantly, no well-articulated theory binds together the individual studies, just as the Yale program did not have a comprehensive theory integrating its efforts and the assumptions made about influence are basically unrelated to current social psychological theorizing. These studies are a long way from contributing to the development of a thorough social influence therapy.

Despite their limitations, the existing studies of attitude change in psychotherapy may eventually contribute to a two-phase view of therapeutic influence (Goldstein, 1971; Levy, 1963; Levy & House, 1970; Meland, 1974; Strong, 1968; Strong & Matross, 1973; Truax, 1966). Each of the two-phase approaches has in common the notion that one phase of therapy should be devoted to the establishment of conditions optimal for having an impact on the patient. Attempts to induce meaningful changes in the patient's life—the other phase—are undertaken only when a good basis for influence has been established. Research on source variables can be thought of as dealing with the first phase of therapy. The development of initial credibility and attractiveness in the eyes of the patient enhances the probability that other therapist influence attempts will be successful. In themselves these variables do not directly affect therapy outcomes, but instead operate on factors affecting the patient's acceptance of constructive changes. Some support for the basic logic of the two-phase view is furnished by the finding of a significant positive correlation between initial credibility and patients' ratings of outcome (Beutler et al., 1972) and significant negative correlations between therapist attractiveness and patient resistance and silence (Goldstein, 1971).

Viewing therapeutic influence in terms of phases clarifies areas where further research is needed. To date, extrapolations of social influence concepts to psychotherapy have focused almost entirely on developing the preparatory phase of the influence process. The "work" of therapy—the actual induction of outcome-directed patient change—has received scant attention. The development of a comprehensive therapy based on principles of social influence requires a great deal of research on ways in which therapists can use their influence to foster the psychological health of their patients. In the two decades since the Yale program was at its height social psychology has largely abandoned the static trait/factor approach. The remainder of this chapter will present an integration of more recent dynamic approaches to influence as they might be applied to psychotherapy.

DYNAMIC INTERDEPENDENCE APPROACH TO INFLUENCE

From the dynamic interdependence approach to influence, psychotherapy is conceptualized as consisting of the therapist and the client establishing mutual goals and cooperating to achieve those goals. The *goals* for therapy are a combination of the individual goals of the persons involved. The client's goals are based upon his needs, wants, and self-interests and may or may not be clearly known to him; the client may be completely aware, partially aware, or totally unaware of his personal goals for therapy when therapy begins. The goals of the therapist are based upon his model of psychological health and the process of therapy. The client may want to feel better, to change his sexual practices, or to have someone confirm that his spouse is mean and unreasonable. The therapist considers such desires within the context of the normative model of psychological health which guides his diagnoses and interventions and the normative model of the process of therapy which guides his behavior. The client and the therapist then explicitly or implicitly negotiate the goals they can mutually commit themselves to achieve.

Goals for therapy are important as they provide guides for action, the basis for evaluating the success of therapy, and the motivating force for both the client and the therapist to promote client growth and change (Johnson & F. P. Johnson, 1975). As the therapist and the client commit themselves to achieving a set of explicit or implicit mutual goals, an inner tension system is aroused which continues until the goal has been accomplished or until some sort of psychological closure is achieved concerning the goals (Lewin, 1935). It is this internal tension system that motivates both the therapist and the client to work toward goal accomplishment and directs their efforts in doing so. There are usually one set of goals for the immediate therapy situation (such as clearly understanding the client's problems) and a set of environmental goals concerning the client's relationships and behaviors outside the context of therapy (such as finding a set of friends at work).

It is within the framework of cooperative effort toward goal accomplishment that influence in the therapy relationship takes place.[1] Influence in a dyadic relationship is based upon persons' affecting each others' goal accomplishment. When interdependence exists between two persons, each has resources upon which the other is dependent. The therapist may control resources directly mediating the client's goal accomplishment (such as when the client wants the therapist to love him or confirm his perception of the world) or affecting the way in which the client attempts to achieve his goal (such as information about the skills or opportunities needed to solve the client's problems). A *resource* is a property of a person which enables him to effect the goal accomplishment and costs experienced by another person. Most contemporary views of power and influence recognize, either implicitly or explicitly, that the ability of person A to influence person B requires the

dependence of B upon A for resources needed for B's goal accomplishment and the alternatives for acquiring such resources open to B (Cartwright, 1959; Emerson, 1962; Second & Backman, 1964; Strong & Matross, 1973; Strupp, 1973; Thibaut & Kelley, 1959; Watson & Johnson, 1972). Obtaining needed resources from others always involves some cost; obtaining a therapist's confirmation of one's perception of the world, for example, costs time, money (usually), and the risks of rejection, ridicule, and exploitation involved in disclosing one's perception of the world. In order to define influence and discuss the therapist's use of influence within the therapeutic relationship, therefore, it is necessary to consider goals, resources, and costs.

Within social psychology, the terms "power," "control," and "influence" are sometimes defined differently and sometimes defined synonymously. "Power" has been defined variously as the actual control of another's behavior, as the capacity to influence another's behavior, and as the capacity to affect another's goal accomplishment. "Influence" has been defined as an attempt to use power to change another person in a desired direction, and "control" has been defined as having the influencee behaving as the influencer intended (Cartwright, 1959). For the purposes of this chapter, however, *influence* and *power* will be defined as one person's control over resources valued by another. More specifically, individual A has power with respect to individual B when B perceives that A controls resources that B values. In turn, B's valuing these resources depends upon (1) the availability of alternative sources of these or similar resources at a similar or lower cost level and (2) the importance B attaches to the goals whose attainment is mediated by A's resources. *A therapist influences a client to the extent that the therapist furnishes resources needed by the client for the accomplishment of highly valued goals and to the extent that the client cannot obtain these resources at a lower cost from other relationships.*

From these definitions, it is apparent that influence is not a stable and unchanging reality in a relationship but is constantly changing and fluctuating. It is the timely and appropriate therapist expression of the resources needed by the client which determines the therapist's influence, not just the possession of the resources. Having expertise in psychotherapy does not ensure a therapist's being able to help a client; it is the skillful use of the expertise in interaction with the client which results in the client's being influenced. *The therapist's ability to influence the client (and vice versa) is clearly an aspect of the ongoing relationship, not an aspect of personal qualities of the persons involved.*

Under certain conditions, the therapist's attempts to influence the client can generate client resistance. A client may resist therapist influence when he distrusts the therapist, when he is so demoralized that he has difficulty in comprehending and responding to influence attempts, when he is so defensive that he perceives all attempts to influence him as threats, or when he perceives the influence as being manipulative rather than as facilitating his goal accomplishment. *Resistance* is defined as the psychological forces aroused in a person which keep him from accepting influence (Johnson & F. P. Johnson, 1975). One key to reducing client resistance resides in the client's locus of causality of the influence attempt. The client can attribute the influence as stemming from himself or from the therapist. The direct use of reward and punishment by the therapist, for example, would lead to the attribution that the therapist is trying to influence the client. By providing expertise, previously unavailable information, a constructive model within a problem-solving discussion, the client is likely to attribute the pressure for change as originating within himself (Liberman, 1974; Raven & Kruglanski, 1970). It is generally assumed that a person is less resistant to his own influence attempts than to the influence attempts of others (Watson & Johnson, 1972).

In discussing the therapist's influence on the client there are two ways in which influence attempts may be classified: (a) according to the type of resource possessed by the therapist and (b) according to the resources needed by the client. From the influencer's point of view, the five most commonly listed resources (Strong & Matross, 1973) are ability (1) to mediate the client's rewards and punishments, (2) to be an authority figure to whom the client believes he is obligated to comply, (3) to be an expert to whom the client attributes superior knowledge or ability, (4) to be a model for the client to identify with, and (5) to provide information previously unavailable to the client.

From the influencee's point of view, the two most commonly listed sources of dependence are outcome dependence and information dependence. Within therapy, the client depends upon the therapist for help in accomplishing his goals (outcome dependence) and for information about how to achieve his goals (information dependence). *Outcome dependence* concerns the therapist's perceived ability to affect the client's goal accomplishment and the client's costs for engaging in goal-directed behavior. It may be defined as the client's belief that the therapist can facilitate the client's goal accomplishment and reduce the client's costs for attempting to achieve his goals. The total "goodness" of outcomes perceived by the client is the sum of the costs incurred and the rewards experienced by achieving his goals. It is usually assumed that the client will try to maximize his goodness of outcome by trying to obtain the most facilitative behavior possible from the therapist while minimizing his own costs. Thibaut and Kelley (1959) stress that the reward-cost value of goal accomplishment depends upon the person's expectations; that is, whether the therapist's behavior is facilitative or costly to the client depends upon what the client expects the therapist to do.

Information dependence concerns the therapist's perceived ability to supply the client with the information needed for deciding which strategies to use in attempting to achieve his goals, the costs of each strategy, and the client's ability to implement the strategies. Information dependence can be defined as the situation in which the client relies upon the therapist for information about the nature of the environment, its meaning, and the possibilities of action within it (Jones & Gerard, 1967). Information dependence includes the client's dependence upon the therapist for expertise, previously unavailable information, and a model of constructive skills, attitudes, and values.

Since therapists are usually not in a position to control clients' achievement of goals (such as meaningful relationships and better job performance), and since therapists do not usually physically punish clients or increase the costs of goal-directed behavior, therapy is usually conceptualized as involving information dependence and the resources of expertise, being a referent for identification, and information distribution. This does not mean that the therapist does not directly mediate the achievement of the immediate goals for the therapy situation, but therapy usually is viewed as providing tools for the client to use in his own attainment of his environmental goals.[2]

The remainder of this chapter deals with the applications to psychotherapy of three major theoretical conceptions in social psychology. The first, social cooperation theory, deals with the preparatory phase of influence in terms of the conjoint interaction between therapist and patient, rather than considering therapist and patient variables as separate entities. It thus emphasizes the dynamic/interdependence view of influence recommended earlier in the discussion of source variables. Further, it suggests methods by which patients and therapist negotiate the goals of therapy and the means of attaining these goals. The two other conceptions, cognitive consistency theory and causal attribution theory, are discussed in terms of their potential for elucidating the ways in which therapist interpretations can induce attitudinal and behavioral change by the patient.

The Negotiation Analogue to Therapy

Therapy can be viewed as a negotiation process between the therapist and the client aimed at influencing the client to change destructive attitude and behavior patterns to self-enhancing attitude and behavior patterns. Views of therapy which emphasize the therapist's ability to influence the client (e.g., Strong, 1968) recognize either implicitly or explicitly the need for the therapist to be able to induce client cooperation in changing the client's attitudes and behaviors. An important set of therapist skills, therefore, are the skills of establishing the conditions under which the client's patterns of attitudes and behaviors can be modified and of intervening to influence the nature and direction of such changes. These skills revolve around the induction of cooperation in mixed-motive situations. A mixed-motive situation is one in which both cooperative and competitive motives are present simultaneously.

Research in social psychology on the induction of cooperation in mixed-motive situations is, therefore, relevant to the examination of therapist influence on a client. This section will discuss the research studies in this area which are most directly relevant to therapy.

The negotiation analogue to therapy focuses upon research in which:

(1) two persons, with different goals and positions, enter a relationship in which they want to reach an agreement (cooperative orientation) which is as favorable to themselves as possible (competitive orientation);

(2) there is an attempt to establish the conditions for cooperative problem solving to facilitate constructive negotiations;

(3) there is an attempt to influence the other's attitudes and behaviors in order to reach a mutually satisfying agreement.

This research analogue is comparable to the processes of therapy, which are:

1. The therapist and the client, each with personal goals and positions, enter a relationship in which there is client ambivalence. Client ambivalence consists of the client both wishing to change to more self-enhancing patterns of attitudes and behaviors (which gives him a cooperative orientation in relation to the therapist) and to keep the security and protection of current but destructive patterns of attitudes and behaviors (which gives him a competitive orientation in relation to the therapist).

2. The therapist attempts to establish the conditions necessary for cooperative problem solving. These include building and maintaining trust while decreasing client egocentrism and demoralization, and establishing the therapist as a reference person to promote client identification with the therapist.

3. The therapist and the client seek to define and diagnose the client's problems by: (a) identifying the current consequences of the client's functioning, including the current feelings of the client, (b) identifying current client destructive attitude and behavior patterns which are "causing" these consequences, and (c) understanding the continuity among the ways in which the client's patterns of attitudes and behaviors were originally learned, the ways in which they became crystallized in his general personality structure, and the ways in which they operate in his current life.

4. The therapist and the client seek to influence the client to: (a) change to more self-enhancing patterns of attitudes and behaviors which will improve the quality of the consequences of the client's functioning (including the feeling state of the client), (b) learn the basic social competencies necessary for building productive and fulfilling relationships within the context of social systems, and (c) apply and integrate the new patterns of attitudes, behaviors, and social competencies into the client's ongoing life.

In contrast to the trait/factor approach to influence, which assumes a linear causal relationship between the traits of the communicator, message, and receiver and subsequent attitude change, and dynamic/interdependence approach, which focuses on the relationship between two persons over time, views influence in its true multivariate complexity, involving a great deal of parallel processing, bidirectional relationships, and feedback loops. In actual interpersonal interaction, effects are the out-come of multiple causes which are often in complex interaction; moreover, it is the rule rather than the exception that the effects act back on the causal variables and are constantly influencing each other; the goals, conditions, and outcomes of therapy all interact and mutu-ally affect each other. Instead of a static view of influence in which one person acts and another responds, the dynamic interdependence con-ceptualization of therapy emphasizes a view in which both persons act and respond at the same time and all relationship variables are in a state of flux and change.

There are several advantages to investigating influence processes within the negotiation situ-ation and generalizing the results to the therapy situation. The first is the increased freedom and protection of subjects that derives from recruit-ing subjects to participate in a negotiation situa-tion as opposed to recruiting subjects to partic-ipate in a therapy situation. The second advant-age of the negotiation situation is that the ex-perimental nature of the research clearly de-monstrates causal relationships between the behaviors and the consequences of the influence attempts. Although there has been considerable correlation research on the relationships be-tween therapist behaviors and client responses, there is little experimental research which clearly demonstrates causal relationships. Third, the experimental realism of negotiation studies increases the internal validity of such research which supports its generalization to applied situations such as therapy. (This issue is dis-cussed in the section on methodology.) Finally, the negotiation approach to the study of psycho-therapy is congruent with contemporary social-psychological theories of power and influence. Within negotiations between the client and the therapist, the goals of the client are clarified, compared with the goals of the therapist, and the nature and cost of the resources of the thera-pist are assessed. Thus, the goals of the client can be directly related to the skills of the thera-pist in providing the resources needed to facilit-ate the accomplishment of the client's goals at a cost acceptable to the client.

In the sections below we shall discuss the negotiation of cooperative goals for therapy, the establishment of the conditions under which cooperative problem solving can take place, and the influencing of client attitudes and behavior.

Establishing Therapeutic Goals

When a client enters therapy, both the client and the therapist have a set of goals for the rela-tionship. A client may wish to improve his feeling state and find a more meaningful career and the therapist may wish to improve the client's general interpersonal functioning. Given that the goals of the client and therapist may or may not have a large overlap, the two must negotiate a set of goals which they can mutually commit them-selves to achieve.

When the client and the therapist first begin in-teracting, their goals may be cooperative (when their goals are positively correlated so that work-ing to achieve one person's goals facilitates the accomplishment of the other person's goals) or competitive (when their goals are negatively correlated so that working to achieve one per-son's goals interferes with the accomplishment of the other person's goals). Given that both the client and the therapist have several goals, some of their goals can be cooperative and some can be competitive. Examples of cooperative goals are when both the client and the therapist wish to alleviate the client's suffering, find constructive solutions to his problems, and improve his psychological health so he can better handle future crises. Yet there are instances when the therapist and the client have competitive goals, such as when a client wishes to remain in the hospital or on disability insurance and the thera-pist wishes to improve the patient's functioning so he can leave the hospital and return to a job, or when a client wishes to keep destructive pat-terns of behavior in order to punish others and the therapist wishes to promote constructive behavior patterns which are reinforcing to others. Some of the most difficult therapy cases involve clients who have goals which are nega-tively correlated with the traditional thera-peutic goals of therapists. There are studies which provide interesting evidence on competi-tive interdependence between client and thera-pist goals (Braginsky, Braginsky, & Ring, 1969; Braginsky & Braginsky, 1971). Perhaps the failure of the Syracuse group to replicate studies with non-YAVIS clients is due to competition between client and therapist goals more com-monly found in institutional settings.

Psychological Health

The therapist's goals are heavily influenced by his normative model of psychological health. Influence is always directional, and the direction of therapist influence attempts is toward im-proving the psychological health of the client. Different therapists have different normative models as to what constitutes psychological health and illness and these models are influenced by medicine, personality theory, and social psychology. A normative model is needed for a diagnosis of the current state of client functioning, for making hypotheses about the origins of the client's difficulties, and for providing a direction for client change. The normative model being developed by Johnson (1974; 1975a) focuses upon the basic cooperative nature of human society and of the humanization process. While still in the developmental stages, it provides an example of a direction for influencing clients in psychotherapy and helps illustrate the point that *a model of psychological health is needed to provide goal direction to the study of therapist influence attempts.*

There are several definitions of psychological health which focus upon a person's ability to interact effectively with other persons (Fromm-Reichman, 1960; Sullivan, 1953). Yet such definitions seem vague as to why persons need to interact with others and what interpersonal competencies are most central to psychological health. More specificity can be added to the definition by focusing upon the keystone of human evolution and all aspects of human society: cooperation. All human social systems and all interpersonal relations exist on a foundation of cooperation (Johnson, 1975c). *Cooperation* can be defined as the coordinated interdependent effort to accomplish mutually desired goals. The most important and frequent type of interdependence among persons is cooperation. A number of noted scientists have taken the position that cooperative interaction is a biological, ecological, anthropological, economic, sociological, and psychological necessity for humans (Asch, 1952; Bruner, 1966; Deutsch, 1962a; Farb, 1963; Horowitz, 1968; Johnson, 1973a; Mead, 1934; Montagu, 1966; Nisbet, 1968; Von Mises, 1949; Went, 1963). Thus, in the fields of biology, ecology, anthropology, economics, sociology, and psychology it is hypothesized that there is a deep human need to respond to others and to operate jointly with others toward achieving mutual goals. Human society and biology are constructed so that this has always been absolutely necessary for the survival of every individual member of our species. Without cooperation among persons, no social systems (such as families, groups, organizations, or societies) could exist. Without high levels of cooperation, there would be no communication, no conception of new persons, no child care, no socialization, no exchange of products and services, no development of the norms and laws

to regulate interaction, and so forth. There is no aspect of human experience more important than cooperation with others and the recognition of this fact helps focus definitions of psychological health dealing with interpersonal relationships.

A central aspect of psychological health, therefore, is the ability to join with other persons in coordinated, interdependent efforts to achieve mutually desired goals. This involves establishing satisfying family, career, leisure, and other relationships with other persons. The advantages of focusing upon cooperative competencies as opposed to general relationship skills is that it provides a context within which to specify the most relevant relationship skills and attitudes. There are literally hundreds of studies comparing the effects of cooperative, competitive, and individual efforts toward achieving goals (Johnson & R. T. Johnson, 1974a, 1974b, 1975). These studies have focused on the consequences of cooperative, competitive, and individualistic interaction among persons. The overall results indicate that cooperation, in comparison with competition and individualization, promotes positive interpersonal relationships characterized by mutual liking, positive attitudes toward each other, mutual concern, friendliness, attentiveness, feelings of obligation to each other, and a desire to earn the respect of others. In addition, cooperation promotes lower levels of personal anxiety; greater feelings of personal security; more mutual support, assistance, helping, and sharing; open, effective, and accurate communication; high levels of trust among persons; more mutual influence; more prosocial behavior; more constructive management of conflicts; more positive self-attitudes; greater task orientation, coordination of efforts, involvement in task, satisfaction from efforts, and achievement; and more empathy and ability to take the emotional perspective of others in a situation. The empirically demonstrated effects of cooperativeness on building and maintaining positive and productive relationships with other persons makes it a central aspect of psychological health.

Although there is a large body of research on the consequences of cooperation, there is a lack of research on the competencies necessary for a person to engage in cooperative efforts with others. In order to develop and maintain cooperative relationships and to join into cooperative endeavors a person needs to develop a set of basic social competencies. The competencies which seem most relevant to the authors are discussed below. These competencies are not by any means unique to the authors of this chapter nor are they to be taken as a final statement of what is required for cooperative interaction with others. They do represent the current normative model being used by the authors, but they are constantly being modified by the research, scholarship, and therapy experiences of the authors. The authors hypothesize that persons who receive faulty socialization and do not develop these social competencies will experience psychological difficulties. Finally, it should be noted that the following is not a developmental stage model specifying independent stages of development; the competencies are developed concurrently and are interrelated.

In order to cooperate effectively with others a person must develop an integrated and coherent self-identity. A lack of such an identity results in dissociation from other persons, cooperative interdependence, and growth-producing experiences (Breger, 1974). In order to engage in cooperative interaction, in order to assume the social roles and mores required by society while at the same time keeping one's personal sense of integrity, a person needs to formulate a distinct image of himself as a certain kind of person who has an identity differentiated and discernible from others, and who is autonomous and independent from others (Breger, 1974; Erikson, 1950; Hamachek, 1971; Johnson, 1975c; Maslow, 1954; Millon, 1969; Perls, 1973; Rogers, 1951). In every healthy person there must be a coherent sense of self, a consistent set of attitudes which define "who I am." One's identity includes (1) self-awareness, awareness of others, and the ability to maintain the proper boundaries between oneself and other persons, (2) the identifications the person makes during his development, and (3) the social roles assumed in the social systems to which he belongs. The differentiation of oneself and others, identifications, and social roles are given a basic unity and wholeness through one's identity. Persons without a coherent self-identity will feel anxiety, insecurity, depression, dissociation, defensiveness, and self-rejection; they will be characterized by transient values and interests and a search for a set of beliefs to cling to. Such feelings and characteristics interfere with the person's participation in stable systems of cooperation with others. In addition, a well-developed identity is necessary for the autonomy needed to promote growth and change in the social systems within which people live.

In order to participate in stable systems of cooperation a person must have the attitude that there is a meaningful purpose and direction in his life which is valued by others and which correlates positively with the goals of valued others. Such an attitude is characterized by such things as intentionality (directing one's attention toward a desired goal), awareness of one's choices, goal-directedness, psychological success (satisfaction from achieving meaningful goals), and self-actualization (the development and utilization of one's potentialities). A set of general goals and purposes gives a person a sense of "where I am going" and is a requirement for a productive and fulfilling life. Since all cooperative efforts are goal-directed, without a sense of direction and purpose the cooperation among persons breaks down. The purposelessness, alienation, meaninglessness, apathy, and depression resulting from a lack of directionality are often seen as signs of psychological illness (Argyris, 1964; Buhler, 1971; DeCharms, 1968; Erikson, 1950; Frankl, 1955; Johnson, 1975c; Lewin, 1935; Maslow, 1954; Millon, 1969; Rogers, 1965; White, 1959).

In order to cooperate with others a person needs the ability to perceive his interdependence with others. In order to work toward accomplishing mutual goals a person must be aware of the relationship between his goal attainment and the goal attainment of others. This involves such things as a perception of common fate, an awareness of mutual causation (that the outcomes of the situation depend upon the behavior of both oneself and others), a long-term time perspective (in order to plan long-range strategies for interaction and coordination of behavior), and an awareness of one's fate so that one can take the initiative in applying one's resources toward the accomplishment of desired goals), and an awareness of the relevant resources of others and of one's dependency upon them. A number of psychologists have discussed the importance of this competency (Bruner, 1966; DeCharms, 1968; Deutsch, 1962a; Erikson, 1950; Freud, 1916–1917; Johnson, 1975c; Millon, 1969; Rotter, 1954, 1966; Sullivan, 1953; White, 1959). Persons who are low on this competency may suffer from chronic feelings of inadequacy, worthlessness, helplessness, powerlessness, failure, and the attitude that they cannot accomplish desired goals.

Trust is a central requirement for cooperation. (Deutsch, 1962a; Marwell & Schmitt, 1975). The attitude that one can rely upon the affection and support of other people is a requirement for successful and prolonged cooperation with others. This attitude includes all aspects of generalized and interpersonal trust. Distrustful attitudes that others are harsh and undependable have been postulated to lead to habitual affective states of depression, anxiety, fear, and apprehension and to beliefs that others are critical, rejecting, humiliating, inconsistent, unpredictable, undependable and exploitative (Deutsch, 1962a; Erikson, 1950; Freud, 1916–1917, Johnson, 1975c; Millon, 1969).

Integrated and Coherent Identity:

> Self-awareness, awareness of others, and the maintenance of proper boundaries
> Identifications during development
> Social roles assigned and chosen in the social systems to which one belongs

Directionality: Meaningful purpose and direction in one's life

> Intentionality
> Awareness of choices
> Goal-directedness
> Psychological success
> Self-actualization

Interdependence: Relationship between own and other's goal attainments

> Perception of common fate
> Perception of mutual causality
> Long-term time perspective
> Awareness of own resources relevant to goal achievement
> Personal causation
> Awareness of others' resources relevant to goal achievement
> Awareness of dependency on others' resources

Trust: Reliance upon the affection, support, and cooperation of other people

Perspective-Taking: Understanding and cognitive and affective reactions of others to a mutual situation

Fig. 1. A Social Competence Model of Psychological Health

In order to cooperate effectively with others a person must be able to understand how a situation appears to another person and how that person is reacting cognitively and affectively. This competency includes all aspects of perspective taking or role taking and is the opposite of egocentrism. Research on perspective taking indicates that there is a general relationship between social perspective taking and (1) social adjustment (Bell & Hall, 1954; Dymond, 1950; Dymond, Hughes, & Raabe, 1952; Rose, Frankel, & Kerr, 1956; Rothenberg, 1970), (2) the development of the ability to communicate effectively (Flavell, 1968; Johnson, 1973b, 1974; Krauss & Glucksberg, 1969), (3) autonomous moral judgment and decision making based upon mutual reciprocity and justice (Kohlberg, 1969; Selman, 1971; Stuart, 1967), (4) cooperation with others (Johnson, 1975b, 1975c), (5) open-mindedness and the acceptance of differences (Falk, 1974; Johnson & Johnson, 1974b), (6) small-group problem solving (Falk, 1974), (7) constructive conflict management (Johnson, 1971b), and (8) cognitive and intellectual development (Looft, 1972). It has also been hypothesized to be related to (1) personal identity and self-awareness (Kinch, 1963; Mead, 1934), (2) reflective thought to make sense out of one's experiences (Mead, 1934), and (3) ability to predict the effects of one's behavior (Flavell, 1963; Mead, 1934).

To summarize the above discussion, psychological health is based upon a person's ability to manage effectively his cooperative interactions with others on both an interpersonal and social system level. In order to do so he must establish a firm sense of identity to integrate his efforts with the efforts of others, establish a sense of direction positively correlated with that of his reference groups to guide his behavior, accurately perceive his interdependence with others in order to join in cooperative efforts, trust others to interact cooperatively with him, and be able to take the perspective of others in striving for mutually desired goals. This model is summarized in Fig. 1. A therapist may use this normative model to guide his definition and diagnosis of client problems and to determine the present competency level of a client. A normative model is needed to establish the therapeutic goals to which the client and therapist can commit themselves. For a more complete discussion of this normative model, see Johnson (1975c).

Conditions for Therapeutic Change

While the goals for therapy are being negotiated by the therapist and the client, the therapist will be concerned with establishing the conditions necessary for cooperative problem solving.

These conditions include the development of trust, the reduction of client egocentrism and demoralization, and the promotion of the client's identification with the therapist. Each of these conditions is in a constant state of change in therapy and must be continually attended to. Trust, for example, is not a stable characteristic of a relationship or of a person (although the willingness to trust others may be); it changes with every contact and must be maintained once it is developed. These conditions affect a client's ability to generate alternative solutions to his problems and process information, affect the communication patterns between the therapist and the client, influence the level and amount of self-disclosure and risk-taking the client engages in, influence the client's openmindedness and flexibility of thinking and his willingness to consider points of view other than his own, increase the client's susceptibility to being influenced by the therapist, and many more aspects of therapy necessary for its success. Each of these conditions will be discussed below.

Much of the *clinical* literature on the establishment of the conditions needed for cooperative problem solving is not discussed in this chapter. There are three reasons for this. First, much of the clinical literature is reviewed in other chapters and does not need to be reiterated here. Second, much of the clinical literature is correlational rather than experimental and has methodological flaws which make its findings questionable. The authors of this chapter prefer discussing research in which causal relationships are clearly demonstrated and in which the validity of the studies is adequate. Finally, the studies reviewed are for the most part the result of a coordinated research effort by one of the authors over a period of years and, therefore, are more related and corroborate each other more than do studies conducted as parts of unrelated programs of research. Even in discussing the experimental literature in social psychology there has been no attempt to be exhaustive and complete. The following evidence is taken as confirmation of the relationships hypothesized. The space limitations of this chapter have precluded a fuller examination of all the empirical support for the hypotheses presented.

Building and Maintaining Trust

The first issue in building a therapeutic relationship is the extent to which the client trusts the therapist. Although the attitude that one can rely upon the affection and support of other people is a predisposition which varies from person to person (and tends to be low or unrealisticly high in some types of therapy patients), within any specific therapy relationship trust has to be built and maintained, and it is constantly changing and varying as the relationship changes and varies. A certain level of trust between the therapist and the client has to be established and maintained in order for constructive problem solving to take place, as all cooperative situations are affected by the trust existing among the participants. Several studies, for example, have demonstrated that communication will not be as effective under low-trust conditions as it is under high-trust conditions (Deutsch, 1957, 1962a; Deutsch & Krauss, 1962; Gahagan & Tedeschi, 1968; Krauss & Deutsch, 1966; Mellinger, 1956; Schlenker, Helm, Nacci, & Tedeschi, 1972; Schlenker, Helm, & Tedeschi, 1972). A series of other studies has demonstrated that trust affects the open discussion of problems and attitudes, participants' openness to change and influence, and the success of problem solving (Argyris, 1965; Deutsch, 1958, 1960a, 1962b; Friedlander, 1970; Gibb, 1964; Johnson & Noonan, 1972). Walton and McKersie (1965) state on the basis of their review of the literature, that trust is a precondition for effective problem solving. Rogers (1951, 1961), Gibb (1964), and Blocher (1966) have all stressed the importance of trust in therapy.

Yet, with all the emphasis on the importance of trust in cooperative situations, almost no research has been conducted on how trust may be developed. Perhaps the only operational model specifying how a person can build and maintain trust in a cooperative problem-solving situation such as therapy is as follows (Johnson, 1972b; Johnson & F. P. Johnson, 1975; Johnson & Noonan, 1972):

1. The client takes a risk by disclosing his problems, feelings, behavior and ideas.
2. The therapist responds with warmth, accurate understanding, and cooperative intentions.
3. The therapist reciprocates to some extent the client's disclosures by disclosing such information as his perceptions of the client, his reactions to what is taking place within the therapy situation, and appropriate information about himself.

Self-disclosure is an implied, if not explicit, client behavior in most therapy relationships

(Jourard, 1964; Mowrer, 1964a; Rogers, 1961). *Self-disclosure* may be defined as revealing how one is reacting to current situations and giving information about the past that is relevant to understanding how one is reacting to the present (Johnson, 1972b). If a client will not discuss his problems and attitudes openly and fully it becomes difficult for most types of therapy to take place. Self-disclosure makes a person vulnerable to possible rejection, scorn, ridicule, shame, or exploitation. In a trusting situation the person self-disclosing is dependent upon the other not to take advantage of his vulnerability. Vulnerability exists when a person has taken a risk which exposes him to potentially harmful consequences. Because of the initiator's vulnerability, the receiver temporarily has power over the initiator's feelings. He can make the initiator feel badly by responding with rejection or ridicule or he can make the initiator feel good by responding with acceptance and understanding. Trust is built when the receiver does not exploit the initiator's vulnerability; trust is damaged when the receiver uses or is seen as using his power to harm the initiator. This is reflected in research which indicates that when a person feels rejected the frequency and depth of his self-disclosures will decrease (Colson, 1968; Johnson & Noonan, 1972; Taylor, Altman, & Sorrentino, 1969).

The client's choosing to self-disclose is only the initial and partial step toward building trust in a therapy relationship. The client's self-disclosures must be responded to by the therapist. In a series of studies, Johnson and his associates have demonstrated that the expression of warmth, accurate understanding, and cooperative intentions increases trust in a relationship, even when there are unresolved conflicts between the two persons involved (Johnson, 1971b; Johnson, McCarty, & Allen, 1975; Johnson & Noonan, 1972). Generalizing from these negotiation studies to the therapy situation, it may be hypothesized that the therapist expression of warmth, accurate understanding, and cooperative intentions in response to client self-disclosures will increase client-therapist trust.

The reciprocation of self-disclosures is the third step in building and maintaining trust in a therapy relationship. Social penetration theory (Taylor, 1968) and social exchange theory (Homans, 1961; Thibaut & Kelley, 1959) suggest that reciprocity is rewarding. The results of several studies indicates that high-disclosing confederates elicit greater self-disclosure than do low-disclosing confederates (Chittick &

Himelstein, 1967; Murdoch, Chenowith, & Rissman, 1969; Taylor, 1964). Jourard (1959) and Jourard and Landsman (1960) found that self-disclosure in dyads tends to be reciprocal. Worthy, Gary, and Kahn (1969) found that increasingly more intimate disclosures were given to the other as the other increased the intimacy of his disclosures. The interviewer who discloses elicits greater disclosures from respondents and is rated as more trustworthy (Drag, 1968) and more positively in general (Jourard & Friedman, 1970) than the interviewer who does not disclose. Sermat and Smyth (1973) found that the confederate's self-disclosure level and the level of intimate disclosure the confederate asked of the subject in his questions significantly affected the subject's self-disclosure level. They also found that the attitudes toward the confederate were more positive when the confederate matched the subject's level of self-disclosure than when the confederate gave minimal self-disclosures. Bierman (1969) reviews a series of studies demonstrating a positive relationship between therapist self-disclosure and client self-disclosure. Johnson and Noonan (1972) conducted a study in which trained confederates either reciprocated or did not reciprocate a person's disclosures; they found that the subjects trusted and liked the confederates in the reciprocation condition significantly more than did the subjects in the nonreciprocation condition. On the basis of these studies, *it may be hypothesized that a client will trust the therapist who appropriately reciprocates the client's self-disclosures.*[3]

Reduction of Egocentrism

In order for the therapist to influence the client to change his destructive and inappropriate attitudes and behavioral patterns the therapist must reduce the client's egocentrism. *Egocentrism* is the defensive adherence to one's own point of view and frame of reference; it is the inability or unwillingness to take the perspective of another person to understand the other's messages, and it is highly related to *closed-mindedness*, which is the withdrawal (psychologically or physically) from opportunities to explore attitudes and perspectives which are discrepant from one's own and the search to bolster one's attitudes and perspective by seeking out others with similar views (Rokeach, 1960). Egocentrism is often promoted by the anxiety and defensiveness generated when one believes that the other is evaluating one's statements and is unwilling to consider one's point of view (Johnson, 1971d; Rapaport, 1960; Rogers, 1965). When a person is feeling defensive, he will protect himself by stubbornly adhering to his present attitudes and behavioral patterns and he will feel threatened by other points of view. Johnson (1973b, 1974) reviews research which indicates that the more defensive the person the more the person will refuse to communicate with others who have opposing points of view. Rokeach (1960) and others present data that indicate that defensiveness reduces the tolerance of ambiguity as well as one's openness to the new and unfamiliar, and there is some evidence that the anxiety generated by being defensive leads to a primitivization and stereotyping of thought processes as well as a reduction of the ability to solve problems (Johnson & R. T. Johnson, 1974a, 1974b, 1975).

The client will be influenced by the therapist's verbal messages to the extent that he attends to the therapist's messages, accurately comprehends his statements, and accepts their content as valid. In order for the client to change his attitudes and behavior he needs to become sufficiently detached from his original viewpoint in order to see the situation from new perspectives. The basis of rational problem solving is a clear understanding of all sides of an issue and an accurate assessment of their validity and relative merits. In order to do this the client must be able to understand the perspectives of other people (including the therapist). A therapist facilitates the perspective-taking ability of the client in order to reduce the client's egocentrism which prevents constructive problem solving. Perspective taking is the opposite of egocentrism and it is crucial for the client to view his problems and actions from a variety of points of view, which will allow him to gain insight into the destructiveness of current attitudes and behavioral patterns. *Perspective taking* is the ability to understand how a situation appears to another person and how the person is reacting cognitively and affectively. It is highly related to *open-mindedness*, which is the willingness to attend to, comprehend, and gain insight into attitudes and viewpoints which are discrepant from one's own (Rokeach, 1960). It is safe to hypothesize that, *as long as the client is locked into his own egocentric point of view, the therapist will be able to exert little influence.*

There are three types of therapist behavior which may be hypothesized to decrease a client's egocentrism and promote client perspective taking: communications indicating that he accurately understands the client, expressions of cooperative intentions, and promotions of client role-reversal with others. The defensiveness and closed-mindedness of a person may be reduced by his beliefs that he has been clearly heard and understood and accepted as a person and that the other person is clearly cooperatively oriented. Johnson (1971b) found that accurately restating the other's cognitive and affective messages results in the other's believing that one accurately understands the other's position, is attempting to understand the other's position, and is an understanding person. Johnson *et al.*, (1975) found that the congruent expression of verbal and nonverbal messages indicating cooperative intentions affected the other's comprehension and retention of one's position, the other's perception that one accurately understands the other's position and is an understanding and accepting person, and the other's belief that one is a person he would like to confide in.

A procedure for directly reducing the defensiveness and closed-mindedness of a client and increasing the client's perspective taking and open-mindedness is role reversal. *Role reversal* takes place when the client takes the role of another person and presents the viewpoint of that person as if the client were he. To initiate the use of role reversal, the therapist identifies another person involved in the client's problems (this may be a current person, a past person, or it can even be a different part of the client). Once the different positions or roles have been identified, the therapist asks the client to present the position and attitudes of the other person. The use of role reversal has been found to increase a person's understanding of the content and frame of reference of others' positions (Johnson, 1966, 1967, 1968, 1971a, 1972a). The more incompatible the positions of the client and the person being role played and the more defensive and committed the client is to his position and attitudes, the harder it may be to achieve insight into the positions and attitudes of others (Johnson, 1968). Many times the client, due to his defensiveness and biases, will misperceive the actions and attitudes of others with whom he is interacting. In order for successful problem solving and productive change to take place, such misunderstandings and misperceptions need to be clarified. Johnson (1966, 1967, 1968) found strong support for the notion that role reversal will clarify misunderstandings and misperceptions. On the basis of this research and the research on the use of role playing (see

Watson & Johnson, 1972) and procedures such as psychodrama, it may be hypothesized that *when a therapist wishes to increase the client's understanding of the feelings, position, thoughts, assumptions, attitudes, perceptions, or perspective of another person in order to facilitate the client's constructive attitude and behavior change and problem solving, a procedure which can be effectively used is role reversal.*

Reduction of Demoralization

When a person finds himself continually unable to act, feel, and think as he believes he should, he usually becomes demoralized (Frank, 1973). To be *demoralized* is to be deprived of courage, to be disheartened, bewildered, confused, and disordered. To various degrees, the demoralized person feels isolated, hopeless, and helpless. Besides being painful, demoralization blocks effective problem solving by keeping the client from perceiving reasonable solutions (demoralized persons are prone to plunge into drastic and rash solutions to their difficulties) and by compounding the problem and making it worse. Storms and Nisbett (1970) describe the latter as a vicious cycle of symptoms, worry about symptoms, and subsequent intensified symptoms. All problems involving a large component of fear and anxiety feed and grow on demoralization.

Frank (1973) contends that almost all therapies attempt to combat demoralization through the rationales they develop for explaining client's symptoms. Although some therapies, most notably European therapies, are less optimistic than others, nearly all therapies conceive of psychological symptoms as basically unstable or changeable, however long the process might take. Even where obvious physical and mental deficits result in symptoms, many therapies, such as Kelly's (1955) personal construct approach, attempt to minimize the number of symptoms which the individual attributes to the clear, stable cause.

Controlled studies of the comparative utility of attributing deviant behavior to stable versus unstable causes are very much needed. Two previous studies have addressed the issue, both supporting the proposition that attributions of symptoms to unstable causes is desirable. Levy and House (1970) found that college student subjects had a greater expectancy for change for attitudes attributed to learned, unstable origins than for attitudes attributed to unlearned, stable

origins. Meichenbaum and Smart (1971) found that near-failing college students did better when they were led to attribute their academic difficulties to the unstable cause of "late blooming" than when they attributed their problems to other causes. Thus *a key to decreasing a client's demoralization seems to be an interpretation of the problem which attributes its causes to unstable causes which the client can influence.*

The Therapist as a Reference Individual

A *reference individual* is a person the client uses as a standard to evaluate his attitudes, abilities, behavior, or current situation. A reference person influences the client through the process of identification. *Identification* is a general process whereby the client takes on the attributes (such as attitude and behavior patterns) of another person. Identification for psychoanalytic theorists includes believing that one *is* the reference person and that one has absorbed the reference person into one's own personality. Such an identification is hypothesized to occur by identifying with the aggressor, by withdrawal of love (analytic identification—Freud, 1946), or as an outcome of the Oedipus complex. To behaviorists, identification consists of imitating models who are more powerful than oneself and being reinforced for such imitation (Bandura, 1969; Maccoby, 1959). Other psychologists argue that a person imitates persons who are perceived to be more competent or more moral (Kohlberg, 1969; White, 1959). In addition to imitation, identification is defined as including (Tjosvold, 1974): (1) emotional attachment, (2) conformity to the reference person's expectations, (3) perceived similarity, (4) idealization of the reference person, and (5) self-esteem due to the reference person's approval. In general theories of identification focus on either the reference person's control of resources and the person's need for these resources or the reference person's superior competence and the person's effort to be competent and to be perceived as being competent. Thus, the client's identification with the therapist clearly relates to the amount of influence the therapist can exert on the client.

The importance of client identification with the therapist is perhaps most clearly stated by Perls (1973). He stated that therapy consists of rectifying false identifications. He believed that neurosis was the product of "bad" identifications and health was the product of "good" identifications. Bad identifications are those which result in stunting or thwarting the person, or promote destructive behavior toward his environment. Good identifications are those which promote the satisfactions and goal-fulfillments of the person and his environment. Through identifying with the therapist (a "good" identification) the past "bad" identifications of the client can be rectified.

If the client identifies with the therapist and uses the therapist as a reference individual, the therapist will be able to exercise a great deal of influence over the client's incorporation of more appropriate and constructive attitudes and behaviors. Johnson and Neale (1970), for example, found that altruistic students identified with persons within and outside their families who were also altruistic. The primary ways in which a therapist encourages client identification with the therapist in order for the therapist to be a constructive model and reference person for the client is through facilitating the accomplishment of the client's goals for therapy and expressing warmth toward the client.

When a client comes to a therapist for help, he expects and hopes to receive it. The client and the therapist become a cooperative dyad in which certain goals are negotiated. The therapist then tries to facilitate the accomplishment of these goals. A person's expectation that the other will facilitate the accomplishment of the person's goals and the resulting cooperative problem solving produces liking for the other (Johnson & S. Johnson, 1972; Johnson & R. T. Johnson, 1974b; S. Johnson & Johnson, 1972). In addition, there is considerable evidence that the other's expression of warmth toward the person will result in the person liking the other (Greenberg, 1968; Johnson, 1971b, 1971c; Johnson & Noonan, 1972; Simonson, 1968). Thus, by cooperatively working toward constructive changes in the client's attitudes and behavior and by expressing warmth for the client as a person, the therapist will facilitate the client's liking for and identification with the therapist. That liking and identification are related is indicated by the finding that the expression of warmth also produces perceptions by the person that the other is similar to oneself in attitudes and values and as a person (Johnson, 1971b, 1971c; Johnson & Noonan, 1972); in order to keep such a perception valid the person will often have to modify his attitudes, values, and behavior to make them more congruent with those of the other. On the basis of this research, *it may be hypothesized that the therapist's expression of warmth toward the client and*

the therapist's facilitation of the client's goal accomplishment will lead to client liking for and identification with the therapist.

Defining and Diagnosing the Client's Problems

While the therapist and the client are exploring the client's goals and establishing the conditions needed for productive therapy, they will be negotiating a definition and a diagnosis of the client's problems. Through identifying the current consequences of the client's functioning (including his feelings), through identifying current client destructive attitude and behavior patterns which are "causing" these consequences, and through attempting to understand the continuity among the ways in which the client's patterns of attitudes and behaviors were originally learned, the ways in which they became crystallized in his general personality structure, and the ways in which they operate in his current life, a therapist and a client arrive at a conceptualization of what the client's problems are and how they were originated and are sustained. From this definition and diagnosis, the client and the therapist ideally arrive at a negotiated agreement as to what the goals of therapy should be.

The most relevant theory in social psychology for a therapist concerned with influencing a client's diagnosis and definition of his problems is attribution theory, which is broadly concerned with the origins, nature, and consequences of a person's perceptions of causality (Jones & Davis, 1965; Jones, Kanouse, Kelley, Nisbett, & Valins, 1971; Kelley, 1967). In many respects attribution theory is more a field of study than a theory *per se*. Interest in the area stems chiefly from Heider (1958), whose "naive psychology" was concerned with the cause-effect analyses made by the "man in the street." Since the publication of theoretical statements by Jones and Davis (1965) and Kelley (1967), research on causal attributions has been extensive. This work has been ordered by three general propositions (Jones *et al.*, 1971, p. xi): (a) people assign causes for important instances of their own behavior and that of others, and actively seek causally relevant information; (b) the attribution of causes follows systematic rules; and (c) causal attributions have important affective and behavioral consequences. A fundamental component of the meaning of an event is the cause to which it is attributed. While research in social psychology has focused on all three of these assumptions, it is consideration of the third area which potentially may have the most immediate impact on psychotherapy research and practice. The study of the consequences of causal attributions is potentially important to therapy because of the possibility that it could lead to an improved understanding of the concept of insight in psychotherapy. Despite the central position given to insight in many psychotherapies, very little systematic research has been devoted to the topic (Luborsky, Chandler, Auerbach, Cohen, & Bachrach 1971; Matross, 1975a). One reason for the paucity of research on insight may be the wide differences in definitions of the concept. Different psychotherapy systems promote very divergent and often conflicting explanations of the nature of psychological symptoms with almost no data available on the comparative utility of different explanatory systems (Hobbs, 1962; Levy, 1963; Urban & Ford, 1971). For instance, no firm data exist to tell us whether it is more useful for patients to attribute their symptoms to "deep" personality dynamics or to "accidental" conditioning processes. Causal attribution theory may be quite helpful in addressing such issues. If any consensus can be reached about the nature of "insight," it is that insight involves the patient's perception of the causes of important instances of his behavior, most often his symptomatic behavior. If the essence of insight is an understanding of causal relationships, then the methods and hypotheses used for studying causal attributions can be applied to the study of insight.

The most common way of conceptualizing causal attributions has been in terms of bipolar dimensions. By far the most heavily studied of these dimensions is that of internal/external (or personal/environmental) causation: whether the cause of a given action is attributed to something within the actor or outside of him. It may be hypothesized that insights developed by clients and many interpretations given by therapists can be meaningfully categorized along the internal/external dimension. Many behavior therapists stress an *external* rationale for the development of maladaptive behavior—namely, that it is conditioned by features of the environment. While internal (particularly genetic) factors are seen as interacting with the environmental factors, external conditioning remains the central process. For example, Wolpe and Lazarus (1966, p. 17) advocate "schooling the patient" to regard his symptoms as the result of conditioned behavioral and emotional habits induced in the same way as experimental neuroses among laboratory animals. The logic of

such "corrective statements" is to put the client into a proper frame of mind for problem solving by inducing him to feel less anxious and guilty about his deviant behavior than if he attributed this behavior to internal personality factors. Laboratory research on the affective consequences of causal attributions provides some support for this position. A number of studies have found that individuals are less aroused and anxious when they can explain unusual or disturbing behavior in terms of external (environmental) causes rather than internal (personal) causes (Dienstbier & Munter, 1971; Hanson & Blechman, 1970; Nisbett & Schachter, 1966; O'Neal, 1972; Schachter & Singer, 1962; Valins, 1966; Valins & Ray, 1967). Two of the studies in this vein are especially relevant to psychotherapy. Ross, Rodin, and Zimbardo (1969) found a relationship between attribution and problem-solving behavior. Individuals were found to engage in more active problem-solving behavior when they attributed arousal symptoms to an external sound than when they attributed their arousal to an internal fear of shock. Storms and Nisbett (1970) also found a relationship between attributions and symptoms. Insomniacs who attributed their symptoms to an external, placebo stimulant went to sleep faster than insomniacs who attributed their symptoms to internal causes.

While some clinical and experimental findings support a case for external problem attributions, other evidence suggests the desirability of internal or personal attributions. In particular, at least four therapy systems emphasize the client's personal responsibility for his problem behavior. Glasser's (1965) Reality Therapy, Mowrer's (1964a) Integrity Therapy, Greenwald's (1973) Decision Therapy, and the existential views of Frankl (1955) and May (1969) contend that the therapist should reject a client's external attributions of his problems (e.g., "I don't get along with people because they don't understand me"). These therapies advocate inducing the client to see that he has *chosen* to do bad things through his own volition. In a related position, Menninger (1973) has called for a fresh examination of the concept of sin, asserting that many troubled people have more need for clergymen who will help them accept responsibility for their misbehavior than for psychotherapists who will absolve them of their responsibility.

Some research findings lend credence to the therapeutic emphasis on personal responsibility. In a study of individuals receiving client-centered counseling, Schroeder (1960) found that initial acceptance of responsibility was positively related to ratings of therapeutic movement. Also in client-centered counseling, Kirtner and Cartwright (1958) found that verbal acceptance of responsibility for problem behavior within the interview was positively related to therapeutic success. Those whose statements were rated as showing acceptance of responsibility for their difficulties had shorter and more successful treatments than did those whose statements were rated as "dealing with problems as though they were always external."

Thus, research findings and major therapy systems support the utility of both internal and external attributions of problem behavior. How can these apparently contradictory positions be reconciled? One possibility is that external problem attributions facilitate problem solving for certain types of problems, while internal attributions are the more helpful for solving others. The therapy system which most clearly emphasizes external attributions, Wolpe's Reciprocal Inhibition Therapy, was developed primarily from work with highly anxious phobic clients. In contrast, the system most clearly emphasizing internal attributions, Reality Therapy, was developed from Glasser's experiences in working with teen-age delinquents. Likewise, the research demonstrating the facilitative effect of external attributions utilized subjects with high levels of anxiety. The research showing the helpful effects of internal attributions utilized clients in client-centered therapy, individuals who were probably not characterized by highly specific fears or intense anxiety states. It might be hypothesized that an optimal level formulation can account for the discrepant findings concerning internal versus external attributions. In general, external attributions might tend to reduce anxiety and other kinds of affect, while internal attributions will tend to heighten affective arousal. For a person who has a problem in which anxiety is hurting his performance, an external attribution can help reduce his arousal to a point which is optimal for effective problem solving. Reducing anxiety can break the cycle of symptoms, worry about symptoms, and intensification of symptoms (Storms & Nisbett, 1970).

External attributions might also be called for in crisis-intervention situations where a client might take a rash or precipitous action (Skilbeck, 1973). For the person about to flee or commit suicide, an external attribution might defuse the immediate crisis enough so that constructive action could then be undertaken.

On the other hand, there may be times when it would be helpful to increase an individual's feeling of concern about his problems in order to motivate him to take effective action. If an individual has been avoiding operating on his difficulties, or feels apathetic and helpless, attributing his difficulties to his own volition may prompt therapeutic movement. Problems like smoking, losing weight, and delinquency are examples of difficulties which might be helped by an emphasis on the individual's personal responsibility in bringing about the dilemma.

Thus, research might examine the hypothesis that external attributions of symptoms depend on the nature of the symptoms. For some problems, it may be useful to increase a client's concern about the problem by inducing the insight that he is personally responsible for the situation. For other problems, it may be best to decrease the client's concern by inducing the insight that his difficulties were caused by circumstances over which he had little control.

In order to negotiate an agreed-upon description of the client's problems the client must attribute the causes of his problems to himself or to his environment. Through asking diagnostic questions (Kelly, 1955) and through making interpretations as to the causal factors involved in a client's problems, a therapist can influence the client to adopt an explanatory system which facilitates the achievement of the goals of therapy. Instead of focusing upon the "truth" of an explanatory definition of the client's problems, attribution theory focuses the therapist upon providing explanatory systems which facilitate the client's acceptance of responsibility for positive change and the client's belief in his own ability to use his resources to achieve meaningful changes in his life. Such a sense of personal causation is an essential ingredient of psychological health.

Negotiating Changes in Client's Attitudes

Whenever persons begin therapy, they have certain attitudes about themselves and their situation. Part of most therapy processes involves clarifying the client's current attitudes, determining how they are affecting his feelings and interaction with others, strengthening constructive attitudes, and changing destructive attitudes which lead to self-defeating cycles of behavior and which cause such feelings as guilt, depression, anxiety, and resentment. Both the therapist and the client will want to change destructive attitudes which contribute to the client's problems and anguish.

Attitudes may be defined as a combination of feelings and beliefs which result in a predisposition to respond favorably or unfavorably toward particular persons, groups, ideas, events, or objects (Watson & Johnson, 1972). The affective component of attitudes consists of the evaluation, liking, or emotional response. The cognitive component consists of the beliefs a client has about the attitude target. Attitudes are relatively enduring predispositions which give continuity to behavior over time; they are learned rather than innate; they are susceptible to change. *Attitude change* is the acquisition, reversal, or intensification of an attitude. Some attitudes facilitate, while other attitudes defeat and frustrate a person's psychological health. From the viewpoint of the model of psychological health described earlier, *appropriate attitudes* are attitudes which promote the person's ability to cooperate effectively with others, while *inappropriate attitudes* are attitudes which make for a more painful and troubled life through decreasing a person's ability to effectively cooperate. In order to live an enjoyable and fulfilling life a person needs a set of constructive attitudes which promote the development and use of the competencies necessary for cooperative interaction.

There are five major approaches in social psychology to the area of attitude acquisition and change (Watson & Johnson, 1972). The application of each of these approaches to therapy is discussed by Johnson and Matross (1975). In this chapter only the effects of certain therapist behaviors on attitude change will be discussed: the structuring of role-reversal situations and therapist expression of accurate understanding, affect, cooperative intentions, and statements arousing cognitive dissonance in the client.

When a person role reverses, he enacts the behavior of another person or assumes and publicly espouses a set of attitudes with which he disagrees. By engaging in role reversal, the client often modifies his attitudes. There are a number of studies which demonstrate greater modification of attitudes after active role reversal than after passive exposure to the same persuasive materials (e.g., Culbertson, 1957; Greenwald & Albert, 1968; Janis & Gilmore, 1965; Janis & King, 1954; King & Janis, 1956; Zimbardo, 1965). Although a variety of explanations have been hypothesized to explain such findings, it seems evident that by "taking the role of the other" the person increases his understanding of others' perspective, thus achieving a reorienta-

tion which allows him to arrive at broader and more productive solutions to his problems. Whatever the mediating process, the evidence is clear that attitudes are modified more by active role reversal than by passive exposure to other points of view.

Wanting to verify this finding is a dyadic problem-solving situation in which face-to-face persuasion and role reversal takes place. Johnson (1966, 1967) found that subjects who role reversed (compared with subjects who negotiated without role reversing) changed their attitudes significantly more on the issue under negotiation. These results were corroborated by Muney and Deutsch (1968). From these experiments, it may be concluded that the use of role reversal does result in attitude change, but the results do not indicate whether the effect comes from listening to one's opponent role reverse or from engaging in role reversal. Johnson (1971a) compared the effects of engaging in role reversal, listening to role reversal, and negotiating without role reversal. He found that the most attitude change took place in the condition where the subjects engaged in role reversal. From these studies, it may be concluded that engaging in role reversal will result in changed attitudes, even when taking the position of others with whom one is negotiating a conflict.

In addition to influencing a client's attitudes and beliefs through structuring a role-reversal episode, the therapist may wish to influence the client's attitudes and beliefs through a variety of therapist behaviors. Three common therapist behaviors are the expression of accurate understanding, the expression of affect such as warmth, coldness, or anger, and the expression of cooperative intentions of wanting to help the client. In his studies on role reversal Johnson (1971a) found that less attitude change took place when subjects listened to their opponent role reverse than when the subjects engaged in role reversal or when they negotiated without role reversal. Role reversal was operationalized in this study as the warm and accurate restatement of the subject's position. The results indicate that listening to another representative warmly restate one's position seems to reinforce one's attitudes and helps to convince one that he is right. Johnson (1971b) conducted a subsequent study in which the warmth and accuracy of another's response were varied independently in order to directly test their effects on the listener. He found that when a cold affective response is given, accurate restatements of the other's position result in more attitude change than do inaccurate restatements. His results also indicate that subjects who listened to a warm affective response believed that (1) their position was superior to the position of the other participant, (2) the other participant agreed with the subject's position, and (3) the other participant was accepting of the subject's position and of the subject as a person. Thus, it seems that when one listens to another person coldly and accurately restating one's position, attitude change will result; but when one listens to the other person warmly responding to one's attitudes, they will be reinforced and will not be modified. This research implies that when a therapist wishes to change the attitudes and beliefs of a client, the expression of coldness along with the accurate restatement of the client's current attitudes and beliefs are effective therapist behaviors, but, when the therapist wishes to strengthen the client's attitudes, the expression of warmth will be effective.

Johnson (1971c) conducted a further study comparing the effects of the expression of combinations of warmth and anger in negotiations. He found that the expression of anger decreases the likelihood of attitude change by the receiver, while it also communicates rejection of the receiver's position. Thus, the expression of anger (compared with warmth) may create resistance to attitude change. He also found that the expresser tends to underestimate the alienating effect of anger on the receiver and, therefore, it probably should be used cautiously by therapists.

Finally, the expression of cooperative intentions will result in client attitude change (Johnson, 1971b; Johnson et al., 1975). An explanation for this finding is that by expressing cooperative intentions the defensiveness and egocentrism of the person decreases, thus allowing the consideration of other points of view and subsequent attitude change. This explanation is supported by the finding that the expression of cooperative intentions results in a reduction of the felt importance to have the "right" ideas (Johnson et al., 1975).

Thus, there is evidence that the use of client role reversal and the expression of therapist accurate understanding, coldness, and cooperativeness are effective methods for inducing change of inappropriate client attitudes. The expression of warmth will strengthen appropriate client attitudes while increasing client liking for the therapist, and the expression of anger will create resistance to attitude change and decrease client liking for the therapist.

Changing Client Attitudes by Introducing Dissonance

A second approach to changing a client's maladaptive attitudes is by creating dissonance among the client's attitudes and cognitions. Dissonance theory (Festinger, 1957) is one of a number of cognitive consistency theories (Heider, 1944, 1958; Newcomb, 1953; Osgood & Tannenbaum, 1955) which postulate that there is a need for consistency among attitudes or between attitudes and behavior. Most of the theories further assume that the presence of inconsistency produces aversive psychological tensions which a person is motivated to reduce by rearranging his psychological world to make it consistent once more. Although dissonance theory has been widely criticized within social psychology (e.g., Chapanis & Chapanis, 1964), several authors have noted the potential for explaining important psychotherapeutic phenomena (Goldstein, Heller, & Sechrest, 1966; Goldstein & Simonson, 1971; Levy, 1963; Strong, 1968). The bulk of the research stemming from these speculations was described earlier and considered the prediction of a linear relationship between attitude discrepancy and change for credible and attractive therapists. Another dissonance phenomenon to receive research attention is the predicted relationship between the amount of effort exerted on a task and attraction to the task. Goldstein (1971) operationalized patient effort experimentally by having patients listen to therapy tapes between sessions, with the findings that among YAVIS patients but not among non-YAVIS patients, those who listened to the tapes were more attracted to therapy than those who did not. With a correlational approach, Beutler et al. (1972) operationalized effort as geographic distance between a patient's home and the hospital where he was receiving treatment and did not find the predicted linear relationship between effort and attraction to treatment.

Surprisingly little research has been devoted to what may be the most distinctive and powerful application of dissonance theory to psychotherapy: the relationship between an individual's behavior and his self-conception. Aronson's (1968, 1972) modification of dissonance theory hypothesizes that the clearest and most important source of cognitive dissonance is that which arises when an individual's actions do not fit his view of himself. The potential application of his hypothesis is in the development of outcome-oriented change procedures, integrating behavioral techniques with interpretation procedures. Although not directly inspired by dissonance theory, Beck's (1974) cognitive modification procedures for chronically depressed patients are the best current example of the way in which discrepancies between behavior and self-perception can be put to therapeutic use. Beck's premise is that many instances of depression involve a basic cognitive reorganization such that negative concepts of oneself and one's future come to dominate the individual's consciousness. Thus, symptoms such as passivity and suicidal wishes tend to be associated with the individual's beliefs that his actions are futile, that he is incompetent and socially undesirable, and that he has lost things of importance to him. The depressed patient's negative self-view and behavioral symptoms form a balanced, consonant system. The individual avoids constructive action because he feels worthless and incompetent, and the more he avoids constructive action, the more incompetent and worthless he feels.

Changing this consonant system requires the therapist to introduce dissonance by inducing a discrepancy between the individual's behavior and his self-view. One way to introduce the needed discrepancy is to persuade, cajole, or otherwise induce the patient to attempt a patently constructive action where success is unavoidable. The discrepancy between the beliefs "I am worthless" and "I performed successfully" will create cognitive dissonance. The dissonance can be dissipated in several ways, including devaluing the task, producing tangible evidence of failure, or changing the belief that one is worthless. If the therapist can forcefully demonstrate that success on the task is worthwhile and if he thwarts efforts to fail, the individual should begin to feel that he is competent, and his depression should be helped. Further improvement will come as the person successfully engages in increasingly more challenging tasks, through "graded task assignments." Beck and his colleagues have conducted some experiments to support their cognitive treatment. One study found that depressed outpatients had significantly lower expectations of success on a card-sorting task than did a group of nondepressed patients, although subsequently both groups performed equally well. Moreover, while initial failure improved the performance of the nondepressed group, initial success improved the performance of the depressed group. The finding that success improved performance was replicated with depressed inpatients. Additionally, measures of mood, expectancy for the future, self-perceived attractiveness, ability to communicate, and social interests indicated success experiences produced generalized improvements in outlook. A third study of depressed individuals found significant improvements in ratings of self-concept, optimism, and mood after patients had successfully progressed through a hierarchy of verbal interaction tasks ranging from reading out loud to attempting to persuade the experimenter to adopt a certain opinion. Cognitive dissonance theory would predict each of these findings.

Besides changing attitudes through changes in behavior, dissonance can also be produced by altering the relationships between cognitions. Beck suggests that some of the unhealthful assumptions of the depressed individual can be undermined by using systematic questioning to highlight discrepancies in the individual's belief system. For example, someone who believes himself to be worthless can be questioned about specific instances indicating worth in the past and then questioned about how one can become suddenly worthless. A similar use of questioning to change attitudes was supported by an analogue study with college student volunteers by Matross (1975b). Questioning students about specific instances of achievement in a simulated counseling interview was found to change students' ratings of their achievement motivation either upward or downward, depending on the nature of the questions. Several of Ellis' (1962) Rational Emotive procedures can also be interpreted as attempts to induce dissonance by pointing out inconsistencies in the patient's assumptive system.

Irrespective of their utilization of dissonance principles, the clinical theories of both Beck and Ellis incorporate a conceptual paradigm which should be quite instructive for researchers inclined to the application of social psychological theories. The foundation for both their approaches are theories about what kinds of attitudes or beliefs are dysfunctional and what kinds of attitudes are associated with psychological health. Attitude change techniques are then directed toward these specific goals. *The single greatest deficiency of social psychological research as well as other research in psychotherapy has been the lack of a theory of psychological health to give coherence to individual techniques.* Researchers have gone to social psychology for aid in investigating the *how* to influence without also exploring *what* to influence.

Changing Client Behaviors

There are often times when a therapist wishes to influence the client to change his behavior patterns in order to increase his ability to relate cooperatively with others. The therapist will wish to eliminate destructive cycles of client behavior and to facilitate the development by the client of the cooperative competencies needed to manage future crises successfully. There are two ways in which the therapist may influence client behavior change: (1) negotiate new patterns of behavior and the development of new cooperative competencies with the client and (2) obtain behavioral compliance from the client to the prescriptions of the therapist in hopes that the reinforcements received from the new behaviors will then influence the client to integrate the new behavior patterns into his ongoing life. Behavior therapies have developed many approaches to obtaining behavioral compliance. Since these approaches are discussed in Chapter 20, the present discussion will focus primarily on the negotiation of client behavior change. The therapist behaviors influencing the negotiation of client behavior change are the expression of (1) accurate understanding, (2) warm, cold, and angry affect, and (3) cooperative intentions followed by cooperative behavior aimed at facilitating the accomplishment of the client's goals.

There is reason to believe that the client's willingness to negotiate an agreement as to how his behavior should change is affected by the therapist's expression of accurate understanding of the client's position, feelings, and perspective. Under highly competitive conditions, Johnson (1966, 1967) found that, of the pairs of subjects in the role-reversal conditions who reached an agreement, the vast majority had at least one person who was highly accurate in restating the position, feelings, and perspective of the other. A later study verified that the more competitive the negotiator, the less likely it is that he will be influenced by listening to the other accurately restate his position, feelings, and perspective (Johnson & Dustin, 1970). Johnson (1971b) systematically varied the accuracy of understanding being expressed by one of the negotiators and found that subjects listening to the other accurately restating their position, feelings, and perspective reached significantly more agreements than did subjects listening to inaccurate restatements.

How cooperatively oriented the other is will affect the extent to which a person will agree to behavior changes. Proposing compromises is a way of demonstrating one's cooperative intentions in a negotiation situation. Johnson (1971b) contrasted the effects of proposing compromises with not proposing compromises and found that more agreements were reached in shorter periods of time when compromises were proposed. Johnson *et al.* (1975) found that the verbal expression of cooperative intentions resulted in more agreements being reached in a shorter period of time. Krauss and Deutsch (1966) found similar results. These results imply that a therapist will successfully influence the client to agree to changes in behavior patterns when the therapist successfully communicates cooperative intentions of wanting to help the client.

There is evidence suggesting that the therapist's expression of affect will influence the successful negotiation of an agreement with the client. In negotiation studies the reaching of an agreement is the clearest indication available of interpersonal influence. Johnson (1971b) found no significant differences in number of agreements reached when listening to the expression of warmth was compared with listening to the expression of coldness. Johnson (1971c), however, found that when subjects listened to affective expressions of others, the invariant expression of warmth resulted in the most agreements, the expression of anger followed by warmth the next, the expression of invariant anger the third, and the expression of warmth followed by anger the least. Thus, while the expression of warmth (compared to coldness) will not influence the successful negotiation of an agreement, the expression of warmth (compared with anger) will. These results imply that the more rejecting of the client the therapist is the less the likelihood of the therapist inducing client cooperation and behavioral change.

Johnson (1971c) also found some interesting effects of *engaging* in the expression of warmth and anger. The expresser was most influenced to reach an agreement when the expression of anger was followed by warmth, next in the invariant anger condition, next in the invariant warmth condition, and least in the condition where the expression of warmth was followed by the expression of anger. These results give some indication that the expression of anger by the therapist may result in later therapist compromises to reach an agreement with the client, perhaps to reduce feelings of guilt about expressing anger.

When it is not possible to negotiate an agreement with the client to change destructive patterns of behavior by the client, the therapist may wish to obtain behavioral compliance by the client to the prescriptions of the therapist. Certain expressions of affect appear to be especially effective in this regard. Johnson (1971c) measured behavioral compliance by whether a person would publicly state acceptance of the other's arguments or would publicly state rejection of his own arguments. The results of this study indicate that the receiver was most complying when the other expressed anger followed by warmth, next in the warmth-anger condition, next in the invariant anger conditions, and least in the invariant warmth condition. Thus, to obtain behavioral compliance, anger is the most effective, especially when it is followed by warmth for compliance. Anger also, however, results in the least private attitude change; this creates the possibility that a therapist may use anger to obtain client overt compliance and perceive that compliance as positive growth when in fact it hides increasing resistance to accepting the therapist's point of view! Johnson and Noonan (1972) found similar results; a person will feel more influenced by (but will dislike and distrust) a rejecting, non-self-disclosing individual. Thus, it may be hypothesized that when the therapist is interested only in influencing the client's behavior, being angry at and rejecting of present client behavior will be useful to obtain behavioral compliance to the therapist's prescriptions, but the price will be a decrease in client trust for, liking for, and actual agreement with the therapist. In such a case the therapist can only hope that the increase in goal accomplishment experienced by the client will encourage the use of new behavior patterns in the future.

Resocialization to Change Attitudes and Behaviors

The resocialization of clients into groups promoting more self-enhancing patterns of attitudes and behaviors has been used with delinquents (Empey & Rabow, 1961; McCorkle, Elias, & Bixby, 1958; Pilnick, et al., 1966), drug dependent clients (Yablonsky, 1962), and other clients with patterns of attitudes and behaviors especially destructive to others and themselves. Such a resocialization approach is based upon social evaluation theory which subsumes reference group theory and social comparison theory (Pettigrew, 1967). The basic tenets of social evaluation theory are that persons learn about themselves by comparing themselves to others and that the process of social evaluation leads to positive, neutral, or negative self-ratings which are relative to the standards set by the persons employed for comparison. The clinical use of this theory is based on the proposition that if the client changes the persons he uses for social evaluation purposes his attitudes and behaviors will change. Everyone is socialized into reference groups and such socialization is always being renegotiated and is subject to change. There has been a great deal of research on social evaluation processes which can be summarized as follows (Pettigrew, 1967; Watson & Johnson, 1972):

1. The patterns of a person's attitudes and behaviors are strongly influenced by the groups to which he belongs and those to which he wants to belong.

2. If a person's attitudes and behaviors conform to group standards and norms, he is reinforced; if they deviate, he is punished.

3. Those persons who are most attached to the group are the least influenced by attempts to change their patterns of attitudes and behaviors.

4. The support of even one other member weakens the powerful effect of a group majority upon a person's attitudes and behaviors.

5. A minority of two persons who are consistent in the expression of their attitudes can influence the majority of other group members.

6. If a group decides to adopt new attitudes and behaviors, its members will also adopt new attitudes and behaviors; participation in group discussions and group decision making helps to overcome resistance to change.

7. As a person's reference groups and sources for social evaluation change, so do his attitudes and behaviors.

When a client is a member of social systems which reinforce his destructive attitude and behavior patterns, the therapist has the choice of changing the entire social system or changing the client's membership. Alcoholics Anonymous is an example of a new reference group which puts great pressure on members to conform to self-enhancing patterns of behaviors and attitudes. Yet even families can support a person's destructiveness. Often social system members have the same ambivalence toward constructive change by a fellow member as the client. Another therapeutic use of social evaluation theory is that withdrawn clients who isolate themselves and their thoughts from others have distorted views of what others believe, which can be corrected when exposed to a constructive reference group and socialized into its membership.

Integrating the New, Eliminating the Old

After more effective behavior patterns are learned, including the development of the basic social competencies needed to cooperate effectively with others, the client must integrate the new patterns of behavior into his ongoing life. There are several ways in which a therapist may encourage such integration. The first is to discuss and demonstrate the new attitudes, behaviors, and competencies enough so that they become embedded in larger systems of attitudes, behaviors, and competencies. Frequency and depth of discussion of the new client patterns is crucial. A second way is to highlight the relationship between the new patterns and more effective goal accomplishment and positive consequences (along with the decrease in pain and depression, etc.). The more clearly the positive consequences are perceived to be resulting from the new patterns, the more integrated the new patterns will become in the client's life.

A third method is to inoculate the client against change (McGuire, 1964). By challenging the client's new patterns with mild arguments against them, a therapist can stimulate a defense against the old patterns and can provide the client with arguments supporting the new patterns. By preparing the client to defend the new patterns against opposition, he becomes inoculated against change. Structuring short role-reversal sessions in which the client takes the role of one of the persons who helped build the old, destructive patterns and attacks his new patterns of attitudes, behaviors, and competencies will be helpful. A mild form of this can be summarized in the question, "What will you say when x says to you, 'you do not have the ability to do y'?"

Finally, a therapist can help integrate the new patterns of attitudes and behaviors into the client's ongoing life by enhancing the client's attributions of being personally responsible for the positive changes. If a client attributes beneficial change to his own efforts, he is more likely to maintain that change than if he attributes it to external forces such as a fantastic therapist or a magic technique. Two studies support this hypothesis. In a laboratory study Davison and Valins (1969) found that subjects who were led to attribute increased shock tolerance to themselves subsequently tolerate higher levels of shock than those who attributed their initial tolerance to a drug (actually a placebo). Using actual clients, Liberman (1974) replicated the maintenance effects of an internal attribution of

constructive behavior. A group of outpatients received eight weekly sessions of placebo therapy in which any improvement was strongly attributed to the treatment; other outpatients received a "mastery" treatment in which improvement was strongly attributed to the client's own efforts. Immediately after treatment, all the clients showed improvement. However, a 3-month follow-up demonstrated that clients who had received the mastery treatment had maintained their improvement significantly better than those who had received the "placebo" treatment. By emphasizing the cooperativeness of therapy, minimizing overt pressure on the client, and emphasizing how the client has *chosen* to implement positive changes in attitudes and behaviors, the therapist can influence the client's attribution of positive change to the client's own efforts. A therapist can convey this attitude of client causation by specifically pointing out all the self-defeating actions the client could have taken but did not.

Summary of Dynamic/Interdependence Approach

The dynamic interdependence approach to the study of influence assumes that it is within the framework of cooperative effort toward goal accomplishment that influence within therapy takes place. Based upon the presenting complaints of the client and the therapist's goals of promoting psychological health and constructive patterns of attitudes and behaviors, the client and the therapist negotiate a set of cooperative goals which both can commit themselves to achieving. The negotiation model of therapy presented in this chapter consists of a set of interrelated processes involving such goal negotiation, definition, and diagnosis of client problems, establishing the conditions for successful problem solving, modifying destructive to self-enhancing patterns of attitudes and behaviors, learning the social competencies necessary for productive cooperative interaction with others, and integrating the new attitude and behavior patterns and social competencies into the client's ongoing life. All of these processes interact and are worked on simultaneously (they are *not* a sequence of activities) and together they define the process of therapy. Figure 2 summarizes the dynamic interdependence approach to influence within therapy. Figure 3 summarizes the therapist behaviors studied which are involved in the process of therapy and lists the client responses which have been empirically validated. From Fig. 3, and the research upon which it is based, it is evident that the needed research on therapy is at the beginning stages and, hopefully, will be conducted during the next few years.

RESEARCH DIRECTIONS

The application of social influence theory within social psychology to psychotherapy has just begun, and a great deal of further research is needed. The approach recommended by the authors of this chapter is to build a model delineating a continuum of psychological health and illness, explore the relationships among variables by associating attitude and behavioral patterns with indicants of the health-illness continuum, and design experimental and multivariate studies validating the use of the processes of interpersonal influence to move persons from illness toward health. *The important point is that interpersonal influence in psychotherapy should not be studied in isolation of goals of change; interpersonal influence needs to be studied in outcome-oriented change studies.* As part of such a research program, models of health-illness can be validated, and the ways in which cooperative relationships build needed social competencies (such as perspective-taking, directionality, and identity) can be illuminated. This type of research program lends itself as readily to prevention of illness as it does to the treatment of psychological illness.

Methodology

In order to generalize the results of experimental research to the therapy situation both the internal and external validity of the experiments have to be demonstrated. *Internal validity* is determined by the *experimental realism*—that is, the extent to which the experimental session is taken seriously by the subject, has impact on the subject, is involving, and is perceived as being realistic (Aronson & Carlsmith, 1968). External validity refers to the generalizability of demonstrated effects—that is, to what settings and to what populations they are applicable. Of the two, internal validity is the more important for if the experimental effect does *not* occur there is no need to worry about its generality.

External validity of research studies is always an empirical question which may be answered only by systematic replications of an experiment in a variety of settings with procedures which adequately operationalize the conceptual variables in each setting. *The findings of a study using actual therapists and clients has no more external validity than does a study on negotiations in a laboratory using confederates and subjects.* The therapy sessions do, however, have greater mundane realism. *Mundane realism* is the extent to which the experimental session resembles the situation to be generalized to (Aronson & Carlsmith, 1968). Generality is not guaranteed simply by providing an experiment with a certain amount of mundane realism. Labeling an experimental session a therapy session provides some mundane realism but it does not increase the probability that the results can be generalized to other therapy sessions. In deciding how generalizable the results of an experiment are the relevant questions are: Did the behavior of the confederates adequately operationalize the concepts being studied? Are the dependent variable measures an adequate operationalization of the concepts? Did the experimental session have experimental realism? Was the demonstrated relationship powerful enough to hold under less controlled situations? Are the subjects used in some significant and relevant way different from the population to be generalized to?

Probably the most effective way to ensure generalizability of results of studies to therapy situations is to replicate the studies a number of times in a variety of settings in different parts of the country and with different types of subjects. Parallel studies in both clinical and experimental settings would greatly enhance the generalizability of the results of both.

Manipulation, Ethics, and Pragmatism

There are psychotherapists who have made rather flippant and sensational comments about a therapist's manuevering clients into believing that therapy is beneficial and that therapy has helped solve the client's problems (e.g., Gillis, 1974). Such comments tend to give the area of social influence in psychotherapy an undesirable reputation. The idea of playing games with a person's pain and suffering, viewing the client as an object to be toyed with, and taking an egocentric view toward the process of therapy is not

provocative. Clients are often in distressed states in which their problem-solving capabilities are diminished and in which they are vulnerable to be manipulated by unethical persons[4]. When a client asks a therapist for help, the client is asking to be influenced in a way which carries heavy and important ethical responsibilities for the therapist. For clients who are forced into therapy, the ethical responsibility is even heavier. The authors wish to again make the point that influence and manipulation are *not* identical and that social influence theories in social psychology support the use of influence as part of a process of cooperative problem solving seeking beneficial change in the client's patterns of attitudes and behaviors; they do not support the efficacy of manipulation[5].

Attempting to manipulate a client, trying to sell the client on the greatness of the therapist, attempting to "con" the client into believing that he feels better, all are deadends conceptually as they do not clarify the interaction processes involved in therapy; also they are deadends practically as they do not create the psychological commitment, conditions, and problem solving needed for the client to discover the more self-enhancing patterns of attitudes and behaviors to be implemented in his ongoing life to manage the current and future crises. The research discussed in this chapter and specifically the studies of Davison and Valins (1969) and Liberman (1974) clearly imply that while short-

---

CLIENT'S GOALS:

Presenting complaints

THERAPIST'S GOALS:
1. Facilitate client developments of self-enhancing patterns of attitudes and behaviors
2. Facilitate psychological health:
   a. differentiation
   b. directionality
   c. interdependence
   d. trust
   e. perspective taking
   f. identity
3. Facilitate integration of 1 and 2 into client's ongoing life

---

Cooperative or competitive interdependence and interaction
Negotiated conceptualization of what the client's problems are, how they originated, and how they are sustained
Negotiated agreement of therapy goals and processes

CONDITIONS FOR CHANGE AND GROWTH:
Development and maintenance of trust
Reduction of egocentrism
Reduction of demoralization
Identification with therapist

THERAPY OUTCOMES:
Client attitude change
Client behavior change
Client learning of cooperative competencies

Fig. 2. Summary of the Dynamic-Interdependence Approach to Influence Within Psychotherapy

---

THERAPIST BEHAVIORS	CLIENT RESPONSES
Expression of warmth, coldness, anger	Perceptions of Therapist: —trustworthy —understanding
Expression of accurate understanding	—accepting
Expression of cooperative intentions	—accurately understands —attempting to understand
Congruity of verbal and nonverbal messages	—someone to confide in
Self-disclosure	Attitudes toward Therapist: —liking
Facilitation of achieving client's goals	—similar in attitudes, values, personally —identification with
Structure role-reversal situations	Attitudes toward Self: —self-confidence
Interpretations which attribute problem's causes to unstable factors	—positive self-esteem —responsible for positive change —personal causation: able to affect changes in one's life
Problem elaboration through questioning	Conceptualization of Problem: —attributes causes of negative affective states to external factors
Interpretations ascribing causes of problems to external or internal causes, depending on the problem and the affective arousal state of client	—attributes causes of problem behaviors to internal factors to increase motivation to change
Introduce discrepancy between client's behavior and self-view	—attributes causes of problem to unstable factors
	Client Responses: —open-mindedness —comprehension of content and perspective of therapist's messages —clarification of misunderstandings of therapist's perspective and messages —frequency and depth of self-disclosure —cooperativeness —problem solving —attitude change —behavioral compliance —behavior change —maintenance of improvements

Fig. 3. Therapist Behaviors and Client Responses

term improvement may be achieved by manipulating clients into believing they are being helped, long-term maintenance of positive change is not achieved. Ethically, conceptually, and practically, manipulation is not desirable. Lying to clients about their improvement is not only unethical, it is also futile.

REFERENCES

ARGYRIS, C. *Integrating the individual and the organization.* New York: Wiley & Sons, 1964.

ARGYRIS, C. *Organization and innovation.* Homewood, Ill.: Dorsey Press, 1965.

ARGYRIS, C. The incompleteness of social-psychological theory: Examples from small group, cognitive consistency, and attribution research. *American Psychologist*, 1969, **24**, 893–908.

ARONSON, E. Dissonance theory: Progress and problems. In R. P. ABELSON, E. ARONSON, T. M. NEWCOMB, W. J. MCGUIRE, M. J. ROSENBERG, & P. H. TANNENBAUM (Eds.), *Source book on cognitive consistency.* New York: Rand McNally, 1968. Pp. 5–27.

ARONSON, E. *The social animal.* San Francisco: Freeman, 1972.

ARONSON, E., & CARLSMITH, J. M. Experimentation in social psychology. In G. LINDZEY & E. ARONSON (Eds.), *The handbook of social psychology.* Vol. II. Reading, Mass.: Addison-Wesley, 1968. Pp. 1–75.

ARONSON, E., TURNER, J. A., & CARLSMITH, J. M. Communicator credibility and communication discrepancy as determinants of opinion change. *Journal of Abnormal Psychology*, 1963, **67**, 31–36.

ASCH, S. E. *Social psychology.* Englewood Cliffs, N. J.: Prentice-Hall, 1952.

ASHBY, J. D., FORD, D. H., GUERNEY, B. G., JR., & GUERNEY, L. Effects on clients of a reflective and a leading type of psychotherapy. *Psychological Monographs*, 1957, **7**, 1–32.

BANDURA, A. *Principles of behavioral modification.* New York: Holt, Rinehart & Winston, 1969.

BARON, R. S., BARON, P. H., & MILLER, N. The relation between distraction and persuasion. *Psychological Bulletin*, 1973, **80**, 310–323.

BECK, A. T. Cognitive modification in depressed, suicidal patients. Paper presented at the Conference of the Society for Psychotherapy Research, Denver, Colorado, 1974.

BELL, G. B., & H. E. HALL. The relationship between leadership and empathy. *Journal of Abnormal and Social Psychology*, 1954, **49**, 156–157.

BEM, D. J. Self-perception: An alternative interpretation of cognitive dissonance phenomena. *Psychological Review*, 1967, **74**, 183–200.

BERGIN, A. E. The effect of dissonant persuasive communications upon changes in a self-referring attitude. *Journal of Personality*, 1962, **30**, 423–438.

BERSCHEID, E., & WALSTER, E. H. *Interpersonal attraction.* Reading, Mass.: Addison-Wesley, 1969.

BERSCHEID, E., & WALSTER, E. Physical attractiveness. In L. BERKOWITZ (Ed.), *Advances in experimental social psychology.* Vol. 7. New York: Academic Press, 1974. Pp. 157–215.

BEUTLER, L. E. Predicting outcomes of psychotherapy: A comparison of predictions from two attitude theories. *Journal of Consulting and Clinical Psychology*, 1971, **37**, 411–416.

BUETLER, L. E. Value and attitude change in psychotherapy: A case for dyadic assessment. *Psychotherapy: Theory, Research and Practice*, 1972, **9**, 362–367.

BEUTLER, L. E., JOBE, A. M., & ELKINS, D. Outcomes in group psychotherapy: Using persuasion theory to increase treatment efficiency. *Journal of Consulting and Clinical Psychology*, 1974, **42**, 547–553.

BEUTLER, L. E., JOHNSON, D. T., NEVILLE, C. W., JR., FLKINS, D., & JOBE, A. M. Attitude similarity and therapist credibility as predictors of attitude change and improvement in psychotherapy. *Journal of Consulting and Clinical Psychology*, 1975, **43**, 90–92.

BEUTLER, L. E., JOHNSON, D. T., NEVILLE, C. W., JR., & WORKMAN, S. N. Effort expended as a determiner of treatment evaluation and outcome: The honor of a prophet in his own country. *Journal of Consulting and Clinical Psychology*, 1972, **39**, 495–500.

BIERMAN, R. Dimensions for interpersonal facilitation in psychotherapy and child development. *Psychological Bulletin*, 1969, **72**, 338–352.

BIGELOW, R. The evolution of cooperation, aggression, and self-control. In J. K. COLE & D. D. JENSEN (Eds.), *Nebraska symposium on motivation.* Lincoln: University of Nebraska Press, 1972. Pp. 1–58.

BINDERMAN, R. M., FRETZ, B. R., SCOTT, N. A., & ABRAMS, M. C. Effects of interpreter credibility and discrepancy level of results on responses to test results. *Journal of Counseling Psychology*, 1972, **19**, 399–403.

BLANCHARD, F. A., WEIGEL, R. H., & COOK, S. W. The effect of relative competence of group members upon interpersonal attraction in cooperating interracial groups, 1976.

BLECHMAN, E. Attribution theory and family therapy. Paper presented at the Convention of the American Psychological Association, Montreal, Quebec, 1973.

BLOCHER, D. *Developmental counseling.* New York: Ronald Press, 1966.

BRAGINSKY, B. M., BRAGINSKY, D. D., & RING, K. *Methods of madness.* New York: Holt, Rinehart & Winston, 1969.

BRAGINSKY, D. D., & BRAGINSKY, B. M. *Hansels and Gretels.* New York: Holt, Rinehart & Winston, 1971.

BREGER, L. *From instinct to identity.* Englewood Cliffs, N.J.: Prentice-Hall, 1974.

BRUNER, J. S. *Toward a theory of instruction.* Cambridge: Harvard University Press, 1966.

BUHLER, C. Basic theoretical concepts of humanistic psychology. *American Psychologist*, 1971, **26**, 378–387.

BYRNE, D. Interpersonal attraction and attitude similarity. *Journal of Abnormal and Social Psychology*, 1961, **62**, 713–715.

BYRNE, D. Attitudes and attraction. In L. BERKOWITZ (Ed.), *Advances in experimental social psychology.* Vol. 4. New York: Academic Press, 1969.

CAMPBELL, P. B. School and self-concept. *Educational Leadership*, 1967, **29**, 510–515.

CARTWRIGHT, D. A field theoretical conception of power. In D. CARTWRIGHT (Ed.), *Studies in social power.* Ann Arbor: University of Michigan, Institute for Social Research, 1959.

CARTWRIGHT, D. Influence, leadership, control. In J. G. MARCH (Ed.), *Handbook of organizations.* Chicago: Rand McNally, 1965. Pp. 1–47.

CHAPANIS, N. P., & CHAPANIS, A. Cognitive dissonance: Five years later. *Psychological Bulletin*, 1964, **61**, 1–22.

CHITTICK, E. V., & HIMELSTEIN, P. The manipulation of self-disclosure. *Journal of Psychology*, 1967, **65**, 117–121.

COLSON, W. N. Self-disclosure as a function of social approval. Unpublished master's thesis, Howard University, 1968.

CULBERTSON, F. Modification of an emotionally held attitude through role playing. *Journal of Abnormal and Social Psychology*, 1957, **54**, 230–233.

DAVIDOFF, L. L. Schizophrenic patients in psychotherapy: The effects of degree of information and compatibility expectations on behavior in the interview setting: An operant conditioning analogue. Unpublished doctoral dissertation, Syracuse University, 1969.

DAVISON, G. C., & VALINS, S. Maintenance of self-attributed and drug-attributed behavior change. *Journal of Personality and Social Psychology*, 1969, **11**, 25–33.

DeCHARMS, R. *Personal causation: The internal affective determinants of behavior*. New York: Academic Press, 1968.

DEUTSCH, M. A theory of cooperation and competition. *Human Relations*, 1949, **2**, 129–152.

DEUTSCH, M. Conditions affecting cooperation. Final Technical Report for the Office of Naval Research, Contract NONR-285, 1957.

DEUTSCH, M. Trust and suspicion. *J. Conflict Resolution*, 1958, **2**, 265–279.

DEUTSCH, M. The effect of motivational orientation upon trust and suspicion. *Human Relations*, 1960a, **13**, 123–139.

DEUTSCH, M. Trust, trustworthiness, and the F scale. *Journal of American Social Psychology*, 1960b, **61**, 138–140.

DEUTSCH, M. Cooperation and trust: Some theoretical notes. In M. R. JONES (Ed.), *Nebraska Symposium on Motivation*. Lincoln: University of Nebraska Press, 1962a. Pp. 275–319.

DEUTSCH, M. Psychological alternatives to war. *Journal of Social Issues*, 1962b, **18**, 97–119.

DEUTSCH, M., & KRAUSS, R. Studies in interpersonal bargaining. *Journal of Conflict Resolution*, 1962, **6**, 52–76.

DIENSTBIER, R. A., & MUNTER, P. O. Cheating as a function of the labeling of natural arousal. *Journal of Personality and Social Psychology*, 1971, **17**, 208–213.

DRAG, L. R. Experimenter-subject interaction: A situational determinant of differential levels of self-disclosure. Unpublished master's thesis, University of Florida, 1968.

DYMOND, R. Personality and empathy. *Journal of Consulting Psychology*, 1950, **14**, 343–350.

DYMOND, R., HUGHES, A., & RABBE, V. Measurable changes in empathy with age. *Journal of Consulting Psychology*, 1952, **16**, 202–206.

ELLIS, A. *Reason and emotion in psychotherapy*. New York: Lyle Stuart, 1962.

EMERSON, R. M. Power-dependence relations. *American Sociological Review*, 1962, **27**, 31–40.

EMPEY, L. T., & RABOW, J. The Provo experiment in delinquency rehabilitation. *American Sociological Review*, 1961, **26**, 679–695.

EPSTEIN, A. The self-concept revisited. Or a theory of a theory. *American Psychologist*, 1973, **28**, 404–416.

ERIKSON, E. H. *Childhood and society*. New York: Norton, 1950.

FALK, D. R. The effects of perspective taking on heterogeneous and homogeneous problem solving groups. Unpublished doctoral dissertation, University of Minnesota, 1974.

FARB, P. *Ecology*. New York: Time, 1963.

FESTINGER, L. A. *A theory of cognitive dissonance*. Evanston. Ill.: Row, Peterson, 1957.

FLAVELL, J. H. *The development psychology of Jean Piaget*. Princeton, N.J.: Van Nostrand, 1963.

FLAVELL, J. H. *The development of role taking and communication skills in children*. New York: Wiley, 1968.

FRANK, J. D. *Persuasion and healing. A comparative study of psychotherapy*. (Rev. Ed.) Baltimore: The Johns Hopkins University Press, 1973.

FRANKL, V. E. *The doctor and the soul*. New York: Knopf, 1955.

FREUD, A. *The ego and the mechanisms of defense*. New York: International Universities Press, 1946.

FREUD, S. Introductory lectures on psychoanalysis (1916–1917). In J. STRACHEY (Ed.), *Standard edition of the complete psychological works of Sigmund Freud*. Vols. 15 and 16. London: Hogarth Press, 1963.

FRIEDLANDER, F. The primacy of trust as a facilitator of further group accomplishment. *Journal of Applied Behavioral Science*, 1970, **6**, 387–400.

FROMM-REICHMAN, F. *Principles of intensive psychotherapy*. Chicago: Phoenix Books, 1960.

GAHAGAN, J. P., & TEDESCHI, J. T. Strategy and the credibility of promises in the Prisoner's Dilemma game. *Journal of Conflict Resolution*, 1968, **12**, 224–234.

GENDLIN, E. T. A theory of personality change. In P. WORCHEL & D. BYRNE (Eds.), *Personality Change*. New York: Wiley, 1964. Pp. 102–148.

GIBB, J. R. Climate for trust formation. In L. P. BRADFORD, J. R. GIBB, & K. D. BENNE (Eds.), *T-group theory and laboratory method*. New York: Wiley, 1964.

GIFFIN, K. The contribution of studies of source credibility to a theory of interpersonal trust in the communication process. *Psychological Bulletin*, 1967, **68**, 104–121.

GILLIS, J. S. Social influence therapy: The therapist as manipulator. *Psychology Today*, 1974, **8**, 91–95.

GLASSER, W. *Reality therapy: A new approach to psychiatry*. New York: Harper, 1965.

GOLDSTEIN, A. P. *Psychotherapeutic attraction*. Elmsford, N.Y.: Pergamon Press, 1971.

GOLDSTEIN, A. P., HELLER, K., & SECHREST, L. B. *Psychotherapy and the psychology of behavior change*. New York: Wiley, 1966.

GOLDSTEIN, A. P., & SIMONSON, N. R. Social psychological approaches to psychotherapy research. In A. E. BERGIN & S. L. GARFIELD (Eds.), *Handbook of psychotherapy and behavior change*. New York: Wiley, 1971. Pp. 154–195.

GREENBERG, R. Effects of pre-session information on perception of the therapist and receptivity to influence in a psychotherapy analogue. Unpublished doctoral dissertation, Syracuse University, 1968.

GREENWALD, A. G., & ALBERT, R. D. Acceptance and recall of improvised arguments. *Journal of Personality and Social Psychology*, 1968, **8**, 31–35.

GREENWALD, H. *Decision therapy*. New York: Wyden, 1973.

GRUDER, C. L. Social power in interpersonal negotiation. In P. SEINGLE (Ed.), *The structure of conflict*. New York: Academic Press, 1970. Pp. 111–154.

HALEY, J. *Strategies of psychotherapy*. New York: Grune & Stratton, 1963.

HAMACHEK, D. E. *Encounters with the self*. New York: Holt, Rinehart & Winston, 1971.

HANSON, L. R., & BLECHMAN, E. The labeling process during sexual intercourse. Unpublished manuscript, U.C.L.A., 1970.

HEIDER, F. Social perception and phenomenal causality. *Psychological Review*, 1944, **51**, 358–374.

HEIDER, F. *The psychology of interpersonal relations*. New York: Wiley, 1968.

HOBBS, N. Sources of gain in psychotherapy. *American Psychologist*, 1962, **17**, 741–747.

HOMANS, G. C. *Social behavior: Its elementary forms*. New York: Harcourt, Brace & World, 1961.

HOROWITZ, I. L. *Professing sociology*. Chicago: Aldine, 1968.

HOVLAND, C. I., LUMSDAINE, A. A., & SHEFFIELD, F. D. *Experiment in Mass Communication*. Princeton, N.J.: Princeton University Press, 1949.

HOVLAND, C. I., LUMSDAINE, A. A., & SHEFFIELD, F. D. *Studies in social psychology in World War II*. Vol. III. *Experiments in mass communication*. Princeton, N.J.: Princeton University Press, 1949.

JANIS, I. L., & GILMORE, J. B. The influence of incentive conditions on the success of role-playing modifying attitudes. *Journal of Personality and Social Psychology*, 1965, **1**, 17–27.

JANIS, I. L., & KING, B. T. The influence of role-playing on opinion change. *Journal of Abnormal and Social Psychology*, 1954, **49**, 211–218.

JOHNSON, D. W. The use of role reversal in intergroup competition. Unpublished doctoral dissertation, Columbia University, 1966.

JOHNSON, D. W. The use of role reversal in intergroup competition. *Journal of Personality and Social Psychol-*

ogy, 1967, **7**, 135–141.

JOHNSON, D. W. The effects upon cooperation of commitment to one's position and engaging in or listening to role reversal. Unpublished research report, University of Minnesota, 1968.

JOHNSON, D. W. The effectiveness of role reversal: The actor or the listener. *Psychological Reports*, 1971a, **28**, 275–282.

JOHNSON, D. W. The effects of warmth of interaction, accuracy of understanding, and the proposal of compromises on the listener's behavior. *Journal of Counseling Psychology*, 1971b, **18**, 207–216.

JOHNSON, D. W. The effects of the order of expressing warmth and anger upon the actor and the listener. *Journal of Counseling Psychology*, 1971c, **18**, 571–578.

JOHNSON, D. W. Role reversal: A summary and review of the research. *International Journal of Group Tensions*, 1971d, **1**, 318–334.

JOHNSON, D. W. The effects of role reversal on seeing a conflict from the opponent's frame of reference. Unpublished manuscript, University of Minnesota, 1972a.

JOHNSON, D. W. *Reaching out: Interpersonal effectiveness and self-actualization*. Englewood Cliffs, N.J.: Prentice-Hall, 1972b.

JOHNSON, D. W. *Contemporary social psychology*. Philadelphia: Lippincott, 1973a.

JOHNSON, D. W. Communication in conflict situations: A critical review of the research. *International Journal of Group Tensions*, 1973b, **3**, 46–67.

JOHNSON, D. W. Students attitudes toward cooperation and competition in a mid-western school district. Unpublished report, University of Minnesota, 1973c.

JOHNSON, D. W. Communication and the inducement of cooperative behavior in conflicts: A critical review. *Speech Monographs*, 1974, **41**, 64–78.

JOHNSON, D. W. Cooperativeness and social perspective taking. *Journal of Personality and Social Psychology*, 1975a, **31**, 241–244.

JOHNSON, D. W. Educational social systems, socialization, and the quality of life. In C. BLONG (Ed.), Proceedings on Systems Thinking and the Quality of Life. Washington, D.C.: Society for General Systems Research, 1975.

JOHNSON, D. W. A model of social effectiveness. Paper presented at the annual convention of the American Educational Research Association, Washington, March, 1975c.

JOHNSON, D. W. Affective perspective taking and cooperative predisposition. *Developmental Psychology*, 1975, **11**, 869–870.

JOHNSON, D. W., & BARRON, H. Role reversal and understanding of the opponent's position: Double exposure, attention, or rehearsal? Unpublished research report, University of Minnesota, 1972.

JOHNSON, D. W., & DUSTIN, R. The initiation of cooperation through role reversal. *Journal of Social Psychology*, 1970, **82**, 193–203.

JOHNSON, D. W., and JOHNSON, F. P. *Joining together: Group theory and group skills*. Englewood Cliffs, N.J.: Prentice-Hall, 1975.

JOHNSON, D. W., & JOHNSON, R. T. The goal structure of open schools. *Journal of Research and Development in Education*, 1974a, **8**, 30–46.

JOHNSON, D. W., & JOHNSON, R. T. Instructional structure: Cooperative, competitive, or individualistic. *Review of Educational Research*, 1974b, **44**, 213–240.

JOHNSON, D. W., & JOHNSON, R. T. *Learning together and alone: Cooperation, and individualization*. Englewood Cliffs, N.J.: Prentice-Hall, 1975.

JOHNSON, D. W., & JOHNSON, S. The effects of attitude similarity, expectation of goal facilitation, and actual goal facilitation on interpersonal attraction. *Journal of Experimental Social Psychology*, 1972, **8**, 197–206.

JOHNSON, D. W., & MATROSS, R. Attitude change methods of helping people change. In F. H. KANFER & A. P.

GOLDSTEIN (Eds.), *Helping people change: Methods and materials*. Elmsford, N.Y.: Pergamon Press, 1975.

JOHNSON, D. W., MCCARTY, K., & ALLEN, T. Congruent and contradictory verbal and nonverbal communication of cooperativeness and competitiveness in negotiations. *Communication Research*, 1976, **3**, 275–292.

JOHNSON, D. W., & NEALE, D. The effects of models, reference groups, and social responsibility norms upon participation in prosocial action activities. *Journal of Social Psychology*, 1970, **81**, 87–92.

JOHNSON, D. W., & NOONAN, M. P. The effects of acceptance and reciprocation of self-disclosures on the development of trust. *Journal of Counseling Psychology*, 1972, **19**, 411–416.

JOHNSON, S., & JOHNSON, D. W. The effects of other's actions, attitude similarity, and race on attraction towards the other. *Human Relations*, 1972, **25**, 121–130.

JONES, E. E., & DAVIS, K. E. From acts to dispositions: The attribution process in person perception. In L. BERKOWITZ (Ed.), *Advances in experimental social psychology*. Vol. II. New York: Academic Press, 1965. Pp. 219–266.

JONES, E. E., & GERARD, H. B. *Foundations of social psychology*. New York: Wiley, 1967.

JONES, E. E., KANOUSE, D. E., KELLEY, H. H., NISBETT, R. E., VALINS, S., & WEINER, B. *Attribution: Perceiving the causes of behavior*. Morristown, N.J.: General Learning Press, 1971.

JOURARD, S. M. Self-disclosure and other cathexis. *Journal of Abnormal and Social Psychology*, 1959, **59**, 428–431.

JOURARD, S. M. *The transparent self*. Toronto: Van Nostrand, 1964.

JOURARD, S. M., & FRIEDMAN, R. Experimenter-subject 'distance' and self-disclosure. *Journal of Personality and Social Psychology*, 1970, **15**, 278–282.

JOURARD, S. M., & LANDSMAN, M. J. Cognition, cathexis and the "dyadic effect" in men's self-disclosing behavior. *Merrill-Palmer Quarterly*, 1960, **6**, 178–186.

KAUL, T., & SCHMIDT, L. Dimensions of interviewer trustworthiness. *Journal of Counseling Psychology*, 1971, **18**, 542–548.

KELLEY, H. H. Attribution theory in social psychology. *Nebraska symposium on motivation*, 1967, **15**, 192–210.

KELLY, G. A. *The psychology of personal constructs*. Vol. II. New York: Norton, 1955.

KINCH, J. W. A formalized theory of the self-concept. *The American Journal of Sociology*, 1963, **68**, 481–486.

KING, B. T., & JANIS, I. L. Comparison of the effectiveness of improvised versus nonimprovised role-playing in producing opinion changes. *Human Relations*, 1956, **9**, 177–186.

KIRTNER, W. L., & CARTWRIGHT, D. S. Success and failure in client-centered therapy as a function of initial in-therapy behavior. *Journal of Consulting Psychology*, 1958, **22**, 329–333.

KOHLBERG, L. Stage and sequence: The cognitive-developmental approach to socialization. In D. A. GOSLIN (Ed.), *Handbook of socialization theory and research*. Chicago: Rand-McNally, 1969. Pp. 347–480.

KRAUSS, R. M., & DEUTSCH, M. Communication in interpersonal bargaining. *Journal of Personality and Social Psychology*, 1966, **4**, 572–577.

KRAUSS, R. M., & GLUCKSBERG, S. The development of communication: Competence as a function of age. *Child Development*, 1969, **40**, 255–266.

LEVY, L. H. *Psychological interpretation*. New York: Holt, Rinehart & Winston, 1963.

LEVY, L. H., & HOUSE, W. C. Perceived origins of beliefs as determinants of expectancy for their change. *Journal of Personality and Social Psychology*, 1970, **14**, 329–334.

LEWIN, K. *A dynamic theory of personality*. New York: McGraw-Hill, 1935.

LIBERMAN, B. Patterns of change and maintenance of improvement: Long-term follow-up investigations of psychotherapeutic effectiveness. Paper presented at

Annual Meeting of the Society for Psychotherapy Research, Denver, June 1974.

London, Perry. *Behavior control*. New York: Harper and Row, 1969.

Looft, W. R. Egocentrism and social interaction across the life span. *Psychological Bulletin*, 1972, **78**, 73–92.

Luborsky, L., Chandler, M., Auerbach, A. H., Cohen, J., & Bachrach, H. M. Factors influencing the outcome of psychotherapy: A review of quantitative research. *Psychological Bulletin*, 1971, **75**, 145–185.

Maccoby, E. Role-taking in childhood and its consequences for social learning. *Child Development*, 1959, **30**, 239–252.

Marwell, G., & Schmitt, D. R. *Cooperation: An experimental analysis*. New York: Academic Press, 1975.

Maslow, A. H. *Motivation and personality*. New York: Harper & Row, 1954.

Matross, R. P. Insight and attribution in counseling and psychotherapy. *Office for Student Affairs Research Bulletin, University of Minnesota*, 1975.

Matross, R. P. Socratic methods in counseling and psychotherapy. *Office for Student Affairs Research Bulletin, University of Minnesota*, 1975b.

May, R. *Love and will*. New York: Norton, 1969.

McCorkle, L. W., Elias, A., & Bixby, F. L. *The Highfields story: A unique experiment in the treatment of juvenile delinquency*. New York: Holt, 1958.

McGuire, W. J. Inducing resistance to persuasion: Some contemporary approaches. In L. Berkowitz (Ed.), *Advances in experimental social psychology*. Vol. 1. New York: Academic Press, 1964. Pp. 191–229.

McGuire, W. J. The nature of attitudes and attitude change. In G. Lindzey & E. Aronson (Eds.), *The handbook of social psychology*. Vol. 3. (2nd Ed.) Reading, Mass.: Addison-Wesley, 1969a.

McGuire, W. J. Personality and susceptibility to social influence. In E. F. Borgassa & W. W. Lambert (Eds.), *Handbook of personality theory and research*. Chicago: Rand McNally, 1969b.

McGuire, W. J. Suspiciousness of experimenter's intent. In R. Rosenthal and R. Rosnow (Eds.), *Artifact in behavioral research*. New York: Academic Press, 1969c. Pp. 13–60.

Mead, G. H. *Mind, self, and society*. Chicago: University of Chicago Press, 1934.

Meehl, P. *Clinical vs. statistical prediction*. Minneapolis: University of Minnesota Press, 1954.

Meichenbaum, D. H., & Smart, I. Use of direct expectancy to modify academic performance and attitudes of college students. *Journal of Counseling Psychology*, 1971, **18**, 531–535.

Meland, J. *Counter influence and counselor effectiveness*. Unpublished doctoral dissertation, University of Minnesota, 1974.

Mellinger, G. D. Interpersonal trust as a factor in communication. *Journal of Abnormal and Social Psychology*, 1956, **52**, 304–309.

Menninger, K. *Whatever became of sin?* New York: Hawthorn, 1973.

Millon, T. *Modern psychopathology*. Philadelphia: Saunders, 1969.

Montagu, A. *On being human*. New York: Hawthorn, 1966.

Mowrer, O. H. Freudianism, behavior therapy and "self-disclosure." *Behavior Research and Therapy*, 1964a, **1**, 321–337.

Mowrer, O. H. *The new group therapy*. Princeton, N.J.: Van Nostrand, 1964b.

Muney, B., & Deutsch, M. The effects of role reversal during the discussion of opposing viewpoints. *Journal of Conflict Resolution*, 1968, **12**, 345–356.

Murdoch, P., Chenowith, R., & Rissman, K. Eligibility and intimacy effects on self-disclosure. Paper presented at the meeting of the Society of Experimental Social Psychology, Madison, Wisconsin, October 31–November 1, 1969.

Newcomb, T. M. An approach to the study of communicative acts. *Psychological Review*, 1953, **60**, 393–404.

Nisbet, R. Cooperation. In *International encyclopedia of the social sciences*. Vol. 3. New York: Macmillan and The Free Press, 1968.

Nisbett, R. E., & Schachter, S. Cognitive manipulation of pain. *Journal of Experimental Social Psychology*, 1966, **2**, 227–236.

O'Neal, E. The influence of future choice importance and arousal upon the Halo Effect. In H. London & R. Nisbett (Eds.), *The cognitive alteration of feeling states*. Chicago: Aldine, 1972.

Osgood, C. E., & Tannenbaum, P. H. The principle of congruity in the prediction of attitude change. *Psychological Review*, 1955, **62**, 42–55.

Patton, M. J. Attraction, discrepancy, and response to psychological treatment. *Journal of Counseling Psychology*, 1969, **16**, 317–324.

Pepinsky, H. B., & Pepinsky, P. *Counseling: Theory and practice*. New York: Ronald, 1954.

Perls, F. *Gestalt therapy verbatim*. Lafayette, CA.: Real People Press, 1969.

Pettigrew, T. F. Social evaluation theory: Convergence and application. In D. Levine (Ed.), *Nebraska Symposium on motivation*. Lincoln, Neb.: University of Nebraska Press, 1967.

Pilnick, F., Elias, A., & Clapp, N. The Essex Fields Concept: A new approach to the social treatment of juvenile delinquents. *Journal of Applied Behavioral Science*, 1966, **2**, 109–130.

Rapaport, A. *Fights, games, and debates*. Ann Arbor: The University of Michigan Press, 1960.

Raven, B. H., & Kruglanski, A. W. Conflict and power. In P. Swingle (Ed.), *The structure of conflict*. New York: Academic Press, 1970. Pp. 69–110.

Rogers, C. R. *Client-centered therapy*. Boston: Houghton Mifflin, 1951.

Rogers, C. *On becoming a person*. Boston: Houghton Mifflin, 1961.

Rogers, C. R. Dealing with psychological tensions. *Journal of Applied Behavioral Science*, 1965, **1**, 6–25.

Rokeach, M. *The open and closed mind*. New York: Basic Books, 1960.

Rokeach, M. *Beliefs, attitudes, and values*. San Francisco: Jossey Bass, 1968.

Rose, G., Frankel, N., & Kerr, W. Empathic and sociometric status among teenagers. *Journal of Genetic Psychology*, 1956, **89**, 277–278.

Ross, L. D., Rodin, J., & Zimbardo, P. G. Toward an attribution therapy: The reduction of fear through induced cognitive-emotional misattribution. *Journal of Personality and Social Psychology*, 1969, **12**, 279–288.

Rothenberg, B. B. Children's social sensitivity and the relationship to interpersonal competence, intrapersonal comfort, and intellectual level. *Developmental Psychology*, 1970, **2**, 335–350.

Rotter, J. B. *Social learning and clinical psychology*. Englewood Cliffs, N.J.: Prentice-Hall, 1954.

Rotter, J. B. Generalized expectancies for internal versus external control of reinforcement. *Psychological Monographs*, 1966, **80** (Whole No. 609).

Schachter, S. The interaction of cognitive and physiological determinants of emotional state. In L. Berkowitz (Ed.), *Advances in experimental social psychology*. New York: Academic Press, 1964.

Schachter, S., & Singer, J. Cognitive, social and physiological determinants of emotional state. *Psychological Review*, 1962, **69**, 379–399.

Schlenker, B. R., Helm, B., Nacci, P., & Tedeschi, J. T. The generalization of credibility across influence modes: Compliance to threats as a function of promise credibility. Mimeo, State University of New York at Albany, 1972.

Schlenker, B. R., Helm, B., & Tedeschi, J. T. The effects of personality and situational variables on behavioral trust. *Journal of Personality and Social Psychology*, 1973, **25**, 419–427.

SCHMIDT, L. D., & STRONG, S. R. "Expert" and "inexpert" counselors. *Journal of Counseling Psychology*, 1970, **17**, 115–118.

SCHMIDT, L. D., & STRONG, S. R. Attractiveness and influence in counseling. *Journal of Counseling Psychology*, 1971, **18**, 348–351.

SCHROEDER, P. Client acceptance of responsibility and difficulty of therapy. *Journal of Consulting Psychology*, 1960, **24**, 467–471.

SCHUTZ, W. C. *Firo: A three dimensional theory of interpersonal behavior*. New York: Holt, Rinehart & Winston, 1958.

SECOND, P. F., & BACKMAN, C. W. *Social psychology*. New York: McGraw-Hill, 1964.

SELMAN, R. L. The relation of role-taking to the development of moral judgement in children. *Child Development*, 1971, **42**, 79–91.

SERMAT, V., & SMYTH, M. Content analysis of verbal communication in the development of a relationship: Conditions influencing self-disclosure. *Journal of Personality and Social Psychology*, 1973, **26**, 332–346.

SIMONSON, N. R. The impact of warm and cold self-disclosing therapists. Unpublished manuscript, Syracuse University, 1968.

SKILBECK, W. M. Attribution theory and crisis intervention therapy. Paper presented at the convention of the American Psychological Association, Montreal, Quebec, 1973.

SPRAFKIN, R. P. Communicator expertness and changes in word meanings in psychological treatment. *Journal of Counseling Psychology*, 1970, **17**, 191–196.

STORMS, M. D., & NISBETT, R. E. Insomnia and the attribution process. *Journal of Personality and Social Psychology*, 1970, **16**, 319–328.

STRONG, S. R. Counseling: An interpersonal influence process. *Journal of Counseling Psychology*, 1968, **15**, 215–224.

STRONG, S. R. Causal attribution in counseling and psychotherapy. *Journal of Counseling Psychology*, 1970, **17**, 388–399.

STRONG, S. R., & DIXON, D. N. Expertness, attractiveness, and influence in counseling. *Journal of Counseling Psychology*, 1971, **18**, 562–570.

STRONG, S. R., & MATROSS, R. P. Change processes in counseling and psychotherapy. *Journal of Counseling Psychology*, 1973, **20**, 25–37.

STRONG, S. R., & SCHMIDT, L. D. Expertness and influence in counseling. *Journal of Counseling Psychology*, 1970a, **17**, 81–87.

STRONG, S. R., & SCHMIDT, L. D. Trustworthiness and influence in counseling. *Journal of Counseling Psychology*, 1970b, **17**, 197–204.

STRUPP, H. H. Toward a reformulation of the psychotherapeutic influence. *International Journal of Psychiatry*, 1973, **11**, 263–354.

STRUPP, H. H., & BERGIN, A. E. Some empirical and conceptual bases for coordinated research in psychotherapy: A critical review of issues, trends, and evidence. *International Journal of Psychiatry*, 7, 1969, 18–90.

STUART, R. B. Decentration in the development of children's concepts of moral and causal judgment. *Journal of Genetic Psychology*, 1967, **111**, 59–68.

SULLIVAN, H. S. *The interpersonal theory of psychiatry*. New York: Norton, 1953.

TAYLOR, D. A. The effects of social reinforcement and self-disclosure patterns on interpersonal behavior. Unpublished manuscript, University of Delaware, 1964.

TAYLOR, D. A. The development of interpersonal relationships: Social penetration processes. *Journal of Social Psychology*, 1968, **75**, 79–90.

TAYLOR, D. A., ALTMAN, I., & SORRENTINO, R. Interpersonal exchange as a function of rewards and costs and situational factors: Expectancy confirmation-discon-

firmation. *Journal of Experimental Social Psychology*, 1969, **5**, 324–339.

THIBAUT, J. W., & KELLEY, H. H. *The social psychology of groups*. New York: Wiley, 1959.

TJOSVOLD, D. Unequal power and status relationships: A critical review of the literature. Mimeographed report, Pennsylvania State University, 1974.

TRUAX, C. B., & CARKHUFF, R. R. *Toward effective counseling and psychotherapy: Training and practice*. Chicago: Aldine, 1967.

TRUAX, C. B., & WARGO, D. G. Psychotherapeutic encounters that change behavior: For better or for worse. *American Journal of Psychotherapy*, 1966, **22**, 499–520.

URBAN, H. B., & FORD, D. H. Some historical and conceptual perspectives on psychotherapy and behavior change. In A. F. BERGIN & S. L. GARFIELD (Eds.), *Handbook of psychotherapy and behavior change: An empirical Analysis*. New York: Wiley, 1971. Pp. 3–35.

VALINS, S. Cognitive effects of false heart-rate feedback. *Journal of Personality and Social Psychology*, 1966, **4**, 400–408.

VALINS, S., & NISBETT, R. E. *Attribution processes in the development and treatment of emotional disorders*. Morristown, N.J.: General Learning Press, 1971. Also in E. E. JONES, D. E. KANOUSE, H. H. KELLEY, R. E. NISBETT, S. VALINS, & B. WEINER, *Attribution: Perceiving the causes of behavior*. Morristown, N.J.: New General Learning Press, 1971.

VALINS, S., & RAY, A. Effects of cognitive desensitization on avoidance behavior. *Journal of Personality and Social Psychology*, 1967, **7**, 345–350.

VON MISES, L. *Human action: A treatise on economics*. New Haven: Yale University Press, 1949.

WALTON, R. E., & MCKERSIE, R. B. *A behavioral theory of labor negotiations*. New York: McGraw-Hill, 1965.

WATSON, G., & JOHNSON, D. W. *Social psychology: Issues and insights*. Philadelphia: Lippincott, 1972.

WENT, F. W. *The plants*. New York: Time, 1963.

WHITE, R. W. Motivation reconsidered: The concept of competence. *Psychological Review*, 1959, **66**, 297–333.

WOLPE, J., & LAZARUS, A. A. *Behavior therapy techniques*. New York: Pergamon Press, 1966.

WORTHY, M., GARY, A. L., & KAHN, G. M. Self-disclosure as an exchange process. *Journal of Personality and Social Psychology*, 1969, **13**, 59–63.

YABLONSKY, L. The anticriminal society: Synanon. *Federal Probation*, 1962, **26**, 50–57.

ZIMBARDO, P. G. The effect of effort and improvisation on self-persuasion produced by role-playing. *Journal of Experimental Social Psychology*, 1965, **1**, 103–120.

EDITORS' REFERENCES

BIERMAN, R. Dimensions for interpersonal facilitation in psychotherapy and child development. *Psychological Bulletin*, 1969, **72**, 338–352.

ERICKSON, M. H., & ROSSI, E. L. Varieties of double bind. *American Journal of Clinical Hypnosis*, 1975, **17**, 143–157.

HALEY, J. *Uncommon therapy: The psychiatric techniques of Milton H. Erickson, M.D.* New York: Ballantine, 1973.

NOTES

1. *Editors' Footnote.* Here and throughout this chapter the authors argue that therapy is a "cooperative" relationship. Perhaps the authors are describing an *ideal* model for therapy since certainly a good deal of therapy is anything but cooperative, as the authors seem to implicitly acknowledge in their reference (page 8) to therapy as "ostensibly cooperative." Based on this model, the authors emphasize the establishment of mutual goals. Our feeling is that such mutuality of goal setting is often quite difficult to achieve; in addition, many therapists

intentionally do not attempt to verbally explicate goals with patients. Such overt focused goal setting is far more characteristic of behavioral, rational-emotive, and time-limited therapies than of psychoanalytic, client-centered, and existential therapies. Thus, the sources of influence in the latter therapies are likely to be somewhat different as emphasized by Strupp in Chapter 1 (this volume).

2. *Editors' Footnote.* Again, this appears to us not to be universally true, but to be more descriptive of supportive, crisis-oriented, and behavioral therapies than of depth therapies.

3. *Editors' Footnote.* This may be true, but the literature cited up to this point, except from Bierman (1968), used *peer* confederates; thus, reciprocation of self-disclosure may *not* occur in unequal status relationships (i.e., much of actual psychotherapy). For a further discussion of this issue, see Emrick, Lassen, and Edwards (Chapter 7, this volume).

4. *Editors' Footnote.* Unless our clinical and teaching experiences are tremendously different from those of the authors, such behavior of the part of therapists seems to represent very infrequent exceptions, not commonplace occurrences. We agree with the authors' position on the ethical responsibilities of therapists but also feel that they are striking a biting blow against largely nonexistent straw therapists.

5. *Editors' Footnote.* We thank John Neill, M.D., for pointing out to us that much of the authors' stance on the use of influence in therapeutic settings seems to be based on an acceptance of the efficacy of a model of rational persuasion. In this context, we would wonder how the philosophy of cooperativeness of mutual goal setting might accommodate the influence strategies of Milton Erickson (Erickson & Rossi, 1975; Haley, 1973). Erickson clearly does not verbalize his goals to patients (i.e., goals are rarely negotiated and overt), yet they also clearly *are* established in the patient's best interest. Thus, following Johnson and Matross' definition of "manipulation" at the beginning of this chapter, it is uncertain whether they would consider Erickson's tactics "manipulative" or "constructively influential." By the authors' definition, they are manipulative in that patients usually do not "understand" what Erickson is doing or why, yet, were the rationale of the therapeutic double-bind or para-doxical intention to be exposed, it would usually lose its power to influence!

CHAPTER 16

COUNTERTRANSFERENCE: THE STATUS OF CLINICAL VERSUS QUANTITATIVE RESEARCH[1]

BARTON A. SINGER AND LESTER LUBORSKY

THROUGH the 65 years since Freud's (1910) first writing on the issue, there have been many review articles on countertransference (Baum, 1969–1970; Kernberg, 1965; Orr, 1954; Sandler, Holder, & Dare, 1970). Those reviews concentrate mainly on the papers written during the 1950s, the heyday of interest in countertransference. While we shall also comment on some of the early articles, we shall emphasize the clinical literature since 1960. In addition, we shall discuss the existing quantitative work on the subject, for there is no extensive review where both the clinical and quantitative studies are compared, contrasted, and integrated.

CLINICAL STUDIES OF COUNTERTRANSFERENCE

Much discussion and controversy in the clinical field centers around the definitions of countertransference—whether the term should be reserved for the original, limited, and specific definition based on Freud's view that it is concerned with the unconscious response of the analyst to the patient's transference, or whether it should involve all the conscious and unconscious responses of the analyst. As one will see in the survey, there are a number of workers in the field who feel that the orthodox view is much too constricted and unrealistic, conveying an unnecessary fear of countertransference. On the other hand, many feel that too loose a concept loses its value as a tool for thought and discussion. It is important to note, however, that the narrower position is generally not accepted by present-day analysts who see the need to recognize and work with the therapist's feelings as well as the patient's feelings.

The original view was that of Freud (1910), who first used the term "countertransference" in stating, "We have become aware of the countertransference, which arises in him [the physician] as a result of the patient's influence on his unconscious feelings, and we are almost inclined to assert that he shall recognize this countertransference in himself and overcome it" (pp. 144–145). He made it clear that he considered countertransference as having an adverse effect on the ability of the therapist to function effectively and to understand his patient. In short, it was something to be avoided as much as possible. While there was discussion and elaboration of the concepts by Stern (1924), Fenichel (1941), Glover (1955), and others, two of the more extensive papers supporting the classical view were those written by Reich (1951, 1960). In her 1951 paper she presented one of the clearest definitions of the classical view of countertransference, stating that it "comprises the effects of the analyst's own unconscious needs and conflicts on his understanding or technique" (p. 26). In such cases the patient represents for the analyst an object of the past onto whom past feelings and wishes are projected, analogous to the patient's transference relationship with the analyst. The eliciting factor for such an occurrence may be something in the patient's personality or something in the current analytic situation. This is countertransference in the proper sense. In her later paper, Reich explains that many kinds of phenomena can reflect countertransference responses. These can include sexual and/or aggressive and related feelings toward the patient or defenses against such feelings. Identification with the patient can occur because of similar conflicts in the therapist that are related to past relationships with important people in his own life. She points out that the therapist is not aware of these kinds of responses but can become aware of their consequences by recognizing, for example, that he is being made too anxious or upset by the patient or that he finds himself unable to concentrate on the therapy hour or to understand the patient.

According to Reich, countertransference has

such an adverse effect on therapy because it can so strongly influence the therapist's primary source of influence—his intuitive understanding of the patient. In analytically oriented therapy, intuition or emotional understanding is extremely important, often as important as logical conclusions or active thinking. Insight into the patient's concerns is often arrived at by using the analyst's own unconscious by a process of partially or temporarily identifying with the patient. Through this identification and through experiencing what the patient is experiencing, the analyst gains an understanding of the patient's unconscious mechanisms. Freud commented on using the analyst's own unconscious as a tool for understanding when he advised the analyst to listen with free-floating attention so that what the patient says is absorbed by the therapist's unconscious. It is clear that when an unconscious conflict on the part of the therapist is activated in the hour, it can affect his ability to concentrate, to listen, to understand, and to respond correctly to the patient and not to the therapist's own needs.

Because of the problems of countertransference and because the analyst has to be the object of the patient's transference, a "neutral" stance is required. According to the classical theory of analytic therapy, the therapist functions partly as a screen onto which the patient projects his conflictual relationships. In this way the patient can reexperience in his relationship with the therapist aspects of significant early relationships, and thereby learn to recognize how these early patterns of relating still influence his present relationship with the therapist. In order to make these transferences possible, the analyst must remain neutral. The concept of therapeutic neutrality denotes that he does not respond to the patient's emotional pull with the normal or expected responsiveness. He must remain impartial and unmoved, not personally affected by the patient's feelings. For example, he must attempt to refrain from anger in response to a patient's behavior that might ordinarily make one angry. Yet it is recognized that "neutrality" is a relative term and is often difficult to achieve. But, to the extent that it can be achieved, the analysis will progress most effectively.

One cannot say, however, that even in a "classical" analysis the therapist should not show any emotion. Unfortunately, Freud's (1912) dictum that "the doctor should be opaque to his patients and like a mirror, should show them nothing but what is shown to him" (p. 118) has often been misinterpreted to mean that he should not show *any* feelings, that there should be no emotional interaction between the therapist and the patient. Reich (1951) clarifies this point:

> To be neutral in relationship to the patient, to remain the screen does not of course imply that the analyst has no relationship at all to the patient. We expect him to be interested in the patient, to have a friendly willingness to help him. He may like or dislike the patient. As far as these attitudes are conscious they have not yet anything to do with countertransference. If these feelings increase in intensity, we can be fairly certain that the unconscious feelings of the analyst, his own transferences onto the patient, i.e., countertransferences, are mixed in. (p. 25)

In her later paper (Reich, 1960) she adds, "Conscious responses should be regarded as countertransference only if they reach an inordinate intensity or are strongly tainted by inappropriate sexual or aggressive feelings, thus revealing themselves to be determined by unconscious infantile strivings" (p. 390). She expands on the notion of a response's indicating countertransference by including behavior on the part of the therapist that has an unconscious meaning for him; for example, when what he does with the patient is "motivated by hidden unconscious tendencies," so that the patient serves some need of the therapist, such as reducing guilt or anxiety or increasing his self-esteem.

Reich also makes an important distinction between acute and chronic countertransference. The former includes those responses that "occur suddenly under specific circumstances and with specific patients" (1951, p. 26); they are based on an identification with the patient. The therapist continues to feel or behave like the patient because in doing so he derives gratification; for example, he begins to support and reinforce aggressive behavior in the patient because of the pleasure it gives him to feel these impulses acted upon. Another example of acute countertransference is seen in the therapist who responds directly to the feelings of a particular patient, returning a patient's love or responding with hate to a patient's hostility. These kinds of reactions are especially seen as reflecting countertransference when they are very intense. The chronic form of countertransference is manifested in behavior that represents an habitual need of the analyst and is a part of the therapist's basic character structure; it generally occurs with most of his patients rather than in relation to a particular kind of conflictual situation. An example of such chronic countertransference is the therapist who has difficulty dealing with his aggressive impulses, is always overly kind, and is unable to be firm even when firmness is appropriate.

As stated before, the broadened view of countertransference includes all conscious and unconscious emotional responses of the analyst. This position is adopted most clearly by Heimann (1950); countertransference, she says, "covers all the feelings which the analyst experiences towards his patient" (p. 81). In this and in another work (Heimann, 1960) she supports the value of the therapist's using his own emotional response to the patient (what she calls his countertransference) as the main means of understanding the patient:

> Along with his freely and evenly hovering attention which enables the analyst to listen simultaneously on many levels, he needs a freely roused emotional sensibility so as to receive and follow closely his patient's emotional movements and unconscious fantasies. By comparing the feelings aroused in himself with the content of his patient's associations and the qualities of his mood and behavior, the analyst has the means for checking whether he has understood or failed to understand his patient. (p. 10)

Heimann takes a definite position that the main use of countertransference is to help the *therapist* empathize with the patient more completely and thereby contribute to the efficacy of his therapeutic interventions.

Agreeing with Heimann's general position on the therapeutic use of countertransference, Grossman (1965) is also in concordance with her specific point that it is most useful to limit the term to the response to a transference feeling. He defines countertransference as a "universal human psychological reaction which occurs in one person towards another as a result of exposure to the transference feelings of that other person" (p. 252). By seeing it as an appropriate, expected reaction to the stimulus situation, the therapist can better modulate his defensiveness, allowing himself to recognize what otherwise might be perceived as unacceptable feelings.

Little (1951, 1960) is the primary psychoanalytic advocate of the notion that the communication of the analyst's countertransference reactions to the patient often can be an extremely valuable therapeutic tool. (This position is not accepted by most analysts who believe the patient would usually be burdened by the showing.) She explains that when, for example, the therapist says or does something motivated by his countertransference feelings that may be mistaken or poorly timed, not only should he correct it but he should also "explain its origin

in the unconscious countertransference unless there is some definite contraindication for doing so, in which case it should be postponed until a suitable time comes, as it surely will. Such explanations may be essential for the further progress of the analysis and it will have only beneficial results. Only harm can come from withholding such an interpretation" (p. 37). She expands the point that countertransference is a fact of analysis and can be both good and bad, depending on how it is used. But it is a powerful tool when employed judiciously and skillfully.

Kernberg (1965) summarizes the classical versus the "totalistic" controversy succinctly and calls for a more clearly defined view of the broadened definition. According to Kernberg, proponents of the classical view criticize the broadening of the definition of countertransference because it makes the term very confusing; it covers a number of clinical phenomena and makes it difficult for a reader to know just what a particular author has in mind. Furthermore, the broadened definition emphasizes detrimentally the importance of the therapist's own feelings. While neutrality does not mean detachment, the "classicists" believe that too much weight given to the therapist's emotional reactivity can interfere with effective treatment. The "totalists," on the other hand, support the need to broaden the countertransference definition because they feel that its value as a therapeutic tool can be hidden by the older viewpoint.

> The fusion of influences of the patient's transference and his reality on the one hand and of the therapist's past and present reality on the other hand gives much important information about the nonverbal communication between patient and analyst which tends to get lost when the efforts center on eliminating the analyst's emotional reaction rather than focusing on it and on its sources. When the analyst feels that his emotional reaction is an important technical instrument for understanding and helping the patient, the analyst feels freer to face his positive and negative emotions evoked in the transference situation, has less need to block these reactions and utilize them for his analytic work. (Kernberg, 1965, p. 40)

This is particularly important when working with patients with low ego strength who can evoke strong countertransference feelings. The totalists also criticize the classicists' "phobic" attitude towards countertransference, an attitude which implies that there is something basically wrong with having countertransference, thus influencing a therapist to deny or avoid recognizing such feelings.

Adopting the definition that countertransference is the "total emotional reaction of the psychoanalyst to the patient in the treatment situation" including "the analyst's conscious and unconscious reactions to the patient's reality as well as to his transference and also to the analyst's own reality needs as well as to his neurotic needs," Kernberg (1965, p. 38) expands aspects of the "totalist's" view. He especially focuses on the problem of identification in the countertransference. Transient trial identification is a key process involved in empathy; the therapist identifies with a patient in a partial and temporary way as a means of attempting to understand him. However, as Reich (1951, 1960) and others have discussed, countertransference can interfere with this process. Kernberg explains the problem in terms of a concept called "projective identification." He sees this as an early form of the mechanism of projection, but differing from projection in that

> the impulse projected onto an internal object does not appear as something alien and distant from the ego because the connection of the ego with that projected impulse still continues and thus the ego empathizes with the object. The anxiety which provoked the projection of the impulse onto the object in the first place now becomes fear of that object, accompanied by the need to control the object in order to prevent it from attacking the ego when under the influence of that impulse. (p. 45)

For example, a patient's intense anger may be projected onto another person, like his analyst, so that he fears him. Yet, because of the weakness of his ego boundaries, the patient is inclined to identify with the therapist, which increases his fear. This condition leads the patient to feel that he must control and fight the therapist before he himself is attacked. Kernberg proposes that when the therapist identifies with the patient who is regressed and consequently undergoes some regression himself, some of his own early identifications and the mechanism of projective identification become activated, severely interfering with the therapy; the therapist experiences anxiety and primitive impulses which can become directed toward the patient, arousing a need to control the patient. While there can be many problems resulting from the unmodulated effects of such a process, when the therapist can control the experience, it can be quite useful to him—feeling something parallel to what the patient experiences can help him to know more about the kind of fears and fantasies the patient is having.

While Kernberg (1965) clearly advocates the utilization of these primitive transference-countertransference phenomena, he does address himself to the need not to let these powerful forces get out of control. Recognizing that this can happen all too easily, he describes the concept of "concern" as a way to focus on and check them. "Concern in this context involves awareness of the serious nature of destructive and self-destructive impulses in the patient, the potential development of such impulses in the analyst, and the awareness by the analyst of the limitations necessarily inherent in his therapeutic efforts with this patient" (p. 51). More specifically, he suggests some guidelines to help the therapist avoid getting into untherapeutic circumstances. He stresses the need to have a constantly critical attitude toward what one is doing so that one is always able to look for and try new ways of dealing with a problem that is not improving in the expected way. The therapist should also check himself from time to time to determine if he is withdrawing and not feeling enough involvement. And, finally, he should be open to consulting with colleagues when he becomes aware of obstacles in the progress of the case.

Such suggestions, while often taken for granted, actually need to be stressed. Especially for the overworked therapist who practices in relative isolation from colleagues, it is all too easy to dismiss such important matters as luxuries, thus often perpetuating untherapeutic conditions. Professional self-criticism as well as communication with co-workers usually is essential for effective psychotherapy.

Sandler et al. (1970), after reviewing much of the literature on countertransference, do not advocate as open and ready use of countertransference in the therapy as Kernberg. However, they do conclude that the term should cover a broader range of phenomena than just those aspects of the therapist's emotional response that interfere with his effectiveness. They believe that countertransference also involves "normal" responses in the therapist and that by carefully examining his own reactions about the patient, he can learn much about what the patient is feeling and attempting to communicate.

A useful endeavor to come to an understanding of the various points of view about countertransference is presented by Baum (1969–1970), who achieves an organized and clinically practical overview of this area. Believing that there is more agreement than disagreement, he first outlines the points of consensus such as the notion that "the analyst is not merely a neutral observer"—due to the many stresses in the therapy situation he is at least occasionally bound to react in ways that will interfere with optimal understanding of what is going on in the patient. All authors seem to agree, however, that the therapist should have sufficient emotional maturity so that his own needs enter as little as possible into the relationship. The ability to identify with the patient in a controlled, systematic way is an important prerequisite; the therapist should be able to empathize but then use the empathy to help the patient to understand himself better. It is also generally agreed that it is important for the therapist to recognize when he is experiencing difficulty in determining if what he is feeling is due to the patient's behavior or due to a personal reaction. When countertransference is having a strong adverse effect and is blocking the therapist's capacity for empathy, the necessity for him to work it through and resolve it is generally accepted.

Yet Baum recognizes that there are some significant differences between classical and totalist approaches, especially in the extent to which countertransference responses are an issue in the therapy. He believes that these differences are largely due to the fact that proponents of the broader definition generally work with "sicker" patients, so that the therapist must be more active and consequently would be more inclined to use his own emotional responses as part of his therapeutic technique. Furthermore, because the transference reactions of such patients are more intense, they are more likely to evoke countertransference responses which must be dealt with, hopefully in a therapeutic way. It is Baum's position that countertransference responses "are undesirable and the analysis would be better off without them" (p. 635). However, as long as these blocks to effective therapy are understood and resolved, they do not have to be considered as something bad. "The important thing is to identify them, work through the countertransference, and once more allow the empathic process to operate" (p. 635).

It is clear that almost all workers in this field stress the importance of becoming consciously aware of countertransference feelings so that they can be worked through within the treatment. Two papers have directly addressed themselves to this issue and offer new ways of looking at the problem. The usual method of exploring countertransference as described in the literature is through self-analysis or discussing the matter with a supervisor or colleague. Ross and Kapp (1962) have developed a new technique which provides an efficient and interesting way of addressing the problem. The method involves having the analyst focus on the visual images that emerge when he hears the patient's dreams; these images then become starting points for associations in self-analysis, either in the session or afterwards. Often these images occur clearly to the analyst as he is listening to the patient's reporting. At other times they may be more fleeting and require some conscious effort to capture them. The images are frequently related to past or recent memories of the therapist; associating to them can often bring to mind important insights into what is occurring in the therapy, making certain countertransference phenomena conscious so that they can be worked with.

Sherman (1965) focuses on the way that countertransference feelings are transmitted to the patient, and believes it clinically useful to pay more attention to what he calls the "peripheral cues" of the psychotherapeutic situation which can be vehicles of communication of countertransference in order to allow the countertransference to be understood and thereby controlled. He makes a distinction between the main aspects of the relationship (such as, for example, interpretation of the patient's transference feelings) and the general context and atmosphere which is "usually considered peripheral to the main business" of therapy. These peripheral elements consist of matters such as nonverbal cues (body movements, changes in the therapist's tone of voice, facial expressions) or in the way that he handles administrative matters such as canceled appointments or vacation plans. The form or way that the therapist presents his interventions can have a major effect on the patient such as reinforcing and conditioning the kinds of patient behavior that fit in with the therapist's own expectations. They can also have a striking influence on the way an interpretation is accepted by the patient. For example, a voice inflection which may connote disapproval can be the deciding factor moving the patient to reject the comment. Sherman's main point is that these peripheral cues often transmit the emotional attitude that the therapist has toward the patient and they can easily be unconscious, hidden from the therapist's awareness, and yet significantly influencing the treatment. By paying closer attention to these more peripheral aspects, the therapist may be able to keep them as a more visible, controlled part of the therapy situation.

QUANTITATIVE STUDIES OF COUNTERTRANSFERENCE

In this section we shall review research which attempts to investigate countertransference in a controlled and systematic way. These studies do not rely mainly on clinical observation and theorizing as those in the first section do, but rather they stress rigorous, scientific exploration.

As Luborsky (1969) has pointed out, quantitative research has had all too little effect on clinical work. Part of the reason for this gap has been the difficulty of focusing on and devising controlled studies of clinical phenomena. Many clinicians feel that

> research is justified so long as it remains within the treatment setting. Any analogue or attempt to simulate treatment conditions or to single out one variable at the expense of others is misleading and suspect. These restrictions seem circular. But attempts to quantify and systematize necessarily segment the complex clinical situation and usually unduly simplify it. Thus there is no way out. Attempts to understand treatment by controlled studies are discouraged by its very richness. (Luborsky & Spence, 1971, p. 409)

Most psychotherapy researchers, however, feel that a scientific orientation requires controlling certain variables even if doing so means that the phenomena studied are not in their most natural form. Consequently, much psychotherapy research deals only with approximations of the actual clinical experience. Most studies of countertransference have this drawback, too, because the problems involved in quantifying such complex phenomena are numerous. There is no agreed-upon unit scale or set of variables with which we can analyze the wide range of clinical phenomena we are continually confronting, nor are there any specimen sets of clinical interviews as agreed-upon objects of study that can be investigated by all workers. It is clear that very few investigations deal with countertransference in the sense of exploring the unconscious response of the therapist to the patient's transference. However, many of the studies to be described below do deal with clinically relevant situations and seem to overlap with the broader definition, which includes *all* the therapist's conscious and unconscious reactions to the patient. Our organizing rationale for this section is first to present those papers which most closely approximate the clinical entity and explore it in some depth. Then we describe investigations dealing with circumstances that appear further away from actual therapy situations.

Several attempts have been made to study countertransference systematically and yet retain its clinical character. One of these endeavors was part of the Menninger Foundation's Psychotherapy Project. When the treatment was ended, the researchers tried to evaluate the extent to which countertransference had hindered the therapy by using a series of questions described by Luborsky, Fabian, Hall, Ticho, and Ticho (1958). Even with a large amount of information—such as post-treatment interviews with the patient, the therapist, and the supervisor, and the complete process notes—it was difficult to determine the influence of countertransference feelings. To help the therapist remember his thoughts and feelings at the end of the session, Alexander (1950) introduced the idea of providing the therapist with a key to press in order to record the time of a personal reaction so that he could find these points later and reconstruct them. While this technique might catch some of the conscious responses, it would not be too sensitive to unconscious responses, which would include the majority of countertransference reactions. A related approach was developed by Bergman (1966) who, as a member of the National Institute of Mental Health Psychotherapy Research Project, recorded his personal reactions after each psychotherapy session. The techniques of Bergman and Alexander suggest some systematic ways that the therapist can note his introspections associated with countertransference during the therapy process. However, as Luborsky and Spence (1971) point out, "a danger is of distraction in the conduct of the treatment. A further drawback is that the actual countertransference reactions often need to be pointed out by a third person" (p. 423).

The investigations described above attempted to study countertransference within the context of the therapy situation using controlled observations beyond the usual form of clinical observations. But no quantitative techniques were utilized. The next series of studies describes efforts to examine countertransference more precisely. With more precision, unfortunately, the nature of the clinical variables change; the examination of therapist and patient personality factors moves away in depth and breadth from what is described in the clinical literature.

Nevertheless, Bandura's (1956) paper is relevant to some of the clinical work of Reich (1951, 1960) and Little (1951, 1960) regarding the way the analyst reacts to unrecognized countertransference feelings. When the therapist is threatened and made anxious by something the patient says or does, he is motivated to behave defensively, often in a way that will avoid, or at least reduce, his anxiety. The clinical literature has detailed a number of such avoidance responses: interrupting the discussion, interpreting prematurely, being too reassuring, or showing disapproval. These reactions are untherapeutic and have as much to do with the therapist's unresolved conflicts as with the patient's behavior. Bandura focuses on the effect that the patient's expression of hostility can have on the therapist who has difficulty handling his own hostility. He assumes that the patient's expression of hostility, either generally or in the transference relationship, will arouse countertransference feelings in the therapist, who has conflicts about his own hostility, which will lead him to respond with avoidance behavior. While the experimenters were not able to obtain the kind of detailed information about the therapist's personality that is often discussed in the clinical studies, they did arrive at some assessment of conflict over hostility, or "hostility anxiety," using a rating system. The 12 therapists, advanced graduate students, were rated on a scale by four clinical psychology staff members who had considerable social and professional contact with them. Assuming that high anxiety over anger would result in more indirect than direct expressions of hostility, they rated the therapists on the degree to which they tended to inhibit hostile reactions and respond in indirect ways when they were provoked in interactions with others. The therapists were also rated on their need for approval and dependency. In order to determine the amount of approach and/or avoidance behavior, tape recordings of therapy sessions were analyzed, focusing on an "interaction sequence" beginning with the patient's statement, the therapist's response, and the next response by the patient. Patients' hostile responses were noted. The therapists' responses were categorized into approach or avoidance types. For example, approach reactions were those that would tend to encourage further expressions of angry feelings or thoughts such as approval, further exploration, or refocusing on a hostile theme. Avoidance responses covered interventions that had the effect of discouraging or inhibiting hostile expressions. These included direct disapproval, silence, and ignoring. The content analysis produced an account of the number of interaction sequences in which the therapist responded with an approach or avoidance reaction to the patient's anger, and the number of sequences in which patient's anger followed the therapist's approach and avoidance. In order to evaluate the relationship between the therapist's personality and the use of approach or avoidance responses, the therapists were divided into high and low scorers on the hostility, dependency,

and approval rating scales, and the ratio of the number of approach responses to the number of avoidance responses (relative preference) was compared for the two groups by a Mann-Whitney U Test. The results showed that therapists who tended to express their own anger directly and who had a low need for approval were more likely to respond with approach reactions to the patient's expression of anger. Another interesting finding was that therapists generally were significantly more inclined to avoid patients' anger when it was directed against the therapist than when it was expressed toward someone else. Furthermore, when patients' anger is responded to with approach or acceptance, this increased the frequency of these behaviors. Conversely, avoidance responses discouraged patients' anger responses.

Closely allied to the Bandura studies, a paper by Yulis and Kiesler (1968) investigated the therapist's defensive and countertherapeutic behavior that is induced by countertransference feelings. They suggested that when a therapist experiences anxiety related to countertransference, one of the main indications is an increase in rigid, defensive interventions. This is especially clear when the patient directs feelings toward the therapist; the latter is inclined to become less emotionally involved with the patient and to avoid dealing with these feelings. Stated another way, the therapist is predisposed to avoid transference interpretations when the transference feelings arouse countertransference. The authors speculated that the therapist who is habitually more tense and conflicted will tend to respond more anxiously and defensively during psychotherapy—especially when confronted by transference feelings—than the less anxious therapist. More specifically, they hypothesized that therapists who are chronically anxious will respond to patients' references to them with more countertransference responses of avoiding personal involvement than therapists who are rated as low in anxiety. They also hypothesized that patient statements involving sex and aggression will bring out many more countertransference responses than neutral statements. Twenty-four graduate students in psychology were divided into two groups of high and low chronically anxious subjects by rating them on a 5-minute speech sample, according to the anxiety scale developed by Gleser, Gottschalk, and Springer (1961). All the subjects listened to three client tape recordings that were categorized as consisting of either sexual, aggressive, or neutral (with respect to sex and aggression) remarks, and at designated spots they were required to select one of a pair of possible statements that would best represent the way they would respond to the patient at that point in the therapy. The 30 pairs of statements differed principally in the extent to which the therapists showed or avoided personal involvement with the patient, or in the extent to which the therapist was openly recognizing or denying that the patient was directing feelings at him. Each personal involvement interpretation received a score of 1, while the interpretation that reflected countertransference received a zero. The data was subjected to an analysis of variance and indicated a significant relationship between anxiety and the countertransference-type responses; that is, a high-anxious therapist showed significantly more responses reflecting defensiveness than the low-anxiety therapist; the low-anxiety therapist more often clearly acknowledged and dealt with the patient-therapist interaction in a therapeutically useful way. Sexual and aggressive patient statements did not elicit more countertransference responses than neutral statements.

Milliken and Kirchner (1971) also found that the therapeutic effectiveness of highly anxious counselors in contrast to less anxious counselors was markedly adversely affected by client feelings (especially anger) directed at them. Using simulated interviews of actor-clients expressing different emotions, the authors demonstrated that those counselors who scored higher on the I.P.A.T. Anxiety Scale Questionnaire were more defensive, as reflected in their being significantly less accurate in recalling what had occurred during the interview—recall was evaluated by an objective true-false test.

In general, the results of these studies of therapist-patient interactions address two issues that are described at length in the clinical literature: therapists who have less anxiety and less conflict about their own feelings are not as personally affected by the patient's expression of emotions and are able to deal with their patients more therapeutically, allowing the patient to continue to explore his threatening feelings; the therapist's countertransference is not aroused to the extent that he must behave in a way that will discourage the patient's free expression.[2]

One of the more ambitious and frequently cited experimental studies of countertransference was done by Cutler (1958). This study is related to Bandura's work in that it examines the extent to which the therapist's behavior is influenced by his personality characteristics and conflicts, but it explores the area in somewhat

greater detail and depth. Assuming that countertransference phenomena can be seen as a special case of personal needs influencing how the therapist perceives the psychotherapy situation, the author hypothesized that the therapist would be more inclined to perceptual distortions when dealing with patient problems that coincide with his own conflicts than when handling neutral areas. More specifically, he evolved a method to show that when a therapist reports what is happening in therapy, he will over- or underemphasize the issues related to his conflicts significantly more often than issues for which he is relatively free of conflict. Cutler identified conflict areas in two therapists by first having them fill out an extensive self-rating scale which evaluated their personality in terms of 16 interpersonal behavioral categories such as submissiveness, dependency, domination, etc. Next, he had nine or more judges who were well acquainted with the two therapists rate them on the same scale. Those personality variables on which there was a significant discrepancy between the therapist's and the judge's ratings were assumed to be indicative of conflict; similarity between judge's and therapist's ratings reflected a lack of conflict. Tape recordings of a series of therapy sessions were made and were then scored by independent judges for the number of indications of the 16 interpersonal behavioral categories shown in the interview by the patient and the therapist. This was assumed to represent an objective account of what had actually occurred in the sessions. In addition, after each of the sessions, the therapist wrote an extensive and detailed account of what he thought had happened in the hour. Scoring of these reports according to the categories provided a measure of the therapist's own perception of his and the patient's behavior. An additional measure involved scoring the therapist's interventions according to their effectiveness in helping the patient to continue to discuss relevant material. The data indicated that the therapist was much less accurate in reporting his own and his patient's behavior in psychotherapy when the topics were related to personality conflicts of his own; there was a significantly greater discrepancy between his own report and the judge's report of what had occurred. Threatening material made defensive operations necessary and affected the accuracy of his perceptions. Another important result to emerge was that when the therapist was working with the patient on issues that were also a problem for him, his interventions were judged to be significantly less effective than when he was working with neutral material. Not only was the study able to provide experimental evidence of the distortions that are assumed to take place and are described in the clinical literature when the therapist is under the influence of countertransference feelings, but it also supported the clinical position that uncontrolled countertransference is usually a hindrance to the conduct of effective psychotherapy.

The last few papers described efforts to delineate the therapist's area of conflicts and to explore how they may influence his attitude and behavior toward patients. While the evaluations of personality factors may have been limited, they were, at least, attempts to examine this complex matter. Most other investigations have not assessed the therapist's personality but, rather, endeavored to study countertransference phenomena from other perspectives.

One of the earliest efforts to examine countertransference in a systematic and quantified way was Fiedler's (1951) study based on the Q-sort technique. Assuming that countertransference involved unrealistic feelings and perceptions on the part of the therapist in his relationship with the patient, he attempted to measure these misconceptions. This was accomplished by requesting therapists and patients to describe themselves by sorting 76 statements into eight categories, ranking them from most to least descriptive of themselves. In addition, the therapist was asked to describe how he ideally would like to be and also to describe how the patient would describe himself. From these sortings, Fiedler derived four variables: (1) the "real similarity" (RS) between the therapist's and the patient's self-description; (2) the "assumed similarity" (AS), or the amount of similarity that the therapist believes to exist between the patient and himself, based on the correlation between the therapist's self-sort and his prediction of the patient; (3) the "real similarity to the therapist's ideal" (RSI) derived from the correlation between the patient's self-sort and the therapist's ideal-sort; (4) the "assumed similarity to the therapist's ideal" (ASI), based on the correlation between the therapist's prediction of the patient and the therapist's ideal-sort. Focused measures of countertransference involved the therapist's misperceptions based on the extent to which he over- or underestimated the patient's similarity to himself or to his ideal. "Unwarranted assumed similarity," derived by subtracting the "real similarity" from the "assumed similarity," gave an estimate of how accurately the therapist saw

himself as similar to the patient. When the therapist overestimated the patient's similarity to himself, or saw himself as more similar than he really was, this was interpreted by Fiedler as meaning that the therapist wanted the patient to be more like himself than the patient really was. Such a condition suggested that the therapist accepted him as being a person like himself and could, therefore, better understand his feelings and thoughts; he could be more empathic. On the other hand, an underestimation indicated that the therapist saw the patient as less like himself, reflecting a negative attitude which would lead the therapist to distance himself. Likewise, the "unwarranted assumed similarity to the ideal" was calculated by subtracting the real similarity to the therapist's ideal from the assumed similarity to the therapist's ideal. An overestimation would mean that the therapist saw the patient as being more like his ideal than the patient really was; he overestimated the patient's adjustment and saw him as stronger than he really was. This attitude would lead the therapist to expect and demand more than the patient was capable of doing, which would usually be untherapeutic. When the therapist saw the patient as less like his ideal, less well adjusted, he saw him as needing help and would be more ready to offer support,[3] usually leading to a good therapy relationship.

While Fiedler focused only on these limited aspects of countertransference, he was able to use his method to distinguish more competent from less competent therapists. He first assumed that the effective therapists would demonstrate more empathy and positive regard and would be more supportive and less demanding. Next, he derived the various Q sorts and obtained for 22 therapists the "unwarranted assumed similarity to self" (UAS), and the "unwarranted assumed similarity to the ideal" (UASI). Finally, he obtained a rating of the therapist's competence by a very experienced supervisor. He found that the very competent therapists had significantly more UASI and UAS patterns which were interpreted as therapeutic. In addition, there was a significant correlation ($r = .59$) between competence and a high positive UAS (reflecting empathy and liking).

Fiedler has presented a way of quantifying countertransference attitudes and relating the results to clinically meaningful descriptions of therapists' behavior. While the technique focuses on only one aspect of this complex issue, it does show that a systematic approach can be employed in this area in which quantification is so difficult.

442   EFFECTIVE PSYCHOTHERAPY

Very similar to the Fiedler (1951) work is the series of studies done at Giessen on the stereotypes in diagnostic judgments of patients (Beckmann & Richter, 1968), and a similar series on diagnostic and prognostic interference distortions based upon personality characteristics and level of training of the therapist (Heising & Beckmann, 1971).

Also akin to some of Fiedler's work is a method developed by Snyder and Snyder (1961), who were able to delineate emotional patterns similar to countertransference in the therapy session and to measure them as they changed over a series of sessions. Defining countertransference broadly as "all affect of the therapist for the client," they obtained information about the therapist's emotional reaction by means of the "Therapist Affect Scale," a 200-item questionnaire which they developed to evaluate the therapist's reactions to therapy. A "Client Affect Scale" was also devised to measure the client's feelings about therapy. In 20 treatments conducted by one of the authors, he and the client filled out the questionnaires after each session. In addition, the therapist filled out the client questionnaire as he believed the client had filled it out in order to evaluate the therapist's perception of how the client felt about the therapist and the therapy. The author believed that he was able to measure countertransference in a few different ways. First, he evaluated it by means of the Therapist's Affect Scale itself. Second, he assumed that the correlation between Client Affect Scale completed by the client and that completed by the therapist would reflect the therapist's accuracy of perception which could be seen as an index of countertransference. Using these measures, the author was able to show that he had significantly more negative countertransference effects with the patients with whom he had poorer therapeutic results. There was a trend for the countertransference to increase as the sessions continued.

While there is some value in attempting to systematically evaluate the therapist's attitudes and feelings toward the patient, it is doubtful that he was able, with these measures, to hone in on many of the important aspects of his feelings, especially those that were unconscious, since such feelings would not be tapped with a self-report type of questionnaire. Furthermore, his conception of countertransference is so broad and superficial that it bears little resemblance to the term as it is used in the clinical literature.

In a series of studies concerned with phenomena that fit within the broader definition of countertransference, Strupp (1958) explored the extent to which the therapist's personality and attitudes—especially his attitude toward the patient—significantly affected his behavior in diagnosis and treatment. More precisely, he was able to provide experimental evidence that conscious and unconscious feelings about a patient influenced the way he diagnosed the case, planned the treatment, estimated the prognosis, and interacted with the patient in the psychotherapy session. In order to explore the psychotherapy variables under systematic and controlled conditions, Strupp decided to provide a common experience for a large number ($N=134$) of therapists. He showed a sound film of a patient undergoing an initial interview to a sample of experienced and inexperienced therapists with instructions to behave as if they themselves were interviewing the patient. This approach assumed that the way the therapist responded to the patient on the film reflected the way he would respond to a patient in real life. The film was interrupted at strategic spots and the subjects were requested to record the comments they would make if they were the patient's therapist. After the film, all the therapists were given a questionnaire which focused on their diagnosis of the patient, the treatment goals and plans, problems that might be encountered, and their attitudes toward the patient. Additional information was gathered about the therapists' training and clinical work. Strupp was able to explore the relationship between the therapist's attitude toward the patient, and various patient, therapist, and treatment variables. For example, he found a significant relationship between prognosis and attitude. Therapists who indicated a dislike for the patient tended to choose more pejorative diagnostic labels, such as psychopathic, paranoid, or character disorder. They also saw the patient as less insightful, more immature, and having a poor prognosis. They anticipated encountering certain kinds of problems in treatment, such as countertransference feelings of anger and resentment. These therapists were more inclined to be strict, active, and to suggest a briefer and more supportive type of therapy which might be terminated by unworkable, countertransference reactions. Their interventions were rated as colder and less empathic. On the other hand, therapists who expressed a positive attitude toward the patient tended to diagnose him as an "hysteric" and to describe him as experiencing much anxiety, and as capable of some introspection and insightfulness. They felt he had a good prognosis with treatment and suggested a more long-term, intensive, insight-oriented therapy that would bring about characterological changes. While these therapists could predict some countertransference responses, they felt that they could deal with them therapeutically. They indicated a preference for handling the patient in a permissive and passive way, and their comments were rated as more warm and empathic. To summarize, there was a significant dichotomy in the sample of therapists, with one group tending to be more "therapeutic, permissive, tolerant, and warm," and the other group appearing more "directive, disciplinarian, moralistic, and harsh."

It is not entirely clear how the results of this study shed light on the issues of countertransference since Strupp was dealing mostly with conscious attitudes and attitudes that the therapists were willing to admit. Most conceptions of countertransference involve unconscious feelings in the therapist that are aroused by the patient. Yet, while the subjects might be somewhat aware of their dislike of the patient and their reluctance to work with him because of this, it is less likely that they would be aware of certain manifestations of their dislike. For example, Strupp found that the group that disliked the patient had three times more verbalizations rated as cold than the group that was favorable to him. Another sidelight to this issue was the fact that while a personal analysis had little effect on the therapists' readiness to dislike the patient, it had a significant effect on the degree to which that attitude was conveyed to the patient. Psychoanalyzed therapists who disliked the patient were rated as significantly more warm and empathic than the unanalyzed ones who communicated their feelings with cold and unempathic interventions. While the study did not delve into the personal aspects and conflicts of the therapist that are aroused by the patient, it did clearly demonstrate that his initial impressions and feelings about the patient can strongly and adversely affect his clinical work. Obviously it is clear, too, that some of a therapist's diagnostic evaluations are shaped by his attitudes and personality.

There are a number of studies which, while not precisely dealing with countertransference, are, nevertheless, relevant because they focus on the powerful effects that patients can have on therapists. They relate to the important clinical problem of the pull of patients' transference feelings on the therapist which often can be the stimulus for countertransference reactions. Butler (1963) explored the concept of the therapist's capacity for expressiveness or openness in his thinking and feeling, and the extent to which that can have a stimulating effect on the patient, encouraging the patient's expansion of his range of new experiences. However, a situation analogous to a transference-countertransference paradigm can arise when the patient's constricted style can inhibit the therapist's openness and spontaneity. The therapist's responsiveness can be dampened by the patient's closedness. It can be hypothesized, then, that when a patient's anxiety and repressiveness about a conflict area stimulate a conflict in the therapist, the latter is not able to deal effectively with the situation; one way that the anxiety may affect him is by his becoming more inhibited and generally defensive. Butler also points out that this process can operate in the opposite direction so that a stimulating patient can contribute to the freedom of the relationship and the openness of the therapist, thereby contributing significantly to a more therapeutic environment. He feels that the more self-aware the therapist is, the less influenced he is by the patient's level of expressiveness and the more he can provide a favorable climate.

Butler cites a series of controlled process studies of psychotherapy (Rice, 1965; Rice, Wagstaff, & Butler, 1961; Wagstaff, Rice, & Butler, 1960) that support his contentions. Patient and therapist interactions in client-centered psychotherapy sessions were studied (Rice, 1965) with a classification system that focused on the aspects of participation such as voice quality, choice of words, and vividness of imagery that reflected what they termed "expressiveness." They worked with variables such as "freshness of words and combinations"—that is, the use of language that conveyed imagery and that tended to stimulate associations and feelings. Another factor, "expressiveness in voice quality," was characterized by high energy used in a controlled but not constricted way. After classifying the patient-therapist behavior, they analyzed the data by a method similar to factor analysis, and related the results to outcome criteria such as therapist ratings of improvement and changes in test scores such as the Butler and Haigh Q sort, the Taylor Manifest Anxiety Scale, and the Barron Ego-Strength Scale. In addition to finding that more expressive patients had better outcomes and that patients with more expressive therapists tended to have more favorable outcomes, there was a strong relationship between patient expressiveness and therapist expressiveness; expressive therapists tended to be associated with expressive patients. The direction of the influence was touched upon in another study in which the experimenter was able to show that both the therapist and the patient influenced the expressive level of the other, although the patient changed more slowly than the therapist. Patient-therapist sessions were divided into three sections, and each third was rated according to the degree to which it resembled the criterion of a maximally expressive client type and a maximally expressive therapist type. When in the first third of the interview there was more expressiveness on the part of the therapist, the patient's expressiveness went up on the second third and the therapist's level tended to decrease toward the patient's level. This phenomenon also occurred when the patient's expressiveness on the first third was higher than the therapist's; in the second third the therapist's level went up and the patient's went down. While both participants affected each other, the change for the therapist was more distinct than the change for the patient, reflecting the significant extent to which the therapist can be influenced by his patient.

One of the more clinically relevant studies in the area of patient-therapist interaction was done by Tourney, Bloom, Lowinger, Schorer, Auld, and Grisell (1966), who examined, among other things, the different kinds of emotional and behavioral responses that therapists have toward schizophrenic and neurotic patients. Twenty-eight patient and therapist variables were scored on 9-point Likert-type rating scales. Patient variables included factors such as thinking disturbance, anxiety, depression, hostility, etc. Therapists were rated on kinds of interpretation, reassurance given patients, errors of commission, errors of omission, anxiety, depression, hostility, positive feelings, etc. The investigators studied 10 schizophrenic and seven neurotic patients who were being seen in psychotherapy by 10 psychiatric residents. Two experienced therapist-judges sat behind a one-way mirror and also listened to the taped sessions before using the rating scale. Each interview was divided into 5-minute segments, and each segment was scored for all 28 variables. Correlation analysis on all the patient and therapist variables found therapist's anxiety to be significantly related to thought disorder, anxiety, and silence in the schizophrenic patient. With the neurotic patient, therapist's anxiety was related to hostility directed at the therapist and to patient resist-

ance. Therapists tended to respond with anger to the neurotic patient's hostility and to the schizophrenic patient's withdrawal. It would appear that while he was frustrated with the schizophrenic's withdrawal, he reciprocated the neurotic's hostility. Differential patient variables also affected the therapist's depression. Therapists tended to be depressed when the neurotic patients were depressed and when the schizophrenic patients were showing a thought disorder. The general trend seemed to be that therapists tended to react by reciprocating the neurotic patient's feelings toward them, but with the schizophrenic patient, they appeared to be responding to the serious signs of psychopathology. The feelings of the therapists were reflected in their behavior as well. When therapists were anxious and hostile, they tended to talk too much; when they were depressed, they were too inactive.

Howard, Orlinsky, and Hill (1969) were also concerned with exploring what the therapist feels during therapy hours and how that is related to the patient's experience and behavior. They developed a Therapy Session Report (TSR), consisting of 167 patient items and 166 therapist items, to be filled out by the patient and therapist after each therapy session. These questions focused on how the participants perceived various aspects of the session such as the therapeutic relationship, the topics of conversation, the feelings that occurred, and how the session developed. Drawing from a sample of 19 male and female therapists and 60 female patients, they found 28 cases where both the patient and the therapist filled out a minimum of eight questionnaires. Using a multivariate factor-analysis technique, the authors described nine therapist factors involved in therapist's feelings (such as withdrawn versus involved, disturbing sexual arousal, nurturant warmth) and 11 dimensions of patient experience (such as painful self-exploration, erotic transference resistance, and hostile provocation with noncommittal therapist). In order to investigate the relationship between patient experience and therapist feelings, correlations were computed between the patient variables and the therapist variables. While a number of relationships were discerned, there were two patterns of interaction that were particularly significant, especially with regard to therapist sex differences. In relation to erotic transference resistance (when the patient was experiencing embarrassing sexual feelings), male therapists had a strong tendency to feel uncomfortable and respond to items like "disturbing sexual arousal," whereas the female therapists tended to describe their positive feeling state with items such as "uneasy intimacy" and "feeling good." The patient dimension of intrusive dependence with embarrassed, tense therapist also produced some interesting results. When dependency demands were expressed openly and strongly, the male therapists did not appear to show any particular pattern of reaction, whereas the female therapists were clearly disturbed as reflected in their marked tendency to respond to items such as "withdrawn" and "suffering." Through the use of systematic evaluation of patient and therapist affective states and sophisticated statistical procedures, the authors were able to explore clinically relevant aspects of the therapy process and investigate therapist feelings in relation to and in reaction to patient behaviors that can be characterized as reflecting countertransference.

Heller, Myers, and Kline (1963) showed that when interviewers dealt with specific kinds of client behavior, they responded in a predictable way. The interviewers were in training and were asked to speak with clients who were actually actors behaving in prescribed roles: (a) dominant-friendly, (b) dominant-hostile, (c) dependent-friendly, (d) dependent-hostile. Interviews were observed and rated by four advanced graduate students in psychology on the Leary Interpersonal Checklist and an anxiety checklist constructed by the investigators. The authors found that the interviewers systematically responded with friendliness to the friendly client, with hostility to the hostile client, with passivity to the dominant client, and with activity and dominance to the passive client. Bohn (1965) also found that the passive-dependent client elicited a significant degree of directiveness on the part of the counselor.

Another study (Beery, 1970) showing that therapist's behavior is differentially affected by different kinds of patients presented a tape of an actress playing the role of either a friendly or a hostile patient to experienced and inexperienced therapists. The author asked them to respond to the actress-patient with their usual therapeutic style. These therapist responses were taped and rated on the dimensions of warmth-acceptance versus rejection-hostility. While the author found that experienced therapists responded more positively—both to the friendly and to the hostile patient—than did the inexperienced therapists, both groups of therapists were clearly affected by the patient's attitude (that is, both experienced and inexperienced therapists re-

sponded more positively to the friendly patient tape than to the unfriendly tape).

Patient-therapist interaction was studied by Russell and Snyder (1963) in a way that was similar to the work of Heller et al. (1963). They hypothesized that therapists would become more anxious with hostile than with friendly clients. In order to test this prediction, they used two actors who played the roles of either a hostile or a friendly individual, and had 10 more experienced and 10 less experienced graduate students interview them. Anxiety was measured by judges' ratings of the counselor behavior, by palmar sweating, and by eye-blink rates. They found that the counselors were significantly more anxious with the hostile type of client, but that the experience level of the counselors was not an important factor. Another study using actors portraying different kinds of patients was that of Gaminsky and Fairwell (1966), who examined the effects of hostile clients on the verbal behavior of the counselor. Actors were instructed to take either a hostile or a friendly role; when hostile, to first direct it at people in general and then at the counselor. Again graduate students were employed as counselors. Interviews were recorded and scored by a modification of the Bales System of Interaction Process Analysis. Using an analysis of variance of the data, the experimenters showed a clear difference in counselor behavior when they interviewed the two kinds of clients. In response to client hostility, the counselors used more avoidance behavior such as suggestion, disapproval, and information-giving, and less interpretation, elaboration, and reflection. This differential response was more marked when client hostility was directed at the counselor than when it was directed at others.

Finally, an effort by Luborsky and Singer (1974) to explore an aspect of the transference-countertransference interaction will be mentioned. Transference-countertransference phenomena were described by utilizing the concept of the therapist's behavior fitting into the patient's negative expectations as expressed in his important relationships. This core concept emerged from the process of rating recorded psychotherapy sessions as part of a larger project (Luborsky, Chandler, Auerbach, Cohen, & Bachrach, 1971). The first author noted that in a significant number of cases therapists tended to respond to the patient in ways that fit the patient's negative expectations. "Negative fit" is defined as the degree to which the therapist actually responds in ways that fit the patient's

negative preconceptions (his fears and expectations) about how people who have been important to him have responded to him. The clinical
judge listens to a tape recording of the psychotherapy session, first identifies the patient's main
fears or expectations of important people, and
then rates the degree to which the therapist is
behaving in that "expected" way in that session.

It appears to us that the therapist's negative
fit behavior describes a phenomenon that partly
involves a reaction between the patient's transference and the therapist's countertransference.
But other explanations may apply. It may not
always be clear whether the therapist is responding to the strong transference pull of
the patient's fear or wish, or to his countertransference feelings toward the particular patient,
or in accordance with some character trait
that coincides with the patient's fear, or to
some combination of these factors. But in
any case, to the extent that the therapist's reactions coincide with the patient's expectation,
we assume that "negative fit" is present in the
relationship.

and Singer, 1974) to explore systematically
(1) how often such "negative fit" behavior
occurs; (2) what kinds of "fit" commonly occur;
(3) how well clinical judges can agree when "fit"
has occurred; (4) to what patient variables,
therapist variables, and treatment variables
"fit" relates.

This work is part of a larger project which is
exploring many patient variables and therapist
variables, and relating these to clinical and
empirical assessment of therapy outcome (Luborsky, Mintz and associates, in prep.)

Forty experienced psychotherapists had tape-
recorded sessions of two of their patients. From
two early sessions, often the third and fifth, from
each patient, 4-minute segments were extracted
from each of the sessions. The segments were
sampled so as to be nearly as possible evenly
spaced throughout the session. The therapists
were all experienced beyond the residency.
Experience ranged from 2 to 20 years, with a
median of 9 years. Psychoanalytic and eclectic
orientations were most common. The treatments
ranged in duration and approach from a 1-
month treatment conducted in conjunction with
the training of psychiatric residents to a $4\frac{1}{2}$-year
psychoanalysis. The average patient seen
once a week for about a year.

Two raters independently listened to tape
recordings of entire psychotherapy sessions and
to the 4-minute segments of therapy sessions and
then rated them.

In addition to "fit," 39 variables for rating
therapist and patient behavior from tape recordings of psychotherapy sessions were used, such
as "patient anxiety," "patient reflectiveness,"
"therapist empathy," and "therapist directiveness." These variables were presented in terms
of 5-point scales. The two raters were experienced clinicians—both psychologists, one with
analytic training. The procedure was for each
judge to listen to the tape or the segment and
then rate it for all 40 variables.

A number of conclusions have emerged so
far from studying the available data:

First, while it is generally acknowledged that
countertransference behavior does occur at
times, the findings show that its frequency is
much greater than is commonly supposed. The
two judges found "fit" in a significantly large
proportion of the taped sessions and segments
that they rated.

Secondly, although there are many possible
types of "fit" patterns described in the countertransference literature (Orr, 1954; Reich, 1951)
two major types were most frequent in this study.
The first type consisted of the therapist's
confirmation of the patient's fear of rejection by
being critical, disapproving, condescending, ungiving, cold, detached, emotionally removed,
and indifferent. Such therapist behavior consisted of more than being "neutral," but rather
involved an active lack of acceptance or a
definite attitude of disinterest. The second type
focused on the therapist's confirmation of the
patient's expectations of being made weak and
dependent by being too directive, domineering,
and controlling; this style was judged to show
"fit" when it was seen as fostering or reinforcing
passivity and discouraging more independent
behavior on the part of the patient. Both forms
were considered by the judges to be at least
untherapeutic, if not anti-therapeutic.

With regard to the question of how well
clinical judges agree in estimating "fit," agreement on the part of two clinical judges is
moderate in judgments for sessions. It seems to
be better for judgments of segments. Most
disagreements seem to be "honest" disagreements—that is, the judges estimate the expectations of the patient similarly but evaluate the
therapist's response differently in terms of how
negative it is for the therapy. Furthermore, the
pattern of correlations which shows the concept
of fit appears to have a great deal of consistency
across judges. (The agreement of the clinical
judges with the analyst and supervisor has not
yet been explored.)

While statistical analyses are incomplete at this writing, four therapist variables have been found to have a significant relationship with "fit": *directiveness*, defined as the extent to which the therapist is deliberately trying to influence the direction of the interaction in the hour; *assertiveness*, defined as how forthrightly, confidently, and forcefully he presents his views to the patient; *warm and giving*, defined as how personally interested in the patient's problems the therapist appears; and *sensitivity*, defined as being sharply attuned to the patient's indirectly expressed feelings, ideas, and expectations. It seems clear that the first three variables have a close relationship with the two kinds of "fit" found in this study, and that therapists who are associated with much "fit" would be too directive and assertive or cold and ungiving. These variables appear to interconnect and be involved in the definition of "fit." The significant relationship between "fit" and sensitivity, however, is consistent with the notion that countertransference interferes with clinical sensitivity. When "fit" is occurring in the relationship, the therapist is rated as unaware of subtleties, not in tune with the patient, and having difficulty grasping the undercurrents of what is happening with the patient. The findings suggest that the therapist who reinforces his patient's fears is also seen as one who is less skillful, sensitive, and effective.

This study adds to the clinical-theoretical literature on countertransference by providing a more systematic way of studying the phenomenon. It is systematic in the sense that it delineates some of the factors involved in this complex matter and also in the sense that an effort has been made to achieve interjudge agreement and evaluate the phenomenon across a sizeable group of therapists. There were some statistically significant relationships between "fit" and certain clinically relevant variables, and more significant findings are anticipated on the nature of the relationship between "fit" and successful therapy results.

To be able to evaluate systematically the extent to which "fit" is occurring in the psychotherapy relationship is important from the standpoint of clinical training as well as research. This framework provides a way of looking at an aspect of the patient-therapist interaction that can be of direct use to the novice therapist as well as the expert. It can help the therapist to look more clearly at his own behavior and the degree to which he is being affected by transference and countertransference.

This last group of studies supports the hypothesis that therapists have differential responses to different types of patients and types of patient responses; yet it would be difficult to determine from these papers whether this differential behavior would necessarily be countertherapeutic in the countertransference sense. We do not know if the behavior would be continued in therapy or whether the responses are only initial responses.[4] Nevertheless, while these studies do not deal with the more specific kinds of classical countertransference phenomena, they do shed light on the more extended or totalistic view. They explore dimensions of the total treatment situation including the realistic aspects that can evoke negative feelings in the therapist. *These studies, taken together, support the position that therapists' differential behavior is also a function of the real stimulus qualities of the psychotherapy relationship. They also underline the importance of viewing countertransference as operating in a reciprocal relationship to transference* —that is, the influence of the patient's transference relations on the therapist can be considerable, arousing strong feelings and stimulating distinct behaviors that can adversely affect his therapeutic style.

Before offering some final, general reflections, it would be valuable to summarize both the clinical and quantitative literature in the form of specific propositions which may stimulate further research on countertransference.

Propositions Emerging from the Clinical Literature

1. Countertransference is a hindrance to effective treatment of the patient.

2. Countertransference hinders the treatment by preventing the therapist from properly identifying with the patient, a necessary part of the process of understanding.

3. One of the marks of the occurrence of countertransference is an inordinate intensity or inappropriateness of sexual or aggressive feelings toward the patient.

4. Countertransference can be of two kinds, acute and chronic. Acute countertransference is in response to specific circumstances and specific patients. The chronic type is based upon an habitual need of the therapist; it occurs with most of his patients and not in reaction to a particular conflict.

5. Countertransference (the *general* definition) can be a valuable therapeutic tool since it can help in empathizing with the patient

(Heimann, 1950, 1960). It can be useful if one keeps a constantly critical attitude toward what one is doing and uses it to try new ways of dealing with a problem which has not been improving as expected (Kernberg, 1965).

6. All authors stress the importance of having countertransference under conscious awareness and control.

7. The therapist's emotional maturity is a deterrent to his potential countertransference needs which might interfere with the relationship (Baum, 1969–1970) and psychotherapy or psychoanalysis is usually necessary to achieve this emotional maturity.

8. Avoiding countertransference problems can be aided by self-analysis or by discussion with a supervisor or colleague.

9. Countertransference can often be communicated peripherally—that is, through non-verbal cues such as body movement or changes in tone of the therapist's voice.

Propositions and Conclusions Emerging from the Quantitative Literature

1. Therapists who tend to express their anger directly and have a low need for approval are more likely to respond appropriately to the patient's anger (Bandura, 1956).

2. Therapists are more inclined to avoid patient's feelings, especially anger, when they are directed against the therapist than when they are expressed toward someone else (Bandura, 1956; Gaminsky & Fairwell, 1966).

3. Therapists are much less accurate in reporting their own and their patients' behavior in psychotherapy when the issues are related to personality conflicts of their own—less accurate in terms of a greater discrepancy between their own report and a judge's report of what occurred (Cutler, 1958).

4. When the therapist works with a patient on areas that are also problematic for himself, his interventions are judged to be less effective than when he works with neutral material (Cutler, 1958).

5. More negative countertransference effects appear with patients with whom the therapist had poorer therapeutic results. There is also a trend for countertransference to increase as sessions continue (Snyder & Snyder, 1961).

6. Therapists indicating a dislike for a patient tend to choose more pejorative diagnostic labels and see the patient as less insightful, more immature, and having a poorer prognosis (Strupp, 1958).

7. More experienced therapists tend to show fewer indications of countertransference in their work than do inexperienced therapists (Beery, 1970; Strupp, 1958).

8. Therapists judged as competent by other therapists or supervisors show fewer signs of countertransference (Fiedler, 1951).

9. Patients with more expressive therapists tend to have more favorable treatment outcomes (Butler, 1963).

10. Both therapists and patients influence the expressive level of each other, although the patient changes more slowly than the therapist (Butler, 1963).

11. Interviewers respond with friendliness to friendly clients, with hostility to hostile clients, with passivity to dominant clients, and with activity and dominance to passive clients (Bohn, 1965; Heller et al., 1963).

12. In response to client hostility (versus friendliness), counselors use more avoidance behavior such as suggestion, disapproval, and information giving, and less interpretation, elaboration, and reflection (Gaminsky & Fairwell, 1966).

GENERAL REFLECTIONS

In reviewing both the clinical and quantitative literature on countertransference, one of the broad conclusions to be drawn is that the clinical literature assumes that countertransference is a given and an intrinsic phenomenon in psychotherapy; it is mostly concerned with exploring its many aspects as completely as possible, presenting theories of its operation, and suggesting ways to avoid it or use it appropriately. On the other hand, the quantitative literature has been mostly concerned with determining evidence for its existence and for its effects, devising procedures whereby one can systematically analyze the phenomenon.

A second conclusion is that there has not been enough overlap between the clinical and research fields; quantitative investigations have not been able to focus in on the detailed problems discussed in clinical studies. The difficulties involved in controlling variables in such a complex field as psychotherapy research have been so enormous that investigators have not been able to work very well with the more subtle, yet substantial, aspects of countertransference. Rather, these studies have been limited to more simplified and superficial problems, and restricted in terms of what could be measured.

Third, because of research obstacles, most

quantitative studies have dealt mainly with the general definition of countertransference, while the clinical papers have emphasized the classical version. Although a few workers (Bandura, 1956; Cutler, 1958) have tried to investigate the therapist's unconscious conflicts, their efforts have been, by and large, superficial endeavors. Consequently, most of the quantitative studies dealt mainly with conscious feelings and attitudes. How does one systematically study the core unconscious conflicts of the therapist and the extent to which they are aroused and influence his behavior in psychotherapy? Taken to an extreme, it would almost have to require an investigator lying hidden under the couch of the patient and the analyst (under the analyst's couch during his own treatment) in order to attempt to analyze the phenomenon in systematic detail. Until some scientific, yet clinically relevant, methods of analysis of patient and therapist personality and interactional variables are achieved, it would appear that the clinical and quantitative literature will remain relatively far apart, with the latter contributing little to help the clinician in his daily work with patients.

While recognizing this problem does not solve it, it may be asked what similarities and points of commonality can be drawn by looking at the two bodies of literature. *Perhaps the most clear-cut and important area of congruence between the clinical and quantitative literatures is the widely agreed-upon position that uncontrolled counter-transference has an adverse effect on therapy outcome.* Not only does it have a markedly detrimental influence on the therapist's technique and interventions, but it also interferes with the optimal understanding of the patient. The need to be consciously aware of counter-transference and have it under control is recognized in both areas. Related to this issue is the principle that *more experienced and more competent therapists tend to be aware of their counter-transference feelings and are more able to prevent them from influencing their behavior with their patients.* Psychotherapy or psychoanalysis may contribute to this greater awareness and control.

Another interesting point of convergence is related to Sherman's (1965) observations that a significant way in which countertransference is conveyed to the patient is through peripheral cues such as tone of voice and other nonverbal modes of communication. It is noteworthy that the quantitative studies utilize to a major degree these peripheral cues when evaluating evidence of countertransference. Especially in those papers where judges are rating therapy sessions for variables such as warmth, rejection, positive regard, empathy, etc., peripheral cues are focused on to a considerable extent.

In addition to these important aspects of overlap between the two fields of study, the quantitative literature not only verifies what the clinical literature describes, but it also opens up some new observations and different points of emphasis. For example, while the general definition of countertransference considers the reality of the patient's personality and the reality of the therapy situation, *the results of a number of quantitative studies present what seems to be a new and qualitatively different weight to the real stimulus value of the patient. These realistic aspects must be taken into account when evaluating countertransference feelings in order to try to determine the effect due to the patient and the effects contributed by the personality conflicts of the therapist. More than the clinical literature would suggest, the patient influences the therapist to a marked degree and in predictable ways.*

Another important observation to emerge from the experimental domain is the extent to which avoidance responses comprise the therapist's countertransference-related behavior. Although there is some clinical discussion of the therapist's tendency to be defensive about certain topics that impinge on his own conflicts, experimental studies have been able to explore the phenomenon more thoroughly and delineate the various kinds of avoidance responses and their consequences. While it may be somewhat obvious that a therapist is inclined to avoid personally threatening material in a therapy session, the resulting effect of this avoidance generally is not so apparent. However, a number of controlled studies have been able to demonstrate a verbal conditioning paradigm; *the therapist's endeavor to avoid conflictual topics has a direct relationship to the frequency of expression of such conflict-related responses by the patient.* For example, if the therapist avoids the patient's anger either by some form of disapproval or by some attempt to ignore it, the patient will tend to decrease expressions of anger in the session. It would appear that the therapist's behavior either aversively diminishes or extinguishes the patient's response, although the former seems more likely. In any case, this condition does not allow the patient to work through the feelings therapeutically.

In conclusion, the quantitative research has shown an advantage in terms of contributing more specific information about the conditions under which countertransference operates. In this sense, we do not agree entirely with Waelder's (1960) somewhat pessimistic conclusion about the quantitative approach—that the quantitative studies tend to show things that already are well-known clinically. Our own conclusions show that the quantitative studies have added a significant range in terms of specificity of detailed relationships.

REFERENCES

ALEXANDER, F. Unpublished report, Los Angeles, 1950.

AUERBACH, A. H., & LUBORSKY, L. Accuracy of judgments of psychotherapy and the nature of the "good hour." In J. SHLIEN, H. F. HUNT, J. P. MATARAZZO, & C. SAVAGE (Eds.), *Research in psychotherapy*. Vol. III. Washington, D.C.: American Psychological Association, 1968. Pp. 4, 5–18.

BANDURA, A. Psychotherapists' anxiety level, self-insight, and psychotherapeutic competence. *Journal of Abnormal and Social Psychology*, 1956, **52**, 333–337.

BANDURA, A., LIPSHER, D. H., & MILLER, P. E. Psychotherapists' approach-avoidance reactions to patients' expression of hostility. *Journal of Consulting Psychology*, 1960, **24**, 1–8.

BAUM, O. E. Countertransference. *Psychoanalytic Review*, 1969–1970, **56**, 621–637.

BECKMANN, D. Psychologische determinanten in der arzt-patient-beziehung. *Munchener Medizinische Wochenschrift*, 1972, **114**, 2–18.

BECKMANN, D., & RICHTER, H. E. Selbstkontrolle einer klinischen Psychoanalytiker-Gruppe durch ein Forschungsprogramm. *Zeitschrift für Psychotherapie und medizinische Psychologie*, 1968, **18**, 201–208.

BEERY, J. W. Therapists' responses as a function of level of therapist experience and attitude of the patient. *Journal of Consulting and Clinical Psychology*, 1970, **34**, 239–243.

BERGMAN, P. An experiment in film psychotherapy. In L. A. GOTTSCHALK & A. H. AUERBACH (Eds.), *Methods of research in psychotherapy*. New York: Appleton-Century-Crofts, 1966. Pp. 35–49.

BOHN, M. J. Counselor behavior as a function of counselor dominance, counselor experience and client type. *Journal of Counseling Psychology*, 1965, **12**, 346–351.

BUTLER, J. M., & RICE, L. N. Adience, self-actualization and drive theory. In J. WEPMAN & R. HEINE (Eds.), *Concepts of personality*. Chicago: Aldine, 1963. Pp. 79–112.

CUTLER, R. L. Countertransference effects in psychotherapy. *Journal of Consulting Psychology*, 1958, **22**, 349–356.

FENICHEL, O. Problems of psychoanalytic technique. *Psychoanalytic Quarterly*, 1941, 27 ff.; 71–75.

FIEDLER, F. E. A method of objective quantification of certain countertransference attitudes. *Journal of Clinical Psychology*, 1951, **7**, 101–107.

FREUD, S. *The future prospects of psychoanalytic therapy* (1910). *Standard edition*, **11**, 139–151. London: Hogarth Press, 1957.

FREUD, S. *Recommendations for physicians on the psychoanalytic method of treatment* (1912). *Standard edition*, **12**, 109–120. London: Hogarth Press, 1957.

GAMINSKY, N. R., & FAIRWELL, G. F. Counselor verbal behavior as a function of client hostility. *Journal of Counseling Psychology*, 1966, **13**, 184–190.

GLESER, G., GOTTSCHALK, L. A., & SPRINGER, K. J. An anxiety scale applicable to verbal samples. *Archives of General Psychiatry*, 1961, **5**, 103–114.

GLOVER, E. *The technique of psychoanalysis*. New York: International Universities Press, 1955.

GROSSMAN, C. M. Transference, countertransference and being in love. *Psychoanalytic Quarterly*, 1965, **34**, 249–256.

HEIMANN, P. On countertransference. *International Journal of Psychoanalysis*, 1950, **31**, 81–84.

HEIMANN, P. Countertransference. *British Journal of Medical Psychology*, 1960, **33**, 9–15.

HEISING, G., & BECKMANN, D. Gegenübetragungsreaktionen bei diagnose-und indikationsstellung. *Zeitschrift für Psychotherapie und Medizinische Pschologie*, 1971, **21**, 2–8.

HELLER, K., MYERS, R. A., & KLINE, L. V. Interviewer behavior as a function of standardized client roles. *Journal of Consulting Psychology*, 1963, **27**, 117–122.

HOWARD, K. I., ORLINSKY, D. E., & HILL, J. A. The therapist's feelings in the therapeutic process. *Journal of Clinical Psychology*, 1969, **25**, 83–93.

KERNBERG, O. Notes on countertransference. *Journal of the American Psychoanalytic Association*, 1965, **13**, 38–56.

LITTLE, M. Countertransference and the patient's response to it. *International Journal of Psychoanalysis*, 1951, **32**, 32–40.

LITTLE, M. Countertransference. *British Journal of Medical Psychology*, 1960, **33**, 29–31.

LUBORSKY, L. Research cannot yet influence clinical practice (An evaluation of Strupp & Bergin's "Some empirical and conceptual bases for coordinated research in psychotherapy: A critical review of issues, trends, and evidence"). *International Journal of Psychiatry*, 1969, **7**, 135–140.

LUBORSKY, L., CHANDLER, M., AUERBACH, A. H., COHEN, J., & BACHRACH, H. M. Factors influencing the outcome of psychotherapy: A review of quantitative research. *Psychological Bulletin*, 1971, **75**, 145–185.

LUBORSKY, L., FABIAN, M., HALL, B. H., TICHO, E., & TICHO, G. Treatment variables. *Bulletin of the Menninger Clinic*, 1958, **22**, 126–147.

LUBORSKY, L. B., & SINGER, B. *The fit of therapist's behavior into patient's negative expectations: A study of transference-countertransference contagion.* Unpublished manuscript, University of Pennsylvania School of Medicine, 1974.

LUBORSKY, L. B., LUBORSKY, L. B., MINTZ, J. and associates. *Who benefits from psychotherapy: The factors influencing the outcome of psychotherapy*. Book in progress.

LUBORSKY, L., & SPENCE, D. P. Quantitative research on psychoanalytic therapy. In A. E. BERGIN & S. L. GARFIELD (Eds.), *Handbook of psychotherapy and behavior change: An empirical analysis*. New York: Wiley, 1971. Pp. 408–437.

MILLIKEN, R. L., & KIRCHNER, R. Counselor's understanding of student's communication as a function of the councelor's perceptual defense. *Journal of Counseling Psychology*, 1971, **18**, 14–18.

ORR, D. W. Transference and countertransference: A historical survey. *American Journal of Psychoanalysis*, 1954, **2**, 621–670.

PARKER, G. V. C. Some concomitants of therapist dominance in the psychotherapy interview. *Journal of Counseling Psychology*, 1967, **31**, 313–318.

REICH, A. On countertransference. *International Journal of Psychoanalysis*, 1951, **32**, 25–31.

REICH, A. Further remarks on countertransference. *International Journal of Psychoanalysis*, 1960, **41**, 389–395.

RICE, L. N. Therapist's style of participation in case outcome. *Journal of Consulting Psychology*, 1965, **29**, 155–160.

RICE, L. N., WAGSTAFF, A. K., & BUTLER, J. M. Some relationships between therapist's style of participation and measure of case outcome. *Counseling Center Discussion Papers*. Vol. 7, No. 5, University of Chicago Library, 1961.

ROSS, D., & KAPP, F. T. A technique for self-analysis of countertransference: Use of the psychoanalyst's visual images in response to the patient's dreams. *Journal of the American Psychoanalytic Association*, 1962, **10**, 645–657.

RUSSELL, P. D., & SNYDER, W. U. Counselor anxiety in relation to amount of clinical experience and quality of affect demonstrated by clients. *Journal of Consulting Psychology*, 1963, **27**, 358–363.

SANDLER, J., HOLDER, A., & DARE, C. Basic psychoanalytic concepts: Countertransference. *British Journal of Psychiatry*, 1970, **117**, 83–88.

SHERMAN, M. Peripheral cues and the invisible countertransference. *American Journal of Psychotherapy*, 1965, **19**, 280–292.

SNYDER, W. U., & SNYDER, B. J. *The psychotherapy relationship*. New York: Macmillan, 1961.

STERN, A. On the countertransference in psychoanalysis. *Psychoanalytic Review*, 1924, **11**, 166–174.

STRUPP, H. H. The psychotherapist's contribution to the treatment process. *Behavioral Science*, 1958, **3**, 34–67.

TOURNEY, G., BLOOM, V., LOWINGER, P. L., SCHORER, C., AULD, F., & GRISELL, J. A study of psychotherapeutic process variables in psychoneurotic and schizophrenic patients. *American Journal of Psychotherapy*, 1966, **20**, 112–124.

WAELDER, R. *Basic theory of psychoanalysis*. New York: International Universities Press, 1960.

WAGSTAFF, A. K., RICE, L. N., & BUTLER, J. M. Factors of client verbal participation in therapy. *Counseling Center Discussion Papers*, Vol. 6, No. 9, University of Chicago Library, 1960.

YULIS, S., & KIESLER, D. J. Countertransference response as a function of therapist anxiety and content of patient talk. *Journal of Consulting and Clinical Psychology*, 1968, **32**, 413–419.

NOTES

1. Support for this study was provided by United States Public Health Service Grant MH-15442, and Research Scientist Award MH-40710 to Dr Lester Luborsky. The authors wish to thank Drs. Henry Bachrach, Alan Gurman, and Andrew Razin for their suggestions on the manuscript, and Marjorie Cohen for assistance in its preparation.

2. *Editors' Footnote*. We wish to emphasize the authors' conclusion here and perhaps to state its importance even more strongly. These studies have clearly documented the clinically held but previously unproven notion that countertransference can interfere with the work of the therapist. Although such documentation may at first seem very unstartling, it should be kept in mind that what has been demonstrated is a link between a presumably unconscious process and complex interpersonal behavior. Such demonstrations, though not surprising to clinicians, should not be dismissed as trivial nor forgotten in discussions of the inaccessibility of the unconscious to empirical, clinically relevant research.

3. *Editors' Footnote*. We question the generality of these assumptions by Fiedler. That is, it does not seem to follow necessarily that overestimating patients leads to demanding too much, and that underestimating leads to offering more support, rather than to opposite tendencies under some circumstances. Furthermore, our clinical experience leads us to believe that countertransference difficulties may lead to both overestimating and underestimating the same patient—i.e., at different times and/or in different areas.

4. *Editors' Footnote*. Particularly in relation to "fit," it is clinically useful to remember that any patient-precipitated bit of un- or anti-therapeutic piece of therapist behavior is potential grist for the therapeutic mill. Just as many behavior therapists actually encourage the performance of problematic behavior within therapy, in order to enable therapist and patient to gain control over it, so in dynamic therapy, problematic interpersonal behavior such as eliciting the anticipated, dreaded (yet sought) "fit" behavior by the therapist provides an ideally immediate opportunity for therapeutic work, provided, of course, that the therapist recognizes what has occurred and skillfully takes his own responsibility for "fit" behavior.

CHAPTER 17

THERAPIST-INDUCED DETERIORATION IN PSYCHOTHERAPY

MICHAEL J. LAMBERT, ALLEN E. BERGIN, and JOHN L. COLLINS

DETERIORATION and the process of worsening in psychotherapy patients is a concern to us all. In the present chapter, the empirical basis for deterioration in psychotherapy patients will be detailed. An attempt will be made to place this phenomenon in its historical perspective, to answer questions concerning its occurrence, and to identify patient-therapist characteristics which appear to be its causal agents. The relationship of deterioration to school, therapeutic procedure, and the like, as well as the implications of therapist-induced deterioration for research, training, and practice, will be discussed.

HISTORICAL OVERVIEW

Clinicians have long been aware of the possible deleterious effects of psychotherapy. Dating back to the earliest psychotherapeutic interventions, there were concerns with who was qualified to facilitate change via psychotherapy, what kind of training would be necessary, and even whether there was a need to undergo treatment as a precondition for practice. In fact, some of our most deeply ingrained training practices may be traced to an awareness of the potential damage an unqualified practitioner may cause.

The earliest and crudest research efforts into the effects of psychotherapy have acknowledged the possibility of deterioration by at times providing a designation of "worse" in gross ratings of patient change. And yet researchers have paid relatively little attention to the fact that the condition of a portion of patients worsens during the course of psychotherapy. Even those empirical assessments which have included a "worse" category have seldom emphasized or even discussed these negative results. Current studies show no marked trend toward identifying clients who deteriorate during psychotherapy or in studying these negative results for the potential learnings they offer.

Despite the general trend to avoid this unpleasant issue, allusions to it have been made repeatedly over the years. Powers and Witmer (1951) were among the earliest to discuss empirical evidences of improvement or deterioration as a consequence of psychotherapy. Rogers and Dymond (1954) alluded to it and called for the study of decreases in behavioral maturity. Cartwright (1956) reanalyzed data from Barron and Leary (1955) and noted the probability of therapy-induced negative change. These observations stirred little interest or controversy' in the professional community at large.

Later, in a symposium at the annual meeting of the American Psychological Association in 1962, attention was directed more precisely to the topic of negative effects in psychotherapy. Two of the four papers presented at this symposium dealt in part with the possible harmful effects of psychotherapy. Subsequently, these papers were published in the *Journal of Counseling Psychology* (Bergin, 1963; Truax, 1963). Each author approached the topic from a different perspective.

Truax (1963) mentioned deterioration and emphasized the effects of therapist-offered conditions such as empathy, regard and genuineness. He also referred to the yet unpublished results of the Wisconsin Study, which suggested that the absence of these therapist qualities were responsible for deterioration in a portion of schizophrenic patients studied. Truax had earlier presented some preliminary data on deterioration during a meeting of the psychotherapy research group at the University of Wisconsin in the spring of 1961. The group was led by Carl Rogers and included Allen Bergin. Truax's hypothesis was put forth after it was found that treated patients had fared no better than those who were receiving routine hospital treatment. A closer examination of the data indicated that therapeutic effects could be detected when therapists were pooled according to the levels of empathy, unconditional positive regard, and genuineness they offered clients. Therapists who offered these conditions at a high level had a high degree of successful outcomes, while those who offered these conditions at low levels had patients who got worse, in contrast to showing no change at all.

Perhaps it was the Wisconsin Project and the sensitivity of the researchers connected with it which marked the opening of serious inquiry into the possible harmful effects of psychotherapy. Bergin (1967) acknowledged that Truax's 1961 verbal report influenced his thinking. But Bergin (1963) approached the topic of deterioration from a much broader base and dealt with it more extensively as a possible answer to the more general question raised by Eysenck of whether therapy had any unique effects. He summarized the results of six controlled outcome studies which employed diverse criteria and included a variety of patient populations. Besides the work of the Wisconsin Project group, he reported five other studies which showed deterioration in a proportion of their research clients. It is interesting to note that this particular paper was entitled "The Effects of Psychotherapy: Negative Results Revisited" and was intended to explain the failure of empirical research to demonstrate the efficacy of traditional psychotherapy.

The empirical basis for deterioration was further strengthened in an article published in the *Journal of Abnormal Psychology* (Bergin, 1966) and reprinted in the *International Journal of Psychiatry* (1967) along with critical reviews written by Eysenck, Frank, Matarazzo, and Truax. In this paper Bergin (1966) proposed the term "deterioration effect" to describe the general finding that a certain proportion of psychotherapy patients were worse after treatment. Such an effect was suggested by the tendency for treated groups to show an increase in variance over control groups on outcome measures. A diagram illustrating this phenomenon along with the seven studies reported in 1966 was later reproduced by Bergin (1971) with 23 additional studies which showed deterioration in a proportion of patients studied. These data will be studied in detail in the next section of this chapter.

Since the early studies connected with the Wisconsin Project were published, researchers connected with the client-centered approach have continued to collect and report data related to this issue. During the 1960s, several reports

on this topic appeared. Much of this work was summarized by Truax and Carkhuff (1967). Reviewing again the results of the schizophrenic project, they wrote: "Using the clinicians' 'blind' analysis of pre- and post-test battery information to establish levels of overall psychological functioning, the findings indicated that patients receiving high levels of the three conditions showed an overall gain in psychological functioning; but those patients who received rather low levels showed a loss in psychological functioning. Control patients showed moderate gains" (p. 96).

More recently, Truax and Mitchell (1971) have summarized the bulk of outcome studies published in the area of the therapists' interpersonal skills. Based on the available evidence, they again conclude that some counselors and therapists are significantly helpful, while others are significantly harmful and that this is determined in large part by such interpersonal skills as empathy, genuineness, and warmth.

The views expressed by Bergin (1963, 1966, 1971), Truax (1963), and Truax and Carkhuff (1967) have not gone unchallenged. Earliest resistance to the notion of a "deterioration effect" came from Eysenck (1967). He wrote: "I would be the last person to argue that psychotherapy may not produce deleterious effects on neurotic and psychotic patients, but I am not sure that the evidence is as strong as it might be" (p. 152). In addition, he argued that such an important conclusion must also be shown to have more than a passing effect and rather long-lasting effects of real-life significance. Matarazzo (1967) and Frank (1967) responded to Bergin's paper but found the same evidence much more convincing. A rejoinder to the arguments of Eysenck was published by Bergin (1967). He stated that the evidence did support the presence of a deterioration effect, that potent variables are in operation in psychotherapy, and that in fact three of the seven studies cited presented data on long-term effects of psychotherapy.

In addition to the criticisms of Eysenck (1967), Bergin's views have prompted other comments. Braucht (1970) replied to Bergin's (1966) article, and argued essentially that the studies quoted by Bergin had too many methodological weaknesses to be considered suitable as evidence. Bergin (1970) defended the evidence he had presented earlier and restated his opinion: "There is an abundance of both clinical and statistical evidence, including the studies Braucht critiques, that deterioration occurs during psychotherapy" (p. 300). May (1971) followed a tack similar to

Braucht's and argued that the evidence in support of the deterioration effect offered by Bergin and others was flimsy because it was based upon studies with various methodological weaknesses. He wrote: "Although it is important to realize that psychotherapy, like any other treatment, may have adverse effects, there is no convincing evidence that, in situations where psychotherapy is on the average ineffective, there is greater outcome variation than in a control group" (p. 184).

Even more recently in response to Bergin (1971), Rachman (1973) has written and emphasized that no cause-effect relationship can be drawn between therapy and deterioration. Rachman concluded that at best the evidence quoted by Bergin in support of a deterioration effect is scanty and incomplete.

This ongoing debate has many ramifications, not the least of which is the efficacy of psychotherapy, for the history of deterioration research is closely linked with the debate over the effectiveness of psychotherapy. Its investigation and elaboration are inseparably connected with this broader issue because the discovery that led to an elaboration of harmful effects also revealed stronger evidence for improvement effects.

Another motive for studying this phenomenon is the desire to identify variables in the therapeutic relationship which lead to negative results so that they may be eliminated.

Psychoanalytic therapy has given us the concept of countertransference, the client-centered school has studied extensively the place of therapist-offered conditions, and other researchers have developed additional concepts to explain patient worsening. The analysis of expectations (see Wilkins, Chapter 13, this volume), therapeutic "fit" (see Singer & Luborsky, Chapter 16, this volume), and "pathogenesis" (see Vandenbos & Karon, 1971) are examples of these lines of inquiry. The future appears bright for an elucidation of the mechanisms whereby some patients improve significantly while others, it appears, are damaged by their contact with "therapeutic" agents.

Toward a Definition of Therapist-Induced Deterioration

Deterioration implies an impairment of vigor, resilience, or usefulness from a previously higher state. Patient deterioration has not in the past nor can it presently be limited to a set definition. It might generally be regarded as a worsening of the patient's symptomatic picture as determined from at least two observations at different times. For the purpose of the present discussion, we are concerned with patients who are judged worse at treatment termination or follow-up.

The precise meaning of this change will be defined by the particular criterion employed in a given study. Later in the chapter, an attempt will be made to compare, analyze, and order the varied definitions used by researchers. As the title of this chapter implies, it is deterioration related to the therapeutic process and particularly to the therapist, which is our focus. We shall attempt to discriminate that part of the worsening which can be attributed to his inappropriate application of therapeutic techniques, "countertransference," a psychonoxious personality, or an interaction of patient and therapist characteristics.

The most sophisticated definition of deterioration will take into account the complexity of the phenomenon of change. Going beyond group averages, such *a definition of deterioration would include not only worsening symptoms but also lack of significant improvement when it is expected and even the acceleration of ongoing deterioration.* It is clear from the empirical evidence that a portion of control patients do deteriorate and therefore it must be assumed that a portion of the deterioration observed in psychotherapy patients is unrelated to therapy variables. Only evidence of worsening in psychotherapy which exceeds that expected from life stress, negative experiences, or an ongoing process of deterioration can be considered part of the "deterioration effect." The controlled studies which support this view will be briefly discussed and criticized. This definition implies the use of criteria that are thorough and comprehensive enough to predict reactions to future events based on the behavioral history of the person and may well exceed our current abilities.

EMPIRICAL EVIDENCE

In this section we shall concern ourselves with the elaboration and clarification of research reports which have allowed us to examine the process and state of deterioration. We shall proceed by discussing particularly important studies and then by attempting to answer questions on issues raised by the occurrence of deterioration. We shall endeavor to specify mechanisms of therapist-induced deterioration and their implications for training, research, and practice.

Bergin (1966) coined the phrase "deterioration effect" to describe the tendency for controlled outcome studies to show an increase in outcome score variability after treatment. Figure 1 is an updated, revised representation of this phenomenon. It was suggested and revised on the basis of nine well-designed outcome studies and the repeated observation that outcome measures show patients to be both more and less disturbed than untreated control subjects. Current renderings, however, show that increased variance in post-test criterion scores of treated groups is not a necessary consequence of deterioration even though it occurs often. Therapy effects, including negative ones, can be distributed so as to show no change or even a restriction in variance. Figure 1 is therefore a convenient but not essential way of showing the diverse effects of therapy interventions as summarized across a large number of studies.

Table 1 summarizes the nine studies mentioned. It is felt that collectively these studies provide a strong empirical base for deterioration in psychotherapy even though, individually, there are weaknesses in each of them.

Powers and Witmer. The Cambridge-Somerville Youth Study of delinquency prevention (Powers & Witmer, 1951) was an impressive, well-designed study of 650 boys, 325 experimental and 325 control, over approximately an 8-year period. The results did not support the notion that the treated subjects fared better than untreated controls. If anything, the controls may have been slightly better off than the experimentals at the conclusion of the experiment. They report a significant improvement in some

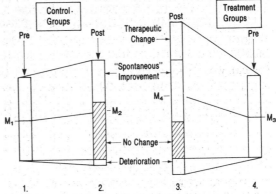

Fig. 1. The diverse effects of psychotherapy: a schematic illustration of changes in pathology for control and treatment groups.*

Bar 1   Distribution of test scores for disturbed control groups at beginning of studies.

Bar 2   Distribution of test scores for disturbed control group at end of study showing increased spread of scores due to "spontaneous" improvement and "spontaneous" deterioration.

Bar 3   Distribution of test scores for disturbed treatment group at beginning of therapy.

Bar 4   Distribution of test scores for disturbed treatment group at end of therapy showing increased spread of scores due to therapeutic change, "spontaneous" improvement, "spontaneous" deterioration, and therapy-induced deterioration.

M_1, M_2

M_3, M_4 Median points, pre and post, which show greater change for therapy groups than control groups.

*Note: Lengths of bars are approximations.

experimental subjects whose matched counterparts did not change. In addition, at the time of follow-up a significant proportion of boys with whom the counselors failed were more socially maladjusted than their matched control. They

TABLE 1. STUDIES DEMONSTRATING BOTH DETERIORATION AND POSITIVE CHANGE AS A RESULT OF PSYCHOTHERAPY.

Authors	Date	Population	N	Therapy Type	Average Therapy Duration	Relevant Criteria
Powers & Witmer	1951	Pre-delinquent boys	325	Directed friendship: social work counseling	6 years	Test battery Delinquency data Adjustment ratings Case record
Rogers & Dymond	1954	Young adults	25	Client-centered	8 months	Q sort; behavior ratings
Barron & Leary	1955	Outpatient neurotics	42	Eclectic-analytic	8 months	MMPI
Mink & Isaksen	1959	Jr. high school students	96	Client-centered (48) Directive-insight (48)	4 months	Calif. Test of Personality
Fairweather, Simon, Gebhard, Weingarten, Holland, Sanders, Stone, & Reahl	1960	Long-term psychotics; short-term psychotics	72	Eclectic-analytic	3–5 months	Q Sort
Cartwright & Vogel	1960	Young adults	22	Client-centered	33 sessions	Q Sort; TAT
Truax	1963	Hospitalized schizophrenics	16	Client-centered Eclectic, analytic	6 months $3\frac{1}{2}$ years	Multiple tests and ward behavior
Volsky, Magoon, Norman, & Hoyt	1965	College students	80	Eclectic, directive	3 sessions	Anxiety, defensiveness, and problem-solving scales
Carkhuff & Truax	1965	Hospitalized psychotics	74	Lay client-centered	24 sessions	Ward behavior

entertain the possibility that some boys were hurt and that some were helped, leaving the average adjustment the same. In 42% of the cases the effort of counselors was judged "clearly ineffectual." This was attributed in some cases to mistakes by counselors (50%), and in others to a lack of motivation in the subjects (2%), or such strongly negative home environments that no known treatment would help.

There are three methodological difficulties with this study which have been raised, although none of them specifically affects the deterioration findings. First, it is hard to assume that the independent variable (directed social work friendship) was the only difference between the treatment and control groups. It is known that at least 10% of the control subjects sought and received help outside the study. Furthermore, over time, a significant number of subjects were lost to the study during its lengthy duration, rendering control and experimental samples biased in unknown ways. It has also been argued that the treatment cannot be termed psychotherapy. It was to be a long-lasting friendship or sustained "big brother" system which was contrasted with typical social casework. It is difficult to assess the degree to which it was like or different from humanistic, client-centered, or relationship therapies.

More relevant to deterioration, May (1971) has pointed out that the method Powers and Witmer used for selecting those who were and were not benefited makes it difficult to be sure that the controls had an equal chance to be judged worse. Despite the ambiguity this point introduces into the findings, this study is the first occasion we know of where carefully gathered empirical data pointed to deterioration and where the authors were astute enough to identify it, even though they held to a contrary hypothesis.

Rogers and Dymond. Rogers and Dymond (1954) edited an important volume on the effects of client-centered therapy. The classic features of this study overshadowed the passing references to a client-deterioration phenomenon. It does, however, provide some supporting evidence for the thesis that negative change in psychotherapy is not an isolated or chance event. The report indicates that of 25 clients treated, six or 24% declined in self-ideal correlation between pretherapy and follow-up testing. In addition, computing the mean change in self-ideal correlation indicates that those who increased averaged an increment of .49 in their correlations, whereas those who decreased averaged a decrement of —.40, while the mean correlations for these two

subgroups were equivalent at the beginning of therapy. Although Butler and Haigh (1954) did not examine these possibilities in the data, they do allude to them in passing: "It is of interest, though it does not bear directly upon the hypothesis, that there has also been a marked increase in the degree of variation of correlations (self-ideal) over this period" (p. 63).

In another section of the Rogers and Dymond study, analysis of behavioral observations made of the clients (independent of therapist progress ratings) yielded results similar to those found with the self-ideal measure: "During the whole period from pre-therapy to follow-up, observers saw a definite increase in the maturity of behavior of those clients whose therapy was rated as successful and a sharp decrease in the maturity of behavior of those clients rated as unsuccessful. The relationship was statistically significant" (p. 228).

While the data, as extracted and summarized above, do show strong deterioration effects, reservations have been expressed by critics in regard to this study. First, the study, while exemplary for its time, did not contain a comparable control group of neurotic subjects but, rather, the no-treatment control was made up of normal subjects, leaving unanswered the question of how large the outcome variance for a comparable group of neurotics not receiving treatment would have been. Of course, later studies indicate that "spontaneous" deterioration is usually lower than the 24% obtained in this study. Secondly, Q-sort relationships provide the basic data under consideration and may be a lenient measure of deterioration. Third, the exact relationship between self-ideal correlation and other measures of health, including behavioral indices, may not be as high as was once assumed. It can be argued, though it is unlikely in this study, that an increase in self-ideal discrepancy is a positive change. Finally, the data presented relate to changes which are apparent at follow-up but not as significant at treatment termination.

Such criticisms must be taken seriously for they prevent the report from being clearly definitive with respect to harmful effects. Nevertheless, it is difficult to find methodologically pure and definitive studies on any topic or modality of therapy.

Barron and Leary. The study by Barron and Leary (1955) has perhaps received the most attention in regard to deterioration (Cartwright, 1956). They studied 150 outpatient neurotics assigned to three groups: 42 to individual therapy, 85 to group psychotherapy, and 23 to a waiting list control. While they did not report improvement in the treatment group exceeding that found in a comparable control group, Cartwright's reanalysis of these data has proved interesting. Table 2, reproduced from Cartwright (1956), shows the difference in variance of difference scores for the psychotherapy and control subjects.

Cartwright comments on the data as follows:

> For many scales the variance results suggest that mean differences between the groups are absent because differences of two kinds, opposed in sign, are present. It seems that some therapy patients *deteriorated* to a greater extent than did the waiting list controls, while some therapy patients *did improve* significantly more than the control. (pp. 403–404)

TABLE 2. VARIANCES OF DISCREPANCY SCORES ON MMPI SCALES FOR INDIVIDUAL PSYCHOTHERAPY AND NONTREATMENT GROUPS.

Scale	Individual psychotherapy (N=42) V^a	Non treatment group (N=23) V	F
L	19.89	23.43	1.18
F	215.21	22.94	9.38**
K	55.95	31.70	1.76
Hs	127.46	64.16	1.99**
D	244.30	93.32	2.62**
Hy	113.21	87.80	1.29
Pd	155.00	89.68	1.73
Pa	111.94	68.06	1.64
Pt	208.51	73.27	2.85**
Sc	272.91	74.13	3.68**
Ma	126.79	75.34	1.68
Es	43.56	14.82	2.94**

^{a}Variance computed from SD data reported by Barron and Leary (1955, table 2, p. 146). From Cartwright (1956), copyright by the American Psychological Association and reproduced by permission.
*p<.05.
**p<.01.

It should be noted in passing that the results were not consistent in group therapy, in that the test variance of those treated by this method did not increase significantly. This difference, of course, is not an argument against a deterioration effect in individual psychotherapy and perhaps even strengthens the case for therapist-induced deterioration.

Mink and Isaksen. Mink and Isaksen (1959) studied the effects of "clinical" and "non-directive" counseling on junior high school students. One-half of the total group of 96 was assigned equally to the two experimental treatments and one-half was assigned to a wait list control. Treatment length appeared to be 4 months in duration after which students were reevaluated via the California Test of Personality. No significant differences were found between ex-

perimental and control subjects. However, the authors point out that the retest scores for the experimental groups varied from the mean significantly more than those of the students who were not counseled. They conclude, "Counseling affected the expression of social adjustments on the California Test of Personality. The forms of expression indicate both improvement and recession" (p. 14).

These results are weakened by the fact that the authors did not state whether subjects were assigned to groups randomly and by the fact that only a single change criterion was employed.

Fairweather et al. Fairweather, Simon, Gebhard, Weingarten, Holland, Sanders, Stone, and Reahl (1960) assigned 32 neurotics and 66 psychotics to one of three treatment programs or a control group. Tests of significance between change score medians revealed only one significant difference between treatment groups. At the same time, significantly different variance occurred on most instruments as a function of treatment groups and between diagnostic categories. The control group usually had the smallest variance with the three treatment groups having the largest variance. Individual psychotherapy and "group living" showed the greatest variance. The authors concluded, "Thus, as far as the scales are concerned, the long-term psychotics, and to a lesser but usually significant extent, the short-term psychotics, change in either a positive or negative scale direction in psychotherapy while the same diagnostic groups remain comparatively unchanged without psychotherapy" (p. 21). One explanation of this finding considered by the authors was that "... patients in therapy get better or worse but generally do not remain the same, whereas patients not in therapy remain about the same" (p. 21).

Several points can further clarify these results. First, the major differences in variance for experimental and control subjects were due to the chronic psychotic patients. Such a finding suggests that psychotherapy, or "group treatment," is more harmful to them than to controls but is not as harmful to neurotics. Second, as with other studies which have employed multiple criteria, not all the measures in this study correspond to one another. For example, on ward behavior, individual psychotherapy patients had about the same variance as the control patients. This equivalence of variability makes the deterioration which did occur appear to be less pronounced. Furthermore, it makes patient worsening related more to diagnostic classification than to therapist variables. Drugs were administered to a significant portion of acute and chronic psychotic patients but their effect did not appear as potent as treatment conditions. At any rate, the results of this report, though complex, do support in many ways the notion of therapy-induced deterioration.

Cartwright and Vogel. Cartwright and Vogel (1960) studied changes in the Q score and the TAT in 22 neurotic outpatients. They reported, among other things, that adjustment changes, as measured by the Q score, regardless of direction, were significantly greater during a therapy period than during a no-therapy period. In addition, they note that: "The post-therapy tests showed those in therapy with experienced therapists to have improved significantly on both tests, whereas those in therapy with inexperienced therapists not to have improved .... in fact they bordered on a significant decrease in health on the TAT" (p. 127).

It should be noted that patients were not randomly assigned to experienced and inexperienced therapists and, therefore, this latter conclusion is not as sound as it might be. In addition, the results did not hold up across criterion measures. For example, more patients changed Q scores in a positive direction with inexperienced therapists than with experienced therapists. While these ambiguities do not interfere with the deterioration hypothesis, they do make it difficult to specify the ways or areas in which people were hurt and the mechanism of these negative effects.

Truax. Truax (1963) reported some of the data collected in the Wisconsin Project. A total of 14 schizophrenics and 14 matched controls (randomly assigned) was selected for analysis of overall change in psychological functioning. A battery of psychological tests was administered initially and again at the end of treatment. They investigated the level of combined facilitative conditions (therapist empathy, regard, and congruence) on patient functioning. Of the eight patients who were judged to have received rather low levels, all were judged to have fallen below the median for the entire group. Thus, it was concluded that high conditions facilitate constructive personality change, while low conditions produce negative personality change.

Reporting on another sample of patients studied with the same design, Truax (1963) examined 'the effects of conditions offered in therapy and change in anxiety experienced by the patient. The Anxiety Reaction Scale was used, yielding results on interpersonal anxiety, som-atic anxiety, and general anxiety. Again, the results were reported as suggesting a tendency for patients receiving high therapeutic conditions to show a drop in anxiety and those receiving low conditions to increase in anxiety. The controls, on the other hand, showed almost no change on this measure. Q-sort data on the same patients indicated a similar trend with low-condition patients changing toward a less "well-adjusted" self-concept. These same trends held on other diverse outcome measures (including intelligence tests) as either statistically significant (as the above results) or as near-significant.

The results of these studies have been questioned by May (1971), Rachman (1973), and Braucht (1970). They made two legitimate criticisms of Truax's work: (1) the original division of subjects into high and low conditions after the fact makes the results questionable, and (2) the number of cases ($N = 14$) was small. While these shortcomings tend to weaken the conclusions which might be drawn, they are not enough to make us consider ignoring the data. In fact, current research with larger samples and random assignment to high and low conditions has replicated the findings in this study (Truax & Mitchell, 1971).[1]

Volsky, Magoon, Norman, and Holt. Volsky et al. (1965) reported the results of a well-designed study with 80 experimental and 20 control subjects. The authors concerned themselves with college counseling center clients and the variables of manifest anxiety, defensiveness, and problem-solving effectiveness. Randomly assigning clients to treatment or control conditions, these authors reported data on the degree of change on outcome variables and their relation to client expectations of counseling and their motivation for change. Significant differences were found between the experimental (individual therapy) and control clients on co-varied scores for problem-solving skills. This change, however, was not in the predicted direction. The authors, aware that "no significant difference" could be a function of co-occurring client improvement and deterioration within the experimental group, tested the hypothesis that the adjusted post-test scores would have equal variance. Using Welch's L_1 test, they considered a rejection of their hypothesis to result from the fact that persons changed in ways not expected on the basis of statistical regression phenomena alone. That is, while no systematic and uniform differences in variance were found, several significant increases in variance were apparent at post-testing.

Jewell (1968) followed up this study by examining the outcomes of 20 randomly selected cases in detail. He found that 10% of these clients became less skillful in problem solving, 35% became more defensive, and 20% were found to be more anxious at treatment end. Jewell's follow-up is limited because he did not also follow a no-treatment control group.

The data of the Volsky et al. (1965) study can be said to give modest support for the presence of deterioration. The authors point out alternate hypotheses which might account for the significant increase in variance noted, and they were not able to identify specific therapist characteristics or treatment conditions which led to deterioration in subjects.

Carkhuff and Truax. Carkhuff and Truax (1965) studied the effects of group counseling on eight groups of 10 hospitalized mental patients who met twice a week and were treated for 24 sessions. Therapists were five trained lay personnel (attendants) who were trained to offer a facilitative environment and encourage self-exploration. A control population consisted of 70 "untreated" hospital patients. Outcome measures were ratings of degree of disturbance, inter- and intra-personal concerns and overall degree of improvement. While the treated patients did show improvement which exceeded that found in controls on all the outcome measures, the authors also report: "It is clear from the other scale values that control group members tended to remain unchanged, while there was a greater variability in the treatment group ratings" (p. 430). The authors did not elaborate further on this result except to mention additional studies with similar findings.

Some control patients were lost during the study, which may have lowered slightly the number of deteriorated cases in this sample. No mention was made as to whether the ward personnel's pre-post test ratings were blind. Subjects in both treatment and control groups comprised very similar populations but were not randomly assigned to these conditions. Even so, the evidence that greater benefit and deterioration occurred in their subjects is hard to ignore in light of the large number of reports in which it appears (Truax & Carkhuff, 1967; Truax & Mitchell, 1971).

Other Empirical Evidence

In addition to the nine studies already discussed, the data base which supports the notion of a deterioration effect is much broader. Bergin (1971), for example, listed 23 studies in which deterioration was discussed by the authors or in which it was possible to deduce its presence or absence from the data reported. These studies and more recent additional ones are summarized in Table 3.

It is clear from the studies in Table 3 that a median deterioration rate in treated groups would be nothing more than a conglomeration of diverse figures which would have very little predictive value. They include a mixture of patient populations, criteria, and rigor in design. Aside from demonstrating that the phenomenon is widespread, few of them add to our understanding of the mechanisms of client deterioration. The few exceptions include the studies by Lieberman et al. (1973), Ricks (1974), and Sloane et al. (1975).

Lieberman et al. One of the best evidences to date of deterioration as a function of treatment is the study reported by Lieberman et al. (1973). These authors investigated the effects of a variety of encounter group experiences on group members. In all, 17 groups with a total of 206 participants were contrasted with one another and with a control population ($N = 69$). The type or area of change was examined by comparing participants and controls on 33 measures at treatment termination and at two follow-up periods. Changes were rated by participants, leaders, significant others, and observers with a variety of change measures which tapped behavior as well as attitudes and values. The lack of correspondence among various perspectives on amount of change led to the development of a cumulative index. Based upon the summary index, it was judged that about one-third of the participants benefited, one-third remained unchanged, and one-third experienced some form of negative consequence, where dropping out was counted as negative. More importantly, 16 severe casualties were directly attributable to the group effects, as well as 17 specific negative changers. In contrast, two-thirds of the control subjects remained unchanged with the other one-third being divided unequally between those who improved and those who deteriorated. Comparable evaluation of deterioration across therapy and control groups was not possible with the data available. Summarizing, the authors write:

> Based both on the number of individuals who experienced benefit from the groups and on the comparison of the different areas in participants and their controls, it was concluded that, overall, encounter groups show a modest positive impact, an impact much less than has been portrayed by their supporters and an impact significantly lower than participants' view of their own change would lead one to assume.

TABLE 3. ADDITIONAL OCCURRENCES OF DETERIORATION IN PSYCHOTHERAPY AND CONTROL GROUPS

Authors	Date	N	In Treated Group	N	In Control Group
Aronson & Weintraub	1968	127	2% to 8% depending on criterion and diagnosis		No control group
Feifel & Eells	1963	63	8%		No control group
Garfield & Bergin	1971	38	3% to 6%		No control group
Horwitz	1974	22	45%		No control group
Imber, Frank, Nash, Stone, & Bliedman	1968	34	44%		No control group
Jonckheere	1965	186	5% average, though as high as 44% among psychotics in psycho-analysis		No control group
Koegler & Brill (brief)	1967	162	3%		No control group
Lieberman, Yalom, & Miles	1973	206 (total) 175 (completed)	9% to 19% depending on criterion		No control group
Ling, Zausmer, & Hope	1952	115	18%		No control group
Ricks	1974	28	Shows harmful effect of one therapist		No control group
Rosenbaum, Friedlander, & Kaplan	1956	210	1%		No control group
Rosenthal	1955	12	25%		No control group
Sager, Riess, & Gundlach	1964	103	2% to 14% same or worse, but categories lumped together		No control group
Strupp, Wallach, & Wogan	1964	44	0%		No control group
Stuart & Lott	1972	79	Increased outcome variability attributed to therapist		No control group
Truax, Wargo, Frank, Imber, Battle, Hoehn-Saric, Nash, & Stone	1966	40	5% on global ratings 25% on discomfort scale		No control group
Uhlenhuth & Duncan	1968	128	26%, though not stated how much worse		No control group
Weber, Elinson, & Moss	1965	55	Increased criterion variability, but not clear evidence of deterioration		No control group
Berleman & Steinburn (at follow-up)	1967	28	36%	33	0%
DiLoreto	1971	60	Minimal deterioration not greater than control subjects	40	Minimal
Feighner, Brown, & Olivier	1973	23	17% all with primary depression	23	0%
Gottschalk, Mayerson, & Gottlieb	1967	34	6%	14	36% among non-equivalent dropouts
Henry & Shlien	1958	14	Significant mean decline at follow-up for time-limited patients on TAT	26	
Koegler & Brill (analytic)	1967	27	4%	116	3% in drug and placebo groups
Paul (individual)	1967	13	Desensitization 0%	14	Attention placebo 0%
		12	Insight 0%	18	No treatment 5%
Paul (group)	1968	9	Desensitization 0%	10	Attention placebo 0%
		8	Insight 0%–13%	11	No treatment 0% to 10%
		10	Group desensitization 0%		
Rogers, Gendlin, Kiesler, & Truax	1967	24	Limited evidence of deterioration	24	
Sloane, Staples, Cristol, Yorkston, & Whipple	1975	30 30	Psychotherapy 3% Behavior therapy 0%	30	3%
Varble & Landfield	1969	36	6%	35	0%
Warne, Canter (inexp), & Wiznia (exp)	1953	30	1% significantly worse 60% slightly worse	30	13% significantly worse
		30	0% significantly worse 7% slightly worse		53% slightly worse
Wispe & Parloff	1965	55	Increased criterion variability, but not clear evidence of deterioration		
Agras, Chapin, & Oliveau	1970		No treatment group	26	24%
Endicott & Endicott	1963		No treatment group	40	12%
Giel, Knox, & Carstairs	1964		No treatment group	100	1%
Jurjevich	1968		No treatment group	62	29%
Kringlen	1965		No treatment group	91	5%

Table 3. *Contd.*

Authors	Date	N	In Treated Group	N	In Control Group
Masserman & Carmichael	1938		No treatment group	32	5%–14%
Saslow & Peters	1956		No treatment group	83	12%
Subotnik	1972		No treatment group	166	21%–37%

[a]The wide range of deterioration rates presented in this table defies precise interpretation of the phenomenon. We have attempted to group studies according to rigor or nature of criteria in the hope of arriving at more reliable figures for baseline rates. Our view now is that the measurements are too crude for this and that we must accept them as simply ambiguous; however, we invite the motivated reader to try his own hand at extracting precision from the present array of data.

To a considerable extent, the modesty of the gain can be attributed to the wide differences among the various groups studied. Some groups were highly productive learning environments, others were innocuous, providing a certain degree of pleasurable stimulation but little learning as measured here. Still others were on balance destructive leaving more of their participants psychologically harmed than psychologically benefited. Differences among groups were more substantial both in the number of people affected and in the type or area of change than were differences between those who participated in them and those who did not. (p. 130)

The Lieberman *et al.* (1973) study is a very detailed and thorough report which repays inspection. It goes beyond most past reports of outcome by specifying therapist and participant variables which are related to deterioration. We find in it strong support for the kind of argument which Bergin (1971), Truax and Carkhuff (1967), and others have made regarding therapy outcomes. These results are presented here in terms of group averages; later, in the sections on therapist factors, a case is made for specific therapist effects.

Ricks. Ricks (1974) studied the adult status on a group of disturbed adolescent boys who had been seen by either of two therapists in a major child guidance clinic. While the long-term outcomes of these two therapists were not different for less disturbed clients, there were striking differences in their therapeutic styles and outcomes with the more disturbed boys. The more successful therapist was labeled "supershrink" by the boys, and Ricks retains this label in describing his techniques versus those of therapist B—whom Bergin and Suinn (1975) have called "pseudoshrink"—most of whose cases became schizophrenic. The outcome of their cases are shown in Table 4. The differences here are clear and statistically significant, though the therapists were selected *post hoc* on the basis of discrepant outcomes. The differences in therapist styles that apparently lead to these outcomes are discussed later in the sections on therapist factors.

Sloane et al. The study by Sloane *et al.* (1975) was designed to compare outcomes of psycho-analytic therapy, behavior therapy, and a waiting list control group. Major differences between therapies were not obtained but their outcomes were significantly better than those of the control group. Only one of 60 therapy cases was worse at the conclusion of treatment, which probably indicates the value of using highly experienced and carefully selected expert therapists. One of 30 control cases was worse. This well-designed and executed study suggests a rather low deterioration rate for well-qualified therapists.

In addition to these studies, numerous others indicate widespread awareness of this phenomenon (Bowden, Endicott, & Spitzer, 1972; Friedman & Lipsedge, 1971; O'Brien, Hamm, Ray, Pierce, Luborsky, & Mintz, 1972), but they do not present data in a form that allows for specification of the deterioration variables. Since the intent of all the above mentioned projects was to demonstrate the value of therapy, the question of negative effects was not usually entertained. This makes their inadvertent appearance all the more persuasive. From an examination of these studies and additional bits of empirical evidence, some interesting and sound conclusions can be drawn in regard to therapist, patient, and situational characteristics which lead to deterioration. Some additional studies and important issues will be considered first.

How General is the Finding of Increased Outcome Variability?

It should be recalled that client deterioration has often been associated with increased variance in outcome scores and, like spontaneous remission, has been linked with issues and polemics on the efficacy of psychotherapy. Thus, the existence of a deterioration effect necessarily implies an opposite "improvement effect"; and those who argue against the significance of patient deterioration often do so to negate the possibility of an improvement effect. The most amusing argument has been offered by Rachman

(1973). He writes about the implication of increased variance in the following way: "one of two conclusions given here must follow: either psychotherapy is capable of helping a lot of people and also making an approximately equal number of people worse; or, most therapists are relatively ineffective and also relatively harmless" (p. 839). Of course, his argument makes the false assumption that increased variance requires equal amounts of change in positive and negative directions. He also assumes that if the variance-increase phenomenon is absent, then therapy is ineffective. Actually, if most therapists were highly effective, post-test variance could be the same, smaller, or larger, than pre-test variance.

While the increased variance phenomenon originally called attention to the possibility of deterioration, it does not occur in every study where deterioration exists, nor does it appear on all criterion measures in a single study. For example, Cartwright and Vogel (1960) report increased variance on Q-score adjustment changes but not adjustment changes as measured by the TAT. They have been absent at treatment termination but present at follow-up (Rogers & Dymond, 1954). Variance in post-test or change scores has been significantly related to diagnostic category (Fairweather *et al.*, 1960) and on occasion the mean variance of control groups has been found to be significantly larger than those obtained by treated subjects. In regard to this issue, Schuldt and Truax (1970) published a review in which they specifically tested the generality of the conclusion that psychotherapy leads to a significantly greater increase in variability of post-test outcome measures within treatment groups than within control groups. Studying the variance in five of their own studies, they found that neither therapy nor control situations had much effect upon variability in outcome measures. However, at least two of the five studies used therapists selected for high competence who would not be expected to yield variance increases. Also, these authors acknowledge the importance of the variance phenomenon in other studies.

Viewing the large number of individual and group therapy outcome studies, increased variance is apparently absent in some cases with certain groups of therapists. This has been observed by Truax (1967) as well as May (1971) and is to be expected when there is a preponderance of "good" therapists or a preponderance of psychonoxious ones.

Gottman (1973) has also critiqued the vari-

ance evidence. While portions of his statistical argument do not seem relevant to the point, he correctly indicates that there are multiple causes of variance changes during psychotherapy. He also properly notes that when we examine the variance of *change* scores rather than *post-test* scores *per se*, a treatment group can have a larger variance than a control group under quite varied circumstances.

Our own view at this time is that: (1) *Increased variance at post-test initially alerted us to the probability of deterioration, particularly because the increase was associated with both improving and declining scores. As a signal of possible harmful effects, it is still relevant.* (2) *Increased variance is not essential to the deterioration argument because individual cases can get worse regardless of whether the distribution of criterion scores has increased, decreased, or remained the same.* (3) *Increased variance can occur without the presence of deterioration such as when the post-test distribution embraces all of the pre-test distribution plus some improvement scores.* (4) *Decreased variance can arise from deterioration effects where the change is uniformly negative but restricted in range (decreased variance can similarly arise from uniformly positive effects). Finally,* (5) *decreased variance can also occur where both positive and negative effects are present such as when clients high on pre-test depression come out lower while those low on pre-test depression come out higher. Such regression toward the mean can also occur when therapy is uniformly effective as Gottman pointed out in an example using aggression as a criterion. Persons who are either too aggressive or not aggressive enough at the beginning may move toward a middle position, thus reducing variance when therapy is effective.*[2]

In the future it would be of help for researchers to study and report both increases and decreases in variance in both treatment and control groups. It would then be useful to specify the sources of the observed changes. Where large increases in variance occur, there is always the possibility that bipolar changes have been produced.

Is There a Baseline for Deterioration in Untreated Subjects?

This is a question which is akin to that of "spontaneous remission" and has been studied by following those who are identified as "patients" either by applying for but not receiving treatment or through epidemiological surveys. What can be expected in relation to "getting

TABLE 4. ADULT OUTCOME OF CHILDREN SEEN BY THERAPISTS A AND B.

	Schizophrenic				Not Schizophrenic				Total
	Chronic		Released		Socially Inadequate		Socially Adequate		
	Raw	Percent	Raw	Percent	Raw	Percent	Raw	Percent	
A	0	(0)	4	(27)	5	(33)	6	(40)	15
B	3	(23)	8	(61)	2	(15)	0	(0)	13
Total	10	(14)	24	(35)	17	(25)	17	(25)	68

Note. There are no differences in any major characteristic at the time of clinic contact between the cases seen by A and B. The only known differences between them is their adult status and the therapist they saw.

The totals shown are for all cases studied, including those seen by therapists other than A or B. This provides a rough baseline of expected change.

(Adapted from Ricks, 1974.)

worse" by observing changes in these subjects? If a reliable baseline could be established, perhaps this would serve as a benchmark against which negative outcomes in treated subjects could be compared. Looking at the figures in Table 3, it can be noted that rates of deterioration in control groups vary widely, just as they do in treatment groups.

As with spontaneous remission (see Lambert, 1976), these figures are so variable as to be a somewhat untrustworthy baseline. Unfortunately, firm evidence for specific baselines of deterioration in treated and untreated groups is not available. The problems involved, mainly those of diverse criterion measures and sampling procedures, will be discussed in detail later.

Do Deterioration Effects Vary with School?

One would hope that differing theories and approaches to change would show marked tendencies for differential effects on patients and that these effects would be apparent in patient deterioration rates. This has not been borne out by the empirical evidence. Lambert and Bergin (1973) summarized the evidence relating to behavioristic and humanistic approaches to psychotherapy and concluded that the evidence is slightly but not convincingly on the side of the behavioral approaches. A subsequent review (Bergin & Suinn, 1975) supported the notion of limited differences between therapies when applied to neurotics. Despite this trend, our expectation is that some approaches may lead to greater deterioration in some patients. Thus far, most of the data are on traditional analytic, client-centered, and eclectic techniques. Unfortunately, systematic examination of this question has been limited in behavior therapy

studies. There is, however, considerable reason to believe that therapy-induced deterioration occurs in behavior therapy as well.

It can be expected that such techniques as flooding, implosive therapy, aversive conditioning, and the like may well have a deteriorative effect, especially in the hands of a novice. Rachman and Teasdale (1969) have discussed the tendency to "leave treatment" as a problem of considerable proportion in aversive conditioning. Marks (1971), among others, has reported the development of significant depression in a proportion of phobic cases treated by desensitization.[3] A number of other studies, such as Bruch's (1974) report on the perils of behavior modification in treating anorexia nervosa, further confirm and extend our understanding of behavioral deterioration effects, including the possibility of suicide.[4]

The widespread concern about some behavioral technology certainly is reminiscent of the stir caused by T groups, but is clearly a source of greater concern to many. Portrayals of patients treated by these methods in books such as *A Clockwork Orange* have not done much for the public's expectations about behavioral methods. Their use in prisons, etc., has been criticized and certainly this is at least in part connected with their potential for harm.

Objections to their use have been raised by humanistic practitioners such as Jourard (1973): "there is a sense in which I regard efforts to foster change in another by environmental control or by shaping techniques or by any means that are not part of an authentic dialogue as in some ways pernicious and mystifying and probably not good for the well being and growth of the persons to whom these efforts are addressed; and probably not very enobling for the people who practice them" (p. 10).

Case study material does imply that some patients being treated by behavior therapy (Palmer, 1970) get worse. Frequently this appears to be related to the focus upon a specific symptom to the exclusion of more-difficult-to-define, internal feeling states which are significant to the patient. Additional evidence of relapse and symptom substitution following the misapplication of behavioral methods has been reported by Hersen (Hersen, Eisler, & Miller, 1975). Stuart and Lott (1972) also sound a warning on possible damaging effects of behavioral contracting with delinquents: "some Project families . . . show marked improvement and others a moderate amount of deterioration" (p. 167). We look forward with interest to the day when there is an accumulation of evidence relating to deterioration in behavioral approaches such that indications and contraindications for certain treatment methods are supported. Current interest in behavior therapy as indicated by the large number of research reports appearing in recent years along with the decline of "miracle cures" makes this a likely possibility.

Client-centered psychotherapy has, to date, produced the most literature on patient deterioration. The therapist qualities which are related to positive and negative behavioral change have received considerable attention. While some have argued (Garfield & Bergin, 1971) that these skills may not generalize across therapies, there is still considerable support that they are not school-specific but that therapeutic encounters which are highly loaded with these positive relationship factors produce much higher positive outcome rates than those which are low in these conditions. At the same time, therapeutic encounters which are characterized by low levels can be expected to sustain a higher casualty rate.[5]

The low frequency of empirical investigations of psychoanalytic psychotherapy limits comparisons based on research evidence. Some data recently published (Kernberg, 1973) give some specificity to client and therapist variables as they relate to positive and negative outcome. Conclusions from these data will be presented in the discussion of client and therapist variables. It appears from this study, as well as others, that there are large numbers of cases who are unsuitable for psychoanalytic treatment and for whom the analytic method may be harmful. In fact, it may be the treatment of choice in only about 5% of the patient population (Malan, 1973).

Most of the work done in this area relates to patient characteristics rather than therapist behavior. Psychoanalysts are, of course, well aware of the importance of the therapist. Still, as Luborsky (1971) points out, no systematic research has been published in regard to therapist empathy, neutrality, affective distance, etc. The term "countertransference" implies possible ill consequences to the patient as a function of the therapist's feelings and unconscious reactions. Quantitative data have been published which show a relationship between countertransference phenomena and client deterioration (see Singer & Luborsky, Chapter 16, this volume).

Little in the way of comparative studies has been produced which would allow comparison of these three main schools of psychotherapy in regard to deterioration. It has been pointed out that viewing change from the point of view of theoretical orientation has not been productive, because, among other reasons, professed orientation actually often tells us very little about what a therapist actually does in therapy.[6]

From a researcher's point of view, traditional approaches like psychoanalytic (Freud), behavioral (Wolpe), humanistic-relationship (Rogers), and cognitive (Kelly) therapies have generally shown positive effects, provided they are implemented by a competent, experienced therapist and not a psychonoxious one. These therapies rest upon a solid tradition of scholarship and research. It is their misapplication that creates most of the problems. Many other therapies derive from an anti-intellectual tradition that spurns scholarly evidence, and they have the appearance of gimmickry, faddism, etc. Approaches like Reichian orgone therapy, primal therapy, Rolfian massage, scientology, and much of the Encounter Movement rest upon a spurious or nonexistent substantive base. One would expect misapplications to be easier and thus more frequent in these approaches. Other approaches, like transactional analysis or reality therapy, derive from a more substantial history but they lie in limbo from an empirical standpoint because their claims have not been verified experimentally, though it is conceivable that they might be eventually. *It is regrettable, however, that so many of these innovations are promoted prior to a reasonable objective test of their effects in the hands of a competent, well-adjusted therapist.* This lack of outcome data on nearly all of them precludes any assessment of deterioration rates resulting from their use, and, of course, equally precludes evaluation of any possible improvement effects.

Do Deterioration Effects Vary with Treatment Modality?

T groups and the like have stirred up more than their share of controversy. In fact, Gibb (1971) suggests that the concern about negative effects has been a barrier to innovation. Therefore, questions regarding negative effects have been more broadly examined than in most other treatment modalities. Some very interesting and helpful information has been discovered. The controversy over casualties in experiential groups became apparent in the late 1960s. Campbell and Dunnett (1968) reviewed the research literature regarding the effectiveness of T-group experiences. They emphasized the use of these groups for business and organizational behavior. As they point out, much of the research to that time had focused upon group process and the influence of groups on organizational development, participant perception, and attitude change. Some hint of negative changes was discovered nonetheless. For example, Boyd and Ellis (1962), investigating the effects of T-groups on 42 managers compared to 24 control subjects, found those attending groups to have made more behavioral changes than control subjects. Ratings of changes were collected from supervisor, peers, and subordinates; 351 statements of perceived change were reported and 137 were agreed upon by two or more observers. Of 22 reported changes judged to be unfavorable (e.g., increase in irritability, lack of tolerance), 20 were attributed to laboratory participation. Observers apparently knew that subjects had been involved in T-group training and so these ratings are open to an apparent bias.

Underwood (1965) studied 15 T-group participants and 15 matched controls. Nine experimental and seven control subjects were reported by observers (with whom they worked) to have changed. There were two and one-half times as many changes reported in the experimental group. In the control group, the ratio of changes judged to be productive to those judged unproductive was 4:1, while the ratio for the experimental group was 2:1. Despite a small sample size and the possibility of rater bias, the authors concluded that T-groups produce more changes and a higher percentage of unfavorable changes with respect to job effectiveness.

More recently, Hartley, Roback, and Abramowitz (1976) have specifically examined the question of deterioration in encounter groups by reviewing the empirical literature. Summarizing nine studies appearing since 1966, they report large variation in estimated casualty rates—from less than 1% to almost 50%. The median casualty rate was about 6%. These varying rates are a function of the casualty criteria employed, varying member characteristics and perhaps the diverse nature of the treatment employed. For example, the definition of casualty ranged from "negative feelings about the experience" and "stressed enough to leave the workshop" to clinical judgment that a "psychotic reaction was precipitated or aggravated" in a T group.

From the research literature, it is difficult to identify deteriorative variables which relate specifically to this mode of "treatment." Lieberman et al. (1973) indicate that generic labels identifying the group do not have differential process or outcome correlates. For example, one of the Gestalt groups evaluated was found to produce the most casualties, while another Gestalt group was among the most beneficial. Lieberman et al. (1973) suggested that, rather than global labels, specific mechanisms of injury were related to deterioration, such as the encouragement of confrontation, expression of anger, rejection by group or leader, and feedback overload. Others have stressed the potential negative consequences of coercive group norms for participation, and Lieberman et al. (1973) have also found some empirical support for this factor.

Continuing efforts need to be made in this area in order to make more accurate predictions about casualties. Delineation of therapist and client variables, discussed in another section, will enable us to screen subjects for treatment and train group leaders more effectively. Further research is needed in regard to facilitative group norms, optimal structure, and the interaction of these treatment variables with leader and participant variables.

Despite the fact that experiential and laboratory groups have different purposes than traditional therapy and frequently exclude psychiatric patients, the parallels in outcome are obvious. *In general, we conclude that groups are often less deleterious but can produce more deterioration than individual psychotherapy.*

Marital Therapy

Various forms of marital therapy might be expected to produce different levels of psychological disturbance. Gurman (1973) reviewed the effectiveness of marital therapy. Summarizing 15 outcome studies, he reported an improvement rate of 66%. Of the 11 studies which listed a "worse" category, only three reported a portion of their clients deteriorated. Preston, Mudd, and Froscher (1953), studying 211 husbands and wives treated separately but concurrently found 10 (5%) to be worse at termination. Reding, Charles, and Hoffman (1967) reported outcomes for 10 couples treated conjointly and reported one (10%) couple to be "worse." Finally, Targow and Zweber (1969), studying 15 couples who had conjoint therapy, reported outcome based on individual change rather than dyadic change and found that five (17%) were considered worse. Overall, the rate of 2% was determined as the casualty rate for these 11 studies of marital outcome.

In a later report Gurman (1975) found even more evidence for deterioration in couples therapy and was more specific about its meanings. His survey is summarized here:

1. Of 17 studies using a "worse" category, eight or 47% have found deterioration.

2. Deterioration rates in different types of marital therapy were: conjoint, 7% (48/702); concurrent, 5% (10/211); group, 8% (7/90); individual, 12% (26/224).

3. Stated otherwise, the deterioration rate for marital therapies where both spouses are involved in treatment in some way (conjoint, concurrent, group) is 6% (65/1003), or one-half that of individual therapy for marital problems—i.e. 12% (26/224).

Although Gurman (1975) does not speculate at length about the reasons for this difference, it does appear that treating the "relationship" rather than the "person" results in less deterioration.[7]

4. The deterioration rate across all studies and all treatment types is 8% ($N = 1638$) but probably higher—i.e., 10% to 12%—since several studies have lumped "no change" and "worse" together and the 8% figure does not include them.

No data were available on the level of deterioration in control couples, and the definition of deterioration in these studies was somewhat unclear.[8] As yet no one has studied the mechanisms of deterioration in marital therapy as it relates to the therapist and his techniques. In addition, group marital therapy has no existing empirical base from which to draw conclusions about the indications and contraindications for this form of treatment (Gurman, 1971). On the other hand, clinical judgment has produced some guidelines. In a related area, Guttman (1973), for example, has cautioned against the use of conjoint family

therapy with extremely anxious young patients who are on the verge of decompensating or just recovering from an acute psychotic breakdown. The author presents four cases of deterioration which were felt to be due to the process of family therapy. The approach used was one which assumed a capacity for insight and autonomous action, was affectively oriented and not as directive as crisis-oriented techniques. It was felt that the deterioration was related to facing unpleasant conflicts, mainly ambivalence toward parents and dependency upon them. This type of intervention was considered helpful with other patient groups but produced harmful consequences when "fragile" patients were treated.

Interventions in marital relationships are proving a fertile ground for the curious researcher. Efforts to identify both positive and negative forces in this type of therapy are needed.

Is There Evidence of Deterioration in Related Areas?

The study of facilitative conditions offered by therapists to clients has been expanded to include questions of broader social significance. These same conditions have been studied in relation to the growth of clinical and counseling graduate students specifically, and to a lesser extent to students in general. This development has led some researchers to the conclusion that graduate schools and, more importantly, teachers can exert a strong negative influence upon students.

Pierce and Schauble (1970) studied changes in counseling intern behavior on the dimensions of empathy, regard, genuineness, and concreteness as it related to those dimensions in their supervisors. Their results showed that trainees whose supervisors were functioning at high levels of empathy, regard, genuineness, and concreteness changed significantly and positively while those interns who had supervisors that were functioning at low levels on these dimensions did not increase but, in fact, tended to decline slightly. Desrosiers (1968) also found a relationship between level of conditions offered in supervision and trainee self-concept changes with some trainees decreasing in self-concept.

Along similar lines, Abramowitz, Wietz, and James (1974) studied changes in trainee self-concept as a function of supervisor self-concept. Signs of trainee deterioration were "marginally reliable" but apparent and seemed to be related to two supervisors with deviant self-concept scores. There are, however, several competing hypotheses which might be put forward to account for the results, all of which are about as plausible as the conclusion that it was caused by the supervisor. This study included several weaknesses (including the criterion measure itself) and the fact that the authors report results on only one of 12 or more subscales of the Tennessee Self-Concept Scale.

Further evidence for the broad facilitative or deteriorative influence of teachers, parents, etc., has been documented by Carkhuff (1969). Although it appears that his conclusions go beyond the data which he quotes as supporting them, this work promises to be a stimulating if not sobering line of inquiry.

The scope of the present chapter does not permit a review of all the possible literature on deterioration. New innovations as well as past practices using such diverse methods as chemotherapy, hypnotherapy, surgical procedures, electroshock, and the like cannot be dealt with here. Some of these methods, in fact, are likely to produce results which are destructive enough to cause permanent negative behavior change. These past and present treatment procedures need continuing documentation since it is likely that they produce their fair share of harmful results.

Are There Certain Patient Characteristics which Can Be Linked to Deterioration?

Unfortunately, patient characteristics have rarely been studied in relation to deterioration. A few studies tersely comment on deterioration by the notation "worse," while most lump "unimproved" and "worse" together. Such generality limits the degree to which psychotherapeutic prescription can take place. As an analogy, penicillin may be the treatment of choice for pneumonia, but if the patient is allergic to penicillin it may do him more harm than good. The medical profession is able to prescribe a treatment that is effective because it recognizes the importance of deteriorative treatments as well as the importance of specifying for which patients and under what conditions it occurs. Likewise, psychotherapeutic techniques may be viewed as facilitative, neutral, or regressive depending upon the patients' characteristics. Despite this lack of specificity, certain patient variables do indeed seem to be related to deterioration.

Patient diagnosis is one such variable. The evidence favors the position that schizophrenic and psychotic individuals are more likely to sustain higher rates of negative change. This has been demonstrated by a number of research reports including one by Fairweather et al. (1960) who found deterioration in a variety of diagnostic categories but none which exceeded that in psychotic subjects. Some have attributed this trend to the more diverse response alternatives available to these individuals. It is not yet possible to arrange a hierarchy for deterioration via diagnostic category. This hierarchy may take a form opposite to that for spontaneous remission proposed by Rachman (1973). In that case, reactive depression and anxiety states would have the lowest occurrence of deterioration and obsessional states and hypochondriasis would have the highest rates of deterioration, except for psychoses.

It appears that related variables such as past history of the disorder may exert a more powerful influence on deterioration than diagnostic label, although this has yet to be documented. This variable has been shown to greatly affect spontaneous remission rates. Along these same lines, past psychological disturbance has been shown to be an important variable time and again in experiential groups. This has been noted by Yalom and Lieberman (1971), Joffe and Scherl (1969), Crawshaw (1969), and N. T. L. (1969).

Returning again to the studies by Yalom and Lieberman (1971) and Lieberman et al. (1973) of encounter group casualties, these researchers began by selecting 18 encounter group styles. Of a total of 209 subjects, Yalom and Lieberman (1971) found 16 casualties whom the group seemed responsible for creating. Eight criteria were used in order to assess deterioration in subjects: (1) request for psychiatric aid, (2) dropouts from group, (3) peer evaluation, (4) self-esteem drop, (5) subject testimony, (6) psychotherapy, (7) leaders' ratings, and (8) miscellaneous sources.

In their study, characteristics of those subjects who deteriorated were specified. It was found that such variables as involvement in the group, low levels of self-esteem, low positive self-concept, higher growth orientation, and greater anticipation or need for fulfillment were positively related to deterioration. Likewise, casualties were more likely to use escape modes of coping and conversely to be less likely to use interpersonal skills in their ego defenses. As Yalom and Lieberman (1971) state: "The entire picture is a consistent one: individuals with generally less favorable mental health, with greater growth needs and higher anticipation for their group experiences and yet who lacked self-esteem and the interpersonal skills to operate effectively in the group situation were more likely to become casualties" (p. 27).

Despite the 16 casualties noted in this study, it should be recognized that there were six groups in which no casualties occurred despite similar group composition. Different leader styles may be responsible for such a finding and will be discussed in a subsequent section.

The data presented by Yalom and Lieberman (1971) are complemented by data gathered in the Menninger Foundation's Psychotherapy Research Project. Kernberg (1973) emphasized the relationship of Initial Ego Strength to outcome. This patient variable taps three separate qualities, including (1) integration of ego structure; (2) degree of deep, satisfying relations with others; and (3) symptom severity. Some very interesting conclusions regarding this variable, patient motivation, and anxiety tolerance are summarized here.

First, patients with low initial ego strength treated by therapists with high skill improved significantly more when the focus on transference was high. Kernberg writes: "A purely supportive approach that does not focus on the transference would be contraindicated in patients with significant ego weaknesses." It can be added that psychoanalytic treatment would also be contraindicated. Presumably, these clients cannot tolerate the regression inherent in psychoanalysis and do not develop a viable relationship in supportive treatment.

Like the work of Lieberman et al. (1973), Kernberg (1973) reports that low quality of interpersonal relationships was a prognostically poor sign and that this coupled with low initial anxiety tolerance and low motivation yielded poor outcomes in psychoanalysis and supportive psychotherapies but better outcomes in supportive-expressive treatments.

In a further report of this project (Horwitz, 1974) the indications and contraindications for psychoanalytic treatment were spelled out in more detail. Of 22 cases starting out in psychoanalysis, four were dropped and shifted to a different treatment because it was felt that psychoanalysis was "too stressful" for the patient. Another six were considered by the research team to have been poorly selected for this type of treatment. Three others were considered "questionable" as to their suitability.

It would appear from this report that at least 10/22 patients originally considered suitable for psychoanalysis were eventually not so considered. Again, ego weaknesses were listed as the primary contraindication. Borderline person-

ality organizations with potential for psychotic reactions, plus a high proportion of patients with "predominant oral fixations" were among those considered hurt by the experience. All of the 13 cases where psychoanalysis was considered unsuitable or questionable demonstrated initial levels of low frustration tolerance.

This project has provided some very interesting information about both positive and negative changes. The fact that Horwitz (1974) devotes an entire chapter to a discussion of negative effects is to be applauded and demonstrates the current trend for researchers to attend to the double-edged sword of treatment. Within the conceptual framework of analytic thinking, this is an important contribution to the patient characteristic variables which might be expected to interact with therapist and choice of treatment. It is unfortunate that these researchers did not also focus on the actual behavior of therapists within the therapeutic hour. The failure to connect patient change with process variables leaves many unanswered questions about the mediating and actual therapist behaviors involved.

What Therapist Factors are Influential in Causing Deterioration?

To believe that deterioration is based solely on patient weakness is to oversimplify an extremely complex phenomenon. One of the variables under intense investigation is the role of the therapist himself; his skill, training, and his personal characteristics deserve careful scrutinizing.

Early attempts to investigate the role of the therapist is typified by the research of Whitehorn and Betz (1960). These two investigators conducted a series of experiments to determine what therapist characteristics were related to high success (type A therapists) in therapy and which variables were related to a low success rate (type B therapists). According to our definition of deterioration, a low success rate can be equivalent to harming patients if a more favorable outcome can be expected. Thus, low-success physicians in the Whitehorn and Betz studies tended to view the patient as "a wayward mind needing correction, an approach likely to alienate him further ... " These physicians also tended to be rigid and to expect deference and conformity to established social patterns. Such an attitude constituted a "hindrance to the development of self-trust and social spontaneity ... "[9]

Unfortunately, the results of studies of the A-B variable have been equivocal. Often those studies that do support the A-B dichotomy are plagued by ambiguities and are frequently poorly conducted. Bowden *et al.* (1972) in a review of the A-B dichotomy have come to much the same conclusion.

Exploitation

A recent attempt to relate therapeutic effectiveness to personality dimensions has been proposed by Vandenbos and Karon (1971). Their basic hypothesis was that "pathogenic" therapists are those who consciously or unconsciously utilize dependent individuals (in this case, their clients) to satisfy the therapists' own personal needs. They further assert that "such therapists were less clinically effective than therapists who put the legitimate needs of the client first."

In order to test their hypothesis, Vandenbos and Karon (1971) conducted an experiment in which degree of pathogenesis in the therapist was related to the outcome of therapy with 15 schizophrenic patients. To assess a therapist's pathogenesis, each took the TAT, which was then scored for pathogenic indicators. Assessment of outcome was based upon a substantial number of tests which included behavioral, projective, intellectual, and interview assessments. "The results show the same relationship between therapist pathogenesis and patient outcome regardless of whether outcome is measured by intellectual tests, clinical status interviews, or hospitalization data; the patients of more benign therapists are functioning at higher levels after six months of treatment than are patients treated by more pathogenic therapists" (p. 116). Thus, it appears that those therapists who utilize dependent individuals to satisfy their own needs are not effective with schizophrenics and may even cause deterioration. Such a hypothesis is completely tenable when accounts such as the following are considered.

Mrs. D (deteriorated) described her therapist as "sadistic." Dr. PN (psycho-noxious) demanded that she reveal deep personal material immediately. He was so threatening to her that she began consuming several alcoholic drinks prior to each session in order to relax enough to disclose material about which she felt very anxious. After therapy was underway, he repeatedly threatened to cut her off from treatment if she did not talk in the manner he prescribed. This was especially disturbing because of her strong need at the time for nonthreatening emotional support. Later, when she discussed feelings of pessimism about her marriage, his response was "You mean you'd commit suicide?"—a thought that she declares was furthest from her mind. Finally, she complained of several physical problems, including excessive fatigue. His reply was: "You are not working efficiently because you don't want to." Although the therapist was an M.D., no physical assessment was done. Subsequent medical investigation after leaving this therapist revealed that Mrs. D suffered from anemia and a low basal metabolic rate. She was ultimately able to find a more suitable therapist and reported significant improvement in her emotional condition. Despite the fact that Dr. PN was well known through his numerous publications, he obviously lacked the capacity to relate to this client in a professional and humane manner. Further informal testimony to this effect was provided by two therapists who were trained by him (Bergin, 1971).

A second provocative example was related by a woman whose therapist began to dwell more and more on her sex life and sexual fantasies. At one point, he began to stroke her body and pressed her face against his. She had been admittedly provocative at times but both she and, eventually, her husband firmly resisted these direct responses on his part. Although there had been a positive relationship up to this point, things abruptly deteriorated and their subsequent encounters were reduced to verbal battles. In a climactic session he screamed that she was insane, hit her across the face, and physically pushed her out. This series of episodes left her in a state of emotional shock and devastation. After years of therapy and thousands of dollars in fees, her analysis had left her in a worse state than when she had begun. She was disoriented and, even more disturbing, was so subject to the therapist's influence that she blamed herself for the outcome!

Experience Level

Another difference which is commonly examined is therapist experience. Although Meltzoff and Kornreich (1970) find it a curious phenomenon that this subject has been investigated, they nevertheless conduct an extensive review of the research in this area. They quote one study by Myers and Auld (1955) where patient outcomes of experienced therapists were compared to outcomes for a group of psychiatric residents who served as the inexperienced group. They found that experienced therapists had more successful terminations and fewer failures. While the psychiatric residents averaged a client drop-out rate of 25% after 10 or more sessions, none of the patients treated by the experienced staff terminated prematurely.

Cartwright and Vogel (1960) found that experienced therapists were no more effective than inexperienced ones in effecting changes in Q scores. On the other hand, they did find that experience was important in producing positive change in TAT mental health ratings. Likewise, t tests between pre- and post-treatment were significant for the experienced therapists but not for the inexperienced ones. McNair, Lorr, and Callahan (1963) found that therapists with more than 4 years of experience held 97 of their 135 clients (72%) in therapy, while those therapists with less than 4 years experience were able to hold only 72 of the 120 clients (60%).

The research data imply that therapist inexperience is a contributing factor in producing negative effects. Thus, while a beginning therapist may have appropriate personal assets, he may mismanage techniques due to unfamiliarity with procedures. Such is the case in this account:

> I was assigned to conduct individual therapy with a middle-aged, hospitalized schizophrenic who was in remission and able to converse lucidly. This was my first attempt at therapy with a psychotic in the VA neuropsychiatric facility to which I had been assigned for internship experience. This patient had been seen previously by my supervisor and I was given a brief account of his history but no suggestions regarding therapy except an allusion to the idea that the patient was now ready for some self-exploration and insight. I took this to mean that a dynamically oriented approach was in order and so I began. I suggested to him that he tell me something about his history. Apparently he had been through this type of thing many times before, so, in the first session the personal recollections came readily. In the second meeting, this continued. It felt good to be in direction of the process and to see significant material unfold and a nice picture of his dynamics form. I began to feel like a supershrink. I pressed him for more material about his early family life in the hope of learning more about the basis of dependency and sexual conflicts he presently experienced with his wife. I encouraged him to tell me about his dreams, fantasies, and early memories. He seemed to warm up to me and to the task. Thoughts flowed more and more freely and I was pleased by his trust and by the dynamic richness of his outpourings. I pressed him further and began to make explicit connections between his past life and the current disarray in his marital relations. He unburdened his sexual experiences and problems in detail. I felt as though I were rediscovering the insights of Sigmund Freud.
>
> Late in that second session I was stunned by the intensity of his growing feelings of involvement with me. I wondered: 'Transference so soon?' Within minutes he seemed to shift more and more into his fantasies. First, he wanted to have sex with me. Then, he wanted to sit on my lap and be my baby. He wanted to be cuddled and stroked in the most immediate way. I began to feel that maybe I had been rushing him. I was relieved when the hour ended.
>
> Upon arriving at my building for the third session, I was informed that my patient had relapsed into a completely psychotic state after our last session. He was considered to be out of control and had been placed on the maximum security ward. I never saw him again. It was as though his usefulness had ended—a fatality of the clinical training program. But, maybe my supervisor resurrected him again for the next trainee who came along.

This case illustrates the pseudo-sophistication of the novice therapist. Apparently blind to the fragility of his patient's adjustment, he enthusiastically pursued his new role as super analyst. His interventions were too vigorous, too fast, and dwelt too much upon intrapsychic dynamics; consequently the patient's defenses collapsed and he reverted to a regressed, psychotic state. The therapist's warmth and interest are admirable; but they did little to stem the tide of pathology; indeed, they may even have stimulated it. The notion of strengthening controls and enhancing concrete reality contact was apparently not considered, or was seen as less interesting. The role of the supervisor and the training program must also be taken into account here as contributing factors to the patient's deterioration. It is as though the priority belonged to education rather than treatment, a common but unfortunate view to which beginning therapists are too often exposed.

The weight of evidence suggests that experience or practice is an important factor in success in therapy.[10] But what about training or the formal education one receives? Although the area has not been thoroughly researched, there is some evidence on both sides of this question.[11] Thus, in a study by Carkhuff and Truax (1965) it was found that only five out of 50, or 10%, of the control group became more psychologically disturbed while 19 of 74, or 26%, of the group treated by lay counselors deteriorated. On the other hand, Bergin and Jasper (1969) found no correlation between therapist empathy and any index of intellectual ability or graduate academic achievement. It may be that supervised experience is a more crucial form of training than traditional didactic education.

Therapist Personality and Behavior

While experience and training may be important therapist characteristics, most studies have not specifically examined deterioration in ways that linked therapist behaviors with harmful outcome. One exception has been the study conducted by Yalom and Lieberman (1971). They studied the ideological orientation of leaders as well as their behavior during encounter group sessions, finding these two dimensions "unrelated."

Each leader was rated both by participant questionnaires and by observer schedules. The participant and observer ratings were reduced to four basic dimensions of leader behavior—emotional stimulation, caring, meaning attribution, and execution functions. The leaders were then grouped into seven types.

Type A Leaders: "*Aggressive stimulators*" were described as intrusive, confrontive, challenging, caring, and self-revealing. They were also termed charismatic, authoritarian, and as focusing upon the individual.

Type B Leaders: "*Love Leaders*" were described as caring, individually focused leaders who gave love as well as information about how to change.

Type C Leaders: "*Social Engineers*" focused on the group as a whole rather than upon individuals. They rarely confronted individuals and were perceived as low on authoritarianism and not charismatic. Often, they were thought of as being close to the participants.

Type D Leaders: "*Laissez-Faire*" were generally distant and cool. They were seen by participants as technicians who offered very little structure to the members of the group.

Type E Leaders: "*Cool, aggressive stimulators*" were aggressive, offered little positive support, were nonauthoritarian, and tended to focus more upon the group.

Type F Leaders: "*High structure*" were extremely controlling and authoritarian. Generally, structured exercises or group games were used throughout the meeting.

Type G Leaders: "*The Tape Leaders*" involved groups structured via audiotape recordings. The tapes focused upon learning how to give and to receive feedback, to contact others emotionally, and to self-disclose. In general, they foster a warm, supportive climate among the group members.

While the data showed that characteristics of some participants made them more vulnerable to negative changes than others, the main finding was that the style of the group leader was the major cause of casualties. The most damaging style, "aggressive stimulator," was characterized by an intrusive, aggressive approach that involved considerable challenging and confronting of the group members. These leaders were impatient and authoritarian in approach, and they insisted on immediate self-disclosure, emotional expression, and attitude change. There were five leaders of this type and all produced casualties except one (and, in fact, nearly half of the most severe casualties). The one exception stated that he realized that there were fragile persons in his group, so he deviated from his usual style and "pulled his punches." For his insight and humanity, this man's name should be published. Another leader, whose group had three casualties commented that "it was a stubborn group, full of people 'too infantile to take responsibility for themselves and to form an adult contrast'... 'I saw that most of the group didn't want to do anything so what I did was to just go ahead and have a good time for myself'" (Yalom & Lieberman, 1971, p. 28). This man's name should also be published. It should be noted that the leaders chosen for this study were among the most experienced and highly recommended in northern California.

An example of a casualty resulting from one of the aggressive, confronting groups where the leader holds center stage in a charismatic manner described by Yalom and Lieberman (1971):

> This subject was unequivocal in her evaluation of her group as a destructive experience. Her group, following the model and suggestions of the leader, was an intensely aggressive one which undertook to help this subject, a passive, gentle individual, to "get in touch with" her anger. Although the group attacked her in many ways, including a physical assault by one of the female members, she most of all remembers the leader's attack on her. At one point he cryptically remarked that she 'was on the verge of schizophrenia.' He would not elaborate on this statement and it echoed ominously within her for many months. For several months she remained extremely uncomfortable. She withdrew markedly from her family and friends, was depressed and insomniac; she was so obsessed with her leader's remark about schizophrenia that she dreaded going to bed because she knew her mind would focus on this point of terror. Often she lapsed into daydreams in which she relived, with a more satisfying ending, some event in the group. The only benefit of the experience, she said, was to help her appreciate how lonely she was; her discomfort has been so great, however, that she has been unable to make use of this knowledge. We consider this subject a severe and long-term casualty; at the interview eight months after the end of the group, she felt that she was gradually reintegrating herself but was not yet back to the point she was before the group began. Her negative experience was a function of aggressive, intrusive leadership style which attempted to change her according to the leader's own values by battering down her characterologic defenses (p. 24).

In addition, Yalom and Lieberman mention five modes of injury: (1) attack by leader or by the group, (2) rejection by leader or by the group, (3) failure to attain unrealistic goals, (4) "input overload", and (5) group pressure. All appear to be under the norm-setting influence of the leader.

Several other studies have also found some leader characteristics which induce deterioration. Feifel and Eells (1963), for instance, conducted a survey of terminated patients in which they found that therapists' feelings of irritation, anger, and boredom, frequent change of therapists, interpretation and confrontation, and termination problems contributed to the non-helpful or deteriorative aspects of therapy. The similarity between the Lieberman *et al.* and Feifel and Eells studies is striking.

Powers and Witmer (1951) also noted deterioration in some of the delinquents in their study. In a few of these cases the counselor's mistakes were seen as a precipitating factor. In several instances, the counselor became so preoccupied in working with other family members that the delinquent was neglected even though in some instances the boy gave definite evidence of liking the counselor and seeking his favor. Such an error is very likely related to Yalom and Lieberman's finding that rejection by leaders or groups can cause deterioration. The second type of error which Powers and Witmer focused on was a punitive attitude toward the boy on the counselor's part. Again, such an attitude relates to both the Yalom and Lieberman and the Feifel and Eells studies which found that attack and therapists' feelings of irritation contribute to deterioration or, at least, were nonhelpful.

Along these same lines, Ricks (1974), in a study previously quoted, was able to distinguish behavioral and attitudinal differences between two therapists who saw 28 disturbed boys. The successful A-therapist devoted more time to those who were most disturbed; the less successful B-therapist did the opposite. A also made more use of resources outside of the immediate therapy situation, was firm and direct with parents, supported movement toward autonomy, and facilitated problem solving in everyday life. This is the context of a strong therapeutic relationship. The author further states:

> ... supportive ego strengthening methods produced much more profound changes than the methods of Therapist B, who moved too precipitously into presumably deep material. Successful therapy with adolescents requires a continuous process of diagnosis, with modification of "opening up" methods, whenever the child, or the therapist, becomes incapable of coping with the material brought out.
>
> If the results achieved by successful therapists such as A argue against the cynical belief that therapy never helps, the apparently destructive effect of intervention by Therapist B also suggests that the potential harmfulness of therapeutic efforts can hardly be ignored.
>
> The children considered here were already experiencing nearly intolerable degrees of anxiety, vulnerability, feelings of unreality, and isolated alienation. When the therapist increased those feelings, without being at the same time able to help the boy develop ways of coping with them, he may well have played a part in the subsequent psychotic developments. Therapy may lead

one into health, but it may also be a part of the complex process that ends up driving one crazy (p. 291).

While A had risen to the occasion and devoted far more time, energy, and involvement to the "sicker" boys, B seemed to be frightened by their pathology and withdrew from them. The case notes reveal this strikingly in that B frequently commented upon the difficulties of cases and seemed to become depressed when confronted with a particularly unpromising case. Among many notes revealing this reaction is an instance in which B ignored the hopeful elements in a client's communication and emphasized the depressed aspects: "I tell him my impression that his spirit has been broken . . . . At the present time it is certainly impossible to get him interested in any occupation, and there doesn't seem to be anything else to do but have him come in for psychotherapy and perhaps if his condition is ameliorated we might get him to do something later on." Later, the therapist noted that: "He is still very depressed and hardly said anything to me at all. The case certainly has an ominous aspect" (p. 282).

The therapist was thus caught up in the boy's depressed and hopeless feelings. He thereby reinforced the client's sense of self-rejection and futility. Detailed examples of the influence of therapist personality problems upon deterioration are uncommon. We are particularly indebted to Ricks for this account, which is worth reading in its entirety. Suffice it to say here that careful studies like this give strong support to traditional clinical beliefs regarding the effects of therapist personality and countertransference phenomena upon outcomes.

The most prolific area of research on therapist characteristics has been that coming from the client-centered orientation. Since this research has been so widely disseminated, only a summary of results will be presented here. When the process variables of therapist accurate empathy, positive regard, and genuineness (congruence) are studied, they have been associated with both improvement and deterioration in patients. Truax and Mitchell (1971), reviewing much of the published research in the area, write: "the patients seen by therapists low in accurate empathy, non-possessive warmth, and genuineness account for the vast majority of deteriorated cases, while therapists high in these conditions account for the majority of the benefited and 'no change' patients" (p. 312). This conclusion is based upon several controlled outcome studies employing both individual and group treatment, and a diversity of patient populations; however, they have not been replicated yet by other investigators (cf. Garfield & Bergin, 1971).

The question often arises as to exactly how the deteriorative process takes place. What is happening when harm is done? Is there such a thing as a moment of negative change in the same sense that Rogers, Gendlin, Kiesler, & Truax (1967) describes moments or "molecules" of positive change? While we do not presently have the same array of verbatim examples of poor therapy that we have for good therapy, there are several good leads toward such a description.

The early Truax scales were anchored at each scale point by transcribed excerpts from tape recordings. Since low scores on these therapist behavior scales are purported to raise the probability of deterioration effects, the examples probably come close to "live" illustrations of deterioration in process. Level One of the 9-point Accurate Empathy Scale (Truax & Carkhuff, 1967) is defined as one in which the

> Therapist seems completely unaware of even the most conspicuous of the client's feelings; his responses are not appropriate to the mood and content of the client's statements. There is no determinable quality of empathy, and hence no accuracy whatsoever. The therapist may be bored and disinterested or actively offering advice, but he is not communicating an awareness of the client's current feelings (p. 47).

One of the examples of this level is reproduced below:

C: I wonder if it's my educational background or if it's me.
T: Mhm.
C: You know what I mean.
T: Yeah.
C: (Pause) I guess if I could just solve that I'd know just about where to hit, huh?
T: Mhm, mhm. Now that you know, a way, if you knew for sure, that your, your lack, if that's what it is—I can't be sure of that yet.
(C: No)
T: (Continuing) ... is really so, that is, it might even feel as though it's something that you just couldn't receive, that is, if, that would be it?
C: Well—I—I didn't, uh, I don't quite follow you— clearly.
T: Well (pause), I guess, I was, I was thinking that— that you perhaps thought that, that if you could be sure that, the uh, that there were tools that, that you didn't have, that, perhaps that could mean that these—uh—tools that you had lacked—way back there in, um, high school
(C: Yah)
T: (Continuing) ... and perhaps just couldn't perceive now and, ah ...
C: Eh, yes, or I might put it this way, um (pause). If I knew that it was, um, let's just take it this way. If I knew that it was my educational background, there would be a possibility of going back.
T: Oh, so, I missed that now, I mean now, and, uh ...
C: ... and really getting myself equipped.
T: I see, I was—uh—I thought you were saying in some ways that, um, um, you thought that, if, if that was so, you were just kind of doomed.

C: No, I mean ...
T: I see.
C: Uh, *not doomed*. Well let's take it this way, um, as I said, if, uh, it's my educational background, then I could go *back* and, catch myself up.
T: I see.
C: And come up.
T: Um.

For an experienced therapist, the foregoing cannot be viewed as a superlative therapeutic moment by any means. The harmful possibility here is that the patient struggles to express himself and to solve a problem; despite his efforts, in the end he feels misunderstood and frustrated. This aversive experience is presumably actively harmful and may be contrasted with therapist neutrality or inertia as depicted in the excerpt below:

C: Now that you're ... know the difference between girls; I think they were about 9 to 8 years old and, uh, they were just like dolls, you know, and (laughs) uh, I used to spend a lot of time with 'em. I used to go over there and would spend more time with these kinds than what would with ...
T: Mhm, hm.
C: But nobody ever told me why I was dragged in here. And I own my own place, I have my, my ... and my farm, I think I still own them. Because that, there was a little mortgage on it. And, uh, (pause) my ex-wife but I don't see how in the world they could change that.
T: Mhm, hm.
C: But they sold my livestock and, uh, I, I worked with horses, and they sold them all, and ah ...
T: I think probably, should I cross this microphone? (Noises)
C: And then I had a bunch of sheep.
T: Mhm, hm.
C: And they sold that stuff off, and the social worker, Mrs. L., says to me, she says that, uh, she says I was ill when I was brought in here.
T: Mhm, hm.
C: And that, which I know that I was not ill. Now, I'll tell you what she might've meant in what way I was ill. How I'll tell 'ya, I botched it out there on the farm and I maybe just didn't get such too good food at the time. Now, whether she wanted to call that ill, or whether she wanted to call it mentally ill, that she didn't say.
T: Mhm, hm.
C: But she says I was ill, well, they could put that I was sick that I didn't have the right kind of food because I gained quite a bit of weight after I was brought in here.
T: Mhm, hm.
C: Yeah, but she didn't say which way she meant or how she meant that.
T: Uh, huh.
C: And she wouldn't give me any explanation and then I got mad at her ...
T: Mhm, hm.

This example may illustrate an absence of therapeutic effect, but it is probably not a psychonoxious event. It is an important task of future research to detail the verbalizations and nonverbal cues that signify a negative change process.

Therapist-Patient Interaction

In the previous discussion we have examined some of the characteristics of patients which make them more susceptible to deterioration than other patients. Likewise, we have examined psychotherapist variables which seem detrimental to the healing process. Despite the seeming simplicity with which the subject has been handled, there is actually a complex interaction which takes place between therapist and client characteristics. Lazarus (1971) describes the variation in response to his follow-up question asking how his former clients felt that their therapy could have been improved:

> Some people felt that they should have been seen more than once a week; others stated that longer intervals between sessions would have been better for them. Some wanted more examples drawn from my own personal experience; others would have preferred less self-disclosure on my behalf. Several people felt that therapy would have been more helpful if I had involved more of their family members. Others wished that I had left their spouses, parents, or siblings out of therapy. This simply bears out that there are few valid general therapeutic roles. What one patient finds especially helpful another considers distinctly harmful. (p. 18)

Although it is debatable whether a client actually knows what is best therapeutically for him, it is a fact that what is best therapeutically for one client is not necessarily good for another client.

Another relevant issue concerns whether the patient, the therapist, or a combination of the two are the main determinants of the interview content. This question arose in the Truax research in terms of who is responsible for levels of therapeutic conditions, or, more specifically, whether there are interaction effects between these therapist-offered conditions and client characteristics. The answer to such a question is complex. Truax (1963) has shown that different therapists produced different levels of accurate empathy across clients, while different patients did not receive significantly different levels of conditions when interacting with the same therapist. Still another hypothesis seems to be that there is little or no interaction with client behavior for counselors offering high conditions. On the other hand, counselors who offer low conditions on the average are affected considerably by client behaviors such as verbal aggression or changes in level of self-exploration (Carkhuff, 1969). While these results have been demonstrated experimentally in that a "client," when instructed, can affect the therapist, these findings have not yet been confirmed in the natural setting. For the moment, at least, it appears that the evidence is strongest in support of the hypothesis that the practitioner is the primary determinant of conditions. A number of other interactional factors must also be considered in a comprehensive analysis of the interaction question.

Race. One easily examined and tangible aspect of any psychotherapeutic relationship is the race of both participants.[12] Banks (1972), for instance, found that rapport was greatest when both client and therapist were of the same race; however, therapist empathy levels were more related to client rapport ratings than to racial similarities. Rogers and Dymond (1954) were interested in a similar question and concluded from their studies that there may be an optimal range of functioning for verbal therapy with respect to ethnocentrism. The possibility that some individuals may be good therapeutic risks and some not seems to be indicated. Bryson and Cody (1973) came to much the same conclusion. Concerning deterioration, however, two recent studies have not found deleterious effects resulting from interracial pairing. Indeed, Krebs (1971) could find no significant negative effects upon blacks treated by a white hospital staff when compared with their Caucasian counterparts. Likewise, Winston, Pardes, and Papernick (1972) discovered that black inpatients did as well or better than whites with white therapists.

Sex. The sex of the client and therapist have also been frequently studied. Typically, sex differences in outcome have not been found. Although Cartwright and Lerner (1963) found differences in empathy levels between same sex and opposite sex client-therapist combinations, their differences disappeared by the end of treatment. Likewise, Sines, Silver, and Lucero (1961) could find no differences between males and females in outcome. Regarding premature termination, however, there is some evidence that early termination occurs with therapists of the opposite sex (Heilbrun, 1971, 1973; McNair et al., 1963; Mendelsohn & Geller, 1967; Reiss, 1973). When and why opposite sex pairings should be deleterious is not clear.

Class. Another frequently studied aspect of the client-therapist relationship is the socio-economic status of each. In a recent study, Mayer and Timms (1970) reported that working class patients preferred therapists who were directive but who also had some good interpersonal skills. The aloof, nondirective, insight-centered counselors were disliked. The crux of the matter may lie in the fact that therapists prefer to treat psychologically sophisticated patients. Unfortunately for Mr. Workingclass, opportunities to become so are quite limited and, even if available, are not sought after. The issue then becomes one of the therapist's negative reaction to such patients. Several investigations (Heller, Myers, & Kline, 1963; Snyder, 1961; Wallach, 1962) have shown that such negative reactions are communicated to the client which often results in subsequent premature termination of therapy. On the other hand, status can improve a relationship when it makes the therapist more attractive to the client. Goldstein (1971) suggests several methods of enhancing therapist attractiveness through increasing his status. Thus, status can be beneficial or negative in its consequences depending upon how it is used— whether pathogenically or facilitatively.

The Criterion Problem

Attempts to specify improvement criteria have been fraught with difficulties for years. Eysenck (1952), for instance, has claimed that traditional psychotherapy is not more effective than no treatment. Bergin (1971), examining similar data, determined that psychotherapy has a positive effect. The difficulty lies in the fact that the relevant criteria which constitute improvement in psychotherapy are subject to value decisions that are difficult to agree upon.

Perhaps the greatest hindrance to observer agreement has been an emphasis upon general classificatory schemes of improvement. Thus, a judge, the therapist, or the client is requested to rate overall improvement in psychotherapy. Such a scheme, based upon a multitude of variables, cannot help but be imprecise. Compounding this problem is the fact that as of yet no satisfactory diagnostic classificatory method has been developed. Except for disorders of organic etiology and the distinction between psychosis and neurosis, the standard diagnostic classifications have provided low reliability.

Another important source of disagreement has come from the use of specific tests which emphasize particular areas of ego functioning. Thus, Q sorts, the MMPI, self-disclosure tests, discomfort scales, etc., have been used to rate improvement. Although, as operational definitions of improvement, tests can achieve a great deal of reliability, there is considerable disagreement as to which tests do indeed measure improvement or whether they do so at all (Bandura, 1969). Some have therefore adopted multiple criterion measures as a preferred method of determining improvement. Unfortunately, the large number of variables often

obscure rather than clarify changes in level of functioning. Likewise, unimportant variables may be examined, while many which are significant go unmeasured. Also, it should be apparent that a limited diagnostic scheme which does not allow the natural course of a given disorder to be followed can offer little guidance in the application of tests.

Our conclusion is that one test, a battery of tests, or a behavioral assessment procedure administered to a group of people cannot precisely indicate improvement or deterioration unless the variables relevant to a specific disorder are linked precisely to the criterion. For example, a person with a sexual dysfunction such as transsexualism might be expected to fulfill a behav)oral test by performing adequately in a previously feared situation. If the subject is able to do so, whereas before he was not, improvement could be said to have occurred. On the other hand, if the client were now more fearful of the situation, one could conclude that deterioration had occurred. Although it is recognized that such an example is quite simplistic, there are real advantages to such a strategy in criterion measurement.

Thus far we have primarily discussed criteria related to improvement and not to deterioration. The same discussion can be applied to a determination of deterioration. The typical method of determining deterioration is with criteria used to assess improvement. Such a situation has arisen because *it is implicitly assumed that deterioration and improvement are opposite sides of the same coin. Such may not be the case!* Consider the example of the student who is so relaxed that he feels no drive to study. On a measure of anxiety he may score quite low, whereas after treatment he may demonstrate a modest amount of anxiety. If one arbitrarily defines deterioration as an increase in anxiety, then this individual has deteriorated. On the other hand, if this subject is now studying because of his increased anxiety and is meeting the demands that life is putting upon him in a more productive manner, one might consider him improved. *Deterioration must be viewed, then, relative to valued directions and degrees of change just as is the case with improvement.*

In examining deterioration in the present review, different rates of change can be seen to occur as a function of the criteria employed. Studies using instruments such as the Q sort, MMPI, or adjective checklists (e.g., Gottschalk, 1966; Jurjevich, 1968; Subotnik, 1972) report high rates of deterioration. This is a result of considering an increased scale score or additional complaints on an adjective checklist as evidence of worsening.

There is no agreement on how much change in a negative scale direction equals substantial deterioration, though some have argued for an operational definition of at least one standard deviation of negative change. Where such a definition is used or where more comprehensive judgments are employed, rates are lower. Even though global judgments of combined indices are open to question, they tend to make the reader more confident that a person judged "worse" is demonstrably worse.

One very promising use of complex and thorough criteria is that reported by Malan and his associates (Malan, Bacal, Heath, & Balfour, 1968; Malan, Heath, Bacal, & Balfour, 1975). These researchers have divided change criteria into 'symptomatic' and 'dynamic' categories. Symptomatic change was defined in the usual manner—i.e., that the complaints of a patient are improved or have disappeared; while dynamic change included both the patients' "disturbances" as well as connecting these to specific types of stress. Thus, a person's history of dealing with stress, frustration, and loss, along with the way he has handled these situational variables since treatment, are involved in the assessment of dynamic change. Using this procedure, an improvement rate of 69%, employing symptomatic criteria, changed to 26% when dynamic change was considered. While either method could be used to report outcome in a study, the second appears more thorough and perhaps more likely to lead to effective therapy. Lazarus (1971) reported work with his own clients and studied relapse in symptoms following treatment. Surprisingly, he found 36% had relapsed anywhere from 1 week to 6 years after therapy. Although in some cases the reasons for relapse were obscure, the majority deteriorated following some new stress-producing situation. Lazarus (1971) reports that *clients who were able to handle this stress without deterioration had undergone a change in outlook and philosophy of life, increased self-esteem and interpersonal skills. It may be argued that ti is these kinds of changes in psychotherapy which mitigate against deterioration during follow-up periods. Researchers would do well to study criteria of these types.*

Future studies need to employ change criteria which are both stringent and optimistic but not irrelevant or gross. Change measures which tap different areas of functioning cannot be expected to show identical outcomes. As has been noted earlier, the examination of variance in pre-test and post-test designs may enable the researcher to identify significant negative changes.

IMPLICATIONS FOR RESEARCH, TRAINING, AND CLINICAL PRACTICE

The many articles listed and discussed here, as well as the clinical material alluded to, lead to a number of concrete recommendations. Those for future research are most apparent. As the attention of researchers turns from studies of overall effects to more specific causal chains or cycles, the evidence for and information about negative therapeutic effects increase. Aside from general recommendations about psychotherapy research which have been expounded upon adequately elsewhere, the following suggestions are offered:

1. Researchers should examine and report the nature and extent of negative change in their therapeutic and control groups as a matter of course.

2. Studies which are sensitive to the presence of deterioration should be conducted, including experimental case studies with criteria that are individualized and related to causal factors.

3. There should be a more complete specification of outcome, which includes the examination of possible "side effects," much like those reported in chemotherapy—for example, positive change on one variable and negative on another.

4. Continued attempts should be made to identify therapist and patient types which interact to produce a negative outcome. While work in this area has yet to result in predictive information, continued efforts may someday repay the investment. The work on pathogenesis seems most promising to date.

5. There should be continued study of untreated subjects. It is hoped that the course of a disorder may be so well defined that deviations from the typical course can indicate either therapeutic or deteriorative processes depending upon the direction of the change.

6. There should be continued studies of innovations and the use of unskilled or inexperienced "therapists" such as paraprofessionals.

It is more difficult to state the recommendations for training and selection. The fact that the earliest work in psychotherapy provided for careful selection and didactic training as well as experiential learning informs one of the early concerns and cautions in this area. We favor the collection and continued publication of predictive work in this area.

Training programs in the helping professions,

by and large, continue to use primarily academic criteria to select candidates for graduate training. This is reasonable given the difficulties in agreeing upon personal qualities which would disqualify a person from the helping role. The difficulty in predicting a deteriorative relationship and the lack of specificity in attributing causality in the process are additional perplexing problems. And yet even our current shallow understanding of this process can offer some guidelines.

Some core personal attitudes are well recognized and accepted as necessary. Such therapist variables as empathy, warmth, acceptance, and the like have been and can continue to be assessed in the selection procedure through role-play, interview, or by a number of other devices. Continued experimentation with these procedures using subjects from a variety of professions and theoretical orientations and with diverse measuring instruments is needed. Too many conclusions have been based upon the research efforts of a few. The work of Karon and Vandebos (1972) represents a divergent but promising method of selection and prediction. We view the current trend for encounter group leaders and the like (requiring more psychologically oriented, professional backgrounds) as necessary but by no means sufficient.

There is a need to help trainees become aware of their strengths and weaknesses and to encourage them to develop their skills rather than to mold them in the way of their supervisors along cherished theoretical lines. While all recommend selection of trainees who are "mentally healthy," the research on variables such as having had therapy, high intelligence, etc., is contradictory. This area promises to be a difficult and challenging research domain.

A Final Note

When deterioration is examined from the perspective of increased variance, therapist traits, and the like, it is too easy to miss the very real pain and waste which are at the core of such an experience.

Unfortunately, the present situation is almost totally out of control. Despite the existence of laws regulating the practice of psychology, social work, and psychiatry, essentially nothing prevents a licensed practitioner from originating a new technique, claiming cures, and using it widely on clients. Even more distressing is the fact that thousands of unlicensed persons are now practicing their own versions of psycho-logical therapy under titles and guises that are not legally controlled. For example, in most states there is little or no legal control over such titles as psychotherapist, counselor, group leader, interpersonal relations consultant, marital therapist, hypnotherapist, analyst, etc. Many individuals with such titles may be perfectly legitimate, but the looseness of legal controls has made it possible for both the charlatan and the well-intentioned but inadequately trained person to operate under such professional sounding but misleading rubrics.

There is a real danger in this for those who are seeking improved adjustment—namely, that commercialization of therapy will lead to the idea that one can trade in an old self or lifestyle for new ones just as one might exchange an old car for the new model. Such simplifications of reality are already evident in the so-called human potential movement of which the Stanford encounter groups are one example. Unfortunately, such ideas lead one to believe that change is easier than it is and that the outcomes will be rosier than they are likely to be. Some of the Stanford casualties were persons whose expectations of salvation by therapy were so exaggerated that their hopes eventually had to be dashed by reality. A more sober analysis reveals that answers to life's problems are not simple, that change is not easy, and that lasting resilient adjustment is gained more by persistent effort than by brief episodes of therapeutic ecstasy.

Regrettably, there is no psychological equivalent of a Food and Drug Administration to monitor therapy methods and root out unproven claims or mispractices. University selection procedures, standards of professional societies, and state licensing laws accomplish this to some degree but these efforts too often are inadequate to cope with the problem. Fortunately, many universities and training programs now screen potential therapists for personal qualities in addition to the traditional academic credentials, and state licensing exams are increasingly devoted to field tests under observation rather than paper-and-pencil exams. It is important to keep the pressure on for the expansion of such procedures.

In the meantime, it is vital that professionals and the public press for uniform state licensing laws that demand quality therapeutic performance prior to licensure and that restrict unlicensed use of therapy techniques. Until that is done, it is a "buyer beware" situation that calls for educated judgment. The best that the therapy consumer can do is select a person duly licensed or certified by the state in one of the major professions like psychology, social work, or psychiatry and who has a local reputation among knowledgeable people for getting good results. Fortunately, there are enough good therapists around so that careful selection should yield a high chance of positive outcomes.

Finally, it is imperative that we continue looking at the process of psychotherapy from various viewpoints. The study of negative effects, although distasteful, has proven instructive. Continued work in this area will repay the effort.

REFERENCES

ABRAMOWITZ, S. I., WIETZ, L. J., & JAMES, C. R. Supervisor self-concept and self-concept deterioration among psychotherapy trainees. Unpublished manuscript, Vanderbilt University, 1974.

AGRAS, W. S., CHAPIN, H. N., & OLIVEAU, D. C. The natural history of phobia: Course and prognosis. *Archives of General Psychiatry*, 1970, **26**, 315–317.

ARONSON, H., & WEINTRAUB, W. Patient changes during classical psychoanalysis as a function of initial status and duration of treatment. Unpublished manuscript, Psychiatric Institute, University of Maryland School of Medicine, 1968.

BANDURA, A. *Principles of behavior modification*. New York: Holt, Rinehart & Winston, 1969.

BANKS, W. M. The differential effects of race and social class in helping. *Journal of Clinical Psychology*, 1972, **28**, 90–92.

BARRON, F., & LEARY, T. F. Changes in psychoneurotic patients with and without psychotherapy. *Journal of Consulting Psychology*, 1955, **19**, 239–245.

BERGIN, A. E. The effects of psychotherapy: Negative results revisited. *Journal of Counseling Psychology*, 1963, **10**, 244–250.

BERGIN, A. E. Some implications of psychotherapy for therapeutic practice. *Journal of Abnormal Psychology*, 1966, **71**, 235–246.

BERGIN, A. E. Further comments on psychotherapy research and therapeutic practice. *International Journal of Psychiatry*, 1967, **3**, 317–323.

BERGIN, A. E. The deterioration effect: A reply to Braucht. *Journal of Abnormal Psychology*, 1970, **75**, 300–302.

BERGIN, A. E. The evaluation of therapeutic outcomes. In A. E. BERGIN & S. L. GARFIELD (Eds.), *Handbook of psychotherapy and behavior change*. New York: Wiley, 1971.

BERGIN, A. E., & JASPER, L. G. Correlates of empathy in psychotherapy: A replication. *Journal of Abnormal Psychology*, 1969, **74**, 477–481.

BERGIN, A. E., & SUINN, R. M. Individual psychotherapy and behavior therapy. *Annual Review of Psychology*, 1975, **26**, 509–556.

BERLEMAN, W. C., & STEINBURN, T. W. The execution and evaluation of a delinquency prevention program. *Social Problems*, 1967, **14**, 413–423.

BOWDEN, C. I., ENDICOTT, J., & SPITZER, R. L. A-B therapist variable and psychotherapeutic outcome. *Journal of Nervous and Mental Disease*, 1972, **154**, 276–286.

BOYD, J. B., & ELLIS, J. D. Findings of research into senior management seminars. Toronto: Hydro-Electric Power Commission of Ontario, 1962.

BRAUCHT, G. N. The deterioration effect: A reply to Bergin. *Journal of Abnormal Psychology*, 1970, **75**, 293–299.

BRUCH, H. Perils of behavior modification in anorexia nervosa. *Journal of the American Medical Association*, 1974, **230**, 1419–1422.

BRYSON, S., & CODY, J. Relationships of race and level of understanding between counselor and client. *Journal of Counseling Psychology*, 1973, **10**, 495–498.

BUTLER, J. M., & HAIGH, G. Changes in the relation between self-concepts consequent upon client-centered counseling. In C. R. ROGERS & R. DYMOND (Eds.), *Psychotherapy and personality change*. Chicago: University of Chicago Press, 1954.

CAMPBELL, J. P., & DUNNETT, M. D. Effectiveness of T-group experiences in managerial training and development. *Psychological Bulletin*, 1968, **70**, 73–104.

CARKHUFF, R. R. *Helping and human relations: Practice and research*. New York: Holt, Rinehart & Winston, 1969.

CARKHUFF, R. R., & TRUAX, C. B. Lay mental health counseling: The effects of lay group counseling. *Journal of Consulting Psychology*, 1965, **29**, 426–431.

CARTWRIGHT, D. S. Note on "changes of psychoneurotic patients with and without psychotherapy." *Journal of Consulting Psychology*, 1956, **20**, 403–404.

CARTWRIGHT, R. D., & LERNER, B. Empathy, need to change, and improvement with psychotherapy. *Journal of Consulting Psychology*, 1963, **27**, 138–144.

CARTWRIGHT, R. D., & VOGEL, J. L. A comparison of changes in psychoneurotic patients during matched periods of therapy and no therapy. *Journal of Consulting Psychology*, 1960, **24**, 121–127.

CRAWSHAW, R. How sensitive is sensitivity training? *American Journal of Psychiatry*, 1969, **124**, 868–873.

DESROSIERS, R. Y. A study of the personal growth of counseling trainees as a function of the level of facilitative conditions offered by their supervisors. Unpublished doctoral dissertation, University of Oregon, 1968.

DI LORETO, A. O. *Comparative psychotherapy*. Chicago: Aldine, 1971.

ENDICOTT, N. A., & ENDICOTT, J. "Improvement" in untreated psychiatric patients. *Archives of General Psychiatry*, 1963, **9**, 575–585.

EYSENCK, H. J. The effects of psychotherapy: An evaluation. *Journal of Consulting Psychology*, 1952, **16**, 319–324.

EYSENCK, H. J. The non-professional psychotherapist. *International Journal of Psychiatry*, 1967, **3**, 150–153.

FAIRWEATHER, G., SIMON, R., GEBHARD, M. E., WEINGARTEN, E., HOLLAND, J. L., SANDERS, R., STONE, G. B., & REAHL, J. E. Relative effectiveness of psychotherapeutic programs: A multicriteria comparison of four programs for three different patient groups. *Psychological Monographs: General and Applied*, 1960, **74** (5, Whole No. 492).

FEIFEL, H., & EELLS, J. Patients and therapists assess the same psychotherapy. *Journal of Consulting Psychology*, 1963, **27**, 310–318.

FEIGHNER, J. P., BROWN, S. L., & OLIVIER, J. E. Electrosleep therapy. *Journal of Nervous and Mental Disease*, 1973, **157**, 121–128.

FRANK, J. D. Does psychotherapy work? *International Journal of Psychiatry*, 1967, **3**, 153–155.

FRIEDMAN, D. E., & LIPSEDGE, M. S. Treatment of phobic anxiety and psychogenic impotency by systematic desensitization employing methohexitone-induced relaxation. *British Journal of Psychiatry*, 1971, **118**, 87–90.

GARFIELD, S. L., & BERGIN, A. E. Therapeutic conditions and outcome. *Journal of Abnormal Psychology*, 1971, **77**, 108–114.

GIBB, J. R. The effects of human relations training. In A. E. BERGIN & S. L. GARFIELD (Eds.), *Handbook of psychotherapy and behavior change*. New York: Wiley, 1971.

GIEL, R., KNOX, R., & CARSTAIRS, G. A 5-year follow-up of 100 neurotic out-patients. *British Medical Journal*, 1964, **2**, 160–163.

GOLDSTEIN, A. P. *Psychotherapeutic attraction*. New York: Pergamon Press, 1971.

GOTTMAN, J. M. N-of-one and N-of-two research in psychotherapy. *Psychological Bulletin*, 1973, **80**, 90–105.

GOTTSCHALK, A. Psychoanalytic notes on T-groups at the

human relations laboratory, Bethel, Maine. *Comprehensive Psychiatry*, 1966, **7**, 472–487.

GOTTSCHALK, L. A., MAYERSON, P., & GOTTLIEB, A. A. Prediction and evaluation of outcome in an emergency brief psychotherapy clinic. *Journal of Nervous and Mental Disease*, 1967, **144**, 77–96.

GURMAN, A. S. Group marital therapy: Clinical and empirical implications for outcome research. *International Journal of Group Psychotherapy*, 1971, **11**, 174–189.

GURMAN, A. S. The effects and effectiveness of marital therapy: A review of outcome research. *Family Process*, 1973, **12**, 145–170.

GURMAN, A. S. Evaluating the outcomes of marital therapy. In A. S. GURMAN (chair), *Research in marital and family therapy*. Workshop presented at the Sixth Annual Meeting of the Society for Psychotherapy Research, Boston, June 1975.

GUTTMAN, H. A. A contraindication for family therapy. The prepsychotic or postpsychotic young adult and his parents. *Archives of General Psychiatry*, 1973, **29**, 352–355.

HARTLEY, D., ROBACK, H. B., & ABRAMOWITZ, S. I. Deterioration effects in encounter groups. *American Psychologist*, 1976, **31**, 247–255.

HEILBRUN, A. B. Female preference for therapist interview style as a function of "client" and therapist social role variables. *Journal of Counseling Psychology*, 1971, **18**, 285–291.

HEILBRUN, A. B. History of self-disclosure in females and early defection from psychotherapy. *Journal of Counseling Psychology*, 1973, **20**, 250–257.

HELLER, K., MYERS, R. A., & KLINE, L. Interviewer behavior as a function of standardized client roles. *Journal of Consulting Psychology*, 1963, **27**, 117–122.

HENRY, W. E., & SHLIEN, J. M. Affective complexity and psychotherapy: Some comparisons of time-limited and unlimited treatment. *Journal of Projective Techniques*, 1958, **22**, 153–162.

HERSEN, M., EISLER, R. M., & MILLER, P. M. (Eds.) *Progress in behavior modification*. Vol. 1. New York: Academic Press, 1975.

HORWITZ, L. *Clinical prediction in psychotherapy*. New York: Aronson, 1974.

IMBER, S. D., FRANK, J. D., NASH, E. H., STONE, A. R., & BLIEDMAN, L. H. Improvement and amount of therapeutic contact: An alternative to the use of no-treatment controls in psychotherapy. *Journal of Consulting Psychology*, 1957, **21**, 309–315.

JEWELL, W. O. Differential judgments of manifest anxiety, defensiveness, and effective problem solving in counseling. Unpublished doctoral dissertation, University of Minnesota, 1968.

JOFFE, S. L., & SCHERL, D. J. Acute psychosis precipitated by T-group experience. *Archives of General Psychiatry*, 1969, **21**, 443–448.

JONCKHEERE, P. Considerations sur la psychotherapie. *Acta Neurologica et Psychiatria Belgica*, 1965, **65**, 667–684.

JOURARD, S. M. Changing personal worlds. *Cornell Journal of Social Relations*, 1973, **8**, 1–11.

JURJEVICH, R. M. Changes in psychiatric symptoms without psychotherapy. In S. LESSE (Ed.), *An evaluation of the results of the psychotherapies*. Springfield, Ill.: Thomas, 1968.

KARON, B. D., & VANDENBOS, G. R. The consequences of psychotherapy for schizophrenic patients. *Psychotherapy: Theory, Research and Practice*, 1972, **9**, 111–119.

KERNBERG, O. F. Summary and conclusion of "psychotherapy and psychoanalysis, final report of the Menninger Foundation's Psychotherapy Research Project. *International Journal of Psychiatry*, 1973, **11**, 62–77.

KOEGLER, R., & BRILL, N. *Treatment of psychiatric outpatients*. New York: Appleton-Century-Crofts, 1967.

KREBS, R. L. Some effects of a white institution on black psychiatric outpatients. *American Journal of Orthopsychiatry*, 1971, **41**, 589–596.

KRINGLEN, E. Obsessional neurosis: A long-term follow-up. *British Journal of Psychiatry*, 1965, **111**, 709–714.

LAMBERT, M. J. Spontaneous remission in adult neurotic disorder: A summary and revision. *Psychological Bulletin*, 1976, **83**, 107–119.

LAMBERT, M. J., & BERGIN, A. E. Psychotherapeutic outcomes and issues related to behavioral and humanistic approaches. *Cornell Journal of Social Relations*, 1973, **8**, 47–61.

LAZARUS, A. A. *Behavior therapy and beyond*. New York: McGraw-Hill, 1971.

LIEBERMAN, M. A., YALOM, I. D., & MILES, M. B. *Encounter groups: First facts*. New York: Basic Books, 1973.

LING, T. M., ZAUSMER, D. M., & HOPE, M. Occupational rehabilitation of psychiatric cases: A follow-up study of 115 cases. *American Journal of Psychiatry*, 1952, **109**, 172–176.

LUBORSKY, L. Perennial mystery of poor agreement among criteria for psychotherapy outcome. *Journal of Consulting and Clinical Psychology*, 1971, **37**, 316–319.

MALAN, D. H. Therapeutic factors in analytical oriented brief psychotherapy. In R. GOSLING (Ed.), *Support, innovation and autonomy: Tavistock Clinic golden jubilee papers*. London: Tavistock, 1973.

MALAN, D. H., BACAL, H. A., HEATH, E. S., & BALFOUR, F. H. G. A study of psychodynamic changes in untreated patients—I. *British Journal of Psychiatry*, 1968, **114**, 525–551.

MALAN, D., HEATH, E. S., BACAL, H. A., & BALFOUR, F. H. G. Psychodynamic changes in untreated neurotic patients—II. Apparently genuine improvements. *Archives of General Psychiatry*, 1975, **32**, 110–126.

MARKS, I. Phobic disorders four years after treatment: A prospective follow-up. *British Journal of Psychiatry*, 1971, **118**, 683–688.

MASSERMAN, J. H., & CARMICHAEL, H. T. Diagnosis and prognosis in psychiatry: With a follow-up study of the results of short term and general hospital therapy of psychiatric cases. *Journal of Mental Science*, 1938, **84**, 893–896.

MATARAZZO, J. D. Some psychotherapists make patients worse! *International Journal of Psychiatry*, 1967, **3**, 156–157.

MAY, R. R. A. For better or for worse? Psychotherapy and variance change: A critical review of the literature. *The Journal of Nervous and Mental Disease*, 1971, **152**, 184–192.

MAYER, J., & TIMMS, J. E. *The client speaks: Workingclass impression of casework*. London: Routledge and Kegan Paul, 1970.

McNAIR, D. M., LORR, M., & CALLAHAN, D. M. Patient and therapist influences on quitting psychotherapy. *Journal of Consulting Psychology*, 1963, **27**, 10–17.

MELTZOFF, J., & KORNREICH, M. *Research in psychotherapy*. New York: Atherton Press, 1970.

MENDELSOHN, G. A., & GELLER, M. H. Similarity, missed sessions, and early termination. *Journal of Counseling Psychology*, 1967, **14**, 210–215.

MINK, O. G., & ISAKSEN, H. L. A comparison of effectiveness of nondirective therapy and clinical counseling in the junior high school. *School Counselor*, 1959, **6**, 12–14.

MYERS, J. K., & AULD, F., JR. Some variables related to outcome of psychotherapy. *Journal of Clinical Psychology*, 1955, **11**, 51–54.

N.T.L. *Institute News and Reports*, 1969, **3**, 1.

O'BRIEN, C. P. HAMM, K. B., RAY, B. A., PIERCE, J. F., LUBORSKY, L., & MINTZ, J. Group vs. individual psychotherapy with schizophrenics. *Archives of General Psychiatry*, 1972, **27**, 474–478.

PALMER, J. O. *The psychological assessment of children*. New York: Wiley, 1970.

PAUL, G. L. Insight versus desensitization in psychotherapy two years after termination. *Journal of Consulting Psychology*, 1967, **31**, 333–348.

PAUL, G. L. Two-year follow-up of systematic desensitization in therapy groups. *Journal of Abnormal Psychology*, 1968, **73**, 119–130.

PIERCE, R. M., & SCHAUBLE, P. G. Graduate training of facilitative counselors: The effect of individual supervision. *Journal of Counseling Psychology*, 1970, **17**, 210–215.

POWERS, E., & WITMER, H. *An experiment in the prevention of delinquency.* New York: Columbia University Press, 1951.

PRESTON, M. G., MUDD, E. H., & FROSCHER, H. B. Factors affecting movement in casework. *Social Casework*, 1953, **34**, 103–111.

RACHMAN, S. J. The effects of psychological treatment. In H. EYSENCK (Ed.), *Handbook of abnormal psychology.* New York: Basic Books, 1973.

RACHMAN, S., TEASDALE, J. *Aversion therapy and behavior disorders: An analysis.* Coral Gobles, Fla.: University of Miami Press, 1969.

REDING, G. R., CHARLES, L. A., & HOFFMAN, M. B. Treatment of the couple by a couple II. Conceptual framework, case presentation and follow-up study. *British Journal of Medical Psychology*, 1967, **40**, 243–251.

RICKS, D. F. Supershrink: Methods of a therapist judged successful on the basis of adult outcome of adolescent patients. In D. RICKS, M. ROFF, & A. THOMAS (Eds.), *Life history research in psychopathology.* Vol. III. Minneapolis: University of Minnesota Press, 1974.

RIESS, B. F. Some causes and correlates of psychotherapy termination: A study of 500 cases. *International Mental Health Research Newsletter*, 1973, **15**, 4–7.

ROGERS, C. R., and DYMOND, R. *Psychotherapy and personality change.* Chicago: University of Chicago Press, 1954.

ROGERS, C. R., GENDLIN, E. T., KIESLER, D., & TRUAX, C. B. *The therapeutic relationship and its impact: A study of psychotherapy with schizophrenics.* Madison: University of Wisconsin Press, 1967.

ROSENBAUM, M., FRIEDLANDER, J., & KAPLAN, S. M. Evaluation of results of psychotherapy. *Psychosomatic Medicine*, 1956, **18**, 113–132.

ROSENTHAL, D. Changes in some moral values following psychotherapy. *Journal of Consulting Psychology*, 1955, **19**, 431–436.

SAGER, C. J., RIESS, B. F., & GUNDLACH, R. Follow-up study of the results of extramural analytic psychotherapy. *American Journal of Psychotherapy*, 1964, **18**, 161–173.

SASLOW, G., & PETERS, A. Follow-up of 'untreated' patients with behavior disorders. *Psychiatric Quarterly*, 1956, **30**, 283–302.

SCHULDT, W. J., & TRUAX, C. B. Variability of outcome in psychotherapeutic research. *Journal of Counseling Psychology*, 1970, **17**, 405–408.

SINES, L., SILVER, R., & LUCERO, R. The effect of therapeutic intervention by untrained "therapists." *Journal of Clinical Psychology*, 1961, **17**, 394–396.

SLOANE, R. B., STAPLES, F. R., CRISTOL, A. H., YORKSTON, N. J., & WHIPPLE, K. *Psychotherapy versus behavior therapy.* Cambridge, Mass.: Harvard University Press, 1975.

SNYDER, W. U. *The psychotherapy relationship.* New York: MacMillan, 1961.

STRUPP, H. H., WALLACH, M. S., & WOGAN, M. Psychotherapy experience in retrospect: Questionnaire survey of former patients and their therapists. *Psychological Monographs*, 1964, **78**, (11, Whole No. 588).

STUART, R. B., & LOTT, L. A. Behavioral contracting with delinquents: A cautionary note. *Journal of Behavior Therapy and Experimental Psychiatry*, 1972, **3**, 161–169.

SUBOTNIK, L. "Spontaneous Remission" of deviant MMPI profiles among college students. *Journal of Consulting and Clinical Psychology*, 1972, **38**, 191–201.

TARGOW, J. G., & ZWEBER, R. V. Participants' reactions to treatment in a married couples' group. *International Journal of Group Psychotherapy*, 1969, **19**, 221–225.

TRUAX, C. B. Effective ingredients in psychotherapy. *Journal of Counseling Psychology*, 1963, **10**, 256–263.

TRUAX, C. B. Research findings: Translations and premature translations into practice. *International Journal of Psychiatry*, 1967, **3**, 158–160.

TRUAX, C. B., & CARKHUFF, R. R. *Toward effective counseling and psychotherapy: Training and practice.* Chicago: Aldine, 1967.

TRUAX, C. B., & MITCHELL, K. M. Research on certain therapist interpersonal skills in relation to process and outcome. In A. E. BERGIN & S. L. GARFIELD (Eds.), *Handbook of psychotherapy and behavior change.* New York: Wiley, 1971. Pp. 299–334.

TRUAX, C. B., WARGO, D. G., FRANK, J. C., IMBER, S. D., BATTLE, C. C., HOEHN-SARIC, R., NASH, E. H., & STONE, A. R. Therapist empathy, genuineness, and warmth and patient outcome. *Journal of Consulting Psychology*, 1966, **30**, 395–401.

TRUAX, C. B., WARGO, D. G., & SILBER, L. Effects of high accurate empathy and non-possessive warmth during group psychotherapy upon female institutionalized delinquents. *Journal of Abnormal Psychology*, 1966, **71**, 267–274.

UHLENHUTH, E. H., & DUNCAN, D. B. Subjective change in psychoneurotic outpatients with medical students I. The kind, amount, and course of change. Unpublished manuscript, Johns Hopkins University, 1968.

UNDERWOOD, W. J. Evaluation of laboratory method training. *Training Directors Journal*, 1965, **19**, 34–40.

VANDENBOS, G. R., & KARON, B. P. Pathogenesis: A new therapist personality dimension related to therapeutic effectiveness. *Journal of Personality Assessment*, 1971, **35**, 252–260.

VARBLE, D. L., & LANDFIELD, A. W. Validity of the self-ideal discrepancy as a criterion measure for success in psychotherapy—a replication. *Journal of Counseling Psychology*, 1969, **16**, 150–156.

VOLSKY, T., JR., MAGOON, T. J., NORMAN, W. T., & HOYT, D. P. *The outcomes of counseling and psychotherapy.* Minneapolis: University of Minnesota Press, 1965.

WALLACH, M. S. Therapists' patient preferences and their relationship to two patient variables. *Journal of Clinical Psychology*, 1962, **18**, 497–501.

WARNE, M. M., CANTER, A. H., & WIZNIA, B. Analysis and follow-up of patients with psychiatric disorders. *American Journal of Psychotherapy*, 1953, **7**, 278–288.

WEBER, J. J., ELINSON, J., & MOSS, L. M. The application of ego strength scales of psychoanalytic clinic records. In G. S. GOLDMAN & D. SHAPIRO (Eds.), *Development in psychoanalysis at Columbia University: Proceedings of the 20th anniversary conference.* New York: Columbia Psychoanalytic Clinic for Training and Research, 1965.

WHITEHORN, J. C., & BETZ, B. Further studies of the doctor as a crucial variable in the outcome of treatment with schizophrenic patients. *American Journal of Psychiatry*, 1960, **117**, 215–223.

WINSTON, A., PARDES, H., & PAPERNICK, D. In-patient treatment of blacks and whites. *Archives of General Psychiatry*, 1972, **26**, 405–409.

WISPE, L. G., & PARLOFF, M. B. Impact of psychotherapy on the productivity of psychologists. *Journal of Abnormal Psychology*, 1965, **70**, 188–193.

YALOM, I. D., & LIEBERMAN, M. A. A study of encounter group casualties. *Archives of General Psychiatry*, 1971, **25**, 16–30.

EDITORS' REFERENCES

GURMAN, A. S., & RICE, D. G. (Eds.) *Couples in conflict: New directions in marital therapy.* New York: Aronson, 1975.

KIRESUK, T. J., & SHERMAN, R. E. Goal attainment scaling: A general method of evaluating comprehensive community mental health programs. *Community Mental Health Journal*, 1968, **4**, 443–453.

MINUCHIN, S. *Families and family therapy.* Cambridge, Mass.: Harvard University Press, 1974.

MINUCHIN, S., BAKER, L., ROSMAN, B. L., LIEBMAN, R., MILMAN, L., & TODD, T. C. A conceptual model of psychosomatic illness in children. Family organization and family therapy. *Archives of General Psychiatry*, 1975, **32**, 1031–1038.

NOTES

1. *Editors' Footnote.* In fact, even more recent research has found that the evidence long believed to be largely supportive of the client-centered "facilitative skills-outcome hypothesis" contains *major* methodological and theoretical flaws. Mitchell, Bozarth, and Krauft argue persuasively elsewhere in this volume (Chapter 18) that the client-centered hypothesis has never been adequately tested in that such theory speaks of *high* and *low* therapeutic conditions whereas, in reality, all the research in this area has examined outcome as a function of *high*er and *low*er levels of therapist interpersonal skill—i.e., no more than a handful of studies have actually included therapists who were *high* in these styles of relating. The reader interested in these variables as part of the "therapist's contribution" to deterioration is encouraged to consider Mitchell *et al.*'s argument carefully.

2. *Editors' Footnote.* We think that this is the most enlightened view of the variance issue yet put forth. The methodological-empirical implications of the Lambert-Bergin-Collins position are clear; moreover, we think that their views should indirectly serve as an important reminder to researchers of the idiosyncratic nature of therapeutic change, both positive and negative. When we speak of deterioration as clinicians, we are concerned not with group averages, but with the phenomenology and experience of unique individuals. A relatively recently developed research methodology for assessing change that allows the specification of treatment goals and outcomes in an individualized yet standardized fashion is that of Kiresuk and his colleagues (Kiresuk & Sherman, 1968), whose work is recommended to the reader.

3. *Editors' Footnote.* It is implied here that the treatment (desensitization) "caused" the development of significant depression. In fact, Marks explicitly stated in his report, "It should also be noted that *many patients had had depressive episodes before they ever had treatment*" (emphasis supplied). Thus, an equally likely explanation of the outcomes found by Marks would be not that desensitization "caused" depression, but that pre-existing depressive illness (in the patients who worsened) was either improperly diagnosed or inappropriately treated. It is a well-known clinical fact that severe phobic reactions are often manifestations of a more basic depressive picture and are often responsive to tricyclic antidepressants. Thus, rather than standing as evidence for the possible harmful effects of behavioral therapies, this study impresses us as an excellent example of both the limitations of single modality therapies and the misapplications of potentially powerful treatment techniques.

4. *Editors' Footnote.* Bruch's study, like that of Marks noted above, similarly strikes as persuasive not so much of the lack of power of particular behavioral techniques and principles or of the dangers inherent therein, but as indicative of the poorly conceived *use* of these techniques. Thus, for example, the same behavioral techniques criticized by Bruch are used by Minuchin, Baker, Rosman, Liebman, Milman, & Todd, (1975) as *one component* in this impressively successful family therapy treatment of anorectics. Thus, we would argue that most of the evidence for the deteriorative effects of behavioral interventions speaks primarily to the issue of the *therapist's* (rather than the technique's) contribution to deterioration, deriving from deficiencies in the therapist's diagnostic acumen (e.g., misdiagnosis of the underlying depression in Marks' subjects), or too narrow or inappropriate conceptualizations of specific disorders (e.g., insensitivity to the complex but predictable behavior-maintaining systems dynamics of anorectic families). It is not our intention here to defend the behavior therapies, but to underscore the salience of the human side of the most "technical" of psychotherapeutic interventions.

5. *Editors' Footnote.* As noted earlier, see Mitchell *et al.* (Chapter 18, this volume) for a sobering analysis of this area.

6. *Editors' Footnote.* See Sundland (Chapter 9, this volume) for a thorough empirical documentation of this fact.

7. *Editors' Footnote.* Readers who are conversant with the properties and dimensions of marital and family *systems* will readily understand the meaning of this finding. Several excellent recent texts consider this issue in detail (see, e.g., Gurman & Rice, 1975; Minuchin, 1974).

8. *Editors' Footnote.* Deterioration was defined in different ways in these studies; some focused on negative change within individuals (e.g., increased depression, lower self-esteem), while others involved dyadic or system changes (e.g., decreased role flexibility). In any case, it is certainly true that the rationales for considering changes to have been negative were rarely explicit and often were theoretically deficient. Because of the value-laden nature of marriage, it is extremely important that more refined criteria for both positive and negative change in couple's therapy be developed.

9. *Editors' Footnote.* While we accept this definition of deterioration, it is not as clear as is implied here that a higher success rate should have been expected for Whitehorn and Betz' schizophrenic patients. Furthermore, there is no evidence in the Whitehorn-Betz work that the *attitudes* of the low-success physicians accounted for the rates of change. More importantly, it is highly questionable that there are real outcome differences between As and Bs; see Razin (Chapter 12, this volume) for a comprehensive critical analysis of the A-B research.

10. *Editors' Footnote.* See Auerbach and Johnson (Chapter 5, this volume) for a persuasive argument that challenges this commonly held belief.

11. *Editors' Footnote.* For a fuller discussion of this issue, see Garfield's (Chapter 4) review of research on the training of professional therapists and Anthony and Carkhuff's (Chapter 6) analysis of the effectiveness of functional (nonprofessional) therapeutic agents in this volume.

12. *Editors' Footnote.* For a comprehensive analysis of this area, see Sattler (Chapter 11, this volume).

CHAPTER 18

A REAPPRAISAL OF THE THERAPEUTIC EFFECTIVENESS OF ACCURATE EMPATHY, NONPOSSESSIVE WARMTH, AND GENUINENESS

Kevin M. Mitchell, Jerold D. Bozarth,
and
Conrad C. Krauft

Following upon the pioneering work of Carl Rogers (1951, 1957, 1962), a large amount of research was generated by his students and others during the 1960s which focused, in particular, upon the effectiveness of levels of accurate empathy, nonpossessive warmth, and genuineness.

Truax and Mitchell's (1971) summary of the literature was reflective of the research dealing with empathy, warmth, and genuineness through 1970. They concluded that:

> therapists or counselors who are accurately empathic, non-possessively warm in attitude and genuine are indeed effective. Also, these findings seem to hold with a wide variety of therapists and counselors, regardless of their training or theoretic orientation, and with a wide variety of clients or patients, including college under-achievers, juvenile delinquents, hospitalized schizo-phrenics, college counselees, mild to severe outpatient neurotics, and a mixed variety of hospitalized patients. Further, the evidence suggests that these findings hold in a variety of therapeutic contexts and in both individual and group psychotherapy or counseling. (p. 310)

These earlier studies, then, have been adequately summarized elsewhere (Carkhuff, 1969a, 1969b; Truax & Mitchell, 1971) and need not be examined again, *per se*, in this chapter. However, that *body* of research needs comment in light of more recent work. Most were *outcome* studies. Indeed, Truax and Mitchell (1971) wrote: "Throughout, we have kept outcome in clear view. In our opinion, process studies are important if and only if the process variables can be related to positive or negative client change" (p. 301). The importance of the early outcome studies cannot be exaggerated. Not only are they to this day the clearest answer to Eysenck's (1966) criticisms of the effectiveness of psychotherapy, but they comprise, in a very real sense, the introduction of the *scientific* study of psychotherapy.

Nevertheless, there was an unwarranted em-phasis on gross outcome studies, and a con-comitant lack of an orderly examination of the precise correlates of the relationship between empathy, warmth, and genuineness and out-come. For example, demographic and process studies were ignored which might have answered the question: "Which therapists, under what conditions, with which clients in what kinds of specific predicaments, need to reach what levels of these interpersonal skills to effect what kinds of client changes?" The extent of the emphasis on outcome led to two conclusions which, it was implied, were unequivocal: (1) the therapist's interpersonal skills are both necessary and sufficient conditions for positive client change, and (2) this holds, to one degree or another, across all major therapist orientations and client problems.

There were, however, early reservations about this position (Matarazzo, 1971; Meltzoff & Kornreich, 1970). They questioned the validity of many of the studies. They suggested that, in many cases, the number of therapists was small and, in an unknown number of instances, the therapists may have been aware of the particular hypotheses and even associated with the re-search effort. An additional problem of the ut-most importance is the degree to which the therapists in these studies valued the interper-sonal skills in question. No attempt has been made to determine this in the earlier outcome studies or in any of those cited in this chapter.

More recent outcome studies, based on samples of therapists of widely divergent orient-ations, and including therapist characteristics in addition to empathy, warmth, and genuine-ness, would seem to indicate that neither con-clusion can stand without qualification. As we shall see, evaluating the effectiveness of any single therapist, client, or situational variable is a highly complex endeavor. As outcome studies examine the relationships among therapist orientations, client predicaments, and therapist settings in increasing detail, it seems to us to be increasingly clear that *the mass of data neither supports nor rejects the overriding influence of such variables as empathy, warmth, and genuineness in all cases.* The studies supporting this conclusion will be described in more detail later in this chapter. *The recent evidence, although equivocal, does seem to suggest that empathy, warmth, and genuineness are related in some way to client change but that their potency and generalizability are not as great as once thought.*

AN OVERVIEW OF THE PRESENT CHAPTER

Much of the research from 1970 to early 1975 has a narrower focus. We feel, however, that the endeavor has been quite fruitful. One question raised in the recent research, for example, is: In precisely what situations and in association with what other variables are empathy, warmth, and genuineness related to client change during, at the termination of, and following psychotherapy? Another basic consideration is the construct validity of the most commonly used measures of these skills.

The areas of greatest interest to us are: (1) recent conflicting outcome studies, (2) methodological problems (e.g., questions of construct validity; statistical and conceptual independence of empathy, warmth, and genuineness), (3) therapist-determined and/or "other"-determined skills stability (i.e., are levels of empathy, warmth, and genuineness primarily a function of the therapist or an interaction among therapist, type of client, and therapy context), (4) training effects, (5) the interpersonal skills as reinforcers, and (6) the potency of the interpersonal skills in contexts other than traditional psychotherapy (e.g., behavior therapy).

DEFINITIONS OF EMPATHY, WARMTH, AND GENUINENESS

Only brief definitions of the Truax[1] scales (Truax & Carkhuff 1967) are given in this chapter. The more complete, level-by-level definitions are available in Truax and Carkhuff (1967), Truax and Mitchell (1971), Bozarth and Krauft (1972b), and Bozarth (1974).

These therapist conditions can be defined briefly as:

Accurate Empathy—the extent to which the therapist (1) is sensitive to the current feelings and thoughts of the helpee (both those in and those out of awareness), (2) has the ability to communicate his understanding of his client's feelings and thinking, and (3) has the ability to use language attuned to that of the client.

Nonpossessive Warmth—the extent to which the therapist communicates a nonevaluative caring and positive regard for the client as a person, although not necessarily condoning his behavior.

Genuineness—the extent to which the therapist is not "defensive" or "phony" in his interactions with his client.

Carkhuff and his colleagues (1969a, 1969b) have made some changes in the Truax scales. However, it is questionable whether these differences are as substantive as has been claimed. The majority of the studies in this chapter used as measures of empathy, warmth, and genuineness independent ratings of tape-recorded psychotherapy excerpts based on either the Truax or Carkhuff scales.

RECENT OUTCOME STUDIES

A brief summary statement of our understanding of the recent literature relating to *adult* individual psychotherapy might be helpful. We shall describe some of these studies in more detail below. Some studies continue to support the earlier findings that one or more of the interpersonal skills are related directly to positive client outcome (Bozarth & Rubin, in press; Cairns, 1972; Minsel, Bommert, Bastine, Langer, Nickel, & Tausch, 1972; Truax, 1970; Truax & Wittmer, 1971; Truax, Wittmer, & Wargo, 1971). Additional studies can be taken as offering some support (Altmann, 1973; Mitchell, Truax, Bozarth, & Krauft, 1973; Truax, Altmann, Wright, & Mitchell, 1973). Finally, there is a growing body of research which appears to be consistent in finding little or no direct relationship between the interpersonal skills and outcome (Beutler, Johnson, Neville, & Workman, 1972; Beutler, Johnson, Neville, Workman, & Elkins, 1973; Garfield & Bergin, 1971; Kurtz & Grummon, 1972; Mintz, Luborsky, & Auerbach, 1971; Mullen & Abeles, 1971; Sloane, Staples, Cristol, Yorkston, & Whipple, 1975).

Many of these findings need some qualification, however. Mintz *et al.* (1971) did not use either the Truax or Carkhuff empathy scales but, instead, used one which in another study (Bachrach, Mintz, & Luborsky, 1971) was found to correlate nearly perfectly with the

Truax scale. The therapists in the Garfield and Bergin (1971) and Mitchell *et al.* (1973) studies were markedly lower on the interpersonal skills than most of the therapists in the early studies. Most of the latter study's "high-functioning" therapists, in fact, were nonfacilitative (i.e., below the scales' midpoints). Thus, it could be argued that such studies do not test the general hypothesis in question. On the other hand, therapists in the Kurtz and Grummon (1972) and Sloane *et al.* (1975) studies generally were higher than the average reported in the literature. The Kurtz and Grummon therapists were not facilitative, however, according to the criteria promulgated by Carkhuff (1969a, 1969b) (i.e., 3.0 or above on 5-point scales), whereas the Sloane *et al.* therapists were facilitative according to the operational scale definitions (Truax & Mitchell, 1971).

Possible explanations for the lowered interpersonal skill scores will be offered later. One possibility which needs further research is that the proportion of therapists scoring lower than the average on empathy, warmth, and genuineness may tend to increase as the sample of therapists becomes more heterogeneous.

Turning to individual child psychotherapy, although very little work has been done in this area, what has been done is largely consistent with the most recent outcome studies dealing with adult psychotherapy. Siegel (1972) found improvement among children with learning disabilities in both verbal and behavioral spheres related to time in play therapy and therapist levels of empathy, warmth, and genuineness. Truax *et al.* (1973) found, at best, mixed results. Independent psychometrists' assessment of change failed to indicate significant improvement as a function of either the therapy or the therapeutic conditions. Although the therapists themselves were quite enthusiastic in their assessment of their clients' improvement, improvement was, at best, modestly related to the three therapeutic conditions. Interestingly, the children's parents also perceived improvement, and they were more likely to relate that improvement to therapists' levels of empathy, warmth, and genuineness. Clearly, a problem with this study is that those sources who saw the most improvement were also those persons who likely had the greatest investment in seeing the therapy as effective. The finding that the parents' perception of improvement was related to the interpersonal skills is quite interesting. On what basis did the parents perceive improvement *differentially* as a function of the interpersonal

skills? Perhaps we should reexamine possible relationships between child therapists and parents, despite the fact that therapist-parent contact usually is minimal.

The Arkansas Psychotherapy Study[2]

We would like to describe one outcome study in greater detail because it was designed specifically to examine the relationship between differential *levels* of empathy, warmth, and genuineness and client change. The study had an unusually large sample of experienced therapists and clients who appeared to be reasonably representative of those populations of therapists and clients engaged in psychotherapy during the late 1960s (Mitchell *et al.*, 1973).

Therapists. From the 1966 American Psychological and Psychiatric Association Directories, a large number of psychologists and psychiatrists were asked to participate in an NIMH-supported psychotherapy project. They were chosen randomly from both directories if they indicated that the practice of psychotherapy was a primary interest. Demographic characteristics of the 75 therapists who generated data for the outcome portion of the project included: 95% had a PhD or MD; median age was 42; 49% were in private practice. Approximately 55% had had at least 3 years of supervised psychotherapy experience, and 44% reported that they tape-recorded their psychotherapy either "frequently" or "routinely." Finally, with respect to *present* practice orientation, 36% referred to themselves as primarily eclectic and 34% were psychoanalytically oriented. The remaining 30% described their orientation as behavioral, existential, Sullivanian, transactional, rational-emotive, and Gestalt. Only 7% were client-centered.[3]

Regarding representativeness of the sample of therapists, they were compared on a number of demographic characteristics with four groups of therapists who varied along a continuum that might best be described as willingness to participate in the study: (1) those who responded to the initial invitation by indicating definitely that they would not participate ($n=80$); (2) those who initially indicated that they might participate and subsequently did not ($n=47$); (3) those who did not respond to the initial invitation to participate in the research project, but who did complete a second biographical information form (BI) sent specifically for the purpose of determining the demographic representativeness of the project sample ($n=60$); and (4) those who did not complete either the first or second BI but who agreed to answer the items during a telephone interview ($n = 61$).

The five groups of therapists were compared on (1) age, (2) sex, (3) marital status, (4) therapist paternal socioeconomic background, (5) present social class of the therapist's typical client, (6) training orientation, (7) practice orientation, (8) number of years of supervised psychotherapy experience, (9) degree, (10) type of practice or setting, (11) amount of past tape recording, and (12) diagnosis of the therapist's *typical* client. Only *age* ($F = 3.53$, $p < .01$) and *mean number of years of supervised psychotherapy training* ($F = 2.42$, $p < .05$) were significantly differentiated among the five groups. The project participants were younger than those therapists who responded to the initial invitation by indicating that they definitely would not participate. Such a difference, however, must be viewed in light of the fact that the present therapists were experienced therapists whose median age was 42. The present therapists were also those who, on the average, had received the least amount of supervised psychotherapy training, but the largest difference between any two groups was less than 1 year.

It should be mentioned that, despite the fact that the present therapists appeared to be quite representative of the population of therapists from whom they were drawn as far as relevant demographic variables were concerned, they made up only 5% of all those therapists who were asked initially to participate. No doubt they differed along some dimensions which were not measured.

Clients. Demographic characteristics of the 120 outcome clients included: 80% under age 35; 99% white; 59% female; and 80% reporting an income of $7,000 or less per year. Diagnostically, 37% were schizophrenic, 5% manic-depressive, 29% neurotic, 13% sociopathic personality, and 16% were judged to be "normal." For 22%, the length of therapy was 1 to 2 months and for another 22% from 3 to 6 months; 28% were in therapy for 6 to 12 months, while another 22% were in therapy for 12 to 36 months. In other words, 50% of the outcome clients were in therapy for at least 6 months and 22% for more than 1 year. Approximately 50% had 20 sessions or less; 43% had between 20 and 100 sessions; and 7% had more than 100 sessions.

Comparisons were made between the study's private practice and public clinic outpatients, who made up the largest single group of clients (72%), and the sample of outpatients reported by Strupp, Fox, and Lessler (1969). These investig-

ators felt that the group they obtained was representative of all outpatients in the United States who had received psychotherapy during the late 1950s and early 1960s. Taking into consideration some qualifications which make the comparison a fairly gross one, the two groups of outpatients seemed to be reasonably similar with regard to age, sex, marital status, income, and number of sessions.

Results. Differential statistical analyses of the data were used, depending upon how the clients were grouped: (1) quartiles separately as a function of the levels of empathy, warmth, or genuineness received; (2) clients showing the greatest positive and greatest negative (or least positive) change; and (3) diagnostic categories—i.e., neurotics and psychotics. In no instance was either empathy or warmth found to be related to client change. Genuineness was found to be related to client change in a sufficient number of analyses to allow us to say that minimal levels of genuineness were related modestly to outcome.

The major conclusions drawn from the *Arkansas* study are:

1. The relatively higher interpersonal skills therapists were *not* more effective overall than the lower skills therapists. However, as noted in the next conclusion, there were severe restrictions on the skills levels. Almost all therapists in this sample were below minimal levels and, as a group, were not facilitative, as operationally defined by the process scales used in the study.

2. The interpersonal interaction levels of the therapists with their clients were relatively superficial. As noted, the therapists interacted with their clients in a relatively nonthreatening and nonrisking manner. The therapists were, as we have said, below minimally facilitative levels on the central therapeutic skills of empathy, warmth, and genuineness.

3. Psychotherapy as practiced by the therapists represented in the sample was, *at best*, moderately effective. In contrast to the 30% spontaneous remission rate which currently is seen as reasonably accurate[4] (Bergin, 1971), improvement rates in the study ranged from 43% to 70% on representative global measures. In all, however, consideration of measurement error, regression effect, etc., suggest to us that client improvement was moderate at best.

4. The psychotherapy was not "for better *or* for worse." Overall, only approximately 2% of the clients showed any signs of deterioration.

5. The relative lack of genuineness of the psy-

chotherapists not only mitigated directly against positive client outcome but also may have lessened whatever helpful effects empathy and warmth, despite their low levels, might have had. We offer this suggestion because both Rogers (1957) and Truax (Truax & Carkhuff, 1967) have theorized about the central role of genuineness in potentiating the effects of empathy and warmth. A rather clear indication of a lack of therapist genuineness mitigating against positive client outcome did occur in the analyses. With the truncated scale range utilized by the raters, high genuineness as described by the scale was not much in evidence, but within the restricted range, the lower genuineness group was consistently and markedly associated with poorer client outcome.

6. Attempts to relate differential effects of certain client variables to psychotherapeutic outcome was also not achieved. For example, prior levels of client adjustment and anxiety as well as length of psychotherapy, were not found to be related to outcome in this study. However, in a study of rehabilitation counselors (Bozarth & Rubin, in press) some limited evidence suggests that the skills may apply differentially to type of client and "helping" setting.

The obvious conclusion to be drawn from the Arkansas *as well as* the other outcome studies reviewed above is that the relationship of empathy, warmth, and genuineness to client outcome is much more complex than the earlier studies have suggested. The evidence suggests that the relationship of these skills to client outcome may occur primarily when the therapists are client-centered in orientation, or they may apply differentially to various kinds of clients or to clients in different therapy settings. Bergin and Suinn (1975) offer the view that the interpersonal skills are not related to client outcome except when the therapists are client-centered in orientation.[5] In our judgment, the evidence with respect to such a hypothesis is equivocal. In some respects it is surprising that higher interpersonal skills levels were found to be related to positive outcome as often as they were, given such problems as the low levels of most psychotherapists' functioning, marginally rigorous measurement criteria, the difficulties inherent in training raters, etc. On the other hand, the failure to replicate the earlier positive findings in the several recent well-designed studies highlights the necessity for caution in offering definitive conclusions. It should be repeated

that the relationship between empathy, warmth, and genuineness and outcome is exceedingly more complex than was thought earlier. The nature of the complexity will be examined in more detail below. Briefly, it may be that the interpersonal skills are related differentially to client change as a function of the different stages of therapy, the nature of the client's problems, and the integration of the interpersonal skills with other therapist variables.

A point which is central to the thrust of this chapter bears scrutiny. We have been speaking of the *overall* relationship between the three interpersonal skills and outcome. Strictly speaking, however, the hypothesis of greatest importance to Truax, Carkhuff, Mitchell, Bozarth and others has been that *high* levels of the skills lead to client improvement. In other words, a reasonable proportion of therapists in any particular study *must* provide *at least* minimally facilitative levels before the study can be seen as even testing the central hypothesis.

As rough estimates of *minimally* facilitative levels of functioning, Truax (Truax & Carkhuff, 1967; Truax & Mitchell, 1971) seems to suggest the midpoints (2.5) on his 5-point warmth and genuineness scales and perhaps 3.5–4.0 on his 9-point empathy scale. Similarly, Carkhuff (e.g., Carkhuff, 1969b) seems to suggest the minimally facilitative therapist must function at 3.0 and above on each of his 5-point scales. A corollary is that even if truly high and truly low groups of therapists are identified and contrasted, the two groups of therapists must be significantly different from each other.

Table 1 is a summary of a number of the outcome studies cited in this chapter. Included are data related to number of clients, measurement of the interpersonal skills (when available), and the number of analyses supporting or not supporting the hypotheses of significant relationships between higher levels of empathy, warmth, and genuineness and positive outcome.

The following criteria were used to include a study in this table.
1. actual psychotherapy sessions were used—not analogue studies, coached clients, practicum students, etc.;
2. only ratings of tape segments or transcripts of interpersonal skills were used, not client or therapist perceptions;
3. only Truax and/or Carkhuff scales or slight modifications (Garfield & Bergin, 1971) were used to rate the therapy sessions; and
4. outcome measures (not process measures—Depth of Self-Exploration, etc.) were used

TABLE 1. RECENT OUTCOME STUDIES OF THERAPISTS' INTERPERSONAL SKILLS.

	Number of Clients	Therapist Skills Measured					Number of Analyses Supporting Hypothesis	
		Type	Reliability	X	SD	Range	Significant	Nonsignificant
Altmann (1973)	19	AE		5.5[a]			1	0
		NPW		2.8[a]			0	1
		G		2.9[a]			0	1
Beutler, Johnson, Neville, & Workman (1972)	54	AE	.54	3.8[b]	1.7[b]	1.0–9.0[b]	0	2
Beutler, Johnson, Neville, Workman, & Elkins (1973)	49	AE	.86				0[c]	1[c]
		NPW	.60					
		G	.68					
Bozarth & Rubin (in press)		AE	.84	3.2[f]		1.8–4.0	15	90
	245	NPW	.87	3.1		1.5–4.0	11	94
		G	.85	3.1		1.7–4.7	11	94
Garfield & Bergin (1971)	38	AE[d]	.91	3.6	1.0		0	13
		NPW	.73	2.8	.5		0	13
		G	.74	3.3	.9		0	13
Kurtz & Grummon (1972)	25	AE	.96	2.3[f]	.5	1.6–3.4	1	5
Mintz, Luborsky, & Auerbach (1971)	27	AE	.89				0	2
Mitchell, Truax, Bozarth, & Krauft (1973)		AE	.67	2.3	.7	1.3–5.0	2	560
	120	NPW	.63	2.1	.3	1.5–3.1	11	551
		G	.79	2.3	.4	2.0–3.1	39	523
Mullen & Abeles (1971)	36	AE	.76	5.0[b]			1	0
		NPW	.73	3.0[b]			0[c]	4[c]
Siegel (1972)	8	AE	.81	6.8[e]				
		NPW	.70	4.6[e]			5[c]	64[c]
		G	.84	4.5[e]				
Sloane, Staples, Cristol, Yorkston, & Whipple (1975)	92	AE		5.6	1.10	1.8–8.0	0	1
		NPW	.58–.74	3.7	.92	1.8–5.0	0	1
		G		5.8	.79	2.9–7.0	0	1
Truax (1970)	31	AE	.82				1[c]	3[c]
		NPW	.81					
		G	.70					
Truax, Altmann, Wright, & Mitchell (1973)		AE	.72	3.6[e]				
	16	NPW	.53	3.5[e]			12[c]	32[c]
		G	.34	3.2[e]				
Truax & Wittmer (1971)	40	AE	.63				2	3
Truax, Wittmer, & Wargo (1971)	160	AE	.81				3	24
		NPW	.76				2	25
		G	.80				2	25
							6[c]	21[c]

Note. Dashes indicate that data were not reported. All means, standard deviations, and ranges have been rounded off to one decimal place (5 or above rounded up). Data in the table not reported in the articles were obtained through personal communications from Abeles (1975), Beutler (1975), and Sloane (1975).
[a] Median values for entire sample.
[b] Not in original article but obtained by personal communication.
[c] Composite of therapist skills.
[d] Used the Bergin and Solomon (1970) 10-point scale.
[e] Mean of the means for the highest and lowest groups.
[f] A 5-point empathy scale (Carkhuff, 1969a, 1969b) was used; all the other studies used a 9-point scale.

(e.g., global improvement, pre-post change on MMPI, etc.).

In light of our concern about the lack of appropriate testing of the "*facilitative skills levels—positive outcome hypothesis*," perhaps the central point to be made is the paucity of relevant data available either from the published reports or from personal communication.

From the available data, it may seem that, based on *mean* levels of the interpersonal skills, eight of the 15 studies tested the "*facilitative skills levels—positive outcome*" hypothesis. However, the *proportions* of truly high and truly low therapists are unknown in *all* of the studies. It may be that the seemingly mean facilitative levels reflect a small number of unusually high-functioning therapists, but that *both* high- and low-functioning groups included therapists who were less than minimally facilitative. A variation of this possibility occurs in Siegel's (1972) study. Siegel was the only therapist; however, we do not know the proportion of children who received at least facilitative and less than facilitative conditions.

Thus, based on the data provided in Table 1, it seems fair to conclude that *none* of the studies actually tested the hypothesis of central concern (i.e., the "facilitative skills levels—positive outcome" hypothesis). *In this sense, our conclusion must be that the relationship between the interpersonal skills and client outcome has not been investigated adequately and, consequently, nothing definitive can be said about the relative efficacy of high and low levels of empathy, warmth, and genuineness.*

It is another thing, however, although quite difficult, to make a judgment, on the basis of the data generated by the studies in Table 1, to what extent any support is or is not provided for a different set of hypotheses—i.e., for the three separate hypotheses of positive relationships between *higher* levels of empathy, warmth, genuineness and client outcome. Looked at overall and quite simply, only 6% of *all* statistical analyses reported in the 15 studies offered statistically significant support for any of the three hypotheses. Another unit of analysis is *each* of the 15 studies. Again, using the admittedly simple criterion of the proportion of statistically significant analyses favoring one or more of the three hypotheses, but viewing each outcome study as an independent replication (to one extent or another) of the early studies, it seems fair to say that perhaps seven (Altmann, 1973; Bozarth & Rubin, in press; Kurtz & Grummon, 1972; Mullen & Abeles, 1971; Truax, 1970; Truax & Wittmer, 1971; Truax et al., 1971) offer at least minimal support for the hypothesis of a statistically significant relationship between *higher* levels of empathy (whether truly facilitative or not) and positive client outcome.

Similarly, perhaps four studies (Bozarth & Rubin, in press; Siegel, 1972; Truax et al., 1973; Truax et al., 1971) offer such support for *higher* levels of warmth, and perhaps three studies (Bozarth & Rubin, in press; Mitchell et al., 1973; Truax et al., 1971) offer such support for *higher* levels of genuineness.[6]

OTHER ASPECTS OF EMPATHY, WARMTH, GENUINENESS, AND OUTCOME

Other research has emphasized different aspects of the empathy warmth, and genuineness dimensions. In a lively exchange (Chinsky & Rappaport, 1970; Rappaport & Chinsky, 1972;

Truax, 1972) questions have been raised regarding the psychometric qualities of the Truax scales, particularly Accurate Empathy (*AE*). Chinsky and Rappaport questioned the reliability of the scales, particularly with respect to the use of taped segments versus therapists and the number of therapists used. It seems to us that Bozarth and Krauft (1972a) responded adequately to that issue. They found that reliability remained stable when more therapists were used and one segment versus several segments were sampled.

Further methodological considerations were raised with respect to the construct validity of the Truax Accurate Empathy Scale—i.e., does the scale measure what it purports to measure? Some recent studies (e.g., Bachrach, Mintz, & Luborsky, 1971; Bellucci, 1971) found that the Truax scale was related to other empathy scales. On the other hand, Kurtz and Grummon (1972) found very few significant correlations among six measures of therapist empathy.[7] Mintz et al. (1971) factor-analyzed a number of therapist variables, finding a first factor which included empathy, warmth, skill, relaxed style, spontaneity, sensitivity, and perceptiveness.

Relationships among empathy, warmth, and genuineness present additional problems. Some of the earlier studies reviewed by Truax and Mitchell (1971) as well as the study by Mitchell et al. (1973) found empathy to be highly correlated with either warmth or genuineness. Indeed, Muehlberg, Pierce, and Drasgow (1969) found high correlations among all three interpersonal skills, as did Gurman (1973b) in a later study. Thus, not only is there conflicting data with respect to whether or not the Truax Accurate Empathy Scale exhibits construct validity but also with respect to whether or not it exhibits independence or correlates highly with the other Truax interpersonal skill measures of warmth and genuineness.

Carkhuff and Burstein (1970), Mitchell et al. (1973), and Berenson and Mitchell (1974) have generated data which suggest that the three interpersonal skills may or may not be highly correlated, depending upon (1) the different sources (therapists, clients, independent raters), (2) the level of functioning of the sources, (3) the specific form of the *scale* (e.g., 9- or 5-point scales), (4) the more general nature of the measure (e.g., tape-rated excerpts or paper-and-pencil tests), and (5) how the therapists are grouped (e.g., high or low facilitative).

The issue is far from settled. It may be that the Truax empathy scale, for example, is not "pure" (that is, raters may be responding to a more global "good therapist" construct encompassing a number of therapist dimensions in addition to empathy) or, the Truax empathy scale may measure one aspect of a more global empathy construct. A third possibility is that empathy is but one of a number of *conceptually* if not statistically different therapist variables which constitute attitudinal and behavioral options open to the effective psychotherapist.

The latter notion strikes us as a particularly reasonable way of looking at the problem. Why should it be surprising that therapists high on empathy are also high on warmth and genuineness, and also confront their clients in ways that appear to be differentially helpful?

Indeed, although Gurman (1973b) presents data which suggest that when the number of rated segments per session are increased therapists varied considerably both across and within sessions with the same patient, he also found that high-functioning therapists had high scores on all three interpersonal skill measures and, generally, functioned at higher levels throughout than low-functioning therapists.

With respect to confrontation, for example, Mitchell and Berenson (1970) found that during the first therapy session high-facilitative therapists significantly more often than low-facilitative therapists used confrontations which provided significant information about the therapist, focused on the here-and-now relationship between therapist and client, and emphasized the client's resources. On the other hand, low-facilitative therapists were significantly more likely to confront their clients with their pathology rather than their resources.

Mitchell and Hall (1971) found that, in addition, the same high-and low-facilitative therapists confronted their clients in a significantly different sequence over time in the first interview. Indeed the high-facilitative therapists *within the first 15 minutes* used significantly more confrontations which focused on the therapist-client relationship, and *within the first half hour* used significantly more confrontations which focused on client resources rather than pathology, and on client action rather than passivity. These data are interesting in their own right, but the point to be made here is that levels of the interpersonal skills and type and frequency of confrontation were related both in a statistical and applied clinical sense. Yet, conceptually these are quite different variables.

Returning to the interpersonal skills themselves, a similar view might obtain. In a few studies (e.g., Truax & Carkhuff· 1967) either genuineness or warmth was found to be unrelated or negatively related to the other two skills. At this point, we have no explanation for this. However, in most of the early and recent research the interpersonal skills are related and in many instances, significantly so; frankly, this does not surprise us. Except for a few idiosyncratic therapists, perhaps as a function of orientation (although more likely as a function of personality), it is inconceivable to us that a therapist who understands his client's many facets including his suffering and despair could fail to care about and respect him, and be responsibly honest and open with him.

One hypothesis of particular interest to us is fashioned after Carkhuff's (1969a, 1969b) model which makes a distinction between a helper's *responsive* and *initiative* responses—that is, certain therapist behaviors are responsive to the helpee's predicament. They are more important in the early as opposed to the later stages of therapy in establishing rapport and reducing the client's anxiety about his predicament by expressing understanding, concern, and a willingness to help. However, in order to effect change in a client's behavior, the therapist must himself engage in initiative responses, behaviors which are more action- (and behavior) oriented, and problem solving. This brings us back to those earlier conclusions (Truax & Mitchell, 1971) which, in our view, need revamping as a result of the recent research: that empathy, warmth, and genuineness are related *directly* to client outcome, *and* that they are necessary and sufficient conditions for client change in all cases.

A number of hypotheses occur to us which, of course, require further investigation. One reason why empathy, warmth, and genuineness have not been found to be related directly to positive client change is that all the outcome research, early and recent, in computing mean scores assign equal weight to segments selected over the entire course of therapy. However, if we follow Carkhuff's reasoning, empathy, warmth, and genuineness may be related to client change differentially as a function of when they are sampled in the course of therapy.

A description of a hypothetical "phase" model of the psychotherapy process might be helpful. An elaboration of Carkhuff's model which appeals to us involves three rather than two phases. Empathy, warmth, and genuineness quite likely are *necessary* and perhaps even *sufficient* in establishing an optimal therapeutic context early in therapy. In this connection, however, we are mindful of Sullivan's excellent suggestion that the client leave each interview with something tangible—some advice, a plan of action. At any rate, once such a context has been established, *the interpersonal skills may continue to be necessary, perhaps one more than another, in either of the succeeding phases, but most likely none is sufficient in either phase.*

The second phase involves the therapist's pushing his client to explore and test the heretofore unspoken dimensions of their relationship (perhaps partly through immediacy, Mitchell, 1971), and, subsequently, examine those very painful, guilt- and anxiety-provoking parts of his self (perhaps partly through confrontation, Berenson & Mitchell, 1974). Finally, the initiative (or perhaps a better term would be the reconstructive) phase occurs.

Here, the therapist as an effective therapist, and equally important as a *person who lives effectively*, is a model and potent reinforcer for his client, and participates actively in the problem-solving and decision-making processes which result in his client's being more tolerant of himself and owning a larger repertoire of effective interpersonal behaviors.

Or, empathy, warmth, and genuineness might be used differentially depending on client diagnosis. Clinical wisdom suggests that high levels of empathy might overwhelm a schizophrenic client early in therapy and that, instead, empathy might best be increased slowly over time within the context of uniformly high levels of warmth. On the other hand, with a neurotic initially high levels of warmth might best be lowered somewhat in the middle phase of therapy in order to heighten negative aspects of the "transference" and increase anxiety sufficiently so it becomes an excellent stimulus for change.

Of particular relevance here is Gurman's (1973b) "empathic specificity" hypothesis. Essentially, the hypothesis is that a therapist's *overall* level of functioning is less predictive of his client's outcome than "his level of functioning around issues that are more central to his patient's experience of dissatisfaction and suffering" (p. 22). A similar notion has been suggested by Mitchell (1975) regarding a more clinically meaningful classification of therapist-initiated confrontations. He suggested that, although by definition all confrontations run the risk of aborting the therapeutic alliance, those pose a greater threat which force a client to doubt certain "myths" about himself, his family, etc., which he considers central to his functioning, no matter how precarious. Such core confron-

tations may cause the client to leave therapy, but they also may result in a major therapeutic breakthrough where an impasse had existed. With respect to the interpersonal skills, it is most likely that such confrontations could be successful only in the context of truly high, perhaps even peak, levels of empathy, warmth, and genuineness. Another, not unrelated, possibility is that therapists have a number of therapeutic options at their disposal, and, consequently, no single variable is going to be found to be related to outcome except in conjunction with other variables.

Perhaps a more balanced view is that our understanding of not only the potency but of the very nature of the relationship between empathy, warmth, and genuineness and outcome must be changed. Two examples might be helpful. Berenson and Mitchell (1974) reported the results of a number of studies referring to the interrelatedness, before and after confrontation, of empathy, warmth, genuineness, and concreteness (Carkhuff, 1969a, 1969b), as well as immediacy (Mitchell, 1971) and reference to significant others (Mitchell, Mitchell, & Berenson, 1970). For our purposes, the findings of interest were: (1) the number, strength, and direction of the correlations among the variables were vastly different for high as opposed to low facilitators; and (2) factor analyses of the data provided different factors, and different loadings of these therapist variables on the factors, for high and low facilitators. Therapists rated high and low on empathy, warmth, and genuineness provided very different encounters for their clients. These groups of therapists differed not only experientially but, of greater importance, structurally. For the truly high-facilitative therapist, for example, structure refers to the fact that the interpersonal skills, themselves intertwined, are integrated with *all* helping attitudes and behaviors so that the facilitative therapist has a wide array of helping skills which he orchestrates, emphasizing one, then another, according to his client's moment-by-moment needs. The point to be made here is that casting the therapists into two groups based on empathy, warmth, and genuineness led to two different matrices which we believe more accurately characterized the integration of skills and behaviors which are unique to these two distinct groups of therapists.

R. Mitchell (1971) studied the relationship between empathy, warmth, genuineness, outcome and a variable she termed "immediacy." Based on a communication model of psychotherapy, Mitchell postulated that *all* client statements include covert if not overt references to the therapist. Some references are fairly trivial, but many more than we realize, many of which are covert, convey important client feelings about the therapist and must be dealt with if therapy is to progress. Of a number of findings, one has particular relevance to our thesis. Mitchell divided the therapists in her study into four groups: (1) those who were significantly higher on all four variables; (2) those who were significantly higher on empathy, warmth, and genuineness, but significantly lower on immediacy; (3) those who were significantly higher on immediacy, but lower on the other three variables; and (4) those who were significantly lower on all four variables. Although none of the four variables was a particularly good predictor of client outcome taken singly or in three of the four clusters described above, additional analyses of the data indicated that only the clients of those therapists in group (3) showed significant deterioration from pre-therapy test scores.

With respect to immediacy, we should be cautious in making too much of the findings of one study.[8] Nevertheless, the concept has great intuitive appeal for us and the findings intrigue us. One possibility is that immediacy is related strongly to *positive* outcome only within the context of exceptionally high levels of the interpersonal skills. It may be that high levels of immediacy so enhance the potential of the here-and-now therapist-client relationship for *therapeutic benefit or harm* that such therapist demands to intensify the alliance must be accompanied by highly therapeutic levels of empathy, warmth, and genuineness. On the other hand, clinical wisdom suggests to us that a therapist who demands an intense relationship in the context of nonfacilitative levels of the interpersonal skills moves his client toward intimacy with a person who is unable (or unwilling) to understand him, who remains unconcerned about him and lacking in respect, and who deals with him in a caricature of the professional relationship, in a distant, stereotyped, and phony relationship. It seems to us that, under such conditions, only the client who is healthy and, therefore, angry enough to leave therapy would fail to deteriorate. One general conclusion, then, is that client deterioration very likely is the result of a number of therapist attitudes and behaviors and, therefore, the antecedents of deterioration will be reliably identified only when we analyze therapist variables in conjunction with one another rather than singly.

It is patently obvious to those of us engaged in psychotherapy research, both process and outcome, that not only therapist variables but also client and situational factors must be examined in concert with each other. However, the vast majority of the outcome research has not been carried out at such a level of sophistication. One example of the kind of complexity that can be attained, at least in analogue research, is a study by Barnett (1971). She found that levels of empathy and genuineness were affected by (1) therapist-client similarity on self-actualization, (2) experimental manipulation of visual cues in different interviews, and (3) interview sequence.

In any event, it seems clear that more recent research strongly suggests that *the relationship between empathy, warmth, and genuineness and outcome is much more complex than had been understood earlier.* For that matter, in an ingenious series of experiments, Mintz (1972) has demonstrated just how complex and "arbitrary" the measurement of outcome can be. We need more "basic" research of this kind which aims at understanding not so much the process of psychotherapy but the process of psychotherapy *research.*

INTERPERSONAL SKILLS STABILITY

Another area of interest is of methodological and, even more important, etiological and training significance. The question is whether the therapist interpersonal skills reflect "relatively permanent attitudinal and personality characteristics as well as specific interpersonal skills . . . (of the therapist)" (Truax & Mitchell, 1971, p. 326). The latter was the position taken by Truax and Mitchell in their earlier review, despite the fact that Carkhuff and his associates in a series of experimental studies (Alexik & Carkhuff, 1967; Carkhuff & Alexik, 1967; Friel, Kratochvil, & Carkhuff, 1968) demonstrated that when an experimental "client" was instructed to do so, he was able to manipulate, although differentially, the facilitative offerings of high- and low-functioning therapists.

In response to the research of Carkhuff and his colleagues, Truax and Mitchell (1971) argued that, "although it has been demonstrated that a "client" *can* manipulate a therapist's offering of these conditions, the earlier research seems to indicate that in practice, clients do not" (p. 326).

Research completed subsequent to the Truax and Mitchell review generally has been contradictory and, as a result, the issue remains unresolved. One bit of progress is that the recent studies have been addressed to more specific aspects of the problem—i.e., under what conditions the interpersonal skills are stable and not stable.

The question, then, is whether the interpersonal skills reflect relatively permanent attitudinal and personality characteristics or are largely situationally determined. All the studies we know of address the problem in two ways: (1) by looking at skills stability over time with the same client or (2) by looking at similarity of levels of skills offered by one therapist to two or more clients. It should be noted that these procedures are completely inferential and based on the assumption, perhaps erroneous, that such data are relevant to the question. A therapist may characteristically offer high levels of empathy but may *choose*, for clinical reasons, not to do so with a particular client. The best way to approach the problem is to interview therapists directly, something which has not been done with respect to empathy, warmth, and genuineness.

Studies Favoring Skills Stability

Representative studies which seem to support the skills stability position include: Pengel (1970), Prager (1970), Cochrane (1972), Bleyle (1973), Mitchell *et al.* (1973), and Taylor (1973). These studies, taken as a whole, suggest that therapist levels of empathy, warmth, and genuineness either remain stable over time or (and this represents another way of approaching the same problem) that the interpersonal skills are unrelated to differential levels of client-therapist similarity or to such client characteristics as sex or diagnosis.

As one way of getting at the problem, Mitchell *et al.* (1973) utilized pair analysis, a procedure rarely used in psychotherapy research, and which perhaps needs further description. The question was: "Did clients seen by the same therapist receive similar levels of the interpersonal skills?" Correlations were computed separately for empathy, warmth, and genuineness. They were based on the first two clients of that sample of therapists included in the outcome analyses who saw two or more clients. If the correlations were high and positive, it meant that the levels of the interpersonal skills received were consistent across clients. And, furthermore, although causality cannot be inferred from correlations, the hypothesis was felt to be at least tenable that the therapists were primarily responsible for the levels of interpersonal skills received by their clients. Further research, of

course, is needed to address directly the cause and effect nature of the association. In our judgment, evidence bearing on this question may be taken as shedding light on the therapist-as-person, his professional skills, wisdom, and judgment, particularly because in the Arkansas study the therapists saw *clients they normally saw*—rather than randomly assigned clients with whom they may not usually have worked. Thus, the question to be answered reflected on therapy and counseling *as it was actually practiced.*

As we noted earlier, most of the studies cited in the Truax and Mitchell (1971) review suggested that the therapist is the primary determinant of the levels of empathy, warmth, and genuineness. However, most of the studies used small, relatively *homogeneous* samples of therapists and clients. Thus, it was particularly important to examine the issue with more heterogeneous therapist and client samples. Separate Pearson product-moment correlations were computed between the therapists' levels of empathy, warmth, and genuineness offered to the first two clients. It should be noted that the number of unique client pairs ($n = 41$) was half the N (82) used in the statistical analyses. Clients were included twice because the order of clients was reversed (i.e., client A, then client B, and client B, then client A). As a check on non-independence, it was found that the correlations between the pairs of clients were virtually unaffected when we doubled the sample size. Statistically significant correlations were found for empathy ($r = .48$, $p < .01$), warmth ($r = .42$, $p < .01$), and genuineness ($r = .34$, $p < .01$).

In the Mitchell *et al.* (1973) study, then, in which the clients were chosen for therapy by their therapists, the levels of empathy, warmth, and genuineness received by the pairs of clients of the therapists were moderately consistent. It should be noted, of course, that the percentage of variance accounted for was only 24%, 21%, and 17%, respectively. Clearly, there were other factors which affected the levels of interpersonal skills received by the clients in the Arkansas study.

By the same token, the hypothesis that the interpersonal skills levels were a function of client-therapist interaction did not receive support, at least not with respect to those measures available in the Arkansas study. Based on a similar pair analysis, the same pairs of clients generally did not perceive the same degree of therapist consistency which was noted by the tape raters (empathy, $r = .51$, $p < .01$; warmth,

$r = .13$; and genuineness, $r = .26$). Furthermore, other analyses indicated that neither client pretherapy status (the majority of which were measures of "personality" and "adjustment") nor levels of client Depth of Self-Exploration (DX), a therapy process measure, were related to levels of interpersonal skills received during psychotherapy.

Studies Not Supporting Skills Stability

Moos and MacIntosh (1970) found that empathy was influenced *to a greater extent* by patient and situation than by therapist. A study by Heck and Davis (1973) generated data suggesting a client-therapist interaction effect on empathy, although they also found that therapists who were higher on cognitive complexity expressed significantly higher levels of empathy regardless of the clients they saw. This is similar to Beutler's *et al.* (1972) finding of a main as well as an interaction effect of A and B therapists and client diagnosis on levels of empathy: (1) A-type therapists were more empathic with schizophrenic than with neurotic clients and (2) B-type therapists (who are higher on cognitive complexity) showed no significant increase in empathy levels which was related to diagnosis.

Two studies by Gurman (1973a, 1973b) are of interest in this regard. In one study, Gurman (1973b) found that high- and low-facilitative therapists varied markedly on all three skills across sessions as well as within sessions with the same patients. However, the therapist groups generally functioned at higher or lower levels, respectively. In the second study, Gurman (1973a) found that high- and low-facilitative therapists functioned differentially depending upon their mood. The high-facilitative therapists were more facilitative under dysphoric mood, whereas the low-facilitative therapists were more effective under a positive mood. Thus, in the first study Gurman demonstrated marked variation in therapist functioning without specifying any particular reason. In the second study Gurman again demonstrated therapist variation, this time relating variation to level of therapist functioning and therapist mood.

The issue remains unresolved although there are some specific hypotheses which seem especially promising: (1) high- and low-functioning therapists are affected differently by client, situational, and "other" therapist factors, and (2) the interpersonal skills may be more stable across clients *with whom therapists choose to work* and, therefore, increased emphasis on selection and

matching processes may increase psychotherapy effectiveness.

Perhaps the following speculations regarding not only empathy, warmth, and genuineness but all so-called "therapist variables" may be helpful:

1. It is probably as important to look at the level of therapist functioning for therapist stability as it is for outcome. Some of Carkhuff's (1969b) research suggests that therapists are more stable above the minimally facilitative conditions and less stable below the minimally facilitative conditions. As a general suggestion for further skills stability research, it is crucial that data on the levels of therapist functioning in terms of average and range should be reported because in most of the studies we have reviewed the levels of therapist functioning have been low and therefore would be subject to more variability if Carkhuff's position is correct.

2. If certain generally effective therapist characteristics exist, it may be of value to keep certain distinctions in mind. Therapist variables may be categorized as attitudes, personality characteristics, or behavior and these may be differentially related to variation with different clients and in different therapy situations. Furthermore, therapist variables may be a function of professional training or they may have been learned quite early in life and in many different kinds of interpersonal situations (e.g., the notion of the "inherently helpful person"). These also may vary differentially depending on the client or therapy situation.

3. One should distinguish between therapist variables measured before, as opposed to during, therapy. The latter likely are subject to greater variation, perhaps some more than others, but our guess is that there are no purely "therapist variables."

4. The distinction between a therapist's *capacity* to be empathic, for example, and the *actual* level of empathy he offers each client may be important.

5. This is certainly suggested by the Gurman (1973b) study. Therapists very likely differ among themselves with respect to certain interpersonal skills regardless of the client. While each therapist may vary his level of empathy, for example, *within a certain range*, as a function of the client, one therapist may be consistently higher with all his clients than other therapists, *all other things being equal.*

6. If outcome findings based on therapist functioning at high levels of the skills are also quite variable, then it may be that the most

effective "therapist variables" are those which are uniquely relevant to each particular therapist-client dyad. If this is the case, then it would be a mistake to continue to attempt to identify broad "therapist variables" which are effective in most if not all psychotherapy, or which are effective even for one therapist with most of his clients.[9]

7. Carkhuff (1969b) suggests that extraneous variables are more likely to affect low facilitators to a greater extent regardless of the helping situation, affect minimally facilitative therapists to a lesser degree and under some conditions but not others, and affect high facilitators very little. In addition, Bozarth and Rubin (in press) found that minimally facilitative therapists may be able to work better with males than females, and in certain situations but not others.

8. Our judgment about skills stability is that the issue remains unresolved. The next step might be to attack the problem more directly and rate *all* 3- or 5-minute segments over the entire course of a feasible number of therapy cases. *If marked variability is demonstrated, even if there is no overlap between truly high- and truly low-functioning therapists, and if the variability seems to make clinical sense, and, finally, if the variability is related to client change, then all future studies of empathy, warmth, and genuineness must sample sequentially (a formidable undertaking), and all past studies may have to be discarded.*[10]

TRAINING EFFECTS

The initial formal training effort involving empathy, warmth, and genuineness was described by Truax and Carkhuff (1967). They emphasized three key elements in the program:

1) A therapeutic context in which the supervisor communicates high levels of accurate empathy, nonpossessive warmth, and genuineness to the trainees themselves;

2) A highly, specific didactic training, using the research scales for 'shaping' the trainees' responses toward high levels of empathy, warmth, and genuineness; and

3) A focused group therapy experience that allows the emergence of the trainee's own idiosyncratic therapeutic self through self-examination and consequent integration of his didactic training with his personal values, goals, and life styles.

Truax and Mitchell (1971) cited studies indicating that such training increases facilitative functioning. With respect to training, they went on to say:

> The findings that these interpersonal skills can be learned in a short amount of time leads to either of two inferences. Perhaps these skills are relatively superficial and thus can be learned quickly. Since the skills have been related to significant client growth..., however, it does not appear likely that they are superficial.
>
> The second inference is that these skills are learned, either overtly or covertly, in early, formative interpersonal situations...and that focused training capitalizes on what may have been past incidental learning. (p. 327)

A review of Carkhuff (1972b) as well as two more recent studies (Oksanen, 1973; Perlman, 1973) offer additional support for the notion that training programs can be developed which increase the levels of therapist functioning.

Turning to more specific aspects of such training, Pierce and Schauble (1970) found that trainees whose superiors functioned at high levels of interpersonal skills increased their functioning significantly, whereas trainees who had low-functioning supervisors either did not change or tended to decline in their levels of functioning. Collingwood (1971) reported that retraining of previously trained undergraduates had the effect of increasing their functioning to their initial post-training peak levels. These studies suggest that: (1) special training programs in interpersonal skills lead to increased levels of functioning by trainees; (2) trainees tend to increase their own levels of functioning in relation to the level of functioning of their trainers; and (3) decreases in performance levels of trainees after specific interpersonal skills training programs can be reinstated with brief retraining or "booster" sessions.

With respect to a much more important issue —i.e., does successful training lead to successful client outcome?—no published studies in *Adult psychotherapy* could be found which were addressed directly to this issue.[11]

It appears that, with respect to professional therapists (the primary focus of this chapter), very little research has addressed itself to whether or not *both* the levels of interpersonal skills increase *and* trainees' clients improve. The recent data regarding paraprofessionals are reviewed by Anthony and Carkhuff in Chapter 6 of this book. The training studies we have found have not used experienced professional psychotherapists. Consequently, a synthesis of those findings reported in the earlier Truax and Mitchell (1971) review, the Carkhuff (1972a, 1972b) reports, and the few relevant studies done since 1970 appear to us to suggest the following conclusions and implications:

1. It would appear that facilitative functioning can be elevated from low levels (less than 1.5) to minimally facilitative levels (3.0) by systematically designed training programs of 100 hours or less. This conclusion is buttressed by the authors' experience with nonpsychotherapy training programs. For example, we were able to increase the levels of empathy of undergraduate resident assistants from 1 to 2.5 in just 6 hours (Mitchell, Bozarth, Pelosi, & Wyrick, 1971). While this was true for empathy, it was not true for warmth, perhaps because trainees need only change specified requirements. It may be that, for empathy, the lower levels can be increased in a way which is similar to how reading speed can often be increased, by merely concentrating on response patterns in a rather mechanistic manner.

2. The above would appear to suggest that warmth and genuineness, which do not consist of somewhat stereotyped response patterns, do not lend themselves to meaningful increase in brief training periods. A corollary may be that warmth and genuineness basically are different *kinds* of interpersonal skills. This hypothesis is supported by studies reporting the lack of significant correlations among tape-rated levels of the three skills. It should be reiterated, of course, that other studies have shown them to be highly correlated. At this point, all that can be said is the familiar refrain that further research is needed. We shall return to this point, however, in a later section.

3. Indirect evidence seems to suggest that trainees who reach minimally facilitative levels have clients who improve to a greater extent than those clients who are not being helped by minimally facilitative helpers. Studies could not be found, however, which directly test the contention that special training programs increase levels of skills and that such trainees have clients who, in turn, significantly improve.

4. One additional point, regarding radically different training programs, deserves mention: perhaps not just any kind of training will do. Myrick and Pare' (1971) found that group sensitivity training increased neither the levels of trainees' interpersonal skills in actual psychotherapy nor their clients' level of improvement in comparison with an appropriate control group.

5. In view of the marked increase in the number of interpersonal skills training programs, it would seem that considerably more information about training effects should be available with respect to: (a) the degree of increase of levels of the interpersonal skills dimensions; (b) which

individuals are more likely to be receptive to such training; and (c) the concomitant degree of effectiveness of persons who increase their levels of functioning. It appears to us unfortunate that training programs developed for the specific purpose of interpersonal skills training have either not built in evaluation components or have not reported such findings (e.g., Bozarth, 1974; Means, 1973; Sydnor & Parkhill, 1973).

THE INTERPERSONAL SKILLS AND BEHAVIOR THERAPY

Assuming that empathy, warmth, and genuineness are at least indirectly related to outcome, the question that arises is: In what specific manner do they affect client change? One possibility, detailed earlier in this chapter and based upon Carkhuff's (1969a, 1969b) distinction between initiative and responsive therapist responses, has been offered. Another possibility is that the interpersonal skills are used, systematically or unsystematically, to reinforce certain client attitudes and behaviors in and out of therapy. Relevant theory, as well as research through mid-1970, has been reviewed by Truax and Mitchell (1971). They concluded that "major revisions are in order for the current client-centered, psychoanalytic, and eclectic views of the therapeutic role of interpersonal skills" (p. 324). Furthermore, "These findings suggest that both the therapist's general level of skills (as proposed by traditional therapists) and his selective differential use of empathy, warmth, and genuineness (as proposed by learning theorists) have separate effects on patient therapeutic outcome" (pp. 324–325).

Only a few studies have examined this issue since mid-1970, at least outside the context of behavior therapy, and the findings have been contradictory. Some laboratory studies (Condiff, 1972; Hodgens, 1970; Vitalo, 1970) are of interest although not related directly to treatment. Vitalo (1970) found that only those *E*s functioning at high levels of the interpersonal skills produced learning rates (with respect to personal reference statements) which differed from the rates of a control group. Hodgens (1970) found that empathy was not a reinforcer of verbal effectiveness with male freshmen. Condiff (1972) found that (1) specific client verbal classes changed in *intensity*, not as a general function of empathy but only as a function of *peak* levels of empathy; (2) the *frequency* of such classes, however, was related to the intensity level of empathy itself; and (3) all client verbal categories receiving high peaks of empathy did not increase uniformly—some increased, while others did not.

It would appear that the surprisingly small number of studies which bear on the reinforcement issue do not offer clear support for Truax's (1966, 1968) initial contention that the interpersonal skills, in fact, serve as specific reinforcers, or for other early studies (reviewed by Truax & Carkhuff, 1967) which suggest that interpersonal skill levels are related to the positive effects of conditioning techniques.[12] However, as has been noted throughout this chapter, an adequate test of the "high conditions-greater change" hypothesis requires that the skills measures be truly high. In these studies this was not the case.

Behaviorally Oriented Therapy

When we turn to the specific behavioral therapies, however, the findings appear to be quite different. A great deal of controversy surrounds present-day behavior therapy with respect to possible relationship or "nonspecific" factors. Much of the discussion remains at the "either/or level," however. For example, Marks and Gelder (1966) have argued that the single most relevant factor in outcome in behavior therapy is the relationship between client and therapist. Crisp's (1966) formulation, however, is probably more palatable to many psychotherapists: "a *combination* of behavior therapy and psychotherapy may be more effective than either one alone" (p. 191). We should add, of course, that one needs to take into account the facilitative levels of the therapist, his competence with respect to behavioral techniques, and a host of other therapist, client, and situational variables, as well as the optimal levels at which these variables interact to produce the most successful outcome. Nevertheless, Crisp's (1966) formulation appears to us to be a good one.[13]

Only three studies we know of have examined the relationship between empathy, warmth, genuineness, behavior therapy, and outcome. The study by Sloane *et al.* (1975), which was mentioned earlier, compared psychoanalytically oriented therapy and a wide range of behavioral techniques, including systematic desensitization, with a no-treatment control group. Both therapy groups improved significantly more than the control group. The finding of particular interest with respect to the present discussion, however, is that in neither treatment group were empathy, warmth, and genuineness related to any of the

outcome measures.[14] Mickelson and Stevic (1971), however, found that high-facilitative behavioral counselors elicited more information-seeking behavior than low facilitators, although the rate of positive verbal reinforcement of such client verbalizations was not different for the two groups of therapists. Furthermore, Ryan and Gizynski (1971), in a retrospective study of clients who had been seen by behaviorally oriented therapists, found that the behavioral techniques were not related to the clients' perceptions of positive outcome. Indeed, those therapists who combined a greater proportion of behavioral to more traditional techniques (e.g., support, interpretation) were less liked by their clients, were seen as less competent, and their techniques were seen as more unpleasant. On the other hand, such variables as therapist confidence and persuasiveness, ability to create positive expectations, as well as the therapist and client's liking of each other were seen by the clients, therapists, and experimenters as related positively and significantly to outcome.

However, both the Mickelson & Stevic and Ryan & Gizynski studies contain certain serious flaws: (1) behavioral therapists were defined very loosely; we suspect that most rigorous behavior therapists would not call them behavior therapists at all; (2) the Ryan and Gizynski study was retrospective, depending upon therapists' and clients' perceptions of outcome some time after therapy; and (3) the Mickelson and Stevic study used high- and low-facilitative graduate student therapists who saw high school students for only one session. In our view, neither study should be seen as providing support for the hypothesis that relationship or "nonspecific" factors are implicated in behavior therapy outcome. Nevertheless, they do suggest that the hypothesis deserves further, more rigorous, investigation.

A word about clients' perception of what matters in therapy is in order. Incidentally, another chapter in this volume (Gurman, chapter 19) examines in detail perceptions of process and outcome by different sources. If indeed clients can correctly identify the necessary and sufficient conditions for positive change, then all research investigating effective therapist variables and techniques should be halted and we should simply rely on clients' reports. However, consider the following: Suppose that a random sample of patients who had undergone successful brain surgery was asked to implicate those variables that were related to improvement. Would they implicate the surgical techniques or so-called "nonspecific" characteristics of the surgeons? Our guess is that few would implicate the surgical techniques. Similarly, behavior therapy clients may implicate relationship or "nonspecific" factors because in past helping situations such factors were believed to be and often were related to effective help. In other words, clients may be less likely to implicate techniques which are foreign to their past experience of being helped. The above does not mean that we should disregard such client perceptions but that they should be viewed with caution.[15]

A number of studies have focused specifically on relationship or "nonspecific" factors in systematic desensitization.

Some behavior therapists have taken the position that the success of taped instructions not only has economic implications (since it appears to eliminate the need for a therapist being present) but indeed may be seen as supporting the conclusion that relationship factors are inoperative (e.g., Lang, 1969).

We would like to examine the therapist-present (TP) versus therapist-absent (TA) issue in systematic desensitization because it strikes us as an excellent behavioral treatment within which to examine the possible importance of relationship factors. We realize, of course, that the application of these techniques applies to a limited array of problems.

In an analogue study, Donner and Guerney (1969) found that both TP and TA groups showed significantly greater improvement in grade point average (GPA) than a group of waiting-list controls. However, in a follow-up study (Donner, 1970) the improvement rate of the TP group was found to be 90%, whereas the TA group maintained an improvement rate of 60%.

Morris and Suckerman (1974a, 1974b) addressed themselves more directly to the complexities involved in the different procedures. In one study (1974a) they compared warm- and cold-therapist groups with a no-treatment control group and found that, on a snake-avoidance task, the warm-therapist group improved significantly more than either the cold-therapist or no-treatment control groups, and that there was no significant difference between the latter two groups.

In a second study, Morris and Suckerman (1974b) varied therapist warmth (based on voice quality) *within an automated desensitization procedure*. That is, subjects were assigned to one of three groups: (1) warm-automated therapist,

(2) cold-automated therapist, and (3) a no-treatment control group. At the end of treatment (4 weeks), they found that, on the same snake-avoidance task, the warm group showed significantly greater improvement than either the cold or no-treatment control group, and that there was no significant difference between the latter two groups. In addition, a 3-week follow-up evaluation found that the warm group performed significantly better than the cold group ($p < .10$). There was no significant difference between the cold and no-treatment control groups. The authors concluded that "this suggests that the manner in which a therapist relates to a client during desensitization is very important for maximally effecting significant positive change" (p. 248). Morris and Suckerman added:

> This is not to say that the therapeutic relationship is a necessary and sufficient factor for producing behavior change, nor that the relationship is at 'the heart of psychotherapeutic change' as Truax and Mitchell (1971) stated. Rather, these results seem to indicate that one aspect of the therapeutic relationship, therapist warmth, is a necessary condition for effecting positive change with desensitization. (pp. 248–249)

There is only one study we know of which examined directly the relationship between the effectiveness of systematic desensitization and the Truax measures of empathy, warmth, and genuineness. Cairns (1972) compared two groups of clients, one of which received higher and the other lower levels of the interpersonal skills. While Cairns found a significant difference from pre- to post-treatment on the *behavioral* measure (approaching a rat in a cage) for the combined high- and low-facilitative groups, she found no significant difference *between* the two groups. Cairns did find, however, that the high-skills group showed significant improvement on two *subjective* change measures: (1) the Fear Survey Schedule III total score and (2) the rating of the specific fear (rats). In addition, the high-skills group was superior with respect to hours of treatment required to complete desensitization.

Despite the Sloane *et al.* (1975) study, the weight of the evidence strikes us as certainly *suggestive* that relationship factors, including warmth in particular, are operative in behavioral therapy generally and specifically in systematic desensitization.[16] It also seems to us likely that empathy and genuineness are related to effective desensitization, probably under conditions as yet not fully specified.

For example, empathy may be particularly useful at at least three points in the systematic desensitization procedure: (1) defining, with the client, those external events which cause him anxiety and which need to be included in a usable hierarchy; (2) specifying the nature, intensity, and frequency of the internal anxiety responses which accompany the external stimuli; and (3) noting the client's feelings during the application of the systematic desensitization procedure.[17] Finally, the nature of desensitization is such that the three interpersonal skills are differentially related to successful outcome.

CONCLUSIONS AND IMPLICATIONS

We have suggested conclusions and implications at various points in the chapter. What we would like to do at this point is indicate those which we feel bear repeating.

Recent research causes us to reexamine a number of positions taken earlier by Truax and his colleagues (Truax & Carkhuff, 1967; Truax & Mitchell, 1971). Briefly, our feeling is that many earlier conclusions need reformulation, that some qualification is necessary, and that much of the earlier and more recent data, when taken together, prove to be surprisingly inconclusive with respect to a number of issues. By the same token, we feel that none of the previous conclusions need to be discarded completely.

Clearly, the nature of the relationship between the interpersonal skills and outcome is more complex than had been realized. Therapist orientation, type of client, and type of therapy as well as a host of more specific variables, must be taken into account.

The *levels* of the interpersonal skills are crucial in understanding outcome. A reexamination of the earlier reports (pre-1970) in this domain indicated that (1) many studies failed to indicate the numerical averages and ranges for therapists classified as "high" or "low" facilitators and (2) many of the studies which did note the numerical scores revealed averages of the "high" facilitative therapists which were "3.0" or lower. It is clear, from the standpoint of the operational definitions of the scales (i.e., that 3.0 on the Carkhuff and Truax scales are minimally facilitative levels), that there are few high-functioning psychotherapists or counselors. Indeed, several of the "high group" mean scores were only slightly above 2.0.

Regardless of the reasons for the low scores, the fact is that most studies have not included high facilitators as defined by the Truax or Carkhuff scales. Instead, most comparisons have been between therapists who are nonfacilitative and those who are barely facilitative. Under such circumstances, it seems to us virtually impossible to explore the full impact of empathy, warmth, and genuineness on client change. In all instances, the hypothesis of *high versus low* skill levels has not been treated. It is of the utmost importance that future research reports include the means and range of the interpersonal skills scores and, furthermore, that researchers include more high-facilitative therapists, as defined by the scales, no matter how rare they may be.

A second issue is the extent to which the measurement scales actually assess the defined constructs; thus, a question arises about the actual constructs being measured which are related to more effective client outcome. It is our view that the research evidence may not negate the construct validity of the scales, but the burden of proof remains with the scale proponents.

Third, we are disappointed with the extent of research on the interpersonal skills as reinforcers and the skills as major factors associated with reinforcement effects. The earlier promise of examining integration of the skills with various reinforcement paradigms (Truax & Mitchell, 1971) has not been carried forward.

Fourth, the research evidence on the effects of training of personnel appears to indicate that the skills levels can be increased from "low" to "high*er*" and, therefore, to minimally facilitative levels. Nevertheless, the effect of training has been quite sparse in psychotherapy research and its effect on *client outcome* has not been examined in sufficient detail. Rather, the conclusion of the effects of training appear to be based primarily on an inductive process: skills levels of trainees can be raised; the interpersonal skills are related positively to client outcome; therefore, training leads to client improvement.

Fifth, looking at the interpersonal skills within the context of the "responsive-initiative" categorization, the levels as differentially related to client change during different time periods in therapy, and the skills in concert with other variables such as confrontation and immediacy strike us as particularly fruitful areas for further research. Such possibilities remain in nascent form but, in our judgment, hold out the potential for finer identification and calibration of the interpersonal skill dimensions.

Finally, we think it fitting, as a reaffirmation, to close the present chapter as the last review closed (Truax & Mitchell, 1971):

> We want to emphasize the therapist-as-person before the therapist-as-expert or therapist-as-technician. We want to emphasize the commonality that psychotherapy has with other aspects of life. *We want to emphasize the therapist as a viable human being engaged in a terribly human endeavor.* (p. 34)

REFERENCES

ABELES, N. Personal communication, March 1975.

ALEXIK, M., & CARKHUFF, R. R. The effects of the manipulation of client depth of self-exploration upon high and low functioning counselors. *Journal of Clinical Psychology*, 1967, **23**, 212–215.

ALTMANN, H. A. Effects of empathy, warmth, and genuineness in the initial counseling interview. *Counselor Education and Supervision*, 1973, **12**, 225–228.

BACHRACH, H., MINTZ, J., & LUBORSKY, L. On rating empathy and other psychotherapy variables: An experience with the effects of training. *Journal of Consulting and Clinical Psychology*, 1971, **36**, 445.

BARNETT, L. C. F. The effect of silent communications upon counseling processes: An experimental study. The relevance of nonverbal behavior and self-actualization for counselor empathy and genuineness and client self-exploration. Doctoral dissertation, University of Missouri, 1971. *Dissertation Abstracts International*, 1971, **31**, 6336A (University Microfilms No. 71-14, 440).

BELLUCCI, J. E. The development and validation of a measure of counselor empathy. Doctoral dissertation, Southern Illinois University, 1971. *Dissertation Abstracts International*, 1971, **32**, 4933A–4934A (University Microfilms No. 72-10, 232).

BERENSON, B. G., & MITCHELL, K. M. *Confrontation for better or worse.* Amherst, Mass.: Human Resource Development Press, 1974.

BERGIN, A. E. The evaluation of therapeutic outcomes. In A. E. BERGIN & S. L. GARFIELD (Eds.), *Handbook of psychotherapy and behavior change: An empirical analysis.* New York: Wiley, 1971. Pp. 299–344.

BERGIN, A. E., & SOLOMON, S. Personality and performance correlates of empathic understanding in psychotherapy. In T. THOMLINSON & J. HART (Eds.), *New directions in client-centered therapy.* Boston: Houghton-Mifflin, 1970.

BERGIN, A. E., & SUINN, R. M. Individual psychotherapy and behavior therapy. *Annual Review of Psychology*, 1975, **26**, 509–556.

BEUTLER, L. E. Personal communication, March 1975.

BEUTLER, L. E., JOHNSON, D. T., NEVILLE, C. W., JR., & WORKMAN, S. N. "Accurate empathy" and the A-B dichotomy. *Journal of Consulting and Clinical Psychology*, 1972, **38**, 372–375.

BEUTLER, L. E., JOHNSON, D. T., NEVILLE, C. W., JR., WORKMAN, S. N., & ELKINS, D. The A-B therapy-type distinction, accurate empathy, non-possessive warmth, and therapist genuineness in psychotherapy. *Journal of Abnormal Psychology*, 1973, **82**, 273–277.

BLEYLE, D. M. The relationship of counselor-client measured value similarity to client self-concept change and client perception of empathy, warmth, and genuineness after brief counseling. Doctoral dissertation, University of Northern Colorado, 1973. *Dissertation Abstracts International*, 1973, **34**, 2277B (University Microfilms No. 73-26, 485).

BORDIN, E. S. *Research strategies in psychotherapy.* New York: Wiley, 1974.

BOZARTH, J. D. *Interpersonal skills training workbook.* Mimeo, University of Iowa, Iowa City, 1974.

BOZARTH, J. D., & KRAUFT, C. C. Accurate empathy ratings: Some methodological considerations. *Journal of Clinical Psychology*, 1972a, **28**, 408–410.

BOZARTH, J. D., & KRAUFT, C. C. *Training manual: Empathy, warmth, and genuineness.* Arkansas Rehabilitation Research and Training Center, University of Arkansas, 1972b.

BOZARTH, J. D., & RUBIN, S. E. Empirical observations of rehabilitation counselor performance and outcome: Some implications. *Rehabilitation Counseling Bulletin*, in press.

CAIRNS, K. V. *Desensitization and relationship quality.* Unpublished master's thesis, University of Calgary, 1972.

CARKHUFF, R. R. *Helping and human relations: A primer for lay and, professional helpers.* Vol. 1. *Selection and training.* New York: Holt, Rinehart & Winston, 1969a.

CARKHUFF, R. R. *Helping and human relations: A primer for lay and professional helpers.* Vol. 2. *Practice and research.* New York: Holt, Rinehart & Winston, 1969b.

CARKHUFF, R. R. The development of systematic human resource development models. *The Counseling Psychologist*, 1972a, **3**, 4–11.

CARKHUFF, R. R. New directions in training for the helping professions: Toward a technology for human and community resource development. *The Counseling Psychologist*, 1972b, **3**, 12–30.

CARKHUFF, R. R., & ALEXIK, M. Effect of client depth of self-exploration upon high and low functioning counselors. *Journal of Counseling Psychology*, 1967, **14**, 350–355.

CARKHUFF, R. R., & BURSTEIN, J. Objective therapist and client ratings of therapist-offered facilitative conditions of moderate to low functioning therapists. *Journal of Clinical Psychology*, 1970, **26**, 394–395.

CHINSKY, J. M., & RAPPAPORT, J. Brief critique of the meaning and reliability of "accurate empathy" ratings. *Psychological Bulletin*, 1970, **73**, 379–382.

COCHRANE, C. T. Effects of diagnostic information on empathic understanding by the therapist in a psychotherapy analogue. *Journal of Consulting and Clinical Psychology*, 1972, **38**, 359–365.

COLLINGWOOD, T. R. Retention and retraining of interpersonal communication skills. *Journal of Clinical Psychology*, 1971, **27**, 294–296.

CONDIFF, D. W. The role of empathy as a reinforcing agent in psychotherapy. Doctoral dissertation, Fuller Theological Seminary Graduate School of Psychology, 1972. *Dissertation Abstracts International*, 1972, **32**, 7304B–7305B (University Microfilms No. 72-15, 861).

CRISP, A. H. Transference 'symptom emergence' and 'social repercussion' in behavior therapy: A study of fifty-four treated patients. *British Journal of Medical Psychology*, 1966, **39**, 179–196.

DONNER, L. Automated group desensitization: A follow-up report. *Behaviour Research and Therapy*, 1970, **8**, 241–247.

DONNER, L., & GUERNEY, B. G. Automated group desensitization for test anxiety. *Behaviour Research and Therapy*, 1969, **7**, 1–13.

EYSENCK, H. J. *The effects of psychotherapy.* New York: International Science Press, 1966.

FRIEL, T., KRATOCHVIL, D., & CARKHUFF, R. R. Effects of client depth of self-exploration on therapists categorized by level of experience and type of training. Unpublished manuscript, State University of New York at Buffalo, 1968.

GARFIELD, S. L., & BERGIN, A. E. Therapeutic conditions and outcome. *Journal of Abnormal Psychology*, 1971, **77**, 108–114.

GURMAN, A. S. Effects of therapist and patient mood on the therapeutic functioning of high- and low-facilitative therapists. *Journal of Consulting and Clinical Psychology*, 1973a, **40**, 48–58.

GURMAN, A. S. Instability of therapeutic conditions in psychotherapy. *Journal of Counseling Psychology*, 1973b, **20**, 16–24.

HECK, E. J., & DAVIS, C. S. Differential expression of empathy in a counseling analogue. *Journal of Counseling Psychology*, 1973, **20**, 101–104.

HODGENS, T. J. An experimental study of the influence of accurate empathy on the verbal operant conditioning of verbal responses. Doctoral dissertation, Boston College, 1970. *Dissertation Abstracts International*, 1970, **31**, 3708B (University Microfilms No. 70-24, 602).

KURTZ, R. R., & GRUMMON, D. L. Different approaches to

the measurement of therapist empathy and their relationship to therapy outcomes. *Journal of Consulting and Clinical Psychology*, 1972, **39**, 106–115.

LANG, P. J. The mechanics of desensitization and the laboratory study of human fear. In C. FRANKS (Ed.), *Behavior therapy: Appraisal and status*. New York: McGraw-Hill, 1969.

MARKS, I. M., & GELDER, M. G. Common ground between behavior therapy and psychodynamic methods. *British Journal of Medical Psychology*, 1966, **39**, 11–23.

MATARAZZO, R. G. Research on the teaching and learning of psychotherapeutic skills. In A. E. BERGIN & S. L. GARFIELD (Eds.), *Handbook of psychotherapy and behavior change: An empirical analysis*. New York: Wiley, 1971. Pp. 895–924.

MEANS, R. Interpersonal Skills Training Programs. *Annual Training Report*, Arkansas Rehabilitation Research and Training Center, University of Arkansas, Arkansas Rehabilitation Services, Hot Springs, Arkansas, 1973.

MELTZOFF, J., & KORNREICH, M. *Research in psychotherapy*. New York: Atherton Press, 1970.

MICKELSON, D., & STEVIC, R. Differential effects of facilitative and nonfacilitative behavioral counselors, *Journal of Counseling Psychology*, 1971, **18**, 314–319.

MINSEL, W., BOMMERT, H., BASTINE, R., LANGER, I., NICKEL, H., & TAUSCH, R. Weitere untersuchung der auswirkung and prozsse klienten-zentrieter gespraschs-psychotherapie zeitsch R. F. *Klinische Psychologie*, 1971, **1**, 232–250.

MINTZ, J. What is 'success' in psychotherapy? *Journal of Abnormal Psychology*, 1972, **80**, 11–19.

MINTZ, J., LUBORSKY, L., & AUERBACH, A. H. Dimensions of psychotherapy: A factor-analytic study of ratings of psychotherapy sessions. *Journal of Consulting and Clinical Psychology*, 1971, **36**, 106–120.

MITCHELL, K. M. Confrontation: Some redefinitions. Unpublished manuscript, New Jersey Medical School, 1975.

MITCHELL, K. M., & BERENSON, B. G. Differential use of confrontation by high and low facilitative therapist. *Journal of Nervous and Mental Disease*, 1970, **151**, 303–309.

MITCHELL, K. M., & HALL, L. A. Frequency and type of confrontation over time within the first therapy interview. *Journal of Consulting and Clinical Psychology*, 1971, **37**, 437–442.

MITCHELL, K. M., MITCHELL, R. M., & BERENSON, B. G. Therapist focus on clients' significant others in psychotherapy. *Journal of Clinical Psychology*, 1970, **26**, 533–536.

MITCHELL, K. M., RUBIN, S. E., BOZARTH, J. D., & WYRICK, T. J. Effects of short-term training on residence hall assistants. *Counselor Education and Supervision*, 1971, **14**, 310–318.

MITCHELL, K. M., TRUAX, C. B., BOZARTH, J. D., & KRAUFT, C. C. *Antecedents to psychotherapeutic outcome*. NIMH Grant Report (12306), Arkansas Rehabilitation Research and Training Center, Arkansas Rehabilitation Services, Hot Springs, Arkansas, March 1973.

MITCHELL, R. M. Relationship between therapist response to therapist-relevant client expressions and therapy process and client outcome. Doctoral dissertation, Michigan State University, 1971. *Dissertation Abstracts International*, 1971, **32**, 1853B (University Microfilms No. 71-23, 216).

MOOS, R. H., & MacINTOSH, S. Multivariate study of the patient-therapist system: A replication and extension. *Journal of Consulting and Clinical Psychology*, 1970, **35**, 298–307.

MORRIS, R. J., & SUCKERMAN, K. R. The importance of the therapeutic relationship to systematic desensitization. *Journal of Consulting and Clinical Psychology*, 1974a, **42**, 148.

MORRIS, R. J., & SUCKERMAN, K. R. Therapist warmth as a

factor in automated systematic desensitization. *Journal of Consulting and Clinical Psychology*, 1974b, **42**, 244–250.

MUEHLBERG, N., PIERCE, R., & DRASGOW, J. A factor analysis of therapeutically facilitative conditions. *Journal of Clinical Psychology*, 1969, **25**, 93–95.

MULLEN, J., & ABELES, N. Relationship of liking, empathy, and therapist's experience to outcome of therapy. *Journal of Counseling Psychology*, 1971, **18**, 39–43.

MYRICK, R. D., & PARE, D. D. A study of the effects of group sensitivity training with student counselor-consultants. *Counselor Education and Supervision*, 1971, **11**, 90–96.

OKSANEN, I. A. The influence of training in the dimensions of empathy, respect, concreteness, and genuineness on counselor effectiveness. Doctoral dissertation, Wayne State University, 1973. *Dissertation Abstracts International*, 1973, **34**, 3067A (University Microfilms No. 73-31, 762).

PENGEL, J. E. The repression-sensitization scale as a predictive measure of certain client and counselor behavior in the initial interview. Doctoral dissertation, University of Connecticut, 1970. *Dissertation Abstracts International*, 1971, **32**, 187A–188A (University Microfilms No. 71-16, 025).

PERLMAN, G. Change in "central therapeutic ingredients" of beginning psychotherapists. *Psychotherapy: Theory, Research and Practice*, 1973, **10**, 48–51.

PIERCE, R. M., & SCHAUBLE, P. G. Graduate training of facilitative counselors: The effects of individual supervision. *Journal of Counseling Psychology*, 1970, **17**, 210–215.

PRAGER, R. A. The relationship of certain client characteristics to therapist-offered conditions and therapeutic outcome. Doctoral dissertation, Columbia University, 1970. *Dissertation Abstracts International*, 1971, **31**, 5634B–5635B (University Microfilms No. 71-6240).

RAPPAPORT, J., & CHINSKY, J. M. Accurate empathy: Confusion of a construct. *Psychological Bulletin*, 1972, **77**, 400–404.

ROGERS, C. R. *Client-centered therapy*. Boston: Houghton Mifflin, 1951.

ROGERS, C. R. The necessary and sufficient conditions of therapeutic personality change. *Journal of Consulting Psychology*, 1957, **21**, 95–103.

ROGERS, C. R. The interpersonal relationship: The core of guidance. *Harvard Educational Review*, 1962, **32**, 416–429.

RYAN, V., & GIZYNSKI, M. Behavior therapy in retrospect: Patients' feelings about their behavior therapists. *Journal of Consulting and Clinical Psychology*, 1971, **37**, 1–9.

SIEGEL, C. L. Changes in play therapy behaviors over time as a function of differing levels of therapist-offered conditions. *Journal of Clinical Psychology*, 1972, **28**, 235–235.

SLOANE, R. B., STAPLES, F. R., CRISTOL, A. H., YORKSTON, N. J., & WHIPPLE, K. *Short-term analytically oriented psychotherapy vs. behavior therapy*. Cambridge, Mass.: Harvard University Press, 1975.

SLOANE, R. B. Personal communication, May 1975.

STRUPP, H. H., FOX, R. E., & LESSLER, K. *Patients view their psychotherapy*. Baltimore: Johns Hopkins Press, 1969.

SYDNOR, G. L., & PARKHILL, N. L. *The analysis of human behavior: A programmed manual*. Human Resources Development Training Institute, Minden, Louisiana, 1973.

TAYLOR, C. E. Counselor's level of empathic understanding of a function of counselor sex and client sex. Doctoral dissertation, University of South Carolina, 1972. *Dissertation Abstracts International*, 1973, **34**, 143A (University Microfilms No. 73-16, 321).

TRUAX, C. B. Reinforcement and nonreinforcement in Rogerian psychotherapy. *Journal of Abnormal Psychology*, 1966, **71**, 1–9.

TRUAX, C. B. Therapist interpersonal reinforcement of client self-exploration and therapeutic outcome in group psychotherapy. *Journal of Counseling Psychology*, 1968, **15**, 225–231.

TRUAX, C. B. Effects of client-centered psychotherapy with schizophrenic patients: Nine years pretherapy and nine years posttherapy hospitalization. *Journal of Consulting and Clinical Psychology*, 1970, **35**, 417–422.

TRUAX, C. B. The meaning and reliability of accurate empathy ratings: A rejoinder. *Psychological Bulletin*, 1972, **77**, 397–399.

TRUAX, C. B., ALTMANN, H., WRIGHT, L., & MITCHELL, K. M. Effects of therapeutic conditions in child therapy. *Journal of Community Psychology*, 1973, **1**, 313–318.

TRUAX, C. B., & CARKHUFF, R. R. *Toward effective counseling and psychotherapy: Training and practice.* Chicago: Aldine, 1967.

TRUAX, C. B., & MITCHELL, K. M. Research on certain therapist interpersonal skills in relation to process and outcome. In A. E. BERGIN & S. L. GARFIELD, (Eds.), *Handbook of psychotherapy and behavior change: An empirical analysis.* New York: Wiley, 1971. Pp. 299–344.

TRUAX, C. B., & WITTMER, J. The effects of therapist focus on patient anxiety source and the interaction with the therapist level of accurate empathy. *Journal of Clinical Psychology*, 1971, **27**, 297–299.

TRUAX, C. B., WITTMER, J., & WARGO, D. G. Effects of the therapeutic conditions of accurate empathy, nonpossessive warmth, and genuineness of hospitalized mental patients during group therapy. *Journal of Clinical Psychology*, 1971, **27**, 137–142.

VITALO, R. L. Effects of facilitative interpersonal functioning in a conditioning paradigm. *Journal of Counseling Psychology*, 1970, **17**, 141–144.

EDITORS' REFERENCES

LAMBERT, M. J. Spontaneous remission in adult neurotic disorder: A revision and summary. *Psychological Bulletin*, 1976, **83**, 107–119.

LIEBERMAN, M. A., YALOM, I. D., & MILES, M. B. *Encounter groups: First facts.* New York: Basic Books, 1973.

ROGERS, C. R. The necessary and sufficient conditions of therapeutic personality change. *Journal of Consulting Psychology*, 1957, **21**, 95–103.

TRUAX, C. B., & MITCHELL, K. M. Research on certain therapist interpersonal skills in relation to process and outcome. In A. E. BERGIN & S. L. GARFIELD, (Eds.), *Handbook of psychotherapy and behavior change: An empirical analysis.* New York: Wiley, 1971. Pp. 299–344.

NOTES

1. The authors were deeply saddened by the untimely death of Dr. Charles B. Truax. We dedicate this chapter to his memory.

2. The Arkansas study was carried out over a 4-year period (1966–1970), supported by National Institute of Mental Health Grant 12306. Dr. Charles B. Truax was principal investigator during 1966–1968; and Dr. Kevin M. Mitchell during 1969–1970. Dr. Jerold Bozarth was principal administrator of the project at the University of Arkansas in 1971 and 1972, during which time he supervised the statistical analyses of the data. The authors are grateful to Drs. Richard C. Bednar, Jeffrey G. Shapiro, and Donald G. Wargo for their help in collecting the data.

3. *Editors' Footnote.* As the reader examines the Arkansas study, it is very important to keep in mind the fact that so few of the therapists who participated were primarily client-centered. Almost all the early studies of therapists'

interpersonal skills and most of the later studies reviewed by Truax and Mitchell (1971) were conducted in client-centered settings. More recently, studies of "therapist conditions" have been broadened to more heterogeneous samples, as noted in the present chapter. Thus, the more equivocal findings on the centrality of these skills as described here may, to an important extent, reflect differences in sampling. If this is the case, and we think it is, it forces a closer look at a basic issue involved in this area of research. The core client-centered proposition argued that these therapist skills are salient regardless of the nature of therapy practiced (Rogers, 1957). The generally negative findings of the Arkansas study, as well as other studies with non-client-centered samples, raises the question of whether (a) these therapist skills are not as important for outcome in non-client-centered therapy or (b) they are just as important, but are not adequately measured in heterogeneous samples by the scales that are typically used. While we know of no data to support the second interpretation, our clinical experience persuades us that this is the more likely explanation. We would be eager to see measures developed that tap the dimensions of empathy, warmth and genuineness within the conceptual framework of other major systems of psychotherapy.

4. *Editors' Footnote.* The reader should note that while this figure appears to have been attributed almost magical qualities by many researchers and clinicians, Bergin himself noted its deficiencies as a usable spontaneous remission rate. Further attempts by Bergin and his colleagues to arrive at more precise and meaningful remission rates are described in Chapter 18 of this volume and by Lambert (1976).

5. *Editors' Footnote.* This is essentially the same position we adopted in Footnote 3. While we agree with Mitchell, Bozarth, and Krauft that the evidence for this hypothesis is quite equivocal, we think our suggestion of developing alternate means of assessing these therapist skills for use in different therapy contexts would be very helpful in resolving this very important issue.

6. *Editors' Footnote.* The argument developed here that the core hypothesis regarding the relationship between these therapist skills and treatment outcome has, in fact, not been investigated is both provocative and, to us, persuasive. It is similar to the position taken by Gurman (Chapter 19, this volume) that, in a different vein, much of the research on these therapist skills has been misguided on theoretical grounds and has failed to test the central tenets of the client-centered position. Gurman argues, in summary, that *all* the research on these skills that has been based on external nonparticipant judges' ratings has been theoretically inappropriate, in that Rogers' (1957) assertion, at its core, was that these therapeutic attitudes had to be *communicated to a client* in order to facilitate therapeutic change. What is perhaps most striking about both Gurman's position and the position adopted here is that it is only after nearly two decades of scientific study on these therapist skills, which have played such a prominent role in theory development and in the training of psychotherapists, that the client-centered hypothesis truly begins to be examined with a methodology that is consonant with theory which begat the hypothesis. It should, therefore, be clear to the reader that, despite the not uncommon view that the client-centered hypothesis has been adequately validated, a good deal more research in this area is called for, along the lines suggested here and by Gurman.

7. *Editors' Footnote.* Among these six measures was that of patients' perception of the therapist skills. As Gurman demonstrates in Chapter 19, there is a very low correlation between patients' ratings and nonparticipant judges' ratings of warmth and genuineness, as well as empathy.

8. *Editors' Footnote.* While we agree that "one swallow doesn't make a summer," we are impressed by the clinical reasonableness of R. Mitchell's study. Her findings are reminiscent of those of Lieberman, Yalom, and Miles (1973), whose "aggressive stimulator" encounter group leaders, characterized by an intrusive, aggressive approach involving a great deal of challenging and confronting of group members, and an insistence on immediate self-disclosure, accounted for the majority of casualties in the group experience. See Lambert, Bergin, and Collins (Chapter 17, this volume) for a further discussion of this "quality" of therapeutic relating.

9. This suggestion was gratefully received from Dr. C. L. Winder, Assistant Provost, Michigan State University.

10. *Editors' Footnote.* The preceding discussion of the stability of these therapist skills strikes us as the methodologically and conceptually clearest and clinically most sophisticated consideration of this issue we have yet read. Its import for researchers in this area is considerable and we encourage the reader to read it again!

11. *Editors' Footnote.* Unfortunately this familiar refrain appears justified in the broader context of the training-in-general of professional therapists. See Garfield (Chapter 4, this volume) for a comprehensive review of this and other issues on research on the training of psychotherapists.

12. *Editors' Footnote.* It does not surprise us that there is a lack of convincing evidence that the interpersonal skills serve as "reinforcers." The nonbehaviorally oriented reader is reminded that "reinforcement" is an *empirical* concept and is defined by the demonstrated effects of a given stimulus on a given response, not by any hedonistic criteria. It seems to us that those workers who have argued in favor of the "reinforcing" value of empathy, etc., have *assumed* that empathic therapist responses have universal and predictable (positive) effects on client (verbal) behavior. Clearly, this is often not the case, as is implied earlier in this chapter by the authors, noting that, for example, high levels of empathy early in therapy may be quite aversive to paranoid or schizophrenic patients. The paradox involved in this issue, then, is that, under certain clinical conditions, a therapist may be truly empathic only by withholding "empathic" responses!

13. *Editors' Footnote.* We largely agree with Crisp's eclectic position but think that Crisp and Marks and Gelder are talking about two different issues. Crisp was speaking of the empirical matter of the efficacy of combined treatment techniques, while Marks and Gelder were arguing that, even in the context of a consistently "behavioral" treatment, relationship factors are the most important elements. The evidence for this latter position, however, is not convincing (see Wilson & Evans, Chapter 20, this volume).

14. *Editors' Footnote.* It should be noted, however, that the generalizability of Sloane *et al.*'s findings are seriously limited by the very small therapist sample ($N=3$ behavior therapists and 3 dynamically oriented therapists). On the other hand, this study is notable in that both groups of therapists functioned at high absolute levels, an issue of major importance as discussed in detail earlier in the present chapter.

15. *Editors' Footnote.* We find the authors' "foreign technique hypothesis" interesting and even deserving of investigation. Still, we find it difficult to believe that their hypothetical surgery patients would attribute treatment effects to their doctors' bedside manner. Moreover, asking patients to note which treatment factors they see as influencing outcome, as in the Ryan and Gizynski study, is an entirely different research strategy from that of asking patients to evaluate, say, therapists' interpersonal skills, and to then correlate these ratings with independent indices of therapeutic change. Thus, patients who are asked to assess their therapists' interpersonal skill levels are *not* being asked to "identify the necessary and sufficient conditions for positive change." While we agree with the authors' criticism of the Ryan and Gizynski study, we think that the format and logic of their critique is not relevant to the literature reviewed in Chapter 19 by Gurman.

16. *Editors' Footnote.* See Wilson and Evans, Chapter 20 of this volume, for a fuller consideration of the role of relationship factors in systematic desensitization and in behavior therapy in general.

17. We are indebted to Dr. Lawrence A. Hall, Assistant Professor of Psychiatry, New Jersey Medical School, for his observations regarding the possible role of relationship factors in systematic desensitization.

CHAPTER 19

THE PATIENT'S PERCEPTION OF THE THERAPEUTIC RELATIONSHIP

ALAN S. GURMAN

DESPITE the existence of a multitude of theories and approaches to the practice of psychotherapy, all major viewpoints have emphasized the importance of the therapeutic relationship. Thus, it was not surprising that Fiedler's (1950a, 1950b, 1951) early studies of the dimensions of an "ideal therapeutic relationship" found that experienced therapists of different orientations concurred in their characterization of such a relationship as warm, accepting, and understanding, and that experienced therapists of different persuasions agreed with each other more than they did with inexperienced therapists of similar orientations. While Fiedler's results have been challenged on methodological grounds (Meltzoff & Kornreich, 1970), subsequent investigations (Gonyea, 1963; Parloff, 1961; Raskin, 1965) have supported his findings.

Furthermore, it is unlikely that practicing clinicians of any theoretical persuasion would disavow the meaningfulness of the relationship construct, though their descriptive languages and explanatory schemas for its importance certainly do vary. Social-psychological arguments for the centrality of the therapist-patient relationship highlight the therapeutic relationship as a construct which mediates the therapist's attractiveness to the patient, thereby heightening the therapist's ability to influence the patient toward 'therapeutic ends (Goldstein, 1973; Goldstein, Heller, & Sechrest, 1966; Goldstein & Simonson, 1971). Behavioral or social-learning theories (Rotter, 1954; Wilson & Evans, Chapter 20, this volume) tend to emphasize the therapist's role in the relationship as that of a salient source for modeling and reinforcement of new patient behavior. Not surprisingly, recent research on the quality of the relationship in studies of behavior therapy (Mickelson & Stevic, 1971; Morris & Suckerman, 1974; Ryan & Gizynski, 1971; Vitalo, 1970) have "reinforced" Rogers' (1957) early assertion that relationship factors are operative, in terms of

treatment outcome, regardless of treatment techniques.

At the other end of the continuum of psychotherapies, psychoanalytically oriented writers have always recognized the importance of the patient-therapist relationship. The neo-analytic writings of Sullivan (1961), Menninger (1958), and Fromm-Reichman (1960) support the common observation that analytically oriented therapists view the therapist-patient relationship and the resolution of neurotic distortions of that relationship as the very cornerstone of their work. More recently, Strupp (1973) has argued that the therapeutic helping relationship, patterned after the parent-child relationship, is the key source of the therapist's interpersonal influence.

Clearly, the most emphatic statement of the necessity of a facilitative therapeutic relationship for positive personality change has been that issued by Rogers (1957), who went so far as to argue for the sufficiency of the therapeutic conditions of empathy, warmth, and genuineness for effective psychotherapy. While nearly two decades of research have now made it clear that such relationship dimensions are rarely sufficient for patient change (see Mitchell, Bozarth, & Krauft, Chapter 18, this volume), their necessity, at least as preconditions for change, seems difficult to impugn. Despite the fact that these therapeutic conditions are neither conceptually nor empirically orthogonal (Kiesler, Mathieu, & Klein, 1967; Rogers, 1957) they do, in theory, represent *somewhat* independent dimensions of the quality of the therapist's "basic feelings" or "underlying attitudes" (Rogers, 1967) toward his patient.

Thus, *accurate empathy* is theoretically described as the "ability of the therapist accurately and sensitively to understand experiences and feelings *and their meaning to the client* during the moment-to-moment encounter of psychotherapy" (Rogers & Truax, 1967). The emphasis of this construct is not upon the therapist's diagnostic understanding of the patient, which might communicate, "I understand the nature of your problem and the forces that make you act or feel that way," but rather focuses on the therapist's sensitive grasp of the phenomenological meaning to the patient of events and experiences and the current experiential impact of the patient's feelings. Thus, empathy goes beyond empathic *inference*—that is, a cognitive-intellectual understanding of the patient—to empathic *communication* "in a language attuned to the client's current feelings" (Rogers & Truax, 1967, p. 104).

Warmth, or unconditional positive regard, is manifest when a "therapist *communicates* to his client a deep and genuine caring for him as a person with human potentialities, a caring uncontaminated by evaluations of his thoughts, feelings or behaviors" (Rogers & Truax, 1967, p. 102) (emphasis supplied). Thus, low levels of warmth are displayed when the therapist expresses dislike or disapproval, or expresses warmth or liking in a selective manner. Warmth also reflects the therapist's responsiveness and active involvement with his patient and his interest and concern for the patient's welfare. It involves the therapist's nonpossessive caring for the patient as a separate person, so that "the patient is free to be himself even if this means that he is temporarily regressing, being defensive, or even disliking or rejecting the therapist himself" (Truax & Mitchell, 1971).

Genuineness, or congruence, describes the degree to which the therapist relates to his patient in a non-"phony," nonprofessionalized, nondefensive manner. Thus, low levels of genuineness occur when, for example, a therapist "presents a facade or defends and denies feelings" and high levels are present when the therapist "is freely and deeply himself" (Truax & Carkhuff, 1967). The incongruent therapist may respond "appropriately" and perhaps even care about and understand his patient, but he does so in a style that gives the impression that "his responses are formulated to sound good rather than being what he really feels and means" (Rogers & Truax, 1967, p. 102).

While in successful therapy all three conditions are assumed to be present to a high degree, it is clear that client-centered theory posits genuineness as the most basic of the conditions and as a precondition for empathy and warmth. As Rogers and Truax (1967) state succinctly,

to be deeply sensitive to the moment-to-moment "being" of another person requires of us as therapists that we first accept and to some degree prize this other person. Consequently, a satisfactory level of empathy can scarcely exist without their being also a considerable degree of unconditional positive regard. But neither of these conditions can possibly be meaningful in the relationship unless they are real. Consequently unless a therapist is, both in these respects and others, integrated and genuine within the therapeutic encounter, the other conditions could scarcely exist to a satisfactory degree. (p. 100)

Measurement of the Quality of the Therapeutic Relationship

Following from these theoretical positions and definitions, a truly immense body of research has emerged (Mitchell *et al.*, Chapter 18, this volume; Truax, 1971b; Truax & Carkhuff, 1967; Truax & Mitchell, 1971). The overwhelming majority of work in this area has focused on relationships between treatment outcome and the level of therapeutic conditions as assessed by trained judges' ratings of audio tape recordings of therapeutic interactions. The earlier enthusiastic writings of Truax (e.g., Truax & Carkhuff, 1967) seemed not only to confirm the theoretical position of Rogers (1957), but also to hold out great evidential promise for the salience and relevance of the conditions triad in most, if not all, psychotherapy. Such asserted universal contingencies rarely, if ever, however, are to be found in the study of human behavior. Not surprisingly, then, more recent evidence (e.g., Bergin & Jasper, 1969; Kurtz & Grummon, 1972; Mitchell *et al.*, Chapter 18, this volume) has suggested that there is no *necessary* (positive) relationship between therapists' conditions levels and measured therapeutic outcome. As Bergin and Jasper (1969) have persuasively argued, such findings do not imply, in and of themselves, that these manners of therapist relating are unnecessary in certain clinical situations. Rather, they argue that outside a client-centered setting, and with therapists of different theoretical orientations, the typical means for assessing these therapist qualities—i.e., via judged tape-ratings—and the nature of their operationalization and definition, closely linked to client-centered theory, probably are irrelevant. Thus, the likelihood exists that these conditions may be displayed in ways that are very discrepant from the models of therapist behavior explicated in the scales usually used for their rating (cf. Rogers, 1967, pp. 555–584). (Albert Ellis would certainly receive very low ratings on "unconditional positive regard," yet he clearly communicates a very deep sense of caring for and "prizing" his patients, albeit not in a manner that would be reflected in *client-centered* criteria.)

Unfortunately, this issue cannot be reduced to one of developing different scales for these conditions for use with different types of therapists. While such work would definitely be a valuable contribution, it would bypass the central notion inherent in the concept of "therapeutic conditions." That is, *Rogers (1957) stated unambiguously that the mere presence, or "offering," of therapeutic conditions to a patient is not sufficient for positive change. Rather, these conditions, attitudes, or styles of relating must be communicated to the patient—the patient must perceive them for change to occur.*[3,4] Thus, Howard and Orlinsky (1972) have appropriately pointed out that most research in the area of "therapeutic conditions" has been tremendously misguided on theoretical grounds. The theoretical inappropriateness of much of this empirical literature is all the more striking in that the majority of it has been conducted by Rogers' own students and by others who adhere to client-centered theory.

The apparent clinical basis for the decision by most researchers to use nonparticipant observers' ratings of the therapeutic relationship, rather than ratings by the patient, may be described. Largely on the basis of Truax' (Truax & Carkhuff, 1967) unequivocal position, it has been argued that, by virtue of the very fact of their patienthood status, patients are unable to perceive accurately the nuances and affective qualities of interpersonal relationships, perhaps especially those of an intimate nature, as in psychotherapy. It follows from this premise that patients, therefore, will "distort" their perceptions of their therapists; hence, the argument goes, assessments of the therapeutic relationship from the patient's point of view or phenomenological experience are poor indices of how facilitative the therapist "really" is.

Even granting the likelihood that such perceptual distortions may occur with a wide variety of patients does not invalidate the proposition that these therapeutic conditions must be perceived by the patient for change to occur. How a therapist communicates these feelings to different types of patients is quite a separate issue.

It should be pointed out that Truax did not disavow the usefulness of the patient's perspective in all cases. Rather, he asserted, such assessments are of "little value with severely disturbed or psychotic individuals," but may be "valuable with juvenile delinquents, outpatient neurotics, and a wide variety of vocational rehabilitation clients" (Truax & Carkhuff, 1967, p. 73). In fact, there exists evidence (Rogers, 1967) that the use of patient ratings is *not* inappropriate in psychotherapy research with chronically hospitalized schizophrenics. Unfortunately, much of the confusion about this issue seems, to this writer, to have derived from Truax' publication of data (Truax, 1971c; Truax & Carkhuff, 1967, pp. 134–135) which were presented somewhat selectively and did not convey the full findings that were available.[5] Moreover, most researchers in this area seem not to have heeded Truax' differential hypothesis about the usefulness of patient ratings as a function of the severity of patient disturbance and, therefore, have generally proceeded to focus on nonparticipant evaluations of the quality of the therapeutic relationship. The important issue of whether, in fact, trained judges and participating patients tend to agree in their evaluations of the relationship will be considered in more detail later in this chapter.[6]

Setting aside this speculative analysis of why the patient's perception of the therapeutic relationship has generally received only passing attention, the key proposition that remains is that it is the patient's perception of the quality of the therapeutic relationship that mediates therapeutic change. Although nearly 100 studies of the perceived qualities of interpersonal relating had been published as of 1972 (Barrett-Lennard, 1972a), no comprehensive review of this literature has yet been undertaken. While this chapter is limited to an examination of research on the patient's perception of "therapeutic conditions" in psychotherapy and counseling, it should be pointed out that such participant evaluations are relevant to a wide variety of encounters beyond psychotherapy. Rogers' (1957) important assertion that his proposed "necessary and sufficient conditions" for positive personality change characterize all important human relationships has received substantial support outside professionalized helping relationships. Thus, these perceived interpersonal conditions have been shown to reflect changes in therapy with married couples (Griffin, 1967; Gurman, 1975; Wells, Figurel, & McNamee, 1975) and to correlate with measures of both marital (Quick & Jacob, 1973; Thornton, 1960) and family (Hollenbeck, 1961; Rosen, 1961; Van Der Veen & Novak, 1970) adjustment. Perceived levels of these conditions also appear to be related to the quality of friendship relationships (Armstrong, 1969; Shapiro,

Krauss, & Truax, 1969; Shapiro & Voog, 1969). Thus, an integrative and critical review of the patient's perception of the therapeutic relationship is likely to have implications that extend beyond formalized "treatment" encounters.

ASSESSING THE PATIENT'S PERCEPTION OF THE RELATIONSHIP

The major instrument used in assessing the patient's perception of the therapeutic relationship is the Relationship Inventory (RI) of Barrett-Lennard (1962). This questionnaire, originally designed for use in individual psychotherapy, has undergone several revisions since its initial publication and has also been adapted for a variety of relationships (group therapy, family interactions, and friendship relations) other than the therapy dyad (Barrett-Lennard, 1972b). Although similar instruments, based on the same theoretical work as the RI, have been used (Gurman, 1973b; Truax & Carkhuff, 1967, pp. 74–79), all but a very small number of studies of the patient's perception have employed the RI; therefore, a detailed description of its construction, reliability, and factor structure seems in order at this point.

Construction of the RI and Definitions of the "Therapeutic Conditions"

As emphasized above, the essential proposition in Rogers' (1957) classical statement on the therapeutic relationship is that "the *client's experience* of his therapist's responses is the primary locus of therapeutic influence in their relationship" (Barrett-Lennard, 1962, p. 2). While Rogers quite properly pointed out that the therapist must first experience certain inward qualities of response to his client, their impact on the client clearly was seen to require the therapist's *communicative expression* of these attitudes. Barrett-Lennard (1962) notes that, "although it is not supposed that a client's conscious perceptions would represent with complete accuracy the way he experiences his therapist, it would seem that his own report, given under suitable conditions, would be the most direct and reliable evidence we could get of his actual experience" (p. 2).

In regard to his descriptions of the dimensions of the therapeutic relationship tapped by the RI, Barrett-Lennard (1962) notes that

> Two of the variables, the concepts of empathic understanding and congruence of the therapist, correspond in essence with the meanings given by Rogers. Two others,

level of regard and unconditionality of regard, represent a division of the concept of unconditional positive regard, originally formulated by Standal (1954), into what are considered by the investigator to be two separate components. They are, therefore, newly defined. (p. 3)

In addition, a fifth variable, the therapist's "willingness to be known" was added by Barrett-Lennard to Rogers' formulation. This scale was dropped from a revision of the RI (Barrett-Lennard, 1969) because of its lack of predictive power in relation to therapeutic outcome (Barrett-Lennard, 1962).

Item Content. Initial items in the RI derived from Rogers' (1957) paper on the conditions of therapy and from Bown's (1954) Relationship Sort. Revisions of item content followed discussion and written comment from staff members at the University of Chicago Counseling Center. Barrett-Lennard (1962) further notes that "The preparation of items involved constant interaction between theory and operational expression and resulted in a continuous growth and progressive refinement of meaning relating to each concept" (p. 6).

Content Validation. A formal content validation procedure was carried out to eliminate nondifferential items. Five judges (client-centered therapists) categorized each item as either a "positive" or "negative" expression of the therapeutic condition it was intended to represent, and used a "neutral" rating for items they regarded as irrelevant or unclear. Following this, each judge rated "positive" items on a scale from $+1$ to $+5$ and "negative" items on a scale from -1 to -5, with regard to their salience as positive or negative expressions of the appropriate variable. The judges' mean ratings were subsequently used in choosing the two half-samples of items for split-half reliability. On the basis of the judges' ratings and some near duplications, six items from the original 92 were eliminated. One other item failed to pass a preliminary empirical item-analysis. The final original version of the RI consisted of 85 items, with each variable represented by 16 to 18 items. The current basic form (Barrett-Lennard, 1964, 1969) contains 64 items, with 16 for each of the four conditions, eight expressed positively and eight expressed negatively.

Endorsement and Scoring. In an attempt to avoid assessing merely the respondent's perception of the presence or absence of therapeutic attitudes, Barrett-Lennard emphasized the importance of determining the clarity and strength of the patient's view. Thus, each item calls for a choice of one of six possible levels of agreement, ranging from $+3$ to -3: "I feel it is probably true (or not true)"; "I feel it is true (or not true)"; "I strongly feel that it is true (or not true)." In the final revision, the items are arranged so that every fourth item taps the same variable. Positive and negative items for each dimension are equally distributed between the two halves of the test.

The scoring procedure has not changed in revisions of the RI. A face-value weighting of the response to each item allows each response for a variable to either add to or detract from the total score on that scale, according to the direction of its theoretical meaning. Thus, on responses to theoretically negative items, the sign is reversed. This method yields a possible scoring range of $+3n$ to $-3n$, where $n = 16$ items per subscale.

Alternate Forms. In addition to the basic RI (Forms OS-64) used for clients to answer in individual counseling and therapy research, and the corresponding form (MO-64) with items worded in the first person for therapists to describe their response to their patients, three alternate forms have been developed: Form OS-G-64 for use in assessing an individual's perception of the conditions presented by a group as a whole (Barrett-Lennard, 1972b);Experimental Form OS-S-42 (containing 42 items) for use in assessing one's view of relationships with family members, friends and personal acquaintances, fellow-workers, and others in one's "public life" (Barrett-Lennard, 1973); and a Teacher-Pupil Relationship Inventory adapted from the basic Form OS-64 (Scheuer, 1969).

The Therapeutic Conditions. Empathic understanding (E) refers to

> the extent to which one person is conscious of the immediate awareness of another ... it is an active process of desiring to know the full present and changing awareness of another person, of reaching out to receive his communication and meaning, and of translating his words and signs into experienced meaning that matches at least those aspects of his awareness that are most important to him at the moment. It is an experiencing of the consciousness "behind" another's outward communication. (Barrett-Lennard, 1962, p. 3)

The empathic process involves both empathic recognition, awareness of feelings directly communicated by the patient, and empathic inference—the sensing of implied or indirectly expressed feelings, perceptions, and attitudes. Examples of items on this scale (Form OS-64) are: "He realizes what I mean even when I have difficulty in saying it" $(+)$; "He appreciates exactly how the things I experience feel to me" $(+)$; "He may understand my words but he does not see the way I feel" $(-)$; "His response to me

is usually so fixed and automatic that I don't really get through to him" $(-)$.

Level of regard (R) refers to

> the affective aspect of one person's response to another ... Positive feelings include respect, liking, appreciation, affection, and any other affectively adient response ... negative feelings include dislike, impatience, contempt and in general affectively abient responses. Level of regard ... may be considered the composite "loading" of all the distinguishable feeling reactions of one person toward another, positive and negative, on a single abstract dimension. The lower extreme ... represents maximum predominance and intensity of negative-type feeling, not merely a lack of positive feeling. (Barrett-Lennard, 1962, p. 9)

Examples of items on this scale are: "He respects me as a person" $(+)$; "He is friendly and warm with me" $(+)$; "He finds me rather dull and uninteresting" $(-)$; "He is impatient with me" $(-)$.

Unconditionality of regard (U) was originally described by Barrett-Lennard (1962) as referring to

> how little or how much variability there is in one person's response to another (regardless of its general level) ... the more A's immediate regard for B varies in response to change in B's feelings toward himself, or toward A, or the different experiences or attitudes that B is communicating to A, or differences in A's mood that are not dependent on B ... the more conditional it is. (p. 4)

The revision of the RI resulted in a more refined definition of UR: "In order for variation in A's response to B to imply conditionality, this variation needs to be linked in the perceiver's experience with some quality or behavior of B" (Barrett-Lennard, 1970, p. 5). Thus, the new definition of UR noted that an inconsistency in the therapist's feelings toward the patient, in order to represent conditionality, had to reflect variability in response to some discernible aspect of the patient. Hence, variability attributable to stimulus sources other than that of the patient (e.g., a therapist's changed mood due to factors extraneous to treatment) would not meet this criterion. Examples of items on this scale are: "I can (or could) be openly critical or appreciative of him without really making him feel any differently about me" $(+)$; "How much he likes or dislikes me is not altered by anything that I tell him about myself" $(+)$; "Depending on my behavior he has a better opinion of me sometimes than he has at other times" $(-)$; "His interest in me depends on the things I say or do" $(-)$.

Congruence (C) refers to

> the degree to which one person is functionally integrated in the context of his relationship with another, such that there is absence of conflict or in-

consistency between his total experience, his awareness, and his overt communication . . . the highly congruent individual is completely honest, direct, and sincere in what he conveys, but he does not feel any compulsion to communicate his perceptions, or any need to withhold them for emotionally self-protective reasons. (Barrett-Lennard, 1962, p. 4)

Noting that C is manifest not only in a therapist's experienced feelings toward the patient, but also in his nonverbal behavior, an extremely important point to be discussed in detail later in this chapter, Barrett-Lennard (1962) adds that

Direct evidence of lack of congruence includes, for example, inconsistency between what the individual says, and what he implies by expression, gestures, or tone of voice. Indications of discomfort, tension, or anxiety are considered to be less direct but equally important evidence of lack of congruence. (p. 4)

The central role of C among the therapeutic conditions, mentioned earlier in reference to Rogers and Truax (1967, p. 100), is conceived by Barrett-Lennard (1962) as setting

an upper limit to the degree to which empathic understanding of another is possible . . . (and) the degree to which an individual can actually respond unconditionally to another is considered a function of his security and integration in relation to the other . . . lack of congruence implies threat and defensiveness and this would tend to reduce overall regard. (p. 5)

Item examples are: "He is comfortable and at ease in our relationship" (+); "He is willing to express whatever is actually in his mind with me, including any feelings about himself or about me" (+); "I feel that he puts on a role or front with me" (−); "I believe that he has feelings he does not tell me about that are causing difficulty in our relationship" (−).

Reliability of the Relationship Inventory

The stability of the RI has been assessed in 14 studies of internal reliability and in 10 studies of test-retest reliability. Five of the studies reporting internal consistencies have been in actual therapy situations, four in therapy analogues, and one in friendship relationships. As can be seen in Table 1, the split-half reliabilities for each of the RI subscales and RI total score are uniformly very high. The mean internal reliability coefficients across these studies are: E, .84; R, .91; U, .74; C, .88; Tot, .91. In addition, Fretz' (1966) partial presentation of internal reliabilities showed correlations ranging from .58 to .76 when the RI was administered after the third counseling session and correlations between .68 to .94 on the second administration, following the sixth interview.

Reports of test-retest reliability similarly show a good deal of stability (Table 1), with mean test-retest correlations of: E, .83; R, .83; U, .80; C, .85; Tot, .90. Thus, the perceptions of therapists by patients, of therapists by themselves, and of parents by children appear highly stable over time. While the majority of these studies used relatively short intervals between testings (approximately one month), three reports did find a high degree of stability over periods of several months. These positive findings assume major methodological importance since the vast majority of studies using the RI have tapped the patient's perception of the therapeutic relationship at only one moment in time, usually around the fourth session in naturalistic studies. Furthermore, many of the studies to be described below are of the one-encounter analogue type. Thus, in considering all these studies together, we may be reassured of the stability of patients' perceptions of their therapists on the basis of the summary data presented in Table 1.

Interrelationships Among RI Scales

As noted earlier, the therapeutic conditions measured by the RI are theoretically assumed to represent different aspects of the therapist's manner of relating to a patient (and, therefore, different dimensions of the patient's experience of that relationship), but to be, nevertheless, conceptually related to each other to some degree. Barrett-Lennard (1962, p. 3) argued that therapist congruence would set upper limits, particularly to the level of his empathic response, and, in addition, affect qualities of regard and unconditionality. Rogers and Truax (1967) also posited the primacy of congruence as a precondition for the communication of warmth and empathy. Thus, in a statistical framework, one would predict significant moderately positive correlations among these conditions. Two sources of data are available for determining the interrelationships among the therapeutic conditions tapped by the RI.

Table 2 presents a summary of studies which have reported intercorrelations among the RI scales. Nine existing studies in this domain have measured the *patient's perception of his therapist* in either naturalistic or analogue settings. The mean intercorrelations, ranges, and standard deviations among RI scales for these studies are presented in Table 3. Thus, despite differences in the degree of disturbance of the patient populations and the level of therapist experience in these studies, three trends emerge: (1) among E, R, and C there is a moderately positive degree

TABLE 1. INTERNAL AND TEST-RETEST RELIABILITIES OF THE RELATIONSHIP INVENTORY

Internal Reliability

Author	Population or Setting	Reliability Measure	RI Scale				
			E	R	U	C	Tot.
Abramowitz & Jackson (1974)	Group therapy outpatients (N = 28)	Alpha coefficient	—	—	—	—	.92
Barrett-Lennard (1962)	Individual therapy outpatients (N = 42)	Split-half	.86	.93	.82	.89	—
Belpaire & Archambault (1973)	Juvenile delinquents: relationship with teachers	Split-half	.91	.92	.49	.90	—
Belpaire & Archambault (1973)	Teachers' relationship with delinquents	Split-half	.87	.95	.79	.90	—
Gurman (1973a)	Individual therapy outpatients (N = 5:39 administrations)	Split-half	—	—	—	—	.86
Hollenbeck (1961)	College students: relationships with parents	Split-half	.86	.95	.89	.87	.97
Lietaer (1974a)[a]	Individual therapy outpatients (N = 96)	Split-half	.81	.88	.67	.87	—
Lietaer (1974a)[a]	Individual outpatient therapists (N = 110)	Split-half	.90	.93	.74	.87	—
Lietaer (1974b)	College students: relationships with parents	Split-half	.92	.91	.68	.90[b]	—
Lin (1973a)	Individual and group counseling analogue (N = 48)	Alpha coefficient	.88	.91	.76	.92	—
McClanahan (1974)	Individual counseling outpatients (N = 86)	Alpha coefficient	.88	.92	.67	.90	.95
Pierce (1971)	Individual therapy analogue (N = 60)	Split-half	.74	—	—	—	—
Snelbecker (1967)	Individual therapy analogue (N = 66)	Split-half	.78	.93	.83	.89	—
Tosi (1970)	Individual counseling analogue (N = 69)	Split-half	—	—	—	—	.82
Wiebe & Pearce (1973)	College students: relationship with friends	Alpha	.64	.83	.73	.80	.93

Test-Retest Reliability

Author	Population or Setting	Time Interval	RI Scale				
			E	R	U	C	Tot.
Barrett-Lennard (1962)	College students: rated close personal relationship (N = 36)	4 weeks	.89	.84	.90	.86	.95
Barrett-Lennard (1969)	College students: rated parents (N = 40)	2–6 weeks	.86	.88	.86	.92	.92
Barrett-Lennard (1969)	Therapists: rated self with most recent client (N = 38)	12 days	.91	.79	.86	.85	.89
Berzon (1964)	Group therapy outpatients (N = 20)	4 weeks	—	—	—	—	.86
Hollenbeck (1961)	College students rated mothers (N = 46)	6 months	.74	.81	.61	.79	.83
Kiesler et al. (1967a)	Individual therapy: hospitalized schizophrenics (N = 8)	4–12 months	.81	.91	.80	.91	.93
Kiesler et al. (1967a)	Therapists: self-rating (N = 11)	4–12 months	.88	.85	.78	.76	.94
Kurtz & Grummon (1972)	Individual therapy outpatients (N = 31)	12 weeks (mean)	.66	—	—	—	—
Mills & Zytowski (1967)	Female college students: mother-child relationship, mothers rated (N = 79)	3 weeks	.90	.74	.80	.88	—
Mills & Zytowski (1967)	Female college students: mother-child relationship, child rates self (N = 79)	3 weeks	.84	.86	.80	.87	—

[a] Lietaer presented reliability data for both "positive regard" and "negative regard," which he had found to be empirically distinguishable. The entries under R here refer to "positive regard;" "negative regard" reliability coefficients were: Therapists, .88; Patients, .82.

[b] Lietaer, in his factor analytic study, found what he called a "transparency" factor, which appears indistinguishable from Barrett-Lennard's (1962) congruence dimension.

TABLE 2. Intercorrelations Among Relationship Inventory Scales of Empathy (E), Regard (R), Unconditionality (U), Congruence (C), and Total Score (T)

Author	E–R	E–U	E–C	R–U	R–C	C–U	E–T	R–T	U–T	C–T	Comments
Barrett-Lennard (1962)	.56	.43	.85	.16	.65	.42	.86	.78	.53	.92	Client ratings after session 5
Barrett-Lennard (1962)	.61	.58	.71	.56	.69	.64	.84	.81	.83	.89	Therapist self-ratings after session 5
Belpaire & Archambault (1973)	.53	.60	.66	.44	.33	.44	—	—	—	—	Most advanced (educationally) delinquents in treatment program
Belpaire & Archambault (1973)	.86	.32	.90	.32	.90	.33	—	—	—	—	Least advanced (educationally) delinquents in treatment program
Berlin (1960)	.37	.54	.70	.52	.55	.71	("positive" relationships)				Female college students' ratings of ongoing interpersonal relationships
	.52	−.04	−.12	.09	−.02	.38	("negative" relationships)				
Carmichael (1970)[b]	.63	−.28	.74	−.36	.84	−.16	.76	.83	.09	.92	Client ratings after session 6 (analogue)
Hollenbeck (1961)	.59	.50	.71	.58	.71	.61	—	—	—	—	College students' ratings of maternal relationship
Hollenbeck (1961)	.65	.49	.72	.52	.72	.53	—	—	—	—	College students' ratings of paternal relationships
Kiesler et al. (1967a)	.43	.39	.48	.68	.83	.77	.64	.95	.73	.88	Initial patient ratings
Kiesler et al. (1967a)	−.13	.22	.26	.40	.27	.38	.58	.66	.68	.70	Terminal patient ratings
Lee (1968)[a]	.60	.41	.55	.45	.70	.56	—	—	—	—	Educational-vocational counseling clients' ratings after one interview
Lewis & Krauss (1971)[c]	(Correlations among E, R, and C ranged from .55 to .74; correlations between U and other scales ranged from .03 to .25)										Client ratings: 7- to 10-minute analogue interview
Lin (1973b)	.70	.31	.71	.23	.74	.10	—	—	—	—	Female student teachers' rating female counselors (analogue)
Lindahl (1973)	.67	—	.60	—	.79	—	.84	.88	—	.87	Patient ratings of group therapists: Study I (Truax Relationship Questionnaire)
Lindahl (1973)	.68	—	.59	—	.61	—	.86	.88	—	.74	Patient rating of group therapists: Study II (Truax Relationship Questionnaire)
Lovejoy (1971)	.75	.57	.67	.52	.67	.56	—	—	—	—	College students' ratings of relationships with friends (high C Ss)
Lovejoy (1971)	.76	.69	.77	.60	.71	.57	—	—	—	—	College students' ratings of relationships with friends (low C Ss)
McClanahan (1974)	.70	.44	.79	.39	.80	.53	—	—	—	—	Client ratings
Mills & Zytowski (1967)	.63	.59	.71	.44	.62	.45	—	—	—	—	Female college students' ratings of their mothers
Mills & Zytowski (1967)	.44	.47	.65	.39	.61	.57	—	—	—	—	Female college students' self-ratings in relationships with mothers
Schoeninger (1965)	.54	—	.63	—	.61	—	—	—	—	—	College students' ratings of therapists (analogue)
Tosi, Frumkin, & Wilson (1968)	.50	.44	.58	.31	.46	.45	.49	.42	.36	.61	Educational-vocational counseling clients' ratings after session 1
Wiebe & Pearce (1973)	.63	.49	.66	.53	.75	.66	—	—	—	—	College students' ratings of relationships with friends

[a] Also included here are data on the Truax-Carkhuff (1967) Relationship Questionnaire.

[b] Appreciation is expressed to Carmichael, who made his raw data available to this author for statistical analysis.

[c] The complete intercorrelation matrix was not included in the Lewis and Krauss report.

of interrelationship or, stated otherwise, these dimensions appear to be relatively dependent; (2) U bears a very low (and in one case negative— Carmichael, 1970) relationship to the other conditions (i.e., it is quite independent); and (3) E, R, and C are all either moderately related or

TABLE 3. MEANS, RANGES, AND STANDARD DEVIATIONS OF INTERCORRELATIONS AMONG RI PATIENT SCALES

		C	R	U	T
E	X̄	.62	.53	.28	.72
	Range	.26 —.85	−.13 —.70	−.28 —.44	.49 —.86
	S.D.	.18	.26	.26	.15
C	X̄		.67	.36	.81
	Range		.27 —.84	−.16 —.77	.61 —.92
	S.D.		.19	.30	.12
R	X̄			.26	.77
	Range			−.36 —.68	.42 —.95
	S.D.			.32	.18
U	X̄				.48
	Range				.09 —.73
	S.D.				.26

Note. E = Empathy, C = Congruence, R = Level of Regard, U = Unconditionality of Regard, T = Total. This table is based on the studies of Barrett-Lennard (1962), Carmichael (1970), Kiesler *et al.* (1967a), Lin (1973b), Lindahl (1973), McClanahan (1974), and Tosi *et al.*, (1968). Lietaer's (1974a) results were quite consistent with those presented in this table; Lietaer's data have not been included here because of both his failure to present a full correlation matrix and because the relationship between his subscales of "positive regard" and "negative regard" and R are uncertain. Lietaer (1974b), in a factor-analytic revision of the RI, found similarly consistent intercorrelations. In addition, Schoeninger (1965), using a modification of the RI, found results consistent with those in this table: E-R, .54; E-C, .63; R-C, .61. U was not included in his questionnaire. Finally, Goby (1973) found the following intercorrelations in a study of 69 inpatient-treated alcoholics: E-R, .79; E-U, .53; E-C, .82; R-U, .42; R-C, .75; C-U, .48.

highly related to T, whereas U accounts for the least variance in T among the four scales. The partial data presented by Lewis and Krauss (1971) is consistent with this trend. Also, in light of Rogers' assertion (Rogers & Traux, 1967) that the level of C sets an upper limit on the other therapeutic conditions, and Barrett-Lennard's (1962) earlier related comments, it is interesting to note that C shows the highest mean correlation with T —.83. In general, studies of nontherapy interactions appear broadly consistent with the findings derived from treatment situations (Table 2).

A comparison of the intercorrelations among the RI scales presented in Table 2 with the internal reliability data on these scales presented in Table 1 shows that the latter uniformly exceed the former. The implication of this comparison is that these scales, while overlapping to some extent, are consistently measuring different dimensions of the patient's perceptions of the therapeutic relationship. Thus, even within the pairing (R-C) with the highest mean correlation (.69), only 47.6% of the variance of either scale can be attributed to the variance of the other scale.

The second, and more powerful, means for assessing the dimensionality of the RI calls for an examination of available factor-analytic studies of the questionnaire. Mills and Zytowski

(1967) factor-analyzed the scale (not item) intercorrelations originally presented by Barrett-Lennard (1962).[7] Using a principal components factor analysis of these data, they extracted three factors. Factor I accounted for about 67% of the total variance, with the subscales loading on it in the following manner: C, .94; E, .91; R, .75; U, .57. Factor II, which accounted for about 15% of the total variance, had a loading of .79 on U, with zero-magnitude loadings on E (−.01) and C (−.08), and a negative loading on R (−.48), suggesting that this was an unconditionality factor. The third factor, accounting for about 10% of the total variance, showed low but positive loadings on R (.45) *and* U (.24) and negative loadings on E (-.33) and C (−.18). This third factor was interpreted by the authors as one of "relationship distortion." Noting that perceptual accuracy and liking for others have been found to be negatively related, Mills and Zytowski argue that a high regard for another person may necessitate some distortion of his characteristics—*too much* regard may influence a therapeutic relationship in an untoward way. On the basis of these findings, Mills and Zytowski (1967) conclude that the presence of a general component accounting for two-thirds of the total variance "seriously questions the presence of multiple (and independent) characteristics of a relationship as measured by the relationship inventory. There appears to be a single dominant characteristic . . . to which all four subtests contribute strongly"

While such a conclusion seems appropriate to the data, it should be pointed out that U was the subscale with the lowest loading (.57) on Factor I and the highest loading (.79) on Factor II, implying that U may represent a separate component of the RI. This possibility will be examined below in reviewing the studies of Gross, Curtin, and Moore (1971), Lewis and Krauss (1971), and Walker and Little (1969).

McClanahan (1974) also performed a principal components analysis of the RI in a study of 83 clients treated in a university counseling center. The RI was administered after three to eight sessions, essentially the same point in counseling as in Barrett-Lennard's (1962) study (fifth session). McClanahan's factor analysis was done on both the RI and the Counseling Evaluation Inventory (CEI) of Linden, Stone, and Shertzer (1965). A one-factor solution for the four RI scales and the three CEI scales of "client satisfaction," "counseling climate," and "counselor comfort" accounted for 57% of the total variance, a finding similar to Mills and Zytowski's (1967) first general component, which accounted for about 67% of the variance. While McClanahan's results thus support those of Mills and Zytowski in arguing for the unidimensionality of the RI, it should be pointed out that in this study the U subscale once again showed the lowest loading (.59) on the general factor (cf: E, .82; R, .84; C, .91).

Lin (1973b) factor-analyzed the RI scales on the basis of the ratings of 48 female student teachers who were randomly assigned to three female counselors for five half-hour sessions. His factor analysis also included ratings after the fifth session on the Sorenson Empathy and Expertness scales (Lin, 1971) and on a revised version of the Truax-Carkhuff Relationship Questionnaire (Truax & Carkhuff, 1967). A One-factor solution, accounting for 65% of the total variance, yielded high positive loadings on E (.85), R (.81), and C (.82), while U loaded only .29.

The study of Gross et al. (1971) has also provided evidence for the possibility of nonindependence among the RI scales. Thirteen staff members of a Veterans Administration Hospital psychiatric ward supplied self-ratings on the RI. Dimensional descriptions of the ward environment were obtained from a principal components vector analysis using the Hotelling iterative procedure (Morrison, 1967). Only the first vector component of the staff's self-descriptions was significant, thus suggesting that the four RI scales may be accounted for by one dimension. This factor accounted for 61% of the total variance of staff ratings. While the loadings on the RI scales were within a narrow range (.70 to .88), once again the U subscale showed the lowest loading on the vector.

Lewis and Krauss (1971), in an analogue study of the relationship between perceived therapeutic conditions and interviewee self-disclosure, found a two-factor solution of the RI. Factor I, accounting for 55% of the total variance, showed all subscales except U having positive loadings between .76 and .87, whereas U loaded only .22 on this factor. Factor II, which accounted for 7% of the total variance, showed a positive loading of .44 for U, with the other subscale loadings ranging from .18 to −.32.

In the study of Gross et al. (1971) described above, patient dimensionality of the RI was also examined. Patient descriptions of the ward staff yielded two dimensions, with E, R, and C contributing to the first vector (.94, .90, and .93, respectively) and U showing a zero-magnitude loading (−.02). Factor II was clearly an unconditionality factor (loading .99), with the other scales being noncontributory (E, .16; R, −.28; C, .14). In this analysis of patient dimensionality, Factor I accounted for 64% of the total variance and Factor II accounted for 28% of the total variance.

All the studies just described (Gross et al., 1971; Lin, 1973b; McClanahan, 1974; Mills & Zytowski, 1967) involved principal component factor analyses based on interscale correlations. In using this method, the distinctive variance of individual items is submerged in the original (Barrett-Lennard, 1962) scales so that the information about what the items do is untapped— that is, only a small part of the information has gone into the analyses and, therefore, yields results of very limited practical use. In addition, the principal components method, without rotation, gathers as much variance as possible into a single factor at the expense of sorting out well-differentiated clusters. The difference between beginning with item (versus scale) intercorrelations is so fundamental that the utility of findings based on this procedure is highly questionable.

Three studies that did begin with item intercorrelations, not subscales, can be described. On the basis of a principal components analysis, Walker and Little (1969) found 10 factored homogeneous item dimensions (FHID) which were then intercorrelated. Rotated maximum-likelihood estimates of factor loadings yielded three components. Factor I was labeled "non-evaluative acceptance," with the highest loadings (.68 and .66) being on two of the three previously determined unconditionality item dimensions. Factor II, "psychological insight," was defined by positive loadings (.56 and .55) on two of the three empathy dimensions found earlier and by positive loadings (.61 and .51) on the two congruence dimensions yielded by the FHID analysis. The third factor was labeled "likability" rather than "positive regard" because the emphasis of the items on the first R dimension (which loaded .83 on the factor), determined by the FHID procedure, was on liking and caring, whereas the second FHID R dimension, which focused on valuing or esteeming, did not contribute as much to this factor (loading .45).

Perhaps the most careful factor-analytic study on the RI since the original Barrett-Lennard (1962) work has been that of Lietaer (1974a, 1974b) in Holland. In the first study Lietaer (1974b) administered an extended form of the RI (the 64-item inventory, plus 20 items from the original [1962] RI, plus 39 items constructed by Lietaer) to 800 college students, half whom rated their relationships with their mothers and half of whom rated their relationships with their fathers. Using a rotated principal components method, Lietaer found the same five meaningful factors for both sets of data: empathy, positive regard, unconditionality, transparency, and directivity. For each of these factors, he then selected the 10 best items to construct a short RI scale, which has since been used as a measure of outcome in marital therapy (Vansteenwegen, 1974).

In the second study Lietaer (1974a) applied the 123-item RI to 100 patient-therapist pairs, half of whom were involved in client-centered therapy and half of whom were involved in psychoanalytically oriented therapy. In this analysis, six factors emerged: empathy, regard, unconditionality, incongruence, transparency, and directivity. Interestingly, unconditionality correlated .49 with a combined score of the empathy, regard, and incongruence scales for the client-centered therapy but was completely independent of them for clients in psycho-dynamically oriented treatment.

In an unpublished study from which only minimal data could be retrieved by the present author, Bebout (1971) carried out Varimax rotations on the RI items (64-item form) from 287 group participants who rated their non-professional encounter group leaders. Bebout found five factors: empathic understanding, positive regard, conditionality, open-genuine, and non-imposing. These leaders were trained to share their immediate positive or negative feelings in their groups in every interpersonal transaction possible. Since those reactions were frequently negative and value-laden, an unconditionality factor could hardly have been expected.

The similarity of the results of Bebout and those of Lietaer is particularly striking in light of the language and cultural differences between their samples.

In summary, *Barrett-Lennard's (1962) stress on the two distinct aspects of regard—the level of regard and the unconditionality of regard—appears to be justified in light of the nine studies reviewed above. The generally high degree of concordance between the E, C, and R subscales found in the studies based on interscale correlations, however, are not supported by the results of studies based on item correlations. On the basis of the existing data deriving from properly conducted factor-analytic studies, it appears that the RI is tapping dimensions that are quite consistent with Barrett-Lennard's original work on the inventory.* While Kiesler (1974) may be correct in stating that "the dimensionality characteristics of the Relationship Inventory remain to be established unequivocally," data appearing since his review rather strongly contradict his conclusion that "there are no more than three factors being measured by the four subtests" (p. 316). Of particular relevance to this chapter is the continuing need for factor-analytic work on the RI in actual treatment settings.

A final note seems in order at this point on the factor structure of the RI conditions in neurotic versus schizophrenic patients. Kiesler *et al.* (1967b) have argued strongly that "perceptions of the therapeutic relationship seem to cluster differently in neurotic and schizophrenic samples. Neurotics associate the therapist's genuineness with his communicated level of empathic understanding while schizophrenics tend to view genuineness and regard factors as related" (p. 172). They further state that this difference may reflect the "relatively greater focus on self-exploration rather than on relationship formation occurring in the initial perceptions of neurotic patients, in contrast to the schizophrenics' placement of more emphasis on the therapist's potential for a genuine understanding of them." While this argument seems clinically sound, the results of the Gross *et al.* (1971) study described earlier may question the Kiesler *et al.* (1967b) position on empirical grounds, in that unconditionality (not level) of regard was found to represent a separate factor dimension. Unfortunately, these two studies are not directly comparable in that Kiesler *et al.* (1967a) studied individual psychotherapy relationships and Gross *et al.* examined perceived relationships between schizophrenic patients and their ward staff as a group. *Further research is clearly needed to determine whether, in fact, the dimensional structure of the RI varies between populations with differing degrees of psychological disturbance.*

PERCEPTION OF THERAPEUTIC CONDITIONS BY PATIENTS, THERAPISTS, AND TRAINED JUDGES

As noted earlier, Rogers' (1957) original conception of the therapeutic dimensions of the patient-therapist relationship emphasized that in order for these attitudes to be communicated to the patient, they must first be experienced by the therapist. Thus, an important issue is whether patients and therapists agree in their perceptions of these qualities in the therapeutic relationship. It is also important to assess the amount of agreement in the rating of these conditions by patients and trained nonparticipant judges, since it has been assumed that trained raters operate out of a frame of reference close to that of the patient (Kiesler *et al.*, 1967a). Hence, as Kiesler *et al.* (1967a) note, "this rating perspective was compatible with Rogers' emphasis on the importance of the patient's perception of therapist conditions as a prerequisite to personality change" (p. 181).

Patients' and Therapists' Perceptions of the Therapeutic Relationship

Table 4 presents a summary of published correlations between patient and therapist ratings on the four RI subscales and the RI total. From the very limited amount of data that has been published in this regard, it is clear that *there is very little agreement between patients' and therapists' perceptions of the quality of the therapeutic relationship.* Nearly a third of the reported correlations are of zero-order magnitude, while the majority of these coefficients are positive but not significant. About one-third

of these reported correlations even show negative relationships between the two rating vantage points. A significant level of agreement on ratings of E is found in three of these eight studies (Anderson, Harrow, Schwarte, & Kupfer, 1972; Hill, 1974; Lietaer, 1974a). It is possible that a slightly different therapist quality (i.e., "therapist understanding") was being measured in two of these studies, rather than empathy. Furthermore, the Burstein and Carkhuff (1968) study, which also used a 5-point rating scale rather than the RI-E scale, failed to find agreement between patients' and therapists' perceptions in two samples (experienced and inexperienced) of therapists. Another analogue study (Shapiro, 1968b) also found similar results. The salience of these largely nonsignificant relationships between patients' and therapists' perceptions of their relationship is heightened by the fact that all but two of the studies reported in Table 4 were conducted under real therapy conditions.

Therapists tend to rate themselves more positively on the RI conditions than do their patients. Thus, Gross *et al.* (1971) and Kiesler *et al.* (1967a), both studying hospitalized schizophrenic patients, found ward staff ratings and individual therapists' ratings to be higher than patient ratings of these same clinicians. This difference was upheld on all scales of the RI in both studies with the exception of patient-perceived C in the Gross *et al.* study, where the difference only approached significance, but in the same direction as on the other scales.

Two studies of individual outpatient psychotherapy yielded more ambiguous comparative results. Kurts and Grummon (1972) found that counselors rated themselves higher on the E scale of the RI than did clients early in therapy (after the third session), but that there was no difference in their mean ratings after the final interview. Barrett-Lennard's (1962) therapists saw themselves as more congruent and as offering higher levels of regard and total conditions than did their patients (after the fifth interview), while patients perceived higher levels of E and U than their therapists experienced themselves as providing.

The two existing analogue studies comparing mean therapist and patient relationship ratings found conflicting results. Grosz' (1968) data, consistent with the trend toward higher therapist ratings noted in the four studies just described, showed counselors' ratings exceeding those of interviewees on the basis of RI total scores. Warren (1973), however, found signifi-

TABLE 4. SUMMARY OF REPORTED CORRELATIONS BETWEEN PATIENT AND THERAPIST RATINGS OF THERAPEUTIC CONDITIONS

Author	Therapeutic Condition				Tot.	Comments
	E	R	U	C		
Anderson, Harrow, Schwartz, & Kupfer (1972)	$p<.01$	$p<.01$	—	N.S.	—	6-point rating scales T "understanding"=E T "interest"=R T "mood"=C
Barrett-Lennard (1962)	.09	.23	.33*	.27	.22	Rating after session 5
Burstein & Carkhuff (1968)	.42	.20	—	.40	.49[b]	Inexperienced T's
Burstein & Carkhuff (1968)	−.22	.47	—	−.67*	−.01	Experienced T's
Hill (1974)	.38*	—	—	—	—	5-point scale from Orlinsky & Howard's (1966) Therapy Session Report: T "understanding"=E
Kiesler et al. (1967a)	−.53	−.07	.14	−.40	−.42	Initial ratings
Kiesler et al. (1967a)	.02	−.16	.06	.12	−.23	Terminal ratings
Kurtz & Grummon (1972)	.20	—	—	—	—	Rating after session 3
Kurtz & Grummon (1972)	.21	—	—	—	—	Rating after final session ($\bar{x}=12$)
Lietaer (1974a)[c]	.46***	.31	.15	.30	.35**	Clients in client-centered therapy
Lietaer (1974a)[c]	.16	−.10	.10	−.03	.28	Clients in analytically oriented therapy
Lietaer (1974a)[c]	.35*	.15	.14	.16	.15	Client-centered and analytic samples combined
Shapiro (1968a)	—	—	—	—	.29	Speech clinicians and standard interviewed

*$p<.01$.

**$p<.05$.

***$p<.001$; all other reported correlations N.S.

[a]The authors did not provide the actual correlations, merely the significance levels.

[b]The authors report this correlation to be significant at $p<.05$, one-tailed; since no directional hypothesis had been advanced, however, this coefficient is not significant at the reported level and should have been based on a two-tailed test, which shows only a trend ($p<.10$) toward significance.

[c]Lietaer, on the basis of a factor-analytic study, reported separate correlations for "positive regard" and "negative regard." The entries under R here refer to "positive regard"; results for "negative regard" were consistent with those shown here. Also, Lietaer's "Total Conditions" were based on the combination of E, C, and his two regard scales; U was not included in his total scores.

cantly higher client ratings on all RI dimensions except U.

In summary, these studies suggest that therapists tend to see themselves as creating a more facilitative therapeutic relationship than do their patients. In addition, the only study (Warren, 1973) finding the opposite to be true was conducted with very inexperienced therapists. This suggests that more experienced therapists tend to overestimate their levels of therapeutic conditions and/or that inexperienced therapists tend to underestimate themselves.[8] Both of these possibilities assume, of course, that patient perceptions of the relationship are more "accurate" than therapist perceptions. Another intriguing possibility is that more experienced therapists do, in fact, experience more positive attitudes toward their patients but are not as able to communicate these feelings as well as more inexperienced therapists!

Patients' and Nonparticipant Judges' Perceptions of the Therapeutic Relationship

Table 5 presents a summary of existing published reports which supply correlational data on the degree of agreement between patients' perceptions of the treatment relationship and nonparticipant judges' ratings of those interactions. Despite the data-based position taken by Kiesler et al. (1967a) that patients and trained tape-rating judges who are naive about psychotherapy show a good deal of agreement in their perceptions of the quality of the therapeutic relationship as reflected in client-centered "conditions," a more comprehensive review of studies relevant to this issue generally fails to support their stance. The studies listed in Table 5 may be viewed from two perspectives. First, among those four studies either using 5-point rating scales rather than the RI to assess the patient's view (Burstein & Carkhuff, 1968; Hill, 1974) or those using the RI but employing the Michigan State Affective Sensitivity Scale (Kagan, Krathwahl, Goldberg, Campbell, Schauble, Greenberg, Danish, Resnikoff, Bowes, & Bondy, 1967) instead of the RI E scale (Kurtz & Grummon, 1972; Zimmerman, 1973), only one significant relationship between perceptual vantage points is found (Hill, 1974). The second framework for assessing the relationships between these raters examines the six studies listed in Table 5 which used both the RI and systematically gathered ratings of empathy, warmth, and genuineness according to standard procedures (Rogers, 1967) for measuring these variables. Clearly, this comparative perspective

is the one most relevant to the present chapter in that both assessment procedures are derived from the same theoretical constructs as described by Rogers (1957). Two of these studies examined only RI-E and judge-rated accurate empathy, with one (Caracena & Vicory, 1969) finding a low but significant positive relationship and the other (Fish, 1970) finding a zero-order correlation. The four remaining studies, which assessed all the conditions variables, yield an equally inconsistent picture. Thus, Kiesler et al. (1967a), studying individual therapy with hospitalized schizophrenics, found highly positive and significant correlations between patient- and judge-rated empathy and total therapeutic conditions both early and late in treatment, and significant

TABLE 5. SUMMARY OF REPORTED CORRELATIONS BETWEEN PATIENT AND JUDGE RATINGS OF THERAPEUTIC CONDITIONS

Author	Therapeutic Condition[a]					Comments
	E	R-NPW	U-NPW	C	Tot.	
Bozarth & Grace (1970)	.36	.20	.47[b]	.07	.48[b]	Experienced T's
Burstein & Carkhuff (1968)[c]	.10	.29	—	.42	.02	Inexperienced T's
	.12	.61*	—	.15	.01	Experienced T's
Caracena & Vicory (1969)	.31*	—	—	—	—	2-session analogue; T experience mixed
Fish (1970)	.03	—	—	—	—	Inexperienced T's
Hill (1974)	.36*	—	—	—	—	5-point scale from Orlinsky & Howard's (1966) Therapy Session Report
Kiesler et al. (1967a)[d]	.88**	.54	.33	.33	.88**	Initial RI and "moment-by-moment" tape ratings
	.71*	—	—	.31	.69**	Initial RI and mean tape ratings, sessions 2–15
	.56*	.62*	.59*	−.21	.57*	Terminal RI and "moment-by-moment" tape ratings
	.38	.60*	.25	.27	.56*	Terminal RI and mean tape ratings of the total course of therapy
Kurtz & Grummon (1972)	.31	—	—	—	—	Rating after session 3
	.00	—	—	—	—	Rating after final session ($\bar{x} = 12$)
McWhirter (1973)	.06	.10	.15	.04	.11	1-session analogue; inexperienced T's
Truax (1966)[e]	.26	.24	.17	.17	—	(TPT) Therapist-patient-therapist samples for tape rating
	.14	.26*	.11	.06	—	(PTP) Patient-therapist-patient samples for tape rating
	.15	.16	.15	.16	—	Time samples for tape rating
Zimmerman (1973)	−.0009	—	—	—	—	Michigan State Affective Sensitivity Scale used to rate E

*$p < .05$.
**$p < .01$.

[a]Since the RI contains separate scales for two dimensions of "nonpossessive warmth," separate columns list relationships between R and tape-rated warmth (R-NPW) and between U and tape-rated warmth (U-NPW).

[b]The authors report the .47 coefficient to be significant at $p < .05$, one-tailed, and the .48 coefficient N.S., two-tailed. Since no directional hypotheses had been advanced, two-tailed tests were called for in both cases; thus, both correlations are N.S. using the more appropriate two-tailed tests.

[c]The authors used 5-point rating scales, not the RI. All other studies listed used the RI unless noted otherwise.

[d]In the Kiesler et al. (1967a) study, patient RI ratings and tape-rated conditions were compared at both early and late points in therapy. "Moment-by-moment" tape ratings refer to the average of tape ratings of brief segments of the three interviews most immediately contiguous to the time of administration of the RI; "mean tape ratings of the total course of therapy" refers to the overall mean of interviews 2–15 and every fifth interview thereafter.

[e]TPT samples refer to those in which the sequence of dyadic interchange rated was therapist, patient x, therapist; PTP samples were those in which the sequence was patient x, therapist, patient x; time samples were randomly selected 3-min. units (in which at least two people spoke).

relationships between the two vantage points late in treatment for ratings of R and "unconditional positive regard." Two other studies of actual psychotherapy (Bozarth & Grace, 1970; Truax, 1966) failed to demonstrate any significant relationships between the two rating perspectives (except for one very low but significant correlation reported by Truax—see Table 5). McWhirter's (1973) analogue study of occupational-vocational counseling failed to reveal any significant correlations between patient RIs and the Truax rating scales. In fact, of the five correlations computed for comparisons of the same therapeutic variable (i.e., C-genuineness, RI total-combined conditions, R-warmth, etc.), all were of near zero-order magnitude, the highest being .15.

Reports by Feitel (1968) and Hansen, Moore, and Carkhuff (1968) similarly found nonsignificant relationships between the two ratings sources, for empathy and for all dimensions, respectively. Finally, while Gurman (1973a) was able reliably to differentiate between "high-facilitative" and "low-facilitative" therapists on the basis of judges' ratings, these differences were not confirmed by patient ratings.

Three other studies of a different nature also deserve examination. Based on the assumption that psychotherapy patients and naive judges not trained in the typical intensive procedures (Rogers, 1967) for ratings tapes would share an implicit understanding of the meaning of therapeutic warmth and genuineness, Gurman (1971a) had 20 female elementary school teachers rank-order five typewritten therapy excerpts presented by Truax and Carkhuff (1967) as representative of five different levels of warmth and five excerpts representative of five levels of genuineness. In effect, then, Gurman's study compared the ratings of people assumed to share the experiential perspective of therapy patients with established examples (used in the training of nonparticipant judges) of judge-perceived warmth and genuineness. Of the 20 rank-order correlations for warmth, 14 were positive, one was zero, and five were negative. The median correlation between subject and Truax ranks was .55. An estimate of the average agreement with the Truax rankings was given by a *rho* of .73. Since the rankings of each subject were not independent, conventional significance tests were inappropriate. Spearman *rho*'s for genuineness showed 14 to be positive and six to be negative, with a median *rho* of −.10. The correlation between the mean rankings for each stage and the Truax ranks was .30. The implica-

tions of these findings were that patient-like subjects' evaluations largely agreed with judge-like ratings for therapist warmth, but not for therapist genuineness.

In a similar preliminary study of empathy by D. Shapiro (1970), naive (untrained) judges' median correlation with the Truax criterion was .62, and the rank-order correlation between his subjects' mean rankings and the Truax rankings was .90, suggesting a substantial degree of agreement between patient-like and judge-like evaluations of therapeutic empathic understanding. In a subsequent replication, D. Shapiro (1973) conducted three further studies of empathy in a similar manner. In two of these three replications, naive judges' perceptions of empathy were significantly in accord with the Truax criterion. Shapiro's (1973) three studies of warmth and genuineness showed two of three correlations indicating agreement between rating sources for warmth but only one indicating positive agreement for genuineness (in fact, in two of the three studies on genuineness, the *rho*s between subjects' mean ranks and the Truax criterion were negative). Thus, Shapiro's second paper essentially confirms Gurman's (1971a) results. These three studies are lent further support by J. Shapiro (1968a), who found that trained expert judges agreed significantly with the ratings of therapeutic conditions provided by naive subjects' (similar to those of both D. Shapiro and Gurman) 7-point rating scale evaluations of therapist empathy, warmth, and genuineness.

Perceptions of Therapeutic Conditions from Different Vantage Points: Conclusions and Implications

The preceding review leads to the following conclusions about the interrelationships among patients', therapists', and judges' assessments of the quality of the therapeutic relationship:

1. Across studies using a variety of instruments to assess patients' and therapists' perceptions of the therapeutic relationship, there is, with the possible exception of therapist empathy, little convincing evidence of agreement between these parties. Even studies using the same relationship measures do not show confirmatory results.

2. This lack of perceptual correspondence between patients and therapists is present under both actual therapy conditions and analogue conditions, and does not appear to be influenced by the severity of patients' psychological disturbance.

3. Therapists and other helping agents tend to rate themselves higher on measures of facilitative therapeutic functioning than do their patients.

4. There is inconsistent yet largely non-confirmatory evidence of the hypothesized positive relationship between ratings of the therapeutic relationship by patients and trained judges. This lack of agreement holds up under both naturalistic and analogue conditions. With the possible exception of therapist empathy, perceptions of therapeutic conditions from these two vantage points seem to be measuring related but importantly different therapist variables.

The major methodological implication of these findings for future research on the therapeutic relationship is that these three evaluative perspectives represent substantially different sources of assessment, each of which may supply relatively unique information about the quality of the interaction between patients and therapists.[9] Therefore, *researchers are cautioned against assuming that evaluation of therapy relationships from any one perspective may speak, by implication, for the persons who may occupy other phenomenological positions.* As a result, patient-perceived therapeutic conditions must not be equated with therapist-perceived or judge-perceived conditions. Discussions and studies of "empathy" for example, must speak with greater specificity, restricting the use of the term to its operationally measured base (e.g., "patient-perceived empathy").

Since the three perceptual vantage points are largely at variance with one another, research employing evaluations of the therapeutic relationship from different perspectives cannot be directly compared. Thus, the review of therapy outcome as a function of the *patient's* perception of the therapeutic relationship, which directly follows this section, represents a body of empirical literature which is best viewed as complementary to, rather than in opposition to, the large body of research on *judge*-rated therapy conditions reviewed by Mitchell *et al.* in the preceding chapter.

THE PATIENT'S PERCEPTION OF THE THERAPEUTIC RELATIONSHIP AND THERAPEUTIC OUTCOMES

The central hypothesis of the relationship between the patient's experience of his therapist's relationship qualities and treatment outcome will be examined in this section. A review of studies of individual therapy and counseling is followed by a similar analysis of group therapy studies.

Perceived Therapeutic Conditions and Outcome: Individual Therapy

Table 6 presents a summary of all available studies that have tested the perceived conditions-outcome hypothesis. Among these 26 studies, all but four were conducted with actual patients or clients, about half of these being college students treated in university counseling centers and about one-fifth seen in university psychiatry clinics. Recent evidence (Mechanic & Greenley, 1974) suggests no appreciable differences between these populations in levels of psychological distress; thus, in terms of severity of disturbance, these groups may be seen as equivalent. Only two of the studies in Table 6 have reported on treatment with severely disturbed (i.e., schizophrenic or psychotic) patients. Experienced and inexperienced therapists are about equally represented. The treatment modalities represented in these studies include a rather balanced mixture of client-centered, psychoanalytically oriented, behavioral, and eclectic therapist orientations. Thus, these studies, taken together, clearly are not restricted to client-centered settings. This fact is very important in light of the argument that the conditions posited by Rogers (1957) for therapeutic change may have questionable relevance outside client-centered settings (Bergin & Jasper, 1969), at least when therapeutic conditions are assessed by nonparticipant (tape-rating) judges.

The studies in Table 6 are about equally divided between relatively brief (two to 20 sessions) and more long-term (20 or more sessions) therapies. In addition, outcome was evaluated by independent judges in over half these studies, with patients also assessing change in the majority of reports, and therapists' judgments used somewhat less often. In sum, the studies described in Table 6 appear to represent a good cross-section of actual outpatient individual therapy, in terms of therapists' orientations and experience levels, length of treatment, and sources of outcome evaluation.

Among the 26 studies in Table 6, 20 report positive findings for the perceived conditions-outcome hypothesis, three report mixed but supportive results, and only three show results clearly failing to demonstrate a relationship between outcome and the quality of the therapist-patient relationship. Despite methodological shortcomings in some of these studies

TABLE 6. STUDIES OF PATIENT PERCEPTIONS OF THE THERAPEUTIC RELATIONSHIP AND TREATMENT OUTCOME: INDIVIDUAL PSYCHOTHERAPY

Author	Therapist N	Patient N	Population	Therapy Type	Average Treatment Length	Naturalistic (N) or Analogue (A)	Therapist Experience Level[a]	Relationship Assessment: Time	Outcome Criteria[b]	Principal Findings[b]
Barrett-Lennard (1962)	21	42	College counseling center clients	Client-centered	33 sess.	N	Inexp.[c]	Session 5 and post-therapy	T: combined pre-post "adjustment" ratings and T component indices; "change" ratings P; combined pre-post Q scale, Taylor MA and MMPI D	More changed P's (combined P component indices) reported higher E, R, U, C, and T at session 5 and higher E, C, and T at post-therapy than less changed P's
Board (1959)	57	88	Psychiatric outpatient clinic	"Supportive"	6 mos. (minimum)	N	Exp.	Post-therapy follow-up (6–21 mos.)	T and P "yes/no" ratings of treatment success	P outcome ratings: 95–100% of successful patients felt liked by T; 57–71% of unsuccessful patients felt liked by T
Bown (1954)[d]	6	6	College counseling center clients	Client-centered	20 sess.	N		Every fifth session	Independent ratings; continuance in therapy	Patient-perceived relationship quality (Q sort) clearly differentiated successful and unsuccessful therapy in predicted direction
Cain (1973)[e]	18	101	College counseling center clients	Mixed		N	Exp.	Session 6 (final interview)	T and P ratings of helpfulness of just-completed interview	P-rated conditions related to interview outcome as rated by both P and T
Carmichael (1970)[f]	3	18	Undergraduate female volunteers (spider phobias)	Client-centered and systematic desensitization (each T conducted both treatments)	6 sess.	A	Inexp.	Session 6 (final interview)	Behavioral avoidance test; P ratings of subjective fear	1. Change in subjective P fear ratings unrelated to RI for both treatment groups 2. Change in behavioral avoidance for desensitization Ss ($N = 8$) negatively related to perceived E ($r = -.54, p < .10$) 3. Change in behavioral avoidance for client-centered Ss ($N = 10$) negatively related to all RI scales except U (mean r, excluding U $= -.81, p < .005$)
Feifel & Eells (1963)	28	63	Outpatient VA clients	Psychoanalytically oriented	65 sess. (approx.)	N	Exp.	Post-therapy and 4-year follow-up		Patients reported that the quality of the T-P relationship was, after "opportunity to talk over problems," the most helpful aspect of treatment

TABLE 6. (Contd.)

Author	Therapist N	Patient N	Population	Therapy Type	Average Treatment Length	Naturalistic (N) or Analogue (A)	Therapist Experience Level[a]	Relationship Assessment: Time	Outcome Criteria[b]	Principal Findings[b]
Feitel (1968)	36	48	University outpatient clinic	Mixed, generally analytically oriented		N	Inexp	Session 5	Supervisors' ratings	Feeling understood related ($r = .59$) to outcome; P-rated E ($r = .34$) and R plus U ($r = .77$) also related to outcome
Fretz (1966)	12	17	Undergraduate outpatients	Educational-vocational counseling	6 sess.	N	Inexp.	Session 3 and Session 6	Client and counselor satisfaction	Satisfaction significantly related to patient-perceived therapeutic conditions
Grigg & Goodstein (1957)	10	52	University counseling center clients	Personal adjustment counseling	12 sess.	N	Mixed	Follow-up (approx. 6 mos., avg.)	P global ratings	P-rated "close" (vs. "distant") T-P relationship significantly differentiated favorable vs. unfavorable outcomes
Gross & De Ridder (1966)	1	8	University counseling center clients	"Personal counseling"	10 sess.	N	Exp.	Session 2	Change in client experiencing (post-pre)	All RI scales except R related to experiencing change (mean correlation between RI and outcome criterion, excluding R, was .78)
Hill (1974)	24	48	University counseling center clients	"Personal counseling"		N	Inexp.	Session 2	P-rated session satisfaction, progress, and helpfulness	P-perceived T "understanding" related to P-rated quality and helpfulness of interview
Jones (1968)	5	60	Community college students		2 sess	A		Session 2	Change in evaluative meaning	No relationship between P-RI and outcome criterion
Kiesler, et al. (1967c)	12	12	Hospitalized schizophrenics	Largely client-centered	74 sess.	N	Exp.	Several assessments	P experiencing level and change; MMPI; Butler-Haigh Q sort; T ratings; hospitalization status; independent ratings; Wittenborn scales	High C patients had most favorable hospitalization status outcomes, but only at 12 mos. follow-up and only in comparison to control P's, not difference compared with low C patients; P experiencing level, but not change, related to level of perceived C and T

Study										
Kurtz & Grummon	31	31	University counseling center clients	General dynamic, phenomenological	12 sess.	N	Half exp., half inexp.	Session 3 (E only)	Self-esteem; MMPI; T and P global ratings; composite measure; depth of self-exploration	P-rated E significantly related to all criteria except P-global ratings
Lesser (1961)	11	22	University counseling center clients	"Personal counseling"	9 sess.	N	Exp.	Post-therapy or session 12 (E only)	Butler-Haigh Q sort	P-rated E unrelated to outcome
Libo (1957)	40	40	Psychosomatic client patients	(not specified)	1–2	N	Inexp.	Session 1	Return for second visit	P perception of T-P relationship (felt attraction-picture Impressions Test) differentiated between return and no-return patients
Lorr (1965)	(not reported)	523	VA outpatients clinics; 50% neurotic; 32% psychotic; 18% personality disorders	Dynamic, general	Min. 3 mos., max. 10 years	N	Exp.		P, T, and judge ratings	P-rated understanding and acceptance related to all raters' outcome evaluations; P-ratings of T "critical-hostile" (i.e., opposite of U) negatively related to P-rated outcome
McClanahan (1974)[c]	11	83	University counseling center clients	Personal adjustment counseling		N N		Sessions 3–8	P satisfaction	Satisfaction significantly related to all RI scales
McNally (1973)	29	52	Junior high, high school, and college students			N	Mixed	Session 2	P, T, and judge ratings of satisfaction/effectiveness	Total RI score best predictor of P-satisfaction (vs. Rotter IE, Marlowe-Crown Social Desirability, and other predictor variables).
Ryan & Gizynski (1971)	13	14	Outpatient neurotics 3 private practice; 11 family service agency	Behavior therapy eclectic		N	Mixed	Post-therapy	P, T, and independent judge ratings of success	P's feeling liked (U) T significantly related to therapy outcome
Sapolsky (1965)	3	16	Hospitalized females, majority schizophrenic	General, plus milieu therapy	6 mos. hospitalization (approx.)	N	Inexp.	Post-discharge	Independent judge's rating of improvement	P's "feeling understood" (E) significantly related to rated improvement
Stanley (1967)[c]	29	125	High school volunteers	Educational-vocational counseling		A	Inexp.		Change in connotative meaning ("College," "My Future," "My Ideal Self," etc.)	Client perception of relationship not related to change criterion

TABLE 6. (Contd.)

Author	Therapist N	Patient N	Population	Therapy Type	Average Treatment Length	Naturalistic (N) or Analogue (A)	Therapist Experience Level[a]	Relationship Assessment: Time	Outcome Criteria[b]	Principal Findings[b]
Strupp, Fox, & Lessler (1969)	79	122	University psychiatry clinic outpatients	Psychoanalytically oriented	25 sess. (min.)	N	Mixed	1 year (min.) post-therapy	P ratings, independent judge ratings	P-rated warmth (R), respect (U), and understanding (E) significantly related to both P and judge outcome evaluation
Tausch, Sander, Bastine, & Friese (1970)g	5	10	Outpatient neurotics	Client-centered		N	Exp.	(Early, but not specified)	P-global ratings	P-rated E and C significantly related to outcome
Truax, Leslie, Smith, Glenn, & Fisher (1966)h	219		Vocational rehabilitation clients	Vocational counseling		N	Exp		Work production, work attitude, dependability, etc.	Perceived empathy, warmth, and genuineness all significantly related to outcome criteria
Zauderer (1967)e	20	20			5 sess.	A	Inexp.	Sessions 1 and 5	Change in self-revealingness, global outcome ratings	Self-revealingness change not related to perceived conditions; level of perceived conditions differentiated high- and low-success cases as rated by both T and P

Note: This table indicates only those findings directly relevant to the primary hypothesized relationship between patient-perceived therapeutic conditions and measured treatment outcome. Other relevant analyses appearing in these studies, e.g., effects of patient disturbance level, therapist experience level, etc., are reported in the text. Empty cells represent unreported data.

[a] In this table and throughout this chapter the present author conceives of therapists and counselors still in training (e.g. graduate students, psychiatric residents) as inexperienced. Experienced therapists, in the writer's view, are those who have at *least* completed their formal training.

[b] The appearance of E, R, U, C, or T in parentheses implies their presumed equivalence with the relationship measure actually used, e.g., "understanding" (E), T = therapist, P = patient.

[c] Although Barrett-Lennard performed several data analyses based on therapists' experience level ("more expert" vs. "less expert"), it is questionable whether either group can be considered to be experienced therapists, since the "more expert" therapists' average number of previously treated clients was only 45 (the mean for "less expert" therapists was 11). Thus, in this table these therapists are considered by the present author to have been inexperienced as a group.

[d] As reported in Goldstein, Heller, and Sechrest (1966, p. 75).

[e] Unpublished doctoral dissertation reported in summary form in *Dissertation Abstracts International*; thus, complete descriptive data not available. The findings reported here for this study did not appear in Carmichael's original report; the raw data were made available by Carmichael and were analyzed by the present author. Both treatments were actually conducted in small groups of about four Ss each; because of the nature of the treatments and the target behavior in question, however, the present author views both treatments as having been essentially individual therapy conducted in a "group-like" setting.

[g] As reported by Barrett-Lennard (1972a).

[h] As reported in Truax and Carkhuff (1967, p. 141). The Truax Relationship Questionnaire (Truax & Carkhuff, 1967, pp. 74–79) was used, not the RI.

(to be discussed below), it is clear from the findings presented in Table 5 that *there exists substantial, if not overwhelming, evidence in support of the hypothesized relationship between patient-perceived therapeutic conditions and outcome in individual psychotherapy and counseling.* The converging evidence for this conclusion is further strengthened by the fact that of the three studies reporting no relationship between perceived conditions and outcome, two (Jones, 1968; Stanley, 1967) utilized analogue designs, and in one of these (Jones, 1968), "treatment" lasted only two sessions. Stated otherwise, only one study (Lesser, 1961) of the 22 conducted with actual help-seeking patients has yielded results that fail to confirm the perceived conditions-outcome hypothesis. Furthermore, only two of these naturalistic studies limited "outcome" ratings to the quality of a just-completed session, while the remainder assessed patient change over an entire course of treatment.

Methodological Limitations. Despite the consistent evidence presented above in support of the perceived conditions-outcome hypothesis, the studies reviewed are not without methodological deficiencies. In lieu of detailed critiques of the methodology of each of these individual therapy studies, three major issues, each relevant to several of these reports, will be considered.

Assessment of pre-post change and the "Law of Initial Values." As many writers (e.g., Fiske, 1971; Luborsky, 1971; Manning & DuBois, 1962; Meltzoff & Kornreich, 1970; Tucker, Damarin, & Messick, 1966) have emphasized, the use of raw pre-post difference scores that are not corrected for initial level creates serious psychometric difficulties. In addition to the low reliability of such scores, these scores may correlate as much as $-.71$ with pre-treatment scores (Fiske, 1971), so that patients with low pre-treatment scores may obtain very high change or "outcome" ratings. Eight of the studies reported in Table 5 can be faulted on this ground (Barrett-Lennard, 1962; Carmichael, 1970; Feitel, 1968; Gross & DeRidder, 1966; Jones, 1968; Kiesler, 1967; Kurtz & Grummon, 1972; Zauderer, 1967).[10] Thus, statistically inappropriate change measures were used over a wide variety of index criteria, including patient self-disclosure, self-esteem, experiencing level, global adjustment, and other variables. The only study using pre- to post-change scores in which there was a correction for initial level was that of Lesser (1961), the only naturalistic study failing to support the perceived conditions-outcome hypothesis. Clearly, the empirical acceptability

of research in this area will be significantly bolstered by attending to this important issue.[11]

Nature and Range of Outcome Criteria. While a moderate range of outcome criteria was used in the studies reported in Table 6, the predominant change measure was a global 5- to 9-point "improvement" rating completed by either the therapist, patient, or both. While such global measures may have a good deal to recommend them (see Mintz, Chapter 22, this volume), outcome criteria that are tailored to the specific needs and goals of each patient may add substantially to the clinical relevance of research in this area of psychotherapy. Standard measures applied across patients (e.g., self-esteem) are of course of value, but are insufficient to tap the unique changes occurring in individual patients.

Time of Assessment of the Perceived Therapeutic Relationship. Barrett-Lennard (1962), in deciding at what point to measure the patient's perception of the therapeutic relationship, argued that "Five therapy interviews was judged to be a safe minimum period of association between client and therapist that would provide the participants with a meaningful basis from which to answer the Relationship Inventory items" (p. 8). Apparently, most subsequent investigators have agreed with Barrett-Lennard's reasoning. Thus, approximately half of the studies listed in Table 6 assessed the patient's perception after the second to the sixth session. While Barrett-Lennard's logic *per se* cannot be faulted, it must be noted that the point at which this assessment is made has very different clinical meanings[12] and methodological consequences. While first session impressions of the therapist by the patient indeed do not allow reports based on a rather full exposure to the therapist, it is quite obvious from everyday clinical experience that first impressions, especially in regard to the quality of the therapist-patient relationship, have enormous practical consequences, such as whether a patient will return for a second visit (see Libo, 1957). Furthermore, the evidence presented earlier in this chapter on the high degree of stability of these patient perceptions over time would argue that future studies of the perceived conditions-outcome hypothesis would add a great deal to our empirical understanding of clinical phenomena by assessing the patient's view after his initial therapy contact. Still, it is possible that measurement of the patient's perception on the basis of a first contact and on the basis of an established, ongoing relationship may differentially predict various process measures and outcome evaluations. The recommendation offered here is that researchers assert an explicit rationale for their chosen time of measuring patient-perceived therapeutic conditions.

Patient-Perceived Versus Judge-Rated Conditions and Therapy Outcome. Despite the arguments of Truax (Truax & Carkhuff, 1967) that judge-rated therapeutic conditions are better predictors of therapeutic change than are patient-rated conditions, very little research bearing directly on this question has actually been conducted. To this writer's knowledge, there exist only four studies of individual psychotherapy or counseling in which both rater vantage points have been assessed and examined in relation to outcome. Kurtz and Grummon (1972) dealt with this issue in a study of outpatient therapy in a university counseling center. Six measures of therapist empathy were used and were classified as follows: (a) situational empathy—the Affective Sensitivity Scale (Kagan *et al.*, 1967); (b) predictive empathy—the Interpersonal Checklist (prediction of client responses) of La Forge and Suczik (1955) and Landfield's (1967) modification of the Kelly Role Concept Repertory Test; (c) judged tape ratings, based on Carkhuff's (1969) Empathic Understanding in Interpersonal Process Scale; (d) perceived empathy—patient and therapist ratings on the RI after the third interview. Among the 36 correlations computed between each empathy measure and the six outcome measures, a third were of zero-order magnitude and half were negative and not significant. Only *client*-rated empathy showed a strong relationship to the various outcome indices, with four of the six correlations being significant.

McNally (1973) studied counseling with a mixed sample of junior high, high school, and college students. Counselor empathy was assessed with patient RI ratings and judge-rated empathic understanding, communication of respect, and facilitative genuineness (Carkhuff, 1969). Counseling effectiveness was rated at termination by counselors, clients, and independent judges on a modified form of the Counseling Evaluation Inventory (Linden *et al.*, 1965). Judge-rated empathy was found to be more predictive *judges*' ratings of counseling effectiveness than were patient RI scores, while total RI scores were better predictors of *client* outcome ratings than were the Carkhuff measures. Since the independent judge's ratings of effectiveness were based on listening to tape recordings of the same interviews on which tape ratings of empathy were based, these two

measures were probably confounded. Therefore, it would appear that patient-perceived therapeutic conditions emerged as superior predictors of outcome.

Feitel (1968; summarized in Bergin & Jasper, 1969) compared the predictive utility of judge-rated Truax empathy scores with RI scores. She found that outcome, based on supervisors' ratings of advanced graduate students in clinical and counseling psychology, correlated significantly with RI-E and RI-R plus U, but was not related to judge-rated empathy.

Kiesler *et al.* (1967), in a comprehensive study of psychotherapy with hospitalized schizophrenics, found judge-rated empathy and patient-rated congruence and total therapeutic conditions to be better predictors of patients' experiencing levels than their counterparts from the other rating vantage point. Among all 10 measures of therapeutic conditions (five judge-rated, five patient-rated), patient-rated C was also the best predictor of percent of time out of the hospital at 12-month follow-up.[13, 14]

In sum, while the existing data on the comparative predictive utility of judge-rated versus patient-rated therapeutic conditions is indeed sparse, *it can be tentatively concluded that patients' ratings of the quality of the therapist-patient relationship are at least as powerful as predictors of therapeutic change as nonparticipant judges' ratings and perhaps even somewhat more powerful.*

Perceived Therapeutic Conditions and Outcome: Group Therapy

In marked contrast to the results of research on the perceived conditions-outcome hypothesis in individual psychotherapy, the existing (and smaller) body of data relevant to this hypothesis in group therapy generally fail to confirm this predictive relationship. A summary of empirical studies of this hypothesis in group therapy and in T groups is presented in Table 7.

Only 10 studies testing the hypothesis in question have been conducted under actual treatment conditions, five with outpatients and five with inpatients. Among the outpatient studies (Abramowitz & Abramowitz, 1974; Hansen *et al.*, 1968; Lindahl, 1973; Truax, Wargo, Tunnell, & Glenn, 1966c) only that of Truax found even tenuous support for the proposed positive relationship between patient-perceived therapeutic conditions and outcome.[15] Of the 69 correlations computed between 23 change measures and therapist empathy, warmth, and genuineness (Truax Relationship Questionnaire, not RI), only nine were statistically significant. Since four correlations would be expected to reach statistical significance ($p < .05$) on the basis of chance alone, the reported positive correlations appear just minimally to exceed this level and, at best, can be interpreted as providing only very weak evidence for the perceived conditions-outcome hypothesis. All but one of these significant correlations were obtained on MMPI change measures, and only one of the 15 conditions X Q-sort correlations was significant. In addition, the obtained significant correlations are quite low (range, .23 to .31), and over a third of the correlations are of zero-order magnitude.

Further support of the *lack* of evidence for the perceived conditions-outcome hypothesis is derived from the overwhelmingly negative results obtained in the outpatient group study with the soundest methodological quality (Abramowitz & Abramowitz, 1974).

Studies testing the hypothesis in question with hospitalized patients report more mixed, yet also largely negative results. Truax's (Truax, Tunnell, & Wargo, 1966) study of hospitalized mental patients showed unequivocally negative results for the perceived conditions-outcome hypothesis. Roback and Strassberg's (1974) results with severely disturbed patients also failed to support the hypothesis. More mixed results were obtained in two studies by Truax, one conducted with hospitalized psychotic patients and institutionalized juvenile delinquents (Truax, 1966) and one conducted with institutionalized delinquents only (Truax, Wargo, Carkhuff, 1966). In the first of these studies, perceived U and C, but not E and R, were significantly related to a composite final outcome criterion (FOC), comprised of eight change indices. The clinical meaning of these positive correlations is largely obscured by the unfortunate inclusion of both behavioral and self-report measures in the FOC. Thus, it is impossible to determine, on the basis of the findings presented, whether perceived therapeutic conditions were differentially associated with these two importantly different sources of change evaluation. Comprehension of even the empirical meaning of Truax' data is even further obfuscated by his failure to report his findings on his two patient populations separately. In the second study (Truax, Wargo, Carkhuffs, 1966), stronger support for the perceived conditions-outcome hypothesis was found. Almost all self-report measures were significantly correlated with perceived conditions (Truax Relationship Questionnaire), while

hospitalization recidivism was unrelated to these perceptions.

Only the group therapy study of Anderson et al. (1972) has found consistently positive relationships between perceived conditions and rated outcome. Studying hospitalized schizophrenic patients with more acute disturbance than in any other of the existing studies of inpatients, Anderson et al. found significant relationships between patient-perceived therapist "understanding" and "interest" (6-point scales) and patient-rated treatment satisfaction.

In sum, *the perceived conditions-outcome hypothesis has generally failed to be confirmed in the context of group therapy with both inpatients and outpatients.* These findings are indeed striking in contrast to the overwhelming support for the hypothesis in a wide variety of individual therapy contexts. Direct evidence in support of any specific interpretations of this difference is meager. Still, a parsimonious explanation that is consistent with both clinical experience and a growing body of empirical research (Bednar & Lawlis, 1971) would suggest that *a group member's perception of the quality of "therapeutic conditions" offered by the group as a whole may be more salient in mediating therapeutic change than is the member's perception of these conditions in the group therapist alone.* Indirect support for this interpretation is offered in two studies of T groups (Clark & Culbert, 1965; Clark, Culbert, & Bobele, 1969), in which it was found that the number of "mutually perceived therapeutic relationships" (MPTR's) experienced by group members significantly differentiated high- and low-changers on a measure of self-awareness. It was also found (Clark et al., 1969) that the combination of experienced MPTRs and non-MPTRs was a better predictor of member change than MPTRs alone.[16,17]

Unfortunately, the inference suggested above regarding the perception of group-offered versus therapist-offered conditions must be said to be very tentative in that, to the writer's knowledge, no direct investigations of this proposition have yet appeared. Studies involving direct comparisons of the predictive utility of therapist-offered versus group-offered perceived conditions would be a welcome addition to the empirical literature and would seem to have enormous implications for clinical practice.[18]

Finally, it should be pointed out that while a number of studies have found significant positive relationships between judge-rated therapist conditions and outcome in group therapy (Truax & Mitchell, 1971), only one study (Truax, 1966)

TABLE 7. STUDIES OF PATIENT PERCEPTIONS OF THE THERAPEUTIC RELATIONSHIP AND TREATMENT OUTCOME: GROUP PSYCHOTHERAPY AND T GROUPS

Author	Therapist N[a]	Patient N	Population	Therapy Type	Average Treatment Length	Naturalistic (N) or Analogue (A)	Outcome Criteria	Principal Findings[b]
Abramowitz & Abramowitz (1974)	1[c] (Exp.)	26 (4 groups)	College students	Insight and non-insight oriented	10 sess.	N[d]	10 measures, including self-esteem, anxiety, alienation, internal control, etc.	Perceived T conditions not related to outcome in either insight or non-insight groups[e]
Anderson et al. (1972)	2 (Inexp.)	61 (4 groups)	Hospitalized-acute treatment service unit; largely schiz. reactions and depressive reactions	Patient-family groups and patient-only groups	30 sess.	N	T and P global ratings of session satisfaction (120 total sessions)	T understanding (E) and interest (R) related to satisfaction
Clark & Culbert (1965)	1 (Exp.)	10 (1 group)	Undergraduate college students	T group	32 sess.	A	"Self-awareness" (Problem Expression Scale)[f]	Number of mutually perceived (member-member, not member-leader) high therapeutic conditions significantly related to process change
Clark, Culbert, & Bobele (1969)	2 (Exp.)	20 (2 groups)	Undergraduate and graduate students	T group plus assigned dyads	14 sess.	A	"Self-awareness" (Problem Expression Scale)[f]	Combination of mutually perceived "therapeutic" and "nontherapeutic" relationships predicts process movement better than no. positive relationships alone
Cooper (1969)	16	107 (12 groups)	(A) Senior-level industrial managers (N = 36) (B) Middle-level industrial managers (N = 28) (C) College students (N = 43)	T group	Group A: 60 hours. Groups B & C: 30 hours.	N	Self-concept consistency between self- and other-perceptions of self, similarity between self-concept and behavior	Group trainer C significantly related to outcome criteria in all three populations
Culbert (1968)	2 (Exp.)	20 (2 groups)	Undergraduate and graduate students	T group	14 sess.	A	"Self-awareness" (Problem Expression Scale)	Member-perceived leader E related to number and rate of members' self-disclosures and to change in self-awareness
Hansen et al. (1968)	9 (Exp.)	70 (9 groups)	8th–12th grade students (school behavior problems)	"Problem-centered"	12 sess.	N	Self-concept change	Perceived T conditions not related to outcome
Lindahl (1973)[g]	2 (Inexp.)	22 (4 groups)	Undergraduate college students[h]	Encounter group	20 sess.	N	Firo-B discrepancy scores, real vs. ideal self, social anxiety, Eysenck Personality Inventory	Perceived T conditions related to some change measures, but generally no support for conditions-change relationship

Study	Therapists[a]	N	Population	Orientation	Sessions	Exp[a]	Outcome measures	Results
Lindahl (1973)[g]	2 (Inexp.)	34 (7 groups)	Undergraduate college students[h]	Encounter group	30 sess.	N	(Same as above)	(Same as above)
Roback & Strassberg (1974)	1 (Inexp.)	18 (3 groups)	Hospitalized schizophrenics	Insight, Interaction & Insight plus Interaction	16–30 sess.	N	Behavioral (e.g. Wittenborn scales) and self-report (e.g., MMPI)	Perceived conditions not related to either behavioral or psychometric change indices
Truax (1966)	8	80[i] (8 groups)	Hospitalized schizophrenics (4 groups); institutionalized juvenile delinquents (4 groups)		24 sess.	N	Composite Final Outcome Criterion (FOC) based on 8 measures, e.g., MMPI, time-out-of institution, Q-sort adjustment	Perceived C and U related to FOC, E and R not related
Truax, Tunnell, & Wargo (1966)[j]		63	Hospitalized psychiatric patients	Eclectic-client-centered		N	Hospitalization states, various Q sorts, MMPI, composite outcome index, etc.	Perceived empathy, warmth, and genuineness not related to outcome
Truax, Wargo, Carkhuff, et al. (1966)[j]		74	Institutionalized male and female juvenile delinquents	Eclectic-client-centered		N	Days institutionalized (1-yr. follow-up), Minnesota Counseling Inventory, various Q sorts, etc.	Perceived empathy, warmth, and genuineness significantly related to all self-report measures, but not related to behavioral criterion (days out of institution)
Truax, Wargo, Tunnell, & Glenn (1966)[j]		52	Outpatients	Eclectic-client centered	(Time-limited; no. sess. not reported)	N	MMPI, various Q sorts, etc.	Perceived conditions significantly related to several, but not all, outcome criteria

Note. Empty cells represent unreported data.

[a] Exp = experienced therapist(s); Inexp = inexperienced therapist(s).

[b] T = therapist, P = patient. E, R, U, C, or T appearing in parentheses implies their presumed equivalence with the relationship measure actually used, e.g., "understanding" (E).

[c] The senior author also served as the therapist.

[d] Patients were not, in fact, typical help-seekers, in that they were recruited for this study via campus posters and newspaper announcements.

[e] Raw data provided by authors in their report were analyzed by the present writer (ASG), comparing composite overall change scores (positive vs. negative) and RI scores (above and below the group median). Results: Insight Group, $X^2 = 1.5$, ns; Non-Insight Group, $X^2 = 0.19$, ns.

[f] Van der Veen, F., & Tomlinson, T. A scale for rating the manner of problem expression. In C. R. Rogers (1967), Appendix C. 3, pp. 599–601.

[g] Used Truax Relationship Questionnaire (Truax & Carkhuff, 1967, pp. 74–79), not RI. The author reports two studies, the second being a replication of the first.

[h] Both "clients" and "non-clients" were included in these groups. "Clients" were defined as members "who were or had been in contact with the student psychiatric clinic or any other equivalent form of institution." "Non-clients" were students "interested in participating in a group experience."

[i] Data for the two patient samples not presented separately.

[j] As reported in Truax and Carkhuff (1967) and Truax (1971a). Used Truax Relationship Questionnaire (Truax & Carkhuff, 1967, pp. 74–79), not RI.

has directly examined outcome as a function of nonparticipant versus patient ratings. While judge-rated conditions in this study were reported to be more related to patient change than were patient-rated conditions, cautious interpretations of these results seem warranted in light of the methodological weaknesses of this study described earlier.

FACTORS INFLUENCING THE PATIENT'S PERCEPTION OF THE THERAPEUTIC RELATIONSHIP

The evidence that has been adduced in support of the perceived conditions-outcome hypothesis in individual psychotherapy is, if not ultimately persuasive, certainly striking. Yet it is true that this literature is largely correlational rather than experimental and, as such, cannot be asserted to substantiate a *causal* relationship between patients' experience of the therapeutic relationship and treatment outcome. This argument is buttressed by the fact that in some of these studies (Board, 1959; Carmichael, 1970; Fretz, 1966; Grigg & Goodstein, 1957; Jones, 1968; Lesser, 1961; Ryan & Gizynski, 1971; Strupp, Fox, & Lessler, 1969) therapy outcome was assessed by the patient at the same moment in time that the relationship was evaluated, thus leaving open the likelihood of confounding measurements. Stated otherwise, it is quite unlikely that a patient will report his therapist to have been understanding and caring yet of little help in the patient's problem-solving or that he will report major therapeutic gains following a relationship with a therapist who is seen as uninvolved and insensitive. On the other hand, the majority of studies reviewed in the previous section of this chapter found significant relationships between patients' relationship perceptions and outcome as assessed from sources other than the patient (Barrett-Lennard, 1962; Bown, 1954; Cain, 1973; Carmichael, 1970; Feitel, 1968; Gross & DeRidder, 1966; Kiesler et al., 1967; Kurtz & Grummon, 1972; Lorr, 1965; Sapolsky, 1965; Truax, Leslie, et al., 1966; Zauderer, 1967). Furthermore, several of these studies reported significant positive relationships between various change criteria from various rater sources and patient perceptions recorded at a moment in time quite distant from the time of outcome assessment—i.e., early in therapy (Barrett-Lennard, 1962; Feitel, 1968; Gross & DeRidder, 1966; Hill, 1974; Kiesler et al., 1967; Kurtz & Grummon, 1972; McClanahan, 1974; McNally, 1973). Thus, while appropriate concerns about the correlational nature of many of these data should not be denied, they can be mitigated to some degree.

It is certainly intellectually satisfying to have found substantial empirical evidence for the salience of posited constructs that have had such a major impact on theory construction in psychotherapy. It is also reassuring that these data support out commonly held clinical beliefs and experiences. Yet such an examination of these studies leaves unmet both a scientific curiosity and, perhaps more importantly, a clinical need to know how patients come to view their therapists as involved or uninvolved, empathic or unempathic, "real" or "phony." Unfortunately for researcher and clinician alike, the work that has been conducted along these lines leaves many questions raised, but few answered. This section will critically examine the state of our empirical knowledge of the factors influencing the patient's perception of the therapeutic relationship and will suggest what appear to be the most fruitful avenues for further study in this realm.

Patient Factors

While it has been commonplace for the therapeutic conditions triad to be described as "therapist-offered" (e.g., Rogers, 1957, 1967; Truax, 1971b; Truax & Carkhuff, 1967; Truax & Mitchell, 1971), it is now more generally acknowledged that while different therapists do display, on the average, different levels of these relationship skills, these therapist qualities are not merely the overt expression of pervasive, static "traits" (cf., Collingwood, Hefele, Muehlberg, & Drasgow, 1970; Hefele, Collingwood, & Drasgow, 1970; Muehlberg, Pierce, & Drasgow, 1969) within the therapist. Therapists vary in their quality of relating both across patients (Beutler, Johnson, Neville, & Workman, 1973) and even over time with the same patient (Beutler et al., 1973; Gurman, 1973b). While a patient cannot elicit therapist responses that do not exist in his repertoire, it is clear from both a logical-scientific perspective (see, e.g., Fiske, Chapter 2, this volume) and from common clinical practice (Singer & Luborsky, Chapter 16, this volume) that any therapist behavior, (e.g., empathic responding) is a function of the interdependent aspects of the patient-therapist *system* (Houts, MacIntosh, & Moos, 1969; Moos & Clemes, 1967; Moos & MacIntosh, 1970; Van Der Veen, 1965) that uniquely characterizes a given therapeutic dyad. The proportion of the variance in patient-perceived therapeutic conditions accounted for by the patient has received scant attention. In fact, only one (unpublished) study[19] known to this writer has attempted to answer this question with the requisite repeated-measures factorial design.

The existing literature on patient variables that may influence their perception of the quality of the therapeutic relationship may be subsumed under the three rubrics of personality traits, psychological states, and directly observed social behavior. *Personality traits* refer here to complex, relatively permanent, and pervasive patterns of perceptual dispositions (including those that are unconscious) and modes of private "inner" experience that are presumed to influence social behavior *across* situations and even to override immediate environmental contingencies (Mischel, 1973a, 1973b; Rioch, 1972; Wachtel, 1973). Such variables have been examined in only four studies of patient perceptions of the treatment relationship. Ashby, Ford, Guerney, & Guerney (1957) studied client "traits" as possible predictors of client perceptions of their therapists in two modes of individual therapy — "leading" (interpretive and analytically oriented) and "reflective" (client-centered). Several pretherapy client characteristics were measured: needs for deference, autonomy, succorance, dominance and aggression (Edwards Personal Preference Schedule), and "tolerance for cognitive ambiguity." The perceived therapeutic relationship was assessed by the "positive subjective reactions" half of the Client Personal Reaction Questionnaire (CPRQ). None of the six "traits" was found to correlate significantly with the CPRQ in either therapeutic modality.

Lin (1973a) examined client "self-confidence" as a possible correlate of perceived therapist relationship qualities. Using a random assignment of high and low self-confidence subjects to three counselors and two treatment settings (individual and group counseling), Lin was unable to find differential perceptions of the therapeutic relationship as a function of either client level of self-confidence or interview type.

The remaining two studies of patient personality trait correlates of perceived therapeutic conditions have been somewhat more encouraging. In an analogue study of the influence of counseling mode (inquiry versus advisory) and patient internal-external locus of control of reinforcement (Rotter, 1966), Broadbent (1971) found that while counseling mode did not affect counselees' perceptions, *externally* oriented subjects experienced higher levels of therapeutic conditions than did internally oriented subjects. This finding would seem to be consistent with evidence (e.g., Switzky & Haywood, 1974) that externally oriented people are more responsive to secondary social reinforcement than internally oriented people.

Abramowitz and Abramowitz (1974) investigated "psychological-mindedness" (PM) as a predictor of outcome in insight- and noninsight-oriented outpatient group therapy. Having determined that high PM clients reaped greater benefit from insight-oriented therapy than did low PM clients (no such differences appeared for the non-insight group therapy members), the authors examined the relationship between therapist "relatability" (based on patient RI scores) and PM. They found that high PM clients reported higher levels of perceived therapeutic conditions than low PM clients in insight-oriented groups, but that this difference was not upheld for the members of the non-insight groups. Moreover, some relevant additional analyses of their data were not performed, which because of the fortunate nature of their data presentation, the present author was able to undertake. On the basis of the "overall change scores" (positive change, negative change, no change) presented in their report for each client, the present author found no difference in therapeutic effectiveness[20] between the two treatment formats ($X^2 = 2.8$, $df = 1$, $p > .05$). On the basis of this finding, it was deemed appropriate to investigate further whether client PM levels (high vs. low) differentiated clients *on-the-whole* on the different scales of the RI. *Chi-square* analyses revealed that while total RI scores, E and U were not differentially associated with PM level ($X^2 = 2.66$, 2.66, 0.67, respectively), R ($X^2 = 6.0$, $p < .02$) and C ($X^2 = 4.1$, $p < .05$) *were* so differentiated, with higher PM subjects reporting higher levels of these therapeutic conditions than low PM subjects. Thus, the original authors' report of a correlation of .70 ($p < .01$) between PM and overall RI scores for insight group clients and a nonsignificant relationship between PM and RI for non-insight clients does not fully convey the fact that, for the sample as a whole, client PM differentially predicted clients' perceptions of their therapist's level of regard and congruence. Because of the theoretical primacy of congruence (Rogers & Truax, 1967), these added findings assume some importance. That is, therapist congruence is probably the "conditions" variable that most severely requires patient perspicacity, in that in order for a patient to discriminate genuine from ingenuine therapist responses, he must be able to identify the lack of correspondence between the therapist's overt behavior and his private experience (e.g., "defensiveness"). That clients who are more motivated toward self-exploration should be able to acutely perceive incongruities between the immediate affective experience of their therapist and his overt behavior certainly is comprehensible and reasonable.

Psychological state variables that may influence patients' perceptions of their therapists may be subdivided into *immediate affective states* and *current degree of emotional* (or behavioral) *disturbance*. Only three studies have examined patients' immediate affective states as predictors of rated therapeutic conditions. Pierce and Mosher (1967) predicted that subjects who were more anxious about communicative interchange would perceive an interviewer as less empathic. Sixty male undergraduates completed a pre-interview anxiety questionnaire and were then interviewed, after being instructed to tell the interviewer what he, the subject, "thinks he is like as a person." The results of this study failed to confirm the authors' prediction. A replication of this study by Pierce (1971) similarly failed to support the hypothesized relationship between interview anxiety and perceived empathy.

Gurman (1973a) investigated the effects of actual patients' pre-session moods on their perceptions of their therapists' quality of relating. Using an intensive design (Chassan, 1967; Dukes, 1965) which included two "high-facilitative" and three "low-facilitative" advanced clinical and counseling psychology graduate student therapists,[21] Gurman had each patient complete the elation vs. depression, tranquility vs anxiety, harmony vs. anger, energy vs. fatigue, and own sociability vs. withdrawal scales of Wessman and Ricks' Personal Feeling Scales (Wessman & Ricks, 1966) immediately before their therapy interviews. Examining between five and 11 sessions for each dyad, Gurman categorized each session as either a high or low session for each reported patient mood by comparing session-by-session moods to the mean pre-session rating for each mood for each patient. Overall (RI total) perceived therapeutic conditions were then examined as a function of patient (high vs. low) pre-session mood. Results indicated that "patients of high-facilitative therapists did not report differential levels of perceived therapeutic facilitativeness under different (patient) pre-session moods, whereas the patients of low-facilitative therapists perceived higher levels of therapeutic functioning when

they, the patients, were in relatively dysphoric pre-session moods" (p. 55). In an attempt to explain these differential results, Gurman speculated that

> Since patients come to therapy hoping to be engaged in a facilitative relationship with their therapists, it is understandable that they might perceive such conditions at higher levels with increased personal discomfort. Since the patients of high-facilitative therapists did not report differential perceptions of their therapists under different moods, it can be inferred that the patients of low-facilitative therapists dealt with the dissonance established by not receiving what they hoped to receive by perceiving what they wanted to perceive. (p. 56)

Current *degree of emotional disturbance* has been examined as a possible predictor of RI ratings in six studies. As noted at earlier points in this chapter, a great deal of controversy has been stimulated by the assumption that more disturbed patients are unable to perceive "accurately" a therapist's relationship qualities (Burstein & Carkhuff, 1968; Hansen et al., 1968). The standard argument *against* the use of patient ratings has been based on data (e.g., Truax & Carkhuff, 1967) showing a lack of correspondence between patient ratings and tape ratings, with the explicit assertion that tape ratings somehow represent *the* "reality" of a therapist's level of therapeutic functioning. That is, if patient and judge ratings disagree in a relatively disturbed sample, it has been *assumed* that this disagreement is sufficient evidence for the irrelevance, or at least, nonutility, of patient ratings. Two analogue studies (Caracena & Vicory, 1969; McWhirter, 1973) have investigated this question with populations demonstrated to be composed of "normal" subjects in each case. Caracena and Vicory (1969) found a nonsignificant correlation $(r = .31)$ between judge-rated and patient-rated therapist empathy and McWhirter (1973) found zero-order correlations between each RI subscale and its tape-rated counterpart. Thus, Caracena and Vicory conclude that,,"*The assumption that low and insignificant relationships (between patient-rated and judge-rated conditions) reported in the literature have been due to the initial perceptual distortion of the troubled respondents does not hold if the same lack of relationship occurs using a group of non-client college freshmen and sophomores*" (p. 513) (emphasis supplied).

Two naturalistic studies of therapy with actual help-seeking populations have also failed to demonstrate that perceived therapist relationship qualities are a function of patient level of disturbance. Ashby *et al.* (1957), in the study of "leading" versus "reflective" therapy described earlier, failed to find significant correlations between client disturbance (number of problems checked on the Mooney Problem Checklist) and perceived positive therapist relationship qualities (Client Personal Reaction Questionnaire) for clients in either treatment modality. Bednar (1970), studying outpatients diagnosed as schizophrenic or neurotic on the basis of their response to the Spitzer Psychiatric Status Schedule, similarly was unable to differentiate patients' rated quality of the therapeutic relationship on the basis of patient degree of disturbance.

The two remaining studies with actual patients have produced results that are inconclusive at best. In his classic monograph, Barrett-Lennard (1962) examined the correlations between outcome and RI scales, from both patient and therapist vantage points, for the "more disturbed" clients in his sample. Not surprisingly, in light of the lack of correspondence between therapists' and patients' perceptions of therapy relationships attested to earlier in this chapter, he found that *all* patient-rated RI scales were significantly correlated with patient change and that *none* of the therapists' RI scales was significantly correlated with change. Unfortunately, the actual range of disturbance of Barrett-Lennard's subjects was so small that dichotomizing them into "more" and "less" disturbed groups seems clinically artificial. Even if Barrett-Lennard's disturbance categorizations are taken at face value, it is certainly striking that the "sicker" clients' perceptions of the treatment relationship were better predictors of outcome than were the perceptions of their assumedly well-adjusted therapists! Since positive therapeutic change *was* demonstrated for this subsample, in order to argue in favor of the Truax (Truax & Carkhuff, 1967) position, one must conclude that (a) the patients' change ratings should be disregarded, (b) the therapist's ratings of the relationship should be disregarded, or (c) perceptions of the relationship by even these "more disturbed" patients were validated as "accurate" insofar as they were the best predictors of outcome. The third interpretation appears to be the most acceptable one.

Kiesler, Klein, Mathieu, and Schoeninger (1967) examined several patient "disturbance" variables in relationship to tape-rated empathy and patient-rated C, the two best conditions predictors of outcome in their research. The present comments are restricted to RI-C, in keeping with the focus of this chapter. The authors found that high versus low RI-C scores could *not* be differentiated on the basis of

whether patients were more acutely or more chronically disturbed ($p \leqslant .10$, Fisher's Exact Test). Further analyses revealed that patient RI-C scores were significantly higher for patients with lower hebephrenic schizophrenia scores (Wittenborn Scales) and for patients with higher WAIS verbal IQs. No significant differences were found on any other Wittenborn scales, on any MMPI scales, or on several other pretherapy adjustment indices. Since 21 probability values were computed and only two reached statistical significance, it must be concluded that these were chance findings. Thus, Kiesler and his associates seem to have gone beyond their data in concluding that "it was clear that patients (receiving and) perceiving high therapist conditions showed less severe symptomatic disturbance at the initiation of therapy" (p. 287). In fact, as noted above, high perceived conditions showed a tendency to be more likely for chronic than for acute cases!

Studies of *observable patient social behavior* as predictors of perceived therapeutic conditions are virtually nonexistent. In the Kiesler, Klein, Mathieu, and Schoeninger (1967) research described above, it was found that patients who talked more during the second therapy session reported higher RI-C ratings than patients who talked less. Lewis and Krauss (1971), in a one-contact analogue study, found that subjects who revealed *more* personal information about themselves perceived the interviewer as *more conditional* in his level of regard than subjects who were less self-disclosing. No statistically significant differences were found for any of the other RI variables. By implication from these studies, patients who, in the first two interviews, talk more but reveal themselves less may be more likely to see their therapists as more accepting and "real." These two studies exhaust the empirical literature on behavioral patient parameters of perceived therapeutic conditions.

Therapist Factors

In light of the predominant ethos that the quality of the therapeutic relationship derives from "therapist-offered" conditions, one would expect to find a substantial amount of empirical data on therapist correlates of patients' perceptions. Yet, even in this domain, the amount of research has been small and the range of research strategies has been narrow. No studies of therapists' current affective states as predictors of patient perceptions have been conducted. The existing literature falls under the two remaining categories of psychological traits and observable social behavior, with the former predominant.

Studies of therapist traits as correlates of patient-perceived therapeutic conditions have focused primarily on the dimensions of expertise-status and dominance. *Expertise* was first investigated by Barrett-Lennard (1962). He compared the RI scores of university counseling center clients seen by "expert" and "nonexpert" therapists and found significant differences in patient perception on RI-E and total score, but not on R, U, C or "willingness to be known." Barrett-Lennard also asserted that his data supported his hypothesis that "expert" therapists would produce greater client change than "nonexpert" therapists. His data, however, showed (p. 22) that, in fact, there was only a nonsignificant trend in this direction ($p < .10$). The second line of evidence purporting to confirm this hypothesis was based on the fact that the clients of "expert" therapists stayed in therapy significantly longer than the clients of "nonexperts" (48 vs. 24.5 interviews). The generally supported relationship between therapy length and outcome is open to several interpretations (Luborsky, Chandler, Auerbach, Cohen, & Bachrach, 1971) and it seems clinically unacceptable to take at face value Barrett-Lennard's conclusion that expertise is *necessarily* reflected in a therapist's ability to keep patients in therapy for longer periods of time. Obviously, the opposite is often true—that more effective therapists are able to conclude their work with patients in shorter amounts of time. In either case, treatment length *per se* would appear to be an unacceptable measure of outcome. Furthermore, as was noted in Table 5 (footnote c), Barrett-Lennard's categorization of his therapists as "expert" and "nonexpert" is highly questionable, in that at the start of his study the "expert" therapists had treated an average of only 45 clients ("nonexperts" had seen an average of 11 clients), a figure easily matched by most 2nd-year psychiatric residents, clinical psychology interns, and MSW trainees (see, e.g., Rice, Gurman, & Razin, 1974), none of whom the author of this chapter considers to be "experienced," let alone "expert."

The differential client perceptions of these therapists' relationship skills may be more attributable to a difference in the therapists' "maturity," in that the "expert" therapists were a good deal older than the "nonexperts" (37.4 vs. 28.4 years). This possibility is supported by the finding of Fish (1970), who, studying advanced graduate student therapists almost identical in age and clinical experience to the therapists of Barrett-Lennard (1962), found patient-rated E to be significantly correlated ($r = .41$, $p < .05$) with therapists' age (note also that E was the only RI subscale found by Barrett-Lennard to differentiate "expert" and "nonexpert" therapists). Since, as Fish argues, empathy may be the result of self-awareness, increasing age may reflect one means by which heightened self-awareness is translated into a more facilitative manner of relating to patients. A recent study of clients' perceptions of the relationship qualities of disabled and non-disabled counselors (Mitchell & Allen, 1975) seems to offer further indirect support for this notion. Disabled counselors received higher scores on all four RI scales than able-bodied counselors, implying that subjects held the former group in higher esteem because they appeared to have "made it" in spite of their disability.

Lin (1973a), in an analogue study referred to earlier in our consideration of patient factors affecting the perceived therapeutic relationship, found that counselor self-confidence was linearly related to interviewees' perceptions of the counselors as empathic, warm, and genuine. Lin speculated that self-confidence may influence patients' perceptions because of non-verbal behaviors that differentiate high- and low-self-confidence counselors. This issue will be examined later in this section.

Fretz (1966) hypothesized a positive relationship between patient-perceived counselor "charisma," defined in Frank's (1961) sense of "mystical healing," and client evaluations of the quality of the therapeutic relationship. While "charisma" was related to client ratings of "satisfaction" after the sixth interview, it was not related to any of the patient RI variables.

Two analogue studies have examined the effects of therapists' status on subjects' perceptions of their relationship skills. Scheid (1972) presented two videotapes to 120 subjects, with one tape presenting excerpts of a counselor functioning at a high facilitative level and one at a low level. Prior to viewing the tape, each subject was given a high-status introduction, a low-status introduction, or no introduction. While perceived counselor competence was affected by the manner of introduction, perceived counselor relatability was more influenced by actual counselor behavior than by status manipulations. Heffernon (1970) also found no differences in RI ratings as a function of counselor status introduction manipulations ("lay citizen" vs. "professional counselor").

Grosz (1968) induced positive and negative expectations about counseling by having half of his subjects listen to tapes describing the positive aspects of counseling and excerpts of "effective" counseling and half listen to tapes describing the negative aspects of counseling and excerpts of "ineffective" counseling. Unlike most studies on patient "expectancy," wherein it is rarely demonstrated that different expectancies have actually been induced (Wilkins, 1973a, 1973b), Grosz did assess the effects of expectancy manipulation before his subjects were assigned to counselors for their interviews. The results of his study indicated no difference in patient-perceived therapeutic conditions as a consequence of induced expectancies.

Warren (1973) and Ziemelis (1974) examined the effects on perceived conditions of assigning subjects to preferred versus nonpreferred interviewers. Warren found no differences in client perceptions as a function of expectancy manipulation, while Ziemelis found that both positive expectancy and no-expectancy conditions resulted in more favorable client evaluations of therapeutic conditions than did negative expectancy conditions. Unfortunately, neither of these studies offered evidence that their expectancy-inducing procedures had actually produced their intended effects.

The studies reviewed above suggest that *what a therapist actually does in interacting with a patient has much greater impact on the patient's perception of his therapist's relationship qualities than how "expert" or "prestigious" the therapist is reputed or portrayed to be.*

Therapist *dominance* in relation to perceived therapeutic relatability was first investigated by Lorr (1965). Five hundred and twenty-three VA psychiatric patients rated their therapists on 4-point scales of 65 items describing their therapists' behavior. Five distinguishable orthogonal factors were extracted from the patient responses. Lorr found small positive intercorrelations among the factors of understanding (e.g., "Realizes and understands how my experiences feel to me"), accepting (e.g., "Shows a real interest in me and my problems"), and authoritarian (e.g., "Seems to try to get me to accept his standards") and suggested that a higher order factor common to the three might be demonstrable.

Other studies, however, have found interpersonal styles similar to authoritarianism to be predictive of patient perceptions of *low* therapist

relatability. Cahoon (1968) and Tosi (1970) both used the Rokeach Scale to assess counselor dogmatism. Both investigators found that more dogmatic counselors were seen by their clients as providing a relatively unfavorable therapeutic climate.[22] These findings are not surprising in that less open or highly dogmatic people are characterized by more defensive behavior in interpersonal transactions (Rokeach, 1960). Furthermore, there is evidence (e.g., Kaplan & Singer, 1963) that dogmatism and sensory discrimination abilities vary negatively with each other. Clearly, a therapist who perceives the world in a rather fixed manner and who responds defensively under (perceived) interpersonal threat or anxiety could hardly be expected to be able to be genuine with patients. Since, as noted earlier, a therapist's level of congruence seems to set an upper limit on his ability to be empathic and accepting, a rigid perceptual scope would severely impair a therapist's relationship skills on all the dimensions of the RI.

A study by Donnan, Harlan, and Thompson (1969) found RI-C to be positively related to counselor "tender-mindedness" (16PF) and client-perceived unconditional positive regard positively related to counselor outgoingness and sociability (16PF). Since 80 correlations were computed in this study and only four were found to be significant ($p < .05$), it must be concluded that these were chance findings.

While there is some evidence (e.g., Passons & Olsen, 1969) that judge-rated empathy is unrelated to counselor dogmatism, it may be hypothesized that the interpersonal behaviors that follow from or are reflected in therapist dogmatism decrease the likelihood of the patient experiencing the therapist as therapeutically facilitative. That Lorr (1965) should have found a low but positive relationship among perceived therapist understanding, acceptance, and authoritarianism is somewhat perplexing. Perhaps unspecifiable differences in his more severely disturbed population, in contrast to the normal and neurotic subjects in other studies, may account for his divergent findings.

Before moving beyond studies of therapist dogmatism, it should also be noted briefly that both therapists' experiencing level (Cahoon, 1968) and certain dimensions of therapists' style of emotional self-report (Fish, 1970) have been found to be predictive of patient-rated empathy. Since a therapist's openness to the nuances of his own emotional experience would seem to be negatively related to dogmatism, these studies offer further, albeit indirect, support for the dogmatism-relatability hypothesis offered above.

The final domain of relatively permanent therapist characteristics that has received at least some attention in its relationship to client perception of facilitative therapist qualities is that of the A-B variable (Razin, 1971). This area is discussed in detail by Razin (Chapter 12, this volume) and will be only briefly summarized here. Nine clinical studies and five analogue studies have examined therapist facilitative conditions; only five of these (Bednar & Mobley, 1971; Kennedy, 1973; Klem, 1971; Kulberg & Franco, 1975; Stern & Bierman, 1973) have used the patient perspective approach. Two clinical studies (Kennedy, 1973; Klem, 1971) found therapist-patient A-B *dis*similarity to be associated with higher patient ratings of therapist functioning, while Bednar and Mobley's (1971) study showed no interaction effects. In the two remaining (analogue) reports, A-therapists were found to be higher on U than were B-therapists, with no differences on E, R, C, or T (Stern & Bierman, 1973), and B-therapists were rated higher on E and R, with no differences on U, C, or T (Kulberg & Franco, 1975). In general, studies of therapeutic conditions using the RI have yielded more, though rather weak, significant findings than those based on judges' ratings. The tentative implication from these studies is that complementary A-B dyads *may* function with greater (patient-perceived) facilitativeness.

Relatively little research and largely conflicting findings characterize our empirical knowledge of *observable correlates* of perceived therapist relatability. This area is one of the most potentially fruitful in the entire literature on "therapeutic conditions" in psychotherapy. Recall that the predominant format for assessing a therapist's relationship qualities has involved the use of nonparticipant ratings of audiotapes. The lack of correspondence between tape-rated and patient-rated conditions has already been attested to earlier in this chapter. The issue that arises in this context is whether the lack of agreement between these vantage points may be, at least in part, accounted for by the different nature of the "information" available to judges and patients; that is, by the very nature of their task, nonparticipant judges are restricted to therapist behavior that is manifest in verbal and vocal channels only. On the other hand, patients have direct exposure to a wealth of nonverbal and nonvocal cues, the most important among these being kinesic and proxemic cues. Chinsky and Rappaport (1970; Rappaport & Chinsky,

1972) offer searing methodological critiques of the usual tape-rating procedures. While most of the issues they raise are beyond the scope of this chapter, they do note that trained raters probably do respond to therapist qualities not implied in the definition of tape-rated empathy (e.g., voice quality, tone, inflection, and language style). They fail to mention that bodily cues may also influence a patient's perception of the therapist's relatability.

J. Shapiro (1966, 1968c) has noted the questionable degree of agreement in ratings of therapist relatability (as judged by nonparticipants) that is conveyed by visual and auditory cues. Considerable research from outside psychotherapy quarters (e.g., Mehrabian, 1968; Mehrabian & Ferris, 1967) has emphasized the large proportion of variance accounted for by nonverbal cues in a receiver's inference of attitudes of the sender of a communication. In addition, several studies have found results that strongly suggest the importance of nonverbal cues in the communication of empathy and warmth (Bayes, 1972; Haase & Tepper, 1972; Hargrove, 1974; Shapiro, Foster, & Powell, 1968; Strong, Taylor, Bratton, & Looper, 1971; Truax, 1971a). Since none of these studies examined *patient* perceptions of therapists' relatability, they are not reviewed here.

Studies of therapist *verbal cues* in relation to patient perceptions of the therapeutic relationship have reported the following findings:

1. *Latency* time per therapist response was unrelated to perceived C (Barrington, 1961) and E (Barrington, 1961; Caracena & Vicory, 1969).

2. *Number of words* spoken by the therapist was unrelated to E or U (Feitel, 1968).

3. *Number of therapist responses* was unrelated to E (Barrington, 1961; Caracena & Vicory, 1969; Feitel, 1968) or C (Barrington, 1961) but bore a significant *positive* relationship to U (Feitel, 1968).

4. *Number of words per therapist response* was unrelated to E (Barrington, 1961; Caracena & Vicory, 1969) but was significantly *negatively* related to U (Feitel, 1968).

5. *Similarity of therapist and patient rate of speech* (words per minute) was positively related to E (Barrington, 1961).

6. *Number of breaks in therapist responses* was unrelated to E (Barrington, 1961; Caracena & Vicory, 1969) or C (Barrington, 1961).

7. *Number of accepting statements* (Feitel, 1968), *proportion of first-person wordings* (Barrington, 1961; Caracena & Vicory, 1969), and *proportion of emotional words* (Barrington,

1961; Caracena & Vicory, 1969) were all un-related to RI variables.

8. *Therapist interruptions of client speech* resulted in lower perceived E than noninterruptive therapist comments (Pierce, 1971; Pierce & Mosher, 1967).

Moreover, Barrington (1961) found that the mean frequencies of nine discrete and objective verbal indices in the first two sessions of counseling were less predictive of patient ratings of the relationship after the fifth interview than were the directional *changes* from the first to second interviews on some of these measures. For example, an *increase* in the percentage of therapists' emotional words was positively related to perceived E, and a *decrease* in the number of breaks in the therapists' speech was positively related to perceived C. Barrington concludes that the latter results suggest that the "measure of disorganization in verbal behavior may be related to various manifestations of a lack of congruence and perhaps in itself functions as one of the cues which influence the client's perception in this area" (p. 41). Examinations of directional trends in an emerging and developing therapeutic relationship, as in Barrington's study, would seem to deserve recommendation beyond the usual static, single-moment-in-time measurement of therapists' behavior and patients' relationship perceptions.

Vocal cues of therapist behavior that have received support as predictors of perceived therapeutic conditions are "expression of interest and involvement" (Caracena & Vicory, 1969), "concerned vocal intonation" (Tepper, 1973), and "clarity of expression" (Caracena & Vicory, 1969). Ratings by nonparticipant judges of counselors' "voice gentleness" and "voice confidence" were found by Caracena and Vicory (1969) to bear zero-order relationships with client-perceived E.

Studies of therapist *kinesic and proxemic cues* as factors influencing patients' relationship perceptions are rare. Tepper (1973) found that role-played interactions between an actor-counselor and an actor-client were rated as significantly higher in therapist-empathy, respect, and genuineness when the "counselor" showed a "concerned facial expression" and maintained direct eye contact with the "client." D'Augelli (1974), in a small-group analogue study, found that "helpee"-rated empathic understanding and warmth-acceptance were positively related to the frequency of "helper" head nods. Tepper (1973) also found that higher levels of all three counselor attitudes were communicated when

the counselor was in a forward trunk lean position. Finally, Pattison (1973) found that while therapists who physically touched their patients (e.g., "usher her down the hall ahead of you and place your hand and wrist on her back or shoulder as you tell here where to go" (p. 161) produced deeper levels of client self-exploration; there were no differences between touched and untouched clients in their ratings of their therapists' relationship qualities, although touched clients rated their therapists higher, but not significantly so, on all RI dimensions.

Patient-therapist similarity in relation to the perceived quality of the therapeutic relationship has been studied in terms of broad-scale "personality" dimensions and demographic characteristics. Although some studies (Broadbent, 1971; Mendelsohn & Geller, 1965; Tosi, 1970) have produced findings supporting a positive relationship between similarity (on variables such as dogmatism and internal-external locus of control) and perceived therapist relatability, an equal number of studies have failed to confirm such relationships (Jones, 1968; Lesser, 1961; Wallace, 1971). Two recent reviews of the effects of therapist-patient *racial similarity* (Gardner, 1971; Sattler, 1970) have concluded that more facilitative relationships are usually established in intraracial dyads than in interracial dyads. All the studies cited by Gardner and Sattler involved assessments of the relationship quality by nonparticipant judges. While evidence on this issue derived from participating clients is limited, same-race pairings do appear to yield better therapeutic relationships (Heffernon, 1970; Mulozzi, 1972; Taylor, 1971; Young, 1973).

The effects of therapist-patient *gender similarity* on perceptions of the relationship has similarly received little attention. Orlinsky and Howard (1974) and Persons, Persons, and Newmark (1974) have found evidence suggesting that female clients experience female therapists as warmer than male therapists and Kiesler et al. (1967) have found that male patients rated male therapists as more genuine than did female patients.[23] Moreover, there is some evidence that female patients tend to rate therapists of *either* sex more positively than do male patients (McClanahan, 1974; Snelbecker, 1967). In addition, differences in gender pairings may be mediated to some degree by the dimension of the therapeutic relationship that is examined. Thus, Persons *et al.* (1974) found that female clients were more responsive to empathic therapist responding than male clients, regardless of the therapist's gender, and that male clients were more responsive to their therapists' genuineness than female clients, also regardless of the therapist's gender.

Comment

In light of the very strong evidence presented earlier in this chapter that, in individual psychotherapy and counseling, patients' perceptions of the quality of the therapeutic relationship are closely linked with treatment outcome, it is disappointing that so little has been empirically established in the domain of therapist and patient variables that increase the probability of a patient's positively experiencing that relationship. In part, the inconclusive status of such research can be attributed to its relative scarcity. More importantly, the *nature* of the research reviewed here presents the most problematic issue. With the exception of the few studies (Barrington, 1961; Caracena & Vicory, 1969; D'Augelli, 1974; Feitel, 1968; Kiesler *et al.*, 1967; Lewis & Krauss, 1971; Pattison, 1973; Pierce, 1971; Pierce & Mosher, 1967; Tepper, 1973) that have taken a molecular approach and have examined discrete, observable therapist and patient *behaviors*, the majority of research in this area has generally failed to explicate how molar "personality" dimensions are directly and immediately manifest in the therapeutic encounter. *A patient's perception of his therapist's relatability is not a direct function of the therapist's "open mindedness" or "self-confidence." It may, however, be influenced by the public behavioral referents of such characterological modes of experience and perception.* Thus, for example, a patient may experience his therapist as "genuine" if there are relatively few breaks in the therapist's speech (Barrington, 1961) and as "warm" if the therapist responds frequently but briefly (Feitel, 1968). Future research must attempt to explicate what it is that the therapist *does* in the therapist-patient transaction that communicates his "attitudes" of involvement, caring, and nondefensiveness. Since these response "styles" have been demonstrated in this chapter to closely correlate with therapeutic outcomes in individual treatment, the future training of effective psychotherapists must have an empirical base which allows specification of the therapist behaviors that are likely to communicate these and other facilitative therapeutic conditions.

CODA

Despite the convincing correlative evidence for the importance of the patient's perception of the therapeutic relationship presented in this chapter, it is clear that such "conditions" are rarely sufficient for constructive personality or behavior change. Nevertheless, their necessity as preconditions for therapeutic influence (see Johnson & Matross, Chapter 15, this volume) seems certain for most patients. It should be pointed out, however, that "empathy, warmth, genuineness" need not have positive effects on patients. Assertions that these "conditions" function as "reinforcers" of certain patient behaviors (e.g., self-exploration) are both scientifically and clinically naive. That is, since "reinforcement" is defined by its effects and not by any apparent hedonistic criteria, it is a mistake to assume that, say, warmth will *necessarily* facilitate the therapeutic process since not a few patients find warmth (or genuineness or empathy) highly aversive because of their interpersonal learning histories. A great deal of research will be needed in order to identify those patients for whom "CARE" (Howard & Orlinsky, 1972) is an *un*necessary and perhaps even countertherapeutic "condition."

Finally, it is anticipated that some readers of this chapter will feel uneasy with the author's apparent acceptance of the validity of conscious patient reports of their perception of their treatment relationships. While common clinical experience persuades that patients do, of course, "perceive" and "experience" their therapists in ways that are not accessible to conscious experience, it is striking that only two empirical examinations of transference phenomena have ever appeared and these only very recently (Lower, Escoll, Little, & Ottenberg, 1973; Luborsky, Graff, Pulver, & Curtis, 1973). Perhaps the most direct response to this issue has been offered very recently by Bordin (1974):

> It should be clear that lack of correspondence between a patient process report and the report of either the therapist or an independent observer does not in itself undermine faith in the veridicality of the patient's report. It is possible that the patient is giving us realistic views of aspects of the process not accessible from other positions. It would take much more subtle and searching evidence to demonstrate that the patient's report is a superimposition of some set of other psychic process rather than a description of therapeutic interactions. (p. 58) (emphasis supplied)

REFERENCES

ABRAMOWITZ, S. I., & ABRAMOWITZ, C. V. Psychological-mindedness and benefit from insight-oriented group therapy. *Archives of General Psychiatry*, 1974, **30**, 610–615.

ABRAMOWITZ, S. I., & JACKSON, C. The comparative effectiveness of there-and-then versus here-and-now therapist interpretations in group psychotherapy. *Journal of Counseling Psychology*, 1974, **21**, 288–293.

ANDERSON, C. M., HARROW, M., SCHWARTZ, A. H., & KUPFER, D. J. Impact of therapist on patient satisfaction in group psychotherapy. *Comprehensive Psychiatry*, 1972, **13**, 33–40.

ARMSTRONG, J. C. Perceived intimate friendship as a quasi-therapeutic agent. *Journal of Counseling Psychology*, 1969, **16**, 137–141.

ASHBY, J. D., FORD, D. H., GUERNEY, B. G., JR., & GUERNEY, L. F. Effects on clients of a reflective and a leading type of psychotherapy. *Psychological Monographs*, 1957, **71** (24, Whole No. 453).

BARRETT-LENNARD, G. T. Dimensions of therapist response as causal factors in therapeutic change. *Psychological Monographs*, 1962, **76** (43, Whole No. 562).

BARRETT-LENNARD, G. T. *The Relationship Inventory: Forms OS-M-64, OS-F-64 and MO-M-64 plus MO-F-64*. Unpublished manuscript, University of New England (Australia), 1964.

BARRETT-LENNARD, G. T. *Technical note on the 64-item revision of the Relationship Inventory*. Unpublished manuscript, University of Waterloo, 1969.

BARRETT-LENNARD, G. T. *The Relationship Inventory: Revision process*. Unpublished manuscript, University of Waterloo, 1970.

BARRETT-LENNARD, G. T. *Resource bibliography of reported studies using the Relationship Inventory. Part A*. Unpublished manuscript, University of Waterloo, 1972a.

BARRETT-LENNARD, G. T. *Revision, applications and further adaptations of the Relationship Inventory*. Unpublished manuscript, University of Waterloo, 1972b.

BARRETT-LENNARD, G. T. *Relationship Inventory—Experimental Form OS-S-42*. Unpublished manuscript, University of Waterloo, 1973.

BARRINGTON, B. L. Prediction from counselor behavior of client perception and of case outcome. *Journal of Counseling Psychology*, 1961, **8**, 37–42.

BAYES, M. A. Behavioral cues of interpersonal warmth. *Journal of Consulting and Clinical Psychology*, 1972, **39**, 333–339.

BEBOUT, J. Unpublished data, Talent in Interpersonal Exploration Groups (TIE), TIE Project, Berkeley, Calif., 1971.

BEDNAR, R. L. Therapeutic relationship of A-B therapists as perceived by client and therapist. *Journal of Counseling Psychology*, 1970, **17**, 119–122.

BEDNAR, R. L., & LAWLIS, G. F. Empirical research in group psychotherapy. In A. E. BERGIN & S. L. GARFIELD (Eds.), *Handbook of psychotherapy and behavior change*. New York: Wiley, 1971.

BEDNAR, R. L., & MOBLEY, M. A-B therapist perceptions and preferences for schizophrenic and psychoneurotic clients. *Journal of Abnormal Psychology*, 1971, **78**, 192–197.

BELPAIRE, F., & ARCHAMBAULT, Y. *Tentative de specifier les elements therapeutiques d'un miliew de reeducation pour jeunes delinquents*. Unpublished manuscript, Section de Recherches du Centre d'Orientation, Montreal, 1973.

BERGIN, A. E., & JASPER, L. G. Correlates of empathy in psychotherapy: A replication. *Journal of Abnormal Psychology*, 1969, **74**, 477–481.

BERLIN, J. I. *Some autonomic correlates of therapeutic conditions in interpersonal relationships*. Unpublished doctoral dissertation, University of Chicago, 1960.

BERZON, B. The self-directed therapeutic group: An evaluative study. Western Behavioral Sciences Institute Reports, 1964.

BEUTLER, L. E., JOHNSON, D. T., NEVILLE, C. W., JR., & WORKMAN, S. N. Some sources of variance in "accurate empathy" ratings. *Journal of Consulting and Clinical Psychology*, 1973, **40**, 167–169.

BOARD, F. A. Patients' and physicians' judgments of outcome of psychotherapy in an outpatient clinic. *Archives of General Psychiatry*, 1959, **1**, 185–196.

BORDIN, E. S. *Research strategies in psychotherapy*. New York: Wiley, 1974.

BOWN, O. H. *An investigation of therapeutic relationship in client-centered psychotherapy*. Unpublished doctoral dissertation, University of Chicago, 1954.

BOZARTH, J. D., & GRACE, D. P. Objective ratings and client perception of therapeutic conditions with university counseling center clients. *Journal of Clinical Psychology*, 1970, **26**, 117–118.

BROADBENT, B. C. Internal-external control and two modes of counseling. *Dissertation Abstracts International*, 1971, **31** (7-A), 3260.

BURSTEIN, J. W., & CARKHUFF, R. R. Objective, therapist and client ratings of therapist-offered facilitative conditions of moderate to low functioning therapists. *Journal of Clinical Psychology*, 1968, **24**, 240–241.

CAHOON, R. A. *Some counselor attitudes and characteristics related to the counseling relationship*. Unpublished doctoral dissertation, Ohio State University, 1968.

CAIN, D. J. The therapist's and client's perceptions of therapeutic conditions in relation to perceived interview outcome. *Dissertation Abstracts International*, 1973, **33** (12-B), 6071.

CARACENA, P. F., & VICTORY, J. R. Correlates of phenomenological and judged empathy. *Journal of Counseling Psychology*, 1969, **16**, 510–515.

CARKHUFF, R. R. *Helping and human relations*. Vol. 2. *Practice and research*. New York: Holt, Rinehart & Winston, 1969.

CARMICHAEL, J. A. *Perception of self-as-object as a consequence of systematic desensitization and client-centered therapy*. Unpublished masters thesis, University of Victoria (British Columbia), 1970.

CHASSAN, J. B. *Research design in clinical psychology and psychiatry*. New York: Appleton-Century-Crofts, 1967.

CHINSKY, J. M., & RAPPAPORT, J. Brief critique of the meaning and reliability of "accurate empathy" ratings. *Psychological Bulletin*, 1970, **73**, 379–382.

CLARK, J. V., & CULBERT, S. A. Mutually therapeutic perception and self-awareness in a T group. *Journal of Applied Behavioral Science*, 1965, **1**, 180–194.

CLARK, J. V., CULBERT, S. A., & BOBELE, H. K. Mutually therapeutic perception of self-awareness under variable conditions. *Journal of Applied Behavioral Science*, 1969, **5**, 65–72.

COLLINGWOOD, T., HEFELE, T., MUEHLBERG, N., & DRASGOW, J. Toward identification of the therapeutically facilitative factor. *Journal of Clinical Psychology*, 1970, **26**, 119–120.

COOPER, G. L. The influence of the trainer on participant change in T-groups. *Human Relations*, 1969, **22**, 515–530.

CULBERT, S. A. Trainer self-disclosure and member growth in two T-groups. *Journal of Applied Behavioral Science*, 1968, **4**, 47–73.

D'AUGELLI, A. R. Nonverbal behavior of helpers in initial helping interactions. *Journal of Counseling Psychology*, 1974, **21**, 360–363.

DONNAN, H. H., HARLAN, G. E., & THOMPSON, S. A. Counselor personality and level of functioning as perceived by clients. *Journal of Counseling Psychology*, 1969, **16**, 482–485.

DUKES, W. F. N=1. *Psychological Bulletin*, 1965, **64**, 74–79.

FEIFEL, H., & EELLS, J. Patients and therapists assess the same psychotherapy. *Journal of Consulting Psychology*, 1963, **27**, 310–318.

FEITEL, B. S. *Feeling understood as a function of a variety of therapist activities*. Unpublished doctoral dissertation, Teachers College, Columbia University, 1968.

FIEDLER, F. E. A comparison of therapeutic relationships in psychoanalytic, nondirective and Adlerian therapy.

Journal of Consulting Psychology, 1950a, **14**, 436–445.

FIEDLER, F. E. The concept of an ideal therapeutic relationship. *Journal of Consulting Psychology*, 1950b, **14**, 239–245.

FIEDLER, F. E. Factor analyses of psychoanalytic, nondirective, and Adlerian therapeutic relationships. *Journal of Consulting Psychology*, 1951, **15**, 32–38.

FISH, J. M. Empathy and the reported emotional experiences of beginning psychotherapists. *Journal of Consulting and Clinical Psychology*, 1970, **35**, 64–69.

FISKE, D. W. The shaky evidence is slowly put together. *Journal of Consulting and Clinical Psychology*, 1971, **37**, 314–315.

FRANK, J. D. *Persuasion and healing*. Baltimore: Johns Hopkins Press, 1961.

FRETZ, B. R. Postural movements in a counseling dyad. *Journal of Counseling Psychology*, 1966, **13**, 335–343.

FROMM-REICHMAN, F. *Principles of intensive psychotherapy*. Chicago: Phoenix, 1960.

GARDNER, L. H. The therapeutic relationship under varying conditions of race. *Psychotherapy: Theory, Research and Practice*, 1971, **8**, 78–87.

GOBY, M. J. *Perceived dimensions of therapeutic relationships and recovery from alcoholism*. Unpublished doctoral dissertation, Illinois Institute of Technology, 1973.

GOLDSTEIN, A. P. *Psychotherapeutic attraction*. New York: Pergamon Press, 1973.

GOLDSTEIN, A. P., HELLER, K., & SECHREST, L. B. *Psychotherapy and the psychology of behavior change*. New York: Wiley, 1966.

GOLDSTEIN, A. P., & SIMONSON, N. R. Social psychological approaches to psychotherapy research. In A. E. BERGIN & S. L. GARFIELD (Eds.), *Handbook of psychotherapy and behavior change*. New York: Wiley, 1971.

GONYEA, G. G. The "ideal therapeutic relationship" and counseling outcome. *Journal of Clinical Psychology*, 1963, **19**, 481–487.

GRIFFIN, R. W. Change in perception of marital relationship as related to marriage counseling. *Dissertation Abstracts International*, 1967, **27** (1-A), 3956.

GRIGG, A. E., & GOLDSTEIN, L. D. The use of clients as judges of the counselors' performance. *Journal of Counseling Psychology*, 1957, **4**, 31–36.

GROSS, W. F., CURTIN, M. E., & MOORE, K. B. Appraisal of a milieu therapy environment by treatment team and patients. *Journal of Clinical Psychology*, 1971, **26**, 541–545.

GROSS, F., & DeRIDDER, L. M. Significant movement in comparatively short-term counseling. *Journal of Counseling Psychology*, 1966, **13**, 98–99.

GROSZ, R. D. Effect of client expectations on the counseling relationship. *Personnel and Guidance Journal*, 1968, **46**, 797–800.

GURMAN, A. S. Rating of therapeutic warmth and genuineness by untrained judges. *Psychological Reports*, 1971a, **28**, 711–714.

GURMAN, A. S. Relationships between therapist and patient moods and therapeutic functioning. Doctoral dissertation. Columbia University, 1971. *Dissertation Abstracts International*, 1971b, **32**, 3635B (University Microfilms No. 72-1318).

GURMAN, A. S. Effects of therapist and patient mood on the therapeutic functioning of high- and low-facilitative therapists. *Journal of Consulting and Clinical Psychology*, 1973a, **40**, 48–58.

GURMAN, A. S. Instability of therapeutic conditions in psychotherapy. *Journal of Counseling Psychology*, 1973b, **20**, 16–24.

GURMAN, A. S. Couples' facilitative communication skill as a dimension of outcome in marital cotherapy. *Journal of Marriage and Family Counseling*, 1975, **1**, 68–79.

HAASE, R. F., & TEPPER, D. T., JR. Nonverbal components of empathic communication. *Journal of Counseling Psychology*, 1972, **19**, 417–424.

HANSEN, J. C., MOORE, G. D., & CARKHUFF, R. R. The differential relationships of objective and client perceptions of counseling. *Journal of Clinical Psychology*, 1968, **24**, 244–246.

HARGROVE, D. S. Verbal interaction analysis of empathic and nonempathic responses of therapists. *Journal of Consulting and Clinical Psychology*, 1974, **42**, 305.

HEFELE, T. J., COLLINGWOOD, T., & DRASGOW, J. Therapeutic facilitativeness as a dimension of effective living: A factor analytic study. *Journal of Clinical Psychology*, 1970, **26**, 121–123.

HEFFERNON, A. W. The effect of race and assumed professional status of male lay counselors upon eighth grade black males' perceptions of and reactions to the counseling process. *Dissertations Abstracts International*, 1970, **31** (4-A), 1575.

HILL, C. E. A comparison of the perceptions of a therapy session by clients, therapists, and objective judges. *JSAS Catalog of Selected Documents in Psychology*, 1974, **4**, 16 (Ms. No. 564).

HOLLENBECK, G. P. *The use of the Relationship Inventory in the prediction of adjustment and achievement*. Unpublished doctoral dissertation, University of Wisonsin, 1961.

HOUTS, D. S., MacINTOSH, S., & MOOS, R. H. Patient-therapist interdependence: Cognitive and behavioral. *Journal of Consulting and Clinical Psychology*, 1969, **33**, 40–45.

HOWARD, K. I., & ORLINSKY, D. E. Psychotherapeutic processes. *Annual Review of Psychology*, 1972, **23**, 615–668.

JONES, H. *The relationship of counselor-client personality similarity to counseling process and outcome*. Unpublished doctoral dissertation, University of Missouri, 1968.

KAGAN, N., KRATHWOHL, D., GOLDBERG, A. D., CAMPBELL, R. J., SCHAUBLE, P. G., GREENBERG, B. S., DANISH, S. J., RESNIKOFF, J., BOWES, J., & BONDY, S. B. *Studies in human interaction: Interpersonal process recall stimulated by videotape*. East Lansing: Educational Publication Services, 1967.

KAPLAN, M. F., & SINGER, E. Dogmatism and sensory alienation: An empirical investigation. *Journal of Consulting Psychology*, 1963, **27**, 486–491.

KENNEDY, J. A-B therapist and client matching: A process study of the A-B variable in actual clinical situations. *Dissertation Abstracts International*, 1973, 33B, 3308.

KIESLER, D. J. *The process of psychotherapy*. Chicago: Aldine, 1973.

KIESLER, D. J., KLEIN, M. H., & MATHIEU, P. L. Therapist conditions and patient process. In C. R. ROGERS (Ed.), *The therapeutic relationship and its impact: A study of psychotherapy with schizophrenics*. Madison: University of Wisconsin Press, 1967b.

KIESLER, D. J., KLEIN, M. H., MATHIEU, R. L., & SCHOENINGER, D. Constructive personality change for therapy and control patients. In C. R. ROGERS (Ed.), *The therapeutic relationship and its impact: A study of psychotherapy with schizophrenics*. Madison: University of Wisconsin Press, 1967c.

KIESLER, D. J., MATHIEU, P. L., & KLEIN, M. H. Measurement of conditions and process variables. In C. R. ROGERS (Ed.), *The therapeutic relationship and its impact: A study of psychotherapy with schizophrenics*. Madison: University of Wisconsin Press, 1967a.

KLEM, R. The A-B variable and interpersonal perceptions in peer dyadic interactions. *Dissertation Abstracts International*, 1971, 32 B, 3641.

KULBERG, F., & FRANCO, E. The effects of A-B similarity and dissimilarity in a dyadic interaction. *Psychological Reports*, 1975, in press.

KURTZ, R. R., & GRUMMON, D. L. Different approaches to the measurement of therapist empathy and their relationship to therapy outcomes. *Journal of Consulting and Clinical Psychology*, 1972, **39**, 106–115.

LA FORGE, R., & SUCZIK, R. The interpersonal dimension of personality: An interpersonal checklist. *Journal of Personality*, 1955, **24**, 94–112.

LANDFIELD, A. W. Grid relationship scoring used with a Rep Test modification. *Psychological Reports*, 1967, **21**, 19–23.

LEE, D. C. *Brief educational-vocational counseling effects of perceived therapist conditions and client rigidity on change in self-acceptance.* Unpublished master's thesis, University of Waterloo, Ontario, Canada, 1968.

LESSER, W. M. The relationship between counseling progress and empathic understanding. *Journal of Counseling Psychology*, 1961, **8**, 330–336.

LEWIS, P., & KRAUSS, H. H. Perceived therapeutic regard as a function of interviewee self-disclosure. *Proceedings of the 79th Annual Convention of the American Psychological Association*, 1971, 581–582 (Summary).

LIBO, L. M. The projective expression of patient-therapist attraction. *Journal of Clinical Psychology*, 1957, **13**, 33–36.

LIETAER, G. *The relationship as experienced by clients and therapist in client-centered and psychoanalytically-oriented therapy.* Paper presented at the Fifth Annual Meeting of the Society for Psychotherapy Research, Denver, June, 1974a.

LIETAER, G. Nederlandstalige revisie van Barrett-Lennard's Relationship Inventory: Een faktoranalytische benadering van de student-ouderrelatie (Dutch revision of Barrett-Lennard's Relationship Inventory: A factor analytic approach to the student-parent relationship). *Nederlands Tjdschrift voor de Psychologie (Dutch Journal of Psychology)*, 1974b, **29**, 191–212.

LIN, T. T. The interaction effects among counselor, client, and counseling settings within the Guided Inquiry Mode: An empirical approach. Doctoral dissertation, University of California, Los Angeles (University Microfilms, 1971, No. 71-14, 004).

LIN, T. T. Counseling relationship as a function of counselor's self-confidence. *Journal of Counseling Psychology*, 1973a, **20**, 293–297.

LIN, T. T. Revision and validation of the Truax-Carkhuff Relationship Inventory. *Measurement and Evaluation in Guidance*, 1973b, **6**, 82–86.

LINDAHL, L. *The FIRO-theory: Some empirical findings: Interpersonal compatability, perception of therapeutic conditions and outcome in group therapy.* Unpublished manuscript, Uppsala University (Sweden) 1973.

LINDEN, J. E., STONE, S. G., & SHERTZER, B. Development and evaluation of an inventory for rating counseling. *Personnel and Guidance Journal*, 1965, **44**, 267–276.

LORR, M. Client perceptions of therapists: A study of therapeutic relation. *Journal of Consulting Psychology*, 1965, **29**, 146–149.

LOVEJOY, L. W. S. *Congruence: Intrapersonal or interpersonal.* Unpublished doctoral dissertation, University of Waterloo, Canada, 1971.

LOWER, R. B., ESCOLL, P. J., LITTLE, R. B., & OTTENBERG, B. P. An experimental examination of transference. *Archives of General Psychiatry*, 1973, **29**, 738–741.

LUBORSKY, L. Perennial mystery of poor agreement among criteria for psychotherapy outcome. *Journal of Consulting and Clinical Psychology*, 1971, **37**, 316–319.

LUBORSKY, L. B., CHANDLER, M., AUERBACH, A. H., COHEN, J., & BACHRACH, H. M. Factors influencing the outcome of psychotherapy: A review of quantitative research. *Psychological Bulletin*, 1971, **75**, 145–185.

LUBORSKY, L., GRAFF, H., PULVER, S., & CURTIS, H. A clinical-quantitative examination of consensus on the concept of transference. *Archives of General Psychiatry*, 1973, **29**, 69–75.

MANNING, W. H., & DUBOIS, P. H. Correlational methods in research on human learning. *Perceptual and Motor Skills*, 1962, **15**, 287–321.

McCLANAHAN, L. D. A comparison of counseling techniques and attitudes with client evaluations of the counseling relationship. Doctoral dissertation, Ohio University. *Dissertation Abstracts International*, 1974, **34** (9-A), 5637.

McCLERNAN, J. L. Implications of sexual attraction (feeling) in the counselor-client relationship. *Dissertation Abstracts International*, 1973, **33** (9-A), 4844.

McNALLY, H. A. An investigation of selected counselor and client characteristics as possible predictors of counseling effectiveness. *Dissertation Abstracts International*, 1973, **33** (12-A), 6672–6673.

McWHIRTER, J. J. Two measures of the facilitative conditions: A correlation study. *Journal of Counseling Psychology*, 1973, **20**, 317–320.

MECHANIC, D., & GREENLEY, J. R. *The prevalence of psychological distress and help-seeking in a college student population.* Unpublished manuscript, Center for Medical Sociology and Health Services Research, University of Wisconsin, 1974.

MEHRABIAN, A. Inference of attitudes from the posture, orientation and distance of a communicator. *Journal of Consulting and Clinical Psychology*, 1968, **32**, 296–308.

MEHRABIAN, A., & FERRIS, S. R. Inference of attitudes from nonverbal communication is two channels. *Journal of Consulting and Clinical Psychology*, 1967, **31**, 248–252.

MELTZOFF, J. & KORNREICH, M. *Research in psychotherapy*, New York: Atherton, 1970.

MENDELSOHN, G. A., & GELLER, M. H. Structure of client attitudes toward counseling and their relation to counselor-client similarity. *Journal of Consulting Psychology*, 1965, **29**, 63–72.

MENNINGER, K. *Theory of psychoanalytic technique.* New York: Harper & Row, 1958.

MICKELSON, D. J., & STEVIC, R. R. Differential effects of facilitative and nonfacilitative behavioral counselors. *Journal of Counseling Psychology*, 1971, **18**, 314–319.

MILLS, D. H., & ZYTOWSKI, D. G. Helping relationship: A structural analysis. *Journal of Counseling Psychology*, 1967, **14**, 193–197.

MISCHEL, W. Toward a cognitive social learning reconceptualization of personality. *Psychological Review*, 1973a, **80**, 252–283.

MISCHEL, W. On the empirical dilemmas of psychodynamic approaches: Issues and alternatives. *Journal of Abnormal Psychology*, 1973b, **82**, 335–344.

MITCHELL, J., & ALLEN, H. Perception of a physically disabled counselor in a counseling session. *Journal of Counseling Psychology*, 1975, **22**, 70–73.

MOOS, R. H., & CLEMES, S. R. Multivariate study of the patient-therapist system. *Journal of Consulting Psychology*, 1967, **31**, 119–130.

MOOS, R. H., & MACINTOSH, S. Multivariate study of the patient-therapist system: A replication and extension. *Journal of Consulting and Clinical Psychology*, 1970, **35**, 298–307.

MORRIS, R. J., & SUCKERMAN, K. R. Therapist warmth as a factor in automated systematic desensitization. *Journal of Consulting and Clinical Psychology*, 1974, **42**, 244–250.

MORRISON, D. F. *Multivariate statistical methods.* New York: McGraw-Hill, 1967.

MUEHLBERG, N., PIERCE, R., & DRASGOW, J. A factor analysis of therapeutically facilitative conditions. *Journal of Clinical Psychology*, 1969, **25**, 93–95.

MULLOZZI, A. D. Interracial counseling: Clients' ratings and counselors' ratings in a first session. *Dissertation Abstracts International*, 1972, **33** (5-A), 2175–2176.

ORLINSKY, D. E., & HOWARD, K. I. *Therapy session report.* Unpublished questionnaire, Institute for Juvenile Research, 1966.

ORLINSKY, D. E., & HOWARD, K. I. *The effects of sex of therapist on the therapeutic experience of women.* Paper presented at the Fifth Annual Meeting of the Society for Psychotherapy Research, Denver, June 1974.

PARLOFF, M. B. Therapist-patient relationships and outcome of psychotherapy. *Journal of Consulting Psychology*, 1961, **25**, 29–38.

PASSONS, W. R., & OLSEN, L. C. Relationship of counselor characteristics and empathic sensitivity. *Journal of Counseling Psychology*, 1969, **16**, 440–445.

PATTISON, J. E. Effects of touch on self-exploration and the therapeutic relationship. *Journal of Consulting and Clinical Psychology*, 1973, **40**, 170–175.

PERSONS, R. W., PERSONS, M. K., & NEWMARK, I. Perceived helpful therapists' characteristics, client improvements, and sex of therapist and client. *Psychotherapy: Theory, Research and Practice*, 1974, **11**, 63–65.

PIERCE, W. D. Anxiety about the act of communicating and perceived empathy. *Psychotherapy: Theory, Research and Practice*, 1971, **8**, 120–123.

PIERCE, W. D., & MOSHER, D. L. Perceived empathy, interviewer behavior, and interviewee anxiety. *Journal of Consulting Psychology*, 1967, **31**, 101.

QUICK, E., & JACOB, T. Marital disturbance in relation to role theory and relationship theory. *Journal of Abnormal Psychology*, 1973, **82**, 309–316.

RAPPAPORT, J., & CHINSKY, J. M. Accurate empathy: Confusion of a construct. *Psychological Bulletin*, 1972, **77**, 400–404.

RASKIN, N. J. The psychotherapy research project of the American Academy of Psychotherapists. *Proceedings of the 73rd Annual Convention of the American Psychological Association*, 1965, **1**, 253–254.

RAZIN, A. M. A-B variable in psychotherapy: A critical review. *Psychological Bulletin*, 1971, **75**, 1–22.

RICE, D. G., GURMAN, A. S., & RAZIN, A. M. Therapist sex, style and theoretical orientation. *Journal of Nervous and Mental Disease*, 1974, **159**, 413–421.

RIOCH, D. "Personality." *Archives of General Psychiatry*, 1972, **27**, 575–580.

ROBACK, H. B., & STRASSBERG, D. S. Relationship between perceived therapist-offered conditions and therapeutic movement in group psychotherapy with hospitalized mental patients. *Small Group Behavior*, 1975, **6**, 345–352.

ROGERS, C. R. The necessary and sufficient conditions of therapeutic personality change. *Journal of Consulting Psychology*, 1957, **21**, 95–103.

ROGERS, C. R. (Ed.) *The therapeutic relationship and its impact: A study of psychotherapy with schizophrenics.* Madison: University of Wisconsin Press, 1967.

ROGERS, C. R., & TRUAX, C. B. The therapeutic conditions antecedent to change: A theoretical view. In C. R. ROGERS (Ed.), *The therapeutic relationship and its impact: A study of psychotherapy with schizophrenics.* Madison, Wisc.: University of Wisconsin Press, 1967.

ROKEACH, M. *The open and closed mind.* New York: Basic Books, 1960.

ROSEN, H. H. *Dimensions of the perceived parent-relationship as related to juvenile delinquency.* Unpublished master's thesis, Auburn University, 1961.

ROTTER, J. B. *Social learning and clinical psychology.* New York: Prentice-Hall, 1954.

ROTTER, J. B. Generalized expectancies for internal versus external control of reinforcement. *Psychological Monographs*, 1966, **80** (1, Whole No. 609).

RYAN, V. L., & GIZYNSKI, M. N. Behavior therapy in retrospect: Patients' feelings about their behavior therapies. *Journal of Consulting and Clinical Psychology*, 1971, **37**, 1–9.

SAPOLSKY, A. Relationship between patient-doctor compatability, mutual perception, and outcome of treatment. *Journal of Abnormal Psychology*, 1965, **70**, 70–76.

SATTLER, J. M. Racial "experimenter effects" in experimentation, testing, interviewing, and psychotherapy. *Psychological Bulletin*, 1970, **73**, 137–160.

SCHEID, A. B. Levels of the facilitative core conditions and status of counselor introduction as critical variables in client perception of the counselor. *Dissertation Abstracts International*, 1972, **32** (7-B), 4228.

SCHEUER, A. L. *A study of the relationship between personal attributes and effectiveness in teachers of the emotionally disturbed and socially maladjusted in a residential school setting.* Unpublished doctoral dissertation, Columbia University, 1969.

SCHOENINGER, D. W. *Client experiencing as a function of therapist self-disclosure and pre-therapy training in experiencing.* Unpublished doctoral dissertation, University of Wisconsin, 1965.

SHAPIRO, D. A. The rating of psychotherapeutic empathy: A preliminary study. *British Journal of Social and Clinical Psychology*, 1970, **9**, 148–151.

SHAPIRO, D. A. Naive British judgements of therapeutic conditions. *British Journal of Social and Clinical Psychology*, 1973, **12**, 289–294.

SHAPIRO, J. G. Agreement between channels of communication in interviews. *Journal of Consulting Psychology*, 1966, **30**, 535–538.

SHAPIRO, J. G. Perception of therapeutic conditions from different vantage points. *Journal of Counseling Psychology*, 1968a, **15**, 346–350.

SHAPIRO, J. G. Relationships between expert and neophyte ratings of therapeutic conditions. *Journal of Consulting and Clinical Psychology*, 1968b, **32**, 87–89.

SHAPIRO, J. G. Relationships between visual and auditory cues of therapeutic effectiveness. *Journal of Clinical Psychology*, 1968c, **24**, 236–239.

SHAPIRO, J. G., FOSTER, C. P., & POWELL, T. Facial and bodily cues of genuineness, empathy and warmth. *Journal of Clinical Psychology*, 1968, **24**, 233–236.

SHAPIRO, J. G., KRAUSS, H. H., & TRUAX, C. B. Therapeutic conditions and disclosure beyond the therapeutic encounter. *Journal of Counseling Psychology*, 1969, **16**, 290–294.

SHAPIRO, J. G., & VOOG, T. Effect of the inherently helpful person on student academic achievement. *Journal of Counseling Psychology*, 1969, **16**, 505–509.

SNELBECKER, G. E. Influence of therapeutic techniques on college students' perceptions of therapists. *Journal of Consulting Psychology*, 1967, **31**, 614–618.

STANDAL, S. W. *The need for positive regard: A contribution to client-centered theory.* Unpublished doctoral dissertation, University of Chicago, 1954.

STANLEY, C. L. "Relationship orientation" of counselor-trainees as related to client perception of the counseling relationship and client change in connotative meanings. *Dissertation Abstracts International*, 1967, **27** (11-A), 3699–3700.

STERN, M., & BIERMAN, R. Facilitative functioning of A-B therapist types. *Psychotherapy: Theory, Research and Practice*, 1973, **10**, 44–47.

STRONG, S. R., TAYLOR, R. G., BRATTON, J. C., & LOOPER, R. G. Nonverbal behavior and perceived counselor characteristics. *Journal of Counseling Psychology*, 1971, **18**, 554–561.

STRUPP, H. H. On the basic ingredients of psychotherapy. *Journal of Consulting and Clinical Psychology*, 1973, **41**, 1–8.

STRUPP, H. H., FOX, R. E., & LESSLER, K. *Patients view their psychotherapy.* Baltimore: Johns Hopkins Press, 1969.

SULLIVAN, H. S. *The psychiatric interview.* New York: Norton, 1961.

SWITZKY, H. N., & HAYWOOD, H. C. Motivational orientation and the relative efficacy of self-monitored and externally imposed reinforcement systems in children. *Journal of Personality and Social Psychology*, 1974, **30**, 360–366.

TAUSCH, R., SANDER, K., BASTINE, R., & FRIESE, H. Variablen und ergebnisse bei client-centered psychotherapie mit alternierenden psychotherapeuten. *Sonderdruck aus Psychologische Rundschau*, 1970, **21**, 29–37.

TAYLOR, V. K. Black adults' perceptions of counselors within the counselor-client relationship. *Dissertation Abstracts International*, 1971, **31** (7-A), 3281–3282.

TEPPER, D. T. The communication of counselor empathy, respect and genuineness through verbal and non-verbal channels. *Dissertation Abstracts International*, 1973, **33** (9-A), 4858.

THORNTON, B. M. *Dimensions of perceived relationship as related to marital adjustment*. Unpublished master's thesis, Auburn University, 1960.

TOSI, D. J. Dogmatism within the counselor-client dyad. *Journal of Counseling Psychology*, 1970, **17**, 284–288.

TOSI, D. J., FRUMKIN, R. M., & WILSON, M. E. Intercorrelations of four relationship components of the Barrett-Lennard Relationship Inventory. *Psychological Reports*, 1968, **23**, 641–642.

TRUAX, C. B. The relationship between the patient's perception of the level of therapeutic conditions offered in psychotherapy and constructive personality change. *Brief Research Reports*, Wisconsin Psychiatric Institute, University of Wisconsin, 1962, No. 1.

TRUAX, C. B. Therapist empathy, warmth, and genuineness and patient personality change in group psychotherapy: A comparison between interaction unit measures, time sample measures, patient perception measures. *Journal of Clinical Psychology*, 1966, **22**, 225–229.

TRUAX, C. B. Length of therapist response, accurate empathy and patient improvement. *Journal of Clinical Psychology*, 1971a, **26**, 539–541.

TRUAX, C. B. The outcome effects of counselor or therapist accurate empathy, nonpossessive warmth and genuineness. *Vocational Guidance*, 1971b, **7**, 61–79.

TRUAX, C. B. Perceived therapeutic conditions and client outcome. *Comparative Group Studies*, 1971c, **2**, 301–310.

TRUAX, C. B., & CARKHUFF, R. R. *Toward effective counseling and psychotherapy*. Chicago: Aldine, 1967.

TRUAX, C. B., LESLIE, G. R., Smith, F. W., Glenn, A. W., & FISHER, G. H. *Empathy, warmth and genuineness and progress in vocational rehabilitation*. Unpublished manuscript, Arkansas Rehabilitation Research and Training Center, 1966.

TRUAX, C. B., & MITCHELL, K. M. Research on certain therapist interpersonal skills in relation to process and outcome. In A. E. BERGIN & S. L. GARFIELD (Eds.), *Handbook of psychotherapy and behavior change*. New York: Wiley, 1971.

TRUAX, C. B., TUNNELL, B. T., JR., & WARGO, D. G. *Prediction of group psychotherapeutic outcome*. Unpublished manuscript, Arkansas Rehabilitation Research and Training Center, 1966.

TRUAX, C. B., WARGO, D. G., CARKHUFF, R. R., TUNNELL, B. T., JR., & GLENN, A. W. *Client perception of therapist empathy, warmth and genuineness and therapeutic outcome in group counseling with juvenile delinquents*. Unpublished manuscript, Arkansas Rehabilitation Research and Training Center, 1966.

TRUAX, C. B., WARGO, D. G., TUNNELL, B. T., JR., & GLENN, A. W. *Patient perception of therapist empathy, warmth and genuineness and therapeutic outcome in outpatient group therapy*. Unpublished manuscript, Arkansas Rehabilitation Research and Training Center, 1966.

TUCKER, L., DAMARIN, F., & MESSICK, S. A base-free measure of change. *Psychometrika*, 1966, **31**, 457–473.

VAN DER VEEN, F. Effects of the therapist and the patient on each other's therapeutic behavior. *Journal of Consulting Psychology*, 1965, **29**, 19–26.

VAN DER VEEN, F. Basic elements in the process of psychotherapy: A research study. *Journal of Consulting Psychology*, 1967, **31**, 295–303.

VAN DER VEEN, F. Client perception of therapist conditions as a factor in psychotherapy. In J. T. HART & T. M. TOMLINSON (Eds.), *New directions in client-centered therapy*. Boston: Houghton-Mifflin, 1970.

VAN DER VEEN, F., & NOVAK, A. L. Perceived parental attitudes and family concepts of disturbed adolescents, normal siblings, and normal controls. *Institute for Juvenile Research Reports*, 1970, **7**, No. 3.

VAN DER VEEN, F., & STOLER, N. Therapist judgments, interview behavior and case outcome. *Psychotherapy: Theory, Research and Practice*, 1965, **2**, 158–163.

VAN DER VEEN, F., & TOMLINSON, T. A scale for rating the manner of problem expression. In C. R. ROGERS (Ed.), *The therapeutic relationship and its impact*. Madison: University of Wisconsin Press, 1967.

VANSTEENWEGEN, A. Het communicatiecentrum voor echtparen te Lovenjoel-Leuven: Onderzoek naar de resultaten van het drie weken durend therapie programma. *Bevolking en Gezin*, 1974, **1**, 105–120.

VITALO, R. L. Effects of facilitative interpersonal functioning in a conditioning paradigm. *Journal of Counseling Psychology*, 1970, **17**, 141–144.

WACHTEL, P. L. Psychodynamics, behavior therapy, and the implacable experimenter: An inquiry into the consistency of personality. *Journal of Abnormal Psychology*, 1973, **82**, 324–334.

WALKER, B. S., & LITTLE, D. F. Factor analysis of the Barrett-Lennard relationship inventory. *Journal of Counseling Psychology*, 1969, **16**, 516–521.

WALLACE, C. J. The effects of perceived similarity on perception of the therapeutic relationship. *Dissertation Abstracts International*, 1971, **31** (7-B), 4349.

WARREN, B. E. Client expectations and the client-counselor relationship in a counseling analogue. *JSAS Catalog of Selected Documents in Psychology*, 1973, **3**, 31.

WELLS, R. A., FIGUREL, J. A., & McNAMEE, P. Group facilitative training with conflicted marital couples. In A. S. GURMAN & D. G. RICE (Eds.), *Couples in conflict: New directions in marital therapy*. New York: Aronson, 1975.

WESSMAN, A. E., RICKS, D. F. *Mood and personality*. New York: Holt, Rinehart & Winston, 1966.

WIEBE, B., & PEARCE, W. B. An item-analysis and revision of the Barrett-Lennard Relationship Inventory. *Journal of Clinical Psychology*, 1973, **29**, 495–497.

WILKINS, W. Client's expectancy of therapeutic gain: Evidence for the active role of the therapist. *Psychiatry*, 1973a, **36**, 184–190.

WILKINS, W. Expectancy of therapeutic gain: An empirical and conceptual critique. *Journal of Consulting and Clinical Psychology*, 1973b, **40**, 69–77.

YOUNG, A. H. Race of psychotherapist and client and perception of variables relevant to therapy outcome. *Dissertation Abstracts International*, 1973, **33** (10-A), 5506.

ZAUDERER, E. S. *The relationship of some counselor characteristics to revealingness in clients*. Unpublished doctoral dissertation, Ohio State University, 1967.

ZIEMELIS, A. Effects of client preference and expectancy upon the initial interview. *Journal of Counseling Psychology*, 1974, **21**, 23–30.

ZIMMERMAN, F. The relationship between counselor accuracy in perceiving affect and client-perceived empathy. *Dissertation Abstracts International*, 1973, **33** (8-A), 4109.

EDITORS' REFERENCES

BARRETT-LENNARD, G. T. *Empathy in human relationships: Significance, nature and measurement*. Unpublished manuscript, University of Waterloo, Ontario, Canada, 1975.

GURMAN, A. S., & GUSTAFSON, J. P. *Patients' perceptions of the therapeutic relationship and group therapy outcome: An empirical and clinical analysis*. Unpublished manuscript, University of Wisconsin Medical School, 1975.

HANSEN, J. C., SIMPFER, D. G., & EASTERLING, R. E. A study of the relationships in multiple counseling. *Journal of Educational Research*, 1967, **60**, 461–463.

WRIGHT, W. Counselor dogmatism, willingness to disclose, and clients' empathy ratings. *Journal of Counseling Psychology*, 1975, **22**, 390–394.

YALOM, I. D. *The theory and practice of group psychotherapy.* New York: Basic Books, 1970.

NOTES

1. The author wishes to thank Andrew M. Razin, Marjorie H. Klein, and Donald W. Fiske for their helpful comments on the manuscript. Special thanks are offered to G. T. Barrett-Lennard for his careful and thoughtful reading of the chapter and his many important suggestions. Thanks are also extended to John Carmichael (Mental Health Centre, Kamloops, British Columbia), Lars Lindahl (Uppsala University, Sweden), and L. D. McClanahan (Athens, Ohio Mental Health Center) for sharing their unpublished data reported in this chapter.

2. *Editors' Footnote.* As co-editors, we each have written "editors'" footnotes for the other's chapter. Thus, Andrew M. Razin is responsible for the notes in this chapter, except for numbers 4, 15, 17, 18, 22, and 23, which were added by Gurman.

3. *Editors' Footnote.* Gurman is really making two methodological points here, neither of which should be lost. Above, he argues for the construction of facilitativeness measures that would be applicable and meaningful with non-client-centered therapists. Secondly, however, he points out that such construction would not correct a problem of at least equal magnitude (i.e., insuring that any measures of facilitativeness must be based on *patient* perceptions).

4. *Editors' Footnote.* Very recently, Barrett-Lennard (1975) has offered a most useful reconceptualization of empathy in human relationships. In brief, he conceives of empathic relating as involving at least three distinct phases, each different in locus and content; these are (1) the "inner" process of empathic listening, resonation and personal understanding, (2) *expressed* empathic understanding, and (3) *received* empathy, or empathy as experienced by the person being empathized with. This view of empathy, with analogous theoretical possibilities for warmth and genuineness, has major methodological implications, most relevant among which for this chapter are (1) that expressed, manifest, or verbalized empathy represents an importantly different subprocess of empathic communication from that of received (roughly equivalent to "perceived") empathy, and (2) that the effect of expressed empathy is highly contingent on the "receiver." These issues will be examined empirically later in this chapter.

5. Fortunately, the present author has been able to retrieve these data from the files of the Wisconsin Psychiatric Institute. They will be presented later in this chapter.

6. *Editors' Footnote.* Further discussion of the utility and problems of patient ratings of process can be found in the early part of Fiske's chapter in this volume, where we also comment on the issue (Footnotes 4 and 5).

7. Factor analyses were also conducted on the therapist RI data presented in Barrett-Lennard (1962) and on the authors' own data consisting of 79 female college students' ratings of their mothers in their parent-child relationship and of themselves in that relationship; since the results of these three other analyses were all confirmatory of the Barrett-Lennard patient RI analysis, they are not described here in detail.

8. *Editors' Footnote.* This interpretation is quite consistent with that in the Auerbach and Johnson chapter in this volume, where we suggest (Footnote 6) that experienced therapists may come to see therapeutic gains that are not seen by inexperienced therapists.

9. *Editors' Footnote.* This strongly supports the point made in Fiske's chapter—namely, that, ideally, ratings from all three vantage points are to be made in process and outcome research.

10. In fairness, Carmichael cannot be faulted in this regard, since the present writer (ASG) performed these analyses.

11. *Editors' Footnote.* Of course, the use of improper outcome measures, such as uncorrected change scores, is a serious problem that needs attention (not only here but in psychotherapy research in general). Here, nevertheless, no clear reason appears for the use of this inadequate measure to exert a *systematic* effect (i.e., such that patient ratings correlate highly with outcome as rated by several sources). In fact, if there is a strong relationship in these studies between initial patient diagnosis or severity and outcome, we should expect all the less outcome variance to be accounted for by patient RI ratings.

12. The writer thanks David G. Rice for suggesting this issue.

13. Truax (Truax & Carkhuff, 1967), reporting on the same research project, argues that there is essentially no relationship between patient-perceived conditions and therapy outcome assessed by more than 30 measures. Unfortunately, Truax failed in the text of his book to comment on other data which he also presented. These data (p. 135) yielded more equivocal results, in that, based on initial RI scores, test-improved (Rorschach, MMPI, Truax Anxiety Scale, Q sort for adjustment) patients showed significantly higher R scores than test-deteriorated patients, while the reverse was true for E ratings. Truax also failed, without explanation, to publish all the results of his data analysis. An in-house research report (Truax, 1962) also showed that these test-improved patients reported significantly more positive *changes* in all RI scores except U from early- to late-therapy than did test-deteriorated subjects. These results, then, implied that improvement was related to the degree to which therapeutic conditions *increased* in the patient's phenomenology.

14. Because the "official" final summary of this research project was published in a book edited by Rogers (1967), independent publication of results from that study by other project members (van der Veen, 1967, 1970; van der Veen & Stoler, 1965) are not reviewed separately in this chapter.

15. *Editors' Footnote.* After this chapter was completed, the author discovered an 11th group therapy study. Hansen, Simpfer, and Easterling (1967), using exactly the same design and client population as in a later study by Hansen *et al.* (1968), found a significant rank-order correlation (.83) between group members' perceptions of their leader's therapeutic conditions and self-concept change based on a Q sort. The authors' data analysis was based on the *mean* perceived conditions and *mean* self-concept change *within* each of their therapy groups, yielding an N of 6. The more appropriate analysis, and the only one which would have allowed direct testing of the client-centered hypothesis, would have involved the product-moment correlation of individual members' scores on these two measures. Unfortunately, therefore, the authors' inappropriate data analysis obscures the meaning of their finding and may explain why this result failed to be replicated in the later study by Hansen *et al.* (1968), in which the appropriate correlational analysis was used.

16. *Editors' Footnote.* Furthermore, therapeutic conditions offered by a group may be something very different from therapeutic conditions offered by an individual therapist. Most groups, after all, are not set up with the expectation that each member will be a facilitative therapist. Unconditionality of regard from one's peers, for example, may serve to prevent receiving useful feedback and may thus be quite countertherapeutic in a group.

17. *Editors' Footnote*. Gurman and Gustafson (1975), in a recent clinical critique of this literature, have argued that the perceived conditions-outcome hypothesis is likely to be confirmed in group therapy only to the extent to which the group experience approximates individual psychotherapy. That is, many schools of group therapy systematically attempt to influence the group members through variables other than the leader's empathy, warmth, genuineness, etc. Yalom (1970), for example, while using the leader-patient relationship, relies heavily on the "social engineering" of the group situation. Such an approach is obviously quite different from those schools of group therapy that rely almost entirely on an intense pairing relationship between therapist and patient, with the group used as a chorus. In summary, Gurman and Gustafson argue that the client-centered hypothesis probably can be confirmed only in groups that center on leader-client relations, that idealize the leader, and that are relatively untroubled by major group difficulties, such as an acting-out patient. Thus, an important direction for further research in this area will involve testing the perceived conditions-outcome hypothesis in the context of different group structures.

18. *Editors' Footnote*. After this chapter had been completed, the author and a colleague (J. P. Gustafson) initiated just such a study.

19. K. Howard and D. Orlinsky (personal communication, December 1974) studied 32 therapists, with two patients per therapist and three sessions per patient. The ANOVA of patient RI's, completed after each session, indicated that about 29% of the variance was due to the therapist and about 49% was due to the patient.

20. "Negatively changed" and "no change" client groups were combined and compared with "positively changed" clients.

21. "High" and "low" functioning therapists were chosen on the basis of *judge*-rated therapeutic conditions in earlier therapy sessions. Despite the lack of agreement between judge-rated and patient-rated conditions that has been described earlier in this chapter, it is clear that the therapists designated as "high" and "low" facilitative differed tremendously in their interpersonal skills: the mean judge-rated therapeutic conditions levels were: Empathy—"high" therapists, 5.61, "low" therapists, 2.33 (10-point scale); Warmth—"high" therapists, 5.67, "low" therapists, 3.37 (9-point scale); Genuineness—"high" therapists, 5.70, "low" therapists, 3.56 (9-point scale).

22. *Editors' Footnote*. In both these studies, empathy was the interpersonal skill rated. A more recent study by Wright (1975) found high-dogmatic counselors to be perceived by their clients as significantly lower in regard, congruence, and unconditionality, but *not* in empathy.

23. *Editors' Footnote*. In contrast, Wright (1975) found that male therapists were perceived as significantly higher in levels of regard, congruence, and empathy (but not unconditionality) by *female* clients than by male clients. Because of patient diagnostic differences in the Wright and Kiesler *et al*. studies, it is impossible to separate out the effects of patient diagnosis and gender on perceived therapist relatability.

CHAPTER 20

THE THERAPIST-CLIENT RELATIONSHIP IN BEHAVIOR THERAPY[1,2]

G. Terence Wilson and Ian M. Evans

INTRODUCTION: A DEVELOPMENTAL PERSPECTIVE

Close to a decade ago, we[3] wrote an article on behavior therapy and the therapist-client relationship in response to the two major criticisms of a behavioral approach that we had encountered. Although these came from the profoundly psychodynamic establishment which dominated clinical psychology and psychiatry in South Africa at the time, similar opinions were being voiced elsewhere. Behavior therapy was seen as a dangerous, mechanistic approach, which debased the essential nature of the therapeutic relationship. The few who accepted the alleged success of behavior therapists such as Wolpe and Lazarus attributed it to the role of factors inadvertently inherent in the therapeutic relationship rather than to the specific conditioning techniques employed. Our intention, therefore, was to expose the incorrectness of these objections and, in addition, to illustrate how a behavioral approach might open up promising conceptual and research avenues to a clearer understanding of the critical interpersonal variables which were, perhaps, being underplayed by behavior therapists (Wilson, Hannon, & Evans, 1968).

Since then, behavior therapy's status has changed from that of a beleaguered minority group to a prospering section of the therapeutic establishment (Franks & Wilson, 1973, 1974). In the process, the field has matured considerably. A brazen confidence has given way to an optimism more cautious; clinical conceptualizations have grown in sophistication; and an open-minded, empirical approach to unresolved issues is increasingly evident. Consequently, while a minority of current-day critics still reiterate the early condemnations of behavior

therapy, behavior therapists themselves are more than ever concerned with the social learning processes of the therapeutic relationship and, more specifically, the therapist's contribution to effective behavior therapy. This sharpened focus appears certain to further our knowledge of psychological processes in general, and promises to result in the development of more efficacious methods of therapeutic behavior change.

Before discussing these methods, it is worth considering briefly the developmental changes that have taken place within behavior therapy. The historical antecedents of behavior therapy are diverse and can be traced to the turn of the century and even beyond. The contemporary origins of behavior therapy date from the 1950s: the pioneering clinical studies of Wolpe and his associates Lazarus and Rachman in South Africa; the contributions of Eysenck and his students at the Maudsley Hospital in London; and the applied operant tradition in the USA. (For a discussion of these developments see Krasner, 1971; O'Leary & Wilson, 1975; Yates, 1970). The original definition of behavior therapy was in terms of the application of "modern learning theory," or conditioning principles, to abnormal behavior (e.g., Eysenck, 1959; Wolpe, 1958). However rigorously those early papers may have attempted to describe treatment in stimulus-response (S-R) terms, the importance of the interpersonal relationship between therapist and client was generally acknowledged. Lazarus (1958, 1960) had always stressed this point, and Wolpe (1958) had reported his strong impression that clients who seemed to like him in the early interviews showed some improvement *before* special treatment methods had been applied (p. 194). In their 1966 text, Wolpe and Lazarus took the view that close rapport between therapist and client was often necessary but not sufficient for effective treatment. They suggested that nonjudgmental acceptance by the therapist would engender a positive emotional response resulting in the "nonspecific reciprocal inhibition" of the anxiety aroused during therapy sessions. This interpretation was quite similar to one suggested by Skinner (1953) in which he had argued that psychotherapy involved a nonpunishing situation in which suppressed behavior could be emitted freely. In both cases, the direct influence of the therapist was interpreted according to the same learning principles that would be used in planning more specific treatment strategies. As such, it was in the tradition of Dollard and Miller (1950) in which complex aspects of therapy were translated into "liberated" S-R principles.

In his seminal paper on behavior therapy, Eysenck (1959) asserted that "personal relations are not essential for cures of neurotic disorder, although they may be useful in certain circumstances" (p. 67). He subsequently stressed that therapists require "a very special ability to understand the difficulties and troubles of the neurotic, and to devise ways and means of getting them out of these difficulties" (1965, p. 157). Eysenck did not single out social influence, although his own theory of personality and behavior therapy (Eysenck & Rachman, 1965) explicitly proposed that for some clients, notably neurotic extraverts, social rewards are potent agents for behavior change; it awaited the Skinnerian group of "applied behavior analysts" to first self-consciously manipulate the social behavior of the therapist in order to effect change in the client.

A factor which doubtless contributed to the misconception of behavior therapy as impersonal was the early rejection of the significance of the psychoanalytic concept of transference. *It is not assumed that the client displaces onto the therapist the attitudes, wishes, and impulses which had been directed toward his parents during childhood and which now irrationally characterize his mode of interacting with significant persons. Similarly, it is not felt that changes in the therapist-client relationship necessarily transfer to the client's relations with other people in his everyday environment (e.g., family or friends).* Referring to Franz Alexander's (1956) own observations, Bandura (1969) has noted that the relatively artificial nature of the therapeutic situation and the diverse social characteristics of the therapist may not present a suitable stimulus for eliciting strong generalized respons-

es. It is highly improbable that the client's behavioral problems can be effectively modified solely in relation to the therapist. As Bandura concludes on the basis of outcome research on psychotherapy, "whatever clients may reenact with their psychotherapists relatively few beneficial effects of these reenactments trickle down to daily interpersonal living. Most likely the artificial relationship provides substitute gratifications for those lacking in the clients' natural relationships instead of serving as a major vehicle for personality change" (p. 79). Accordingly, the emotional experiences which transpire between the therapist and client, and which are the essential change-producing agents in psychoanalysis (Kaplan, 1974; Moore & Fine, 1967), are *not* regarded as the essence of behavior therapy.

A second reason for the impersonal image behavior therapy acquired was that when studies first began to appear in which the contingency of the therapist's response to the client was the treatment strategy, they were not perceived as involving the therapeutic relationship. Behavior therapists' heritage is, after all, learning theory, and the preference for logical positivism is deeply rooted (Kendler & Spence, 1971). *"Relationship" is not easily defined operationally, unlike contingencies of social attention.* Not only could these social contingencies be defined and measured, but they could also be altered, and with them the client's behavior. So to some, behavior therapists were "behavioral engineers" (Ayllon & Michael, 1959), and they were quickly dubbed "mechanistic," in keeping with their own metaphors.

Although recognized, the therapeutic relationship was clearly deemphasized relative to specific conditioning techniques. It was not until the more sophisticated social learning formulation of behavior therapy that the full importance of the relationship was to be appreciated. In 1965, against a backdrop of social learning and behavior influence, Ullmann and Krasner provided a view of behavior therapy more encompassing than any previously offered. They described behavior therapy as "treatment deducible from the sociopsychological model that aims to alter a person's behavior directly through the application of general psychological principles" (1969, p. 244). Staats (1970) similarly criticized the narrow belief that behavior therapy was the application of simple conditioning principles, and coined the term "social behaviorism" to convey the necessity for the behavior therapist to be concerned with the richness of human social processes, language, perception, and sensory-motor skills. Staats (1970) has attempted to preserve some theoretical unity by extending S-R (neo-behavioral) interpretations of simple learning to complex human behavior. Bandura (1969), however, in his scholarly formulation of the social learning conceptualization of behavior modification, considers cognitive mediational processes fundamental. Social learning theory explicitly includes experimentally derived principles of behavior change from social and developmental psychology. Social influence processes such as persuasion, expectancy, attitude change, and interpersonal attraction are integral features of behavior modification thus conceived. Within this expanded context, the reciprocal influence processes which define the therapist-client relationship are viewed as being of the utmost importance to the understanding and effective use of behavioral treatment methods. In current behavior therapy the relationship developed between therapist and client is seen as facilitating the modification of clients' cognitive, affective, and motor patterns so as to enable them to secure greater emotional and interpersonal satisfactions from their natural environments. The remainder of this chapter discusses the therapist's role in accomplishing these objectives.

BEHAVIORAL ASSESSMENT

Conducting an adequate behavioral assessment of any clinical case is perhaps the most important, and assuredly the most difficult, aspect of behavior therapy. Several thorough discussions of the nature of behavior assessment are available (e.g., Evans & Nelson, 1974; Goldfried & Sprafkin, 1974; Kanfer & Saslow, 1969; Mischel, 1968). To summarize, behavioral assessment, while not limited to these activities, is designed to (a) identify target behaviors for modification (i.e., those response patterns which are to be strengthened and those behaviors which require elimination), (b) isolate whatever psychological and environmental factors are currently maintaining the problem behavior, and (c) determine which technique or combination of techniques might most effectively produce the desired therapeutic improvement. Each of these activities will be discussed in turn.

The importance of setting the goals of therapy can hardly be overemphasized. Contrary to the charge that behavior therapists deliberately impose goals on unresisting clients, it has been proposed that the *client* should have the major

say in ultimately deciding on treatment goals in behavior therapy (Bandura, 1969; Franks & Wilson, 1975). Selecting effective techniques with which to modify behavior is an empirical question which is the province and expertise of the therapist. The choice of therapeutic goals is a matter of value judgment and must be mainly determined by the client. Consider the alteration of sexual preferences (Wilson & Davison, 1974). Psychodynamic thinking assumes that homosexuality represents a pathological or "abnormal" deviation from the "normal" heterosexual psychosexual developmental process (e.g., Bieber, 1962). In terms of the social learning approach, "normal" and "abnormal" are viewed as labels which reflect society's prevailing value judgments; they tell us more about the labeler's behavior than about the person being labeled. There is no evidence to contradict the assumption that homosexual responsiveness is socially acquired in the same manner as heterosexuality. Accordingly, behavior therapists appear open to helping homosexuals adjust more satisfactorily to a permanent homosexual identity (Davison & Wilson, 1973a). This willingness to accept the client's goal, albeit unconventional, is illustrated by Kohlenberg (1974), whose successful treatment of a homosexual pedophile had as its goal teaching the client to be sexually responsive to other adult male partners.

Of course, while ideally the client has decision-making primacy, it would be foolish to imagine that in practice the therapist plays no part in the setting of treatment goals. Some of the more obvious ways in which this happens should be briefly mentioned. One very common influence arises when the therapist attempts to define, in behavioral terms, goals which are relatively specific but which carry surplus meaning. It is quite common, for example, for a client to express a wish to be "less frigid," which usually translates into a more mundane goal of achieving orgasm with her partner at least a certain percentage of the time. Often the goals have to be set at a less ambitious level—the nonorgasmic client who wishes to become multiply orgasmic, for instance, might be persuaded to settle for the more realistic goal of achieving orgasm by any method of stimulation. Or, again, the therapist can modify the client's goal in a direction that he did not know was feasible: suggesting to a client with a drinking problem that he aim for moderate drinking rather than total abstinence would be one example.

It is when the client has *no* clear goals, and has undertaken therapy out of diffuse personal dissatisfaction or when his current behavior is generally condemned (e.g., homosexuality) that the influence of the therapist is likely to be most marked. In this instance the therapist's contribution is in helping the client develop appropriate problem-solving strategies whereby he learns to establish realistic and personally satisfying goals for himself (see later section). The therapist's discussion of alternative courses of action open to the client, and his evaluation of their likely consequences unavoidably reflect his own values and life experiences. But even here the behavior therapist attempts to declare honestly his personal biases. The analogy is that of a stock broker: it is when the client has no ideas about what to do with his money that the broker's own favored investments are most likely to be suggested. Even so, a good broker presents only pros and cons—it is up to the investor to make the decision. If the therapist's value-system is sufficiently at variance with the client's and they disagree about which goals are most important or feasible, referral to a more appropriate therapist, or even complete refusal to endorse the proposed treatment goal is indicated. In the last resort, the therapist's actions are governed by his personal and professional values, and he is not obliged to work toward client-determined goals if he believes them to be ill-advised.[4]

Establishing treatment objectives with institutionalized populations such as prisoners and mental hospital inmates, or with respect to children, involves more complex ethical and legal questions which are beyond the scope of this chapter (but see Bandura, 1974; Franks & Wilson, 1975; Friedman, 1975; Goldiamond, 1974). Suffice it to say that, among other organizations, the American Psychological Association has created a special Commission on Behavior Modification which is responsible for developing guidelines governing the use of behavioral treatment methods with these populations. At present, the role of the therapist in these situations varies considerably, according to his own personal style, and no course of action can be prescribed. Personally, in our own work, we weave a delicate course between attempting to match societal values and occasionally attempting to influence them. In a vocational rehabilitation setting, for example, we know from experience that the handicapped clients are most likely to lose their first jobs because of tardiness or lack of punctuality; these, therefore, must become the primary target behaviors in the behavior modification program in the sheltered workshop, regardless

of our own feelings about the importance of such things. On the other hand, if ward aides in a mental retardation setting request help in persuading an adolescent to stop masturbating, we might instead encourage the aides to teach the boy to masturbate in private. In parent-training programs it is usually claimed that parents are given effective procedures which will increase their ability to achieve their *own* child-rearing goals. In practice, however, even recommending reward over punishment represents a cultural bias; recognizing this, Evans, Dubanoski, and Higuchi (1974) have suggested that a legitimate treatment goal for physically abusive parents from a subculture in which punishment is common might be simply a more moderate use of punishment—this goal is about as popular with children's protective services as the goal of moderate drinking is with most agencies serving the alcoholic.

The second major task of assessment is to identify the complex variables surrounding and sustaining the goal behaviors. This demands much clinical acumen and challenges the therapist's ingenuity no less than do alternative approaches to assessment. Although often misleadingly portrayed as simple, behavior therapy is deceptively intricate. "To select desensitization hierarchies, to find effective reinforcers, or to isolate target behaviors requires not only technical skill but the qualities of a *menschenkenner* who is sensitive to human behavior beyond his academic knowledge" (Kanfer & Phillips, 1966, p. 126). It is extremely useful to have knowledge or experience of the problem domain; for us, constructing a hierarchy to deal with a fear of flying is much easier than imagining the possible stimuli surrounding the panic attacks of a scuba diver. Sensitivity to the complex interaction of behaviors is also important. Wolpe (1969) describes a case in which he initially used systematic desensitization with a claustrophobic female client without success; he subsequently chanced upon the fact, however, that the psychological factors controlling the claustrophobia were long-suppressed anger and frustration at her husband for his domination over her every activity. A switch in therapeutic tactics to a program of assertion training resulted in the speedy elimination of her phobia.

As the interview is a major vehicle for obtaining information on controlling variables, the behavior therapist's ability to make the client feel at ease and talk about anxiety-provoking, embarrassing, or distressing material is critical. Except for therapy-wise clients, initial inter-

views which are focused upon the most private
and personal details demand, for most, novel
roles proscribed in many subcultures. The
behavior therapist needs to be an acute observer.
Being able to read between the lines, being able
to pick up cues and hints, or being able to
recognize potential sources of stress in individual lives is as important for a behavior therapist as for any other therapist. Following H. S.
Sullivan's approach, Goldfried and Davison
(1976) have noted that the relationship can often
provide the alert therapist with a useful sample,
despite some distortions, of the client's interpersonal behavior in the natural environment.
The therapist should recognize the biases which
might impair his gathering of information
(Lazarus, 1971) and should realize his potential
for wielding adverse and improper influence in
the interview (Thomas, 1973). In general, we
recognize that the client is in a quite well-defined
role and his behavior is at least partly a function
of that setting; *the behavior therapist does not
accept every verbal statement at face value, as is
commonly supposed.*

Once the target behaviors have been identified
and some of the controlling variables uncovered,
the therapist's third task in assessment is to
select the appropriate therapeutic strategy. A
particular advantage of the social learning approach is that it offers the behavior therapist
several alternative methods for the modification
of psychological problems. Yet relatively little
attention has been paid to the problem of assessing clients in order to choose the most appropriate therapeutic technique, and *there is very
little research done on the kinds of clients most
likely to benefit from particular treatments. By
and large, the matching of different techniques to
different problems is still a matter of informed
guesswork or trial and error.* While there are
clinical indications and contraindications for
many behavioral methods (cf. Bandura, 1969;
Lazarus, 1971; O'Leary & Wilson, 1975), the
a priori guidelines governing their use are often
too general or imprecise.

One reason for this generality is that *behavior
therapy does not involve the fixed application of
techniques,but a problem-solving strategy in which
each client may be regarded as the subject of an
informal experiment* (see Yates, 1970, for a more
elaborate discussion of this concept). *Rather
than artificially molding the client's problems to
suit preconceived theoretical notions, behavior
therapy is predicated on tailoring the diverse
principles and procedures of social learning theory
to the individual's need.* A clinical illustration of

this problem-solving process is described by
Wilson (1973), in adapting the orgasmic recon-
ditioning paradigm to the treatment of a case
of vaginismus in which neither imaginal nor *in
vivo* desensitization (the usually recommended
technique—Masters & Johnson, 1970) had produced any improvement. Since the client did
reliably achieve orgasm during mutual masturbation with her fiance, she was instructed to
associate this powerful reinforcer systematically
with symbolic representation of vaginal penetration in the necessary graduated sequence (cf.
Davison, 1968). Once she was able to maintain
arousal with this imagery the procedure was
repeated *in vivo* with first finger and then penile
insertion. Again, of course, this creative problem-
solving approach represents the ideal, and most
behavior therapists have their preferred methods
and techniques. This whole discussion is excel-
lently summarized by Ullmann:

> Simply handing out tokens does not mean a person
> has a token economy; and shocking a person con-
> tingent upon some behavior does not mean a person is a
> behavior therapist. To say this is equivalent to saying
> that anybody who runs rats is an experimenter. In
> both instances it is the design of the situation and not
> the implementation that is a crucial element. (1971,
> p. 373).

SOCIAL INFLUENCE

It is not surprising, given the historical developments discussed in the Introduction, that
factors primarily associated with relationship
experiences have commonly been designated
"nonspecific" influences in behavior therapy;
concepts such as placebo effects, demand characteristics, suggestion, expectation, empathy,
and rapport are accommodated by this convenient category and contrasted with the "specific," conditioning-based technique. Yet, as
Bandura (1969) and Mahoney (1974) have
properly pointed out, social influence factors
which invariably characterize human interactions are quite specific in their mode of operation. It would be most accurate to say that nonspecific really means unspecified rather than
unspecifiable. Moreover, it should be apparent
that in the broader conceptualization of behavior therapy within the social learning framework, these social influence factors are an
integral part of behavior therapy; it is particularly illogical to separate social influence and
the more formal learning techniques when social
variables can be fruitfully interpreted according
to learning principles (Staats, 1970). This type
of theoretical integration allows the relationship

experience to be geared to achieving well-defined treatment goals (Wilson *et al.*, 1968); it also renders highly relevant to behavior therapy the extensive experimental literature in social psychology suggesting just how the therapist's personal influence may be enhanced (Feldman, 1974b; Goldstein, 1973). In this next section possible learning interpretations of the therapist's influence will be considered and a few of the determining variables examined.

Social Reinforcement

In a very general way, explicit social reinforcement has been a primary behavior therapy technique:

> grossly deviant behavior in both children and adults —including infantile behavior, self-destructive tendencies, hypochondriacal and delusional behavior, extreme withdrawal, chronic anorexia, psychogenic seizures, psychotic tendencies and other deleterious behaviors— can be eliminated, reinstated, and substantially increased depending upon the amount of interest, attention and solicitous concern such behaviors elicit from others. (Bandura, 1969, p. 78)

Countless studies of more minor problem behaviors responding successfully to contingent attention of teachers, parents, siblings, and others significant to the client, further attest to the necessary ubiquity of social reinforcement in behavior therapy. Where the reinforcing value of the professional therapist is not great, the basic strategy has been to rely entirely upon these nonprofessional mediators (Tharp & Wetzel, 1969); with severely withdrawn clients, attempts have sometimes been made to deliberately establish cuddling, smiling, and praise as secondary reinforcers by pairing with food (e.g., Davison, 1964) or with termination of aversive events (Lovaas, Schaeffer, & Simmons, 1965).

Much more complex and controversial is the role of therapist reinforcement in incidental learning during therapy. Truax's (1966) analysis of Rogers' use of contingent social approval in what was supposedly "nondirective" therapy is the commonly cited example of what we mean, although there was no experimental demonstration that the contingency detected *did* influence the client. The influence of reinforcement has been frequently demonstrated elsewhere, however, in both therapeutic (see, e.g., Goldiamond & Dyrud, 1968; Kanfer & Phillips, 1970) and contrived (e.g., Salzinger, 1959) settings. In most of the experimental studies, the target behavior has been some class of the subject's verbal repertoire, but eye-contact and other nonverbal responses have sometimes provided the measure of interest. The reinforcing stimuli have ranged from psychoanalytic interpretations—although these may function as punishments (Kanfer, Phillips, Matarazzo, & Saslow, 1960)—and Rogerian reflections to simple smiles, nods of the head, and murmured "uh-huhs." [5]

The initial enthusiasm for verbal operant conditioning and its presumed significance for psychotherapy was reflected in Krasner's (1962) tongue-in-cheek use of the phrase "social reinforcement machine" to describe the psychotherapist. Today, however, the limitations of verbal conditioning are more in evidence. Although clients' verbal behavior during therapy has been altered, generalization to either verbal or nonverbal behavior in the natural environment is difficult to effect and rarely reported (Tracey, Briddell, & Wilson, 1974). The value of verbal conditioning as an analogue of psychotherapy depends upon one's being able to specify the critical variables much more precisely than at present. For instance, how will awareness of a social contingency affect the client's response to it? As early as 1958 Krasner and Ullmann reported a case in which a paranoid patient spontaneously identified the contingency—mother-related statements were being reinforced—and thereafter never mentioned "mother" again. Davison (1973) has labeled such oppositional behavior "counter-control," and has attempted to analyze it within the conceptual framework of social learning theory. He cites a study by Davis (1971) in which more verbal conditioning was obtained if the experimenter first disagreed with what the subject was saying and then agreed, as opposed to agreeing or disagreeing all the time. These results were taken to indicate the importance of the subject perceiving himself in a position where he was not manipulated. Presumably, the inconsistency of the experimenter's behavior suggested to the subject that he was exerting greater power over the experimenter than vice versa.

These and other similar findings (e.g., Resnick & Schwartz, 1973) create difficulties only if, as Bandura (1974) observes, it is believed that reinforcement acts as an automatic strengthener of human behavior rather than an informative and motivating influence. It has become increasingly difficult to argue that verbal conditioning is possible without subjects' awareness of what is being reinforced (e.g., Page, 1972, 1974; Spielberger & DeNike, 1966). Recent studies of verbal conditioning using improved methodology strongly suggest that man actively interprets input from his social environment rather than automatically or unconsciously responding to reinforcement contingencies. Whether a client emits the targeted behavior or engages in countercontrol actions will depend on a number of complex, interacting factors, including the situational context, the nature of the incentive, personal characteristics of both therapist and client, and so on (e.g., Bates, 1972; Sarason, 1965).

One final problem with verbal conditioning as an analogue of psychotherapy should be noted. Moos and his colleagues (Moos & Clemes, 1967; Moos & MacIntosh, 1970) have used multivariate analyses of therapist-client dyads in demonstrating that the therapist-client relationship needs to be conceptualized as an interacting system of mutual social influence. Verbal conditioning studies have assumed a one-way influence process in which the therapist has predetermined which responses will be reinforced on what schedule and in what manner. Moos found that patients exercised significantly greater influence over the behavior of nonbehavioral therapists (psychiatric residents) than vice versa. Therapist behavior was not a function of any "behavioral traits" or consistently applied technique, but was situationally or client determined. Indeed, Moos suggests that these data raise the novel question of whether therapists are more open to change than patients during therapy. It would be interesting to know if one would find similar results with behaviorally trained therapists.

Elicitation of client behavior

In our 1968 paper we proposed, following Staats' conceptions (Staats & Staats, 1963), that in addition to being a source of social reinforcement, the therapist can be considered an important source of discriminative stimuli. Since then, Staats (1968) has used the secondary reinforcement principle to propose an A-R-D theory of human motivation—a given stimulus has attitudinal, reinforcing, and discriminative properties; altering the value of one of these properties will affect the others. (In the next section the importance of this for the client's attitude toward the therapist will be elaborated upon.) As a great deal of behavior therapy involves asking clients to *do* something—imagine a scene, relax in a chair, self-monitor daily caloric intake, ask the woman for a date, squeeze a partner's penis—the powerful nature of these verbal requests is very important.

Our emphasis on ability to elicit overt approach behaviors should not be construed as neglect of the eliciting of emotional responses; these are equally important when and if they contribute to change which can be sustained outside the therapeutic relationship. It is fairly easy to arouse anxiety, grief, anger, sexual desire, and a host of other emotions during therapy, both deliberately and accidentally, but in behavior therapy it is rare that there is a good cause for doing so. *Often in behavior therapy an intense emotional experience is aroused, not for the client to get in touch with it, but to extinguish it.* Vivid verbal powers, good acting ability, and a certain flamboyant insensitivity to the absurd seem to be necessary, at least somewhat, to carrying out successfully techniques such as implosion or covert sensitization. The behavior therapist, like any other individual, will inadvertently elicit, by casual remark, appearance, dress, or mannerism, a set of complex emotional responses in his client, as, of course, will happen in reverse. On the whole, these are random factors and there is nothing much that can be done about them except to be aware of their omnipresence.[6]

When the therapist's eliciting power fails, or when he evokes a strong antipathy in his client, two possible factors contributing to "resistance" have been identified. If the therapist becomes aware of resentment or anger that was not expressed directly by the client, it is often useful to turn the occasion into an opportunity for assertion training. If the client persistently fails to carry out assigned tasks or to follow instructions, logical analysis of the possible causes is urgently required. The behavior may simply not be in the client's repertoire, or it may be impractical for the present situation and mood of the client: asking an obese client to self-monitor her daily caloric intake and eating habits might be too demanding because of concomitant anxiety and depression.[7] Anxieties, guilt-feelings, or fear of societal disapproval often counteract the eliciting power of the therapist: a more careful successive approximation procedure must then be used. Motivation to carry out the assigned tasks may be low because failure is anticipated: clients may have a history of failure leading to minimal expectancies, or a history of failure with one specific technique—recently one of our clients had been inadequately instructed by a urologist in the squeeze technique for premature ejaculation and he and his wife were understandably reluctant to repeat the procedure under more careful guidance.

Clearly, expectancy is a crucial aspect of elicitation failure and this will be discussed at greater length presently. In addition, there are other important ways to overcome these failures. One strategy concerns client commitment (e.g., Feldman, 1974b). Social psychological research leads to the prediction that there is a greater probability of the client carrying out an assigned task if he commits himself to do so than if commanded to do so. A number of complex variables influence commitment strategies (e.g., Kanfer & Karoly, 1972). One method of obtaining commitment is to suggest a pair of equally important therapeutic assignments which the client is asked to go away and think about and announce at the next session the choice he has made. Mahoney (1974) has similarly suggested that the presence or absence of choice may moderate countercontrol behavior. A second factor implicated by Mahoney is the conspicuousness of the therapist's influence attempts. The discussion of Davis' results in the previous section illustrates how this might operate to produce oppositional behavior in the client. Interestingly, both these factors are key features of Erikson's strategic therapy (Haley, 1973). The choice option, for example, is reflected in the method known as "providing a worse alternative." Since strategic therapy involves a deliberate attempt to use social influence in order to have the client follow the therapist's clinical directives, the various clinical procedures to overcome resistance which Haley describes might, as Davison (1973) and Lazarus and Rosen (in press) have suggested, reward more systematic attention from behavior therapists.

In clients who show no resistance to external direction, contingency contracting might be used to overcome elicitation failure. In this procedure various reinforcements are worked out in advance for participation in therapy or successful completion of an assignment. In the behavioral treatment of obesity, for example, Romanczyk, Tracey, Wilson, and Thorpe (1973) eliminated the notorious tendency of obese clients of dropping out of ongoing therapy programs by making a refundable deposit contingent upon attendance at group sessions. Lobitz and LoPiccolo (1972) specify "treatment rules" in a "penalty contract" which clients sign at the beginning of their program for the treatment of sexual dysfunction. The rules are that clients must keep appointments, keep daily record forms of their progress, and engage in only those forms of sexual activity prescribed by the therapists. Violations result in progressive financial loss, with the sixth viola-

tion resulting in the termination of treatment. Lobitz and LoPiccolo report that this procedure was very successful with older, middle-class couples, but less effective in motivating younger couples, especially those in the counterculture for whom money was not a major reinforcer. Once again this highlights the importance of therapist flexibility in devising different methods for different clients. In another variation of the same theme, behavior therapists often contract with clients to have post-dated checks sent off to their most disliked organization if therapeutic directives which have been mutually agreed upon are not followed (e.g., Boudin, 1972; Wilson & Rosen, 1976).

Finally, the most fundamental strategy of all is to enhance the discriminative stimulus value of the therapist by enhancing his attractiveness to the client. This will be discussed next.

Attitude toward the therapist

According to A-R-D theory, the more positive the emotional responses in the client evoked by the therapist, the greater will be the therapist's reinforcing and discriminative stimulus value— the significance of which has been shown. It is in this context that the voluminous literature on interpersonal attractiveness is so relevant to planned strategies of behavior change. Lott and Lott (1972) have proposed a similar notion: "a liked person will evoke a wide variety of overt and covert responses classifiable as approach... A liked person can function as an incentive and raise general drive level in the individual who responds with liking" (p. 112). In reviewing their own and other work, the Lotts have amassed the evidence supporting these interacting functions: for instance, there is experimental evidence that people sit closer to those they like, communicate more effectively, learn to understand emotional states more accurately, pay more attention to and remember more vividly liked individuals, and imitate more readily (see following section). Of special importance are those studies showing that reinforcing agents who are positively valued are more effective in changing behavior (e.g., Patterson & Anderson, 1964; Wahler, 1967). In experimental situations, those who first spend time in warm social interactions with the subjects produce better, more persistent learning (e.g., Allen, Spear, & Johnson, 1969; Berkowitz & Zigler, 1965). Verbal conditioning is more effective when the reinforcing agent is liked (Krasner, Knowles, & Ullmann, 1965) or has previously spent time establishing rapport (Gelder, 1968). Although there is little specific information on this, we might also surmise that a liked individual can punish or give critical feedback more effectively than disliked individuals from whom negative comment is likely to elicit resentment or anger.

It can be argued that *there are essentially two ways of ensuring that the attitudes of the client toward the therapist are favorable. One is to attempt to make the client and the therapist more similar, by matching the therapist to the client according to criteria likely to increase interpersonal attractiveness. The other is to provide the therapist with a variety of behaviors likely to increase his attractiveness to the client.* (Obviously the positive regard that the client feels for the therapist can take various subtle forms—admiration, respect, feelings of comfort, physical attraction, and so forth. As any of these is likely to result in general positive regard, or halo effect, we will talk of attractiveness or positive attitudinal value of the therapist for the sake of simplicity.) These two general strategies are considered next.

Generally, behavior therapists have not considered therapist-client matching to be either feasible or overridingly important. Essentially this is because of the reliance on the triadic model of nonprofessional mediators (Tharp & Wetzel, 1969). The use of parents, teachers, peers, and even former clients, who have special abilities and invaluable experience with different clients has unique advantages; it ensures "more genuine and enduring relationship experiences than those derived from a purchased relationship provided by a busy professional therapist at brief weekly intervals" (Bandura, 1971, p. 697). This model is particularly appropriate with clients traditionally difficult to engage in interpersonal psychotherapy—the non-YAVIS client (see Goldstein, 1973). It is well known that psychotherapists are prejudiced against such clients (Garfield, 1971; Goldstein, 1971). Yet trained behavior therapists might not show this biased labeling effect as they appear to respond more to objective behavioral descriptions than to labels (Langer & Abelson, 1974). Behavior therapists are probably not without bias, however; those who reported that they did not view homosexuality as a sickness nevertheless rated it as less good, less moral, and less rational than heterosexuality (Davison & Wilson, 1973a). Another subtle source of bias in behavior therapists, it has been suggested, is their experimental training. This tends to cause the student therapist to

focus on target behaviors which are observable and measurable—such emphases are strongly reinforced in graduate settings valuing laboratory research, but may well result in the therapist searching too soon for an observable behavior to change that is only trivially related to the client's subjective experiences and thus emotionally unsatisfying.

Although often accepted as fact, the real value of relying on nonprofessional therapists who are similar to the client has never been systematically determined. Self-help groups such as AA (Alcoholics Anonymous), TOPS (Take Off Pounds Sensibly), and Mothers Anonymous (for child-abusing mothers) swear by this effect, and behavioral programs with alcoholics (Wiens, Montague, Manaugh, & English, 1976) and obese clients (Levitz & Stunkard, 1974) have employed recovered alcoholics and TOPS chapter leaders respectively. Yet Levitz and Stunkard (1974) found that their weight reduction program was significantly more effective when administered by professional behavior therapists. In their behavioral consultation program for parents and teachers of children with conduct problems, Kent and O'Leary (1975) found no difference between the effectiveness of PhD-level behavior therapists and BA-level paraprofessionals (e.g., former teachers) who had been trained in the use of behavioral principles and procedures. Subjective ratings, however, showed that teachers significantly preferred working with the paraprofessionals.

Emphasizing the importance of therapist-client similarity, Masters and Johnson (1970) have advocated the necessity of dual-sex therapy teams for treating sexually-dysfunctional couples. They claim that no man can ever fully understand a woman's sexual functioning because "he can never experience orgasm as a woman.... The exact converse applies to any woman... because she will never experience ejaculatory demand or seminal fluid release" (p. 4). However, the clinical experience of many individual therapists does not bear this out (e.g., Annon, 1974; Brady, 1971; Kaplan, 1974), and data in support of Masters and Johnson's assertion are lacking. On the contrary, recent experimental evidence indicates that a series of educational videotapes (featuring a male therapist and a young married couple with largely unidentified sex problems as models) can be used successfully to treat women with primary orgasmic dysfunction (Robinson, 1974). Lazarus (1974) has delineated different therapeutic situations which indicate whether a woman seeking treatment is best served by consulting a male or female therapist. Ideally, this decision is made on the basis of the specific nature of the particular woman's problems—for example, is it critical to have another woman as a role model? In any event, client-therapist matching is a tricky business as the decisive dimensions are so infuriatingly volatile. One of the authors recalls seeing a disaffected black client who was understandably hostile on discovering that the therapist grew up in South Africa; but on learning he was not a racist, formed a positive relationship in which both could poke good-natured fun at the dominant white American society of which neither felt himself a total part.

The best solution, then, is for the therapist to have a certain facility in relating to a number of different types of person. These interpersonal skills have the consequence of increasing attractiveness and thus ability to influence: it is in this way that such therapist characteristics as empathy, warmth, and so forth, are considered important in behavior therapy. It must be remembered that the A-R-D functions of a stimulus are mutually interdependent—a stimulus paired with reinforcement will become a secondary reinforcer and also be positively evaluated. A therapist who successfully deals with his client's problems will almost certainly be described subsequently in warm, positive terms. Studies showing that empathic therapists (as rated by the clients) are also successful, have, as a major design problem, this chicken-egg limitation.[8] Clients, on the whole, like their therapists: a remarkable 96% of parents in a child guidance clinic rated their behavior therapists as understanding, warm, sincere, and interested (O'Leary, Turkewitz, & Taffel, 1973).

Interpersonal skills seem to come easily to some people; others need guidance, and this raises the question of whether personal therapy is desirable in the training of behavioral clinicians. Unlike other approaches, behavior therapists are not required to enter into therapy. However, students of behavior therapy will sometimes require corrective feedback and assistance if their own personal difficulties and social behavior interfere with effective clinical functioning. Davison and Goldfried (1973), for example, report that they recommend a course of desensitization for students who are unduly sensitive to criticism. To the extent that empathy, communication competencies, and other clinically important characteristics can be operationally defined, therapists can be taught to develop such skills. Other very real clinical considerations include the therapist's being authentic, self-disclosing where appropriate, using humor judiciously, and modeling his own acceptance of the fact that he is a fallible human being by candidly acknowledging lapses and errors without trying to persuade the client that they were deliberate therapeutic strategies (cf. Lazarus, 1971).

The therapist as a role model

Thus far we have attempted to point to ways in which a variety of factors traditionally attributed to the therapist-client relationship come to effect therapeutic change through principles of social learning. Imitative learning can be thought of as a very basic mechanism of behavior change. Much of what has already been discussed under increasing interpersonal attractiveness is highly relevant to modeling, as the degree to which an observer imitates a model is partly a function of similarity and attractiveness, partly a function of rewards available, and so forth.

There are a number of direct situations in behavior therapy in which the therapist deliberately uses himself as a model. Working with children who are behavior problems, we typically involve the entire family in the therapy sessions so that we can model for the parents appropriate ways of responding to the child. Many techniques rely heavily on modeling. In participant modeling (Bandura, 1971; Rachman, 1972) and assertion training (Alberti & Emmons, 1974), for instance, suitable behaviors often have to be modeled, although, of course, this can be done by prepared audio and videotapes (Hersen, Eisler, & Miller, 1973; McFall & Twentyman, 1973). The producers of commercial teaching films for clients are becoming increasingly aware that the model's characteristics are important; in the filmed sexual material we use, for instance, the people demonstrating coital positions, masturbatory techniques, or simply loving, shared enjoyment, are now rather ordinary looking and a far cry from the stars of the pornographic material we once had to use, who largely display abnormalities of bodily parts or sexual functioning.

Model similarity is not critical in producing a therapeutic effect such as reduction of fearful behavior (Bandura & Barab, 1973), but it can be extremely useful. Phobics who observed a model progressively overcome fear through perseverance demonstrated greater improvement than their counterparts who witnessed a daring performance by a totally fearless model (e.g.,

Meichenbaum, 1971). It is possible to reduce the importance of model-observer matching by having the observer (the client) direct his attention to the relevant behaviors being modeled. Sloggett (1972) demonstrated that having the observers (teachers) *code* the behavioral interactions of the model teacher was more effective than simply having them watch the model in changing their subsequent behavior in a simulated classroom. Another important way of avoiding the mismatch problem is to have the client observe some *other* individual who is more suitable as a role model—D'Zurilla and Goldfried (1971) utilized competent, successful students as the models for less competent, freshman students.

D'Zurilla and Goldfried (1971) actually encouraged their student clients to learn to imitate appropriate models as part of a more general training in coping and problem-solving strategies. Along similar lines, Mahoney (1974) has recently advocated that behavior therapy should emphasize the development of coping skills to negotiate an adaptive course and independently deal with future adjustment difficulties. He suggests that this might be best accomplished if behavior therapists would

> share their commitment to empiricism and view therapy as an apprenticeship designed to train *personal* scientists—individuals who are skillful in the functional analysis and systematic improvement of their own behavior.... If the clinician considers the scientific approach a useful paradigm for his own problem solving endeavors, he can hardly discourage a personal science paradigm for his client. (p. 274)

Mahoney observes that this emphasizes the importance of the therapist as a personal model for his client. Multimodal modeling of affective, behavioral, and cognitive reactions is required, and *appropriate* self-disclosure by the therapist of his own coping strategies is regarded as a necessary aspect of the influence process. The significance of cognitive modeling is underscored since it is rarely available in nontherapeutic settings. "By 'thinking out loud' and sharing his meditational skills, the therapist may provide valuable assistance in the development, integration, and adaptive revision of client cognitions" (Mahoney, 1974, p. 280).

What this reasoning entails, of course, is making systematic what undoubtedly goes on in an unstructured and often inadvertent manner in many forms of therapy, including behavior therapy. For example, one of the authors was treating an agoraphobic woman by means of a combination of Ellis's (1970) rational-emotive therapy and systematic desensitization. One

therapeutic goal was to enable the client to fly to Europe for a vacation. She was elated at being able to undertake the trip, and upon her return recounted to the therapist how, although the effects of therapy had not generalized to the natural situation, she had nonetheless coped with frequently occurring anxiety by imagining how *he* would have behaved in those situations. The basis for this fortuitous modeling effect appeared to be some anecdotal comments the therapist once made during casual conversation about his own experiences traveling in Europe. *If he is to function as a personal role model for clients, the therapist must necessarily be an adequately adjusted, reasonably effective problem-solver in his own right.* This need not place an intolerable strain on the personal qualities of the therapist. As Mahoney (1974) notes, the modeling research on the coping-versus-mastery distinction suggests that *the clinician who tries to appear as the perfectly adjusted individual may actually reduce his therapeutic influence. The behavior therapist is not to be regarded as the new high priest to be emulated in all situations —like parents, we usually want our clients to do what we say, not what we do.*

Developing therapeutic expectancies

This is the last, and in some ways the most complex, of the topics to be considered in this section, as expectancy is not a term in the usual behavioral language of human learning research. The behavior therapist can do one of three things with expectancy: he can keep faith and interpret it according to behavioral principles; he can accept it as a powerful force worth adding to his collection of therapeutic deities; or he can dismiss the whole heretical topic. The third approach flies in the face of a considerable body of empirical data. Jerome Frank (1961) suggested that "part of the success of all forms of psychotherapy may be attributed to the therapist's ability to mobilize the patient's expectation of help" (pp. 70–71) and behavior therapy seems to be no exception to this clinical rule (Borkovec, 1973; Lazarus, 1971; Mahoney, 1974; Ryan & Gyzinski, 1971). Anyone watching behavior therapists at work will notice systematic attempts to increase expectancies in the clients (Klein, Dittman, Parloff, & Gill, 1969). But expectancy, as we will show, is a double-edged sword, and our preference, therefore, is for the first of the three courses of action so that it is possible to tie the expectancy effect rationally to the formal techniques and to the variables that influence expectancy. Ullmann and Krasner (1969) defined expectancy as a "verbal description of a role enactment likely to be reinforced in a given situation" (p. 72). This definition refers to the aspect of expectancy in which role-appropriate behaviors occur. Mahoney (1974) offers a more cognitive learning conceptualization of expectancy as "a complex of meditational processes which influence selective attention, response utilization, and anticipated consequences" (p. 275). Following Bandura's (1969) social learning model, this approach emphasizes that the therapist's actions which induce expectancies operate via their effect on the client's covert perceptual processes, which then mediate changes in overt behavior and attitudes.

By encouraging strong impressions of ultimate success, the client is able to bridge the gap between the immediate arduous tasks required by the therapist and the ultimate positive benefit (Mischel, 1974). Another important mechanism is the elicitation of positive emotional states, such as hope, delight, and so on, that may well counteract the anxiety, depression, and hopelessness experienced by the client. A somewhat more subtle process is one which serves to maintain the client in therapy—the client comes with expectations not only of getting better but of what to expect during treatment, and incongruity might well cause the client to terminate prematurely. Related to this latter process is Rosen's (1972) identification of two variables which he suggests affect clients' satisfaction and continuation with the therapeutic relationship. The first is stimulus-response congruence—the extent to which the therapist's responses inform clients that their communications are understood. Congruence is viewed as a generalized secondary reinforcer, incongruence as a secondary aversive stimulus. The second is content relevance—the extent that the content of the therapist's responses is perceived by clients as pertinent to their ideas of crucial therapeutic issues.

Expectancy may bring about a relabeling of the individual by others. The classroom teacher and harassed parent may change their behavior radically toward a problem child once the therapist has assured them that the child is sure to become more manageable—this phenomenon has been shown in social psychological research on teacher expectancies and relabeling of children's behavior (Rosenthal & Jacobson, 1968). We have frequently noticed occasions in our own work in which a behavioral explanation of the origins of the problematic behavior (describing it in matter-of-fact rather than illness, terms) and assurances that it can be altered, bring about a decrease in anxiety. Davison (1969) has called this "assessment therapy," and it is, in itself, very beneficial when anxiety about the problem behavior is a maintaining variable (Evans, 1973) or when the parent's anxiety is a maintaining factor.

The social psychology literature suggests a host of different ways in which expectancy effects can be enhanced (Goldstein, Heller, & Sechrest, 1966). One obvious technique is to spend a little time discussing the value of the procedures and the literature proving their efficacy. A second possible strategy might be to make it initially somewhat difficult for the client to be accepted into therapy; another is to require the client to pay a fee. The problem is that if the client's expectancies are built up too high, and success does not immediately follow, one has a serious negative reaction as both client and therapist attempt to reduce dissonance. Feldman (1974a) has suggested that when confronted with failure, the therapist reduces dissonance by such methods as denigrating the client, seeing at least some successful change somewhere, denying that the behavior is alterable, or extolling the advances in knowledge gained from failures. As for the client, he might well be left with a strong conviction that his problems are insoluble, with concomitant feelings of depression, futility in further attempts, and other counterproductive consequences.

We propose that the best solution, both in ensuring a productive degree of expectancy and avoiding the client's overconfidence, is to structure the treatment for the client. This has been described in very practical terms by Goldfried and Davison (1976). Essentially the strategy is, as Goldstein *et al.* (1966) recommended, to provide clients with information which will produce a cognitive structure whereby they can organize their experiences in therapy. Structuring would include an explanation of the development, maintenance, and modification of the client's problems, a persuasive rationale for the specific treatment methods to be employed, a description of the procedural steps involved and the client's own responsibilities in actively participating in the treatment. This latter point is very important as it not only strengthens the client's attribution of change to his own efforts but helps define for him the client role he is expected to adopt. Discussion of previously successful results with a particular technique can also be tempered with mention of possible pitfalls. Anticipating difficulties and how they can be overcome is especially important since many clients are often insufficiently persistent in the face of initial failure.

In an earlier exposition of the same basic approach, Rotter (1954) stated that the purpose of structuring is to have the client "attend to, react to, or concern himself with the 'right' things in therapy" (p. 352). Frank (1961) has speculated how the development of a shared conceptual framework between therapist and client might facilitate attitude change. Fish (1973) described a variety of ways in which behavior therapy techniques can be presented to clients, based partly on the therapist's knowledge of his client's interests, attitudes, and belief structure. An engineer with a very mechanistic view of the world might be given a conditioning interpretation of systematic desensitization; a young college student might best profit from an analogy with hypnotic or "altered states of consciousness" phenomena. In general, this ability to structure his procedures, evaluations, and attitudes into a systematic whole gives the therapist considerable credibility—perhaps, as Mahoney (1974) posits, this process underlies the superiority of systems of therapy which offer formal paradigms and rationales rather than isolated techniques.

BEHAVIORAL TREATMENT TECHNIQUES: THE THERAPIST'S SPECIFIC CONTRIBUTION

If our theoretical models were more complete, there would be no need for this section. In the preceding discussion we attempted to show some of the mechanisms of social influence, and it would simply follow logically that these interact with the components of the specific techniques. Thus, systematic desensitization will be *enhanced* if the therapist has good verbal control over the client so that he carries out the procedures, if the therapist has skillfully identified the significant themes for the hierarchy, if the therapist has reinforcing power and has generated some anxiety-inhibiting hopes for success, and so on. Yet it would be incorrect to think that the therapeutic outcome can be attributed, causally, to such variables, even if they are proven *necessary* for success (Evans, 1973). What has to be done is to relate social influence variables precisely to the active ingredients of various "techniques" so that they may be modified, refined, and their efficiency and efficacy enhanced. In this respect we are in fundamental disagreement with the increasingly common

argument (e.g., London, 1972) that behavior therapists should be technicians and that, therefore, only formal procedures must be evaluated. We divide this next section into techniques only for convenience of organization in response to what is actually typical in the literature. It should be remembered that we see little value in separating social influence variables and examining their interaction with formal techniques unless the consistent theoretical integration is made as well.

Systematic desensitization

Alternative explanations to the conditioning conceptualization of systematic desensitization have emphasized relationship factors like suggestion, empathy, and the therapist's skill in developing expectancies of therapeutic gain and acting as a social reinforcing agent of improvement (e.g., Marmor, 1971; Murray & Jacobson, 1971; Wilkins, 1971). However, in a detailed critique of this interpretation, Davison and Wilson (1973b) concluded that experiments purporting to demonstrate the role of the desensitizer as a social reinforcer for a reduction in fear or avoidance behavior were either "inappropriate in conception, confounded in design, or productive of inconclusive results" (p. 1). Moreover, systematic desensitization has been shown to be successful even when client contact with the therapist was intentionally minimized. Lang, Melamed, and Hart (1970) found that a computer-programmed apparatus known as DAD (Device for Automated Desensitization) was as effective as a live therapist in producing fear reduction through desensitization. Other studies using automated, tape-recorded stimulus presentation have similarly shown that self-directed desensitization and its more orthodox therapist-administered counterpart can be equally effective (Baker, Cohen, & Saunders, 1973; Kahn & Baker, 1968; Nawas, Fishman, & Pucel, 1970). Since these studies used nonclinical volunteer subjects, caution should be had in generalizing these findings to desensitization with actual clients.[9] On the other hand, Robinson's (1974) successful treatment of sexual dysfunction using an automated modeling procedure involved only clients who had been medically referred. Of course, the clinical use of automated methods always necessitates *some* human contact, but certainly not a relationship in the conventional sense.

It has also been shown that therapist-produced expectancy of favorable treatment outcome and attention-placebo factors can enhance the therapeutic effects of systematic desensitization but cannot account for all improvement (Davison & Wilson, 1973b; Wilson & Davison, 1975). Controlled studies by Gelder, Bancroft, Gath, Johnston, Mathews, and Shaw (1973) and Paul (1966), among others, have unequivocally established that systematic desensitization produces significantly greater change than relationship factors alone. Borkovec's (1973) comprehensive review of the role of expectancy in desensitization research showed that all studies which have demonstrated that desensitization is equally effective with or without therapeutic instructions or expectancy manipulations used only highly fearful subjects, whereas those studies which indicated an expectancy effect employed low fearful subjects. He concluded that the latter effect is most simply interpreted as the influence of external demand characteristics which are not sufficient for modifying genuinely phobic behavior. With *clinical* populations, then, expectancy effects in desensitization would appear to play an auxiliary or facilitative role.

It must be reiterated that to conclude that the effects of desensitization under controlled laboratory conditions cannot be attributed only to subjects' expectations is not to say that they do not foster at least some of the therapeutic improvement which is produced (Rosen, 1974). The most constructive strategy would be to determine *how* expectancies facilitate outcome,[10] as Spanos, DeMoor & Barber (1973) have done in drawing a parallel between social influence factors in hypnosis and desensitization. Bandura (1969) has suggested that subjects' expectancies influence their involvement in required therapeutic participation (e.g., selective attention, response effort, etc.). However, Rosen's (1974) findings are inconsistent with this position, and he has hypothesized that therapy set or expectancy helps subjects relax, thereby facilitating nonreinforced exposure to the aversive stimuli without directly affecting subjects' compliance with the procedures.

Evidence indicating that the manner in which the therapist relates to the client is important for effecting improvement has been reported by Morris & Suckerman (1974a, 1974b).[11] In both live and automated (tape-recorded) desensitization a *warm* therapist ("soft, melodic, and pleasant voice") achieved significantly superior results than a *cold* therapist ("harsh, impersonal, and businesslike voice"). The authors suggest that the relatively profound effect of this seemingly subtle factor of therapist voice quality may be explained by its possible influence on the interpersonal attraction of subjects to the therapist (Goldstein *et al.*, 1966), or by motivating subjects to try harder. An alternative explanation is provided by Rosen's (1974) analysis of the expectancy effect in desensitization as noted above.

Hemingway (reported in Goldstein, 1971) compared group systematic desensitization under conditions of high versus moderate subject interpersonal attraction to the therapist. Subjects assigned to the high-attraction condition were informed that they had been exceptionally well matched with their therapist with whom they would get along very well. Moderate-attraction subjects were told that there was "no reason to believe that you will not get on well together." Consistent with a previous study by Cohen (1967), Hemingway found that the high-attraction condition resulted in a lower attrition rate and less absenteeism from therapy sessions. However, there were no significant differences in terms of objective outcome measures in either study. Despite the fact that Goldstein (1971) has shown some effect on process measures during desensitization, any causal relationship between structuring clients for high levels of interpersonal attraction to the therapist and positive treatment outcome has yet to be demonstrated.

The foregoing discussion has emphasized that relationship variables are not necessarily critical ingredients within the boundary conditions of the specific systematic desensitization procedure (Evans, 1973). It is also clear that, in clinical practice, desensitization should be used in the context of an appropriate therapist-client relationship. Furthermore, as we have stressed above in the section on behavioral assessment, the most crucial and difficult feature of the successful clinical application of systematic desensitization revolves around the therapist's decision of whether or not desensitization is the technique of choice, and if so, the subsequent task of determining relevant stimulus hierarchies. Even in the Baker *et al.* (1973) and Lang *et al.* (1970) studies demonstrating the success of automated or self-directed desensitization, the therapist initially determined the appropriateness of desensitization as the preferred behavioral method and constructed the hierarchy. Systematic desensitization is not routine for all anxiety-related problems. The method is often adopted prematurely (see also Lazarus, 1971; Lazarus, & Serber, 1968), and greater attention

558 EFFECTIVE PSYCHOTHERAPY

by therapists to the guidelines for its application would undoubtedly make for more effective treatment (O'Leary & Wilson, 1975; Paul & Bernstein, 1973).

Aversion therapy

Rapid smoking is a technique which has been convincingly shown to be effective in decreasing cigarette smoking in controlled outcome studies (Kopel, 1973; Lichtenstein, Harris, Birchler, Wahl, & Schmahl, 1973). In this method, clients are instructed to smoke every 6 seconds. A trial terminates when the client cannot tolerate another inhalation, and trials usually continue until the client cannot abide another cigarette. The client experiences intense nausea and dizziness, and it is assumed that the aversion *per se* is the decisive factor in reducing subsequent cigarette smoking. Lichtenstein *et al.* (1973) found that an attention-placebo treatment, included to control for the "nonspecific components of the treatment package" was equally effective in producing abstinence at the end of treatment, but that the rapid smoking technique resulted in significantly superior maintenance of abstinence over a 6-month follow-up. Furthermore, differences among therapists who administered the procedure (two experienced, one experienced) failed to influence the outcome results. In Kopel's (1973) study, subject-administered rapid smoking proved as effective as experimenter-administered treatment in essentially replicating the therapeutic success reported by Lichtenstein *et al.* (1973).

Yet Harris and Lichtenstein (1971) have reported a study in which "nonspecific social variables" exerted a powerful influence on the results achieved with the typical rapid smoking technique. Half the subjects (high social condition) were treated by an experimenter who was warm and friendly, interacted on a first-name basis, and self-disclosed his own experiences at stopping smoking. He also fostered a positive expectancy of successful outcome by describing rapid smoking as a proven technique, and he provided positive social reinforcement contingent on subjects' efforts at reducing smoking. The remaining subjects (low social condition) were exposed to an experimenter who was impersonal, indifferent, and failed to self-disclose; who described the technique as an experimental method which was being tested; and who provided no positive social reinforcement for subjects' efforts at reducing smoking. Independent measures of this manipulation showed that the two groups differed significantly in terms of these social variable conditions.

High social subjects were significantly more abstinent at the end of treatment and over a 1-month follow-up, demonstrating that these three therapist influences contribute directly to the successful use of rapid smoking. The superiority of the high social subjects is the more impressive given that the low social condition included all three "nonspecific" variables (motivated subjects, structure, and self-monitoring) which McFall and Hammen (1971) have shown to produce results comparable to those reported by most behavioral treatment programs.

The contribution of the wider social influence factors to treatment successes achieved with other aversion conditioning methods has been stressed by Marmor (1971), among others. He cites two of Birk's cases in which male homosexuals, who, as a result of treatment with the anticipatory avoidance conditioning technique (cf. Birk, Huddleston, Miller, & Cohler, 1971), had shown markedly reduced homosexual behavior. For different reasons, both patients became angry with their therapist and immediately "regressed" to a number of homosexual encounters. Marmor claims that a simple conditioning explanation cannot accommodate these phenomena, and that there is "something that goes on centrally in the patient that is a very important factor in the therapeutic modifications achieved" (p. 65). A basic aspect of this central process, Marmor suggests, is the therapist-client relationship.

To emphasize the importance of central processes is to underscore a central tenet of social learning theory. As Bandura pithily comments, "so-called conditioned reactions are largely self-activated on the basis of learned expectations rather than automatically evoked" (1974, p. 859). The myth that automatic deconditioning is readily reproducible has characterized much of the behavior therapy literature. It is not difficult then to understand how public apprehension is aroused by misleading science fiction as, for example, portrayed in "A Clockwork Orange." Available evidence not only suggests that conditioned aversion reactions cannot be developed all that easily (Evans, 1975), but these cannot be developed without the client's deliberate, conscious cooperation (Davison, 1973). Also clients can rapidly desensitize themselves to successfully created conditioned aversions (e.g., Hammersley, 1957; Wiens *et al.*, 1976). To conclude this section, it is clear that considerations of *both ethics and efficacy* demand that if aversion therapy is to be employed, the client's freely given, informed consent to a therapist he trusts and respects is a minimum necessity.

Other behavioral techniques

The increasing use of contingency contracting procedures has reemphasized the importance of the therapist-client relationship in behavior therapy (Kanfer & Karoly, 1972). Issuing a cautionary note on the use of behavioral contracting with delinquent youths and their families, Stuart and Lott (1972) reported that therapist differences were a more significant determinant of contract contents than either client characteristics or intervention structure. Nor was this therapist effect related to global factors such as therapist sex or professional status. Rather, it appeared that specific skills in individual circumstances made the difference. Likening contingency contracting to labor mediation, Stuart and Lott point out the importance of what Franks and Wilson (1974) dubbed the "Kissinger effect"—the therapist's skill in negotiating compromises in which no one loses face. This talent for assuming responsibility for decisive shifts of position in order to promote behavioral change is hardly limited to behavioral contracting with families. It also looms large in the use of behavioral strategies in marital therapy, and is a classic example of the fact that some behavior therapists will be more successful than others regardless of technical expertise.

One of behavior therapy's strongest claims to fame involves the repeated successes which have been achieved in the treatment of enuresis with the bell and pad conditioning method (Baker, 1969; O'Leary & Wilson, 1975; Young & Morgan, 1972). James and Foreman (1973) investigated the relationship between the therapist's A-B status (Betz, 1962) and treatment outcome using the bell and pad device. The results indicated that A-B scale scores of the mothers of enuretic children, who served as "behavior therapy technicians" (i.e., *mediators* according to the triadic model mentioned earlier), were significantly correlated with therapeutic efficacy, B-status mothers proving superior.

James and Foreman explain their data by accepting the interaction hypothesis as an established fact. This hypothesis is that A-B therapist "type" interacts with patient variables related to diagnostic category such that As and Bs achieve greater success with schizophrenic and neurotic patients respectively. However, in an evaluative review of the psychotherapy literature, Chartier (1971) has concluded that "the interaction hypothesis has not only remained undemonstrated in the clinical studies, but is actually *contraindicated by* comparable success rates of As and Bs with neurotics" (p. 24, italics ours). James and Foreman fail to suggest what the critical behavioral correlates of the apparently more effective Bs were, other than to point to their presumed "mechanical ability and interest." In fact, it is unclear what the A-B variable, described as a "mysterious measure" by Howard and Orlinsky (1972), means, and in the absence of subsequent replications of these findings, it would be premature to think of using it to screen prospective behavioral mediators as James and Foreman propose. Correlating randomly chosen personality trait variables with specific behavioral techniques without any logical connection is essentially futile (e.g., Evans & Nelson, 1974; Mischel, 1968).

There exist as yet few relevant data on how the personal characteristics of the behavioral mediator might influence treatment programs in the natural environment. O'Donnell and Fo (1974) have described an effective community intervention program for problem youth—the Buddy System in which indigenous nonprofessionals were trained to modify the youths' troublesome behaviors through the use of their interpersonal relationship and the techniques of contingency management. They found a significant association between amount of behavioral improvement and the internal-external locus of control (I-E) of buddy-youth pairs (Rotter, 1966). Specifically, the greater the relative external nature of the mediator, the less the behavioral change. Further research is necessary to identify the specific behavioral correlates of this mediator effect. For example, Goodstadt and Hjelle (1973) showed that externals resorted to coercive power in coping with a problem worker, while internals relied on personal persuasive power. It is possible that the youths in O'Donnell and Fo's program resisted similar coercive influence attempts by their buddies.

It is perhaps important to note that these youths were distinctly external in nature themselves. As such, the relatively adverse impact of more external mediators is inconsistent with the well-documented finding that external individuals are highly responsive to external social influence whereas internals respond favorably to intrinsic reinforcers (e.g., Baron & Ganz, 1972; Switzky & Haywood, 1974). This incon-

560   Effective Psychotherapy

sistency is less surprising if I-E differences are viewed not as a transsituational personality trait, but as malleable, situation-specific effects (Mahoney, 1974).

Other scattered clinical observations suggest the importance of the mediators' personal qualities. In their evaluation of the use of behavior therapy with autistic children, for example, Lovaas, Koegel, Simmons, and Long (1973) concluded that some parents were more successful mediators than others. Anecdotal observations indicated that characteristics common to effective parents included the capacity to be emotionally expressive; the willingness to use strong behavioral consequences (e.g., food and spankings); the attribution of responsibility to the child and the denial of the "sick" role; and the commitment, requiring considerable personal sacrifice, of a major part of their lives to the child. Emotionally unresponsive parents, who were more permissive, and who passively preferred to let their children "grow," were less successful. Systematic investigation of these subjective impressions would carry great practical significance for the treatment of psychotic children.

CONCLUSION

In marked contrast to virtually all other forms of therapy, the primary emphasis in behavior therapy has been on specific behavior change techniques. And the rather impressive facts are that many behavioral methods have been demonstrated to be effective even when administered by therapists of varied personal style, sex, and socioeconomic background—e.g., systematic desensitization (Paul, 1969), token reinforcement programs (O'Leary & Drabman, 1971). The emphasis on efficacious techniques has been further highlighted by their successful self-or client-administration which has facilitated self-regulated improvement in naturalistic settings—e.g., self-directed desensitization by acrophobics (Baker et al., 1973), self-control treatment of obesity and other behavioral and emotional problems (Stunkard & Mahoney, 1976; Watson & Tharp, 1972), and academic and social self-counseling through a branching programmed manual (Gilbert & Ewing, 1971). Other behavioral procedures have been so explicitly described that some of them can be applied by people who simply read about them in programmed texts—e.g., toilet-training procedures detailed in parent manuals (Foxx & Azrin, 1973), etc.

Despite these technical advances in the development of self-administered procedures, bibliographic material, and tape-recorded programs, behavior therapy, as we have attempted to show, still requires considerable therapist skill, sensitivity, and clinical acumen for successful application. Judging by their success in treating even complex clinical disorders (cf. O'Leary & Wilson, 1975), behavior therapists generally possess the requisite skills. Yet the conviction persists in some quarters that behavior therapy is an impersonal, mechanistic approach, as, in general, relatively little attention is devoted to these therapist activities in published accounts of treatment successes. Articles in scientific journals where most behavior therapists publish have, understandably, concentrated on descriptions of single techniques frequently applied to straightforward problems, with the attendant therapist's clinical expertise simply assumed. *Some behavior therapists have specifically shied away from considerations of therapist variables on the mistaken assumption that they are not measurable variables of the kind they prefer to study.*

In this paper we have suggested that *a shift in emphasis is needed. The realistic reporting of multifaceted treatment of complicated clinical cases will do much to revise inaccurate stereotypes of the practice of behavior therapy. It would be useful, too, if the language of behavior therapy were humanized in accord with what are, predominantly, its socially beneficial consequences. The figurative use of terms describing the behavior therapist as a "social reinforcement machine," a "behavioral engineer," or a behavioral "programmer" should be abandoned, as they tend to perpetuate the inaccurate image of man dominated by environmental events beyond his control* (Bandura, 1974).

Most importantly, however, the conceptual basis of behavior therapy should reflect more sophisticated formulations of behavior theory. The explicit recognition of cognitive mediation, of self-regulatory capacities, and of the limited role of automatic behavior change processes has significant implications for the field. The therapist ceases to be a simple "shaper" of attitudes and behavior, although his influence on the client remains profound. Rather, *the therapist becomes more of a consultant than a controller, skillfully directing consciously involved clients in active problem-solving strategies, instead of conditioning passive responders to external forces.* Students of behavior therapy viewed in this way can then be encouraged to explore further the reciprocal social influence processes which characterize the therapist-client relationship for the greater benefit of all who seek therapy.

REFERENCES

ALBERTI, R. E., & EMMONS, M. L. *Your perfect right: A guide to assertive behavior.* (2nd Ed.) San Luis Obispo, Calif.: Impact, 1974.

ALEXANDER, F. *Psychoanalysis and psychotherapy; Developments in theory, techniques, and training.* New York: Norton, 1956.

ALLEN, S. S., SPEAR, P. S., & JOHNSON, J. Experimenter role effects on children's task performance and perception. *Child Development,* 1969, **40,** 1–10.

ANNON, J. S. *The behavioral treatment of sexual problems.* Honolulu, Hawaii: Kapiolani Health Services, 1974.

AYLLON, T., & MICHAEL, J. The psychiatric nurse as a behavioral engineer. *Journal of the Experimental Analysis of Behavior,* 1959, **2,** 323–334.

BAKER, B. L. Symptom treatment and symptom substitution in enuresis. *Journal of Abnormal Psychology,* 1969, **74,** 42–49.

BAKER, B. L., COHEN, D. C., & SAUNDERS, J. T. Self-directed desensitization of acrophobia. *Behaviour Research and Therapy,* 1973, **11,** 79–89.

BANDURA, A. *Principles of behavior modification.* New York: Holt, Rinehart & Winston, 1969.

BANDURA, A. Psychotherapy based upon modeling principles. In A. E. BERGIN & S. L. GARFIELD (Eds.), *Handbook of psychotherapy and behavior change: An empirical analysis.* New York: Wiley, 1971.

BANDURA, A. Behavior theory and the models of man. *American Psychologist,* 1974, **29,** 859–869.

BANDURA, A., & BARAB, P. G. Processes governing disinhibitory effects through symbolic modeling. *Journal of Abnormal Psychology,* 1973, **82,** 1–9.

BARON, R. M., & GANZ, R. L. Effects of locus of control and type of feedback on the task performance of lower-class black children. *Journal of Personality and Social Psychology,* 1972, **21,** 124–130.

BATES, H. D. The effects of dispositional and contextual social desirability on verbal conditioning. In J. B. ROTTER, J. E. CHANCE, & E. J. PHARES (Eds.), *Applications of a social learning theory of personality.* New York: Holt, Rinehart & Winston, 1972.

BERKOWITZ, H., & ZIGLER, E. Effects of preliminary positive and negative interactions and delay conditions on children's responsiveness to social reinforcement. *Journal of Personality and Social Psychology,* 1965, **2,** 500–505.

BETZ, B. J. Experiences in research in psychotherapy with schizophrenic patients. In H. H. STRUPP & L. LUBORSKY (Eds.), *Research in psychotherapy.* Vol. 2. Washington, D.C.; American Psychological Association, 1962.

BIEBER, I. *Homosexuality.* New York: Basic Books, 1962.

BIRK, L., HUDDLESTON, W., MILLER, E., & COHLER, B. Avoidance conditioning for homosexuality. *Archives of General Psychiatry,* 1971, **25,** 314–325.

BORKOVEC, T. D. The role of expectancy and physiological feedback in fear research: A review with special reference to subject characteristics. *Behavior Therapy,* 1973, **4,** 491–505.

BOUDIN, H. M. Contingency contracting as a therapeutic tool in the deceleration of amphetamine use. *Behavior Therapy,* 1972, **3,** 604–608.

BRADY, J. P. Brevital-aided systematic desensitization. In R. RUBIN, H. FENSTERHEIM, A. A. LAZARUS, & C. M. FRANKS (Eds.), *Advances in behavior therapy 1969.* New York: Academic Press, 1971.

CHARTIER, G. M. A-B therapist variable: Real or imagined? *Psychological Bulletin,* 1971, **75,** 22–33.

COHEN, R. Group desensitization of test anxiety. Unpublished doctoral dissertation, Syracuse University, 1967.

DAVIS, J. D. *The interview as arena.* Stanford, Calif.: Stanford University Press, 1971.

DAVISON, G. C. A social learning therapy programme with an autistic child. *Behaviour Research and Therapy,* 1964, **2,** 149–159.

DAVISON, G. C. Elimination of a sadistic fantasy by a client-controlled counterconditioning technique. *Journal of Abnormal and Social Psychology,* 1968, **73,** 84–90.

DAVISON, G. C. An appraisal of behavior modification techniques with adults in institutional settings. In C. M. FRANKS (Ed.), *Behavior therapy: Appraisal and status.* New York: McGraw-Hill, 1969.

DAVISON, G. C. Counter-control in behavior modification. In L. A. HAMMERLYNCK, L. C. HANDY, & E. J. MASH (Eds.), *Behavior change: Methodology, concepts, and practice.* Champaign, Ill.: Research Press, 1973.

DAVISON, G. C., & GOLDFRIED, M. R. Postdoctoral training in clinical behavior therapy. *Menninger Clinic Bulletin,* 1973, No. 17.

DAVISON, G. C., & WILSON, G. T. Attitudes of behavior therapists towards homosexuality. *Behavior Therapy,* 1973a, **4,** 686–696.

DAVISON, G. C., & WILSON, G. T. Processes of fear-reduction in systematic desensitization: Cognitive and social reinforcement factors in humans. *Behavior Therapy,* 1973b, **4,** 1–21.

DOLLARD, J., & MILLER, N. E. *Personality and psychotherapy.* New York: McGraw-Hill, 1950.

D'ZURILLA, T., & GOLDFRIED, M. R. Problem-solving and behavior modification. *Journal of Abnormal Psychology,* 1971, **78,** 107–126.

ELLIS, A. *The essence of rational psychotherapy: A comprehensive approach to treatment.* New York: Institute for Rational Living, 1970.

EVANS, I. M. The logical requirements for explanations of systematic desensitization. *Behavior Therapy,* 1973, **4,** 506–514.

EVANS, I. M. Classical conditioning. In M. P. FELDMAN and A. BROADHURST (Eds.), *The theoretical and experimental bases of behavior therapy.* London: Wiley, 1976.

EVANS, I. M., DUBANOSKI, R. A., & HIGUCHI, A. A. Behavior therapy with child-abusing parents: Initial concepts underlying predictive, preventive, and analogue studies. Paper presented at the annual meeting of the Association for Advancement of Behavior Therapy, Chicago, November 1974.

EVANS, I. M., & NELSON, R. O. A curriculum for the teaching of behavior assessment. *American Psychologist,* 1974, **29,** 598–606.

EYSENCK, H. J. Learning theory and behaviour therapy. *Journal of Mental Science,* 1959, **105,** 61–75.

EYSENCK, H. J. *Fact and fiction in psychology.* Baltimore: Penguin, 1965.

EYSENCK, H. J., & RACHMAN, S. *The causes and cures of neurosis.* London: Routledge and Kegan Paul, 1965.

FELDMAN, M. P. Social psychology and behavior therapy: A cognitive dissonance based theory of behavior in the clinical situation. Unpublished manuscript, University of Birmingham, 1974a.

FELDMAN, M. P. Social psychology and behavior therapy: Social influence processes. Unpublished manuscript, University of Birmingham, 1974b.

FISH, J. M. *Placebo therapy.* San Francisco: Jossey Bass, 1973.

FOXX, R. M., & AZRIN, N. H. Dry pants: A rapid method of toilet training. *Behaviour Research and Therapy,* 1973, **11,** 435–442.

FRANK, J. D. *Persuasion and Healing.* Baltimore: Johns Hopkins University Press, 1961.

FRANKS, C. M., & WILSON, G. T. *Annual review of behavior therapy: Theory and practice.* Vol. 1. New York: Brunner/Mazel, 1973.

FRANKS, C. M., & WILSON, G. T. *Annual review of behavior therapy: Theory and practice*. Vol. 2. New York: Brunner/Mazel, 1974.

FRANKS, C. M., & WILSON, G. T. *Annual review of behavior therapy: Theory and practice*. Vol. 3. New York: Brunner/Mazel, 1975.

FRIEDMAN, P. R. Legal regulation of applied behavior analysis in mental institutions and prisons. Paper presented at the National Conference on Behavior Modification in Closed Institutions and Prisons, Washington, D.C., 1975.

GARFIELD, S. L. Research on client variables in psychotherapy. In A. E. BERGIN & S. L. GARFIELD (Eds.), *Handbook of psychotherapy and behavior change: An empirical analysis*. New York: Wiley, 1971.

GELDER, M. G. Verbal conditioning as a measure of interpersonal influence in psychiatric interviews. *British Journal of Social and Clinical Psychology*, 1968, 7, 194–209.

GELDER, M. G., BANCROFT, J. H. J., GATH, D. H., JOHNSTON, D. W., MATHEWS, A. M., & SHAW, P. Specific and non-specific factors in behaviour therapy. *British Journal of Psychiatry*, 1973, 123, 445–462.

GILBERT, W. M., & EWING, T. N. Programmed versus face-to-face counseling. *Journal of Counseling Psychology*, 1971, 18, 413–427.

GOLDFRIED, M. R., & DAVISON, G. C. *Clinical behavior therapy*. New York: Holt, Rinehart & Winston, 1976.

GOLDFRIED, M. R., & SPRAFKIN, J. *Behavioral personality assessment*. Morristown, N.J.: General Learning Press, 1974.

GOLDIAMOND, I. Toward a constructional approach to social problems. Ethical and constitutional issues raised by applied behavior analysis. *Behaviorism*, 1974, 2, 1–84.

GOLDIAMOND, I., & DYRUD, J. E. Some applications and implications of behavior analysis of psychotherapy. In J. M. SHLIEN (Ed.), *Research in psychotherapy*. Vol. III. Washington, D.C.: American Psychological Association, 1968.

GOLDSTEIN, A. P. *Psychotherapeutic attraction*. New York: Pergamon Press, 1971.

GOLDSTEIN, A. P. *Structured learning therapy*. New York: Pergamon Press, 1973.

GOLDSTEIN, A. P., HELLER, K., & SECHREST, L. B. *Psychotherapy and the psychology of behavior change*. New York: Wiley, 1966.

GOODSTADT, B. E., & HJELLE, L. A. Power to the powerless: Locus of control and the use of power. *Journal of Personality and Social Psychology*, 1973, 27, 190–196.

HALEY, J. *Uncommon therapy*. New York: Norton, 1973.

HAMMERSLEY, D. W. Conditioned reflex therapy. In R. S. WALLERSTEIN (Ed.), *Hospital treatment of alcoholism*. *Menninger Clinic Monographs*, 1957, 11, 11–18.

HARRIS, D. E., & LICHTENSTEIN, E. The contribution of non-specific social variables to a successful behavioral treatment of smoking. Paper presented at the annual meeting of the Western Psychological Association, San Francisco, April 1971.

HERSEN, M., EISLER, R. M., & MILLER, P. M. Development of assertive responses: Clinical, measurement and research considerations. *Behaviour Research and Therapy*, 1973, 11, 505–521.

HOWARD, K. L., & ORLINSKY, D. E. Psychotherapeutic process. In P. H. MUSSEN & M. R. ROSENZWEIG (Eds.), *Annual review of psychology*. Vol. 23. Palo Alto, Calif.: Annual Reviews, 1972. Pp. 615–668.

JAMES, L. E., & FOREMAN, M. E. A-B status of behavior therapy technicians as related to success of Mowrer's conditioning treatment of enuresis. *Journal of Consulting and Clinical Psychology*, 1973, 41, 224–229.

KAHN, M., & BAKER, B. Desensitization with minimal therapist contact. *Journal of Abnormal Psychology*, 1968, 73, 198–200.

KANFER, F. H., & KAROLY, P. Self-control: A behavioristic

excursion into the lion's den. *Behavior Therapy*, 1972, 3, 398–416.

KANFER, F. H., & PHILLIPS, J. S. Behavior therapy: A panacea for all ills or a passing fancy? *Archives of General Psychiatry*, 1966, 15, 114–128.

KANFER, F. H., & PHILLIPS, J. S. *Learning foundations of behavior therapy*. New York: Wiley, 1970.

KANFER, F. H., PHILLIPS, J. S., MATARAZZO, J. D., & SASLOW, G. Experimental modification of interviewer content in standardized interviews. *Journal of Consulting Psychology*, 1960, 24, 528–536.

KANFER, F. H., & SASLOW, G. Behavioral diagnosis. In C. M. FRANKS (Ed.), *Behavior therapy: Appraisal and status*. New York: McGraw-Hill, 1969.

KAPLAN, H. S. *The new sex therapy*. New York: Brunner/Mazel, 1974.

KENDLER, H. H., & SPENCE, J. T. Tenets of neobehaviorism. In H. H. KENDLER & J. T. SPENCE (Eds.), *Essays in neobehaviorism*. New York: Appleton-Century-Crofts, 1971.

KENT, R. N., & O'LEARY, K. D. Personal communication, 1975.

KLEIN, M. H., DITTMAN, A. T., PARLOFF, M. B., & GILL, M. M. Behavior therapy: Observations and reflections. *Journal of Consulting and Clinical Psychology*, 1969, 33, 259–266.

KOHLENBERG, R. J. Treatment of a homosexual pedophiliac using in vivo desensitization. *Journal of Abnormal Psychology*, 1974, 83, 192–195.

KOPEL, S. A. Self-applied rapid smoking procedures. Unpublished doctoral dissertation, University of Oregon, 1973.

KRASNER, L. The therapist as a social reinforcement machine. In H. H. STRUPP & L. LUBORSKY (Eds.), *Research in psychotherapy*. Vol. II. Washington, D.C.: American Psychological Association, 1962.

KRASNER, L. Behavior therapy. In P. H. MUSSEN & M. R. ROSENZWEIG (Eds.), *Annual review of psychology*. Vol. 22. Palo Alto, Calif.: Annual Reviews, 1971.

KRASNER, L., KNOWLES, J. B., & ULLMANN, L. P. Effect of verbal conditioning of attitudes on subsequent motor performance. *Journal of Personality and Social Psychology*, 1965, 1, 407–412.

KRASNER, L., & ULLMANN, L. P. Variables in the verbal conditioning of schizophrenic subjects. *American Psychologist*, 1958, 13, 358 (Abstract).

LANG, P. J., MELAMED, B. G., & HART, J. A psychophysiological analysis of fear modification using an automated desensitization procedure. *Journal of Abnormal Psychology*, 1970, 76, 220–234.

LANGER, E. J., & ABELSON, R. P. A patient by any other name . . . : Clinician group difference in labeling bias. *Journal of Consulting and Clinical Psychology*, 1974, 42, 4–9.

LAZARUS, A. A. New methods in psychotherapy: A case study. *South African Medical Journal*, 1958, 32, 660–664.

LAZARUS, A. A. The elimination of children's phobias by deconditioning. In H. J. EYSENCK (Ed.), *Behaviour therapy and the neuroses*. London: Pergamon, 1960.

LAZARUS, A. A. *Behavior therapy and beyond*. New York: McGraw-Hill, 1971.

LAZARUS, A. A. Women in behavior therapy. In V. FRANKS & V. BURTLE (Eds.), *Women in therapy: New psychotherapies for a changing society*. New York: Brunner/Mazel, 1974.

LAZARUS, A. A., & ROSEN, R. C. Behavior therapy techniques in the treatment of sexual disabilities. In J. K. MAYER (Ed.), *Forms of direct intervention in sexual disabilities*. New York: Medcom, in press.

LAZARUS, A. A., & SERBER, M. Is systematic desensitization being misapplied? *Psychological Reports*, 1968, 23, 215–218.

LEVITZ, L. S., & STUNKARD, A. J. A therapeutic coalition

for obesity: Behavior modification and patient self-help. *American Journal of Psychiatry*, 1974, **131**, 424–427.

LICHTENSTEIN, E., HARRIS, D. E., BIRCHLER, G., WAHL, J. M., & SCHMAHL, D. P. Comparison of rapid smoking, warm, smoky air, and attention placebo in the modification of smoking behavior. *Journal of Consulting and Clinical Psychology*, 1973, **40**, 92–98.

LOBITZ, W. C., & LoPICCOLO, J. New methods in the behavioral treatment of sexual dysfunction. *Journal of Behavior Therapy and Experimental Psychiatry*, 1972, **3**, 265–271.

LONDON, P. The end of ideology in behavior modification. *American Psychologist*, 1972, **27**, 913–920.

LOTT, A. J., & LOTT, B. E. The power of liking: Consequences of interpersonal attitudes derived from a liberalized view of secondary reinforcement. In L. BERKOWITZ (Ed.), *Advances in experimental social psychology*. Vol. 6. New York: Academic Press, 1972.

LOVAAS, O. I., KOEGEL, R., SIMMONS, J. Q., & LONG, J. S. Some generalization and follow-up measures of autistic children in behavior therapy. *Journal of Applied Behavior Analysis*, 1973, **6**, 131–164.

LOVAAS, O. I., SCHAEFFER, B., & SIMMONS, J. Q. Building social behavior in autistic children using electric shock. *Journal of Experimental Studies in Personality*, 1965, **1**, 99–109.

MAHONEY, M. J. *Cognition and behavior modification*. Cambridge, Mass.: Ballinger, 1974.

MARMOR, J. Dynamic psychotherapy and behavior therapy: Are they irreconcilable? *Archives of General Psychiatry*, 1971, **24**, 22–28.

MASTERS, W. H., & JOHNSON, V. E. *Human sexual inadequacy*. Boston: Little Brown, 1970.

McFALL, R. M., & HAMMEN, C. L. Motivation, structure, and self-monitoring: The role of nonspecific factors in smoking reduction. *Journal of Consulting and Clinical Psychology*, 1971, **37**, 80–86.

McFALL, R. M., & TWENTYMAN, C. Four experiments on the relative contributions of rehearsal, modeling, and coaching to assertion training. *Journal of Abnormal Psychology*, 1973, **81**, 199–218.

MEICHENBAUM, D. Examination of model characteristics in reducing avoidance behavior. *Journal of Personality and Social Psychology*, 1971, **14**, 298–307.

MISCHEL, W. *Personality and assessment*. New York: Wiley, 1968.

MISCHEL, W. Processes in delay of gratification. In L. BERKOWITZ (Ed.), *Advances in experimental social psychology*. Vol. 7. New York: Academic Press, 1974.

MOORE, B. E., & FINE, B. D. *A glossary of psychoanalytic terms and concepts*. New York: American Psychoanalytic Association, 1967.

MOOS, R. H., & CLEMES, S. R. Multivariate study of the patient-therapist system. *Journal of Consulting Psychology*, 1967, **31**, 119–130.

MOOS, R. H., & MacINTOSH, S. Multivariate study of the patient-therapist system. *Journal of Consulting and Clinical Psychology*, 1970, **35**, 298–307.

MORRIS, R. J., & SUCKERMAN, K. R. The importance of the therapeutic relationship in systematic desensitization. *Journal of Consulting and Clinical Psychology*, 1974a, **42**, 147.

MORRIS, R. J., & SUCKERMAN, K. R. Therapist warmth as a factor in automated systematic desensitization. *Journal of Consulting and Clinical Psychology*, 1974b, **42**, 244–250.

MURRAY, E. J., & JACOBSON, L. I. The nature of learning in traditional and behavioral psychotherapy. In A. E. BERGIN & S. L. GARFIELD (Eds.), *Handbook of psychotherapy and behavior change: An empirical analysis*. New York: Wiley, 1971.

NAWAS, M. M., FISHMAN, S. T., & PUCEL, J. C. A standardized desensitization program applicable to groups and individual treatments. *Behaviour Research and Therapy*, 1970, **8**, 49–56.

O'DONNELL, C. R., & FO, W. S. O. The buddy system: Mediator-target locus of control and behavioral outcome. Unpublished manuscript, University of Hawaii, 1974.

O'LEARY, K. D., & DRABMAN, R. Token reinforcement programs in the classroom: A review. *Psychological Bulletin*, 1971, **75**, 379–398.

O'LEARY, K. D., TURKEWITZ, H., & TAFFEL, S. J. Parent and therapist evaluation of behavior therapy in a child psychological clinic. *Journal of Consulting and Clinical Psychology*, 1973, **41**, 279–283.

O'LEARY, K. D., & WILSON, G. T. *Behavior therapy: Application and outcome*. Englewood Cliffs, N.J.: Prentice-Hall, 1975.

PAGE, M. M. Demand characteristics and the verbal operant conditioning experiment. *Journal of Personality and Social Psychology*, 1972, **23**, 372–378.

PAGE, M. M. Demand characteristics and the classical conditioning of attitudes experiment. *Journal of Personality and Social Psychology*, 1974, **30**, 468–476.

PATTERSON, G. R., & ANDERSON, D. Peers as social reinforcers. *Child Development*, 1964, **35**, 951–960.

PAUL, G. L. *Insight versus desensitization in psychotherapy: An experiment in anxiety reduction*. Stanford, Calif.: Stanford University Press, 1966.

PAUL, G. L. Behavior modification research: Design and tactics. In C. M. FRANKS (Ed.), *Behavior therapy: Appraisal and status*. New York: McGraw-Hill, 1969.

PAUL, G. L., & BERNSTEIN, D. A. *Anxiety and clinical problems; Systematic desensitization and related techniques*. Morristown, N.J.: General Learning Press, 1973.

RACHMAN, S. Clinical applications of observational learning, imitation and modeling. *Behavior Therapy*, 1972, **3**, 379–397.

RESNICK, J. H., & SCHWARTZ, T. Ethical standards as an independent variable in psychological research. *American Psychologist*, 1973, **28**, 134–139.

ROBINSON, C. H. The effects of observational learning on the masturbation patterns of preorgasmic females. Paper presented at the annual meeting of the Society for the Scientific Study of Sex, Las Vegas, November, 1974.

ROMANCZYK, R. G., TRACEY, D. A., WILSON, G. T., & THORPE, G. L. Behavioral techniques in the treatment of obesity: A comparative analysis. *Behaviour Research and Therapy*, 1973, **11**, 629–640.

ROSEN, A. The treatment relationship: A conceptualization. *Journal of Consulting and Clinical Psychology*, 1972, **38**, 329–337.

ROSEN, G. M. Therapy set: Its effect on subjects' involvement in systematic desensitization and treatment outcome. *Journal of Abnormal Psychology*, 1974, **83**, 291–300.

ROSENTHAL, R., & JACOBSON, L. F. Teacher expectations for the disadvantaged. *Scientific American*, 1968, **218**, 19–23.

ROTTER, J. B. *Social learning and clinical psychology*. New York: Prentice-Hall, 1954.

ROTTER, J. B. Generalized expectancies for internal versus external control of reinforcement. *Psychological Monographs*, 1966, **80** (1, Whole No. 609).

RYAN, V. L., & GIZYNSKI, M. N. Behavior therapy in retrospect: Patients' feelings about their behavior therapies. *Journal of Consulting and Clinical Psychology*, 1971, **37**, 1–9.

SALZINGER, K. Experimental manipulation of verbal behavior: A review. *Journal of General Psychology*, 1959, **61**, 65–94.

SARASON, I. G. The human reinforcer in verbal behavior research. In L. KRASNER & L. P. ULLMANN (Eds.), *Research in behavior modification*. New York: Holt, Rinehart & Winston, 1965.

EP—T*

SKINNER, B. F. *Science and human behavior*. New York: Macmillan, 1953.

SLOGGETT, B. B. The comparative effects of verbal information, passive observation, and active observation on the acquisition of classroom management skills. Unpublished doctoral dissertation, University of Hawaii, 1972.

SPANOS, N. P., DEMOOR, W., & BARBER, T. X. Hypnosis and behavior therapy: Common denominators. *American Journal of Clinical Hypnosis*, 1973, **16**, 45–64.

SPIELBERGER, C. D., & DENIKE, L. D. Descriptive behaviorism versus cognitive theory in verbal operant conditioning. *Psychological Review*, 1966, **73**, 306–326.

STAATS, A. W. Social behaviorism and human motivation: Principles of the attitude-reinforcer-discriminative system. In A. G. GREENWALD, T. C. BROCK, & T. M. OSTROM (Eds.), *Psychological foundations of attitudes*. New York: Academic Press, 1968.

STAATS, A. W. Social behaviorism, human motivation, and the conditioning therapies. In B. MAHER (Ed.), *Progress in experimental personality research*. New York: Academic Press, 1970.

STAATS, A. W., & STAATS, C. K. *Complex human behavior*. New York: Holt, Rinehart & Winston, 1963.

STUART, R. B., & LOTT, L. A. Behavioral contracting with delinquents: A cautionary note. *Journal of Behavior Therapy and Experimental Psychiatry*, 1972, **3**, 161–169.

STUNKARD, A. J., & MAHONEY, M. J. Behavioral treatment of eating disorders. In H. LEITENBERG (Ed.), *Handbook of behavior modification*. New York: Prentice-Hall, 1976.

SWITZKY, H. N., & HAYWOOD, H. C. Motivational orientation and the relative efficacy of self-monitored and externally imposed reinforcement systems in children. *Journal of Personality and Social Psychology*, 1974, **30**, 360–366.

THARP, R. G., & WETZEL, R. J. *Behavior modification in the natural environment*. New York: Academic Press, 1969.

THOMAS, E. J. Bias and therapist influence in behavioral assessment. *Journal of Behavior Therapy and Experimental Psychiatry*, 1973, **4**, 107–112.

TRACEY, D. A., BRIDDELL, D., & WILSON, G. T. Group therapy with chronic psychiatric patients: Generalization of verbal conditioning to verbal and nonverbal behavior. *Journal of Applied Behavior Analysis*, 1974, **7**, 391–402.

TRUAX, C. B. Reinforcement and nonreinforcement in Rogerian psychotherapy. *Journal of Abnormal and Social Psychology*, 1966, **71**, 1–9.

ULLMANN, L. P. The major concepts taught to behavior therapy trainees. In A. M. GRAZIANO (Ed.), *Behavior therapy with children*. Chicago: Aldine Atherton, 1971.

ULLMANN, L. P., & KRASNER, L. *Case studies in behavior modification*. New York: Holt, Rinehart & Winston, 1965.

ULLMANN, L. P., & KRASNER, L. *A psychological approach to Abnormal behavior*. Englewood Cliffs, N.J.: Prentice-Hall, 1969.

WAHLER, R. G. Infant social attachments: A reinforcement theory interpretation and investigation. *Child Development*, 1967, **38**, 1079–1088.

WATSON, D. L., & THARP, R. G. *Self-directed behavior: Self-modification for personal adjustment*. Monterey, Calif.: Brooks/Cole, 1972.

WIENS, A. H., MONTAGUE, J. R., MANAUGH, T. S., & ENGLISH, C. J. Pharmacologic aversive counterconditioning to alcohol in a private hospital: One year follow-up. *Journal of Studies on Alcohol*, 1976, **37**, 1320–1324.

WILKINS, W. Desensitization: Social and cognitive factors underlying the effectiveness of Wolpe's procedure. *Psychological Bulletin*, 1971, **76**, 311–317.

WILSON, G. T. Innovations in the modification of phobic behaviors in two clinical cases. *Behavior Therapy*, 1973, **4**, 426–430.

WILSON, G. T., & DAVISON, G. C. Behavior therapy and homosexuality: A critical perspective. *Behavior Therapy*, 1974, **5**, 16–28.

WILSON, G. T., & DAVISON, G. C. "Effects of expectancy on systematic desensitization and flooding": A critical analysis. *European Journal of Behavioural Analysis and Modification*, 1975, **1**, 12–14.

WILSON, G. T., HANNON, A. E., & EVANS, W. I. M. Behavior therapy and the therapist-patient relationship. *Journal of Consulting and Clinical Psychology*, 1968, **32**, 103–109.

WILSON, G. T., & ROSEN, R. C. Training controlled drinking in an alcoholic through a multifaceted behavioral treatment program: A case study. In J. D. KRUMBOLTZ & C. E. THORESEN (Eds.), *Counseling methods*. New York: Holt, Rinehart & Winston, 1976.

WOLPE, J. *Psychotherapy by reciprocal inhibition*. Stanford, Calif.: Stanford University Press, 1958.

WOLPE, J. *The practice of behavior therapy*. New York: Pergamon Press, 1969.

WOLPE, J., & LAZARUS, A. A. *Behavior therapy techniques*. New York: Pergamon Press, 1966.

YATES, A. *Behavior therapy*. New York: Wiley, 1970.

YOUNG, G. C., & MORGAN, R. T. T. Overlearning in the conditioning treatment of enuresis: A long-term follow-up study. *Behaviour Research and Therapy*, 1972, **10**, 419–420.

EDITORS' REFERENCES

GURMAN, A. S. Treatment of a case of public-speaking anxiety by in vivo desensitization and cue-controlled relaxation. *Journal of Behavior Therapy and Experimental Psychiatry*, 1973, **4**, 51–54.

MAHONEY, M. J. *Cognition and behavior modification*. Cambridge, Mass.: Ballinger, 1974.

MICKELSON, D. J., & STEVIC, R. R. Differential effects of facilitative and nonfacilitative behavioral counselors. *Journal of Counseling Psychology*, 1971, **18**, 314–319.

NOWICKI, S., BONNER, J., & FEATHER, B. Effects of locus of control and differential analog interview procedures on the perceived therapeutic relationship. *Journal of Consulting and Clinical Psychology*, 1972, **38**, 434–438.

SUINN, R. M., & RICHARDSON, F. Anxiety management training: A non-specific behavior therapy program for anxiety control. *Behavior Therapy*, 1971, **2**, 498–510.

VITALO, R. L. Effects of facilitative interpersonal functioning in a conditioning paradigm. *Journal of Counseling Psychology*, 1970, **17**, 141–144.

NOTES

1. "Behavior therapy" and "behavior modification" are terms used synonymously throughout this chapter.

2. We are grateful to the editors of this volume, as well as to Gerald C. Davison for their helpful comments on the manuscript.

3. We are permanently indebted to Alma E. Hannon, our coauthor of this earlier paper, whose enlightened teaching has so greatly influenced us.

4. *Editors' Footnote*. An alternative strategy, which one of us (ASG) has used on occasion, is for the therapist to treat the "presented" problem at face value when the client denies any motivation to work on what the therapist considers a more salient issue in the hope that the client, his "admission ticket" having been honored, will then feel more comfortable discussing these other issues. For example, one of our clients with a long history of diarrhea initially requested "behavior modification" for this complaint and during the first three history-taking and exploratory sessions steadfastly refused to acknowledge the relevance and problematic nature of his rela-

tionship with his girlfriend and his excessive and unrealistic academic performance standards. An 8-week program of training in the use of self-controlled relaxation procedures (based on Gurman, 1973; Suinn & Richardson, 1971) substantially reduced the frequency and intensity of these distressing gastrointestinal episodes. At this point, the patient stated that he was glad that a therapist had finally (there had been three previous therapists) responded directly to his complaint and that he then felt comfortable "getting into my other problems," which the therapist had, of course, initially seen as the sources of the variables controlling his psychosomatic difficulty.

5. *Editors' Footnote.* It must be remembered, of course, that "reinforcers" are defined by their effects on behavior, not on the basis of hedonistic criteria. Thus, for some clients what is typically thought of as an "empathic" response may be highly aversive (e.g., the feeling of "being understood" is anxiety-arousing).

6. *Editors' Footnote.* While such factors are random in the sense of not being predictable or controllable pre-treatment, we would argue that while a therapist cannot *change* them, he would be wise to *use* (the client's reaction to) them as an in vivo means of helping the client understand (become able to identify contingencies regarding) his impact on other people and vice versa. Obviously, the extent to which such experiences are "used" should be a function of the nature of client problems being addressed.

7. *Editors' Footnote.* Some clients, of course, may fail to carry out assigned tasks or to follow instructions for still a third, broader reason—i.e., because of characteristic "resistance" in the face of attempts by certain classes of people (e.g., "authority figures") to influence their behavior. While assertiveness training, rational-emotive instruction, etc., may resolve the impasse between a given therapist and client, we doubt that such a focal resolution often generalizes. Again, it must be the individually tailored treatment goals that are being sought that should determine how such "resistances" are responded to, or, in Mahoney's (1974) terms, the therapist must be more committed to the person than to the paradigm.

8. *Editors' Footnote.* While we agree with the authors' point here in general, it should be pointed out that, as Gurman notes (Chapter 19 this volume), client ratings of empathy *early* in therapy are quite consistently predictive of outcome assessed from multiple sources. Thus, we feel that this particular chicken and this particular egg are readily discriminable.

9. *Editors' Footnote.* We think this point deserves emphasizing.

10. *Editors' Footnote.* See Wilkins (Chapter 13, this volume) for further consideration of this issue.

11. *Editors' Footnote.* Also, see Mickelson and Stevic (1971), Nowicki, Bonner and Feather (1972), and Vitalo (1970).

CHAPTER 21

THE THERAPIST'S EXPERIENCE OF PSYCHOTHERAPY

David E. Orlinsky and Kenneth I. Howard

IN DEFENSE OF RESEARCH ON THE THERAPIST'S EXPERIENCE

What reason is there to be interested in how the therapist experiences psychotherapy? Ordinarily one would say that the therapist *does* therapy, while the patient *experiences* therapy. Experience seems to imply a receptive, not a contributive, mode of participation. To experience, one must be affected; one must undergo something. Clearly, the aim of therapy is to affect the patient, not to affect the therapist. The therapist conducts the therapy, the patient undergoes it. Interest in the character and quality of the patient's experience is thus readily comprehensible, and studies implementing this interest have not been lacking (e.g., Orlinsky & Howard, 1975; Snyder, 1961; Strupp, Fox, & Lessler, 1969). Yet, to many people, the basis for interest in the therapist's experience of psychotherapy as a legitimate area of scientific work remains obscure. There has been considerable research on the effects of therapist personality and attitudes (e.g., the A-B variable), but there has been little systematic study of the experiences of psychotherapists in the actual conduct of psychotherapy.

The clinical literature, of course, abounds with informal accounts of particular experiences—usually subsumed under the broad and somewhat tendentious heading of countertransference—but these are unsystematic and of unknown generalizability.[1] Aside from our own work (Orlinsky & Howard, 1975) only two major empirical studies have included a focus on therapist experience. Snyder (1961) developed questionnaires to be completed by the participants after each therapy session: the Client's Post-Interview Attitudes Toward Therapy and the Therapist's Personal Reaction Questionnaires. Unfortunately, however, although he studied 20 clients over a period of time, he was the only therapist in the sample and his results are therefore difficult to generalize. In another study with a larger number of therapists, Meyer, Borgatta, and Fanshel (1964) used a brief questionnaire to assess caseworkers' reactions in initial interviews. They derived several empirical dimensions from their data, but again there is a problem of generalizability in that initial casework interviews are probably not very representative of the typical psychotherapy session.

Because of the situation that exists, it is important at the outset to clarify the reasons for (and to understand the prejudices against) scientific study of the therapist's experience. It is a very common view that therapy is "for" the patient and "by" the therapist. Basically, the therapist is conceived as the agent, and the patient as the object, of treatment. From this perspective, one is constrained to see the therapist as an active participant in the process, and is prompted to study his techniques, skills, even personality and social background as sources of his contribution to therapy. One is not predisposed by this view to think very much about the therapist's experiences in psychotherapy, or if one does think about them at all they are too likely to be seen as idle curiosities or as unwanted intrusions.

Two seriously misleading biases are contained in this common view. One is found most often in the research literature and is based on an image of the therapist as an impersonal *instrument* of treatment. This image suggests that the therapist, qua therapist, does not participate as a person—that, in effect, he has no subjective experiences in psychotherapy that are worth studying. It implies that the therapist's experience, such as it is, is not truly integral to the events of the therapeutic process.

A second prejudice (often held by "technique"-oriented clinicians) might concede the existence of the therapist's experience as meaningful but would imply that it really does not matter. Only his technical interventions matter, because they affect the patient's experience (for good or ill) and *that* is what therapy is about. These biases are widely held though commonly unstated, and may even be denied by some who nevertheless behave in accordance with them. The beliefs in question appeal to the philosophical puritanism of researchers and to the ambivalence of therapists concerning their own involvement in therapy.

Yet the inescapable fact of the matter is that the therapist is a *person*, however much he may strive to make himself an instrument of his patient's treatment. As a person, the therapist is necessarily both acting and experiencing in the therapeutic process. Further, the therapist's actions to a very large extent represent an adaptation to his ongoing experience of therapy. The matter is illustrated in the accompanying diagram (Fig. 1) showing the therapist and the patient relating to one another in their common situation. In this scheme, "the behavior of each towards the other is mediated by the *experience* by each of the other, just as the experience of each is mediated by the behavior of each" (Laing, Phillipson, & Lee, 1966, p. 13). The therapist's actions in therapy are, in part, a function of his experience of the patient (and himself) in their common situation—and, thus, the therapist's experience of psychotherapy is an integral element in the events of therapy.

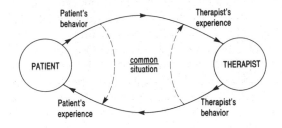

Fig. 1. Interrelations of Experience and Behavior in Psychotherapy (adapted from Laing, Phillipson, & Lee, 1966).

Moreover, insofar as consequences of importance for the outcome of therapy actually follow from the therapist's actions, the experiences that condition his actions have an eminently practical relevance. The therapist is often in a position to offer opinions and to make decisions that can have far-reaching effects on the life and social network of his patient. These opinions and decisions are necessarily based on his experiences with the patient in psychotherapy. Research on the ways in which therapists experience psychotherapy, and on the factors that influence their experiences, should shed light on their reactions to patients, and thus potentially may have considerable practical value.

Another point that may be made in favor of research on the therapist's experience of psychotherapy relates to matters of theory rather than practice. The earliest and most influential of modern theories of personality were created by psychotherapists—Freud, Adler, Jung, Horney, Sullivan, Rogers, etc., etc. These theories of personality, and the theories of therapy that are associated with them, were mainly derived from the experiences of their authors in the course of working with patients. In an important, but for the most part informal and implicit, sense, the therapist's experience of psychotherapy has constituted the principal data base for such theories. Systematic research on the therapist's experience should help to clarify the still apparently intuitive connection between the therapist's working theory of personality and its clinical data base.

With these justifications, we turn for the moment from studies of the therapist's contribution to psychotherapy to consider psychotherapy's contribution to the therapist as an experiencing, reactive individual. We first describe a method for empirical research on therapists' (and patients') experiences in therapy, and then present analyses of data on the therapist's experience collected by this method. Finally, we discuss the implications of our findings for gaining a better understanding of the therapist's contribution to treatment.

METHOD OF RESEARCH ON THE THERAPIST'S EXPERIENCE

The Therapy Session Report

The Therapy Session Report was developed as an instrument for studying patients' and therapists' experiences in psychotherapy. The Therapist Form of the Therapy Session Report (Orlinsky & Howard, 1966) is a structured response questionnaire containing 152 items. Generally, the response alternatives for these items were either "none—some—a lot" or "slightly or not at all—some—pretty much—very much." The questionnaire was designed so that it could be completed after a therapy session in 10–15 minutes. The 152 items, listed in Tables 2–11, were designed to cover 10 facets of a therapist's experiences during a session—six focusing on the patient (Tables 2–7) and four on the therapist (Tables 8–11).

With regard to the therapist's experience of the patient, there were 19 items which surveyed the topics that were talked about during the session (*dialogue*—Table 2); 14 items covered the therapist's appraisal of what the patient seemed to want from the session (*motives*—Table 3); 12 items were designed to survey the patient's current worries (*concerns*—Table 4); 32 items were selected to cover the patient's affective states (*feelings*—Table 5); 8 items focused on the patient's interpersonal *behavior* (Table 6); and 8 items were designed to cover the patient's self-experience (*self-adaptation*—Table 7).

With regard to the therapist's experience of himself, 14 items surveyed his goals during the session (*aims*—Table 8); 8 items covered his interpersonal *behavior* (Table 9); and 27 items focused on the therapist's *feelings* (Table 10). Finally, there were 10 multiple-choice items which focused on the therapist's perception of the session as an ongoing interpersonal act and on his evaluation of it (*session development and evaluation*—Table 11).

Subjects: The Therapists and Their Patients

There were 17 therapists in our sample who completed Therapy Session Reports for at least five sessions with from one to three patients. As indicated in Table 1, the number of sessions studied ranged from five to 64 per therapist-case. For some cases, the initial phase of therapy was included; for others, the middle or last phase; for some, the entire course of treatment. Results from an earlier study (Hill, Howard, & Orlinsky, 1970) based on preliminary data suggest that the dimensions of therapist experience are not significantly affected by the period of treatment. The data reported in this chapter were analyzed in such a way as to eliminate systematic effects of treatment phase by random selection of five sessions from each case for each of the analyses. Table 1 displays some selected characteristics of this sample. An inclusive selection procedure was used—i.e., we included everyone who would cooperate who was engaged in treatment during the period of data collection. That included virtually all patients and a majority of the therapists at the Katherine Wright Mental Health Clinic (Chicago). The 13 male and four female therapists ranged in age from 29 to 50 (median = 36). They were psychiatrists, clinical psychologists, and psychiatric social workers with a median of 6 years experience in the practice of psychotherapy; 59% had had personal therapy. Their general theoretical orientation was dynamic-eclectic. In most respects this sample is quite representative of the

population of metropolitan therapists (see Henry, Sims, & Spray, 1971).

The 32 patients treated by these therapists were all women in once-weekly outpatient therapy. They ranged in age from 19 to 52 (median = 25). Most were unmarried and employed. Eighty-seven percent had at least completed high school and 37% were college graduates. Forty-one percent were diagnosed

TABLE 1. SAMPLE CHARACTERISTICS

Characteristic	Therapists	Patients Treated
N	17	32
Sessions reported		
Total	1091	—
Range	5–64	—
Median	14	—
Age		
Range	29–50	19–52
Median	36	25
Sex		
Male	76%	0%
Female	24%	100%
Marital status		
Single	35%	61%
First marriage	53%	13%
Second or later marriage	6%	3%
Separated or divorced	6%	23%
Parental status		
No children	59%	72%
At least one child	41%	28%
Occupation		
Employed	100%	72%
Psychiatrist	53%	—
Psychologist	24%	—
Social Worker	24%	—
Education		
Some H.S. or less	0%	13%
H.S. graduate	0%	16%
Some college	0%	34%
College graduate	0%	28%
Graduate school	0%	28%
Graduate school	100%	9%
Religious background		
Protestant	29%	25%
Catholic	12%	59%
Jewish	41%	13%
None or other	18%	3%
Social class of origin		
Upper middle and above	12%	10%
Middle	47%	24%
Lower middle	29%	28%
Upper lower and below	12%	38%
Professional experience		
Years of practice: range	2–20	—
median	6	—
Personal therapy	59%	100%
Diagnosis		
Depressive reaction	—	41%
Anxiety reaction	—	19%
Personality disturbance	—	22%
Schizoid/schizophrenic	—	19%
Previous psychotherapy	—	56%

as neurotic depressive reactions, 19% anxiety reactions, 22% personality disturbances, and 19% schizoid or ambulatory schizophrenic. Fifty-six percent had had previous therapy. The patients were generally rather similar to those described in previous surveys of outpatients (e.g., Ryan, 1969).

Forms of Data Analysis

Responses to the Therapist Form of the Therapy Session Report were subjected to a series of analyses that involved (1) the estimation of the endorsement frequencies for each item, (2) the determination of the factor structure of each set of items (facet), and (3) the description of multifaceted dimensions of therapist experience.

Endorsement frequencies. Of the 17 therapists who completed forms for at least five sessions with a particular patient, several reported on two or more patients. In order to preserve some balance in the results, three patients were sampled from those therapists who reported on four or more patients. In this way a "therapist-case" sample was constructed which consisted of the reports of the 17 therapists on 32 patients ($N = 621$ sessions). Endorsement frequencies were calculated by randomly selecting five sessions from each therapist-case and counting the frequency of each response to each item in the questionnaire. These frequencies were then converted to percentages, as shown in Tables 2 through 11.

Facet factor analyses. The items in the Therapy Session Report were organized into 10 sets in terms of the facets of experience which were surveyed (dialogue, motives, concerns, etc.). Each of these sets was factor-analyzed, separately, in order to reduce the number of variables carried into subsequent analyses, and to ensure greater clinical meaningfulness and reliability of the variables.

The factor-analytic procedure employed was the same for each of the 10 facets. Five sessions were randomly selected from each of the 32 therapist-cases. Using one session at a time from each case, the items which constituted a facet were intercorrelated ($N = 32$). This yielded five statistically independent estimates of the correlation between every pair of items in the facet. These correlations were converted to Fisher's (1954, p. 198) z, averaged for each item pair, and the average z was reconverted to a correlation coefficient. In this manner more precise and stable estimates of the relationships among items within a facet (within a session) were obtained.

These "average" correlation matrices were then factor-analyzed with unities in the major diagonals. Varying numbers of factors were rotated (Varimax) in order to determine the number of factors to be retained for each facet. Examination of the decomposition of the factors augmented the general criterion of retaining the maximum number of common factors (Howard & Gordon, 1963). In this way, 53 facet factors were determined and each questionnaire was scored on these factors by adding (with unit weight) those items which defined each factor. These facet factors are displayed in Tables 2 through 10, and 12.

Dimensions of therapist experience. Three separate factor analyses were used to explore the overall dimensionality of therapist experience: (1) a session analysis, (2) a sequence analysis, and (3) a person analysis. In each, the procedures for factoring, rotation, and determination of number of factors were the same as those described above.

For the session analysis, five sessions were selected randomly from the 32 therapist-cases, and five 53×53 correlation matrices were computed. These were averaged and factored as above. In this way 11 factors were defined which accounted for 63% of the total variance (Tables 13 through 23).

For the sequence factors, all of the 621 sessions for the 32 therapist-cases were employed. A one-way multivariate analysis of variance was computed—the "way" being therapist-case and the dependent variables being the 53 facet factor scores. The residual correlation matrix (53×53) was then factor-analyzed. This residual correlation matrix consists of the correlations among the 53 scores, over sessions (time), and is equivalent to that which would have been obtained by standard scoring each therapist-case (to remove level differences between cases) and then intercorrelating these standard scores ($N = 621$). Ten factors emerged from this factor analysis accounting for 51% of the total variance.

For the person factors, averages were computed for each therapist-case, for the 53 facet factor scores, over the entire set of sessions for that case. These averages were intercorrelated to form a single 53×53 matrix ($N = 32$), and this matrix was factor-analyzed. Nine factors were retained, accounting for 76% of the total variance.

FACETS OF THE THERAPIST'S EXPERIENCE

How Do Therapists View Their Patients?

The Therapy Session Report asks the therapist to consider his experience of the patient from a variety of perspectives, some observational and others inferential. The therapist is asked to report what his patient talked about with him during the session, and what the patient seemed to want. The therapist is also asked for his impression of the problematic concerns and themes expressed in the patient's discourse, and his impression of the patient's behavioral stance in relating to him during the session. Inquiry is also directed to the therapist's perception of his patient's feeling states during the session, his patient's self-experience in the session, and the effectiveness of his patient's current coping with life. What follows is a description of the contents and the organization of the therapist's experience of the patient in each of these several respects.

Dialogue. Therapist's perceptions of the topics discussed with them by their patients were organized into seven discrete areas, as shown in Table 2. As might be expected, one of the more commonly discussed was (1) *parental family* (mother, father, brothers or sisters, childhood and adolescence). There were two clusters of content relating to conjugal rather than parental family: (7) *domestic relationships* (relations with the opposite sex, marriage, and children) and (2) *domestic affairs* (household responsibilities and finances). Relations with the opposite sex—a salient issue for married and unmarried alike—was the single most frequently discussed topic of the 19 listed in the Therapy Session Report. Also very frequently discussed were work or education and relations with others of the same sex, which together defined a cluster called (4) *work and peers*. Another interesting cluster, (6) *personal fate*, was composed of very rarely discussed religious ideas, together with very frequently discussed hopes and fears about the future, and bodily symptoms, functions, and appearance. The final two areas of dialogue were more uniquely relevant to the therapeutic situation. These were (5) *therapy and therapist*, discussed on the average in half of the sessions observed (i.e., about as often as *parental family*!), and (3) *fantasy* (which consisted of dreams and fantasies together with strange or unusual ideas and experiences), discussed about a third of the time.

Motives. Why did patients talk about these things? What did they want or hope to get in their therapy sessions? The patterning of motives attributed to their patients by therapists, together with the relative frequency with which they are noted in therapy sessions, are shown in Table 3. The largest, and on the average most frequently perceived cluster of patient aims was the desire for (9) *insight*: to explore emerging

TABLE 2. THERAPISTS' PERCEPTIONS OF PATIENT DIALOGUE IN THERAPY SESSIONS

During this session my patient talked about:	% Endorsement	Factor Structure							h²
		1	2	3	4	5	6	7	
I-2. Mother.	52ᵃ	81ᵇ							68
I-5. Childhood memories and experiences.	60	80							75
I-3. Father.	42	79							73
I-4. Brothers or sisters.	29	65							53
I-6. Adolescence.	26	65	−38						63
I-12. Household responsibilities or activities.	36		83						75
I-11. Financial resources or problems with money.	30		77						66
I-18. Dreams or fantasies.	41			76					65
I-16. Strange or unusual ideas and experiences.	28			61					51
I-9. Relations with others of same sex.	66				82				70
I-8. Work, career, or education.	74				74				70
I-19. Perceptions or feelings about me (therapist).	45					80			71
I-20. Therapy: feelings and progress as a patient.	55					77			67
I-7. Religious feelings, activities or experiences.	16						82		71
I-17. Hopes or fears about the future.	72		38				55		63
I-15. Body functions, symptoms, or appearance.	49					−45	51		57
I-13. Feelings about spouse or about being married.	41							84	76
I-10. Relations with the opposite sex.	78							65	64
I-14. Feelings about children or being a parent.	32							62	59
Percent of total variance		15.0	10.2	6.9	8.4	9.0	7.5	9.2	66.2

ᵃEndorsement frequencies represent a combination of alternatives "some" and "a lot."
ᵇDecimals omitted. Underlined loadings indicate items used for factor scoring. Unless the highest for an item, only loadings .35 or above are shown.

TABLE 3. THERAPISTS' PERCEPTIONS OF PATIENT MOTIVES IN THERAPY SESSIONS

This session my patient seemed to want:	% Endorsement	Factor Structure						h²
		8	9	10	11	12	13	
I-22. A chance to let go and express feelings.	56ᵃ	76ᵇ						72
I-23. To learn more about what to do in therapy, and what to expect from it.	40	−61		36				61
I-29. To explore emerging feelings and experiences.	64		72					64
I-26. To understand the reasons behind problematic feelings or behavior.	72		71					63
I-33. Help in evaluating feelings and reactions.	66		68					68
I-34. To work through a particular problem.	66		52			42		52
I-31. To get a personal response from me.	62			77				70
I-35. My frank opinion or evaluation.	48		35	67				65
I-27. Reassurance, sympathy, or approval from me.	82			58	40			65
I-32. Help in controlling feelings or impulses.	32				81			77
I-25. Relief from tension or unhappy feelings.	67				69			64
I-30. To get advice on how to deal more effectively with self or others.	52					79		66
I-24. To avoid dealing with anxiety-arousing concerns.	48						86	77
I-28. To evade or withdraw from effective contact with me.	32						85	78
Percent of total variance		7.8	15.4	12.2	10.9	8.8	12.3	67.3

ᵃEndorsement frequencies represent a combination of alternatives "some" and "a lot."
ᵇDecimals omitted. Underlined loadings indicate items used for factor scoring. Unless the highest for an item, only loadings .35 or above are shown.

feelings and experiences; to understand the reasons for feelings and actions; to get help in evaluating experiences; and to resolve specific problems. This motivational attribution, of course, is most congruent with expectations of the patient role in therapy. Insight, in the broad sense indicated, is the traditional stock-in-trade of psychotherapy. It is probably the patient motivation that most therapists wish to see in their patients[2], and (to the extent that patients have been properly socialized to their role in therapy) it is probably a desire that most patients actually have.

Insight, however, is not the only thing that therapists see their patients as wanting. Also frequently noted were wishes for (8) *catharsis versus orientation* (to let go and express feeling versus to learn what to do in therapy); (11) *emotional relief and control* (e.g., relief from tension and unhappiness); and (12) *advice* on how to deal more effectively with self and others. All of these, too, are congruent with common conceptions of the patient role—i.e., would tend to be viewed as legitimate desires on the patient's part.

Two other patterns of motivation are of a more personal nature. One was the desire for (10) *therapist involvement*, in which the patient was seen as wanting a personal response from the therapist, the therapist's frank opinion or evaluation, and his reassurance, sympathy, or approval. The last (reassurance, etc.) was the most frequently noted of the 14 items in this section of the Therapy Session Report, observed on the average in 82% of the sessions studied! Less frequently noted was the desire to (13) *avoid therapeutic involvement* (*resistance*), although this was still seen as a factor that therapists must deal with in more than a third of their sessions with patients. Resistance takes the form of wishing to avoid dealing with anxiety-arousing concerns, and of wishing to evade or withdraw from effective contact with the therapist.

Reference to item 51 in Table 11 (see below) will show that therapists viewed their patients as strongly or very strongly motivated to attend their sessions in 60% of the occasions studied.

Concerns. What were the areas of problematic concern that therapists perceived their patients to be struggling with? The 12 relevant items in the Therapy Session Report clustered in five thematic areas, as shown in Table 4. Almost all were very frequently encountered in sessions; each was, on the average, observed in about 50% or more of the sessions studied. The single most frequently endorsed item was concern over personal identity and aspirations, which together with angry feelings and behavior, and fearful or panicky experiences, defined a cluster of concerns called (15) *identity conflict*. Another large cluster focused on problems relating to (14) *isolation and intimacy*: concern over meaning little or being worthless to others; being lonely and isolated; being dependent on others; and being able to give lovingly of oneself to others. It is not clear that *identity conflict* and concern over *isolation and intimacy* are problems that

TABLE 4. THERAPISTS' PERCEPTIONS OF PATIENT CONCERNS IN THERAPY SESSIONS

This session my patient was concerned about:	% Endorsement	Factor Structure					h^2
		14	15	16	17	18	
I-48. Meaning little or nothing to others: being worthless or unlovable.	52[a]	73[b]					66
I-41. Being lonely or isolated.	68	70					59
I-37. Being dependent on others.	59	65					59
I-44. Loving: being able to give of her (his) self to others.	59	59					57
I-45. Angry feelings or behavior.	68		76				59
I-46. Personal identity and aspirations.	79		58				45
I-47. Fearful or panicky experiences.	36	38	47	−40			65
I-43. Expressing her (his) self to others.	67			72			68
I-39. Being assertive or competitive.	55		36	65			65
I-42. Sexual feelings and experiences.	43				87		76
I-38. Meeting obligations and responsibilities.	61					86	80
I-40. The demands of conscience: shameful or guilty feelings.	58				41	69	70
Percent of total variance		17.6	12.4	11.0	9.9	13.2	64.1

[a]Endorsement frequencies represent a combination of alternatives "some" and "a lot."

[b]Decimals omitted. Underlined loadings indicate items used for factor scoring. Unless the highest for an item, only loadings .35 or above are shown.

only women deal with, but these are certainly problem areas that are very much discussed in contemporary women's literature. So, too, is the area of (16) *self-assertion*, which in therapy was most frequently manifested in terms of expressing oneself to others, but also in terms of being overtly assertive and competitive. Two other areas are broadly applicable and familiar problematic themes: concerns over matters of (18) *conscience* (meeting obligations, and shameful or guilty feelings) and (17) *sexuality*.

Feelings. The patient's feelings are another prime focus of the therapist's attention, in particular those feelings which the patient manifests during the therapy session. A list of 32 feeling states was included in the Therapy Session Report for the therapist's use in describing the nature of his patient's affect. Nine patterns of feeling were found, as shown in Table 5. The largest and generally most frequently noted pattern was that of patient feeling (20) *confident*—i.e., feeling accepted, hopeful, relaxed, confident, pleased, close, affectionate, and likable. Therapists saw their patients as feeling "accepted" in 82% of the sessions observed, second only to their feeling "serious" as a constant element in the affective tone of therapy. However, another rather common patient feeling pattern was (25) *anxious* (feeling anxious and guilty, as well as inadequate and serious), with "anxious" present in 71% of the reported sessions. Two other dysphoric patterns that were fairly commonly noted were patient feeling (24) *depressed* (helpless, tearful, depressed, discouraged, hurt, inadequate) and (23) *inhibited* (cautious, inhibited, hurt, withdrawn, frustrated). Patients were also seen as feeling (22) *angry* in about a third of their

sessions—i.e., angry, tired, discouraged, impatient, and frustrated. Therapists viewed their patients about equally often, however, as feeling (19) *relieved* (relieved, grateful, determined, pleased) perhaps as a function of catharsis of these dysphoric states.

Some interesting but relatively infrequent feeling states were also noted. A cluster defined by feeling sexually attracted, affectionate, likable, embarrassed, and close, was called patient feeling (21) *eroticized affection*. Another was feeling (27) *confused* (confused, strange, embarrassed, inadequate, helpless, and inhibited), which occurred in less than one-third of the sessions. Finally, a single item defined the very rarely occurring feeling of being (26) *ill*.

Behavior. Behavior in the sense of instrumental activity in therapy consists for the most part of the conversation that is carried on between patient and therapist (the contents of which have already been described under the heading of Dialogue). There is, however, another sense of behavior as interpersonal adaptation or style of relating. This latter sense appears largely in the form of expressive manner, and defines not so much *what* a person does as *how* he does it. Eight items in the Therapy Session Report were designed to survey this facet of the therapist's experience of his patient. From these, three distinct modes of relating were discerned, as shown in Table 6. Therapists generally saw their patients as very much (29) *structuring* interaction in the session, mainly by talking and by taking initiative in bringing up the subjects of conversation. The patient's *structuring* tended to focus on what the patient was feeling, and was friendly in tone. Patients were also fairly typic-

TABLE 5. THERAPISTS' PERCEPTIONS OF PATIENT FEELINGS IN THERAPY SESSIONS

My patient seemed to feel:	% Endorsement	Factor Structure									h^2
		19	20	21	22	23	24	25	26	27	
II-8. Relieved	41[a]	82[b]									73
II-7. Grateful	37	56	39								53
II-6. Determined	60	42					-36		-36		71
II-26. Accepted	82		69								57
II-29. Hopeful	68		67								70
II-3. Relaxed	64		66								64
II-1. Confident	61		64				-40				66
II-22. Pleased	39	35	59								63
II-10. Close	54		59	41							67
II-15. Likable	71		46	43							63
II-32. Sexually attracted	18			82							70
II-18. Affectionate	43		57	58							69
II-21. Angry	45				67						60
II-30. Tired	29				61						57
II-11. Impatient	31				49						63
II-25. Discouraged	41				54		52				74
II-27. Cautious	61					80					73
II-23. Inhibited	53					66					75
II-4. Withdrawn	31					53				40	63
II-28. Frustrated	58				41	50	38				73
II-16. Hurt	28					55	45				71
II-5. Helpless	38						70			36	74
II-9. Tearful	24						67				59
II-17. Depressed	60						66				61
II-14. Inadequate	60					37	42	36		39	66
II-20. Anxious	71							67			65
II-12. Guilty	48							60			57
II-19. Serious	90					35		35			54
II-31. Ill	3								77		64
II-24. Confused	39									78	70
II-13. Strange	21									77	71
II-2. Embarrassed	48			37						47	65
Percent of total variance		6.1	11.4	5.6	6.5	9.1	9.4	6.0	4.3	7.3	65.7

[a]Endorsement frequencies represent a combination of alternatives "some" and "a lot."

[b]Decimals omitted. Underlined loadings indicate items used for factor scoring. Unless the highest for an item, only loadings .35 or above are shown.

ally seen by their therapists as relating in an (28) *accepting* manner—i.e., as attentive to the therapist, as tending to agree with the therapist, and as acting in a warm and friendly fashion. Both of these modes of relating are expectable and virtually normative aspects of the patient role.[3] A much less frequently occurring, and socially deviant, mode of relating for patients was acting in a (30) *domineering* manner toward the therapist, taking a negative or critical stance and trying to persuade the therapist to view things differently. We shall see later that this mode of relating in patients typically entailed an open confrontation with the therapist.

Self-Adaptation. In addition to striking a certain balance in relating to the therapist, the patient also must attempt to maintain an appropriate equilibrium in adapting to himself, as he reflexively experiences himself during the session. The results of the patient's efforts to maintain equilibrium *vis-à-vis* himself, successful or otherwise, are observable by the therapist in the patient's expressive behavior. Eight items in the Therapy Session Report permitted the therapist to comment on this aspect of the patient's presence with him, as shown in Table 7. Factor analysis of these items resulted in the definition of three modes of patient self-adaptation, as viewed by therapists. Most salient of these was (31) *self-possession* (*control and coherence*); in less than one-fifth of the sessions observed did therapists find their patients to be less than substantially self-possessed. Therapists also for the most part found their patients to be (32) *open* (*focusing and expressive*) with them during sessions, though more moderately. No doubt openness tended to give way to reserve when it threatened the individual's self-possession, as it does in most social situations. A third dimension of self-adaptation noted by therapists in their patients was (33) *self-critical arousal versus self-satisfaction*, reflecting variations both in self-esteem and in emotionality. As Table 7 indicates, therapists saw their patients varying con-

TABLE 6. THERAPISTS' PERCEPTIONS OF PATIENT BEHAVIOR IN THERAPY SESSIONS

During this session, how much:	% Endorsement		Factor Structure			
	Some	Much[a]	28	29	30	h²
II-46. Was your patient attentive to what you were trying to get across?	33	63	87[b]			78
II-47. Did your patient tend to agree with or accept your comments or suggestions?	54	34	75		-38	71
II-43. Was your patient warm and friendly towards you?	42	46	47	45		46
II-35. Did your patient talk?	15	81		82		70
II-37. Did your patient take initiative in bringing up the subjects that were talked about?	26	68		82		69
II-40. Did your patient talk about what she (he) was feeling?	48	44		65		42
II-45. Did your patient try to persuade you of her (his) own point of view?	36	22			77	62
II-49. Was your patient negative or critical toward you?	19	7			77	65
Percent of total variance			20.3	25.0	17.5	62.8

[a]Endorsement frequencies represent a combination of alternatives "pretty much" and "very much."

[b]Decimals omitted. Underlined loadings indicate items used for factor scoring. Unless the highest for an item, only loadings .35 or above are shown.

TABLE 7. THERAPISTS' PERCEPTIONS OF PATIENT SELF-ADAPTATION IN THERAPY SESSIONS

During this session, how much:	% Endorsement		Factor Structure			
	Some	Much[a]	31	32	33	h²
II-48. Did your patient retain effective control over her (his) actions and expressions?	16	82	89[b]			80
II-38. Was your patient logical and organized in expressing thoughts and feelings?	16	83	58	47		61
II-42. Was your patient able to freely produce ideas and associations?	42	36		86		76
II-44. Was your patient spontaneous?	33	58		84		71
II-36. Was your patient able to focus on what was of present concern to her (him)?	30	64		73		57
II-41. Was your patient self-critical or self-rejecting?	49	13			83	70
II-39. Were your patient's feelings stirred up?	45	45	-36		58	55
II-50. Was your patient satisfied or pleased with her (his) own behavior?	57	17		48	-68	71
Percent of total variance			16.7	31.6	19.4	67.6

[a]Endorsement frequencies represent a combination of alternatives "pretty much" and "very much."

[b]Decimals omitted. Underlined loadings indicate items used for factor scoring. Unless the highest for an item, only loadings .35 or above are shown.

siderably in self-esteem, but as tending strongly to being at least "moderately" self-critically stirred-up, during the sessions studied.

Coping and Progress. Finally, therapists were asked to estimate after each session how well their patients were currently coping with the exigencies of life, and how much progress they had made on that occasion toward resolving their problems. Reference to item 53 in Table 11 (see below) indicates that, in general, therapists viewed their patients as coping "fairly well"—having their "ups and downs." On only 5% of the occasions did therapists feel that their patients were having serious trouble coping, while on 25% of the occasions they saw their patients as doing "quite well" or "very well" in their adaptive functioning. Item 52 in Table 11 suggests that therapists for the most part see (or claim) only slight progress in any particular session. On 13% of the occasions observed, "considerable" or greater progress was noted, while another 13% of the sessions seemed to therapists an exercise in futility (or worse). Reference to Table 12 (see below) will reveal that the therapist's view of the patient's progress during the session was bound up with his own sense of (50) *therapeutic effectiveness,* and also that the better the therapist felt his patient to be functioning, the more positively he himself looked forward to their sessions!

How Do Therapists View Themselves?

While the patient is undoubtedly the prime focus of the therapist's attention in treatment, the therapist is most unlikely to be completely unself-conscious during their sessions. He is aware—if only in a proximal and subsidiary manner—of relating interactively with his patient, of having intentions for their meetings, of being affectively responsive to what transpires, and of having evaluative reactions to his own performance. These facets of the therapist's self-experience are surveyed in four sections of the Therapy Session Report.

Aims. What do therapists strive to achieve with their patients during therapy sessions? What are the goals or aims that guide their interventions? A list of 14 therapist aims was included in the Therapy Session Report, the empirical structure and saliences of which are shown in Table 8. The most prevalent of the five patterns of intention that emerged from the factor analysis was the therapist's aim to provide (35) *insight*—i.e., cognitive understanding and realistic evaluation. Nearly as constant a theme among the therapist's goals was his desire to (36) *enhance the relationship* by helping the patient to feel accepted and by responding personally and empathically to what he understood the patient's actions and communications to mean. Another common goal of the therapist was the wish to give the patient an opportunity for (34) *catharsis*, by helping the patient focus on, talk about, and get relief from emergent and dysphoric emotional states. These three clusters of therapeutic intent were reported for an average of three-fourths to four-fifths of the sessions observed.

Therapists also worked to (38) *promote behavioral change* in their patients by offering encouragement, suggestions, and stimulation. The fifth pattern, aiming to provide (37) *control versus support*, suggests that therapists had to chose between supplementing the patient's self-control and supporting the patient's self-confidence—i.e., that it was difficult or impossible to seek both aims at one time. Perhaps it is a reflection of the outpatient setting of these therapeutic sessions that therapists sought to support self-esteem in their patients about three times more often than they felt the need to reinforce the patient's self-control.

It is interesting to compare the therapists' perceptions of their patients' wants with what they themselves hoped to offer. Thus, *insight* was sought (9) and offered (35); *catharsis* was sought (8) and offered (34); and patients' desire for *therapist involvement* (10) was partially matched by the therapists' aim to *enhance the relationship* (36). Various elements of the patients' desire for *emotional relief and control* (11) were corresponded to by therapists' goals of providing *catharsis* (34) and *control versus support* (37). Patients' wishes to receive *advice* (12) were not directly matched by any therapist intention, but might to some extent be indirectly

TABLE 8. SELF-REPORTS OF THERAPIST AIMS IN THERAPY SESSIONS

			Factor Structure					
	I was working toward:	% Endorsement	34	35	36	37	38	h²
III-3.	Helping my patient talk about her (his) feelings and concerns.	86[a]	72[b]					62
III-4.	Helping my patient get relief from tensions or unhappy feelings.	50	64					46
III-8.	Moving my patient closer to experiencing emergent feelings.	70	61					53
III-5.	Helping my patient understand the reasons behind her (his) reactions.	78		77				63
III-12.	Helping my patient realistically evaluate reactions and feelings.	86		77				65
III-1.	Helping my patient feel accepted in our relationship.	64			76			62
III-10.	Establishing a genuine person-to-person relationship with my patient.	70			73			61
III-2.	Getting a better understanding of my patient, of what was really going on.	85			68			57
III-13.	Sharing empathically in what my patient was experiencing.	75			54			39
III-11.	Helping my patient get better self control over feelings and impulses.	26				74		73
III-6.	Supporting my patient's self-esteem and confidence.	77			42	−61		70
III-7.	Encouraging attempts to change and try new ways of behaving.	61					84	76
III-9.	Helping my patient learn new ways for dealing with self and others.	61		42			65	63
III-14.	Getting my patient to take a more active role and responsibility for progress in therapy.	54				43	49	52
	Percent of total variance		10.8	12.4	16.0	8.8	12.2	60.2

[a]Endorsement frequencies represent a combination of alternatives "some" and "a lot."
[b]Decimals omitted. Underlined loadings indicate items used for factor scoring. Unless the highest for an item, only loadings .35 or above are shown.

TABLE 9. SELF-REPORTS OF THERAPIST BEHAVIOR IN THERAPY SESSIONS

During this session, how much:	% Endorsement		Factor Structure			
	Some	Much[a]	39	40	41	h²
III-22. Were you attentive to what your patient was trying to get across?	5	94	84[b]			71
III-27. Were you warm and friendly towards your patient?	31	67	80			71
III-25. Did you take initiative in defining the issues that were talked about?	43	26		84		72
III-21. Did you talk?	68	27		81		69
III-28. Did you express feeling?	59	29	40	49		41
III-24. Were you critical or disapproving towards your patient?	34	2			65	54
III-26. Did you try to change your patient's point of view or way of doing things?	40	25	38		59	55
III-23. Did you tend to agree with or accept your patient's ideas or suggestions?	61	27			−76	60
Percent of total variance			21.6	22.3	17.7	61.7

[a] Endorsement frequencies represent a combination of alternatives "pretty much" and "very much."

[b] Decimals omitted. Underlined loadings indicate items used for factor scoring. Unless the highest for an item, only loadings .35 or above are shown.

satisfied through the therapists' desire to *promote behavioral change* (38).

Behavior. The therapists' modes of relating to patients were assessed by an application of essentially the same items that were used to survey therapists' perceptions of their patients' behavior. The empirical structure and saliences of these are shown in Table 9. Clearly the dominant mode of relating which therapists saw in themselves was (39) *warmth*, as defined by friendly attention. Therapists regarded themselves as doing "much" (40) *structuring* in only about one-fourth of the sessions studied, although they confessed to "some" talking and expression of feeling in about two-thirds of the sessions. Another therapist mode of relating that is mainly in the background of self-awareness was acting in a (41) *domineering versus accepting* manner toward patients.

Feelings. Although patients on occasion express some doubt about it, therapists very clearly recognize that they, too, have feelings in the therapy session. What these feelings tend to be is revealed in Table 10, where the analysis of a 27-item section of the Therapy Session Report is presented. Therapists most often and most easily felt "interested" and "involved"—(45) *detached versus interested*—and (43) *alert (versus tired)*. One may take these as signs of effective personal commitment to enacting the therapist role. Another very frequently reported affective pattern was (42) *expansive confidence*—i.e., therapist feeling confident, optimistic, cheerful, relaxed, playful, effective, and pleased. Less constantly, but still in about a half to three-fourths of the sessions, therapists reported feeling (44) *intimate* (sympathetic, close, and affectionate), while they reported feeling (46) *inadequate (un-*

certain) on about a quarter of the occasions observed. Therapists felt (47) *demanding*, (49) *ill*, and (48) *disturbing sexual arousal* (sexually stimulated, annoyed, and attracted) quite rarely by their own report, generally in about 10% of the sessions observed. This profile of therapist affective states gives us a glimpse of the human person "behind" the professional role—generally involved to the point that little distance or discrepancy is felt between person and role: the therapist was often quite warmly and personally responsive to the patient, sometimes frustrated and distressed, and, infrequently, struggling with inappropriate or interfering feelings.

Session Development and Evaluation. Another aspect of the therapist's experience of the psychotherapy session is his perception of it as an episodic social act unfolding through time. This act may be viewed as progressively composed by the participants through sequential steps or stages. G. H. Mead (1954) defined "stages in the act" as impulse, perception, manipulation, and consummation. Regarding the individual session, the stage of "impulse" entails the eagerness or reluctance of each participant to encounter the other. The "perceptions" of each are mainly focused on the patient and his problems, as these become manifest during the session. The patient's "manipulative" task is to report honestly and fully on his experience to the therapist, and the therapist's "manipulative" task involves his informed and helpful intervention in the patient's problems. Ideally, "consummation" of the psychotherapeutic session occurs in progress toward resolving the problems for which the patient is in treatment. How far that ideal is realized depends on the prior stages in the act: the intensity and direction of the participants' motiva-

TABLE 10. SELF-REPORTS OF THERAPIST FEELINGS IN THERAPY SESSIONS

During this session, I felt:	% Endorsement	Factor Structure 42	43	44	45	46	47	48	49	h²
III-44. Confident	84ᵃ	79ᵇ								71
III-48. Optimistic	73	67				−42				71
III-34. Cheerful	46	65								62
III-45. Relaxed	91	62								66
III-37. Playful	14	55								54
III-40. Effective	76	55								66
III-29. Pleased	69	53								54
III-51. Alert	94		53		−35					56
III-53. Tired	55		−81							70
III-49. Distracted	22		−50					47		61
III-33. Sympathetic	78			75						67
III-52. Close	62			62						64
III-50. Affectionate	48	41		56						65
III-42. Detached	24				52	38				47
III-46. Interested	97				−81					73
III-36. Involved	87				−76					68
III-30. Thoughtful	86				−49	35	−35			66
III-41. Perplexed	28					83				72
III-47. Unsure	24					81				66
III-35. Frustrated	24					61				71
III-39. Apprehensive	13					57				42
III-38. Demanding	28						77			64
III-32. Bored	11				39		39			41
III-54. Sexually stimulated	10							73		55
III-31. Annoyed	14							63		74
III-43. Attracted	52	40						46		58
III-55. Headachey or ill	8								69	54
Percent of total variance		12.6	6.2	6.8	9.2	10.0	6.0	6.3	5.1	62.2

ᵃEndorsement frequencies represent a combination of alternatives "some" and "a lot."

ᵇDecimals omitted. Underlined loadings indicate items used for factor scoring. Unless the highest for an item, only loadings .35 or above are shown.

tions; the sensitivity and accuracy of their respective perceptions; and the effectiveness of their interactive performances. Satisfying progress will cause the session to be spontaneously evaluated in positive terms; lack of progress, or deterioration, will result in a spontaneous negative evaluation. One would expect this general aspect of therapeutic experience to be particularly salient for the therapist, since it is largely his job to monitor explicitly his own and his patients' conduct of their sessions.

Ten questions in the Therapy Session Report surveyed the facet of session development and evaluation. The frequencies of response to these are shown in Table 11, and their structure in the therapist's experience is shown in Table 12. One dimension of session development that was quite salient for therapists focused primarily on their own perceptiveness toward the patient: they tended in most sessions to view themselves as (53) *empathically understanding*, and only rarely to feel any considerable lapse of rapport and comprehension. They were, on the other hand, much more modest in viewing themselves as (50) *therapeutically effective*, a dimension combining evaluations of "consummation" with an estimate of their own "manipulative" efficacy

(i.e., helpfulness). Table 11 indicates that 58% of the sessions studied were rated by therapists as "fair" or "pretty good" (25% as "very good"), and in 68% of the sessions therapists reported that they had been "somewhat" or "pretty" helpful. However, they felt that their own states of mind or personal reactions interfered with their therapeutic efforts "moderately" or "considerably" in only 10% of the sessions—suggesting that the difficulty of translating empathic understanding into effectively helpful interventions was viewed as being inherent to the task rather than a result of their own failings.

Two other dimensions of session development revealed patterns of interrelation between the therapist's view of his own and his patient's participation. One involved the therapist's sense of being (51) *open with a motivated patient*—i.e., his tendency to disclose more of his spontaneous impressions and reactions to patients whom he saw as eager for therapeutic contact. Therapists were, on average, only "slightly" to "moderately" self-disclosing, even though they viewed their patients as "moderately" to "very strongly" motivated.

The remaining dimension of session development linked the therapist's evaluation of his

TABLE 11. THERAPISTS' PERCEPTIONS AND EVALUATIONS OF SESSION DEVELOPMENT—ENDORSEMENT FREQUENCIES

Therapist TSR items	Percent Endorsement
II-51. How motivated for coming to therapy was your patient this session?	
1. Very strongly motivated.	11
2. Strongly motivated.	49
3. Moderately motivated.	29
4. Just kept her appointment.	10
5. Had to make herself keep the appointment.	1
II-52. How much progress did your patient seem to make in this session?	
1. A great deal of progress.	1
2. Considerable progress.	12
3. Moderate progress.	28
4. Some progress.	47
5. Didn't get anywhere this session	12
6. Seems to have gotten worse.	1
II-53. How well does your patient seem to be getting along at this time?	
1. Very well; seems in really good condition.	6
2. Quite well; no important complaints.	19
3. Fairly well; has ups and downs.	58
4. So-so; manages to keep going with some effort.	12
5. Fairly poorly; having a rough time.	4
6. Quite poorly; seems in really bad condition.	1
III-15. How much were you looking forward to seeing your patient this session?	
1. I definitely anticipated a meaningful or pleasant session.	6
2. I had some pleasant anticipation.	49
3. I had no particular anticipations but found myself pleased to see my patient when the time came.	22
4. I felt neutral about seeing my patient this session.	14
5. I anticipated a trying or somewhat unpleasant session.	9
III-16. To what extent did your own state of mind or personal reactions tend to interfere with your therapeutic efforts during this session?	
1. Considerably.	2
2. Moderately.	8
3. Somewhat.	19
4. Slightly.	38
5. Not at all.	33

Therapist TSR items	Percent Endorsement
III-17. To what extent did you reveal your spontaneous impressions or reactions to your patient this session?	
1. Considerably.	12
2. Moderately.	26
3. Somewhat.	32
4. Slightly.	24
5. Not at all.	6
III-18. To what extent were you in rapport with your patient's feelings?	
1. Completely	4
2. Almost completely.	21
3. A great deal.	37
4. A fair amount.	24
5. Some.	12
6. Little.	2
III-19. How much do you feel you understood of what your patient said and did?	
1. Everything.	4
2. Almost all.	35
3. A great deal.	31
4. A fair amount.	22
5. Some.	6
6. Little.	2
III-20. How helpful do you feel that you were to your patient this session?	
1. Completely helpful.	0
2. Very helpful.	12
3. Pretty helpful.	37
4. Somewhat helpful.	31
5. Slightly helpful.	17
6. Not at all helpful.	4
I-1. How do you feel about the session which you have just completed? This session was:	
1. Perfect.	2
2. Excellent.	8
3. Very good.	25
4. Pretty good.	34
5. Fair.	24
6. Pretty poor.	8
7. Very poor.	1

TABLE 12. THERAPISTS' PERCEPTIONS AND EVALUATIONS OF SESSION DEVELOPMENT—FACTOR STRUCTURE

Items		50	51	52	53	h²
I-1.	How do you feel about the session which you have just completed?	71[a]			36	73
III-20.	How helpful do you feel that you were to your patient this session?	64			36	70
II-52.	How much progress did your patient seem to make in this session?	63		35		64
III-16.	To what extent did your own state of mind or personal reactions tend to interfere with your therapeutic efforts during this session?	−77				70
III-17.	To what extent did you reveal your spontaneous impressions or reactions to your patient this session?		86		35	87
II-51.	How motivated for coming to therapy was your patient this session?	47	68			76
II-53.	How well does your patient seem to be getting along at this time?			83		79
III-15.	How much were you looking forward to seeing your patient this session?			72		63
III-18.	To what extent were you in rapport with your patient's feelings?				83	81
III-19.	How much do you feel you understood of what your patient said and did?				75	70
	Percent of total variance	24.2	14.5	16.1	18.6	73.3

[a]Decimals omitted. Underlined loadings indicate items used for factor scoring. Unless the highest for an item, only loadings .35 or above are shown.

patient's psychological functioning with his own motivation for meeting, in a pattern called (52) *looking forward to a session with a patient who is doing well versus dreading a session with a patient who is doing poorly*. (This may be simply another demonstration of the ubiquity of the pleasure principle in human affairs.) In general, therapists viewed their patients as getting along "fairly well," and felt "some pleasant anticipation" of their sessions.

Salient Features of the Therapist's Experience

A summary impression of the several facets of therapist's experience may be formed by noting the most salient items within each. The salient features will be taken to be those that were relatively often *intensely present* in the therapists' reports—i.e., rated "a lot" or "very much" in at least 25% of the sessions studied. These salient items represent the most striking characteristics of psychotherapy, as perceived by the present group of therapists.

Therapists heard their patients talk "a lot" about relations with *the opposite sex* in a third of the sessions studied, and "a lot" about relations with *others of the same sex* nearly as often (28% of the sessions). In terms of salience, therefore, current interpersonal relations appear as the most striking focus of patients' "dialogue." No particular "motive" was especially striking, although patients were perceived as "strongly" or "very strongly" *motivated for sessions* 60% of the time (Table 11, item 51). Two areas of "concern" were salient, and help to understand the focus on current relationships in dialogue. Intense concern with *personal identity and aspirations* was reported 36% of the time, and with *being lonely or isolated* 29% of the time. These concerns point to adaptational problems in satisfying, and in balancing, the frequently opposite needs for autonomy and affiliation.

The most salient aspect of patients' "behavior" was, naturally enough, their verbal output. Therapists viewed them as *talking* "very much" 26% of the time. Therapists also saw their patients as "feeling" intensely *serious* in 30% of the sessions (twice as often as the next most salient feeling). In terms of "self-adaptation," patients were perceived as "very much" having *a sense of control* over their feelings and behavior 26% of the time. One cannot help wondering if patients would agree with this impression! In the same vein, therapists viewed their patients as getting along "quite well" or "very well" in 25% of the sessions studied (Table 11, item 53).

The emphatic conative orientation of the therapist's participation is indicated by the fact that fully half of the 14 "aims" were experienced as salient. Most dramatically striking was the therapist's intense striving to *help the patient talk about her feelings and concerns* (48% of the sessions) and, for his own part, to *get a better understanding of the patient* (41% of the sessions). These may be characterized as process goals, aimed at facilitating the therapeutic interaction rather than at changing the patient. Other salient process goals were those of *establishing a genuine person-to-person relationship with the patient* (34% of the time) and *helping the patient to feel accepted* (25% of the time). Salient goals that were more directly aimed at making some positive change in the patient were: *helping the patient understand the reasons for emotional reactions* (32% of the time); *helping the patient realistically evaluate reactions and feelings* (26% of the time); and *supporting the patient's self-esteem and confidence* (25% of the time).

Complementing all this effort on the therapist's part was one salient mode of interpersonal "behavior" and three salient "feeling" states. Therapists were "very much" *attentive to what the patient was trying to get across* in 38% of the sessions studied, and felt very *interested* (47% of the time), *alert* (34% of the time), and *thoughtful* (31% of the time). In other words, therapists saliently experienced themselves as genuinely involved in their work. Reference to Table 11 supports this view, as therapists there may be seen to have positively anticipated meeting their patients 55% of the time (item 15), felt "completely" or "almost completely" in rapport with their patients in 25% of the sessions (item 18), and sensed that they had understood "everything" or "almost all" the patient had said and done 39% of the time (item 20). Nor was the therapist's involvement solely attentive and receptive: 38% of the time therapists revealed their own spontaneous impressions and reactions to a "moderate" or "considerable" degree (item 17).

The overall picture that emerges in reviewing the statistically most salient aspects of therapist experience is one of two people hard at work in an effort to understand and resolve interpersonal problems. Obviously (as Tables 2 through 11 show) this effort is not always experienced as a successful or as a comfortable one by the participants. The factor analyses, to which we now turn, will document the variety of forms encompassed within the average picture of therapist experience that has been presented.

DIMENSIONS OF THERAPIST EXPERIENCE

The various facets of therapist experience that we have surveyed separately do not, of course, exist in isolation from each other. Together they define the complex multifaceted reality of the therapy session, as it is experienced by the psychotherapist. Consequently, our methodology demands a resynthesis for the sake of verisimilitude of that which has been analytically fragmented for the sake of descriptive and conceptual clarity. Having discerned the empirical structure of each facet, we turn next to a study of the interrelations among different facets. This analysis entailed use of scores for each facet of therapeutic experience, based on the empirically defined dimensions just reviewed, in a single intercorrelation matrix which was then factor-analyzed according to the procedures described above. Three separate factor analyses were performed: one, focusing on the structure of individual differences in therapist experience within the session; a second, analyzing dimensions of temporal variation across sessions; and a third, analyzing dimensions of individual differences among therapists summing over blocks of sessions. The results of the first analysis will be presented in detail below, and the results of the latter two will then be briefly summarized and compared with the first.

The Session as a Unit

Eleven dimensions of therapist experience *within* the therapeutic session emerged from the first factor analysis. Upon inspection, these dimensions were grouped into those which focused primarily upon patterns of patient participation, of therapist participation, or of mutual involvement in the session.

Patterns of patient participation. The first and largest of the dimensions that focused on the patient centered on the degree of distress the therapist perceived in the patient during the session. The facets emphasized were patient feelings and problematic concerns, as shown in Table 13. High scores on this dimension occurred when therapists viewed their patients as feeling (25) anxious, (27) confused, (24) depressed and (23) inhibited, and as concerned about (18) conscience, (17) sexuality, and (15) identity conflicts. Completing the picture were the thera-

TABLE 13. SESSION FACTOR I. DISTRESSED, ANXIOUSLY DEPRESSED PATIENT

Therapist views patient as:	
(25) Feeling *anxious*	.80[a]
(11) wanting *emotional relief and control*	.75
(27) feeling *confused*	.69
(18) concerned about *conscience*	.67
(24) feeling *depressed*	.64
(33) being *self-critically aroused*	.62
(23) feeling *inhibited*	.51
(17) concerned about *sexuality*	.48
(15) concerned about *identity conflict (fears and anger)*	.45
(3) talking about *fantasy*	(.39)

[a]Only loadings .35 or higher are shown. Entries in parentheses are not salient.

pists' perceptions that their patients were (33) self-critically aroused, wanted (11) emotional relief and control, and talked about unrealistic experience or (3) fantasy. Session Factor I was called *Distressed, Anxiously Depressed Patient.*

Session Factor II, the therapist's view of an *Open, Actively Expressive Patient,* delineates a perception of effective role performance on the patient's part. The patient was seen as (29) structuring the interaction in a way that was genuinely (32) open (i.e., "focusing" and expressive), and the therapist in a complementary manner refrained from intruding his own (40) structuring of the session (see Table 14).

TABLE 14. SESSION FACTOR II. OPEN, ACTIVELY EXPRESSIVE PATIENT

Therapist views patient as:	
(29) relating in a *structuring* manner	.77[a]
(32) being *open (focusing and expressive)*	.76
(8) wanting *catharsis*	.61
(23) *not* feeling *inhibited*	(.40)
Therapist views self as:	
(40) *not* relating in a *structuring* manner	.62
(52) *looking forward to session with a patient who is doing well*	(.35)

[a]Only loadings .35 or higher are shown. Entries in parentheses are not salient.

Session Factor III also reflects a quality of the patient's role performance, but in this case in a negative light (see Table 15). The therapist perceived the patient as wanting to (13) avoid therapeutic involvement, as wanting neither (9) insight nor (12) advice, and as relating in a (30) domineering manner. This dimension, called *Obstructive Resistive Patient,* seems to reflect cooperativeness or uncooperativeness of the patient, in contrast to ability to perform effectively in the patient role.

The four remaining patterns of patient participation focus mainly on the content of what was

TABLE 15. SESSION FACTOR III. OBSTRUCTIVE, RESISTIVE
PATIENT

Therapist views patient as:	
(13) wanting to *avoid therapeutic involvement*	.79[a]
(9) *not* wanting *insight*	.56
(30) relating in a *domineering* manner	.48
(12) *not* wanting *advice*	.46
(23) feeling *inhibited*	(.36)
Therapist views self as:	
(36) aiming to *enhance relationship*	.33[b]

[a]Only loadings .35 or higher are shown. Entries in parentheses are not salient.
[b]Salient on this factor.

discussed by the patient during therapy. In the largest of these, Session Factor IV, the therapist viewed his patient as an *Autonomous, Socially Effective Patient* (see Table 16). The patient was

TABLE 16. SESSION FACTOR IV. AUTONOMOUS, SOCIALLY
EFFECTIVE PATIENT

Therapist views patient as:	
(4) talking about *work and peers*	.69[a]
(16) concerned about *self-assertion*	.62
(31) being *self-possessed*	.60
(19) feeling *relieved*	.51
(20) feeling *confident*	.45
(9) wanting *insight*	(.37)
(15) concerned about *identity conflict (fears and anger)*	(.36)
Therapist views self as:	
(26) *not* feeling *ill*	.43
(52) *looking forward to session with a patient who is doing well*	(.40)
(42) feeling *expansive confidence*	(.37)
(38) aiming to *promote behavioral change*	(.36)

[a]Only loadings .35 or higher are shown. Entries in parentheses are not salient.

viewed as talking about issues of (16) self-assertion in (4) work and peer relations, in a (31) self-possessed manner accompanied by feelings of (20) confidence and (19) relief. Session Factor V was called *Patient Discussing Prospects in Marital and Domestic Involvements* (see Table 17), and Session Factor VI was called *Patient Focusing on Therapist* (see Table 18). These titles are descriptive and seem to require no amplification. Session Factor VII was interpreted as a bipolar dimension, one "end" of which primar-

TABLE 17. SESSION FACTOR V. PATIENT DISCUSSING
PROSPECTS IN MARITAL AND DOMESTIC INVOLVEMENTS

Therapist views patient as:	
(7) talking about *domestic relationships*	.73[a]
(2) talking about *domestic affairs (household and finances)*	.62
(6) talking about *personal fate*	.59

[a]Only loadings .35 or higher are shown. Entries in parentheses are not salient.

TABLE 18. SESSION FACTOR VI. PATIENT FOCUSING
ON THERAPIST

Therapist views patient as:	
(3) talking about *fantasy*	.63[a]
(5) talking about *therapy and therapist*	.53
(10) wanting *therapist involvement*	.50

[a]Only loadings .35 or higher are shown. Entries in parentheses are not salient.

ily reflected patient participation and the other therapist participation. Session Factor VII+ was called *Patient Exploring Family Background* (see Table 19): talking about (1) parental family (past and present); relating in an (28) accepting manner; (12) not wanting advice from the therapist; and the therapist (38) not seeking to promote any particular change in the patient's behavior.

TABLE 19. SESSION FACTOR VII+. PATIENT EXPLORING
FAMILY BACKGROUND

Therapist views patient as:	
(1) talking about *parental family (past and present)*	.63[a]
(28) relating in an *accepting* manner	(.48)
(12) *not* wanting *advice*	(.41)
Therapist views self as:	
(38) *not* aiming to *promote behavioral change*	.55

SESSION FACTOR VII−. THERAPIST PROMOTING BEHAVIORAL CHANGE	
Therapist views patient as:	
(1) *not* talking about *parental family (past and present)*	.63
(28) *not* relating in an *accepting* manner	(.48)
(12) wanting *advice*	(.41)
Therapist views self as:	
(38) aiming to *promote behavioral change*	.55

[a]Only loadings .35 or higher are shown. Entries in parentheses are not salient.

Patterns of therapist participation. In addition to the pattern of therapist participation reflected in Session Factor VII−, two other dimensions emphasized aspects of the therapist's self-experience in treatment. The largest of these was Session Factor VIII, called *Warmly Involved, Empathic, Effective Therapist.* Here (see Table 20) therapists saw themselves as (53) empathically understanding and (50) therapeutically effective (the "perception" and "manipulation-consummation" stages of session development). This effectiveness in role performance was supplemented on the personal side by a very positive affective involvement: therapists reported feeling (45) involved, (42) expansively confident, (43) alert, and (44) intimate, and as relating with (39) warmth. Patients were understandably seen as responding in an (28) accepting manner.

The obverse of this pattern, represented by low

TABLE 20. SESSION FACTOR VIII. WARMLY INVOLVED, EMPATHIC, EFFECTIVE THERAPIST

Therapist views patient as:	
(28) relating in an *accepting* manner	.50[a]
Therapist views self as:	
(50) *therapeutically effective*	.78
(53) *empathically understanding*	.77
(45) feeling *involved* (*vs. detached*)	.70
(39) relating with *warmth*	.70
(42) feeling *expansive confidence*	.67
(43) feeling *alert* (*vs. tired*)	.66
(46) *not* feeling *inadequate* (*uncertain*)	.57
(44) feeling *intimate*	(.56)
(52) *looking forward to session with a patient who is doing well*	(.38)
(51) being *open with a motivated patient*	.36
(34) aiming to provide *catharsis*	.31[b]

[a]Only loadings .35 or higher are shown. Entries in parentheses are not salient.
[b]Salient on this factor.

scores on Session Factor VIII, is also worth considering. Here the therapist experienced himself as unempathic and ineffective, feeling primarily (45) detached, (43) tired, and (46) inadequate and uncertain, with a marked absence of any of the close and positive feelings noted above. In other words, experiences of failure and of alienation tended to be associated for therapists. Whether one causes the other, or whether both are the result of something else, remains an intriguing question for further study.

In Session Factor IX the therapist experienced himself in an uncharacteristically (41) domineering attitude, feeling (47) demanding, and attempting to (40) structure the interaction to provide (37) control and (35) insight for a patient who was perceived to be equally (30) domineering in manner (see Table 21). This dimension (which, but for the nonsalient loading of (30), might be classed as a pattern of mutual involvement) was called *Forceful, Confronting Therapist*: a head-on collision between the participants in which conative and affective elements seemed to predominate over any particular contents that might have occasioned the conflict.

TABLE 21. SESSION FACTOR IX. FORCEFUL, CONFRONTING THERAPIST

Therapist views patient as:	
(30) relating in a *domineering* manner	(.45)[a]
Therapist views self as:	
(41) relating in a *domineering* (*vs. accepting*) manner	.74
(47) feeling *demanding*	.73
(37) aiming to provide *control* (*vs. support*)	.66
(35) aiming to provide *insight*	.54
(40) relating in a *structuring* manner	(.41)

[a]Only loadings .35 or higher are shown. Entries in parentheses are not salient.

Finally, among therapist-centered patterns of the therapists' experience, there is Session Factor VII—, called *Therapist Promoting Behavioral Change* (see Table 19, above). This reflects the extent to which the therapist actively attempted to suggest and encourage new ways of dealing with self or with others to the patient, and seems to be at least partially responsive to the therapist's perception of his patient's desire to receive (12) advice. The bipolarity of Session Factor VII suggests that this mode of therapist involvement was inhibited by the patient's exploration of familial relations, and reciprocally that "pushing" the patient in this way tended to inhibit that more reflective, self-exploratory activity in the patient.

Patterns of mutual involvement. Two dimensions of therapist experience appear to focus principally on some state of relation between patient and therapist in the particular session (a third of this sort has already been mentioned in Session Factor IX). One pattern of mutual involvement perceived by therapists was positive in tone but disturbing in impact; it was called *Erotic Transference-Countertransference*. Table 22 shows the predominance of emotional elements in this pattern: patient seen as feeling (21) erotized affection and (20) confident, while seeking greater (10) therapist involvement; and therapist responding by feeling (44) intimacy and (48) disturbing sexual arousal. Concurrent reports from patients make it clear that this erotization of the therapeutic relationship is not unilaterally perceived by therapists (see Orlinsky & Howard, 1975, especially Chapters 7 and 11).

TABLE 22. SESSION FACTOR X. EROTIC TRANSFERENCE-COUNTERTRANSFERENCE

Therapist views patient as:	
(21) feeling *erotized affection*	.82[a]
(20) feeling *confident*	(.41)
(10) wanting *therapist involvement*	(.38)
Therapist views self as:	
(48) feeling *disturbing sexual arousal*	.59
(44) feeling *intimate*	.58

[a]Only loadings .35 or higher are shown. Entries in parentheses are not salient.

In other words, it is not purely (or even mainly) a projection of the therapist's part. (It was also, one may recall, a relatively rare occurrence.)

The second pattern of mutual involvement perceived by therapists was more unambiguously unpleasant. Table 23 indicates the therapist's view of the patient as feeling (22) angry in relation to concerns about (14) isolation and intimacy. The therapist reported himself as tending

TABLE 23. SESSION FACTOR XI. DREADING A SESSION
WITH A PATIENT SEEN AS ANGRILY CONCERNED
ABOUT ISOLATION AND INTIMACY

Therapist views patient as:	
(22) feeling *angry*	.67[a]
(14) concerned about *isolation and intimacy*	.67
Therapist views self as:	
(52) *dreading session with a patient who is doing poorly*	.44
(30) relating in a *domineering* manner	(.44)

[a]Only loadings .35 or higher are shown. Entries in parentheses are not salient.

to (52) dread having such sessions with a patient he saw as burdened with problems, and as tending (perhaps defensively) to relate in a (30) domineering manner. Session Factor XI was interpreted as the therapists' *Dreading a Session with a Patient Seen as Angrily Concerned About Isolation and Intimacy.*

Sequence and Person Factors

The dimensions of therapist experience just reported characterize individual differences among therapists focused within the single therapeutic session. Two other analyses of the data were also prepared. In one of these, the series of sessions reported by each of the therapists were linked in chain-wise fashion to preserve sequential variations but to effectively eliminate individual differences. The results of this factor analysis will be called "*sequence factors*," indicating the fact that the structure refers to *covariation among* therapist *experiences over time.* The second alternative factor analysis emphasized the variation among therapists over larger blocks of sessions, effectively suppressing sequential effects while maximizing dimensions of individual difference. This was achieved (as noted in the Method section above) by computing a single score for each therapist-case on each of the 53 facet dimensions, averaging across all of the sessions reported by that therapist for that patient. The results of this analysis will be called "*person factors*," indicating the fact that the characteristics entailed in each particular dimension were, on average, *more markedly apparent in some therapists than in others.*

The results of these two additional factor analyses are summarized and compared with the analysis of "*session factors*" in Table 24. Ten sequence factors and nine person factors were retained for interpretation according to the criteria noted in the Method section. The main fact that we wish to emphasize here is that eight of the 11 session factors are closely reflected in

both of the alternative analyses (while two more are reflected in one alternative analysis). This seems to us an impressive stability despite differences in analytic procedures that could be likened to three alternative ways of "slicing through" the data. It suggests to us that these eight patterns discerned in the data are "really there," and tend to characterize both some *periods* in therapy more than others and some *therapists* more than others.

Four of the session factors that focus primarily on the patient's participation were present in slightly varying guises in all three analyses: the extent of emotional distress, perceived largely in terms of anxiety and depression; the degree of effective role performance and of resistiveness to influence; and the amount of focusing on marital and domestic involvements. Two of the other three "content" areas distinguished in session factors, (patient concern with social effectiveness and focusing on the therapist) were noted among sequence factors—suggesting that there were *periods* when these were prominent in all therapists' experiences. One "content" area that distinguished between sessions, but not between periods of therapy or between different therapists, was the patient's exploration of family background. By contrast, therapists as a group experienced their patients as being more angry and upset during some *periods* than during others (Sequence Factor VI); and some *therapists* more than others experienced their patients as motivated and insight-seeking versus resistive and defensive (Person Factor IV).

All three of the patterns of therapist participation that emerged in the session factors also emerged in some form in the sequence and the person factors: therapist personal involvement and effectiveness, open confrontation between therapist and patient, and active efforts to teach and encourage behavioral change in the patient. Interpretively, this congruence across analyses suggests that therapists experience *sessions* differentially along these dimensions, that they experience *periods* differentially along these dimensions, and that on the average *therapists* experience their cases differentially along these dimensions.

One of the two session factors classified as patterns of mutual involvement was also identified among sequence factors and person factors: erotic transference-countertransference. The other session factor (unpleasantly anticipated dealings with angry patients) did not differentiate among periods of therapy or among therapists; all therapists seem to have had their share of this at one

TABLE 24. DIMENSIONS OF THERAPIST EXPERIENCE FOUND IN THREE FACTOR ANALYSES OF THE SAMPLE DATA

Session Factors	Sequence Factors	Person Factors
I. Distressed, Anxiously Depressed Patient	I. Distressed, Anxiously Depressed Patient	I. Distressed, Anxiously Depressed Patient
II. Open, Actively Expressive Patient	II+. Open, Actively Expressive Patient	II. Open, Actively Expressive Patient
III. Obstructive, Resistive Patient	II−. Evasive, Resistive Patient	IV−. Resistive, Defensive Patient
IV. Autonomous, Socially Effective Patient	III. Patient Concerned about Social Effectiveness and Autonomy	
V. Patient Discussing Prospects in Marital/Domestic Involvements	IV. Patient Discussing Prospects in Marital/Domestic Involvements	III. Patient Discussing Marital/Domestic Involvements
VI. Patient Focusing on Therapist	V. Patient Focusing on Therapist	
VII+. Patient Exploring Family Background		
	VI. Angry, Upset Patient	
		IV+. Motivated, Insight-Seeking Patient
VIII. Warmly Involved, Empathic, Effective Therapist	VII. Warmly Involved, Empathic, Effective Therapist	V. Warmly Involved, Empathic, Effective Therapist
IX. Forceful, Confronting Therapist	VIII. Forceful Confrontation with a Critical, Controlling Patient	VI. Forceful Confrontation with a Critical, Controlling Patient
VII−. Therapist Promoting Behavioral Change	IX. Supporting Behavioral Change with a Guidance-Seeking Patient	VII. Promoting Behavioral Change with a Discontented, Guidance-Seeking Patient
X. Erotic Transference-Countertransference	X. Erotic Transference-Countertransference	VIII. Erotic Transference-Countertransference
XI. Dreading Session with a Patient Seen as Angrily Concerned about Isolation and Intimacy		
		IX. Alert, Effective Involvement with a Catharsis-Seeking Patient (+) vs. Tired, Ineffective Detachment with an Involvement-Seeking Patient (−)

time or another. (Therapists' perceptions of their patients' feeling angry did saliently organize one Sequence Factor—VI. *Angry, Upset Patient*)— but the internal evidence seems too sparse to warrant treating these as equivalent forms.)

One bipolar dimension among person factors of therapist experience (i.e., a dimension of variation among therapists) did not have any clear parallels among session factors or sequence factors. Person Factor IX was a pattern of mutual involvement that was called *Alert, Effective Involvement with a Catharsis-Seeking Patient (+) versus Tired, Ineffective Detachment with an Involvement-Seeking Patient (−)*. The latter pole seems to identify therapists who chronically felt that they could not personally muster the resources to cope with a particular patient's needs. Any therapists who approach this extremity of experience ought probably to transfer that patient, for the benefit of all concerned.

Finally, it is interesting to note among person factors that the dimensions of therapist experience are nearly all patterns of mutual involvement, rather than focusing primarily on either the patient or the therapist. Among session factors and among sequence factors, the majority of dimensions seemed to adhere neatly to the typical subject/object organization of the experiential field. In a particular session, or at a particular time in therapy, therapists tended to see patients as doing A, B, C … and themselves (separately) as doing X, Y, Z …. However, in portraits of therapist experience developed by a kind of statistical "time exposure" in which perceptions of several successive sessions are allowed to cumulate, patterns of interrelation between patient and therapist participation received greater emphasis. Perhaps it is from these latter that the deeper lying psychodynamics of the therapeutic process will prove to be most accessible (see e.g., Orlinsky & Howard, 1975, especially Chapters 9 through 12 and 14).

TYPES OF SESSIONS EXPERIENCED BY THERAPISTS

The natural unit of the therapist's experience is the psychotherapeutic session. We have focused on the constituent elements of that experience, and on the multifaceted dimensions in terms of which sessions are differentiated from one another. At this point, we shall carry our analysis one step further, to focus on the therapy session as a whole. When the therapist leaves his office after a session with a patient, he carries with him a global impression of what the session has been like. To capture something of that global impression, we shall construct a typology of session experience based on the empirically derived dimensions that have been presented above.

The various session factors offer several choices for use in developing a typology of session experience. One desideratum in a typology, however, is simplicity, so long as that is consistent with the basic features of the material. For this reason, we have chosen to use what seem to us to be the two major dimensions characteristic of session experience—one predominantly focused on the patient's participation and the other on the therapist's participation. These are Session Factor I (*Distressed, Anxiously Depressed Patient*) and Session Factor VIII (*Warmly Involved, Empathic, Effective Therapist*), which will be referred to respectively as *Patient Distress* and *Therapist Effectiveness*. Statistically, these are the most substantial of the session factors; clinically, they seem the most generally relevant.

To construct a typology of sessions from these dimensions, we dichotomized the range of possible scores on each into a "low" and "high" range (not a median split of obtained scores) and then combined Patient Distress and Therapist Effectiveness as independent coordinates in a fourfold table (see Table 25). By this means, we obtained four session types: *Type A* was defined by low Patient Distress and high Therapist Effectiveness, which from the therapist's point of view we thought might be called "Smooth Sailing"; *Type B*, on the other hand, was defined by high Patient Distress as well as high Therapist Effectiveness, which might result in a successful session but which we thought might be experienced by the therapist as "Heavy Going"; *Type C* was the least fortunate kind of session a therapist might have, defined as it was by high Patient Distress and low Therapist Effectiveness (an experience that was called "Foundering," to continue the sailing metaphor); finally, *Type D* (called "Coasting") might provide some relief to the beleaguered therapist, since the low Therapist Effectiveness that defined it was accompanied by low Patient Distress.

A question naturally arises as to how frequently each type of session is experienced by therapists. To explore this in the sample that we

TABLE 25. TYPES OF SESSIONS EXPERIENCED BY THERAPISTS

PATIENT DISTRESS (Session Factor I—Distressed, Anxiously Depressed Patient)	THERAPIST EFFECTIVENESS (Session Factor VIII—Warmly Involved, Empathic, Effective Therapist)		
	Low (0–10)	High (11–20)	
Low (0–10)	Type D "Coasting" 17 (10.6%)	Type A "Smooth Sailing" 110 (68.8%)	127 (79.4%)
High (11–20)	Type C "Foundering" 6 (3.8%)	Type B "Heavy Going" 27 (16.9%)	33 (20.6%)
	23 (14.4%)	137 (85.6%)	160 (100.0%)

have, five sessions were randomly selected from each therapist-case reported and scores for Session Factors I and VIII were converted to a range of 0 to 20, such that 0 represented "none" of the quality, 10 indicated "some" of the quality, and scores approaching 20 implied "a lot" of the quality. (This partitioning of the range rendered the dimensions of Patient Distress and Therapist Effectiveness similar to many of the individual items on the Therapy Session Report.) With these scores, we could place each of the 160 sessions (32 therapist-cases, 5 sessions from each) in the appropriate quadrant of Table 25, where the cumulative frequencies are presented. For this sample, *Type A* ("Smooth Sailing") was far and away the most frequent kind of session reported by therapists; nearly 70% of the 160 sessions were of this type.[4] This might make psychotherapy sound like rather pleasant and undemanding work; however, it must be remembered that the proportions for each type are a function of the somewhat arbitrary placement of the cutoff between "low" and "high" on each marginal dimension. Also, it must be remembered that what seemed like moderate Patient Distress to the therapist might seem like rather intense distress to the patient. In a significant minority of sessions (approximately one in six) therapists perceived their patients to be in severe distress but also experienced themselves as meeting this challenge effectively. *Type B* ("Heavy Going") is the sort of session in which therapists really earn their money. Reassuringly, *Type C* ("Foundering") is the least frequently occurring type of therapist experience, found in fewer than 4% of the 160 sessions. Finally, in about one out of 10 sessions, therapists found themselves in the potentially vulnerable but fortunate situation of "Coasting" (*Type D*)—not experiencing themselves at their best, but not called upon either for too demanding a performance. A comparison of the marginal frequencies in Table 25 with those for each type suggests that there is no statistically significant association between Patient Distress and Therapist Effectiveness. That is, the level of the patient's emotional distress did not seem to affect that of the therapist's effectiveness (in his experience), and vice versa. Presumably these levels are determined in large measure by causes prior to, and outside of, the therapeutic session.

The typology of sessions as experienced by therapists has for us, as therapists, a familiar and meaningful ring to it. It is a gross typology, and it is easy to suggest other factors (e.g., the effectiveness of the patient's role performance) as significant refinements. The qualifications one might be tempted to add, however, are just those that were recognized in the session factors that were not used as a basis for the typology. Other types might be defined by using them, if the need arose; but as an approximation to the therapist's *global* experience of the therapy session, these four types seem sufficiently serviceable. One might, for example, use them selectively in studying the relation of process to outcome in therapy, hypothesizing that sessions of *Type B* ("Heavy Going"—in which the therapist responds effectively to intense patient distress) are critical for attaining positive outcomes, while sessions of *Type C* ("Foundering"—in which the therapist fails when he is most needed) are differentially productive of negative outcomes.

SUMMARY AND PROSPECT

We have argued that the experiences of the therapist, as well as those of the patient, are integral and relevant aspects of the psychotherapeutic process. We have developed a method by which the experience of therapy may be studied and, to illustrate its use, we presented a series of analyses that delineates the actual experiences of a group of psychotherapists at work.[5] In these analyses, we first examined various facets of therapists' experiences: the dialogue, motives, concerns, feelings, interpersonal behavior, self-adaptation, and coping of the patient; the aims, interpersonal behavior, feelings, and evaluations of the therapist. Then we explored the structure of therapist experience across facets, and found a number of clinically meaningful dimensions replicated in three factor-analytic procedures. Finally, we used two of these empirically determined dimensions to construct a global typology of sessions, and surveyed the therapists' reports to assess the relative frequency of each type.

All of this represents no more than the beginning of a line of inquiry that complements and enhances the power of other, more traditional methods of research on psychotherapy. The necessary next step is quite clear: to consolidate the ground that we have already covered by doing parallel studies of larger and more diverse samples. A stable, general delineation of therapist experience will require reports from a representative variety of therapists treating a variety of patients by varied methods in varied contexts. No one, of course, wants merely to repeat work that even they have done, let alone the work of others. A fruitful line of inquiry is one that will open out into new perspectives and branch sufficiently to accommodate the ramified interests of a research community. Given these needs, the following seem to us to be some promising "growing edges" for research on the therapist's experience.

Interrelations of therapist experience with patient experience. The therapist's experience is, we have argued, no less integral to the events of psychotherapy than the patient's experience, but by the same token is no more integral or important. The patient's experience deserves, and has received, study in its own right. The most exciting prospect, however, and one that is most logical in our analysis, is to study the interrelations of the patient's and the therapist's experiences over a series of common sessions. How do the experiences of the therapist articulate with those of the patient? Are there areas of significant congruence or discrepancy in their reports of the same sessions? What implications are there for understanding the dynamics of the therapeutic relationship and the nature of interpersonal process more generally? Explorations in this direction have already been reported in *Varieties of Psychotherapeutic Experience* (Orlinsky & Howard, 1975), where (a) the structural dimensions and types of *conjoint experience* in therapeutic dyads were determined through factor analysis (Chapters 11 and 12), and (b) the informational value of the therapist's experience as a predictive guide to the patient's concurrent experience was critically assessed (Chapter 13; also see Howard, Orlinsky, & Hill, 1969). The clinical value in developing the latter seems obvious, particularly as it may help the therapist use his experience to anticipate and capitalize on subsequent events in the treatment. The former provides a unique glimpse into the phenomenological interior of a social relationship and, in addition to a deeper understanding of therapeutic dynamics (e.g., the nature of impasses), offers a new model of empirical research that has broad applicability in social psychology.

Comparison of participants' experiences with reports of nonparticipant observers. Evidence of significant discrepancy between the reports of patient and therapist on the same sessions is already available (Orlinsky & Howard, 1975; Orlinsky, Howard, & Hill, 1975). Preliminary research by Mintz, Auerbach, Luborsky, and Johnson (1973), along with several parallel studies of therapist-offered conditions in the Rogerian framework (Bozarth & Grace, 1970; Caracena & Vicory, 1969; Carkhuff & Burstein, 1970; Fish, 1970), suggest that as much divergence may be expected between the accounts of external observers and participants as between the accounts of the participants themselves. These studies all focus on the events of psychotherapy, but it is hard to believe that the effect is peculiar to clinical interaction. If, indeed, it is established as a general condition, what will have become of the consensual standard of "objectivity"? How will one set about to establish what "really happened" in an interactive situation if the accounts of participants and witnesses reach only modest levels of agreement? A methodological Pandora's Box will have been broached whose contents might prove a considerable plague to behavioral science research as we have known it.

Determinants of participants' experiences. Whether or not participants' reports agree with one another, or with those of external observers, an effort to trace the determinants of their experiences seems intriguing and worthwhile. For example, how much of the therapist's experience in therapy is due to stable characteristics of his patients, how much to his own characteristics, how much to interactions between his own and his patient's traits, and how much to the contingencies of the therapeutic process and intercurrent life events? How, in other words, is the variance in a participant's experience to be partitioned? Howard, Orlinsky, and Perilstein (1976) have applied a statistical components-of-variance model to data on patient experience, with results that, for example, "the greatest impact of differences among therapists on patients' experiences is on the affectively satisfying or unsatisfying quality of the patient's relationship with the therapist." (A parallel study of therapist experience is being completed.) Knowledge of the specific factors that determine

specific kinds of experience should enable us to explain and predict their occurrence in treatment and, under favorable circumstances, to prescribe and produce specific therapeutic effects. One hardly need emphasize the importance of this direction for research and clinical practice. As an indication of what may be done, Howard, Orlinsky, and Hill (1970) studied the impact of patient-therapist pairing on patients' experienced satisfaction. More recently, a study of the influence of therapist gender on the experiences of women patients (Orlinsky & Howard, 1976) yielded the conclusion that "while for many patients the sex of the therapist made little difference," patients "who are single women [23 to 28 years old and never married] *and* depressive reactions will feel more support and satisfaction in treatment with a woman therapist." Initial explorations of the impact of other patient and therapist characteristics have also been reported in *Varieties of Psychotherapeutic Experience* (Orlinsky & Howard, 1975).

Differential effects of different types of experience. Perhaps the ultimate reason for studying therapeutic process is the determination of the effects of different kinds of process on treatment outcome. It is clearly not sufficient to compare the results of, for example, psychoanalytic therapy and behavioral therapy for groups of patients without knowing what actually happened—that is, what was experienced—in each case. Different modes of treatment tend to overlap in significant respects, and the "same" type of treatment offered by different therapists (or even by the same therapist to different patients) may be quite varied in form and content. Much greater specificity in the description of treatment process is needed before we can know precisely what factors cause what effects, as we have argued in detail elsewhere (Howard & Orlinsky, 1972). A hypothetical study relating type of session experience (e.g., "Heavy Going" versus "Foundering") to positive and negative outcomes has already been mentioned to illustrate the possibilities of research in this direction. We are, ourselves, currently involved in the assessment of outcomes and the collection of long-term follow-up data on more than 100 patients whose experiences in treatment have been studied. From these data, we may begin to discern the impact of experiences in the therapeutic relationship on personal functioning in other areas of life—"in sickness and in health, for better or for worse," and in whatever measure it exists.

As to the line of research and the data reported in this chapter, clearly no definite conclusions can as yet be drawn with any confidence. We may, however, sketch two summary impressions of what we have found. One impression is that therapists do not, in practice, seem to differentiate among patients as if they represented distinct diagnostic entities (according to patterns of emotional distress, behavior, or problematic concern). There was only one common factor that included all types of distress (Session Factor I)—depression, anxiety, inhibition, agitation, and so forth. Therapists seem to function instead in terms of the patient's level of distress, as well as effectiveness and cooperativeness in role performance. Perceptions of patients are cast more in terms of pragmatic and interactive constructs than in terms of the abstract and impersonal categories familiar from textbooks and formal staff meetings.

A second impression is that the therapist does not "do" therapy as if it were a skilled but detached application of impersonal techniques. On the contrary, therapists tend to feel genuinely and warmly involved precisely when they experience themselves as functioning most effectively (Session Factor VIII). Some forms of involvement, of course, are undoubtedly quite uncomfortable and perhaps counterproductive as well (e.g., erotic transference-countertransference). But the "textbook" image of the therapist as an instrumentally oriented, technical agent whose personal responsiveness is excluded from therapy seems remote from the way therapists actually experience psychotherapy. One desirable result of research on therapists' actual experiences would be the emergence of more realistic conceptions and hypotheses about the therapist's contribution to psychotherapy.

REFERENCES

BOZARTH, J. D., & GRACE, D. P. Objective ratings and client perceptions of therapeutic conditions with university counseling center clients. *Journal of Clinical Psychology*, 1970, **26**, 117–118.

CARACENA, P. F., & VICORY, J. R. Correlates of phenomenological and judged empathy. *Journal of Counseling Psychology*, 1969, **16**, 510–515.

CARKHUFF, R. R., & BURSTEIN, J. W. Objective, therapist and client ratings of therapist-offered facilitative conditions of moderate to low functioning therapists. *Journal of Clinical Psychology*, 1970, **26**, 394–395.

FISH, J. M. Empathy and the reported emotional experiences of beginning psychotherapists. *Journal of Consulting and Clinical Psychology*, 1970, **35**, 64–69.

FISHER, R. A. *Statistical methods for research workers*. New York: Haffner, 1954.

HENRY, W. E., SIMS, J. H., & SPRAY, S. L. *The fifth profession*. San Francisco: Jossey-Bass, 1971.

HILL, J. A., HOWARD, K. I., & ORLINSKY, D. E. The therapist's experience of psychotherapy: Some dimensions and determinants. *Multivariate Behavioral Research*, 1970, **5**, 435–451.

HOWARD, K. I., & GORDON, R. A. An empirical note on the "number of factors" problem in factor analysis. *Psychological Reports*, 1963, **12**, 247–250.

HOWARD, K. I., & ORLINSKY, D. E. Psychotherapeutic processes. *Annual Review of Psychology*, 1972, **23**, 615–668.

HOWARD, K. I., ORLINSKY, D. E., & HILL, J. A. The therapist's feelings in the therapeutic process. *Journal of Clinical Psychology*, 1969, **25**, 83–93.

HOWARD, K. I., ORLINSKY, D. E., & HILL, J. A. Patient satisfactions as a function of patient-therapist pairing. *Psychotherapy: Theory, Research, and Practice*, 1970, **7**, 130–134.

HOWARD, K. I., ORLINSKY, D. E., & PERILSTEIN, J. The contribution of therapists to patients' experiences in psychotherapy: A components of variance model for analyzing process data. *Journal of Consulting and Clinical Psychology*, 1976, **44**, 520–526.

LAING, R. D., PHILLIPSON, H., & LEE, A. R. *Interpersonal perception*. New York: Harper & Row, 1966.

MEAD, G. H. Stages in the act: Preliminary statement. In A. STRAUSS (Ed.), *The social psychology of George Herbert Mead*. Chicago: Phoenix Books, 1954.

MEYER, H. J., BORGATTA, E. F., & FANSHEL, D. A study of the interview process: The caseworker-client relationship. *Genetic Psychology Monographs*, 1964, **69**, 247–295.

MINTZ, J., AUERBACH, A. H., LUBORSKY, L., & JOHNSON, M. Patients', therapists', and observers' views of psychotherapy: A "Rashomon" experience or a reasonable consensus. *British Journal of Medical Psychology*, 1973, **46**, 83–89.

ORLINSKY, D. E., & HOWARD, K. I. *Therapy Session Report, Form T*. Chicago: Institute for Juvenile Research, 1966.

ORLINSKY, D. E., & HOWARD, K. I. *Varieties of psychotherapeutic experience: Multivariate analyses of patients' and therapists' reports*. New York: Teachers College Press, 1975.

ORLINSKY, D. E., & HOWARD, K. I. The effects of sex of therapist on the therapeutic experiences of women. *Psychotherapy: Theory, Research, and Practice*, 1976, **13**, 82–88.

ORLINSKY, D. E., HOWARD, K. I., & HILL, J. A. Conjoint psychotherapeutic experience: Some dimensions and determinants. *Multivariate Behavioral Research*, 1975, **10**, 463–477.

RYAN, W. (Ed.) *Distress in the city*. Cleveland: Case Western Reserve University Press, 1969.

SNYDER, W. U. *The psychotherapy relationship*. New York: MacMillan, 1961.

STRUPP, H. H., FOX, R. E., & LESSLER, K. *Patients view their psychotherapy*. Baltimore: Johns Hopkins Press, 1969.

EDITORS' REFERENCES

ORLINSKY, D. E., & HOWARD, K. I. *Varieties of psychotherapeutic experience: Multivariate analyses of patients' and therapists' reports*. New York: Teachers College Press, 1975.

NOTES

1. *Editors' Footnote*. We wish to reemphasize the authors' point of the scarcity of this type of research. Although this volume is primarily composed of critical reviews, this chapter, which is a report of original research, is included because of its uniqueness as the first systematic study of therapists' experience of sessions. As such, the authors' aim has, appropriately, been descriptive, and the great value of this work in providing such data and methodology will become clearer later in the chapter.

2. *Editors' Footnote*. That insight was the most sought after aim is a bit surprising. From our own clinical work, we would have expected subjective distress relief and/or

advice (which are given below as less frequently cited patient aims) to be more frequently sought. That therapists *wish* to see insight-seeking suggests that we may be seeing what therapist-colored glasses do to our view of the patient. A second explanation is that this patient sample is in certain ways ideal. The evidence for this will become clearer as the authors present their results below.

3. *Editors' Footnote.* As suggested in footnote 2, these patients, at least from their therapists' viewpoints, seem to be near-ideal in doing and saying the "right" things frequently.

4. *Editors' Footnote.* Once again, we note the ideality of the descriptions these therapists provide. Apparently, not only the patients, but also the sessions, proceed quite normatively with surprising frequency. The most likely explanation, which the authors are clearly aware of, is that the therapist's view tends to idealize perceptions and/or to minimize patient distress. Whether this tendency is generally characteristic of therapists, or this sample *is* in some ways atypically ideal must await replicational study with other therapists.

5. *Editors' Footnote.* Again, we want to underline the authors' statement and point out the great value that a carefully done descriptive study such as this one has by virtue of developing this methodology. The possibility of studying the relative frequency of the four types of sessions (A-D) as a function of any of several different independent variables such as therapist-patient sex (dis-)similarity or race (dis-)similarity, therapist experience level, and patient diagnosis is intriguing. Researchers looking for "process-outcome" measures might thus find the authors' scheme to be quite valuable. Furthermore, the patient version of this scheme, developed by Orlinsky and Howard (1975) offers a valuable set of correlative data.

CHAPTER 22

THE ROLE OF THE THERAPIST IN ASSESSING PSYCHOTHERAPY OUTCOME[1]

JIM MINTZ

IN psychotherapy research, a distinction is often drawn between "outcome" and "process" studies (Meltzoff & Kornreich, 1970; Stollak, Guerney & Rothberg, 1966). Outcome studies are those directly focused on the conditions and determinants of therapeutic benefits, while process studies focus on the events which go on within the treatment sessions. But interest in outcome implicitly underlies virtually all research in psychotherapy. There would be little point in learning more about what happens in treatment if those events did not in some way affect outcome.

Measurement of treatment outcome is therefore one of the most important problems for psychotherapy researchers. This chapter deals with the role of the therapist in this area. It begins with an overview of current research practice regarding use of the therapist and summarizes some typical findings. Factors influencing the agreement between therapist outcome ratings and other outcome measures are discussed, and some determinants of therapist outcome judgments are presented. Finally, the assets and liabilities of the therapist as a "measurement instrument" are considered, and some recommendations are made.

USE OF THE THERAPIST IN THE RESEARCH LITERATURE

When Is the Therapist Used?

Two recent broad reviews of the psychotherapy research literature (Luborsky, Chandler, Auerbach, Cohen, & Bachrach, 1971; Meltzoff & Kornreich, 1970) give different pictures of the "state of the scientific art" of assessing therapy outcome. Luborsky's group, reviewing 166 studies over 23 years, concludes that the therapist provides the most frequent measure of outcome. But Meltzoff and Kornreich state

that use of the therapist is infrequent; such measures "rank far down the list."

To resolve this apparent contradiction, a sample of studies from each volume was reviewed. From Luborsky's prepared summaries, every fifth one was selected—a total of 31 studies.[2] From Meltzoff and Kornreich, the 28 "adequate controlled studies with major positive benefits" were selected (pp. 77–105). An additional 10 independent studies of clinical samples were found in another review volume (Stollak et al., 1966). When several published studies by the same authors were based on the same sample, only the first was used in this review. For each study, it was noted whether the therapist was used to assess outcome or not, and some basic characteristics of patients, settings, and treatment types were recorded.

Table 1 presents the results of this mini-review of the reviews. It helps account for the apparent contradiction between them, and provides a background from which to evaluate the role of the therapist in assessment of outcome. The therapist was used to measure outcome in almost 75% of the studies sampled from Luborsky's review, far more frequently than any other criterion. But *none* of the "adequate controlled studies" from Meltzoff and Kornreich's review used the therapist to assess treatment outcome.

The therapist was clearly the instrument of choice in studies of what most people without psychiatric/psychological background would probably think of as psychotherapy—typically, a neurotic adult talking one-to-one with a psychiatrist or psychologist in a clinic or office. Studies of that kind of psychotherapy were usually uncontrolled—i.e., they did not include groups of patients receiving no treatment or alternative treatments. Almost all (88%) of the therapist ratings were global outcome ratings obtained only at the end of treatment.[3]

When was the therapist *not* used to assess

TABLE 1. COMPARISON OF STUDIES THAT USE AND DO NOT USE THE THERAPIST TO ASSESS OUTCOME

	Therapist Used	Therapist Not Used
Number of Studies	25	44
Age % Adult	100%	77%
Setting:		
Clinic	72%	32%
Inpatient	16%	25%
Private practice	8%	0%
Other	4%	39%
Type of Therapy:		
Client-centered	24%	4%
Other individual	56%	25%
Brief	20%	16%
Group	0%	41%
Other	16%	41%
Type of Patient:		
Psychiatric	92%	54%
Behavioral	0%	25%
Nonpatient	8%	20%
Type of Study:		
Psychiatric*	64%	20%
Other	36%	79%
Number of Treatments Studied:		
One treatment only	88%	68%
More than one treatment	12%	32%

*Psychiatric studies were defined as treatments of adult patients in a psychiatric setting with traditional individual psychotherapy.

outcome? Most of these studies involved non-psychiatric settings (e.g., army, institutions for retarded or delinquents, schools, medical treatment settings). The patients were usually being treated for some behavioral disorder. In about one-fourth of these studies, the patients were children. In some cases, the subjects were not psychiatric patients at all. The therapy was often group treatment and was often not traditional individual psychotherapy. In such studies, the most common measures were objective behavioral indices (used in more than 75% of these studies) and psychological tests. Observers' judgments were used in about 20% of these studies to supplement objective measures or tests. Very few studies used only subjective outcome ratings from patients or observers. If outcome assessment was based only on subjective judgment, the overwhelming choice (over 80%) was to use the therapist.

In short, two research populations were observed. Treatment of neurotic and psychotic patients with traditional individual psychotherapy was usually assessed at the end of treatment by the therapist. In other settings, often involving patients with behavioral disorders, behavioral measures or pre- and post-treatment testing predominated.

Typical Findings Based on Therapist Ratings

Although most reports give only summary statistics, frequency distributions of therapist post-treatment ratings of improvement were obtained from five different sources—three published (Fiske, Cartwright, & Kirtner, 1964; Garfield, Prager, & Bergin, 1971; Mintz, Luborsky, & Auerbach, 1971), and two unpublished.[4] In all, therapist ratings of 393 different patients' improvement are summarized in Table 2. Ratings have been categorized as indicating (a) regression (usually points 1–4 on a 9-point scale), (b) no change (point 5 on a 9-point scale), (c) slight to moderate change (covering points 6 and 7 of the usual 9-point scale), or (d) great change or recovery (points 8–9).

The main finding is that most patients are seen as making slight-to-moderate gains (ranging from 52% to 69% of the various samples). In most samples, few patients are seen by the therapist as getting worse. Roughly one-fourth are typically seen as making substantial gains. Improving the precision of the scale in the "very slight" to "moderate" improvement range would undoubtedly be useful. There is probably quite a bit of reliable differentiation obscured by the fact that over one-half the subjects in a study may fall in that range and typically over 40% are rated at the same scale point.

TABLE 2. PROPORTION OF FIVE SAMPLES RATED BY THERAPISTS AS IMPROVED

Sample	Amount of Improvement				
	Worse	No Change	Small to Moderate	Large	% at Mode
Menninger Foundation (N = 200)	2%	9%	64%	24%	34%
Luborsky (N = 39)	2%	0%	69%	28%	46%
Garfield et al. (1971) (N = 34)	3%	6%	56%	35%	44%
Mintz et al. (1971) (N = 27)	7%	26%	52%	15%	44%
Fiske et al. (1964) (N = 93)	3%	15%	59%	22%	59%
All Samples (N = 393)	3%	10%	62%	25%	43%

Agreement of Therapist Ratings with Other Outcome Criteria

The limited range of therapist ratings may be a factor in one of the most usual findings reported with therapist ratings—the low level of agreement between the therapist and other criteria. But how substantial is this finding?

Meltzoff and Kornreich (1970) cite four studies in which patients and therapists did not agree (Battle, Imber, Hoehn-Saric, Stone, Nash, & Frank, 1966; Cartwright, Kirtner, & Fiske, 1963; Cartwright & Roth, 1957; Nichols & Beck, 1960). Luborsky *et al.* (1971), declaring that "many different kinds of changes occur," cite only the Fiske *et al.* (1964) data.

But Meltzoff and Kornreich cite six studies in which significant relationships between patient and therapist ratings *were* found (Bellak, Meyer, Prola, Rosenberg, & Zuckerman, 1965; Board, 1959; Dietz, 1967; Stieper & Wiener, 1965; Storrow, 1960; Yalom, 1966). Moreover, others can be added to the list. Garfield *et al.* (1971) did a study directly focused on evaluation of outcome from various perspectives. They obtained a variety of client, therapist, and supervisor ratings of outcome for 34 clients at a university clinic, as well as the MMPI and Q Disturbance scales at pre- and post-treatment points. Although they stated that there was "little relationship between the various criteria," they did report significant correlations between patients' and therapists' global ratings. That study has been reviewed in this regard by Luborsky (1971). Haskell, Pugatch, and McNair (1969) reported a correlation of .65 between global improvement ratings made by 43 patients at a city university clinic and those of their therapists. Strupp, Wallach, and Wogan (1964) reported a low but significant correlation between patient and therapist retrospective global outcome ratings. In Luborsky's 5-year study of outpatient psychotherapy, substantial overlap between patient and therapist factors of change was found ($r = .60$ with an N of 73).[5]

Studies of single variables have shown equivocal results as far as agreement among viewpoints is concerned (Strupp & Bergin, 1969). Much of the evidence for low consensus as to outcome seems to come from factor-analytic studies. Strupp and Bergin cite five studies to support their contention that "the main factors... tend to be closely associated with the measurement method... rather than... some conceptual variable" (Cartwright *et al.*, 1963; Forsyth & Fairweather, 1961; Gibson, Snyder, & Ray, 1955; Nichols & Beck, 1960; Shore, Massimo, & Ricks, 1965). Because the factor-analytic evidence is the foundation of the belief that psychotherapy outcome has little common ground for the participants, these five studies were carefully reviewed.

Every study had at least one methodological flaw significant enough to seriously question the validity of the findings. The study by Shore *et al.* (1965) of outcome for delinquent boys simply included no therapist measure and is not relevant here. It is noted in passing that that study used 30 variables and included only 20 subjects; and the variables studied were primarily change scores, many experimentally dependent.

The Gibson *et al.* (1955) study included 20 measures on only 30 to 42 subjects (apparently all subjects did not take all the tests). It is not clear whether the correlation matrix used was based on different samples from variable to variable, a poor practice with such a low N and such a high number of missing observations. Seventeen of the scores were change scores.

The Forsyth and Fairweather (1961) study also included no therapist measure and thus is not really relevant here. This study did include 66 variables on 96 patients, analyzed using tetrachoric correlation. Nunnally (1967) has unequivocally stated that there is no mathematical basis for the use of the tetrachoric correlation in factor analysis and noted that tetrachoric correlations may be as much as .20 higher than point biserial (i.e., observed) correlations computed on the same dichotomous data.

The Nichols and Beck (1960) study involved 30 variables and 75 subjects. Most of the variables were change scores from two tests—the California Psychological Inventory and a sentence completion. Therapist and patient ratings were four rated change items filled out by each after treatment. The authors did not present the correlations among items, but they can be estimated by taking the sums of the cross products of the factor loadings shown. This should approximately reproduce the correlations among variables if the factor analysis is an adequate descriptive summary (Harmon, 1967). Of the 16 estimated correlations obtained between the four patient change ratings and the four therapist ratings, 11 would have reached the .05 level of statistical significance with 75 subjects.

The factor analysis of criteria from which Cartwright *et al.* (1963) reported "methods factors" is particularly noteworthy. They present an analysis with 83 tests and 93 subjects. Two distinct factors reported were patient and therapist factors. That factor analysis is the basis of their view that "there are important dimensions of change which are not ordinarily attended to by the therapist," a view which is a commonplace observation (Luborsky *et al.*, 1971; Strupp & Bergin, 1969).

As noted earlier, Donald Fiske made the raw data from that study available for reanalysis.

The two most obvious global outcome measures were the client and therapist post-therapy questionnaire composites. Since they are composites (sums of five items), they are both likely to be quite reliable, unlike most of the difference measures used. The correlation between them was .60 (highly significant statistically), reflecting substantial agreement between patients and therapists in their ratings of outcome. Looking back at the factor matrix, one can observe that the highest loading for the client measure was on the "therapist-method" factor.

Without engaging in a lengthy statistical or methodological critique of these studies, at least a passing reference to some problems will provide a new perspective on them. As Nunnally (1967) forcefully stated, "frequently factor analyses . . . are undertaken with many fewer subjects than the minimum recommended (ten subjects per item). There are some horrible examples in the literature where the number of subjects was approximately the same as the number of items" (p. 257). All the studies cited are at fault in this regard. To compound the problems, most of the measures are change scores (and thus relatively unreliable), and many are experimentally dependent (e.g., Hs and Hy scales of the MMPI, which "define" a factor, have many items in common). All these facts are consistent with the appearance of "methods" factors. In sum, the scientific evidence for the multifactor view of the criterion issue is far from conclusive.

This is not, however, meant to imply that methods factors or "points-of-view" do not exist; probably they do. Therapists' ratings of various aspects of the treatment experience may well show a degree of internal consistency and distinctness from the views of the same events by others, and only to some degree because of shared error of measurement in measurements made by the same instrument.

For one thing, goals of patients and therapists may differ. For example, Nichols and Beck (1960) indicated that patients weighed self-understanding less than therapists did in defining global improvement. Judging the success of a treatment is both a matter of value (e.g., whether the patient's "character," specific behavior, or symptoms, etc., *should* change) and of fact (e.g., whether it actually has changed or not).

Are the patient and therapist scaling in the same terms? To some degree they probably are, and, accordingly, some consensus should be expected. But the psychotherapy experience exists in different contexts for patient, therapist, and researcher. The patient must somehow scale the therapy experience against his other experiences—perhaps his other treatment experiences, if he has had any. The therapist is likely to view each patient against the backdrop of his other patients—perhaps his other patients similar to this one. This perspective is not available to the patient, since he knows nothing about other patients' experiences.[6] Finally, the researcher rescales both patient and therapist ratings in terms of other patients and therapists in the study—a context unavailable to either participant. These scaling issues are important insofar as "bias" exists from individual to individual, and there is evidence that significant bias exists in therapists' rating of treatment outcome (Mintz, 1972). And, of course, ratings scales used are often quite crude. A single line on a piece of paper, anchored at about five points with words like "improved" and "unimproved," is not unusual at all. Finally, patients and therapists may honestly disagree about treatment outcome in some cases and may *know it*.

In view of these factors, it may be unreasonable to expect patient and therapist to behave like "alternate forms" of a test and show perfect agreement. However, there is more evidence for a substantial common evaluative factor than is commonly thought. In many studies, even some of those typically interpreted as showing disparity between patient and therapist views of outcome, the participants were seen to have a significant level of agreement—not total agreement, to be sure, but nevertheless, a common ground. More reliable multi-item measures would undoubtedly help in discovering how important that common ground is.

THE BASES OF THERAPIST RATINGS

Sources of Information

What are the therapist's sources of information about the patient's progress? First and foremost, probably, is the patient's own report as to the status of his problems. In traditional talk therapies, the patient spends much of his time reporting on and describing in detail his difficulties in living.

Of course, in other settings this source of information may be less useful. Behavior modification approaches may involve programs of therapy with little intercurrent discussion of current status. In hospitals or institutional settings, the problems being treated may not have much opportunity to occur—institutional treatment of alcoholics or sexual deviates are two examples.

In some cases, the therapist may use direct observation. This might be a major source of information if the patient's problems were such as to occur with some regularity in the treatment setting itself. Examples come readily to mind. In a hospital setting, ward behavior may be observed. In our outpatient drug clinic, there is ample opportunity, in the case of some of the patients, for counselors to observe directly their patients' interactions with others. Physical manifestations, such as speech problems and nervous tremors, might be seen in the therapist's office. And a host of psychological and interpersonal manifestations of a patient's problems might well appear during the treatment in a way that the therapist may observe. Psychotic patients may react to hallucinations; patients with low self-esteem may deprecate themselves; patients who cannot get along with others may be belligerent; patients who are dissatisfied with life may be dissatisfied with their therapist. All these manifestations may be used by the therapist to assess his work in an ongoing way.

Finally, there may be information available from others not directly involved in the treatment. Relatives are probably the most usual source of this type in the outpatient context. In institutional settings, there is likely to be much input to the therapist from other staff, and perhaps from other patients as well. In our drug clinic, one of the most significant sources of information for counselors is the hospital laboratory, which regularly reports the results of tests on patients' urines for illicit drug use.

The sources of information are not independent of the treatment setting and patient population. Where objective signs or information independent of the treatment sessions are available to the therapist, they may well be available to the researcher as well. When events transpiring only during the treatment are available to the therapist, it may be that the therapist becomes the only resource available to the researcher. This is probably often true in the psychiatric outpatient setting.

Change and the Therapist's Global Assessment

Wherever the therapist gets information and however he assimilates and weighs it, the outcome rating which is the end product of that process should in some way reflect changes which have occurred in the patient, or, in the case of some patients, changes which have not

occurred. Sargent (1961), for example, notes that *absence* of deterioration may be a positive outcome in some cases. In any event, in exploring the determinants of therapist ratings of outcome, it is natural to begin with assessments of pre- and post-treatment functioning, and to ask whether raw change, or some linear function of pre- and post-treatment adjustment, can substantially account for the therapist's view of overall outcome.

Much of the available evidence suggests that post-treatment adjustment status seems to have more importance to the therapist than outcome judgments based on change (Mintz, 1972). That is, patients who end treatment relatively well adjusted tend to be seen as successfully treated, *regardless* of how well or poorly adjusted they were initially. This means that treatment of patients who make small gains in level of adjustment is seen as more successful if the patient ends (and begins) treatment at relatively well-adjusted levels.

But it is also widely observed that change is related to initial level. Patients who are more poorly adjusted tend to improve more, at least in raw numerical terms. Probably this largely reflects ceiling effects—patients initially low in adjustment have more room to move on the measures. For example, a 2-point gain might be better than average for a patient who was relatively well adjusted at the beginning of therapy and, at the same time, might well be worse than average for a patient who was more poorly adjusted initially. Table 3 gives an example of this finding based on the data of Fiske *et al.* (1964).

TABLE 3. RAW GAIN IN THERAPIST-RATED ADJUSTMENT AS A FUNCTION OF INITIAL LEVEL*

Initial Adjustment	Amount Gained			
	Less Than 1 Point	1 to 2 Points	3 or More Points	Modal Gain
Good (7–8) (N = 24)	16 (67%)	8 (33%)		0 points
Fair (5–6) (N = 39)	8 (20%)	25 (64%)	6 (15%)	2 points
Poor (below 5) (N = 30)	4 (13%)	9 (30%)	17 (57%)	3 points
N = 93	28 (30%)	42 (45%)	23 (25%)	

*Ratings were made on a 9-point scale; data from Fiske *et al.* (1964).

The fact that therapists value gains made by better adjusted patients more than similar sized gains made by less well-adjusted patients suggests that the therapists may implicitly be evalu-

basically affecting covert internal processes. Many contemporary psychotherapy researchers believe that what is "wrong" with patients is properly viewed at the level of observable behavior. The behaviorist tradition puts great stress on objective observables (Strupp & Bergin, 1969). And, of course, objective measures are likely to be psychometrically attractive as well. Although modern behavior therapists show increasing interest in covert processes, both as mediational processes and targets for change (Cautela, 1971; Jacobs & Wolpin, 1971), their reliance on behavioral indices of progress is still obvious.

Carl Rogers (1963) cites loss of faith in psycho-analytic dogma, the growth of competing schools of thought, the widespread occurrence of diverg[ence] in basic clinical judgments (what psychometricians call "unreliability"), and the rise of scientific/behavioristic clinical practice as sig[nific]ant factors behind increased interest in objective behavioral measurement and standardized tests, and less reliance on clinicians' judg[ments] in contemporary scientific inquiry into therapy.

[With] regard to research design, attention to [the need] for controls in psychotherapy studies, [raised] originally by Eysenck's (1952) critical [review of] uncontrolled research, has conse[quences for] choosing outcome measures. The [...] unique knowledge of events occurring [...] by situation, which is an asset in [...] is not useful in studies utilizing [cont]rols or waiting list groups, since [such gro]ups have no therapist. There is [...] doubt that therapist ratings from [different treat]ment schools are comparable [... 1974]. Therefore, research[...] with no-treatment, waiting [list tr]eatment groups are likely to [... an] outcome which can be [... in a]ll groups in the study, such [... rating]s, and behavioral criteria.

...N AND ...NDATIONS

...sor of outcome has ...rvey method of re-...chiatric setting. Not ...al choice for prac-...ons, but also many ...d view the thera-...asurer of patient ..., the research

picture may be changing, with increased interest in controls and an increasingly behavioristic view of psychotherapeutic processes.

Abandoning the therapist as an informant about change and its determinants because of measurement problems may be a case of throwing the baby out with the bath water. Obtaining reliability at the cost of validity is a poor trade-off indeed. One would hardly recommend evaluating therapy outcome by weighing the patients. Although this could be done very reliably, it would obviously have no validity for most patients.

Although the therapist has a unique role to play in informing us about the events and outcomes of therapy, little useful knowledge will be gained from poorly defined, unreliable measures. Typical practice has been the casual use of simple-looking rating scales which ask for highly complex judgments which are largely, even primarily, evaluative rather than descriptive, and with little or no precision of definition or training in their use. Tests measuring the therapist's perception of outcome and its determinants deserve the same serious psychometric attention as any other measurement procedures if we are to hope to learn from their use.

Too little research has been focused on methodological considerations of outcome measurement, in the past or currently. A review of the most recent published research (*Journal of Consulting and Clinical Psychology* for 1973 and *Journal of Abnormal Psychology* for 1974, and looking specifically for research pertaining to use of the therapist in research, revealed only two studies which were even remotely relevant here (Chipman & Paykel, 1974; Langer & Abelson, 1974).

Chipman and Paykel explored the extent to which global ratings of severity of illness could be tied to specific symptom ratings, and specified a number of symptoms (e.g., agitation, guilt) which were significantly related to global ratings. Langer and Abelson reported that analytic clinicians were more likely to describe an individual viewed on videotape as disturbed if he was identified as a patient than if called a job applicant. Behavioral clinicians' adjustment ratings were not affected, suggesting at the very least that clinicians of different schools may have different standards for evaluating pre-treatment adjustment.

It was suggested earlier that therapy outcome is often a multilevel phenomenon, permitting a variety of interpretations depending on one's vantage point and one's values. While reasonabl[e]

ating patients relative to a reference group of patients with similar initial pictures. A number of writers have described and recommended the use of the "residual gain" method (Manning & DuBois, 1962) to define criteria in psychotherapy (Fiske, Hunt, Luborsky, Orne, Parloff, Reiser, & Tuma, 1970; Luborsky et al., 1971). In simple terms, this means that a patient's improvement is rescaled so that it is relative not to the average gain in the sample as a whole, but to the average gain made by those with similar initial levels. Patients with high residual gain scores are those who improved more than one would expect on the basis of their initial levels. Their actual numerical gains may vary widely depending on whether they began at high or low levels.

Hammond, Hirsch, and Todd (1964) postulate that concrete cues mediate between the clinical event and the clinical judge and that the nature of the judgment process can be explored by empirical analyses of the relationships between the cues and judgments. In statistical terms, they are referring to multiple regression analyses. In the area of psychotherapy, the patients' pre-treatment and post-treatment adjustment might be viewed as major cues affecting the therapist's ultimate judgment as to treatment outcome. To explore this, the multiple regression method was applied to analysis of therapist outcome ratings as follows. These analyses were based on several studies which published correlations among global outcome ratings and pre- and post-therapy adjustment (Fiske et al., 1964; Strupp et al., 1964) and on some unpublished data.[7] The Fiske et al. (1964) data are based on 93 outpatients at the University of Chicago clinic. The outcome measure is a 9-point rating scale of global outcome completed by the therapist. The adjustment scores were the therapist's ratings of "integration" pre- and post-treatment. The Strupp et al. (1964) study involved 44 patients at a university clinic. Data were taken from the correlation matrix provided by the authors. The clusters used were "overall success" (cluster T1), "remaining disturbance" (cluster T2), and "adjustment before therapy" (cluster T5). The Luborsky study involved 73 outpatients. The outcome score is a sum of several therapist ratings of change and benefits from therapy. The pre- and post-treatment adjustment measures were composites based on patient reports and clinical observers' ratings at pre- and post-treatment evaluation interviews.

For each study, the multiple regression equation for predicting therapist global outcome ratings from the adjustment measures was calculated. The squared multiple correlation (R^2) gives the maximum proportion of the variance in the therapist's global assessment which can be accounted for by a linear function of the adjustment measures (the "best fit" function). The residual variance $(1 - R^2)$ is the part of the variance *not* accounted for by the best fit function. Part of this is measurement error, but as Hammond et al. (1964) point out, residual variance may also reflect the systematic influence of other factors which were not included in the regression analysis, or may reflect the size of nonlinear components in the criterion.

In addition to the "best fit" equation, the extent to which the therapist's overall outcome assessment related to several other measures based on adjustment was examined. These were (a) raw change in adjustment, (b) the residual gain score, and (c) final level of adjustment alone. The similarity of these functions to the "best fit" function was explored. The results are summarized in Table 4.

TABLE 4. SQUARED MULTIPLE CORRELATIONS BETWEEN VARIOUS FUNCTIONS OF PRE- AND POST-TREATMENT ADJUSTMENT AND THERAPIST GLOBAL CHANGE RATINGS

Function	Study Sampled			
	Fiske	Strupp	Luborsky	Average
A: Best Fit	.670	.527	.439	.545
B: Residual Gain	.660	.519	.433	.537
C: Change	.495	.402	.398	.432
D: Post Only	.581	.436	.200	.406
r_{AB}*		.992	.974	.993

*Correlation between Best Fit function and Residual Gain function.

The results from all the studies were highly consistent. First, in each case, the therapist's global outcome rating did prove to be highly predictable from pre- and post-treatment adjustment (R^2 ranged from .44 to .67). Of course, while these values were high, they still left ample room for the operation of other factors. Second, the residual gain score typically was about as good a predictor of the therapist's outcome rating as was the best possible function. In fact, the correlation between the best function and the residual gain score was virtually perfect in each study.

The other functions of adjustment measures were not at all as good at accounting for variation in therapist ratings as the residual gain score was. To a large degree, then, the therapist's global assessment of outcome is a measure of patient improvement, but it is adjusted for the initial level of patient functioning.

That does not describe the entire picture, however. The remaining variance ($1 - R^2$ ranged from .33 to .56) represents therapist criterion ratings which cannot be explained in terms of a simple linear function of pre- and post-treatment adjustment. In clinical terms, this means that two patients may begin at the same level of adjustment, make the same numerical improvement, and yet be rated reliably differently by their therapists.

To some degree, then, the therapist ratings do directly reflect improvement, but this improvement is rescaled to take into account the fact that different performance standards exist for different people. Figuratively, it is suggested that the therapist views the patient's improvement, rescales it relative to his expectations for a patient of that type, and then adds a component of personal evaluation whose determinants are unknown at this time. The result is the global outcome measure.

FACTORS AFFECTING THE USE OF THE THERAPIST

The heterogeneity of the psychiatric population is probably one of the most significant factors in the widespread use of therapist ratings in that context. In the psychiatric outpatient clinic and private practice populations, it is impossible to define standard behavioral indices or tests which meaningfully apply to all or even most patients in the same way. Many psychiatric patients may not even have significant behavioral disturbances on which to base assessment of outcome.

Even if objective criteria or tests exist in some settings, or for some more homogeneous subgroups, there are likely to be practical difficulties. Systematic observation of outpatients may be impossible. Getting patient cooperation in taking tests in these settings may also be a problem. Patients' involvement in treatment is personal and clinical. They typically have little to gain by participating in research, and may experience it as an invasion of privacy.

In addition to such practical and methodological considerations, some clinical researchers would argue that clinicians' judgments are the most reasonable measures to use in the clinical setting. The traditional psychoanalytic view is that the patient's problems are internal—defenses, conflicts, wishes. While overt behaviors and test performances may reflect these underlying and more basic factors, they may also disguise them—a distinction only the analyst can make.

Many clinicians would view specific symptom ratings as a superficial and mechanical way of evaluating a treatment experience.

Even a casual reading of Freud (1937) leaves no doubt that he felt that assessment of outcome was appropriately left in the hands of the authoritative, expert analyst, a view still characteristic in psychoanalytically oriented research. Sargent (1961), for example, contends that Rogerian research methods have limited relevance to psychoanalytic research because "the theory tested is confined to the levels of adjustive behavior and consciousness." She defends the "substitution of routine clinical judgments for 'standardized' ratings" from attacks by what she terms "methods-conscious critics" of the psychoanalytically-oriented Menninger Foundation Psychotherapy Research Project. Her paper provides an extensive consideration of this issue, simultaneously protesting the increasing influence of behavioristic methodology and emphatically defending clinical judgment as a process for examining clinical events.

Assets of the Therapist

The therapist has several assets as an evaluator of psychotherapy outcome. He is usually a highly trained professional, presumably expert in the assessment of behavior, particularly abnormal or deviant behavior. He is often familiar with, if not highly trained in, research methodology. He is uniquely informed about the case, both in terms of presenting problem and course of treatment. As compared to the patient or the patient's family, the therapist is likely to be relatively objective in evaluating the outcome. The therapist, after all, does not begin each treatment experience in a distressed neurotic or psychotic state. The therapist should be in a position to view any one treatment as simply that, one treatment experience among many. Hopefully, his own sense of worth is not too tied up in any particular patient's outcome.

Perhaps most important, the therapist is in a position to organize or evaluate all the clinical data flexibly, weighing the unique features of each case differently. He can evaluate things such as insight, for which no tests may exist, and resistance, which occurs during the treatment and would be difficult to measure apart from detailed study of the sessions. He can realize that goals may shift during the course of treatment, and that presenting problems may not reflect the focus of the therapeutic work as it progresses.

Strupp and Bergin (1969) cite Jewell's finding (from Volsky, Magoon, Norman, & Hoyt, 1965) that clinical judges asked to evaluate clients' anxiety levels felt that ideally anxiety should be decreased in 37% of the cases, not changed in 53%, and actually increased in 10% of the cases; that is, a pre-post increase in anxiety might be a deterioration for one patient, but a sign of improvement for another who was initially seen as pathologically flat in affect. If therapists characteristically see treatment goals in that diverse manner, it is hard to see how standard measurement procedures, uniformly applied to all patients, would be valid.

Liabilities of the Therapist

A major issue is the concern that the therapist, in evaluating the outcome of treatment, may feel that he is in fact evaluating himself as a practitioner. Even where the therapist is not actively concerned about his own personal value, he may well be a committed advocate of the type of therapy he is doing. If he is aware that his "school" is being studied, there is presumably pressure on him to minimize the failures and maximize the successes of his method.

The review of the literature undertaken for this chapter failed to turn up much empirical evidence for such bias, but it is an obvious concern. Meltzoff and Kornreich (1970) warn specifically that unbiased and accurate judgments will be hard to obtain from the therapist because he, like the patient, is "intensely ego-involved in the process." Luborsky et al. (197?) while advocating the use of the therapist in ? regard, warn that the fact that the therapis? "committed participant in the therapeu? change, is a distinct disadvantage." ? interest shown by most psychologists ? ipating in research (Bednar & Sh? may well reflect defensive processe?

To explore this factor, each av? of the clinical staff at the ? Hospital drug clinic with a ? more patients was asked t? clients for inclusion in a p? Five counselors did so. O? with only eight patien? inclusion. The study? counselors with 73 a? ors were told that a cross ? wanted (virtually all of our pa?? addicted veterans), both successfu? cessful, so that a fair picture of treatmen?

clinic would be obtained. The chosen patients were compared with those not chosen in terms of the counselor's own ratings, made one month before our inquiry, of how much each patient was benefiting from therapy. (These ratings a? collected monthly as part of our routine cl? evaluation, and are highly related to wh? or not the patient continues his illicit dr? The average counselor rating of benefi? patients chosen for inclusion was 2.?? point scale (1 = great; 5 = none); the? the patients not chosen was 2.76. ?? counselors had a difference ? chosen; the other showed no d? groups ($p < .05$, one-tailed? zero difference). This findi? the hypothesis that ther? such a way as to reflect w? results are similar to '? finding that *therapist?* *unsuccessful patien?* *study.*[8]

Another liab? spective is lim? In outpatien? patient's se? different ? all are ? Becau? ly f? val? v?

DISCUSSI? RECOMMEN?

The therapist as asse? largely been tied to the s? search in the traditional psy? only is the therapist a natur? tical and methodological reas? clinicians in such settings wou? pist as the most appropriate me? progress. In all these respec?

consensus among judges of outcome may be more common than is usually thought, the picture is clearly not one of unanimity. In this context, the concept of interrater reliability does not make sense when applied to the therapist and another judge. That concept is based on the notion of interchangeable *randomly* selected judges from a population of potential judges. But the therapist is a uniquely informed judge. Reliability in that case is probably best assessed by evaluating the internal consistency of the therapist's multi-item ratings of outcome or by short-term test-retest study of therapist ratings of the same patients. Studies of relationships among different viewpoints are more properly termed studies of concurrent validity.

For several reasons, factor-analytic studies are probably *not* the most useful approach to clarifying the nature of relationships among therapy criteria. They are extremely difficult to do because of the large samples required. This is an area of inquiry in which experimental interdependencies and shared error of measurement among variables are probably inevitable. By now, hopefully, no one still believes that a large number of measures of varying relevance and precision can be factor-analyzed with the computer bearing the responsibility of letting us know what is important and what is not.

The factor-analytic method reveals patterns of shared variance within a set of variables. A traditional psychometric assumption is that error of measurement is not shared from measure to measure. But, when measures in the analysis are adjacent items on a single page with identical response formats filled out by the same person at a single sitting, then substantial correlations among errors of measurement are probably inevitable. As the relative importance of the error component in each variable increases (i.e., as reliability decreases), the likelihood is that "method" factors defined by shared error of measurement will be increasingly significant in accounting for interrelationships among measures.

In other words, this measurement problem should be approached in the same way as any other. What is needed first is much more thoughtful attention to the development, in a straightforward, nonevaluative manner, of highly reliable measures of outcome *within each source*—including measures which accurately indicate where the patient stands on various criteria according to the therapist. Only then should relations to other views be studied.

It is, of course, far easier to define objective, standard criteria when dealing with a relatively homogeneous population. With tightly defined samples presenting certain symptom pictures, it has been relatively easy to develop sound objective outcome measures which straightforwardly apply to all patients in the study. In such cases, the therapist can still provide important information bearing on the issue of whether significant outside events need to be considered, and if and how the process of treatment has directly affected outcome.

The suggestion that homogeneous research populations would make outcome measurement much simpler and clearer is not a new one (Fiske *et al.*, 1964; Luborsky *et al.*, 1971). But within the psychiatric outpatient setting, it is usually impossible for any one researcher to obtain a sufficiently large sample of patients of one type for a study. Perhaps several researchers in outpatient settings, applying the same measurement instruments, might be able to pool and subdivide their samples: researcher A might then analyze the pooled data from all the "distressed students"; researcher B could look at "separation"; researcher C might be interested in "marital discord." Some of these might even overlap. The point is to define samples where there is reason to believe that all the patients can legitimately be evaluated in the same terms. Unfortunately, this idea is probably impracticable. Strupp and Bergin (1969), after proposing collaborative research, abandoned the idea (Bergin & Strupp, 1970) largely because of lack of interest on the part of research workers, a phenomenon more widely noted among psychologists by Bednar and Shapiro (1970).

In sum, then, the therapist has potential in research in two ways directly relevant to the measurement of outcome. First, the therapist may be able to provide reliable and, more importantly, valid measurement of certain events for which no good standard measures exist—events such as the gaining of insight or the increased capacity for intimacy. Obviously, much good psychometric work needs to be done to develop measures of such concepts or to demonstrate convincingly that they cannot be measured. But researchers who dismiss these notions outright as too mystical for consideration should not be surprised when their studies of such things as MMPI responses are dismissed by therapists. In most cases, using the therapist merely to rate specific observable symptoms seems a poor use of his specific assets.

Second, the therapist may give the researcher some good ideas as to how, if at all, the events that went on between the initial and final sessions affected the outcome, however defined. The job of objectively detailing *all* the possibly relevant events in a patient's life is staggering. The therapist may be in a good position to point out which changes in the patient are likely to have resulted from or at least been affected by treatment, and which changes he views as largely independent of therapy.

It was noted earlier that the therapist is in a position to use a different set of criteria for each patient in rating outcome. Is such a flexible weighting system an asset? Clinically, yes. But methodologically speaking, probably not. The psychometrician's goal (Nunnally, 1967) is to have unidimensional measures. A flexible measurement system which permits the clinician to consider different factors in different cases is an instance of a multidimensional scale. Patients may get the same score for different reasons, making interpretation of results difficult.[9]

In any event, does he actually do so? The evidence in the areas of treatment evaluation (Mintz, 1972) and clinical prediction (Gough, 1962) is that linear models are typically adequate to explain the clinician's judgments. The evidence for unique weighting systems or flexible adjustment of criteria to meet the unique situation of the individual case is usually flimsy (e.g., Hammond et al.,1964). But research in this area typically begins by presenting the clinician with a highly "stripped-down" pseudoclinical situation, one contrived to focus on a manageable number of factors. Hoffman et al. (1968), for example, asked physicians to judge the malignancy of ulcers based on hypothetical case records which simply indicated seven cues as present or absent, with no additional information. In a most extreme example, Mintz (1972) presented clinicians with only two rating scales presumably filled out by a psychotherapy patient before and after treatment and asked them to rate the success of the case. In short, clinical judgment in real-life situations is too complex to study, due to the high degree of confounding of factors of interest. But if the clinician behaves simply in highly simplified research situations, to what degree can we generalize these findings? As Hammond et al. (1964) stated, "our scientific knowledge concerning the human's ability to detect nonlinear relations is hardly more than primitive" (p. 446).

Even if the clinician's weighting of factors in scaling outcome is largely additive, and reasonably constant from case to case, his outcome rating is, nevertheless, a sophisticated measure.

To the extent that it represents change, it seems to take into account the fact that changing is harder for some people than it is for others, at least in terms of overall adjustment. The connection noted above between the widely recommended residual gain score and the therapist global rating seems to lend support to both.

The difference between them is, of course, that the therapist rating has a reliable component which *cannot* be accounted for in any linear way on the basis of initial *or* final level of adjustment. Exploration of that component of therapist ratings is needed. While it may turn out to be largely interpretable as bias, it may also reflect the operation of clinical judgment processes. The fact that such processes are complex is hardly a reason to abandon the inquiry.

In the course of reading the research literature for this chapter some distance between the researcher and the clinician was sensed. Particularly in the area of agreement and disagreement among various criteria, the impression was obtained that although researchers were often surprised by their findings, they for some reason did not ask those involved how they would explain what was going on. References were seen to dramatic disagreements between patients and therapists, for example, but no indication was given that the researcher went back to the therapist and said, "In the case of so-and-so, you saw improvement, but he didn't. What's up?" Probably most therapists would not be at a loss for words. Of course, their answers might turn out to be of no scientific value ultimately, but the question has apparently not been asked.

When Mintz (1972) asked clinical judges to defend their "self-fulfilling prophecies" that patients with good prognostic indicators do better than those with poor ones, some of their responses, in retrospect, were crude definitions of the residual gain notion which in fact does turn out statistically to account for clinicians' judgments to a large extent—"change at high levels of adjustment . . . is more difficult and should be weighted more" (Mintz, 1972, p. 15). In short, increased interaction of researcher with clinician is advocated, particularly in the face of puzzling findings.

Perhaps what is needed most is to remove the evaluative connotations from research in psychotherapy and move toward precise descriptive studies. Questions of "good" or "bad" changes—couched in terms of improvement, success, and so on—are largely sociocultural questions, not scientific ones.[10] Obviously, patients and clinicians are engaged in an interpersonal process in which values play one of the major roles. But that should not coerce the research scientist into acceptance of the viewpoint that judgments about the value of what is happening are the essence of outcome research.

As someone to describe the events of treatment and the changes in the patient which occurred, the therapist is uniquely qualified. A judgment that some particular change did or did not take place is legitimately scientific; a judgment as to how "good" or "bad" these changes (or lack of changes) are is more properly a clinical, even a nonscientific one.

REFERENCES

BATTLE, C., IMBER, S., HOEHN-SARIC, R., STONE, A., NASH, E., & FRANK, J. Target complaints as criteria of improvement. *American Journal of Psychotherapy*, 1966, **20**, 184–192.

BEDNAR, R. L., & SHAPIRO, J. G. Professional research commitment: A symptom or a syndrome. *Journal of Consulting and Clinical Psychology*, 1970, **34**, 323–326.

BELLAK, L., MEYER, E. J., PROLA, M., ROSENBERG, S., & ZUCKERMAN, M. A multiple level study of brief psychotherapy in a trouble shooting clinic. In L. BELLAK & L. SMALL (Eds.), *Emergency psychotherapy and brief psychotherapy*. New York: Grune & Stratton, 1965.

BERGIN, A. E., & STRUPP, H. H. New directions in psychotherapy research. *Journal of Abnormal Psychology*, 1970, **76**, 13–26.

BOARD, F. Patients' and physicians' judgments of outcome of psychotherapy in an outpatient clinic: A questionnaire investigation. *Archives of General Psychiatry*, 1959, **1**, 185–196.

CARTWRIGHT, D., KIRTNER, W., & FISKE, D. Method factors in changes associated with psychotherapy. *Journal of Abnormal and Social Psychology*, 1963, **66**, 164–175.

CARTWRIGHT, D., & ROTH, I. Success and satisfaction in psychotherapy. *Journal of Clinical Psychology*, 1957, **13**, 20–26.

CAUTELA, J. Covert conditioning. In A. JACOBS & L. SACHS (Eds.), *The psychology of private events*. New York: Academic Press, 1971.

CHIPMAN, A., & PAYKEL, E. How ill is the patient at this time? Cues determining clinician's global judgments. *Journal of Consulting and Clinical Psychology*, 1974, **42**, 669–674.

DIETZ, D. Relationships between staff and patients in judging criteria for improvement in mental health. *Journal of Clinical Psychology*, 1967, **23**, 41–46.

EYSENCK, H. The effects of psychotherapy: An evaluation. *Journal of Consulting Psychology*, 1952, **16**, 319–324.

FISKE, D., CARTWRIGHT, D., & KIRTNER, W. Are psychotherapeutic changes predictable? *Journal of Abnormal Social Psychology*, 1964, **69**, 418–426.

FISKE, D., HUNT, H., LUBORSKY, L., ORNE, M., PARLOFF, M., REISSER, M., & TUMA, A. H. Planning of research on effectiveness of psychotherapy. *Archives of General Psychiatry*, 1970, **22**, 22–32.

FORSYTH, R., & FAIRWEATHER, G. Psychotherapeutic and other hospital treatment criteria. *Journal of Abnormal Social Psychology*, 1961, **62**, 598–605.

FREUD, S. Analysis terminable and interminable (1937). In J. STRACHEY (Ed.), *Collected Papers*. London: Hogarth Press, 1950.

GARFIELD, S., PRAGER, R., & BERGIN, A. E. Evaluation of outcome in psychotherapy. *Journal of Consulting and Clinical Psychology*, 1971, **37**, 307–313.

GIBSON, R., SNYDER, W., & RAY, W. A factor analysis of measures of change following client-centered psychotherapy. *Journal of Consulting Psychology*, 1955, **2**, 83–90.

GOUGH, H. Clinical vs. statistical prediction in psychology. In L. POSTMAN (Ed.), *Psychology in the making*. New York: Knopf, 1962.

HAMMOND, K., HIRSCH, C., & TODD, F. Analyzing the components of clinical inference. *Psychological Review*, 1964, **71**, 438–456.

HARMON, H. *Modern factor analysis.* (2nd Ed.) Chicago: University of Chicago Press, 1967.

HASKELL, D., PUGATCH, D., & McNAIR, D. Time limited psychotherapy for whom? *Archives of General Psychiatry*, 1969, **21**, 546–552.

HOFFMAN, P., SLOVIC, P., & RORER, L. An analysis of variance model for the assessment of configural cue utilization in clinical judgment. *Psychological Bulletin*, 1968, **69**, 338–349.

JACOBS, A., & WOLPIN, M. A second look at systematic desensitization. In A. JACOBS & L. SACHS (Eds.), *The psychology of private events*. New York: Academic Press, 1971.

LANGER, E., & ABELSON, R. A patient by any other name . . . : Clinician group differences in labeling bias. *Journal of Consulting and Clinical Psychology*, 1974, **42**, 4–9.

LUBORSKY, L. The perennial mystery of poor agreement among criteria for psychotherapy outcome. *Journal of Consulting and Clinical Psychology*, 1971, **37**, 316–319.

LUBORSKY, L., CHANDLER, M., AUERBACH, A., COHEN, J., & BACHRACH, H. Factors influencing the outcome of psychotherapy: A review of quantitative research. *Psychological Bulletin*, 1971, **75**, 145–185.

MANNING, W., & DuBOIS, P. Correlational methods in research on human learning. *Perceptual and Motor Skills*, 1962, **15**, 287–321.

MELTZOFF, J., & KORNREICH, M. *Research in psychotherapy*. New York: Atherton, 1970.

MINTZ, J. What is 'success' in psychotherapy? *Journal of Abnormal Psychology*, 1972, **80**, 11–19.

MINTZ, J., LUBORSKY, L., & AUERBACH, A. H. Dimensions of psychotherapy: A factor-analytic study of ratings of psychotherapy sessions. *Journal of Consulting and Clinical Psychology*, 1971, **36**, 106–120.

NICHOLS, R., & BECK, K. Factors in psychotherapy change. *Journal of Consulting Psychology*, 1960, **24**, 388–399.

NUNNALLY, J. *Psychometric theory*. New York: McGraw-Hill, 1967.

ROGERS, C. Psychotherapy today or where do we go from here? *American Journal of Psychotherapy*, 1963, **17**, 5–16.

SARGENT, H. Intrapsychic change: Methodological problems in psychotherapy research. *Psychiatry*, 1961, **24**, 93–108.

SHORE, M., MASSIMO, J., & RICKS, D. A factor analytic study of psychotherapeutic change in delinquent boys. *Journal of Clinical Psychology*, 1965, **21**, 208–212.

STIEPER, D., & WIENER, D. *Dimensions of psychotherapy: An experimental and clinical approach*. Chicago: Aldine, 1965.

STOLLAK, G., GUERNEY, B., & ROTHBERG, M. (Eds.) *Psychotherapy research: Selected readings*. Chicago: Rand McNally, 1966.

STORROW, H. The measurement of outcome in psychotherapy. *Archives of General Psychiatry*, 1960, **2**, 142–146.

STRUPP, H. H., & BERGIN, A. E. Some empirical and conceptual bases for coordinated research in psychotherapy: A critical review of issues, trends and evidence. *International Journal of Psychiatry*, 1969, **7**, 18–90.

STRUPP, H., WALLACH, M., & WOGAN, M. Psychotherapy experience in retrospect: Questionnaire survey of former patients and their therapists. *Psychological Monographs*, 1964, **78** (11, Whole No. 588).

VOLSKY, T., MAGOON, T. J., NORMAN, W. T., & HOYT, D. P. *The outcomes of counseling and psychotherapy.* Minneapolis: University of Minnesota Press, 1965.

YALOM, I. A study of group therapy dropouts. *Archives of General Psychiatry*, 1966, **14**, 393–414.

EDITORS' REFERENCES

GREEN, B., GLESER, G., STONE, W., & SEIFERT, R. Relationships among diverse measures of psychotherapy outcome. *Journal of Consulting and Clinical Psychology*, 1975, **43**, 689–699.

WASKOW, I., & PARLOFF, M. (Eds.). *Psychotherapy change measures.* Washington, D.C.: United States Government Printing Office, 1975.

NOTES

1. This chapter would not have been possible without the help of others. Much of its content and structure benefited from numerous consultations with Ms. Kate O'Hare. Dr. Lester Luborsky put at my disposal the background research which went into his comprehensive review of the psychotherapy literature. He also made available to me the data of the predictive study (Luborsky & Mintz, "An 80 case predictive study of psychotherapy," in preparation) on which I worked so closely with him for five years, first as apprentice and later as collaborator. Finally, he let me use data he had collected at the Menninger Foundation. I have also used data from Donald Fiske's study (Fiske, Cartwright, & Kirtner, 1964) which Lester Luborsky had obtained to reanalyze in parallel fashion with his own data. The willingness of Dr. Luborsky and Dr. Fiske to share their scientific information is a model of scientific cooperation and responsibility, and I am happy to acknowledge their help. Naturally, the responsibility for any conclusions I have come to in the course of analysis and reanalysis rests with me.

    Dr. Charles P. O'Brien, Chief, Drug Dependence Treatment Center, Philadelphia VA Hospital, was consistently encouraging. The entire staff of the DDTC cooperated from time to time in studies potentially relevant to this paper, many of which showed me that my thinking on some topic was off-base, and which, accordingly, did not merit reporting here. Mrs. Joan Maruyama and Mrs. Dolores Redican carefully prepared the manuscript. Suzanne Malenbaum, Nancy Hanna, and George Woody read the manuscript and made comments. I thank them all.

2. As Luborsky et al. (1971) indicated: "For each study, we first prepared a detailed one-page summary which included sample size, type of patients, treatment mode, and predictive outcome measures" (p. 147). I thank Luborsky for putting these at my disposal.

3. *Editors' Footnote.* For a recent study which suggests that global ratings are useful, and which examines the relationships among several outcome measures, see Green, Gleser, Stone, and Seifert (1975). In addition, an excellent treatment of the selection of outcome measures, with practical suggestions for researchers, is Waskow and Parloff (1975).

4. Only Garfield et al. (1971) actually published the distributions of therapist outcome ratings. The data from Mintz et al. (1971) and Fiske et al. (1964) were made available by the senior authors, through the cooperation of Luborsky, who also provided outcome data he collected in his 5-year predictive study of psychotherapy,

and some evaluation data he collected in 1953 in the Menninger Foundation's annual survey of its functioning.

5. L. Luborsky et al. An 80 case predictive study of psychotherapy. In preparation.

6. *Editors' Footnote.* Furthermore, the patient is likely to compare himself with peers and significant others (many or most of whom are *non*patients)—a perspective unavailable to therapist or researcher.

7. L. Luborsky et al. An 80 case predictive study of psychotherapy. In preparation.

8. *Editors' Footnote.* We do not at all disagree with the substance of Mintz' conclusion (below) that the therapist provides a unique and indispensable set of outcome (and process) data. Nevertheless, we probably differ somewhat in that we weight more highly the evidence suggesting that therapists tend to distort systematically in the direction of presenting both process and outcome more positively (than do patients and probably also judges). As Mintz points out above, there is little evidence for this bias, but this lack seems primarily due to the lack of investigation of this issue. We are inclined to view Board's finding (that therapists *are* systematically selective in including patients for study), for example, as suspiciously suggestive that therapists are similarly selective in recalling and therefore assessing individual patients' behavior and verbalizations. Our suspicions are strengthened by (1) the surprisingly widespread "positivity" of process data derived from therapists in Orlinsky and Howard's study in this volume, and by (2) the evidence cited in Gurman's chapter that therapists rate their own levels of facilitativeness more highly than do their patients.

9. *Editors' Footnote.* We disagree with Mintz here. It is our bias to sacrifice psychometrical purity, when necessary, for clinical relevance. Ideally, of course, a piece of psychotherapy research satisfies both sets of demands, but actually such has not often been the case. As we have indicated elsewhere in this volume (e.g., in our footnotes in Fiske's chapter) the rarely embodied art and creativity of psychotherapy research involves the accurate measurement and association of clinically real and significant processes and events. But where such ideality or artistry has not been materialized, we feel that it is detrimental to both research and practice to have therapists (or patients or judges) consider all patients equally on all dimensions of an outcome scale. Patients may well wind up with the same *overall* improvement score for different reasons, but we feel that outcome considered across patients *is* multidimensional and that outcome measures ought to reflect this multiplicity by attempting, for example, to produce profiles of outcome (analogous, perhaps, to the MMPI), wherein changes in particular spheres of psychological functioning are demonstrable, distinguishable, and quantified. In fact, contrary to Mintz, we feel that interpretation of results is made more difficult by the use of *uni*dimensional scales, which would necessarily avoid focusing in on the specific spheres in which a patient (or therapist) sought or made changes. Furthermore, we think the advocacy of such unidimensional measurement might tend to discourage the current trend in clinical practice toward increasing specificity of treatment goals, and we would regret such a reversal.

10. *Editors' Footnote.* While it is undoubtedly easier in psychotherapy research than in clinical practice to "remove evaluative connotations" from discussion of therapeutic change, it does not seem to be a readily accomplished "removal" in either area. Discussion of this problem is found in Rabkin's chapter (in her text and in our footnotes) in this volume.

NAME INDEX

SUBJECT INDEX